THE COMPACT TOPICAL BIBLE

*A Complete Alphabetical Listing
of Bible Subjects and References*

•Topical Bible • Concordance • Dictionary

JAMES INGLIS

KREGEL PUBLICATIONS
Grand Rapids, Michigan 49501

The Compact Topical Bible, by James Inglis. Published in 1990 by Kregel Publications, a division of Kregel, Inc. P. O. Box 2607, Grand Rapids, MI 49501. All rights reserved.

Library of Congress Cataloging-in-Publication Data

Inglis, James, 1859-1885.
   [Bible text cyclopedia]
   The compact topical Bible / James Inglis.
       p.   cm.
   Reprint. Originally published: The Bible text cyclopedia. Gall & Inglis, 1860.
   Includes index.
   1. Bible—Indexes. I. Title.

BS432.I5   1990   220.3—dc20   90-36535
                                                                                    CIP

ISBN   0-8254-2900-5 (pbk.)

                    1 2 3 4 5 Printing/Year 94 93 92 91 90

PREFACE

This work, it is believed, will be found to differ materially from any cyclopedia, dictionary, or index to the Holy Scriptures hitherto published. Its original title, *The Bible Text Cyclopedia; Being a Complete Classification of Scripture Texts in the Form of an Alphabetical Index of Subjects*, distinctly expresses its character. The following is the general plan which has been observed in its preparation:

1. Every subject will be found in it which has a place in the Sacred Volume, whether doctrinal, devotional, practical, ecclesiastical, historical, biographical, or secular. The name of every person and place connected with any historical event is given, but where such names occur only in topographical or genealogical tables they are omitted. Among the subjects are some of considerable importance which do not appear in any other cyclopedia.

2. The author has attempted to discover every text of Scripture belonging to each topic. For this purpose, the whole Bible was formally indexed, verse by verse and clause by clause, with repeated revisions. The texts thus obtained, amounting to many thousands, were then arranged under their respective heads. Omissions, to some extent, were supplied from concordances, Scripture textbooks, and similar publications. In this work, the author has employed his leisure hours for more than seven years. He cannot expect that he has been perfectly successful, as an absolutely complete collection of Scripture passages on every topic is scarcely attainable; but the utmost care has been taken to secure thoroughness and accuracy, and to make the book a complete, as it is an original, index to the Holy Bible.

On controversial topics, such as baptism and church government, the texts are arranged under their titles without any minor divisions. But on the great doctrinal questions, such a system was neither possible nor desirable, as no faithful index to the Word of God could be made unless prominence were given to the supreme divinity of the Lord Jesus Christ, His death for sinners, and similar doctrines. The texts on doctrinal, devotional, and practical subjects are quoted in full, and are followed by illustrative cases: these are arranged under the headings "exemplified," in which the passages are quoted; and "examples," when there is merely a reference.

Examples of the figurative and symbolical use of certain words such as *day*, *night*, *darkness*, *dove*, *lion*, are appended to them; but it has not been thought necessary to refer to every instance, as they may easily be found in a concordance.

3. The subjects are arranged alphabetically, to facilitate reference. No general titles, such as history, geography, or botany, occur in the work. To find the history of the Israelites, the reader will examine the title *Israelites*; and every plant, tree, or flower will be found under its own name. The same rule applies to all other subjects.

At the end of many of the heads, references are given to similar and opposite subjects in other parts of the work. Thus, there is a reference from *regeneration* to *sanctification*, from *integrity* to *dishonesty*, and from *masters* to *servants*.

In the choice of titles to the different topics—a task which occasioned much thought and anxiety—consideration is given both to appropriateness and practical utility, that title being preferred which would most naturally occur to a reader. At the same time, various titles are given to aid in discovering any subject of which a person may be in search.

4. In some instances the original Hebrew and Greek are given, when necessary to the understanding of the texts; and a short explanation, with the same view, is made occasionally of Greek and Hebrew words.

In the belief that the Scriptures are the fountain-head of all spiritual knowledge, and the ultimate standard of truth and duty, this work is published with the hope that it may direct inquirers to the springs of eternal life, and aid them in modeling their faith and practice by the Word of God. "All Scripture is given by inspiration of God, and is profitable for doctrine, for reproof, for correction, for instruction in righteousness; that the man of God may be perfect, thoroughly furnished unto all good works" (1 Tim. 3:16).

JAMES INGLIS

THE COMPACT TOPICAL BIBLE

AARON

AARON, High-Priest. Son of Amram and Jochebed, of the family of Kohathites, tribe of Levi, Ex. 6.16-20. Jos. 21.4,10. 1 Chr. 6.2,3. 1 Chr. 23.13. Marriage and children, Ex. 6.23,25. Num. 3.2. 1 Chr. 6. 1 Chr. 24.

Call and inspiration, eloquence, character, Ex. 4.14-16. Ex. 7.1. Heb. 5.4. Psa. 106.16. Meets Moses by divine direction, introduces him to the Israelites, Ex. 4.27-31. His interviews with Pharaoh, miracles, Ex. *c.* 4 to 12.

Associated with Moses in leading the Israelites, Ex. 6.26,27. Jos. 24.5. 1 Sam. 12.6,8. Psa. 77.20. Psa. 99.6. Psa. 105.26. Mic. 6.4. Israelites murmur against him, Ex. 5.20,21. Ex. 16.2-10. Num. 14.2-5,10. Num. 16.3-11,41. Num. 20.2. Psa. 106.16.

Lays up a pot of manna in the Ark, Ex. 16.34. With Hur, holds up Moses' hands, Ex. 17.12. Ascends Sinai, Ex. 19.24. Ex. 24.1,9. Is judge while Moses is on the mount, Ex. 24.14.

First High-Priest, his descendants all priests, his consecration, Ex. *c.* 28 and 29. Lev. 8. Num. 3.3. Num. 18. 1 Chr. 23.13. 2 Chr. 26.18. Psa. 99.6. Psa. 133.2. See PRIEST.

Makes the golden calf, Ex. 32. Act. 7.40. Moses intercedes for him, Deu. 9.20. Rod of, buds and is laid up in the Ark, Num. 17. Heb. 9.4.

Blesses the Israelites, Lev. 9.22. Num. 6.23. Forbidden to mourn for his sons' death, Lev. 10.6,19. His jealousy of Moses, Num. 12.1. Intercedes for Miriam, Num. 12.11,12. Stays the plague after Korah's rebellion, Num. 16.

Excluded from Canaan for his sin at Meribah, Num. 20. Age, death, and burial in mount Hor, Ex. 7.7. Num. 33.38,39. Num. 20.23-29. Deu. 10.6. Deu. 32.50.

ABADDON (destroyer), the angel of the bottomless pit, Rev. 9.11.

ABANA (Heb. Amana), a river of Damascus, 2 Kin. 5.12. See Song 4.8.

ABARIM (the passages, see Jer. 22.20), a chain of mountains E. of Jordan, on one of which (Nebo) Moses died, Num. 27.12. Num. 33.47,48. Deu. 32.49.

ABIB

ABBA (father), Mar. 14.36. Rom. 8.15. Gal. 4.6.

ABDON, a Judge of Israel, Jud. 12.13-15.

ABEDNEGO, or AZARIAH, a pious friend of Daniel, delivered from the fiery furnace, made governor by Nebuchadnezzar, Dan. 1.6-20. Dan. 2.17,49. Dan. 3.

ABEL, son of Adam, a shepherd, sacrifice of accepted, slain by Cain, Gen. 4.2-11,25. Mat. 23.35. Luk. 11.51. Heb. 11.4. Heb. 12.24. 1 Jno. 3.12.

———, stone of, near Bethshemesh, ark placed on by Philistines, 1 Sam. 6.18.

ABEL, ABEL-BETHMAACAH, or ABEL-MAIM, a town in the N. of Palestine. Sheba flees to, is slain in, 2 Sam. 20.14-18. Spoiled by Benhadad, 1 Kin. 15.20. 2 Chr. 16.4. Taken by Tiglath, 2 Kin. 15.29.

ABEL-MEHOLAH, a town near the Jordan, Elisha's birthplace, 1 Kin. 19.16. Jud. 7.22. 1 Kin. 4.12.

ABEL-MIZRAIM (mourning of the Egyptians), a place W. of Jordan, where Joseph mourned for his father, Gen. 50.11.

ABEL-SHITTIM. See SHITTIM.

ABIA, or ABIJAH, a descendant of Eleazar, chief of one of the 24 courses of priests, 1 Chr. 24.10. Neh. 12.4,17. Luk. 1.5.

———, Samuel's son, made judge, his wickedness, 1 Sam. 8.1-5.

ABIATHAR, High-Priest. Of the line of Ithamar and Eli, son of Ahimelech, called Ahimelech, 2 Sam. 8.17. 1 Chr. 24.3-6,31. Abimelech, 1 Chr. 18.16.

His father gives David shewbread, 1 Sam. 21. Mar. 2.26. Escapes to David from Nob, 1 Sam. 22.20. 1 Sam. 23.6. Consulted by David, 1 Sam. 23.9. 1 Sam. 30.7.

Joint-priest with Zadok, 2 Sam. 8.17. 2 Sam. 15.35. 2 Sam. 20.25. 1 Kin. 4.4. 1 Chr. 18.16. 1 Chr. 15.11. His fidelity to David, 2 Sam. 15.24,29. Deposed by Solomon for aiding Adonijah, 1 Kin. 1.7. 1 Kin. 2.26. See 1 Sam. 2.31-35.

ABIB, or NISAN, 1st month. Abib signifies ears; see Ex. 9.31. Lev. 2.14. Began with the new moon in April, Ex. 12.2. Departure from Egypt in, Ex. 13.4. Passover kept in, Ex. 23.15. Tabernacle set up in, Ex. 40.2,17.

Israelites reach Zin in, Num. 20.1. Cross Jordan in, Jos. 4.19. Overflow of Jordan in, 1 Chr. 12.15. Haman's decree in, Est. 3.12. Christ's death in, Mat. 27.15. After the captivity, called Nisan, Neh. 2.1. Est. 3.7.

ABIEZER, or JEEZER, founder of the family of Abiezrites, Num. 26.30. Jos. 17.2. Jud. 6.34. Jud. 8.2.

ABIGAIL, Nabal's wife, her reception of David, becomes his wife, 1 Sam. 25. 1 Sam. 27.3. 2 Sam. 2.2. Mother of Chileab, 2 Sam. 3.3. 1 Chr. 3.1.

ABIHU, 2d son of Aaron, Ex. 6.23. Goes up the mount, Ex. 24.9. Is consecrated priest, Ex. 28.1. His death, for offering strange fire, Lev. 10.1,2. Num. 3.4. Num. 26.61.

ABIJAH, son of Jeroboam, his excellence and early death, 1 Kin. 14.1-18.

ABIJAM, or ABIJAH, 2d king of Judah, son of Rehoboam, 1 Kin. 14.31. 1 Kin. 15.2. 2 Chr. 12.16. Mat. 1.7. His sins, God's mercy to him for David's sake, 1 Kin. 15.1-5.

His wars with Jeroboam, 1 Kin. 15.6,7. Upbraids Jeroboam for idolatry, his faith and victory, 2 Chr. 13. His wives and children, 2 Chr. 13.21,22. Death, 1 Kin. 15.8. 2 Chr. 14.1. Chronicles of his reign written by Iddo, 2 Chr. 13.22.

ABILENE, a northern province of Palestine, Luk. 3.1.

ABIMELECH I, king of Gerar, his treatment of Abraham and Sarah, Gen. 20, and covenant at Beersheba, Gen. 21.22-32.

—————— II., king of Gerar, his treatment of Isaac and Rebecca, Gen. 26. and covenant with Isaac, Gen. 26.6-31.

——————. See ACHISH.

——————, son of Gideon, his birth, Jud. 8.31. Murders his brethren, his usurpation and death, Jud. 9. 2 Sam. 11.21.

ABINADAB, a Levite of Kirjath-jearim, or Gibeah. The ark in his house 70 years, 1 Sam. 7.1,2. 2 Sam. 6.3,4. 1 Chr. 13.7.

——————, son of Jesse, follows Saul to battle, 1 Sam. 16.8. 1 Sam. 17.13.

ABIRAM and DATHAN, Reubenites, conspire, with Korah, against Moses and Aaron, destroyed by an earthquake, Num. 16. Num. 26.9. Deu. 11.6. Psa. 106.17.

ABISHAG, wife of David, 1 Kin. 1.1-4. Sought in marriage by Adonijah, 1 Kin. 2.21, 22.

ABISHAI, son of David's sister, Zeruiah, 1 Chr. 2.16. David's captain, 2 Sam. 23.18. Seeks to slay Saul, 1 Sam. 26.6-8. Pursues Abner, 2 Sam. 2.24. Slays him, 2 Sam. 3.30.

Defeats the Edomites, 1 Chr. 18.12, and Ammonites, 2 Sam. 10.10,14. Seeks to slay Shimei, 2 Sam. 16.9. 2 Sam. 19.21. Commands a division in the battle against Absalom, 2 Sam. 18.2,5.

Sent against Sheba, 2 Sam. 20.6,10. Rescues David from a Philistine giant, 2 Sam. 21.17. One of three who procure water for David from Bethlehem, 1 Chr. 11.15-20.

ABLUTION, of the face and body, Ruth 3.3. 2 Sam. 12.20. Eze. 23.40. Mat. 6.17. Of the feet, Gen. 18.4. Gen. 19.2. Gen. 24.32. Gen. 43.24. Jud. 19.21. 2 Sam. 11.8. Song 5.3. Luk. 7.38,44. Jno. 13.5. 1 Tim. 5.10.

Of the dead, Act. 9.37. Of infants, Eze. 16.4. Pouring water on the hands, 2 Kin. 3.11. Washing the hands as a declaration of innocence, Deu. 21.6. Psa. 26.6. Mat. 27.24. See PURIFICATION.

ABNER, son of Ner, and cousin of Saul, 1 Sam. 14.50,51. Captain of Saul's host, 1 Sam. 17.55. 1 Sam. 26.5,14. Introduces David to Saul, 1 Sam. 17.57. Dedicates spoils, 1 Chr. 26.28. Makes Ishbosheth king, slays Asahel, is defeated by Joab, 2 Sam. 2.8-32.

Quarrels with Ishbosheth, is reconciled to David, 2 Sam. 3.6-21. Slain by Joab, 2 Sam. 3.22-38. 1 Kin. 2.5,32. Mourned for by David, 2 Sam. 3.31-39.

ABOMINATION OF DESOLATION, supposed to be the idolatrous ensigns of the Roman army, Dan. 9.27. Dan. 12.11. Mat. 24.15.

ABRAHAM, son of Terah, Gen. 11.26,27. Marries Sarah, Gen. 11.27,29. 1 Pet. 3.6. Departs from Ur, his birthplace, to Haran, Gen. 11.31. Neh. 9.7. Act. 7.4.

Goes to Canaan at the call of God, Gen. 12.1-9. Jos. 24.3. Isa. 51.2. Eze. 33.24. Heb. 11.8-10. Sojourns in Egypt during a famine, deceives Pharaoh respecting his wife, Gen. 12.10-20. Gen. 26.1.

Separates from Lot, dwells at Hebron, Gen. 13. Gen. 14.13. Gen. 35.27. Rescues Lot from captivity, is blessed by Melchizedek, Gen. 14.13-20. Heb. 7.1-10.

His sacrifice and vision, Gen. 15.8-17. Marries Hagar, birth of Ishmael, Gen. 16. Gal. 4.22. Name changed from Abram (high or great father) to Abraham (father of a multitude), Gen. 17.5. Neh. 9.7.

Circumcision instituted, Gen. 17. 9 - 27. Isaac promised, Gen. 15.4. Gen. 17.15-21. Gen. 18.9-15. Entertains 3 angels, prays for Sodom, Gen. 18. Sees it destroyed, Gen. 19.27,28.

Isaac born, Hagar and Ishmael banished, Gen. 21.1-21. 1 Chr. 1.34. Gal. 4.22-30. Dwells in Gerar, his deceit respecting Sarah, Gen. 20.

Covenant with Abimelech at Beersheba, Gen. 21.22-32. Plants a grove and dwells there, Gen. 21.31-33. Offers Isaac, stayed by an angel, Gen. 22.1-19. Heb. 11.17. Jas. 2.21.

Purchases Machpelah, buries Sarah, Gen. 23. Gen. 49.30,31. Gen. 50.13. Sends his servant for a wife for Isaac, Gen. 24. Marries Keturah, sons by her, Gen. 25.1-4. 1 Chr. 1.32,33.

His testament, age, death and burial, Gen. 25.5-10. His riches, Gen. 13.2. Gen. 24.35. Isa. 51.2. Altars built by, Gen. 12.7,8. Gen. 13.4. Gen. 21.33.

His faith and character, Gen. 18.19. Gen. 22. 12. Gen. 26.5. Neh. 9.7,8. Psa. 105.6. Rom. 4. Gal. 3.6-9. Heb. 11.8-19. Jas. 2.21-24. Called the friend of God, 2 Chr. 20.7. Isa. 41.8. Jas. 2.23.

Reverenced by the Jews, Mat. 3.9. Luk. 13.16,28. Luk. 19.9. Jno. 8.33-40, 52-59.

The covenant with him and his posterity, and prophecies concerning them, Gen. 12.1-3 Gen. 13.14-17. Gen. 15. Gen. 17. Gen. 21.12.

ABSALOM, son of David, and Maacah, the daughter of king of Geshur, 2 Sam. 3.3. 1 Chr. 3.2. His personal appearance, 2 Sam. 14.25, 26. Murders his brother Amnon, is banished to Geshur, 2 Sam. 13.2. 2 Sam. 15.8. Returns to Jerusalem, burns Joab's barley, 2 Sam. 14. 21-32.

Restored to David's favour, 2 Sam. 14.33. Rebellion of, 2 Sam. c. 15-17. 2 Sam. 20.6. 1 Kin. 2.7. Psa. 3 (title). Slain by Joab, 2 Sam. 18.9-18. Lament for, by David, 2 Sam. 18.33. 2 Sam. 19.4. Children of, 2 Sam. 14.27. 1 Kin. 15.2. 2 Chr. 11.20. His son dead, 2 Sam. 18.18.

ABSALOM'S PILLAR, in the King's Dale, 2 Sam. 18.18.

ACCESS TO GOD. See GOD, Favour of.

ACCHO, or PTOLEMAIS (now Acre), a town of Phenicia given to Asher. Canaanites remained in, Jud. 1.31. Church at, visited by Paul, Act. 21.7.

ACCURSED. See ANATHEMA.

ACELDAMA (the Field of Blood), or POTTERS' FIELD. Bought for a stranger's burying-ground with the thirty pieces of silver given back by Judas, Mat. 27.8. Act. 1.19.

ACHAIA, a region of Greece. Churches in, visited by Paul, Act. 18. Act. 19.21. Rom. 16.5. 1 Cor. 16.15. Contribute to the saints at Jerusalem, Rom. 15.26. Towns of, see CENCHREA, CORINTH.

ACHAICUS, a Corinthian Christian. Visits Paul at Rome, 1 Cor. 16.17,18.

ACHAN, or ACHAR. Hides a wedge of gold, &c.; stoned to death in the valley of Achor, Jos. 7. Jos. 22.20. 1 Chr. 2.7.

ACHISH, king of the Philistines, called Abimelech, Psa. 34 (title). Receives David when fleeing from Saul; gives him Ziklag, 1 Sam. 21.10-15. 1 Sam. 27.2-12. 1 Sam. 28.1, 2. 1 Sam. 29.

ACHMETHA (Ecbatana), a city of Persia. Cyrus' decree found in, Ezr. 6.2.

ACHOR (trouble), a valley in Palestine, where Achan was stoned, Jos. 7.26. Jos. 15.7. Isa. 65.10. Hos. 2.15.

ACHSA, Caleb's daughter. Married to Othniel on his taking Kirjath-Sepher; obtains a field from her father, Jos. 15.16-19. Jud. 1.9-13. 1 Chr. 2.49.

ACHZIB, a town of Asher, Jos. 19.29. Jud. 1.31. Mic. 1.14.

ACRE. 1 Sam. 14.14. Isa. 5.10. The Hebrew measure signifies what a yoke of oxen can plough in a day. (Two horses can plough from a half to a whole acre daily).

ADAM. Created in the image of God on the sixth day, Gen. 1.26-28. Gen. 2.7. Gen. 5.1,2. 1 Cor. 15.45. 1 Tim. 2.13. Placed in Eden to dress it; tree of knowledge forbidden to be eaten of, Gen. 2.8-17. His food, Gen. 1.29. Gen. 2.16. His dominion, Gen. 1.26,28.

Names animals, &c., Gen. 2.19,20. Eve brought to him, Gen. 2.21-25. 1 Tim. 2.13. His innocence, Gen. 2.25. Blessed by God, Gen. 1.28. Temptation, fall, and expulsion from Eden, Gen. 3. Job. 31.33. Hos. 6.7 (marg.). Rom. 5.14-21. 1 Tim. 2.14.

Condemned to labour, the ground cursed for his sin, Gen. 3.17-19. Coats of skins pro-

vided for, Gen. 3.21. Birth of Cain, Abel, and Seth, Gen. 4.1,2,25. Descendants of, see GENEALOGIES. His age and death, Gen. 5.5. Father of the human race, Gen. 1.28. Deu. 32.8. Mal. 2.10. 1 Cor. 15.22,45. Sin and death introduced by. See FALL OF MAN.

ADAM. The second Adam, an appellation of Christ, 1 Cor. 15.45,47. See Rom. 5.14.

———, a city east of Jordan, opposite Zaretan, Jos. 3.16.

ADAMANT. Eze. 3.9. Zec. 7.12. Translated diamond, Jer. 17.1.

ADAR, the 12th month (March), Est. 3.7. Second temple finished in, Ezr. 6.15. Feast of Purim in, Est. 9.1-26.

ADDER, a poisonous serpent, Gen. 49.17. Psa. 91.13. Psa. 140.3. Pro. 23.32. Deafness of, Psa. 58.4.

ADINO. See JASHOBEAM.

ADMAH, a city in the vale of Siddim, Gen. 10.19. Invaded by Chedorlaomer, Gen. 14.2. Destroyed with Sodom, Deu. 29.23. Hos. 11.8.

ADONIBEZEK, a Canaanitish king; defeated and slain by Judah and Simeon, Jud. 1.4-7.

ADONIJAH, son of David and Haggith, 2 Sam. 3.4. 1 Chr. 3.2. Indulged by David, 1 Kin. 1.6. Made king by Joab and Abiathar, 1 Kin. 1.5-33. Seeks Abishag in marriage; is put to death by Solomon, 1 Kin. 2.13-25.

ADONIRAM, or ADORAM, collector of tribute under David and Solomon, 2 Sam. 20. 24. 1 Kin. 4.6. 1 Kin. 5.14. Stoned by Israel when collecting tribute for Rehoboam, 1 Kin. 12.18.

ADONIZEDEK, king of Jerusalem; defeated and slain by Joshua, Jos. 10.1-27.

ADOPTION. Examples of. Abraham's servant, Gen. 15.3. Ephraim and Manasseh, Gen. 48.5. Moses, Ex. 2.1-10. Heb. 11.24. Hezron, 1 Chr. 2.21-24, with Num. 32.41. Jarha, 1 Chr. 2.34-41. Esther, Est. 2.7.

ADOPTION, SPIRITUAL. Ex. 4.22. Israel is my son, even my firstborn. 23. And I say unto thee, Let my son go, that he may serve me.

Deu. 8.5. As a man chasteneth his son, so the Lord thy God chasteneth thee.

Deu. 14.1. Ye are the children of the Lord your God.

Deu. 32.5. Their spot is not the spot of his children: 6. Is not he thy father that hath bought thee? hath he not made thee?

2 Sam. 7.14. I will be his father, and he shall be my son. If he commit iniquity, I will chasten him with the rod of men.

1 Chr. 28.6. I have chosen him to be my son, and I will be his father.

Pro. 14.26. His children shall have a place of refuge.

Isa. 43.6. Bring my sons from far, and my daughters from the ends of the earth; 7. Even every one that is called by my name: for I have created him for my glory, I have formed him; yea, I have made him. Psa. 45.13.

Isa. 63.16. Thou art our Father, though Abraham be ignorant of us, and Israel acknowledge us not: thou, O Lord, art our Father, our Redeemer.

Jer. 31.9. I am a father to Israel, and Ephraim is my firstborn. 20. Is Ephraim my dear son? *is he* a pleasant child? for since I spake against him, I do earnestly remember him still.

Eze. 16.8. I sware unto thee, and entered into a covenant with thee, saith the Lord God, and thou becamest mine. 21. Thou hast slain my children.

Hos. 1.10. In the place where it was said unto them, Ye *are* not my people, *there* it shall be said unto them, Ye *are* the sons of the living God.

Hos. 11.1. When Israel *was* a child, then I loved him, and called my son out of Egypt.

Mat. 5.9. Blessed *are* the peacemakers: for they shall be called the children of God. 45. That ye may be the children of your Father which is in heaven. 48. Be ye therefore perfect even as your Father which is in heaven is perfect.

Mat. 6.6. Pray to thy Father which is in secret; and thy Father, which seeth in secret, shall reward thee openly. 8. Your Father knoweth what things ye have need of, before ye ask him. 9. After this manner therefore pray ye: Our Father which art in heaven, Hallowed be thy name. *v.* 1,4,14,15,18,26, 32. Mat. 5.16. Mat. 18.14. Mar. 11.25,26.

Mat. 7.11. If ye then, being evil, know how to give good gifts unto your children, how much more shall your Father which is in heaven give good things to them that ask him?

Mat. 10.20. It is not ye that speak, but the Spirit of your Father which speaketh in you.

Mat. 13.43. Then shall the righteous shine forth as the sun in the kingdom of their Father.

Mat. 23.9. Call no *man* your father upon the earth: for one is your Father, which is in heaven.

Luk. 6.35. Ye shall be the children of the Highest: for he is kind unto the unthankful and to the evil. 36. Be ye therefore merciful, as your Father also is merciful.

Luk. 12.32. Fear not, little flock; for it is your Father's good pleasure to give you the kingdom. *v.* 30.

Jno. 1.12. As many as received him, to them gave he power to become the sons of God, *even* to them that believe on his name: 13. Which were born, not of blood, nor of the will of the flesh, nor of the will of man, but of God.

Jno. 8.42. Jesus said unto them, If God were your Father, ye would love me.

Jno. 11.52. He should gather together in one the children of God that were scattered abroad.

Jno. 20.17. Go to my brethren, and say unto them, I ascend unto my Father, and your Father; and *to* my God, and your God.

Rom. 1.7. Beloved of God, called *to be* saints: Grace to you, and peace, from God our Father.

Rom. 8.14. As many as are led by the Spirit of God, they are the sons of God. 15. Ye have received the Spirit of adoption, whereby we cry, Abba, Father. 16. The Spirit itself beareth witness with our spirit, that we are the children of God. 17. And if children, then heirs; heirs of God, and jointheirs with Christ.

Rom. 8.19. The earnest expectation of the creature waiteth for the manifestation of the sons of God. 21. The creature itself also shall be delivered from the bondage of corruption into the glorious liberty of the children of God. 29. He also did predestinate to be conformed to the image of his Son, that he might be the firstborn among many brethren.

Rom. 9.8. They which are the children of the flesh, these *are* not the children of God: but the children of the promise are counted for the seed.

2 Cor. 6.17. Be ye separate, saith the Lord, and touch not the unclean *thing*; and I will receive you, 18. And will be a Father unto you, and ye shall be my sons and daughters, saith the Lord Almighty.

Gal. 3.26. Ye are all the children of God by faith in Christ Jesus. 29. If ye *be* Christ's, then are ye Abraham's seed, and heirs according to the promise.

Gal. 4.5. To redeem them that were under the law, that we might receive the adoption of sons. 6. Because ye are sons, God hath sent forth the Spirit of his son into your hearts, crying, Abba, Father. 7. Wherefore thou art no more a servant, but a son; and if a son, then an heir of God through Christ.

Eph. 1.5. Having predestinated us unto the adoption of children by Jesus Christ to himself, according to the good pleasure of his will.

Eph. 2.19. Fellow-citizens with the saints, and of the household of God.

Eph. 3.6. That the Gentiles should be fellow-heirs, and of the same body, and partakers of his promise in Christ by the gospel. 15. Of whom the whole family in heaven and earth is named.

Eph. 4.6. One God and Father of all, who *is* above all, and through all, and in you all.

Eph. 5.1. Be ye therefore followers of God, as dear children.

Phi. 2.15. Be blameless and harmless, the sons of God, without rebuke, in the midst of a crooked and perverse nation.

Heb. 2.10. It became him, for whom *are* all things, and by whom *are* all things, in bringing many sons unto glory, to make the Captain of their salvation perfect through sufferings.

Heb. 2.11. For both he that sanctifieth and they who are sanctified *are* all of one: for which cause he is not ashamed to call them brethren. 13. Behold I and the children which God hath given me.

Heb. 12.6. Whom the Lord loveth he chasteneth, and scourgeth every son whom he receiveth. 7. If ye endure chastening, God dealeth with you as with sons; 9. Shall we not much rather be in subjection unto the Father of spirits, and live?

1 Jno. 3.1. Behold what manner of love the Father hath bestowed upon us, that we should be called the sons of God! 2. Beloved, now are we the sons of God. 10. In this the children of God are manifest, and the children of the devil: whosoever doeth not righteousness is not of God, neither he that loveth not his brother.

1 Jno. 4.4. Ye are of God, little children, and have overcome them; because greater is he that is in you, than he that is in the world.

Rev. 21.7. He that overcometh shall inherit all things; and I will be his God, and he shall be my son.

See REGENERATION—GOD'S LOVE TO HIS PEOPLE—LIKENESS TO GOD.

ADRAMMELECH, an Assyrian idol introduced into Samaria, 2 Kin. 17.31.

————, son of Sennacherib, murders him, 2 Kin. 19.37. Isa. 37.38.

ADRAMYTTIUM, a seaport of Mysia, Act. 27.2.

ADRIA, the Adriatic Sea, Act. 27.27.

ADRIEL, marries Merab, Saul's daughter, 1 Sam. 18.19. His sons slain, 2 Sam. 21.8 (*marg.*).

ADULLAM, a cave in the mountains near the Dead Sea, David hides in, 1 Sam. 22.1. 2 Sam. 23.13. 1 Chr. 11.15. Psa. 57 (title). Psa. 142 (title).

————, a Canaanitish town, afterwards belonging to Judah, Gen. 38.1. Jos. 12.15. Jos. 15.35. Mic. 1.15. Fortified by Rehoboam, 2 Chr. 11.7. Inhabited after the captivity, Neh. 11.30.

ADULTERY, FORNICATION, UNCLEANNESS. Gen. 20.3. Behold, thou *art but* a dead man, for the woman which thou hast taken ; for she *is* a man's wife.

Ex. 20.14. Thou shalt not commit adultery. Deu. 5.18. Mat. 5.27. Luk. 18.20. Jas. 2.1.

Lev. 19.29. Do not prostitute thy daughter, to cause her to be a whore ; lest the land fall to whoredom, and the land become full of wickedness. Deu. 23.17.

2 Sam. 12.14. By this deed thou hast given great occasion to the enemies of the Lord to blaspheme.

Job 31.9. If mine heart have been deceived by a woman, or *if* I have laid wait at my neighbour's door ; 10. *Then* let my wife grind unto another, and let others bow down upon her. 11. For this *is* an heinous crime ; yea, it *is* an iniquity *to be punished by* the judges. 12. For it *is* a fire *that* consumeth to destruction, and would root out all mine increase. *v.* 1.

Pro. 2.18. Her house inclineth unto death, and her paths unto the dead. 19. None that go unto her return again, neither take they hold of the paths of life. *v.* 16-19.

Pro. 5.3. The lips of a strange woman drop *as* an honeycomb, and her mouth *is* smoother than oil : 4. But her end is bitter as wormwood, sharp as a two-edged sword. *v.* 5-22.

Pro. 6.27. Can a man take fire in his bosom, and his clothes not be burned ? 28. Can one go upon hot coals, and his feet not be burned ? 29. So he that goeth in to his neighbour's wife; whosoever toucheth her shall not be innocent.

Pro. 6.32. *But* whoso committeth adultery with a woman lacketh understanding : he *that* doeth it destroyeth his own soul. 33. A wound and dishonour shall he get ; and his reproach shall not be wiped away. *v.* 24-26. Pro. 7.5-23.

Pro. 9.18. The dead *are* there ; *and that* her guests *are* in the depths of hell. *v.* 13-17. Job 24.15.

Pro. 22 14. The mouth of strange women *is* a deep pit : he that is abhorred of the Lord shall fall therein. Pro. 23.27,28. Pro. 30.20.

Pro. 29.3. He that keepeth company with harlots spendeth *his* substance. Pro. 31.3.

Ecc. 7.26. I find more bitter than death the woman whose heart *is* snares and nets, *and* her hands *as* bands : whoso pleaseth God shall

escape from her ; but the sinner shall be taken by her. *v.* 27,28.

Jer. 3.1. If a man put away his wife, and she go from him, and become another man's, shall he return unto her again ? shall not that land be greatly polluted ?

Jer. 5.9. Shall I not visit for these *things ?* saith the Lord : and shall not my soul be avenged on such a nation as this ? *v.* 7,8.

Jer. 7.9. Will ye commit adultery ; 10. And come and stand before me in this house, which is called by my name, and say, We are delivered to do all these abominations ?

Jer. 29.23. They have committed villany in Israel, and have committed adultery with their neighbours' wives ; even I know, and *am* a witness, saith the Lord. Eze. 22.9-11. Eze. 33.26. Amo. 2.7.

Hos. 4.1. The Lord hath a controversy with the inhabitants of the land. 2. By committing adultery, they break out, and blood toucheth blood. 11. Whoredom, and wine, and new wine, take away the heart.

Mat. 5.28. Whosoever looketh on a woman to lust after.her hath committed adultery with her already in his heart. 32. Whosoever shall put away his wife, saving for the cause of fornication, causeth her to commit adultery : and whosoever shall marry her that is divorced committeth adultery. Luk. 16.18.

Mat. 15.19. Out of the heart proceed evil thoughts, adulteries, fornications.

Act. 15.20. That they abstain from fornication.

Rom. 1.24. God also gave them up to uncleanness through the lusts of their own hearts, to dishonour their own bodies between themselves. *v.* 25-29.

Rom. 7.3. If, while *her* husband liveth, she be married to another man, she shall be called an adulteress.

Rom. 13.13. Let us walk honestly, as in the day ; not in rioting and drunkenness, not in chambering and wantonness.

1 Cor. 3.17. If any man defile the temple of God, him shall God destroy ; for the temple of God is holy, which *temple* ye are.

1 Cor. 5.1. It is reported commonly *that there is* fornication among you, and such fornication as is not so much as named among the Gentiles, that one should have his father's wife.

1 Cor. 5.3. For I, verily, have judged already, *concerning* him that hath so done this deed, 5. To deliver such an one unto Satan for the destruction of the flesh, that the spirit may be saved in the day of the Lord Jesus.

1 Cor. 5.11. I have written unto you not to keep company, if any man that is called a brother be a fornicator, with such an one no not to eat. *v.* 9,10.

1 Cor. 6.9. Be not deceived : neither fornicators, nor adulterers, nor effeminate, nor abusers of themselves with mankind, 10. Shall inherit the kingdom of God. 13. The body *is* not for fornication, but for the Lord, and the Lord for the body.

1 Cor. 6.15. Know ye not that your bodies are the members of Christ ? shall I then take the members of Christ, and make *them* the members of an harlot ? God forbid. 18. Flee fornication. Every sin that a man doeth is without the body ; but he that committeth fornication sinneth against his own body.

1 Cor. 10.8. Neither let us commit fornication, as some of them committed, and fell in one day three and twenty thousand.

2 Cor. 12.21. I shall bewail many which have sinned already, and have not repented of the uncleanness and fornication and lasciviousness which they have committed.

Gal. 5.19. The works of the flesh are manifest, which are *these*; Adultery, fornication, uncleanness, lasciviousness, 21. Of the which I tell you before, as I have also told *you* in time past, that they which do such things shall not inherit the kingdom of God.

Eph. 4.17. Walk not as other Gentiles walk, in the vanity of their mind; 19. Who, being past feeling, have given themselves over unto lasciviousness, to work all uncleanness with greediness. 20. But ye have not so learned Christ.

Eph. 5.3. But fornication, and all uncleanness, let it not be once named among you, as becometh saints; 4. Neither filthiness, nor foolish talking, nor jesting, which are not convenient; 5. Ye know, that no whoremonger, nor unclean person, hath any inheritance in the kingdom of Christ and of God. 6. Let no man deceive you with vain words: for because of these things cometh the wrath of God upon the children of disobedience. 7. Be not ye therefore partakers with them.

Eph. 5.11. Have no fellowship with the unfruitful works of darkness, but rather reprove *them*. 12. For it is a shame even to speak of those things which are done of them in secret.

Col. 3.5. Mortify therefore your members which are upon the earth; fornication, uncleanness, inordinate affection, evil concupiscence: 8. Put off all these; filthy communication out of your mouth. *v.* 6.

1 The. 4.3. This is the will of God, *even* your sanctification, that ye should abstain from fornication: 4. That every one of you should know how to possess his vessel in sanctification and honour; 5. Not in the lust of concupiscence, even as the Gentiles which know not God: 7. For God hath not called us unto uncleanness, but unto holiness.

Heb. 12.16. Lest there *be* any fornicator, or profane person.

Heb. 13.4. Whoremongers, and adulterers, God will judge.

1 Pet. 4.3. The time past of *our* life may suffice us to have wrought the will of the Gentiles, when we walked in lasciviousness, lusts: 4. Wherein they think it strange that ye run not with *them* to the same excess of riot, speaking evil of *you*.

2 Pet. 2.10. Chiefly them that walk after the flesh in the lust of uncleanness. 14. Having eyes full of adultery, and that cannot cease from sin; beguiling unstable souls.

Jude, 7. Even as Sodom and Gomorrah, and the cities about them, in like manner, giving themselves over to fornication, and going after strange flesh, are set forth for an example, suffering the vengeance of eternal fire.

Jude 8. Likewise also these *filthy* dreamers defile the flesh. 10. What they know naturally, as brute beasts, in those things they corrupt themselves.

Rev. 2.14. Balaam, who taught Balac to cast a stumbling-block before the children of Israel, to commit fornication.

Rev. 2.20. Thou sufferest that woman Jezebel, to teach and to seduce my servants to commit fornication. 21. And I gave her space to repent of her fornication; and she repented not. 22. Behold, I will cast her into a bed, and them that commit adultery with her into great tribulation, except they repent of their deeds.

Rev. 9.21. Neither repented they of their fornication.

Rev. 21.8. The abominable, and whoremongers, shall have their part in the lake which burneth with fire and brimstone; which is the second death.

Rev. 22.15. For without *are* dogs, and whoremongers.

ADULTERY, EXAMPLES OF. Sodomites, Gen. 19.5-8. Lot. Gen. 19.31-38. Shechem, Gen. 34.2. Reuben, Gen. 35.22. Judah, Gen. 38.1-24. Potiphar's wife, Gen. 39.7-12. Samson, Jud. 16.1. Eli's sons, 1 Sam. 2.22. David, 2 Sam. 11.1-5. Amnon, 2 Sam. 13.1-20. Absalom, 2 Sam. 16.22. Israelites, Jer. 5.7-9. Jer. 29.23. Eze. 22.9-11. Eze. 33.26. Herod, Mar. 6.17,18. Samaritan woman, Jno. 4.18. A woman, Jno. 8.3-11. Corinthians, 1 Cor. 5.1. Gentiles, Eph. 4.17-19. 1 Pet. 4.3.

————, Jewish Law and Punishment. Ex. 22.16. Lev. 18.20-23. Lev. 19.20-22. Lev. 20.10-21. Lev. 21.9. Num. 5.12-31. Deu. 22. 20-30. Deu. 27.20-23. Jno. 8.5.

ADVENT, SECOND. See CHRIST'S SECOND COMING.

ADVERSITY. See AFFLICTION—POOR.

ADVOCATE. Christ is our advocate, 1 Jno. 2.1. See CHRIST, HIGH-PRIEST.

AFFLICTION, ITS BENEFITS AND DESIGN. Gen. 22.12 Now I know that thou fearest God, seeing thou hast not withheld thy son, thine only *son*, from me. *v.* 1-14.

Deu. 8.2. Remember all the way which the Lord thy God led thee these forty years in the wilderness, to humble thee, *and* to prove thee, to know what *was* in thine heart, whether thou wouldest keep his commandments, or no.

Deu. 8.3. And he humbled thee, and suffered thee to hunger, and fed thee with manna, which thou knewest not, neither did thy fathers know; that he might make thee know that man doth not live by bread only, but by every *word* that proceedeth out of the mouth of the Lord doth man live.

Deu. 8.5. Consider in thine heart, that, as a man chasteneth his son, *so* the Lord thy God chasteneth thee. 16. That he might humble thee, and that he might prove thee, to do thee good at thy latter end.

Deu. 31.17. I will forsake them, and I will hide my face from them, and they shall be devoured, and many evils and troubles shall befall them; so that they will say in that day, Are not these evils come upon us, because our God *is* not among us?

Jud. 2.21. I also will not henceforth drive out any from before them of the nations which Joshua left when he died. 22. That through them I may prove Israel, whether they will keep the way of the Lord to walk therein, as their fathers did keep *it*, or not.

2 Sam. 7.14. If he commit iniquity, I will chasten him with the rod of men, and with the stripes of the children of men.

1 Kin. 8.33. When thy people Israel be smitten down before the enemy, because they have sinned against thee, and shall turn again to thee, and confess thy name, and pray. 47. If they shall bethink themselves in the land whither they were carried captives, and repent, and make supplication unto thee in the land of them that carried them captives, saying, We have sinned, and have done perversely, we have committed wickedness ; 48. And *so* return unto thee with all their heart, and with all their soul, in the land of their enemies, which led them away captive, and pray unto thee toward their land, which thou gavest unto their fathers. *v.* 35. Deu. 4.30,31. Deu. 30.1,2.

Job 5.17. Happy *is* the man whom God correcteth.

Job 23.10. *When* he hath tried me, I shall come forth as gold.

Job 33.17. That he may withdraw man *from his* purpose, and hide pride from man. 19. He is chastened also with pain upon his bed, and the multitude of his bones with strong *pain.*

Job 36.8. If *they* be bound in fetters, *and* be holden in cords of affliction ; 9. Then he sheweth them their work, and their transgressions that they have exceeded. 10. He openeth also their ear to discipline, and commandeth that they return from iniquity.

Psa. 50.15. Call upon me in the day of trouble : I will deliver thee, and thou shalt glorify me.

Psa. 89.30. If his children forsake my law, and walk not in my judgments ; 32. Then will I visit their transgression with the rod, and their iniquity with stripes.

Psa. 94.12. Blessed *is* the man whom thou chastenest, O Lord, and teachest him out of thy law ; 13. That thou mayest give him rest from the days of adversity, until the pit be digged for the wicked.

Psa. 126.5. They that sow in tears shall reap in joy. 6. He that goeth forth and weepeth, bearing precious seed, shall doubtless come again with rejoicing, bringing his sheaves *with him.*

Pro. 3.11. My son, despise not the chastening of the Lord ; neither be weary of his correction : 12. For whom the Lord loveth he correcteth ; even as a father the son *in whom* he delighteth.

Pro. 20.30. The blueness of a wound cleanseth away evil : so *do* stripes the inward parts of the belly.

Ecc. 7.2. *It is* better to go to the house of mourning, than to go to the house of feasting : for that *is* the end of all men ; and the living will lay *it* to his heart. 3. Sorrow *is* better than laughter : for by the sadness of the countenance the heart is made better. 4. The heart of the wise *is* in the house of mourning.

Isa. 1.25. I will turn my hand upon thee, and purely purge away thy dross, and take away all thy tin : 26. Afterward thou shalt be called, The city of righteousness, The faithful city. 27. Zion shall be redeemed with judgment, and her converts with righteousness.

Isa. 4.4. The Lord shall have washed away the filth of the daughters of Zion, by the spirit of judgment, and by the spirit of burning.

Isa. 10.20. The remnant of Israel, and such as are escaped of the house of Jacob, shall no more again stay upon him that smote them ; but shall stay upon the Lord.

Isa. 19.20. It shall be for a sign and for a witness unto the Lord of hosts in the land of Egypt : for they shall cry unto the Lord because of the oppressors. 22. The Lord shall smite Egypt : he shall smite and heal *it :* and they shall return *even* to the Lord, and he shall be entreated of them.

Isa. 26.9. When thy judgments *are* in the earth, the inhabitants of the world will learn righteousness.

Isa. 27.9. By this therefore shall the iniquity of Jacob be purged ; and this *is* all the fruit to take away his sin.

Isa. 48.10. I have refined thee, but not with silver ; I have chosen thee in the furnace of affliction.

Isa. 52.6. My people shall know my name : therefore *they shall know* in that day that I *am* he that doth speak : behold *it is* I. *v.* 4,5.

Jer. 2.27. They have turned *their* back unto me, and not *their* face : but in the time of their trouble they will say, Arise, and save us.

Jer. 9.7. Behold, I will melt them, and try them ; for how shall I do for the daughter of my people ?

Jer. 22.22. The wind shall eat up all thy pastors, and thy lovers shall go into captivity : surely then shalt thou be ashamed and confounded for all thy wickedness. 23. How gracious shalt thou be when pangs come upon thee, the pain as of a woman in travail !

Lam. 3.27. *It is* good for a man that he bear the yoke in his youth. 28. He sitteth alone and keepeth silence, because he hath borne *it* upon him. *v.* 29-33.

Eze. 14.10. They shall bear the punishment of their iniquity : 11. That the house of Israel may go no more astray from me, neither be polluted any more with all their transgressions ; but that they may be my people, and I may be their God.

Eze. 20.37. I will cause you to pass under the rod, and I will bring you into the bond of the covenant : 43. There shall ye remember your ways, and all your doings, wherein ye have been defiled ; and ye shall loathe yourselves in your own sight for all your evils that ye have committed. Eze. 6.9.

Dan. 12.10. Many shall be purified, and made white, and tried. Dan. 11.35.

Hos. 2.6. Behold, I will hedge up thy way with thorns, and make a wall, that she shall not find her paths. 7. Then shall she say, I will go and return to my first husband ; for then *was it* better with me than now.

Hos. 5.15. I will go *and* return to my place, till they acknowledge their offence, and seek my face : in their affliction they will seek me early.

Mic. 6.9. The Lord's voice crieth unto the city: hear ye the rod, and who hath appointed it.

Zec. 13.9. I will bring the third part through the fire, and will refine them as silver is refined, and will try them as gold is tried.

Mal. 2.3. *One* shall take you away with it. 4. And ye shall know that I have sent this commandment unto you, that my covenant might be with Levi.

Mal. 3.3. He shall purify the sons of Levi, and purge them as gold and silver, that they may offer unto the Lord an offering in righteousness.

Mar. 9.49. Every one shall be salted with fire, and every sacrifice shall be salted with salt.

Jno. 9.2. Master, who did sin, this man, or his parents, that he was born blind? 3. Jesus answered, Neither hath this man sinned, nor his parents : but that the works of God should be made manifest in him.

Jno. 11.4. This sickness is not unto death, but for the glory of God, that the Son of God might be glorified thereby.

Jno. 15.2. Every branch that beareth fruit, he purgeth it, that it may bring forth more fruit.

Jno. 21.19. This spake he, signifying by what death he should glorify God.

Act. 14.22. We must through much tribulation enter into the kingdom of God.

Rom. 5.3. Tribulation worketh patience ; 4. And patience, experience ; and experience, hope.

Rom. 8.17. If so be that we suffer with him, that we may be also glorified together. 28. All things work together for good to them that love God.

1 Cor. 11.32. We are chastened of the Lord, that we should not be condemned with the world.

2 Cor. 1.6. Whether we be afflicted, it is for your consolation and salvation, which is effectual in the enduring of the same sufferings which we also suffer.

2 Cor. 4.8. We are troubled on every side, yet not distressed ; we are perplexed, but not in despair ; 9. Persecuted, but not forsaken ; cast down, but not destroyed ; 10. Always bearing about in the body the dying of the Lord Jesus, that the life also of Jesus might be made manifest in our body. 11. For we which live are alway delivered unto death for Jesus' sake, that the life also of Jesus might be made manifest in our mortal flesh. 12. So then death worketh in us. 16. Though our outward man perish, yet the inward man is renewed day by day. 17. Our light affliction, which is but for a moment, worketh for us a far more exceeding and eternal weight of glory.

2 Cor. 12.7. There was given to me a thorn in the flesh, the messenger of Satan to buffet me, lest I should be exalted above measure.

Phi. 1.12. The things which happened unto me have fallen out rather unto the furtherance of the gospel ; 13. So that my bonds in Christ are manifest in all the palace, and in all other places ; 14. And many of the brethren in the Lord, waxing confident by my bonds, are much more bold to speak the word without fear. 19. I know that this shall turn to my salvation through your prayer, and the supply of the Spirit of Jesus Christ.

2 The. 1.5. That ye may be counted worthy of the kingdom of God, for which ye also suffer.

Heb. 12.6. Whom the Lord loveth he chasteneth, and scourgeth every son whom he receiveth. 7. If ye endure chastening, God dealeth with you as with sons ; for what son is he whom the father chasteneth not ?

Heb. 12.9. We have had fathers of our flesh which corrected us, and we gave them rever-

ence : shall we not much rather be in subjection unto the Father of spirits, and live? 10. But he for our profit, that we might be partakers of his holiness.

Heb. 12.11. Now no chastening for the present seemeth to be joyous, but grievous : nevertheless afterward it yieldeth the peaceable fruit of righteousness unto them which are exercised thereby.

Jas. 1.2. Count it all joy when ye fall into divers temptations ; 3. Knowing this, that the trying of your faith worketh patience. 4. But let patience have her perfect work, that ye may be perfect and entire, wanting nothing. 12. Blessed is the man that endureth temptation : for when he is tried, he shall receive the crown of life.

1 Pet. 1.7. That the trial of your faith, being much more precious than of gold that perisheth, though it be tried with fire, might be found unto praise and honour and glory at the appearing of Jesus Christ.

1 Pet. 4.14. If ye be reproached for the name of Christ, happy are ye ; for the Spirit of glory and of God resteth upon you : on their part he is evil spoken of, but on your part he is glorified.

Rev. 2.10. The devil shall cast some of you into prison, that ye may be tried ; and ye shall have tribulation ten days : be thou faithful unto death, and I will give thee a crown of life.

Rev. 3.19. As many as I love, I rebuke and chasten.

AFFLICTION, ITS BENEFITS EXEMPLIFIED. Gen. 42.21. We are verily guilty concerning our brother, in that we saw the anguish of his soul, when he besought us, and we would not hear ; therefore is this distress come upon us.

Ex. 9.27. Pharaoh sent, and called for Moses and Aaron, and said unto them, I have sinned this time : the Lord is righteous, and I and my people are wicked. 28. Entreat the Lord (for it is enough) that there be no more mighty thunderings and hail ; and I will let you go, and ye shall stay no longer. Ex. 10.7,16,17. Ex. 12.31-33.

Num. 21.7. The people came to Moses, and said, We have sinned, for we have spoken against the Lord, and against thee ; pray unto the Lord, that he take away the serpents from us.

Jud. 10.15. We have sinned : do thou unto us whatsoever seemeth good unto thee ; deliver us only, we pray thee, this day.

1 Kin. 13.6. Entreat now the face of the Lord thy God, and pray for me, that my hand may be restored me again.

1 Kin. 17.18. Art thou come unto me to call my sin to remembrance, and to slay my son ?

2 Chr. 15.4. When they in their trouble did turn unto the Lord God of Israel, and sought him, he was found of them.

2 Chr. 33.12. When he was in affliction, he besought the Lord his God, and humbled himself greatly before the God of his fathers, 13. And prayed unto him : and he was entreated of him, and heard his supplication, and brought him again to Jerusalem into his kingdom. Then Manasseh knew that the Lord he was God.

Ezr. 9.13. After all that is come upon us for our evil deeds, and for our great trespass, seeing that thou our God has punished us less than our iniquities deserve.

Neh. 9.33. Thou *art* just in all that is brought upon us ; for thou hast done right, but we have done wickedly.

Job 40.4. Behold, I am vile ; what shall I answer thee ? I will lay mine hand upon my mouth. 5. Once have I spoken, but I will not answer ; yea, twice, but I will proceed no further.

Psa. 66.10. Thou, O God, hast proved us : thou hast tried us, as silver is tried. 11. Thou broughtest us into the net ; thou laidst affliction upon our loins. 12. Thou hast caused men to ride over our heads ; we went through fire and through water : but thou broughtest us out into a wealthy *place*.

Psa. 78.34. When he slew them, then they sought him : and they returned and inquired early after God. 35. And they remembered that God *was* their rock, and the high God their redeemer.

Psa. 105.18. Whose feet they hurt with fetters : he was laid in iron : 19. Until the time that his word came : the word of the Lord tried him.

Psa. 119.67. Before I was afflicted I went astray : but now have I kept thy word. 71. *It is* good for me that I have been afflicted ; that I might learn thy statutes.

Isa. 26.16. Lord, in trouble have they visited thee, they poured out a prayer *when* thy chastening *was* upon them.

Jer. 31.18. I have surely heard Ephraim bemoaning himself *thus* : Thou hast chastised me, and I was chastised, as a bullock unaccustomed *to the yoke :* turn thou me, and I shall be turned ; for thou *art* the Lord my God.

Jer. 31.19. Surely after that I was turned, I repented ; and after that I was instructed, I smote upon *my* thigh : I was ashamed, yea, even confounded, because I did bear the reproach of my youth.

Lam. 3.19. Remembering mine affliction and my misery, the wormwood and the gall. 20. My soul hath *them* still in remembrance, and is humbled in me.

Hos. 6.1. Come, and let us return unto the Lord ; for he hath torn, and he will heal us ; he hath smitten, and he will bind us up.

Luk. 15.17. When he came to himself, he said, How many hired servants of my father's have bread enough, and to spare, and I perish with hunger ! 18. I will arise and go to my father, and will say unto him, Father, I have sinned against heaven, and before thee.

Act. 8.24. Pray ye to the Lord for me, that none of these things which ye have spoken come upon me.

See JUDGMENTS, DESIGN OF—RESIGNATION.

AFFLICTION, COMFORT IN.   Gen. 21.17. Fear not ; for God hath heard the voice of the lad.

Ex. 3.7. I know their sorrows.   *v.* 16.

Deu. 33.27. The eternal God is *thy* refuge, and underneath *are* the everlasting arms.

Job 5.18. He maketh sore, and bindeth up : he woundeth, and his hands make whole.

Job 11.16. Thou shalt forget *thy* misery, *and* remember it as waters *that* pass away.

Job 35.10. God my maker, who giveth songs in the night.

Psa. 9.9. The Lord also will be a refuge for the oppressed, a refuge in times of trouble.

Psa. 23.4. I will fear no evil : for thou *art* with me ; thy rod and thy staff they comfort me.

Psa. 30.5. His anger *endureth but* a moment ; in his favour *is* life : weeping may endure for a night, but joy *cometh* in the morning.

Psa. 31.7. Thou hast considered my trouble ; thou hast known my soul in adversities.

Psa. 41.3. The Lord will strengthen him upon the bed of languishing : thou wilt make all his bed in his sickness.

Psa. 42.5. Hope thou in God : for I shall yet praise him *for* the help of his countenance.

Psa. 55.22. Cast thy burden upon the Lord, and he shall sustain thee : he shall never suffer the righteous to be moved.

Psa. 69.33. The Lord heareth the poor, and despiseth not his prisoners.

Psa. 94.19. In the multitude of my thoughts within me thy comforts delight my soul.

Psa. 103.13. As a father pitieth *his* children, *so* the Lord pitieth them that fear him. 14. He knoweth our frame ; He remembereth that we are dust.

Psa. 112.4. Unto the upright there ariseth light in the darkness.

Psa. 119.50. This *is* my comfort in my affliction : for thy word hath quickened me. 52. I remembered thy judgments of old, O Lord ; and have comforted myself. 54. Thy statutes have been my songs in the house of my pilgrimage. 92. Unless thy law *had been* my delights, I should then have perished in mine affliction. 143. Trouble and anguish have taken hold on me : *yet* thy commandments *are* my delights.

Psa. 147.3. He healeth the broken in heart, and bindeth up their wounds.

Isa. 25.4. Thou hast been a strength to the poor, a strength to the needy in his distress, a refuge from the storm, a shadow from the heat, when the blast of the terrible ones *is* as a storm *against* the wall.

Isa. 27.8. He stayeth his rough wind in the day of the east wind.

Isa. 30.19. Thou shalt weep no more : he will be very gracious unto thee at the voice of thy cry ; when he shall hear it, he will answer thee. 20. And *though* the Lord give you the bread of adversity, and the water of affliction, yet shall not thy teachers be removed into a corner.

Isa. 40.1. Comfort ye, comfort ye my people, saith your God. 2. Speak ye comfortably to Jerusalem, and cry unto her, that her warfare is accomplished. 29. He giveth power to the faint ; and to *them that have* no might he increaseth strength.

Isa. 41.10. I will strengthen thee ; yea, I will help thee ; yea, I will uphold thee with the right hand of my righteousness. 13. I the Lord thy God will hold thy right hand, saying unto thee, Fear not ; I will help thee. 14. Fear not, thou worm Jacob, *and* ye men of Israel ; I will help thee, saith the Lord, and thy redeemer, the Holy One of Israel.

Isa. 41.17. *When* the poor and needy seek water, and *there* is none, *and* their tongue faileth for thirst, I the Lord will hear them, *I* the God of Israel will not forsake them.

Isa. 42.3. A bruised reed shall he not break, and the smoking flax shall he not quench.

Isa. 43.2. When thou passest through the waters, I *will be* with thee; and through the rivers, they shall not overflow thee: when thou walkest through the fire, thou shalt not be burned; neither shall the flame kindle upon thee.

Isa. 49.13. The Lord hath comforted his people, and will have mercy upon his afflicted.

Isa. 50.4. That I should know how to speak a word in season to *him that is* weary. 10. Who *is* among you that walketh *in* darkness, and hath no light? let him trust in the name of the Lord, and stay upon his God.

Isa. 51.3. The Lord shall comfort Zion: he will comfort all her waste places; and he will make her wilderness like Eden, joy and gladness shall be found therein, thanksgiving, and the voice of melody.

Isa. 51.12. I, *even* I, *am* he that comforteth you: who *art* thou, that thou shouldest be afraid of a man *that* shall die, and of the son of man *which* shall be made *as* grass; 13. And forgettest the Lord thy maker. *v.* 3-13.

Isa. 54.4. Fear not; for thou shalt not be ashamed: neither be thou confounded; for thou shalt not be put to shame: for thou shalt forget the shame of thy youth, and shalt not remember the reproach of thy widowhood any more.

Isa. 54.11. O thou afflicted, tossed with tempest, *and* not comforted, behold, I will lay thy stones with fair colours.

Isa. 61.1. He hath sent me to bind up the broken-hearted, to proclaim liberty to the captives. 2. To comfort all that mourn; 3. To appoint unto them that mourn in Zion, to give unto them beauty for ashes, the oil of joy for mourning, the garment of praise for the spirit of heaviness.

Isa. 66.5. He shall appear to your joy, and they shall be ashamed. 13. As one whom his mother comforteth, so will I comfort you; and ye shall be comforted in Jerusalem. 14. And when ye see this, your heart shall rejoice, and your bones shall flourish like an herb: and the hand of the Lord shall be known toward his servants.

Jer. 31.13. I will turn their mourning into joy, and will comfort them, and make them rejoice from their sorrow. 25. I have satiated the weary soul, and I have replenished every sorrowful soul.

Lam. 3.56. Thou hast heard my voice: 57. Thou drewest near in the day *that* I called upon thee: thou saidst, Fear not.

Eze. 11.16. Yet will I be to them as a little sanctuary.

Hos. 2.14. I will allure her, and bring her into the wilderness, and speak comfortably unto her.

Nah. 1.7. The Lord *is* good, a strong hold in the day of trouble; and he knoweth them that trust in him.

Zeph. 3.18. I will gather *them that are* sorrowful for the solemn assembly.

Zec. 1.17. The Lord shall yet comfort Zion.

Mat. 5.4. Blessed *are* they that mourn: for they shall be comforted. 10. Blessed *are* they which are persecuted for righteousness' sake: for their's is the kingdom of heaven.

Mat. 11.28. Come unto me, all *ye* that labour and are heavy laden, and I will give you rest.

Mat. 14.27. Be of good cheer; it is I; be not afraid.

Luk. 6.21 Blessed *are ye* that hunger now: for ye shall be filled. Blessed *are ye* that weep now: for ye shall laugh. 22. Blessed are ye, when men shall hate you. 23. Rejoice ye in that day, and leap for joy: for, behold, your reward *is* great in heaven. Mat. 5. 11, 12.

Luk. 7.13. He had compassion on her, and said unto her, Weep not.

Jno. 14.1. Let not your heart be troubled: ye believe in God, believe also in me. 16. He shall give you another Comforter, that he may abide with you for ever. 18. I will not leave you comfortless: I will come to you. 27. My peace I give unto you: not as the world giveth, give I unto you. Let not your heart be troubled, neither let it be afraid.

Jno. 15.18. If the world hate you, ye know that it hated me before *it hated* you. 20. Remember the word that I said unto you, The servant is not greater than his lord. If they have persecuted me, they will also persecute you.

Jno. 16.20. Your sorrow shall be turned into joy. 22. Ye now therefore have sorrow: but I will see you again, and your heart shall rejoice, and your joy no man taketh from you. 33. In the world ye shall have tribulation: but be of good cheer; I have overcome the world.

Act. 23.11. Be of good cheer, Paul: for as thou hast testified of me in Jerusalem, so must thou bear witness also at Rome.

Rom. 8.32. He that spared not his own Son, but delivered him up for us all, how shall he not with him also freely give us all things?

Rom. 15.4. That we, through patience and comfort of the scriptures, might have hope. *v.* 5.

2 Cor. 1.3. The Father of mercies, and the God of all comfort; 4. Who comforteth us in all our tribulation, that we may be able to comfort them which are in any trouble, by the comfort wherewith we ourselves are comforted of God. 5. As the sufferings of Christ abound in us, so our consolation also aboundeth by Christ. 7. As ye are partakers of the sufferings, so *shall ye be* also of the consolation.

2 Cor. 7.6. God, that comforteth those that are cast down, comforted us.

2 Cor. 12.9. My grace is sufficient for thee: for my strength is made perfect in weakness.

1 The. 4.13. I would not have you to be ignorant, brethren, concerning them which are asleep, that ye sorrow not, even as others which have no hope.

2 The. 1.7. To you who are troubled rest with us.

2 The. 2.16. Our Lord Jesus Christ himself, and God, even our Father, which hath loved us, and hath given *us* everlasting consolation, and good hope through grace. 17. Comfort your hearts.

2 Tim. 4.17. The Lord stood with me, and strengthened me.

Heb. 2.18. In that he himself hath suffered being tempted, he is able to succour them that are tempted.

Heb. 4.15. Not an high-priest which cannot be touched with the feeling of our infirmities; but was in all points tempted like as *we are*.

Heb. 6.18. Strong consolation, who have fled for refuge to lay hold upon the hope set before us.

Heb. 13.5. I will never leave thee, nor forsake thee.

Jas. 5.8. Be ye also patient; stablish your hearts: for the coming of the Lord draweth nigh.

1 Pet. 3.17. Better, if the will of God be so, that ye suffer for well doing, than for evil doing.

1 Pet. 4.12. Think it not strange concerning the fiery trial which is to try you, as though some strange thing happened unto you: 13. But rejoice, inasmuch as ye are partakers of Christ's sufferings; that, when his glory shall be revealed, ye may be glad also with exceeding joy. 14. If ye be reproached for the name of Christ, happy *are ye.*

Rev. 2.9. I know thy tribulation, and poverty, (but thou art rich.) 10. Fear none of those things which thou shalt suffer: behold, the devil shall cast *some* of you into prison, that ye may be tried; and ye shall have tribulation ten days: be thou faithful unto death, and I will give thee a crown of life. 13. I know thy works, and where thou dwellest, *even* where Satan's seat *is.*

See GOD PROTECTOR—POOR, GOD'S CARE OF—WIDOWS.

AFFLICTION, DESCRIPTION OF. Gen. 37.29-35. Gen. 42.36-38. Job 7.2-6. Job. 9.18. Job 16.6-14. Job 17.7-16. Job 19.7-20. Job 30.15-19. Job 33.19-22. Psa. 18.4,5. Psa. 31. 9-13. Psa. 32.3,4. Psa. 39.1-4. Psa. 42.6,7. Psa. 55.4-8. Psa. 69.1-3,20. Psa. 73.10. Psa. 77.2-4. Psa. 80.5,6. Psa. 88.3-18. Psa. 102. 3-11. Psa. 107.4,5,10,18,25-27,39. Psa. 109. 22-24. Psa. 116.3. Psa. 141.7. Psa. 143.3,4. Pro. 12.25. Pro. 13.12. Pro. 14.10. Pro. 15. 13,15. Pro. 17.22. Pro. 18.14. Isa. 1.6. Isa. 16.2. Jer. 8.21. Jer. 9.1. Jer. 22.10. Jer. 31.15. Jer. 49.23. Lam. 1.12. Lam. 3.2-10, 52-54. Eze. 21.7. Eze. 24.16. Mat. 24. 1 Cor. 4.9-13. 2 Cor. 1.8-10. 2 Cor. 2.4. 2 Cor. 4.8-11. 2 Cor. 6.4-10. 2 Cor. 11.23-30.

——— DESPONDENCY IN. See MURMURING.

——— FAITH IN. See FAITH, EXEMPLIFIED.

——— FROM GOD. Deu. 32.39. I kill, and I make alive; I wound, and I heal: neither *is there any* that can deliver out of my hand.

Ruth 1.20. The Almighty hath dealt very bitterly with me. 21. I went out full, and the Lord hath brought me home again empty: why *then* call ye me Naomi, seeing the Lord hath testified against me, and the Almighty hath afflicted me?

1 Sam. 2.6. The Lord killeth, and maketh alive: he bringeth down to the grave, and bringeth up.

2 Sam. 16.10. Let him curse, because the Lord hath said unto him, Curse David.

2 Kin. 6.33. This evil *is* of the Lord.

2 Kin. 15.5. The Lord smote the king, so that he was a leper.

Job 1.21. The Lord gave, and the Lord hath taken away.

Job 5.6. Affliction cometh not forth of the dust. 17. Happy *is* the man whom God correcteth. *v.* 18.

Job 6.4. The arrows of the Almighty *are* within me.

Job 9.12. He taketh away, who can hinder him?

Job 11.10. If he cut off, and shut up, or gather together, then who can hinder him?

Job 19.6. God hath overthrown me. *v.* 8-13.

Job 21.17. *God* distributeth sorrows in his anger.

Job 23.16. God maketh my heart soft, and the Almighty troubleth me.

Job 27.2. God liveth, *who* hath taken away my judgment.

Job 34.29. He hideth *his* face, who then can behold him?

Psa. 66.11. Thou broughtest us into the net; thou laidest affliction upon our loins.

Psa. 71.20. Thou has shewed me great and sore troubles.

Psa. 78.33. Their days did he consume in vanity.

Psa. 88.6. Thou hast laid me in the lowest pit, in darkness. *v.* 7,16. Psa. 89.38-45.

Psa. 90.7. We are consumed by thine anger.

Psa. 102.10. Thou hast lifted me up, and cast me down. 23. He weakened my strength in the way.

Psa. 107.12. He brought down their heart with labour.

Isa. 45.7. I make peace, and create evil.

Jer. 30.15. I have done these things unto thee.

Jer. 45.3. The Lord hath added grief to my sorrow.

Lam. 3.1. I *am* the man *that* hath seen affliction by the rod of his wrath.

Amos 3.6. Shall there be evil in a city, and the Lord hath not done it *?*

Jonah 2.3. All thy billows and thy waves passed over me.

Mic. 1.12. Evil came down from the Lord unto the gate.

Mic. 6.9. The Lord's voice crieth unto the city.

1 The. 3.3. Know that we are appointed thereunto.

See FAMINE—PESTILENCE—WAR—JUDGMENTS, DESIGN OF.

AFFLICTION. GOD DELIVERS FROM. See GOD PROTECTOR.

———, IMPENITENCE IN. Lev. 26.23. If ye will not be reformed by me by these things, but will walk contrary unto me; 24. Then will I also walk contrary unto you, and will punish you yet seven times for your sins. *v.* 27,28.

Job 36.13. They cry not when he bindeth them.

Psa. 78.31. The wrath of God came upon them. 32. For all this they sinned still, and believed not for his wondrous works.

Isa. 8.21. When they shall be hungry, they shall fret themselves, and curse their king and their God, and look upward.

Isa. 9.13. The people turneth not unto him that smiteth them, neither do they seek the Lord of hosts.

Isa. 22.12. Did the Lord God of hosts call to weeping, and to mourning, and to baldness, and to girding with sackcloth: 13. And behold joy and gladness, slaying oxen, and killing sheep, eating flesh, and drinking wine: let us eat and drink; for to-morrow we shall die.

Isa. 26.11. Lord, *when* thy hand is lifted up, they will not see.

Isa. 42.25. It hath set him on fire round about, yet he knew not ; and it burned him, yet he laid *it* not to heart.

Isa. 57.17. I hid me, and was wroth, and he went on frowardly in the way of his heart.

Jer. 2.30. In vain have I smitten your children ; they received no correction. 35. Thou sayest, Because I am innocent, surely his anger shall turn from me : behold, I will plead with thee, because thou sayest, I have not sinned.

Jer. 3.3. The showers have been withholden, and there hath been no latter rain ; and thou hadst a whore's forehead, thou refusedst to be ashamed.

Jer. 5.3. Thou hast stricken them, but they have not grieved ; thou hast consumed them, *but* they have refused to receive correction : they have made their faces harder than a rock ; they have refused to return.

Jer. 7.28. A nation that obeyeth not the voice of the Lord their God, nor receiveth correction.

Dan. 9.13. All this evil is come upon us : yet made we not our prayer before the Lord our God, that we might turn from our iniquities.

Hos. 7.9. Strangers have devoured his strength, and he knoweth *it* not ; yea, gray hairs are here and there upon him, yet he knoweth not. 10. They do not return to the Lord their God, nor seek him for all this. 14. They have not cried unto me with their heart, when they howled upon their beds.

Hos. 9.17. My God will cast them away, because they did not hearken unto him.

Amos 4.6. I also have given you cleanness of teeth in all your cities, and want of bread in all your places ; yet have ye not returned unto me, saith the Lord. *v.* 7-10. 11. I have overthrown *some* of you, as God overthrew Sodom and Gomorrah, and ye were as a firebrand plucked out of the burning : yet have ye not returned unto me.

Zeph. 3.2. She obeyed not the voice ; she received not correction. 7. I said, Surely thou wilt fear me, thou wilt receive instruction ; so their dwelling should not be cut off, howsoever I punished them : but they rose early, *and* corrupted all their doings.

Hag. 2.17. I smote you with blasting and with mildew and with hail in all the labours of your hands ; yet ye *turned* not to me, saith the Lord.

Rev. 9.20. The rest of the men which were not killed by these plagues yet repented not.

Rev. 16.9. Blasphemed the name of God, which hath power over these plagues : and they repented not to give him glory. 10. They gnawed their tongues for pain, 11. And blasphemed the God of heaven because of their pains and their sores, and repented not of their deeds. *v.* 21.

AFFLICTION, IMPENITENCE IN, EXAMPLES OF. Pharaoh, Ex. 8.19. Ex. 9.30-34. Ex. 14.5-9. Asa, 2 Chr. 16.12. Ahaz, 2 Chr. 28.22,23. See IMPENITENCE—MIRACLES, UNBELIEF IN.

————, PRAYER IN. Gen. 32.11. Deliver me, I pray thee, from the hand of my brother, from the hand of Esau : for I fear him.

Gen. 43.14. God Almighty give you mercy before the man.

Ex. 17.4. What shall I do unto this people ? they be almost ready to stone me.

2 Sam. 12.22. While the child was yet alive, I fasted and wept : for I said, Who can tell *whether* God will be gracious to me, that the child may live ? 1 Sam. 1.10,11.

2 Sam. 15.31. O Lord, I pray thee, turn the counsel of Ahithophel into foolishness.

2 Kin. 19.16. Lord, bow down thine ear, and hear : open, Lord, thine eyes, and see ; and hear the words of Sennacherib, which hath sent him to reproach the living God. 19. Now therefore, O Lord our God, I beseech thee, save thou us out of his hand, that all the kingdoms of the earth may know that thou *art* the Lord God, *even* thou only.

1 Chr. 5.20. They cried to God in the battle, and he was entreated of them ; because they put their trust in him.

2 Chr. 6.29. What prayer *or* what supplication soever shall be made of any man, or of all thy people Israel, when every one shall know his own sore and his own grief, and shall spread forth his hands in this house. 30. Then hear thou from heaven thy dwelling-place, and forgive.

2 Chr. 14.11. Help us, O Lord our God ; for we rest on thee, and in thy name we go against this multitude. O Lord, thou *art* our God ; let not man prevail against thee.

2 Chr. 20.12. O our God, wilt thou not judge them? for we have no might against this great company that cometh against us ; neither know we what to do : but our eyes *are* upon thee. *v.* 4-13.

Neh. 4.4. Hear, O our God ; for we are despised : and turn their reproach upon their own head, and give them for a prey in the land of captivity. *v.* 5,9. Neh. 6.9,14.

Neh. 9.32. Let not all the trouble seem little before thee, that hath come upon us, on our kings.

Job 10.2. I will say unto God, Do not condemn me ; shew me wherefore thou contendest with me. 9. Remember, I beseech thee, that thou hast made me as the clay ; and wilt thou bring me into dust again? *v.* 15.

Job 13.21. Withdraw thine hand far from me : and let not thy dread make me afraid.

Job 16.20. My friends scorn me : *but* mine eye poureth out *tears* unto God.

Psa. 3.1. Lord, how are they increased that trouble me ! many *are* they that rise up against me. 2. Many *there be* which say of my soul, *There is* no help for him in God. 7. Arise, O Lord ; save me, O my God.

Psa. 4.1. Hear me when I call, O God of my righteousness : thou hast enlarged me *when I was* in distress ; have mercy upon me, and hear my prayer.

Psa. 5.8. Lead me, O Lord, in thy righteousness because of mine enemies ; make thy way straight before my face.

Psa. 6.1. O Lord, rebuke me not in thine anger, neither chasten me in thy hot displeasure. 2. Have mercy upon me, O Lord ; for I *am* weak : O Lord, heal me ; for my bones are vexed. 3. My soul is also sore vexed : but thou, O Lord, how long? 4. Return, O Lord, deliver my soul : oh save me for thy mercies' sake. *v.* 5-7.

Psa. 7.1. O Lord my God, in thee do I put my trust : save me from all them that persecute me, and deliver me : 2. Lest he tear my soul like a lion, rending *it* in pieces, while *there is* none to deliver. *v.* 6,7.

Psa. 9.13. Have mercy upon me, O Lord; consider my trouble *which I suffer* of them that hate me, thou that liftest me up from the gates of death. *v.* 14.

Psa. 10.1. Why standest thou afar off, O Lord? *why* hidest thou *thyself* in times of trouble? 12. Arise, O Lord; O God, lift up thine hand: forget not the humble. *v.* 13-15.

Psa. 13.1. How long wilt thou forget me, O Lord? for ever? how long wilt thou hide thy face from me? 2. How long shall I take counsel in my soul, *having* sorrow in my heart daily? how long shall mine enemy be exalted over me? 3. Consider *and* hear me, O Lord my God: lighten mine eyes, lest I sleep the *sleep of* death. *v.* 4.

Psa. 14.7. O that the salvation of Israel *were come* out of Zion!

Psa. 16.1. Preserve me, O God: for in thee do I put my trust.

Psa. 17.1. Hear the right, O Lord, attend unto my cry, give ear unto my prayer, *that goeth* not out of feigned lips.

Psa. 17.7. Shew thy marvellous loving-kindness, O thou that savest by thy right hand them which put their trust *in thee* from those that rise up *against* them. 8. Keep me as the apple of the eye, hide me under the shadow of thy wings, 9. From the wicked that oppress me, *from* my deadly enemies, *who* compass me about. 13. Arise, O Lord, disappoint him, cast him down: deliver my soul from the wicked, *which is* thy sword. *v.* 2,14.

Psa. 22.1. My God, my God, why hast thou forsaken me? *why art thou so* far from helping me, *and from* the words of my roaring? 11. Be not far from me; for trouble *is* near; for *there is* none to help. 19. Be not thou far from me, O Lord: O my strength, haste thee to help me. 20. Deliver my soul from the sword: my darling from the power of the dog. 21. Save me from the lion's mouth. Psa. 33.21,22.

Psa. 25.2. O my God, I trust in thee: let me not be ashamed, let not mine enemies triumph over me. 16. Turn thee unto me, and have mercy upon me; for I *am* desolate and afflicted. 17. The troubles of my heart are enlarged: *O* bring thou me out of my distresses. 18. Look upon mine affliction and my pain; and forgive all my sins. 19. Consider mine enemies; for they are many; and they hate me with cruel hatred. 22. Redeem Israel, O God, out of all his troubles.

Psa. 27.11. Teach me thy way, O Lord, and lead me in a plain path, because of mine enemies. 12. Deliver me not over unto the will of mine enemies: for false witnesses are risen up against me, and such as breathe out cruelty.

Psa. 28.1. Unto thee will I cry, O Lord my rock; be not silent to me: lest, *if* thou be silent to me, I become like them that go down into the pit.

Psa. 30.9. What profit *is there* in my blood, when I go down to the pit? Shall the dust praise thee? shall it declare thy truth? 10. Hear, O Lord, and have mercy upon me: Lord, be thou my helper.

Psa. 31.1. In thee, O Lord, do I put my trust; let me never be ashamed: deliver me in thy righteousness.

Psa. 31.2. Bow down thine ear to me; deliver me speedily: be thou my strong rock, for an house of defence to save me. 3. For thou *art* my rock and my fortress; therefore for thy name's sake lead me, and guide me. 4. Pull me out of the net that they have laid privily for me: for thou *art* my strength.

Psa. 31.9. Have mercy upon me, O Lord, for I am in trouble: mine eye is consumed with grief, *yea*, my soul and my belly. 14. But I trusted in thee, O Lord: I said, Thou *art* my God. 15. My times *are* in thy hand: deliver me from the hand of mine enemies, and from them that persecute me. 16. Make thy face to shine upon thy servant: save me for thy mercies' sake. 17. Let me not be ashamed, O Lord; for I have called upon thee.

Psa. 35.1. Plead *my cause*, O Lord, with them that strive with me: fight against them that fight against me. 2. Take hold of shield and buckler, and stand up for mine help. 3. Draw out also the spear, and stop *the way* against them that persecute me: say unto my soul, I *am* thy salvation.

Psa. 35.17. Lord, how long wilt thou look on? rescue my soul from their destructions, my darling from the lions. 19. Let not them that are mine enemies wrongfully rejoice over me: *neither* let them wink with the eye that hate me without a cause.

Psa. 35.22. *This* thou hast seen, O Lord: keep not silence: O Lord, be not far from me. 23. Stir up thyself, and awake to my judgment, *even* unto my cause, my God and my Lord. 25. Let them not say in their hearts, Ah, so would we have it: let them not say, We have swallowed him up.

Psa. 38.1. O Lord, rebuke me not in thy wrath: neither chasten me in thy hot displeasure. 2. For thine arrows stick fast in me, and thy hand presseth me sore.

Psa. 38.9. Lord, all my desire *is before* thee; and my groaning is not hid from thee. 10. My heart panteth, my strength faileth me: as for the light of mine eyes, it also is gone from me. 16. *Hear me*, lest *otherwise* they should rejoice over me: when my foot slippeth.

Psa. 39.10. Remove thy stroke away from me: I am consumed by the blow of thine hand. 12. Hear my prayer, O Lord, and give ear unto my cry; hold not thy peace at my tears: for I *am* a stranger with thee, *and* a sojourner, as all my fathers *were*. 13. O spare me, that I may recover strength, before I go hence, and be no more.

Psa. 40.13. Be pleased, O Lord, to deliver me: O Lord, make haste to help me. 17. I *am* poor and needy; *yet* the Lord thinketh upon me: thou *art* my help and my deliverer; make no tarrying, O my God. Psa. 70.5.

Psa. 42.9. I will say unto God my rock, Why hast thou forgotten me? why go I mourning because of the oppression of the enemy?

Psa. 43.1. Judge me, O God, and plead my cause against an ungodly nation: O deliver me from the deceitful and unjust man. 2. For thou *art* the God of my strength: why dost thou cast me off? why go I mourning because of the oppression of the enemy.

Psa. 44.4. Thou art my King, O God: command deliverances for Jacob. 23. Awake, why sleepest thou, O Lord? arise, cast *us* not off for ever.

Psa. 44.24. Wherefore hidest thou thy face, *and* forgettest our affliction and our oppression? 25. For our soul is bowed down to the dust: our belly cleaveth unto the earth. 26. Arise for our help, and redeem us for thy mercies' sake.

Psa. 54.1. Save me, O God, by thy name, and judge me by thy strength. 2. Hear my prayer, O God; give ear to the words of my mouth. 3. For strangers are risen up against me, and oppressors seek after my soul.

Psa. 55.1. Give ear to my prayer, O God; and hide not thyself from my supplication. 2. Attend unto me, and hear me: I mourn in my complaint, and make a noise; 3. Because of the voice of the enemy.

Psa. 56.1. Be merciful unto me, O God: for man would swallow me up; he fighting daily oppresseth me. 2. Mine enemies would daily swallow *me* up: for *they be* many that fight against me, O thou most High.

Psa. 57.1. Be merciful unto me, O God, be merciful unto me: for my soul trusteth in thee: yea, in the shadow of thy wings will I make my refuge, until *these* calamities be overpast. 2. I will cry unto God most high; unto God that performeth *all things* for me.

Psa. 59.1. Deliver me from mine enemies, O my God: defend me from them that rise up against me. 2. Deliver me from the workers of iniquity, and save me from bloody men. 4. Awake to help me, and behold.

Psa. 60.1. O God, thou hast cast us off, thou hast scattered us, thou hast been displeased; O turn thyself to us again. 2. Thou hast made the earth to tremble; thou hast broken it: heal the breaches thereof; for it shaketh. 3. Thou hast shewed thy people hard things: thou hast made us to drink the wine of astonishment. 11. Give us help from trouble: for vain *is* the help of man. Psa. 108.12.

Psa. 61.1. Hear my cry, O God; attend unto my prayer. 2. From the end of the earth will I cry unto thee, when my heart is overwhelmed: lead me to the rock *that* is higher than I.

Psa. 64.1. Hear my voice, O God, in my prayer: preserve my life from fear of the enemy. 2. Hide me from the secret counsel of the wicked; from the insurrection of the workers of iniquity.

Psa. 69.1. Save me, O God; for the waters are come in unto *my* soul.

Psa. 69.13. As for me, my prayer *is* unto thee, O Lord, *in* an acceptable time: O God, in the multitude of thy mercy hear me, in the truth of thy salvation. 14. Deliver me out of the mire, and let me not sink: let me be delivered from them that hate me, and out of the deep waters. 15. Let not the waterflood overflow me, neither let the deep swallow me up, and let not the pit shut her mouth upon me.

Psa. 69.17. Hide not thy face from thy servant; for I am in trouble: hear me speedily. 18. Draw nigh unto my soul, *and* redeem it: deliver me because of mine enemies. 19. Thou hast known my reproach, and my shame, and my dishonour: mine adversaries *are* all before thee. 29. I *am* poor and sorrowful: let thy salvation, O God, set me up on high.

Psa. 70.1. *Make haste*, O God, to deliver me; make haste to help me, O Lord.

Psa. 70.2. Let them be ashamed and confounded that seek after my soul. *v.* 3-5.

Psa. 71.1. In thee, O Lord, do I put my trust: let me never be put to confusion. 2. Deliver me in thy righteousness, and cause me to escape: incline thine ear unto me, and save me. 4. Deliver me, O my God, out of the hand of the wicked, out of the hand of the unrighteous and cruel man.

Psa. 71.9. Cast me not off in the time of old age; forsake me not when my strength faileth. 12. O God, be not far from me: O my God, make haste for my help.

Psa. 74.1. O God, why hast thou cast *us* off for ever? *why* doth thine anger smoke against the sheep of thy pasture? 3. Lift up thy feet unto the perpetual desolations, *even* all *that* the enemy hath done wickedly in the sanctuary.

Psa. 74.10. O God, how long shall the adversary reproach? shall the enemy blaspheme thy name for ever? 11. Why withdrawest thou thy hand, even thy right hand? pluck *it* out of thy bosom. 19. O deliver not the soul of thy turtle-dove unto the multitude *of the wicked*: forget not the congregation of thy poor for ever. 21. O let not the oppressed return ashamed: let the poor and needy praise thy name. 22. Arise, O God, plead thine own cause: remember how the foolish man reproacheth thee daily. 23. Forget not the voice of thine enemies: the tumult of those that rise up against thee increaseth continually. *v.* 1-23.

Psa. 77.1. I cried unto God with my voice, *even* unto God with my voice; and he gave ear unto me. 2. In the day of my trouble I sought the Lord. 7. Will the Lord cast off for ever? and will he be favourable no more? 8. Is his mercy clean gone for ever? doth *his* promise fail for evermore? 9. Hath God forgotten to be gracious? hath he in anger shut up his tender mercies?

Psa. 79.1. O God, the heathen are come into thine inheritance; thy holy temple have they defiled; they have laid Jerusalem on heaps. 5. How long, Lord? wilt thou be angry for ever? shall thy jealousy burn like fire?

Psa. 79.8. O remember not against us former iniquities: let thy tender mercies speedily prevent us: for we are brought very low. 9. Help us, O God of our salvation, for the glory of thy name: and deliver us, and purge away our sins, for thy name's sake.

Psa. 79.11. Let the sighing of the prisoner come before thee; according to the greatness of thy power preserve thou those that are appointed to die. *v.* 1-11.

Psa. 80.1. Give ear, O Shepherd of Israel, thou that leadest Joseph like a flock; thou that dwellest *between* the cherubims, shine forth.

Psa. 80.3. Turn us again, O God, and cause thy face to shine; and we shall be saved. 4. O Lord God of hosts, how long wilt thou be angry against the prayer of thy people? 5. Thou feedest them with the bread of tears; and givest them tears to drink in great measure. 14. Return, we beseech thee, O God of hosts: look down from heaven, and behold, and visit this vine. *v.* 1-16.

Psa. 83.1. Keep not thou silence, O God: hold not thy peace, and be not still, O God. 2. For, lo, thine enemies make a tumult: and they that hate thee have lifted up the head. *v.* 3-5.

Psa. 85.5. Wilt thou be angry with us for ever? wilt thou draw out thine anger to all generations? 6. Wilt thou not revive us again: that thy people may rejoice in thee? 7. Shew us thy mercy, O Lord, and grant us thy salvation.

Psa. 86.1. Bow down thine ear, O Lord, hear me: for I *am* poor and needy. 2. Preserve my soul; for I *am* holy: O thou my God, save thy servant that trusteth in thee. 3. Be merciful unto me, O Lord: for I cry unto thee daily. 4. Rejoice the soul of thy servant: for unto thee, O Lord, do I lift up my soul.

Psa. 86.16. O turn unto me, and have mercy upon me; give thy strength unto thy servant, and save the son of thine handmaid. 17. Shew me a token for good; that they which hate me may see *it*, and be ashamed: because thou, Lord, hast holpen me, and comforted me.

Psa. 88.9. Lord, I have called daily upon thee, I have stretched out my hands unto thee. 13. Unto thee have I cried, O Lord; and in the morning shall my prayer prevent thee. 14. Lord, why castest thou off my soul? *why* hidest thou thy face from me? *v.* 10-12.

Psa. 89.46. How long, Lord? wilt thou hide thyself for ever? shall thy wrath burn like fire? 47. Remember how short my time is: wherefore hast thou made all men in vain? 49. Lord, where *are* thy former loving-kindnesses, *which* thou swarest unto David in thy truth?

Psa. 89.50. Remember, Lord, the reproach of thy servants; *how* I do bear in my bosom *the reproach of* all the mighty people; 51. Wherewith thine enemies have reproached, O Lord; wherewith they have reproached the footsteps of thine anointed. *v.* 39-51.

Psa. 90.15. Make us glad according to the days *wherein* thou hast afflicted us, *and* the years *wherein* we have seen evil.

Psa. 94.1. O God, to whom vengeance belongeth, shew thyself. 2. Lift up thyself, thou judge of the earth: render a reward to the proud. *v.* 3-5.

Psa. 102.2. Hide not thy face from me in the day *when* I am in trouble; incline thine ear unto me: in the day *when* I call answer me speedily. 24. O my God, take me not away in the midst of my days.

Psa. 106.47. Save us, O Lord our God, and gather us from among the heathen, to give thanks unto thy holy name.

Psa. 108.6. That thy beloved may be delivered: save *with* thy right hand, and answer me.

Psa. 109.1. Hold not thy peace, O God of my praise; 2. For the mouth of the wicked and the mouth of the deceitful are opened against me. 21. But do thou for me, O God the Lord, for thy name's sake: because thy mercy *is* good, deliver thou me.

Psa. 109.26. Help me, O Lord my God: O save me according to thy mercy: 27. That they may know that this *is* thy hand; *that* thou, Lord, hast done it. 28. Let them curse, but bless thou: when they arise, let them be ashamed; but let thy servant rejoice. Psa. 120.2.

Psa. 116.4. Then called I upon the name of the Lord; O Lord, I beseech thee, deliver my soul.

Psa. 119.22. Remove from me reproach and contempt; for I have kept thy testimonies. 28. My soul melteth for heaviness: strengthen thou me according unto thy word. 39. Turn away my reproach which I fear: for thy judgments *are* good.

Psa. 119.41. Let thy mercies come also unto me, O Lord, *even* thy salvation, according to thy word. 42. So shall I have wherewith to answer him that reproacheth me: for I trust in thy word. 76. Let, I pray thee, thy merciful kindness be for my comfort, according to thy word unto thy servant. 77. Let thy tender mercies come unto me, that I may live: for thy law *is* my delight.

Psa. 119.82. Mine eyes fail for thy word, saying, When wilt thou comfort me? 84. How many *are* the days of thy servant? when wilt thou execute judgment on them that persecute me?

Psa. 119.107. I am afflicted very much: quicken me, O Lord, according unto thy word. 121. Leave me not to mine oppressors. 122. Be surety for thy servant for good: let not the proud oppress me. 123. Mine eyes fail for thy salvation, and for the word of thy righteousness.

Psa. 119.134. Deliver me from the oppression of man: so will I keep thy precepts. 153. Consider mine affliction, and deliver me: for I do not forget thy law. 154. Plead my cause, and deliver me: quicken me according to thy word.

Psa. 119.170. Let my supplication come before thee: deliver me according to thy word. 173. Let thine hand help me; for I have chosen thy precepts.

Psa. 123.3. Have mercy upon us, O Lord, have mercy upon us: for we are exceedingly filled with contempt. 4. Our soul is exceedingly filled with the scorning of those that are at ease, *and* with the contempt of the proud.

Psa. 126.4. Turn again our captivity, O Lord, as the streams in the south.

Psa. 130.1. Out of the depths have I cried unto thee, O Lord. 2. Lord, hear my voice: let thine ears be attentive to the voice of my supplications.

Psa. 140.4. Keep me, O Lord, from the hands of the wicked; preserve me from the violent man; who have purposed to overthrow my goings.

Psa. 140.6. I said unto the Lord, Thou *art* my God: hear the voice of my supplications, O Lord. 7. O God the Lord, the strength of my salvation, thou hast covered my head in the day of battle. 8. Grant not, O Lord, the desires of the wicked: further not his wicked device; *lest* they exalt themselves.

Psa. 141.8. Mine eyes *are* unto thee, O God the Lord: in thee is my trust; leave not my soul destitute. 9. Keep me from the snares *which* they have laid for me, and the gins of the workers of iniquity.

Psa. 142.1. With my voice unto the Lord did I make my supplication. 2. I poured out my complaint before him; I shewed before him my trouble.

Psa. 142.5. I cried unto thee, O Lord: I said, Thou *art* my refuge *and* my portion in the land of the living. 6. Attend unto my cry; for I am brought very low: deliver me from my persecutors; for they are stronger than I. 7. Bring my soul out of prison, that I may praise thy name.

Psa. 143.7. Hear me speedily, O Lord: my spirit faileth: hide not thy face from me, lest I be like unto them that go down into the pit.

8. Cause me to hear thy loving-kindness in the morning; for in thee do I trust: cause me to know the way wherein I should walk; for I lift up my soul unto thee.

Psa. 143.9. Deliver me, O Lord, from mine enemies: I flee unto thee to hide me. 11. Quicken me, O Lord, for thy name's sake: for thy righteousness' sake bring my soul out of trouble. *v.* 12. Psa. 144.5-11.

Isa. 33.2. O Lord, be gracious unto us; we have waited for thee: be thou their arm every morning, our salvation also in the time of trouble.

Isa. 38.14. Mine eyes fail *with looking* upward: O Lord, I am oppressed; undertake for me.

Isa. 51.9. Awake, awake, put on strength, O arm of the Lord; awake, as in the ancient days, in the generations of old.

Isa. 63.15. Look down from heaven, and behold from the habitation of thy holiness and of thy glory. 17. Return, for thy servants' sake, the tribes of thine inheritance.

Isa. 64.1. Ch that thou wouldest rend the heavens, that thou wouldest come down, that the mountains might flow down at thy presence.

Isa. 64.9. Be not wroth very sore, O Lord, neither remember iniquity for ever: behold, see, we beseech thee, we *are* all thy people. 10. Thy holy cities are a wilderness, Zion is a wilderness, Jerusalem is a desolation. 11. Our holy and our beautiful house, where our fathers praised thee, is burnt up with fire: and all our pleasant things are laid waste. 12. Wilt thou refrain thyself for these *things*, O Lord? wilt thou hold thy peace, and afflict us very sore?

Jer. 10.24. O Lord, correct me, but with judgment; not in thine anger, lest thou bring me to nothing.

Jer. 14.8. O the hope of Israel, the saviour thereof in time of trouble, why shouldest thou be as a stranger in the land, and as a wayfaring man *that* turneth aside to tarry for a night? 9. Why shouldest thou be as a man astonied, as a mighty man *that* cannot save? yet thou, O Lord, *art* in the midst of us, and we are called by thy name; leave us not.

Jer. 14.19. Hast thou utterly rejected Judah? hath thy soul loathed Zion? why hast thou smitten us, and *there is* no healing for us? we looked for peace, and *there is* no good; and for the time of healing, and behold trouble! 20. We acknowledge, O Lord, our wickedness, *and* the iniquity of our fathers: for we have sinned against thee. 21. Do not abhor *us*, for thy name's sake, do not disgrace the throne of thy glory: remember, break not thy covenant with us. Jer. 32.16-25.

Jer. 15.15. O Lord, thou knowest: remember me, and visit me, and revenge me of my persecutors; take me not away in thy longsuffering: know that for thy sake I have suffered rebuke.

Jer. 17.17. Be not a terror unto me: thou *art* my hope in the day of evil. 18. Let them be confounded that persecute me, but let not me be confounded: let them be dismayed, but let not me be dismayed.

Jer. 18.19. Give heed to me, O Lord, and hearken to the voice of them that contend with me. Jer. 20.7,8.

Lam. 1.20. Behold, O Lord; for I *am* in distress: my bowels are troubled; mine heart is turned within me; for I have grievously rebelled: abroad the sword bereaveth, at home *there is* as death.

Lam. 2.18. Their heart cried unto the Lord, O wall of the daughter of Zion, let tears run down like a river day and night: give thyself no rest; let not the apple of thine eye cease. 19. Arise, cry out in the night: in the beginning of the watches pour out thine heart like water before the face of the Lord: lift up thy hands toward him for the life of thy young children, that faint for hunger in the top of every street.

Lam. 5.1. Remember, O Lord, what is come upon us: consider, and behold our reproach. 16. The crown is fallen *from* our head: woe unto us, that we have sinned! 17. For this our heart is faint; for these *things* our eyes are dim. Lam. *c.* 1-5.

Dan. 6.10. He kneeled upon his knees three times a day, and prayed, and gave thanks before his God, as he did aforetime. ·

Joel 1.19. O Lord, to thee will I cry: for the fire hath devoured the pastures of the wilderness, and the flame hath burned all the trees of the field.

Hab. 1.12. *Art* thou not from everlasting, O Lord my God, mine Holy One? we shall not die. O Lord, thou hast ordained them for judgment; and, O mighty God, thou hast established them for correction. 13. *Thou art* of purer eyes than to behold evil, and canst not look on iniquity: wherefore lookest thou upon them that deal treacherously, *and* holdest thy tongue when the wicked devoureth *the man that is* more righteous than he?

Hab. 3.2. O Lord, revive thy work in the midst of the years, in the midst of the years make known; in wrath remember mercy.

Mat. 8.25. His disciples came to *him*, and awoke him, saying, Lord, save us: we perish.

Mat. 14.30. He was afraid; and beginning to sink, he cried, saying, Lord, save me.

Luk. 23.46. Father, into thy hands I commend my spirit.

Act. 4.29. Now, Lord, behold their threatenings: and grant unto thy servants, that with all boldness they may speak thy word, 30. By stretching forth thine hand to heal.

Act. 7.59. Lord Jesus receive my spirit.

2 Cor. 12.8. For this thing I besought the Lord thrice, that it might depart from me.

See PRAYER, INTERCESSORY.

AFFLICTION, RESIGNATION IN. See RESIGNATION.

———, UNIVERSAL. Gen. 3.16. In sorrow thou shalt bring forth children. 17. Cursed *is* the ground for thy sake; in sorrow shalt thou eat *of* it all the days of thy life.

Job 5.7. Man is born unto trouble, as the sparks fly upward.

Job 9.22. He destroyeth the perfect and the wicked.

Job 14.1. Man *that is* born of a woman *is* of few days, and full of trouble.

Psa. 90.10. If by reason of strength *they be* fourscore years, yet *is* their strength labour and sorrow.

Luk. 13.2. Suppose ye that these Galileans were sinners above all the Galileans, because they suffered such things? 3. I tell you, Nay. *v.* 4,5.

1 Pet. 5.9. The same afflictions are accomplished in your brethren that are in the world.

(Compare PERSECUTION with AFFLICTION.)

AGABUS prophesies a famine, Act. 11.28, and Paul's apprehension at Jerusalem, Act. 21.10.

AGAG, king of Amalek, defeated by Saul and slain by Samuel, 1 Sam. 15.8,33. See Num. 24.7.

AGATE, a precious stone, Isa. 54.12. Eze. 27.16. Set in the high-priest's breastplate, Ex. 28.19.

AGED, THE. See OLD AGE.

AGRICULTURE, practised by Adam, Gen. 2.15. Gen. 3.19,23. Cain, Gen. 4.2. Noah, Gen. 9.20. Elisha, 1 Kin. 19.19. David, 1 Chr. 27.26-31. Uzziah, 2 Chr. 26.10. Solomon, Ecc. 2.4-6.

Operations of. Digging, Isa. 5.6. Isa. 7.25. Luk. 13.8. Luk. 16.3. Gathering out stones, Isa. 5.2. Manuring, Isa. 25.10. Mat. 13.30. Luk. 14.34,35. Weeding, Mat. 13.28. Ingrafting, Rom. 11.17-24. See BARNS, FENCES, HARROW, IRRIGATION, MILLS, MOWING, PLOUGHING, PRUNING, REAPING, SHEPHERDS, SOWING, THRESHING, VINEYARDS.

Implements, &c. See AXE, CART, FAN, FLAIL, FORK, GOAD, HARROW, MATTOCK, PLOUGH, PRUNING-HOOK, SHOVEL, SICKLE, SIEVE.

Animals used in. See ASS, BULLOCK, HEIFER, HORSE. Compare Gen. 42.27. Deu. 11.15. 1 Kin. 18.5. Jer. 50.11. Isa. 15.6. Isa. 11.7.

Produce exported. See CATTLE, CORN, OIL, WINE.

――――――, LAWS REGARDING. Land to lie fallow during the Sabbatical year and Year of Jubilee, Ex. 23.10,11. Lev. 25.4,5,11,12. Sabbath to be kept during harvest, Ex. 34.21. Restitution to be made for cattle trespassing, Ex. 22.5.

Punishment for injuring crops, Ex. 22.6. Deu. 23.25. Strangers allowed to eat corn and fruit, but not to carry it away, Deu. 23.24,25. See Mat. 12.1. Mixed seeds not to be used, Deu. 22.9. Ploughing with an ox and an ass forbidden, Deu. 22.10.

Fruit of trees not to be eaten for 3 years, offered to God the 4th year, eaten by the owner from the 5th year, Lev. 19.23-25.

Planters of vineyards exempted from military service until they had eaten of the fruit, Deu. 20.6. See FIRST-FRUITS, GLEANINGS, LANDMARKS, TITHES.

AGRIPPA, son of Herod III., and king of Chalcis, Galilee, and Perea ; Paul pleads before him, Act. 25. Act. 26. Impressed by Paul's discourse, Act. 26.28.

AGUR, author of the 30th chapter of Proverbs, Pro. 30.1.

AHAB, seventh king of Israel, son and successor of Omri, 1 Kin. 16.29. His wickedness, worship of Baal, &c., 1 Kin. 16.30-33. 1 Kin. 18.18,19. 1 Kin. 21.25,26. 2 Kin. 3.2. 2 Chr. 21.6. 2 Chr. 22.2-4. Mic. 6.16. Marries Jezebel, a Zidonian ; her evil influence, 1 Kin. 16.31. 1 Kin. 21.

Drought predicted by Elijah, 1 Kin. 17. He meets Elijah, the miracle on Carmel, and abundant rain, 1 Kin. 18. Tells Jezebel of Elijah slaying Baal's prophets, 1 Kin. 19.1. Attacked by Benhadad, defeats him twice according to predictions of a prophet, 1 Kin. 20.1-30.

Rebuked for releasing Benhadad, 1 Kin. 20.31-43. Takes Naboth's vineyard, is rebuked by Elijah, his repentance defers the threatened judgments, 1 Kin. 21. League with Jehoshaphat against Syria, imprisons Micaiah, encouraged by false prophets, disguises himself, is slain at Ramoth-gilead, 1 Kin. 22. 2 Chr. 18.

Jericho rebuilt in his reign, 1 Kin. 16.34. Prophecies against him and his posterity, 1 Kin. 20.42. 1 Kin. 21.19-24. 1 Kin. 22.19-28. 2 Kin. 9.8,25,26. His sons murdered, 2 Kin. 10.1-8.

AHAB, a false prophet ; Jeremiah predicts his death, Jer. 29.21,22.

AHASUERUS, king of Persia ; his treatment of Vashti, Esther, Mordecai, Haman, and the Jews, Book of Esther.

――――――. See ARTAXERXES.

――――――, the father of Darius, the Median, Dan. 9.1.

AHAVA, a river in Babylonia, where Ezra gathered the Jews and proclaimed a fast before returning to Judea, Ezr. 8.15,21,31.

AHAZ, eleventh king of Judah, son and successor of Jotham, 2 Kin. 15.38. 2 Kin. 16.1. 1 Chr. 3.13. Attacked by Pekah and Rezin, his son slain, captives taken by Pekah, but afterwards restored, towns taken by Rezin, 2 Kin. 16.5,6. 2 Chr. 28.5-15. Isa. 7.1.

Refuses to ask a sign of Isaiah, Isa. 7.11,12. Subsidizes Tiglath for aiding him against Rezin, 2 Kin. 16.7-9,17,18. 2 Chr. 28.16-21. Invasion by Edomites and Philistines, 2 Chr. 28. 17-19. Idolatry of, 2 Kin. 16.2-4. 2 Chr. 28. 1-4,19,22-25.

Sets up a pagan altar, destroys the sacred vessels, &c., and closes the Temple, 2 Kin. 16.10-18. 2 Chr. 28.24. 2 Chr. 29.3,7,19. Sundial of, 2 Kin. 20.11. Isa. 38.8.

Upper chamber of, with idolatrous altars, 2 Kin. 23.12. Isaiah, Hosea, and Micah prophesied in his reign, Isa. 1.1. Hos. 1.1. Mic. 1.1. Death of, 2 Kin. 16.20. 2 Chr. 28.27. Isa. 6.1. Prophecy against him, Isa. 7.13-25. Against his invaders, Isa. 7.3-9,16.

AHAZIAH, sixth king of Judah, son and successor of Jehoram, 2 Kin. 8.25. 1 Chr. 3.11. Called Azariah, 2 Chr. 22.6, and Jehoahaz, 2 Chr. 21.17. 2 Chr. 25.23. Evil influence of his mother Athaliah, 2 Chr. 22.2-5. 2 Kin. 8.26, 27.

Dedicates treasures, 2 Kin. 12.18. Allied with Joram against Hazael, visits Joram at Jezreel, and is slain by Jehu, 2 Kin. 8.28,29. 2 Kin. 9.16,23. 2 Chr. 22.5-9. Burial of, 2 Chr. 22.9.

――――――, eighth king of Israel, son and successor of Ahab, 1 Kin. 22.40,51. Joins Jehoshaphat in making ships for Tarshish, which were wrecked at Ezion-geber, 1 Kin. 22.49. 2 Chr. 20.35-37.

His wickedness and idolatry, 1 Kin. 22.52,53. 2 Chr. 20.35. Revolt of Moab, 2 Kin. 1.1. Inquires of Baalzebub in his sickness, receives a message from Elijah, sends men to take him, 2 Kin. 1. His death as prophesied, 2 Kin. 1.16,17.

AHIA, high-priest, supposed to be the same as Ahimelech, I Sam.14.3, with 1 Sam. 22.9,11,20.

AHIJAH, the Shilonite, a prophet; predicts that Jeroboam will be king, 1 Kin. 11.29-40; the punishment of Israel's idolatry, 1 Kin. 11. 31-35. 2 Chr. 10.15; the death of Abijah and Jeroboam's overthrow, 1 Kin. 14.5-16.

AHIKAM, son of Shaphan, sent to Huldah by Josiah, 2 Kin. 22.12-14. Saves Jeremiah's life, Jer. 26.24. See Jer. 39.14.

AHIMAAZ, high-priest, son and successor of Zadok, 1 Chr. 6.8. Acts as David's spy, 2 Sam. 15.27,36. 2 Sam. 17.17-21. Brings news of Absalom's death, 2 Sam. 18.27-29.

AHIMELECH, OR AHIA, high-priest, son of Ahitub, of the line of Ithamar and Eli, 1 Sam. 14.3. Father of Abiathar, 1 Sam. 22.20. Gives David shewbread and Goliath's sword, 1 Sam. 21. Slain by Saul, 1 Sam. 22.9-22. See Mar. 2.26.

AHINOAM, wife of David, 1 Sam. 25.43. 1 Sam. 27.3. 2 Sam. 2.2. Taken captive at Ziklag, 1 Sam. 30.5. Mother of Amnon, 2 Sam. 3.2.

AHIO, aids David in removing the Ark, 2 Sam. 6.3,4.

AHITHOPHEL, David's counsellor, joins Absalom, 2 Chr. 27.33. 2 Sam. 15.12. 2 Sam. 16.15-23. See Psa. 41.9. Psa. 55.12-14. His reputed wisdom, 2 Sam. 16.23. Commits suicide on his counsel being rejected, 2 Sam. 17.1-14,23.

AHITUB, high-priest, son of Phinehas and father of Ahia, 1 Sam. 14.3. 1 Sam 22.9.

———, father of Zadok, 2 Sam. 8.17. 1 Chr. 6.8. 1 Chr. 18.16. Ezr. 7.2.

AHOLIAB, divinely instructed to make the Tabernacle, Ex. 31.6. Ex. 35.34. Ex. 36.1.

AHOLIBAH (a tent), Aholah (my tent in in her) symbolical of Judah and Israel, Eze. 23.4.

AI, a city in Canaan, Gen. 12.8. Gen. 13.3. Destroyed by Joshua, Jos. 7. Jos. 8. Rebuilt, Ezr. 2.28. Called Aija, Neh. 11.31, and Aiath, Isa. 10.28.

AIJELETH SHAHAR (hind of the morning), its reference in Psa. 22 (title) is not understood.

AJALON, a Levitical city of Dan, Jos. 19.42, or Zebulun, Jud. 12.12. A city of refuge, Jos. 21.24. 1 Sam. 14.31. 1 Chr. 6.69. Amorites remained in, Jud. 1.35.

———, a city of Judah taken by Philistines, 2 Chr. 28.18. Fenced by Rehoboam, 2 Chr. 11.10.

———, valley of, Joshua commands the sun and moon to stand still in, Jos. 10.12.

ALABASTER, a kind of marble, Mat. 26.7. Mar. 14.3.

ALAMOTH signifies virgins, Psa. 46 (title), a psalm for female voices.

ALEXANDER, son of Simon the Cyrenian, Mar. 15.21.

———, one of the Sanhedrim who imprisoned Peter and John, Act. 4.6.

———, a Jew of Ephesus, persecuted by the worshippers of Diana, Act. 19.33,34.

———, the coppersmith, his heresy and excommunication, 1 Tim. 1.20. 2 Tim. 4.14,15.

ALEXANDRIA, a city of Egypt; men of, dispute with Stephen, Act. 6.9. Ships of, Act. 27.6. Act. 28.11. Birthplace of Apollos, Act. 18.24.

ALGUM, or ALMUG TREES, brought from Ophir, used for the Temple and for musical instruments, 1 Kin. 10.11,12. 2 Chr. 9.10,11. Brought from Lebanon, 2 Chr. 2.8.

ALIEN, a stranger, Eph. 2.12. Heb. 11.34. So translated, Mat. 17.25. Jno. 10.5.

ALLEGORY, Gal. 4.24.

ALLIANCES, POLITICAL. Examples of:—Abraham, Gen. 14.13. Gen. 21.22-32. Isaac, Gen. 26.28. The Gibeonites, Jos. 9. Solomon and Hiram, 1 Kin. 5.12. 1 Kin. 9.27. Amos 1.9. Asa and Benhadad, 1 Kin. 15.19. 2 Chr. 16.3. Jehoshaphat and Ahab, 1 Kin. 22. 2 Chr. 18.1. Jehoshaphat and Ahaziah, 2 Chr. 20.35.

Ahaz and Tiglath, 2 Kin. 16.7,8. 2 Chr. 28.16,21. Rezin and Pekah, 2 Kin. 16.5. Amaziah, 2 Chr. 25.6. Zedekiah, Jer. 37.7. Eze. 17.15-17.

Ratification of. See COVENANTS.

With idolaters forbidden, Ex. 23.32,33. Ex. 34.12-15. Deu. 7.2. Jud. 2.2. 2 Chr. 19.2. 2 Chr. 20.37. 2 Chr. 25.7,8. Isa. 8.11,12. Isa. 30.2. Isa. 31.1. Hos. 4.17. Hos. 12.1.

ALLON-BACHUTH (oak of weeping), the burial-place of Rebekah's nurse, Gen. 35.8.

ALMOND-TREE, and ALMONDS, Gen. 43.11. Aaron's rod of, Num. 17.8. Appearance of, Ecc. 12.5.

ALMS. See POOR, KINDNESS TO.

ALOES, an odoriferous tree, Num. 24.6. Psa. 45.8. Pro. 7.17. Song 4.14. Jno. 19.39.

ALPHA (the first letter of the Greek alphabet), a name of Christ, Rev. 1.8,11. Rev. 21.6. Rev. 22.13. See Isa. 41.4. Isa. 44.6. Isa. 48.12.

ALTARS. To be made of earth, or unhewn stone, and without steps, Ex. 20.24-26. Deu. 27.5-7. Jos. 8.30,31. Groves not to be planted near, Deu. 16.21. Of Noah, Gen. 8.20. Abraham, Gen. 12.7,8. Gen. 13.18. Gen. 22.9.

Of Isaac, Gen. 26.25. Jacob, Gen. 33.20. Gen. 35.1-7. Moses, Ex. 17.15. Ex. 24.4. Balaam, Num. 23.1,14,29. Joshua on Mount Ebal, Deu. 27.4-7. Jos. 8.30-32. Of Reubenites and Gadites, Jos. 22.10,34. Gideon, Jud. 6.26,27. Israel, Jud. 21.4. Samuel, 1 Sam 7.17. Saul, 1 Sam. 14.35. David, 2 Sam. 24.18. Elijah, 1 Kin. 18.31,32.

Idolatrous, Jud. 6.25. 1 Kin. 12.32. 1 Kin. 16.32. 1 Kin. 18.26. 2 Kin. 16.10. 2 Kin. 23.12,15. Isa. 27.9. Hos. 8.11. Of brick, Isa. 65.3. Inscription on, Act. 17.23.

ALTAR OF BURNT-OFFERING, called the brazen altar, Ex. 39.39. 1 Kin. 8.64. Altar of God, Psa. 43.4. Altar of the Lord, Mal. 2.13.

In the Tabernacle, pattern of, shewn to Moses in the Mount; made of shittim-wood, overlaid with brass, with horns at the four corners, 5 cubits in length and breadth, 3 high, Ex. 27.1-8. Ex. 38.1-7.

Placed before the door of the Tabernacle, Ex. 40.6,29. Eze. 8.16. Mat. 23.35.

Vessels, of brass; pans, shovels, basons, flesh-hooks, grate, with rings and staves for carrying it, Ex. 27.3-7. Ex. 38.3-7. 1 Sam. 2.13,14.

Atonement made for it for seven days, Ex. 29. 36,37. Was anointed with oil. Ex. 30.26-28. Ex. 40.10. Lev. 8.10,11. Offerings at the dedication of, Num. 7. Was sanctified by God, Ex. 29.44. Ex. 40.10.

Sanctified whatever touched it, Ex. 29.37. Ex. 30.29. Mat. 23.18,19. Was a place of refuge, Ex. 21.14. 1 Kin. 1.50. 1 Kin. 2.28. 2 Kin. 11.15. See TABERNACLE, Historical Notices of.

In the Temple made by Solomon, of brass, 20 cubits in length and breadth, 10 high, 2 Chr. 4.1. Renewed by Asa, 2 Chr. 15.8. Removed by Ahaz, 2 Kin. 16.14-17. Cleansed by Hezekiah, 2 Chr. 29.18-24. Repaired by Manasseh, 2 Chr. 33.16. Vessels of, taken to Babylon, 2 Kin. 25.14.

In the second Temple, built by Zerubbabel, Ezr. 3.1-6.

In the Temple seen by Ezekiel, Eze. 43.13-27.

Used for sacrifices. See FIRE, SACRED— OFFERINGS, Mode of, Tables 1, 2, 3, and each of the different kinds of offerings.

ALTAR OF INCENSE, called the Golden Altar, Ex. 39.38. Num. 4.11. Altar of sweet incense, Lev. 4.7. Altar before the Lord, Lev. 16.18.

In the Tabernacle, made of shittim-wood, covered with gold, 1 cubit in length and breadth, 2 cubits high, had horns at the four corners, the top bordered with crowns of gold, under which were rings of gold for staves to carry it, Ex. 30.1-10. Ex. 37.25-28. The cover made out of the censers of Korah, &c., Num. 16.36-40.

Placed before the vail in the holy place, Ex. 30.6. Ex. 40.5,26,27.

Anointed with oil, Ex. 30.26,27. Atonement made for it once a year, Ex. 30.10. Lev. 16.18. Covered by the priests before removal, Num. 4.11.

Incense burned on it morning and evening, Ex. 30.7,8. No sacrifice or common incense to be offered on it, Ex. 30.9. The blood of sin-offerings put on its horns, Lev. 4.7,18. Lev. 8.15. Lev. 9.9. Lev. 16.18. Sacred fire only used on, Lev. 16.12. Lev. 10.1,2. See TABERNACLE, Historical Notices of.

In the Temple, made of cedar-wood, overlaid with gold, 1 Kin. 6.20. 1 Kin. 7.48. 1 Chr. 28.18.

Seen by John, Rev. 8.3. Rev. 9.13.
See INCENSE.

AL-TASCHITH (destroy not). Title of Psa. 57 to 59. Psa. 75. Compare 1 Sam. 26.9. Deu. 9.26.

AMALEKITES, descended from Amalek, grandson of Esau, Gen. 36.12,16. 1 Chr. 1.36. Territory of, Gen. 14.7. Num. 13.29. Num. 14.25. 1 Sam. 15.7. 1 Sam. 27.8. 1 Chr. 4.43. Defeated by Joshua, Ex. 17.8-13. De-

feat Israel at Hormah, Num. 14.45. Deu. 1.44.

Israel commanded to destroy, Deu. 25.17-19. 1 Sam. 28.18. Invade Palestine, Jud. 3.13. Jud. 5.14. Defeated by Gideon, Jud. 6. Jud. 7. Jud. 10.12. Defeated by Saul, Agag slain by Samuel, 1 Sam. 14.48. 1 Sam. 15. 1 Sam. 28.18.

Defeated by David, 1 Sam. 27.8,9. 1 Chr. 18.11. Burn Ziklag, and are defeated by David, 1 Sam. 30.1,18. 2 Sam. 1.1. 2 Sam. 8.12. See Psa. 83.7.

Defeated by Simeonites in Hezekiah's reign, 1 Chr. 4.41-43. Prophecies of, Ex. 17.14,16. Num. 24.20. Deu. 25.19.

AMANA, a hill near Damascus, Song 4.8.

AMASA, son of Jether, an Ishmaelite, and Abigail, David's sister, 2 Sam. 17.25. 1 Chr. 2.17. Joins David at Ziklag, 1 Chr. 12.16-18. Joins Absalom, made captain of his army, 2 Sam. 17.25.

Returns to David; made captain instead of Joab, 2 Sam. 19.13. Sent against Sheba, 2 Sam. 20.4,5. Slain by Joab, 2 Sam. 20.8-12. 1 Kin. 2.5,32.

AMAZIAH, eighth king of Judah, son and successor of Joash, 2 Kin. 14.1,2. 1 Chr. 3.12. 2 Chr. 24.27. Slays his father's murderers, 2 Kin. 14.5,6. 2 Chr. 25.3,4. Hires Ephraimites to assist against Edom, but at a prophet's command sends them back, conquers Edom, 2 Chr. 25.5-12. 2 Kin. 14.7.

His idolatry rebuked, is defeated and taken prisoner by Joash, 2 Kin.14.8-15. 2 Chr.25.14-24. Assassinated, 2 Kin. 14.19,20. 2 Chr. 25.25-28. The early part of his reign good, 2 Kin. 14.3,4. 2 Kin. 15.3. 2 Chr. 25.2 2 Chr. 26.4.

————, priest at Bethel under Jeroboam II. Amos prophesies against him, Amos 7. 10-17.

AMBASSADORS, to Edom, Num. 20.14; to the Amorites, Num. 21.21; from Gibeonites, Jos. 9.4; to Ammon, Jud. 11.12; from Hiram, 2 Sam. 5.11; to Ammon, 2 Sam. 10.1-5; from Benhadad, 1 Kin. 20.2; from Amaziah, 2 Kin. 14.8; to Tiglath, 2 Kin. 16.7; to So, 2 Kin. 17.4; from Sennacherib, 2 Kin. 19.9; from Berodach, 2 Kin.20.12. 2 Chr. 32.31; to Egypt, Eze. 17.15.

Custom of sending referred to, Pro. 13.17. Isa. 18.2. Isa. 30.4. Isa. 33.7. Jer. 49.14. Luk. 14.32. Illustrative, 2 Cor. 5.18-20.

AMBER, signifies burnished brass, Eze. 1.4,27. See Eze. 8.2. Rev. 1.15.

AMBITION. See PRIDE.

AMBUSHES, AND STRATAGEMS, at Ai, Jos. 8.2-22; against Midian, Jud. 7.16-22; at Shechem, Jud. 9.34; at Gibeah, Jud. 20.29-41; by Jonathan, 1 Sam. 14.8-14; by David, 2 Sam. 5.23; by Jeroboam, 2 Chr. 13.13; by Jehoshaphat, 2 Chr. 20.22. Allusion to, Jer. 51.12.

AMEN, a strong affirmation, equivalent to an oath, Num. 5.22. Deu. 27.12-26. Neh. 5.13. 2 Cor. 1.20. Rev. 1.18 Rev. 22.20. Used in prayer and praise, 1 Jn. 1.36. 1 Chr. 16.36. Neh. 8.6. Psa. 41.13. Psa. 72.19. Psa. 89.52. Psa. 106.48. Jer. 28.6. Mat. 6.13. 1 Cor. 14.16. Rev. 5.14. Rev. 19.4. A name of Christ. Rev. 3.14.

AMETHYST, a precious stone in the high-priest's breastplate, Ex. 28.19. Ex. 39.12. In the foundations of the new Jerusalem, Rev. 21.20.

AMMAH, a hill near Gibeon, Abner defeated at, 2 Sam. 2.24.

AMMINADIB signifies attendants of the prince, Song 6.12.

AMMONITES, descended from Ben-ammi, son of Lot, Gen. 19.38. Territory of, Num. 21.24. Deu. 2.19. Jos. 12.2. Jos. 13.10,25. Israelites forbidden to attack, Deu. 2.19,37.

Inhospitality to Israel punished by their being shut out from the congregation, Deu. 23. 3-6. Neh. 13.1. Invade Israel, Jud. 3.13. Oppress Israel, defeated by Jephthah, Jud. 10. 7-18. Jud. 11. Jud. 12.1-3. By Saul, 1 Sam. 11. 1 Sam. 14.47.

By David, 2 Sam. 8.12. 2 Sam. 12.26-31. 2 Sam. 17.27. 1 Chr. 18.11. By Joab, 2 Sam. 10. 2 Sam. 11.1-17. 1 Chr. 20.1-3. By Jehoshaphat, 2 Chr. 20. By Jotham, and made tributary, 2 Chr. 27.5. Tributary to Uzziah, 2 Chr. 26.8.

Invade Gilead, &c., Jer. 49.1. Amos 1.13. Assist Nebuchadnezzar against Jehoiakim, 2 Kin. 24.2. See Psa. 83.7,8. Aid in the murder of Gedaliah, Jer. 40.11,14. Jer. 41.10,15. Oppose the building of Jerusalem, Neh. 4.1-12. See TOBIAH.

Intermarriages with, by Solomon, 1 Kin.11.1. 2 Chr. 12.13. Neh. 13.26. By Jews, Ezr. 9.1. Neh. 13.23.

Kings of. See BAALIS, HANUN, NAHASH.
Towns of. See HESHBON, MINNITH, RABBAH.

Idols of. See MILCOM, MOLOCH.

Prophecies of, Isa. 11.14. Jer. 9.25,26. Jer. 25.15-21. Jer. 27.1-11. Jer. 49.1-6. Eze. 21. 20,28-32. Eze. 25.1-11. Dan. 11.41. Amos 1.13-15. Zeph. 2.9-11.

AMNON, eldest son of David and Ahinoam, 2 Sam. 3.2. 1 Chr. 3.1. Slain by Absalom for his conduct to Tamar, 2 Sam. 13.

AMON, fourteenth king of Judah, son and successor of Manasseh, 2 Kin. 21.18,19. 1 Chr. 3.14. 2 Chr. 33.20,21. Mat. 1.10. His wickedness and idolatry, 2 Kin. 21.20-22. 2 Chr. 33.22,23. Assassinated, his murderers punished, 2 Kin. 21.23-26. 2 Chr. 33.24,25.

AMORITES. Descended from Canaan, Gen. 10.15,16. 1 Chr. 1.13,14. Their stature, Deu. 3.11. Amos 2.9. Territory of, Gen. 14.7. Num. 13.29. Num. 21.13. Deu. 1.4,7,19. Deu. 3.8,9. Jos. 5.1. Jos. 10.5. Jos. 11.3. Jos. 12.2-5. Jud. 1.36. Dukes of, Jos. 13.21.

Defeated by Chedorlaomer; Aner and Eshcol allied with Abraham, Gen. 14.7-24. Defeated by Jacob, Gen. 48.22.

Iniquity and idolatry of, Gen. 15.16. Jud. 6.10. 1 Kin. 21.26. 2 Kin. 21.11. Ezr. 9.1. (See CHEMOSH.) Land of, given to Israel, Gen. 15.21. Deu. 7.1. Jos. 3.10. Jud. 11.23. Israel commanded to destroy, Deu. 20.17,18.

Defeat Israel at Hormah, Num. 14.45. Deu. 1.44. King of, defeated. See SIHON. Five kings of, defeated by Joshua, Jos. 10. Jos. 11. Territory of, given to Reuben, Gad, & Manasseh, Num. 32.33-42. Jos. 13.15-21. (See GILEAD.) Partially conquered, Jud. 1.34, 35. Peace with Israel, Jud. 3.5. 1 Sam. 7.14. 2 Sam. 21.2. (See GIBEONITES.) Tributary to Solomon, 1 Kin. 9.20,21. 2 Chr. 8.7. Intermarriages with, by Jews, Ezr. 9.1,2.

AMOS, a herdman of Tekoa, prophesies in the reign of Uzziah, &c., Amos 1.1. Amos 7.14. His boldness when forbidden to prophesy, Amos 7.10-17.

AMPHIPOLIS, a town of Macedonia, Act. 17.1.

AMPLIAS, a Christian at Rome, Rom. 16.8.

AMRAM, son of Kohath, father of Moses, Ex. 6.18,20. Num. 26.58,59. 1 Chr. 6.3,18. 1 Chr. 23.12,13. Heb. 11.23. Head of a family of Kohathites, Num. 3.19,27. 1 Chr. 26.23.

AMRAPHEL, king of Shinar, invades Canaan, Gen. 14.1,9.

AMUSEMENTS. See DANCING, GAMES, MUSIC.

ANAH, finds *mules* in the wilderness, perhaps *warm springs*, Gen. 36.24.

ANAKIM, a race of giants in Canaan, Num. 13.28-33. Deu. 1.28. Deu. 2.10. Deu. 9.2. Defeated by Joshua—a remnant of left among the Philistines, Jos. 11.21,22. Defeated by Caleb, Jos. 14.12,15. Jos. 15.13,14. Jud. 1.20. Hebron their chief city. See HEBRON.

ANAMMELECH, an Assyrian idol, brought to Samaria, 2 Kin. 17.31.

ANANIAS, high-priest, commands Paul to be smitten, Act. 23.2-5 Accuses him to Felix, Act. 24.1, and to Festus, Act. 25.2.

————, his sale of land, falsehood, and death as a judgment, Act. 5.1-11.

————, a Christian of Damascus, his vision, restores Paul's sight and baptizes him, Act. 9.10-18. Act. 22.12-16.

ANATHEMA, meaning accursed or separated, Rom. 9.3. 1 Cor. 16.22. Gal. 1.8,9. A term implying execration, translated accursed, 1 Cor. 12.3. Meaning things devoted to destruction; see VOWS—OATHS.

ANATHOTH, a city of the priests in Benjamin, Jos. 21.13,18. 1 Chr. 6.60. 1 Kin. 2.26. Isa. 10.30. Birthplace and residence of Jeremiah, Jer. 1.1. Jer. 29.27. Jer. 32.7-12. Prophecy against, Jer. 11.21-23. Inhabitants of, return from captivity, Ezr. 2.23. Neh. 7.27.

ANCHOR, Act. 27.29,30,40. Illustrative, Heb. 6.19.

ANCIENTS, same as elders, Psa. 119.100, &c.

ANDREW, an apostle, son of Jonas and brother of Peter, a fisherman of Bethsaida, Mat. 4.18. Jno. 1.44. A disciple of John; he comes to Christ, and brings Peter, Jno. 1.35-42. His call, Mat. 4.18, Mar. 1.16, and Apostleship, Mat. 10.2. Luk. 6.14. Act. 1.13.

His remark before the miracle of feeding five thousand, Jno. 6.9. Brings Greeks to Jesus, Jno. 12.22. Asks Christ of his second coming, Mar. 13.3. Meets with the disciples in the upper room, Act. 1.13.

ANDRONICUS, Paul's kinsman, and fellow-prisoner. Rom. 16.7.

ANER, an Amoritish chief, allied with Abraham against Chedorlaomer, Gen. 14.14-24.

ANGEL OF THE LORD (of JEHOVAH). A divine person. Compare Gen. 16.7 with *v.* 13. Gen. 18.2 with *v.* 22. Gen. 22.11 with *v.* 12.   *v.* 15 with *v.* 16.   Gen. 31.11 with *v.* 13. Gen. 32.24 with *v.* 30.   Gen. 48.16 with *v.* 15. Ex. 3.2 with *v.* 4,6,14, Deu. 33.16, Jos. 5.13-15, & Jos. 6.2.   Ex. 19.19,20 & Ex. 20.1 with Act. 7.38 & Ex. 23.20,21.   Jud. 13.3 with *v.* 18 (*marg.*) and *v.* 19,22.   Called Angel of his Presence, Isa. 63.9 with Ex. 33.14,15.   Called Messenger (angel) of the Covenant, Mal. 3.1. See Jno. 2.13-17.   Called Christ, 1 Cor. 10.9 with Num. 21.5,6.   Ex. 17.2,7.   See Heb. 11.26.

ANGEL, ARCHANGEL (chief angel), 1 The. 4.16.   Jude 9.   See Rev. 8.2—GABRIEL —MICHAEL.

ANGELS. Gen. 3.24.   At the east of the garden of Eden, cherubims, and a flaming sword which turned every way, to keep the way of the tree of life.

Jud. 13.6.   His countenance *was* like the countenance of an angel of God, very terrible.

2 Kin. 6.17.   The mountain *was* full of horses and chariots of fire round about Elisha.

Job 4.18.   He put no trust in his servants ; and his angels he charged with folly.

Psa. 8.5.   Thou hast made him a little lower than the angels.

Psa. 34.7.   The angel of the Lord encampeth round about them that fear him, and delivereth them.

Psa. 68.17.   The chariots of God *are* twenty thousand, *even* thousands of angels : the Lord *is* among them, *as* in Sinai.

Psa. 91.11.   He shall give his angels charge over thee, to keep thee in all thy ways.   12. They shall bear thee up in *their* hands, lest thou dash thy foot against a stone.

Psa. 104.4.   Who maketh his angels spirits ; his ministers a flaming fire.

Isa. 6.2.   Above it stood the seraphims : each one had six wings ; with twain he covered his face, and with twain he covered his feet, and with twain he did fly.

Eze. 1.13.   As for the likeness of the living creatures, their appearance *was* like burning coals of fire, *and* like the appearance of lamps : it went up and down among the living creatures ; and the fire was bright, and out of the fire went forth lightning.   14. And the living creatures ran and returned as the appearance of a flash of lightning.   24. Like the noise of great waters, as the voice of the Almighty, the voice of speech, as the noise of an host : when they stood, they let down their wings.   *v.* 4-25. Eze. 10.

Dan. 4.13.   A watcher and an holy one came down from heaven.   17. This matter *is* by the decree of the watchers, and the demand by the word of the holy ones.

Dan. 8.13.   I heard one saint speaking, and another saint said unto that certain *saint* which spake.

Dan. 10.6.   His body also *was* like the beryl, and his face as the appearance of lightning, and his eyes as lamps of fire, and his arms and his feet like in colour to polished brass, and the voice of his words like the voice of a multitude.

Zec. 6.5.   The angel answered and said unto me, These *are* the four spirits of the heavens, which go forth from standing before the Lord of all the earth.

Mat. 13.39.   The reapers are the angels.   41. The Son of man shall send forth his angels, and they shall gather out of his kingdom all

things that offend, and them which do iniquity.   *v.* 39-42,49.

Mat. 18.10.   In heaven their angels do always behold the face of my Father which is in heaven.

Mat. 24.31.   He shall send his angels with a great sound of a trumpet, and they shall gather together his elect.   36. Of that day and hour knoweth no *man*, no, not the angels of heaven.

Mat. 25.31.   The Son of man shall come in his glory, and all the holy angels with him.

Mat. 26.53.   He shall presently give me more than twelve legions of angels.

Mat. 28.3.   His countenance was like lightning, and his raiment white as snow.   *v.* 1-8.

Luk. 12.8.   Him shall the Son of man also confess before the angels of God :   9. But he that denieth me before men, shall be denied before the angels of God.

Luk. 15.10.   There is joy in the presence of the angels of God over one sinner that repenteth.   *v.* 7.

Luk. 16.22.   The beggar died, and was carried by the angels into Abraham's bosom.

Jno. 1.51.   Ye shall see heaven open, and the angels of God ascending and descending upon the Son of man.

Act. 7.53.   Who have received the law by the disposition of angels.

Gal. 3.19.   *It was* ordained by angels in the hand of a mediator.

Eph. 3.10.   That now, unto the principalities and powers in heavenly *places*, might be known by the church the manifold wisdom of God.

Col. 1.16.   By him were all things created that are in heaven, and that are in earth, visible and invisible, whether *they be* thrones, or dominions, or principalities, or powers.

2 The. 1.7.   The Lord Jesus shall be revealed from heaven with his mighty angels.

1 Tim. 3.16.   God was manifest in the flesh, justified in the Spirit, seen of angels.

Heb. 1.6.   Let all the angels of God worship him.   7. And of the angels he saith, Who maketh his angels spirits, and his ministers a flame of fire.   14. Are they not all ministering spirits, sent forth to minister for them who shall be heirs of salvation ?

Heb. 2.2.   The word spoken by angels was steadfast.

Heb. 12.22.   An innumerable company of angels.   *v.* 4-14.

1 Pet. 1.12.   Which things the angels desire to look into.

1 Pet. 3.22.   Angels, and authorities, and powers ; being made subject unto him.

2 Pet. 2.11.   Angels, which are greater in power and might, bring not railing accusation against them before the Lord.

Rev. 5.11.   I beheld, and I heard the voice of many angels round about the throne, and the beasts, and the elders : and the number of them was ten thousand times ten thousand, and thousands of thousands.

Rev. 10.1.   I saw another mighty angel come down from heaven, clothed with a cloud ; and a rainbow *was* upon his head, and his face *was* as it were the sun, and his feet as pillars of fire : 2. And he had in his hand a little book open : and he set his right foot upon the sea, and *his* left *foot* on the earth,   3. And cried with a loud voice, as *when* a lion roareth : and when he had cried, seven thunders uttered their voices. *v.* 4-11.

Rev. 14.10. He shall be tormented with fire and brimstone in the presence of the holy angels.

Rev. 15.6. The seven angels came out of the temple, having the seven plagues, clothed in pure and white linen, and having their breasts girded with golden girdles.

Rev. 18.1. After these things I saw another angel come down from heaven, having great power; and the earth was lightened with his glory. 2. And he cried mightily with a strong voice, saying, Babylon the great is fallen.

Rev. 22.16. I Jesus have sent mine angel to testify unto you these things in the churches.

ANGELS, THEIR APPEARANCES AND COMMUNICATIONS. To Abraham, Gen. 18.2. Gen. 22.11-18. Hagar, Gen. 16.7. Lot, Gen. 19.1-17. Jacob, Gen. 28.12. Gen. 32.1,24. Moses, Ex. 3.2. Israelites, Ex. 14.19. Jud. 2.1-4. Balaam, Num. 22.31. Joshua, Jos. 5.15.

To Gideon, Jud. 6.11-22. Manoah and his wife Jud. 13.6,15-20. David, 2 Sam. 24.16. 1 Chr. 21.20. Elijah, 1 Kin. 19.5. Elisha, 2 Kin. 6.17. To Ezekiel, Eze. 1. Eze. 9. Eze. 10. Eze. 40.3. Daniel, Dan. 6.22. Dan. 10.5-10,16,18. Dan. 12.5-7. Shadrach, &c., Dan. 3.25. Zechariah, Zec. 2.3. Zec. 3.1,2. Zec. 4.1.

To Joseph, Mat. 1.20. Mat. 2.13,19. Zacharias, Luk. 1.11. The shepherds, Luk. 2.9,13. Christ, Mat. 4.11. Luk. 22.43. The sick at the pool of Siloam, Jno. 5.4.

To the keepers and women at Christ's sepulchre, Mat. 28.2-5. Luk. 24.23. Jno. 20.12. Disciples at Christ's ascension, Act. 1.10,11. Peter and John, Act. 5.19. Philip, Act. 8.26. Cornelius, Act. 10.3. Paul, Act. 27.23. John, Rev. 1.1. Rev. 5.2. Rev. 7.11. Rev. 10.9. Rev. 11.1. Rev. 17.7. Rev. 22.8.

See CHERUBIM — SERAPHIM — GABRIEL— MICHAEL.

——————, JUDGMENTS INFLICTED BY, on Sodom, Gen. 19. Jerusalem, 2 Sam. 24.16. 1 Chr. 21.15,16. Assyrians, Isa. 37.36. Herod, Act. 12.23.

——————, WORSHIP OF, forbidden, Col. 2.18. Rev. 19.10. Rev. 22.8,9.

—————— WORSHIP GOD. See PRAISE IN HEAVEN.

—————— OF THE CHURCHES, Rev. 1.20. Rev. 2.1,8,12,18. Rev. 3.1,7,14.

——————, FALLEN, 2 Pet. 2.4. Jude 6. See DEMONS—SATAN.

ANGER. Gen. 4.6. Why art thou wroth? and why is thy countenance fallen?

Gen. 49.7. Cursed be their anger, for it was fierce; and their wrath, for it was cruel.

2 Chr. 28.9. A rage that reacheth up unto heaven.

Job 5.2. Wrath killeth the foolish man.

Job 18.4. He teareth himself in his anger.

Job 19.29. Wrath bringeth the punishments of the sword.

Psa. 37.8. Cease from anger, and forsake wrath.

Psa. 55.3. In wrath they hate me.

Pro. 6.34. Jealousy is the rage of a man: therefore he will not spare in the day of vengeance.

Pro. 12.16. A fool's wrath is presently known.

Pro. 14.17. He that is soon angry dealeth foolishly. 29. He that is slow to wrath is of great understanding: but he that is hasty of spirit exalteth folly.

Pro. 15.1. A soft answer turneth away wrath: but grievous words stir up anger. 18. A wrathful man stirreth up strife: but he that is slow to anger appeaseth strife.

Pro. 16.14. The wrath of a king is as messengers of death: but a wise man will pacify it. 32. He that is slow to anger is better than the mighty; and he that ruleth his spirit than he that taketh a city.

Pro. 19.11. The discretion of a man deferreth his anger. 12. The king's wrath is as the roaring of a lion. 19. A man of great wrath shall suffer punishment: for if thou deliver him, yet thou must do it again.

Pro. 21.24. Proud and haughty scorner is his name who dealeth in proud wrath.

Pro. 25.28. He that hath no rule over his own spirit is like a city that is broken down, and without walls.

Pro. 27.3. A stone is heavy, and the sand weighty; but a fool's wrath is heavier than them both. 4. Wrath is cruel, and anger is outrageous.

Pro. 29.8. Wise men turn away wrath. 9. If a wise man contendeth with a foolish man, whether he rage or laugh, there is no rest. 22. An angry man stirreth up strife, and a furious man aboundeth in transgression.

Pro. 30.33. The forcing of wrath bringeth forth strife.

Ecc. 7.9. Be not hasty in thy spirit to be angry; for anger resteth in the bosom of fools.

Jer. 48.30. I know his wrath, saith the Lord.

Hos. 7.16. Their princes shall fall by the sword for the rage of their tongue.

Amos 1.11. His anger did tear perpetually, and he kept his wrath for ever.

Jonah 4.4. Doest thou well to be angry?

Mat. 5.22. Whosoever is angry with his brother without a cause shall be in danger of the judgment.

2 Cor. 12.20. Lest there be debates, envyings, wraths, strifes, backbitings, whisperings, swellings, tumults.

Gal. 5.20. The works of the flesh are, wrath, strife.

Eph. 4.26. Be ye angry, and sin not: let not the sun go down upon your wrath. 31. All bitterness, and wrath, and anger, and clamour, and evil speaking, be put away from you.

Col. 3.8. Put off all these; anger, wrath, malice.

1 Tim. 2.8. Lifting up holy hands, without wrath.

Tit. 1.7. Not self-willed, not soon angry.

Jas. 1.19. Slow to speak, slow to wrath. 20. The wrath of man worketh not the righteousness of God.

ANGER, EXAMPLES OF. Pharaoh, Ex. 10.28. Moses, Num. 20.10,11. Balaam, Num. 22.27,29. Balak, Num. 24.10,11. Ephraimites, Jud. 8.1. 2 Chr. 25.10. Saul and Jonathan, 1 Sam. 20.30-34. Ahab, 1 Kin. 21.4. Naaman, 2 Kin. 5.12. Asa, 2 Chr. 16.10. Uzziah, 2 Chr. 26.19. Ahasuerus, Est. 1.12. Est. 7.7. Haman, Est. 3.5. Moab, Isa. 16.6. Nebuchadnezzar, Dan. 3.13. Herod, Mat. 2.16. Men of Nazareth, Luk. 4.28. Paul, Act. 23.3. See MALICE — MEEKNESS — FORGIVENESS. For ANGER, RIGHTEOUS, see ZEAL.

ANIMALS, CLEAN AND UNCLEAN, Lev. 11. Deu. 14.3-20.

ANISE, or DILL, an aromatic plant, Mat. 23.23.

ANNA, an aged prophetess, her prayer and fasting, she discourses of Christ in the Temple, Luk. 2.36-38.

ANNAS, joint high-priest with Caiaphas his son-in-law, Luk. 3.2. Christ brought before Jno. 18.13,19,24, and Peter, Act. 4.6.

ANOINTING of the person, Deu. 28.40. Ruth 3.3. Est. 2.12. Psa. 92.10. Psa. 104.15. Psa. 141.5. Pro. 27.9,16. Ecc. 9.8. Song 1.3. Song 4.10. Isa. 57.9. Amos 6.6. Mic. 6.15. Omitted during mourning, 2 Sam. 12.20. 2 Sam. 14.2. Isa. 61.3. Dan. 10.3.
Of guests, the head and feet, 2 Chr. 28.15. Of Jesus, Luk. 7.37,38,46. Jno. 11.2. Jno. 12.3. Of the sick, Isa. 1.6. Mar. 6.13. Luk. 10.34. Jas. 5.14. Rev. 3.18. For burial, Mat. 26.12. Mar. 14.8. Mar. 16.1. Luk. 23.56. Of weapons of war, Isa. 21.5.

———, SACRED, signifying consecration, Psa. 105.15. Isa. 10.27. Isa. 45.1. Eze. 28.14. Hab. 3.13. Zec. 4.14. Signifying Christ's consecration, Psa. 45.7. Psa. 89.20. Isa. 61.1. Dan. 9.24. Luk. 4.18. Act. 4.27. Act. 10.38. Heb. 1.9. Signifying spiritual gifts, 2 Cor. 1.21. 1 Jno. 2.20,27.
Of the high-priest, Ex. 29.29. Ex. 40.13. Lev. 6.20. Lev. 8.12. Lev. 16.32. Num. 35.25. Psa. 133.2. Of the priests, Ex. 30.30. Ex. 40.15. Lev. 4.3. Lev. 8.30. Num. 3.3.
Of kings, Jud. 9.8,15. Saul, 1 Sam. 9.16. 1 Sam. 10.1. 1 Sam. 15.1. 2 Sam. 1.14,21. David, 1 Sam. 16.3,12,13. 2 Sam. 2.4. 2 Sam. 5.3. 2 Sam. 12.7. 2 Sam. 19.21. 1 Chr. 11.3. Solomon, 1 Kin. 1.39. 1 Chr. 29.22. Jehu, 1 Kin. 19.16. 2 Kin. 9.1-3,12. Hazael, 1 Kin. 19.15. Joash, 2 Kin. 11.12. 2 Chr. 23.11. Jehoahaz, 2 Kin. 23.30.
Of Elisha, the prophet, 1 Kin. 19.16.
Of the Tabernacle, altars, and vessels, Ex. 29.36. Ex. 30.26-29. Ex. 40.9-11. Lev. 8.10. Num. 7,1,10.
Of Jacob's Pillar, Gen. 28.18. Gen. 31.13. Gen. 35.14. See OIL OF OLIVES—OIL, SACRED —OINTMENT.

ANT, its industry, Pro. 6.6-8. Pro. 30.25.

ANTEDILUVIANS, great age of, Gen. 5. Gen. 7.6. Giants among, Gen. 6.4. Polygamy practised by, Gen. 4.19. Religion of, Gen. 4.3,4,26. Arts and occupations of, Gen. 4.2,3. Gen. 4.20-22. Gen. 6.14-22. Dwellings of, Gen. 4.16-20. Food of, Gen. 1.29. Enoch prophesies to, Jude 14,15. Noah preaches to, Heb. 11.7. 1 Pet. 3.18-20. 2 Pet. 2.5. Wickedness and destruction of, Gen. 6.5-7. Gen. 7.1,21-23. Job 22.15-17. Mat. 24,37-39. Luk. 17.26,27. 2 Pet. 2.5. See FLOOD.

ANTELOPE. See DEER.

ANTICHRIST (an opposer of Christ), 1 Jno. 2.18,22. 1 Jno. 4.3. 2 Jno. 7. See APOSTASY OF LAST DAYS.

ANTIOCH, a city in Pisidia, Paul preaches at, and is expelled from, Act. 13.14-52. 2 Tim. 3.11. Jews from, persecute Paul at Lystra, he returns to it, Act. 14.19-22. Revisits, Act. 18.22.

———, a city in Syria, gospel successfully preached at, disciples first called Christians at, Act. 11.19-30. Barnabas and Saul sent from, Act. 13.1-3. Return to, Act. 14.26-28. Dissension in, about circumcision, Paul and Barnabas sent from, to Jerusalem, return with the apostles' letter, Act. 15.1-35. Paul reproves Peter at, Gal. 2.11-15.

ANTIPAS, a martyr, slain in Pergamos, Rev. 2.13.

ANTIPATRIS, a town in Samaria, Paul brought to, Act. 23.31.

ANVIL, Isa. 41.7.

APE, brought by Solomon's ships, 1 Kin. 10.22. 2 Chr. 9.21. See Isa. 13.21. Isa. 34.14.

APELLES, a Christian at Rome, Rom. 16.10.

APHARSACHITES, or APHARSATH-CHITES, colonists from Assyria, settled in Samaria, Ezr. 4.9. Ezr. 5.6. See 2 Kin. 17. 24-41.

APHEK, or APHEKAH, a city of Judah near Ebenezer, Philistines defeat Israel near, 1 Sam. 4.1.

———, a town of Issachar, near Jezreel, where Saul was slain, 1 Sam. 29.1.

———, a town of Syria, Benhadad takes refuge in, 1 Kin. 20.26.

APOLLONIA, a city of Macedonia, visited by Paul, Act. 17.1.

APOLLOS, a Jew, born at Alexandria, a disciple of John, his zeal and preaching, instructed by Aquila and Priscilla, teaches in Corinth, Act. 18.24-28. Act. 19.1. A sect in Corinth follow him as their teacher, 1 Cor. 1.12. 1 Cor. 3.4-7. Declines to return to Corinth, 1 Cor. 16.12. Paul's regard for him, Tit. 3.13.

APOLLYON (a destroyer), the angel of the bottomless pit, Rev. 9.11.

APOSTACY. See BACKSLIDING.

———OF THE LAST DAYS, Dan. 7.25,26. 2 The. 2.3-10. 1 Tim. 4.1-3. 2 Tim. 3.1-5. 2 Tim. 4.3. 2 Pet. 3.3,4. Jude 17-19. Rev. 20.8. See ANTICHRIST, BABYLON THE GREAT.

APOSTLES, imperfect knowledge and faith before Pentecost, Mat. 8.25-27. Mat. 15.23. Mat. 16.8-12,21,22. Mat. 19.25. Mar. 4.13. Mar. 6.51,52. Mar. 8.17,18. Mar. 9.9,10, 31,32. Mar. 10.13,14. Luk. 9.44,45. Luk. 18.34. Luk. 24.19,21. Jno. 4.32,33. Jno. 10.6. Jno. 11.12,13. Jno. 12.16. Jno. 13,6-8. Jno. 14.5-9,22. Jno. 16.6,17,18,32. Jno. 20.9. Jno. 21.12. Act. 1.6.

———, INSPIRATION AND AUTHORITY, Mat. 4.19. Follow me, and I will make you fishers of men. v. 18-22. Mat. 9.9. Jno. 1.43.
Mat. 10.1. When he had called unto *him* his twelve disciples, he gave them power *against* unclean spirits, to cast them out, and to heal all manner of sickness, and all manner of disease. 27. What I tell you in darkness, *that* speak ye in light : and what ye hear in the ear, *that* preach ye upon the house-tops. 40. He that receiveth you receiveth me, and he that receiveth me receiveth him that sent me. Luk. 10.16.
Mat. 16.17. Blessed art thou, Simon Bar-jona : for flesh and blood hath not revealed *it* unto thee, but my Father which is in heaven. 18. And I say also unto thee, That thou *art*

Peter, and upon this rock I will build my church ; and the gates of hell shall not prevail against it. 19. And I will give unto thee the keys of the kingdom of heaven : and whatsoever thou shalt bind on earth shall be bound in heaven : and whatsoever thou shalt loose on earth shall be loosed in heaven.

Mat. 18.18. Whatsoever ye shall bind on earth shall be bound in heaven : and whatsoever ye shall loose on earth shall be loosed in heaven. 19. Again I say unto you, That if two of you shall agree on earth as touching any thing that they shall ask, it shall be done for them of my Father which is in heaven.

Mat. 19.28. Ye which have followed me, in the regeneration when the Son of man shall sit in the throne of his glory, ye also shall sit upon twelve thrones, judging the twelve tribes of Israel.

Mat. 28.19. Go ye therefore, and teach all nations, baptizing them in the name of the Father, and of the Son, and of the Holy Ghost. 20. Teaching them to observe all things whatsoever I have commanded you : and, lo, I am with you alway, *even* unto the end of the world. Amen.

Mar. 3.14. He ordained twelve, that they should be with him, and that he might send them forth to preach, 15. And to have power to heal sicknesses, and to cast out devils. *v.* 13-19.

Mar. 6.7. He called *unto him* the twelve, and began to send them forth by two and two ; and gave them power over unclean spirits.

Mar. 16.15. He said unto them, Go ye into all the world, and preach the gospel to every creature.

Luk. 5.10. Jesus said unto Simon, Fear not ; from henceforth thou shalt catch men.

Luk. 22.28. Ye are they which have continued with me in my temptations. 29. And I appoint unto you a kingdom, as my Father hath appointed unto me ; 30. That ye may eat and drink at my table in my kingdom, and sit on thrones judging the twelve tribes of Israel.

Luk. 24.45. Then opened he their understanding, that they might understand the scriptures.

Jno. 20.23. Whose soever sins ye remit, they are remitted unto them ; *and* whose soever *sins* ye retain, they are retained.

Jno. 21.15. He saith unto him, Feed my lambs. 16. Feed my sheep. *v.* 17.

Act. 1.2. He through the Holy Ghost had given commandments unto the apostles whom he had chosen.

Act. 5.20. Stand and speak in the temple to the people all the words of this life.

Act. 6.2. It is not reason that we should leave the word of God, and serve tables. 4. But we will give ourselves continually to prayer, and to the ministry of the word.

Act. 9.15. He is a chosen vessel unto me, to bear my name before the Gentiles, and kings, and the children of Israel.

Act. 10.33. Now therefore are we all here present before God, to hear all things that are commanded thee of God. 42. He commanded us to preach unto the people, and to testify that it is he which was ordained of God *to be* the Judge of quick and dead.

Act. 13.46. Lo, we turn to the Gentiles. 47. For so hath the Lord commanded us.

Act. 15.7. A good while ago God made choice

among us, that the Gentiles by my mouth should hear the word of the gospel, and believe.

Act. 16.9. There stood a man of Macedonia, and prayed him, saying, Come over into Macedonia, and help us. 10. And after he had seen the vision, immediately we endeavoured to go into Macedonia, assuredly gathering that the Lord had called us for to preach the gospel unto them.

Act. 18.9. Then spake the Lord to Paul in the night by a vision, Be not afraid, but speak, and hold not thy peace : 10. For I am with thee, and no man shall set on thee to hurt thee.

Act. 20.24. The ministry, which I have received of the Lord Jesus, to testify the gospel of the grace of God.

Act. 27.23. There stood by me this night the angel of God, whose I am, and whom I serve.

Rom. 1.1. Paul, a servant of Jesus Christ, called *to be* an apostle, separated unto the gospel of God. 5. By whom we have received grace and apostleship, for obedience to the faith among all nations, for his name.

Rom. 11.13. I speak to you Gentiles, inasmuch as I am the apostle of the Gentiles, I magnify mine office.

Rom. 15.15. Putting you in mind, because of the grace that is given to me of God. 16. That I should be the minister of Jesus Christ to the Gentiles, ministering the gospel of God.

1 Cor. 1.17. Christ sent me not to baptize, but to preach the gospel : not with wisdom of words, lest the cross of Christ should be made of none effect.

1 Cor. 2.7. We speak the wisdom of God in a mystery, *even* the hidden *wisdom*, which God ordained before the world unto our glory. 16. We have the mind of Christ.

1 Cor. 3.9. We are labourers together with God : ye are God's husbandry ; *ye are* God's building. 10. According to the grace of God which is given unto me, as a wise masterbuilder, I have laid the foundation.

1 Cor. 4.1. Let a man so account of us as of the ministers of Christ, and stewards of the mysteries of God.

1 Cor. 5.3. I verily, as absent in body, but present in spirit, have judged already, as though I were present, *concerning* him that hath so done this deed.

1 Cor. 7.17. As God hath distributed to every man, as the Lord hath called every one, so let him walk. So ordain I in all churches. 25. Now concerning virgins I have no commandment of the Lord : yet I give my judgment, as one that hath obtained mercy of the Lord to be faithful.

1 Cor. 9.1. Am I not an apostle ? am I not free ? have I not seen Jesus Christ our Lord ? are not ye my work in the Lord ? 2. If I be not an apostle unto others, yet doubtless I am to you : for the seal of mine apostleship are ye in the Lord.

1 Cor. 9.16. Though I preach the gospel, I have nothing to glory of : for necessity is laid upon me ; yea, woe is unto me, if I preach not the gospel. 17. For if I do this thing willingly, I have a reward : but if against my will, a dispensation *of the gospel* is committed unto me.

1 Cor. 11.2. Now I praise you, brethren, that ye remember me in all things, and keep the ordinances, as I delivered *them* to you.

23. I have received of the Lord that which also I delivered unto you, That the Lord Jesus the *same* night in which he was betrayed took bread.

1 Cor. 12.28. God hath set some in the church, first apostles.

1 Cor. 14.18. I thank my God, I speak with tongues more than ye all.

2 Cor. 1.23. To spare you I came not as yet unto Corinth. 24. Not for that we have dominion over your faith, but are helpers of your joy.

2 Cor. 2.10. To whom ye forgive any thing, I *forgive* also : for if I forgave any thing, to whom I forgave *it*, for your sakes *forgave I it* in the person of Christ. 14. Thanks *be* unto God, which always causeth us to triumph in Christ, and maketh manifest the savour of his knowledge by us in every place.

2 Cor. 3.5. Not that we are sufficient of ourselves to think any thing as of ourselves ; but our sufficiency *is* of God ; 6. Who also hath made us able ministers of the new testament ; not of the letter, but of the spirit : for the letter killeth, but the spirit giveth life.

2 Cor. 4.6. God, who commanded the light to shine out of darkness, hath shined in our hearts, to *give* the light of the knowledge of the glory of God in the face of Jesus Christ. 7. But we have this treasure in earthen vessels, that the excellency of the power may be of God, and not of us. *v.* 1-18.

2 Cor. 5.18. Hath given to us the ministry of reconciliation ; 20. Now then we are ambassadors for Christ, as though God did beseech *you* by us : we pray *you* in Christ's stead, be ye reconciled to God. *v.* 19.

2 Cor. 6.1. We then, *as* workers together *with him*, beseech *you* also that ye receive not the grace of God in vain.

2 Cor. 10.6. Having in a readiness to revenge all disobedience, when your obedience is fulfilled. 8. For though I should boast somewhat more of our authority, (which the Lord hath given us for edification, and not for your destruction,) I should not be ashamed.

2 Cor. 10.11. Let such an one think this, that, such as we are in word by letters when we are absent, such *will we be* also in deed when we are present. 13. We will not boast of things without *our* measure, but according to the measure of the rule which God hath distributed to us, a measure to reach even unto you. *v.* 1-18.

2 Cor. 11.5. I suppose I was not a whit behind the very chiefest apostles. *v.* 1-33.

2 Cor. 12.2. I knew a man in Christ above fourteen years ago, (whether in the body, I cannot tell ; or whether out of the body, I cannot tell : God knoweth ;) such an one caught up to the third heaven. 3. And I knew such a man, (whether in the body, or out of the body, I cannot tell : God knoweth ;) 4. How that he was caught up into paradise, and heard unspeakable words, which it is not lawful for a man to utter.

2 Cor. 12.7. Lest I should be exalted above measure through the abundance of the revelations, there was given to me a thorn in the flesh.

2 Cor. 12.11. In nothing am I behind the very chiefest apostles, though I be nothing. 12. Truly the signs of an apostle were wrought among you in all patience, in signs, and wonders, and mighty deeds. *v.* 1-21.

2 Cor. 13.2. And being absent now I write to them which heretofore have sinned, and to all other, that, if I come again, I will not spare : 3. Since ye seek a proof of Christ speaking in me, which to you-ward is not weak, but is mighty in you. 10. I write these things being absent, lest being present I should use sharpness, according to the power which the Lord hath given me to edification, and not to destruction. *v.* 9.

Gal. 1.1. Paul, an apostle, not of men, neither by man, but by Jesus Christ, and God the Father, who raised him from the dead. 11. I certify you, brethren, that the gospel which was preached of me is not after man. 12. For I neither received it of man, neither was I taught *it*, but by the revelation of Jesus Christ. 15. It pleased God, who separated me from my mother's womb, and called *me* by his grace, 16. To reveal his Son in me, that I might preach him among the heathen. *v.* 17-24.

Gal. 2.2. I went up by revelation. 8. For he that wrought effectually in Peter to the apostleship of the circumcision, the same was mighty in me toward the Gentiles.

Eph. 1.1. Paul, an apostle of Jesus Christ by the will of God.

Eph. 2.20. Are built upon the foundation of the apostles and prophets.

Eph. 3.2. If ye have heard of the dispensation of the grace of God which is given me to you-ward : 3. How that by revelation he made known unto me the mystery ; (as I wrote afore in few words, 4. Whereby, when ye read, ye may understand my knowledge in the mystery of Christ), 5. Which in other ages was not made known unto the sons of men, as it is now revealed unto his holy apostles and prophets by the Spirit.

Eph. 3.7. Whereof I was made a minister, according to the gift of the grace of God given unto me by the effectual working of his power. 8. Unto me, who am less than the least of all saints, is this grace given, that I should preach among the Gentiles the unsearchable riches of Christ ; 9. And to make all *men* see what *is* the fellowship of the mystery.

Eph. 4.11. He gave some, apostles ; and some, prophets. 17. This I say therefore, and testify in the Lord, that ye henceforth walk not as other Gentiles.

Phil. 4.9. Those things, which ye have both learned, and received, and heard, and seen in me, do.

Col 1.25. Whereof I am made a minister, according to the dispensation of God which is given to me for you, to fulfil the word of God. 29. Whereunto I also labour, striving according to his working, which worketh in me mightily.

1 The. 2.6. We might have been burdensome, as the apostles of Christ.

1 The. 4.15. This we say unto you by the word of the Lord.

2 The. 3.4. We have confidence in the Lord touching you, that ye both do and will do the things which we command you. 6. Now we command you, brethren, in the name of our Lord Jesus Christ, that ye withdraw yourselves from every brother that walketh disorderly, and not after the tradition which he received of us.

2 The. 3.14. If any man obey not our word by this epistle, note that man, and

have no company with him, that he may be ashamed.

1 Tim. 1.1. Paul, an apostle of Jesus Christ by the commandment of God our Saviour, and Lord Jesus Christ. 11. According to the glorious gospel of the blessed God, which was committed to my trust. 12. I thank Christ Jesus our Lord, who hath enabled me, for that he counted me faithful, putting me into the ministry.

1 Tim. 1.20. Hymeneus and Alexander; whom I have delivered unto Satan, that they may learn not to blaspheme.

1 Tim. 2.7. I am ordained a preacher and an apostle (I speak the truth in Christ, *and* lie not); a teacher of the Gentiles in faith and verity. 2 Tim. 1.11.

2 Tim. 1.1. Paul, an apostle of Jesus Christ by the will of God, according to the promise of life which is in Christ Jesus.

2 Tim. 4.17. The Lord stood with me, and strengthened me; that by me the preaching might be fully known, and *that* all the Gentiles might hear.

Tit. 1.1. Paul, a servant of God, and an apostle of Jesus Christ, according to the faith of God's elect, and the acknowledging of the truth which is after godliness; 3. But hath in due times manifested his word through preaching, which is committed unto me, according to the commandment of God our Saviour.

Jas. 1.1. James, a servant of God and of the Lord Jesus Christ.

2 Pet. 1.14. I must put off *this* my tabernacle, even as our Lord Jesus Christ hath shewed me.

2 Pet. 3.2. That ye may be mindful of the words which were spoken before by the holy prophets, and of the commandment of us the apostles of the Lord and Saviour. Jude 17.

1 Jno. 4.6. He that knoweth God heareth us; he that is not of God heareth not us. Hereby know we the spirit of truth, and the spirit of error.

2 Jno. 9. I wrote unto the church: but Diotrephes, who loveth to have the preeminence among them, receiveth us not. 10. Wherefore, if I come, I will remember his deeds which he doeth, prating against us with malicious words.

Rev. 10.11. Thou must prophesy again before many peoples, and nations, and tongues, and kings.

Rev. 21.14. The wall of the city had twelve foundations, and in them the names of the twelve apostles of the Lamb. See MINISTERS—(THE) SEVENTY—WORD OF GOD.

APOSTLES, INSPIRATION BY THE HOLY SPIRIT, Mat. 3.11. He shall baptize you with the Holy Ghost and with fire.

Mat. 10.19. When they deliver you up, take no thought how or what ye shall speak: for it shall be given you in that same hour what ye shall speak. 20. For it is not ye that speak, but the Spirit of your Father which speaketh in you. Mar. 13.11. Luk. 21.14,15. Luk. 12.11,12.

Luk. 24.49. Behold, I send the promise of my Father upon you: but tarry ye in the city of Jerusalem, until ye be endued with power from on high.

Jno. 14.16. I will pray the Father, and he shall give you another Comforter, that he may

abide with you for ever; 17. *Even* the Spirit of truth; whom the world cannot receive, because it seeth him not, neither knoweth him: but ye know him; for he dwelleth with you, and shall be in you.

Jno. 14.26. But the Comforter, *which is* the Holy Ghost, whom the Father will send in my name, he shall teach you all things, and bring all things to your remembrance, whatsoever I have said unto you.

Jno. 15.26. But when the Comforter is come, whom I will send unto you from the Father, *even* the Spirit of truth, which proceedeth from the Father, he shall testify of me.

Jno. 16.13. Howbeit when he, the Spirit of truth, is come, he will guide you into all truth: for he shall not speak of himself; but whatsoever he shall hear, *that* shall he speak: and he will shew you things to come. 14. He shall glorify me: for he shall receive of mine, and shall shew *it* unto you. 15. All things that the Father hath are mine: therefore said I, that he shall take of mine, and shall shew *it* unto you.

Jno. 20.21. Then said Jesus to them again, Peace *be* unto you: as *my* Father hath sent me, even so send I you. 22. And when he had said this, he breathed on *them*, and saith unto them, Receive ye the Holy Ghost.

Act. 1.4. Wait for the promise of the Father, which, *saith he*, ye have heard of me. 5. For John truly baptized with water; but ye shall be baptized with the Holy Ghost not many days hence. 8. Ye shall receive power, after that the Holy Ghost has come upon you.

Act. 2.1. When the day of Pentecost was fully come, they were all with one accord in one place. 2. And suddenly there came a sound from heaven, as of a rushing mighty wind, and it filled all the house where they were sitting. 3. And there appeared unto them cloven tongues, like as of fire, and it sat upon each of them: 4. And they were all filled with the Holy Ghost, and began to speak with other tongues, as the Spirit gave them utterance.

Act. 4.8. Peter, filled with the Holy Ghost, said. 31. When they had prayed, the place was shaken where they were assembled together; and they were all filled with the Holy Ghost, and they spake the word of God with boldness.

Act. 9.17. Brother Saul, the Lord, *even* Jesus, that appeared unto thee in the way as thou camest, hath sent me, that thou mightest receive thy sight, and be filled with the Holy Ghost.

Act. 10.19. While Peter thought on the vision, the Spirit said unto him, Behold three men seek thee.

Act. 11.12. The Spirit bade me go with them, nothing doubting.

Act. 13.2. The Holy Ghost said, Separate me Barnabas and Saul for the work whereunto I have called them. 4. They, being sent forth by the Holy Ghost, departed unto Seleucia. 9. Then Saul (who also *is called* Paul), filled with the Holy Ghost.

Act. 15.28. It seemed good to the Holy Ghost, and to us.

Act. 16.6. Were forbidden of the Holy Ghost to preach the word in Asia, 7. After they were come to Mysia, they assayed to go into Bithynia: but the Spirit suffered them not.

Act. 19.21. Paul purposed in the Spirit.

Act. 20.23. The Holy Ghost witnesseth in every city, saying that bonds and afflictions abide me.

1 Cor. 2.4. My preaching *was* not with enticing words of man's wisdom, but in demonstration of the Spirit and of power. 10. God hath revealed *them* unto us by his Spirit : for the Spirit searcheth all things, yea, the deep things of God.

1 Cor. 7.40. I think also that I have the Spirit of God.

Gal. 3.5. He therefore that ministereth to you the Spirit, and worketh miracles among you, *doeth he it* by the works of the law, or by the hearing of faith ?

Eph. 3.5. It is now revealed unto his holy apostles and prophets by the Spirit.

1 The. 4.8. He therefore that despiseth, despiseth not man, but God, who hath also given unto us his holy Spirit.

1 Tim. 4.1. The Spirit speaketh expressly, that in the latter times some shall depart from the faith.

Heb. 10.15. *Whereof* the Holy Ghost also is a witness to us.

1 Pet. 1.12. The things, which are now reported unto you by them that have preached the gospel unto you with the Holy Ghost sent down from heaven.

Rev. 1.10. I was in the Spirit on the Lord's day.

Rev. 4.1. I looked, and, behold, a door *was* opened in heaven : and the first voice which I heard *was* as it were of a trumpet talking with me ; which said, Come up hither, and I will shew thee things which must be hereafter. 2. And immediately I was in the spirit.

Rev. 14.13. I heard a voice from heaven saying unto me, Write, Blessed *are* the dead which die in the Lord from henceforth : Yea, saith the Spirit, that they may rest from their labours.

Rev. 17.3. So he carried me away in the spirit into the wilderness.

Rev. 21.10. He carried me away in the spirit to a great and high mountain, and shewed me that great city, the holy Jerusalem, descending out of heaven from God.

APOSTLES, MIRACULOUS GIFTS bestowed on, Mat. 10.1. Mar. 3.15. Mar. 6.7. Luk. 9.1,2. Luk. 10.9. Act. 2.4,43. Act. 5.12. 1 Cor. 14.18. 2 Cor. 12.12. See MIRACLES.

————, NAMES OF, Mat. 10.2-4. Mar. 3.16-19. Luk. 6.13-16. Act. 1.13,26. See ANDREW, BARTHOLOMEW, JAMES SON OF ZEBEDEE, JAMES SON OF ALPHEUS, JOHN, JUDAS ISCARIOT, JUDAS OF JUDE, MATTHEW or LEVI, PAUL, PETER, PHILIP, SIMON ZELOTES, THOMAS.

————, WITNESSES TO CHRIST, Luk. 24. 48. Ye are witnesses of these things.

Jno. 15.27. Ye also shall bear witness, because ye have been with me from the beginning.

Jno. 19.35. And he that saw *it* bare record, and his record is true : and he knoweth that he saith true, that ye might believe.

Jno. 21.24. This is the disciple which testifieth of these things, and wrote these things : and we know that his testimony is true.

Act. 1.8. Ye shall be witnesses unto me both in Jerusalem, and in all Judea, and in Samaria, and unto the uttermost part of the earth.

Act. 1.21. Of these men which have companied with us all the time that the Lord Jesus went in and out among us, 22. Beginning from the baptism of John, unto that same day that he was taken up from us, must one be ordained to be a witness with us of his resurrection.

Act. 10.39. We are witnesses of all things which he did both in the land of the Jews, and in Jerusalem ; whom they slew, and hanged on à tree : 40. Him God raised up the third day, and shewed him openly ; 41. Not to all the people, but unto witnesses chosen before of God, *even* to us, who did eat and drink with him after he rose from the dead. Act. 2.32. Act. 3.15. Act. 4.33. Act. 5.32. Act. 13.31.

Act. 22.14. The God of our fathers hath chosen thee, that thou shouldst know his will, and see that Just One, and shouldest hear the voice of his mouth. 15. For thou shalt be his witness unto all men of what thou hast seen and heard. Act. 23.11. Act. 26.16.

1 Cor. 9.1. Am I not an apostle ? am I not free ? have I not seen Jesus Christ our Lord ?

1 Cor. 15.8. Last of all he was seen of me also, as of one born out of due time. *v.* 5-9.

1 Pet. 5.1. Who am also an elder, and a witness of the sufferings of Christ.

2 Pet. 1.16. We have not followed cunningly devised fables, when we made known unto you the power and coming of our Lord Jesus Christ, but were eye-witnesses of his majesty. 18. This voice which came from heaven we heard, when we were with him in the holy mount.

1 Jno. 1.1. That which was from the beginning, which we have heard, which we have seen with our eyes, which we have looked upon, and our hands have handled, of the Word of life ; 2. (For the life was manifested, and we have seen *it*, and bear witness, and shew unto you that eternal life which was with the Father, and was manifested unto us:) 3. That which we have seen and heard declare we unto you, that ye also may have fellowship with us : and truly our fellowship *is* with the Father, and with his Son Jesus Christ.

APOSTLES' ZEAL. See ZEAL.

————, FALSE, 2 Cor. 11.13. Rev. 2.2. See FALSE TEACHERS.

APOSTLE (one sent forth, a messenger, Phi. 2.25). A name of Christ, Heb. 3.1. Barnabas so called, Act. 14.4,14.

APOTHECARY (a dealer in perfumes), Ex. 30.25,35. Ex. 37.29. Ecc. 10.1.

APPEAL made by Paul to Cæsar, Act. 25. 10,11. Act. 26.32. Act. 28.19.

APII-FORUM, a town in Italy, where the disciples met Paul, Act. 28.15.

APPLE (Citron), Song 2.3,5. Song 7.8. Song 8.5. Joel 1.12 with Pro. 25.11.

AQUILA and PRISCILLA banished from Rome, and come to Corinth, where Paul abides with them. Work at tent-making, Act. 18.1-3. Sail to Ephesus with Paul, instruct Apollos, Act. 18.18,19,26. Their zeal and attachment to Paul, Rom. 16.3,4. 2 Tim. 4.19. Send a salutation to the Corinthians, 1 Cor. 16.19. Return to Rome, Rom. 16.3.

AR, or RABBATH MOAB, the chief city of the Moabites, S. of the river Arnon, Num.

21.13-15. Deu. 2.9,18,24,29. Burnt by Sihon, king of Heshbon, Num. 21.26-30. Prophecy of, Isa. 15.1.

ARABIANS, descended from Ishmael, Gen. 25.13,14. 1 Chr. 1.29-31 with Isa. 21.11-17. Territory of, Gen. 25.18. 2 Chr. 26.7. Lived in tents, Isa. 13.20. Jer. 3.2. Bring gold to Solomon, 2 Chr. 9.14 ; and flocks to Jehoshaphat, 2 Chr. 17.11.

Invade Judah, slay Jehoram's sons, 2 Chr. 21.16,17. 2 Chr. 22.1. Defeated by Uzziah, 2 Chr. 26.7. Oppose the building of Jerusalem, Neh. 2.19. Neh. 4.7. Commerce of, with Tyre, Eze. 27.21. At Jerusalem on day of Pentecost, Act. 2.11. Paul visits, Gal. 1.17. Prophecies of, Isa. 21.11-17. Isa. 42.11. Isa. 60.7. Jer. 25.23,24. Jer. 49.28-33.

Tribes of. See DEDANIM, DUMAH, HAVILAH, ISHMAELITES, KEDAR, NEBAIOTH, SHEBA, TEMA. Town of, see GUR-BAAL.

ARAD, a Canaanitish king of a city of the same name, defeated by Israel at Hormah, Num. 21.1-3. Num. 33.40. Jos. 12.14. Jude 1.16.

ARAM. See MESOPOTAMIA—SYRIA.

ARARAT, a mountainous region in Armenia, on one of whose hills the ark rested, Gen. 8.4,5. See ARMENIA.

ARAUNAH, or ORNAN, the Jebusite ; his offer to David of his threshing-floor, &c., 2 Sam. 24.16-24. 1 Chr. 21.18-25.

ARBA. See HEBRON.

ARCH (galleries, *marg.*), Eze. 40.16.

ARCHANGEL. See ANGEL.

ARCHELAUS, son and successor of Herod I., governor of Judea, Mat. 2.22.

ARCHER, Gen. 21.20. 1 Sam. 31.3. Isa. 22.3. Jer. 51.3. See ARROW—BOW.

ARCHIPPUS, a Christian minister at Colosse. Paul's exhortation to, Col. 4.17. Philem. 2.

ARCTURUS (Heb. ASH), the Great Bear, a constellation, Job 9.9. Job 38.32.

AREOPAGUS, the supreme court in Athens, held on Mars' Hill. Paul's address to, Act. 17.19.22-34.

ARETAS, king of Syria, 2 Cor. 11.32.

ARGOB, a district in Bashan. See JAIR.

ARIEL, a poetical name of Jerusalem, Isa. 29.1.

ARIMATHEA (Rama ?), the city of Joseph, Mat. 27.57. Mar. 15.43. Luk. 23.51. Jno. 19.38.

ARIOCH, an officer of Nebuchadnezzar, Dan. 2.24.

ARISTARCHUS, a Macedonian, Paul's companion in travel and fellow-prisoner in Rome, Act. 19.29. Act. 20.4. Act. 27.2. Col. 4.10. Philem. 24.

ARISTOBULUS, household of, Christians, Rom. 16.10.

ARK of bulrushes in which Moses was preserved, Ex. 2.3.

—— OF THE COVENANT, called the Ark of the Covenant of the Lord, Num. 10.33. 2 Sam. 6.2. Of the testimony, Ex. 30.6. Of the Lord, Jos. 4.11. Of God, 1 Sam. 3.3. Of God's strength, 2 Chr. 6.41. Holy ark, 2 Chr. 35.3.

Made of shittim-wood, length 2½ cubits, breadth and height 1½, overlaid with gold, bordered with a gold crown, carried on staves passed through four gold rings, Ex. 25.10-15. Ex. 35.12. Ex. 37.1-5. Mercy-seat placed upon it. See MERCY-SEAT.

Contained, the two tables of the law, Ex. 25.16,21. Ex. 40.20. Deu. 10.5. Aaron's rod, Num. 17.10. Heb. 9.4. A golden pot of manna, Ex. 16.33,34. Heb. 9.4. A copy of the law, Deu. 31.26. In Solomon's time it contained only the tables of the law, 1 Kin. 8.9.

Placed in the Tabernacle in the Holy of Holies, Ex. 26.33. Ex. 40.21. 1 Sam. 3.3. 2 Sam. 7.2. 2 Sam. 11.11. 1 Kin. 8.6. 1 Chr. 17.1. Heb. 9.3,4. Was anointed with holy oil, Ex. 30.26. Was sprinkled with blood, and incense offered on it, on the day of atonement, Lev. 16.13-15.

Covered by the priests before removal with the vail of the Holy of Holies and other coverings, Num. 4.5,6. Carried by Kohathites, Num. 3.31. Num. 4.4,15. Deu. 10.8. 2 Sam. 15.24. 1 Chr. 15.2,15. By priests, Jos. 3.6,14. Jos. 8.33. Carried before Israelites in their march, Num. 10.33. Jos. 3.6.

Was sacred, Num. 4.5,15. 1 Sam. 6.19. 1 Chr. 15.2,13. 2 Chr. 35.3. Sanctified its resting-place, 2 Chr. 8.11. Levites ministered before, 1 Chr. 16.4,37. Inquiring of God before, Jud. 20.27. 1 Sam. 14.19. Neglect of, by the people in Saul's time, 1 Chr. 13.3. Worship before, Jos. 7.6. 2 Chr. 5.6-14. Symbolical of God's presence, Num. 14.44. 2 Chr. 6.41. Psa. 132.8. Prophecy of its temporary use, Jer. 3.16.

HISTORICAL NOTICES OF, AND MIRACLES CONNECTED WITH. Made by Bezaleel, Ex. 37.1. Jordan divided before it, Jos. 4.7. The walls of Jericho fall before it, Jos. 6.6-20. Set up at Shiloh, its continuance there, Jos. 18.1. Jos. 19.51. Jos. 21.2. Jud. 20.18,26,27. 1 Sam. 1.3,24.

Taken to battle by Israel, and captured by the Philistines, 1 Sam. 4.3-22. Dagon falls before it, 1 Sam. 5.1-4. The Philistines plagued on its account, 1 Sam. 5.6-12. Returned to Bethshemesh on a cart drawn by milch kine, 1 Sam. 6.1-18.

The men of Bethshemesh smitten for looking into, 1 Sam. 6.19-21. Brought to Abinadab's house in Kirjath-jearim, remains there twenty years, 1 Sam. 7.1,2. 2 Sam. 6.4. With Saul's army, 1 Sam. 14.18.

Fetched from Kirjath-jearim by David, Uzzah struck dead for touching it, 2 Sam. 6.1-8. 1 Chr. 13.3-11. Taken into the house of Obededom, where it remains three months, 2 Sam. 6.9-11. 1 Chr. 13.12-14.

Brought by David to Zion and placed in a tent. 2 Sam. 6.12-17. 1 Chr. 6.31. 1 Chr. 15. 1 Chr. 16.1. Placed in the Temple by Solomon, 1 Kin. 8.6-9. 2 Chr. 5.2-9. Restored by Josiah, 2 Chr. 35.3. Burned by Nebuchadnezzar, 2 Kin. 25.9. 2 Chr. 36.19.

ARK OF NOAH, made by divine direction, of gopher-wood, 300 cubits long, 50 broad, 30 high, Noah and his family saved in, Gen. 6.14-22. Gen. 7. Gen. 8. Mat. 24.38. Heb. 11.7. 1 Pet. 3.20.

ARK of the Testament seen by John in vision, Rev. 11.19.

ARKITES, descended from Canaan, Gen. 10.17. 1 Chr. 1.15.

ARM, illustrative, Ex. 6.6. Isa. 51.9.

ARMAGEDDON, signifying Mount of Mageddon, mentioned only in Rev. 16.16. See MEGIDDO.

ARMENIA, or ARARAT, a country E. of Asia Minor, 2 Kin. 19.37 (marg.). Jer. 51.27. Towns of, see MINNI, TOGARMAH.

ARMIES and WAR. Soldiers summoned by trumpet, see TRUMPET. Punishment for neglecting the summons, Jud. 21.5,8-11. 1 Sam. 11.7. Army numbered, Num. 26.2. 2 Sam. 18.1,2. 1 Kin. 20.15. 2 Sam. 10.6. 2 Chr. 12.3. 2 Chr. 14.9. 1 Sam. 11.8. 1 Sam. 13.2. 1 Sam. 14.17.

Order of March, Ex. 13.18 (marg.). 1 Chr. 12. 38. Joel 2.7,8. Divided into three companies, Jud. 7.16. Jud. 9.43. 1 Sam. 11.11. 1 Sam. 13.17,18. 2 Sam. 18.2. Other divisions, 2 Sam. 10.8,9. Job 1.17. See STANDARDS.

Inquiring of God before battle, Num. 27.21. Jud. 1.1. 1 Sam. 23.2-12. Sacrifices offered, 1 Sam. 13.11,12. Purification after, Num. 31. 19-24. Army preceded by singers, 2 Chr. 20. 21,22. Ark taken to battle, Jos. 6.6,7. 1 Sam. 4.4. 2 Sam. 15.24. Gods of Philistines taken to battle, 1 Chr. 14.12.

Army commanded by the king, 1 Sam. 8.20. 1 Sam. 11.11. 2 Sam. 12.29,30. 2 Chr. 18.29. See CAPTAINS. Battle-cries, signals, orations, and songs, Ex. 32.17,18. Num. 10.35. Deu. 21.2. Jud. 7.18. 1 Sam. 4.9. 1 Sam. 17.20,52. 2 Sam. 10.12. 2 Sam. 20.1. 2 Chr. 20.21.

Triumphs, processions, music, songs, and dances, Ex. 15.20,21. Num. 21.27-30. Jud. 5. 1 Sam. 18.6,7. 2 Chr. 20.27,23. See MUSIC—DANCING. Rewards, Jos.15.16. 1 Sam.17.25. 1 Sam. 18.21-27. 2 Sam. 18.11. 1 Chr. 11.6. Division of spoil, Num. 31.21-47. Deu. 20.14. Jos. 8.2-27. Jud. 5.30. 1 Sam. 21.9. 1 Sam. 30.23-25. 2 Sam. 12.30. Gen. 14.11,12. Ex. 15.9. Zec. 14.1. Slain, treatment of, 1 Sam. 17.54,57. 1 Sam. 31.8-10. 2 Sam. 4.8. 1 Kin. 11.15.

Stones cast on land, 2 Kin. 3.25. Cities sown with salt, Jud. 9.45. Single combat, 1 Sam. 17.4-10. Battle of picked men, 2 Sam. 2.14-16.

Divine aid promised to Israel, Lev. 26.7,8. Jos. 1.5. 1 Kin. 20.13,28. 2 Chr. 20.15-17. Miraculous interpositions, Ex. 14.19-31. Ex. 17.11. Jos. 6. Jos. 10.11-13. Jud. 7.22. 1 Sam. 14.20. 2 Kin. 3.22. 2 Kin. 19.35. 2 Chr. 20,22.

See ARMOUR-BEARER, HORSES, CITIES FENCED, GARRISON, CAPTIVES, HOSTAGES, VOWS, AMBUSH, SIEGE, HERALD, SPIES, AMBASSADOR, WAR, SOLDIERS, STANDARDS.

ARMOUR-BEARER of Abimelech, Jud. 9.54. Of Jonathan, 1 Sam. 14.6,7. Of Saul, 1 Sam. 16.21. 1 Sam. 31.6. Of Goliath, 1 Sam. 17.7. Of Joab, 2 Sam. 18.15.

ARMOURY of David, Song 4.4. Of Rehoboam, 2 Chr. 11.12. Of Hezekiah, Isa. 39.2. Illustrative, Jer. 50.25.

ARMS and ARMOUR. See ARROW, BATTLE-AXE, BATTERING-RAM, BOW, BREASTPLATE, BRIGANDINE, BUCKLER, CHARIOTS (WAR), COAT OF MAIL, DAGGER, DART, ENGINE, GREAVES, HABERGEON, HARNESS,

HELMET, JAVELIN, LANCE, SHIELD, SLING, SPEAR, SWORD.

ARNON, a river east of Jordan, the boundary of Moab and the Amorites, Num. 21. 13,26. Num. 22.36. Deu. 2.24,36. Deu. 3.8,16. Jos. 12.1. Fords of, Isa. 16.2.

AROER, an Amoritish town, possessed by Reubenites, Deu. 2.36. Jos. 12.2. Jos. 13,9. 1 Chr. 5.8. Isa. 17.2. Jer. 48.19.

————, built by Gadites, Num. 32.34. Jos. 13.25. Jud. 11.33. 2 Sam. 24.5.

————, in Judah, 1 Sam. 30.28.

ARPHAD, or ARPAD, a Syrian city, conquered by the Assyrians, 2 Kin. 18.34. 2 Kin. 19.13. Isa. 10.9. Isa. 36.19. Isa. 37.13. Jer. 49.23. See ARVADITES.

ARROWS used in battle, 1 Sam. 20.20,36. Job 41.28. Psa. 11.2. Isa. 5.28. Jer. 50.9,14. Jer. 51.11. Eze. 39.3,9. Ahab killed by, 1 Kin. 22.34 ; and Jehoram, 2 Kin. 9.24. Joash shoots by Elisha's command, 2 Kin. 13.16. See ARCHER—BOW. Employed in divination, Eze. 21.21. Illustrative, Num. 24.8. Job 6.4. Lam. 3.12,13. Eze. 5.16. Psa. 45.5. Jer. 9.8. Psa. 127.4. 2 Sam. 22.15. Hab. 3.11.

ARTAXERXES I., or AHASUERUS, king of Persia; stops the building of the Temple, Ezr. 4.6-24.

———— II., king of Persia, aids Ezra and the Jews, Ezr. 7. Aids Nehemiah and the Jews, Neh. 2. Neh. 5.14.

ARTEMAS, a Christian disciple ; Paul's assistant, Tit. 3.12.

ARTILLERY (weapons), 1 Sam. 20.40.

ARTS and MANUFACTURES. See BEATEN-WORK, BRASS, BREAD, BRICKS, CARPENTER, CARVING, COPPER, DRESS, DYEING, EMBROIDERY, ENGRAVING, FOUNDING, FULLER, GOLD, HOUSES, INK, IRON, LACE, LEATHER, LIME, LINEN, MASON, MINING, MUSIC, PAINTING, PAPER, PARCHMENT, PEN, PICTURES, POTTER, ROPES, SHIPS, SILK, SILVER, SMITH,SOAP, SPINNING, SUN-DIAL, TANNING, TAPESTRY, TENT, WEAVING, WINE, WRITING. See EMPLOYMENTS.

ARUMAH, or RUMAH, a town near Shechem, where Abimelech dwelt, Jud. 9.41. 2 Kin. 23.36.

ARVADITES, descended from Canaan, Gen. 10.18. 1 Chr. 1.16. Mariners and soldiers of, connected with Tyre, Eze. 27.8.11. See ARPHAD.

ASA, third king of Judah, son and successor of Abijah, 1 Kin. 15.8-10. 1 Chr. 3.10. 2 Chr. 14.1. Mat. 1.7. Removes idols and deposes Queen Maachah, 1 Kin. 15.11-14. 2 Chr. 14.2-5. 2 Chr. 15.8,16.

Azariah's prophecy causes him to repair the Temple, and with the people make a covenant with God, 2 Chr. 15. Early part of his reign peaceful ; his forts and garrisons, 2 Chr. 14.6-8. 2 Chr. 15.19.

Invasion of the Ethiopians ; his prayer and victory, 2 Chr. 14.9-15. 2 Chr. 16.8. Invasion of Baasha, Asa subsidizes Benhadad who defeats Baasha, 1 Kin. 15.16-22. 2 Chr. 16.1-6. Jer. 41.9.

Imprisons the prophet Hanani for rebuking him, and oppresses the people, 2 Chr. 16.7-10. His sickness and trust in physicians, 1 Kin. 15.23. 2 Chr. 16.12. Death and burial, 1 Kin.

15.24. 2 Chr. 16.13,14. Prophecies respecting, 2 Chr. 15.1-7. 2 Chr. 16.7-9.

ASAHEL, brother of Joab, one of David's captains, his fleetness, is slain by Abner, 2 Sam. 2.18-24,32. 2 Sam. 3.27. 2 Sam. 23.24. 1 Chr. 2.16. 1 Chr. 11.26.

ASAPH, a Levite, son of Barachias, 1 Chr. 6.39. One of the three leaders of sacred music under David, 1 Chr. 15.16-19. 1 Chr. 16.5-7. 1 Chr. 25.1-9. 2 Chr. 5.12. 2 Chr. 35.15. Neh. 12.46. Played on cymbals, 1 Chr. 16.5.

A prophet, 2 Chr. 29.30. His name attached to Psa. 50 & Psa. 73 to 83.

Sons of, choristers of the Temple, 1 Chr. 25.1,2. 2 Chr. 20.14. 2 Chr. 29.13. Ezr. 2.41. Ezr. 3.10,11. Neh. 7.44. Neh. 11.17,22.

ASENATH, daughter of Potipherah and wife of Joseph, Gen. 41.45. Gen. 46.20.

ASH, Isa. 44.14.

ASHDOD, or AZOTUS, one of the five chief cities of the Philistines, Jos. 13.3. 1 Sam. 6.17. Anakims remained in, Jos. 11.22. Seat of Dagon's temple in which the ark was placed ; inhabitants of plagued, 1 Sam. 5. Dismantled by Uzziah, 2 Chr. 26.6.

Taken by Tartan, Isa. 20.1. Jews married women from, Neh. 13.23. Language of, Neh. 13.24. Visited by Philip, Act. 8.40. Prophecies of. See PHILISTINES.

ASHER, son of Jacob and Zilpah, Gen. 30.13. Gen. 35.26. Ex. 1.4. 1 Chr. 2.2. His children, Gen. 46.17. Blessed by Jacob, Gen. 49.20.

————, TRIBE OF. Numbered at Sinai, Num. 1.41, and in the plains of Moab, Num. 26.44-47. Families of, Num. 26.44-47. 1 Chr. 7.30-40. Encamped north of the Tabernacle, under the standard of Dan, Num. 2.25,27.

Blessing of Moses on, Deu. 33.24. Inheritance in Canaan, Jos. 19.24-31. Did not expel the Canaanites, Jud. 1.31,32. Their shipping, Jud. 5.17. Reproved for not aiding Barak, Jud. 5.17. Assist Gideon against Midian, Jud. 6.35. Jud. 7.23.

Join Ishbosheth, 2 Sam. 2.9. Number of their soldiers in David's time, 1 Chr. 7.40. 1 Chr. 12.36. Keep Hezekiah's passover, 2 Chr. 30.11. See ISRAEL, TRIBES OF, for what is common to the tribes.

ASHES of burnt-offerings to be carried without the camp, Lev. 4.12. Lev. 6.11. Num. 19.9. Of the red heifer used for the water of purification, Num. 19.9. Heb. 9.13.

———— AND DUST in mourning, put on the head, &c., Jos. 7.6. 2 Sam. 13.19. 1 Kin. 20.38. Est. 4.1. Job 2.12. Rev. 18.19. Sitting in, Est. 4.3. Job 2.8. Isa. 58.5. Jer. 6.26. Illustrative, Psa. 102.9. Isa. 61.3. Job 42.6. Dan. 9.3.

ASHIMA, an idol of Hamath introduced into Samaria, 2 Kin. 17.30.

ASHKENAZ, a son of Gomer, Gen. 10.3. A kingdom, Jer. 51.27. See MINNI.

ASHPENAZ, the chief eunuch who had the care of Daniel, Dan. 1.3-10.

ASHTAROTH, or ASHTAROTH-KARNAIM, a town of Bashan belonging to the Rephaim, Gen. 14.5. Deu. 1.4. Jos. 9.10. Jos. 12.4. Given to Manasseh, Jos. 13.31. A Levitical city, 1 Chr. 6.71.

ASHTAROTH, a goddess of the Sidonians, 1 Kin. 11.33. Worshipped by the Israelites, Jud. 2.13. Jud. 10.6. 1 Sam. 7.3. 1 Sam. 12.10. By the Philistines, who put Saul's armour in the temple of, 1 Sam. 31.10. By Solomon, 1 Kin. 11.5,33. High places of, removed by Josiah, 2 Kin. 23.13.

ASIA MINOR, PROVINCES OF. See BITHYNIA, CAPPADOCIA, CILICIA, GALATIA, LYCAONIA, LYCIA, LYDIA, MYSIA, PAMPHYLIA, PISIDIA, PHRYGIA, PONTUS, with their towns. See also other towns—CNIDUS, PHILADELPHIA, TROAS, TROGYLLIUM. History of churches in, will be found under each name.

ASKELON, one of the five chief cities of the Philistines, a seaport. Jos. 13.3. 1 Sam. 6.17. 2 Sam. 1.20. Taken by Judah, Jud. 1.18. Samson slays thirty men at, Jud. 14.19. Prophecies of, see PHILISTINES.

ASNAPPER, an Assyrian prince ; sends colonies to Samaria, Ezr. 4.10.

ASP, a poisonous serpent, Deu. 32.33. Job 20.14,16. Isa. 11.8. Rom. 3.13.

ASS, used for riding, Gen. 22.3. Num. 22.21. Jos. 15.18. 2 Sam. 16.2. Rulers rode on, Jud. 5.10. Jud. 10.4. Jud. 12.14. Zec. 9.9. Used in chariots, Isa. 21.7. For carrying burdens, Isa. 30.6. In agriculture, Isa. 30.24. Isa. 32.20.

Management of, Pro. 26.3. Isa. 1.3. Luk. 13.15. Luk. 14.5. Great numbers of kept, Gen. 12.16. Gen. 30.43. Gen. 47.17. 1 Chr. 27.30. Ezr. 2.67. Job 42.12. Balaam's ass, Num. 22.22-32. Samson's exploit with the jaw-bone of, Jud. 15.16.

Saul's search for, 1 Sam. 9.3. Christ rode on, Mat. 21.2-5. Firstlings of to be redeemed, Ex. 13.13. Not to be yoked with an ox, Deu. 22.10. To rest on Sabbath, Ex. 23.12. Wild, Job 6.5. Job 24.5. Job 39.5. Psa. 104.11. Isa. 32.14. Jer. 2.24. Jer. 14.6. Hos. 8.9.

————, a weight, 2 Kin. 6.25.

ASSHUR, a son of Shem, builds Nineveh, &c., Gen. 10.11,12,22. 1 Chr. 1.17. See ASSYRIA.

ASSOS, a town of Mysia, visited by Paul, Act. 20.13,14.

ASSURANCE of understanding (assured understanding), Col. 2.2. Of faith, Heb. 10.22. Of hope, Heb. 6.11. See FAITH, Exemplified.

ASSYRIA, kingdom of, founded by Asshur and Nimrod, Gen. 10.8-12. Mic. 5.6. Different boundaries as extended by conquests, Gen. 2.14. Gen. 25.18. 2 Kin. 17.6. 2 Kin. 19. 12,13. Isa. 7.20. Isa. 20. Commerce of, Eze. 27.23. King of, warned by Jonah, Jonah 3.

Kings of, invade Israel, Judah, and Ashdod. See PUL, TIGLATH-PILEZER, SHALMANEZER, SARGON, SENNACHERIB, ESARHADDON.

Cities and districts of. See ARPHAD, AVA, CARCHEMISH, CALNEH, CUTHAH, HABOR, HALAH, KIR, NINEVEH (the capital), REHOBOTH, RESEN, REZEPH, SEPHARAD, SEPHARVAIM, TIPHSAH.

Cities built by Nimrod—Babylon, Erech, Accad, Calneh, Gen. 10.9,10. By Asshur—Nineveh, Calah, Rehoboth, and Resen, Gen. 10.11,12.

Idols of. See ADRAMMELECH, ANAMME-LECH, NISROCH, TARTAK. Prophecies of, Num. 24.22,24. 2 Kin. 19.21-34. Isa. 7.17-25. Isa. 8.4-10. Isa. 10.5-34. Isa. 14. 24-27. Isa. 19.23-25. Isa. 20. Isa. 30.27-33. Isa. 31.8,9. Isa. 33.1-12. Isa. 37.21-35. Eze. 31. Jonah 3. 1-4. Nah. c.1 to 3. Zeph. 2,13-15. Zec. 10.11.

ASTROLOGERS, Isa. 47.13. Jer. 10.2. Dan. 1.20. Dan. 2.27. Dan. 4.7. Dan. 5.7.

ASTRONOMY. See MOON—STARS—SUN.

ASYNCRITUS, a Christian at Rome, Rom. 16.14.

ATAD, THRESHING-FLOOR OF. See ABEL-MIZRAIM.

ATHALIAH, daughter of Ahab, wife of Jehoram, king of Judah, and mother of Aha-ziah, 2 Kin. 8.26. 2 Chr. 21.6. 2 Chr. 22.2,10. Her evil influence over her husband and son, 2 Kin. 8.18. 2 Chr. 21.6,13. 2 Chr. 22.3,4. Murders all her grandchildren but Joash; usurps the throne, 2 Kin. 11.1-3. 2 Chr. 22. 10-12. Slain by order of Jehoiada, 2 Kin. 11. 12-16,20. 2 Chr. 23.12-15,21.

ATHENS, a city of Attica, in Greece. Paul preaches at ; Dionysius, &c., converted, Act. 17.15-34. 1 The. 3.1. Athenians' character ; superstition, Act. 17.21-23. See MARS HILL.

ATONEMENT (Heb. *caphar*, to cover) by sacrifices, Ex. 29.36. Ex. 30.10. Lev. 1.4. Lev. 4.20, &c. In money, Ex. 30.15,16. Num. 3.40-50. Num. 18.16. Translated reconcilia-tion, Lev. 6.30. Lev. 8.15. Eze. 45.15. Dan. 9.24.

Different parts of the verb translated—appease, Gen. 32.20. Be merciful, Deu. 21.8. Purge, Psa. 79.9. Forgive, Psa. 78.38. Pacify, Pro. 16.14. Disannul, Isa. 28.18. Cleanse, Num. 35.33.

(Greek, *katallage*), atonement, Rom. 5.11. Translated reconcile and reconciliation, Rom. 5.10. Rom. 11.15. 1 Cor. 7.11. 2 Cor. 5.18, 19,20. See CHRIST'S DEATH, DESIGN OF—PARDON THROUGH CHRIST.

—————, DAY OF, appointed on the 10th day of 7th month, Lev. 23.27. A Sabbath of rest, Lev. 16.29,31. Lev. 23.28-32. Num. 29.7. Humiliation and confession of sin on, Lev. 16.21,29. Lev. 23.27-32. Sacrifices on ; scape-goat sent away on, Lev. 16.3-26. Num. 29. 7-11.

Sacrifices for the high-priest, Lev. 16.3-14,24. Heb. 5.3. For the congregation, Lev. 16.15-24, 30,33,34. Heb. 9.7. Atonement made on, for the holy place, by sprinkling the blood of the sin-offering on the mercy-seat, altar of incense, and Tabernacle, Ex. 30.10. Lev. 16.15-20. Heb. 9.19-22.

Incense offered on before the mercy-seat, Lev. 16.12,13. High-priest entered the Holy of Holies three times on, Lev. 16.12-17. Heb. 9.7 ; wearing a special dress, Lev. 16.4. Jubilee year commenced on, Lev. 25.9.

ATTALIA, a city in Pamphylia, visited by Paul, Act. 14.25.

AUGUSTUS, a Roman emperor, in whose reign Christ was born, Luk. 2.1. Also a title of the Roman emperors, Act. 25.21,25. (Nero was then emperor).

AUTUMN. See HARVEST.

AVA, or IVAH, a state conquered by Sen-nacherib ; colonists sent from to Samaria ;

worship Nibhaz and Tartak, 2 Kin. 17.24. 2 Kin. 18.34. 2 Kin. 19.13. See Ezra 4.9.

AVEN, or LEBANON, a plain in Syria, Jos. 11.17. Amos 1.5.

—————, a town in Egypt, Eze. 30.17 ; same as On, Gen. 41.45. See BETHAVEN.

AVIM, a people inhabiting the south of Palestine ; expelled by the Philistines, Deu. 2.23. Jos. 13.3. See Gen. 36.35.

AVITES. See AVA.

AWL, Ex. 21.6. Deu. 15.17.

AXE, of iron, Deu. 19.5. 1 Sam. 13.20,21. 2 Sam. 12.31. Psa. 74.6,7. Elisha causes an axe-head to swim, 2 Kin. 6.5,6. Illustrative, Jer. 46.22. Mat. 3.10. See BATTLE-AXE.

AZARIAH, or AMARIAH, high-priest in Jehoshaphat's reign, 2 Chr. 19.11.

—————, high-priest in Uzziah's reign ; opposes the king burning incense, 2 Chr. 26. 17-20. 1 Chr. 6.10.

—————, or AMARIAH, high-priest in Hezekiah's reign, 2 Chr. 31.10. 1 Chr. 6.11.

—————, high-priest shortly before the captivity, 1 Chr. 6.14. 1 Chr. 9.11.

—————, king of Judah. See UZZIAH.

—————, son of Oded, a prophet who met king Asa after a victory, and encouraged him to reform Judah, and put down idolatry, 2 Chr. 15.

AZEKAH, a city of Judah, Jos. 15.35. Five kings slain near, Jos. 10.10,11. Goliath slain near, 1 Sam. 17.1. Fortified by Rehoboam, 2 Chr. 11.9. Besieged by Nebuchadnezzar, Jer. 34.7. Rebuilt after the captivity, Neh. 11.30.

AZOTUS. See ASHDOD.

B

BAAL, a Zidonian god, worshipped by the Israelites, Jud. 2.11-13. 1 Sam. 7.3,4. 2 Kin. 17.16. Jer. 2.8,23. Jer. 7.9. Jer. 9.14. Jer. 11.13,17. Jer. 12.16. Jer. 19.45. Jer. 23.13,27. Jer. 32.29. Hos. 2.8,13,17. Hos. 13.1 Zeph. 1.4.

Worshipped by Ahab, 1 Kin. 16.31-33. 1 Kin. 18.18. 1 Kin. 19.18. 2 Kin. 3.2. By Ahaziah, 2 Chr. 24.7 with 2 Chr. 22.2-4. By Ahaz, 2 Chr. 28.2. By Manasseh, 2 Kin. 21.3. 2 Chr. 33.3.

Idols and altars of, destroyed by Gideon, Jud. 6.25-32. By Jehu, 2 Kin. 10.18-28. By Jehoiada, 2 Kin. 11.18. By Josiah, 2 Kin. 23.4,5.

Prophets of, maintained by Jezebel, 1 Kin. 18.19. Slain by Elijah, 1 Kin. 18.40. By Jehu, 2 Kin. 10.18-25.

BAALAH. See KIRJATH-JEARIM.

BAAL-BERITH, an idol worshipped by the Shechemites, Jud. 8.33. Jud. 9.4,46.

BAAL-GAD, a city in the valley of Lebanon, under Mount Hermon, Jos. 11.17. Jos. 12.7. Jos. 13.5. See BAAL-HERMON.

BAAL-HAMON, or HAMMON, a town of Asher, where Solomon had a vineyard, Jos. 19.28. Song 8.11.

BAAL-HAZOR, a place near Ephraim, belonging to Absalom, where he murdered Amnon, 2 Sam. 13.23.

BAAL-HERMON, a town near Mount Hermon, Jud. 3.3. 1 Chr. 5.23. Supposed to be the same as Baal-gad.

BAALIS, king of the Ammonites, instigates Ishmael to slay Gedaliah, Jer. 40.14. Jer. 41.10.

BAAL-MEON, or BETH-MEON, a town in Reuben, Num. 32.38. Jos. 13.17. Afterwards possessed by the Moabites, Jer. 48.23. Eze. 25.9.

BAAL-PEOR, an idol of the Moabites and Midianites, worshipped by the Israelites in Shittim, Num. 25. Num. 31.1-16. Num. 22.41. Deu. 4.3. Deu. 22.17. Psa. 106.28. Hos. 9.10.

BAAL-PERAZIM (the plain of breaches), a place in the valley of Rephaim, so named by David on defeating the Philistines, 2 Sam. 5.20. 1 Chr. 14.11. Called Mount Perazim, Isa. 28.21.

BAAL-SHALISHA, a district or town in Ephraim, 1 Sam. 9.4. 2 Kin. 4.42.

BAAL-TAMAR, a place near Gibeah, where the other tribes defeated Benjamin, Jud. 20.33.

BAAL-ZEBUB. See BEELZEBUB.

BAAL-ZEPHON, a town of Egypt by the Red Sea, Ex. 14.2. Num. 33.7.

BAANAH, a captain, murders Ishbosheth, is slain by David's order, 2 Sam. 4.2-12.

BAASHA, third king of Israel, slays Nadab and all his house, and succeeds him, 1 Kin. 15.27-30. Invades Judah, is defeated by Asa's ally Benhadad, 1 Kin. 15.16-22,32. 2 Chr. 16.1-6. Jer. 41.9. His sins, prophecy against him, his death, 1 Kin. 15.34. 1 Kin. 16.1-7. 1 Kin. 21.22. 2 Kin. 9.9.

BABEL (confusion), TOWER OF, in the land of Shinar, building of stopped by the confusion of tongues, Gen. 11.1-9.

BABYLONIA, or CHALDEA, called Babylon, Isa. 13.19. Merathaim, Jer. 50.21. Sheshak, Jer. 25.26. Land of Shinar, Dan. 1.2. Chaldea, Job 1.17. Isa. 47.1 Eze. 12.13. Division and boundaries, 2 Kin. 17.24. Isa. 23.12,13. Dan. 3.1. Act. 7.4.
Founded by Nimrod, Gen. 10.10. Tower of Babel built in, Gen. 11.1-9. Amraphel, king of, invades Canaan, Gen. 14.1,2. Berodach's embassy to Hezekiah, 2 Kin. 20.12. Isa. 39.1. Relations of, with the Jews, see NEBUCHADNEZZAR, EVIL MERODACH, BELSHAZZAR, MERODACH.
Power of, Isa. 47.5. Jer. 5.15. Wealth of, Jer. 51.13. Commerce of, Jos. 7.21. Isa. 43.14. Eze. 17.4. Towns of, Gen. 10.10. See BABYLON, CALNEH, TEL-ABIB.
Plain of Dura, Dan. 2.1. Rivers of, see AHAVA, EUPHRATES, CHEBAR. Idols of, see BEL, MERODACH, NEBO, SUCCOTH-BENOTH.

BABYLON, THE CITY. Built by Nimrod, Gen. 10.10. Enlarged by Nebuchadnezzar, Dan. 4.30. Fortifications of, Isa. 45.1,2. Jer. 51.58. Splendour of, Isa. 14.4. A church at, Peter writes from, 1 Pet. 5.13.

————, PROPHECIES OF, Psa. 87.4. Psa. 137.8,9. Isa. 13. Isa. 14.4-26. Isa. 21.1-10. Isa. 46.1,2. Isa. 47. Isa. 48.14,20. Jer. 21.4-10. Jer. 25.12-14. Jer. 27.1-11. Jer. 28.14. Jer. 32.28. Jer. 34.2,3. Jer. 42.11,12. Jer. 43. Jer. 46.13-26. Jer. 49.28-30. Jer. 50. Jer. 51.

Eze. 21.19. Eze. 26. Eze. 29.17-20. Eze. 30.10. Eze. 32.11. Dan. 2.21-38. Dan. 4.10-26. Dan. 5.25-29. Dan. 7. Hab. 1.5-11. Zec. 2.7-9.

BABYLON THE GREAT. Predictions against, Rev. 14.8. Rev. 16.19. Rev. 17. Rev. 18.

BACA (valley of weeping), illustrative, Psa. 84.6.

BACKBITING. See SPEAKING EVIL.

BACKSLIDING AND APOSTACY. Deu. 4.9. Keep thy soul diligently, lest thou forget the things which thine eyes have seen, and lest they depart from thy heart all the days of thy life.

Deu. 8.11. Beware that thou forget not the Lord thy God, in not keeping his commandments, 12. Lest *when* thou hast eaten and art full, 14. Then thine heart be lifted up, and thou forget the Lord thy God.

Deu. 28.58. If thou wilt not observe to do all the words of this law that are written in this book, that thou mayest fear this glorious and fearful name, the LORD THY GOD; 59. Then the Lord will make thy plagues wonderful, and the plagues of thy seed, *even* great plagues, and of long continuance, and sore sicknesses, and of long continuance.

Deu. 28.63. And it shall come to pass, *that* as the Lord rejoiced over you to do you good, and to multiply you; so the Lord will rejoice over you to destroy you, and to bring you to nought. *v.* 15-68. Lev. 26.14-39. Deu. 31.16-30. 1 Kin. 9.6-9.

Deu. 29.18. Lest there should be among you man, or woman, or family, or tribe, whose heart turneth away this day from the Lord our God; lest there should be among you a root that beareth gall and wormwood. *v.* 18-28.

Jos. 22.29. God forbid that we should rebel against the Lord, and turn this day from following the Lord. *v.* 22-29. Jos. 24.16.

Jos. 24.27. And Joshua said, Behold, this stone shall be a witness unto us; for it hath heard all the words of the Lord which he spake unto us: it shall be therefore a witness unto you, lest ye deny your God. *v.* 20-27.

1 Chr. 28.9. If thou forsake him, he will cast thee off for ever.

2 Chr. 15.2. The Lord *is* with you, while ye be with him; and if ye seek him, he will be found of you; but if ye forsake him, he will forsake you. Ezr. 8.22.

Job. 34.26. He striketh them as wicked men in the open sight of others; 27. Because they turned back from him, and would not consider any of his ways.

Psa. 44.20. If we have forgotten the name of our God, or stretched out our hands to a strange god; 21. Shall not God search this out? for he knoweth the secrets of the heart.

Psa. 73.27. For, lo, they that are far from thee shall perish: thou hast destroyed all them that go a whoring from thee.

Psa. 85.8. But let them not turn again to folly.

Psa. 125.5. As for such as turn aside unto their crooked ways, the Lord shall lead them forth with the workers of iniquity.

Pro. 2.17. Which forsaketh the guide of her youth, and forgetteth the covenant of her God.

Pro. 14.14. The backslider in heart shall be filled with his own ways.

Isa. 1.28. They that forsake the Lord shall be consumed.

Jer. 17.5. Cursed *be* the man whose heart departeth from the Lord. 6. For he shall be like the heath in the desert, and shall not see when good cometh; but shall inhabit the parched places in the wilderness, *in* a salt land and not inhabited.

Jer. 17.13. O Lord, the hope of Israel, all that forsake thee shall be ashamed, *and* they that depart from me shall be written in the earth, because they have forsaken the Lord, the fountain of living waters.

Eze. 18.24. When the righteous turneth away from his righteousness, and committeth iniquity, *and* doeth according to all the abominations that the wicked *man* doeth, shall he live? All his righteousness that he hath done shall not be mentioned: in his trespass that he hath trespassed, and in his sin that he hath sinned, in them shall he die. *v.* 26. Eze. 3.20. Eze. 33.18.

Mat. 5.13. If the salt have lost his savour, wherewith shall it be salted? it is thenceforth good for nothing, but to be cast out, and to be trodden under foot of men.

Mat. 10.33. Whosoever shall deny me before men, him will I also deny before my Father which is in heaven. Luk. 12.9.

Mat. 12.45. Then goeth he, and taketh with himself seven other spirits more wicked than himself, and they enter in and dwell there: and the last *state* of that man is worse than the first. Luk. 11.24-26.

Mat. 13.20. He that received the seed into stony places, the same is he that heareth the word, and anon with joy receiveth it; 21. Yet hath he not root in himself, but dureth for a while: for when tribulation or persecution ariseth because of the word, by and by he is offended. *v.* 5,6. Mar. 4.5,6,16,17. Luk. 8.6,13.

Mat. 24.10. Then shall many be offended, and shall betray one another, and shall hate one another. 12. Because iniquity shall abound, the love of many shall wax cold.

Mat. 26.31. All ye shall be offended because of me this night: for it is written, I will smite the shepherd, and the sheep of the flock shall be scattered abroad.

Mar. 8.38. Whosoever therefore shall be ashamed of me, and of my words, in this adulterous and sinful generation, of him also shall the Son of man be ashamed.

Luk. 9.62. No man, having put his hand to the plough, and looking back, is fit for the kingdom of God.

Luk. 17.32. Remember Lot's wife.

Jno. 6.67. Then said Jesus unto the twelve, Will ye also go away?

Jno. 15.6. If a man abide not in me, he is cast forth as a branch, and is withered; and men gather them, and cast *them* into the fire, and they are burned.

Gal. 3.1. O foolish Galatians, who hath bewitched you, that ye should not obey the truth, before whose eyes Jesus Christ hath been evidently set forth, crucified among you?

Gal. 5.7. Ye did run well; who did hinder you that ye should not obey the truth?

1 Tim. 1.19. Holding faith, and a good conscience; which some having put away concerning faith have made shipwreck.

1 Tim. 5.15. Some are already turned aside after Satan.

1 Tim. 6.10. The love of money is the root of all evil: which while some coveted after, they have erred from the faith, and pierced themselves through with many sorrows. 20. O Timothy, keep that which is committed to thy trust, avoiding profane *and* vain babblings, and oppositions of science falsely so called: 21. Which some professing, have erred concerning the faith.

2 Tim. 1.8. Be not thou therefore ashamed of the testimony of our Lord, nor of me his prisoner.

2 Tim. 2.12. If we deny him he also will deny us.

2 Tim. 4.10. Hath forsaken me, having loved this present world.

Heb. 3.12. Take heed, brethren, lest there be in any of you an evil heart of unbelief, in departing from the living God.

Heb. 4.1. Let us therefore fear, lest, a promise being left *us* of entering into his rest, any of you should seem to come short of it. 11. Let us labour therefore to enter into that rest, lest any man fall after the same example of unbelief.

Heb. 5.11. Ye are dull of hearing. 12. For when for the time ye ought to be teachers, ye have need that one teach you again which *be* the first principles of the oracles of God; and are become such as have need of milk, and not of strong meat.

Heb. 6.4. *It is* impossible for those who were once enlightened, and have tasted of the heavenly gift, and were made partakers of the Holy Ghost, 5. And have tasted the good word of God, and the powers of the world to come, 6. If they shall fall away, to renew them again unto repentance; seeing they crucify to themselves the Son of God afresh, and put *him* to an open shame. 7. For the earth which drinketh in the rain that cometh oft upon it, and bringeth forth herbs meet for them by whom it is dressed, receiveth blessing from God: 8. But that which beareth thorns and briers *is* rejected, and *is* nigh unto cursing; whose end *is* to be burned.

Heb. 10.26. If we sin wilfully after that we have received the knowledge of the truth, there remaineth no more sacrifice for sins, 27. But a certain fearful looking for of judgment and fiery indignation, which shall devour the adversaries. 28. He that despised Moses' law died without mercy under two or three witnesses: 29. Of how much sorer punishment, suppose ye, shall he be thought worthy, who hath trodden under foot the Son of God, and hath counted the blood of the covenant, wherewith he was sanctified, an unholy thing, and hath done despite unto the Spirit of grace?

Heb. 10.38. If *any man* draw back, my soul shall have no pleasure in him. 39. But we are not of them who draw back unto perdition.

2 Pet. 1.9. He that lacketh these things is blind, and cannot see afar off, and hath forgotten that he was purged from his old sins.

2 Pet. 2.1. Even denying the Lord that bought them, and bring upon themselves swift destruction.

2 Pet. 2.15. Which have forsaken the right way, and are gone astray, following the way of Balaam *the son* of Bosor, who loved the wages of unrighteousness; 17. These are wells without water, clouds that are carried with a

tempest; to whom the mist of darkness is reserved for ever.

2 Pet. 2.20. If after they have escaped the pollutions of the world through the knowledge of the Lord and Saviour Jesus Christ, they are again entangled therein, and overcome, the latter end is worse with them than the beginning. 21. For it had been better for them not to have known the way of righteousness, than, after they have known *it*, to turn from the holy commandment delivered unto them. 22. But it is happened unto them according to the true proverb, The dog *is* turned to his own vomit again; and the sow that was washed to her wallowing in the mire.

2 Pet. 3.17. Seeing ye know *these things* before, beware lest ye also, being led away with the error of the wicked, fall from your own stedfastness.

1 Jno. 2.19. They went out from us, but they were not of us; for if they had been of us, they would *no doubt* have continued with us: but *they went out*, that they might be made manifest that they were not all of us.

2 Jno. 9. Whosoever transgresseth, and abideth not in the doctrine of Christ, hath not God.

Jude 4. Certain men crept in unawares, who were before of old ordained to this condemnation, ungodly men, turning the grace of our God into lasciviousness, and denying the only Lord God, and our Lord Jesus Christ. 5. I will therefore put you in remembrance, though ye once knew this, how that the Lord, having saved the people out of the land of Egypt, afterward destroyed them that believed not. 6. And the angels which kept not their first estate, but left their own habitation, he hath reserved in everlasting chains, under darkness, unto the judgment of the great day.

Rev. 2.4. I have *somewhat* against thee, because thou hast left thy first love.

Rev. 2.21. I gave her space to repent of her fornication; and she repented not. 22. Behold, I will cast her into a bed, and them that commit adultery with her into great tribulation, except they repent of their deeds. 23. And I will kill her children with death.

Rev. 3.2. Be watchful, and strengthen the things which remain, that are ready to die: for I have not found thy works perfect before God. 3. Remember therefore how thou hast received and heard, and hold fast, and repent. If therefore thou shalt not watch, I will come on thee as a thief, and thou shalt not know what hour I will come upon thee.

Rev. 21.8. The fearful, and unbelieving, shall have their part in the lake which burneth with fire and brimstone: which is the second death.

BACKSLIDING, Examples and Punishment of. Saul, 1 Sam. 15.11,26-28. 1 Sam. 28.17. David, 2 Sam. 12.14. Solomon, 1 Kin. 11.4-40. Neh. 13.26. Amon, 2 Kin. 21.22,23. Rehoboam, 2 Chr. 12.1,2. Asa, 2 Chr. 16.7-9. Jehoram, 2 Chr. 21.5-19. Ahaziah, 2 Chr. 22.7. Joash, 2 Chr. 24.24. Amaziah, 2 Chr. 25.27.

The disciples, Mat. 26.56. Peter, Mat. 26. 69-75. Many disciples, Jno. 6.66. Hymeneus and Alexander, 1 Tim. 1.19,20. Phygellus and Hermogenes, 2 Tim. 1.15. Demas, 2 Tim. 4.10. Churches of Asia, 1 Tim. 5.15. Rev. 2.4,14,15,20. Rev. 3.2,3,15-18.

See Apostacy of Last Days.

BACKSLIDING and Apostacy of Israel, Ex. 33.3. I will not go up in the midst of thee; for thou *art* a stiffnecked people: lest I consume thee in the way. Ex. 32.7,8. Deu. 9.12.

Deu. 32.5. They have corrupted themselves, their spot *is* not *the spot* of his children: *they are* a perverse and crooked generation. 6. Do ye thus requite the Lord, O foolish people and unwise? *is* not he thy father *that* hath bought thee? hath he not made thee, and established thee? 15. He forsook God *which* made him, and lightly esteemed the Rock of his salvation. *v.* 18. Num. 14.43. Jud. 2.12. Jud. 10.12-14.

2 Chr. 24.20. Thus saith God, Why transgress ye the commandments of the Lord, that ye cannot prosper? because ye have forsaken the Lord, he hath also forsaken you. 2 Kin. 18.1,12. 2 Chr. 13.11. 2 Chr. 27.2. 2 Chr. 29.6,8.

Ezr. 9.10. Now, O our God, what shall we say after this? for we have forsaken thy commandments, 13. And after all that is come upon us for our evil deeds, and for our great trespass, seeing that thou our God hast punished us less than our iniquities *deserve*, and hast given us *such* deliverance as this; 14. Should we again break thy commandments, and join in affinity with the people of these abominations? wouldest not thou be angry with us till thou hadst consumed *us*, so that *there should be* no remnant nor escaping?

Neh. 9.26. Nevertheless they were disobedient, and rebelled against thee, and cast thy law behind their backs, and slew thy prophets which testified against them to turn them to thee, and they wrought great provocations.

Psa. 78.10. They kept not the covenant of God, and refused to walk in his law; 11. And forgat his works, and his wonders that he had shewed them.

Psa. 78.56. They tempted and provoked the most high God, and kept not his testimonies: 57. But turned back, and dealt unfaithfully like their fathers: they were turned aside like a deceitful bow.

Isa. 1.4. Ah sinful nation, a people laden with iniquity, a seed of evildoers, children that are corrupters: they have forsaken the Lord, they have provoked the Holy One of Israel unto anger, they are gone away backward.

Isa. 1.5. Why should ye be stricken any more? ye will revolt more and more: the whole head is sick, and the whole heart faint. 6. From the sole of the foot even unto the head *there is* no soundness in it; *but* wounds, and bruises, and putrifying sores: they have not been closed, neither bound up, neither mollified with ointment. 7. Your country *is* desolate, your cities *are* burned with fire: your land, strangers devour it in your presence, and *it is* desolate, as overthrown by strangers.

Isa. 1.21. How is the faithful city become an harlot! it was full of judgment; righteousness lodged in it; but now murderers. 22. Thy silver has become dross, thy wine mixed with water. Isa. 50.1.

Isa. 2.6. Thou hast forsaken thy people the house of Jacob, because they be replenished from the east, and *are* soothsayers like the Philistines, and they please themselves in the children of strangers.

Isa. 5.24. As the fire devoureth the stubble

and the flame consumeth the chaff, *so* their root shall be as rottenness, and their blossom shall go up as dust: because they have cast away the law of the Lord of hosts, and despised the word of the Holy One of Israel. *v.* 12-30.

Isa. 9.16. For the leaders of this people cause *them* to err; and *they that are* led of them *are* destroyed. *v.* 13-21.

Isa. 17.10. Because thou hast forgotten the God of thy salvation, and hast not been mindful of the rock of thy strength, therefore shalt thou plant pleasant plants, and shalt set it with strange slips: 11. In the day shalt thou make thy plant to grow, and in the morning shalt thou make thy seed to flourish; *but* the harvest *shall be* a heap in the day of grief and of desperate sorrow.

Isa. 24.5. The earth also is defiled under the inhabitants thereof; because they have transgressed the laws, changed the ordinance, broken the everlasting covenant.' 6. Therefore hath the curse devoured the earth, and they that dwell therein are desolate: therefore the inhabitants of the earth are burned, and few men left.

Isa. 30.9. That this *is* a rebellious people, lying children, children *that* will not hear the law of the Lord. 15. For thus saith the Lord God, the Holy One of Israel; In returning and rest shall ye be saved; in quietness and in confidence shall be your strength: and ye would not.

Isa. 43.22. But thou hast not called upon me, O Jacob; but thou hast been weary of me, O Israel. 24. Thou hast bought me no sweet cane with money, neither hast thou filled me with the fat of thy sacrifices: but thou hast made me to serve with thy sins, thou hast wearied me with thine iniquities.

Isa. 51.17. Awake, awake, stand up, O Jerusalem, which hast drunk at the hand of the Lord the cup of his fury: thou hast drunken the dregs of the cup of trembling, *and* wrung *them* out. *v.* 18-20.

Isa. 65.2. I have spread out my hands all the day unto a rebellious people, which walketh in a way *that was* not good, after their own thoughts; 3. A people that provoketh me to anger continually to my face.

Jer. 2.5. What iniquity have your fathers found in me, that they are gone far from me, and have walked after vanity, and are become vain?

Jer. 2.11. Hath a nation changed *their* gods, which *are* yet no gods? but my people have changed their glory for *that which* doth not profit. 12. Be astonished, O ye heavens, at this, and be horribly afraid, be ye very desolate, saith the Lord. 13. For my people have committed two evils; they have forsaken me the fountain of living waters, *and* hewed them out cisterns, broken cisterns, that can hold no water.

Jer. 2.17. Hast thou not procured this unto thyself, in that thou hast forsaken the Lord thy God, when he led thee by the way? 19. Thine own wickedness shall correct thee, and thy backslidings shall reprove thee: know therefore and see that *it is* an evil *thing* and bitter, that thou hast forsaken the Lord thy God, and that my fear *is* not in thee, saith the Lord God of hosts.

Jer. 2.21. Yet I had planted thee a noble

vine, wholly a right seed: how then art thou turned into the degenerate plant of a strange vine unto me? 27. They have turned *their* back unto me, and not *their* face: but in the time of their trouble they will say, Arise, and save us.

Jer. 2.31. Have I been a wilderness unto Israel? a land of darkness? wherefore say my people, We are lords; we will come no more unto thee? 32. Can a maid forget her ornaments, *or* a bride her attire? yet my people have forgotten me days without number.

Jer. 3.21. They have perverted their way, *and* they have forgotten the Lord their God. *v.* 1-11.

Jer. 5.19. When ye shall say, Wherefore doeth the Lord our God all these *things* unto us? then shalt thou answer them, Like as ye have forsaken me, and served strange gods in your land, so shall ye serve strangers in a land *that is* not your's. 23. But this people hath a revolting and a rebellious heart; they are revolted and gone. *v.* 1-31. Jer. 11.9-17.

Jer. 6.30. Reprobate silver shall *men* call them, because the Lord hath rejected them. Eze. 22.18.

Jer. 7.12. Go ye now unto my place which *was* in Shiloh, where I set my name at the first, and see what I did to it for the wickedness of my people Israel. *v.* 13-34.

Jer. 8.5. Why *then* is this people of Jerusalem slidden back by a perpetual backsliding? they hold fast deceit, they refuse to return. 14. The Lord our God hath put us to silence, and given us water of gall to drink, because we have sinned against the Lord. 15. We looked for peace, but no good *came; and* for a time of health, and behold trouble! *v.* 1-22.

Jer. 10.21. The pastors are become brutish, and have not sought the Lord: therefore they shall not prosper, and all their flocks shall be scattered. *v.* 17-22.

Jer. 12.7. I have forsaken mine house, I have left mine heritage; I have given the dearly beloved of my soul into the hand of her enemies.

Jer. 13.24. Therefore will I scatter them as the stubble that passeth away by the wind of the wilderness. 25. This *is* thy lot, the portion of thy measures from me, saith the Lord; because thou hast forgotten me, and trusted in falsehood.

Jer. 14.7. O Lord, though our iniquities testify against us, do thou *it* for thy name's sake: for our backslidings are many; we have sinned against thee. 10. Thus have they loved to wander, they have not refrained their feet; therefore the Lord doth not accept them: he will now remember their iniquity, and visit their sins.

Jer. 15.1. Though Moses and Samuel stood before me, *yet* my mind *could* not *be* toward this people: cast *them* out of my sight, and let them go forth. *v.* 2-14.

Jer. 18.13. Ask ye now among the heathen, who hath heard such things: the virgin of Israel hath done a very horrible thing. 14. Will *a man* leave the snow of Lebanon *which cometh* from the rock of the field? *or* shall the cold flowing waters that come from another place be forsaken? 15. Because my people hath forgotten me, they have burned incense to vanity, and they have caused them to stumble in their ways *from* the ancient paths, to walk in paths, *in* a way not cast up. Jer. 19.

Jer. 32.31. This city hath been to me *as* a provocation of mine anger and of my fury from the day that they built it even unto this day; that I should remove it from before my face. *v.* 30.

Jer. 50.6. My people hath been lost sheep: their shepherds have caused them to go astray, they have turned them away *on* the mountains : they have gone from mountain to hill, they have forgotten their resting-place.

Eze. 5.6. She hath changed my judgments into wickedness more than the nations, and my statutes more than the countries that *are* round about her : for they have refused my judgments and my statutes, they have not walked in them. *v.* 1-17.

Eze. 11.21. *As for them* whose heart walketh after the heart of their detestable things and their abominations, I will recompense their way upon their own heads, saith the Lord God. *v.* 1-21. [See Parable of the Vine, Eze. 15.]

Eze. 16.43. Because thou hast not remembered the days of thy youth, but hast fretted me in all these *things*; behold, therefore I also will recompense thy way upon *thine* head, saith the Lord God. [See Parables of an Unfaithful Wife, Eze. 16. Eze. 23. Hos. 2. Hos. 3.]

Hos. 1.6. I will no more have mercy upon the house of Israel ; but I will utterly take them away. 9. Ye *are* not my people, and I will not be your *God.* *v.* 1-9.

Hos. 4.6. Because thou hast rejected knowledge, I will also reject thee, that thou shalt be no priest to me : seeing thou hast forgotten the law of thy God, I will also forget thy children.

Hos. 4.10. They shall eat, and not have enough : they shall commit whoredom, and shall not increase : because they have left off to take heed to the Lord. *v.* 16.

Hos. 5.11. Ephraim *is* oppressed *and* broken in judgment, because he willingly walked after the commandment. 12. Therefore *will* I *be* unto Ephraim as a moth, and to the house of Judah as rottenness. *v.* 1-15.

Hos. 6.4. O Ephraim, what shall I do unto thee? O Judah, what shall I do unto thee? for your goodness *is* as a morning cloud, and as the early dew it goeth away. 7. They like men have transgressed the covenant : there have they dealt treacherously against me. *v.* 4-11. Hos. 8.14. Hos. 9.1-17. Hos. 13.16.

Hos. 11.2. As they called them, so they went from them. 7. And my people are bent to backsliding from me : though they called them to the most High, none at all would exalt *him.*

Amos 2.4. For three transgressions of Judah, and for four, I will not turn away *the punishment* thereof ; because they have despised the law of the Lord, and have not kept his commandments.

Zeph. 1.6. Them that are turned back from the Lord ; and *those* that have not sought the Lord, nor inquired for him.

Mal. 1.6. A son honoureth *his* father, and a servant his master : if then I *be* a father, where *is* mine honour? and if I *be* a master, where *is* my fear? saith the Lord of hosts unto you, O priests, that despise my name. And ye say, Wherein have we despised thy name?

Mal. 3.7. Even from the days of your fathers ye are gone away from mine ordinances, and have not kept *them.* Return unto me, and I will return unto you, saith the Lord of hosts. But ye said, Wherein shall we return?

See IDOLATRY, LUKEWARMNESS, DECISION.

BADGERS' SKINS, shoes made of, Eze. 16.10. See TABERNACLE, COVERINGS OF.

BAG. See PURSE.

BAHURIM, a town near Jerusalem, 2 Sam. 3.16. Shimei curses David at, 2 Sam. 16.5. David's two spies hid in a well at, 2 Sam. 17.18.

BAKER OF PHARAOH, imprisonment, dream and execution of, Gen. 40.

BAKING. See BREAD.

BALAAM, a soothsayer of Mesopotamia, Deu. 23.4. Jos. 13.22. Sent for by Balak to curse Israel, Num. 22. Jos. 24.9. Neh. 13.2. Mic. 6.5. Rebuked by the ass, stopped by an angel, Num. 22.22-35. 2 Pet. 2.16.

His sacrifices and prophecies, Num. 22.34-41. Num. 23. Num. 24. His covetousness, Num. 22.21. 2 Pet. 2.15. Jude 11. Instigates Balak to seduce Israel, Num. 31.16. Rev. 2.14,15. Slain by the Israelites, Num. 31.8. Jos. 13.22.

BALAK, king of Moab, sends messengers to Balaam, that he might curse Israel, Num. *c.* 22 to 24. Jos. 24.9. Mic. 6.5. Jud. 11.25 with Num. 24 9. Seduces the Israelites, Num. 25. Rev. 2.14.

BALANCES, or SCALES, Job 31.6. Isa. 40.12,15. Required to be just, Lev. 19.36. Pro. 11.1. Pro. 16.11. Pro. 20.23. Eze. 45.10. Hos. 12.7. Amos 8.5. Mic. 6.11. See WEIGHTS.

BALDNESS, Lev. 13.40,41. As a sign of mourning forbidden, Lev. 21.5. Deu. 14.1. The usage referred to, Job 1.20. Isa. 3.24. Isa. 15.2. Isa. 22.12. Jer. 7.29. Jer. 16.6. Jer. 47.5. Jer. 48.37. Eze. 7.18. Eze. 27.31. Eze. 29.18. Amos 8.10. Mic. 1.16. Elisha mocked for, 2 Kin. 2.23.

BALM, a fragrant balsam, Gilead famous for, Gen. 37.25. Gen. 43.11. Jer. 8.22. Jer. 46.11. Jer. 51.8. Eze. 27.17.

BANISHMENT, Ezr. 7.26. Examples of, Absalom, 2 Sam. 14.13,14,24. Jews, Act. 18.2. John, Rev. 1.9.

BANNER. See STANDARD.

BANQUET. See FEAST.

BAPTISM (Gr. *baptisma, baptismos, baptizo*) generally translated baptism, as Mat. 3.7. Translated wash, Mar. 7.4,8. Luke 11.38. Heb. 9.10.

Mat. 3.6. Baptized of him in Jordan, confessing their sins. 7. But when he saw many of the Pharisees and Sadducees come to his baptism, he said unto them, O generation of vipers, who hath warned you to flee from the wrath to come? 8. Bring forth therefore fruits meet for repentance.

Mat. 3.11. I indeed baptize you with water unto repentance : but he that cometh after me is mightier than I, whose shoes I am not worthy to bear : he shall baptize you with the Holy Ghost, and *with* fire.

Mat. 3.13. Then cometh Jesus from Galilee to Jordan unto John, to be baptized of him. 14. But John forbade him, saying, I have need to be baptized of thee, and comest thou to me? 15. And Jesus answering, said unto him, Suffer *it to be so* now; for thus it becometh us to fulfil all righteousness. Then he suffered him. 16. And Jesus, when he was baptized, went up straightway out of the water: and, lo, the heavens were opened unto him, and he saw the Spirit of God descending like a dove, and lighting upon him. Mar. 1.8-10. Luke 3.7,8. Jno. 10.40.

Mat. 20.22. Are ye able to drink of the cup that I shall drink of, and to be baptized with the baptism that I am baptized with? They say unto him, We are able. 23. And he saith unto them, Ye shall drink indeed of my cup, and be baptized with the baptism that I am baptized with. Mar. 10.38.

Mat. 21.25. The baptism of John, whence was it? from heaven, or of men? Mar. 11.30. Luk. 20.4.

Mat. 28.19. Go ye therefore, and teach all nations, baptizing them in the name of the Father, and of the Son, and of the Holy Ghost.

Mar. 1.4. John did baptize in the wilderness, and preach the baptism of repentance for the remission of sins. 5. And there went out unto him all the land of Judea, and they of Jerusalem, and were all baptized of him in the river of Jordan, confessing their sins.

Mar. 16.16. He that believeth, and is baptized, shall be saved.

Luk. 3.12. Then came also publicans to be baptized, and said unto him, Master, what shall we do? 21. When all the people were baptized, it came to pass, that Jesus also being baptized, and praying, the heaven was opened.

Luk. 7.29. All the people that heard *him*, and the publicans, justified God, being baptized with the baptism of John. 30. But the Pharisees and lawyers rejected the counsel of God against themselves, being not baptized of him.

Luk. 12.50. I have a baptism to be baptized with; and how am I straitened till it be accomplished!

Jno. 1.25. Why baptizest thou then, if thou be not that Christ, nor Elias, neither that prophet? 26. John answered them, saying, I baptize with water: but there standeth one among you, whom ye know not.

Jno. 1.28. In Bethabara, beyond Jordan, where John was baptizing.

Jno. 1.31. I knew him not: but that he should be made manifest to Israel, therefore am I come baptizing with water. 33. I knew him not: but he that sent me to baptize with water, the same said unto me, Upon whom thou shalt see the Spirit descending, and remaining on him, the same is he which baptizeth with the Holy Ghost.

Jno. 3.22. There he tarried with them, and baptized. 23. And John also was baptizing in Ænon, near to Salem, because there was much water there; and they came, and were baptized.

Jno. 3.26. They came unto John, and said unto him, Rabbi, he that was with thee beyond Jordan, to whom thou bearest witness, behold, the same baptizeth, and all *men* come to him.

Jno. 4.1. The Pharisees had heard that Jesus made and baptized more disciples than John. 2. Jesus himself baptized not, but his disciples.

Act. 1.5. John truly baptized with water; but ye shall be baptized with the Holy Ghost not many days hence. 22. Beginning from the baptism of John, unto that same day that he was taken up from us, must one be ordained to be a witness with us.

Act. 2.38. Peter said unto them, Repent, and be baptized every one of you in the name of Jesus Christ for the remission of sins, and ye shall receive the gift of the Holy Ghost. 41. Then they that gladly received his word were baptized: and the same day there were added *unto them* about three thousand souls.

Act. 8.12. When they believed Philip preaching the things concerning the kingdom of God, and the name of Jesus Christ, they were baptized, both men and women. 13. Then Simon himself believed also: and when he was baptized, he continued with Philip.

Act. 8.15. Prayed for them, that they might receive the Holy Ghost. 16. (For as yet he was fallen upon none of them: only they were baptized in the name of the Lord Jesus.)

Act. 8.36. They came unto a certain water: and the eunuch said, See, *here is* water; what doth hinder me to be baptized? 37. Philip said, If thou believest with all thine heart, thou mayest. And he answered and said, I believe that Jesus Christ is the Son of God. 38. And he commanded the chariot to stand still: and they went down both into the water, both Philip and the eunuch; and he baptized him.

Act. 9.18. He received sight forthwith, and arose, and was baptized.

Act. 10.37. That word, *I say*, ye know, which was published throughout all Judea, and began from Galilee, after the baptism which John preached.

Act. 10.47. Can any man forbid water, that these should not be baptized, which have received the Holy Ghost as well as we? 48. And he commanded them to be baptized in the name of the Lord.

Act. 11.16. Then remembered I the word of the Lord, how that he said, John indeed baptized with water; but ye shall be baptized with the Holy Ghost.

Act. 16.14. Whose heart the Lord opened, that she attended unto the things which were spoken of Paul. 15. And when she was baptized, and her household, she besought *us*, saying, If ye have judged me to be faithful to the Lord, come into my house.

Act. 16.33. He took them the same hour of the night, and washed *their* stripes; and was baptized, he and all his, straightway.

Act. 18.8. Many of the Corinthians hearing believed, and were baptized. 25. This man was instructed in the way of the Lord; and, being fervent in the spirit, he spake and taught diligently the things of the Lord, knowing only the baptism of John.

Act. 19.2. He said unto them, Have ye received the Holy Ghost since ye believed? And they said unto him, We have not so much as heard whether there be any Holy Ghost. 3. And he said unto them, Unto what then were ye baptized? And they said, Unto John's baptism. 4. John verily baptized with the baptism of repentance, saying unto the people, that they should believe on him which should come after him, that is, on Christ

Jesus. 5. When they heard *this*, they were baptized in the name of the Lord Jesus. 6. And when Paul had laid *his* hands upon them, the Holy Ghost came on them.

Act. 22.16. Now, why tarriest thou? arise, and be baptized, and wash away thy sins, calling on the name of the Lord.

Rom. 6.3. So many of us as were baptized into Jesus Christ were baptized into his death? 4. Therefore we are buried with him by baptism into death : that like as Christ was raised up from the dead by the glory of the Father, even so we also should walk in newness of life.

1 Cor. 1.13. Were ye baptized in the name of Paul? 14. I thank God that I baptized none of you, but Crispus and Gaius ; 15. Lest any should say that I baptized in mine own name. 16. And I baptized also the household of Stephanas: besides, I know not whether I baptized any other. 17. For Christ sent me not to baptize, but to preach the gospel.

1 Cor. 10.2. Were all baptized unto Moses in the cloud and in the sea.

1 Cor. 12.13. By one Spirit are we all baptized into one body, whether *we be* Jews or Gentiles, whether *we be* bond or free ; and have been all made to drink into one Spirit.

1 Cor. 15.29. What shall they do which are baptized for the dead, if the dead rise not at all? why are they then baptized for the dead?

Gal. 3.27. As many of you as have been baptized into Christ have put on Christ.

Eph. 4.5. One Lord, one faith, one baptism.

Col. 2.12. Buried with him in baptism, wherein also ye are risen with *him* through the faith of the operation of God, who hath raised him from the dead.

1 Pet. 3.18. Christ also hath once suffered for sins, the just for the unjust, that he might bring us to God, being put to death in the flesh, but quickened by the Spirit : 21. The like figure whereunto *even* baptism doth also now save us (not the putting away of the filth of the flesh, but the answer of a good conscience toward God), by the resurrection of Jesus Christ.

BAR AND **BOLT**, 2 Sam. 13.17,18. Brazen, 1 Kin. 4.13. Iron, Isa. 45.2. Wood, Nah. 3.13.

BARABBAS, a murderer released by Pilate, Mat. 27.16-26. Mar. 15.7-15. Luk. 23.18-25. Jno. 18.40. Act. 3.14.

BARAK, a judge of Israel ; with Deborah delivers Israel from Jabin and Sisera, Jud. 4. Heb. 11.32. Song of victory, Jud. 5.

BARBARIAN (signifies stranger or foreigner), Act. 28.2-4. Rom. 1.14. 1 Cor. 14.11. Col. 3.11.

BARBER, Eze. 5.1.

BARLEY in Egypt, Ex. 9.31. In Palestine, Deu. 8.8. 1 Chr. 11.13. Jer. 41.8. Given to horses, 1 Kin. 4.28. Meal of, used in offerings, Num. 5.15. Eze. 45.15. An article of barter, 2 Chr. 2.10. Hos. 3.2 ; and of tribute, 2 Chr. 27.5. Value of, Lev. 27.16. 2 Kin. 7.1. Rev. 6.6. Joab's field of, burnt by Absalom, 2 Sam. 14.30. See BREAD—HARVEST.

BARN, GARNER or GRANARY, 2 Kin. 6.27. Job 39.12. Joel 1.17. Luk. 12.18,24. Illustrative, Mat. 3.12. Mat. 13.30. See TREASURIES.

BARNABAS, or JOSES, called a prophet and teacher, Act. 13.1. An apostle, Act. 14.14. A Levite from Cyprus ; sells his land for the benefit of the church, Act. 4.36,37. Brings Paul to the apostles, Act. 9.27. Is sent by the church to Antioch, Act. 11.22.

Brings Paul to Antioch, Act. 11.25,26. Is sent to Jerusalem with Paul, Act. 11.30. Returns to Antioch, Act. 12.25. Is sent to Seleucia, Act. 13. Preaches at Iconium ; persecuted, Act. 14.1-7. Is called Jupiter at Lystra : departs to Derbe, Act. 14.12-28.

His dispute at Antioch about circumcision ; sent to Jerusalem ; returns with the letter of the apostles, Act. 15.1-35. Gal. 2.1-9. Separates from the Gentiles at Antioch, Gal. 2.13. His dispute and separation from Paul, Act. 15.36, 37. Reconciliation, 1 Cor. 9.6. His character, Act. 11.24. Act. 15.26. 1 Cor. 9.6.

BARREL of meal, miracle, 1 Kin. 17.12-14.

BARSABAS. See JUSTUS.

BARTER, Gen. 47.17. 1 Kin. 5.8,11. 2 Chr. 2.10. Job 28.17. Hos. 3.2.

BARTHOLOMEW (Nathaniel ?), an apostle, Mat. 10.3. Mar. 3.18. Luk. 6.14. Act. 1.13.

BARTIMEUS of Jericho, a beggar cured of blindness by Christ, Mar. 10.46. Luk. 18.35. Mat. 20.29.

BARUCH, a scribe ; writes Jeremiah's prophecy, and reads it publicly, Jer. 36. Receives Jeremiah's deed of purchase, Jer. 32. 12-16. Accompanies him to Egypt, Jer. 43. 6-8. Prophecy regarding, Jer. 45.

BARZILLAI, his kindness to David, 2 Sam. 17.27-29. 2 Sam. 19.31,32. David's gratitude to him, 2 Sam. 19.33-40. 1 Kin. 2.7.

BASHAN, a kingdom of the Rephaim and Amorites, east of Jordan and north of Arnon, Gen. 14.5 with Jos. 13.12. Deu. 4.47. Og, king of, defeated by Israel, and his country taken. See OG. Given to Gad, Reuben, and Manasseh, Num. 32.33. Deu. 3.10-14. Jos. 12.4-6. Jos. 13.29-31. Jos. 17.1.

Hazael invades and takes certain towns of, 2 Kin. 10.32,33. Recovered by Jehoash, 2 Kin. 13.25. Fruitfulness of, Isa. 33.9. Jer. 50.19. Nah. 1.4. Oaks of, famous, Isa. 2.13. Eze. 27.6. Zec. 11.2.

Cattle and flocks of, Deu. 32.14. Psa. 22.12. Eze. 39.18. Amos 4.1. Mic. 7.14. Towns of, conquered by Jair, and called Bashan Havothjair. See ARGOB, ASHTAROTH, EDREI, JAIR. Hill of, Psa. 68.15,22. Jer. 22.20.

BASKET, Gen. 40.16,17. Lev. 8.31. Deu. 28.5. Amos 8.1. Act. 9.25.

BASONS. See BOWL—LAVER.

BAT, Lev. 11.19. Deu. 14.18. Isa. 2.20.

BATH, a measure containing nine gallons, equal to an ephah, or the tenth part of a homer, Eze. 45.11,14. 1 Kin. 7.26,38. 2 Chr. 2.10. 2 Chr. 4.5. Ezr. 7.22. Translated, measure, Luk. 16.6.

BATHING. See ABLUTION — PURIFICATION.

BATHSHEBA, or BATHSHUA (granddaughter of Ahitophel), wife of Uriah ; seduced by David, 2 Sam. 11.2-5. Psa. 51, title. Mourns for Uriah's death, and becomes David's wife ;

her child's death, 2 Sam. 11.26,27. 2 Sam. 12.14-18. Mother of Solomon, &c., 2 Sam. 12.24. 2 Sam. 5.14. 1 Chr. 3.5. Acquaints David with Adonijah's usurpation, 1 Kin. 1.11-31. Intercedes with Solomon for Adonijah, 1 Kin. 2.13-21.

BATTERING-RAM, 2 Sam. 20.15. Eze. 4.2. Eze. 21.22.

BATTLE. See ARMIES—WAR.

BATTLE-AXE, Eze. 26.9. Illustrative, Jer. 51.20.

BATTLEMENTS of houses, Deu. 22.8. Of walls, Jer. 5.10.

BAY-TREE, an evergreen, Psa. 37.35.

BDELLIUM, a precious stone, or perhaps a gum, Gen. 2.12. Num. 11.7.

BEACON, Isa. 30.17. Of fire, Jer. 6,1. See STANDARD.

BEAN, 2 Sam. 17.28. Eze. 4.9.

BEAR, its fierceness, 2 Sam. 17.8. Pro. 17.12. Pro. 28.15. Isa. 11.7. Isa. 59.11. Lam. 3.10. Hos. 13.8. Amos 5.19. One slain by David, 1 Sam. 17.34-37. Two tear forty-two children in Bethel, 2 Kin. 2.24. Symbolical, Dan. 7.5. Rev. 13.2.

BEARD worn long by the Jews, 1 Sam. 21.13. 2 Sam. 20.9. Psa. 133.2. Eze. 5.1. Disgrace of having it shaven, 2 Sam. 10.4,5. Shaved by the Egyptians, Gen. 41.14. Marring of, forbidden in mourning, Lev. 19. 27. Lev. 21.5. Allowed to grow untrimmed in mourning, 2 Sam. 19.24. Also plucked off, Ezr. 9.3. And cut off, Isa. 7.20. Isa. 15.2. Jer. 41.5. Jer. 48.37. Shaved in leprosy, Lev. 13.29-33. Lev. 14.9. See BALDNESS—BARBER.

BEASTS, creation of, Gen. 1.24,25. Gen. 2.19. Psa. 50.10,11. Jer. 27.5. God's care of, Gen. 1.30. Gen. 9.10. Psa. 36.6. Psa. 104.11. Nature, habits, and abodes of, Job 12.7,8. Job 37.8. Job 40.20. Psa. 49.12. Psa. 73.22. Psa. 104.20-25. Ecc. 3.18-21. Isa. 13.21,22. Isa. 34.14. Jer. 50.39. Mar. 1.13. Jas. 3.7.

Named by Adam, Gen. 2.20. Solomon's knowledge of, 1 Kin. 4.33. Clean, offered in sacrifice, Gen. 4.4. Gen. 7.2-8. Gen. 8.20 (see OFFERINGS) ; and given to man for food after the flood, Gen. 9.2-4. Lev. 11. Unclean, Lev. 7.21. Lev. 11. Lev. 20.25. Deu. 14.3-19. Act. 10.14.

Sent in judgment, Lev. 26.22. Deu. 28.26. Eze. 5.17. Eze. 14.15. Eze. 32.4. Rev. 6.8. Preserved in the ark, Gen. 7.14. Gen. 8.19. Suffered in the plagues, Ex. 8.17. Ex. 9.9,19. Ex. 11.5. Forced to fast, Jonah 3.7. Paul fought with, 1 Cor. 15.32.

Symbolical, Isa. 30.6. Dan. 7.11,17,19. Dan. 8.4. Act. 10.12. Rev. 11.7. Rev. 13. Rev. 14.9,11. Rev. 15.2. Rev.16. 2,10-13. Rev. 17. Rev. 19.19,20. Rev. 20.4,10. Symbolical (living creatures), Rev. 4.6-9. Rev. 5.6-14. Rev. 6.1-7. Rev. 7.11. Rev. 14.3. Rev. 15.7. Rev. 19.4. Man's dominion over.—See MAN. Firstlings of.—See FIRST-BORN.

See ANTELOPE, APE, ASS, BADGER, BAT, BEAR, BEHEMOTH, BOAR, BULL, CAMEL, CATTLE, CHAMOIS, CONEY, COW, DEER, DOG, ELEPHANT, FERRET, FOX, GOAT, GREYHOUND, HARE, HEIFER, HORSE, LEOPARD, LION, MOLE, MOUSE, PYGARG, RAM, SATYR, SHEEP, SWINE, UNICORN, WEASEL, WHALE, WOLF.

BEATEN-WORK (not cast but wrought), of metals, Ex. 25.18.

BED, or COUCH, Gen. 47.31. Gen. 49.4. Ex. 8.3. 1 Sam. 19.13-15. Pro. 7.16,17. Song 1.16. Isa. 28.20. Eze. 23.41. Amos 3.12 Mat. 9.6. Mar. 4.21. Luk. 5.19. Act. 5.15. Of Iron, Deu. 3.11. Of wood, Song 3.7-9. Of Ivory, Amos 6.4. Of gold and silver, Est. 1.6.

Of the king guarded, Song 3.7. Used by day, 2 Sam. 4.5. 2 Sam. 11.2. At meals, 1 Sam. 28.23-25. Est. 7.8. Amos 6.4-6. Luk. 7.36-38. Jno. 13.23. Illustrative, Job 17.13. Psa. 139.8. Isa. 57.2. Song 6.2. See PILLOW.

BEE, Deu. 1.44. Jud. 14.8. Psa. 118.12. Isa. 7.18.

BEEL-ZEBUB, the prince of demons, Mat. 10.25. Mat. 12.24,27. Mar. 3.22. Luk. 11. 15,18,19. Baal-zebub, an idol-god of the Philistines at Ekron ; Ahaziah sends to inquire of, 2 Kin. 1.2.

BEER (a well), an encampment of Israel in Moab, where a well was dug, Num. 21.16-18.

———, a town in Judah to which Jotham fled, Jud. 9.21.

BEER-LAHAI-ROI, a well near which the angel of the Lord found Hagar, Gen. 16.7,14. Isaac dwelt near, Gen. 24.62. Gen. 25.11.

BEEROTH, a town of the Gibeonites, Jos. 9.17. Given to Benjamin, Jos. 18.25. 2 Sam. 4.2. Ezr. 2.25.

BEERSHEBA, a city on the south frontier of Palestine, Jud. 20.1. 2 Chr. 19.4. 2 Chr. 30.5. Name given to it by Abraham, who plants a grove and dwells at, Gen. 21.31-33. Gen. 22.19. Isaac dwells at, Gen. 26.23. Jacob quits for Haran, Gen. 28.10. And offers sacrifices at, on his way to Egypt, Gen. 46.1. Given to Judah, Jos. 15.28. 2 Sam. 24.7. Transferred to Simeon, Jos. 19.2. 1 Chr. 4.28. Samuel's sons are judges at, 1 Sam. 8.2. Idolatrous worship at, Amos 5.5. Amos 8.14. Jews return to, from captivity, Neh. 11.27,30.

———, WELL OF, dug by Abraham and Isaac ; their covenants with the Philistines concerning, Gen. 21.25-32. Gen. 26.

———, WILDERNESS OF. An angel appears to Hagar in, Gen. 21.14-19 ; and to Elijah, 1 Kin. 19.3-7.

BEETLE, an insect, supposed to be a kind of locust, Lev. 11.22.

BEEVES, plural of beef, but signifying cattle, Lev. 22.19,21.

BEGGARS AND BEGGING, 1 Sam. 2.8. Psa. 37.25. Psa. 109.10. Pro. 20.4. Luk. 16.3. Bartimeus, Mar. 10.46. Lazarus, Luk. 16.20-22. The blind man, Jno. 9.8. The lame man, Act. 3.2-5. See POOR.

BEHEADING (a Roman punishment) of John, Mat. 14.10. Of James, Act. 12.2. Of the martyrs, Rev. 20.4.

BEHEMOTH (the great beast), Job 40. 15-24.

BEKAH, half a shekel, about 1s. 1½d. Ex. 38.26.

BEL, a Babylonian idol, Isa. 46.1. Jer. 50.2. Jer. 51.44.

BELIAL signifies wickedness, son of Belial, a wicked or worthless person, Deu. 13.13.

1 Sam. 1.16. 1 Sam. 2.12. A name of Satan, 2 Cor. 6.15.

BELIEVER, a New Testament name of saints, Act. 5.14. 1 Tim. 4.12, &c. See SAINTS —CHURCH.

BELIEVING. See FAITH.

BELLOWS, used in smelting, Jer. 6.29.

BELLS (of gold) attached to the high-priest's robe, Ex. 28.33-35. Ex. 39. 25-26. To horses, Zec. 14.20.

BELLY, equivalent to the modern figurative use of the word heart, Job 15.2,35. Job 20.20. Psa. 44.25. Pro. 18.8,20. Pro. 20.27,30. Hab. 3.16. Jno. 7.38. Tit. 1.12.

BELSHAZZAR, king of Babylon, son or grandson of Nebuchadnezzar, feast of; the handwriting on the wall interpreted to, by Daniel; slain by Darius, Dan. 5.5-31.

BENAIAH, one of David's captains, 2 Sam. 8.18. His exploits, 2 Sam. 23.20-23. 1 Chr. 11.22-24. Slays Adonijah, and Joab, and Shimei by Solomon's command; made captain of the host, 1 Kin. 2.30-35,46. 1 Kin. 4.4.

BENCH of ivory, Eze. 27.6. See THRONE—BED.

BENEDICTION by Melchizedec, Heb. 7. 1-7. By Isaac, Gen. 27.23-29. Gen. 28.1-4. By Jacob, Gen. 47.7-10. Gen. 48.15-22. Gen. 49. By Moses, Num. 10.36. Deu. 33. By Aaron, Lev. 9.22,23. Num. 6.23-27. By Balaam, Num. c. 23 & 24. Jos. 24.10. By Joshua, Jos. 14.13. Jos. 22. 6,7. By Eli, 1 Sam. 2.20. By David, 2 Sam. 6.18,20. 2 Sam. 13.25. 2 Sam. 19.39. By Solomon, 1 Kin. 8.14,55. 2 Chr. 6.3. By Simeon, Luk. 2.34. By travellers, Psa. 129.8. The priests and Levites appointed to bless the people, Deu. 10.8. Deu. 21.5.

———, FORMS OF, Num. 6.23. On this wise ye shall bless the children of Israel, saying unto them, 24. The Lord bless thee, and keep thee: 25. The Lord make his face shine upon thee, and be gracious unto thee: 26. The Lord lift up his countenance upon thee, and give thee peace.

Num. 10.35. When the ark set forward, that Moses said, Rise up, Lord, and let thine enemies be scattered; and let them that hate thee flee before thee. 36. And when it rested, he said, Return, O Lord, unto the many thousands of Israel. See SALUTATIONS—PRAYER, INTERCESSORY.

BENEVOLENCE. See LIBERALITY—LOVE —POOR, KINDNESS TO.

BENHADAD I., king of Damascus, alliance with Asa against Baasha, 1 Kin. 15.18-20.

——— **II.**, son of Benhadad I., besieges Samaria in Ahab's reign and is defeated, 1 Kin. 20. Is attacked by Ahab and Jehoshaphat at Ramoth Gilead, Ahab slain, 1 Kin. 22. Sends Namaan to be cured by Elisha, 2 Kin. 5. Invades Israel in Jehoram's reign, his army struck blind, 2 Kin. 6.8-23. Besieges Samaria, his army miraculously put to flight, 2 Kin. 6.24-29. 2 Kin. 7. Sends Hazael to inquire of Elisha, 2 Kin. 8.7-14. Murdered by Hazael, 2 Kin. 8.15.

——— **III.**, son of Hazael, conquered by Jehoash, 2 Kin. 13.24,25. By Jeroboam II., 2 Kin. 14.25-28.

BENJAMIN, youngest son of Jacob and Rachel, Gen. 35.18,24. Gen. 46.19. Jacob's love for, Gen. 42.4,36,38. Gen. 43.6,14. Gen. 44.20-34. Joseph's treatment of, in Egypt, Gen. 43.16-34. Gen. 44. Gen. 45.14,22. Blessed by Jacob, Gen. 49.27. His sons, Gen. 46.21.

———, TRIBE OF. Numbered at Sinai, Num. 1.37. And in the plains of Moab, Num. 26.41. Families of, Num. 26.38-40. 1 Chr. 7.6-12. 1 Chr. 8. Marched and encamped under the standard of Ephraim west of the Tabernacle, Num. 2.18,22. Blessing of Moses on, Deu. 33.12.

Inheritance in Canaan, Jos. 18.11-28. Did not expel the Jebusites, Jud. 1.21. Assisted Deborah, Jud. 5.14. Invaded by Ammonites, Jud. 10.9. War of the other tribes with, Jud. c. 19 & 20. Provided with wives at Shiloh, Jud. 21.

Saul, king of Israel, chosen from, 1 Sam. 9.1,17. 1 Sam. 10.20,21. A band of, with David at Ziklag, 1 Chr. 12.1,2,16. Not numbered by Joab with the rest of Israel, 1 Chr. 21.6. Adhere to Ishbosheth, 2 Sam. 2.9,15,31. 1 Chr. 12.29. Return to David, 2 Sam. 3.19. 2 Sam. 19.16,17. Adhere to Rehoboam. 1 Kin. 12.21. 2 Chr. 11.1.

Armies of, under Asa, 2 Chr. 14.8. Under Jehoshaphat, 2 Chr. 17.17. Skill as bowmen and slingers, Jud. 3.15. Jud. 20.16. 1 Chr. 8.40. 1 Chr. 12.2. Returned from captivity, Ezr. 1.5. For things common to the tribes, see ISRAEL, TRIBES OF.

BERACHAH, a valley where Jehoshaphat gained a victory over Ammon, 2 Chr. 20.26.

BEREA, a city of Macedonia, Paul's success at, Act. 17.10-14. Act. 20.4.

BERNICE present with Agrippa at Paul's trial, Act. 25.13,23. Act. 26.30.

BERODACH-BALADAN. See MERODACH.

BERYL, a precious stone, Song 5.14. Eze. 1.16. Eze. 10.9. Set in the high-priest's breastplate, Ex. 28.20. Ex. 39.13. In the foundation of the New Jerusalem, Rev. 21.20.

BESOM, Isa. 14.23.

BESOR, a brook south of Ziklag, crossed by David, 1 Sam. 30.9,10.

BETHABARA, a town beyond Jordan, Jud. 7.24. John baptizes at, Jno. 1.28. Jesus escapes to, from the Jews; converts at, Jno. 10.39-42.

BETHANY, a village near Jerusalem, Jno. 11.18. Jesus visits the house of Martha in, Luk. 10.38-41. Raises Lazarus, Jno. 11. Feasted by Simon the leper, Mat. 26.6-13. Jno. 12.1-9. Sends his disciples to bring a colt from, Mar. 11.1. Returns from the Temple to, Mat. 21.17. Mar. 11.11,12. Ascends to heaven near, Luk. 24.50.

BETHARBEL, a city of Samaria, taken by Shalmanezer, Hos. 10.14.

BETH-AVEN, a town east of Bethel, Jos. 7.2. Saul's victory near, 1 Sam. 13.5. 1 Sam. 14.23.

——— (house of idols), name given to Bethel (house of God) after the golden calves were set up there, Hos. 4.15. Hos. 5.8. Hos. 10.5.

———, WILDERNESS OF, Jos. 18.12.

BETHEL (house of God), or LUZ, a Canaanitish town 12 miles north of Jerusalem, Jos. 8.17. Jos. 12 16. Jacob's vision, vow, sacrifice and prayer at, Gen. 28.19. Gen. 31.13. Gen. 35.1-15. Hos. 12.4. Deborah buried at, Gen. 35.8.

Assigned to Benjamin, Jos. 18.13,22. Conquered by Ephraim, Jud. 1.22-26. Deborah judges at, Jud. 4.5. The Israelites worship near, Jud. 21.19. 1 Sam. 10.3. Samuel judges at, 1 Sam. 7.16.

Jeroboam sets up calves at, 1 Kin. 12.28-33. 2 Kin. 10.29. See CALVES. Prophecy against the altar at, and Jeroboam's hand withered at, 1 Kin. 13.1-6,32. 2 Kin. 23.4,15-20. The old prophet at, 1 Kin. 13.11-32.

A school of the prophets, 2 Kin. 2.3. Mockers at, destroyed by bears, 2 Kin. 2.23,24. Jeroboam II.'s court at, Amos 7.10-13. Shalmanezer sends a priest to, 2 Kin. 17.27,28. Peopled after the captivity, Ezr. 2.28. See BETHAVEN.

Prophecies against. See CALVES OF BETHEL.

————— MOUNT, 1 Sam. 13.2.

BETHER (mountains of spices), Song 2.17. Song 8.14.

BETHESDA, a pool in Jerusalem where Christ cured an impotent man, Jno. 5.2-4.

BETH-HACCEREM, a mountain a few miles south of Jerusalem, Jer. 6.1.

BETH-HORON, upper and nether, two frontier towns of Benjamin and Ephraim, between which Joshua defeated the Amorites, Jos. 10.10,11. Jos. 16.3,5. Jos. 18.13. 1 Sam. 13 18. 1 Chr. 7.24. Fortified by Solomon, 1 Kin. 9.17. 2 Chr. 8.5.

BETHLEHEM, a city of Judah, Jud. 17.7. Jud. 19.18. Called Ephratah or Ephrath, Gen. 48.7. Psa. 132.6. Mic. 5.2. Rachael dies at, Gen. 35.16,19. Gen. 48.7. Naomi, Ruth and Boaz dwell at, Ruth 1.1,19. Ruth 2.4. Ruth 4.

David born at, 1 Sam. 16.1. 1 Sam. 17.12. Besieged by David, 2 Sam. 23.14-16. Fortified by Rehoboam, 2 Chr. 11.6. Christ born at, Mic. 5.2. Mat. 2. Luk. 2.4,15. Children of, slain by Herod, Mat. 2.16-18.

————— , WELL OF, exploit of three of David's captains to procure water from, 2 Sam. 23.15-18.

————— , a town of Zebulun, Jos. 19.15. Ibzan judges Israel at, Jud. 12.10.

BETHMAACHAH. See ABEL-BETH-MAACHA.

BETH-PEOR, a city of Moab, on the Jordan, given to Reuben; Moses buried over-against it, Deu. 3.29. Deu. 4.46. Deu. 34.6. Jos. 13.20.

BETHPHAGE, a village near Jerusalem, passed by Jesus on his last visit to Jerusalem, Mat. 21.1. Mar. 11.1. Luk. 19.29.

BETH-REHOB. See REHOB.

BETHSAIDA OF GALILEE, the town of Philip, &c., Jno. 1.44. Jno. 12.21. Christ visits, Mar. 6.45. Cures a blind man at, Mar. 8.22. Christ's prophecy against, Mat. 11.21. Luk. 10.13.

————— , east of the Sea of Galilee, Christ feeds 5000 near, Luk. 9.10. Mat. 14.13. Mar. 6.32.

BETHSHAN, a town of Manasseh west of the Jordan, Jos. 17.11. Jud. 1.27. 1 Kin. 4.12. 1 Chr. 7.29. The bodies of Saul and his sons fastened to the wall of, by the Philistines, 1 Sam. 31.10,12. 2 Sam. 21.12.

BETHSHEMESH, a frontier city of Judah, Jos. 15.10. 1 Kin. 4.9. A city of the priests, Jos. 21.16. 1 Chr. 6.59. Men of, smitten for looking into the Ark, 1 Sam. 6.10-15,19-21. Amaziah defeated at, by Jehoash, 2 Kin. 14.11-13. Taken by the Philistines in the reign of Ahaz, 2 Chr. 28.18.

————— , a town of Naphtali, Jos. 19.38. Jud. 1.33.

————— a town of Issachar, Jos. 19.22.

————— , a name of On. See ON.

BETHUEL, son of Abraham's brother Nahor, and father of Laban and Rebecca. Gen. 22.22,23. Gen. 24.15,24. Gen. 25.20. Gen. 28.2.

BETROTHAL considered as sacred as marriage, Gen. 24.51,55. Deu. 20.7. Deu. 22.23,24. Jud. 14.7,8. Mat. 1.18. Luk. 1.27. Luk. 2.5. Illustrative, Jer. 2.2. Hos. 2.19,20. 2 Cor. 11.2. See MARRIAGE.

BEULAH (married), a name given to Palestine, Isa. 62.4.

BEZALEEL, divinely instructed to make the Tabernacle, Ex. 31.2. Ex. 36.1. Ex. 37.1. Ex. 38.22. 1 Chr. 2.20. 2 Chr. 1.5.

BEZEK, ADONIBEZEK, king of, conquered by Joshua, Jud. 1.4. Saul's army mustered at, 1 Sam. 11.8.

BEZER, a Levitical city of refuge in Reuben, Deu. 4.43. Jos. 20.8. Jos. 21.36. 1 Chr. 6.78.

BIBLE. See WORD OF GOD.

BIER. 2 Sam. 3.31. Luk. 7.14. See BURIAL.

BIGOTRY. Num. 11.29. Moses said unto him, Enviest thou for my sake? would God that all the Lord's people were prophets, and that the Lord would put his spirit upon them! Job 13.7. Will ye speak wickedly for God? and talk deceitfully for him? 8. Will ye accept his person? will ye contend for God? Jer. 7.4. Trust ye not in lying words, saying, The temple of the Lord, are these. Luk. 9.55. He turned, and rebuked them, and said, Ye know not what manner of spirit ye are of. 56. For the Son of man is not come to destroy men's lives, but to save them. 1 Cor. 10.27. If any of them that believe not bid you to a feast, and ye be disposed to go; whatsoever is set before you, eat, asking no question for conscience' sake. Col. 2.16. Let no man therefore judge you in meat, or in drink, or in respect of an holyday, or of the new moon, or of the sabbath days: 17. Which are a shadow of things to come; but the body is of Christ.

————— , EXAMPLES OF. Joshua, Num. 11.27-29. Jonah, Jon. 4. Judas, &c., Mat. 26.8,9. Mar. 14.4,5. Jno. 12.4,5. John, Mar. 9.38-40. Luk. 9.49,50. James and John, Luk. 9.54,55. Nathanael, Jno. 1.46. Disciples, Mat. 19.13. Mar. 10.13. Luk. 18.15. Pharisees, Mat. 9.3. Mat. 11.18,19. Mat. 23.15. Luk. 7.39. Luk. 11.38,39. Luk. 19.7. Jno. 7.52. Jno. 9.28,29,34. Jno. 16.2. Jno. 19.15. (See SABBATH, Jewish misconceptions of.) Men of Nazareth, Luk. 4.28.

Samaritans, Luk. 9.53. Jews, Luk. 13.1-5. Jno. 4.9,27. Act. 21.28,29. Act. 22.22. Rom. 10.2. 1 The. 2.15,16. Christians at Jerusalem, Act. 10.45. Act. 11.2,3. Act. 21.20-24 ; and at Antioch, Act. 15.1-10, 24 ; and at Galatia, Gal. 5.1. Gal. 6.13. Saul, Act. 22.3,4. Act. 26.5,9. Gal. 1.13,14. Phil. 3.6.

See LIBERTY, CHRISTIAN—UNCHARITABLE-NESS.

BIGTHAN, a chamberlain of Ahasuerus, his conspiracy discovered by Mordecai, Est. 2.21-23. Est. 6.2.

BILDAD the Shuhite, his discourses with Job, Job 2.11. Job c. 8, 18, & 25. His sacrifice, Job 42.9. See Gen. 25.2.

BILHAH, Rachel's handmaid, given by her as a wife to Jacob, Gen. 29.29. Gen. 30.3,4. Gen. 37.2. Mother of Dan and Naphtali, Gen. 30.1-8. Gen. 35.25. Gen. 46.24,25. Reuben's intercourse with her, Gen. 35.22. Gen. 49.4.

BILL OF **DIVORCEMENT,** a legal deed of separation, Deu. 24.1-4. Mat. 5.31. See DIVORCE.

BIRDS, creation of, Gen. 1.20-30. Man's dominion over, see MAN. Clean, used for food, Deu. 14.11,20 ; and in sacrifice, Gen. 8.20. See OFFERINGS, Tables 1,2,3. Unclean, Lev. 11.13-20. Deu. 14.12-19.

God's care of, Job 38.41. Psa. 147.9. Mat. 10.29, Luk. 12.6,24. Singing of, Ecc. 12.4. Song 2.12. Taming of, Job 41.5. Jas. 3.7. Solomon's knowledge of, 1 Kin. 4.33. Nests of, Psa. 104.17. Mat. 8.20. Mat. 13.32.

The dam not to be taken with the young, Deu. 22.6,7. Kept in cages, Jer. 5.27. Rev. 18.2. Taken in snares. See SNARES. Illustrative, Isa. 46.11. Jer. 12.9. Eze. 39.4. Symbolical, Dan. 7.6.

See BITTERN, CORMORANT, CRANE, CUC-KOO, DOVE, EAGLE, GLEDE, HAWK, HERON, KITE, LAPWING, NIGHT-HAWK, OSPREY, OSSIFRAGE, OSTRICH, OWL, PARTRIDGE, PEACOCK, QUAIL, RAVEN, SPARROW, STORK, SWALLOW, SWAN, VULTURE.

BIRTHDAY, Pharaoh's feast on, Gen. 40.20 ; and Herod's, Mat. 14.6.

BIRTHRIGHT. See FIRST-BORN.

BISHOP (Gr. *episkopos*), translated bishop, Phil. 1.1. 1 Tim. 3.2. Tit. 1.7. 1 Pet. 2.25. Overseer, Act. 20.28. (*Episkopee*), translated bishopric, Act. 1.20. Office of a bishop, 1 Tim. 3.1. Visitation, Luk. 19.44. 1 Pet. 2.12. (*Episkopos*), translated, taking the oversight, 1 Pet. 5.2. Looking diligently, Heb. 12.15.

See CHURCH-GOVERNMENT.

BIT, of a bridle, Psa. 32.9. Jas. 3.3.

BITHYNIA, a province of Asia Minor, Act. 16.7. 1 Pet. 1.1.

BITTER HERBS, eaten with the Passover, Ex. 12.8. Num. 9.11.

BITTERN, a bird, Isa. 14.23. Isa. 34.11. Zeph. 2.14.

BLACKNESS, illustrative of grief, &c., Job 30.30. Joel, 2.6.

BLASPHEMY, Ex. 20.7. Thou shalt not take the name of the Lord thy God in vain; for the Lord will not hold him guiltless that taketh his name in vain. Deu. 5.11.

Lev. 19.12. Ye shall not swear by my name falsely, neither shalt thou profane the name of thy God. Lev. 22.32.

2 Kin. 19.22. Whom hast thou reproached and blasphemed? and against whom hast thou exalted *thy* voice, and lifted up thine eyes on high? *even* against the Holy One of Israel. Isa. 37.23.

2 Chr. 32.19. They spake against the God of Jerusalem, as against the gods of the people.

Psa. 10.7. His mouth is full of cursing. Rom. 3.14.

Psa. 44.15. The shame of my face hath covered me, 16. For the voice of him that reproacheth and blasphemeth.

Psa. 59.12. *For* the sin of their mouth *and* the words of their lips let them even be taken in their pride : and for cursing and lying *which* they speak. 13. Consume *them* in wrath.

Psa. 74.18. The foolish people have blasphemed thy name.

Psa. 109.17. As he loved cursing, so let it come unto him. 18 As he clothed himself with cursing like as with his garment, so let it come into his bowels like water, and like oil into his bones.

Psa. 139.20. They speak against thee wickedly, *and* thine enemies take *thy name* in vain.

Pro. 26.2. As the bird by wandering, so the curse causeless shall not come.

Pro. 30.9. Lest I be full, and deny *thee*, and say, Who is the Lord? or lest I be poor, and steal, and take the name of my God *in vain*.

Isa. 8.21. When they shall be hungry, they shall fret themselves, and curse their king and their God, and look upward. 22. And *they shall be* driven to darkness.

Isa. 52.5. My name continually every day *is* blasphemed.

Isa. 65.7. Blasphemed me upon the hills: therefore will I measure their former work into their bosom.

Jer. 23.10. Because of swearing the land mourneth.

Eze. 20.27. Your fathers have blasphemed me, in that they have committed a trespass against me.

Eze. 35.12. I have heard all thy blasphemies which thou hast spoken. 13. Ye have boasted against me, and have multiplied your words against me : I have heard *them*.

Dan. 7.25. He shall speak *great* words against the most High.

Dan. 11.36. Shall speak marvellous things against the God of gods, and shall prosper till the indignation be accomplished. 37. Neither shall he regard the God of his fathers ; for he shall magnify himself above all.

Hos. 4.2. By swearing, they break out, and blood toucheth blood.

Zec. 5.3. Every one that sweareth shall be cut off. 4. It shall enter into the house of him that sweareth falsely by my name : and it shall remain in the midst of his house, and shall consume it with the timber thereof, and the stones thereof.

Mat. 5.34. Swear not at all; neither by heaven; for it is God's throne : 35. Nor by the earth ; for it is his footstool: neither by Jerusalem ; for it is the city of the great King. 36. Neither shalt thou swear by thy head, because thou canst not make one hair white or black. 37. But let your communication be, Yea, yea ; Nay, nay : for whatsoever is more than these cometh of evil.

Mat. 10.25. They have called the master of the house Beelzebub.

Mat. 12.31. All manner of sin and blasphemy shall be forgiven unto men ; but the blasphemy *against* the *Holy* Ghost shall not be forgiven unto men. Mar. 3.29,30.

Mat. 15.19. Out of the heart proceed blasphemies.

Rom. 2.24. The name of God is blasphemed among the Gentiles through you. 2 Sam. 12.14.

Col. 3.8. Put off all these ; blasphemy, filthy communication out of your mouth.

2 Thes. 2.4. Exalteth himself above all that is called God, or that is worshipped ; so that he as God sitteth in the temple of God, shewing himself that he is God.

2 Tim. 3.2. Men shall be blasphemers. Rev. 16.11.

Jas. 2.7. Do not they blaspheme that worthy name by the which ye are called ?

Jas. 3.10. Out of the same mouth proceedeth blessing and cursing. My brethren, these things ought not so to be.

Jas. 5.12. Above all things, my brethren, swear not ; neither by heaven, neither by the earth, neither by any other oath : but let your yea be yea ; and *your* nay, nay ; lest ye fall into condemnation.

Rev. 13.1. Upon his heads the name of blasphemy. 6. He opened his mouth in blasphemy against God, to blaspheme his name, and his tabernacle, and them that dwell in heaven.

Rev. 16.9. Men were scorched with great heat, and blasphemed the name of God. 21. Men blasphemed God because of the plague of the hail.

Rev. 17.3. I saw a woman sit upon a scarlet-coloured beast, full of names of blasphemy.

BLASPHEMY, Examples of. An Israelite, Lev. 24.11-16. Shimei, 2 Sam. 16.5. Gehazi, 2 Kin. 5.20. Jehoram, 2 Kin. 6.31. Rabshekah, 2 Kin. 18.22. 2 Kin. 19. Job's wife, Job 2.9. Peter, Mat. 26.72,74. Mar. 14.71.

Jews and Herod's soldiers, Mat. 27.26,29-44. Mar. 3.30. Luk. 22.64,65. Luk. 23.35-39. Herod's courtiers, Act 12.22,23. Jews, Act. 13.45. Act. 18.6. Act. 26.11. Rev. 2.9. Saul of Tarsus, 1 Tim. 1.13. Hymeneus and Alexander, 1 Tim. 1.20. See INFIDELITY.

———, Jewish law commanded blasphemers to be stoned to death, Lev. 24.16.

BLASTUS, Herod's chamberlain ; intercedes for the Tyrians, Act. 12.20.

BLEMISH, priests required to be without. See PRIEST. Also animals for sacrifice.—See OFFERING. Illustrative, 2 Pet. 2.13. Jude 12.

BLESSEDNESS. See SPIRITUAL JOY.

BLESSING OF GOD. See GOD'S FAVOUR, SPIRITUAL BLESSINGS, WORSHIP, TEMPORAL BLESSINGS, GOD'S GOODNESS IN PROVIDENCE, RICHES, RIGHT USE OF.

——— AT MEALS. See PRAYER AT MEALS.

———. See BENEDICTIONS — SALUTATIONS.

BLESSING, CUP OF, 1 Cor. 10.16. See Psa. 116.13. Mat. 26.27.

BLIND, The, unkindness to, forbidden, Lev. 19.14. Deu. 27.18.

BLINDNESS, disqualified for the priesthood, Lev. 21.18. Examples of, Isaac, Gen. 27.1. Jacob, Gen. 48.10. Eli, 1 Sam. 4.15. Ahijah, 1 Kin. 14.4. Inflicted miraculously on Sodomites, Gen. 19.11. On Syrians, 2 Kin. 6. 18. On Paul, Act. 9.8. On Elymas, Act. 13.11. Miraculously cured by Christ, Mat. 9.27. Mat. 11.5. Mat. 12.22. Mat. 20.30. Mar. 8.23. Jno. 9.1. In animals, disqualified for sacrifices, Lev. 22.22. Deu. 15.21. Mal. 1.8. See SPIRITUAL BLINDNESS.

BLOOD called the life, Gen. 9.4. Lev. 19.16. Sprinkled on the door-posts at the first passover, Ex. 12.7-23. Sprinkled on the people as a sign of the covenant, Ex. 24.6-8. Zec. 9.11. Heb. 9.19,20. An atonement for sin, and use of, in sacrifices.—See OFFERINGS, Tables 1, 2, 3 —ATONEMENT, DAY OF.

Leaven not to be offered with, Ex. 23.18. Ex. 34.25. Forbidden as food, Gen. 9.4. Lev. 3.17. Lev. 7.26,27. Lev. 17.10-14. Lev. 19.26. Deu. 12.16,23. Deu. 15.23. Act. 15.20,29. Act. 21.25. Eaten by Israelites after the battle of Gibeah, 1 Sam. 14.32-34. Drink-offerings of, by idolaters, Psa. 16.4. Revenge of.—See MURDER, JUDICIAL PUNISHMENT. Waters of Egypt turned into, Ex. 4.9. Ex. 7.17. Symbolical, Luk. 22.20. Jno. 6.55. Rev. 6.12. Rev. 8.8. Rev. 11.6.

BOAR, WILD, Psa. 80.13. See SWINE.

BOASTING. See PRIDE.

BOAT. See SHIPS.

BOAZ, a Bethlehemite ; his kindness and marriage to Ruth, Ruth c. 2 to 4. An ancestor of David and Christ, Ruth 4.17. Mat. 1.5. Luk. 3.32.

———, one of the two brazen pillars of the Temple, 1 Kin. 7.21. 2 Chr. 3.17.

BOCHIM, Israelites rebuked at, by an angel ; their repentance, Jud. 2.1-5.

BOHAN, STONE OF, a boundary of Judah and Benjamin, named from a Reubenite. Jos. 15.6. Jos. 18.17.

BOIL, plague of, in Egypt, Ex. 9.9,10. Deu. 28.27. Of Hezekiah cured, 2 Kin. 20.7.

BOLLED, signifies podded, or nearly ripe, Ex. 9.31.

BOLT. See BAR.

BONDAGE. See CAPTIVITY.

BONDMAN AND BONDMAID. See SERVANTS, BOND.

BONDS. See CHAIN.

BONNET. See DRESS (Head-dress).

BOOKS, made in the form of a roll or scroll, Isa. 34.4. Jer. 36.4. Rev. 6.14. With leaves or folds, Jer. 36.23. Rev. 5.1-3. Written on both sides, Eze. 2.9,10. Rev. 5.1. Sealed, Isa. 29.11. Dan. 12.4. Rev. 5.1. Antiquity of, Gen. 5.1. Job 19.23. Job 31.35. Numerous, Ecc. 12.12. Value of, Act. 19.19. See INK, PAPER, PARCHMENT, SCRIBES, WRITING.

———, LIST OF. Of the generation of Adam, Gen. 5.1. Of the law written by Moses,

Deu. 31.9,19,24,26. Written by the priests, Num. 5.23. By the king, Deu. 17,18. Of the Wars of the Lord, Num. 21.14. Ex. 17.14.

Of Jasher, Jos. 10.13. 2 Sam. 1.18. Describing Palestine, Jos. 18.9. Samuel's book of the kingdom, 1 Sam. 10.25. Of Samuel, Nathan, Gad, 1 Chr. 29.29. Of the Kings, 1 Chr 9.1. 2 Chr. 24.27. Of the Chronicles of David, 1 Chr. 27.24. Of the Acts of Solomon, 1 Kin. 11.41.

Of Nathan, Ahijah, and Iddo, 2 Chr. 9.29. Of Shemaiah and Iddo, 2 Chr. 12.15. Of Iddo, 2 Chr. 13.22. Of the Kings of Judah and Israel, 2 Chr. 16.11. 2 Chr. 25.26. 2 Chr. 27.7. 2 Chr. 28.26. 2 Chr. 35.27. 2 Chr. 36.8.

Of the Kings of Israel, 1 Kin. 14.19. 2 Chr. 20.34. 2 Chr. 33.18. Of Jehu, 2 Chr. 20.34. Of Isaiah, 2 Chr. 26.22. 2 Chr. 32.32. Isa. 8.1. Of Jeremiah, Jer. 30.2-8. Of the Lamentations, 2 Chr. 35.25. Of the purchase, Jer. 32.12. Of the sayings of the seers, 2 Chr. 33.19.

Of records, Ezr. 4.15. Ezr. 6.1.2. Est. 6.1. Est. 9.32. Read by Daniel, Dan. 9.2. Of magic, Act. 19.19. Belonging to Paul, 2 Tim. 4.13.

Figurative names :—God's Book, Ex. 32. 32,33. Psa. 56.8. Psa. 139.16. Rev. 20.12. Of remembrance, Mal. 3.16. Of life, or of the living, Psa. 69.28. Dan. 12.1. Phil. 4.3. Rev. 3.5. Rev. 13.8. Rev. 17.8. Rev. 20.12,15. Rev. 21.27. Rev. 22.19. Symbolical, Zec. 5.1. Rev. 5.1. Eating of, signifying studying carefully, Jer. 15.16. Eze. 2.8. Eze. 3.1-3. Rev. 10.2-10.

BOOTH, or COTTAGE, made of boughs, Jonah 4.5. For cattle, Gen. 33.17. For keepers of gardens and vineyards, Job 27.18. Isa. 1.8. Isa. 24.20. Israelites dwelt in, during the Feast of Tabernacles, Lev. 23.40-43. Neh. 8. 15,16.

BORROWING money on land, Neh. 5.4. On interest, Pro. 22.7.—See USURY, Evils of. Israelites borrowed (asked) of the Egyptians, Ex. 3.22.

BOSSES (studs) of a shield, Job 15.26.

BOTTLES made of skins, Gen. 21.14. Jos. 9.4,13. Job 32.19. Psa. 119.83. Mat. 9.17. Of earthenware, Isa. 30.14 (marg.). Jer. 19. 1,10. Jer. 48.12. Translated pitcher, Lam. 4.2. Illustrative, Job 38.37. Psa. 56.8. See CRUSE—PITCHER.

BOW, Gen. 21.16,20. Gen. 27.3. Used in battle, Jer. 4.29. Zec. 9.13. Zec. 10.4. Made of iron or steel, 2 Sam. 22.35. Job 20.24. Of wood, Eze. 39.9. Mode of using, Isa. 13.18. Lam. 2.4. Eze. 39.3. Hab. 3.9.

Used by Jonathan, 2 Sam. 1.22. Philistines, 1 Sam. 31.3. David's army, 2 Sam. 1.18. 1 Chr. 12.2. Reubenites, &c., 1 Chr. 5.18. Benjamites, 2 Chr. 14.8. Uzziah's army, 2 Chr. 26.14. Nehemiah's guard, Neh. 4.13. Lydians, Jer. 46.9. Illustrative, Gen. 49.24. Job 29.20. Psa. 78.57. Hab. 3.9. Rev. 6 2. See ARCHER—ARROWS.

BOWELS, equivalent to the modern figurative use of the word heart, Gen. 43.30. Isa. 16.11. Jer. 4.19. 2 Cor. 6.12.

BOWING in worship.—See WORSHIP. To men —See SALUTATIONS.

BOWLS AND BASONS, Ex. 12.22. Jud. 6.38. 2 Sam. 17.28. Amos 6.6. Jno. 13.5.

Of gold used in the Tabernacle, Ex. 25.29. Ex. 37.16. Num. 4.7,14. And in the Temple, 1 Kin. 7.40,50. 1 Chr. 28.17. 2 Chr. 4.8,22 (marg.). Zec. 14.20. Illustrative, Ecc. 12.6. See LAVER.

BOX, 2 Kin. 9.1. Of alabaster, Mat. 26.7.

BOX-TREE, Isa. 41.19. Isa. 60.13.

BOZRAH, an Edomitish town, Gen. 36.33. Afterwards belonging to Moab, Jer. 48.24. Sheep of, Mic. 2.12. Prophecies of, Isa. 34.6. Isa. 63.1. Jer. 49.13,22. Amos 1.12.

BRACELET worn by females, Gen. 24.30. Ex. 35.22. Isa. 3.19. Eze. 16.11. By men, Gen. 38.18,25. Num. 31.50. 2 Sam. 1.10.

BRAMBLE, Isa. 34.13. Luk. 6.44. Fable of, Jud. 9.14,15.

BRANCH, illustrative, Gen. 49.22. Pro. 11.28. Hos. 14.6. Isa. 60.21. Jno. 15.2-5. Rom. 11.16. When withered, of the destruction of the wicked, Isa. 18.5. Dan. 4.14. Jno. 15.6. Rom. 11.17,21.

A name of Christ, Psa. 80.15. Isa. 4.2. Isa. 11.1. Jer. 23.5. Jer. 33.15. Zec. 3.8. Zec. 6.12. Luk. 1.78 (marg.). See INGRAFTING.

BRASS, OR COPPER, smelting of, Eze. 22.20. Job 28.2. In Canaan, Deu. 8.9. Jos. 22.8. In Syria, 2 Sam. 8.8. Tyrians traded in, Eze. 27.13. Altar, vessels, &c., of the Tabernacle and Temple made of, Ex. 38.28-31. 1 Kin. 7.14-47. Ezr. 8.27.

Cymbals of, 1 Chr. 15.19; and trumpets, 1 Cor. 13.1. Armour of, 1 Sam. 17.5,6. 2 Chr. 12.10. Fetters of, Jud. 16.21. 2 Kin. 25.7. Gates of, Psa. 107.16. Isa. 45.2. Bars of, 1 Kin. 4.13. Idols of, Dan. 5.4. Rev. 9.20.

Mirrors of, Ex. 38.8. Household vessels of, Mar. 7.4. Money of, Mat. 10.9. Mar. 12.41 (marg.). Workers in, Tubal Cain, Gen. 4 22. Hiram, 1 Kin. 7.14. Alexander, 2 Tim. 4.14. Translated steel, Psa. 18.34.

Illustrative, Lev. 26.19. Deu. 33.25. Isa. 48.4. Jer. 1.18. Symbolical, Dan. 2.32,39. Dan. 7.19. Dan. 10.6. Zech. 6.1. Rev. 1.15.

BRAZEN LAVER. See LAVER.

——— SERPENT, made by Moses, Num. 21.9. Incense burned to it, it is destroyed by Hezekiah, 2 Kin. 18.4. Illustrative of Christ, Jno. 3.14,15.

BREAD, baking of, in ovens. See FURNACE. In pans, Lev. 2.5,7. 2 Sam. 13.6-9. On the hearth, Gen. 18.6. On coals, 1 Kin. 19.6. Isa. 44.19. Jno. 21.9. Kneaded, Ex. 8.3. Ex. 12.34. Jer. 7.18.

Made with oil, Ex. 29.2,23. With honey, Ex. 16.31. Unleavened, Gen. 19.3. Ex. 29.2. Jud. 6.19. 1 Sam. 28.24. Made into loaves, 1 Sam. 10.3. 1 Sam. 17.17. 1 Sam. 25.18. 1 Kin. 14.3. Mar. 8.14. Into cakes, 2 Sam. 6.19. 1 Kin. 17.12; or wafers, Lev. 16.31. Ex. 29.23 ; or cracknels, 1 Kin. 14.3.

Made by men, Gen. 40.2. By women, Lev. 26.26. 1 Sam. 8.13. Sold by bakers, Jer. 37.21. Mar. 6.37. Wheaten, Ex. 29.2 1 Kin. 4.22. 1 Kin. 5.11. Psa. 81.16. Of manna, Num. 11.8. Of meal and oil, 1 Kin. 17.12. Of barley, Jud. 7.13. Elisha's miracle, 2 Kin. 4.42-44. Christ's miracle, Jno. 6.9.

Eating of, in friendship, Psa. 41.9. Jno. 13.18. Principal article of food, Isa. 33.16. Lam. 5.9. Eze. 16.49. Mat. 6.11. Illustrative,

Psa. 80.5. Psa. 127.2. Isa. 30.20. Hos. 9.4. Psa. 132.15. Isa. 55.2. 2 Cor. 9.10. Jno. 6.32-35. 1 Cor. 10.17. Symbolical, Eze. 4.9. Used at the Lord's Supper, Mat. 26.26. Act. 20.7,11.

Bread used in offerings, made by Levites, 1 Chr. 23.29. Offered and eaten by the priests, Lev. 21.6,8,17,21,22. Lev. 22.25. 1 Sam. 2.36. 2 Kin. 23.9. Eze. 13.19. Offering of polluted bread, Mal. 1.7. In idolatry, Jer. 7.18. Jer. 44.19.

See LEAVEN, FEAST OF PASSOVER, OFFERINGS, MEAT-OFFERING, SHEWBREAD.

BREASTPLATE, Rev. 9.9. Translated coat-of-mail, 1 Sam. 17.5,38. Harness, 1 Kin. 22.34. 2 Chr. 18.33. Habergeon, 2 Chr. 26.14. Neh. 4.16. Job 41.26. Illustrative of righteousness, Isa. 59.17. Eph. 6.14. 1 The. 5.8.

—————— OF THE HIGH-PRIEST. See HIGH-PRIEST.

BREECHES, linen, of the high-priest. See HIGH-PRIEST.

BRIBERY, Deu. 16.19. Neither take a gift: for a gift doth blind the eyes of the wise, and pervert the words of the righteous. Ex. 23.8.

Deu. 27.25. Cursed *be* he that taketh reward to slay an innocent person.

Job 15.34. Fire shall consume the tabernacles of bribery.

Psa. 26.10. Their right hand is full of bribes.

Pro. 15.27. He that is greedy of gain troubleth his own house: but he that hateth gifts shall live.

Pro. 17.8. A gift *is as* a precious stone in the eyes of him that hath it ; whithersoever it turneth, it prospereth. 23. A wicked *man* taketh a gift out of the bosom to pervert the ways of judgment.

Pro. 18.16. A man's gift maketh room for him, and bringeth him before great men.

Pro. 21.14. A gift in secret pacifieth anger : and a reward in the bosom strong wrath.

Pro. 25.14. Whoso boasteth himself of a false gift *is like* clouds and wind without rain.

Pro. 28.21. To have respect of persons is not good : for for a piece of bread *that* man will transgress.

Pro. 29.4. The king by judgment establisheth the land : but he that receiveth gifts overthroweth it.

Ecc. 7.7. A gift destroyeth the heart.

Isa. 1.23. Every one loveth gifts, and followeth after rewards.

Isa. 5.23. Woe unto them which justify the wicked for reward.

Eze. 22.12. In thee have they taken gifts to shed blood.

Amos 5.12. They take a bribe, and they turn aside the poor in the gate *from their right.*

Mic. 7.3. That they may do evil with both hands earnestly, the prince asketh, and the judge *asketh* for a reward.

——————, EXAMPLES OF. Samuel's sons, 1 Sam. 8.3. Haman, Est. 3.9. Chief-priests, Mat. 26.15. Mat. 28.12. Felix, Act. 24.26. See RULERS' INJUSTICE.

BRICKS, used in building city and tower of Babel, Gen. 11.3. Treasure cities in Egypt, Ex. 1.11,14. Houses, Isa. 9.10. Idolatrous altars, Isa. 65,3. Making of, 2 Sam. 12.31. Jer. 43.9. Nah. 3.14. By Israelites, Ex. 5.7-19.

BRIDE AND BRIDEGROOM. See MARRIAGE.

BRIDLE, Psa. 32.9. Pro. 26.3. Rev. 14.20. Illustrative, 2 Kin. 19.28. Psa. 39.1. Jas. 1.26. See BIT.

BRIERS. See THORNS.

BRIGANDINE, a piece of armour, Jer. 46.4. Jer. 51.3.

BRIMSTONE, Sodom destroyed by, Gen. 19.24. Illustrative, Psa. 11.6. Isa. 30.33. Isa. 34.9. Rev. 9.17,18. Rev. 14.10. Rev. 19.20. Rev. 20.10. Rev. 21.8.

BROOKS. See RIVERS.

BROTH, Jud. 6.19,20. 2 Kin. 4.38. Isa. 65.4. Symbolical, Eze. 24.5.

BROTHER, besides its ordinary meaning, it signifies near relation, Gen. 14.16. Gen. 29.12. One of the same nation, Neh. 5.7. Jer. 34.9. Of kindred tribes or nations, Deu. 23.7. Jud. 21.6. Obad. 10. Fellow-man, Gen. 9.5. Mat. 18.35. 1 Jno. 3.15.

Friend, 2 Sam. 1.26. 1 Kin. 13.30. 1 Kin. 20.33. Fellow-Christian, Act. 9.17. Act. 21.20. Rom. 16.23. 1 Cor. 7.12. 2 Cor. 2.13. Christ calls his disciples brethren, Mat. 12.50. Mat. 25.40. Heb. 2.11,12.

BROTHERLY KINDNESS. See LOVE.

BUCKET, Num. 24.7. Isa. 40.15.

BUCKLER. See SHIELD.

BUILDER, 1 Kin. 5.18. Neh. 4.5. Eze. 27.4. Illustrative, Psa. 118.22. Heb. 11.10. 1 Cor. 3.10.

BUILDINGS. See BABEL, BRICKS, CITIES, HOUSES, FORTRESS, FOUNDATION, PALACE, STONE, TEMPLE.

BUL, the eighth month (November). The Temple finished in, 1 Kin. 6.38. Jeroboam's idolatrous feast in, 1 Kin. 12.32,33. 1 Chr. 27.11.

BULL, BULLOCK, OX, used as synonymous terms, Num. 7.88. 1 Kin. 7.25 with Jer. 52.20. Used in sacrifice. See OFFERINGS. Sold in the Temple, Jno. 2.14. Sacrificed to idols, Hos. 12.11. Act. 14.13.

Used in the plough, 1 Sam. 14.14. 1 Kin. 19.19. Pro. 14.4. Isa. 32.20. Jer. 31.18. For treading out corn, Deu. 25.4. In waggons, Num. 7.3,7. For burdens, 1 Chr. 12.40. Carried the Ark from Kirjath-jearim, 2 Sam. 6.3,6. Pieces of, sent by Saul to summon Israel to war, 1 Sam. 11.7. Ox goads used for, Jud. 3.31. Caught when wild in nets, Isa. 51.20. Laws respecting, Ex. 21.28-36. Ex. 22.1-10. Ex. 23.4,12. Deu. 22.10. Deu. 25.4.

Illustrative, Psa. 22.12. Psa. 68.30. Deu. 33.17. Symbolical, Eze. 1.10. Rev. 4.7. Brazen bulls of the molten sea in the Temple, 2 Chr. 4.4. Jer. 52.20. See CATTLE.

BULRUSH, Isa. 58.5. Grew beside water, Job 8.11. Isa. 35.7. Ark of, Ex. 2.3. Boats of, Isa. 18.2.

BULWARKS, works thrown up in besieging a city, Deu. 20.20. Of cities.—See FORTRESS —WALLS.

BURDEN, in prophecy, signifies doom, Isa. 13.1. Eze. 12.10.

BURIAL, the body washed before, Act. 9.37. Embalmed, anointed, and laid in spices, Gen. 50.2,3,26. 2 Chr. 16.14. Mar. 14.8. Mar.

16.1. Luk. 23.56. Luk. 24.1. Jno. 19.40. Wrapped in linen cloths, Jno. 11.44. Jno. 19.40.

Burned, 1 Sam. 31.12. Amos 6.10. Egyptians laid in a coffin, Gen. 50.26. First-born of Egyptians buried without embalming, Num. 33.4. Soon after death, Jno. 11.17. Act. 5. 9,10. Accompanied with burning of odours, 2 Chr. 16.14. 2 Chr. 21.19. Jer. 34.5.

Bier used, 2 Sam. 3.31. Luk. 7.14. Body followed by relations and friends, Gen. 50.5-9. 2 Sam. 3.31. 1 Kin. 14.13. Luk. 7.12,13. Act. 8.2. Want of, disgraceful, 2 Kin. 9.10. Pro. 30.17. Isa. 14.19. Jer. 16.4. Jer. 22.19. Eze. 39.15.

Among strangers a punishment, 1 Kin. 13.22. Of criminals on the same day, Deu. 21.23. Jos. 8.29. Jno. 19.31. Of enemies, 2 Sam. 18.17. 1 Kin. 11.15. Eze. 39.11-13. Mourning at.—See MOURNING. Illustrative, Rom. 6.4. Col. 2.12.

BURIAL-PLACES, or SEPULCHRES, prepared during lifetime, Gen. 50.5. 2 Chr. 16.14. Isa. 22.16. Mat. 27.60. Paternal, 2 Sam. 19. 37. 1 Kin. 14.31. 1 Kin. 15.24. Paternal, attachment to, Gen. 47.30. Gen. 49.29. Gen. 50.25. Neh. 2.3. In a man's own house, 1 Sam. 25.1. 1 Kin. 2.34. Or garden, 2 Kin. 21.18,26. Or property, Jos. 24.30,33.

Under a tree, Gen. 35.8. 1 Sam. 31.13. On hills, Deu. 10.6 with Num. 20.28. 2 Kin. 23.16. In caves, 1 Kin. 13.31. Isa. 22.16. With stone at the mouth, Jno. 11.38. Jno. 19.41. Jno. 20.6. And sealed, Mat. 27.60,64. See MACH-PELAH.

Of kings, in the city of David, 1 Kin. 2.10. 2 Chr. 32.33. Burying in, honourable, 2 Chr. 24.16. Exclusion from, dishonourable, 2 Chr. 21.19. 2 Chr. 24.25.

In the valley of Tophet, Jer. 7.32. Of criminals, marked by stones, Jos. 7.26. Of the poor, and strangers, Jer. 26.23. Mat. 27.7. Pillars and tombstones set over, with inscriptions, Gen. 35.20. 2 Kin. 23.17. Tombs painted and garnished, Mat. 23.27,29. Rebuilt, Luk. 11.47.

Were unclean, Num. 19.16,18. Isa. 65.4. Demoniacs abode in tombs, Mat. 8.28. Graves were not visible, Luk. 11.44.

BURNING-BUSH, EX. 3.1-4.

BURNT-OFFERING. See OFFERINGS, BURNT. Altar of. See ALTAR.

BUSHEL (about a peck), Mat. 5.15. Mar. 4.21.

BUSINESS, DILIGENCE IN. See INDUSTRY.

BUTLER, or CUP-BEARER, Gen. 40.1,11. 1 Kin. 10.5. 2 Chr. 9.4. Neh. 1.11. Neh. 2.1.

BUTTER, Gen. 18.8. Jud. 5.25. 2 Sam. 17.29. Churning of, Pro. 30.33.

BUZ, son of Nahor ; people descended from him, Gen. 22.21. Job 32.2. Jer. 25.23.

C

CAB, a measure, about half a gallon, 2 Kin. 6.25.

CABIN (*marg.* cell or vaults), Jer. 37.16. Or stocks, comp. Jer. 20.2.

CABUL (unpleasing), a town in Zebulun, Jos. 19.27. And a district given by Solomon to Hiram, 1 Kin. 9.12,13.

CAIAPHAS, father-in-law to Annas, Jno. 18.13. High-priest when John began his ministry, Luk. 3.2. Counsels Christ's death, Jno. 11.49-51. Jno. 18.14. Jesus brought before, Mat. 26.2,3,57,63-65. Jno. 18.24,28. Peter, &c., brought before, Act. 4.6.

CAIN, birth and occupation, Gen. 4.1,2. Offering not accepted ; his anger, Gen. 4.3-7. Heb. 11.4. Murders Abel ; his punishment, Gen. 4.8-15. 1 Jno. 3.12. Jude 11. Residence in Nod ; his children, Gen. 4.16,17.

CALAMUS. See CANE, SWEET.

CALDRON, 1 Sam. 2.14. Job 41.20. Mic. 3.3. In the Temple, 2 Chr. 35.13. Jer. 52. 18,19. Illustrative, Eze. 11.3-11.

CALEB, son of Jephunneh the Kenezite, Num. 32.12. Jos. 14.6.—See Jos. 15.17. Sent as a spy ; his courage and reward, Num. 13.6, 30. Num. 14.6,24,30,38. Num. 32.12. Deu. 1.36.

A prince of Judah ; he assists in dividing Palestine, Num. 34.19. His inheritance, Jos. 14.6-15. Jos. 15.13-16. His descendants, 1 Chr. 4.15.

CALF. See BULL—CATTLE.

——, **GOLDEN,** made by Aaron, and worshipped ; destroyed by Moses, Ex. 32.4. Deu. 9.16. Neh. 9.18. Psa. 106.19. Act. 7.41.

CALLING, EFFECTUAL. See REGENERATION.

CALNEH, CANNEH, or CALNO, an Assyrian town built by Nimrod ; traded with Tyre, Gen. 10.10. Isa. 10.9. Eze. 27.23. Amos 6.2.

CALVARY (Greek), or GOLGOTHA (Heb.), the place of a scull ; a place in Jerusalem where Christ was crucified, Mat. 27.33. Mar. 15.22. Luk. 23.33. Jno. 19.17.

CALVES of Bethel and Dan ; idolatrous images of gold set up by Jeroboam, and priests appointed for, 1 Kin. 12.28-33. 2 Kin. 10.29. 2 Chr. 13.8. Prophecy against the calf of Bethel fulfilled by Josiah destroying it, 1 Kin. 13.1-5, 32. 2 Kin. 23.4,15-20. Jehu worshipped, 2 Kin. 10.29.

Prophecies against, Jer. 48.13. Hos. 4.15. Hos. 8.5,6. Hos. 10.5,6,15. Hos. 13.2. Amos 3.14. Amos 4.4. Amos 5.5,6. Amos 8.14.

—— OF THE LIPS signifies the sacrifice of the lips, that is, praise, Hos. 14.2. See Heb. 13.15. Psa. 116.17. Jer. 33.11.

CAMEL, or DROMEDARY, Lev. 11.4. Deu. 14.7. Used for riding, Gen. 24.10,61,64. For posts, Est. 8.10,14. Jer. 2.23. In chariots, Isa. 21.7. For burdens, Gen. 37.25. 1 Kin. 10.2. 2 Kin. 8.9. 1 Chr. 12.40. Isa. 30.6. In battle, Jud. 6.5. 1 Sam. 27.9. 1 Sam. 30.17.

Herds of, possessed by Abraham, Gen. 24.35. Jacob, Gen. 30.43. Egyptians, Gen. 12.16. Ex. 9.3. Job, Job 1.3,17. Midianites, Jud. 7.12. Isa. 60.6. Amalekites, 1 Sam. 30.17. Hagarites, 1 Chr. 5.21. Kedarites, Jer. 49.29,32. David, 1 Chr. 27.30. Jews, Ezr. 2.67.

Housings and ornaments of, Gen. 31.34. Jud. 8.21,26. Stabling, &c., Eze. 25.5. 1 Kin. 4.28. Proverbs regarding, Mat. 19.24. Mat. 23.24. Hair of, used for cloth, Mat. 3.4.

CAMELEON, a lizard, Lev. 11.30.

CAMP. See TENTS.

CAMPHIRE, a plant, Song 1.14. Song 4.13.

CANA OF GALILEE, a town near Capernaum; Christ changes water to wine at, Jno. 2.1-11. Cures the son of a nobleman from Capernaum at, Jno. 4.46,47. Residence of Nathanael, Jno. 21.2.

CANAAN, LAND OF. See PALESTINE.

————, son of Ham, the curse on, Gen. 9.25-27.

CANAANITES, seven nations of, descended from Canaan, Gen. 10.15-19. Ex. 3.8. Deu. 7.1. 1 Chr. 1.13-16. Territory of, Gen. 10.19. Gen. 12.6. Num. 13.29. Jud. 4.2. Isaac forbids Jacob to marry a wife of, Gen. 28.1. Judah's wife of, Gen. 38.2. 1 Chr. 2.3.

Wickedness and idolatry of, Lev. 18.28. Deu. 12.31. Ezr. 9.1. Psa. 106.38. Land of, given to Israelites, Gen. 12.6,7. Gen. 15.18. Gen. 17.8. Ex. 23.23. Deu. 7.1-3. Deu. 32.49. Psa. 135.11.

See ADMAH, AMORITES, ANAKIM, ARKITES, ARVADITES, AVIM, BEZEK, CANAANITES, CAPHTORIM, GIRGASHITES, GOMORRHA, HITTITES, HIVITES, JEBUSITES, KADMONITES, KENITES, KENIZZITES, PERIZZITES, PHENICIA, PHILISTINES, REPHAIM, SODOM, ZEBOIM, ZOAR.

————, TRIBE OF. Arad, king of, defeated by Israel, Num. 21.1-3. Jabin, king of, defeated by Joshua, Jos. 11.1-16. Jabin II. subjugates Israelites, who are freed by Barak, Jud. 4. Jud. 5.19. Tributary to Manasseh, &c., Jos. 17.12-18; but imperfectly subdued, Jud. 1.1-33.

Iron chariots of, Jos. 17.18. Defeated by Pharaoh at Gezer, 1 Kin. 9.16. Jews intermarried with, Ezr. 9.2.

CANDACE, queen of Ethiopia, Act. 8.27.

CANDLE AND CANDLESTICK. See LAMP.

CANDLESTICK, GOLDEN, called the lamp of God, 1 Sam. 3.3. The pure candlestick, Lev. 24.4. Made after a divine pattern, Ex. 25.40. Num. 8.4.

Of the Tabernacle, had seven branches, Ex. 25.31-39. Ex. 37.17-24. Of the Temple, had ten branches, 1 Kin. 7.49,50. 1 Chr. 28.15. 2 Chr. 4.20. Had gold snuffers and dishes, Ex. 25.38. Ex. 37.23. Placed in the holy place overagainst the table, Ex. 26.35. Ex. 40. 24,25. Heb. 9.2.

Was lighted every night by the priests, and supplied with olive oil, Ex. 27.20,21. Ex. 30.7,8. Lev. 24.1-4. 2 Chr. 13.11. Directions for its removal by the Kohathites, Num. 4.9,10. Taken to Babylon, Jer. 52.19. Symbolical, Zec. 4.2,11. Rev. 1.12,13,20. Rev. 11.4.

CANE, SWEET, or CALAMUS, a fragrant reed, Song 4.14. Trade in, Jer. 6.20. Eze. 27.19. Used in the sacred anointing oil, Ex. 30.23. Isa. 43.24.

CANKERWORM, Joel 1.4. Joel 2.25. Nah. 3.15,16.

CANNEH. See CALNEH.

CAPERNAUM, a city near the Sea of Galilee, where Christ dwelt after leaving Nazareth, Mat. 4.13. Luk. 4.31. Christ's miracles at,

Mat. 9.1-26. Mat. 17.24-27. Mar. 1.21-45. Mar. 2. Mar. 3.1-6. Luk. 7.1-10. Jno. 4. 46-53. Jno. 6.17-25,59.

Christ's prophecy against, Mat. 11.23. Luk. 10.15.

CAPHTORIM, a people descended from a son of Mizraim, Gen. 10.14. 1 Chr. 1.12. Displaced the Avims in Canaan, joined the Philistines, Deu. 2.23 with Jos. 13.3 & Jer. 47 4. Amos 9.7.

CAPPADOCIA, a province of Asia Minor, Act. 2.9. 1 Pet. 1.1.

CAPTAIN of the host, or general, Deu. 20.9. Jud. 4.2. 1 Sam. 14.50. 1 Kin. 2.35. 1 Kin. 16.16. 1 Chr. 27.34. Of the guard, Gen. 37.36. 2 Kin. 25.8. Of the tribes, Num. 2. Of thousands, Num. 31.48. 1 Sam. 17.18. 1 Chr. 28.1. Of hundreds, 1 Kin. 11.15. See CENTURION. Of fifties, 2 Kin. 1.9. Isa. 3.3. Of the ward, Jer. 37.13.

Signifying king, 1 Sam. 9.16. 2 Kin. 20.5. Leader, 1 Sam. 22.2. 1 Chr. 11.21. Officer, 1 Chr. 12.34. Jno. 18.12.

David's captains, the orders of merit, 2 Sam. 23. 1 Chr. c. 11 & 12. Of Jehoshaphat, 2 Chr. 17.14-19. Appointed by the king, 1 Sam. 18.13. 2 Sam. 17.25. 2 Sam. 18.1.

A name applied to the angel of the Lord and Christ, Jos. 5.14. 2 Chr. 13.12. Heb. 2.10.

CAPTIVES, taken in war, Gen. 14.12. 1 Sam. 30.1,2. Laws and practices in regard to, Num. 31.9-17. Deu. 20.13,14. Jos. 8.29. Jos. 10.15-43. Jos. 11.11. Jud. 7.25. Jud. 8.18-21. Jud. 21.11,12. 1 Sam. 15.3,33. 2 Sam. 8.2.

Cruelty to, Jud. 1.6,7. 2 Kin. 8.12, 2 Kin. 15.16. 2 Chr. 25.12. Lam. 5.11-13. Amos 1.13. Zec. 14.2. Imprisoned, and the eyes of, put out, Jud. 16.21. 2 Kin. 25.7. Jer. 52.11. Enslaved, Ex. 12.29. 2 Sam. 12.31. 2 Kin. 5.2.

Married by captors, Deu. 21.12,13. Est. 2.17. Kindly treated, 2 Kin. 6.22. 2 Kin. 25.27-30. 2 Chr. 28.15. Psa. 106.46. Promoted to honours, Neh. 1.11. Est. 2. Dan. 1. Settled in colonies, 2 Kin. 16.9. 2 Kin. 17.6,24. See RANSOM.

CAPTIVITY, illustrative, Psa. 116.16. Isa. 61.1. Rom. 7.23. 2 Tim. 2.26. 2 Tim. 3.6. 1 Cor. 9.27. 2 Cor. 10.5. Captivity led captive, Jud. 5.12. Psa. 68.18. Eph. 4.8.

————OF ISRAELITES. See ISRAELITES, History of.

CARBUNCLE, a precious stone, Isa. 54.12. Eze. 28.13. Set in the high-priest's breastplate, Ex. 28.17. Ex. 39.10.

CARCHEMISH, an Assyrian town on the Euphrates, 2 Chr. 35.20. Isa. 10.9. Jer. 46.2.

CARE, WORLDLY. See COVETOUSNESS.

CARMEL, a hill on the sea-coast of Palestine, Jer. 46.18. Its fertility, Isa. 33.9. Isa. 35.2. Jer. 50.19. Amos 1.2. Beauty, Song 7.5. Forests, 2 Kin. 19.23. Caves, Amos 9.3. Mic. 7.14. Elijah's sacrifice on, 1 Kin. 18.19-46. Elisha dwells on, 2 Kin. 2.25. 2 Kin. 4.25.

————, a town and district in Judah, Jos. 15.55. Monument erected by Saul at, 1 Sam. 15.12. Nabal lived in, 1 Sam. 25.2. Vineyards of Uzziah in, 2 Chr. 26.10.

CARNAL-MINDEDNESS. See WORLDLINESS, MAN, NATURAL STATE OF, SINNERS.

CARPENTER, 2 Kin. 12.11. Isa. 41.7. Isa. 44.13. Jer. 24.1. David hires from Hiram, 2 Sam. 5.11. Joseph, Mat. 13.55. Jesus called, Mar. 6.3. Symbolical, Zec. 1.20.

CARPUS, a disciple at Troas, 2 Tim. 4.13.

CARRIAGES (baggage), Jud. 18.21. 1 Sam. 17.22. Isa. 46.1. Act. 21.15.

CART, or **WAGGON,** used as a conveyance, Gen. 45.27. For goods, Num. 7.3-9. 2 Sam. 6.3. Amos 2.13. In war, Eze. 23.24. Drawn by oxen, &c., Num. 7.3,6. 1 Sam. 6.7. Translated litter, Isa. 28.27,28. Wheels of, used for threshing, Isa. 28.27,28. See **CHARIOT.**

CART-ROPE, Isa. 5.18.

CARVING of the wood-work of the Temple, 1 Kin. 6.18,29,32,35. Psa. 74.6. Of beds, Pro. 7.16. Of images, Deu. 7.5. Isa. 44.9-17. Isa. 45.20. Hab. 2.18,19. Skill of Bezaleel, in Ex. 31.5; and of Hiram, 2 Chr. 2.14.

CASLUHIM, a son of Mizraim, and progenitor of the Philistines, Gen. 10.14. 1 Chr. 1.12.

CASSIA, an aromatic spice, Psa. 45.8. Eze. 27.19. Used in the sacred anointing oil, Ex. 30.24.

CASTLE. See **FORTRESS.** Signifies, dwelling, 1 Chr. 6.54.

CASTOR AND **POLLUX.** In Greek it is *Dioscuri*; that is, sons of Jupiter, supposed to be the patron gods of sailors, Act. 28.11.

CATERPILLAR, 1 Kin. 8.37. Psa. 78.46. Psa. 105.34. Jer. 51.27. Joel 1.4. Joel 2.25.

CATTLE, creation of, Gen. 1.25. Clean, Deu. 14.4,5. Numbers of, killed at feasts, 1 Kin. 4.23. Neh. 5.18. Isa. 22.13. Fatted calves, 1 Sam. 28.24,25. Luk. 15.23. Large herds of, Gen. 12.16. Gen. 13.2. Gen. 30.43. Ex. 12.38. 2 Chr. 26.10. Job 1.3. Job 42.12. Ecc. 2.7. Jonah 4.11.

Booths made for, Gen. 33.17. Fed in stalls, Pro. 14.4. Pro. 15.17. Hab. 3.17. Watering and care of, Luk. 13.15. Luk. 14.5. Food of, Num. 22.4. Isa. 11.7. Isa. 30.24. Isa. 65.25. Gilead famous for, Num. 32.1-4. 1 Chr. 5.9. And Bashan.—See **BASHAN.**

Of Levites dedicated to God, Num. 3.45. Suffered in the plagues of Egypt, Ex. 9.3,19-21. See **BULL—COW—HEIFER.**

CAUL (braided tresses of hair), Isa. 3.18.

CAVES used as dwellings and hiding-places, Gen. 19.30. Jud. 6.2. 1 Sam. 13.6. 1 Kin. 18.4. 1 Kin. 19.9. Isa. 2.19. Eze. 33.27. Heb. 11.38.—See **ADULLAM—EN-GEDI—MAKKEDAH.** As burial-places.—See **BURIAL-PLACES.**

CEDAR of Lebanon, 2 Kin. 19.23. Psa. 29.5. Isa. 2.13. Its height and beauty, Num. 24.6. Psa. 80.10,11. Psa. 104.16. Eze. 31.8. Amos 2.9. Value of, 2 Chr. 1.15. Isa. 9.10. Jer. 22.7.

Used in the Temple, 1 Chr. 22.4. 2 Chr. 2.3. 1 Kin. 5.6-10. 1 Kin. 9.11. 2 Chr. 2.16. In the second Temple, Ezr. 3.7. Used for David's palace, 2 Sam. 5.11. 1 Chr. 17.1. For Solomon's palace, 1 Kin. 7.2. 1 Kin. 10.21; and chariot (or bed), Song 3.9. For ceilings. See **CEILING.**

For masts, Eze. 27.5. In purification, Lev.

14.4,6,49-52. Num. 19.6. Illustrative, Psa. 72.16. Psa. 92.12. Isa. 2.13. Isa. 14.8. Eze. 31.3. Zec. 11.2.

CEDRON, or **KIDRON,** a brook on the E. of Jerusalem, 1 Kin. 2.37. Neh. 2.15. Jer. 31.40. Crossed by David when fleeing from Absalom, 2 Sam. 15.23. Idols destroyed at, 1 Kin. 15.13. 2 Kin. 23.6,12. 2 Chr. 29.16. Course of, turned by Hezekiah, 2 Chr. 32.4. Crossed by Jesus on his way to Gethsemane, Jno. 18.1.

CEILING of rooms, Hag. 1.4. Of cedar or fir, 1 Kin. 6.15. 2 Chr. 3.5. Jer. 22.14.

CENCHREA, a port of Corinth, whence Paul sailed for Ephesus; Aquila's vow at, Act. 18.18. Phebe, a servant of the church, at, Rom. 16.1.

CENSERS used with live coals for burning incense, Lev. 10.2. Num. 16.46. 2 Chr. 26.19. Made of gold, 1 Kin. 7.50 with Ex. 37.16. Heb. 9.4. Brazen, used by Korah, &c.; made into plates to cover the incense altar, Num. 16.37-39. Used in idolatrous worship, Eze. 8.11. Symbolical, Rev. 8.3,5.

CENSORIOUSNESS. See **UNCHARITABLENESS—SPEAKING EVIL.**

CENTURION (a Roman officer over 100 men), Mar. 15.44,45. Act. 21.32. Act. 22.25, 26. Act. 23.17,23. Act. 24.23. Of Capernaum; built a synagogue; his faith; servant of, healed by Christ, Mat. 8.5,9. Luk. 7.1-10. One present at the cross, Mat. 27.54. Mar. 15.39. Luk. 23.47. Cornelius, Act. 10. Julius, Act. c. 27 & 28.

CEPHAS. See **PETER.**

CEREMONIAL, uncleanness. See **DEFILEMENT.**

CESAR, a title of the Roman emperors; given to Augustus, Luk. 2.1. To Tiberius, Luk. 3.1. Luk. 20.22. To Claudius, Act. 11. 28. To Nero, Phil. 4.22.

CESAREA, IN **PALESTINE,** a seaport; residence of Philip the evangelist, Act. 8.40. Act. 21.8. Peter visits Cornelius at, Act. c. 10 & 11. Herod's death at, Act. 12.19-23. Paul escapes to, Act. 9.30. Visits disciples at, Act. 18.22. Act. 21.8-16. Is taken by soldiers to; his imprisonment and trial in, Act. 23.23-35. Act. c. 24 to 26.

—————— PHILIPPI, in the N. of Galilee; Christ's visit to, Mat. 16.13. Mar. 8.27. Luk. 9.18.

CHAFF, illustrative, Job 21.18. Psa. 1.4. Isa. 5.24. Isa. 17.13. Hos. 13.3. Mat. 3.12. See **THRESHING.**

CHAINS, golden, worn as a badge of office, Gen. 41.42. Dan. 5.7,29. As ornaments, Num. 31.50. Isa. 3.19. Song 1.10. Eze. 16.11. Put on the high-priest's breastplate, Ex. 28.14. Ex. 39.15. In the Temple, 1 Kin. 6.21.

Of brass, in the Temple, 1 Kin. 7.17. Of silver, for idols, Isa. 40.19. On camel's necks, Jud. 8.26. Of iron, for prisoners, Psa. 149.8. Jer. 40.4. Act. 12.7. Act. 28.20. 2 Tim. 1.16. —See **FETTERS.** Illustrative, Psa. 73.6. Pro. 1.9. Lam. 3.7. Eze. 7.23-27. 2 Pet. 2.4. Rev. 20.1.

CHALCEDONY, a precious stone, Rev. 21.19.

CHALDEANS. See BABYLONIA.

CHALK, Isa. 27.9.

CHAMBERS. See HOUSES.

—— OF IMAGERY, Eze. 8.10-12.

CHAMBERLAIN, 2 Kin. 23.11. Est. 1.10. Act. 12.20. Rom. 16.23. The original is variously translated—Officer, Steward, Eunuch, Governor.

CHAMOIS, Deu. 14.5.

CHANCELLOR, the title of the Persian governor in Samaria, Ezr. 4.8,9,17.

CHAPEL, Amos 7.13. Usually translated sanctuary, Amos 7.9, &c.

CHAPITER (the capital of a pillar), Ex. 36.38.

CHARRAN. See HARAN.

CHARASHIM, valley of craftsmen, near Jerusalem, 1 Chr. 4.14. Neh. 11.35.

CHARGER, a dish, Num. 7.13,84. Ezr. 1.9. Mat. 14.8. Translated platter, Luk. 11.39.

CHARIOTS, used in war, Ex. 14.7,25. Deu. 20.1. Jos. 11.4. 1 Kin. 20.1,25. 2 Kin. 6.14. 2 Kin. 9.21. 2 Kin. 10.2,16. Psa. 20.7. Joel 2.5. Nah. 2.3,4. Nah. 3.2. Used for travelling and in state-processions, Gen. 41.43. Gen. 46.29. 2 Kin. 5.9. 2 Chr. 35.24. Jer. 17.25. Act. 8.29.

Drawn by horses, Ex. 14.9. 2 Sam. 15.1. 2 Kin. 7.14. Song 1.9. By asses or camels, Isa. 21.7. Mic. 1.13. Made of, and armed with, iron, Jos. 17.18. Jud. 1.19. Of wood, Song 3.9. Wheels of, Ex. 14.25. 1 Kin. 7.33. Cloths of, Eze. 27.20.

Brought into Judea by David, 2 Sam. 8.4. By Solomon from Egypt, 1 Kin. 10.26,28,29. Drivers employed, 1 Kin. 22.34. Preceded by runners, 1 Sam. 8.11. 2 Sam. 15.1. 1 Kin. 1.5. 1 Kin. 18.46. Idolatrous, of the sun, 2 Kin. 23.11.

Illustrative, 2 Kin. 13.14. Psa. 104.3. Isa. 66.15. Hab. 3.8. Symbolical, Zec. 6.2. 2 Kin. 2.11. 2 Kin. 6.17. Rev. 9.9.

——, cities of Solomon, 1 Kin. 9.19. 2 Chr. 1.14. 2 Chr. 8.6. 2 Chr. 9.25.

CHARITY. See LOVE—POOR, KINDNESS TO.

CHARMERS. See SORCERY—SERPENTS.

CHEBAR, a river of Mesopotamia, to which the Jews were carried captive; Ezekiel's visions there, Eze. 1.1-3. Eze. 3.15. Eze. 10.15,22. Eze. 43.3.

CHEDORLAOMER, king of Elam, invades Canaan; captives rescued from, by Abraham, Gen. 14.

CHEERFULNESS. See CONTENTMENT.

CHEESE, 1 Sam. 17.18. 2 Sam. 17.29. Job 10.10.

CHEMARIM (idolatrous priests), Zeph.1.4. 2 Kin. 23.5. Hos. 10.5.

CHEMOSH, a name of the Moabites, Num. 21.29 ; from their idol, 1 Kin. 11.7,33. 2 Kin. 23.13. Jer. 48.7,13,46. Worshipped by the Amorites, Jud. 11.24.

CHENANIAH, a master of the Temple singing, 1 Chr. 15.22,27.

CHERETHITES, a tribe of Philistines, Eze.25.16. Zeph.2.5. 1 Sam.30.14,16. David's body-guard formed out of, 2 Sam. 8.18. 2 Sam. 15.18. 2 Sam. 20.23.

CHERITH, a brook, near which Elijah was fed by ravens, 1 Kin. 17.3-7.

CHERUBIM, placed at the entrance of Eden, Gen. 3.24. Of gold, over the Ark, Ex. 25.18-20. Ex. 37.7-9. 1 Sam. 4.4. 1 Kin. 8.6,7. 2 Chr. 5.7,8. Heb. 9.5. In the Holy of Holies, 1 Kin. 6.23-28. 2 Chr. 3.10-13.

Representations of, on the Tabernacle curtains, Ex. 26.1. Ex. 36.8. Vail, Ex. 26.31. Ex. 36.35. Temple vail, 2 Chr. 3.14. Doors and walls, 1 Kin. 6.29-35. 2 Chr. 3.7. Brazen lavers, 1 Kin. 7.29,36.

Illustrative, Eze. 28.14,16. Symbolical, Eze. 1. Eze. 9.3. Eze. 10. Psa. 18.10. God's presence between.—See CLOUD OF GLORY.

CHESNUT, Gen. 30.37. Eze. 31.8.

CHILDREN, a blessing, Gen. 30.1. Psa. 113.9. Psa. 127.3-5. Given in answer to prayer, Gen. 15.2-5. Gen. 21.1. Gen. 25.21. Gen. 30.17-22. 1 Sam. 1.27. Luk. 1.13.

Treatment of, after birth, Lam. 2.22. Eze. 16.4. Luk. 2.7,12. Circumcised.—See CIRCUMCISION. Naming of — See NAMES. Weaning of, Gen. 21.8. 1 Sam. 1.22. Isa. 28.9. Tutors of, 2 Kin. 10.1. Gal. 4.1,2. Act. 22.3. Nurses, Gen. 24.59. Ex. 2.7,9. Ruth 4.16. 2 Sam. 4.4. 2 Kin. 11.2. Amusements of, Zec. 8.5. Mat. 11.16,17. Job 21.11.

Attended public worship, Jos. 8.35. 2 Chr. 20.13. Ezr. 8.21. Neh. 8.2,3. Neh. 12.43. Mat. 21.15. Luk. 2.46. From the age of three years, 2 Chr. 31.16. Dedicated to God, Jud. 11.39. Jud. 13.7. 1 Sam. 1.22,28. Prayer for, and blessing of, by parents.—See PARENTS, PRAYERS OF.

Adoption of.—See ADOPTION. First-born, privileges of.—See FIRST-BORN. Inheritance of.—See INHERITANCE. Marriage of.—See MARRIAGE.

Taken as bond-servants for debt, 2 Kin. 4.1. Neh. 5.5. Job 24.9. Mat. 18.25. Offered to idols.—See IDOLATROUS OFFERINGS. Slain in famine, Lev. 26.29. Deu. 28.53-57. 2 Kin. 6.28,29. Jer. 19.9. Lam. 2.20. Lam. 4.10. Eze. 5.10. Slain by Pharaoh, Ex. 1.22. By Herod, Mat. 2.16-18.

Illegitimate, excluded from the congregation, Deu. 23.2. Heb. 12.8. Rebellious, punished with death, Ex. 21.15,17. Lev. 20.9. Deu. 21.18-21. Fatherless.—See WIDOWS and ORPHANS.

Miracles connected with, 1 Kin. 17.17-23. 2 Kin. 4.17-36. Mat. 15.28. Mat. 17.18. Luk. 8.42. Luk. 9.38. Jno. 4.49. Blessed by Christ, Mat. 19.13-15. Mar. 10.13-16. Luk. 18.15,16.

Illustrative, Psa. 131.2. Mat. 18.2-6. Mar. 9.35-37. Mar. 10.15. Luk. 9.46-48. Luk. 18.17. 1 Cor. 14.20. Heb. 12.9. Jer. 1.6,7. 1 Cor. 13.11. 1 Cor. 14.20. Eph. 4.14. 1 Pet. 2.2. Death of.—See DEATH.

CHILDREN AND YOUTH—DUTIES AND PRIVILEGES—Deu. 31.12. Gather the people together, men, and women, and children, that they may hear, and that they may learn, and fear the Lord your God, and observe to do all the words of this law; 13. And *that* their children, which have not known *any thing,* may hear, and learn to fear the Lord your God. Jos. 8.35. 2 Chr. 20.13. Neh. 8.2,3. Neh. 12.43. Ezr. 8.21.

Psa. 34.11. Come, ye children, hearken unto me : I will teach you the fear of the Lord.

Psa. 71.5. Thou *art* my hope, O Lord God : *thou art* my trust from my youth. 17. O God, thou hast taught me from my youth.

Psa. 119.9. Wherewithal shall a young man cleanse his way? by taking heed *thereto* according to thy word.

Psa. 144.12. Our sons *may be* as plants grown up in their youth ; *that* our daughters *may be* as corner stones, polished *after* the similitude of a palace.

Psa. 148.12. Young men and maidens ; old men, and children : 13. Let them praise the name of the Lord.

Pro. 3.1. My son, forget not my law ; but let thine heart keep my commandments : 2. For length of days, and long life, and peace, shall they add to thee. 3. Let not mercy and truth forsake thee : bind them about thy neck ; write them upon the table of thine heart : 4. So shalt thou find favour and good understanding in the sight of God and man.

Pro. 8.17. I love them that love me ; and those that seek me early shall find me. 32. Hearken unto me, O ye children : for blessed *are they that* keep my ways. 33. Hear instruction, and be wise, and refuse it not.

Pro. 20.11. Even a child is known by his doings, whether his work *be* pure, and whether *it be* right.

Pro. 23.15. My son, if thine heart be wise, my heart shall rejoice, even mine. 16. Yea, my reins shall rejoice, when thy lips speak right things. 24. The father of the righteous shall greatly rejoice : and he that begetteth a wise *child* shall have joy of him. 25. Thy father and thy mother shall be glad, and she that bare thee shall rejoice. 26. My son, give me thine heart, and let thine eyes observe my ways.

Pro. 29.3. Whoso loveth wisdom rejoiceth his father.

Ecc. 4.13. Better *is* a poor and a wise child than an old and foolish king, who will no more be admonished.

Ecc. 12.1. Remember now thy Creator in the days of thy youth, while the evil days come not, nor the years draw nigh, when thou shalt say, I have no pleasure in them.

Isa. 40.11. He shall gather the lambs with his arm, and carry *them* in his bosom.

Isa. 54.13. All thy children *shall be* taught of the Lord ; and great *shall be* the peace of thy children.

Jer. 3.4. Wilt thou not from this time cry unto me, My father, thou *art* the guide of my youth?

Lam. 3.27. *It is* good for a man that he bear the yoke in his youth.

Mat. 18.4. Whosoever therefore shall humble himself as this little child, the same is greatest in the kingdom of heaven. 5. And whoso shall receive one such little child in my name receiveth me. 10. Despise not one of these little ones ; for I say unto you, That in heaven their angels do always behold the face of my Father which is in heaven. Mar. 9.37. Luk. 9.48.

Mat. 19.14. Jesus said, Suffer little children,

and forbid them not, to come unto me : for of such is the kingdom of heaven. 15. And he laid *his* hands on them. Luk. 18.15,16.

Mat. 21.15. The chief-priests saw the children crying in the temple, and saying, Hosanna to the son of David ; 16. Out of the mouth of babes and sucklings thou hast perfected praise. Psa. 8.2.

Mat. 23.37. How often would I have gathered thy children together, even as a hen gathereth her chickens under *her* wings, and ye would not !

Mar. 10.16. He took them up in his arms, put *his* hands upon them, and blessed them. *v.* 13-15.

Jno. 21.15. Feed my lambs.

Act. 2.39. The promise is unto you, and to your children.

1 Tim. 4.12. Let no man despise thy youth ; but be thou an example of the believers, in word, in conversation, in charity, in spirit, in faith, in purity.

2 Tim. 2.22. Flee also youthful lusts : but follow righteousness, faith, charity, peace, with them that call on the Lord out of a pure heart.

Tit. 2.6. Young men likewise exhort to be sober minded.

1 Jno. 2.12. Little children, your sins are forgiven you for his name's sake. 13. Young men, ye have overcome the wicked one. Little children, ye have known the Father.

CHILDREN AND YOUTH, DUTIES TO PARENTS, Ex. 20. 12. Honour thy father and thy mother : that thy days may be long upon the land which the Lord thy God giveth thee. Deu. 5.16. Mat. 15.4. Mat. 19.19.

Lev. 19. 3. Fear every man his mother, and his father. 32. Rise up before the hoary head, and honour the face of the old man.

Pro. 1.8. My son, hear the instruction of thy father, and forsake not the law of thy mother : 9. For they *shall be* an ornament of grace unto thy head, and chains about thy neck.

Pro. 4.1. Hear, ye children, the instruction of a father, and attend to know understanding. 20. My son, attend to my words ; incline thine ear unto my sayings. 21. Let them not depart from thine eyes ; keep them in the midst of thine heart. 22. For they *are* life unto those that find them, and health to all their flesh.

Pro. 5.1. My son, attend unto my wisdom, *and* bow thine ear to my understanding : 2. That thou mayest regard discretion, and *that* thy lips may keep knowledge.

Pro. 6.20. My son, keep thy father's commandment, and forsake not the law of thy mother : 21. Bind them continually upon thine heart, *and* tie them about thy neck.

Pro. 10.1. A wise son maketh a glad father.

Pro. 13.1. A wise son *heareth* his father's instruction.

Pro. 15.5. He that regardeth reproof is prudent. 20. A wise son maketh a glad father.

Pro. 17.6. The glory of children *are* their fathers.

Pro. 23.22. Hearken unto thy father that begat thee, and despise not thy mother when she is old.

Pro. 27.11. My son, be wise, and make my heart glad, that I may answer him that reproacheth me.

Pro. 28.7. Whoso keepeth the law *is* a wise son.

Mal. 1.6.　A son honoureth his father.

Mal. 4.6.　He shall turn the heart of the children to their fathers, lest I come and smite the earth with a curse.

Eph. 6.1.　Children, obey your parents in the Lord: for this is right.　2. Honour thy father and mother; which is the first commandment with promise;　3. That it may be well with thee, and thou mayest live long on the earth.

Col. 3.20.　Obey your parents in all things: for this is wellpleasing unto the Lord.

1 Tim. 5.4.　If any widow have children or nephews, let them learn first to shew piety at home, and to requite their parents: for that is good and acceptable before God.　8. But if any provide not for his own, and specially for those of his own house, he hath denied the faith, and is worse than an infidel.　16. If any man or woman that believeth have widows, let them relieve them, and let not the church be charged; that it may relieve them that are widows indeed.

Heb. 12.9.　Fathers of our flesh which corrected us, and we gave them reverence.

CHILDREN AND YOUTH, DUTIFUL, EXAMPLES OF, Shem and Japheth, Gen. 9.23. Isaac. Gen. 22.6-12. Esau, Gen. 28.6-9. Judah, Gen. 44.18-34.　Joseph, Gen. 45.9-13.　Gen. 46.29.　Gen. 47.11,12. Gen. 48.12.　Gen. 50.1-13. Moses, Ex. 18.7. Jephthah's daughter, Jud. 11.36.　Ruth, Ruth 1.15-17.　Elihu, Job 32. 4-7.　Saul, 1 Sam. 9.5.　David, 1 Sam. 22.3,4. Solomon, 1 Kin. 2.19,20.　Rechabites, Jer. 35. 18,19.　Jesus, Luk. 2.51.

――――, PIOUS, EXAMPLES OF. Samson, Jud. 13.24.　Samuel, 1 Sam. 2.26.　1 Sam. 3.10. Abijah, 1 Kin. 14.13.　Obadiah, 1 Kin. 18.12. Jehoshaphat. 1 Kin. 22.43.　2 Chr. 17.3.

Jewish children, 2 Chr. 20.13.　Neh. 12.43. Job, Job 29.4.　David, Psa. 71.5,17.　Solomon, 1 Kin. 3.3-13.　Josiah, 2 Chr. 34.1-3.　Children in the Temple, Mat. 21.15.　John, Luk. 1.80. Jesus, Luk. 2.52. Timothy, 2 Tim. 1.5.　2 Tim. 3.15.

―――― AND YOUTH, WICKED.　SINS OF THE YOUNG.　Gen. 8.21. The imagination of man's heart is evil from his youth.

Num. 32.14.　Ye are risen up in your fathers' stead, an increase of sinful men.

Deu. 27.16.　Cursed be he that setteth light by his father or his mother. And all the people shall say, Amen.

Job 13.26.　Makest me to possess the iniquities of my youth.

Job. 19.18.　Yea, young children despised me; I arose, and they spake against me.

Job 20.11.　His bones are full of the sin of his youth, which shall lie down with him in the dust.

Job 30.1.　They that are younger than I have me in derision.　12. The youth; they push away my feet, and they raise up against me the ways of their destruction.

Psa. 25.7.　Remember not the sins of my youth.

Pro. 7.7.　Among the simple ones, I discerned among the youths, a young man void of understanding.

Pro. 10.1.　The proverbs of Solomon.　A wise son maketh a glad father: but a foolish son is the heaviness of his mother.

Pro. 13.1.　A wise son heareth his father's

instruction: but a scorner heareth not rebuke.

Pro. 15.5.　A fool despiseth his father's instruction: but he that regardeth reproof is prudent.　20. A wise son maketh a glad father: but a foolish man despiseth his mother.

Pro. 17.2.　A wise servant shall have rule over a son that causeth shame.　21. He that begetteth a fool doeth it to his sorrow: and the father of a fool hath no joy.　25. A foolish son is a grief to his father, and bitterness to her that bear him.　Pro. 19.12.

Pro. 19.26.　He that wasteth his father, and chaseth away his mother, is a son that causeth shame, and bringeth reproach.

Pro. 20.20.　Whoso curseth his father or his mother, his lamp shall be put out in obscure darkness.

Pro. 22.15.　Foolishness is bound in the heart of a child.

Pro. 23.22.　Hearken unto thy father that begat thee, and despise not thy mother when she is old.

Pro. 28.7.　Whoso keepeth the law is a wise son: but he that is a companion of riotous men shameth his father.　24. Whoso robbeth his father or his mother, and saith, It is no transgression; the same is the companion of a destroyer.

Pro. 30.11.　A generation that curseth their father, and doth not bless their mother.　17. The eye that mocketh at his father, and despiseth to obey his mother, the ravens of the valley shall pick it out, and the young eagles shall eat it.

Ecc. 11.9.　Rejoice, O young man, in thy youth; and let thy heart cheer thee in the days of thy youth, and walk in the ways of thine heart, and in the sight of thine eyes: but know thou, that for all these things God will bring thee into judgment.　10. For childhood and youth are vanity.

Jer. 3.25.　We have sinned against the Lord our God, we and our fathers, from our youth.

Jer. 7.18.　The children gather wood, to make cakes to the queen of heaven.

Jer. 32.30.　The children of Israel and the children of Judah have only done evil before me from their youth.

Eze. 22.7.　They set light by father and mother.

CHILDREN AND YOUTH, WICKED, EXAMPLES OF.　Canaan, Gen. 9.25.　Eli's sons, 1 Sam. 2.12.　Samuel's sons, 1 Sam. 8.3. Absalom, 2 Sam. 15.　Adonijah, 1 Kin. 1.5. Abijam, 1 Kin. 15.3.　Ahaziah, 1 Kin. 22.52. Children at Bethel, 2 Kin. 2.23,24.　Samaritans' descendants, 2 Kin. 17.41.　Amon, 2 Kin. 21.21. Sennacherib's sons, 2 Kin. 19.37.

―――― OF SAINTS BLESSED BY GOD. Gen. 7.1.　Come thou and all thy house into the ark.　Gen. 6.18.

Gen. 17.7.　I will establish my covenant between me and thee and thy seed after thee in their generations for an everlasting covenant, to be a God unto thee, and to thy seed after thee.　v. 8.

Gen. 19.12.　Hast thou here any besides? son in law, and thy sons, and thy daughters, and whatsoever thou hast in the city, bring them out of this place.　v. 15, 16.

Gen. 21.13.　Of the son of the bond-woman will I make a nation, because he is thy seed.

Gen. 26.24. Will bless thee, and multiply thy seed for my servant Abraham's sake.

Deu. 4.37. Because he loved thy fathers, therefore he chose their seed after them. Deu. 10.15.

Deu. 12.28. That it may go well with thee, and with thy children after thee for ever. Deu. 29.29.

1 Kin. 11.13. I will not rend away all the kingdom; but will give one tribe to thy son, for David my servant's sake.

1 Kin. 15.4. For David's sake did the Lord his God give him a lamp in Jerusalem, to set up his son after him.

2 Kin. 8.19. The Lord would not destroy Judah for David his servant's sake, as he promised him to give him alway a light, and to his children.

Psa. 37.26. His seed is blessed.

Psa. 102.28. The children of thy servants shall continue, and their seed shall be established before thee.

Psa. 103.17. His righteousness unto children's children.

Psa. 112.2. His seed shall be mighty upon earth: the generation of the upright shall be blessed. 3. Wealth and riches shall be in his house.

Pro. 3.33. He blesseth the habitation of the just.

Pro. 11.21. The seed of the righteous shall be delivered.

Pro. 12.7. The house of the righteous shall stand.

Pro. 13.22. A good man leaveth an inheritance to his children's children : and the wealth of the sinner is laid up for the just.

Pro. 20.7. His children are blessed after him.

Isa. 44.3. I will pour my spirit upon thy seed, and my blessing upon thine offspring: 4. And they shall spring up as among the grass, as willows by the water courses. 5. One shall say, I am the Lord's; and another shall call himself by the name of Jacob ; and another shall subscribe with his hand unto the Lord, and surname himself by the name of Israel.

Isa. 65.23. They are the seed of the blessed of the Lord, and their offspring with them.

Jer. 31.1. The God of all the families of Israel.

Jer. 32.39. That they may fear me for ever, for the good of them, and of their children after them.

Act. 2.39. The promise is unto you and to your children

1 Cor. 7.14. The unbelieving husband is sanctified by the wife, and the unbelieving wife is sanctified by the husband : else were your children unclean ; but now are they holy. Mal. 2.15.

CHILDREN OF THE WICKED. See SIN, FRUITS OF, HEREDITARY CONSEQUENCES.

CHIMHAM, son of Barzillai, David takes him into his household, 2 Sam. 19.37,40, and recommends him to Solomon, 1 Kin. 2.7. See Jer. 41.17.

CHIMNEY, Hos. 13.3.

CHINNERETH. See CINNEROTH.

CHIOS, an island in the Mediterranean, Act. 20.15.

CHISLEU, the ninth month (December), Ezr. 10.9. Neh. 1.1. Jer. 36.22,23. Zec. 7.1.

CHITTIM, a people descended from Javan, Gen. 10.4. Isles or coasts of, in the Mediterranean, Isa. 23.1,12. Jer. 2.10. Commerce of, Eze. 27.6. Prophecies respecting, Num. 24.24. Dan. 11.30.

CHIUN, or REMPHAN (Saturn), a Phenician idol, worshipped by Israelites, Amos 5.26. Act. 7.43.

CHLOE, house of, Corinthian disciples, 1 Cor. 1.11.

CHORAZIN, a town near the Sea of Galilee, Christ's miracles in, Mat. 11.21. Luk. 10.13.

CHRIST, ASCENSION OF. Psa. 24.7. Lift up your heads, O ye gates ; and be ye lift up, ye everlasting doors ; and the King of glory shall come in. v. 8-10.

Psa. 68.18. Thou hast ascended on high, thou hast led captivity captive. Eph. 4.8.

Mar. 16.19. After the Lord had spoken unto them, he was received up into heaven, and sat on the right hand of God.

Luk. 24.26. Ought not Christ to have suffered these things, and to enter into his glory? 50. He led them out as far as to Bethany, and he lifted up his hands, and blessed them. 51. And it came to pass, while he blessed them, he was parted from them, and carried up into heaven.

Jno. 1.51. Hereafter ye shall see heaven open, and the angels of God ascending and descending upon the Son of man. See Act. 1.10.

Jno. 6.62. What and if ye shall see the Son of man ascend up where he was before?

Jno. 7.33. Yet a little while am I with you, and then I go unto him that sent me. 34. Ye shall seek me, and shall not find me: and where I am, thither ye cannot come. 39. The Holy Ghost was not yet given ; because that Jesus was not yet glorified.

Jno. 13.31. Now is the Son of man glorified, and God is glorified in him. 32. If God be glorified in him, God shall also glorify him in himself, and shall straightway glorify him.

Jno. 14.2. I go to prepare a place for you. 12. Greater works than these shall he do ; because I go unto my Father. 28. Ye have heard how I said unto you, I go away, and come again unto you. If ye loved me, ye would rejoice, because I said, I go unto the Father : for my Father is greater than I.

Jno. 16.5. Now I go my way to him that sent me. 7. It is expedient for you that I go away : for if I go not away, the Comforter will not come unto you ; but if I depart, I will send him unto you. 10. I go to my Father, and ye see me no more.

Jno. 16.16. A little while, and ye shall not see me : and again, a little while, and ye shall see me, because I go to the Father. 25. The time cometh, when I shall no more speak unto you in proverbs, but I shall shew you plainly of the Father. 28. I came forth from the Father, and am come into the world : again, I leave the world, and go to the Father.

Jno. 17.5. Now, O Father, glorify thou me with thine own self with the glory which I had with thee before the world was.

Jno. 20.17. Touch me not ; for I am not yet ascended to my Father: but go to my brethren.

and say unto them, I ascend unto my Father, and your Father; and *to* my God, and your God.

Act. 1.9.   When he had spoken these things, while they beheld, he was taken up; and a cloud received him out of their sight.

Act. 2.33.   Being by the right hand of God exalted, and having received of the Father the promise of the Holy Ghost.

Act. 3.21.   Whom the heaven must receive until the times of restitution of all things.

Act. 5.31.   Him hath God exalted with his right hand *to be* a Prince and a Saviour, for to give repentance to Israel, and forgiveness of sins.

Act. 7.55.   Looked up stedfastly into heaven, and saw the glory of God, and Jesus standing on the right hand of God, 56. And said, Behold, I see the heavens opened, and the Son of man standing on the right hand of God.

Rom. 8.17. We may be also glorified together. 34. Who is even at the right hand of God.

Eph. 1.20.   He raised him from the dead, and set *him* at his own right hand in the heavenly *places*.

Eph. 4.10.   He that descended is the same also that ascended up far above all heavens, that he might fill all things.

Phil. 2.9. God also hath highly exalted him.

Col. 2.15.   Having spoiled principalities and powers, he made a show of them openly, triumphing over them in it.

Col. 3.1.   Sitteth on the right hand of God.

1 Tim. 3.16.   God was manifest in the flesh, received up into glory.

Heb. 1.3.   When he had by himself purged our sins, sat down on the right hand of the Majesty on high.

Heb. 2.9.   We see Jesus, who was made a little lower than the angels for the suffering of death, crowned with glory and honour.

Heb. 4.10.   He that is entered into his rest, he also hath ceased from his own works, as God *did* from his.   14. We have a great highpriest, that is passed into the heavens, Jesus the Son of God.

Heb. 6.20.   The forerunner is for us entered, *even* Jesus, made an.high-priest for ever.

Heb. 7.26.   Such an high-priest became us, *who is* holy, harmless, undefiled, separate from sinners, and made higher than the heavens.

Heb. 8.1.   We have such an high-priest, who is set on the right hand of the throne of the Majesty in the heavens.

Heb. 9.12.   By his own blood he entered in once into the holy place, having obtained eternal redemption *for us.*   24. Christ is not entered into the holy places made with hands, *which are* the figures of the true; but into heaven itself, now to appear in the presence of God for us.

Heb. 10.12.   After he had offered one sacrifice for sins, for ever sat down on the right hand of God; 13. From henceforth expecting till his enemies be made his footstool.

Heb. 12.2.   Who for the joy that was set before him endured the cross, despising the shame, and is set down at the right hand of the throne of God.

1 Pet. 3.22.   Who is gone into heaven, and is on the right hand of God.

Rev. 1.5.   *Who is* the faithful witness, *and* the first begotten of the dead.

Rev. 3.21   To him that overcometh will I grant to sit with me in my throne, even *as* I also overcame, and am set down with my Father in his throne.

See CHRIST, HEAD OF THE CHURCH — CHRIST, KING.

CHRIST, COMPASSION OF. See CHRIST, LOVE OF.

———, CONFESSING OF. See DECISION.

CHRIST CREATOR. Jno. 1.3. All things were made by him; and without him was not anything made that was made.   10. He was in the world, and the world was made by him.

1 Cor. 8.6.   *There is but* one God, the Father, of whom *are* all things, and we in him; and one Lord Jesus Christ, by whom *are* all things, and we by him.

Eph. 3.9.   God, who created all things by Jesus Christ.

Col. 1.16.   By him were all things created, that are in heaven, and that are in earth, visible and invisible, whether *they be* thrones, or dominions, or principalities, or powers: all things were created by him, and for him: 17. And he is before all things, and by him all things consist.

Heb. 1.2.   *His* Son, whom he hath appointed heir of all things, by whom also he made the worlds.   *v.* 3, compare Gen. 1.26.

CHRIST DEATH OF, ITS DESIGN. Gen. 3.15. I will put enmity between thee and the woman, and between thy seed and her seed; it shall bruise thy head, and thou shalt bruise his heel.

Isa. 53.4.   Surely he hath borne our griefs, and carried our sorrows: yet we did esteem him stricken, smitten of God, and afflicted. 5. But he *was* wounded for our transgressions, *he was* bruised for our iniquities: the chastisement of our peace *was* upon him; and with his stripes we are healed.   6. All we like sheep have gone astray; we have turned every one to his own way; and the Lord hath laid on him the iniquity of us all.   8. He was cut off out of the land of the living: for the transgression of my people was he stricken.

Isa. 53.10. It pleased the Lord to bruise him; he hath put *him* to grief: when thou shalt make his soul an offering for sin, he shall see *his* seed, he shall prolong *his* days, and the pleasure of the Lord shall prosper in his hand. 11. He shall see of the travail of his soul, *and* shall be satisfied: by his knowledge shall my righteous servant justify many; for he shall bear their iniquities.   12. Therefore will I divide him *a portion* with the great, and he shall divide the spoil with the strong; because he hath poured out his soul unto death: and he was numbered with the transgressors; and he bare the sin of many, and made intercession for the transgressors.   *v.* 1-12.

Dan. 9.24.   To finish the transgression, and to make an end of sins, and to make reconciliation for iniquity, and to bring in everlasting righteousness, and to seal up the vision and prophecy, and to anoint the most Holy. 26. After three score and two weeks shall Messiah be cut off, but not for himself.

Zec. 9.11.   By the blood of my covenant I have sent forth thy prisoners out of the pit wherein is no water.

Zec. 13.1.   There shall be a fountain opened to the house of David and to the inhabitants of Jerusalem for sin and for uncleanness. 7. Awake, O sword, against my shepherd, and against the man *that is* my fellow, saith the Lord of hosts : smite the shepherd.

Mat. 20.28. The Son of man came not to be ministered unto, but to minister, and to give his life a ransom for many. Mar. 10.45.

Mat. 26.28. This is my blood of the new testament, which is shed for many for the remission of sins. Mar. 14.24.

Luk. 22.19. He took bread, and gave thanks, and brake *it*, and gave unto them, saying, This is my body which is given for you : this do in remembrance of me. 20. Likewise also the cup after supper, saying, This cup *is* the new testament in my blood, which is shed for you.

Luk. 24.26. Ought not Christ to have suffered these things, and to enter into his glory ?

Jno. 1.29. Behold the Lamb of God, which taketh away the sin of the world.

Jno. 3.14. As Moses lifted up the serpent in the wilderness, even so must the Son of man be lifted up : 15. That whosoever believeth in him should not perish, but have eternal life. 16. For God so loved the world, that he gave his only-begotten Son, that whosoever believeth in him should not perish, but have everlasting life. 17. For God sent not his Son into the world to condemn the world ; but that the world through him might be saved.

Jno. 6.51. The bread that I will give is my flesh, which I will give for the life of the world.

Jno. 10.11. The good shepherd giveth his life for the sheep. 15. I lay down my life for the sheep. 17. Therefore doth my Father love me, because I lay down my life, that I might take it again.

Jno. 11.50. It is expedient for us, that one man should die for the people, and that the whole nation perish not. 51. Jesus should die for that nation ; 52. And not for that nation only, but that also he should gather together in one the children of God that were scattered abroad.

Jno. 12.24. Except a corn of wheat fall into the ground and die, it abideth alone : but if it die, it bringeth forth much fruit. 31. Now is the judgment of this world : now shall the prince of this world be cast out. 32. And if I be lifted up from the earth, will draw all *men* unto me. 33. This he said, signifying what death he should die.

Jno. 14.19. Yet a little while, and the world seeth me no more ; but ye see me : because I live, ye shall live also.

Jno. 15.13. Greater love hath no man than this, that a man lay down his life for his friends.

Act. 5.30. The God of our fathers raised up Jesus, whom ye slew and hanged on a tree. 31. Him hath God exalted with his right hand *to be* a Prince and a Saviour, for to give repentance to Israel, and forgiveness of sins.

Act. 20.28. Feed the church of God, which he hath purchased with his own blood.

Act. 26.23. That Christ should suffer, *and* that he should be the first that should rise from the dead, and should shew light unto the people, and to the Gentiles.

Rom. 3.24. Justified freely by his grace through the redemption that is in Christ Jesus. 25. Whom God hath set forth *to be* a propi-

tiation through faith in his blood, to declare his righteousness for the remission of sins that are past, through the forbearance of God.

Rom. 4.25. Who was delivered for our offences, and was raised again for our justification.

Rom. 5.6. When we were yet without strength, in due time Christ died for the ungodly. 7. Scarcely for a righteous man will one die : yet peradventure for a good man some would even dare to die. 8. But God commendeth his love toward us, in that, while we were yet sinners, Christ died for us. 9. Much more then, being now justified by his blood, we shall be saved from wrath through him. 10. For if, when we were enemies, we were reconciled to God by the death of his Son, much more, being reconciled, we shall be saved by his life. 11. We also joy in God through our Lord Jesus Christ, by whom we have now received the atonement.

Rom. 6.3. Know ye not, that so many of us as were baptized into Jesus Christ were baptized into his death ? 4. Therefore we are buried with him by baptism into death ; that like as Christ was raised up from the dead by the glory of the Father, even so we also should walk in newness of life. 5. For if we have been planted together in the likeness of his death, we shall be also *in the likeness of his* resurrection. 9. Christ being raised from the dead dieth no more ; death hath no more dominion over him. 10. For in that he died, he died unto sin once.

Rom. 8.3. God sending his own Son in the likeness of sinful flesh, and for sin, condemned sin in the flesh. 32. He that spared not his own son, but delivered him up for us all, how shall he not with him also freely give us all things ? 34. Who *is* he that condemneth ? *It is* Christ that died. 39. Nor height, nor depth, nor any other creature, shall be able to separate us from the love of God, which is in Christ Jesus our Lord.

Rom. 14.9. To this end Christ both died, and rose, and revived, that he might be Lord both of the dead and living. 15. Destroy not him with thy meat, for whom Christ died.

1 Cor. 5.7. Even Christ our passover is sacrificed for us.

1 Cor. 6.20. Ye are bought with a price : therefore glorify God in your body, and in your spirit, which are God's.

1 Cor. 8.11. Through thy knowledge shall the weak brother perish, for whom Christ died ?

1 Cor. 15.3. Christ died for our sins according to the scriptures.

2 Cor. 5.14. The love of Christ constraineth us ; because we thus judge, that if one died for all, then were all dead : 15. And *that* he died for all, that they which live should not henceforth live unto themselves, but unto him which died for them, and rose again. 19. God was in Christ, reconciling the world unto himself, not imputing their trespasses unto them ; and hath committed unto us the word of reconciliation. 21. He hath made him *to be* sin for us, who knew no sin ; that we might be made the right ousness of God in him.

2 Cor. 8.9. Ye know the grace of our Lord Jesus Christ, that, though he was rich, yet for your sakes he became poor, that ye through his poverty might be rich.

Gal. 1.3.   Our Lord Jesus Christ.   4. Who gave himself for our sins, that he might deliver us from this present evil world, according to the will of God and our Father.

Gal. 2.20.   I am crucified with Christ: nevertheless I live; yet not I, but Christ liveth in me: and the life which I now live in the flesh I live by the faith of the Son of God.

Gal. 3.13.   Christ hath redeemed us from the curse of the law, being made a curse for us: for it is written, Cursed *is* every one that hangeth on a tree.

Gal. 4.4.   When the fulness of the time was come, God sent forth his Son, made of a woman, made under the law, ¶ 5. To redeem them that were under the law, that we might receive the adoption of sons.

Eph. 1.6.   He hath made us accepted in the beloved.   7. In whom we have redemption through his blood, the forgiveness of sins, according to the riches of his grace.

Eph. 2.13.   Now in Christ Jesus ye who sometimes were far off are made nigh by the blood of Christ.   14. He is our peace, who hath made both one, and hath broken down the middle wall of partition *between us*;   15. Having abolished in his flesh the enmity, *even* the law of commandments *contained* in ordinances; for to make in himself of twain one new man, *so* making peace;   16. And that he might reconcile both unto God in one body by the cross, having slain the enmity thereby.

Eph. 5.2.   Christ also hath loved us, and hath given himself for us an offering and a sacrifice to God for a sweet-smelling savour. 25. Christ also loved the church, and gave himself for it;   26. That he might sanctify and cleanse it with the washing of water by the word;   27. That he might present it to himself a glorious church, not having spot, or wrinkle, or any such thing; but that it should be holy and without blemish.

Col. 1.14.   In whom we have redemption through his blood, *even* the forgiveness of sins. 20. Having made peace through the blood of his cross, by him to reconcile all things unto himself; by him, *I say*, whether *they be* things in earth, or things in heaven.   21. Now hath he reconciled,   22. In the body of his flesh through death, to present you holy and unblameable and unreproveable in his sight.

Col. 2.14.   Blotting out the handwriting of ordinances that was against us, which was contrary to us, and took it out of the way, nailing it to his cross;   15. *And* having spoiled principalities and powers, he made a show of them openly, triumphing over them in it.

1 The. 1.10.   Jesus, which delivered us from the wrath to come.

1 The. 5.9.   God hath not appointed us to wrath, but to obtain salvation by our Lord Jesus Christ,   10. Who died for us, that, whether we wake or sleep, we should live together with him.

1 Tim. 2.6.   Who gave himself a ransom for all, to be testified in due time.

Tit. 2.14.   Who gave himself for us, that he might redeem us from all iniquity, and purify unto himself a peculiar people, zealous of good works.

Heb. 1.3.   When he had by himself purged our sins.

Heb. 2.9.   We see Jesus, who was made a little lower than the angels for the suffering of death, crowned with glory and honour; that he by the grace of God should taste death for every man.   10. To make the captain of their salvation perfect through sufferings.   14. As the children are partakers of flesh and blood, he also himself likewise took part of the same; that through death he might destroy him that had the power of death, that is, the devil; 15. And deliver them who through fear of death were all their lifetime subject to bondage. 18. In that he himself hath suffered being tempted, he is able to succour them that are tempted.

Heb. 7.27.   Who needeth not daily, as those high-priests, to offer up sacrifice, first for his own sins, and then for the people's: for this he did once, when he offered up himself.

Heb. 9.12.   Neither by the blood of goats and calves, but by his own blood he entered in once into the holy place, having obtained eternal redemption *for us*.   13. For if the blood of bulls and of goats, and the ashes of an heifer sprinkling the unclean, sanctifieth to the purifying of the flesh: 14. How much more shall the blood of Christ, who through the eternal Spirit offered himself without spot to God, purge your conscience from dead works to serve the living God?   15. And for this cause he is the mediator of the new testament, that by means of death, for the redemption of the transgressions *that were* under the first testament, they which are called might receive the promise of eternal inheritance.

Heb. 9.16.   For where a testament *is*, there must also of necessity be the death of the testator.   17. For a testament *is* of force after men are dead: otherwise it is of no strength at all while the testator liveth.   25. Nor yet that he should offer himself often, as the high-priest entereth into the holy place every year with blood of others;   26. For then must he often have suffered since the foundation of the world: but now once in the end of the world hath he appeared to put away sin by the sacrifice of himself.   28. Christ was once offered to bear the sins of many

Heb. 10.10.   We are sanctified through the offering of the body of Jesus Christ once *for all*.   12. This man, after he had offered one sacrifice for sins for ever, sat down on the right hand of God.   14. By one offering he hath perfected for ever them that are sanctified. 17. Their sins and iniquities will I remember no more.   18. Now where remission of these *is*, there *is* no more offering for sin. 19. Having therefore, brethren, boldness to enter into the holiest by the blood of Jesus,   20. By a new and living way, which he hath consecrated for us, through the vail, that is to say, his flesh.

Heb. 12.2.   Who for the joy that was set before him endured the cross, despising the shame, and is set down at the right hand of the throne of God.   24. To Jesus the mediator of the new covenant, and to the blood of sprinkling, that speaketh better things than *that of* Abel.

Heb. 13.11.   The bodies of those beasts, whose blood is brought into the sanctuary by the high-priest for sin, are burned without the camp.   12. Wherefore Jesus also, that he might sanctify the people with his own blood, suffered without the gate.

1 Pet. 1.2.   Elect according to the fore-

knowledge of God the Father, through sanctification of the Spirit, unto obedience and sprinkling of the blood of Jesus Christ. 18. Ye know that ye were not redeemed with corruptible things, *as* silver and gold, from your vain conversation *received* by tradition from your fathers; 19. But with the precious blood of Christ, as of a lamb without blemish and without spot: 20. Who verily was foreordained before the foundation of the world, but was manifest in these last times for you, 21. Who by him do believe in God, that raised him up from the dead, and gave him glory; that your faith and hope might be in God.

1 Pet. 2.21.   Christ also suffered for us, leaving us an example, that ye should follow his steps: 24. Who his own self bare our sins in his own body on the tree, that we, being dead to sins, should live unto righteousness: by whose stripes ye were healed.

1 Pet. 3.18.   Christ also hath once suffered for sins, the just for the unjust, that he might bring us to God, being put to death in the flesh, but quickened by the Spirit.

1 Pet. 4.1.   Christ hath suffered for us in the flesh.

1 Jno. 1.7.   The blood of Jesus Christ his Son cleanseth us from all sin.

1 Jno. 2.2.   He is the propitiation for our sins: and not for our's only, but also for *the sins of* the whole world.

1 Jno. 3.16.   Hereby perceive we the love *of God*, because he laid down his life for us.

1 Jno. 4.10.   Herein is love, not that we loved God, but that he loved us, and sent his Son *to be* the propitiation for our sins.

Rev. 1.5.   Unto him that loved us, and washed us from our sins in his own blood, 6. And hath made us kings and priests unto God and his Father.

Rev. 5.9.   Thou wast slain, and hast redeemed us to God by thy blood out of every kindred, and tongue, and people, and nation; 10. And hast made us unto our God kings and priests: and we shall reign on the earth.

Rev. 7.14.   These are they which came out of great tribulation, and have washed their robes, and made them white in the blood of the Lamb. 15. Therefore are they before the throne of God.

Rev. 13.8.   The Lamb slain from the foundation of the world.

See CHRIST, SUFFERINGS OF.

CHRIST, DEATH OF, PREDICTED BY HIMSELF.   Mat. 12.40. As Jonas was three days and three nights in the whale's belly: so shall the Son of man be three days and three nights in the heart of the earth.   Luk. 11.30.

Mat. 16.21.   From that time forth began Jesus to shew unto his disciples, how that he must go unto Jerusalem, and suffer many things of the elders and chief priests and scribes, and be killed.   Mar. 8.31.   Luk. 9.22.

Mat. 17.22.   Jesus said unto them, The Son of man shall be betrayed into the hands of men: 23. And they shall kill him.   Mar. 9.31,32.   Luk. 9.44,45.   Luk. 24.7.   Mat. 21. 33-45.   Parable of the Wicked Husbandmen.

Mat. 26.2.   After two days is *the feast of* the passover, and the Son of man is betrayed to be crucified.

Mar. 10.33. Behold, we go up to Jerusalem; and the Son of man shall be delivered unto the chief priests, and unto the scribes; and they shall condemn him to death, and shall deliver him to the Gentiles: 34. And they shall mock him, and shall scourge him, and shall spit upon him, and shall kill him: and the third day he shall rise again. Mat. 20.18,19. Luk. 18.31-33.

Luk. 17.25.   First must he suffer many things, and be rejected of this generation.

Luk. 22.15.   With desire I have desired to eat this passover with you before I suffer. 37. This that is written must yet be accomplished in me, And he was reckoned among the transgressors: for the things concerning me have an end.

Jno. 10.11.   I am the good shepherd: the good shepherd giveth his life for the sheep. 15. I lay down my life for the sheep. 17. Therefore doth my Father love me, because I lay down my life, that I might take it again.   18. No man taketh it from me, but I lay it down of myself.   I have power to lay it down, and I have power to take it again.

Jno. 12.7.   Let her alone: against the day of my burying hath she kept this.   32. I, if I be lifted up from the earth, will draw all *men* unto me.   33. This he said, signifying what death he should die.   Mat. 26.12.   Mar. 14.9.

Jno. 13.18.   He that eateth bread with me hath lifted up his heel against me.   19. Now I tell you before it come, that, when it is come to pass, ye may believe that I am *he.* 21. Verily, verily, I say unto you, that one of you shall betray me.   Mat. 26.21.   Mar. 14.18.   Luk. 22.21.

Jno. 14.19.   Yet a little while, and the world seeth me no more.

Jno. 15.13.   Greater love hath no man than this, that a man lay down his life for his friends.

Jno. 16.20.   Ye shall weep and lament, but the world shall rejoice: and ye shall be sorrowful, but your sorrow shall be turned into joy.

CHRIST, DEATH OF, VOLUNTARY.   Isa. 50.6.   I gave my back to the smiters, and my cheeks to them that plucked off the hair: I hid not my face from shame and spitting.

Isa. 53.12.   He poured out his soul unto death.

Mat. 26.24.   The Son of man goeth as it is written of him.   39. O my Father, if it be possible, let this cup pass from me; nevertheless not as I will, but as thou *wilt.*   42. O my Father, if this cup may not pass away from me, except I drink it, thy will be done.   Mar. 14.36,39.

Mat. 26.53.   Thinkest thou that I cannot now pray to my Father, and he shall presently give me more than twelve legions of angels? 54. But how then shall the scriptures be fulfilled, that thus it must be?

Luk. 9.51.   When the time was come that he should be received up, he stedfastly set his face to go to Jerusalem.

Luk. 12.50.   I have a baptism to be baptized with: and how am I straitened till it be accomplished!   Luk. 22.15.

Luk. 22.42.   Father, if thou be willing, remove this cup from me: nevertheless not my will, but thine be done.

Jno. 10.17.   Therefore doth my Father love me, because I lay down my life, that I might take it again.   18. No man taketh it from me, but I lay it down of myself.   I have power to lay it down, and I have power to take it again.

Jno. 18.5. They answered him, Jesus of Nazareth. Jesus saith unto them, I am he. 8. I have told you that I am he : if therefore ye seek me, let these go their way. 11. Put up thy sword into the sheath : the cup which my Father hath given me, shall I not drink it ?

Phil. 2.8. Being found in fashion as a man, he humbled himself, and became obedient unto death, even the death of the cross.

CHRIST, Denial of. See Backsliding.

————, Eternal. Pro. 8.22. The Lord possessed me in the beginning of his way, before his works of old. 23. I was set up from everlasting, from the beginning, or ever the earth was. 24. When there were no depths, I was brought forth ; when there were no fountains abounding with water. 25. Before the mountains were settled, before the hills was I brought forth.

Isa. 9.6. The everlasting Father.

Mic. 5.2. Out of thee shall he come forth unto me that is to be ruler in Israel ; whose goings forth have been from of old, from everlasting.

Jno. 1.1. In the beginning was the Word, and the Word was with God, and the Word was God. 2. The same was in the beginning with God. 4. In him was life. 15. He that cometh after me is preferred before me : for he was before me.

Jno. 6.62. What and if ye shall see the Son of man ascend up where he was before ?

Jno. 8.23. I am from above : I am not of this world. 58. Before Abraham was, I am.

Jno. 17.5. The glory which I had with thee before the world was.

2 Cor. 8.9. He was rich, yet for your sakes he became poor.

Eph. 4.10. He that descended is the same also that ascended up far above all heavens, that he might fill all things.

Col. 1.17. He is before all things, and by him all things consist.

Heb. 1.10. Thou, Lord, in the beginning hast laid the foundation of the earth ; and the heavens are the works of thine hands : 11. They shall perish ; but thou remainest ; and they all shall wax old as doth a garment ; 12. And as a vesture shalt thou fold them up, and they shall be changed : but thou art the same, and thy years shall not fail. Psa. 102. 24-27.

Heb. 7.16. Made, not after the law of a carnal commandment, but after the power of an endless life. 24. He continueth ever. 25. He ever liveth to make intercession for them. Heb. 6.20.

Heb. 13.8. Jesus Christ the same yesterday, and to-day, and for ever.

1 Jno. 1.1. That which was from the beginning, which we have heard, which we have seen with our eyes, which we have looked upon, and our hands have handled, of the Word of life ; 2. For the life was manifested, and we have seen it, and bear witness, and shew unto you that eternal life, which was with the Father, and was manifested unto us.

Rev. 1.8. I am Alpha and Omega, the beginning and the ending, saith the Lord, which is, and which was, and which is to come, the Almighty. 11. I am Alpha and Omega, the first and the last. 17. I am the first and the last : 18. I am he that liveth, and was dead ;

and, behold, I am alive for evermore. Rev. 21.6. Rev. 22.13.

Rev. 2.8. These things saith the first and the last, which was dead, and is alive.

CHRIST, Example of. See Likeness to God and Christ.

————, Faith in. See Faith.

————, Genealogy of. See Genealogies.

CHRIST God. Psa. 24.10. Who is this King of glory ? The Lord of hosts ; he is the King of glory. 1 Cor. 2.8.

Psa. 45.6. Thy throne, O God, is for ever and ever : the sceptre of thy kingdom is a right sceptre. 7. Thou lovest righteousness, and hatest wickedness : therefore God, thy God, hath anointed thee with the oil of gladness above thy fellows. Heb. 1.8.

Isa. 6.1. I saw also the Lord sitting upon a throne, high and lifted up, and his train filled the temple. Jno. 12.41.

Isa. 8.13. Sanctify the Lord of hosts himself ; and let him be your fear, and let him be your dread. 14. And he shall be for a sanctuary ; but for a stone of stumbling and for a rock of offence. 1 Pet. 2.8.

Isa. 9.6. His name shall be called Wonderful, Counseller, The mighty God, The everlasting Father, The Prince of Peace.

Isa. 40.3. Prepare ye the way of the Lord, make straight in the desert a highway for our God. 9. Say unto the cities of Judah, Behold your God ! 10. Behold, the Lord God will come with strong hand, and his arm shall rule for him. Mat. 3.3.

Mal. 3.1. The Lord, whom ye seek, shall suddenly come to his temple, even the messenger of the covenant, whom ye delight in : behold, he shall come, saith the Lord of hosts.

Mat. 1.23. Behold, a virgin shall be with child, and shall bring forth a son, and they shall call his name Emmanuel, which being interpreted is, God with us. Isa. 7.14.

Mat. 22.43. How then doth David in spirit call him Lord, saying, 44. The Lord said unto my Lord, Sit thou on my right hand, till I make thine enemies thy footstool ? 45. If David then call him Lord, how is he his son ? Psa. 110.1.

Jno. 1.1. In the beginning was the Word, and the Word was with God, and the Word was God. 2. The same was in the beginning with God.

Jno. 5.17. Jesus answered them, My Father worketh hitherto, and I work. 18. Therefore the Jews sought the more to kill him, because he not only had broken the sabbath, but said also that God was his Father, making himself equal with God.

Jno. 10.30. I and my Father are one. 31. Then the Jews took up stones again to stone him. 32. Jesus answered them, Many good works have I shewed you from my Father : for which of those works do ye stone me ? 33. For a good work we stone thee not ; but for blasphemy ; and because that thou, being a man, makest thyself God.

Jno. 20.28. Thomas answered and said unto him, My Lord and my God.

Act. 20.28. Feed the church of God, which he hath purchased with his own blood.

Rom. 9.5. Of whom as concerning the flesh

Christ *came*, who is over all, God blessed for ever.

1 Cor. 10.9. Neither let us tempt Christ, as some of them also tempted, and were destroyed of serpents. See Num. 21.6.

1 Cor. 15.47. The second man *is* the Lord from heaven.

Phil. 2.5. Christ Jesus, 6. Who, being in the form of God, thought it not robbery to be equal with God.

Col. 2.9. In him dwelleth all the fulness of the Godhead bodily.

1 Tim. 3.16. God was manifest in the flesh.

Tit. 2.13. The glorious appearing of the great God and our Saviour Jesus Christ.

Heb. 1.8. But unto the Son *he saith,* Thy throne, O God, *is* for ever and ever ; a sceptre of righteousness *is* the sceptre of thy kingdom. 10. And, Thou, Lord, in the beginning hast laid the foundation of the earth ; and the heavens are the works of thine hands. *v.* 1-14. Psa. 102.24-27.

1 Jno. 5.20. This is the true God and eternal life.

See CHRIST, SON OF GOD — GOD THE FATHER, SON, AND HOLY SPIRIT.

CHRIST, GOD GLORIFIED BY. See GOD GLORIFIED.

————, HEAD OF THE CHURCH. Isa. 33.22. The Lord *is* our judge, the Lord *is* our lawgiver, the Lord *is* our king ; he will save us.

Isa. 55.4. I have given him *for* a witness to the people, a leader and commander to the people.

Mat. 12.6. In this place is *one* greater than the temple. 8. The Son of man is Lord even of the sabbath-day. Mar. 2.28. Luk. 6.5.

Mat. 23.8. Be not ye called Rabbi : for one is your Master, *even* Christ ; and all ye are brethren. 10. Neither be ye called masters : for one is your Master, *even* Christ.

Jno. 13.13. Ye call me Master and Lord : and ye say well ; for *so* I am.

Act. 2.36. Let all the house of Israel know assuredly, that God hath made that same Jesus, whom ye have crucified, both Lord and Christ.

Rom. 8.29. The first-born among many brethren.

1 Cor. 11.3. I would have you know, that the head of every man is Christ.

1 Cor. 12.5. There are differences of administrations, but the same Lord.

Eph. 1.10. That in the dispensation of the fulness of times, he might gather together in one all things in Christ, both which are in heaven, and which are on earth, *even* in him. 22. Hath put all *things* under his feet, and gave him *to be* the head over all *things* to the church, 23. Which is his body, the fulness of him that filleth all in all.

Eph. 2.20. Are built upon the foundation of the apostles and prophets, Jesus Christ himself being the chief corner *stone ;* 21. In whom all the building fitly framed together groweth unto an holy temple in the Lord : 22. In whom ye also are builded together for an habitation of God through the Spirit.

Eph. 4.15. Speaking the truth in love, may grow up into him in all things, which is the head, *even* Christ.

Eph. 5.23. Christ is the head of the church :

and he is the saviour of the body. 24. The church is subject unto Christ.

Col. 1.13. Hath translated *us* into the kingdom of his dear Son. 18. He is the head of the body, the church : who is the beginning, the first-born from the dead ; that in all *thing* he might have the pre-eminence.

Col. 2.10. And ye are complete in him, which is the head of all principality and power. 19. The Head, from which all the body by joints and bands having nourishment ministered, and knit together, increaseth with the increase of God. Jno. 15.1-8—Parable of the Vine.

Heb. 3.3. This *man* was counted worthy of more glory than Moses, inasmuch as he who hath builded the house hath more honour than the house. 6. Christ as a son over his own house ; whose house are we.

1 Pet. 2.7. The stone which the builders disallowed, the same is made the head of the corner. Psa. 118.22. Mat. 21.42.

Rev. 1.13. And in the midst of the seven candlesticks *one* like unto the Son of man. 20. The seven candlesticks which thou sawest are the seven churches. *v.* 12-20.

Rev. 2.1. These things saith he that holdeth the seven stars in his right hand, who walketh in the midst of the seven golden candlesticks. 9. I know thy works, and tribulation, and poverty, (but thou art rich) and *I know* the blasphemy of them which say they are Jews, and are not, but *are* the synagogue of Satan. 12. These things saith he which hath the sharp sword with two edges ; 13. I know thy works, and where thou dwellest, *even* where Satan's seat *is* : and thou holdest fast my name, and hast not denied my faith, even in those days wherein Antipas *was* my faithful martyr, who was slain among you, where Satan dwelleth.

Rev. 2.18. The Son of God, who hath his eyes like unto a flame of fire, and his feet *are* like fine brass ; 19. I know thy works, and charity, and service, and faith, and thy patience, and thy works ; and the last *to be* more than the first.

Rev. 3.1. He that hath the seven Spirits of God, and the seven stars. 7. These things saith he that is holy, he that is true, he that hath the key of David, he that openeth, and no man shutteth ; and shutteth, and no man openeth.

Rev. 5.6. Lo, in the midst of the throne and of the four beasts, and in the midst of the elders, stood a Lamb as it had been slain, having seven horns and seven eyes, which are the seven Spirits of God sent forth into all the earth.

Rev. 21.22. I saw no temple therein : for the Lord God Almighty and the Lamb are the temple of it. 23. And the city had no need of the sun, neither of the moon, to shine in it : for the glory of God did lighten it, and the Lamb *is* the light thereof.

Rev. 22.16. I Jesus have sent mine angel to testify unto you these things in the churches. I am the root and the offspring of David, *and* the bright and morning star.

See CHRIST, KING—UNION TO CHRIST.

CHRIST, HIGH-PRIEST AND MEDIATOR. Psa. 110.4. The Lord hath sworn, and will not repent, Thou *art* a priest for ever after the order of Melchizedek.

Isa. 53.12. He bare the sin of many, and made intercession for the transgressors.

Zec. 6.13. He shall be a priest upon his throne: and the counsel of peace shall be between them both.

Luk. 22.32. I have prayed for thee that thy faith fail not.

Luk. 23.34. Father, forgive them; for they know not what they do.

Jno. 14.6. I am the way, and the truth, and the life: no man cometh unto the Father, but by me.

Jno. 17.9. I pray for them: I pray not for the world, but for them which thou hast given me; for they are thine. 11. Holy Father, keep through thine own name those whom thou hast given me, that they may be one, as we *are*. 20. Neither pray I for these alone, but for them also which shall believe on me through their word. *v.* 1-26.

Rom. 8.34. Who also maketh intercession for us.

Eph. 2.13. But now, in Christ Jesus, ye who sometimes were far off are made nigh by the blood of Christ. 18. For through him we both have access by one Spirit unto the Father.

1 Tim. 2.5. *There is* one God, and one mediator between God and men, the man Christ Jesus.

Heb. 2.17. In all things it behoved him to be made like unto *his* brethren, that he might be a merciful and faithful high-priest in things *pertaining* to God, to make reconciliation for the sins of the people.

Heb. 3.1. The Apostle and High-priest of our profession, Christ Jesus; 2. Who was faithful to him that appointed him, as also Moses *was faithful* in all his house.

Heb. 4.14. Seeing then that we have a great high-priest, that is passed into the heavens, Jesus the Son of God, let us hold fast *our* profession. 15. For we have not an high-priest which cannot be touched with the feeling of our infirmities; but was in all points tempted like as *we are, yet* without sin.

Heb. 5.5. Christ glorified not himself to be made an high-priest; but he that said unto him, Thou art my Son, to-day have I begotten thee. 6. As he saith also in another *place*, Thou *art* a priest for ever after the order of Melchisedec. 10. Called of God an high-priest after the order of Melchisedec. *v.* 1-6.

Heb. 6.20. The forerunner is for us entered, *even* Jesus, made an high-priest for ever after the order of Melchisedec.

Heb. 7.3. Without father, without mother, without descent, having neither beginning of days, nor end of life; but made like unto the Son of God; abideth a priest continually. 24. This *man*, because he continueth ever, hath an unchangeable priesthood. 25. Wherefore he is able also to save them to the uttermost that come unto God by him, seeing he ever liveth to make intercession for them. 26. For such an high-priest became us, *who is* holy, harmless, undefiled, separate from sinners, and made higher than the heavens;

Heb. 7.27. Who needeth not daily, as those high-priests, to offer up sacrifice, first for his own sins, and then for the people's: for this he did once, when he offered up himself. 28. For the law maketh men high-priests which have infirmity; but the word of the oath, which was since the law, *maketh* the Son, who is consecrated for evermore. *v.* 1-28.

Heb. 8.1. We have such an high-priest, who is set on the right hand of the throne of the Majesty in the heavens; 2. A minister of the sanctuary, and of the true tabernacle, which the Lord pitched, and not man. 6. He obtained a more excellent ministry, by how much also he is the mediator of a better covenant, which was established upon better promises.

Heb. 9.11. Christ being come an high-priest of good things to come, by a greater and more perfect tabernacle, not made with hands, that is to say, not of this building; 12. Neither by the blood of goats and calves, but by his own blood he entered in once into the holy place, having obtained eternal redemption *for us*. 15. For this cause he is the mediator of the new testament, that by means of death, for the redemption of the transgressions *that were* under the first testament, they which are called might receive the promise of eternal inheritance.

Heb. 9.24. Christ is not entered into the holy places made with hands, *which are* the figures of the true; but into heaven itself, now to appear in the presence of God for us. *v.* 11-28. See Rev. 8.3,4.

Heb. 10.11. Every priest standeth daily ministering and offering oftentimes the same sacrifices, which can never take away sins: 12. But this man, after he had offered one sacrifice for sins for ever, sat down on the right hand of God. 21. An high-priest over the house of God. *v.* 1-21.

Heb. 12.24. Jesus the mediator of the new covenant, and to the blood of sprinkling, that speaketh better things than *that of* Abel.

1 Jno. 2.1. If any man sin, we have an advocate with the Father, Jesus Christ the righteous.

CHRIST, HOLINESS AND PERFECTIONS OF.

Job 33.23. One among a thousand.

Psa. 40.8. I delight to do thy will, O my God: yea, thy law *is* within my heart.

Psa. 45.2. Thou art fairer than the children of men: grace is poured into thy lips. 7. Thou lovest righteousness, and hatest wickedness. (Song of Solomon throughout). Heb. 1.9.

Psa. 89.19. Thou speakest in vision to thy holy one.

Isa. 11.5. Righteousness shall be the girdle of his loins, and faithfulness the girdle of his reins. *v.* 2-5.

Isa. 32.1. Behold, a king shall reign in righteousness.

Isa. 42.21. The Lord is well pleased for his righteousness' sake; he will magnify the law, and make *it* honourable.

Isa. 49.2. A polished shaft.

Isa. 50.5. The Lord God hath opened mine ear, and I was not rebellious, neither turned away back.

Isa. 53.9. He had done no violence, neither *was any* deceit in his mouth.

Isa. 59.17. He put on righteousness as a breastplate, and an helmet of salvation upon his head; and he put on the garments of vengeance *for* clothing, and was clad with zeal as a cloke.

Jer. 23.5. I will raise unto David a righteous Branch.

Eze. 34.29. I will raise up for them a plant of renown.

Mic. 5.4. He shall stand and feed in the strength of the Lord, in the majesty of the name of the Lord his God.

Hag. 2.7. The desire of all nations.

Zec. 9.9. He is just, and having salvation; lowly.

Mat. 3.15. Suffer it to be so now: for thus it becometh us to fulfil all righteousness. 17. This is my beloved Son, in whom I am well pleased.

Mat. 5.17. I am not come to destroy, but to fulfil.

Mat. 12.41. A greater than Jonas is here. 42. A greater than Solomon is here.

Mat. 17.27. Lest we should offend them, take, and give unto them for me and thee.

Mat. 27.4. I have betrayed the innocent blood. 19. Have thou nothing to do with that just man.

Mar. 15.14. Why what evil hath he done?

Luk. 1.35. That holy thing which shall be born of thee shall be called the Son of God.

Luk. 2.49. Wist ye not that I must be about my Father's business?

Luk. 3.16. One mightier than I cometh, the latchet of whose shoes I am not worthy to unloose. Mat. 3.11. Mar. 1.7,8.

Luk. 4.34. I know thee who thou art; the Holy One of God. Mar. 1.25.

Luk. 23.41. This man hath done nothing amiss. 47. Certainly this was a righteous man.

Jno. 1.14. We beheld his glory, the glory as of the only-begotten of the Father, full of grace and truth. 18. The only-begotten Son, which is in the bosom of the Father.

Jno. 4.34. My meat is to do the will of him that sent me, and to finish his work.

Jno. 5.30. My judgment is just; because I seek not mine own will, but the will of the Father which hath sent me. 34. I receive not testimony from man. 41. I receive not honour from men.

Jno. 6.38. I came down from heaven, not to do mine own will, but the will of him that sent me.

Jno. 7.18. He that seeketh his glory that sent him, the same is true, and no unrighteousness is in him.

Jno. 8.29. I do always those things that please him. 46. Which of you convinceth me of sin? 55. I know him, and keep his saying.

Jno. 14.30. The prince of this world cometh, and hath nothing in me. (See the Temptation, Mat. 4.1-10). 31. I love the Father; and as the Father gave me commandment, even so I do.

Jno. 15.10. I have kept my Father's commandments, and abide in his love. 15. All things that I have heard of my Father I have made known unto you.

Jno. 16.10. Of righteousness, because I go to my Father, and ye see me no more.

Jno. 17.4. I have glorified thee on the earth: I have finished the work which thou gavest me to do.' 14. I am not of the world. v. 16.

Jno. 18.20. I spake openly to the world; I ever taught in the synagogue, and in the temple, whither the Jews always resort; and in secret have I said nothing. 21. Why askest thou me? ask them which heard me, what I have said unto them: behold, they know what I said.

Jno. 19.6. I find no fault in him. 30. He said, It is finished. Luk. 23.14.

Act. 3.14. The Holy One and the Just.

Act. 4.27. Thy holy child Jesus.

Act. 13.28. They found no cause of death in him.

Act. 22.14. That Just One.

Rom. 5.19. By the obedience of one shall many be made righteous. v. 15-21.

1 Cor. 1.24. Christ the power of God, and the wisdom of God.

1 Cor. 15.45. The last Adam was made a quickening spirit. 47. The second man is the Lord from heaven.

2 Cor. 1.19. The Son of God, Jesus Christ, was not yea and nay, but in him was yea.

2 Cor. 4.4. Who is the image of God.

2 Cor. 5.21. Who knew no sin.

2 Cor. 9.15. His unspeakable gift.

Eph. 3.8. The unsearchable riches of Christ.

Col. 1.19. It pleased the Father that in him should all fulness dwell.

2 The. 3.3. The Lord is faithful.

2 Tim. 2.13. He abideth faithful: he cannot deny himself.

Heb. 1.3. The brightness of his glory, and the express image of his person.

Heb. 3.2. Who was faithful to him that appointed him.

Heb. 4.15. We have not an high-priest which cannot be touched with the feeling of our infirmities; but was in all points tempted like as we are, yet without sin.

Heb. 7.26. Such an high-priest became us, who is holy, harmless, undefiled, separate from sinners.

Heb. 9.14. Christ, who through the eternal Spirit offered himself without spot to God.

Jas. 2.7. That worthy name by the which ye are called.

1 Pet. 1.19. A lamb without blemish and without spot.

1 Pet. 2.22. Who did no sin, neither was guile found in his mouth: 23. Who, when he was reviled, reviled not again; when he suffered, he threatened not; but committed himself to him that judgeth righteously.

1 Jno. 2.29. Ye know that he is righteous.

1 Jno. 3.5. In him is no sin.

Rev. 3.7. He that is holy, he that is true. 21. I also overcame.

CHRIST, Humility of. See CHRIST, MEEKNESS OF.

————, Incarnation of. Gen. 3.15. I will put enmity between thee and the woman, and between thy seed and her seed; it shall bruise thy head, and thou shalt bruise his heel.

1 Chr. 5.2. Judah prevailed above his brethren, and of him came the chief ruler.

Psa. 80.17. Let thy hand be upon the man of thy right hand, upon the son of man whom thou madest strong for thyself.

Psa. 89.19. Thou spakest in vision to thy Holy One, and saidst, I have laid help upon one that is mighty; I have exalted one chosen out of the people.

Isa. 9.6. Unto us a child is born, unto us a son is given.

Isa. 11.1. There shall come forth a rod out of the stem of Jesse, and a Branch shall grow out of his roots. See GENEALOGIES. Mat. 1.1-17. Luk. 3.23-38.

Isa. 32.2. And a man shall be as an hiding-place from the wind, and a covert from the tempest; as rivers of water in a dry place, as the shadow of a great rock in a weary land.

Jer. 23.5. Behold, the days come, saith the Lord, that I will raise unto David a righteous Branch, and a King shall reign and prosper, and shall execute judgment and justice in the earth.

Mic. 5.2. Out of thee shall he come forth unto me *that is* to be ruler in Israel.

Mat. 1.18. The birth of Jesus Christ was on this wise: When as his mother Mary was espoused to Joseph, before they came together, she was found with child of the Holy Ghost. 23. Behold, a virgin shall be with child, and shall bring forth a son, and they shall call his name Emmanuel, which being interpreted is, God with us. Isa. 7.14.

Mat. 8.20. The Son of man hath not where to lay *his* head.

Mat. 13.55. Is not this the carpenter's son? is not his mother called Mary? and his brethren, James, and Joses, and Simon, and Judas? 56. And his sisters, are they not all with us?

Mat. 22.45. If David then call him Lord, how is he his son?

Luk. 1.30. Fear not, Mary: for thou hast found favour with God. 31. And, behold, thou shalt conceive in thy womb, and bring forth a son, and shalt call his name JESUS. 43. Whence *is* this to me, that the mother of my Lord should come to me?

Luk. 2.7. She brought forth her firstborn son, and wrapped him in swaddling clothes, and laid him in a manger. *v.* 12. 40. The child grew, and waxed strong in spirit, filled with wisdom: and the grace of God was upon him. 52. Jesus increased in wisdom and stature, and in favour with God and man. *v.* 40-52.

Luk. 24.39. Behold my hands and my feet, that it is I myself: handle me, and see; for a spirit hath not flesh and bones, as ye see me have.

Jno. 1.14. The Word was made flesh, and dwelt among us, (and we beheld his glory, the glory as of the only-begotten of the Father,) full of grace and truth.

Jno. 4.22. Salvation is of the Jews.

Jno. 7.28. Ye both know me, and ye know whence I am.

Jno. 20.27. Reach hither thy finger, and behold my hands; and reach hither thy hand, and thrust *it* into my side: and be not faithless, but believing.

Act. 2.30. Knowing that God had sworn with an oath to him, that of the fruit of his loins, according to the flesh, he would raise up Christ to sit on his throne. 2 Sam. 7.12. Psa. 89.35,36.

Act. 3.22. Moses truly said unto the fathers, A prophet shall the Lord your God raise up unto you of your brethren, like unto me. Deu. 18.15-19.

Act. 13.23. Of this man's seed hath God according to *his* promise raised unto Israel a Saviour, Jesus.

Rom. 1.3. His Son Jesus Christ our Lord, which was made of the seed of David according to the flesh.

Rom. 8.3. God sending his own Son in the likeness of sinful flesh, and for sin, condemned sin in the flesh.

Rom. 9.5. Of whom as concerning the flesh Christ *came*.

Gal. 3.16. To Abraham and his seed were the promises made. He saith not, And to seeds, as of many; but as of one, And to thy seed, which is Christ. Gen. 12.3. Gen. 17.7. Gen. 22.18.

Gal. 4.4. When the fulness of the time was come, God sent forth his Son, made of a woman, made under the law.

Eph. 4.9. Now that he ascended, what is it but that he also descended first into the lower parts of the earth?

Phil. 2.7. Made himself of no reputation, and took upon him the form of a servant, and was made in the likeness of men: 8. And being found in fashion as a man, he humbled himself, and became obedient unto death.

Col. 2.9. In him dwelleth all the fulness of the Godhead bodily.

1 Tim. 2.5. One mediator between God and men, the man Christ Jesus.

1 Tim. 3.16. Great, is the mystery of godliness: God was manifest in the flesh.

Heb. 2.9. We see Jesus, who was made a little lower than the angels for the suffering of death. 14. As the children are partakers of flesh and blood, he also himself likewise took part of the same. 16. He took not on *him the nature of* angels; but he took on *him* the seed of Abraham.

Heb. 2.17. In all things it behoved him to be made like unto *his* brethren, that he might be a merciful and faithful high-priest in things *pertaining* to God, to make reconciliation for the sins of the people. 18. For in that he himself hath suffered being tempted, he is able to succour them that are tempted. *v.* 9-17.

Heb. 4.15. For we have not an high-priest which cannot be touched with the feeling of our infirmities; but was in all points tempted like as *we are, yet* without sin.

Heb. 7.14. *It is* evident that our Lord sprang out of Juda. Psa. 40.6,7.

Heb. 10.5. A body hast thou prepared me.

1 Jno. 1.1. That which was from the beginning, which we have heard, which we have seen with our eyes, which we have looked upon, and our hands have handled, of the Word of life; 2. For the life was manifested, and we have seen *it,* and bear witness, and shew unto you that eternal life, which was with the Father, and was manifested unto us.

1 Jno. 4.2. Every spirit that confesseth that Jesus Christ is come in the flesh is of God: 3. And every spirit that confesseth not that Jesus Christ is come in the flesh is not of God: and this is that *spirit* of antichrist, whereof ye have heard that it should come; and even now already is it in the world.

Rev. 22.16. I am the root and the offspring of David.

CHRIST, INTERCESSION OF. See CHRIST, HIGH-PRIEST.

————, JEWS' RECEPTION OF. JEWISH VIEWS RESPECTING. Isa. 8.14. He shall be for a sanctuary; but for a stone of stumbling and for a rock of offence to both the houses of Israel, for a gin and for a snare to the inhabitants of Jerusalem.

Isa. 49.4. I have laboured in vain, I have spent my strength for nought, and in vain.

Isa. 53.1. Who hath believed our report? and to whom is the arm of the Lord revealed? 2. For he shall grow up before him as a tender plant, and as a root out of a dry ground: he hath no form nor comeliness; and when we shall see him, *there is* no beauty that we should desire him. 3. He is despised and rejected of men; a man of sorrows, and acquainted with grief: and we hid as it were *our* faces from him; he was despised, and we esteemed him not. 4. We did esteem him stricken, smitten of God, and afflicted.

Mat. 4.25. There followed him great multitudes of people from Galilee.   Mat. 8.1. Mat. 19.1,2.   Mar. 10.1.   Mar. 3.7.   Mar. 5.21.

Mat. 7.28. When Jesus had ended these sayings, the people were astonished at his doctrine: 29. For he taught them as *one* having authority, and not as the scribes. Mar. 1.22.   Luk. 4.32.

Mat. 9.8. When the multitudes saw *it*, they marvelled, and glorified God, which had given such power unto men. 27. Two blind men followed him, crying, and saying, *Thou* son of David, have mercy on us. 33. The multitudes marvelled, saying, It was never so seen in Israel. 34. But the Pharisees said, He casteth out devils through the prince of the devils.

Mat. 12.22. The blind and dumb both spake and saw. 23. And all the people were amazed, and said, Is not this the son of David?

Mat. 13.2. Great multitudes were gathered together unto him, so that he went into a ship, and sat; and the whole multitude stood on the shore. 54. They were astonished, and said, Whence hath this *man* this wisdom, and *these* mighty works?   Mar. 4.1.   Mar. 6.2.

Mat. 14.33. Came and worshipped him, saying, Of a truth thou art the Son of God. Mar. 6.51,52.

Mat. 16.1. The Pharisees also with the Sadducees came, and tempting desired him that he would shew them a sign from heaven. 14. Some *say that thou art* John the Baptist: some, Elias; and others, Jeremias, or one of the prophets. Mat. 12.38. Mar. 8.11. Luk. 11.16.   Mar. 8.28.   Luk. 9.19.

Mat. 17.10. His disciples asked him, saying, Why then say the scribes that Elias must first come?   Mar. 9.11.

Mat. 21.8. A very great multitude spread their garments in the way; others cut down branches from the trees, and strawed *them* in the way. 9. And the multitudes that went before, and that followed, cried, saying, Hosanna to the son of David: Blessed *is* he that cometh in the name of the Lord; Hosanna in the highest. 10. And when he was come into Jerusalem, all the city was moved, saying, Who is this? Mar. 11.8-10. Luk. 19. 36-38.   Jno. 12.12,13.

Mat. 21.11. And the multitude said, This is Jesus the prophet of Nazareth of Galilee. 15. When the chief priests and scribes saw the wonderful things that he did, and the children crying in the temple, and saying, Hosanna to the son of David; they were sore displeased. 45. When the chief priests and Pharisees had heard his parables, they perceived that he spake of them. 46. But when they sought to lay hands on him, they feared the multitude,

because they took him for a prophet. Mar. 12.12.   Luk. 20.19.

Mat. 22.42. What think ye of Christ? whose son is he? They say unto him, *The son* of David. 46. No man was able to answer him a word, neither durst any *man* from that day forth ask him any more *questions.*

Mat. 26.5. They said, Not on the feast *day*, lest there be an uproar among the people. 63. The high-priest said unto him, I adjure thee by the living God, that thou tell us whether thou be the Christ, the Son of God. Mar. 14.2,61.

Mat. 27.54. When the centurion, and they that were with him, watching Jesus, saw the earthquake, and those things that were done, they feared greatly, saying, Truly this was the Son of God.   Mar. 15.39.   Luk. 23.47.

Mar. 1.37. When they had found him, they said unto him, All *men* seek for thee.

Mar. 2.2. Many were gathered together, insomuch that there was no room to receive *them*, no, not so much as about the door: and he preached the word unto them. 12. They were all amazed, and glorified God, saying, We never saw it on this fashion. 15. As Jesus sat at meat in his house, many publicans and sinners sat also together with Jesus and his disciples: for there were many, and they followed him.   Mar. 1.33.

Mar. 3.20. The multitude cometh together again, so that they could not so much as eat bread. 21. When his friends heard *of it*, they went out to lay hold on him: for they said, He is beside himself.

Mar. 5.42. They were astonished with a great astonishment. Luk. 8.56.

Mar. 6.33. The people saw them departing, and many knew him, and ran afoot thither out of all cities, and outwent them, and came together unto him. 55. Ran through that whole region round about, and began to carry about in beds those that were sick, where they heard he was. 56. And whithersoever he entered, into villages, or cities, or country, they laid the sick in the streets, and besought him that they might touch if it were but the border of his garment. Mat. 14.13,35. Luk. 9.11.   Jno. 6.2.

Mar. 7.37. Were beyond measure astonished, saying, He hath done all things well: he maketh both the deaf to hear, and the dumb to speak. Mat. 15.31.

Mar. 12.37. The common people heard him gladly.

Luk. 4.14. There went out a fame of him through all the region round about. 15. And he taught in their synagogues, being glorified of all. 22. All bare him witness, and wondered at the gracious words which proceeded out of his mouth. And they said, Is not this Joseph's son? 36. They were all amazed, and spake among themselves, saying, What a word *is* this! for with authority and power he commandeth the unclean spirits, and they come out. 42. The people sought him, and came unto him, and stayed him, that he should not depart from them. Mar. 1.27.

Luk. 5.1. The people pressed upon him to hear the word of God. 17. As he was teaching, there were Pharisees and doctors of the law sitting by, which were come out of every town of Galilee, and Judæa, and Jerusalem. 19. When they could not find by what *way* they might bring him in because of the multitude, they went upon the house-top, and let him down through the tiling, with *his* couch, into the midst before Jesus. 26. They were all amazed, and they glorified God, and were filled with fear, saying, We have seen strange things to-day.

Luk. 6.17. He came down with them, and stood in the plain, and the company of his disciples, and a great multitude of people out of all Judæa and Jerusalem, and from the sea-coast of Tyre and Sidon, which came to hear him, and to be healed of their diseases ; 18. And they that were vexed with unclean spirits : and they were healed. 19 And the whole multitude sought to touch him : for there went virtue out of him, and healed *them* all.

Luk. 7.16. There came a fear on all : and they glorified God, saying, That a great prophet is risen up among us ; and, That God hath visited his people. 17. And this rumour of him went forth throughout all Judea, and throughout all the region round about. 18. And the disciples of John shewed him of all these things. 29. All the people that heard *him*, and the publicans, justified God, being baptized with the baptism of John.

Luk. 7.30. But the Pharisees and lawyers rejected the counsel of God against themselves, being not baptized of him. 34. The Son of man is come eating and drinking ; and ye say, Behold a gluttonous man, and a winebibber, a friend of publicans and sinners !

Luk. 8.19. Then came to him *his* mother and his brethren, and could not come at him for the press. 25. They being afraid wondered, saying one to another, What manner of man is this ! for he commandeth even the winds and water, and they obey him. 35. They went out to see what was done ; and came to Jesus, and found the man, out of whom the devils were departed, sitting at the feet of Jesus, clothed, and in his right mind : and they were afraid. 37. Then the whole multitude of the country of the Gadarenes round about besought him to depart from them ; for they were taken with great fear. 40. When Jesus was returned, the people *gladly* received him : for they were all waiting for him. Mat. 8.15-34. Mar. 4.41. Mar. 5.17-21.

Luk. 9.7. Herod the tetrarch heard of all that was done by him : and he was perplexed, because that it was said of some, that John was risen from the dead ; 8. And of some, that Elias had appeared ; and of others, that one of the old prophets was risen again. 9. And Herod said, John have I beheaded : but who is this, of whom I hear such things ? And he desired to see him. Mar. 6.14-16.

Luk. 12.1. There were gathered together an innumerable multitude of people, insomuch that they trode one upon another.

Luk. 13.17. All the people rejoiced for all the glorious things that were done by him.

Luk. 18.43. Immediately he received his sight, and followed him, glorifying God : and all the people, when they saw *it*, gave praise unto God.

Luk. 19.37. When he was come nigh, even now at the descent of the mount of Olives, the whole multitude of the disciples began to rejoice, and praise God with a loud voice, for all the mighty works that they had seen. 48.

Could not find what they might do ; for all the people were very attentive to hear him. Mar. 11.18.

Luk. 21.38. And all the people came early in the morning to him in the temple, for to hear him. Jno. 8.2.

Luk. 23.27. There followed him a great company of people, and of women, which also bewailed and lamented him.

Jno. 2.11. This beginning of miracles did Jesus in Cana of Galilee, and manifested forth his glory ; and his disciples believed on him. 23. When he was in Jerusalem at the passover, in the feast *day*, many believed in his name, when they saw the miracles which he did.

Jno. 3.2. Rabbi, we know that thou art a teacher come from God : for no man can do these miracles that thou doest, except God be with him. 26. The same baptizeth, and all *men* come to him.

Jno. 4.25. I know that Messias cometh, which is called Christ : when he is come, he will tell us all things. 29. Come, see a man, which told me all things that ever I did : is not this the Christ ? 39. Many of the Samaritans of that city believed on him for the saying of the woman, which testified, He told me all that ever I did. 45. When he was come into Galilee, the Galileans received him, having seen all the things that he did at Jerusalem at the feast. 53. The father knew that *it was* at the same hour, in the which Jesus said unto him, Thy son liveth : and himself believed, and his whole house.

Jno. 6.14. When they had seen the miracle that Jesus did, said, This is of a truth that Prophet that should come into the world.

Jno. 7.3. His brethren therefore said unto him, Depart hence, and go into Judea, that thy disciples also may see the works that thou doest. 4. For *there is* no man *that* doeth any thing in secret, and he himself seeketh to be known openly. If thou do these things, shew thyself to the world. 5. For neither did his brethren believe in him. 12. There was much murmuring among the people concerning him : for some said, He is a good man : others said, Nay ; but he deceiveth the people.

Jno. 7.13. Howbeit no man spake openly of him for fear of the Jews. 15. The Jews marvelled, saying, How knoweth this man letters, having never learned ? 25. Then said some of them of Jerusalem, Is not this he, whom they seek to kill ? 26. But, lo, he speaketh boldly, and they say nothing unto him. Do the rulers know indeed that this is the very Christ ? 27. Howbeit we know this man whence he is : but when Christ cometh, no man knoweth whence he is.

Jno. 7.31. Many of the people believed on him, and said, When Christ cometh, will he do more miracles than these which this *man* hath done ? 40. Many of the people therefore, when they heard this saying, said, Of a truth this is the Prophet. 41. Others said, This is the Christ. But some said, Shall Christ come out of Galilee ? 42. Hath not the scripture said, That Christ cometh of the seed of David, and out of the town of Bethlehem, where David was ? 43. So there was a division among the people because of him. 44. And some of them would have taken him ; but no man laid hands on him. 46. Never man spake like this man.

Jno. 8.13. The Pharisees therefore said unto him, Thou bearest record of thyself; thy record is not true. 22. Then said the Jews, Will he kill himself? because he saith, Whither I go, ye cannot come. 30. As he spake these words, many believed on him. 53. Art thou greater than our father Abraham, which is dead? and the prophets are dead: whom makest thou thyself?

Jno. 9.16. Said some of the Pharisees, This man is not of God, because he keepeth not the sabbath day. Others said, How can a man that is a sinner do such miracles? And there was a division among them. 17. They say unto the blind man again, What sayest thou of him, that he hath opened thine eyes? He said, He is a prophet. 24. Give God the praise: we know that this man is a sinner. 25. He answered and said, Whether he be a sinner *or* no, I know not: one thing I know, that, whereas I was blind, now I see. 29. We know that God spake unto Moses: *as for* this *fellow*, we know not from whence he is. 30. Ye know not from whence he is, and *yet* he hath opened mine eyes. 33. If this man were not of God, he could do nothing.

Jno. 10.20. Many of them said, He hath a devil, and is mad; why hear ye him? 21. Others said, These are not the words of him that hath a devil. Can a devil open the eyes of the blind? 24. How long dost thou make us to doubt? If thou be the Christ, tell us plainly. 32. For a good work we stone thee not; but for blasphemy; and because that thou, being a man, makest thyself God. 41. Many resorted unto him, and said, John did no miracle: but all things that John spake of this man were true. 42. And many believed on him there.

Jno. 11.37. Some of them said, Could not this man, which opened the eyes of the blind, have caused that even this man should not have died? 45. Many of the Jews which came to Mary, and had seen the things which Jesus did, believed on him. 46. But some of them went their ways to the Pharisees, and told them what things Jesus had done. 47. Then gathered the chief priests and the Pharisees a council, and said, What do we? for this man doeth many miracles. 48. If we let him thus alone, all *men* will believe on him.

Jno. 12.9. Much people of the Jews therefore knew that he was there: and they came not for Jesus' sake only. 11. By reason of him many of the Jews went away, and believed on Jesus. 18. For this cause the people also met him, for that they heard that he had done this miracle. 19. The Pharisees therefore said among themselves, Perceive ye how ye prevail nothing? behold, the world is gone after him.

Jno. 12.20. There were certain Greeks among them that came up to worship at the feast: 21. The same came therefore to Philip, which was of Bethsaida of Galilee, and desired him, saying, Sir, we would see Jesus. 34. We have heard out of the law that Christ abideth for ever: and how sayest thou, The Son of man must be lifted up? who is this Son of man? 37. Though he had done so many miracles before them, yet they believed not on him.

See Christ, Messiah. Christ, sufferings of. Pharisees.

CHRIST, King and Judge—His Justice.
Gen. 49.10. The sceptre shall not depart from

Judah, nor a lawgiver from between his feet, until Shiloh come; and unto him *shall* the gathering of the people *be.*

Num. 24.17. I shall see him, but not now: I shall behold him, but not nigh: there shall come a Star out of Jacob, and a Sceptre shall rise out of Israel.

1 Sam. 2.10. He shall give strength unto his king, and exalt the horn of his anointed.

Psa. 2.6. Yet have I set my king upon my holy hill of Zion.

Psa. 18.43. Thou hast made me the head of the heathen: a people *whom* I have not known shall serve me. 44. As soon as they hear of me, they shall obey me: the strangers shall submit themselves unto me.

Psa. 24.8. Who *is* this King of glory? The Lord strong and mighty, the Lord mighty in battle. *v.* 7-10.

Psa. 45.3. Gird thy sword upon *thy* thigh, O *most* mighty, with thy glory and thy majesty. 4. And in thy majesty ride prosperously because of truth and meekness *and* righteousness; and thy right hand shall teach thee terrible things. 5. Thine arrows *are* sharp in the heart of the king's enemies; *whereby* the people fall under thee. 6. Thy throne, O God, *is* for ever and ever: the sceptre of thy kingdom *is* a right sceptre. 7. Thou lovest righteousness, and hatest wickedness: therefore God, thy God, hath anointed thee with the oil of gladness above thy fellows. Song 1.4,12.

Psa. 72.2. He shall judge thy people with righteousness, and thy poor with judgment. 4. He shall judge the poor of the people, he shall save the children of the needy, and shall break in pieces the oppressor. 5. They shall fear thee as long as the sun and moon endure, throughout all generations. 8. He shall have dominion also from sea to sea, and from the river unto the ends of the earth. 11. Yea, all kings shall fall down before him: all nations shall serve him.

Psa. 72.17. His name shall endure for ever: his name shall be continued as long as the sun: and *men* shall be blessed in him: all nations shall call him blessed.

Psa. 75.2. When I shall receive the congregation I will judge uprightly. 3. The earth and all the inhabitants thereof are dissolved: I bear up the pillars of it.

Psa. 89.3. I have made a covenant with my chosen, I have sworn unto David my servant. 4. Thy seed will I establish for ever, and build up thy throne to all generations. 19. Thou spakest in vision to thy holy one, and saidst, I have laid help upon *one that is* mighty; I have exalted *one* chosen out of the people. 20. I have found David my servant; with my holy oil have I anointed him: 21. With whom my hand shall be established: mine arm also shall strengthen him. 23. And I will beat down his foes before his face, and plague them that hate him.

Psa. 89.27. I will make him *my* firstborn, higher than the kings of the earth. 29. His seed also will make *to endure* for ever, and his throne as the days of heaven. 36. His seed shall endure for ever, and his throne as the sun before me. 37. It shall be established for ever as the moon, and *as* a faithful witness in heaven.

Psa. 96.13. He cometh to judge the earth

he shall judge the world with righteousness, and the people with his truth.

Psa. 110.1. The Lord said unto my Lord, Sit thou at my right hand, until I make thine enemies thy footstool. 2. The Lord shall send the rod of thy strength out of Zion : rule thou in the midst of thine enemies. Heb. 10.12,13.

Psa. 132.11. The Lord hath sworn *in* truth unto David ; he will not turn from it ; Of the fruit of thy body will I set upon thy throne. 17. There will I make the horn of David to bud : I have ordained a lamp for mine anointed. 18. His enemies will I clothe with shame: but upon himself shall his crown flourish.

Isa. 2.4. He shall judge among the nations, and shall rebuke many people : and they shall beat their swords into plowshares, and their spears into pruninghooks. Mic. 4.3.

Isa. 6.1. I saw also the Lord sitting upon a throne, high and lifted up, and his train filled the temple. *v.* 2,3. Jno. 12.41.

Isa. 9.6. The government shall be upon his shoulder : and his name shall be called Wonderful, Counsellor, The mighty God, The everlasting Father, The Prince of Peace. 7. Of the increase of *his* government and peace *there shall be* no end, upon the throne of David, and upon his kingdom, to order it, and to establish it with judgment and with justice from henceforth even for ever.

Isa. 11.3. He shall not judge after the sight of his eyes, neither reprove after the hearing of his ears : 4. But with righteousness shall he judge the poor, and reprove with equity for the meek of the earth. He shall smite the earth with the rod of his mouth, and with the breath of his lips shall he slay the wicked. 10. In that day there shall be a root of Jesse, which shall stand for an ensign of the people : to it shall the Gentiles seek : and his rest shall be glorious.

Isa. 32.1. Behold, a king shall reign in righteousness, and princes shall rule in judgment.

Isa. 33.17. Thine eyes shall see the king in his beauty.

Isa. 40.10. Behold, the Lord God will come with strong *hand*, and his arm shall rule for him : behold, his reward *is* with him, and his work before him.

Isa. 52.7. How beautiful upon the mountains are the feet of him that bringeth good tidings, that publisheth peace ; that bringeth good tidings of good, that publisheth salvation ; that saith unto Zion, Thy God reigneth ! 13. Behold, my servant shall deal prudently, he shall be exalted and extolled, and be very high.

Isa. 59.18. According to *their* deeds, accordingly he will repay, fury to his adversaries, recompence to his enemies ; to the islands he will repay recompence.

Jer. 23.5. I will raise unto David a righteous Branch, and a King shall reign and prosper, and shall execute judgment and justice in the earth. 6. In his days Judah shall be saved, and Israel shall dwel, safely : and this *is* his name whereby he shall be called, THE LORD OUR RIGHTEOUSNESS. Jer. 33. 15,16.

Jer. 30.9. They shall serve the Lord their God, and David their king, whom I will raise up unto them.

Eze. 17.22. I will also take of the highest branch of the high cedar, and will set *it* ; I will crop off from the top of his young twigs a tender one, and will plant *it* upon an high mountain and eminent : 23. In the mountain of the height of Israel will I plant it : and it shall bring forth boughs, and bear fruit, and be a goodly cedar : and under it shall dwell all fowl of every wing ; in the shadow of the branches thereof shall they dwell. 24. And all the trees of the field shall know that I the Lord have brought down the high tree, have exalted the low tree, have dried up the green tree, and have made the dry tree to flourish · I the Lord have spoken and have done *it.*

Eze. 21.27. I will overturn, overturn, overturn, it : and it shall be no *more*, until he come whose right it is ; and I will give it *him.*

Eze. 34.23. I will set up one shepherd over them, and he shall feed them, *even* my servant David ; he shall feed them, and he shall be their shepherd. 24. And I the Lord will be their God, and my servant David a prince among them ; I the Lord have spoken *it.*

Eze. 37.24. David my servant *shall be* king over them ; and they all shall have one shepherd : they shall also walk in my judgments, and observe my statutes, and do them. 25. And they shall dwell in the land that I have given unto Jacob my servant, wherein your fathers have dwelt ; and they shall dwell therein, *even* they, and their children, and their children's children for ever : and my servant David *shall be* their prince for ever.

Dan. 2.35. The stone that smote the image became a great mountain, and filled the whole earth. 44. And in the days of these kings shall the God of heaven set up a kingdom, which shall never be destroyed : and the kingdom shall not be left to other people, *but* it shall break in pieces and consume all these kingdoms, and it shall stand for ever.

Dan. 7.13. Behold, *one* like the Son of man came with the clouds of heaven, and came to the Ancient of days, and they brought him near before him. 14. There was given him dominion, and glory, and a kingdom, that all people, nations, and languages, should serve him : his dominion *is* an everlasting dominion, which shall not pass away, and his kingdom *that* which shall not be destroyed.

Dan. 8.25. He shall also stand up against the Prince of princes ; but he shall be broken without hand.

Dan. 9.25. From the going forth of the commandment to restore and to build Jerusalem unto the Messiah the Prince *shall be* seven weeks, and threescore and two weeks.

Hos. 3.5. Afterward shall the children of Israel return, and seek the Lord their God, and David their king ; and shall fear the Lord and his goodness in the latter days.

Mic. 5.1. They shall smite the judge of Israel with a rod upon the cheek. 2. Out of thee shall he come forth unto me *that is* to be ruler in Israel ; whose goings forth *have been* from of old, from everlasting. 4. And he shall stand and feed in the strength of the Lord, in the majesty of the name of the Lord his God ; and they shall abide : for now shall he be great unto the ends of the earth. Mat. 2.6.

Zec. 6.13. He shall build the temple of the Lord ; and he shall bear the glory, and shall sit and rule upon his throne ; and he shall be a priest upon his throne : and the counsel of peace shall be between them both.

Zec. 9.9. Rejoice greatly, O daughter of Zion; shout, O daughter of Jerusalem: behold, thy king cometh unto thee: he *is* just, and having salvation. 10. He shall speak peace unto the heathen: and his dominion *shall be* from sea *even* to sea, and from the river *even* to the ends of the earth. Mat. 21.5.

Mal. 3.2. Who may abide the day of his coming? and who shall stand when he appeareth? for he *is* like a refiner's fire, and like fuller's sope: 3. He shall sit *as* a refiner and purifier of silver: and he shall purify the sons of Levi, and purge them as gold and silver, that they may offer unto the Lord an offering in righteousness.

Mat. 2.2. Where is he that is born King of the Jews? for we have seen his star in the east, and are come to worship him.

Mat. 3.12. Whose fan *is* in his hand, and he will thoroughly purge his floor, and gather his wheat into the garner; but he will burn up the chaff with unquenchable fire. Luk. 3.17.

Mat. 12.6. In this place is *one* greater than the temple.

Mat. 13.41. The Son of man shall send forth his angels, and they shall gather out of his kingdom all things that offend, and them which do iniquity.

Mat. 16.27. The Son of man shall come in the glory of his Father with his angels; and then he shall reward every man according to his works. 28. There be some standing here which shall not taste of death till they see the Son of man coming in his kingdom.

Mat. 19.28. In the regeneration when the Son of man shall sit in the throne of his glory, ye also shall sit upon twelve thrones.

Mat. 25.31. When the Son of man shall come in his glory, and all the holy angels with him, then shall he sit upon the throne of his glory: 32. And before him shall be gathered all nations: and he shall separate them one from another, as a shepherd divideth *his* sheep from the goats: 33. And he shall set the sheep on his right hand, but the goats on the left. 34. Then shall the King say unto them on his right hand, Come, ye blessed of my Father.

Mat. 26.64. Hereafter shall ye see the Son of man sitting on the right hand of power, and coming in the clouds of heaven. Mar. 14.62. Luk. 22.69.

Mat 28.18. All power is given unto me in heaven and in earth.

Luk. 1.32. He shall be great, and shall be called the Son of the Highest: and the Lord God shall give unto him the throne of his father David. 33. He shall reign over the house of Jacob for ever; and of his kingdom there shall be no end.

Luk. 10.22. All things are delivered to me of my Father. Mat. 11.27.

Luk. 19.27. Those mine enemies, which would not that I should reign over them, bring hither, and slay *them* before me.

Luk. 22.29. I appoint unto you a kingdom, as my Father hath appointed unto me; 30. That ye may eat and drink at my table in my kingdom, and sit on thrones judging the twelve tribes of Israel.

Luk. 23.42. Lord remember me when thou comest into thy kingdom.

Jno. 1.49. ... Thou art the King of Israel.

Jno. 3.31. He that is of the earth is earthly, and speaketh of the earth: he that cometh from heaven is above all. 35. The Father loveth the Son, and hath given all things into his hand.

Jno. 5.22. The Father judgeth no man, but hath committed all judgment unto the Son: 23. That all *men* should honour the Son, even as they honour the Father. 27. Hath given him authority to execute judgment also, because he is the Son of man. 30. I can of mine own self do nothing: as I hear, I judge: and my judgment is just.

Jno. 8.16. If I judge, my judgment is true: for I am not alone, but I and the Father that sent me.

Jno. 12.13. Hosanna: Blessed *is* the King of Israel that cometh in the name of the Lord. 15. Fear not, daughter of Sion: behold, thy King cometh, sitting on an ass's colt.

Jno. 13.3. Jesus knowing that the Father had given all things into his hands.

Jno. 18.36. My kingdom is not of this world: if my kingdom were of this world, then would my servants fight, that I should not be delivered to the Jews: but now is my kingdom not from hence. 37. Pilate therefore said unto him, Art thou a king then? Jesus answered, Thou sayest that I am a king. To this end was I born.

Jno. 19.19. Pilate wrote a title, and put *it* on the cross. And the writing was, JESUS OF NAZARETH THE KING OF THE JEWS.

Act. 2.30. Knowing that God had sworn with an oath to him, that of the fruit of his loins, according to the flesh, he would raise up Christ to sit on his throne.

Act. 3.15. And killed the Prince of life, whom God hath raised from the dead.

Act. 5.31. Him hath God exalted with his right hand *to be* a Prince and a Saviour.

Act. 10.36. Jesus Christ he is Lord of all. 42. It is he which was ordained of God *to be* the Judge of quick and dead. Rom. 10.12.

Act. 17.31. He hath appointed a day, in the which he will judge the world in righteousness by *that* man whom he hath ordained; *whereof* he hath given assurance unto all *men*, in that he hath raised him from the dead.

Rom. 2.16. God shall judge the secrets of men by Jesus Christ according to my gospel.

Rom. 9.5. Christ, who is over all, God blessed for ever.

Rom. 14.9. To this end Christ both died, and rose, and revived, that he might be Lord both of the dead and living. 10. We shall all stand before the judgment-seat of Christ.

1 Cor. 2.8. Had they known *it*, they would not have crucified the Lord of glory. Jas. 2.1.

1 Cor. 4.4. He that judgeth me is the Lord. 5. Judge nothing before the time, until the Lord come, who both will bring to light the hidden things of darkness, and will make manifest the counsels of the hearts.

1 Cor. 15.24. He shall have put down all rule and all authority and power. 25. For he must reign, till he hath put all enemies under his feet. 26. The last enemy *that* shall be destroyed *is* death. 27. For he hath put all things under his feet. 28. All things shall be subdued unto him.

2 Cor. 5.10. We must all appear before the judgment-seat of Christ; that every one may receive the things *done* in *his* body, according to that he hath done, whether *it be* good or bad.

Eph. 1.20. Set *him* at his own right hand in the heavenly *places*, 21. Far above all principality, and power, and might, and dominion, and every name that is named, not only in this world, but also in that which is to come : 22. And hath put all *things* under his feet.

Eph. 4.10. He that descended is the same also that ascended up far above all heavens, that he might fill all things.

Phil. 2.9. God also hath highly exalted him, and given him a name which is above every name : 10. That at the name of Jesus every knee should bow, of *things* in heaven, and *things* in earth, and *things* under the earth ; 11. And *that* every tongue should confess that Jesus Christ *is* Lord, to the glory of God the Father.

Col. 1.15. Who is the image of the invisible God, the firstborn of every creature : 16. All things were created by him, and for him.

2 The. 1.7. And to you who are troubled rest with us, when the Lord Jesus shall be revealed from heaven with his mighty angels, 8. In flaming fire taking vengeance on them that know not God, and that obey not the gospel of our Lord Jesus Christ.

1 Tim. 6.15. *Who is* the blessed and only Potentate, the King of kings, and Lord of lords ; 16. To whom be honour and power everlasting.

2 Tim. 4.1. The Lord Jesus Christ, who shall judge the quick and the dead at his appearing and his kingdom. 8. There is laid up for me a crown of righteousness, which the Lord, the righteous Judge, shall give me at that day.

Heb. 1.2. *His* Son, whom he hath appointed heir of all things. 3. Who being the brightness of *his* glory, and the express image of his person, and upholding all things by the word of his power, when he had by himself purged our sins, sat down on the right hand of the Majesty on high ; 4. Being made so much better than the angels, as he hath by inheritance obtained a more excellent name than they.

Heb. 2.7. Thou madest him a little lower than the angels : thou crownedst him with glory and honour, and didst set him over the works of thy hands. 8. Thou hast put all things in subjection under his feet. For in that he put all in subjection under him, he left nothing *that is* not put under him.

Heb. 7.26. Made higher than the heavens.

Jas. 5.9. Behold, the Judge standeth before the door.

1 Pet. 3.22. Is on the right hand of God ; angels and authorities and powers being made subject unto him.

Jude 14. Behold, the Lord cometh with ten thousand of his saints, 15. To execute judgment upon all, and to convince all that are ungodly among them of all their ungodly deeds which they have ungodly committed, and of all their hard *speeches* which ungodly sinners have spoken against him.

Rev. 1.5. Jesus Christ, *who is* the faithful witness, *and* the first-begotten of the dead, and the prince of the kings of the earth. Unto him that loved us, and washed us from our sins in his own blood, 6. And hath made us kings and priests unto God and his Father ; to him *be* glory and dominion for ever and ever. Amen. 7. Behold, he cometh with clouds ; and every eye shall see him, and they *also* which pierced him : and all kindreds of the earth shall wail because of him. 18. *I am* he that liveth, and was dead ; and, behold, I am alive for evermore, Amen ; and have the keys of hell and of death.

Rev. 2.23. I will kill her children with death ; and all the churches shall know that I am he which searcheth the reins and hearts : and I will give unto every one of you according to your works.

Rev. 3.7. He that hath the key of David, he that openeth, and no man shutteth ; and shutteth, and no man openeth. 14. These things saith the Amen, the faithful and true witness, the beginning of the creation of God. 21. To him that overcometh will I grant to sit with me in my throne, even as I also overcame, and am set down with my Father in his throne.
Isa. 22.22.

Rev. 5.5. The Lion of the tribe of Juda. 12. Worthy is the Lamb that was slain to receive power, and riches, and wisdom, and strength, and honour, and glory, and blessing.

Rev. 6.16. Hide us from the face of him that sitteth on the throne, and from the wrath of the Lamb : 17. For the great day of his wrath is come ; and who shall be able to stand ?

Rev. 11.15. The kingdoms of this world are become *the kingdoms* of our Lord, and of his Christ ; and he shall reign for ever and ever.

Rev. 12.10. Now is come salvation, and strength, and the kingdom of our God, and the power of his Christ : for the accuser of our brethren is cast down.

Rev. 14.14. Behold a white cloud, and upon the cloud *one* sat like unto the Son of man, having on his head a golden crown, and in his hand a sharp sickle.

Rev. 17.14. These shall make war with the Lamb, and the Lamb shall overcome them : for he is Lord of lords, and King of kings.

Rev. 19.11. I saw heaven opened, and behold a white horse : and he that sat upon him *was* called Faithful and True, and in righteousness he doth judge and make war. 12. His eyes *were* as a flame of fire, and on his head *were* many crowns ; and he had a name written, that no man knew, but he himself. 15. Out of his mouth goeth a sharp sword, that with it he should smite the nations : and he shall rule them with a rod of iron : and he treadeth the winepress of the fierceness and wrath of Almighty God. 16. He hath on *his* vesture and on his thigh a name written, KING OF KINGS, AND LORD OF LORDS.

Rev. 20.4. I saw thrones, and they sat upon them, and judgment was given unto them : and *I saw* the souls of them that were beheaded for the witness of Jesus, and for the word of God, and which had not worshipped the beast, neither his image, neither had received *his* mark upon their foreheads, or in their hands ; and they lived and reigned with Christ a thousand years. 6. Blessed and holy *is* he that hath part in the first resurrection : on such the second death hath no power ; but they shall be priests of God and of Christ, and shall reign with him a thousand years.

CHRIST, KINGDOM OF. See **CHURCH, PROPHECIES OF.**

CHRIST, LIFE OF. (*From Robinson's Harmony*).	MATT.	MARK.	LUKE.	JOHN.
I. EVENTS CONNECTED WITH HIS BIRTH AND CHILDHOOD. Time: *About thirteen years and a half*.				
Preface to Luke's Gospel.			1. 1-4	
An angel appears to Zacharias.—*Jerusalem; in the Temple.*			1. 5-25	
The same angel appears to Mary.—*Nazareth.*			1. 26-38	
Mary visits Elizabeth.—*Jutta?*			1. 39-56	
Birth of John the Baptist.—*Jutta?*			1. 57-80	
An angel appears to Joseph.—*Nazareth.*	1. 18-25			
The birth of Jesus.—*Bethlehem.*			2. 1-7	
An angel appears to the shepherds.—*Near Bethlehem.*			2. 8-20	
The circumcision of Jesus, and his presentation in the Temple.—*Bethlehem. Jerusalem.*			2. 21-38	
The Magi.—*Jerusalem. Bethlehem.*	2. 1-12			
The flight into Egypt. Herod's cruelty. The return. —*Bethlehem. Nazareth.*	2. 13-23		2. 39,40	
At twelve years of age Jesus goes to the passover.—*Jerusalem.*			2. 41-52	
The Genealogies.	1. 1-17		3. 23-38	
II. ANNOUNCEMENT AND INTRODUCTION OF HIS PUBLIC MINISTRY. Time: *About one year.*				
The ministry of John the Baptist.—*The Desert. The Jordan.*	3. 1-12	1. 1-8	3. 1-18	
The baptism of Jesus.—*The Jordan.*	3. 13-17	1. 9-11	3. 21-23	
The temptation.—*Desert of Judea.*	4. 1-11	1. 12,13	4. 1-13	
Preface to John's Gospel.				1. 1-18
Testimony of John the Baptist to Jesus.—*Bethabara beyond Jordan.*				1. 19-34
Jesus gains disciples.—*The Jordan. Galilee?*				1. 35-51
The marriage at Cana of Galilee.				2. 1-12
III. HIS FIRST PASSOVER, AND THE SUBSEQUENT TRANSACTIONS UNTIL THE SECOND. Time: *One year.*				
At the passover Jesus drives the traders out of the Temple.—*Jerusalem.*				2. 13-25 3. 1-21
Our Lord's discourse with Nicodemus.—*Jerusalem.*				
Jesus leaves Jerusalem, but remains in Judea and baptizes. Further testimony of John the Baptist. —*Ænon.*				3. 22-36
Jesus departs into Galilee after John's imprisonment.	4. 12; 14. 3-5	1. 14; 6. 17-20	4. 14; 3. 19,20	4. 1-3
Our Lord's discourse with the Samaritan woman. Many of the Samaritans believe on him.—*Sychar, that is, Shechem or Neapolis.*				4. 4-42
Jesus teaches publicly in Galilee.	4. 17	1. 14,15	4. 14,15	4. 43-45
Jesus again at Cana, where he heals the son of a nobleman lying ill at Capernaum.—*Cana of Galilee.*				4. 46-54
Jesus at Nazareth; he is there rejected; and fixes his abode at Capernaum.	4. 13-16		4. 16-31	
The call of Simon Peter and Andrew, and of James and John, with the miraculous draught of fishes.—*By the Sea of Galilee; near Capernaum.*	4. 18-22	1. 16-20	5. 1-11	
The healing of a demoniac in the synagogue.—*Capernaum.*		1. 21-28	4. 31-37	
The healing of Peter's wife's mother, and many others.—*Capernaum.*	8. 14-17	1. 29-34	4. 38-41	
Jesus with his disciples goes from Capernaum throughout Galilee.	4. 23-25	1. 35-39	4. 42-44	
The healing of a leper.—*Galilee.*	8. 2-4	1. 40-45	5. 12-16	
The healing of a paralytic.—*Capernaum.*	9. 2-8	2. 1-12	5. 17-26	
The call of Matthew.—*Capernaum.*	9. 9	2. 13,14	5. 27,28	
IV. HIS SECOND PASSOVER, AND THE SUBSEQUENT TRANSACTIONS UNTIL THE THIRD. Time: *One year.*				
The pool of Bethesda; the healing of the infirm man; and our Lord's subsequent discourse.—*Jerusalem.*				5. 1-47
The disciples pluck ears of grain on the sabbath.— *On the way to Galilee?*	12. 1-8	2. 23-28	6. 1-5	

CHRIST, LIFE OF—Continued.	MATT.	MARK.	LUKE.	JOHN.
The healing of the withered hand on the sabbath.— *Galilee: Capernaum?*	12. 9-14	3. 1-6	6. 6-11	.
Jesus arrives at the sea of Tiberias, and is followed by multitudes.	12. 15-21	3. 7-12	.	.
Jesus withdraws to the mountain, and chooses the twelve; the multitudes follow him.—*Near Capernaum.*	10. 2-4	3. 13-19	6. 12-19	.
The sermon on the mount.—*Near Capernaum.*	c. 5-7	.	6. 20-49	.
The healing of the centurion's servant.—*Capernaum.*	8. 5-13	.	7. 1-10	.
The raising of the widow's son.—*Nain.*	.	.	7. 11-17	.
John the Baptist in prison sends disciples to Jesus.—*Galilee: Capernaum?*	11. 2-19	.	7. 18-35	.
Reflections of Jesus on appealing to his mighty works.—*Capernaum?*	11. 20-30	.	.	.
While sitting at meat with a Pharisee, Jesus is anointed by a woman who had been a sinner.—*Capernaum?*	.	.	7. 36-50	.
Jesus, with the twelve, makes a second circuit in Galilee.	.	.	8. 1-3	.
The healing of a demoniac. The scribes and Pharisees blaspheme.—*Galilee.*	12. 22-37	3. 19-30	11. 14,15, 17-23	.
The scribes and Pharisees seek a sign. Our Lord's reflections.—*Galilee.*	12. 38-45	.	11. 16, 24-36	.
The true disciples of Christ his nearest relatives.—*Galilee.*	12. 46-50	3. 31-35	8. 19-21	.
Jesus discourses to his disciples and the multitude.—*Galilee.*	.	.	11. 37-54	.
The slaughter of certain Galileans. Parable of the barren fig-tree.—*Galilee.*	.	.	12. 1-59	.
Parable of the sower.—*Sea of Galilee: near Capernaum?*	.	.	13. 1-9	.
Parable of the tares. Other parables.—*Near Capernaum?*	13. 1-23	4. 1-25	8. 4-18	.
Jesus directs to cross the lake. Incidents. The tempest stilled.—*Sea of Galilee.*	13. 24-53	4. 26-34	.	.
The two demoniacs of Gadara.—*S. E. coast of the Sea of Galilee.*	8. 18-27	4. 35-41	8. 22-25	.
Levi's feast. Discourse concerning fasting.—*Capernaum.*	8. 28-34 9. 1	5. 1-21	8. 26-40	.
The raising of Jairus's daughter. The woman with an issue of blood.—*Capernaum.*	9. 10-17	2. 15-22	5. 29-39	.
Two blind men healed, and a dumb spirit cast out.—*Capernaum?*	9. 18-26	5. 22-43	8. 41-56	.
Jesus again at Nazareth, and again rejected.	9. 27-34	.	.	.
A third circuit in Galilee. The twelve instructed and sent forth.—*Galilee.*	13. 54-58	6. 1-6	.	.
	9. 35-38			
	10. 1,5-42	6. 6-13	9. 1-6	.
	11. 1			
Herod holds Jesus to be John the Baptist, whom he had just before beheaded.—*Galilee? Peræa.*	14. 1,2, 6-12	6. 14-16, 21-29	9. 7-9	.
The twelve return, and Jesus retires with them across the lake. Five thousand are fed.—*Capernaum. N. E. coast of the Sea of Galilee.*	14. 13-21	6. 30-44	9. 10-17	6. 1-14
Jesus walks upon the water.—*Night on the Sea of Galilee. Gennesareth.*	14. 22-36	6. 45-56	.	6. 15-21
Our Lord's discourse to the multitude in the synagogue at Capernaum. Many disciples turn back. Peter's profession of Faith.—*Capernaum.*	.	.	.	6. 22-71 7. 1
V. FROM THE THIRD PASSOVER DURING OUR LORD'S MINISTRY UNTIL HIS FINAL DEPARTURE FROM GALILEE AT THE FESTIVAL OF TABERNACLES. Time: *Six months.*				
Our Lord justifies his disciples for eating with unwashen hands. Pharisaic traditions.—*Capernaum.*	15. 1-20	7. 1-23	.	.
The daughter of a Syrophenician woman is healed.—*Region of Tyre and Sidon.*	15. 21-28	7. 24-30	.	.
A deaf and dumb man healed; also many others. Four thousand are fed.—*The Decapolis.*	15. 29-38	7. 31-37 8. 1-9	.	.

CHRIST, LIFE OF—Continued.	MATT.	MARK.	LUKE.	JOHN.
The Pharisees and Sadducees again require a sign.—Near Magdala.	15. 39 16. 1-4 }	8. 10-12	.	.
The disciples cautioned against the leaven of the Pharisees, &c.—N. E. coast of the Sea of Galilee.	16. 4-12	8. 13-21	.	.
A blind man healed.—Bethsaida (Julias).	.	8. 22-26	.	.
Peter and the rest again profess their faith in Christ.—Region of Cæsarea Philippi.	16. 13-20	8. 27-30	9. 18-21	.
Our Lord foretells his own death and resurrection, and the trials of his followers.—Region of Cæsarea Philippi.	16. 21-28	{ 8. 31-38 9. 1 }	9. 22 27	.
The transfiguration. Our Lord's subsequent discourse with the three disciples.—Region of Cæsarea Philippi.	17. 1-13	9. 2-13	9. 28-36	.
The healing of a demoniac, whom the disciples could not heal.—Region of Cæsarea Philippi.	17. 14-21	9. 14-29	9. 37-43	.
Jesus again foretells his own death and resurrection.—Galilee.	17. 22,23	9. 30-32	9. 43-45	.
The tribute-money miraculously provided.—Capernaum.	17. 24-27	9. 33	.	.
The disciples contend who should be the greatest. Jesus exhorts to humility, forbearance, and brotherly love.—Capernaum.	18. 1-35	9. 33-50	9. 46-50	.
Jesus goes up to the festival of tabernacles. His final departure from Galilee. Incidents in Samaria.	.	.	9. 51-62	7. 2-10
The seventy instructed and sent out.—Samaria.	.	.	10. 1-16	.
Ten lepers cleansed.—Samaria?	.	.	17. 11-19	.
VI. THE FESTIVAL OF TABERNACLES, AND THE SUBSEQUENT TRANSACTIONS UNTIL OUR LORD'S ARRIVAL AT BETHANY SIX DAYS BEFORE THE FOURTH PASSOVER. Time: Six months, less one week.				
Jesus at the festival of tabernacles. His public teaching.—Jerusalem.	.	.	.	{ 7. 11-53 8. 1
The woman taken in adultery.—Jerusalem.	.	.	.	8. 2-11
Further public teaching of our Lord. He reproves the unbelieving Jews, and escapes from their hands.—Jerusalem.	.	.	.	8. 12-59
A lawyer instructed. Love to our neighbour defined. Parable of the good Samaritan.—Near Jerusalem.	.	.	10. 25-37	.
Jesus in the house of Martha and Mary.—Bethany.	.	.	10. 38-42	.
The disciples again taught how to pray.—Near Jerusalem.	.	.	11. 1-13	.
The seventy return.—Jerusalem?	.	.	10. 17-24	.
A man born blind is healed on the sabbath. Our Lord's subsequent discourses.—Jerusalem.	.	.	.	{ 9. 1-41 10. 1-21
Jesus in Jerusalem at the festival of dedication. He retires beyond Jordan.—Jerusalem. Bethabara beyond Jordan.	.	.	.	10. 22-42
The raising of Lazarus.—Bethany.	.	.	.	11. 1-46
The counsel of Caiaphas against Jesus. He retires from Jerusalem.—Jerusalem. Ephraim.	.	.	.	11. 47-54
Jesus beyond Jordan is followed by multitudes. The healing of the infirm woman on the sabbath.—Valley of Jordan. Peræa.	19. 1,2	10. 1	13. 10-21	.
Our Lord goes teaching and journeying towards Jerusalem. He is warned against Herod.—Peræa.	.	.	13. 22-35	.
Our Lord dines with a chief Pharisee on the sabbath. Incidents.—Peræa.	.	.	14. 1-24	.
What is required of true disciples.—Peræa.	.	.	14. 25-35	.
Parable of the lost sheep, &c. Parable of the prodigal son.—Peræa.	.	.	15. 1-32	.
Parable of the unjust steward.—Peræa.	.	.	16. 1-13	.
The Pharisees reproved. Parable of the rich man and Lazarus.—Peræa.	.	.	16. 14-31	.
Jesus inculcates forbearance, faith, humility.—Peræa.	.	.	17. 1-10	.
Christ's coming will be sudden.—Peræa.	.	.	17. 20-37	.
Parables: The importunate widow. The Pharisee and publican.—Peræa.	.	.	18. 1-14	.
Precepts respecting divorce.—Peræa.	19. 3-12	10. 2-12	.	.
Jesus receives and blesses little children.—Peræa.	19. 13-15	10. 13-16	18. 15-17	.

CHRIST, Life of—Continued.	MATT.	MARK.	LUKE.	JOHN.
The rich young man. Parable of the labourers in the vineyard.—*Peræa.*	19. 16-30 20. 1-16	10. 17-31	18. 18-30	.
Jesus a third time foretells his death and resurrection.—*Peræa.*	20. 17-19	10. 32-34	18. 31-34	.
James and John make their ambitious request.—*Peræa.*	20. 20-28	10. 35-45	.	.
The healing of two blind men near Jericho.	20. 29-34	10. 46-52	18. 35-43 19. 1	.
The visit to Zaccheus. Parable of the ten pounds.—*Jericho.*	.	.	19. 2-28	.
Jesus arrives at Bethany six days before the passover.—*Bethany.*	.	.	.	{ 11. 55-57 { 12. 1,9-11
VII. His public entry into Jerusalem, and the subsequent transactions before the fourth Passover. Time: *Five days.*				
Our Lord's public entry into Jerusalem.—*Bethany. Jerusalem. (1st day of the week, Sunday).*	21. 1-11, 14-17	11. 1-11	19. 29-44	12. 12-19
The barren fig-tree. The cleansing of the Temple.—*Bethany. Jerusalem. (2d day of the week, Monday).*	21. 12,13, 18,19	11. 12-19	19. 45-48 21. 37,38	.
The barren fig-tree withers away.—*Between Bethany and Jerusalem. (3d day of the week, Tuesday).*	21. 20-22	11. 20-26	.	.
Christ's authority questioned. Parable of the two sons.—*Jerusalem.*	21. 23-32	11. 27-33	20. 1-8	.
Parable of the wicked husbandmen.—*Jerusalem.*	21. 33-46	12. 1-12	20. 9-19	.
Parable of the marriage of the king's son.—*Jerusalem.*	22. 1-14	.	.	.
Insidious question of the Pharisees and Herodians : tribute to Cæsar.—*Jerusalem.*	22. 15-22	12. 13-17	20. 20-26	.
Insidious question of the Sadducees : the resurrection.—*Jerusalem.*	22. 23-33	12. 18-27	20. 27-40	.
A lawyer questions Jesus. The two great commandments.—*Jerusalem.*	22. 34-40	12. 28-34	.	.
How is Christ the Son of David?—*Jerusalem.*	22. 41-46	12. 35-37	20. 41-44	.
Warnings against the evil example of the scribes and Pharisees.—*Jerusalem.*	23. 1-12	12. 38,39	20. 45,46	.
Woes against the scribes and Pharisees. Lamentation over Jerusalem.—*Jerusalem.*	23. 13-39	12. 40	20. 47	.
The widow's mite.—*Jerusalem.*	.	12. 41-44	21. 1-4	.
Certain Greeks desire to see Jesus.—*Jerusalem.*	.	.	.	12. 20-36
Reflections upon the unbelief of the Jews.—*Jerusalem.*	.	.	.	12. 37-50
Jesus, on taking leave of the temple, foretells its destruction and the persecution of his disciples.—*Jerusalem. Mount of Olives.*	24. 1-14	13. 1-13	21. 5-19	.
The signs of Christ's coming to destroy Jerusalem, and put an end to the Jewish state and dispensation.—*Mount of Olives.*	24. 15-42	13. 14-37	21. 20-36	.
Transition to Christ's final coming at the day of judgment. Exhortation to watchfulness. Parables : the ten virgins ; the five talents.—*Mount of Olives.*	24. 43-51 } 25. 1-30 }	.	.	.
Scenes of the judgment-day.—*Mount of Olives.*	25. 31-46	.	.	.
The rulers conspire. The supper at Bethany. Treachery of Judas.—*Jerusalem. Bethany. (4th day of the week, Wednesday).*	26. 1-16	14. 1-11	22. 1-6	12. 2-8
VIII. The fourth Passover ; our Lord's passion ; and the accompanying events until the end of the Jewish sabbath. Time: *Two days.*				
Preparation for the passover.—*Bethany. Jerusalem. (5th day of the week, Thursday).*	26. 17-19	14. 12-16	22. 7-13	.
The passover meal. Contention among the twelve. *Jerusalem. (Evening, introducing the 6th day of the week, Friday).*	26. 20	14. 17	{ 22. 14-18, { 24-30	.
Jesus washes the feet of his disciples.—*Jerusalem.*	.	.	.	13. 1-20
Jesus points out the traitor. Judas withdraws.—*Jerusalem.*	.	.	.	.
Jesus foretells the fall of Peter, and the dispersion of the twelve.—*Jerusalem.*	26. 21-25	14. 18-21	22. 21-23	13. 21-35
The Lord's supper.—*Jerusalem.* 1 Cor. 11. 23-25.	26. 31-35 26. 26-29	14. 27-31 14. 22-25	22. 31-38 22. 19,20	13. 36-38

CHRIST, LIFE OF—Continued.	MATT.	MARK.	LUKE.	JOHN.
Jesus comforts his disciples. The Holy Spirit promised.—Jerusalem.				14. 1-31
Christ the true vine. His disciples hated by the world.—Jerusalem.				15. 1-27
Persecution foretold. Further promise of the Holy Spirit. Prayer in the name of Christ.—Jerusalem.				16. 1-33
Christ's last prayer with his disciples.—Jerusalem.				17. 1-26
The agony in Gethsemane.—Mount of Olives.	26. 30, 36-46	14. 26, 32-42	22. 39-46	18. 1
Jesus betrayed, and made prisoner.—Gethsemane.	26. 47-56	14. 43-52	22. 47-53	18. 2-12
Jesus before Caiaphas. Peter thrice denies him.—Jerusalem. (Night introducing the 6th day of the week, Friday).	26. 57,58, 69-75	14. 53,54 66-72	22. 54-62	18. 13-18, 25-27
Jesus before Caiaphas and the Sanhedrim. Declares himself to be the Christ; is condemned and mocked. Jerusalem. (Morning of the 6th day of the week).	26. 59-68	14. 55-65	22. 63-71	18. 19-24
The Sanhedrim lead Jesus away to Pilate.—Jerusalem. (6th day of the week).	27. 1,2, 11-14	15. 1-5	23. 1-5	18. 28-38
Jesus before Herod.—Jerusalem.			23. 6-12	
Pilate seeks to release Jesus. The Jews demand Barabbas.—Jerusalem.	27. 15-26	15. 6-15	23. 18-25	18. 39,40
Pilate delivers up Jesus to death. He is scourged and mocked.—Jerusalem.	27. 26-30	15. 15-19		19. 1-3
Pilate, after again seeking to release Jesus, delivers him to be crucified.—Jerusalem.				19. 4-16
Judas repents and hangs himself.—Jerusalem. Act. 1. 18,19.	27. 3-10			
Jesus is led away to be crucified.—Jerusalem.	27. 31-34	15. 20-23	23. 26-33	19. 16,17
The crucifixion.—Jerusalem.	27. 35-38	15. 24-28	23. 33,34, 38	19. 18-24
The Jews mock at Jesus on the cross. He commends his mother to John.—Jerusalem.	27. 39-44	15. 29-32	23. 35-37, 39-43	19. 25-27
Darkness prevails. Christ expires on the cross.—Jerusalem.	27. 45-50	15. 33-37	23. 44-46	19. 28-30
The veil of the temple rent, and graves opened. Judgment of the centurion. The women at the cross.—Jerusalem.	27. 51-56	15. 38-41	23. 45, 47-49	
The taking down from the cross. The burial.—Jerusalem.	27. 57-61	15. 42-47	23. 50-56	19. 31-42
The watch at the sepulchre.—Jerusalem. (Seventh day of the week, or Sabbath).	27. 62-66			
IX. OUR LORD'S RESURRECTION, HIS SUBSEQUENT APPEARANCES, AND HIS ASCENSION. Time: Forty days.				
Morning of the resurrection.—Jerusalem. (1st day of the week).	28. 2-4	16. 1		
Visit of the women to the sepulchre. Mary Magdalene returns.—Jerusalem.	28. 1	16. 2-4	24. 1-3	20. 1,2
Vision of angels in the sepulchre.—Jerusalem.	28. 5-7	16. 5-7	24. 4-8	
The women return to the city. Jesus meets them.—Jerusalem.	28. 8-10	16. 8	24. 9-11	
Peter and John run to the sepulchre.—Jerusalem.			24. 12	20. 3-10
Our Lord is seen by Mary Magdalene at the sepulchre.—Jerusalem.		16. 9-11		20. 11-18
Report of the watch.—Jerusalem.	28. 11-15			
Our Lord is seen by Peter. Then by two disciples on the way to Emmaus.—Jerusalem. Emmaus. 1 Cor. 15. 5.		16. 12,13	24. 13-35	
Jesus appears in the midst of the apostles, Thomas being absent.—Jerusalem. 1 Cor. 15. 5. (Evening following the 1st day of the week, or the Lord's day).		16. 14-18	24. 36-49	20. 19-23
Jesus appears in the midst of the apostles, Thomas being present.—Jerusalem. (Evening following the 1st day of the week. The second Lord's day).				20. 24-29
The apostles go away into Galilee. Jesus shews himself to nine of them at the sea of Tiberias.—Galilee.	28. 16			21. 1-24
Jesus meets his apostles and about five hundred brethren on a mountain in Galilee. 1 Cor. 15. 6.	28. 16-20			
Our Lord is seen by James; then by all the apostles.—Jerusalem. Act. 1. 3-8. 1 Cor. 15. 7.				
The ascension.—Bethany. Act. 1. 9-12.		16. 19,20	24. 50-53	
Conclusion of John's Gospel.				20. 30-31 21. 25

CHRIST, Likeness of Saints to. See Likeness to God and Christ.

————, Love, Compassion, and Sympathy of. Psa. 72.14. He shall redeem their soul from deceit and violence : and precious shall their blood be in his sight.

Pro. 8.17. I love them that love me ; and those that seek me early shall find me. 31. Rejoicing in the habitable part of his earth ; and my delights *were* with the sons of men. (See Song of Solomon throughout.)

Isa. 40.11. He shall feed his flock like a shepherd : he shall gather the lambs with his arm, and carry *them* in his bosom, *and* shall gently lead those that are with young.

Isa. 42.3. A bruised reed shall he not break, and the smoking flax shall he not quench.

Isa. 63.9. In all their affliction he was afflicted, and the angel of his presence saved them : in his love and in his pity he redeemed them ; and he bare them, and carried them all the days of old. *v.* 7,8.

Mic. 5.4. He shall stand and feed in the strength of the Lord, in the majesty of the name of the Lord his God : and they shall abide.

Mat. 8.17. Himself took our infirmities, and bare *our* sicknesses. Isa. 53.4.

Mat. 9.36. When he saw the multitudes, he was moved with compassion on them, because they fainted, and were scattered abroad, as sheep having no shepherd.

Mat. 12.49. And he stretched forth his hand toward his disciples, and said, Behold my mother and my brethren ! 50. For whosoever shall do the will of my Father which is in heaven, the same is my brother, and sister, and mother. Mar. 3.31-35. Luk. 8.19-21.

Mat. 14.14. Jesus went forth, and saw a great multitude, and was moved with compassion toward them, and he healed their sick.

Mat. 15.32. I have compassion on the multitude, because they continue with me now three days, and have nothing to eat : and I will not send them away fasting, lest they faint in the way.

Mat. 18.6. But whoso shall offend one of these little ones which believe in me, it were better for him that a millstone were hanged about his neck, and *that* he were drowned in the depth of the sea. 10. Take heed that ye despise not one of these little ones ; for I say unto you, That in heaven their angels do always behold the face of my Father which is in heaven. Mar. 9.37,42. Luk. 9.48.

Mat. 23.37. O Jerusalem, Jerusalem, *thou* that killest the prophets, and stonest them which are sent unto thee, how often would I have gathered thy children together, even as a hen gathereth her chickens under *her* wings, and ye would not !

Mat. 28.10. Go tell my brethren that they go into Galilee.

Mar. 3.5. Being grieved for the hardness of their hearts.

Mar. 8.12. He sighed deeply in his spirit, and saith, Why doth this generation seek after a sign ?

Mar. 9.36. He took a child, and set him in the midst of them : and when he had taken him in his arms, he said unto them, 37. Whosoever shall receive one of such children in my name, receiveth me. Mat. 18.2-5. Luk. 9.48.

Mar. 10.13. They brought young children to him, that he should touch them : and *his* disciples rebuked those that brought *them.* 14. But when Jesus saw *it,* he was much displeased, and said unto them, Suffer the little children to come unto me, and forbid them not : for of such is the kingdom of God. 16. And he took them up in his arms, put *his* hands upon them, and blessed them. 21. Jesus beholding him loved him. Mat. 19.13-15. Luk. 18.15,16.

Luk. 7.13. When the Lord saw her, he had compassion on her, and said unto her, Weep not.

Luk. 22.32. I have prayed for thee, that thy faith fail not : and when thou art converted, strengthen thy brethren.

Luk. 23.28. Jesus turning unto them said, Daughters of Jerusalem, weep not for me, but weep for yourselves, and for your children.

Luk. 24. 38. He said unto them, Why are ye troubled ? and why do thoughts arise in your hearts ? 39. Behold my hands and my feet, that it is I myself : handle me, and see ; for a spirit hath not flesh and bones, as ye see me have. 40. And when he had thus spoken, he shewed them *his* hands and *his* feet.

Jno. 10.3. The sheep hear his voice : and he calleth his own sheep by name, and leadeth them out. 4. And when he putteth forth his own sheep, he goeth before them, and ·the sheep follow him : for they know his voice. 11. I am the good shepherd : the good shepherd giveth his life for the sheep. 14. I am the good shepherd, and know my *sheep,* and am known of mine. 15. I lay down my life for the sheep. 16. And other sheep I have, which are not of this fold : them also I must bring, and they shall hear my voice ; and there shall be one fold, *and* one shepherd.

Jno. 11.5. Jesus loved Martha, and her sister, and Lazarus. 33. When Jesus therefore saw her weeping, and the Jews also weeping which came with her, he groaned in the spirit, and was troubled, 34. And said, Where have ye laid him ? They said unto him, Lord, come and see. 35. Jesus wept. 36. Then said the Jews, Behold how he loved him !

Jno. 13.1. Having loved his own which were in the world, he loved them unto the end. 23. There was leaning on Jesus' bosom one of his disciples, whom Jesus loved. 34. As I have loved you, that ye also love one another.

Jno. 14.1. Let not your heart be troubled : ye believe in God, believe also in me. 2. In my Father's house are many mansions : if *it were* not so, I would have told you. I go to prepare a place for you. 3. And if I go and prepare a place for you, I will come again, and receive you unto myself ; that where I am, *there* ye may be also. 18. I will not leave you comfortless : I will come to you. 21. He that loveth me shall be loved of my Father, and I will love him, and will manifest myself to him. 27. Peace I leave with you, my peace I give unto you :·not as the world giveth, give I unto you. Let not your heart be troubled, neither let it be afraid.

Jno. 15.9. As the Father hath loved me, so have I loved you : continue ye in my love. 10. If ye keep my commandments, ye shall abide in my love : 11. These things have I spoken unto you, that my joy might remain in you, and *that* your joy might be full. 12. This is my commandment, That ye love one another, as I have loved you. 13. Greater love hath no man than this, that a man lay down his life for his friends. 15. I call you not servants ; for the servant knoweth not what his lord doeth : but I have called you friends ; for all things that I have heard of my Father I have made known unto you.

Jno. 17.12. While I was with them in the world, I kept them in thy name : those that thou gavest me I have kept, and none of them is lost. 15. I pray not that thou shouldest take them out of the world, but that thou shouldest keep them from the evil. 19. For their sakes I sanctify myself, that they also might be sanctified through the truth.

Jno. 18.8. If therefore ye seek me, let these go their way : 9. That the saying might be fulfilled, which he spake, Of them which thou gavest me have I lost none.

Jno. 19.26. When Jesus therefore saw his mother, and the disciple standing by, whom he loved, he saith unto his mother, Woman, behold thy son ! 27. Then saith he to the disciple, Behold thy mother !

Jno. 20.17. Go to my brethren, and say unto them, I ascend unto my Father, and your Father ; and to my God, and your God. 27. Reach hither thy finger, and behold my hands ; and reach hither thy hand, and thrust it into my side : and be not faithless, but believing.

Jno. 21.15. Jesus saith to Simon Peter, Simon, son of Jonas, lovest thou me more than these? He saith unto him, Yea, Lord ; thou knowest that I love thee. He saith unto him, Feed my lambs. v. 16,17.

Act. 9.4. Saul, Saul, why persecutest thou me ? 5. And he said, Who art thou, Lord ? And the Lord said, I am Jesus whom thou persecutest.

Act. 10.38. Who went about doing good, and healing all that were oppressed of the devil.

Rom. 8.35. Who shall separate us from the love of Christ ? 37. Nay, in all these things we are more than conquerors through him that loved us. 39. Nor height, nor depth, nor any other creature, shall be able to separate us from the love of God, which is in Christ Jesus our Lord.

Rom. 15.3. Even Christ pleased not himself ; but, as it is written, The reproaches of them that reproached thee fell on me.

2 Cor. 5.14. The love of Christ constraineth us.

2 Cor. 8.9. Ye know the grace of our Lord Jesus Christ, that, though he was rich, yet for your sakes he became poor, that ye through his poverty might be rich.

Gal. 2.20. The Son of God, who loved me, and gave himself for me.

Eph. 3.18. May be able to comprehend with all saints what is the breadth, and length, and depth, and height ; 19. And to know the love of Christ, which passeth knowledge.

Eph. 5.2. Christ also hath loved us, and hath given himself for us an offering and a sacrifice to God for a sweet-smelling savour. 25. Christ also loved the church, and gave himself for it. 29. No man ever yet hated his own flesh ; but nourisheth and cherisheth it, even as the Lord the church : 30. For we are members of his body, of his flesh, and of his bones.

2 The. 2.13. Brethren beloved of the Lord.

Heb. 2.11. Both he that sanctifieth and they who are sanctified are all of one : for which cause he is not ashamed to call them brethren. 18. In that he himself hath suffered being tempted, he is able to succour them that are tempted.

Heb. 4.15. We have not an high-priest which cannot be touched with the feeling of our infirmities ; but was in all points tempted like as we are, yet without sin.

1 Jno. 3.16. Hereby perceive we the love of God, because he laid down his life for us.

Rev. 1.5. Unto him that loved us, and washed us from our sins in his own blood. 17. And when I saw him, I fell at his feet as dead. And he laid his right hand upon me, saying unto me, Fear not ; I am the first and the last.

Rev. 2.24. I will put upon you none other burden.

Rev. 3.9. I will make them to come and worship before thy feet, and to know that I have loved thee. 19. As many as I love, I rebuke and chasten.

CHRIST, LOVE TO. See LOVE TO GOD AND CHRIST.

————, MERCY OF. See CHRIST, PARDON FROM.

————, MEEKNESS AND HUMILITY OF. Psa. 45.4. Ride prosperously, because of truth and meekness.

Isa. 42.2. He shall not cry, nor lift up, nor cause his voice to be heard in the street.

Isa. 50.5. The Lord God hath opened mine ear, and I was not rebellious, neither turned away back. 6. I gave my back to the smiters, and my cheeks to them that plucked off the hair : I hid not my face from shame and spitting.

Isa. 52.13. My servant shall deal prudently.

Isa. 53.7. He was oppressed, and he was afflicted, yet he opened not his mouth : he is brought as a lamb to the slaughter, and as a sheep before her shearers is dumb, so he openeth not his mouth.

Zec. 9.9. Lowly, and riding upon an ass, and upon a colt, the foal of an ass. Mat. 21.5.

Mat. 9.10. As Jesus sat at meat in the house, behold, many publicans and sinners came and sat down with him and his disciples. Mar. 2.14. Luk. 5.27,28.

Mat. 11.29. Learn of me ; for I am meek and lowly in heart.

Mat. 26.49. Forthwith he came to Jesus, and said, Hail, master ; and kissed him. 50. And Jesus said unto him, Friend, wherefore art thou come?

Mat. 27.12. When he was accused of the chief priests and elders, he answered nothing. 14. He answered him to never a word ; insomuch that the governor marvelled greatly.

Luk. 22 27. I am among you as he that serveth.

Luk. 23.34. Then said Jesus, Father, forgive them ; for they know not what they do.

Jno. 8.48. The Jews said unto him, Say we not well that thou art a Samaritan, and hast a devil ? 49. Jesus answered, I have not a devil ; but I honour my Father, and ye do dishonour me. 50. And I seek not mine own glory.

Jno. 13.5. He poureth water into a bason, and began to wash the disciples' feet, and to wipe *them* with the towel wherewith he was girded. 14. If I then, *your* Lord and master, have washed your feet; ye also ought to wash one another's feet.

2 Cor. 10.1. The meekness and gentleness of Christ.

Phil. 2.7. Made himself of no reputation, and took upon him the form of a servant, and was made in the likeness of men; 8. And being found in fashion as a man, he humbled himself, and became obedient unto death, even the death of the cross.

Heb. 12.3. Consider him that endured such contradiction of sinners against himself.

1 Pet. 2.23. Who, when he was reviled, reviled not again; when he suffered, he threatened not; but committed *himself* to him that judgeth righteously.

CHRIST, MESSIAH [Messiah is Hebrew, and Christ is Greek, both signifying *anointed*, and so translated Psa. 2.2. See Act. 4.26. Jno. 1.41 *marg.*]. Dan. 9.25. From the going forth of the commandment to restore and to build Jerusalem unto the Messiah the Prince *shall be* seven weeks, and threescore and two weeks: 26. And after threescore and two weeks shall Messiah be cut off, but not for himself.

Mat. 11.3. Art thou he that should come, or do we look for another? 4. Jesus answered and said unto them, Go and shew John again those things which ye do hear and see: 5. The blind receive their sight, and the lame walk; the lepers are cleansed, and the deaf hear; the dead are raised up, and the poor have the gospel preached to them. 6. And blessed is *he*, whosoever shall not be offended in me.

Mat. 16.15. But whom say ye that I am? 16. And Simon Peter answered and said, Thou art the Christ, the Son of the living God.

Mat. 26.63. I adjure thee by the living God, that thou tell us whether thou be the Christ, the Son of God. 64. Jesus saith unto him, Thou hast said: nevertheless, I say unto you, Hereafter shall ye see the Son of man sitting on the right hand of power, and coming in the clouds of heaven.

Luk. 2.38. She, coming in that instant, gave thanks likewise unto the Lord, and spake of him to all them that looked for redemption in Jerusalem.

Luk. 20.41. How say they that Christ is David's son? 42. And David himself saith in the book of Psalms, the·Lord said unto my Lord, Sit thou on my right hand, 43. Till I make thine enemies thy footstool. 44. David therefore calleth him Lord, how is he then his son? Mat. 22.42-45. Mar. 12.35-37.

Luk. 24.25. O fools, and slow of heart to believe all that the prophets have spoken! 26. Ought not Christ to have suffered these things, and to enter into his glory? 27. And beginning at Moses and all the prophets, he expounded unto them in all the scriptures the things concerning himself.

Jno. 1.41. We have found the Messias, which is, being interpreted, The Christ. 45. We have found him, of whom Moses in the law, and the prophets, did write, Jesus of Nazareth, the son of Joseph.

Jno. 4.26. Jesus saith unto her, I that speak unto thee am *he*. 29. Come, see a man which told me all things that ever I did: is not this the Christ? 42. Now we believe, not because of thy saying: for we have heard *him* ourselves, and know that this is indeed the Christ, the Saviour of the world.

Jno. 5.33. Ye sent unto John, and he bare witness unto the truth. 36. I have greater witness than *that* of John: for the works which the Father hath given me to finish, the same works that I do, bear witness of me, that the Father hath sent me. 37. The Father himself, which hath sent me, hath borne witness of me. Ye have neither heard his voice at any time, nor seen his shape. 39. Search the scriptures; for in them ye think ye have eternal life: and they are they which testify of me. 46. Had ye believed Moses, ye would have believed me: for he wrote of me.

Jno. 6.27. Him hath God the Father sealed.

Jno. 8.14. Though I bear record of myself, *yet* my record is true: for I know whence I came, and whither I go. 17. It is also written in your law, that the testimony of two men is true. 18. I am one that bear witness of myself, and the Father that sent me beareth witness of me. 25. Then said they unto him, Who art thou? And Jesus saith unto them, Even *the same* that I said unto you from the beginning.

Jno. 8.28. When ye have lifted up the Son of man, then shall ye know that I am *he*, and *that* I do nothing of myself; but as my Father hath taught me, I speak these things. 56. Your father Abraham rejoiced to see my day: and he saw *it*, and was glad.

Jno. 13.19. I tell you before it come, that, when it is come to pass, ye may believe that I am *he*.

Act. 3.18. Those things, which God before had shewed by the mouth of all his prophets, that Christ should suffer, he hath so fulfilled. 20. He shall send Jesus Christ, which before was preached unto you: 24. All the prophets from Samuel and those that follow after, as many as have spoken, have likewise foretold of these days.

Act. 4.26. The kings of the earth stood up, and the rulers were gathered together against the Lord, and against his Christ. 27. For of a truth against thy holy child Jesus, whom thou hast anointed, both Herod and Pontius Pilate, with the Gentiles, and the people of Israel, were gathered together. Psa. 2.2.

Act. 9.22. Saul confounded the Jews which dwelt at Damascus, proving that this is very Christ.

Act. 10.43. To him give all the prophets witness.

Act. 13.27. Because they knew him not. nor yet the voices of the prophets which are read every sabbath day, they have fulfilled *them* in condemning *him*.

Act. 17.3. Alleging, that Christ must needs have suffered, and risen again from the dead; and that this Jesus, whom I preach unto you, is Christ.

Act. 26.6. I stand and am judged for the hope of the promise made of God unto our fathers: 7. Unto which *promise* our twelve tribes, instantly serving *God* day and night, hope to come. 22. Witnessing both to small and great, saying none other things than those which the prophets and Moses did say should come: 23. That Christ should suffer, *and* that he should be the first that should rise from the dead, and should shew light unto the people, and to the Gentiles.

Act. 28.23. He expounded and testified the kingdom of God, persuading them concerning Jesus, both out of the law of Moses, and *out of* the prophets.

Rom. 1.1. Paul, a servant of Jesus Christ, separated unto the gospel of God, 2. Which he had promised afore by his prophets in the holy scriptures, 3. Concerning his Son Jesus Christ our Lord, which was made of the seed of David according to the flesh.

1 Cor. 15.3. I delivered unto you first of all that which I also received, how that Christ died for our sins according to the scriptures.

1 Pet. 1.10. Of which salvation the prophets have inquired and searched diligently, who prophesied of the grace *that should come* unto you: 11. Searching what, or what manner of time the Spirit of Christ which was in them did signify, when it testified beforehand the sufferings of Christ, and the glory that should follow.

2 Pet. 1.16. We have not followed cunningly devised fables, when we made known unto you the power and coming of our Lord Jesus Christ, but were eyewitnesses of his majesty. 17. For he received from God the Father honour and glory, when there came such a voice to him from the excellent glory, This is my beloved Son, in whom I am well pleased. 18. And this voice which came from heaven we heard, when we were with him in the holy mount.

1 Jno. 5.6. This is he that came by water and blood, *even* Jesus Christ ; not by water only, but by water and blood. And it is the Spirit that beareth witness, because the Spirit is truth. 7. There are three that bear record in heaven, the Father, the Word, and the Holy Ghost : and these three are one. 8. And there are three that bear witness in earth, the spirit, and the water, and the blood: and these three agree in one. 9. If we receive the witness of men, the witness of God is greater : for this is the witness of God which he hath testified of his Son.

See CHRIST, SON OF GOD.—MIRACLES.

CHRIST, MIRACLES OF, CHRONOLOGICALLY ARRANGED.—

Water made wine, Jno. 2.1-11.

Healing the nobleman's son, Jno. 4.46-54.

First miraculous draught of fishes, Luk. 5. 1-11.

Demoniac in the synagogue cured, Mar. 1. 23-26. Luk. 4.33-36.

Healing of Simon's wife's mother, Mat. 8.14-17. Mar. 1.29-31. Luk. 4.38,39.

Cleansing of the leper, Mat. 8.1-4. Mar. 1. 40-45. Luk. 5.12-16.

Healing of the paralytic, Mat. 9.1-8. Mar. 2. 1-12. Luk. 5.17-26.

Healing of the impotent man, Jno. 5.1-16.

Restoring the withered hand, Mat. 12.9-13. Mar. 3.1-5. Luk. 6.6-11.

Healing of the centurion's servant, Mat. 8. 5-13. Luk. 7.1-10.

Raising of the widow's son, Luk. 7.11-16.

Healing of a demoniac, Mat. 12.22-37. Mar. 3.19-30. Luk. 11.14,15,17-23.

Stilling of the tempest, Mat. 8.23-27. Mar. 4.35-41. Luk. 8.22-25. Mat. 14.32.

The demoniacs in Gadara healed, Mat. 8. 28-34. Mar. 5.1-20. Luk. 8.26-39.

Raising of Jairus' daughter, Mat. 9.18,19,23-26. Mar. 5.22-24,35-43. Luk. 8.41,42,49-56.

Woman with the issue of blood cured, Mat. 9.20-22. Mar. 5.25-34. Luk. 8.43-48.

Opening the eyes of two blind men in the house, Mat. 9.27-31.

A devil cast out and a dumb man cured, Mat. 9.32,33.

Five thousand fed, Mat. 14.15-21. Mar. 6.35-44. Luk. 9.12-17. Jno. 6.5-14.

Walking on the sea, Mat. 14.22-33. Mar. 6. 45-52. Jno. 6.14-21.

The daughter of the Syrophenician healed, Mat. 15.21-28. Mar. 7.24-30.

Four thousand fed, Mat. 15.32-39. Mar. 8.1-9.

One deaf and dumb cured, Mar. 7.31-37.

One blind cured, Mar. 8.22-36.

Lunatic child healed, Mat. 17.14-21. Mar. 9. 14-29. Luk. 9.37-43.

Piece of money in the fish's mouth, Mat. 17.24-27.

The ten lepers cured, Luk. 17.11-19.

Opening the eyes of one born blind, Jno. 9.

Raising of Lazarus, Jno. 11.1-54.

Woman with the spirit of infirmity cured, Luk. 13.10-17.

The dropsy cured, Luk. 14.1-6.

Two blind men cured near Jericho, Mat. 20. 29-34. Mar. 10.46-52. Luk. 18.35-43.

The fig-tree blighted, Mat. 21.17-22. Mar. 11. 12-14,20-24.

Healing of Marcus' ear, Luk. 22.49-51.

Second draught of fishes, Jno.21.6.

Various miracles, Mat. 4.23,24. Mat. 14.14. Mat. 15.30. Mar. 1.34. Luk. 6.17-19. Luk. 7.21,22.

CHRIST, NAMES, TITLES, AND APPELLATIONS OF. Adam, 1 Cor. 15.45. Advocate, 1 Jno. 2.1. Almighty, Rev. 1.8. Alpha and Omega, Rev. 1.8. Amen, Rev. 3.14. Angel, Isa. 63.9. Anointed, Psa. 2.2. Apostle, Heb. 3.1. Author and Finisher of our faith, Heb. 12.2.

Beginning of the Creation of God, Rev. 3.14. Beloved, Eph. 1.6. Bishop, 1 Pet. 2.25. Blessed and only Potentate, 1 Tim. 6.15. Branch, Jer. 23.5. Bread of life, Jno. 6.48. Bridegroom, Mat. 9.15. Brightness of the Father's glory, Heb. 1.3.

Captain of the Lord's host, Jos. 5.14. Captain of salvation, Heb. 2.10. Chief Shepherd, 1 Pet. 5.4. Christ, Mat. 1.16. Luk. 9.20. Commander, Isa. 55.4. Consolation of Israel, Luk. 2.25. Corner-stone, Eph. 2.20. Counsellor, Isa. 9.6. Covenant of the people, Isa. 42.6.

David, Jer. 30.9. Day's-man, Job 9.33. Dayspring, Luk. 1.78. Day-star, 2 Pet. 1.19. Deliverer, Rom. 11.26. Desire of all nations, Hag. 2.7. Door, Jno. 10.7.

Elect, Isa. 42.1. Emmanuel, Isa. 7.14. Ensign, Isa. 11.10. Eternal life, 1 Jno. 5.20. Everlasting Father, Isa. 9.6.

First-begotten, Heb. 1.6. First-begotten of the dead, Rev. 1.5. Firstborn, Psa. 89.27. First and the Last, Rev. 2.8. Foundation, Isa. 28.16. Fountain, Zec. 13.1. Forerunner, Heb. 6.20.

Gift of God, Jno. 4.10. God, Jno. 1.1. Governor, Mat. 2.6.

Head of the church, Eph. 5.23. Heir of all things, Heb. 1.2. High-priest, Heb. 4.14. Holy

Child Jesus, Act. 4.30. Holy One, Psa. 16.10. Holy One of God, Mar. 1.24. Hope (our), 1 Tim. 1.1. Horn of salvation, Luk. 1.69.

I Am, Jno. 8.58. Image of God, Heb. 1.3. Israel, Isa. 49.3. Jehovah, Isa. 40.3. Jehovah's Fellow, Zec. 13.7. Jesus, Mat. 1.21, Judge, Act. 10.42. Just One, Act. 7.52.

King, Mat. 21.5. King of Israel, Jno. 1.49. King of the Jews, Mat. 2.2. King of saints, Rev. 15.3. King of kings, Rev. 17.14.

Lamb, Rev. 14.4. Lamb of God, Jno. 1.29. Rev. 13.8. Lawgiver, Isa. 33.22. Leader, Isa. 55.4. Life, Jno. 14.6. Light, Jno. 8.12. Lion of the tribe of Judah, Rev. 5.5. Lord, Rom. 1.3. Lord of lords, Rev. 17.14. Lord of all, Act. 10.36. Lord of glory, 1 Cor. 2.8. Lord our Righteousness, Jer. 23.6. Lord God Almighty, Rev. 15.3, Lord from heaven, 1 Cor. 15.47.

Man, Act. 17.31. Master, Mat. 23.8. Mediator, 1 Tim. 2.5. Messenger of the Covenant, Mal. 3.1. Messiah, Jno. 1.41. Mighty God, Isa. 9.6. Minister of the sanctuary, Heb. 8.2. Morning-star, Rev. 22.16.

Nazarene, Mat. 2.23. Offspring of David, Rev. 22.16. Only-begotten, Jno. 1.14.

Passover, 1 Cor. 5.7. Plant of renown, Eze. 34.29. Potentate, 1 Tim. 6.15. Power of God, 1 Cor. 1.24. Physician, Mat. 9.12. Priest, Heb. 7.17. Prince, Act. 5.31. Prince of life, Act. 3.15. Prince of peace, Isa. 9.6. Prince of the kings of the earth, Rev.1.5. Prophet, Luk. 24.19. Propitiation, 1 Jno. 2.2.

Ransom, 1 Tim. 2.6. Redeemer, Isa. 59.20. Resurrection and life, Jno. 11.25. Rock, 1 Cor. 10.4. Root of David, Rev. 22.16. Root of Jesse, Isa. 11.10. Rose of Sharon, Song 2.1. Ruler in Israel, Mic. 5.2.

Salvation, Luk. 2.30. Sanctuary, Isa. 8.14. Saviour, Luk. 2.11. Sceptre, Num. 24.17. Seed of the woman, Gen. 3.15. Servant, Isa. 42.1. Shepherd, Jno. 10.11 ; 1 Pet. 5.4 ; Jno. 10.14. Shiloh, Gen. 49.10. Son of God, Luk. 1.35. Son of man, Mat. 8.20. Son of the Blessed, Mar. 14.61. Son of the Highest, Luk. 1.32. Son of David, Mat. 9.27. Star, Num. 24.17. Sun of righteousness, Mal. 4.2. Surety, Heb. 7.22.

Teacher, Jno. 3.2. Truth, Jno. 14.6.

Vine, Jno. 15.1. Way, Jno. 14.6. Wisdom, Pro. 8.12. Witness, Isa. 55.4 ; Rev. 1.5. Wonderful, Isa. 9.6. Word, Jno. 1.1. Word of God, Rev. 19.13. Word of Life, 1 Jno. 1.1.

CHRIST, OMNIPOTENCE OF. See CHRIST, POWER OF.

————, OMNIPRESENCE OF. Mat. 18.20. Where two or three are gathered together in my name, there am I in the midst of them.

Mat. 28.20. Lo, I am with you alway, even unto the end of the world.

Jno. 3.13. No man hath ascended up to heaven, but he that came down from heaven, even the Son of man which is in heaven.

Eph. 1.23. Him that filleth all in all.

————, OMNISCIENCE AND WISDOM OF. Pro. 8.14. Counsel is mine, and sound wisdom : I am understanding ; I have strength. 15. By me kings reign, and princes decree justice. 16. By me princes rule, and nobles, even all the judges of the earth.

Isa. 11.2. The spirit of the Lord shall rest upon him, the spirit of wisdom and understanding, the spirit of counsel and might, the spirit of knowledge and of the fear of the Lord ; 3. And shall make him of quick understanding in the fear of the Lord : and he shall not judge after the sight of his eyes, neither reprove after the hearing of his ears.

Isa. 50.4. The Lord God hath given me the tongue of the learned, that I should know how to speak a word in season to him that is weary : he wakeneth morning by morning, he wakeneth mine ear to hear as the learned.

Mat. 11.27. No man knoweth the Son, but the Father ; neither knoweth any man the Father, save the Son, and he to whomsoever the Son will reveal him.

Mat. 13.54. They were astonished, and said, Whence hath this man this wisdom, and these mighty works?

Mat. 24.25. Behold, I have told you before.

Mat. 26.46. Behold, he is at hand that doth betray me. Mar. 14.42.

Mar. 2.8. Immediately when Jesus perceived in his spirit that they so reasoned within themselves, he said unto them, Why reason ye these things in your hearts?

Mar. 5.30. Jesus, immediately knowing in himself that virtue had gone out of him, turned him about in the press, and said, Who touched my clothes?

Luk. 2.40. The child grew, and waxed strong in spirit, filled with wisdom : and the grace of God was upon him. 47. And all that heard him were astonished at his understanding and answers. 52. Jesus increased in wisdom and stature.

Luk. 5.22. When Jesus perceived their thoughts, he answering said unto them, What reason ye in your hearts?

Luk. 6.8. He knew their thoughts.

Luk. 9.47. Jesus, perceiving the thought of their heart, took a child, and set him by him.

Luk. 22.10. When ye are entered into the city, there shall a man meet you, bearing a pitcher of water ; follow him into the house where he entereth in. 11. And ye shall say unto the goodman of the house, The Master saith unto thee, Where is the guestchamber, where I shall eat the passover with my disciples? 12. And he shall shew you a large upper room furnished : there make ready. Mar. 14.13-15.

Jno. 1.48. Before that Philip called thee, when thou wast under the fig-tree, I saw thee.

Jno. 2.24. Jesus did not commit himself unto them, because he knew all men, 25. And needed not that any should testify of man : for he knew what was in man.

Jno. 3.32. What he hath seen and heard, that he testifieth.

Jno. 4.16. Jesus saith unto her, Go, call thy husband, and come hither. 17. The woman answered and said, I have no husband. Jesus said unto her, Thou hast well said, I have no husband : 18. For thou hast had five husbands ; and he whom thou now hast is not thy husband : in that saidst thou truly. 19. The woman saith unto him, Sir, I perceive that thou art a prophet. 29. Come, see a man which told me all things that ever I did : is not this the Christ?

Jno. 5.30. As I hear, I judge : and my judgment is just ; because I seek not mine own will, but the will of the Father which hath sent me. 42. I know you, that ye have not the love of God in you.

Jno. 6.64. Jesus knew from the beginning who they were that believed not, and who should betray him.

Jno. 7.29. I know him: for I am from him, and he hath sent me.

Jno. 8.16. Yet if I judge, my judgment is true: for I am not alone, but I and the Father that sent me. Jno. 5.30.

Jno. 13.1. Jesus knew that his hour was come that he should depart out of this world unto the Father. 10. Ye are clean, but not all. 11. He knew who should betray him; therefore said he, Ye are not all clean.

Jno. 16.30. Now are we sure that thou knowest all things, and needest not that any man should ask thee.

Jno. 18.4. Jesus therefore, knowing all things that should come upon him, went forth.

Jno. 20.27. Then saith he to Thomas, Reach hither thy finger, and behold my hands; and reach hither thy hand, and thrust it into my side: and be not faithless, but believing. Compare v. 25.

Jno. 21.17. Lord, thou knowest all things; thou knowest that I love thee.

Act. 1.24. They prayed, and said, Thou, Lord, which knowest the hearts of all men, shew whether of these two thou hast chosen.

Col. 2.3. In whom are hid all the treasures of wisdom and knowledge.

Heb. 4.12. The word of God is quick, and powerful, and sharper than any two-edged sword, piercing even to the dividing asunder of soul and spirit, and of the joints and marrow, and is a discerner of the thoughts and intents of the heart. 13. Neither is there any creature that is not manifest in his sight: but all things are naked and opened unto the eyes of him with whom we have to do.

Rev. 2.18. The Son of God, who hath his eyes like unto a flame of fire. 23. All the churches shall know that I am he which searcheth the reins and hearts: and I will give unto every one of you according to your works.

Rev. 5.5. Behold, the Lion of the tribe of Juda, the Root of David, hath prevailed to open the book, and to loose the seven seals thereof. 12. Worthy is the Lamb that was slain to receive power, and riches, and wisdom.

CHRIST, PARABLES OF, CHRONOLOGI-CALLY ARRANGED—

The wise and foolish builders, Mat. 7.24-27. Luk. 6.48,49.

Two debtors, Luk. 7.41-47.

The rich fool, Luk. 12.16-21.

The servants waiting for their Lord, Luk. 12.35-40.

Barren fig-tree, Luk. 13.6-9.

The sower, Mat. 13.3-9,18-23. Mar. 4.1-9, 14-20. Luk. 8.5-8,11-15.

The tares, Mat. 13.24-43.

Seed growing secretly, Mar. 4.26-29.

Mustard seed, Mat. 13.31,32. Mar. 4.30-32. Luk. 13.18,19.

Leaven, Mat. 13.33. Luk. 13.20,21.

Hid treasure, Mat. 13.44.

Pearl of great price, Mat. 13.45,46.

Draw-net, Mat. 13.47-50.

Unmerciful servant, Mat. 18.23-35.

Good Samaritan, Luk. 10.30-37.

Friend at midnight, Luk. 11.5-8.

Good shepherd, Jno. 10.1-16.

Great supper, Luk. 14.15-24.

Lost sheep, Luk. 15.3-7. Mat. 18.12-14.

Lost pece of money, Luk. 15.8-10.

The prodigal and his brother, Luk. 15.11-32.

The unjust steward, Luk. 16.1-9.

Rich man and Lazarus, Luk. 16.19-31.

Importunate widow, Luk. 18.1-8.

Pharisee and publican, Luk. 18.9-14.

Labourers in the vineyard, Mat. 20.1-16.

The pounds, Luk. 19.11-27.

The two sons, Mat. 21.28-32.

Wicked husbandmen, Mat. 21.33-44. Mar. 12.1-12. Luk. 20.9-18.

Marriage of the king's son, Mat. 22.1-14.

Fig-tree leafing, Mar. 13.28,29. Mat. 24.32.

Man taking a far journey, Mar. 13.34-37.

Ten virgins, Mat. 25.1-13.

Talents, Mat. 25.14-30.

The vine, Jno. 15.1-5.

CHRIST, PARDON FROM. Isa. 42.3. A bruised reed shall he not break, and the smoking flax shall he not quench.

Mat. 9.2. Jesus seeing their faith said unto the sick of the palsy; Son, be of good cheer; thy sins be forgiven thee. 6. The Son of man hath power on earth to forgive sins. Mar. 2.5,10. Luk. 5.20,24.

Luk. 7.47. Her sins, which are many, are forgiven; for she loved much. 48. And he said unto her, Thy sins are forgiven. 49. They that sat at meat with him began to say within themselves, Who is this that forgiveth sins also? 50. He said to the woman, Thy faith hath saved thee; go in peace.

Act. 5.31. Him hath God exalted with his right hand to be a Prince and a Saviour, for to give repentance to Israel, and forgiveness of sins.

Rom. 16.24. The grace of our Lord Jesus Christ be with you all.

Col. 3.13. As Christ forgave you, so also do ye.

1 Tim. 1.14. The grace of our Lord was exceeding abundant with faith and love which is in Christ Jesus. 16. For this cause I obtained mercy, that in me first Jesus Christ might shew forth all longsuffering, for a pattern to them which should hereafter believe on him to life everlasting.

1 Pet. 2.3. If so be ye have tasted that the Lord is gracious.

See PARDON THROUGH CHRIST.

CHRIST, POWER AND OMNIPOTENCE OF.

Psa. 45.3. Gird thy sword upon thy thigh, O most mighty, with thy glory and thy majesty. 4. And in thy majesty ride prosperously because of truth and meekness and righteousness: and thy right hand shall teach thee terrible things. 5. Thine arrows are sharp in the heart of the king's enemies; whereby the people fall under thee.

Psa. 110.3. Thy people shall be willing in the day of thy power.

Isa. 9.6. The government shall be upon his shoulder: and his name shall be called Wonderful, Counsellor, The mighty God, The Everlasting Father, The Prince of Peace.

Isa. 40.10. Behold, the Lord God will come with strong hand, and his arm shall rule for him: behold, his reward is with him, and his work before him.

Isa. 50.2. Is my hand shortened at all, that

it cannot redeem? or have I no power to deliver? behold, at my rebuke I dry up the sea, I make the rivers a wilderness: their fish stinketh, because *there is* no water, and dieth for thirst. 3. I clothe the heavens with blackness, and I make sackcloth their covering. See *v*. 4.

Isa. 63.1. Who *is* this that cometh from Edom, with dyed garments from Bozrah? this *that is* glorious in his apparel, travelling in the greatness of his strength? I that speak in righteousness, mighty to save.

Mat. 8.3. Jesus put forth *his* hand, and touched him, saying, I will; be thou clean. And immediately his leprosy was cleansed. 16. And he cast out the spirits with *his* word. 27. The men marvelled, saying, What manner of man is this, that even the winds and the sea obey him!

Mat. 10.1. When he had called unto *him* his twelve disciples, he gave them power *against* unclean spirits, to cast them out, and to heal all manner of sickness and all manner of disease. Mar. 6.7. Luk. 9.1.

Mat. 12.13. Stretch forth thine hand. And he stretched *it* forth; and it was restored whole, like as the other. 28. If I cast out devils by the Spirit of God, then the kingdom of God is come unto you. 29. Or else how can one enter into a strong man's house, and spoil his goods, except he first bind the strong man? and then he will spoil his house. Mar. 3.27. Luk. 11.20-22.

Mat. 28.18. All power is given unto me in heaven and in earth.

Luk. 5.17. The power of the Lord was *present* to heal them.

Jno. 2.19. Destroy this temple, and in three days I will raise it up.

Jno. 5.21. As the Father raiseth up the dead, and quickeneth *them;* even so the Son quickeneth whom he will. 28. Marvel not at this: for the hour is coming, in the which all that are in the graves shall hear his voice, 29. And shall come forth.

Jno. 10.18. No man taketh it from me, but I lay it down of myself: I have power to lay it down, and I have power to take it again. 28. I give unto them eternal life; and they shall never perish, neither shall any pluck them out of my hand.

Jno. 17.2. As thou hast given him power over all flesh, that he should give eternal life to as many as thou hast given him.

Jno. 18.6. As soon then as he had said unto them, I am *he*, they went backward, and fell to the ground.

Phil. 3.21. Who shall change our vile body, that it may be fashioned like unto his glorious body, according to the working whereby he is able even to subdue all things unto himself.

2 The. 1.9. Punished with everlasting destruction from the presence of the Lord, and from the glory of his power.

1 Tim. 6.16. To whom *be* honour and power everlasting. Amen.

Heb. 1.3. Upholding all things by the word of his power.

Heb. 7.25. He is able also to save them to the uttermost that come unto God by him.

2 Pet. 1.16. We have not followed cunningly devised fables, when we made known unto you the power and coming of our Lord Jesus Christ.

Rev. 1.8. I am Alpha and Omega, the beginning and the ending, saith the Lord, which is, and which was, and which is to come, the Almighty.

Rev. 3.7. He that hath the key of David, he that openeth, and no man shutteth; and shutteth, and no man openeth.

Rev. 5.12. Worthy is the Lamb that was slain to receive power, and riches, and wisdom, and strength, and honour, and glory, and blessing.

See CHRIST, MIRACLES OF.—CHRIST, KING.

CHRIST, PRAYERS OF. Mat. 11.25. I thank thee, O Father, Lord of heaven and earth, because thou hast hid these things from the wise and prudent, and hast revealed them unto babes. 26. Even so, Father; for so it seemed good in thy sight.

Mat. 14.23. He went up into a mountain apart to pray: and when the evening was come, he was there alone. Mar. 6.46.

Mat. 15.36. And he took the seven loaves and the fishes, and gave thanks, and brake *them*.

Mat. 19.13. Then were there brought unto him little children, that he should put *his* hands on them, and pray.

Mat. 26.26. And as they were eating, Jesus took bread, and blessed *it*, and brake *it*, and gave *it* to the disciples, and said, Take, eat; this is my body. 27. And he took the cup, and gave thanks. 1 Cor. 11.24.

Mat. 26.36. Then cometh Jesus with them unto a place called Gethsemane, and saith unto the disciples, Sit ye here, while I go and pray yonder. 39. And he went a little farther, and fell on his face, and prayed, saying, O my Father, if it be possible, let this cup pass from me: nevertheless not as I will, but as thou *wilt*. 42. He went away again the second time, and prayed, saying, O my Father, if this cup may not pass away from me, except I drink it, thy will be done. 44. And he left them, and went away again, and prayed the third time, saying the same words. Mar. 14. 32-39.

Mat. 27.46. Jesus cried with a loud voice, saying, Eli, Eli, lama sabachthani? That is to say, My God, my God why hast thou forsaken me?

Mar. 1.35. In the morning, rising up a great while before day, he went out, and departed into a solitary place, and there prayed.

Mar. 6.41. When he had taken the five loaves and the two fishes, he looked up to heaven, and blessed, and brake the loaves.

Luk. 3.21. Jesus also being baptized, and praying, the heaven was opened.

Luk. 5.16. He withdrew himself into the wilderness, and prayed.

Luk. 6.12. He went out into a mountain to pray, and continued all night in prayer to God.

Luk. 9.18. As he was alone praying, his disciples were with him. 28. He took Peter and John and James, and went up into a mountain to pray. 29. And as he prayed, the fashion of his countenance was altered, and his raiment *was* white *and* glistering.

Luk. 11.1. As he was praying in a certain place, when he ceased, one of his disciples said unto him, Lord, teach us to pray.

Luk. 22.32. I have prayed for thee, that thy faith fail not. 41. And he was withdrawn from them about a stone's cast, and kneeled down, and prayed. 43. There appeared an angel unto him from heaven, strengthening him. 44. Being in an agony he prayed more earnestly: and his sweat was as it were great drops of blood falling down to the ground.

Luk. 23.34. Then said Jesus, Father, forgive them; for they know not what they do. 46. When Jesus had cried with a loud voice, he said, Father, into thy hands I commend my spirit: and having said thus, he gave up the ghost.

Jno. 11.41. Jesus lifted up *his* eyes, and said, Father, I thank thee that thou hast heard me. 42. And I knew that thou hearest me always.

Jno. 12.27. Now is my soul troubled; and what shall I say? Father, save me from this hour: but for this cause came I unto this hour. 28. Father, glorify thy name. Then came there a voice from heaven, *saying,* I have both glorified *it,* and will glorify *it* again.

Jno. 17.1. These words spake Jesus, and lifted up his eyes to heaven, and said, Father, the hour is come; glorify thy Son, that thy Son also may glorify thee. *v.* 1-26.

Heb. 5.7. Who in the days of his flesh, when he had offered up prayers and supplications with strong crying and tears unto him that was able to save him from death, and was heard in that he feared.

CHRIST, Prayer and Praise in Name of. Mat. 18.20. Where two or three are gathered together in my name, there am I in the midst of them.

Jno. 14.13. Whatsoever ye shall ask in my name, that will I do, that the Father may be glorified in the Son. 14. If ye shall ask any thing in my name, I will do *it.*

Jno. 16.23. Whatsoever ye shall ask the Father in my name, he will give *it* you. 24. Hitherto have ye asked nothing in my name: ask, and ye shall receive, that your joy may be full. 26. At that day ye shall ask in my name. Jno. 15.16.

Rom. 1.8. I thank my God through Jesus Christ for you all.

Rom. 10.13. Whosoever shall call upon the name of the Lord shall be saved.

Eph. 2.18. Through him we both have access by one Spirit unto the Father.

Eph. 5.20. Giving thanks always for all things unto God and the Father in the name of our Lord Jesus Christ.

Col. 3.17. Whatsoever ye do in word or deed, *do* all in the name of the Lord Jesus, giving thanks to God and the Father by him.

Heb. 10.19. Having therefore, brethren, boldness to enter into the holiest by the blood of Jesus.

Heb. 13.15. By him therefore let us offer the sacrifice of praise to God continually, that is, the fruit of *our* lips, giving thanks to his name.

1 Pet. 2.5. An holy priesthood, to offer up spiritual sacrifices, acceptable to God by Jesus Christ.

CHRIST, Prophecies of. These will be found quoted under the subdivisions of the title Christ. Thus, for Prophecies of Christ as the Messiah, see Christ, Messiah. Prophecies of Christ the Saviour, see Christ the Saviour, and so on.

CHRIST Prophet. Deu. 18.15. The Lord thy God will raise up unto thee a Prophet from the midst of thee, of thy brethren, like unto me; unto him ye shall hearken; 18. I will raise them up a Prophet from among their brethren, like unto thee, and will put my words in his mouth; and he shall speak unto them all that I shall command him. Act. 3.23.

Luk. 7.16. They glorified God, saying, That a great prophet is risen up among us; and, That God hath visited his people.

Luk. 13.33. It cannot be that a prophet perish out of Jerusalem.

Luk. 24.19. Jesus of Nazareth, which was a prophet mighty in deed and word before God and all the people.

Jno. 3.2. Rabbi, we know that thou art a teacher come from God: for no man can do these miracles that thou doest, except God be with him.

See Christ, Omniscience of, Zeal of, Love of, Head of the Church, Messiah, Miracles of, Parables of, Christ, Son of God, God the Father, Son, and Holy Spirit.

CHRIST, Prophet. His Predictions. Mat. 8.11,12. Mat. 10.23,34. Mat. 11.23. Luk. 10.15. Mat. 13.30-50. Mar. 9.1. Luk. 9.27. Mat. 19.28. Mar. 10.30. Luk. 18.30. Mat. 21.43,44. Mat. 23.35-39. Mat. 24. Mat. 13. Luk. 21. Mat. 25. Mar. 11.1-6,14. Mat. 21. 1-3,19. Jno. 13.18-27,36-38. Jno. 16.32. Mar. 14.12-31,42,62. Mat. 26.17-35,46,64. Luk. 22. 10-13,31-38. Mar. 16.17. Luk. 12.40-53. Luk. 13.24-35. Luk. 17.20-37. Luk. 19.30-34,42-44. Luk. 23.28-31,43. Luk. 24.49. Jno. 14.16,26. Jno. 15.26. Jno. 16.7-14,28. Act. 1.4-8. Jno. 4.21,23. Jno. 5.25-29. Jno. 6.39,54. Jno. 7.39. Jno. 11.4,11,23,40. Jno. 12.32. Jno. 20.17. Jno. 21.18-23.

See Christ, Death of, predicted.

CHRIST, Regeneration from. See Regeneration.

———, Resurrection of. Psa. 2.7. The Lord hath said unto me, Thou *art* my Son; this day have I begotten thee. Act. 13.33.

Psa. 16.9. My flesh also shall rest in hope. 10. For thou wilt not leave my soul in hell; neither wilt thou suffer thine Holy One to see corruption. (See Psa. 2.7). Isa. 26.19.

Mat. 12.40. As Jonas was three days and three nights in the whale's belly; so shall the Son of man be three days and three nights in the heart of the earth.

Mat. 16.21. Began Jesus to shew unto his disciples, how that he must go unto Jerusalem, and be killed, and be raised again the third day. Mat. 17.23. Luk. 9.22. Luk. 24.7.

Mat. 20.19. Shall deliver him to the Gentiles to mock, and to scourge, and to crucify *him* : and the third day he shall rise again. Mat. 26.32. After I am risen again, I will go before you into Galilee. Mar. 14.28.

Mat. 27.52. Many bodies of the saints which slept arose, 53. And came out of the graves after his resurrection. 63. Sir, we remember that that deceiver said, while he was yet alive, After three days I will rise again. Mar. 8.31.

Mar. 9.9. Till the Son of man were risen from the dead. 10. And they kept that saying with themselves, questioning one with another what the rising from the dead should mean.

Luk. 24.46. Thus it is written, and thus it behoved Christ to suffer, and to rise from the dead the third day.

Jno. 2.19. Destroy this temple, and in three days I will raise it up. 21. But he spake of the temple of his body. v. 22.

Jno. 12.23. The hour is come, that the Son of man should be glorified.

Act. 1.3. To whom also he shewed himself alive after his passion by many infallible proofs, being seen of them forty days, and speaking of the things pertaining to the kingdom of God. 22. Must one be ordained to be a witness with us of his resurrection.

Act. 2.24. Whom God hath raised up, having loosed the pains of death: because it was not possible that he should be holden of it. 31. He seeing this before spake of the resurrection of Christ, that his soul was not left in hell, neither his flesh did see corruption. 32. This Jesus hath God raised up, whereof we all are witnesses. Psa. 16.9,10.

Act. 3.15. And killed the Prince of life, whom God hath raised from the dead; whereof we are witnesses.

Act. 4.10. Jesus Christ of Nazareth, whom ye crucified, whom God raised from the dead. 33. With great power gave the apostles witness of the resurrection of the Lord Jesus.

Act. 10.40. Him God raised up the third day, and shewed him openly; 41. Not to all the people, but unto witnesses chosen before of God, even to us, who did eat and drink with him after he rose from the dead.

Act. 13.30. God raised him from the dead: 31. And he was seen many days of them which came up with him from Galilee to Jerusalem, who are his witnesses unto the people. 33. He hath raised up Jesus again; as it is also written in the second psalm, Thou art my Son, this day have I begotten thee. 34. And as concerning that he raised him up from the dead, now no more to return to corruption, he said on this wise, I will give you the sure mercies of David. Psa. 2.7.

Act. 17.31. He will judge the world in righteousness by that man whom he hath ordained; whereof he hath given assurance unto all men, in that he hath raised him from the dead.

Act. 26.23. That Christ should suffer, and that he should be the first that should rise from the dead. v. 26.

Rom. 1.4. Declared to be the Son of God with power, according to the spirit of holiness, by the resurrection from the dead.

Rom. 4.24. Him that raised up Jesus our Lord from the dead. 25. Was raised again for our justification.

Rom. 5.10. If, when we were enemies, we were reconciled to God by the death of his Son, much more, being reconciled, we shall be saved by his life.

Rom. 6.4. Christ was raised up from the dead by the glory of the Father. 5. If we have been planted together in the likeness of his death, we shall be also in the likeness of his resurrection. 9. Christ being raised from the dead dieth no more; death hath no more dominion over him. 10. In that he died, he died unto sin once: but in that he liveth, he liveth unto God.

Rom. 8.11. The Spirit of him that raised up Jesus from the dead. 34. Who is he that condemneth? It is Christ that died, yea rather, that is risen again, who is even at the right hand of God.

Rom. 10.9. If thou shalt confess with thy mouth the Lord Jesus, and shalt believe in thine heart that God hath raised him from the dead, thou shalt be saved.

1 Cor. 6.14. God hath both raised up the Lord, and will also raise up us by his own power.

1 Cor. 15.4. That he was buried, and that he rose again the third day according to the scriptures. 20. Now is Christ risen from the dead, and become the firstfruits of them that slept. 21. For since by man came death, by man came also the resurrection of the dead. 22. For as in Adam all die, even so in Christ shall all be made alive. 23. But every man in his own order: Christ the firstfruits; afterward they that are Christ's at his coming. v. 5-8, 12-20.

2 Cor. 13.4. He was crucified through weakness, yet he liveth by the power of God.

Eph. 1.20. He raised him from the dead, and set him at his own right hand in the heavenly places.

Phil. 3.10. That I may know him, and the power of his resurrection.

Col. 1.18. The firstborn from the dead; that in all things he might have the preeminence.

Col. 2.12. God who hath raised him from the dead.

2 Tim. 2.8. Remember that Jesus Christ of the seed of David was raised from the dead according to my gospel.

Heb. 13.20. The God of peace, that brought again from the dead our Lord Jesus.

1 Pet. 1.3. The God and Father of our Lord Jesus Christ, which according to his abundant mercy hath begotten us again unto a lively hope by the resurrection of Jesus Christ from the dead. 21. Who by him do believe in God, that raised him up from the dead, and gave him glory.

1 Pet. 3.18. Put to death in the flesh, but quickened by the Spirit. 21. The like figure whereunto even baptism doth also now save us, by the resurrection of Jesus Christ.

Rev. 1.5. Jesus Christ, who is the faithful witness, and the first begotten of the dead. 18. I am he that liveth, and was dead; and, behold, I am alive for evermore, Amen; and have the keys of hell and of death.

For historical references to the Resurrection, see CHRIST, LIFE OF, IX.

CHRIST, RESURRECTION BY. See RESURRECTION.

———, SALVATION BY. See CHRIST, SAVIOUR—FAITH IN CHRIST.

———, SANCTIFICATION BY. See REGENERATION.

CHRIST THE SAVIOUR. Gen. 12.3. In thee shall all families of the earth be blessed.

Gen. 49.18. I have waited for thy salvation, O Lord.

Job 33.23. If there be a messenger with him, an interpreter, one among a thousand, to shew unto man his uprightness: 24. Then he is gracious unto him, and saith, Deliver him from going down to the pit; I have found a ransom.

Psa. 14.7. Oh that the salvation of Israel were come out of Zion!

Psa. 72.4. He shall judge the poor of the people, he shall save the children of the needy, and shall break in pieces the oppressor. 12. For he shall deliver the needy when he crieth; the poor also, and *him* that hath no helper. 13. He shall spare the poor and needy, and shall save the souls of the needy. 14. He shall redeem their soul from deceit and violence: and precious shall their blood be in his sight. 17. *Men* shall be blessed in him: all nations shall call him blessed.

Psa. 80.17. Let thy hand be upon the man of thy right hand, upon the son of man *whom* thou madest strong for thyself.

Psa. 89.19. I have laid help upon *one that is* mighty; I have exalted *one* chosen out of the people.

Psa. 118.26. Blessed *be* he that cometh in the name of the Lord.

Isa. 8.14. He shall be for a sanctuary.

Isa. 28.16. Behold, I lay in Zion for a foundation a stone, a tried stone, a precious corner *stone*, a sure foundation: he that believeth shall not make haste.

Isa. 32.2. A man shall be as an hiding-place from the wind, and a covert from the tempest; as rivers of water in a dry place, as the shadow of a great rock in a weary land.

Isa. 40.10. The Lord God will come with strong *hand*, and his arm shall rule for him: behold, his reward *is* with him, and his work before him. 11. He shall feed his flock like a shepherd: he shall gather the lambs with his arm, and carry *them* in his bosom, *and* shall gently lead those that are with young.

Isa. 42.6. Give thee for a covenant of the people, for a light of the Gentiles; 7. To open the blind eyes, to bring out the prisoners from the prison, *and* them that sit in darkness out of the prison-house.

Isa. 49.6. It is a light thing that thou shouldest be my servant to raise up the tribes of Jacob, and to restore the preserved of Israel: I will also give thee for a light to the Gentiles, that thou mayest be my salvation unto the end of the earth. 8. I will preserve thee, and give thee for a covenant of the people, to establish the earth, to cause to inherit the desolate heritages; 9. That thou mayest say to the prisoners, Go forth; to them that *are* in darkness, Shew yourselves. Act. 13.47.

Isa. 50.2. Wherefore, when I came, *was there* no man? when I called, *was there* none to answer? Is my hand shortened at all, that it cannot redeem? or have I no power to deliver? 8. *He is* near that justifieth me; who will contend with me? let us stand together: who *is* mine adversary? let him come near to me. 9. Behold, the Lord God will help me; who *is* he *that* shall condemn me?

Isa. 53.10. It pleased the Lord to bruise him; he hath put *him* to grief: when thou shalt make his soul an offering for sin, he shall see *his* seed, he shall prolong *his* days, and the pleasure of the Lord shall prosper in his hand. 11. He shall see of the travail of his soul, *and* shall be satisfied: by his knowledge shall my righteous servant justify many; for he shall bear their iniquities.

Isa. 59.16. He saw that there *was* no man, and wondered that *there was* no intercessor: therefore his arm brought salvation unto him;

and his righteousness, it sustained him. 17. For he put on righteousness as a breastplate, and an helmet of salvation upon his head; and he put on the garments of vengeance *for* clothing, and was clad with zeal as a cloke. 20. The Redeemer shall come to Zion, and unto them that turn from transgression in Jacob.

Isa. 61.1. The Spirit of the Lord God *is* upon me; because the Lord hath anointed me to preach good tidings unto the meek; he hath sent me to bind up the broken-hearted, to proclaim liberty to the captives, and the opening of the prison to *them that are* bound: 2. To proclaim the acceptable year of the Lord, and the day of vengeance of our God; to comfort all that mourn; 3. To appoint unto them that mourn in Zion, to give unto them beauty for ashes, the oil of joy for mourning, the garment of praise for the spirit of heaviness; that they might be called trees of righteousness, the planting of the Lord, that he might be glorified.

Isa. 62.11. The Lord hath proclaimed unto the end of the world, Say ye to the daughter of Zion, Behold, thy salvation cometh; behold, his reward *is* with him, and his work before him.

Isa. 63.1. Who *is* this that cometh from Edom, with dyed garments from Bozrah? this *that is* glorious in his apparel, travelling in the greatness of his strength? I that speak in righteousness, mighty to save. 5. I looked, and *there was* none to help; and I wondered that *there was* none to uphold: therefore mine own arm brought salvation unto me; and my fury, it upheld me. 8. He said, Surely they *are* my people, children *that* will not lie: so he was their Saviour. 9. In all their affliction he was afflicted, and the angel of his presence saved them: in his love and in his pity he redeemed them; and he bare them, and carried them all the days of old.

Jer. 23.5. I will raise unto David a righteous Branch, and a King shall reign and prosper, and shall execute judgment and justice in the earth. 6. In his days Judah shall be saved, and Israel shall dwell safely; and this *is* his name whereby he shall be called, THE LORD OUR RIGHTEOUSNESS. Jer. 33.15,16.

Eze. 34.23. I will set up one shepherd over them, and he shall feed them, *even* my servant David; he shall feed them, and he shall be their shepherd.

Mic. 5.4. He shall stand and feed in the strength of the Lord, in the majesty of the name of the Lord his God; and they shall abide: for now shall he be great unto the ends of the earth.

Hag. 2.7. The desire of all nations shall come.

Zec. 4.7. He shall bring forth the headstone *thereof with* shoutings, *crying*, Grace, grace unto it.

Zec. 9.9. Shout, O daughter of Jerusalem: behold, thy king cometh unto thee: he *is* just, and having salvation.

Mal. 4.2. Unto you that fear my name shall the Sun of righteousness arise with healing in his wings; and ye shall go forth, and grow up as calves of the stall.

Mat. 1.21. Thou shalt call his name JESUS: for he shall save his people from their sins.

Mat. 15.24. I am not sent but unto the lost sheep of the house of Israel.

Mat. 18.11. The Son of man is come to save that which was lost. 12. How think ye? if a man have an hundred sheep, and one of them be gone astray, doth he not leave the ninety and nine, and goeth into the mountains, and seeketh that which is gone astray? 13. And if so be that he find it, verily I say unto you, he rejoiceth more of that *sheep*, than of the ninety and nine which went not astray. Luk. 15.1-6.

Mat. 21.42. Did ye never read in the scriptures, The stone which the builders rejected, the same is become the head of the corner: this is the Lord's doing, and it is marvellous in our eyes? Psa. 118.22,23. Mar. 12.10,11. Luk. 20.17.

Luk. 1.68. Blessed *be* the Lord God of Israel; for he hath visited and redeemed his people, 69. And hath raised up an horn of salvation for us in the house of his servant David. 76. Thou shalt go before the face of the Lord to prepare his ways; 77. To give knowledge of salvation unto his people by the remission of their sins.

Luk. 2.11. Unto you is born this day in the city of David a Saviour, which is Christ the Lord. 30. Mine eyes have seen thy salvation, 31. Which thou hast prepared before the face of all people; 32. A light to lighten the Gentiles, and the glory of thy people Israel. 34. Behold, this *child* is set for the fall and rising again of many in Israel.

Luk. 5.31. They that are whole need not a physician; but they that are sick. 32. I came not to call the righteous, but sinners to repentance. Mat. 9.12,13.

Luk. 9.56. The Son of man is not come to destroy men's lives, but to save *them*.

Luk. 19.10. The Son of man is come to seek and to save that which was lost. (Luk. 15.4-10. The Parables.)

Jno. 1.9. *That* was the true Light, which lighteth every man that cometh into the world.

Jno. 3.16. God so loved the world, that he gave his only-begotten Son, that whosoever believeth in him should not perish, but have everlasting life. 17. God sent not his Son into the world to condemn the world; but that the world through him might be saved.

Jno. 4.14. Whosoever drinketh of the water that I shall give him shall never thirst; but the water that I shall give him shall be in him a well of water springing up into everlasting life. 42. This is indeed the Christ, the Saviour of the world.

Jno. 5.26. As the Father hath life in himself; so hath he given to the Son to have life in himself. 34. These things I say, that ye might be saved. 39. Search the scriptures; for in them ye think ye have eternal life: and they are they which testify of me. 40. And ye will not come to me, that ye might have life.

Jno. 6.27. Labour not for the meat which perisheth, but for that meat which endureth unto everlasting life, which the Son of man shall give unto you. 32. My Father giveth you the true bread from heaven. 33. For the bread of God is he which cometh down from heaven, and giveth life unto the world. 35. I am the bread of life: he that cometh to me shall never hunger; and he that believeth on me shall

never thirst. 37. Him that cometh to me I will in no wise cast out.

Jno. 6.39. Of all which he hath given me I should lose nothing, but should raise it up again at the last day. 50. I am the living bread which came down from heaven: if any man eat of this bread, he shall live for ever: and the bread that I will give is my flesh, which I will give for the life of the world. 53. Except ye eat the flesh of the Son of man, and drink his blood, ye have no life in you. 54. Whoso eateth my flesh, and drinketh my blood, hath eternal life; and I will raise him up at the last day.

Jno. 6.55. For my flesh is meat indeed, and my blood is drink indeed. 56. He that eateth my flesh, and drinketh my blood, dwelleth in me, and I in him. 57. He that eateth me, even he shall live by me. 58. This is that bread which came down from heaven: not as your fathers did eat manna, and are dead: he that eateth of this bread shall live for ever. 68. Lord, to whom shall we go? thou hast the words of eternal life.

Jno. 8.12. I am the light of the world: he that followeth me shall not walk in darkness, but shall have the light of life.

Jno. 9.5. As long as I am in the world, I am the light of the world. 39. For judgment I am come into this world, that they which see not might see.

Jno. 10.7. I am the door of the sheep. 9. I am the door: by me if any man enter in, he shall be saved, and shall go in and out, and find pasture. 10. I am come that they might have life, and that they might have *it* more abundantly. 11. I am the good shepherd: the good shepherd giveth his life for the sheep. 14. I am the good shepherd, and know my *sheep*, and am known of mine. 27. My sheep hear my voice, and I know them, and they follow me: 28. And I give unto them eternal life; and they shall never perish; neither shall any *man* pluck them out of my hand.

Jno. 12.27. Now is my soul troubled; and what shall I say? Father, save me from this hour: but for this cause came I unto this hour. 47. I came not to judge the world, but to save the world.

Jno. 14.6. I am the way, and the truth, and the life: no man cometh unto the Father, but by me. 19. Because I live, ye shall live also.

Jno. 16.33. Be of good cheer, I have overcome the world.

Jno. 17.2. As thou hast given him power over all flesh, that he should give eternal life to as many as thou hast given him. 3. This is life eternal, that they might know thee the only true God, and Jesus Christ, whom thou hast sent.

Jno. 18.37. For this cause came I into the world, that I should bear witness unto the truth.

Act. 2.36. Let all the house of Israel know assuredly, that God hath made that same Jesus, whom ye have crucified, both Lord and Christ.

Act. 3.15. Killed the Prince of life. 26. God, having raised up his Son Jesus, sent him to bless you, in turning away every one of you from his iniquities.

Act. 4.11. This is the stone which was set at nought of you builders, which is become the head of the corner. 12. Neither is there salvation in any other: for there is none other name under heaven given among men, whereby we must be saved.

Act. 5.31. Him hath God exalted with his right hand to be a Prince and a Saviour, for to give repentance to Israel, and forgiveness of sins.

Act. 13.23. Of this man's seed hath God, according to his promise, raised unto Israel a Saviour, Jesus.

Act. 15.11. Through the grace of the Lord Jesus Christ we shall be saved.

Act. 16.31. Believe on the Lord Jesus Christ, and thou shalt be saved, and thy house.

Rom. 5.15. The grace of God, and the gift by grace, which is by one man, Jesus Christ, hath abounded unto many. 17. They which receive abundance of grace and of the gift of righteousness shall reign in life by one, Jesus Christ. 18. By the righteousness of one the free gift came upon all men unto justification of life. 19. For as by one man's disobedience many were made sinners, so by the obedience of one shall many be made righteous. 21. As sin reigned unto death, even so might grace reign through righteousness unto eternal life by Jesus Christ our Lord.

Rom. 6.23. The gift of God is eternal life through Jesus Christ our Lord.

Rom. 10.9. If thou shalt confess with thy mouth the Lord Jesus, and shalt believe in thine heart that God hath raised him from the dead, thou shalt be saved.

Rom. 15.7. Christ also received us to the glory of God. 8. Jesus Christ was a minister of the circumcision for the truth of God, to confirm the promises made unto the fathers: 9. And that the Gentiles might glorify God for his mercy.

1 Cor. 1.30. Of him are ye in Christ Jesus, who of God is made unto us wisdom, and righteousness, and sanctification, and redemption.

1 Cor. 3.11. Other foundation can no man lay than that is laid, which is Jesus Christ.

1 Cor. 6.11. Ye are washed, but ye are sanctified, but ye are justified in the name of the Lord Jesus.

1 Cor. 10.3. And did all eat the same spiritual meat; 4. And did all drink the same spiritual drink: for they drank of that spiritual Rock that followed them: and that Rock was Christ.

1 Cor. 15.17. If Christ be not raised, your faith is vain; ye are yet in your sins. 57. Thanks be to God, which giveth us the victory through our Lord Jesus Christ.

2 Cor. 5.18. All things are of God, who hath reconciled us to himself by Jesus Christ, and hath given to us the ministry of reconciliation; 19. To wit, that God was in Christ, reconciling the world unto himself, not imputing their trespasses unto them; and hath committed unto us the word of reconciliation.

Gal. 4.7. Thou art no more a servant, but a son; and if a son, then an heir of God through Christ.

Eph. 1.10. That in the dispensation of the fulness of times, he might gather together in one all things in Christ, both which are in heaven, and which are on earth, even in him: 11. In whom also we have obtained an inheritance.

Eph. 2.20. Built upon the foundation of the apostles and prophets, Jesus Christ himself being the chief corner-stone.

Eph. 4.8. When he ascended up on high, he led captivity captive, and gave gifts unto men.

Eph. 5.23. Christ is the head of the church: and he is the saviour of the body.

Phil. 3.20. We look for the Saviour, the Lord Jesus Christ.

Col. 1.27. Christ in you, the hope of glory.

Col. 2.8. Beware lest any man spoil you through philosophy, and not after Christ. 10. Ye are complete in him.

Col. 3.3. Ye are dead, and your life is hid with Christ in God. 4. When Christ, who is our life, shall appear, then shall ye also appear with him in glory. 11. Christ is all, and in all.

1 The. 1.10. Jesus, which delivered us from the wrath to come.

2 The. 1.12. That the name of our Lord Jesus Christ may be glorified in you, and ye in him, according to the grace of our God, and the Lord Jesus Christ.

1 Tim. 1.1. Lord Jesus Christ, which is our hope. 15. This is a faithful saying, and worthy of all acceptation, that Christ Jesus came into the world to save sinners; of whom I am chief.

2 Tim. 1.1. The promise of life which is in Christ Jesus. 9. Who hath saved us, and called us with an holy calling, not according to our works, but according to his own purpose and grace, which was given us in Christ Jesus before the world began, 10. But is now made manifest by the appearing of our Saviour Jesus Christ, who hath abolished death, and hath brought life and immortality to light through the gospel. 12. I know whom I have believed, and am persuaded that he is able to keep that which I have committed unto him against that day.

2 Tim. 2.10. The salvation which is in Christ Jesus with eternal glory.

2 Tim. 3.15. Salvation through faith which is in Christ Jesus.

Tit. 2.13. The great God and our Saviour Jesus Christ; 14. Who gave himself for us, that he might redeem us from all iniquity, and purify unto himself a peculiar people, zealous of good works.

Heb. 2.3. How shall we escape, if we neglect so great salvation: which at the first began to be spoken by the Lord. 17. In all things it behoved him to be made like unto his brethren, that he might be a merciful and faithful highpriest in things pertaining to God, to make reconciliation for the sins of the people.

Heb. 5.9. Being made perfect, he became the author of eternal salvation unto all them that obey him.

Heb. 7.22. By so much was Jesus made a surety of a better testament. 25. He is able also to save them to the uttermost that come unto God by him, seeing he ever liveth to make intercession for them.

Heb. 13.10. We have an altar, whereof they have no right to eat which serve the tabernacle. 20. The God of peace, that brought again from the dead our Lord Jesus, that great Shepherd of the sheep, through the blood of the everlasting covenant.

1 Pet. 1.3. Hath begotten us again unto a lively hope, by the resurrection of Jesus Christ from the dead.

1 Pet. 2.4. To whom coming, *as unto* a living stone, disallowed indeed of men, but chosen of God, *and* precious, 5. Ye also, as lively stones, are built up a spiritual house, an holy priesthood, to offer up spiritual sacrifices, acceptable to God by Jesus Christ. 6. Behold, I lay in Sion a chief corner-stone, elect, precious : and he that believeth on him shall not be confounded. 7. Unto you therefore which believe *he is* precious. The stone which the builders disallowed, the same is made the head of the corner.

1 Pet. 2.25. Ye were as sheep going astray ; but are now returned unto the Shepherd and Bishop of your souls.

1 Pet. 3.21. The like figure whereunto *even* baptism doth also now save us (not the putting away of the filth of the flesh, but the answer of a good conscience toward God), by the resurrection of Jesus Christ.

1 Pet. 5.10. The God of all grace, who hath called us unto his eternal glory by Christ Jesus.

2 Pet. 1.3. His divine power hath given unto us all things that *pertain* unto life and godliness, through the knowledge of him that hath called us to glory and virtue.

1 Jno. 3.5. Ye know that he was manifested to take away our sins. 8. For this purpose the Son of God was manifested, that he might destroy the works of the devil.

1 Jno. 4.9. God sent his only-begotten Son into the world, that we might live through him. 14. We have seen and do testify that the Father sent the Son *to be* the Saviour of the world.

1 Jno. 5.11. This is the record, that God hath given to us eternal life, and this life is in his Son. 12. He that hath the Son hath life ; *and* he that hath not the Son of God hath not life. 13. These things have I written unto you that believe on the name of the Son of God ; that ye may know that ye have eternal life, and that ye may believe on the name of the Son of God. 20. We know that the Son of God is come, and hath given us an understanding, that we may know him that is true ; and we are in him that is true, *even* in his Son Jesus Christ. This is the true God, and eternal life.

Jude 1. To them that are sanctified by God the Father, and preserved in Jesus Christ.

Rev. 2.7. To him that overcometh will I give to eat of the tree of life, which is in the midst of the paradise of God.

Rev. 3.18. I counsel thee to buy of me gold tried in the fire, that thou mayest be rich ; and white raiment, that thou mayest be clothed, and *that* the shame of thy nakedness do not appear ; and anoint thine eyes with eye-salve, that thou mayest see.

Rev. 7.10. Salvation to our God which sitteth upon the throne, and unto the Lamb.

Rev. 14.4. These are they which follow the Lamb whithersoever he goeth. These were redeemed from among men, *being* the firstfruits unto God and to the Lamb.

Rev. 21.27. There shall in no wise enter into it any thing that defileth ; but they which are written in the Lamb's book of life.

Rev. 22.1. He shewed me a pure river of water of life, clear as crystal, proceeding out of the throne of God and of the Lamb. 2. In the midst of the street of it, and on either side of the river, *was there* the tree of life, which bare twelve *manner of* fruits, *and* yielded her fruit every month : and the leaves of the tree *were* for the healing of the nations.

See FAITH IN CHRIST.—PARDON.—CHRIST, DEATH OF.—CHRIST, HIGH-PRIEST.

CHRIST, SECOND COMING OF. Job 19.25. I know *that* my redeemer liveth, and *that* he shall stand at the latter *day* upon the earth : 26. And *though* after my skin *worms* destroy this *body*, yet in my flesh shall I see God.

Mat. 16.27. The Son of man shall come in the glory of his Father with his angels ; and then he shall reward every man according to his works. 28. There be some standing here, which shall not taste of death, till they see the Son of man coming in his kingdom. Mar. 9.1. Luk. 9.27.

Mat. 24.27. As the lightning cometh out of the east, and shineth even unto the west ; so shall also the coming of the Son of man be. 30. Then shall appear the sign of the Son of man in heaven : and then shall all the tribes of the earth mourn, and they shall see the Son of man coming in the clouds of heaven with power and great glory. 31. And he shall send his angels with a great sound of a trumpet, and they shall gather together his elect from the four winds, from one end of heaven to the other.

Mat. 24.37. As the days of Noe *were*, so shall also the coming of the Son of man be. 38. As in the days that were before the flood they were eating and drinking, marrying and giving in marriage, until the day that Noe entered into the ark, 39. And knew not until the flood came, and took them all away ; so shall also the coming of the Son of man be.

Mat. 24.42. Watch therefore : for ye know not what hour your Lord doth come. 43. If the goodman of the house had known in what watch the thief would come, he would have watched, and would not have suffered his house to be broken up. 44. Therefore be ye also ready : for in such an hour as ye think not the Son of man cometh. *v.* 1-44. Mar. 13.1-37. Luk. 21.5-35. Luk. 17.22-37. Luk. 12.40.

Mat. 25.6. At midnight there was a cry made, Behold, the bridegroom cometh ; go ye out to meet him. 10. While they went to buy, the bridegroom came ; and they that were ready went in with him to the marriage : and the door was shut. 13. Watch therefore, for ye know neither the day nor the hour wherein the Son of man cometh. 19. After a long time the lord of those servants cometh, and reckoneth with them. 31. When the Son of man shall come in his glory, and all the holy angels with him, then shall he sit upon the throne of his glory. *v.* 1-13, 31-46.

Mat. 26.64. Hereafter shall ye see the Son of man sitting on the right hand of power, and coming in the clouds of heaven.

Mar. 13.27. Then shall he send his angels, and shall gather together his elect from the four winds, from the uttermost part of the earth to the uttermost part of heaven. 32. But of that day and *that* hour knoweth no man, no, not the angels which are in heaven, neither the Son, but the Father. 35. Watch ye therefore : for ye know not when the master of the house cometh, at even, or at midnight, or at the cockcrowing, or in the morning :

36. Lest coming suddenly he find you sleeping. Mat. 24.36.

Luk. 9.26. Whosoever shall be ashamed of me and of my words, of him shall the Son of man be ashamed, when he shall come in his own glory, and *in his* Father's, and of the holy angels. Mar. 8.38.

Luk. 12.37. Blessed *are* those servants, whom the lord when he cometh shall find watching: verily I say unto you, that he shall gird himself, and make them to sit down to meat, and will come forth and serve them. 38. And if he shall come in the second watch, or come in the third watch, and find *them* so, blessed are these servants.

Luk. 18.8. Nevertheless when the Son of man cometh, shall he find faith on the earth?

Luk. 19.12. A certain nobleman went into a far country to receive for himself a kingdom, and to return. 15. And it came to pass, that when he was returned, having received the kingdom, then he commanded these servants to be called unto him.

Luk. 21.35. As a snare shall it come on all them that dwell on the face of the whole earth.

Jno. 14.3. If I go and prepare a place for you, I will come again, and receive you unto myself; that where I am, *there ye* may be also.

Act. 1.11. This same Jesus, which is taken up from you into heaven, shall so come in like manner as ye have seen him go into heaven.

Act. 3.20. He shall send Jesus Christ, which before was preached unto you: 21. Whom the heaven must receive until the times of restitution of all things, which God hath spoken by the mouth of all his holy prophets since the world began.

1 Cor. 1.7. Come behind in no gift; waiting for the coming of our Lord Jesus Christ. 8. Who shall also confirm you unto the end, *that ye may be* blameless in the day of our Lord Jesus Christ.

1 Cor. 4.5. Judge nothing before the time, until the Lord come, who both will bring to light the hidden things of darkness, and will make manifest the counsels of the hearts.

1 Cor. 11.26. As often as ye eat this bread, and drink this cup, ye do shew the Lord's death till he come.

1 Cor. 15.23. Christ the firstfruits; afterward they that are Christ's at his coming.

Phil. 3.20. Our conversation is in heaven; from whence also we look for the Saviour, the Lord Jesus Christ: 21. Who shall change our vile body.

Phil. 4.5. The Lord *is* at hand.

Col. 3.4. When Christ, *who is* our life, shall appear, then shall ye also appear with him in glory.

1 The. 1.10. Wait for his Son from heaven, whom he raised from the dead, *even* Jesus.

1 The. 2.19. What *is* our hope, or joy, or crown of rejoicing? *Are* not even ye in the presence of our Lord Jesus Christ at his coming?

1 The. 3.13. He may stablish your hearts unblameable in holiness before God, even our Father, at the coming of our Lord Jesus Christ with all his saints.

1 The. 4.15. We which are alive *and* remain unto the coming of the Lord shall not prevent them which are asleep. 16. For the Lord himself shall descend from heaven with a shout, with the voice of the archangel, and with the trump of God; and the dead in Christ shall rise first: 17. Then we which are alive *and* remain shall be caught up together with them in the clouds, to meet the Lord in the air: and so shall we ever be with the Lord.

1 The. 5.2. Yourselves know perfectly that the day of the Lord so cometh as a thief in the night. 3. For when they shall say, Peace and safety; then sudden destruction cometh upon them, as travail upon a woman with child; and they shall not escape. 23. *I pray God* your whole spirit and soul and body be preserved blameless unto the coming of our Lord Jesus Christ.

2 The. 1.7. To you who are troubled rest with us, when the Lord Jesus shall be revealed from heaven with his mighty angels. 10. He shall come to be glorified in his saints, and to be admired in all them that believe in that day.

2 The. 2.1. We beseech you, brethren, by the coming of our Lord Jesus Christ, and *by* our gathering together unto him, 2. That ye be not soon shaken in mind, or be troubled, neither by spirit, nor by word, nor by letter as from us, as that the day of Christ is at hand. 3. Let no man deceive you by any means: for *that day shall not come*, except there come a falling away first, and that man of sin be revealed, the son of perdition; 5. Remember ye not, that, when I was yet with you, I told you these things? 8. Then shall that Wicked be revealed, whom the Lord shall consume with the spirit of his mouth, and shall destroy with the brightness of his coming.

2 The. 3.5. The Lord direct your hearts into the love of God, and into the patient waiting for Christ.

1 Tim. 6.14. Keep *this* commandment without spot, unrebukable, until the appearing of our Lord Jesus Christ: 15. Which in his times he shall shew.

2 Tim. 4.1. The Lord Jesus Christ, who shall judge the quick and the dead at his appearing and his kingdom. 8. There is laid up for me a crown of righteousness, which the Lord, the righteous Judge, shall give me at that day; and not to me only, but unto all them also that love his appearing.

Tit. 2.13. Looking for that blessed hope, and the glorious appearing of the great God and our Saviour Jesus Christ.

Heb. 9.28. Unto them that look for him shall he appear the second time without sin unto salvation.

Jas. 5.7. Be patient therefore, brethren, unto the coming of the Lord. Behold, the husbandman waiteth for the precious fruit of the earth, and hath long patience for it, until he receive the early and latter rain. 8. Be ye also patient; stablish your hearts: for the coming of the Lord draweth nigh. 9. The judge standeth before the door.

1 Pet. 1.7. Praise and honour and glory at the appearing of Jesus Christ. 13. Wherefore gird up the loins of your mind, be sober, and hope to the end, for the grace that is to be brought unto you at the revelation of Jesus Christ.

1 Pet. 4.13. When his glory shall be revealed, ye may be glad also with exceeding joy.

1 Pet. 5.4. When the chief Shepherd shall appear, ye shall receive a crown of glory that fadeth not away.

2 Pet. 1.16. We have not followed cunningly devised fables, when we made known unto you the power and coming of our Lord Jesus Christ.

2 Pet. 3.12. Looking for and hasting unto the coming of the day of God, wherein the heavens being on fire shall be dissolved, and the elements shall melt with fervent heat? *v.* 3,4,8-14.

1 Jno. 2.28. Little children, abide in him; that, when he shall appear, we may have confidence, and not be ashamed before him at his coming.

1 Jno. 3.2. But we know that, when he shall appear, we shall be like him; for we shall see him as he is.

Jude 14. Enoch also, the seventh from Adam, prophesied of these, saying, Behold, the Lord cometh with ten thousands of his saints, 15. To execute judgment upon all.

Rev. 1.7. Behold, he cometh with clouds; and every eye shall see him, and they *also* which pierced him: and all kindreds of the earth shall wail because of him.

Rev. 16.15. Behold I come as a thief.

Rev. 22.12. behold, I come quickly; and my reward *is* with me, to give every man according as his work shall be. 20. He which testifieth these things saith, Surely I come quickly. Amen. Even so, come, Lord Jesus.

See JUDGMENT OF THE LAST DAY—RESURRECTION.

CHRIST. SON OF GOD.—CHRIST AND THE FATHER. Deu. 18.18. I will raise them up a Prophet from among their brethren, like unto thee, and will put my words in his mouth; and he shall speak unto them all that I shall command him.

Psa. 2.6. Yet have I set my King upon my holy hill of Zion. 7. I will declare the decree: the Lord hath said unto me, Thou *art* my Son; this day have I begotten thee.

Psa. 40.6. Sacrifice and offering thou didst not desire; mine ears hast thou opened: burnt-offering and sin-offering hast thou not required. 7. Then said I, Lo, I come: in the volume of the book *it is* written of me, 8. I delight to do thy will, O my God: yea, thy law *is* within my heart.

Psa. 45.2. Grace is poured into thy lips: therefore God hath blessed thee for ever. 6. Thy throne, O God, *is* for ever and ever: the sceptre of thy kingdom *is* a right sceptre. 7. Thou lovest righteousness, and hatest wickedness: therefore God, thy God, hath anointed thee with the oil of gladness above thy fellows.

Psa. 89.19. Thou spakest in vision to thy holy one, and saidst, I have laid help upon *one that is* mighty; I have exalted *one* chosen out of the people. 20. I have found David my servant; with my holy oil have I anointed him: 21. With whom my hand shall be established: mine arm also shall strengthen him.

Psa. 110.1. The Lord said unto my Lord, Sit thou at my right hand, until I make thine enemies thy footstool.

Pro. 8.22. The Lord possessed me in the beginning of his way, before his works of old. 30. Then I was by him, *as* one brought up

with him; and I was daily *his* delight, rejoicing always before him.

Isa. 28.16. Behold, I lay in Zion for a foundation a stone, a tried stone, a precious corner *stone*, a sure foundation.

Isa. 42.1. Behold my servant, whom I uphold; mine elect, *in whom* my soul delighteth; I have put my spirit upon him. 6. I the Lord have called thee in righteousness, and will hold thine hand, and will keep thee, and give thee for a covenant of the people, for a light of the Gentiles.

Isa. 48.16. I have not spoken in secret from the beginning; from the time that it was, there *am* I: and now the Lord God, and his Spirit, hath sent me.

Isa. 49.1. The Lord hath called me from the womb; from the bowels of my mother hath he made mention of my name. 3. Thou *art* my servant, O Israel, in whom I will be glorified. 4. Then I said, I have laboured in vain, I have spent my strength for nought, and in vain: *yet* surely my judgment *is* with the Lord, and my work with my God.

Isa. 49.5. Now, saith the Lord that formed me from the womb *to be* his servant, to bring Jacob again to him, Though Israel be not gathered, yet shall I be glorious in the eyes of the Lord, and my God shall be my strength. 7. Thus saith the Lord, the Redeemer of Israel, *and* his Holy One, to him whom man despiseth, to him whom the nation abhorreth, to a servant of rulers, Kings shall see and arise, princes also shall worship, because of the Lord that is faithful, *and* the Holy One of Israel, and he shall choose thee.

Isa. 50.4. The Lord God hath given me the tongue of the learned, that I should know how to speak a word in season to *him that is* weary: he wakeneth morning by morning, he wakeneth mine ear to hear as the learned. 5. The Lord God hath opened mine ear, and I was not rebellious, neither turned away back. 7. The Lord God will help me; therefore shall I not be confounded: therefore have I set my face like a flint, and I know that I shall not be ashamed. 8. *He is* near that justifieth me; who will contend with me? let us stand together: who *is* mine adversary? let him come near to me. 9. Behold, the Lord God will help me; who *is* he *that* shall condemn me?

Isa. 51.16. I have put my words in thy mouth, and I have covered thee in the shadow of mine hand, that I may plant the heavens, and lay the foundations of the earth, and say unto Zion, Thou *art* my people.

Isa. 53.10. It pleased the Lord to bruise him; he hath put *him* to grief: when thou shalt make his soul an offering for sin, he shall see *his* seed, he shall prolong *his* days, and the pleasure of the Lord shall prosper in his hand.

Isa. 55.3. I will make an everlasting covenant with you, *even* the sure mercies of David. 4. Behold, I have given him *for* a witness to the people. 5. Nations *that* knew not thee shall run unto thee because of the Lord thy God, and for the Holy One of Israel; for he hath glorified thee.

Isa. 61.1. The Spirit of the Lord God *is* upon me; because the Lord hath anointed me to preach good tidings unto the meek; he hath sent me to bind up the broken-hearted.

Eze. 21.27. I will overturn, overturn, overturn, it: and it shall be no *more*, until he come whose right it is; and I will give it *him*.

Eze. 34.23. I will set up one Shepherd over them, and he shall feed them, *even* my servant David; he shall feed them, and he shall be their shepherd. 24. And I the Lord will be their God, and my servant David a prince among them: I the Lord have spoken *it*.
Eze. 37.24.

Dan. 7.13. Behold, *one* like the Son of man came with the clouds of heaven, and came to the Ancient of days, and they brought him near before him. 14. And there was given him dominion, and glory, and a kingdom, that all people, nations, and languages, should serve him.

Mic. 5.4. He shall stand and feed in the strength of the Lord, in the majesty of the name of the Lord his God; and they shall abide.

Zec. 13.7. Awake, O sword, against my shepherd, and against the man *that* is my fellow, saith the Lord of hosts: smite the shepherd, and the sheep shall be scattered.

Mat. 1.18. The birth of Jesus Christ was on this wise: When as his mother Mary was espoused to Joseph, before they came together, she was found with child of the Holy Ghost. 20. Fear not to take unto thee Mary thy wife: for that which is conceived in her is of the Holy Ghost.

Mat. 3.17. Lo a voice from heaven, saying, This is my beloved Son, in whom I am well pleased. Mar. 1.11. Luk. 3.22.

Mat. 10.40. He that receiveth me receiveth him that sent me.

Mat. 11.27. All things are delivered unto me of my Father: and no man knoweth the Son, but the Father; neither knoweth any man the Father, save the Son, and *he* to whomsoever the Son will reveal *him*. Luk. 10.22.

Mat. 16.16. Thou art the Christ, the Son of the living God.

Mat. 17.5. This is my beloved Son, in whom I am well pleased; hear ye him. Mar. 9.7. Luk. 9.35.

Mat. 20.23. To sit on my right hand, and on my left, is not mine to give, but *it shall be given to them* for whom it is prepared of my Father.

Mat. 26.63. I adjure thee by the living God, that thou tell us whether thou be the Christ, the Son of God. 64. Jesus saith unto him, Thou hast said.

Luk. 1.35. The Holy Ghost shall come upon thee, and the power of the Highest shall overshadow thee: therefore also that holy thing which shall be born of thee shall be called the Son of God.

Luk. 22.29. I appoint unto you a kingdom, as my Father hath appointed unto me. 70. Art thou then the Son of God? And he said unto them, Ye say that I am. Mar. 14.61.

Jno. 1.1. In the beginning was the Word, and the Word was with God, and the Word was God. 2. The same was in the beginning with God. 14. The Word was made flesh, and dwelt among us (and we beheld his glory, the glory as of the only-begotten of the Father), full of grace and truth. 18. No man hath seen God at any time; the only-begotten Son, which is in the bosom of the Father, he hath declared *him*. 34. I saw, and bare record that this is

the Son of God. 49. Rabbi, thou art the Son of God; thou art the King of Israel.

Jno. 3.16. God so loved the world that he gave his only-begotten Son. 34. He whom God hath sent speaketh the words of God: for God giveth not the Spirit by measure *unto him*. 35. The Father loveth the Son, and hath given all things into his hand.

Jno. 5.19. The Son can do nothing of himself, but what he seeth the Father do: for what things soever he doeth, these also doeth the Son likewise. 20. The Father loveth the Son, and sheweth him all things that himself doeth: and he will shew him greater works than these. 21. As the Father raiseth up the dead, and quickeneth *them*; even so the Son quickeneth whom he will. 23. All *men* should honour the Son, even as they honour the Father. He that honoureth not the Son, honoureth not the Father which hath sent him.

Jno. 5.26. As the Father hath life in himself; so hath he given to the Son to have life in himself; 27. And hath given him authority to execute judgment also, because he is the Son of man. 30. I can of mine own self do nothing: as I hear, I judge: and my judgment is just; because I seek not mine own will, but the will of the Father which hath sent me. 32. There is another that beareth witness of me; and I know that the witness which he witnesseth of me is true.

Jno. 5.36. The works which the Father hath given me to finish, the same works that I do, bear witness of me, that the Father hath sent me. 37. The Father himself, which hath sent me, hath borne witness of me. Ye have neither heard his voice at any time, nor seen his shape.

Jno. 6.27. Him hath God the Father sealed. 30. I came down from heaven, not to do mine own will, but the will of him that sent me. 46. Not that any man hath seen the Father, save he which is of God, he hath seen the Father. 57. The living Father hath sent me, and I live by the Father. 69. We believe and are sure that thou art that Christ, the Son of the living God.

Jno. 7.16. My doctrine is not mine, but his that sent me. 28. I am not come of myself, but he that sent me is true, whom ye know not. 29. But I know him: for I am from him, and he hath sent me.

Jno. 8.16. I am not alone, but I and the Father that sent me. 19. Then said they unto him, Where is thy Father? Jesus answered, Ye neither know me, nor my Father: if ye had known me, ye should have known my Father also. 26. He that sent me is true; and I speak to the world those things which I have heard of him. 28. When ye have lifted up the Son of man, then shall ye know that I am *he*, and *that* I do nothing of myself; but as my Father hath taught me, I speak these things. 29. And he that sent me is with me: the Father hath not left me alone; for I do always those things that please him.

Jno. 8.38. I speak that which I have seen with my Father. 40. A man that hath told you the truth, which I have heard of God. 42. If God were your Father, ye would love me: for I proceeded forth and came from God; neither came I of myself, but he sent me. 49. I honour my Father, and ye do dishonour me. 50. And I seek not mine own glory : there is one that seeketh and judgeth. 54. If I honour myself, my honour is nothing : it is my Father that honoureth me ; of whom ye say, that he is your God : 55. Yet ye have not known him ; but I know him : and if I should say, I know him not, I shall be a liar like unto you : but I know him, and keep his saying.

Jno. 9.35. He said unto him, Dost thou believe on the Son of God? 36. He answered and said, Who is he, Lord, that I might believe on him ? 37. Jesus said unto him, Thou hast both seen him, and it is he that talketh with thee.

Jno. 10.15. As the Father knoweth me, even so know I the Father. 17. Therefore doth my Father love me, because I lay down my life, that I might take it again. 18. This commandment have I received of my Father. 29. My Father, which gave *them* me, is greater than all ; and no *man* is able to pluck *them* out of my Father's hand. 30. I and *my* Father are one.

Jno. 10.34. Is it not written in your law, I said, Ye are gods? 35. If he called them gods, unto whom the word of God came, and the scripture cannot be broken ; 36. Say ye of him, whom the Father hath sanctified, and sent into the world, Thou blasphemest ; because I said, I am the Son of God ? 37. If I do not the works of my Father, believe me not. 38. But if I do, though ye believe not me, believe the works : that ye may know, and believe, that the Father *is* in me, and I in him.

Jno. 11.41. Father, I thank thee that thou hast heard me. 42. And I knew that thou hearest me always : but because of the people which stand by I said *it*, that they may believe that thou hast sent me.

Jno. 12.49. I have not spoken of myself ; but the Father which sent me, he gave me a commandment, what I should say, and what I should speak. 50. And I know that his commandment is life everlasting : whatsoever I speak therefore, even as the Father said unto me, so I speak.

Jno. 13.3. Jesus knowing that the Father had given all things into his hands, and that he was come from God, and went to God. 31. Now is the Son of man glorified, and God is glorified in him. 32. If God be glorified in him, God shall also glorify him in himself, and shall straightway glorify him.

Jno. 14.7. If ye had known me, ye should have known my Father also : and from henceforth ye know him, and have seen him. 14. He that hath seen me hath seen the Father ; and how sayest thou *then*, Shew us the Father? 10. Believest thou not that I am in the Father, and the Father in me? the words that I speak unto you I speak not of myself : but the Father that dwelleth in me, he doeth the works. 11. Believe me that I *am* in the Father, and the Father in me.

Jno. 14.13. Whatsoever ye shall ask in my name, that will I do, that the Father may be glorified in the Son. 16. I will pray the Father, and he shall give you another Comforter, that he may abide with you for ever. 20. At that day ye shall know that I *am* in my Father, and ye in me, and I in you. 24. The word which ye hear is not mine, but the Father's which sent me. 28. If ye loved me, ye would rejoice,

because I said, I go unto the Father : for my Father is greater than I. 31. That the world may know that I love the Father ; and as the Father gave me commandment, even so I do.

Jno. 15.1. I am the true vine, and my Father is the husbandman. 9. As the Father hath loved me, so have I loved you. 10. I have kept my Father's commandments, and abide in his love. 23. He that hateth me hateth my Father also. 24. Now have they both seen and hated both me and my Father.

Jno. 16.5. I go my way to him that sent me. 15. All things that the Father hath are mine. 27. The Father himself loveth you, because ye have loved me, and have believed that I came out from God. 28. I came forth from the Father, and am come into the world : again, I leave the world, and go to the Father. 32. I am not alone, because the Father is with me.

Jno. 17.1. Father, the hour is come ; glorify thy Son, that thy Son also may glorify thee. *v.* 1-26.

Jno. 20.17. I am not yet ascended to my Father : but go to my brethren, and say unto them, I ascend unto my Father, and your Father ; and *to* my God, and your God. 21. As *my* Father hath sent me, even so send I you.

Act. 2.22. Jesus of Nazareth, a man approved of God among you by miracles and wonders and signs, which God did by him in the midst of you. 23. Him, being delivered by the determinate counsel and foreknowledge of God, ye have taken. 24. Whom God hath raised up, having loosed the pains of death.

Act. 3.13. The God of our fathers, hath glorified his Son Jesus.

Act. 10.38. God anointed Jesus of Nazareth with the Holy Ghost and with power : who went about doing good, and healing all that were oppressed of the devil ; for God was with him. 42. It is he which was ordained of God *to be* the Judge of quick and dead.

Act. 13.37. He, whom God raised again, saw no corruption.

Rom. 1.4. Declared *to be* the Son of God with power, according to the spirit of holiness, by the resurrection from the dead.

Rom. 8.32. He that spared not his own Son, but delivered him up for us all.

1 Cor. 1.30. Of him are ye in Christ Jesus, who of God is made unto us wisdom, and righteousness, and sanctification, and redemption.

1 Cor. 3.23. Ye are Christ's ; and Christ *is* God's.

1 Cor. 8.6. *There is but* one God, the Father, of whom *are* all things, and we in him ; and one Lord Jesus Christ, by whom *are* all things, and we by him.

1 Cor. 11.3. The head of Christ *is* God.

1 Cor. 15.24. When he shall have delivered up the kingdom to God, even the Father. 27. He hath put all things under his feet. But when he saith all things are put under *him, it is* manifest that he is excepted, which did put all things under him. 28. And when all things shall be subdued unto him, then shall the Son also himself be subject unto him that put all things under him, that God may be all in all.

2 Cor. 1.3. God, even the Father of our Lord Jesus Christ.

2 Cor. 4.6. The light of the knowledge of the glory of God in the face of Jesus Christ. 14. He which raised up the Lord Jesus shall raise up us also by Jesus.

Gal. 1.3. Our Lord Jesus Christ, 4. Who gave himself for our sins, that he might deliver us from this present evil world, according to the will of God and our Father.

Gal. 4.4. God sent forth his Son, made of a woman.

Eph. 1.3. The God and Father of our Lord Jesus Christ. 6. The Beloved. 17. The God of our Lord Jesus Christ, the Father of glory. 19. The working of his mighty power, 20. Which he wrought in Christ, when he raised him from the dead, and set *him* at his own right hand in the heavenly *places*.

Eph. 3.9. God, who created all things by Jesus Christ.

Phil. 2.6. Being in the form of God, thought it not robbery to be equal with God. 9. God also hath highly exalted him, and given him a name which is above every name.

Col. 1.15. Who is the image of the invisible God, the firstborn of every creature. 19. It pleased *the Father* that in him should all fulness dwell.

Col. 2.2. The mystery of God, and of the Father, and of Christ.

1 The. 3.11. God himself and our Father, and our Lord Jesus Christ, direct our way unto you.

Heb. 1.2. Hath in these last days spoken unto us by *his* Son, whom he hath appointed heir of all things, by whom also he made the worlds; 3. Who being the brightness of *his* glory, and the express image of his person, and upholding all things by the word of his power, when he had by himself purged our sins, sat down on the right hand of the Majesty on high.

Heb. 3.2. Who was faithful to him that appointed him.

Heb. 5.5. Christ glorified not himself to be made an high-priest; but he that said unto him, Thou art my Son, to-day have I begotten thee. 10. Called of God an high-priest after the order of Melchisedec.

Heb. 13.20. The God of peace, that brought again from the dead our Lord Jesus.

1 Pet. 1.21. God, that raised him up from the dead, and gave him glory.

1 Pet. 2.4. A living stone, disallowed indeed of men, but chosen of God, *and* precious.

2 Pet. 1.17. He received from God the Father honour and glory, when there came such a voice to him from the excellent glory. This is my beloved Son, in whom I am well pleased.

1 Jno. 1.2. That eternal life, which was with the Father, and was manifested unto us.

1 Jno. 4.9. God sent his only-begotten Son into the world, that we might live through him. 14. The Father sent the Son *to be* the Saviour of the world.

1 Jno. 5.9. This is the witness of God, which he hath testified of his Son.

See CHRIST, GOD.—GOD THE FATHER, SON, AND HOLY SPIRIT.

CHRIST, SUFFERINGS, PERSECUTION, AND DEATH OF. Gen. 3.15. I will put enmity between thee and the woman, and between thy seed and her seed; it shall bruise thy head, and thou shalt bruise his heel.

Psa. 21.1. My God, my God, why hast thou forsaken me? *why art thou so* far from helping me, *and from* the words of my roaring? 2. O my God, I cry in the daytime, but thou hearest not; and in the night season, and am not silent.

Psa. 22.6. I *am* a worm, and no man; a reproach of men, and despised of the people. 7. All they that see me laugh me to scorn: they shoot out the lip, they shake the head, *saying,* 8. He trusted on the Lord *that* he would deliver him: let him deliver him, seeing he delighted in him. 11. Be not far from me; for trouble *is* near; for *there is* none to help. 12. Many bulls have compassed me: strong *bulls* of Bashan have beset me round. 13. They gaped upon me *with* their mouths, *as* a ravening and a roaring lion.

Psa. 22.14. I am poured out like water, and all my bones are out of joint: my heart is like wax; it is melted in the midst of my bowels. 15. My strength is dried up like a potsherd; and my tongue cleaveth to my jaws; and thou hast brought me into the dust of death. 16. For dogs have compassed me: the assembly of the wicked have inclosed me: they pierced my hands and my feet.

Psa. 22.17. I may tell all my bones: they look *and* stare upon me. 18. They part my garments among them, and cast lots upon my vesture. 19. But be not thou far from me, O Lord: O my strength, haste thee to help me. 20. Deliver my soul from the sword: my darling from the power of the dog. 21. Save me from the lion's mouth: for thou hast heard me from the horns of the unicorns.

Psa. 69.7. For thy sake I have borne reproach; shame hath covered my face. 8. I am become a stranger unto my brethren, and an alien unto my mother's children. 9. For the zeal of thine house hath eaten me up; and the reproaches of them that reproached thee are fallen upon me. 20. Reproach hath broken my heart; and I am full of heaviness: and I looked *for some* to take pity, but *there was* none; and for comforters, but I found none. 21. They gave me also gall for my meat; and in my thirst they gave me vinegar to drink. 26. They persecute *him* whom thou hast smitten; and they talk to the grief of those whom thou hast wounded. *v.* 1-21.

Psa. 109.25. I became also a reproach unto them: *when* they looked upon me they shaked their heads.

Isa. 49.7. Thus saith the Lord, the Redeemer of Israel, *and* his Holy One, to him whom man despiseth, to him whom the nation abhorreth, to a servant of rulers.

Isa. 50.6. I gave my back to the smiters, and my cheeks to them that plucked off the hair: I hid not my face from shame and spitting.

Isa. 52.14. As many were astonied at thee; his visage was so marred more than any man, and his form more than the sons of men.

Isa. 53.2. He shall grow up before him as a tender plant, and as a root out of a dry ground: he hath no form nor comeliness; and when we shall see him, *there is* no beauty that we should desire him. 3. He is despised and rejected of men; a man of sorrows, and acquainted with grief: and we hid as it were *our* faces from him; he was despised, and we esteemed him not. 4. Surely he hath borne our griefs, and carried our sorrows: yet we did esteem him stricken, smitten of God, and afflicted.

Isa. 53.5. But he *was* wounded for our transgressions, *he was* bruised for our iniquities: the chastisement of our peace *was* upon him; and with his stripes we are healed. 7. He was oppressed, and he was afflicted, yet he opened not his mouth: he is brought as a lamb to the slaughter, and as a sheep before her shearers is dumb, so he openeth not his mouth.

Isa. 53.8. He was taken from prison and from judgment: and who shall declare his generation? for he was cut off out of the land of the living: for the transgression of my people was he stricken. 9. And he made his grave with the wicked, and with the rich in his death; because he had done no violence, neither *was any* deceit in his mouth. 10. Yet it pleased the Lord to bruise him: he hath put *him* to grief.

Mic. 5.1. They shall smite the judge of Israel with a rod upon the cheek.

Zec. 13.6. *One* shall say unto him, What *are* these wounds in thine hands? Then he shall answer, *Those* with which I was wounded *in* the house of my friends. 7. Awake, O sword, against my shepherd, and against the man *that is* my fellow, saith the Lord of hosts: smite the shepherd, and the sheep shall be scattered.

Mat. 4.1. Then was Jesus led up of the spirit into the wilderness to be tempted of the devil. 2. And when he had fasted forty days and forty nights, he was afterward an hungred.

Mat. 8.17. Himself took our infirmities, and bare *our* sicknesses. 20. The foxes have holes, and the birds of the air *have* nests; but the Son of man hath not where to lay *his* head. Luk. 9.58.

Mat. 12.14. The Pharisees went out, and held a council against him, how they might destroy him. 24. When the Pharisees heard *it*, they said, This *fellow* doth not cast out devils, but by Beelzebub the prince of the devils. Mat. 21.46. Mar. 3.6,22. Luk. 6.11. Luk. 11.15.

Mat. 16.1. The Pharisees also with the Sadducees came, and tempting desired him that he would shew them a sign from heaven.

Mat. 21.18. In the morning as he returned into the city, he hungered.

Mat. 26.4. Consulted that they might take Jesus by subtilty, and kill *him*. 14. Judas Iscariot went unto the chief priests, 15. And said *unto them*, What will ye give me, and I will deliver him unto you? And they covenanted with him for thirty pieces of silver. 16. And from that time he sought opportunity to betray him. Mar. 14.1. Luk. 22.2.

Mat. 26.38. My soul is exceeding sorrowful, even unto death: tarry ye here, and watch with me. 39. He went a little farther, and fell on his face, and prayed, saying, O my Father, if it be possible, let this cup pass from me: nevertheless not as I will, but as thou *wilt*. 55. Jesus said to the multitudes, Are ye come out as against a thief with swords and staves for to take me? 59. Now the chief priests, and elders, and all the council, sought false witness against Jesus, to put him to death. Mar. 14.34,48. Luk. 22.52.

Mat. 27.25. Then answered all the people, and said, His blood *be* on us, and on our children. 26. Then released he Barabbas unto them: and when he had scourged Jesus, he delivered *him* to be crucified. 28. They stripped him, and put on him a scarlet robe. 29. And when they had platted a crown of thorns, they put *it* upon his head, and a reed in his right hand: and they bowed the knee before him, and mocked him, saying, Hail, King of the Jews!

Mat. 27.30. And they spit upon him, and took the reed, and smote him on the head. 39. They that passed by reviled him, wagging their heads, 40. And saying, Thou that destroyest the temple, and buildest *it* in three days, save thyself. If thou be the Son of God, come down from the cross. 41. Likewise also the chief priests mocking *him*, with the scribes and elders, said, 42. He saved others; himself he cannot save. If he be the King of Israel, let him now come down from the cross, and we will believe him. 43. He trusted in God; let him deliver him now, if he will have him: for he said, I am the Son of God. 44. The thieves also, which were crucified with him, cast the same in his teeth. Mar. *c.* 15. Jno. *c.* 19.

Mar. 3.21. When his friends heard *of it*, they went out to lay hold on him: for they said, He is beside himself.

Mar. 15.34. At the ninth hour Jesus cried with a loud voice, saying, Eloi, Eloi, lama sabachthani? which is, being interpreted, My God, my God, why hast thou forsaken me?

Luk. 2.34. Behold, this *child* is set for a sign which shall be spoken against.

Luk. 4.28. All they in the synagogue, when they heard these things, were filled with wrath, 29. And rose up, and thrust him out of the city, and led him unto the brow of the hill whereon their city was built, that they might cast him down headlong.

Luk. 7.34. The Son of man is come eating and drinking; and ye say, Behold a gluttonous man, and a winebibber, a friend of publicans and sinners!

Luk. 11.53. The scribes and the Pharisees began to urge *him* vehemently, and to provoke him to speak of many things: 54. Laying wait for him, and seeking to catch something out of his mouth, that they might accuse him.

Luk. 12.50. I have a baptism to be baptized with; and how am I straitened till it be accomplished!

Luk. 13.31. There came certain of the Pharisees, saying unto him, Get thee out, and depart hence: for Herod will kill thee.

Luk. 19.14. His citizens hated him, and sent a message after him, saying, We will not have this *man* to reign over us. 47. The chief priests and the scribes and the chief of the people sought to destroy him. Mar. 11.18.

Luk. 20.20. They watched *him*, and sent forth spies, which should feign themselves just men, that they might take hold of his words, that so they might deliver him unto the power and authority of the governor. Mat. 22.15. Mar. 12.13.

Luk. 22.2. The chief priests and scribes sought how they might kill him; for they feared the people. 3. Then entered Satan into Judas surnamed Iscariot, being of the number of the twelve. 4. And he went his way, and communed with the chief priests and captains, how he might betray him unto them. 5. And they were glad, and covenanted to give him money.

Luk. 22.44. Being in an agony he prayed more earnestly : and his sweat was as it were great drops of blood falling down to the ground. 53. This is your hour, and the power of darkness. '63. The men that held Jesus mocked him, and smote *him.* 64. And when they had blindfolded him, they struck him on the face, and asked him, saying, Prophesy, who is it that smote thee? 65. And many other things blasphemously spake they against him. Mat. 26.67. Mar. 14.65.

Luk. 23.11. Herod with his men of war set him at nought, and mocked *him,* and arrayed him in a gorgeous robe. 23. They were instant with loud voices, requiring that he might be crucified. Mat. 27.23. Mar. 15.14.

Jno. 4.6. Jesus therefore, being wearied with *his* journey, sat thus on the well.

Jno. 5.16. Therefore did the Jews persecute Jesus, and sought to slay him, because he had done these things on the Sabbath-day.

Jno. 7.1. He would not walk in Jewry, because the Jews sought to kill him. 7. The world cannot hate you; but me it hateth, because I testify of it, that the works thereof are evil. 19. Why go ye about to kill me? 20. The people answered and said, Thou hast a devil : who goeth about to kill thee? 30. Then they sought to take him : but no man laid hands on him, because his hour was not yet come. 32. The Pharisees and the chief priests sent officers to take him.

Jno. 8.37. Ye seek to kill me, because my word hath no place in you. 40. Ye seek to kill me, a man that hath told you the truth, which I have heard of God. 48. Say we not well that thou art a Samaritan, and hast a devil ? 52. Now we know that thou hast a devil. 59. Then took they up stones to cast at him. Jno. 10.31.

Jno. 10.20. Many of them said, He hath a devil, and is mad ; why hear ye him? 39. They sought again to take him : but he escaped out of their hand.

Jno. 11.33. When Jesus therefore saw her weeping, and the Jews also weeping which came with her, he groaned in the spirit, and was troubled. 35. Jesus wept. 53. From that day forth they took counsel together for to put him to death. 57. The chief priests and the Pharisees had given a commandment, that, if any man knew where he were, he should shew *it,* that they might take him. Jno. 12.10.

Jno. 12.27. Now is my soul troubled ; and what shall I say ? Father, save me from this hour : but for this cause came I unto this hour.

Jno. 14.30. The prince of this world cometh, and hath nothing in me.

Jno. 15.18. If the world hate you, ye know that it hated me before *it hated* you. 24. Now have they both seen and hated both me and my Father. 25. But *this cometh to pass,* that the word might be fulfilled that is written in their law, They hated me without a cause.

Jno. 18.11. The cup which my Father hath given me, shall I not drink it? 22. One of the officers which stood by struck Jesus with the palm of his hand, saying, Answerest thou the high-priest so? 23. Jesus answered him, If I

have spoken evil, bear witness of the evil : but if well, why smitest thou me? 30. If he were not a malefactor, we would not have delivered him up unto thee.

Jno. 19.6. They cried out, saying, Crucify *him,* crucify *him.* Pilate saith unto them, Take ye him, and crucify *him* : for I find no fault in him. 15. They cried out, Away with *him,* away with *him,* crucify him. 28. Jesus knowing that all things were now accomplished, that the scripture might be fulfilled, saith, I thirst.

Act. 2.23. Him, being delivered by the determinate counsel and foreknowledge of God, ye have taken, and by wicked hands have crucified and slain.

Act. 4.27. Against thy holy child Jesus, whom thou hast anointed, both Herod and Pontius Pilate, with the Gentiles, and the people of Israel, were gathered together. Psa. 2.1,2.

1 Cor. 2.8. Have crucified the Lord of glory.

2 Cor. 8.9. Though he was rich, yet for your sakes he became poor, that ye through his poverty might be rich.

2 Cor. 13.4. He was crucified through weakness, yet he liveth by the power of God.

Gal. 3.13. Christ hath redeemed us from the curse of the law, being made a curse for us : for it is written, Cursed *is* every one that hangeth on a tree.

Eph. 4.9. He also descended first into the lower parts of the earth.

Phil. 2.7. Made himself of no reputation, and took upon him the form of a servant, and was made in the likeness of men : 8. And being found in fashion as a man, he humbled himself, and became obedient unto death, even the death of the cross.

Heb. 2.9. Jesus, who was made a little lower than the angels for the suffering of death.

Heb. 4.15. In all points tempted like as *we are, yet* without sin.

Heb. 5.7. Who in the days of his flesh, when he had offered up prayers and supplications with strong crying and tears unto him that was able to save him from death, and was heard in that he feared ; 8. Though he were a Son, yet learned he obedience by the things which he suffered.

Heb. 12.2. Endured the cross, despising the shame, and is set down at the right hand of the throne of God. 3. For consider him that endured such contradiction of sinners against himself, lest ye be wearied and faint in your minds.

1 Pet. 4.1. Christ hath suffered for us in the flesh.

Rev. 5.6. Stood a Lamb as it had been slain.

Rev. 19.13. He *was* clothed with a vesture dipped in blood : and his name is called The Word of God.

CHRIST, Union to. See Union to Christ.

———, Wisdom of. See Christ, Omniscience of.

———, Wisdom from. See Wisdom.

———, Worship of. Psa. 45.11. He *is* thy Lord ; and worship thou him. 17. I will make thy name to be remembered in all generations : therefore shall the people praise thee for ever and ever.

Psa. 72.15. Prayer also shall be made for him continually ; *and* daily shall he be praised.

Mat. 28.9. Jesus met them, saying, All hail. And they came and held him by the feet, and worshipped him. 17. When they saw him, they worshipped him.

Mar. 11.9. They that went before, and they that followed, cried, saying, Hosanna ; Blessed *is* he that cometh in the name of the Lord : 10. Blessed *be* the kingdom of our father David, that cometh in the name of the Lord : Hosanna in the highest. Mat. 21.9. Jno. 12.13.

Luk. 23.42. He said unto Jesus, Lord, remember me when thou comest into thy kingdom.

Luk. 24.52. They worshipped him, and returned to Jerusalem with great joy.

Jno. 5.23. All *men* should honour the Son, even as they honour the Father. He that honoureth not the Son honoureth not the Father which hath sent him.

Act. 7.59. They stoned Stephen, calling upon *God*, and saying, Lord Jesus, receive my spirit. Act. 1.24.

Rom. 16.24. The grace of our Lord Jesus Christ *be* with you all. Amen.

1 Cor. 1.2. With all that in every place call upon the name of Jesus Christ our Lord, both their's and our's.

2 Cor. 12.8. I besought the Lord thrice, that it might depart from me. 9. And he said unto me, My grace is sufficient for thee : for my strength is made perfect in weakness.

Phil. 2.10. At the name of Jesus every knee should bow, of *things* in heaven, and *things* in earth, and *things* under the earth ; 11. And *that* every tongue should confess that Jesus Christ is Lord, to the glory of God the Father.

Heb. 1.6. When he bringeth in the first-begotten into the world, he saith, And let all the angels of God worship him.

Rev. 5.8. The four beasts and four *and* twenty elders fell down before the Lamb, having every one of them harps, and golden vials full of odours, which are the prayers of saints. 9. And they sung a new song, saying, Thou art worthy to take the book, and to open the seals thereof. 12. Worthy is the Lamb that was slain to receive power, and riches, and wisdom, and strength, and honour, and glory, and blessing.

Rev. 5.13. And every creature which is in heaven, and on the earth, and under the earth, and such as are in the sea, and all that are in them, heard I saying, Blessing, and honour, and glory, and power, *be* unto him that sitteth upon the throne, and unto the Lamb, for ever and ever. 14. And the four beasts said, Amen. And the four *and* twenty elders fell down and worshipped him that liveth for ever and ever.

Rev. 7.10. Salvation to our God which sitteth upon the throne, and unto the Lamb.

CHRIST, ZEAL OF. Psa. 69.9. The zeal of thine house hath eaten me up.

Isa. 59.17. He put on the garments of vengeance *for* clothing, and was clad with zeal as a cloke.

Mat. 4.23. Jesus went about all Galilee, teaching in their synagogues, and preaching the gospel of the kingdom, and healing all manner of sickness and all manner of disease among the people. Mat. 9.35. Mar. 6.6.

Mar. 3.20. The multitude cometh together again, so that they could not so much as eat bread. 21. And when his friends heard *of it*, they went out to lay hold on him : for they said, He is beside himself.

Luk. 2.49. How is it that ye sought me? wist ye not that I must be about my Father's business?

Luk. 4.43. I must preach the kingdom of God to other cities also : for therefore am I sent. Mar. 1.38.

Luk. 8.1. He went throughout every city and village, preaching and shewing the glad tidings of the kingdom of God.

Luk. 9.51. When the time was come that he should be received up, he stedfastly set his face to go to Jerusalem.

Luk. 12.50. I have a baptism to be baptized with ; and how am I straitened till it be accomplished !

Luk. 13.32. Behold, I cast out devils, and I do cures to-day and to-morrow, and the third *day* I shall be perfected. 33. Nevertheless I must walk to-day, and to-morrow, and the *day* following.

Jno. 2.17. His disciples remembered that it was written, The zeal of thine house hath eaten me up. Psa. 69.9.

Jno. 4.32. I have meat to eat that ye know not of. 34. Jesus saith unto them, My meat is to do the will of him that sent me, and to finish his work.

Jno. 9.4. I must work the works of him that sent me, while it is day : the night cometh, when no man can work.

Act. 10.38. Who went about doing good, and healing all that were oppressed of the devil ; for God was with him.

Rom. 15.3. Even Christ pleased not himself ; but, as it is written, The reproaches of them that reproached thee fell on me.

1 Tim. 6.13. Jesus, who before Pontius Pilate witnessed a good confession.

CHRISTIANS, name first given at Antioch, Act. 11.26. See CHURCH, SAINTS, NAZARENE, DISCIPLE.

CHRONICLES. See BOOKS.

CHRYSOLITE AND CHRYSOPRASUS, precious stones in the foundation of the New Jerusalem, Rev. 21.20.

CHURCH (Gr. *ecclesia*), signifies the congregation of the Israelites, Act. 7.38. Heb. 2.12. Mat. 18.17. The Christian Church, Mat. 16.18. 1 Cor. 12.28. 1 Cor. 11.22. 1 Cor. 15.9. Gal. 1.13. Eph. 1.22. Eph. 3.10. 1 Tim. 3.15. Heb. 12.23, &c. Particular Christian churches, as Jerusalem, Act. 8.1. Corinth, 1 Cor. 1.2, &c. The original is translated an assembly, Act. 19.32,39,41.

Church signifies temple (Gr. *ieron*), in Act. 19.37.

―――― DISCIPLINE. Mat. 18.15. If thy brother shall trespass against thee, go and tell him his fault between thee and him alone : if he shall hear thee, thou hast gained thy brother. 16. But if he will not hear *thee, then* take with thee one or two more, that in the mouth of two or three witnesses every word may be established. 17. And if he shall neglect to hear them, tell *it* unto the church : but if he

neglect to hear the church, let him be unto thee as an heathen man and a publican.
18. Whatsoever ye shall bind on earth shall be bound in heaven: and whatsoever ye shall loose on earth shall be loosed in heaven.

Rom. 14.1. Him that is weak in the faith receive ye, but not to doubtful disputations.

Rom. 15.1. We then that are strong ought to bear the infirmities of the weak. *v.* 1-3.

Rom. 16.17. Mark them which cause divisions and offences, contrary to the doctrine which ye have learned ; and avoid them.

1 Cor. 4.19. I will come to you shortly, if the Lord will, and will know, not the speech of them which are puffed up, but the power. 21. What will ye ? shall I come unto you with a rod, or in love, and *in* the spirit of meekness ?

1 Cor. 5.2. Ye are puffed up, and have not rather mourned, that he that hath done this deed might be taken away from among you. 4. In the name of our Lord Jesus Christ, when ye are gathered together, and my spirit, with the power of our Lord Jesus Christ, 5. To deliver such an one unto Satan for the destruction of the flesh, that the spirit may be saved in the day of the Lord Jesus. 6. Know ye not that a little leaven leaveneth the whole lump ? 7. Purge out therefore the old leaven, that ye may be a new lump, as ye are unleavened.

1 Cor. 5.11. I have written unto you not to keep company, if any man that is called a brother be a fornicator, or covetous, or an idolater, or a railer, or a drunkard, or an extortioner ; with such an one no not to eat. 12. What have I to do to judge them also that are without ? do not ye judge them that are within ? 13. Therefore put away from among yourselves that wicked person.

1 Cor. 16.22. If any man love not the Lord Jesus Christ, let him be Anathema Maran-atha.

2 Cor. 2.6. Sufficient to such a man *is* this punishment, which *was inflicted* of many. 7. Ye *ought* rather to forgive *him*, and comfort *him*, lest perhaps such an one should be swallowed up with overmuch sorrow. 8. Wherefore I beseech you that ye would confirm *your* love toward him. 10. To whom ye forgive any thing, I *forgive* also : for if I forgave any thing, to whom I forgave *it*, for your sakes *forgave I it* in the person of Christ ; 11. Lest Satan should get an advantage of us : for we are not ignorant of his devices.

2 Cor. 6.14. Be ye not unequally yoked together with unbelievers : for what fellowship hath righteousness with unrighteousness ? and what communion hath light with darkness ? 15. And what concord hath Christ with Belial ? or what part hath he that believeth with an infidel ?

2 Cor. 7.7. He told us your earnest desire, your mourning, your fervent mind toward me ; so that I rejoiced the more. 8. For though I made you sorry with a letter, I do not repent, though I did repent : for I perceive that the same epistle hath made you sorry, though *it were* but for a season. 2 Cor. 10.1-11.

2 Cor. 13.1. In the mouth of two or three witnesses shall every word be established. 2. I write to them which heretofore have sinned, and to all other, that, if I come again, I will not spare. 10. I write these things, being absent, lest being present I should use sharpness, according to the power which the Lord hath given me to edification, and not to destruction.

Gal. 5.10. He that troubleth you shall bear his judgment, whosoever he be. 12. I would they were even cut off which trouble you.

Gal. 6.1. Brethren, if a man be overtaken in a fault, ye which are spiritual, restore such an one in the spirit of meekness ; considering thyself, lest thou also be tempted.

2 The. 3.6. We command you, brethren, in the name of our Lord Jesus Christ, that ye withdraw yourselves from every brother that walketh disorderly, and not after the tradition which he received of us. 14. If any man obey not our word by this epistle, note that man, and have no company with him, that he may be ashamed. 15. Yet count *him* not as an enemy, but admonish *him* as a brother.

1 Tim. 1.19. Some having put away concerning faith have made shipwreck : 20. Of whom is Hymenæus and Alexander ; whom I have delivered unto Satan, that they may learn not to blaspheme.

1 Tim. 5.1. Rebuke not an elder, but entreat *him* as a father ; *and* the younger men as brethren ; 2. The elder women as mothers ; the younger as sisters, with all purity. 19. Against an elder receive not an accusation, but before two or three witnesses. 20. Them that sin rebuke before all, that others also may fear.

1 Tim. 6.5. Perverse disputings of men of corrupt minds, and destitute of the truth, supposing that gain is godliness : from such withdraw thyself.

2 Tim. 4.2. Reprove, rebuke, exhort with all longsuffering and doctrine.

Tit. 1.13. Rebuke them sharply, that they may be sound in the faith.

Tit. 2.15. These things speak, and exhort, and rebuke with all authority. Let no man despise thee.

Tit. 3.10. A man that is an heretick after the first and second admonition reject ; 11. Knowing that he that is such is subverted, and sinneth, being condemned of himself.

2 Jno. 10. If there come any unto you, and bring not this doctrine, receive him not into *your* house, neither bid him God speed : 11. For he that biddeth him God speed is partaker of his evil deeds.

See ANATHEMA—EXCOMMUNICATION.

CHURCH, DUTY OF, TO MINISTERS. Mal. 2.7. They should seek the law at his mouth : for he *is* the messenger of the Lord of hosts.

Mat. 10.40. He that receiveth you, receiveth me ; and he that receiveth me, receiveth him that sent me. 41. He that receiveth a prophet in the name of a prophet, shall receive a prophet's reward ; and he that receiveth a righteous man in the name of a righteous man, shall receive a righteous man's reward.

Mat. 14.12. His disciples came, and took up the body, and buried it, and went and told Jesus.

Mat. 23.2. The scribes and the Pharisees sit in Moses' seat : 3. All therefore whatsoever they bid you observe, *that* observe and do. 9. Call no *man* your father upon the earth : for one is your Father, which is in heaven.

Act. 16.15. She besought *us*, saying, If ye have judged me to be faithful to the Lord, come into my house, and abide *there.* And she constrained us.

Act. 20.37. They all wept sore, and fell on Paul's neck, and kissed him; 38. Sorrowing most of all for the words which he spake, that they should see his face no more. And they accompanied him unto the ship.

Act. 21.5. They all brought us on our way, with wives and children, till we were out of the city: and we kneeled down on the shore, and prayed. 6. And when we had taken our leave one of another, we took ship; and they returned home again.

Act. 28.10. Who also honoured us with many honours; and when we departed, they laded us with such things as were necessary.

Rom. 16.2. She hath been a succourer of many, and of myself also. 3. Greet Priscilla and Aquila my helpers in Christ Jesus; 4. Who have for my life laid down their own necks: unto whom not only I give thanks, but also all the churches of the Gentiles. 9. Salute Urbane, our helper in Christ, and Stachys my beloved.

1 Cor. 4.1. Let a man so account of us, as of the ministers of Christ, and stewards of the mysteries of God.

1 Cor. 16.10. If Timotheus come, see that he may be with you without fear: for he worketh the work of the Lord, as I also do. 11. Let no man therefore despise him: but conduct him forth in peace. 16. Submit yourselves unto such, and to every one that helpeth with us, and laboureth. 17. I am glad of the coming of Stephanas, and Fortunatus, and Achaicus: for that which was lacking on your part they have supplied. 18. For they have refreshed my spirit and yours: therefore acknowledge ye them that are such.

2 Cor. 1.14. Ye have acknowledged us in part, that we are your rejoicing, even as ye also are our's in the day of the Lord, having confidence in you all, that my joy is the joy of you all. 2 Cor. 6.12.

2 Cor. 8.5. This they did, not as we hoped; but first gave their own selves to the Lord, and unto us by the will of God. 7. Ye abound in your love to us.

Gal. 4.14. My temptation which was in my flesh ye despised not, nor rejected; but received me as an angel of God, even as Christ Jesus. 15. Where is then the blessedness ye spake of? for I bear you record, that, if it had been possible, ye would have plucked out your own eyes, and have given them to me.

Phil. 1.26. That your rejoicing may be more abundant in Jesus Christ for me by my coming to you again.

Phil. 2.28. That, when ye see him again, ye may rejoice, and that I may be the less sorrowful. 29. Receive him therefore in the Lord with all gladness; and hold such in reputation: 30. For the work of Christ he was nigh unto death, not regarding his life; to supply your lack of service toward me.

Phil. 4.3. I entreat thee also, true yokefellow, help those women which laboured with me in the gospel, with Clement also, and with other my fellow-labourers.

1 The. 3.6. That ye have good remembrance of us always, desiring greatly to see us.

1 The. 5.12. Know them which labour among you, and are over you in the Lord, and admonish you; 13. And to esteem them very highly in love for their work's sake.

1 Tim. 5.17. Let the elders that rule well be counted worthy of double honour, especially they who labour in the word and doctrine.

2 Tim. 1.16. The Lord give mercy unto the house of Onesiphorus; for he oft refreshed me, and was not ashamed of my chain: 17. But, when he was in Rome, he sought me out very diligently, and found me. 18. The Lord grant unto him that he may find mercy of the Lord in that day: and in how many things he ministered unto me at Ephesus, thou knowest very well.

Tit. 2.15. Let no man despise thee.

Phlm. 19. I do not say to thee how thou owest unto me even thine own self besides. 20. Yea, brother, let me have joy of thee in the Lord: refresh my bowels in the Lord.

Heb. 13.7. Remember them which have the rule over you, who have spoken unto you the word of God: whose faith follow, considering the end of their conversation. 17. Obey them that have the rule over you, and submit yourselves: for they watch for your souls, as they that must give account, that they may do it with joy, and not with grief: for that is unprofitable for you.

1 Pet. 5.5. Ye younger, submit yourselves unto the elder. Yea, all of you be subject one to another, and be clothed with humility.

See MINISTERS, MAINTENANCE OF.—MINISTERS, PRAYER FOR.

CHURCH, ENEMIES OF. See PERSECUTION.—SAINTS, ENMITY TO.—AFFLICTION, PRAYER IN.

———, GLORIFIES GOD. See GOD GLORIFIED IN THE CHURCH.

———, GOD'S CARE OF, AND PRESENCE IN. See GOD PROTECTOR.—GOD, FAVOUR OF.—GOD, LOVE OF.

———, GOVERNMENT. Act. 1.15. Peter stood up in the midst of the disciples, and said (the number of the names together were about an hundred and twenty). 23. They appointed two, Joseph called Barsabas, who was surnamed Justus, and Matthias. 24. And they prayed, and said, Thou, Lord, which knowest the hearts of all men, shew whether of these two thou hast chosen, 25. That he may take part of this ministry and apostleship, from which Judas by transgression fell, that he might go to his own place. 26. And they gave forth their lots: and the lot fell upon Matthias; and he was numbered with the eleven apostles.

Act. 6.2. The twelve called the multitude of the disciples unto them, and said, It is not reason that we should leave the word of God, and serve tables. 3. Brethren, look ye out among you seven men of honest report, full of the Holy Ghost and wisdom, whom we may appoint over this business. 5. The saying pleased the whole multitude: and they chose Stephen, a man full of faith and of the Holy Ghost, and Philip, &c., 6. Whom they set before the apostles: and when they had prayed, they laid their hands on them.

Act. 11.22. Tidings of these things came unto the ears of the church which was in Jerusalem: and they sent forth Barnabas, that he should go as far as Antioch. 29. The disciples, every man according to his ability, determined to send relief unto the brethren which dwelt in Judea: 30. Which also they did, and sent it to the elders by the hands of Barnabas and Saul.

Act. 13. 1. There were in the church that was at Antioch certain prophets and teachers; as Barnabas, and Simeon. 3. When they had fasted and prayed, and laid *their* hands on them, they sent *them* away. 5. They had also John to *their* minister.

Act. 14. 23. When they had ordained them elders in every church, and had prayed with fasting, they commended them to the Lord.

Act. 15. 2. They determined that Paul and Barnabas, and certain other of them, should go up to Jerusalem unto the apostles and elders about this question. 4. When they were come to Jerusalem, they were received of the church, and *of* the apostles and elders, and they declared all things that God had done with them. 6. The apostles and elders came together for to consider of this matter.

Act. 15. 22. Then pleased it the apostles and elders, with the whole church, to send chosen men of their own company to Antioch with Paul and Barnabas, *namely*, Judas surnamed Barsabas, and Silas, chief men among the brethren : 23. And they wrote *letters* by them after this manner; The apostles and elders and brethren *send* greeting unto the brethren which are of the Gentiles in Antioch and Syria and Cilicia. 25. It seemed good unto us, being assembled with one accord, to send chosen men unto you with our beloved Barnabas and Paul.

Act. 15. 28. For it seemed good to the Holy Ghost, and to us, to lay upon you no greater burden than these necessary things. 36. Paul said unto Barnabas, Let us go again and visit our brethren in every city where we have preached the word of the Lord, *and see* how they do. 40. Paul chose Silas, and departed, being recommended by the brethren unto the grace of God. 41. He went through Syria and Cilicia, confirming the churches.

Act. 20. 17. From Miletus he sent to Ephesus, and called the elders of the church. 28. Take heed therefore unto yourselves, and to all the flock, over the which the Holy Ghost hath made you overseers, to feed the church of God.

1 Cor. 7. 17. As God hath distributed to every man, as the Lord hath called every one, so let him walk. And so ordain I in all churches.

1 Cor. 11. 2. I praise you, brethren, that ye remember me in all things, and keep the ordinances, as I delivered *them* to you. 33. When ye come together to eat, tarry one for another. 34. And if any man hunger, let him eat at home; that ye come not together unto condemnation. And the rest will I set in order when I come.

1 Cor. 12. 5. There are differences of administrations, but the same Lord. 28. God hath set some in the church, first apostles, secondarily prophets, thirdly teachers, after that miracles, then gifts of healings, helps, governments, diversities of tongues.

1 Cor. 14. 26. How is it then, brethren? when ye come together, every one of you hath a psalm, hath a doctrine, hath a tongue, hath a revelation, hath an interpretation. Let all things be done unto edifying. 33. God is not *the author* of confusion, but of peace, as in all churches of the saints. 40. Let all things be done decently and in order.

1 Cor. 16. 3. When I come, whomsoever ye shall approve by *your* letters, them will I send to bring your liberality unto Jerusalem. 16. Submit yourselves unto such, and to every one that helpeth with *us*, and laboureth.

2 Cor. 2. 6. Sufficient to such a man *is this* punishment, which *was inflicted* of many. 7. So that contrariwise, ye *ought* rather to forgive *him*, and comfort *him*, lest perhaps such an one should be swallowed up with overmuch sorrow. *v.* 2-11.

Gal. 2. 9. When James, Cephas, and John, who seemed to be pillars, perceived the grace that was given unto me, they gave to me and Barnabas the right hands of fellowship; that we should go to the heathen, and they unto the circumcision. 10. Only they would that we should remember the poor.

Eph. 4. 11. He gave some, apostles; and some, prophets; and some, evangelists; and some, pastors and teachers; 12. For the perfecting of the saints, for the work of the ministry, for the edifying of the body of Christ.

Phil. 1. 1. All the saints in Christ Jesus which are at Philippi, with the bishops and deacons.

1 Tim. 3. 1. If a man desire the office of a bishop, he desireth a good work. 2. A bishop then must be blameless. 5. For if a man know not how to rule his own house, how shall he take care of the church of God? 8. *Must* the deacons *be* grave, not doubletongued, not given to much wine, not greedy of filthy lucre; 9. Holding the mystery of the faith in a pure conscience.

1 Tim. 3. 10. And let these also first be proved; then let them use the office of a deacon, being *found* blameless. 11. Even so *must their* wives *be* grave, not slanderers, sober, faithful in all things. 12. Let the deacons be the husbands of one wife, ruling their children and their own houses well. 13. For they that have used the office of a deacon well purchase to themselves a good degree, and great boldness in the faith which is in Christ Jesus. *v.* 1-13.

1 Tim. 4. 14. Neglect not the gift that is in thee, which was given thee by prophecy, with the laying on of the hands of the presbytery.

1 Tim. 5. 1. Rebuke not an elder, but entreat *him* as a father; *and* the younger men as brethren. 17. Let the elders that rule well be counted worthy of double honour, especially they who labour in the word and doctrine. 22. Lay hands suddenly on no man, neither be partaker of other men's sins.

2 Tim. 1. 6. I put thee in remembrance, that thou stir up the gift of God, which is in thee by the putting on of my hands.

Tit. 1. 5. For this cause left I thee in Crete, that thou shouldest set in order the things that are wanting, and ordain elders in every city, as I had appointed thee.

Heb. 13. 17. Obey them that have the rule over you, and submit yourselves. 24. Salute all them that have the rule over you, and all the saints.

Jas. 5. 14. Is any sick among you? let him call for the elders of the church; and let them pray over him, anointing him with oil in the name of the Lord : 15. And the prayer of faith shall save the sick.

1 Pet. 5. 1. The elders which are among you I exhort, who am also an elder. 2. Feed the flock of God which is among you, taking the oversight *thereof*, not by constraint, but willingly; not for filthy lucre, but of a ready

mind; 3. Neither as being lords over God's heritage, but being ensamples to the flock.

3 Jno. 9. I wrote unto the church: but Diotrephes, who loveth to have the pre-eminence among them, receiveth us not. 10. Wherefore, if I come, I will remember his deeds which he doeth, prating against us with malicious words: and not content therewith, neither doth he himself receive the brethren, and forbiddeth them that would, and casteth them out of the church.

See ANGELS OF THE CHURCHES, APOSTLES, BISHOP, DEACON, ELDER, EVANGELIST, HELPS, ORDINATION, PASTOR, PRESBYTERY, TEACHER, CHRIST HEAD OF THE CHURCH.

CHURCH, HISTORY OF. See under the name of each church, as JERUSALEM—CO-RINTH, &c.; also PETER—PAUL.

———— MEMBERS. See SAINTS' CHA-RACTER.—SAINTS, COMMUNION OF.

————, NAMES AND DESCRIPTION OF. Ex. 15.17. The mountain of thine inheritance, in the place, O Lord, which thou hast made for thee to dwell in, in the Sanctuary, O Lord, which thy hands have established.

Deu. 32.9. The Lord's portion is his people; Jacob is the lot of his inheritance.

Psa. 2.6. My holy hill of Zion.

Psa. 45.13. The king's daughter is all glorious within: her clothing is of wrought gold. (See Song of Songs throughout.)

Psa. 46.4. The city of God, the holy place of the tabernacles of the most High.

Psa. 48.1. The city of our God, in the mountain of his holiness. 2. Beautiful for situation, the joy of the whole earth, is mount Zion, on the sides of the north, the city of the great King. 12. Walk about Zion, and go round about her: tell the towers thereof. 13. Mark ye well her bulwarks, consider her palaces.

Psa. 50.2. Out of Zion, the perfection of beauty, God hath shined.

Psa. 78.60. He forsook the tabernacle of Shiloh, the tent which he placed among men; 61. And delivered his strength into captivity, and his glory into the enemy's hand. 62. He gave his people over also unto the sword; and was wroth with his inheritance.

Psa. 87.3. Glorious things are spoken of thee, O city of God.

Psa. 89.7. The assembly of the saints.

Psa. 111.1. The assembly of the upright.

Psa. 114.2. Judah was his sanctuary, and Israel his dominion.

Psa. 149.1. The congregation of saints.

Isa. 2.3. Let us go up to the mountain of the Lord, to the house of the God of Jacob.

Isa. 11.10. His rest shall be glorious.

Isa. 19.25. Israel mine inheritance.

Isa. 60.21. The branch of my planting, the work of my hands.

Isa. 62.12. The holy people, The redeemed of the Lord: and thou shalt be called, Sought out, A city not forsaken.

Jer. 12.10. Many pastors have destroyed my vineyard, they have trodden my portion under foot, they have made my pleasant portion a desolate wilderness.

Jer. 31.23. The Lord bless thee, O habitation of justice, and mountain of holiness.

Eze. 43.7. The place of my throne, and the place of the soles of my feet, where I will dwell in the midst of the children of Israel for ever.

Zec. 8.3. Jerusalem shall be called a city of truth; and the mountain of the Lord of hosts the holy mountain.

Mat. 13.24. The kingdom of heaven.

Act. 20.28. The church of God.

1 Cor. 3.9. Ye are God's husbandry; ye are God's building.

Gal. 4.26. Jerusalem which is above is free, which is the mother of us all.

Gal. 6.16. The Israel of God.

Eph. 1.22. The church, 23. Which is his body, the fulness of him that filleth all in all.

Eph. 2.19. The household of God. 21. In whom all the building, fitly framed together, groweth unto an holy temple in the Lord: 22. In whom ye also are builded together for an habitation of God through the Spirit.

Eph. 3.15. The whole family in heaven and earth.

2 The. 1.1. The church of the Thessalonians in God our Father and the Lord Jesus Christ.

1 Tim. 3.15. The house of God, which is the church of the living God, the pillar and ground of the truth.

Heb. 3.6. Christ as a Son over his own house; whose house are we.

Heb. 12.22. Ye are come unto mount Sion, and unto the city of the living God, the heavenly Jerusalem, and to an innumerable company of angels, 23. To the general assembly and church of the firstborn, which are written in heaven, and to God the Judge of all, and to the spirits of just men made perfect.

1 Pet. 2.5. Ye also, as lively stones, are built up a spiritual house, an holy priesthood, to offer up spiritual sacrifices.

1 Pet. 5.2. The flock of God. 3. God's heritage.

Rev. 1.20. The seven candlesticks which thou sawest, are the seven churches.

Rev. 21.2. I John saw the holy city, new Jerusalem, coming down from God out of heaven, prepared as a bride adorned for her husband. 9. The bride, the Lamb's wife. Rev. 19.7.

See SAINTS, CHARACTER OF.

CHURCH, PRAYER FOR. See PRAYER INTERCESSORY, EXAMPLES OF.

————, PROPHECIES OF. KINGDOM OF CHRIST. GOSPEL DISPENSATION. Gen. 12.3. In thee shall all families of the earth be blessed.

Gen. 49.10. Unto him shall the gathering of the people be.

Deu. 32.21. I will move them to jealousy with those which are not a people; I will provoke them to anger with a foolish nation.

Psa. 2.8. Ask of me, and I shall give thee the heathen for thine inheritance, and the uttermost parts of the earth for thy possession.

Psa. 22.27. All the ends of the world shall remember and turn unto the Lord: and all the kindreds of the nations shall worship before thee. 28. For the kingdom is the Lord's: and he is the governor among the nations. 29. All they that be fat upon earth shall eat and worship: all they that go down to the dust shall bow before him: and none can keep alive his own soul.

Psa. 22.30. A seed shall serve him; it shall

be accounted to the Lord for a generation. 31. They shall come, and shall declare his righteousness unto a people that shall be born, that he hath done *this*.

Psa. 46.4. *There is* a river, the streams whereof shall make glad the city of God, the holy *place* of the tabernacles of the most High. 10. Be still, and know that I *am* God: I will be exalted among the heathen, I will be exalted in the earth.

Psa. 65.2. O thou that hearest prayer, unto thee shall all flesh come.

Psa. 66.4. All the earth shall worship thee, and shall sing unto thee; they shall sing *to* thy name.

Psa. 67.5. Let the people praise thee, O God; let all the people praise thee. 6. *Then* shall the earth yield her increase; *and* God, *even* our own God, shall bless us. *v.* 1-7.

Psa. 68.31. Princes shall come out of Egypt; Ethiopia shall soon stretch out her hands unto God. 32. Sing unto God, ye kingdoms of the earth; O sing praises unto the Lord.

Psa. 69.35. God will save Zion, and will build the cities of Judah : that they may dwell there, and have it in possession. 36. The seed also of his servants shall inherit it : and they that love his name shall dwell therein.

Psa. 72.2. He shall judge thy people with righteousness, and thy poor with judgment. 3. The mountains shall bring peace to the people, and the little hills, by righteousness. 4. He shall judge the poor of the people, he shall save the children of the needy, and shall break in pieces the oppressor. 7. In his days shall the righteous flourish ; and abundance of peace so long as the moon endureth. 8. He shall have dominion also from sea to sea, and from the river unto the ends of the earth.

Psa. 72.9. They that dwell in the wilderness shall bow before him ; and his enemies shall lick the dust. 10. The kings of Tarshish and of the isles shall bring presents: the kings of Sheba and Seba shall offer gifts. 11. Yea, all kings shall fall down before him: all nations shall serve him. 16. There shall be an handful of corn in the earth upon the top of the mountains ; the fruit thereof shall shake like Lebanon: and *they* of the city shall flourish like grass of the earth. 19. Blessed *be* his glorious name for ever: and let the whole earth be filled *with* his glory; Amen, and Amen. *v.* 1-20.

Psa. 85.10. Mercy and truth are met together ; righteousness and peace have kissed *each other*. 11. Truth shall spring out of the earth ; and righteousness shall look down from heaven. 12. Yea, the Lord shall give *that which is* good ; and our land shall yield her increase.

Psa. 86.9. All nations whom thou hast made shall come and worship before thee, O Lord ; and shall glorify thy name.

Psa. 87.4. I will make mention of Rahab and Babylon to them that know me.

Psa. 89.25. I will set his hand also in the sea, and his right hand in the rivers. 29. His seed also will I make *to* endure for ever, and his throne as the days of heaven. 36. His seed shall endure for ever, and his throne as the sun before me. 37. It shall be established for ever as the moon, and *as* a faithful witness in heaven. *v.* 1-37.

Psa. 96.11. Let the heavens rejoice, and let the earth be glad ; let the sea roar, and the fulness thereof. 12. Let the field be joyful, and all that *is* therein : then shall all the trees of the wood rejoice 13. Before the Lord : for he cometh, for he cometh to judge the earth : he shall judge the world with righteousness, and the people with his truth. *v.* 1-13.

Psa. 102.13. Thou shalt arise, *and* have mercy upon Zion : for the time to favour her, yea, the set time, is come. 14. For thy servants take pleasure in her stones, and favour the dust thereof. 15. So the heathen shall fear the name of the Lord, and all the kings of the earth thy glory. 16. When the Lord shall build up Zion, he shall appear in his glory.

Psa. 110.3. Thy people *shall be* willing in the day of thy power, in the beauties of holiness from the womb of the morning : thou hast the dew of thy youth. *v.* 1-7.

Psa. 113.3. From the rising of the sun unto the going down of the same the Lord's name *is* to be praised.

Psa. 118.24. This *is* the day *which* the Lord hath made ; we will rejoice and be glad in it.

Psa. 126.5. They that sow in tears shall reap in joy. 6. He that goeth forth and weepeth, bearing precious seed, shall doubtless come again with rejoicing, bringing his sheaves *with him*.

Psa. 132.15. I will abundantly bless her provision : I will satisfy her poor with bread. 16. I will also clothe her priests with salvation : and her saints shall shout aloud for joy. 17. There will I make the horn of David to bud : I have ordained a lamp for mine anointed. 18. His enemies will I clothe with shame : but upon himself shall his crown flourish.

Psa. 138.4. All the kings of the earth shall ·praise thee, O Lord, when they hear the words of thy mouth. 5. Yea, they shall sing in the ways of the Lord : for great *is* the glory of the Lord.

Psa. 145.10. All thy works shall praise thee, O Lord ; and thy saints shall bless thee. 11. They shall speak of the glory of thy kingdom, and talk of thy power.

Isa. 2.2. It shall come to pass in the last days, *that* the mountain of the Lord's house shall be established in the top of the mountains, and shall be exalted above the hills ; and all nations shall flow unto it. 3. Many people shall go and say, Come ye, and let us go up to the mountain of the Lord, to the house of the God of Jacob ; and he will teach us of his ways, and we will walk in his paths: for out of Zion shall go forth the law, and the word of the Lord from Jerusalem. 4. He shall judge among the nations, and shall rebuke many people: and they shall beat their swords into plowshares, and their spears into pruninghooks : nation shall not lift up sword against nation, neither shall they learn war any more. *v.* 5.

Isa. 4.2. In that day shall the branch of the Lord be beautiful and glorious, and the fruit of the earth *shall be* excellent and comely for them that are escaped of Israel. 3. And it shall come to pass, *that he that is* left in Zion, and *he that* remaineth in Jerusalem, shall be called holy, *even* every one that is written among the living in Jerusalem.

Isa. 4.5. And the Lord will create upon every dwelling-place of Mount Zion, and upon her assemblies, a cloud and smoke by day, and the shining of a flaming fire by night: for upon all the glory *shall be* a defence. 6. And there shall be a tabernacle for a shadow in the day-time from the heat, and for a place of refuge, and for a covert from storm and from rain.

Isa. 9.2. The people that walked in darkness have seen a great light: they that dwell in the land of the shadow of death, upon them hath the light shined. 6. The government shall be upon his shoulder: and his name shall be called Wonderful, Counsellor, The mighty God, The everlasting Father, The Prince of Peace. 7. Of the increase of *his* government and peace *there shall be* no end, upon the throne of David, and upon his kingdom, to order it, and to establish it with judgment and with justice from henceforth even for ever. *v.* 1-7.

Isa. 11.6. The wolf also shall dwell with the lamb, and the leopard shall lie down with the kid; and the calf and the young lion and the fatling together; and a little child shall lead them. 7. And the cow and the bear shall feed; their young ones shall lie down together: and the lion shall eat straw like the ox. 8. And the sucking child shall play on the hole of the asp, and the weaned child shall put his hand on the cockatrice' den.

Isa. 11.9. They shall not hurt nor destroy in all my holy mountain: for the earth shall be full of the knowledge of the Lord, as the waters cover the sea. 10. And in that day there shall be a root of Jesse, which shall stand for an ensign of the people; to it shall the Gentiles seek: and his rest shall be glorious. *v.* 1-10.

Isa. 18.7. In that time shall the present be brought unto the Lord of hosts of a people scattered and peeled, and from a people terrible from their beginning hitherto; a nation meted out and trodden under foot, whose land the rivers have spoiled, to the place of the name of the Lord of hosts, the mount Zion.

Isa. 19.24. In that day shall Israel be the third with Egypt and with Assyria, *even* a blessing in the midst of the land: 25. Whom the Lord of hosts shall bless, saying, Blessed *be* Egypt my people, and Assyria the work of my hands, and Israel mine inheritance.

Isa. 24.16. From the uttermost part of the earth have we heard songs.

Isa. 25.6. In this mountain shall the Lord of hosts make unto all people a feast of fat things, a feast of wines on the lees, of fat things full of marrow, of wines on the lees well refined. 7. And he will destroy in this mountain the face of the covering cast over all people, and the vail that is spread over all nations. 8. He will swallow up death in victory; and the Lord God will wipe away tears from off all faces; and the rebuke of his people shall he take away from off all the earth: for the Lord hath spoken *it.*

Isa. 29.18. In that day shall the deaf hear the words of the book, and the eyes of the blind shall see out of obscurity, and out of darkness. 19. The meek also shall increase *their* joy in the Lord, and the poor among men shall rejoice in the Holy One of Israel. *v.* 18-24.

Isa. 30.20. And *though* the Lord give you the bread of adversity, and the water of affliction, yet shall not thy teachers be removed into a corner any more, but thine eyes shall see thy teachers.

Isa. 32.3. The eyes of them that see shall not be dim, and the ears of them that hear shall hearken. 4. The heart also of the rash shall understand knowledge, and the tongue of the stammerers shall be ready to speak plainly. 15. Until the Spirit be poured upon us from on high, and the wilderness be a fruitful field, and the fruitful field be counted for a forest. 16. Then judgment shall dwell in the wilderness, and righteousness remain in the fruitful field. 17. And the work of righteousness shall be peace; and the effect of righteousness, quietness and assurance for ever. *v.* 1-20.

Isa. 33.20. Look upon Zion, the city of our solemnities: thine eyes shall see Jerusalem a quiet habitation, a tabernacle *that* shall not be taken down; not one of the stakes thereof shall ever be removed, neither shall any of the cords thereof be broken. 21. But there the glorious Lord *will be* unto us a place of broad rivers *and* streams; wherein shall go no galley with oars, neither shall gallant ship pass thereby. *v.* 5, 13-24.

Isa. 35.1. The wilderness and the solitary place shall be glad for them; and the desert shall rejoice, and blossom as the rose. 2. It shall blossom abundantly, and rejoice even with joy and singing: the glory of Lebanon shall be given unto it, the excellency of Carmel and Sharon, they shall see the glory of the Lord, *and* the excellency of our God. 5. The eyes of the blind shall be opened, and the ears of the deaf shall be unstopped.

Isa. 35.6. Then shall the lame *man* leap as an hart, and the tongue of the dumb sing: for in the wilderness shall waters break out, and streams in the desert. 7. And the parched ground shall become a pool, and the thirsty land springs of water: in the habitation of dragons, where each lay, *shall be* grass with reeds and rushes. *v.* 1-10.

Isa. 40.5. The glory of the Lord shall be revealed, and all flesh shall see *it* together: for the mouth of the Lord hath spoken *it.* *v.* 4-11.

Isa. 42.3. He shall bring forth judgment unto truth. 4. He shall not fail nor be discouraged, till he have set judgment in the earth: and the isles shall wait for his law. *v.* 1-12.

Isa. 44.3. I will pour water upon him that is thirsty, and floods upon the dry ground: I will pour my spirit upon thy seed, and my blessing upon thine offspring: 4. And they shall spring up *as* among the grass, as willows by the water courses. 5. One shall say, I *am* the Lord's; and another shall call *himself* by the name of Jacob; and another shall subscribe *with* his hand unto the Lord, and surname *himself* by the name of Israel.

Isa. 45.8. Drop down, ye heavens, from above, and let the skies pour down righteousness: let the earth open, and let them bring forth salvation, and let righteousness spring up together; I the Lord have created it. 23. I have sworn by myself, the word is gone out of my mouth *in* righteousness, and shall not return, That unto me every knee shall bow, every tongue shall swear. 24. Surely, shall *one* say, In the Lord have I righteousness and strength: *even* to him shall *men* come. *v.* 6.

Isa. 46.12. Hearken unto me, ye stouthearted, that *are* far from righteousness: 13. I bring near my righteousness; it shall not be far off, and my salvation shall not tarry: and I will place salvation in Zion for Israel my glory.

Isa. 49.6. It is a light thing that thou shouldest be my servant, to raise up the tribes of Jacob, and to restore the preserved of Israel; I will also give thee for a light to the Gentiles, that thou mayest be my salvation unto the end of the earth. 7. Thus saith the Lord, the Redeemer of Israel, *and* his Holy One, to him whom man despiseth, to him whom the nation abhorreth, to a servant of rulers, Kings shall see and arise, princes also shall worship, because of the Lord that is faithful, *and* the Holy One of Israel, and he shall choose thee.

Isa. 49.8. Thus saith the Lord, In an acceptable time have I heard thee, and in a day of salvation have I helped thee: and I will preserve thee, and give thee for a covenant of the people, to establish the earth, to cause to inherit the desolate heritages: 9. That thou mayest say to the prisoners, Go forth; to them that *are* in darkness, Shew yourselves: they shall feed in the ways, and their pastures *shall be* in all high places.

Isa. 49.10. They shall not hunger nor thirst; neither shall the heat nor sun smite them: for he that hath mercy on them shall lead them, even by the springs of water shall he guide them. 11. And I will make all my mountains a way, and my highways shall be exalted. 12. Behold, these shall come from far: and, lo, these from the north and from the west; and these from the land of Sinim. 18. Lift up thine eyes round about, and behold: all these gather themselves together, *and* come to thee. *As* I live, saith the Lord, thou shalt surely clothe thee with them all, as with an ornament, and bind them *on thee*, as a bride *doeth*. *v.* 18-23.

Isa. 51.3. The Lord shall comfort Zion: he will comfort all her waste places; and he will make her wilderness like Eden, and her desert like the garden of the Lord; joy and gladness shall be found therein, thanksgiving, and the voice of melody. 5. My righteousness *is* near; my salvation is gone forth, and mine arms shall judge the people; the isles shall wait upon me, and on mine arm shall they trust.

Isa. 51.6. Lift up your eyes to the heavens, and look upon the earth beneath: for the heavens shall vanish away like smoke, and the earth shall wax old like a garment, and they that dwell therein shall die in like manner: but my salvation shall be for ever, and my righteousness shall not be abolished. 8. For the moth shall eat them up like a garment, and the worm shall eat them like wool: but my righteousness shall be for ever, and my salvation from generation to generation. *v.* 3-16.

Isa. 52.1. Awake, awake; put on thy strength, O Zion; put on thy beautiful garments, O Jerusalem, the holy city: for henceforth there shall no more come into thee the uncircumcised and the unclean. 2. Shake thyself from the dust; arise, *and* sit down, O Jerusalem: loose thyself from the bands of thy neck, O captive daughter of Zion. 7. How beautiful upon the mountains are the feet of him that bringeth good tidings, that publisheth peace; that bringeth good tidings of good,

that publisheth salvation: that saith unto Zion, Thy God reigneth!

,Isa. 52.8. Thy watchmen shall lift up the voice; with the voice together shall they sing: for they shall see eye to eye, when the Lord shall bring again Zion. 10. The Lord hath made bare his holy arm in the eyes of all the nations; and all the ends of the earth shall see the salvation of our God. 15. So shall he sprinkle many nations; the kings shall shut their mouths at him: for *that* which had not been told them shall they see; and *that* which they had not heard shall they consider. *v.* 1-15.

Isa. 53.10. When thou shalt make his soul an offering for sin, he shall see *his* seed, he shall prolong *his* days, and the pleasure of the Lord shall prosper in his hand. 11. He shall see of the travail of his soul, *and* shall be satisfied: by his knowledge shall my righteous servant justify many; for he shall bear their iniquities. 12. Therefore will I divide him *a portion* with the great, and he shall divide the spoil with the strong.

Isa. 54.1. Sing, O barren, thou *that* didst not bear; break forth into singing, and cry aloud, thou *that* didst not travail with child: for more *are* the children of the desolate than the children of the married wife, saith the Lord. 2. Enlarge the place of thy tent, and let them stretch forth the curtains of thine habitations: spare not, lengthen thy cords, and strengthen thy stakes; 3. For thou shalt break forth on the right hand and on the left; and thy seed shall inherit the Gentiles, and make the desolate cities to be inhabited.

Isa. 54.4. Thou shalt forget the shame of thy youth, and shalt not remember the reproach of thy widowhood any more. 5. The God of the whole earth shall he be called. 11. O thou afflicted, tossed with tempest, *and* not comforted, behold, I will lay thy stones with fair colours, and lay thy foundations with sapphires. 12. And I will make thy windows of agates, and thy gates of carbuncles, and all thy borders of pleasant stones. 13. And all thy children *shall be* taught of the Lord; and great *shall be* the peace of thy children.

Isa. 54.14. In righteousness shalt thou be established: thou shalt be far from oppression; for thou shalt not fear: and from terror; for it shall not come near thee. *v.* 1-17.

Isa. 55.5. Behold, thou shalt call a nation *that* thou knowest not, and nations *that* knew not thee shall run unto thee because of the Lord thy God, and for the Holy One of Israel; for he hath glorified thee. 10. For as the rain cometh down, and the snow from heaven, and returneth not thither, but watereth the earth, and maketh it bring forth and bud, that it may give seed to the sower, and bread to the eater: 11. So shall my word be that goeth forth out of my mouth; it shall not return unto me void, but it shall accomplish that which I please, and it shall prosper *in the thing* whereto I sent it.

Isa. 55.12. Ye shall go out with joy, and be led forth with peace: the mountains and the hills shall break forth before you into singing, and all the trees of the field shall clap *their* hands. 13. Instead of the thorn shall come up the fir tree, and instead of the brier shall come up the myrtle tree: and it shall be to the Lord for a name, for an everlasting sign *that* shall not be cut off. *v.* 1-13.

Isa. 56.7. Mine house shall be called an house of prayer for all people. 8. The Lord God which gathereth the outcasts of Israel saith, Yet will I gather *others* to him, beside those that are gathered unto him. *v.* 3-8.

Isa. 59.19. So shall they fear the name of the Lord from the west, and his glory from the rising of the sun. When the enemy shall come in like a flood, the Spirit of the Lord shall lift up a standard against him. *v.* 19-21.

Isa. 60.1. Arise, shine; for thy light is come, and the glory of the Lord is risen upon thee. 3. The Gentiles shall come to thy light, and kings to the brightness of thy rising. 4. Lift up thine eyes round about, and see: all they gather themselves together, they come to thee: thy sons shall come from far, and thy daughters shall be nursed at *thy* side. 5. Then thou shalt see, and flow together, and thine heart shall fear, and be enlarged; because the abundance of the sea shall be converted unto thee, the forces of the Gentiles shall come unto thee.

Isa. 60.7. All the flocks of Kedar shall be gathered together unto thee, the rams of Nebaioth shall minister unto thee: they shall come up with acceptance on mine altar, and I will glorify the house of my glory. 8. Who *are* these *that* fly as a cloud, and as the doves to their windows? 9. Surely the isles shall wait for me, and the ships of Tarshish first, to bring thy sons from far, their silver and their gold with them, unto the name of the Lord thy God, and to the Holy One of Israel, because he hath glorified thee.

Isa. 60.19. The sun shall be no more thy light by day; neither for brightness shall the moon give light unto thee: but the Lord shall be unto thee an everlasting light, and thy God thy glory. 20. Thy sun shall no more go down; neither shall thy moon withdraw itself: for the Lord shall be thine everlasting light, and the days of thy mourning shall be ended. *v.* 1-22.

Isa. 61.1. The Spirit of the Lord God *is* upon me; because the Lord hath anointed me to preach good tidings unto the meek; he hath sent me to bind up the broken-hearted, to proclaim liberty to the captives, and the opening of the prison to *them that are* bound; 2. To proclaim the acceptable year of the Lord, and the day of vengeance of our God; to comfort all that mourn; 3. To appoint unto them that mourn in Zion, to give unto them beauty for ashes, the oil of joy for mourning.

Isa. 61.6. But ye shall be named the Priests of the Lord: *men* shall call you the Ministers of our God: ye shall eat the riches of the Gentiles, and in their glory shall ye boast yourselves. 9. Their seed shall be known among the Gentiles, and their offspring among the people: all that see them shall acknowledge them, that they *are* the seed *which* the Lord hath blessed. 11. As the earth bringeth forth her bud, and as the garden causeth the things that are sown in it to spring forth; so the Lord God will cause righteousness and praise to spring forth before all the nations. *v.* 1-11.

Isa. 62.2. The Gentiles shall see thy righteousness, and all kings thy glory: and thou shalt be called by a new name, which the mouth of the Lord shall name. 3. Thou shalt also be a crown of glory in the hand of the Lord, and a royal diadem in the hand of thy God. 12. They shall call them, The holy people, The redeemed of the Lord: and thou shalt be called, Sought out, A city not forsaken. *v.* 1-12.

Isa. 65.1. I am sought of *them that* asked not *for me;* I am found of *them that* sought me not: I said, Behold me, behold me, unto a nation *that* was not called by my name. 17. For, behold, I create new heavens, and a new earth: and the former shall not be remembered, nor come into mind. 18. But be ye glad and rejoice for ever *in that* which I create: for, behold, I create Jerusalem a rejoicing, and her people a joy. 19. And I will rejoice in Jerusalem, and joy in my people: and the voice of weeping shall be no more heard in her, nor the voice of crying.

Isa. 65.23. They shall not labour in vain, nor bring forth for trouble: for they *are* the seed of the blessed of the Lord, and their offspring with them. 24. And it shall come to pass, that before they call, I will answer; and while they are yet speaking, I will hear. 25. The wolf and the lamb shall feed together, and the lion shall eat straw like the bullock: and dust *shall be* the serpent's meat. They shall not hurt nor destroy in all my holy mountain, saith the Lord. *v.* 1-25.

Isa. 66.12. Behold, I will extend peace to her like a river, and the glory of the Gentiles like a flowing stream: then shall ye suck, ye shall be borne upon *her* sides, and be dandled upon *her* knees. 19. I will set a sign among them, and I will send those that escape of them unto the nations, *to* Tarshish, Pul, and Lud, that draw the bow, *to* Tubal, and Javan, *to* the isles afar off, that have not heard my fame, neither have seen my glory; and they shall declare my glory among the Gentiles. 23. It shall come to pass, *that* from one new moon to another, and from one Sabbath to another, shall all flesh come to worship before me, saith the Lord. *v.* 7-23.

Jer. 3.17. They shall call Jerusalem the throne of the Lord; and all the nations shall be gathered unto it, to the name of the Lord, to Jerusalem: neither shall they walk any more after the imagination of their evil heart.

Jer. 4.2. The nations shall bless themselves in him, and in him shall they glory.

Jer. 16.19. The Gentiles shall come unto thee from the ends of the earth, and shall say, Surely our fathers have inherited lies, vanity, and *things* wherein *there is* no profit. 20. Shall a man make gods unto himself, and they *are* no gods? 21. Therefore, behold, I will this once cause them to know, I will cause them to know mine hand and my might; and they shall know that my name *is* The Lord.

Jer. 31.34. They shall teach no more every man his neighbour, and every man his brother, saying, Know the Lord: for they shall all know me, from the least of them unto the greatest of them, saith the Lord: for I will forgive their iniquity, and I will remember their sin no more.

Jer. 33.22. As the host of heaven cannot be numbered, neither the sand of the sea measured: so will I multiply the seed of David my servant, and the Levites that minister unto me.

Ezk. 17.22. I will also take of the highest branch of the high cedar, and will set *it*; I will crop off from the top of his young twigs a tender one, and will plant *it* upon an high mountain and eminent: 23. In the mountain of the height of Israel will I plant it: and it shall bring forth boughs, and bear fruit, and be a goodly cedar: and under it shall dwell all fowl of every wing; in the shadow of the branches thereof shall they dwell. 24. And all the trees of the field shall know that I the Lord have brought down the high tree, have exalted the low tree, have dried up the green tree, and have made the dry tree to flourish: I the Lord have spoken and have done *it*.

Ezk. 34.26. I will make them and the places round about my hill a blessing; and I will cause the shower to come down in his season: there shall be showers of blessing. 29. And I will raise up for them a plant of renown, and they shall be no more consumed with hunger in the land, neither bear the shame of the heathen any more. 30. Thus shall they know that I the Lord their God *am* with them, and *that* they, *even* the house of Israel, *are* my people, saith the Lord God. 31. And ye my flock, the flock of my pasture, *are* men, *and* I *am* your God, saith the Lord God. *v.* 28-31.

Ezk. 47.3. When the man that had the line in his hand went forth eastward, he measured a thousand cubits, and he brought me through the waters; the waters *were* to the ancles. 4. Again he measured a thousand, and brought me through the waters; the waters *were* to the knees. Again he measured a thousand, and brought me through; the waters *were* to the loins. 5. Afterward he measured a thousand; *and it was* a river that I could not pass over: for the waters were risen, waters to swim in, a river that could not be passed over.

Ezk. 47.7. Now when I had returned, behold, at the bank of the river *were* very many trees on the one side and on the other. 8. Then said he unto me, These waters issue out toward the east country, and go down into the desert, and go into the sea: *which being* brought forth into the sea, the waters shall be healed. 9. And it shall come to pass, *that* every thing that liveth, which moveth, whithersoever the rivers shall come, shall live: and there shall be a very great multitude of fish, because these waters shall come thither: for they shall be healed; and every thing shall live whither the river cometh.

Ezk. 47.12. And by the river upon the bank thereof, on this side and on that side, shall grow all trees for meat, whose leaf shall not fade, neither shall the fruit thereof be consumed: it shall bring forth new fruit according to his months, because their waters they issued out of the sanctuary: and the fruit thereof shall be for meat, and the leaf thereof for medicine. *v.* 1-12.

Dan. 2.35. And the stone that smote the image became a great mountain, and filled the whole earth. 44. In the days of these kings shall the God of heaven set up a kingdom, which shall never be destroyed: and the kingdom shall not be left to other people, *but* it shall break in pieces and consume all these kingdoms, and it shall stand for ever. *v.* 45.

Dan. 7.13. I saw in the night visions, and, behold, *one* like the Son of man came with the clouds of heaven, and came to the Ancient of days, and they brought him near before him. 14. And there was given him dominion, and glory, and a kingdom, that all people, nations, and languages, should serve him: his dominion *is* an everlasting dominion, which shall not pass away, and his kingdom *that* which shall not be destroyed.

Dan. 7.18. But the saints of the most High shall take the kingdom, and possess the kingdom for ever, even for ever and ever. 22. Until the Ancient of days came, and judgment was given to the saints of the most High; and the time came that the saints possessed the kingdom. 27. The kingdom and dominion, and the greatness of the kingdom under the whole heaven, shall be given to the people of the saints of the most High, whose kingdom *is* an everlasting kingdom, and all dominions shall serve and obey him.

Dan. 12.4. Seal the book, *even* to the time of the end: many shall run to and fro, and knowledge shall be increased. *v.* 1-13.

Joel 2.26. Ye shall eat in plenty, and be satisfied, and praise the name of the Lord your God, that hath dealt wondrously with you: and my people shall never be ashamed. 27. And ye shall know that I *am* in the midst of Israel, and *that* I *am* the Lord your God, and none else: and my people shall never be ashamed.

Joel 2.28. And it shall come to pass afterward, *that* I will pour out my Spirit upon all flesh; and your sons and your daughters shall prophesy, your old men shall dream dreams, your young men shall see visions: 29. And also upon the servants and upon the handmaids in those days will I pour out my Spirit. 30. And I will shew wonders in the heavens and in the earth, blood, and fire, and pillars of smoke. 31. The sun shall be turned into darkness, and the moon into blood, before the great and the terrible day of the Lord come.

Joel 2.32. And it shall come to pass, *that* whosoever shall call on the name of the Lord shall be delivered: for in mount Zion and in Jerusalem shall be deliverance, as the Lord hath said, and in the remnant whom the Lord shall call. Act. 2.16-21.

Joel 3.18. It shall come to pass in that day, *that* the mountains shall drop down new wine, and the hills shall flow with milk, and all the rivers of Judah shall flow with waters, and a fountain shall come forth of the house of the Lord, and shall water the valley of Shittim.

Amos 9.11. In that day will I raise up the tabernacle of David that is fallen, and close up the breaches thereof; and I will raise up his ruins, and I will build it as in the days of old: 12. That they may possess the remnant of Edom, and of all the heathen, which are called by my name, saith the Lord that doeth this.

Mic. 4.3. He shall judge among many people, and rebuke strong nations afar off; and they shall beat their swords into plow-shares, and their spears into pruning-hooks: nation shall not lift up a sword against nation, neither shall they learn war any more. 4. But they shall sit every man under his vine and under his fig tree; and none shall make *them* afraid: for the mouth of the Lord of hosts hath spoken *it*. *v.* 1-7.

Mic. 5.2. But thou, Beth-lehem Ephratah, *though* thou be little among the thousands of Judah, *yet* out of thee shall he come forth unto me *that is* to be ruler in Israel; whose goings forth *have been* from of old, from everlasting. 4. And he shall stand and feed in the strength of the Lord, in the majesty of the name of the Lord his God; and they shall abide: for now shall he be great unto the ends of the earth. 7. And the remnant of Jacob shall be in the midst of many people as a dew from the Lord, as the showers upon the grass, that tarrieth not for man, nor waiteth for the sons of men. *v.* 2-15.

Hab. 2.14. The earth shall be filled with the knowledge of the glory of the Lord, as the waters cover the sea.

Zeph. 2.11. The Lord *will be* terrible unto them: for he will famish all the gods of the earth; and *men* shall worship him, every one from his place, *even* all the isles of the heathen.

Zeph. 3.9. Then will I turn to the people a pure language, that they may all call upon the name of the Lord, to serve him with one consent. *v.* 9-20.

Hag. 2.7. And I will shake all nations, and the Desire of all nations shall come: and I will fill this house with glory, saith the Lord of hosts. 8. The silver *is* mine, and the gold *is* mine, saith the Lord of hosts. 9. The glory of this latter house shall be greater than of the former, saith the Lord of hosts: and in this place will I give peace, saith the Lord of hosts.

Zech. 2.10. Sing and rejoice, O daughter of Zion: for, lo, I come, and I will dwell in the midst of thee, saith the Lord. 11. And many nations shall be joined to the Lord in that day, and shall be my people: and I will dwell in the midst of thee, and thou shalt know that the Lord of hosts hath sent me unto thee.

Zech. 4.10. Who hath despised the day of small things? for they shall rejoice.

Zech. 6.15. They *that are* far off shall come and build in the temple of the Lord.

Zech. 8.20. *It shall* yet *come to pass*, that there shall come people, and the inhabitants of many cities: 21. And the inhabitants of one *city* shall go to another, saying, Let us go speedily to pray before the Lord, and to seek the Lord of hosts: I will go also. 22. Yea, many people and strong nations shall come to seek the Lord of hosts in Jerusalem, and to pray before the Lord.

Zech. 8.23. Thus saith the Lord of hosts; In those days *it shall come to pass*, that ten men shall take hold out of all languages of the nations, even shall take hold of the skirt of him that is a Jew, saying, We will go with you: for we have heard *that* God *is* with you.

Zech. 9.1. The eyes of man, as of all the tribes of Israel, *shall be* toward the Lord. 10. I will cut off the chariot from Ephraim, and the horse from Jerusalem, and the battle bow shall be cut off: and he shall speak peace unto the heathen: and his dominion *shall be* from sea *even* to sea, and from the river *even* to the ends of the earth. *v.* 9-17.

Zech. 14.8. It shall be in that day, *that* living waters shall go out from Jerusalem; half of them toward the former sea, and half of them toward the hinder sea: in summer and in winter shall it be. 9. And the Lord shall be king over all the earth: in that day shall there be one Lord, and his name one.

16. Every one that is left of all the nations which came against Jerusalem shall even go up from year to year to worship the King, the Lord of hosts, and to keep the feast of tabernacles. *v.* 8-21.

Mal. 1.11. From the rising of the sun even unto the going down of the same my name *shall be* great among the Gentiles; and in every place incense *shall be* offered unto my name, and a pure offering: for my name *shall be* great among the heathen, saith the Lord of hosts.

Mat. 8.11. Many shall come from the east and west, and shall sit down with Abraham, and Isaac, and Jacob, in the kingdom of heaven.

Mat. 11.11. There hath not risen a greater than John the Baptist: notwithstanding he that is least in the kingdom of heaven is greater than he.

Mat. 13.16. But blessed *are* your eyes, for they see: and your ears, for they hear. 17. For verily I say unto you, That many prophets and righteous *men* have desired to see *those things* which ye see, and have not seen *them*; and to hear *those things* which ye hear, and have not heard *them*.

Mat. 13.31. The kingdom of heaven is like to a grain of mustard seed, which a man took, and sowed in his field: 32. Which indeed is the least of all seeds: but when it is grown, it is the greatest among herbs, and becometh a tree, so that the birds of the air come and lodge in the branches thereof. 33. The kingdom of heaven is like unto leaven, which a woman took, and hid in three measures of meal, till the whole was leavened.

Mat. 16.18. Upon this rock I will build my church; and the gates of hell shall not prevail against it.

Mark 4.26. So is the kingdom of God, as if a man should cast seed into the ground; 27. And should sleep, and rise night and day, and the seed should spring and grow up, he knoweth not how. 28. For the earth bringeth forth fruit of herself; first the blade, then the ear, after that the full corn in the ear. 29. But when the fruit is brought forth, immediately he putteth in the sickle, because the harvest is come. *v.* 30-32.

Luk. 7.22. Tell John what things ye have seen and heard; how that the blind see, the lame walk, the lepers are cleansed, the deaf hear, the dead are raised, to the poor the gospel is preached. Mat. 11.5.

Jno. 8.35. The servant abideth not in the house for ever: *but* the Son abideth ever.

Jno. 10.16. Other sheep I have, which are not of this fold: them also I must bring, and they shall hear my voice; and there shall be one fold, *and* one shepherd.

1 Cor. 15.24. Then *cometh* the end, when he shall have delivered up the kingdom to God, even the Father; when he shall have put down all rule and all authority and power. 25. For he must reign, till he hath put all enemies under his feet. 26. The last enemy *that* shall be destroyed *is* death. 27. For he hath put all things under his feet. But when he saith all things are put under *him, it is* manifest that he is excepted, which did put all things under him. 28. And when all things shall be subdued unto him, then shall the Son also himself be subject unto him that

put all things under him, that God may be all in all.

Eph. 1.10. That in the dispensation of the fulness of times he might gather together in one all things in Christ, both which are in heaven, and which are on earth; *even* in him.

Heb. 12.23. To the general assembly and church of the firstborn, which are written in heaven, and to God the Judge of all, and to the spirits of just men made perfect, 24. And to Jesus the mediator of the new covenant, and to the blood of sprinkling, that speaketh better things than *that* of Abel. 27. This *word*, Yet once more, signifieth the removing of those things that are shaken, as of things that are made, that those things which cannot be shaken may remain. 28. Wherefore we receiving a kingdom which cannot be moved, let us have grace.

Rev. 5.10. Hast made us unto our God kings and priests: and we shall reign on the earth. 13. Every creature which is in heaven, and on the earth, and under the earth, and such as are in the sea, and all that are in them, heard I saying, Blessing, and honour, and glory, and power, *be* unto him that sitteth upon the throne, and unto the Lamb for ever and ever. 14. And the four beasts said, Amen. And the four *and* twenty elders fell down and worshipped him that liveth for ever and ever.

Rev. 11.15. The seventh angel sounded; and there were great voices in heaven, saying, The kingdoms of this world are become *the kingdoms* of our Lord, and of his Christ; and he shall reign for ever and ever.

Rev. 12.10. I heard a loud voice saying in heaven, Now is come salvation, and strength, and the kingdom of our God, and the power of his Christ: for the accuser of our brethren is cast down, which accused them before our God day and night.

Rev. 15.4. All nations shall come and worship before thee.

Rev. 20.4. And I saw thrones, and they sat upon them, and judgment was given unto them: and *I saw* the souls of them that were beheaded for the witness of Jesus, and for the word of God, and which had not worshipped the beast, neither his image, neither had received *his* mark upon their foreheads, or in their hands; and they lived and reigned with Christ a thousand years. 5. But the rest of the dead lived not again until the thousand years were finished. This *is* the first resurrection.

Rev. 20.6. Blessed and holy *is* he that hath part in the first resurrection: on such the second death hath no power, but they shall be priests of God and of Christ, and shall reign with him a thousand years.

See SALVATION.

CHURCH, UNITY OF. Jno. 10.16. Other sheep I have, which are not of this fold: them also I must bring, and they shall hear my voice; and there shall be one fold, *and* one shepherd.

Jno. 17.11. Holy Father, keep through thine own name those whom thou hast given me, that they may be one, as we *are*. 21. That they all may be one; as thou, Father, *art* in me, and I in thee, that they also may be one in us: that the world may believe that thou hast sent me. 22. And the glory which thou gavest me I have given them; that they may

be one, even as we are one: 23. I in them, and thou in me, that they may be made perfect in one; and that the world may know that thou hast sent me, and hast loved me, as thou hast loved me.

Rom. 12.4. As we have many members in one body, and all members have not the same office: 5. So we, *being* many, are one body in Christ, and every one members one of another.

1 Cor. 10.17. We *being* many are one bread, *and* one body: for we are all partakers of that one bread.

1 Cor. 12.5. There are differences of administrations, but the same Lord. 12. As the body is one, and hath many members, and all the members of that one body, being many, are one body: so also *is* Christ. 13. For by one Spirit are we all baptised into one body, whether *we be* Jews or Gentiles, whether *we be* bond or free; and have been all made to drink into one Spirit. 26. And whether one member suffer, all the members suffer with it; or one member be honoured, all the members rejoice with it. 27. Now ye are the body of Christ, and members in particular. *v.* 12-27.

Gal. 3.26. Ye are all the children of God by faith in Christ Jesus. 27. For as many of you as have been baptised into Christ have put on Christ. 28. There is neither Jew nor Greek, there is neither bond nor free, there is neither male nor female: for ye are all one in Christ Jesus.

Eph. 1.10. That in the dispensation of the fulness of times, he might gather together in one all things in Christ, both which are in heaven, and which are on earth, *even* in him.

Eph. 2.15. Having abolished in his flesh the enmity, *even* the law of commandments *contained* in ordinances; for to make in himself of twain one new man, *so* making peace. 19. Ye are no more strangers and foreigners, but fellow-citizens with the saints, and of the household of God. 21. In whom all the building, fitly framed together, groweth unto an holy temple in the Lord.

Eph. 3.6. The Gentiles should be fellow-heirs, and of the same body, and partakers of his promise in Christ by the gospel. 15. Of whom the whole family in heaven and earth is named.

Eph. 4.4. *There is* one body, and one Spirit, even as ye are called in one hope of your calling; 5. One Lord, one faith, one baptism, 6. One God and Father of all, who *is* above all, and through all, and in you all. 12. For the perfecting of the saints, for the work of the ministry, for the edifying of the body of Christ: 13. Till we all come in the unity of the faith, and of the knowledge of the Son of God, unto a perfect man, unto the measure of the stature of the fulness of Christ.

Eph. 4.16. From whom the whole body fitly joined together and compacted by that which every joint supplieth, according to the effectual working in the measure of every part, maketh increase of the body, unto the edifying of itself in love. 25. We are members one of another.

Col. 3.11. There is neither Greek nor Jew, circumcision nor uncircumcision, Barbarian, Scythian, bond *nor* free: but Christ *is* all, and in all. 15. Let the peace of God rule in your hearts, to the which also ye are called in one body.

See CHRIST, HEAD OF THE CHURCH.— UNION TO CHRIST.

CHURCH AND COUNTRY, LOVE OF. Num. 24.9. Blessed is he that blesseth thee, and cursed is he that curseth thee. Gen. 12.3. Gen. 27.29.

Psa. 74.3. Lift up thy feet unto the perpetual desolations; *even all that* the enemy hath done wickedly in the sanctuary. 7. They have cast fire into thy sanctuary, they have defiled *by casting down* the dwelling-place of thy name to the ground. 8. They said in their hearts, Let us destroy them together: they have burned up all the synagogues of God in the land. 10. O God, how long shall the adversary reproach? shall the enemy blaspheme thy name for ever? 11. Why withdrawest thou thy hand, even thy right hand? pluck *it* out of thy bosom.

Psa. 102.14. Thy servants take pleasure in her stones, and favour the dust thereof.

Psa. 122.6. Pray for the peace of Jerusalem: they shall prosper that love thee. 9. Because of the house of the Lord our God I will seek thy good.

Psa. 128.5. The Lord shall bless thee out of Zion: and thou shalt see the good of Jerusalem all the days of thy life. 6. Yea, thou shalt see thy children's children, *and* peace upon Israel.

Psa. 137.1. By the rivers of Babylon, there we sat down, yea, we wept, when we remembered Zion. 2. We hanged our harps upon the willows in the midst thereof. 3. For there they that carried us away captive required of us a song; and they that wasted us *required of us* mirth, *saying,* Sing us *one* of the songs of Zion. 4. How shall we sing the Lord's song in a strange land? 5. If I forget thee, O Jerusalem, let my right hand forget *her cunning.* 6. If I do not remember thee, let my tongue cleave to the roof of my mouth; if I prefer not Jerusalem above my chief joy.

Isa. 22.4. Look away from me; I will weep bitterly, labour not to comfort me, because of the spoiling of the daughter of my people. 5. For *it is* a day of trouble, and of treading down, and of perplexity by the Lord God of hosts.

Isa. 58.12. *They that shall be* of thee shall build the old waste places: thou shalt raise up the foundations of many generations; and thou shalt be called, The repairer of the breach, The restorer of paths to dwell in.

Isa. 62.1. For Zion's sake will I not hold my peace, and for Jerusalem's sake I will not rest, until the righteousness thereof go forth as brightness, and the salvation thereof as a lamp *that* burneth. 6. I have set watchmen upon thy walls, O Jerusalem, *which* shall never hold their peace day nor night: ye that make mention of the Lord, keep not silence; 7. And give him no rest, till he establish, and till he make Jerusalem a praise in the earth.

Isa. 66.10. Rejoice ye with Jerusalem, and be glad with her, all ye that love her: rejoice for joy with her, all ye that mourn for her. 13. Ye shall be comforted in Jerusalem. 14. And when ye see *this,* your heart shall rejoice, and your bones shall flourish like an herb.

Jer. 9.1. Oh that my head were waters, and mine eyes a fountain of tears, that I

might weep day and night for the slain of the daughter of my people!

Jer. 14.17. Let mine eyes run down with tears night and day, and let them not cease: for the virgin daughter of my people is broken with a great breach, with a very grievous blow.

Jer. 51.50. Remember the Lord afar off, and let Jerusalem come into your mind. 51. We are confounded, because we have heard reproach: shame hath covered our faces: for strangers are come into the sanctuaries of the Lord's house.

Lam. 2.11. Mine eyes do fail with tears, my bowels are troubled, my liver is poured upon the earth, for the destruction of the daughter of my people; because the children and the sucklings swoon in the streets of the city.

Lam. 3.48. Mine eye runneth down with rivers of water for the destruction of the daughter of my people. 49. Mine eye trickleth down, and ceaseth not, without any intermission, 50. Till the Lord look down, and behold from heaven. 51. Mine eye affecteth mine heart because of all the daughters of my city. See LAMENTATIONS, c. 1-5.

CHURCH AND COUNTRY, LOVE OF, EXAMPLES OF. Moses, Ex. 2.11,12. Act. 7.23-25. Heb. 11.24,25. Num. 27.15-17. Reubenites, Num. 32.18. Israelites, Jud. 5.2,18. Jud. 21.2-4. Eli, 1 Sam. 4.13,18. Phinehas' wife, 1 Sam. 4.21. Saul, 1 Sam. 11.4-9. David, 2 Sam. 1.20. Philistines, 2 Sam. 10.12. Lepers, 2 Kin. 7.9. Nehemiah, Neh. 1.2-4. Neh. 2. Jews, Neh. 11.2. Mordecai, Est. 4. Est. 10.3. Esther, Est. 4.16. Est. 7.3,4. Est. 8.6.
See LOVE and KINDNESS—ZEAL.

CHURNING. See BUTTER.

CHUSHAN-RISHATHAIM, king of Mesopotamia, subjugates Israel, and is defeated by Othniel. Jud. 3.8-10.

CILICIA, a province of Asia Minor. Jews from, dispute with Stephen, Act. 6.9. The apostles send a letter to the churches in, Act. 15.23. Paul visits the churches in, Act. 15.41. Gal. 1.21. See TARSUS.

CINNAMON. Ex. 30.23. Pro. 7.17. Song 4.14. Rev. 18.13.

CINNEROTH, a city and district in the tribe of Naphtali, supposed to be the same as Gennesareth. Deu. 3.17. Jos. 11.2. Jos. 19.35. Sea of, see GALILEE.

CIRCUMCISION. Of divine appointment, Gen. 17.10-14. Lev. 12.3. Jno. 7.22. Act. 7.8. Rom. 4.11. Performed on the 8th day of all males home-born or bought, Gen. 17.12,13. Lev. 12.3. Phi. 3.5. When necessary, on Sabbath, Jno. 7.23. Necessary to the observance of the passover, Ex. 12.48. Accompanied with naming the child, Gen. 21.3,4. Luk. 1.59. Luk. 2.21. Punishment for neglecting, Gen. 17.14. Ex. 4.24.

Observed by Abraham, Gen. 17.23-27. Gen. 21.3,4. Shechemites, Gen. 34.24. Moses, Ex. 4.25. Joshua at Gilgal, Jos. 5.2-9. Parents of John, Luk. 1.59. Of Christ, Luk. 2.21. Of Paul, Phi. 3.5. Timothy circumcised, Act. 16.3.

Omitted by Israel in the wilderness, Jos. 5.7. Promises connected with, Gen. 17.4-14. Act. 7.8. Rom. 3.1. Rom. 4.11. Rom. 9.7-13. Gal. 5.3. Erroneous views of, Act. 15.1. Did not secure spiritual blessings, Rom. 2.25,28. Gal. 6.13. Abolished, Act. 15.5-29. Rom. 3.30.

Rom. 4.9-11. 1 Cor. 7.18,19. Gal. 2.3,4. Gal. 5.2-11. Gal. 6.12. Eph. 2.11,15. Col. 2.11. Col. 3.11.

Illustrative, Ex. 6.12. Deu. 10.16. Deu. 30.6. Jer. 6.10. Jer. 9.26. Rom. 2.28,29. Rom. 15.8. Phi. 3.3. Col. 2.11. Col. 3.11.

THE CIRCUMCISION, a name of the Jews, Act. 10.45. Act. 11.2. Gal. 2.9. Col. 4.11. Tit. 1.10. Of Christians, Phi. 3.3.

CISTERN, illustrative, 2 Kin. 18.31. Pro. 5.15. Ecc. 12.6. See WELLS.

CITIES AND TOWNS, antiquity of, Gen. 4.17. Gen. 10.10-12. Naming of, see NAMES. Fenced and garrisoned, Deu. 9.1. Jos. 10.20. Jos. 14.12. 2 Chr. 8.5. 2 Chr. 11.10-12. 2 Chr. 17.2,19. 2 Chr. 21.3. Isa. 23.11. See FORTRESS, WALLS, GATES.

Royal cities, Jos. 10.2. 1 Sam. 27.5. 2 Sam. 12.26. 1 Chr. 11.7. Treasure and store cities, Gen. 41.48. Ex. 1.11. 1 Kin. 9.19. 2 Chr. 8.4. 2 Chr. 16.4. 2 Chr. 17.12. Chariot cities, 2 Chr. 1.14. 2 Chr. 8.6. 2 Chr. 9.25. Merchant cities, Isa. 23.11. Eze. 17.4. Eze. 27.3. Of Priests and Levites, see PRIESTS, LEVITES.

Built of brick, see BRICKS. Of stone, 2 Sam. 17.13. Psa. 102.14. Eze. 26.12. Streets of, see STREETS. Governors and magistrates of, see ELDERS. Town-clerk, Act. 19.35. Supplied with water, see WELLS.

Suburbs of, for cattle, Num. 35.3-5. Jos. 14.4. Watchmen of, see WATCHMEN. Adjacent villages belonged to, see VILLAGES. Illustrative, Heb. 11.10,16. Heb. 12.22. Heb. 13.14. For lists of cities, see PALESTINE and other countries.

CITIES OF REFUGE, from the avenger of blood, for manslayers not murderers, who were tried, and obliged to remain in the city till the high-priest's death; were all Levitical cities, Ex. 21.13,14. Num. 35.11-32. Deu. 4.41-43. Deu. 19.2-13. Jos. 20.

Roads made to, Deu. 19.3. Names of, see BEZER, GOLAN, HEBRON, KEDESH-NAPHTALI, RAMOTH-GILEAD, SHECHEM.

CITIZEN of Rome, Act. 21.39. Privileges of, Act. 16.37,38. Act. 22.25-29. Act. 23.27. Act. 25.10,12,25,27. Act. 26.32. Illustrative, Eph. 2.19. See SUBJECTS.

CLAUDA, an island off the coast of Crete, Act. 27.16.

CLAUDIA, a Christian female of Rome, 2 Tim. 4.21.

CLAUDIUS, emperor of Rome, dearth in his reign, Act. 11.28. Banishes Jews from Rome, Act. 18.2.

—— **LYSIAS**, general at Jerusalem, apprehends Paul, Act. 21.31-40. Act. 22.23-30. And sends him to Felix, Act. 23.10-35.

—— **FELIX**. See FELIX.

CLAY, used for seals, Job 38.14. By the potter, Isa. 29.16. Christ anoints a blind man with, Jno. 9.6-15. Illustrative, Job 4.19. Isa. 45.9. Isa. 64.8. Rom. 9.21. Symbolical, Dan. 2.33-41.

CLEAN AND UNCLEAN ANIMALS, Lev. 11. Deu. 14. See DEFILEMENT.

CLEANSING. See ABLUTION—PURIFICATION.

CLEMENT, a Christian at Philippi, Phi. 4.3.

CLEOPAS, a disciple to whom Jesus appeared on the way to Emmaus, Luk. 24.18.

CLEOPHAS. See ALPHEUS.

CLOAK. See DRESS.

CLOUD OF GLORY. A pillar of cloud by day and fire by night, guiding Israel in the wilderness, Ex. 13.21,22. Num. 10.33-36. Num. 14.14. Deu. 1.33. Neh. 9.19. Psa. 78.14. Defended Israel, Ex. 14.19,20,24. When it rested, Israel rested; when taken up, they journeyed, Ex. 40.36-38. Num. 9.17-23. Num. 10.11,12.

Appearances of—First at the Red Sea, Ex. 13.21. Ex. 14.19. When Israel murmured for bread, Ex. 16.10. At the giving of the law, Ex. 19.9,16. Ex. 24.16-18. Ex. 34.5. At the appointment of seventy elders, Num. 11.25. At the sedition of Miriam and Aaron, Num. 12.5,10. When Israel murmured on the report of the spies, Num. 14.10. At the rebellion of Korah, Num. 16.19,42.

Over the tabernacle, Num. 9.15-22. At the tabernacle door, Ex. 33.9,10; Num. 12.5; Deu. 31.15. Filling the tabernacle, Ex. 40.34,35. On the mercy-seat, Lev. 16.2. See MERCY-SEAT. In Solomon's temple, 1 Kin. 8.10,11. Eze. 10.4.

CNIDUS, a town of Asia Minor, Act. 27.7.

COAL. Pro. 26.21. Job 41.21. Psa. 18.8,12. Isa. 44.12. Signifying charcoal, Psa. 120.4. Jno. 18.18. Jno. 21.9. Live coal, illustrative, 2 Sam. 14.7.

COAT. See DRESS. COAT OF MAIL, see BREASTPLATE.

COCKATRICE, a venomous serpent, Isa. 11.8. Illustrative, Isa. 14.29. Isa. 59.5. Jer. 8.17.

COCK-CROWING (the third watch, about 3 o'clock morning), Mar. 13.35. Peter warned by, Mar. 14.30,68,72.

COCKLE, a plant, Job 31.40.

COFFER, or CHEST, 1 Sam. 6.8,15. Eze. 27.24. See TREASURY.

COFFIN, used in Egypt, Gen. 50.26.

COIN. See MONEY.

COLLEGE (literally, second part, a division of Jerusalem), 2 Kin. 22.14. 2 Chr. 34.22.

COLOSSE, a city of Phrygia, Epaphras minister at, Col. 1.7,8. Paul's epistle to the church at, Col. 1.2.

COMFORT. See AFFLICTION, COMFORT IN.

COMFORTER, THE. See HOLY SPIRIT.

COMMANDMENTS, THE. 1st, See IDOLATRY, GOD THE ONLY GOD. 2d, See IDOLATRY, GOD JEALOUS. 3d, See BLASPHEMY, WORSHIP. 4th, See SABBATH, WORSHIP. 5th, See CHILDREN, DUTIES OF. 6th, See MURDER, MALICE, PERSECUTION. 7th, See ADULTERY, SENSUALITY. 8th, See DISHONESTY, INTEGRITY. 9th, See FALSEHOOD, SPEAKING EVIL, TREACHERY. 10th, See COVETOUSNESS, CONTENTMENT, ENVY. THE TEN COMMANDMENTS, see LAW OF GOD.

COMMERCE AND TRADE carried on with money, Gen. 23.16. Gen. 47.14. Ecc. 10.19.

See MONEY, BARTER. By caravans, Gen. 37.25,27. 2 Chr, 9.14. Isa. 21.13. By ships, 1 Kin. 9.27,28. Pro. 31.14. Rev. 18.19. See SHIPS. In shops, Jer. 37.21. At fairs, see MARKET. By the Arabians (Sheba), 1 Kin. 10.10-15. Isa. 60.6. Jer. 6.20. Eze. 27.21-24. Egyptians, Gen. 42.2-34. Ethiopians, Isa. 45.14. Ishmaelites, Gen. 37.27,28. Israelites, 1 Kin. 9.26. Eze. 27.17. Ninevites, Nah. 3.16. Syrians, Eze. 27.16,18. Tarshish, Jer. 10.9. Eze. 27.25. Tyrians, 2 Sam. 5.11. 1 Kin. 5.6. Isa. 23.8. Eze. 27. Eze. 28.5. Zidonians, Isa. 23.2. Eze. 27.8. Articles of, see ARTS AND MANUFACTURES.

COMMUNION, CHRISTIAN. See SAINTS, COMMUNION OF.—GOD, FAVOUR OF.— PRAYERFULNESS.—SPIRITUAL DILIGENCE.

COMPANY, EVIL. See EVIL COMPANY. GOOD, see SAINTS, COMMUNION OF.

CONCISION (a cutting), a by-name for circumcision. Phi. 3.2.

CONCUBINE. See POLYGAMY.

CONCUPISCENCE, Rom. 7.8. Col. 3.5. Usually translated, lust, as Jno. 8.44. Desire, Luk. 22.15. Phi. 1.23.

CONDUIT. See GIHON.

CONEY, a wild animal, Lev. 11.5. Deu. 14.7. Psa. 104.18. Pro. 30.26.

CONFECTIONER, a compounder of spices, 1 Sam. 8.13. See APOTHECARY.

CONFESSING CHRIST. See DECISION.

CONFESSION OF SIN. See REPENTANCE.

CONFIDENCE IN GOD. See FAITH. Confidence in man, self-confidence, see FALSE CONFIDENCE.

CONFUSION OF TONGUES. See BABEL.

CONIAH. See JEHOIACHIN.

CONSCIENCE. Pro. 20.27. The spirit of man is the candle of the Lord, searching all the inward parts.

Rom. 2.14. When the Gentiles, which have not the law, do by nature the things contained in the law, these, having not the law, are a law unto themselves: 15. Which shew the work of the law written in their hearts, their conscience also bearing witness, and *their* thoughts the mean while accusing or else excusing one another.

Rom. 14.14. To him that esteemeth any thing to be unclean, to him *it is* unclean. 22. Happy *is* he that condemneth not himself in that thing which he alloweth. 23. And he that doubteth is damned if he eat, because *he eateth* not of faith: for whatsoever *is* not of faith is sin.

1 Cor. 8.7. Howbeit *there is* not in every man that knowledge: for some with conscience of the idol unto this hour eat *it* as a thing offered unto an idol; and their conscience being weak is defiled.

Tit. 1.15. Unto the pure all things *are* pure: but unto them that are defiled and unbelieving *is* nothing pure; but even their mind and conscience is defiled.

Tit. 3.11. He that is such is subverted, and sinneth, being condemned of himself.

1 Jno. 3.20. If our heart condemn us, God is greater than our heart, and knoweth all things. 21. Beloved, if our heart condemn us not, *then* have we confidence toward God. See CONVICTION OF SIN.

CONSCIENTIOUSNESS. See INTEGRITY.

CONSECRATION. See PRIEST, LEVITES, DEDICATION.

CONSOLATION IN AFFLICTION. See AFFLICTION, COMFORT IN.

CONSPIRACY. See SUBJECTS, REBELLION OF.

CONTENTMENT. Psa. 16.6. The lines are fallen unto me in pleasant *places*; yea, I have a goodly heritage.

Psa. 37.7. Rest in the Lord, and wait patiently for him: fret not thyself because of him who prospereth in his way. 16. A little that a righteous man hath *is* better than the riches of many wicked.

Pro. 14.14. A good man *shall be satisfied* from himself. *v.* 10.

Pro. 15.13. A merry heart maketh a cheerful countenance. 15. A merry heart *hath* a continual feast. 16. Better *is* little with the fear of the Lord, than great treasure, and trouble therewith. 17. Better *is* a dinner of herbs where love is, than a stalled ox and hatred therewith. 30. The light of the eyes rejoiceth the heart: *and* a good report maketh the bones fat.

Pro. 16.8. Better *is* a little with righteousness, than great revenues without right.

Pro. 17.1. Better is a dry morsel and quietness therewith, than a house full of sacrifices with strife. 22. A merry heart doeth good *like* a medicine.

Pro. 30.8. Give me neither poverty nor riches; feed me with food convenient for me.

Ecc. 2.24. *There is* nothing better for a man *than* that he should eat and drink, and *that* he should make his soul enjoy good in his labour. Ecc. 3.12,13. Ecc. 8.15.

Ecc. 4.6. Better *is* an handful *with* quietness, than both the hands full *with* travail and vexation of spirit.

Ecc. 5.12. The sleep of a labouring man *is* sweet, whether he eat little or much.

Ecc. 6.9. Better *is* the sight of the eyes than the wandering of the desire. *v.* 7, 8.

Ecc. 9.7. Eat thy bread with joy, and drink thy wine with a merry heart; for God now accepteth thy works. 8. Let thy garments be always white; and let thy head lack no ointment. 9. Live joyfully with the wife whom thou lovest all the days of the life of thy vanity, which he hath given thee under the sun.

Luk. 3.14. And be content with your wages.

1 Cor. 7.17. As God hath distributed to every man, as the Lord hath called every one, so let him walk. 20. Let every man abide in the same calling wherein he was called. 21. Art thou called *being* a servant? care not for it: but if thou mayest be made free, use *it* rather. *v.* 24.

Gal. 5.26. Let us not be desirous of vain glory, provoking one another, envying one another.

Phi. 4.11. I have learned, in whatsoever state I am, *therewith* to be content. 12. I know both how to be abased, and I know how to abound: every where and in all things I am instructed both to be full and to be hungry, both to abound and to suffer need.

1 Tim. 6.6. Godliness with contentment is great gain. 7. For we brought nothing into *this* world, *and it is* certain we can carry

nothing out. 8. And having food and raiment let us be therewith content.

Heb. 13.5. *Be* content with such things as ye have: for he hath said, I will never leave thee, nor forsake thee.

CONTENTMENT, EXAMPLES OF. Esau, Gen. 33.9. Barzillai, 2 Sam. 19.33-37. Shunemite, 2 Kin. 4.13. See RESIGNATION, THANKFULNESS, COVETOUSNESS, MURMURING.

CONTRITION. See REPENTANCE.

CONVERSATION. 1. (Gr. *anastrophe*), mode of life, behaviour, Gal. 1.13. Eph. 4.22. 1 Tim. 4.12. Heb. 13.7. Jas. 3.13. 1 Pet. 2.12. 1 Pet. 3.1,2,16. 2. (Gr. *politeuma*), citizen life, Phi. 3.20. 3. (Gr. *tropos*), disposition, Heb. 13.5. See SPEAKING FOOLISHLY—SPEAKING WITH WISDOM.

CONVERSION. See REGENERATION—ZEAL FOR CONVERSION.

CONVICTION OF SIN. DREAD OF GOD. SINNERS' MISERY. Gen. 4.13. Cain said unto the Lord, My punishment *is* greater than I can bear.

Lev. 26.36. The sound of a shaken leaf shall chase them; and they shall flee, as fleeing from a sword. 39. They that are left of you shall pine away in their iniquity in your enemies' lands. *v.* 37.

Deu. 28.34. Thou shalt be mad for the sight of thine eyes which thou shalt see. 65. And among these nations shalt thou find no ease, neither shall the sole of thy foot have rest: but the Lord shall give thee there a trembling heart, and failing of eyes, and sorrow of mind: 66. And thy life shall hang in doubt before thee; and thou shalt fear day and night, and shalt have none assurance of thy life: 67. In the morning thou shalt say, Would God it were even! and at even thou shalt say, Would God it were morning! for the fear of thine heart wherewith thou shalt fear, and for the sight of thine eyes which thou shalt see.

1 Sam. 6.20. Who is able to stand before this holy Lord God? and to whom shall he go up from us?

Job. 18.11. Terrors shall make him afraid on every side, and shall drive him to his feet.

Job 24.17. The morning *is* to them even as the shadow of death: if one know them, *they are in* the terrors of the shadow of death.

Job 27.20. Terrors take hold on him as waters, a tempest stealeth him away in the night.

Job 30.15. Terrors are turned upon me: they pursue my soul as the wind; and my welfare passeth away as a cloud.

Job 37.20. Shall it be told him that I speak? if a man speak, surely he shall be swallowed up.

Job 40.4. Behold, I am vile; what shall I answer thee? I will lay mine hand upon my mouth. 5. Once have I spoken, but I will not answer; yea, twice, but I will proceed no further.

Psa. 31.10. My life is spent with grief, and my years with sighing: my strength faileth because of mine iniquity, and my bones are consumed.

Psa. 38.2. Thine arrows stick fast in me, and thy hand presseth me sore. 3. *There is* no soundness in my flesh because of thine anger; neither *is there any* rest in my bones because of my sin. 4. For mine iniquities

are gone over mine head: as an heavy burden they are too heavy for me. 5. My wounds stink, *and* are corrupt because of my foolishness. 6. I am troubled; I am bowed down greatly; I go mourning all the day long.

Pro. 1.27. When your fear cometh as desolation, and your destruction cometh as a whirlwind; when distress and anguish cometh upon you.

Pro. 5.11. Thou mourn at the last, when thy flesh and thy body are consumed, 12. And say, How have I hated instruction, and my heart despised reproof; 13. And have not obeyed the voice of my teachers, nor inclined mine ear to them that instructed me! 14. I was almost in all evil in the midst of the congregation.

Pro. 28.1. The wicked flee when no man pursueth.

Isa. 2.19. They shall go into the holes of the rocks, and into the caves of the earth, for fear of the Lord, and for the glory of his majesty, hen he ariseth to shake terribly the earth. *v.* 21.

Isa. 6.5. Woe *is* me! for I am undone; because I *am* a man of unclean lips, and I dwell in the midst of a people of unclean lips: for mine eyes have seen the King, the Lord of hosts.

Isa. 57.20. The wicked *are* like the troubled sea, when it cannot rest, whose waters cast up mire and dirt. 21. *There is* no peace, saith my God, to the wicked. Isa. 48.22.

Lam. 1.20. I *am* in distress; my bowels are troubled: mine heart is turned within me; for I have grievously rebelled.

Eze. 7.16. Shall be on the mountains like doves of the valleys, all of them mourning, every one for his iniquity. 17. All hands shall be feeble, and all knees shall be weak *as* water. 18. They shall also gird *themselves* with sackcloth, and horror shall cover them; and shame *shall be* upon all faces, and baldness upon all their heads. 25. They shall seek peace; and *there shall be* none. 26. Mischief shall come upon mischief, and rumour shall be upon rumour: then shall they seek a vision of the prophet: but the law shall perish from the priest, and counsel from the ancients.

Eze. 33.10. If our transgressions and our sins *be* upon us, and we pine away in them, how should we then live?

Mic. 7.17. They shall lick the dust like a serpent, they shall move out of their holes like worms of the earth: they shall be afraid of the Lord our God, and shall fear because of thee.

Mat. 24.30. Then shall all the tribes of the earth mourn, and they shall see the Son of man coming in the clouds.

Luk. 5.8. He fell down at Jesus' knees, saying, Depart from me; for I am a sinful man, O Lord.

Luk. 13.28. There shall be weeping and gnashing of teeth, when ye shall see Abraham, and Isaac, and Jacob, and all the prophets, in the kingdom of God, and you *yourselves* thrust out.

Act. 2.37. They were pricked in their heart, and said unto Peter, and to the rest of the apostles, Men *and* brethren, what shall we do?

Act. 9.6. He, trembling and astonished, said, Lord, what wilt thou have me to do?

Act. 16.29. He called for a light, and sprang

in, and came trembling, and fell down before Paul and Silas, 30. And brought them out, and said, Sirs, what must I do to be saved?

Rom. 2.15. Their conscience also bearing witness, and *their* thoughts the meanwhile accusing or else excusing one another.

Rom. 7.10. The commandment, which *was ordained* to life, I found *to be* unto death. 11. For sin, taking occasion by the commandment, deceived me, and by it slew *me*. 24. O wretched man that I am! who shall deliver me from the body of this death?

2 Cor. 7.10. The sorrow of the world worketh death.

1 Jno. 3.20. If our heart condemn us, God is greater than our heart, and knoweth all things.

1 Jno. 4.18. There is no fear in love; but perfect love casteth out fear: because fear hath torment. He that feareth is not made perfect in love.

Rev. 1.17. When I saw him, I fell at his feet as dead.

Rev. 6.15. Every bondman; and every freeman, hid themselves in the dens and in the rocks of the mountains; 16. And said to the mountains and rocks, Fall on us, and hide us from the face of him that sitteth on the throne, and from the wrath of the Lamb: 17. For the great day of his wrath is come; and who shall be able to stand? Hos. 10.8. Luk. 23.30.

Rev. 9.6. In those days shall men seek death, and shall not find it; and shall desire to die, and death shall flee from them.

CONVICTION, EXAMPLES OF. Adam and Eve, Gen. 3.8-10. Joseph's brethren, Gen. 44.16. Gen. 45.3. Gen. 50.15-18. Pharaoh, Ex. 9.27,28. Ex. 10.16,17. Ex. 12.31-33. Egyptians, Ex. 10.7. Ex. 12.33. Ex. 14.25. Israelites, Ex. 20.19. Ex. 33.4. Num. 14.39,40. Num. 17.12,13. Num. 21.7. Deu. 18.16. Manoah, Jud. 13.22. Saul, 1 Sam. 15.24. 1 Sam. 24.16-20. 1 Sam. 26.21. David, 2 Sam. 6.9. 1 Chr. 21.30. Widow, 1 Kin. 17.18. Princes of Judah, Jer. 36.16. Belshazzar, Dan. 5.6. Darius, Dan. 6.18. Herod, Mat. 14.2. Gadarênes, Mar. 5.17. Jews, Jno. 8.9. Judas, Mat. 27.3-5. Felix, Act. 24,25. See REPENTANCE.—AFFLICTION, BENEFITS OF.—JUDGMENTS, DESIGN OF.

COOKING. See BREAD, FOOD, FURNACE.

COOS, an island of the Mediterranean, Act. 21.1.

COPPER AND COPPERSMITH. See BRASS.

COR, a measure of 10 ephahs or baths, about 90 gals., 1 Kin. 4.22 (*marg.*) Eze. 45.14.

CORAL, Job 28.18. Eze. 27.16.

CORBAN (dedicated), Mar. 7.11.

CORD. See ROPES.

CORIANDER, a plant, Ex. 16.31. Num. 11.7.

CORINTH, a city of Achaia, Paul visits, Act. 18. 2 Cor. 12.14. 2 Cor. 13.1. Apollos visits, Act. 19.1. Church, schism in, 1 Cor. 1.12. 1 Cor. 3.4. Church, immoralities in, 1 Cor. 5. 1 Cor. 11. Church of, writes to Paul, 1 Cor. 7.1. Alienation from Paul, 2 Cor. 10.

Abuse of ordinances, 1 Cor. 11.22. 1 Cor. 14. Heresies in, 1 Cor. 15.12. 2 Cor. 11. Lawsuits in, 1 Cor. 6. Liberality of the church, 2 Cor. 9.

Visited by Titus, 2 Cor. 8. 2 Cor. 12. 18. Erastus, a Christian of, Rom. 16.23. 2 Tim. 4.20.

CORMORANT, an unclean bird, Lev. 11.17. Deu. 14.17. Isa. 34.11. Zeph. 2.14.

CORN, growth of, Psa. 65.13. Mar. 4.28. Abounded in Egypt, Gen. 41.47-49. In Palestine, Deu. 33.28. Eze. 27.17. Parched, Ruth 2.14. 1 Sam. 17.17. 1 Sam. 25.18. 2 Sam. 17.28. Israelites ate corn of the country, Jos. 5.11,12. Samson burnt the shocks of, Jud. 15.5. Ears of, plucked by Christ's disciples, Mat. 12.1. Laws regarding, Ex. 22.6. Deu. 23.25.

Illustrative, Psa. 72.16. Hos. 14.7. Jno. 12.24. Symbolical, Gen. 41.5. See BARLEY, BREAD, RYE, WHEAT, BARNS, FIRST-FRUITS, GLEANING, HARVEST, REAPING, THRESHING, TITHES.

CORNELIUS, a pious centurion; his vision, sends for Peter, is baptized, Act. 10.

CORNER-STONE, Job 38.6. Psa. 144.12. Illustrative, Psa. 118.22. Isa. 28.16. Eph. 2.20. 1 Pet. 2.6.

CORNET. See TRUMPET.

CORRUPTION, MOUNT OF. See OLIVES, MOUNT OF.

COTTAGE. See BOOTH, TENT.

COUNCIL. See SANHEDRIM.

COUNSELLOR. Of kings, 1 Chr. 27.32, 33. Ezr. 4.5. Ezr. 7.14,15,28. Job 12.17. Dan. 6.7. A member of the Sanhedrim, Mar. 15.43. A name of Christ, Isa. 9.6.

COURT. See HOUSES, TEMPLE, TABERNACLE.

COURTS OF JUSTICE. See JUSTICE, ADMINISTRATION OF. COURT OF KINGS, see KINGS.

COURTESY. See SALUTATIONS.

COVENANTS. Sacredness of, Jos. 9.18-21. Gal. 3.15. Breach of, punished, 2 Sam. 21.1-6. Jer. 34.8-22. Eze. 17.13-19. National, see ALLIANCES.

Ratified by oath, see OATHS. Giving the hand, Ezr. 10.19. Lam. 5.6. Eze. 17.18. Loosing the shoe before witnesses, Ruth 4.7-11. Writing and sealing the agreement, Neh. 9.38. Jer. 32.10-12. Presents, Gen. 21.27-30. 1 Sam. 18.3. Feasting, Gen. 26.30. Raising a pillar, Gen. 31.45,46. By salt, Lev. 2.13. Num. 18.19. 2 Chr. 13.5. Passing between the divided parts of a sacrifice, Gen. 15.9-17. Jer. 34.18,19.

———— OF GOD WITH MAN. With Adam, Gen. 2.16,17. Noah, Gen. 8.16. Of circumcision with Abraham, Gen. 17.13. Rom. 9.7-13. See CIRCUMCISION. With Isaac, Gen. 17.19. Jacob, Gen. 28.13-15. With the Israelites to deliver them from Egypt, Ex. 6.4-8.

Of the Sabbath, Ex. 31.16. Of the Ten Commandments, Ex. 34.28. Deu. 5.2,3. Deu. 9.9. Of the priesthood with Phinehas, Num. 25.12,13. With Levi, Neh. 13.29. Mal. 2.4,5. With Israel in the land of Moab, Deu. 29.1-15. With David and his children, 2 Sam. 23.5. Psa. 89.20-37. Jer. 33.21. With believers, Isa. 55.3.

To give the Holy Spirit, Isa. 59.21. A new covenant, Jer. 31.31-34. The covenant's renewal, Eze. 30.37. The covenant's confirmation, Dan. 9.27. Covenant of mercy to the Jews, Jer. 32.38-40. Eze. 37.26. Rom. 11.27. The better covenant, Heb. 8.6. The new covenant, Heb. 8.13. Heb. 12.24. The everlasting covenant, Heb.13.20.

COVENANTS WITH GOD. Joshua, Jos. 24.25. Jehoiada and Joash, 2 Kin. 11.17. Josiah, 2 Kin. 23.3. Asa, 2 Chr. 15.12-15. Nehemiah, Neh. 9.38. Neh. 10. Israelites, Jer. 50.5.

COVETOUSNESS. WORLDLY CARE. LOVE OF RICHES. Ex. 18.21. Provide men of truth, hating covetousness.

Ex. 20.17. Thou shalt not covet thy neighbour's house, thou shalt not covet thy neighbour's wife, nor his man-servant, nor his maid-servant, nor his ox, nor his ass, nor any thing that is thy neighbour's. Deu. 5.21.

Deu. 8.12. Lest when thou hast eaten and art full, and hast built goodly houses, and dwelt therein; 13. And when thy herds and thy flocks multiply, and thy silver and thy gold is multiplied, and all that thou hast is multiplied; 14. Then thine heart be lifted up, and thou forget the Lord thy God. v. 17. Deu. 6.10-12.

Deu. 31.20. Eaten and filled themselves, and waxen fat; then will they turn unto other gods.

Neh. 5.7. Ye exact usury every one of his brother.

Job 20.15. He hath swallowed down riches, and he shall vomit them up again : God shall cast them out of his belly. 22. In the fulness of his sufficiency he shall be in straits. 23. When he is about to fill his belly, God shall cast the fury of his wrath upon him, and shall rain it upon him while he is eating.

Job 21.13. Spend their days in wealth, and in a moment go down to the grave. 14. Therefore they say unto God, Depart from us.

Job 27.16. Though he heap up silver as the dust, and prepare raiment as the clay ; 17. He may prepare it, but the just shall put it on, and the innocent shall divide the silver. 18. He buildeth his house as a moth, and as a booth that the keeper maketh. 19. The rich man shall lie down, but he shall not be gathered : he openeth his eyes, and he is not.

Job 29.18. I said, I shall die in my nest, and I shall multiply my days as the sand. v. 19,20.

Job 31.24. If I have made gold my hope, or have said to the fine gold, Thou art my confidence ; 25. If I rejoiced because my wealth was great, and because mine hand had gotten much.

Psa. 10.3. The covetous, whom 'the Lord abhorreth.

Psa. 17.14. Men of the world, which have their portion in this life, and whose belly thou fillest with thy hid treasure.

Psa. 30.6. In my prosperity I said, I shall never be moved.

Psa. 37.16. A little that a righteous man hath is better than the riches of many wicked.

Psa. 39.6. Every man walketh in a vain show : surely they are disquieted in vain : he heapeth up riches, and knoweth not who shall gather them.

Psa. 49.11. Their inward thought is, that their houses shall continue for ever, and their dwelling-places to all generations ; they call their lands after their own names. 12. Nevertheless man being in honour abideth not : he is like the beasts that perish. 13. This their way is their folly : yet their posterity approve their sayings. 14. Like sheep they are laid in the grave. 16. Be not thou afraid when one is made rich, when the glory of his house is increased ; 17. For when he dieth he shall carry nothing away : his glory shall not descend after him. 18. Though while he lived he blessed his soul.

Psa. 52.7. Lo, this is the man that made not God his strength ; but trusted in the abundance of his riches.

Psa. 62.10. If riches increase, set not your heart upon them.

Psa. 73.5. They are not in trouble as other men ; neither are they plagued like other men. 7. Their eyes stand out with fatness : they have more than heart could wish.

Psa. 119.36. Incline my heart unto thy testimonies, and not to covetousness.

Pro. 1.19. So are the ways of every one that is greedy of gain; which taketh away the life of the owners thereof. 32. The prosperity of fools shall destroy them.

Pro. 10.2. Treasures of wickedness profit nothing.

Pro. 11.4. Riches profit not in the day of wrath. 24. There is that withholdeth more than is meet, but it tendeth to poverty. 26. He that withholdeth corn, the people shall curse him. 28. He that trusteth in his riches shall fall.

Pro. 13.7. There is that maketh himself rich, yet hath nothing : there is that maketh himself poor, yet hath great riches. 11. Wealth gotten by vanity shall be diminished.

Pro. 15.6. In the revenues of the wicked is trouble. 16. Better is little with the fear of the Lord than great treasure and trouble therewith. 17. Better is a dinner of herbs where love is, than a stalled ox and hatred therewith. 27. He that is greedy of gain troubleth his own house.

Pro. 16.8. Better is a little with righteousness, than great revenues without right.

Pro. 17.1. Better is a dry morsel, and quietness therewith, than an house full of sacrifices with strife.

Pro. 18.11. The rich man's wealth is his strong city, and as an high wall in his own conceit. Pro. 10.15.

Pro. 20.21. An inheritance may be gotten hastily at the beginning ; but the end thereof shall not be blessed.

Pro. 21.6. The getting of treasures by a lying tongue is a vanity tossed to and fro of them that seek death. 25. The desire of the slothful killeth him. 26. He coveteth greedily all the day long.

Pro. 22.16. He that oppresseth the poor to increase his riches, and he that giveth to the rich, shall surely come to want.

Pro. 23.4. Labour not to be rich. 5. Wilt thou set thine eyes upon that which is not? for riches certainly make themselves wings ; they fly away as an eagle toward heaven.

Pro. 27.24. Riches are not for ever : and doth the crown endure to every generation?

Pro. 28.8. He that by usury and unjust gain increaseth his substance, he shall gather it for him that will pity the poor. 16. He that hateth covetousness shall prolong his days.

20. He that maketh haste to be rich shall not be innocent. 22. He that hasteth to be rich *hath* an evil eye.

Pro. 30.8. Give me neither poverty nor riches ; feed me with food convenient for me : 9. Lest I be full, and deny *thee*, and say, Who *is* the Lord ?

Ecc. 1.8. All things *are* full of labour ; man cannot utter *it* : the eye is not satisfied with seeing, nor the ear filled with hearing. *v.* 2-8.

Ecc. 2.18. I hated all my labour which I had taken under the sun : because I should leave it unto the man that shall be after me. 19. And who knoweth whether he shall be a wise *man* or a fool ? 22. What hath man of all his labour, and of the vexation of his heart, wherein he hath laboured under the sun ? 23. For all his days *are* sorrows, and his travail grief ; yea, his heart taketh not rest in the night. This is also vanity. 26. To the sinner he giveth travail, to gather and to heap up, that he may give to *him that is* good before God.

Ecc. 4.6. Better *is* an handful *with* quietness, than both the hands full *with* travail and vexation of spirit. 8. There is one *alone*, and *there is* not a second ; yea, he hath neither child nor brother : yet *is there* no end of all his labour ; neither is his eye satisfied with riches ; neither *saith he*, For whom do I labour, and bereave my soul *of* good ?

Ecc. 5.10. He that loveth silver shall not be satisfied with silver ; nor he that loveth abundance with increase : this *is* also vanity. 11. When goods increase, they are increased that eat them : and what good *is there* to the owners thereof, saving the beholding *of them* with their eyes ? 12. The sleep of a labouring man *is* sweet, whether he eat little or much : but the abundance of the rich will not suffer him to sleep. 13. There is a sore evil *which* I have seen under the sun, *namely*, riches kept for the owners thereof to their hurt.

Ecc. 5.15. He shall take nothing of his labour, which he may carry away in his hand. 16. And this also *is* a sore evil, *that* in all points as he came, so shall he go : and what profit hath he that hath laboured for the wind ? 17. All his days also he eateth in darkness.

Ecc. 6.2. A man to whom God hath given riches, wealth, and honour, so that he wanteth nothing for his soul of all that he desireth, yet God giveth him not power to eat thereof, but a stranger eateth it : this *is* vanity, and it *is* an evil disease. 7. All the labour of man *is* for his mouth, and yet the appetite is not filled. *v.* 1-7.

Isa. 5.8. Woe unto them that join house to house, *that* lay field to field, till *there be* no place, that they may be placed alone in the midst of the earth !

Isa. 55.2. Wherefore do ye spend money for *that which is* not bread ? and your labour for *that which* satisfieth not ?

Isa. 56.11. *They are* greedy dogs *which* can never have enough : they all look to their own way, every one for his gain, from his quarter.

Isa. 57.17. For the iniquity of his covetousness was I wroth, and smote him.

Jer. 6.13. From the least of them even unto the greatest of them every one *is* given to covetousness.

Jer. 9.23. Let not the rich *man* glory in his riches.

Jer. 17.11. *As* the partridge sitteth *on* eggs, and hatcheth *them* not ; *so* he that getteth riches, and not by right, shall leave them in the midst of his days, and at his end shall be a fool.

Jer. 22.17. Thine eyes and thine heart *are* not but for thy covetousness.

Jer. 48.36 The riches *that* he hath gotten are perished.

Jer. 51.13. Abundant in treasures, thine end is come, *and* the measure of thy covetousness.

Eze. 7.19. They shall cast their silver in the streets, and their gold shall be removed : their silver and their gold shall not be able to deliver them in the day of the wrath of the Lord : they shall not satisfy their souls, neither fill their bowels : because it is the stumblingblock of their iniquity.

Eze. 13.19. Will ye pollute me among my people for handfuls of barley and for pieces of bread.

Eze. 22.12. They have taken gifts to shed blood ; thou hast taken usury and increase, and thou hast greedily gained of thy neighbours by extortion, and hast forgotten me, saith the Lord God. 13. I have smitten mine hand at thy dishonest gain which thou hast made.

Eze. 28.5. By thy great wisdom *and* by thy traffick hast thou increased thy riches, and thine heart is lifted up because of thy riches.

Eze. 33.31. With their mouth they shew much love, *but* their heart goeth after their covetousness.

Hos. 10.1. Israel *is* an empty vine, he bringeth forth fruit unto himself.

Hos. 12.8. I am become rich, I have found me out substance : *in* all my labours they shall find none iniquity in me.

Amos 8.5. When will the new moon be gone, that we may sell corn ? and the sabbath, that we may set forth wheat.

Mic. 2.2. They covet fields, and take *them* by violence ; and houses, and take *them* away : so they oppress a man and his house.

Mic. 3.11. The heads thereof judge for reward, and the priests thereof teach for hire, and the prophets thereof divine for money.

Hab. 1.16. They sacrifice unto their net, and burn incense unto their drag ; because by them their portion *is* fat, and their meat plenteous.

Hab. 2.5. *He is* a proud man, neither keepeth at home, who enlargeth his desire as hell, and *is* as death, and cannot be satisfied, but gathereth unto him all nations, and heapeth unto him all people.

Hab. 2.6. Woe to him that increaseth *that which is* not his ! that ladeth himself with thick clay ! 9. That coveteth an evil covetousness to his house, that he may set his nest on high ! 13. *Is it* not of the Lord of hosts that the people shall labour in the very fire, and the people shall weary themselves for very vanity ?

Zeph. 1.18. Neither their silver nor their gold shall be able to deliver them in the day of the Lord's wrath.

Hag. 1.6. Ye have sown much, and bring in little ; ye eat, but ye have not enough ; ye drink, but ye are not filled with drink ; ye clothe you, but there is none warm ; and he that earneth wages, earneth wages *to put it* into a bag with holes.

Mal. 1.10. Who *is there* even among you that would shut the doors *for nought ?* neither do ye kindle *fire* on mine altar for nought.

Mat. 6.19. Lay not up for yourselves treasures upon earth. 24. No man can serve two masters : for either he will hate the one, and love the other ; or else he will hold to the one, and despise the other. Ye cannot serve God and mammon. 25. Take no thought for your life, what ye shall eat, or what ye shall drink ; nor yet for your body, what ye shall put on. Is not the life more than meat, and the body than raiment ? *v.* 24-34. Luk. 12.22-31.

Mat. 13.22. The care of this world, and the deceitfulness of riches, choke the word, and he becometh unfruitful. *v.* 7. Mar. 4.7,18,19. Luk. 8.7,14.

Mat. 16.26. What is a man profited, if he shall gain the whole world, and lose his own soul?

Mat. 19.24. It is easier for a camel to go through the eye of a needle, than for a rich man to enter into the kingdom of God. *v.* 23. Luk. 18.24,25.

Mat. 22.5. They made light of *it*, and went their ways, one to his farm, another to his merchandise. *v.* 1-14.

Mar. 7.21. Out of the heart proceed . . . 22. Covetousness . . . these evil things come from within, and defile the man.

Mar. 10.24. How hard is it for them that trust in riches to enter into the kingdom of God !

Luk. 6.24. Woe unto you that are rich ! for ye have received your consolation. 25. Woe unto you that are full ! for ye shall hunger.

Luk. 10.41. Thou art careful and troubled about many things.

Luk. 12.15. Take heed, and beware of covetousness : for a man's life consisteth not in the abundance of the things which he possesseth. [See Parable of rich man, *v.* 16-21.] 33. Provide yourselves bags which wax not old, a treasure in the heavens that faileth not, where no thief approacheth, neither moth corrupteth. 34. For where your treasure is, there will your heart be also. Mat. 6.21.

Luk. 14.18. They all with one *consent* began to make excuse. The first said unto him, I have bought a piece of ground, and I must needs go and see it : I pray thee have me excused. *v.* 16-24.

Jno. 6.27. Labour not for the meat which perisheth.

Rom. 1.29. Being filled with all unrighteousness, covetousness.

1 Cor. 5.11. If any man that is called a brother be covetous, or an extortioner, with such an one no not to eat.

1 Cor. 7.30. They that buy, as though they possessed not ; 31. And they that use this world, as not abusing *it* : for the fashion of this world passeth away.

2 Cor. 9.6. He which soweth sparingly shall reap also sparingly ; and he which soweth bountifully shall reap also bountifully. 7. Every man according as he purposeth in his heart, *so let him give* ; not grudgingly, or of necessity : for God loveth a cheerful giver.

Eph. 5.3. Covetousness, let it not be once named among you, as becometh saints. 5. Nor covetous man, who is an idolater, hath any inheritance in the kingdom of Christ and of God. 1 Cor. 6.10.

Phil. 3.19. Who mind earthly things.

Phil. 4.6. Be careful for nothing.

Col. 3.2. Set your affection on things above, not on things on the earth. 5. Mortify therefore your members which are upon the earth ; covetousness, which is idolatry : 6. For which things' sake the wrath of God cometh on the children of disobedience.

1 Tim. 3.3. Not greedy of filthy lucre ; but patient, not a brawler, not covetous. Tit. 1.11.

1 Tim. 6.5. Supposing that gain is godliness : from such withdraw thyself. 9. They that will be rich fall into temptation and a snare, and *into* many foolish and hurtful lusts, which drown men in destruction and perdition. 10. For the love of money is the root of all evil : which while some coveted after, they have erred from the faith, and pierced themselves through with many sorrows. 11. But thou, O man of God, flee these things. 17. Charge them that are rich in this world, that they be not high-minded, nor trust in uncertain riches.

2 Tim. 2.4. No man that warreth entangleth himself with the affairs of *this* life.

2 Tim. 3.2. Men shall be lovers of their own selves, covetous.

Heb. 13.5. *Let your* conversation *be* without covetousness ; *and be* content with such things as ye have.

Jas. 1.11. So also shall the rich man fade away in his ways.

Jas. 4.2. Ye lust, and have not ; ye kill, and desire to have, and cannot obtain. 13. Go to now, ye that say, To-day or to-morrow we will go into such a city, and continue there a year, and buy and sell, and get gain : 14. Whereas ye know not what *shall be* on the morrow. *v.* 13-17.

Jas. 5.1. Go to now, *ye* rich men, weep and howl for your miseries that shall come upon *you.* 2. Your riches are corrupted, and your garments are motheaten. 3. Your gold and silver is cankered ; and the rust of them shall be a witness against you, and shall eat your flesh as it were fire. Ye have heaped treasure together for the last days.

1 Pet. 1.7. Gold that perisheth.

1 Pet. 5.2. Taking the oversight *thereof*, not by constraint, but willingly ; not for filthy lucre.

2 Pet. 2.3. Through covetousness shall they with feigned words make merchandise of you : whose judgment now of a long time lingereth not. 14. An heart they have exercised with covetous practices. *v.* 15,16.

1 Jno. 2.15. Love not the world, neither the things *that are* in the world. If any man love the world, the love of the Father is not in him. *v.* 16,17.

COVETOUSNESS, EXAMPLES OF. Eve, Gen. 3.6. Lot, Gen. 13.10-13. Laban, Gen. 24.30. Achan, Jos. 7.21. Eli's sons, 1 Sam. 2.13-17. Samuel's sons, 1 Sam. 8.3. Saul, 1 Sam. 15.8,9. Ahab, 1 Kin. 21.2-16. Gehazi, 2 Kin. 5.20-27. Jews, Neh. 5.1-11. Neh. 13.10. Hag. 1.4-9. Jno. 6.26. Tyrians, Eze. 28.1-19. Priests, Mal. 1.10. Ruler, Mat. 19.22. Money-changers, Mat. 21.12,13. Jno. 2.14-16. Judas, Mat. 26.15,16. Jno. 12.6. Steward, Luk. 16.1-8. Pharisees, Luk. 16.14. Men of Sodom, Luk. 17.28-30. Simon Magus, Act. 8.18-23. Sorcerers, Act. 16.19.

Demetrius, Act. 19.24-27. Festus, Act. 24.26.
Demas, 2 Tim. 4.10. Balaam, 2 Pet. 2.15.

See BRIBERY — CONTENTMENT — LIBER-
ALITY—MURMURING—RICHES, RIGHT USE
OF—WORLDLINESS.

COW, or KINE, yoked by the Philistines in
sending back the ark, 1 Sam. 6.7-12. Sacrificed, 1 Sam. 6.14. Pharaoh's dream of, Gen.
41.2-7,26-30. Illustrative, Amos 4.1. See
CATTLE.

COWARDICE. See FEAR OF MAN.

CRACKNELS. See BREAD.

CRANE, a bird of passage, Isa. 38.14.
Jer. 8.7.

CREATION. See GOD CREATOR—CHRIST
CREATOR—HOLY SPIRIT CREATOR.

CREDITORS. Took pledges, Deu. 24.10.
Pro. 22.27. Sureties, Pro. 11.15. Pro. 22.26.
Mortgages, Neh. 5.3. Bills, Luk. 16.6. En-
forced payment by selling the debtor or surety's property, or taking him and his family
for bond-slaves, Ex. 21.2. 2 Kin. 4.1. Neh.
5.5. Job 24.9. Pro. 22.26,27. Mat. 18.25.
By imprisonment, Mat. 5.26. Mat. 18.30.

Forbidden to take millstones in pledge, Deu.
24.6. To take pledges violently, Deu. 24.10.
Job 22.6. Job 24.9. To exact debts on the
sabbatical year, Deu. 15.2,3. To exact usury
from Israelites, Ex. 22.25. Lev. 25.36. Deu.
23.20. To retain garments as pledges after
sunset, Ex. 22.26,27. Deu. 24.12,13. Eze.
18.7,12. Eze. 33.15. Amos 2.8. To take a
widow's garment in pledge, Deu. 24.17. Or a
widow's ox, Job 24.3.

CREEPING THINGS, Gen. 1.26. Rom.
1.23. The original is applied to beasts generally, Psa. 104.20. Aquatic animals, Psa. 104.25.
The smaller quadrupeds, as weasels, &c., Lev.
11.29-31. Insects, &c., Lev. 11.20-23. Many-
footed animals, Lev. 11.42. Reptiles that
crawl on their bellies, Lev. 11.42.

Were unclean, Lev. 5.2. Lev. 11.20-44. Deu.
14.19. Exceptions, Lev. 11.21,22. Idolatrous
representations of, Eze. 8.10.

CRESCENS, a companion of Paul, 2 Tim.
4.10.

CRETE (CANDIA), an island in the
Mediterranean, Act. 2.11. Act. 27.7,12,13,21.
Titus left at, Tit. 1.5. Cretians' character, Tit.
1.12. Towns of, see FAIR-HAVENS, LASEA,
PHENICE. Cape of, see SALMONE.

CRIB. See MANGER.

CRISPUS, chief ruler of the synagogue at
Corinth, Act. 18.8. Baptized by Paul, 1 Cor.
1.14.

CROSS. Illustrative of self-denial, Mat.
10.38. Mat. 16.24. Mar. 10.21. Luk. 9.23.
Of the Gospel, 1 Cor. 1.17,18. Gal. 5.11,24.
Gal. 6.12,14. Phi. 3.18. See CRUCIFIXION.

CROWN. Of Kings, 2 Sam. 1.10. 2 Sam.
12.30. 2 Kin. 11.12. Est. 6.8. Psa. 21.3.
Song 3.11. Rev. 6.2. Of Queen, Est. 1.11. Est.
2.17. On the high-priest's mitre, Ex. 29.6. Lev.
8.9. Zec. 6.11. Upon the ark, &c., Ex.
25.11,25. Ex. 30.3.

Of honour, Est. 8.15. Zec. 6.14. 1 Cor.
9.25. 2 Tim. 2.5. An ornament, Eze. 23.42.
Eze. 16.12. Set with precious stones, Zec.

9.16. Isa. 62.3. Of thorns, Jno. 19.5. Illustrative, Pro. 12.4. Pro. 16.31. Isa. 28.5.
Lam. 5.16. Phil. 4.1. 1 Thess. 2.19. 2 Tim.
4.8. Jas. 1.12. 1 Pet. 5.4. Rev. 3.11. Symbolical, Rev. 6.2. Rev. 9.7. Rev. 12.1,3. Rev.
13.1. Rev. 14.14. Rev. 19.12. Rev. 4.4,10.

CRUCIFIXION, a Roman punishment,
Mat. 20.19 with Jno. 18.31,32. Of two thieves,
Mat. 27.38. Of disciples, Mat. 23.34. Termed
cursed, Gal. 3.13. An offence, Gal. 5.11. Illus-
trative, Gal. 5.24. See CROSS—CHRIST'S
SUFFERINGS—CHRIST, DEATH OF.

CRUELTY. See MALICE, MURDER.

CRUSE, a bottle or pitcher, 1 Sam. 26.11.
1 Kin. 14.3. 2 Kin. 2.20.

CRYSTAL, a transparent stone, Job 28.17.
Eze. 1.22. Rev. 4.6. Rev. 21.11. Rev. 22.1.

CUBIT, a measure of length, 18 or 21 inches,
Gen. 6.16. Called the cubit of a man, Deu.
3.11. Rev. 21.17. A longer cubit, 3 inches
more, Eze. 43.13. A measure of time, stature,
or age, Mat. 6.27. Luk. 12.25.

CUCKOO, Lev. 11.16. Deu. 14.15.

CUCUMBER, a plant, Num. 11.5. Isa. 1.8.

CUMMIN, a plant, Isa. 28.25,27. Mat.
23.23.

CUP, Gen. 40.11. 2 Sam. 12.3. 1 Kin. 7.26.
Mat. 23.25. Silver, Gen. 44.2. Golden in the
Temple, 1 Chr. 28.17. Jer. 52. 19. Of consolation, Jer. 16.7. Of the Lord's Supper,
Luk. 22.20. Of devils, 1 Cor. 10.21. Illustrative, Psa. 23.5. Psa. 73.10. Psa. 116.13.
Mat. 20.22,23. Mat. 26.39. Psa. 75.8. Isa.
51.22. Jer. 25.15-28. Eze. 23.31-34. Rev.
14.10. Rev. 17.4.

CUP-BEARER. See BUTLER.

CURIOSITY. Forbidden, and examples
of, Gen. 32.29. Ex. 19.21,24. Num. 4.20,21.
Deu. 29.29. Jud. 13.17,18. 1 Sam. 6.19. Pro.
27.20. Ecc. 7.21,22. Dan. 12.9. Luk. 13.23,24.
Luk. 23.8. Jno. 21.21,22. Act. 1.7. Act.
17.21. Col. 2.18.

CURSE. See ANATHEMA, OATHS. Cursing,
see BLASPHEMY.

CURTAINS, or HANGINGS, for rooms,
Est. 1.6. For tents, Song 1.5. Isa. 54.2. Jer.
4.20. Jer. 10.20. Jer. 49.29. Hab. 3.7. For
groves, 2 Kin. 23.7. Illustrative, Isa. 40.22.
See TABERNACLE.

CUSH, eldest son of Ham, and father of
Nimrod, Gen. 10.6-8. 1 Chr. 1.8-10. See
ETHIOPIA.

CUSHI, brings David word of Absalom's
death, 2 Sam. 18.21-32.

CUTHAH, a district from which colonists
were brought to Samaria. They worship
Nergal, 2 Kin. 17.24-30. Ezr. 4.10.

CYMBALS, made of brass, 1 Cor. 15.19,28.
1 Cor. 13.1. Used by David in bringing up
the ark, 2 Sam. 6.5. 1 Chr. 13.8. 1 Chr.
15.16,19,28. And by Solomon, 2 Chr. 5.12,13.
Levites appointed by David to play on, for
the temple service, 1 Chr. 16.5,37,42. 1 Chr.
25.1,6. Psa. 150.5.

Used on the day of atonement, 2 Chr. 29.25.
On laying the foundation of the second temple,
Ezr. 3.10,11. At the dedication of the wall,
Neh. 12.27,36.

CYPRESS, Isa. 44.14. Song 1.14 (*marg.*) Song 4.13 (*marg.*) Translated fir-tree, 2 Sam. 6.5. 1 Kin. 5.8.

CYPRUS, an island in the Mediterranean, Act. 21.3. Act. 27.4. Barnabas, a native of, Act. 4.36. Gospel preached at, Act. 11.19,20. Visited by Barnabas and Saul, Elymas struck blind, Sergius Paulus converted at, Act. 13.4-12. Barnabas and Mark visit, Act. 15.39. Mnason, a disciple of, Act. 21.16. See **PAPHOS**, **SALAMIS**.

CYRENE, a city in Libya, Act. 2.10. Synagogue of, Act. 6.9. Simon belonged to, Mar. 15.21. And Lucius, &c., Act. 11.20. Act. 13.1.

CYRENIUS, Roman governor of Syria, Luk. 2.2.

CYRUS, king of Persia, his decree for rebuilding the Temple, 2 Chr. 36.22,23. Ezr. 1. Ezr. 3.7. Ezr. 4.3. Ezr. 5.13,14. Ezr. 6.3. Daniel, an officer of, Dan. 1.21. Dan. 6.28. Dan. 10.1. Prophecies respecting, Isa. 41.2. Isa. 44.28. Isa. 45.1-4,13. Isa. 46.11. Isa. 48.14,15.

D

DAGGER, Jud. 3.16-22.

DAGON, an idol of the Philistines. Sacrifices offered to, Jud. 16.23. Image of, broken, when the ark was set in the house of, 1 Sam. 5. Saul's head put in the temple of, 1 Chr. 10.10.

DALMANUTHA, a town near Magdala, on the W. of the Sea of Galilee, Mar. 8.10 with Mat. 15.39.

DALMATIA, a province near Macedonia, visited by Titus, 2 Tim. 4.10.

DAMARIS, a woman of Athens, converted by Paul, Act. 17.34.

DAMASCUS, a city of Syria. Antiquity of, Gen. 14.15. Gen. 15.2. Paul's journey to ; he recovers his sight at ; preaches at, is persecuted, and escapes from, Act. 9. Act. 22.5-16. Act. 26.12-20. 2 Cor. 11.32. Revisits, Gal. 1.17. See **SYRIA**.

———, **WILDERNESS OF**, 1 Kin. 19.15.

DAN, son of Jacob and Bilhah, Gen. 30.6. Gen. 35.25. His children, Gen. 46.23. Blessed by Jacob, Gen. 49.16,17.

———, **TRIBE OF**. Numbered at Sinai, Num. 1.39; and in the plains of Moab, Num.26.42,43. Blessing of Moses on, Deu. 33.22. Inheritance of, Jos. 19.40-46. Encamped N. of the tabernacle, Num. 2.25. Led the 4th and last division of Israel in journeying, Num. 2.31. Num. 10.25.

Driven to the hills by the Amorites, Jud. 1.34,35. Reproved for not aiding against Sisera, Jud. 5.17. Conquer new territory, and build Dan, Jos. 19.47. Jud. 18. Steal Micah's idol and ephod, set it up in Dan, Jud. 18. Commerce of, Eze. 27.19.

For things common to the tribes, see **ISRAEL**, **TRIBES OF**.

———, or **LAISH**, a city, the northern limit of Palestine, Gen. 14.14. Deu. 34.1. Jno. 20.1. Jer. 8.16. Captured by the Danites ; name changed from Laish ; idolatry established at, Jos. 19.47. Jud. 18.

A golden calf set up at, 1 Kin. 12.28,29.

Captured by Benhadad, 1 Kin. 15.20. 2 Chr. 16.4. Prophecies against, see **CALVES OF BETHEL**.

DANCING to music, an act of rejoicing, Psa. 30.11. Ecc. 3.4. Lam. 5.15. Luk. 15.25. By men alone, 1 Sam. 30.16. Jer. 31.13. By women alone, Jer. 31.4,13. By Herodias' daughter, Mat. 14.6. By children, Job 21.11. Mat. 11.17.

In war-triumphs, by women alone, Jud. 11.34. 1 Sam. 18.6. 1 Sam. 21.11. In worship, Psa. 149.3. Psa. 150.4. By women alone, Ex. 15.20. Jud. 21.19,21. By David, 2 Sam. 6.14. Idolatrous, Ex. 32.19.

DANIEL, taken captive to Babylon with Jehoiakim, named Belteshazzar, Dan. 1.1-7. His abstemiousness, Dan. 1.8-16. Dan. 10.2,3. Relates and interprets Nebuchadnezzar's dreams, Dan. 2. Dan. 4. Interprets the handwriting on the wall to Belshazzar, Dan. 5.

Cast into the lions' den by Darius, and delivered, Dan. 6. His rank in Babylon, Dan. 2.48,49. Dan. 5.11,29. Dan. 6.2. A prophet, Dan. 1.17-20. Dan. 4.8,9. Eze. 28.3. Mat. 24.15. Visions of, Dan. c. 7 to 12.

Piety of, Dan. 1.8. Dan. 6.22. Dan. 10.11. Dan. 12.13. Eze. 14.14. Prayerfulness of, Dan. 2.18-23. Dan. 6.10,11. Dan. 9.3-19. His courage and fidelity, Dan. 4.27. Dan. 5.17-23. Dan. 6.10-23.

DARIUS I., the Median, king of Persia, conquers Babylon, Dan. 5.31. Dan. 9.1. His treatment of Daniel, Dan. 6.

——— **II.**, his decree in favour of the Jews, Ezr. 5. Ezr. 6. Hag. 1.1. Zec. 1.1.

——— **III.**, the Persian, Neh. 12.22.

DARKNESS of the earth, Gen. 1.2. Job 38.9. In Egypt, Ex. 10.21,22. At Sinai, Ex. 20.21. At Christ's death, Mat. 27.45. Illustrative, Isa. 8.22. Jno. 1.5. Eph. 5.11. 1 Jno. 2.11.

DART, or **JAVELIN**, Num. 25.7. 1 Sam. 18.10. 2 Sam. 18.14. Job 41.29. Illustrative, Eph. 6.16.

DATE, the fruit of the palm-tree, 2 Chr. 31.5 (*marg.*)

DATHAN. See **ABIRAM**.

DAVID, second king of Israel, his genealogy, of the tribe of Judah, son of Jesse, Ruth 4.18-22. 1 Sam. 16.11. 1 Sam. 17.12. 1 Chr. 2.3-15. Mat. 1.1-6. A shepherd, kills a lion and a bear, 1 Sam. 16.11. 1 Sam. 17.15,34.

Anointed king by Samuel at Bethlehem; the Spirit of the Lord comes upon him, 1 Sam. 16.1,13. Psa. 89.20. His prowess exaggerated, 1 Sam. 16.18 with 1 Sam. 17.34-36,39. Sent for by Saul ; plays on a harp before him ; loved by him, 1 Sam. 16.21-23.

Sent to his brethren at the army ; interview with Saul ; slays Goliath, 1 Sam. 17. Beloved by Jonathan, 1 Sam. 18.1-4. Appointed an officer ; his prudence, valour, popularity, 1 Sam. 18.

Incurs the jealousy of Saul, who plots against him ; Merab promised in marriage, but given to Adriel, 1 Sam. 18.8-30. Slays 200 Philistines ; marries Michal, 1 Sam. 18.27. Saul pacified by Jonathan, 1 Sam. 19.1-7. David defeats the Philistines, 1 Sam. 19.8.

Saul casts a javelin at him ; sends to seize him ; Michal saves his life ; he flees to Ramah ;

Saul seeks him there, 1 Sam. 19.9-24. Covenant with Jonathan, 1 Sam. 20. Comes to Nob; eats shewbread, 1 Sam. 21. Mat. 12.3.

Flees to Gath; feigns madness, 1 Sam. 21.10-15. Gathers a band at Adullam; goes to Moab; returns to Hareth; shelters Abiathar, 1 Sam. 22. Rescues Keilah; Saul seeks him in Maon, 1 Sam. 23. And Engedi; he spares Saul's life, 1 Sam. 24.

His covenant with Jonathan, 1 Sam. 23.16-18. Saul seeks him in Ziph; spares Saul's life; their reconciliation, 1 Sam. 26. Expedition against Nabal; marries Abigail and Ahinoam, 1 Sam. 25. Withdraws to Achish, who gives him Ziklag, 1 Sam. 27.

Joined by soldiers, 1 Chr. 12.1-22. Expeditions against Amalek, &c.; his falsehood to Achish, 1 Sam. 27.8. 1 Chr. 12.15. Is refused permission to join the Philistines, 1 Sam. 28.1,2. 1 Sam. 29. Leaves Philistia after one year four months' residence, 1 Sam. 27 7.

Rescues the captives of Ziklag; sends presents to the Israelites, 1 Sam. 30. Receives news of Saul's death; slays the Amalekite; his lament for Saul, 2 Sam. 1. Anointed king at Hebron, 2 Sam. 2.1-4, 11. 2 Sam. 5.5. 1 Kin. 2.11. 1 Chr. 3.4. 1 Chr. 11.1-3.

His regard for Saul, 2 Sam. 2.4-7. Civil war; successes against Abner, 2 Sam. c. 2 & 3. Michal restored to him, 2 Sam. 3.14-16. Reconciliation with Abner; Abner murdered; his lament for him, 2 Sam. 3.17-39. Ishbosheth murdered; his murderers punished, 2 Sam. 4.

Anointed king of all Israel after seven years' reign, 2 Sam. 5.1-5. 1 Chr. 11.1-3. 1 Chr. 12.23-40. Conquers Jerusalem; makes it his capital, and fortifies it, 2 Sam. 5.6-9. 1 Chr. 11.4-8. Isa. 29.1. Builds a house, 2 Sam. 5.11. 2 Chr. 2.3.

Friendship with Hiram, 2 Sam. 5.11. 1 Kin. 5.1 (see Amos 1.9). His prosperity and fame, 2 Sam. 5.10. 1 Chr. 11.9. 1 Chr. 14.17. 1 Chr. 29.28-30. Defeats Philistines at Rephaim; burns their images, 2 Sam. 5.17-25.

Brings the ark to Obed-edom's house, and to the city of David; Michal taunts him for dancing before it, 2 Sam. 6. 1 Chr. 13. 1 Chr. c. 13,15, & 16. Purposes to build a temple, but is forbidden, 2 Sam. 7. 1 Chr. 17.

Conquers the Philistines, Moabites, Syrians, Edomites, 2 Sam. 8. 1 Chr. 18. 1 Chr. 20.4-8. Kindness to Mephibosheth, 2 Sam. 9. 2 Sam. 19.24-30. Defeats the Ammonites and Syrians, 2 Sam. 10. 1 Chr. 19. Adultery with Bathsheba; murder of Uriah, 2 Sam. 11.

Nathan's parable; punishment predicted; his repentance, 2 Sam. 12.1-14. Psa. 51. Death of his son; birth of Solomon, 2 Sam. 12.19,24,25. Takes Rabbah; enslaves the Ammonites, 2 Sam. 12.26-31.

Amnon murdered; Absalom banished; David's love for him, 2 Sam. 13. Joab effects his recall, 2 Sam. 14. Absalom's rebellion, 2 Sam. 15. David leaves Jerusalem; sends back Zadok and the ark, 2 Sam. 15.13-37. Met by Ziba; cursed by Shimei, 2 Sam. 16.

Crosses the Jordan; Barzillai's hospitality, 2 Sam. 17.21-29. Absalom's defeat and death, 2 Sam. 18. David's lament, 2 Sam. 18.33. 2 Sam. 19.1-4. Reinstated in the kingdom, 2 Sam. 19.9-43. Forbearance to Shimei, 2 Sam. 19.23.

Gratitude to Barzillai, 2 Sam. 19.31-43. Sheba's conspiracy; Amasa made general;

Joab murders him; Sheba slain, 2 Sam. 20. Three years' famine; Saul's sons executed, 2 Sam. 21.1-21. Saul's bones buried, 2 Sam. 21.12-14.

Philistine giants defeated, 2 Sam. 21.15-22. 1 Chr. 20.4-8. David pours out water at the well of Bethlehem; exploits of his captains, 2 Sam. 23.8-39. 1 Chr. 11. Numbers Israel; is offered the choice of three evils; the pestilence; his prayers and sacrifice, 2 Sam. 24. 1 Chr. 21. 1 Chr. 27.24.

Purchases the threshing-floor of Araunah, 2 Sam. 24.18-25. 1 Chr. 21.18-28. Marries Abishaig, 1 Kin. 1.1-4. Adonijah usurps the throne; Solomon appointed David's successor, 1 Kin. 1. 1 Chr. 23.1.

His charge to Solomon and Israel, 1 Kin. 2.1-11. 1 Chr. 22.6-19. 1 Chr. c. 28 & 29. His last words, 2 Sam. 23.1-7. Death after forty years' reign, 1 Kin. 2.10. 1 Chr. 29.28. Act. 2.29,34. His wives and children, 2 Sam. 3.2-5. 2 Sam. 5.14-16. 1 Chr. 3.1-9. 1 Chr. 14.3-7.

Preparations for building the temple, see TEMPLE. Arrangements for temple-service, 1 Chr. c. 23 to 26. 2 Chr. 7.6. 2 Chr. 8.14. 2 Chr. 23.18. 2 Chr. 29.27-30. 2 Chr. 35.15. Ezr. 3.10. Ezr. 8.20.

His justice, 1 Chr. 18.14. 2 Sam. 8.15. Prudence, 1 Sam. 18.14,30. Mercy, 1 Sam. 24.7. 1 Sam. 26.11. 2 Sam. 16.11. 2 Sam. 19.22,23. Piety, 1 Sam. 13.14. 2 Sam. 24.25. 1 Kin. 3.14. 1 Chr. 29.10. 2 Chr. 7.17. Zec. 12.8. Act. 13.22. Prayers, 2 Sam. 7.18-29. 1 Chr. 17.16-27.

His musical skill, 1 Sam. 16.23. 1 Chr. 15.16. 1 Chr. 23.5. 2 Chr. 7.6. Neh. 12.36. Amos 6.5. A psalmist, 2 Sam. 22.1. 1 Chr. 23.1. See the PSALMS. A prophet, 1 Chr. 28.19. Act. 2.30. Act. 4.25.

Prophecies respecting himself and his kingdom, Num. 24.17,19. 2 Sam. 7.11-16. 1 Chr. 17.9-14. 1 Chr. 22. 2 Chr. 6.5-17. 2 Chr. 13.5. 2 Chr. 21.7. Isa. 9.7. Isa. 16.5. Isa. 22.20-25. Jer. 23.5. Jer. 33.15-26. Luk. 1.32,33.

History of, written by Samuel, Nathan, and Gad, 1 Chr. 29.29,30. Officers of, see CAPTAIN.

DAVID, a prophetical name of Christ, Jer. 30.9. Eze. 37.24,25. Eze. 34.23,24. Hos. 3.5.

DAY, reckoned from evening to evening, Gen. 1.5. Lev. 22.7. Lev. 23.32. Neh. 13.19. Mat. 27.62-64. Dan. 8.14 (marg.) And divided into four parts, Neh. 9.3 with Neh. 8.3.

Reckoned from morning to evening, divided into morning, noon, evening, Gen. 43.16. Deu. 28.67. 1 Kin. 18.26. Psa. 55.17. Eze. 24.18. Act. 22.6. Divided into hours, Jno. 11.9. See HOURS. Reckoned from evening to morning, Mar. 14.30. See NIGHT.

Representing a year, Num. 14.34. Eze. 4.4-6. In prophecy, Dan. 8.14. Dan. 12.11,12. Rev. 11.3. Rev. 12.6. Rev. 9.15. See PROPHETIC PERIODS. Illustrative, 1 The. 5.5,8. Pro. 4.18. Rev. 21.25.

——, LAST. See JUDGMENT-DAY.

——, LORD'S. See SABBATH.

—— OF ATONEMENT. See ATONEMENT, DAY OF.

DAYS OF THE WEEK, called the six working-days, Eze. 46.1. Numbered, Ex. 20.9,10. Mar. 16.2. The seventh day called

Sabbath, see SABBATH. Sixth day called Preparation-day, Mar. 15.42. Jno. 19.14,31,42. First day called the Lord's Day, Rev. 1.10.

DAY'S JOURNEY, a measure of distance, Ex. 3.18. 1 Kin. 19.4. Jonah 3.4. Sabbath-day's journey, Act. 1.12.

DAYSMAN (*marg.* umpire), Job 9.33.

DAY-STAR (Gr. *phosphorus*), the morning-star, or the sun. Illustrative, 2 Pet. 1.19.

DEACON. Phi. 1.1. 1 Tim. 3.8-12. Elsewhere translated servant and minister, Mat. 23.11. Mar. 10.43. Jno. 12.26. 1 Cor. 3.5. 1 The. 3.2. In Rom. 16.1, Phebe is called *diakonos*, servant of the church. See also Act. 6.1-6. See CHURCH GOVERNMENT.

DEAD, THE. See BURIAL.

DEAD SEA (modern name), called Salt Sea, occupying the valley of Sodom and Gomorrah, Gen. 14.3. Num. 34.3,12. Jos. 15.5. Called Sea of the Plain, Deu. 3.17. Deu. 4.49. Jos. 3.16. East Sea, Joel 2.20. Former sea, Zec. 14.8. Prophecy of, Eze. 47.7-10,18.

DEAF, the ill-treatment of, forbidden, Lev. 19.14. Miraculous cure of, Mat. 11.5. Mar. 7.32. Mar. 9.25. Illustrative, Isa. 29.18. Isa. 43.8. See IMPENITENCE—SPIRITUAL BLINDNESS.

DEATH. Gen. 2.17. In the day that thou eatest thereof thou shalt surely die.

Gen. 3.19. Till thou return unto the ground; for out of it wast thou taken: for dust thou *art*, and unto dust shalt thou return.

Gen. 5.27. The days of Methuselah were nine hundred sixty and nine years: and he died.

Gen. 27.2. I know not the day of my death.

Jos. 23.14. This day I *am* going the way of all the earth.

1 Sam. 2.6. The Lord killeth, and maketh alive: he bringeth down to the grave.

1 Sam. 20.3. *There is* but a step between me and death.

2 Sam. 1.23. In their death they were not divided.

2 Sam. 3.33. Died Abner as a fool dieth? 34. As a man falleth before wicked men, *so* fellest thou.

2 Sam. 12.23. Now he is dead, wherefore should I fast? can I bring him back again? I shall go to him, but he shall not return to me.

2 Sam. 14.14. We must needs die, and *are* as water spilt on the ground, which cannot be gathered up again.

2 Sam. 19.37. That I may die in mine own city.

Job 3.13. Now should I have lain still and been quiet, I should have slept: then had I been at rest. 17. There the wicked cease *from* troubling; and there the weary be at rest. 18. *There* the prisoners rest together; they hear not the voice of the oppressor. 19. The small and great are there; and the servant *is* free from his master.

Job 7.1. An appointed time to man upon earth? *are not* his days also like the days of an hireling? 8. The eye of him that hath seen me shall see me no *more*: thine eyes *are* upon me, and I *am* not. 9. *As* the cloud is consumed and vanisheth away; so he that

goeth down to the grave shall come up no *more.* 10. He shall return no more to his house, neither shall his place know him any more. 21. Now shall I sleep in the dust; and thou shalt seek me in the morning, but I *shall* not *be.* Job 14.6.

Job 10.21. I go *whence* I shall not return, *even* to the land of darkness, and the shadow of death.

Job 14.2. He cometh forth like a flower, and is cut down: he fleeth also as a shadow, and continueth not. 5. His days *are* determined, the number of his months *are* with thee; thou hast appointed his bounds that he cannot pass. 7. Hope of a tree, if it be cut down, that it will sprout again. 10. But man dieth, and wasteth away: yea, man giveth up the ghost, and where *is* he? 12. Man lieth down, and riseth not: till the heavens *be* no more, they shall not awake, nor be raised out of their sleep.

Job 14.14. If a man die, shall he live *again?* All the days of my appointed time will I wait, till my change come. 19. Thou destroyest the hope of man. 20. Thou prevailest for ever against him, and he passeth; thou changest his countenance, and sendest him away. 21. His sons come to honour, and he knoweth *it* not; and they are brought low, but he perceiveth *it* not.

Job 16.22. When a few years are come, then I shall go the way *whence* I shall not return.

Job 17.13. The grave *is* mine house: I have made my bed in the darkness. 14. I have said to corruption, Thou *art* my father; to the worm, *Thou art* my mother, and my sister. 16. They shall go down to the bars of the pit, when *our* rest together *is* in the dust.

Job 21.23. One dieth in his full strength, being wholly at ease and quiet. 25. Another dieth in the bitterness of his soul. 26. They shall lie down alike in the dust, and the worms shall cover them. 32. Yet shall he be brought to the grave, and shall remain in the tomb. 33. The clods of the valley shall be sweet unto him, and every man shall draw after him, as *there are* innumerable before him.

Job 30.23. Thou wilt bring me to death, and *to* the house appointed for all living.

Job 34.14. *If* he gather unto himself his spirit and his breath; 15. All flesh shall perish together, and man shall turn again unto dust.

Job 36.18. Lest he take thee away with *his* stroke: then a great ransom cannot deliver thee. 19. Will he esteem thy riches? *no,* not gold, nor all the forces of strength.

Job 38.17. Have the gates of death been opened unto thee? or hast thou seen the doors of the shadow of death?

Psa. 30.9. What profit *is there* in my blood, when I go down to the pit? Shall the dust praise thee? shall it declare thy truth? Psa. 6.5. Psa. 88.9-14. Psa. 115.17. Isa. 38.18.

Psa. 39.13. O spare me, that I may recover strength, before I go hence, and be no more.

Psa. 49.7. None *of them* can by any means redeem his brother, nor give to God a ransom for him. 9. That he should still live for ever, *and* not see corruption. 10. Wise men die, likewise the fool and the brutish person perish.

Psa. 82.7. Ye shall die like men, and fall like one of the princes.

Psa. 89.48. What man *is he that* liveth, and shall not see death? shall he deliver his soul from the hand of the grave?

Psa. 90.3. Thou turnest man to destruction; and sayest, Return, ye children of men.

Psa. 103.14. He remembereth that we *are* dust. 15. *As for* man, his days *are* as grass: as a flower of the field, so he flourisheth: 16. For the wind passeth over it, and it is gone; and the place thereof shall know it no more.

Psa. 104.29. Thou takest away their breath, they die, and return to their dust.

Psa. 143.3. To dwell in darkness, as those that have been long dead. Lam. 3.6.

Psa. 144.4. Man is like to vanity: his days *are* as a shadow that passeth away.

Psa. 146.4. His breath goeth forth, he returneth to his earth; in that very day his thoughts perish.

Ecc. 2.14. One event happeneth to them all. 16. No remembrance of the wise more than of the fool. How dieth the wise *man?* as the fool.

Ecc. 3.2. A time to die. 19. That which befalleth the sons of men befalleth beasts; even one thing befalleth them: as the one dieth, so dieth the other; yea, they have all one breath. 20. All go unto one place: all are of the dust, and all turn to dust again. Ecc. 6.6.

Ecc. 4.2. I praised the dead which are already dead, more than the living.

Ecc. 5.15. As he came forth of his mother's womb, naked shall he return to go as he came, and shall take nothing of his labour, which he may carry away in his hand. Job 1.21.

Ecc. 6.10. Neither may he contend with him that is mightier than he.

Ecc. 7.2. Better to go to the house of mourning than to go to the house of feasting: for that *is* the end of all men. 15. A just *man* that perisheth in his righteousness.

Ecc. 8.8. No man that hath power over the spirit, to retain the spirit; neither *hath he* power in the day of death: and *there is* no discharge in *that* war.

Ecc. 9.3. They live, and after that *they go* to the dead. 5. The living know that they shall die: but the dead know not any thing, neither have they any more a reward: for the memory of them is forgotten. 6. Also their love, and their hatred, and their envy, is now perished; neither have they any more a portion for ever in any *thing* that is done under the sun. 10. No work, nor device, nor knowledge, nor wisdom, in the grave, whither thou goest.

Ecc. 12.5. Man goeth to his long home, and the mourners go about the streets. 7. Then shall the dust return to the earth as it was; and the spirit shall return unto God who gave it.

Isa. 38.1. Set thine house in order; for thou shalt die, and not live. 10. I said in the cutting off of my days, I shall go to the gates of the grave: I am deprived of the residue of my years. 11. I said, I shall not see the Lord, *even* the Lord, in the land of the living: I shall behold man no more with the inhabitants of the world. 12. Mine age is departed, and is removed from me as a shepherd's tent: I have cut off like a weaver my life.

Isa. 40.7. The grass withereth, the flower fadeth; because the Spirit of the Lord bloweth upon it: surely the people *is* grass. 1 Pet. 1.24.

Isa. 51.12. Afraid of a man *that* shall die, and of the son of man *which* shall be made *as* grass.

Jer. 9.21. Death is come up into our windows, *and* is entered into our palaces, to cut off the children from without, *and* the young men from the streets.

Jer. 34.5. Thou shalt die in peace.

Eze. 24.16. I take away from thee the desire of thine eyes with a stroke.

Zec. 1.5. Your fathers, where *are* they? and the prophets, do they live for ever?

Mat. 10.28. Fear not them which kill the body, but are not able to kill the soul.

Luk. 23.41. We receive the due reward of our deeds.

Jno. 6.49. Your fathers are dead.

Jno. 9.4. The night cometh, when no man can work.

Rom. 5.12. Death passed upon all men, for that all have sinned. 14. Death reigned from Adam to Moses, even over them that had not sinned after the similitude of Adam's transgression.

Rom. 8.10. The body *is* dead because of sin.

1 Cor. 15.21. By man *came* death. 22. In Adam all die. 26. The last enemy shall be destroyed, death. 56. The sting of death *is* sin.

1 Tim. 6.7. We brought nothing into *this* world, *and it is* certain we can carry nothing out.

Heb. 2.14. Through death he might destroy him that had the power of death, that is, the devil. 15. Through fear of death were all their lifetime subject to bondage.

Heb. 9.27. It is appointed unto men once to die.

Heb. 13.14. Here have we no continuing city.

Jas. 1.10. As the flower of the grass he shall pass away. 11. For the sun is no sooner risen with a burning heat, but it withereth the grass, and the flower thereof falleth, and the grace of the fashion of it perisheth: so also shall the rich man fade away in his ways.

Rev. 20.14. Death and hell were cast into the lake of fire.

DEATH OF CHILDREN, EXAMPLES OF. First-born of the Egyptians, Ex. 12.29,30. The child of David, 2 Sam. 12.14-23. Of Jeroboam, 1 Kin. 14.13. Of the widow, 1 Kin. 17.17. Of the Shunemite, 2 Kin. 4.19,20. Of Jairus, Mat. 9.18,24.

———, escaped by Enoch, Gen. 5.24; and Elijah, 2 Kin. 2; and saints at Christ's coming, 1 Cor. 15.51. 1 The. 4.15,17.

——— ETERNAL. See HELL.

———, PREPARATION FOR. Deu. 32.29. O that they were wise, *that* they understood this, *that* they would consider their latter end!

2 Kin. 20.1. Thus saith the Lord, Set thine house in order; for thou shalt die, and not live.

Psa. 39.4. Lord, make me to know mine end, and the measure of my days, what it *is;* *that* I may know how frail I *am.* 13. O spare me, that I may recover strength, before I go hence, and be no more.

Psa. 90.12. So teach us to number our days, that we may apply our hearts unto wisdom.

Ecc. 9.4. To him that is joined to all the living there is hope: for a living dog is better than a dead lion. 10. Whatsoever thy hand findeth to do, do it with thy might: for there is no work, nor device, nor knowledge, nor wisdom, in the grave, whither thou goest.

Ecc. 11.7. Truly the light is sweet, and a pleasant thing it is for the eyes to behold the sun: 8. But if a man live many years, and rejoice in them all; yet let him remember the days of darkness; for they shall be many.

Isa. 38.18. The grave cannot praise thee, death can not celebrate thee: they that go down into the pit cannot hope for thy truth. 19. The living, the living, he shall praise thee, as I do this day: the father to the children shall make known thy truth.

Luk. 12.37. Blessed are those servants, whom the Lord, when he cometh, shall find watching.

Jno. 9.4. I must work the works of him that sent me, while it is day: the night cometh, when no man can work.

Rom. 14.8. Whether we live, we live unto the Lord; and whether we die, we die unto the Lord: whether we live therefore, or die, we are the Lord's.

Phil. 1.21. To me to live is Christ, and to die is gain.

Heb. 13.14. Here have we no continuing city, but we seek one to come.

Jas. 4.15. Ye ought to say, If the Lord will, we shall live, and do this, or that.

1 Pet. 1.17. Pass the time of your sojourning here in fear.

DEATH OF SAINTS. Gen. 15.15. Thou shalt go to thy fathers in peace; thou shalt be buried in a good old age. Gen. 49.33. Num. 20.26. 2 Kin. 22.20.

Num. 23.10. Let me die the death of the righteous, and let my last end be like his!

2 Sam. 12.23. I shall go to him, but he shall not return to me.

Psa. 23.4. Though I walk through the valley of the shadow of death, I will fear no evil: for thou art with me; thy rod and thy staff they comfort me.

Psa. 37.37. Mark the perfect man, and behold the upright: for the end of that man is peace.

Psa. 49.15. God will redeem my soul from the power of the grave: for he shall receive me.

Psa. 116.15. Precious in the sight of the Lord is the death of his saints.

Pro. 14.32. The righteous hath hope in his death.

Ecc. 7.1. Better the day of death than the day of one's birth.

Isa. 57.1. The righteous perisheth, and no man layeth it to heart: and merciful men are taken away, none considering that the righteous is taken away from the evil to come. 2. He shall enter into peace: they shall rest in their beds, each one walking in his uprightness.

Dan. 12.13. Thou shalt rest, and stand in thy lot at the end of the days.

Luk. 2.29. Now lettest thou thy servant depart in peace.

Luk. 16.22. The beggar died, and was carried by the angels into Abraham's bosom.

Luk. 23.43. To-day shalt thou be with me in paradise.

Jno. 11.11. Our friend Lazarus sleepeth.

Jno. 21.19. By what death he should glorify God.

Act. 7.59. They stoned Stephen, calling upon God, and saying, Lord Jesus, receive my spirit.

Rom. 14.7. No man dieth to himself. 8. Whether we die, we die unto the Lord: whether we live therefore, or die, we are the Lord's. v. 9.

1 Cor. 3.22. Or life, or death, or things present, or things to come; all are yours.

1 Cor. 15.51. We shall not all sleep, but we shall all be changed. 55. O death, where is thy sting? O grave, where is thy victory? 57. Thanks be to God, which giveth us the victory through our Lord Jesus Christ.

2 Cor. 1.9. We had the sentence of death in ourselves, that we should not trust in ourselves, but in God which raiseth the dead.

2 Cor. 5.1. If our earthly house of this tabernacle were dissolved, we have a building of God, an house not made with hands, eternal in the heavens. 4. We that are in this tabernacle do groan, being burdened: not for that we would be unclothed, but clothed upon, that mortality might be swallowed up of life. 8. We are confident, I say, and willing rather to be absent from the body, and to be present with the Lord.

Phil. 1.20. Christ shall be magnified in my body, whether it be by life, or by death. 21. To me to live is Christ, and to die is gain. 23. I am in a strait betwixt two, having a desire to depart, and to be with Christ; which is far better.

1 The. 4.13. Them which are asleep, that ye sorrow not, even as others which have no hope. 14. Them also which sleep in Jesus will God bring with him.

1 The. 5.10. Whether we wake or sleep, we should live together with him.

2 Tim. 4.6. Now ready to be offered, and the time of my departure is at hand. 7. I have fought a good fight, I have finished my course, I have kept the faith: 8. Henceforth there is laid up for me a crown of righteousness.

Heb. 2.15. Deliver them who through fear of death were all their lifetime subject to bondage.

Heb. 11.13. All died in faith, not having received the promises, but having seen them afar off.

2 Pet. 1.11. An entrance shall be ministered unto you abundantly. 14. Shortly I must put off this my tabernacle, even as our Lord Jesus Christ hath shewed me.

Rev. 14.13. Blessed are the dead which die in the Lord from henceforth: Yea, saith the Spirit, that they may rest from their labours.

DEATH OF SAINTS, EXAMPLES OF. Abraham, Gen. 15.15. Gen. 25.8. Jacob, Gen. 49.33. Heb. 11.21. Joseph, Gen. 50.24. Heb. 11.22. Aaron, Num. 20.25-28. Moses, Deu. 34.5,6. Eli, 1 Sam. 4.18. David, 1 Kin. 2.1,2. Jehoiada, 2 Chr. 24.16. Hezekiah, 2 Kin. 22.20. 2 Chr. 32.33. Josiah, 2 Chr. 35.24,25. The penitent thief, Luk. 23.43. Stephen, Act. 7.59. Act. 8.2. Dorcas, Act. 9.39.

DEATH OF SINNERS. Num. 16.29. If these men die the common death of all men, or if they be visited after the visitation of all men, the Lord hath not sent me.

1 Sam. 25.38. The Lord smote Nabal, that he died.

2 Chr. 21.20. (Jehoram) departed without being desired.

Job 4.21. Doth not their excellency which is in them go away? they die, even without wisdom.

Job 18.14. His confidence shall be rooted out of his tabernacle, and it shall bring him to the king of terrors. 18. He shall be driven from light into darkness, and chased out of the world.

Job 20.5. The triumphing of the wicked is short, and the joy of the hypocrite but for a moment? 8. He shall fly away as a dream, and shall not be found: yea, he shall be chased away as a vision of the night. 11. His bones are full of the sin of his youth, which shall lie down with him in the dust.

Job 21.17. How oft is the candle of the wicked put out! and how oft cometh their destruction upon them! God distributeth sorrows in his anger. 18. They are as stubble before the wind, and as chaff that the storm carrieth away.

Job 24.20. The worm shall feed sweetly on him; he shall be no more remembered; and wickedness shall be broken as a tree. 24. They are exalted for a little while, but are gone and brought low; they are taken out of the way as all other, and cut off as the tops of the ears of corn.

Job 27.8. What is the hope of the hypocrite, though he hath gained, when God taketh away his soul? 19. The rich man shall lie down, but he shall not be gathered: he openeth his eyes, and he is not. 20. Terrors take hold on him as waters, a tempest stealeth him away in the night. 21. The east wind carrieth him away, and he departeth: and as a storm hurleth him out of his place. 22. God shall cast upon him, and not spare: he would fain flee out of his hand. 23. Men shall clap their hands at him, and shall hiss him out of his place.

Job 34.20. In a moment shall they die, and the people shall be troubled at midnight, and pass away: and the mighty shall be taken away without hand.

Job 36.12. If they obey not, they shall perish by the sword, and they shall die without knowledge. 14. They die in youth, and their life is among the unclean. 18. Because there is wrath, beware lest he take thee away with his stroke: then a great ransom cannot deliver thee. 20. The night, when people are cut off in their place.

Psa. 37.2. They shall soon be cut down like the grass, and wither as the green herb. 9. Evildoers shall be cut off. 10. Yet a little while, and the wicked shall not be: yea, thou shalt diligently consider his place, and it shall not be. 35. I have seen the wicked in great power, and spreading himself like a green bay tree. 36. Yet he passed away, and, lo, he was not: yea, I sought him, but he could not be found.

Psa. 49.7. None of them can give to God a

ransom for him: 9. That he should still live for ever, and not see corruption. 10. The fool and the brutish person perish, and leave their wealth to others. 14. Like sheep they are laid in the grave; death shall feed on them; and the upright shall have dominion over them in the morning; and their beauty shall consume in the grave from their dwelling. 17. When he dieth he shall carry nothing away: his glory shall not descend after him. 19. He shall go to the generation of his fathers; they shall never see light. 20. Man that is in honour, and understandeth not, is like the beasts that perish.

Psa. 55.15. Let death seize upon them, and let them go down quick into hell: for wickedness is in their dwellings, and among them. 23. Thou, O God, shalt bring them down into the pit of destruction: bloody and deceitful men shall not live out half their days.

Psa. 58.9. Before your pots can feel the thorns, he shall take them away as with a whirlwind, both living, and in his wrath.

Psa. 73.4. There are no bands in their death: but their strength is firm. 17. Then understood I their end. 18. Surely thou didst set them in slippery places: thou castedst them down into destruction. 19. How are they brought into desolation, as in a moment! they are utterly consumed with terrors. 20. As a dream when one awaketh; so, O Lord, when thou awakest, thou shalt despise their image.

Psa. 78.50. He made a way to his anger; he spared not their soul from death, but gave their life over to the pestilence.

Psa. 92.7. When the wicked spring as the grass, and when all the workers of iniquity do flourish; it is that they shall be destroyed for ever.

Pro. 2.22. The wicked shall be cut off from the earth, and the transgressors shall be rooted out of it.

Pro. 5.23. He shall die without instruction.

Pro. 10.25. As the whirlwind passeth, so is the wicked no more. 27. The years of the wicked shall be shortened.

Pro. 11.7. When a wicked man dieth, his expectation shall perish: and the hope of unjust men perisheth. 10. When the wicked perish, there is shouting.

Pro. 13.9. The lamp of the wicked shall be put out.

Pro. 14.32. The wicked is driven away in his wickedness.

Pro. 21.16. The man that wandereth out of the way of understanding shall remain in the congregation of the dead.

Pro. 24.20. There shall be no reward to the evil man; the candle of the wicked shall be put out.

Pro. 29.1. He, that being often reproved hardeneth his neck, shall suddenly be destroyed, and that without remedy. 16. When the wicked are multiplied, transgression increaseth.

Ecc. 8.10. I saw the wicked buried, who had come and gone from the place of the holy, and they were forgotten in the city where they had so done.

Isa. 14.11. Thy pomp is brought down to the grave, and the noise of thy viols: the worm is spread under thee, and the worms cover thee. 15. Thou shalt be brought down to hell, to the sides of the pit.

Isa. 17.14. Behold at eveningtide trouble; *and* before the morning he *is* not.

Isa. 26.14. *They are* dead, they shall not live; *they are* deceased, they shall not rise: therefore hast thou visited and destroyed them, and made all their memory to perish.

Jer. 15.9. She hath given up the ghost; her sun is gone down while it *was* yet day.

Jer. 16.4. They shall die of grievous deaths: they shall not be lamented, neither shall they be buried.

Eze. 28.8. They shall bring thee down to the pit, and thou shalt die the deaths of *them that are* slain in the midst of the seas. 10. Thou shalt die the deaths of the uncircumcised by the hand of strangers. Eze. 31.14.

Amos 9.10. All the sinners of my people shall die by the sword.

1 The. 5.3. When they shall say, Peace and safety; then sudden destruction cometh upon them, as travail upon a woman with child; and they shall not escape. Act. 5.5-10.

See SIN, PUNISHMENT OF—HELL—MIRACLES.

DEATH, SPIRITUAL. See MAN, NATURAL STATE OF.—FALL, THE.

DEBIR, KIRJATH-SEPHER, or KIRJATH-SANNAH, a city of Judah. Anakim defeated at, by Joshua, Jos. 11.21. Taken by Othniel, Jos. 15.15-17,49. A Levitical city of refuge, Jos. 21.15.

DEBORAH, Rebekah's nurse, Gen. 24.59. Gen. 35.8.

————, the prophetess, judges Israel, Jud. 4.4,5. Jud. 5.7. With Barak delivers Israel from Sisera, Jud. 4.6-16. Song of triumph, Jud. 5.

DEBTORS. See CREDITORS.

DECAPOLIS, ten cities near the Sea of Galilee, Christ's preaching and miracles in, Mat. 4.25. Mar. 5.20. Mar. 7.31.

DECEIT. See FALSEHOOD—FLATTERY—TREACHERY.

DECISION—PERSEVERANCE—FIDELITY TO GOD—PROFESSION OF FAITH—CONFESSING CHRIST. Deu. 10.20. Fear the Lord thy God; him shalt thou serve, and to him shalt thou cleave, and swear by his name. Deu. 13.4.

Deu. 11.22. To love the Lord your God, to walk in all his ways, and to cleave unto him. Jos. 22.5.

Deu. 30.19. Choose life, that both thou and thy seed may live.

Jos. 1.7. Be thou strong, and very courageous, that thou mayest observe to do according to all the law which Moses my servant commanded thee: turn not from it *to* the right hand or *to* the left, that thou mayest prosper whithersoever thou goest.

Jos. 23.8. Cleave unto the Lord your God, as ye have done unto this day.

Jos. 24.15. If it seem evil unto you to serve the Lord, choose you this day whom ye will serve.

1 Sam. 12.20. Turn not aside from following the Lord, but serve the Lord with all your heart. *v.* 21.

1 Kin. 18.21. How long halt ye between two opinions? if the Lord *be* God, follow him.

1 Chr. 16.15. Be ye mindful always of his covenant.

2 Chr. 19.11. Deal courageously, and the Lord shall be with the good.

Psa. 37.34. Wait on the Lord, and keep his way, and he shall exalt thee to inherit the land.

Pro. 4.25. Let thine eyes look right on, and let thine eyelids look straight before thee. 26. Ponder the path of thy feet, and let all thy ways be established. 27. Turn not to the right hand nor to the left: remove thy foot from evil.

Ecc. 7.18. *It is* good that thou shouldest take hold of this; yea, also from this withdraw not thine hand: for he that feareth God shall come forth of them all.

Isa. 40.31. They that wait upon the Lord shall renew *their* strength; they shall mount up with wings as eagles; they shall run, and not be weary; *and* they shall walk, and not faint.

Isa. 56.6. The sons of the stranger, that join themselves to the Lord, to serve him, and to love the name of the Lord, to be his servants, every one that keepeth the sabbath from polluting it, and taketh hold of my covenant; 7. Even them will I bring to my holy mountain, and make them joyful in my house of prayer.

Isa. 65.16. He who blesseth himself in the earth shall bless himself in the God of truth; and he that sweareth in the earth shall swear by the God of truth.

Hos. 6.3. Then shall we know, *if* we follow on to know the Lord.

Mat. 6.24. No man can serve two masters: for either he will hate the one, and love the other; or else he will hold to the one, and despise the other. Ye cannot serve God and mammon. Luk. 16.13.

Mat. 10.32. Whosoever therefore shall confess me before men, him will I confess also before my Father which is in heaven.

Mat. 24.13. He that shall endure unto the end, the same shall be saved. Mar. 13.13. Mat. 10.22.

Mat. 25.23. Well done, good and faithful servant; thou hast been faithful over a few things, I will make thee ruler over many things: enter thou into the joy of thy Lord.

Luk. 7.23. Blessed is *he,* whosoever shall not be offended in me. Mat. 11.6.

Luk. 9.26. Whosoever shall be ashamed of me and of my words, of him shall the Son of man be ashamed, when he shall come in his own glory, and *in his* Father's, and of the holy angels. Mar. 8.38.

Luk. 9.59. He said unto another, Follow me. But he said, Lord, suffer me first to go and bury my father. 60. Jesus said unto him, Let the dead bury their dead: but go thou and preach the kingdom of God. Mat. 8.21,22.

Luk. 9.61. And another also said, Lord, I will follow thee; but let me first go bid them farewell, which are at home at my house. 62. And Jesus said unto him, No man, having put his hand to the plough, and looking back, is fit for the kingdom of God.

Luk. 11.23. He that is not with me is against me: and he that gathereth not with me scattereth. Mat. 12.30.

Luk. 12.8. Whosoever shall confess me

before men, him shall the Son of man also confess before the angels of God.

Luk. 17. 32. Remember Lot's wife. 33. Whosoever shall seek to save his life shall lose it; and whosoever shall lose his life shall preserve it.

Luk. 21. 19. In your patience possess ye your souls.

Jno. 8. 31. If ye continue in my word, *then* are ye my disciples indeed; 32. And ye shall know the truth, and the truth shall make you free.

Jno. 15. 4. Abide in me, and I in you. As the branch cannot bear fruit of itself, except it abide in the vine; no more can ye, except ye abide in me. 5. I am the vine, ye *are* the branches: he that abideth in me, and I in him, the same bringeth forth much fruit; for without me ye can do nothing. 7. If ye abide in me, and my words abide in you, ye shall ask what ye will, and it shall be done unto you. 9. Continue ye in my love.

Act. 11. 23. Exhorted them all, that with purpose of heart they would cleave unto the Lord.

Act. 13. 43. Persuaded them to continue in the grace of God.

Act. 14. 22. Confirming the souls of the disciples, *and* exhorting them to continue in the faith.

Rom. 2. 7. To them who, by patient continuance in well-doing, seek for glory, and honour, and immortality, eternal life.

Rom. 6. 13. Yield yourselves unto God, as those that are alive from the dead, and your members *as* instruments of righteousness unto God.

Rom. 10. 9. If thou shalt confess with thy mouth the Lord Jesus, and shalt believe in thine heart that God hath raised him from the dead, thou shalt be saved. 10. With the heart man believeth unto righteousness; and with the mouth confession is made unto salvation.

Rom. 11. 22. But toward thee, goodness, if thou continue in *his* goodness: otherwise thou also shalt be cut off.

Rom. 12. 1. I beseech you therefore, brethren, by the mercies of God, that ye present your bodies a living sacrifice, holy, acceptable unto God, *which is* your reasonable service.

Rom. 14. 7. None of us liveth to himself, and no man dieth to himself. 8. For whether we live, we live unto the Lord; and whether we die, we die unto the Lord: whether we live therefore, or die, we are the Lord's. 9. For to this end Christ both died, and rose, and revived, that he might be Lord both of the dead and living.

1 Cor. 7. 32. I would have you without carefulness. He that is unmarried careth for the things that belong to the Lord, how he may please the Lord. *v.* 33-35.

1 Cor. 12. 3. No man can say that Jesus is the Lord, but by the Holy Ghost.

1 Cor. 15. 1. The gospel which I preached unto you, which also ye have received, and wherein ye stand; 2. By which also ye are saved, if ye keep in memory what I preached unto you, unless ye have believed in vain.

1 Cor. 15. 58. Be ye stedfast, unmoveable, always abounding in the work of the Lord,

forasmuch as ye know that your labour is not in vain in the Lord.

1 Cor. 16. 13. Watch ye, stand fast in the faith, quit you like men, be strong.

2 Cor. 1. 24. By faith ye stand.

2 Cor. 4. 10. Always bearing about in the body the dying of the Lord Jesus, that the life also of Jesus might be made manifest in our body.

2 Cor. 5. 9. We labour, that, whether present or absent, we may be accepted of him. 15. They which live should not henceforth live unto themselves, but unto him which died for them, and rose again.

2 Cor. 10. 5. Casting down imaginations, and every high thing that exalteth itself against the knowledge of God, and bringing into captivity every thought to the obedience of Christ. 17. He that glorieth, let him glory in the Lord.

Gal. 5. 1. Stand fast therefore in the liberty wherewith Christ hath made us free, and be not entangled again with the yoke of bondage. 10. I have confidence in you through the Lord, that ye will be none otherwise minded.

Gal. 6. 9. Let us not be weary in well-doing: for in due season we shall reap, if we faint not.

Eph. 4. 14. Be no more children, tossed to and fro, and carried about with every wind of doctrine, by the sleight of men, *and* cunning craftiness, whereby they lie in wait to deceive.

Eph. 6. 13. Take unto you the whole armour of God, that ye may be able to withstand in the evil day, and having done all, to stand.

Phil. 1. 27. Let your conversation be as it becometh the gospel of Christ: that whether I come and see you, or else be absent, I may hear of your affairs, that ye stand fast in one spirit, with one mind striving together for the faith of the gospel.

Phil. 2. 11. Every tongue should confess that Jesus Christ *is* Lord, to the glory of God the Father.

Phil. 3. 16. Whereto we have already attained, let us walk by the same rule, let us mind the same thing.

Phil. 4. 1. Stand fast in the Lord, *my* dearly beloved.

Col. 1. 10. That ye might walk worthy of the Lord unto all pleasing, being fruitful in every good work, and increasing in the knowledge of God. 23. Continue in the faith grounded and settled, and *be* not moved away from the hope of the gospel, which ye have heard.

Col. 2. 2. The acknowledgment of the mystery of God, and of the Father, and of Christ. 6. As ye have therefore received Christ Jesus the Lord, *so* walk ye in him: 7. Rooted and built up in him, and stablished in the faith. 19. The Head, from which all the body by joints and bands having nourishment ministered, and knit together, increaseth with the increase of God.

Col. 3. 17. Whatsoever ye do in word or deed, *do* all in the name of the Lord Jesus. 23. Whatsoever ye do, do *it* heartily, as to the Lord, and not unto men.

Col. 4. 12. Stand perfect and complete in all the will of God.

1 The. 3. 8. We live, if ye stand fast in the Lord. 13. He may stablish your hearts unblameable in holiness before God, even our

Father, at the coming of our Lord Jesus Christ with all his saints.

1 The. 4.1. As ye have received of us how ye ought to walk and to please God, *so* ye would abound more and more.

1 The. 5.21. Prove all things; hold fast that which is good.

2 The. 2.15. Stand fast, and hold the traditions which ye have been taught, whether by word, or our epistle. 16. Our Lord Jesus Christ himself, 17. Stablish you in every good word and work.

2 The. 3.13. Brethren, be not weary in well-doing.

1 Tim. 1.18. War a good warfare; 19. Holding faith, and a good conscience.

1 Tim. 6.12. Fight the good fight of faith, lay hold on eternal life. 14. Keep *this* commandment without spot, unrebukeable, until the appearing of our Lord Jesus Christ.

2 Tim. 1.8. Be not thou therefore ashamed of the testimony of our Lord, nor of me his prisoner: but be thou partaker of the afflictions of the gospel according to the power of God. 13. Hold fast the form of sound words, which thou hast heard of me, in faith and love which is in Christ Jesus. 14. That good thing which was committed unto thee keep by the Holy Ghost which dwelleth in us.

2 Tim. 2.1. Thou therefore, my son, be strong in the grace that is in Christ Jesus. 3. Endure hardness, as a good soldier of Jesus Christ.

2 Tim. 2.12. If we suffer, we shall also reign with *him*: if we deny *him*, he also will deny us.

2 Tim. 3.14. Continue thou in the things which thou hast learned and hast been assured of, knowing of whom thou hast learned *them*.

Tit. 1.9. Holding fast the faithful word as he hath been taught.

Heb. 2.1. Give the more earnest heed to the things which we have heard, lest at any time we should let *them* slip.

Heb. 3.6. Whose house are we, if we hold fast the confidence and the rejoicing of the hope firm unto the end. 14. We are made partakers of Christ, if we hold the beginning of our confidence stedfast unto the end.

Heb. 4.14. Seeing then that we have a great high-priest, that is passed into the heavens, Jesus the Son of God, let us hold fast *our* profession.

Heb. 6.1. Leaving the principles of the doctrine of Christ, let us go on unto perfection. *v*. 9.

Heb. 10.23. Let us hold fast the profession of *our* faith without wavering; for he *is* faithful that promised. 35. Cast not away therefore your confidence, which hath great recompense of reward.

Heb. 12.1. Seeing we also are compassed about with so great a cloud of witnesses, let us lay aside every weight, and the sin which doth so easily beset *us*, and let us run with patience the race that is set before us.

Heb. 13.9. Be not carried about with divers and strange doctrines: for *it is* a good thing that the heart be established with grace. 13. Let us go forth therefore unto him without the camp, bearing his reproach.

Jas. 1.4. Let patience have *her* perfect work, that ye may be perfect and entire, wanting nothing. 12. Blessed *is* the man that

endureth temptation: for when he is tried, he shall receive the crown of life. 25. Whoso looketh into the perfect law of liberty, and continueth *therein*, he being not a forgetful hearer, but a doer of the work, this man shall be blessed in his deed.

1 Pet. 1.13. Gird up the loins of your mind, be sober, and hope to the end for the grace that is to be brought unto you at the revelation of Jesus Christ.

1 Pet. 3.15. *Be* ready always to *give* an answer to every man that asketh you a reason of the hope that is in you with meekness and fear. 17. *It is* better, if the will of God be so, that ye suffer for well-doing, than for evil-doing.

1 Pet. 5.9. Whom resist stedfast in the faith.

2 Pet. 1.10. Give diligence to make your calling and election sure: for if ye do these things, ye shall never fall: 11. For so an entrance shall be ministered unto you abundantly into the everlasting kingdom of our Lord.

2 Pet. 3.17. Seeing ye know *these things* before, beware lest ye also, being led away with the error of the wicked, fall from your own stedfastness. 18. Grow in grace, and *in* the knowledge of our Lord and Saviour.

1 Jno. 2.23. *He that acknowledgeth the Son hath the Father also.* 24. Let that therefore abide in you, which ye have heard from the beginning. If that which ye have heard from the beginning shall remain in you, ye also shall continue in the Son, and in the Father. 28. Little children, abide in him; that, when he shall appear, we may have confidence, and not be ashamed before him at his coming.

1 Jno. 4.2. Every spirit that confesseth that Jesus Christ is come in the flesh is of God. 15. Whosoever shall confess that Jesus is the Son of God, God dwelleth in him, and he in God.

1 Jno. 5.13. These things have I written unto you that believe on the name of the Son of God; that ye may know that ye have eternal life, and that ye may believe on the name of the Son of God.

2 Jno. 8. Look to yourselves, that we lose not those things which we have wrought, but that we receive a full reward.

Jude 20. Building up yourselves on your most holy faith, 21. Keep yourselves in the love of God.

Rev. 2.7. To him that overcometh will I give to eat of the tree of life, which is in the midst of the paradise of God. 10. Be thou faithful unto death, and I will give thee a crown of life. 11. He that overcometh shall not be hurt of the second death.

Rev. 2.17. To him that overcometh will I give to eat of the hidden manna, and will give him a white stone, and in the stone a new name written. 25. That which ye have *already* hold fast till I come. 26. He that overcometh, and keepeth my works unto the end, to him will I give power over the nations.

Rev. 3.5. He that overcometh, the same shall be clothed in white raiment; and I will not blot out his name out of the book of life, but I will confess his name before my Father, and before his angels. 11. Hold that fast which thou hast, that no man take thy crown. 12. Him that overcometh will I make a pillar in the temple of my God, and he shall go no more out. 21. To him that overcometh will I grant to sit with me in my throne, even as I also overcame.

Rev. 14.12. Here is the patience of the saints : here *are* they that keep the commandments of God, and the faith of Jesus.

Rev. 15.2. I saw them that had gotten the victory over the beast, and over his image, and over his mark, *and* over the number of his name, stand on the sea of glass, having the harps of God.

Rev. 21.7. He that overcometh shall inherit all things ; and I will be his God, and he shall be my son.

Rev. 22.11. He that is righteous, let him be righteous still : and he that is holy, let him be holy still.

DECISION, PERSEVERANCE, &c., EXEMPLIFIED. Gen. 4.26. Then began men to call upon the name of the Lord.

Gen. 28.20. If God will be with me, and will keep me in this way that I go, and will give me bread to eat, and raiment to put on, 21. So that I come again to my father's house in peace, then shall the Lord be my God.

Gen. 39.9. How then can I do this great wickedness, and sin against God ?

Gen. 48.15. God, before whom my fathers Abraham and Isaac did walk. Gen. 24.40.

Num. 12.7. My servant Moses *is* not so, who *is* faithful in all mine house. Heb. 3.5.

Num. 14.24. My servant Caleb, because he had another spirit with him, and hath followed me fully, him will I bring into the land. *v.* 6-10,37,38. Deu. 1.36. Jos. 14.14.

Deu. 4.4. Ye that did cleave unto the Lord your God *are* alive every one of you this day.

Deu. 5.27. Speak thou unto us all that the Lord our God shall speak unto thee, and we will hear *it*, and do *it*. Ex. 24.3,7. Ex. 19.8.

Deu. 26.17. Thou hast avouched the Lord this day to be thy God, and to walk in his ways, and to keep his statutes, and his commandments, and his judgments, and to hearken unto his voice. Deu. 29.12.

Deu. 33.9. Neither did he acknowledge his brethren, nor knew his own children : for they have observed thy word, and kept thy covenant. Ex. 32.26.

Jos. 2.11. The Lord your God, he *is* God in heaven above, and in earth beneath.

Jos. 22.34. The children of Reuben and the children of Gad called the altar *Ed* : for it *shall be* a witness between us that the Lord *is* God.

Jos. 24.15. As for me and my house, we will serve the Lord. 22. Ye *are* witnesses against yourselves that ye have chosen you the Lord, to serve him. And they said, We *are* witnesses. *v.* 18-24.

Ruth 1.16. Thy people *shall be* my people, and thy God my God.

2 Sam. 22.21. I have kept the ways of the Lord, and have not wickedly departed from my God. 22. For all his judgments *were* before me, and I did not put away his statutes from me. 23. I was also upright before him, and I kept myself from mine iniquity.

1 Kin. 13.8. If thou wilt give me half thine house, I will not go in with thee, neither will I eat bread nor drink water in this place : 9. For so was it charged me by the word of the Lord. 10. So he went another way, and returned not by the way that he came to Beth-el.

1 Kin. 18.22. Then said Elijah unto the people, I, *even* I only, remain a prophet of the Lord.

1 Kin. 19.18. I have left *me* seven thousand in Israel, all the knees which have not bowed unto Baal, and every mouth which hath not kissed him.

1 Kin. 22.7. Jehoshaphat said, *Is there* not here a prophet of the Lord besides, that we might enquire of him ? 2 Chr. 18.6.

2 Kin. 5.15. Now I know that *there is* no God in all the earth, but in Israel. 17. Thy servant will henceforth offer neither burnt-offering nor sacrifice unto other gods, but unto the Lord.

2 Kin. 18.6. He clave to the Lord, *and* departed not from following him, but kept his commandments, which the Lord commanded Moses. 2 Chr. 15.17.

2 Kin. 22.2. He did *that which was* right in the sight of the Lord, and walked in all the way of David his father, and turned not aside to the right hand or to the left.

2 Kin. 23.3. The king stood by a pillar, and made a covenant before the Lord, to walk after the Lord, and to keep his commandments and his testimonies and his statutes with all *their* heart and all *their* soul, to perform the words of this covenant that were written in this book. And all the people stood to the covenant. 2 Chr. 34.31.

2 Kin. 23.25. Like unto him was there no king before him, that turned to the Lord with all his heart, and with all his soul, and with all his might, according to all the law of Moses ; neither after him arose there *any* like him.

2 Chr. 11.16. Such as set their hearts to seek the Lord God of Israel, came to Jerusalem, to sacrifice unto the Lord God of their fathers.

2 Chr. 13.10. As for us, the Lord *is* our God, and we have not forsaken him. 11. We keep the charge of the Lord our God.

2 Chr. 15.12. They entered into a covenant to seek the Lord God of their fathers with all their heart and with all their soul : 15. And all Judah rejoiced at the oath : for they had sworn with all their heart, and sought him with their whole desire ; and he was found of them. 2 Chr. 23.16. 2 Kin. 11.17. 2 Chr. 29.10. Ezr. 10.3-44. Neh. 9.38. Jer. 34.15.

Ezr. 5.11. We are the servants of the God of heaven and earth.

Neh. 6.11. Should such a man as I flee ? and who *is there*, that, *being* as I *am*, would go into the temple to save his life ? I will not go in.

Neh. 10.28. All they that had separated themselves from the people of the lands unto the law of God, their wives, their sons, and their daughters, every one having knowledge, and having understanding ; 29. They clave to their brethren, their nobles, and entered into a curse, and into an oath, to walk in God's law. *v.* 1-39.

Est. 4.16. I go in unto the king, which *is* not according to the law : and if I perish, I perish.

Job 2.3. One that feareth God, and escheweth evil ? and still he holdeth fast his integrity, although thou movedst me against him.

Job 23.11. My foot hath held his steps, his way have I kept, and not declined. 12. Neither have I gone back from the commandment of his lips; I have esteemed the words of his mouth more than my necessary *food.*

Psa. 17.3. Thou hast proved mine heart; thou hast visited *me* in the night; thou hast tried me, *and* shalt find nothing: I am purposed *that* my mouth shall not transgress.

Psa. 26.6. I will wash mine hands in innocency: so will I compass thine altar, O Lord. 11. As for me, I will walk in mine integrity.

Psa. 40.9. I have preached righteousness in the great congregation: lo, I have not refrained my lips, O Lord, thou knowest. 10. I have not hid thy righteousness within my heart; I have declared thy faithfulness and thy salvation: I have not concealed thy lovingkindness and thy truth from the great congregation.

Psa. 50.5. My saints that have made a covenant with me by sacrifice.

Psa. 56.12. Thy vows *are* upon me, O God: I will render praises unto thee.

Psa. 66.16. Come *and* hear, all ye that fear God, and I will declare what he hath done for my soul.

Psa. 71.17. Hitherto have I declared thy wondrous works.

Psa. 86.11. I will walk in thy truth: unite my heart to fear thy name.

Psa. 101.2. I will behave myself wisely in a perfect way. O when wilt thou come unto me? I will walk within my house with a perfect heart. 3. I will set no wicked thing before mine eyes: I hate the work of them that turn aside; *it* shall not cleave to me.

Psa. 108.1. O God, my heart is fixed; I will sing and give praise, even with my glory. Psa. 57.7,8.

Psa. 116.9. I will walk before the Lord in the land of the living. 13. I will take the cup of salvation, and call upon the name of the Lord. 14. I will pay my vows unto the Lord now in the presence of all his people. 16. O Lord, truly I *am* thy servant; I *am* thy servant, *and* the son of thine handmaid.

Psa. 119.8. I will keep thy statutes: O forsake me not. 30. I have chosen the way of truth: thy judgments have I laid *before me.* 31. I have stuck unto thy testimonies. 38. Thy servant, who *is devoted* to thy fear. 44. So shall I keep thy law continually for ever and ever. 45. And I will walk at liberty: for I seek thy precepts. 46. I will speak of thy testimonies also before kings, and will not be ashamed. 57. *Thou art* my portion, O Lord: I have said that I would keep thy words. 94. I *am* thine, save me; for I have sought thy precepts.

Psa. 119.106. I have sworn, and I will perform *it,* that I will keep thy righteous judgments. 115. Depart from me, ye evildoers: for I will keep the commandments of my God. 125. I *am* thy servant; give me understanding, that I may know thy testimonies. 145. I cried with *my* whole heart; hear me, O Lord: I will keep thy statutes. 143. I cried unto thee; save me, and I shall keep thy testimonies. Psa. 31.3.12.

Isa. 44.5. One shall say, I *am* the Lord's; and another shall call *himself* by the name of Jacob; and another shall subscribe *with* his hand unto the Lord.

Isa. 45.14. Surely God *is* in thee; and *there is* none else, *there is* no God.

Jer. 4.2. Thou shalt swear, The Lord liveth, in truth, in judgment, and in righteousness; and the nations shall bless themselves in him, and in him shall they glory.

Jer. 42.5. The Lord be a true and faithful witness between us, if we do not even according to all things for the which the Lord thy God shall send thee to us. 6. Whether *it be* good, or whether *it be* evil, we will obey the voice of the Lord our God.

Jer. 50.5. They shall ask the way to Zion with their faces thitherward, *saying,* Come, and let us join ourselves to the Lord in a perpetual covenant *that* shall not be forgotten.

Dan. 4.37. Now I Nebuchadnezzar praise and extol and honour the King of heaven. *v.* 34. Dan. 6.26,27.

Hos. 11.12. Judah yet ruleth with God, and is faithful with the saints.

Jonah 1.9. I fear the Lord, the God of heaven, which hath made the sea and the dry *land.* Gen. 42.18.

Mic. 4.5. We will walk in the name of the Lord our God for ever and ever.

Mat. 9.9. And he saith unto him, Follow me. And he arose, and followed him.

Mar. 15.43. Joseph of Arimathea went in boldly unto Pilate, and craved the body of Jesus.

Luk. 2.37. Which departed not from the temple, but served *God* with fastings and prayers night and day.

Luk. 18.28. Lo, we have left all, and followed thee.

Jno. 1.49. Nathaniel saith unto him, Rabbi, thou art the Son of God; thou art the King of Israel.

Jno. 6.68. Simon Peter answered him, Lord, to whom shall we go? thou hast the words of eternal life. 69. We believe, and are sure, that thou art that Christ, the Son of the living God.

Jno. 9.33. If this man were not of God, he could do nothing.

Jno. 11.27. I believe that thou art the Christ, the Son of God, which should come into the world.

Act. 2.42. They continued stedfastly in the apostles' doctrine and fellowship, and in breaking of bread, and in prayers.

Act. 9.29. He spake boldly in the name of the Lord Jesus, and disputed against the Grecians.

Act. 26.6. I stand and am judged for the hope of the promise made of God unto our fathers.

Rom. 1.16. I am not ashamed of the gospel of Christ.

2 Cor. 4.1. As we have received mercy we faint not.

2 Cor. 8.5. First gave their own selves to the Lord, and unto us by the will of God.

Phil. 1.7. Both in my bonds, and in the defence and confirmation of the gospel, ye all are partakers of my grace. 20. That in nothing I shall be ashamed, but *that* with all boldness, as always, *so* now also Christ shall be magnified in my body, whether *it be* by life, or by death. 21. For to me to live *is* Christ, and to die *is* gain.

Col. 2.5. Joying and beholding your order, and the stedfastness of your faith in Christ.

2 The. 1.3. Your faith groweth exceedingly.

1 Tim. 6.12. Hast professed a good profession before many witnesses.

2 Tim. 4.7. I have fought a good fight, I have finished my course, I have kept the faith.

Heb. 11.17. By faith Abraham, when he was tried, offered up Isaac: and he that had received the promises offered up his only-begotten son. Heb. 6.15.

Rev. 2.2. I know thy works, and thy labour, and thy patience, 3. And hast borne, and hast patience, and for my name's sake hast laboured, and hast not fainted.

Rev. 3.4. Thou hast a few names even in Sardis, which have not defiled their garments ; and they shall walk with me in white : for they are worthy. 8. Thou hast a little strength, and hast kept my word, and hast not denied my name. 10. Because thou hast kept the word of my patience, I also will keep thee from the hour of temptation, which shall come upon all the world.

Rev. 14.4. These are they which were not defiled with women ; for they are virgins. These are they which follow the Lamb whithersoever he goeth.

See SPIRITUAL DILIGENCE—PERSECUTION —SELF-DENIAL—ZEAL.

DECISION, VALLEY OF. See JEHOSHAPHAT, VALLEY OF.

DECREES OF GOD. See PREDESTINATION.

DEDAN, grandson of Cush, Gen. 10.7. 1 Chr. 1.9.

———— grandson of Abraham and Keturah, Gen. 25.3. 1 Chr. 1.32. Dedanites, merchants, Isa. 21.13. Eze. 27.20. Prophecies of, Jer. 25.23. Jer. 49.8. Eze. 25.13. Eze. 38.13.

DEDICATION. Of tabernacle and its contents, Num. 7. Of Solomon's temple, 1 Kin. 8. 2 Chr. 7.5. Of second temple, Ezr. 6.16,17. Of Jerusalem's wall, Neh. 12.27-43. Of houses, Deu. 20.5. Psa. 30 (title). Of persons and property, see VOWS, FIRST-BORN, FIRST-FRUITS.

Dedicated things placed in treasuries of the temple, see TREASURIES. Applied to the maintenance of the temple and priests, Num. 18.14. 1 Chr. 26.26,27.

————, FEAST OF. See FEASTS.

DEER. Fallow deer, Deu. 14.5. 1 Kin. 4.23. Hart and roe, Deu. 12.15. Psa. 42.1. Song 8.14. Isa. 35.6. Roe, 2 Sam. 2.18. 1 Chr. 12.8. Pro. 6.5. Roebuck, Deu. 14.5. 1 Kin. 4.23. Hind, Pro. 5.19. Jer. 14.5. 2 Sam. 22.34.

DEFILEMENT AND PURIFICATION. Purification of persons defiled by leprosy, Lev. 13.3,44-46. Lev. 14. Lev. 22.4-7. By various diseases, Lev. 15. Lev. 22.4. By child-birth, Lev. 12.2-8. Luk. 2.22. By being with a dead body, touching a bone or a grave, Num. 19.11-22. Num. 31.19,20. By touching the carcase of a clean animal that died of itself, Lev. 11.39,40. Lev. 17.15,16. Lev. 22.8. Or any unclean thing, Lev. 5.2-13. Lev. 11.8.24-28. Lev. 14.46-57. Lev. 15.5-11. Deu. 23.10,11. By leading the scapegoat into the wilderness, Lev. 16.26. By burning the sin-offering on the day of atonement, Lev. 16.28. By sacrificing the red heifer, Num. 19.7-10.

DEGREES (literally steps), title of Psa. 120-134. Probably so called because the sense ascends, as it were, by degrees or steps, the first or last words of a preceding clause being repeated at the beginning of the succeeding one. Comp. Psa. 122.2,3,4 ; Psa. 123.3,4 ; Psa. 126.2,3 ; Psa. 129.1,2. See Jud. 5.3,19,30.

DEHAVITES, Ezr. 4.9. Supposed to be the same as Avites. See AVA.

DELIGHTING IN GOD. See LOVE TO GOD — SPIRITUAL DILIGENCE — SPIRITUAL PEACE AND JOY.

DELILAH, the woman who betrayed Samson to the Philistines, Jud. 16.

DELIVERANCE FROM GOD. See GOD PROTECTOR—GOD SAVIOUR.—AFFLICTION, PRAYER IN.

DELUGE. See FLOOD.

DEMAS, a fellow-labourer of Paul, Col. 4.14. Phlm. 24. Forsakes Paul and goes to Thessalonica, 2 Tim. 4.10.

DEMETRIUS, a silversmith, opposes Paul at Ephesus, Act. 19.24-38.

————, a Christian commended by John, 3 Jno. 12.

DEMONS (Gr. daimonion or daimon). Called devils, Lev. 17.7. Evil spirits, 1 Sam. 16.14. Evil angels, Psa. 78.49. Unclean spirit, Mat. 12.43. Angels of the devil, Mat. 25.41. Foul spirit, Mar. 9.25. Rev. 18.2. Spirit of divination, Act. 16.16. Lying spirit, 1 Kin. 22.22. Principalities, powers, &c., Eph. 6.12.

Worship of, forbidden, Lev. 17.7. Examples of, Deu. 32.17. 2 Chr. 11.15. Psa. 106.37. Zec. 13.2. 1 Cor. 10.20. 1 Tim. 4.1. Rev. 9.20. Saul possessed by an evil spirit, 1 Sam. 16.14-23. 1 Sam. 18.10,11. 1 Sam. 19.9,10. Comp. Jud. 9.23. 1 Kin. 22.21-23.

Cast out by Christ, Mat. 4.24. Mat. 8.16,28-34. Mat. 9.32,33. Mat. 12.22-29. Mat. 15.22,28. Mat. 17.14-21. Mar. 1.23-26. Luk. 4.41. Luk. 8.2. Power over, given to the Apostles, &c., Mat. 10.1. Mar. 16.17.

Cast out by a disciple, Mar. 9.38. By the seventy, Luk. 10.17. By Peter, Act. 5.16. By Paul, Act. 16.16-18. Act. 19.12. By Philip, Act. 8.7. Disciples unable to cast out, Mar. 9.18,28,29. And Sceva's sons, Act. 19.13-16. Parable regarding, Mat. 12.43-45.

Work false miracles, Rev. 16.13,14. Punishment of, Mat. 25.41. Mat. 8.29. Luk. 8.28. 1 Cor. 6.3. Jas. 2.19. 2 Pet. 2.4. Jude 6. Rev. 12.7-9. Rev. 16.13,14. See SATAN.

DENYING CHRIST. See BACKSLIDING.

DEPRAVITY. See MAN, NATURAL STATE OF. — THE FALL — GODLESSNESS — IMPENITENCE—SIN—SINNERS—CHILDREN, WICKED.

DEPUTY, a governor, 1 Kin. 22.47 ; or pro-consul, Act. 13.7,8. Act. 18.12.

DERBE, a city of Lycaonia. Paul and Barnabas flee to, from Iconium, Act. 14.6 ; and from Lystra, Act. 14.20. Paul and Silas visit, Act. 16.1. The birthplace of Gaius, Act. 20.4.

DESERTS AND WILDERNESSES. Barrenness of, Ex. 17.1. Lev. 16.22. Num. 20.5. Deu. 8.15. Deu. 32.10. Jer. 2.2,6. Vegetation of, Ex. 3.1. Jer. 17.6. Hos. 9.10. Mar. 6.39. Names of deserts, see EDOM,

Damascus, Kadesh, Paran, Red Sea, Shur, Sin, Sinai, Zin.—Palestine, Deserts of.

DESPAIR. See Conviction of Sin.

DESPONDENCY. See Murmuring — Doubting.

DEVIL. See Satan—Demons.

DEVOTEDNESS to God. See Love to God — Decision — Spiritual Diligence — Glorifying God.

DEVOTED THINGS. See Vows.

DEW. Abundance of, Deu. 33.13. 2 Sam. 17.12. Job 29.19. Pro. 3.20. Dan. 4.15. Miracle of, Jud. 6.36-40. Illustrative, Psa. 110.3. Isa. 26.19. Hos. 6.4. Hos. 14.5.

DIAL of Ahaz, 2 Kin. 20.11. Isa. 38.8.

DIAMOND, Ex. 28.18. Eze. 28.13. Jer. 17.1.

DIANA, an Ephesian goddess. Temple and silver shrines of, Act. 19.24,27,28,35. See Shrine.

DIBON, or Dimon, a town of Moab, N. of the Arnon, Num. 21.30. Israelites encamp at, Num. 33.45. Given to Gad and Reuben, Num. 32.3,34. Jos. 13.17. Re-possessed by Moab, Isa. 15.2,9. Jer. 48.18,22.

DILIGENCE in Business, see Industry. Diligence, spiritual, see Spiritual Diligence—Decision.

DINAH, daughter of Jacob and Leah, Gen. 30.21. Seduced by Shechem, Gen. 34.

DINNER. See Feasts.

DIONYSIUS, the Areopagite of Athens, converted by Paul, Act. 17.34.

DIOTREPHES, a false teacher, condemned by John, 3 Jno. 9.

DISCERNING of Spirits, signifies discriminating between true and false prophetical gifts, 1 Cor. 12.10. 1 Jno. 4.1.

DISCIPLE, a name of the 12 apostles, Mat. 10.1. Mat. 20.17. Of Christians, Act. 9.26. Act. 14.22. Act. 21.4. Of John's followers, Mat. 9.14.

DISCONTENT. See Murmuring—Contentment.

DISEASES. Kinds of, Lev. 26.16. Deu. 28.22,27,35. Lev. 21.18,20. Lev. 22.22. Ulcers, Isa. 1.6. Sun-stroke, Psa. 121.6. 2 Kin. 4.19,20. Isa. 49.10. Dropsy, Luk. 14.2. Dysentery, Act. 28.8. Issue, Mat. 9.20. Lunacy, Mat. 4.24. Worms, Act. 12.23. Palsy, Mar. 2.3.

See Blindness, Boils, Deafness, Demons, Fever, Lameness, Leprosy, Madness, Palsy, Pestilence.

Physicians employed, 2 Chr. 16.12. Jer. 8.22. Mat. 9.12. Mar. 5.26. Luk. 4.23. Medicine used, Pro. 17.22. Pro. 20.30 (marg.) Jer. 30.13. Jer. 46.11. Balsams and plasters, 2 Kin. 20.7. Isa. 1.6. Jer. 8.22. Treatment of wounds, Isa. 1.6. Luk. 10.34. Of fractures, Eze. 30.21. See Miracles—Anointing.

DISH. Jud. 5.25. 2 Kin. 21.13. Mat. 26.23. Used in the tabernacle, Ex. 25.29. Num. 4.7. See Charger.

DISHONESTY, Fraud, Theft. Ex. 20.15. Thou shalt not steal. Deu. 5.19. Mat. 19.18. Rom. 13.9.

Lev. 19.11. Ye shall not steal, neither deal falsely.

Lev. 19.13. Thou shalt not defraud thy neighbour, neither rob. *him*: the wages of him that is hired shall not abide with thee all night. Deu. 24.15. Jas. 5.4.

Lev. 25.14. If thou sell ought or buyest *ought* of thy neighbour's hand, ye shall not oppress one another. *v.* 17.

Deu. 25.13. Thou shalt not have in thy bag divers weights, a great and a small. 14. Thou shalt not have in thine house divers measures, a great and a small. 15. *But* thou shalt have a perfect and just weight, a perfect and just measure shalt thou have: that thy days may be lengthened. 16. For all that do such things, *and* all that do unrighteously, *are* an abomination unto the Lord thy God. Lev. 19.35,36. Pro. 11.1. Pro. 20.10,23.

Job 24.16. In the dark they dig through houses, *which* they had marked for themselves in the daytime: they know not the light. *v.* 14-18.

Job 31.39. If I have eaten the fruits thereof without money, or have caused the owners thereof to lose their life: 40. Let thistles grow instead of wheat.

Psa. 37.21. The wicked borroweth, and payeth not again.

Psa. 50.18. When thou sawest a thief, then thou consentedst with him.

Psa. 62.10. Trust not in oppression, and become not vain in robbery.

Psa. 119.61. The bands of the wicked have robbed me.

Pro. 3.27. Withhold not good from them to whom it is due, when it is in the power of thine hand to do *it*. 28. Say not unto thy neighbour, Go, and come again, and to-morrow I will give; when thou hast it by thee.

Pro. 6.30. *Men* do not despise a thief, if he steal to satisfy his soul when he is hungry: 31. But *if* he be found, he shall restore sevenfold; he shall give all the substance of his house.

Pro. 20.14. *It is* naught, saith the buyer: but when he is gone his way, then he boasteth.

Pro. 21.7. The robbery of the wicked shall destroy them.

Pro. 23.10. Remove not the old landmark; and enter not into the fields of the fatherless. Deu. 19.14. Deu. 27.17. Pro. 22.28.

Pro. 29.24. Whoso is partner with a thief hateth his own soul.

Pro. 30.8. Feed me with food convenient for me: 9. Lest I be poor and steal.

Isa. 61.8. I the Lord love judgment, I hate robbery for burnt-offering.

Jer. 2.26. The thief is ashamed when he is found.

Jer. 7.9. Will ye steal, 10. And come and stand before me in this house, and say, We are delivered to do all these abominations? 11. Is this house, which is called by my name, become a den of robbers in your eyes? Behold, even I have seen *it*, saith the Lord.

Jer. 22.13. Woe unto him that buildeth his house by unrighteousness, and his chambers by wrong; *that* useth his neighbour's service without wages.

Eze. 22.29. The people used oppression, and exercised robbery, and have vexed the poor and needy; yea, they have oppressed the stranger wrongfully.

Hos. 4.1. The Lord hath a controversy with the inhabitants of the land, because *there is* no truth, nor mercy, nor knowledge of God in the land. 2. By stealing, they break out.

Hos. 12.7. The balances of deceit *are* in his hand: he loveth to oppress.

Amos 3.10. They know not to do right, saith the Lord, who store up violence and robbery in their palaces.

Amos 8.5. Making the ephah small, and the shekel great, and falsifying the balances by deceit.

Mic. 6.10. Are there yet the treasures of wickedness in the house of the wicked, and the scant measure *that is* abominable? 11. Shall I count *them* pure with the wicked balances, and with the bag of deceitful weights?

Nah. 3.1. Woe to the bloody city! it *is* all full of lies *and* robbery.

Zeph. 1.9. Will I punish all those which fill their masters' houses with violence and deceit.

Zec. 5.3. This *is* the curse that goeth forth over the face of the whole earth: for every one that stealeth shall be cut off. 4. I will bring it forth, saith the Lord of hosts, and it shall enter into the house of the thief; and it shall remain in the midst of his house, and shall consume it with the timber thereof and the stones thereof.

Mat. 15.19. Out of the heart proceed thefts.

Rom. 2.21. Thou that preachest a man should not steal, dost thou steal?

Rom. 13.8. Owe no man anything.

1 Cor. 6.8. Ye do wrong, and defraud, and that *your* brethren. 10. Nor thieves, nor covetous, nor extortioners, shall inherit the kingdom of God.

Eph. 4.28. Let him that stole steal no more.

1 The. 4.6. That no *man* go beyond and defraud his brother in *any* matter: because that the Lord *is* the avenger of all such.

Tit. 2.10. Not purloining, but shewing all good fidelity.

1 Pet. 4.15. Let none of you suffer as a thief.

Rev. 9.21. Neither repented they of their thefts.

DISHONESTY. Restitution to be made, Ex. 22.1-13. See Lev. 6.2-5. Pro. 6.31.

————, EXAMPLES OF. Abimelech's servants, Gen. 21.25. Gen. 26.15-22. Jacob, Gen. 25.29-33. Laban, Gen. 29.23-26. Gen. 31.41. Rachel, Gen. 31.19. Achan, Jos. 7.11-26. Micah, Jud. 17.2. Danites, Jud. 18.14-21. Ahab, 1 Kin. 21.2-16. Judas, Jno. 12.6.

See INTEGRITY—MASTERS—RULERS—SERVANTS—POOR.

DISOBEDIENCE TO SPECIAL COMMANDS, EXAMPLES OF. Adam and Eve, Gen. 3.6,11. Lot's wife, Gen. 19.26. Moses, Ex. 4.13,14. Num. 20.11,24. Pharaoh, Ex. 4.23. Ex. 10.1-4. Israelites, Ex. 16.19,20. Num. 33.55,56. Deu. 1.26. Jos. 5.6. Nadab and Abihu, Lev. 10.1,2. Balaam, Num. 22.22. Achan, Jos. 7.15-26. Saul, 1 Sam. 13.8-14. 1 Sam. 15.8-23. 1 Sam. 28.17,18. The young prophet, 1 Kin. 13.20-26. An Israelite, 1 Kin. 20.36. Ahab,

1 Kin. 20.42. Priests, 1 Chr. 15.13. The Jews, Jer. 43.7. Jer. 44.12-14. Jonah, Jon. 1.3-12. The leper, Mar. 1.45.

DISOBEDIENCE TO PARENTS. See CHILDREN, DUTIES OF.—CHILDREN, WICKED.

DISPERSION OF NATIONS, after the Flood, Gen. 10. At Babel, Gen. 11.1-9. Deu. 32.8.

DISTAFF, Pro. 31.19. Ex. 35.25,26.

DIVINATION. See SORCERY.

DIVISIONS. See STRIFE—HERESY.

DIVORCE. Permitted on account of adultery, given in writing, Deu. 24.1. Jer. 3.1. Mat. 5.31,32. Mat. 19.7-9. To bond-servants, Ex. 21.7-11. To captives, Deu. 21.11-14. Commanded from idolatrous wives, Ezr. 10.2-17. Neh. 13.23-30.

Practised illegally by the Jews, Mic. 2.9. Mal. 2.14. Mat. 19.3,9. When a divorced woman might marry, Deu. 24.1,2. When she might not marry, Deu. 24.3,4. Mat. 5.32. Mat. 19.9. Luk. 16.18. 1 Cor. 7.11. Illustrative, Isa. 50.1. Jer. 3.8. See MARRIAGE.

DOCTOR. (Gr. *didaskos*), a teacher of the Jewish law, Luk. 2.46. Luk. 5.17. Act. 5.34. 1 Tim. 1.7. Usually translated *master*, as Mat. 8.19.

DOCTRINES, FALSE. See FALSE TEACHERS.

DOEG, an Edomite, tells Saul of Ahimelech helping David, 1 Sam. 21.7. 1 Sam. 22.9,22. Psa. 52 (*title*). Slays Ahimelech and 85 priests, 1 Sam. 22.18,19.

DOG, Deu. 23.18. Sheep-dogs, Job 30.1. Street-dogs, Psa. 59.6. 1 Kin. 21.19. 1 Kin. 22.38. Luk. 16.21. House-dog, Mat. 15.27. Held in contempt, 1 Sam. 17.43. 2 Sam. 3.8. 2 Sam. 16.9. Illustrative, Phil. 3.2. Isa. 56.10.

DOOR, Gen. 19.9. Posts and lintels of, Ex. 12.22. Ex. 21.6. Hinges of, 1 Kin. 7.50. Mode of opening, Song 5.4. Texts written on, Deu. 11.20. Temple, doors of, two leaves, and carved, 1 Kin. 6.33-35. Illustrative, Pro. 26.14. Hos. 2.15. Jno. 10.1,7. 1 Cor. 16.9. Rev. 3.8. See BAR—KEY—LOCK.

DOORKEEPER. See LEVITES—PORTERS.

DOR, a town and district in the W. coast of Palestine, Jos. 11.2. Jos. 12.23. 1 Kin. 4.11. Given to Manasseh, Jos. 17.11. Jud 1.27.

DORCAS, or TABITHA, a female convert at Joppa; her alms deeds; raised to life by Peter, Act. 9.36-42.

DOTHAN, a district and town near Samaria, where Joseph buys his brethren, Gen. 37.17. The Syrians struck with blindness at, 2 Kin. 6.13-19.

DOUBT. DESPONDENCY—WEAK FAITH. Job 30.20. I cry unto thee, and thou dost not hear me: I stand up, and thou regardest me *not*. 21. Thou art become cruel to me: with thy strong hand thou opposest thyself against me. Job 3. Job 4.5. Job 16. Job 17. Job 23.15-17.

Psa. 22.2. O my God, I cry in the daytime, but thou hearest not; and in the night season, and am not silent.

Psa. 31.22. I said in my haste, I am cut off from before thine eyes.

Psa. 42.5. Why art thou cast down, O my soul? and *why* art thou disquieted in me?

hope thou in God: for I shall yet praise him *for* the help of his countenance. 6. O my God, my soul is cast down within me.

Psa. 49.5. Wherefore should I fear in the days of evil, *when* the iniquity of my heels shall compass me about?

Psa. 73.13. Verily I have cleansed my heart *in* vain, and washed my hands in innocency. 14. For all the day long have I been plagued, and chastened every morning. 15. If I say, I will speak thus; behold, I should offend *against* the generation of thy children. 16. When I thought to know this, it *was* too painful for me; 17. Until I went into the sanctuary of God.

Psa. 77.3. I remembered God, and was troubled: I complained, and my spirit was overwhelmed. 7. Will the Lord cast off for ever? and will he be favourable no more? 8. Is his mercy clean gone for ever? doth *his* promise fail for evermore? 9. Hath God forgotten to be gracious? hath he in anger shut up his tender mercies?

Pro. 24.10. If thou faint in the day of adversity, thy strength *is* small.

Isa. 40.27. Why sayest thou, O Jacob, and speakest, O Israel, My way is hid from the Lord, and my judgment is passed over from my God? 28. Hast thou not known? hast thou not heard, *that* the everlasting God, the Lord, the Creator of the ends of the earth, fainteth not, neither is weary? *there is* no searching of his understanding. Isa. 50.2.

Isa. 49.14. Zion said, The Lord hath forsaken me, and my Lord hath forgotten me. 15. Can a woman forget her sucking child, that she should not have compassion on the son of her womb? yea, they may forget, yet will I not forget thee.

Jer. 8.18. *When* I would comfort myself against sorrow, my heart *is* faint in me.

Jer. 15.18. Why is my pain perpetual, and my wound incurable, *which* refuseth to be healed? wilt thou be altogether unto me as a liar, *and* as waters *that* fail?

Jer. 45.3. Woe is me now! for the Lord hath added grief to my sorrow; I fainted in my sighing, and I find no rest.

Lam. 3.8. When I cry and shout, he shutteth out my prayer. 17. Thou hast removed my soul far off from peace: I forgat prosperity. 18. And I said, My strength and my hope is perished from the Lord.

Lam. 5.20. Wherefore dost thou forget us for ever, *and* forsake us so long time? Lam. c. 1-5.

Hos. 10.3. We have no king, because we feared not the Lord; what then should a king do to us?

Mat. 8.26. Why are ye fearful, O ye of little faith? Mar. 4.40. Luk. 8.25.

Mat. 14.31. O thou of little faith, wherefore didst thou doubt?

Mat. 17.17. O faithless and perverse generation, how long shall I be with you? how long shall I suffer you? Mar. 9.18,19,28. Luk. 9.40.

Mar. 4.38. Master, carest thou not that we perish?

1 Pet. 1.6. Ye are in heaviness through manifold temptations.

DOUBT, EXAMPLES OF. Abraham, Gen. 12.12,13. Gen. 17.17. Gen. 20.11. Sarah, Gen. 18.12-14. Isaac, Gen. 26.6,7. Lot, Gen. 19.30 Moses Ex. 3.11. Ex. 4.1,10,13.

Ex. 5.22,23. Ex. 6.12,30. Num. 11.21-23 Israelites, Ex. 6.9. Ex. 14.10. 1 Sam. 17.11,24.

Gideon, Jud. 6.13,15. Samuel, 1 Sam. 16.1,2. David, 1 Sam. 21.12,13. 1 Sam. 27.1. David's men, 1 Sam. 23.3. Obadiah, 1 Kin. 18.9-14. Elijah, 1 Kin. 19.13,14,18. Joash, 2 Kin. 13.18,19. Jeremiah, Jer. 1.6. Jer. 32.24,25. Lam. c. 1-5.

The disciples, Mat. 8.25,26. Mat. 17.16,20. Mar. 4.38,40. Mar. 9.18. Mar. 16.10-14. Luk. 8.25. Luk. 9.40. John the Baptist, Mat. 11.2,3. Peter, Mat. 14.29,31. Ananias, Act. 9.13,14.

See UNBELIEF—MURMURING—FEAR OF MAN.

DOVE, TURTLE DOVE, and PIGEON, Isa. 59.11. Isa. 60.8. Nah. 2.7. Mat. 10.16. Used in sacrifice by Abraham, Gen. 15.9. By the poor at the purification of women, Lev. 12.6. Luk. 2.24. And of Nazarites, Num. 6.10. And lepers, Lev. 14.22.

Used as a burnt-offering, Lev. 1.14-17. A trespass-offering, Lev. 5.7-10. A sin-offering, Num. 6.11. Sent from the ark, Gen. 8.8-11. Sold in the temple, Mat. 21.12. Jno. 2.14. Illustrative, Mat. 3.16.

DOWRY. See MARRIAGE CUSTOMS.

DRAG. See FISHES.

DRAGON. The original signifies—A poisonous serpent, Deu. 32.33. A serpent of the desert, Psa. 91.13. Isa. 34.13. Jer. 9.11. Jer. 51.37. Mal. 1.3. Of the sea, Isa. 27.1. Psa. 74.13. A crocodile (symbolical of Egypt), Eze. 29.3. Eze. 32.2.

A wolf, Mic. 1.8. A name of Satan, Rev. 20.2. Symbolical, Rev. 12. Rev. 13. Rev. 16.13. The Hebrew is translated 'great whale' in Gen. 1.21. Job 7.12. Serpent, Ex. 7.9.

DRAM, a Persian gold coin, value about 14s., 1 Chr. 29.7. Ezr. 2.69.

DREAMS, Job. 20.8. Ecc. 5.3,7. Sent from God, to Abimelech, Gen. 20.3. Jacob, Gen. 28.12. Gen. 31.11-13. Gen. 46.2. Laban, Gen. 31.24. Joseph, Gen. 37.5-10. The Midianite, Jud. 7.13. Solomon, 1 Kin. 3.5-15.

Eliphaz, Job 4.12. Daniel, Dan. 7. Joseph, Mat. 1.20. Mat. 2.13,19,22. Pilate's wife, Mat. 27.19. Paul, Act. 16.9. Act. 23.11. Of Pharaoh's officers and Pharaoh, interpreted by Joseph, Gen. c. 40 & 41. Of Nebuchadnezzar, interpreted by Daniel, Dan. 2. Dan. 4.

Prophets received revelations in, Num. 12.6. Job 33.15. Jer. 23.28. 1 Sam. 28.6. Joel 2.28. False prophets pretended to revelations in, Deu. 13.1-5. Jer. 23.25-32. Jer. 27.9. Jer. 29.8. Zec. 10.2. Interpretation of, from God, Gen. 40.8. Gen. 41.16. Dan. 2.18-23,28-30. See VISIONS.

DRESS. First clothing of skins, Gen. 3.21 (10 Hebrew and Greek words are translated as follows): (1.) Mantle, 1 Kin. 19.13. 2 Kin. 2.13. Translated garment, Gen. 25.25. Jos. 7.21. Robe, Jonah 3.6.

(2.) Mantle, 1 Sam. 15.27. Ezr. 9.3. Job 1.20. Worn by women, Isa. 3.22. Translated cloak, Isa. 59.17. Coat, 1 Sam. 2.19. Robe, 1 Sam. 18.4. 1 Chr. 15.27. And worn

by women, 2 Sam. 13.18.   Robe of the ephod,
Ex. 29.5.   Lev. 8.7.

(3.) Mantle, Jud. 4.18 (*marg.* rug).   (4.) Garment in which a poor man slept, Ex. 22.27.
(5.) Coat, Gen. 3.21.   Gen. 37.3.   Job 30.18.
Worn by priests, Ex. 28.4,40.   Translated
robe, Isa. 22.21.   Garment of women, 2 Sam.
13.18.   (6.) Coats, Dan. 3.21.   (7.) Hosen
(under-garments), Dan. 3.21.

(8.) Upper garment, translated cloak, Mat.
5.40.   Robe, Jno. 19.2,5.   Garment, Mat.
9.20.   Mat. 23.5.   Mar. 10.50.   Jno. 13.4.
Jno. 19.23.   Act. 9.39.   Act. 12.8.   Act. 18.6.
Raiment, Mat. 17.2.   Mat. 27.31.   Act. 22.20.
Rev. 4.4.   Clothes, Mat. 21.7.   Mat. 24.18.
Mat. 26.65.   Luk. 8.27.   Act. 7.58.   Act.
22.23.   Vesture, Mat. 27.35.   Rev. 19.13.
Apparel, 1 Pet. 3.3.

(9.) Cloak, 2 Tim. 4.13.   (10.) Coat, Mat.
5.40.   Luk. 6.29.   Jno. 19.23.   Act. 9.39.
Translated garment, Jude 23.   (Female attire,
Isa. 3.18-24.)

[Twenty different words are variously rendered apparel, attire, clothes, clothing, covering, garments, lap, raiment, vestment, vesture, wardrobe.   It is impossible to make the
distinction between them apparent.]

See Embroidery — Ephod — Fringes —
Girdle — Habergeon — Mourning. —
Priest, dress of.—Prophets, dress of.—
Purse—Shoe—Stomacher—Towel.

Not to be of mixed materials, Deu. 22.11.
Men and women not to exchange, Deu. 22.5.
Purification of, from leprosy or plague, Lev.
13.47-59.   From ceremonial defilement, Lev.
11.32.   Num. 31.20.   Rending of, see Mourning.   Moderation in, enjoined, 1 Tim. 2.9.
1 Pet. 3.3.

Changes of Raiment. Stores of kept, Job
27.16.   Isa. 3.6.   Jas. 5.2.   2 Kin. 10.22.   And
presents of made, Gen. 45.22.   1 Sam. 18.4.
2 Kin. 5.5.   Dan. 5.7.   Est. 6.8.   At marriages,
Mat. 22.11.   Jud. 14.12.

Colours of. White, Ecc. 9.8.   Est. 8.15.
Purple, Jud. 8.26.   Pro. 31.22.   Jer. 10.9.
Eze. 27.16.   Act. 16.14.   Scarlet, 2 Sam. 1.24.
Pro. 31.21.   Lam. 4.5.   Dan. 5.7.   Blue, Est.
8.15.   Eze. 23.6.   Eze. 27.24.   Party-coloured,
Gen. 37.3.   Jud. 5.30.   2 Sam. 13.18.

Materials used in.   See Camels' Hair—
Goats' Hair—Leather—Linen—Sackcloth—Silk—Skins—Wool.

Head-dress.   Worn by priests ; bonnet or
turban of linen, Ex. 28.40.   Ex. 29.9.   Ex.
39.28.   Lev. 8.13.   Eze. 44.18.   Worn by
men ; hats or turbans, Dan. 3.21.   Worn by
women ; bonnet, Isa. 3.20.   Hood, Isa. 3.23.
Kerchief, Eze. 13.18,21.   Head-bands, Isa.
3.20.   See Caul, Hair, Muffler, Tires,
Veil, Phylactery.

DRINK-OFFERING. See Offering.

DRINK, Strong.   See Wine.

DROMEDARY. See Camel.

DROUGHT, Psa. 32.4.   Gen. 31.40.   Deu.
28.23.   Hag. 1.10,11.   1 Kin. *c.* 17 & 18.   See
Rain.

DRUNKENNESS. Deu. 21.20.   This our
son *is* a glutton and a drunkard.   21.   And all
the men of his city shall stone him with stones,
that he die : so shalt thou put evil away from
among you ; and all Israel shall hear, and
fear.

Deu. 29.19.   I shall have peace, though I
walk in the imagination of mine heart, to add
drunkenness to thirst.

Psa. 69.12.   I was the song of the drunkards.

Pro. 20.1.   Wine *is* a mocker, strong drink
is raging : and whosoever is deceived thereby
is not wise.

Pro. 21.17.   He that loveth wine shall not
be rich.

Pro. 23.20.   Be not among winebibbers.
21.   The drunkard and the glutton shall come
to poverty.   29.   Who hath woe ? who hath
sorrow ? who hath contentions ? who hath
babbling ? who hath wounds without cause ?
who hath redness of eyes ? 30.   They that
tarry long at the wine ; they that go to seek
mixed wine.   31.   Look not thou upon the
wine when it is red, when it giveth his colour
in the cup, *when* it moveth itself aright.   32.
At the last it biteth like a serpent, and sting-
eth like an adder.   *v.* 33-35.

Pro. 31.4.   *It is* not for kings, O Lemuel, *it
is* not for kings to drink wine ; nor for princes
strong drink :   5.   Lest they drink, and forget
the law.

Isa. 5.11.   Woe unto them that rise up
early in the morning, *that* they may follow
strong drink ; that continue until night, *till*
wine inflame them !   12.   And the harp, and
the viol, the tabret, and pipe, and wine, are
in their feasts : but they regard not the work
of the Lord.   22.   Woe unto *them that are*
mighty to drink wine, and men of strength to
mingle strong drink.

Isa. 28.1.   Woe to the drunkards of Ephraim, whose glorious beauty *is* a fading flower,
which *are* on the head of the fat valleys of
them that are overcome with wine !   3.   The
crown of pride, the drunkards of Ephraim,
shall be trodden under feet.   7.   The priest
and the prophet have erred through strong
drink, they are swallowed up of wine, they
are out of the way through strong drink ; they
err in vision, they stumble *in* judgment.

Isa. 56.12.   I will fetch wine, and we will
fill ourselves with strong drink.

Hos. 4.11.   Wine and new wine take away
the heart.

Hos. 7.5.   The princes have made *him* sick
with bottles of wine : he stretched out his
hand with scorners.   14.   They assemble themselves for corn and for wine.

Joel 1.5.   Awake, ye drunkards, and weep ;
and howl, all ye drinkers of wine, because of
the new wine ; for it is cut off from your
mouth.

Joel 3.3.   Sold a girl for wine, that they
might drink.

Amos 2.8.   They drink the wine of the condemned *in* the house of their god.   12.   Ye
gave the Nazarites wine to drink.

Amos 6.6.   That drink wine in bowls : but
they are not grieved for the affliction of Joseph.

Mic. 2.11.   Do lie, *saying*, I will prophesy
unto thee of wine and of strong drink ; he
shall even be the prophet of this people.

Nah. 1.10.   While they are drunken *as*
drunkards, they shall be devoured as stubble
fully dry.

Hab. 2.15.   Woe unto him that giveth his
neighbour drink, that puttest thy bottle to
him, and makest *him* drunken also.

Mat. 24.49.   To eat and drink with the
drunken.   50.   The Lord of that servant

shall come in a day when he looketh not for *him*.

Luk. 21.34. Lest at any time your hearts be overcharged with surfeiting, and drunkenness, and *so* that day come upon you unawares.

Rom. 13.13. Not in rioting and drunkenness.

1 Cor. 5.11. If any man that is called a brother be a drunkard, with such an one no not to eat.

1 Cor. 6.10. Nor drunkards shall inherit the kingdom of God.

1 Cor. 11.21. One is hungry, and another is drunken.

Gal. 5.21. Drunkenness, revellings, and such like : of the which I tell you before, as I have also told *you* in time past, that they which do such things shall not inherit the kingdom of God.

Eph. 5.18. Be not drunk with wine, wherein is excess.

1 The. 5.7. They that be drunken are drunken in the night. 8. But let us, who are of the day, be sober.

DRUNKENNESS, EXAMPLES OF. Noah, Gen. 9.21. Lot, Gen. 19.33. Nabal, 1 Sam. 25.36. Elah, 1 Kin. 16.9. Benhadad, 1 Kin. 20.16. Ahasuerus, Est. 1.10,11. Belshazzar, Dan. 5.1-5. See SENSUALITY.

DRUSILLA, wife of Felix, Act. 24.24.

DUKE, a title of the Edomite chiefs, Gen. 36.15-43. 1 Chr. 1.51-54. Of the Amorites, Jos. 13.21. Translated governor, Zec. 9.7.

DULCIMER (Chal. *symphonia*, a bagpipe?), Dan. 3.5,10,15.

DUMAH, a tribe of Ishmaelites, Gen. 25.14. 1 Chr. 1.30. Prophecy of, Isa. 21.11,12.

DUMB, THE. Zacharias struck dumb, Luk. 1.20,64. See DEAF.

DURA, PLAIN OF, near Babylon. The golden image set up in, by Nebuchadnezzar, Dan. 3.1.

DUST. Casting of, in anger, 2 Sam. 16.13. Act. 22.23. Shaking off from the feet, Mat. 10.14. Act. 13.51. Rain of—that is, clouds of sand—Deu. 28.24. See Ex. 8.16. Psa. 78.27. See ASHES.

DWELLINGS. See HOUSES — TENTS — PALACES.

DYEING, Ex. 25.5. Ex. 26.14. Eze. 23.15. Nah. 2.3 (*marg.*)

E

EAGLE, Lev. 11.13. Mat. 24.28. Its swiftness, Deu. 28.49. Pro. 30.19. 2 Sam. 1.23. Care of its young, Deu. 32.11. Ex. 19.4. Moulting of, Psa. 103.5. Nest of, Jer. 49.16. The bald eagle, or vulture, Mic. 1.16. Giereagle, a kind of vulture, Lev. 11.18. Symbolical, Eze. 1.10. Eze. 10.14. Eze. 17.3. Dan. 7.4. Rev. 4.7. Rev. 12.14.

EAR, boring of, as a sign of servitude, Ex. 21.5,6. See Psa. 40.6.

EARING (ploughing), 1 Sam. 8.12. Gen. 45.6. Ex. 34.21. Isa. 30.24.

EARNEST. Illustrative, 2 Cor. 1.22. 2 Cor. 5.5. Eph. 1.14.

EARNESTNESS. See PRAYERFULNESS—SPIRITUAL DILIGENCE.

EAR-RINGS. See RINGS.

EARTH, THE. Primitive state of, Gen. c. 1 to 3. Form and condition of, Gen. 1.6,7. Job. 26.7. 1 Sam. 2.8. Ecc. 1.4. Isa. 40.22. Destroyed by a flood, Gen. c. 7 & 8. Early divisions of, Gen. c. 10 & 11. Deu. 32.8. Not to be destroyed again by water, Gen. 9.11. To be dissolved by fire, and renewed, Isa. 51.6-16. Psa. 102.26. Isa. 65.17. 2 Pet. 3.7-13. Rev. 21.1. See JUDGMENT.

Creation of. See GOD CREATOR—CHRIST CREATOR—HOLY SPIRIT CREATOR.

EARTHENWARE. See POTTER.

EARTHQUAKES. Description of, Job 9.6. Psa. 18.7,15. Psa. 46.2,3. Psa. 60.2. Psa. 104.32. Isa. 13.13,14. Isa. 24.19,20. Jer. 4.24. Nah. 1.5. Zec. 14.4. At Sinai, Ex. 19.18. Psa. 68.8. Psa. 77.18. Psa. 114.4-7. Heb. 12.26.

At the destruction of Korah, Num. 16.31,32. At Gibeah, 1 Sam. 14.15. When Elijah fled from Jezebel, 1 Kin. 19.11. In Uzziah's reign, Amos 1.1. Zec. 14.5. At Christ's death, Mat. 27.51 ; and resurrection, Mat. 28.2. At Philippi, Act. 16.26. Symbolical, Rev. 6.12-14. Rev. 11.13. Rev. 16.18,20.

EAST SEA. See DEAD SEA. East wind, see WIND.

EASTER, Act. 12.4. The Greek word is *paska*, everywhere else translated *passover ;* as Mat. 26.2.

EBAL, a mountain in Samaria, on which six of the tribes stood to say Amen to the curses, Deu. 11.29. Deu. 27.4,13. Joshua's altar on, Jos. 8.30,33.

EBED-MELECH, the Ethiopian, rescues Jeremiah, Jer. 38.7-13. Prophecy respecting, Jer. 39.16-18.

EBENEZER, a name given by Samuel to a memorial stone near Mizpeh on the defeat of the Philistines, 1 Sam. 7.12. Israelites defeated at, 1 Sam. 4.1. Ark brought from, 1 Sam. 5.1.

EBER, or HEBER, a descendant of Shem, and ancestor of the Hebrews, Gen. 10.21-25. Gen. 11.14. 1 Chr. 1.19,25. Luk. 3.35. Prophecy respecting, Num. 24.24.

EBONY, Eze. 27.15.

ECONOMY. See INDUSTRY.

EDAR, TOWER OF, near Bethlehem. Jacob sojourned near, Gen. 35.21. Mic. 4.8 (*marg.*)

EDEN, LAND OF, near the *confluence* (not *source*) of the 4 rivers Euphrates, Gen. 2.10-14. See PARADISE.

——, HOUSE OF, or Beth-eden, a place in Syria, Amos 1.5.

EDOMITES, descended from Esau, Gen. 36. Dukes of, Gen. 36,9-43. Ex.15.15. 1 Chr. 1.51-54. Kings of, Gen. 36.31-39. Num. 20. 14. 1 Chr. 1.43-50. Eze. 32.29. Amos 2.1. See HADAD. Territory of, Gen. 32.3. Deu. 2.4,5,12.

Israel forbidden to hate or spoil, Deu. 2.4-6. Deu. 23.7. Refuse passage to Israel, Num. 20.18-21. Received into the congregation at the third generation, Deu. 23.8. Defeated by

Saul, 1 Sam. 14.47. Subdued by David, 2 Sam. 8.14. 1 Kin. 11.16. 1 Chr. 18.11-13. Psa. 60 (title). Psa. 108.9. Hadad, of the seed-royal, flees to Egypt, 1 Kin. 11.14-22,25.

Under a regent, 1 Kin. 22.47. Jehoshaphat defeats them, 2 Chr. 20.22. They join him in war with Moab, 2 Kin. 3.9,26. Revolt against Joram, and are defeated, 2 Kin. 8.20-22. 2 Chr. 21.8-10.

Defeated by Amaziah, 2 Kin. 14.7,10. 2 Chr. 25.11,12. Invade Judah, 2 Chr. 28.17. Aid Babylon against Israel, Eze. 35.5. Amos 1. 9-11. Obd. 11-16. Hatred of, to Israel, Psa. 137.7. Eze. 25.12-14. Eze. 35.3-10.

Towns of, see BOZRAH, ELATH, EZION-GABER, SELAH. Mountains of, see HALAK, HOR, SEIR. Wilderness of Edom, 2 Kin. 3.8. Districts and tribes of, see HORITES, TEMAN, UZ.

EDOMITES. Idumea and Esau, prophecies of, Gen. 25.23. Gen. 27.29,37-40. Num. 24. 18. Isa. 11.14. Isa. 21.11,12. Isa. 34. Isa. 63.1-4. Jer. 9.25,26. Jer. 27.1-11. Jer. 49.7-22. Lam. 4.21,22. Eze. 25.12-14. Eze. 32.29,30. Eze. 35. Eze. 36.5. Joel 3.19. Amos 1.11,12. Amos 9.12. Obd. v. 1-21. Mal. 1.2-5.

EDREI, a town of Bashan, where Joshua defeated Og, Num. 21.33-35. Deu. 1.4. Deu. 3.1-3. Given to Manasseh, Jos. 13.31.

EGLON, king of Moab, subjugates Israel; is slain by Ehud, Jud. 3.12-30.

EGYPT (Heb. *Mizraim*), called Pathros, Isa. 11.11. Rahab, Psa. 87.4. Land of Ham, Psa. 105.23. Peopled by Mizraim's descendants, Gen. 10.6,13,14. Boundaries of, Jos. 15. 4. 2 Kin. 24.7. Isa. 27.12. Eze. 29.10.

Fertility and productions of, Gen. 13.10. Num. 11.5. Isa. 19.5-9. Irrigation of, Deu. 11.10. Commerce, Gen. 37.25,36. 1 Kin. 10. 28,29. Eze. 27.7. Armies, Ex. 14.7. Isa. 31.1. The Magi; their learning, Gen. 41.8. Ex. 7.11. 1 Kin. 4.30. Act. 7.22. Priests of, Gen. 41.45. Gen. 47.22.

The king's property in the land, Gen. 47. 18-26. Embalming practised in, Gen. 50.3. Shepherds abhorred in, Gen. 46.34; and sacrifice of cattle, Ex. 8.26. People of, would not eat with Hebrews, Gen. 43.32. Not to be hated by Israelites; to be received into the congregation in the 3d generation, Deu. 23.7,8. Israelites, alliances with, forbidden, Isa. 30.2. Isa. 31.1. Isa. 36.6. Eze. 17.15. Eze. 29.6.

Relations of, with Abraham, see PHARAOH I.; with Joseph, Jacob, &c., PHARAOH II.; with Moses, &c., PHARAOH III.; with David, PHARAOH IV.; with Solomon, PHARAOH V.; with Jeroboam and Rehoboam, SHISHAK; with Hoshea, So; with Hezekiah, PHARAOH VI.; with Assyria, Josiah, Jehoahaz, PHARAOH NECHO; with Zedekiah and the Jews, PHARAOH HOPHRA. Joseph takes Christ to, Mat. 2.13-20.

Towns and districts of, Eze. 30.13-18. See ALEXANDRIA, AVEN, BAAL-ZEPHON, GOSHEN, MEMPHIS, MIGDOL, NO, NOPH, ON, PATHROS, PITHOM, RAMESES, SUCCOTH, SYENE, TAHPANES, ZOAN.

Prophecies of, Gen. 15.13,14. Isa. 19. Isa. 20.2-6. Isa. 45.14. Jer. 9.25,26. Jer. 43.8-13. Jer. 44.30. Jer. 46. Eze. c. 29-32. Joel 3.19. Zec. 10.11.

————, RIVER OF, southern boundary of Palestine (not the Nile, see NILE), Gen. 15.18. Num. 34.5. Jos. 15.4,47. 1 Kin. 8.65. 2

Kin. 24.7. Isa. 27.12. Eze. 47.19. Eze. 48.28. Called Sihor, Jos. 13.3. 1 Chr. 13.5. See SIHOR.

EHUD, a judge of Israel, slays Eglon, Jud. 3.12-30. Jud. 4.1.

EKRON, the most northern city of the Philistines, Jos. 13.3. Conquered by Judah, Jos. 15.11,45. Jud. 1.18. Given to Dan, Jos. 19.43. Possessed by the Philistines; the ark sent to Israel from, 1 Sam. 5.10. 1 Sam. 6.1-8. Baalzebub's temple in, 2 Kin. 1.2.

ELAH, 4th king of Israel, son and successor of Baasha, drunkenness and idolatry of; murdered with all his relatives, by Zimri, 1 Kin. 16.6-14. 2 Kin. 9.31.

————, VALLEY OF, David slays Goliath in, and the Israelites rout the Philistines, 1 Sam. 17.2,19. 1 Sam. 21.9.

ELAM. Elamites descended from Shem, Gen. 10.22. 1 Chr. 1.17. Chedorlaomer, king of, invades Canaan, Gen. 14.1. A province of Persia, Dan. 8.2. Eze. 4.9. Elamites in Jerusalem at Pentecost, Act. 2.9. Prophecies of, see PERSIA.

ELATH, a city of Idumea, near the Red Sea, Deu. 2.8. 1 Kin. 9.26. Taken from the Edomites by Uzziah, 2 Chr. 26.2. Taken by the Syrians, 2 Kin. 16.6.

ELDAD AND MEDAD, prophesy in the camp of Israel, Num. 11.26-29.

ELDERS, of the family, Gen. 50.7. 70 Elders of Israel, Ex. 24.1,9,14. Num. 11.16,24,25. Elders of Israel or the tribes, Ex. 3.16. Ex. 4.29. Lev. 4.15. Deu. 27.1. Deu. 31.28. Jos. 8.33. Jos. 23.2. 1 Sam. 30.26. 2 Sam. 5 3.

Of the Jews, Ezr. 6.14. Of the city, Deu. 25.7. Jud. 8.14. 1 Kin. 21.11. Of the priests, 2 Kin. 19.2. 1 Chr. 24.31. Ezr. 8.29. Jer. 19.1. Mat. 2.4. Of the Sanhedrim, see SANHEDRIM. Of the synagogue, see SYNAGOGUE. Jewish teachers or rabbis, Mar. 7.3-5.

Elders (Gr. *Presbuteros*) of the church, Act. 11.30. Act. 14.23. 1 Tim. 5.17,19. Tit. 1.5. Jas. 5.14. 1 Pet. 5.1. In Jerusalem, Act. 15.2,4,6,22,23. Act. 16.4. Act. 21.18. In Ephesus, Act. 20.17.

Elders (Gr. *Presbuterion*) of the Jews, Luk. 22.66. Act. 22.5. Of the church, translated *presbytery*, 1 Tim. 4.14. Apostles call themselves, 1 Pet. 5.1. 2 Jno. 1. 3 Jno. 1. Old Testament saints, Heb. 11.2. Symbolical, Rev. 4.4,10. Rev. 5.5-8,14. Rev. 7.11,13. Rev. 11.16. Rev. 14.3. Rev. 19.4.

ELEALEH, a town of Reuben, east of Jordan, Num. 32.3,37. Possessed by the Moabites, Isa. 15.4. Isa. 16.9.

ELEAZAR, OR ELIEZER, high-priest; Aaron's 3d son, and chief of the tribe of Levi, Ex. 6.23,25. Num. 3.2-4,32. Made priest, Ex. 28.1. Takes up the censers of Korah, &c., Num. 16.39. Succeeds Aaron as high-priest, Num. 20.26-28.

Assists Moses to number Israel, Num. 26.63. Divides Palestine with Joshua, Num. 34.17. His death, Jos. 24.33. Descendants, 1 Chr. 24.1-19.

————, son of Abinadab, set apart to keep the ark at Kirjath-jearim, 1 Sam. 7.1.

————, one of David's captains, 2 Sam. 23.9-12. 1 Chr. 11.12-14.

ELECTION. See PREDESTINATION.

EL-ELOHE-ISRAEL (God the God of Israel), the name of Jacob's altar at Salem, Gen. 33.20.

ELEPHANT. See IVORY.

ELHANAN, one of David's captains, slays a giant, 2 Sam. 21.19. 1 Chr. 20.5.

ELI, judge and high-priest. Of the line of Ithamar, 1 Sam. 1.9. 1 Chr. 24.3,6, with 1 Kin. 2.27. Blesses Hannah, 1 Sam. 1.14-17. 1 Sam. 2.20. His inefficient restraint of his sons, 1 Sam. 2.22-25,29. 1 Sam. 3.13. Is rebuked, and the extinction of his family predicted by a prophet, 1 Sam. 2.27-36 ; and by Samuel ; his submission, 1 Sam. 3. Fulfilled, 1 Kin. 2.27. Trembles for the ark ; his age and death, after being judge 40 years, 1 Sam. 4.13-18.

ELIAB, eldest son of Jesse, 1 Sam. 16.6,7. His displeasure at David, 1 Sam. 17.28,29. Called Elihu, chief of the tribe of Judah, 1 Chr. 27.18. His grand-daughter marries Rehoboam, 2 Chr. 11.18.

ELIAKIM, son of Hilkiah, overseer of Hezekiah's household ; his conference with Rab-shakeh, 2 Kin. 18.18,26. Prophecy respecting him, Isa. 22.20-25.

————. See JEHOIAKIM.

ELIAS. See ELIJAH.

ELIASHIB, a high-priest after the captivity, Neh. 3.1. Neh. 12.10. Allied to Tobiah ; gives him a chamber of the temple, Neh. 13. 4-9.

ELIEZER of Damascus, Abraham's steward, Gen. 15.2. See Gen. 24.

————, the second son of Moses, Ex. 18.4. 1 Chr. 23.15,17.

————, a prophet, predicts the destruction of Jehoshaphat's ships, 2 Chr. 20.37.

ELIHU the Buzite, his converse with Job, Job c. 32 to 37.

ELIJAH, or ELIAS, predicts a drought, 1 Kin. 17.1-7. Jas. 5.17. Is fed with ravens by the brook Cherith, 1 Kin. 17.6. Is fed by a widow; her oil and meal miraculously increased, 1 Kin. 17.9-16. Luk. 4.26. Raises a widow's son, 1 Kin. 17.17-24.

Sends Obadiah to Ahab, 1 Kin. 18.1-16. His sacrifice on Carmel, 1 Kin. 18.17-39. Commands Baal's prophets to be slain, 1 Kin. 18.40. Prays for rain, 1 Kin. 18.41-45. Jas. 5.17,18. Runs before Ahab, 1 Kin. 18.46.

Flees from Jezebel to the wilderness ; prays for death ; is fed by an angel ; and is 40 days without food, 1 Kin. 19.1-8. An earthquake, &c., at Horeb ; God commands him to anoint Hazael, Jehu, and Elisha, 1 Kin. 19.11-18. Casts his mantle on Elisha, who becomes his servant, 1 Kin. 19.19-21. 2 Kin. 3.11.

His predictions against Ahab and Jezebel, 1 Kin. 21.17-29. 2 Kin. 9.25-37. Against Ahaziah, 2 Kin. 1.2-4,16,17. His prophecy in writing against Jehoram, 2 Chr. 21.12-15. Brings fire from heaven on Ahaziah's soldiers, 2 Kin. 1.10-12. Luk. 9.54.

Divides Jordan, 2 Kin. 2.8. His translation ; unbelief of the sons of the prophets, 2 Kin. 2.1-18. His dress, &c., 2 Kin. 1.8. Character and prayerfulness, 1 Kin. 17.20-24. 1 Kin.

18.36,37. 1 Kin. 19.14. Luk. 1.17. Rom. 11.2. Jas. 5.17.

Appears in the Mount of Transfiguration, Mat. 17.3,4. Mar. 9.4. Luk. 9.30. Prophecy respecting John the Baptist under the name of, Mal. 4.5. Mat. 11.14. Mat. 17.10-12. Mar. 9.12,13. Luk. 1.17. The Jews mistake John for, Jno. 1.21-25 ; and also Jesus, Mat. 16.14.

ELIM, an encampment of the Israelites ; its wells and palm-trees, Ex. 15.27.

ELIMELECH, the husband of Naomi, Ruth 1.1-3. Ruth 4.9.

ELIPHAZ, the Temanite. His converse with Job, Job 2.11. Job c. 4, 5, 15, & 22. Commanded to offer a sacrifice, Job 42.7-9.

ELISHA, or ELISEUS. His call to follow Elijah, 1 Kin. 19.16-21. Serves Elijah ; his fidelity ; witnesses Elijah's translation ; receives a double portion of his spirit, 2 Kin. 2.1-15. 2 Kin. 3.11. Divides Jordan, 2 Kin. 2.14. Heals the waters of Jericho, 2 Kin. 2.19-22.

Children mock him, and are destroyed by bears, 2 Kin. 2.23,24. Prophesies to Jehoshaphat the defeat of Moab, 2 Kin. 3. Multiplies a widow's oil, 2 Kin. 4.1-7. Predicts a son to the Shunemite, 2 Kin. 4.8-17. Restores the Shunemite's child to life, 2 Kin. 4.18-37. 2 Kin. 8.5.

Miracle of the meal and pottage, 2 Kin. 4.38-41. Feeds 100 men with 20 loaves, 2 Kin. 4.42-44. Cures Naaman's leprosy, 2 Kin. 5.1-19. Luk. 4.27. Smites Gehazi with leprosy, 2 Kin. 5.26,27. Causes iron to swim, 2 Kin. 6.6. Discloses the King of Syria's counsel, 2 Kin. 6.12.

Prays that his servant's eyes may be opened, 2 Kin. 6.17. Smites with blindness the army sent to take him, 2 Kin. 6.18. Jehoram sends to slay him, 2 Kin. 6.31-33. Predicts plenty during the famine in Samaria, and the death of the unbelieving lord, 2 Kin. 7. And a famine of 7 years, 2 Kin. 8.1-3.

His interview with Hazael, and prediction, 2 Kin. 8.9-13. Sends a prophet to anoint Jehu king, 2 Kin. 9.1-3. Predicts to Jehoash victory over the Syrians, 2 Kin. 13.14-19. His death, 2 Kin. 13.14-20. A dead man restored to life on touching his bones, 2 Kin. 13.21.

ELISHAH, a son of Javan, Gen. 10.4. 1 Chr. 1.7. His name given to islands of the Mediterranean, Gen. 10.5. Eze. 27.7.

ELISHEBA, daughter of Amminadab, and wife of Aaron, Ex. 6.23.

ELIZABETH, wife of Zacharias. Her character, Luk. 1.5,6. Visited by Mary, her cousin ; her prophecies of Christ, Luk. 1.40-45,56. Mother of John the Baptist, Luk. 1.

ELKANAH, the father of Samuel, 1 Sam. 1.19,20.

ELKOSH, the birthplace of Nahum, Nah. 1.1.

ELLASAR, Arioch king of, invades Canaan, Gen. 14.1.

ELM, Hos. 4.13. Translated oak, Gen. 35.4. Jud. 6.11.

ELNATHAN, an officer of Jehoiakim, Jer. 36.12. Brings Urijah from Egypt, Jer. 26.22,23. Opposes the burning of Jeremiah's roll, Jer. 36.25.

ELOI (my God), Mar. 15.34.

ELON, a judge of Israel, Jud. 12.11,12.

ELUL, 6th month (September). Wall of Jerusalem finished in, Neh. 6.15. Temple built in, Hag. 1.14,15.

ELYMAS, or BARJESUS, the sorcerer. Struck with blindness by Paul, Act. 13.6-11.

EMBALMING. See BURIAL.

EMBROIDERY, or NEEDLE-WORK. On the tabernacle curtains, Ex. 26.36. Ex. 27.16. On the high-priest's coat and girdle, Ex. 28.4,39. On the garments of men, Jud. 5.30. Eze. 26.16. Of women, Psa. 45.14. Eze. 16.10,13,18. Aholiab's skill in, Ex. 35.35. See TAPESTRY.

EMERALD. Eze. 27.16. Eze. 28.13. Rev. 4.3. In the high-priest's breastplate, Ex. 28.18. Symbolical, Rev. 21.19.

EMIM. Giants who occupied the country afterwards possessed by the Moabites, Gen. 14.5. Deu. 2.10,11.

EMMAUS, a village near Jerusalem. Jesus appears to two disciples in, Luk. 24.13-33.

ENCHANTMENT. See SORCERY.

ENDOR, a town of Manasseh, west of Jordan, Jos. 17.11. Deborah and Barak's victory at, Jud. 4 with Psa. 83.10. Saul consults a witch at, 1 Sam. 28.7-25.

ENEAS, a paralytic at Lydda, cured by Peter, Act. 9.32-35.

EN-EGLAIM, a town of Moab, Eze. 47.10.

EN-GEDI, a town of Judah, Jos. 15.62. Near the Dead Sea, Eze. 47.10. Called Hazezon-tamar, and originally inhabited by Amorites, Gen. 14.7 with 2 Chr. 20.2. Vineyards of, Song 1.14.

——, wilderness of. David and his army take refuge in, from Saul, 1 Sam. 23.29. 1 Sam. 24. David finds Saul in a cave of, 1 Sam. 24.3.

ENGRAVING. Of metals, Ex. 32.4. 1 Kin. 7.31. 2 Chr. 2.7,14. Of gems or seals, Ex. 28.9-11,21,36. Ex.39.6,14,30. Zec. 3.9.

EN-HAKKORE (the well of him that cried), the well provided by God in answer to Samson's prayer, Jud. 15.18,19.

ENGINES for casting stones, &c., 2 Chr. 26.15.

ENGRAFTING. Illustrative, Rom. 11.17-24. Jas. 1.21.

ENOCH, son of Jared, and father of Methuselah. His life, piety, and translation, Gen. 5.21-24. Heb. 11.5. Prophecy by, Jude 14,15.

——, son of Cain. A city called after him, Gen. 4.17.

ENON, a place near Salem, at which John baptized, Jno. 3.23.

ENQUIRING OF GOD. By Rebekah, Gen. 25.22. By Israelites, Jud. 1.1. 1 Sam. 10.22. By David, 2 Sam. 2.1. 2 Sam. 5.19,23. 2 Sam. 21.1. 1 Chr. 14.10,14.
Of the high-priest. By Israelites, Jud. 20.18-27. By Saul, 1 Sam. 14.19,37-41. By David, 1 Sam. 22.10. 1 Sam. 30.8. See URIM. In the temple, 2 Sam. 16.23. 1 Chr. 21.30. Psa. 27.4. 2 Kin. 16.15.
Of the prophets, Eze. 14.7. By Saul, 1 Sam.

9.6-9. By David, 1 Sam. 23.2,4 with 1 Sam. 22.5. By Jehoshaphat, 1 Kin. 22.7. 2 Kin. 3.11. By Ben-hadad, 2 Kin. 8.8. By Josiah, 2 Kin. 22.13. By Zedekiah, Jer. 21.1,2. Jer. 37.7. By elders of Israel, Eze. 20.1.

EN-ROGEL, or FULLER'S FOUNTAIN, near Jerusalem, on the boundary between Judah and Benjamin, Jos. 15.7. Jos. 18.16. 2 Sam. 17.17. Adonijah's coronation-feast at, 1 Kin. 1.9.

ENSIGNS. See STANDARDS.

ENVY AND JEALOUSY. Ex. 20.17. Thou shalt not covet.
Psa. 37.1. Fret not thyself because of evil-doers, neither be thou envious against the workers of iniquity. 7. Fret not thyself be-cause of him who prospereth in his way, because of the man who bringeth wicked devices to pass. Pro. 24.19.
Psa. 49.16. Be not thou afraid when one is made rich.
Psa. 73.3. I was envious at the foolish, when I saw the prosperity of the wicked.
Psa. 112.10. The wicked shall see it, and be grieved ; he shall gnash with his teeth, and melt away.
Pro. 3.31. Envy thou not the oppressor.
Pro. 14.30. Envy is the rottenness of the bones.
Pro. 23.17. Let not thine heart envy sin-ners.
Pro. 24.1. Be not thou envious against evil men.
Pro. 27.4. Who is able to stand before envy?
Ecc. 4.4. All travail, and every right work, that for this a man is envied of his neighbour. 5. The fool foldeth his hands together, and eateth his own flesh.
Song 8.6. Jealousy is cruel as the grave : the coals thereof are coals of fire.
Isa. 26.11. They shall see, and be ashamed for their envy at the people.
Eze. 35.11. I will even do according to thine envy, which thou hast used out of thy hatred against them.
Rom. 13.13. Not in strife and envying.
1 Cor. 3.3. Whereas there is among you envying, and strife, and divisions, are ye not carnal, and walk as men?
1 Cor. 13.4. Charity envieth not.
2 Cor. 12.20. Lest there be debates, envy-ings.
Gal. 5.19. The works of the flesh are mani-fest. 20. Variance, emulations, 21. Envyings, they which do such things shall not inherit the kingdom of God. 26. Let us not be de-sirous of vain glory, provoking one another, envying one another.
Phil. 1.15. Some indeed preach Christ even of envy and strife.
1 Tim. 6.4. Doting about questions and strifes of words, whereof cometh envy.
Tit. 3.3. Living in malice and envy.
Jas. 3.14. If ye have bitter envying and strife in your hearts, glory not, and lie not against the truth. 16. Where envying and strife is, there is confusion and every evil work.
Jas. 4.5. The spirit that dwelleth in us lusteth to envy.
Jas. 5.9. Grudge not one against another, brethren, lest ye be condemned : behold, the judge standeth before the door.
1 Pet. 2.1. Laying aside all malice, and all guile, and hypocrisies, and envies.

ENVY AND JEALOUSY, EXAMPLES OF. Cain, Gen. 4.4-8. 1 Jno. 3.12. Sarah, Gen. 16.5,6. Gen. 21.9,10. Philistines, Gen. 26.14. Rachel, Gen. 30.1. Leah, Gen. 30.15. Laban's sons, Gen. 31.1. Joseph's brethren, Gen. 37.4-11,19,20. Act. 7.9. Miriam and Aaron, Num. 12.1-10. Korah, &c., Num. 16.3. Psa. 106.16-18. Saul, 1 Sam. 18.8,9,29. 1 Sam. 20.31. Darius' princes, Dan. 6.4. Priests, &c., Mat. 27.18. Jno. 11.47. Jews, Act. 13.45.

EPÆNETUS, an early convert of Achaia, Rom. 16.5.

EPAPHRAS, a minister of the Colossian church, Col. 1.7,8. Col. 4.12,13. Imprisoned at Rome with Paul, Philm. 23.

EPAPHRODITUS, a companion and fellow-labourer of Paul. Sent by the Philippians to minister to him when imprisoned at Rome, Phil. 2.25-30. Phil. 4.18.

EPHAH, a tribe of Midianites, Gen. 25.4. Isa. 60.6.

———, a dry measure, containing about 9 gals., equal to the bath for liquids, Eze. 45.11. Ex. 16.36. Isa. 5.10. Symbolical, Zec. 5.6-8.

EPHESUS, capital of Ionia. Paul visits, Act. 18. 19-21. Aquila and Priscilla reside in, and instruct Apollos, Act. 18.18-28. Paul baptizes John's disciples ; resides two years at ; his success ; persecution by Demetrius and worshippers of Diana, Act. 19. 1 Cor. 15.32. 1 Cor. 16.8.

Sceva's sons attempt to expel a demon, Act. 19.13-16. Elders of the church addressed by Paul at Miletus, Act. 20.16-38. Timothy left at, 1 Tim. 1.3. Tychicus sent to, 2 Tim. 4.12. Onesiphorus ministers to Paul at, 2 Tim. 1.18. Epistle to, by Christ, Rev. 1.11. Rev. 2.1-7. Paul's epistle to the Ephesians.

EPHOD. Worn by the high-priest ; a richly coloured linen garment, with gold clasps and precious stones, Ex. 25.7. Ex. 28.4-14. Breast-plate fastened to it, Ex. 28.15-30. Robe of, made of blue, and ornamented with gold bells and pomegranates, Ex. 28.31-35. Ex. 29.5. Ex. 35.9. Ex. 39.2-26. Lev. 8.7. 1 Sam. 14.3. 1 Sam. 21.9. 1 Sam. 23.6,9. 1 Sam. 30.7.

Worn by priests ; of linen. Called coats, Ex. 28.40. Ex. 29.8. Ex. 39.27. Ex. 40.14. Lev. 8.13. Lev. 10.5. Called ephods, 1 Sam. 2.28. 1 Sam. 22.18. Worn by Samuel, 1 Sam. 2.18. By David before the ark, 2 Sam. 6.14.

EPHRAIM, second son of Joseph, adopted by Jacob, Gen. 41.52. Gen. 48.5. Blessed by Jacob before Manasseh, Gen. 48.14-20. His children, Num. 26.35-37. 1 Chr. 7.20-27. Mourns for his sons' death, 1 Chr. 7.21,22.

———, TRIBE OF. Numbered at Sinai, Num. 1.33. And in the plains of Moab, Num. 26.37. Encamped west of the tabernacle, Num. 2.18. Led the 3d division of Israel, Num. 2.24. Num. 10.22. Blessing of Moses on, Deu. 33.13-17.

Inheritance of, Jos. 16.5-9. Jos. 17.10,15-19. 1 Chr. 7.28,29. Did not drive out the Canaanites, Jos. 16.10. Jud. 1.29. 1 Kin. 9.16. Assisted by Manasseh ; take Bethel, Jud. 1.22-25. The tabernacle in their city, Shiloh, Jos. 18.1. Their jealousy of Gideon, Jud. 8.1.

Defeated by Jephthah and the Gileadites, Jud. 12.1-6. Adhere to Ish-bosheth, 2 Sam. 2.9. One of Jeroboam's calves set up in Bethel, 1 Kin. 12. 29. Some of, joined Judah under Asa, 2 Chr. 15.9. Kept Hezekiah's passover, 2 Chr. 30.18 ; and destroyed idols, 2 Chr. 31.1.

Dwelt in Jerusalem after the captivity, 1 Chr. 9.3 with Neh. 11. Was the leading tribe in the kingdom of Israel, Isa. 11.13. Jer. 7.15. Eze. 37.16,19.

For things common to the tribes, see ISRAEL, TRIBES OF.

EPHRAIM, a name for the ten tribes, 2 Chr. 17.2. 2 Chr. 25.6,7. Prophecies of, see ISRAELITES (the Ten Tribes).

———, a town north of Jerusalem. Absalom resides near, 2 Sam. 13.23. Taken by Abijah, 2 Chr. 13.19. Jesus retires to, Jno. 11.54.

———, MOUNT, a range of hills in Central Palestine, Jos. 17.15-18. Joshua buried in, Jud. 2.9. Residence of Micah, Jud. c. 17 & 18. Jonathan, &c., defeat the Philistines near, 1 Sam. 14.22-27. Residence of Sheba, 2 Sam. 20.21. Shechem in, see SAMARIA.

———, WOOD OF, east of Jordan, 2 Sam. 18.6-8 with 2 Sam. 17.24, and Jud. 12.4-6.

EPHRATAH and EPHRATH. See BETH-LEHEM.

EPHRON, the Hittite. Sells a field containing the cave of Machpelah to Abraham, Gen. 23.8-20.

EPHRON, MOUNT, between Judah and Benjamin, Jos. 15.9. See 2 Chr. 13.19.

EPICUREANS. Athenian philosophers, dispute with Paul, Act. 17.18-20.

EPISTLES. See LETTERS.

ER, eldest son of Judah, died for his wickedness, Gen. 38.3,7. Gen. 46.12.

ERASTUS, chamberlain at Corinth, and a Christian convert, Rom. 16.23. 2 Tim. 4.20. An assistant of Paul, sent to Macedonia with Timothy, Act. 19.22.

ESARHADDON, king of Assyria, succeeds Sennacherib, 2 Kin. 19.37. Isa. 37.38. Colonises Samaria, &c., Ezr. 4.2,10.

ESAU, or EDOM, eldest son of Isaac and Rebekah. His birth, Gen. 25.19-26. 1 Chr. 1.34. His character and occupation, Gen. 25.27. Sells his birthright, Gen. 25.29-34. Mal. 1.2. Rom. 9.13. Heb. 12.16. His marriage, Gen. 26.34,35. Enmity to Jacob for obtaining the blessing, Gen. 27.30-41.

Blessed by his father, Gen. 27.39,40. Heb. 11.20. Second marriage, Gen. 28.6-9. Reconciliation with Jacob, Gen. 33. His prosperity, Gen. 33.1. Gen. 36.6,7. Buries his father, Gen. 35.29. His wives and descendants, Gen. 36. 1 Chr. 1.35-57. Prophecies of, see EDOMITES.

ESDRAELON, PLAIN OF. See MEGIDDO.

ESEK (contention), a well dug by Isaac, Gen. 26.20.

ESHCOL, an Amoritish chief allied with Abraham, Gen. 14.13,24.

———, VALLEY or BROOK OF. Grapes brought from, by the 12 spies, Num. 13.23,24. Num. 32.9. Deu. 1.24,25.

ESHTAOL, a town in the plain of Judah, Jos. 15.33. Inhabited by Danites, Jos. 19.41. Jud. 13.2,8,11. Samson dwelt near, Jud. 13.25. Was buried near, Jud. 16.31.

ESTHER, or HADASSAH, daughter of Abihail, the uncle of Mordecai. Brought up by her cousin, Mordecai, Est. 2.7,15. Married to King Ahasuerus, Est. 2. Acquaints the king with Mordecai's discovery of a plot against him, Est. 2.22. Accuses Haman to the king, and defeats his plot against the Jews, Est. c. 4-9.

ETAM, a rock where Samson was taken and delivered to the Philistines, Jud. 15. 8-13.

ETERNAL LIFE. See SALVATION—SOUL IMMORTAL.

—— PUNISHMENT. See HELL—JUDGMENT—SIN, PUNISHMENT OF.

ETHAN, the Ezrahite, of the tribe of Judah, 1 Chr. 2.6. His wisdom, 1 Kin. 4.31. Author of Psalm 89, see title.

——, a Levite. See JEDUTHUN.

ETHANIM (month of streaming rivers), the 7th month (October). Feast of atonement and tabernacles held in, Lev. 23.24,27. Jubilee proclaimed in, Lev. 25.9. Dedication of the temple in, 1 Kin. 8.2. Altar rebuilt and offerings renewed in, Ezr. 3.1,6.

ETHIOPIA (Heb. Cush). People of, descended from Cush, Gen. 10.6. 1 Chr. 1.9. Territory and boundaries, Gen. 2.13. 2 Chr. 21.16. Est. 1.1. Isa. 18.1. Eze. 29.10. Eze. 30.5. Complexion of its people, Jer. 13.23. Their warlike character, Jer. 46.9.

Merchandise of, Isa. 45.14. Precious stones of, Job 28.19. Moses' wife from, Num. 12.1. Part of Shishak's army from, 2 Chr. 12.3. Zerah, king of, defeated by Asa, 2 Chr. 14.9-15. 2 Chr. 16.8. Tirhakah, king of, attacks Assyria, 2 Kin. 19.9.

Ebed-melech the Ethiopian's kindness to Jeremiah, Jer. 38.7-13. Jer. 39.15-18. Candace, queen of; the Ethiopian eunuch's conversion, Act. 8.27-39. Prophecies of, Psa. 68.31. Psa. 87.4. Isa. 20.2-6. Isa. 45.14. Eze. 30.4-9. Dan. 11.43. Hab. 3.7. Zeph. 2.12.

EUBULUS, a Roman Christian, 2 Tim. 4.21.

EUNICE, Timothy's mother. Her piety, 2 Tim. 1.5.

EUODIAS, a female Philippian disciple, admonished by Paul, Phi. 4.2.

EUPHRATES. Called the River, 1 Kin. 4.21. Ezr. 4.10,16. The fourth river of Eden, Gen. 2.14. Boundary of Israel by prophecy, Gen. 15.18. Ex. 23.31. Deu. 1.7. Deu. 11.24. Jos. 1.4. Of the Reubenites, 1 Chr. 5.9. Of David's kingdom, 2 Sam. 8.3. 1 Chr. 18.3. Of Solomon's, 1 Kin. 4.21. Of Egypt, 2 Kin. 24.7. Jer. 46.2-10.

Jeremiah buries his girdle in, Jer. 13.1-7. And casts his book into, Jer. 51.63,64. Symbolical, Isa. 8.7. Rev. 9.14. Rev. 16.12.

EUROCLYDON, name of a wind, Act. 27.14.

EUTYCHUS, a youth at Troas, who was restored to life by Paul, Act. 20.9-11.

EVANGELIST, Eph. 4.11. 2 Tim. 4.5. Philip, an evangelist, Act. 21.8. The verb euangelizo is translated, to preach the gospel,

or bring glad tidings, Rom. 10.15. Shew glad tidings, Luk. 8.1. Declare glad tidings, Act. 13.32. The noun euangelion is rendered gospel, Mat. 4.23.

EVE. Her creation, Gen. 1.26-28. Gen. 2.21-24. 1 Tim. 2.13. Named by Adam (Isha) woman, Gen. 2.23; and Eve (Living), Gen. 3.20. Temptation and fall, Gen. 3. 2 Cor. 11.3. 1 Tim. 2.14. Clothing of, Gen. 3.7,21.

Curse pronounced on, Gen. 3.16. Promise made to, of Messiah, Gen. 3.15. Birth of Cain and Abel, Gen. 4.1,2. Of Seth, Gen. 4.25. Children of, Gen. 5.4.

EVIL COMPANY AND EXAMPLE. Gen. 19.15. Arise, lest thou be consumed in the iniquity of the city.

Gen. 49.6. Come not thou into their secret; unto their assembly, mine honour, be not thou united.

Ex. 23.2. Thou shalt not follow a multitude to do evil. 32. Make no covenant with them, nor with their gods. 33. They shall not dwell in thy land, lest they make thee sin against me: for if thou serve their gods, it will surely be a snare unto thee. Ex. 34.12-15. Deu. 7.2-4. Jos. 23.6-13.

Lev. 18.3. After the doings of the land of Egypt, wherein ye dwelt, shall ye not do; and after the doings of the land of Canaan, whither I bring you, shall ye not do; neither shall ye walk in their ordinances. Lev. 20.23.

Num. 16.26. Depart, I pray you, from the tents of these wicked men, and touch nothing of their's, lest ye be consumed in all their sins. v. 21-26.

Num. 33.55. If ye will not drive out the inhabitants of the land from before you; then it shall come to pass, that those which ye let remain of them shall be pricks in your eyes, and thorns in your sides. Jud. 2.1-3.

Deu. 12.30. Be not snared by following them, after that they be destroyed from before thee; and that thou enquire not after their gods, saying, How did these nations serve their gods? even so will I do likewise.

2 Sam. 23.6. The sons of Belial shall be all of them as thorns thrust away, because they cannot be taken with hands: 7. But the man that shall touch them must be fenced with iron and the staff of a spear.

2 Chr. 19.2. Shouldest thou help the ungodly, and love them that hate the Lord?

Ezr. 9.14. Should we again break thy commandments, and join in affinity with the people of these abominations? wouldest not thou be angry with us till thou hadst consumed us.

Psa. 1.1. Blessed is the man that walketh not in the counsel of the ungodly, nor standeth in the way of sinners, nor sitteth in the seat of the scornful.

Psa. 6.8. Depart from me, all ye workers of iniquity.

Psa. 15.4. In whose eyes a vile person is contemned.

Psa. 26.4. I have not sat with vain persons, neither will I go in with dissemblers. 5. I have hated the congregation of evil doers; and will not sit with the wicked. 9. Gather not my soul with sinners, nor my life with bloody men.

Psa. 28.3. Draw me not away with the wicked, and with the workers of iniquity.

Psa. 31.6. I have hated them that regard lying vanities.

Psa. 50.18. When thou sawest a thief, then thou consentedst with him, and hast been partaker with adulterers.

Psa. 101.4. A froward heart shall depart from me: I will not know a wicked *person*. 7. He that worketh deceit shall not dwell within my house: he that telleth lies shall not tarry in my sight.

Psa. 106.34. They did not destroy the nations, concerning whom the Lord commanded them: 35. But were mingled among the heathen, and learned their works.

Psa. 119.115. Depart from me, ye evildoers: for I will keep the commandments of my God.

Psa. 120.5. Woe is me, that I sojourn in Mesech, *that* I dwell in the tents of Kedar! 6. My soul hath long dwelt with him that hateth peace.

Psa. 139.19. Depart from me therefore, ye bloody men. 21. Do not I hate them, O Lord, that hate thee? and am not I grieved with those that rise up against thee? 22. I hate them with perfect hatred; I count them mine enemies.

Psa. 141.4. Incline not my heart to *any* evil thing, to practise wicked works with men that work iniquity: and let me not eat of their dainties.

Pro. 1.10. My son, if sinners entice thee, consent thou not. 11. If they say, Come with us. 14. Cast in thy lot among us: let us all have one purse: 15. My son, walk not thou in the way with them; refrain thy foot from their path.

Pro. 2.11. Understanding shall keep thee; 12. To deliver thee from the way of the evil *man*, from the man that speaketh froward things. 16. To deliver thee from the strange woman, *even* from the stranger *which* flattereth with her words. 19. None that go unto her return again, neither take they hold of the paths of life.

Pro. 4.14. Enter not into the path of the wicked, and go not in the way of evil *men*. 15. Avoid it, pass not by it, turn from it, and pass away.

Pro. 5.8. Remove thy way far from her, and come nigh the door of her house.

Pro. 9.6. Forsake the foolish, and live.

Pro. 12.11. He that followeth vain *persons is* void of understanding. 26. The way of the wicked seduceth them.

Pro. 13.20. A companion of fools shall be destroyed.

Pro. 14.7. Go from the presence of a foolish man, when thou perceivest not *in him* the lips of knowledge.

Pro. 16.29. A violent man enticeth his neighbour, and leadeth him into the way that *is* not good.

Pro. 17.12. Let a bear robbed of her whelps meet a man, rather than a fool in his folly.

Pro. 20.19. Meddle not with him that flattereth.

Pro. 22.5. Thorns *and* snares *are* in the way of the froward: he that doth keep his soul shall be far from them. 10. Cast out the scorner, and contention shall go out. 24. Make no friendship with an angry man; and with a furious man thou shalt not go: 25. Lest thou learn his ways, and get a snare to thy soul.

Pro. 23.6. Eat thou not the bread of *him that hath* an evil eye, neither desire thou his dainty meats. 20. Be not among winebibbers; among riotous eaters of flesh.

Pro. 24.1. Be not thou envious against evil men, neither desire to be with them.

Pro. 28.7. He that is a companion of riotous *men* shameth his father. 19. He that followeth after vain *persons* shall have poverty enough.

Pro. 29.16. When the wicked are multiplied, transgression increaseth. 24. Whoso is partner with a thief hateth his own soul: he heareth cursing, and bewrayeth *it* not.

Ecc. 9.18. One sinner destroyeth much good.

Isa. 1.23. Thy princes *are* companions of thieves.

Isa. 8.11. Instructed me that I should not walk in the way of this people. 12. Say ye not, A confederacy, to all *them to* whom this people shall say, A confederacy.

Jer. 2.25. There is no hope: no; for I have loved strangers, and after them will I go.

Jer. 9.2. Oh that I had in the wilderness a lodging-place of wayfaring men; that I might leave my people, and go from them! for they *be* all adulterers, an assembly of treacherous men.

Jer. 15.17. I sat not in the assembly of the mockers, nor rejoiced; I sat alone because of thy hand.

Jer. 51.6. Flee out of the midst of Babylon, and deliver every man his soul: be not cut off in her iniquity. 45. Go ye out of the midst of her, and deliver ye every man his soul from the fierce anger of the Lord.

Hos. 4.17. Ephraim *is* joined to idols: let him alone.

Hos. 7.8. He hath mixed himself among the people. 9. Strangers have devoured his strength, and he knoweth *it* not.

Mic. 6.16. Ye walk in their counsels; that I should make thee a desolation.

Mat. 24.12. Because iniquity shall abound, the love of many shall wax cold.

Rom. 16.17. Mark them which cause divisions and offences contrary to the doctrine which ye have learned; and avoid them. 18. By good words and fair speeches deceive the hearts of the simple.

1 Cor. 5.6. A little leaven leaveneth the whole lump. 9. Not to company with fornicators. 10. Yet not altogether with the fornicators of this world, or with the covetous, or extortioners, or with idolaters; for then must ye needs go out of the world. 11. If any man that is called a brother be a fornicator, or covetous, or an idolater, or a railer, or a drunkard, or an extortioner, with such an one no not to eat. Gal. 5.9.

1 Cor. 15.33. Be not deceived: evil communications corrupt good manners.

2 Cor. 6.14. Be ye not unequally yoked together with unbelievers: for what fellowship hath righteousness with unrighteousness? and what communion hath light with darkness? 15. And what concord hath Christ with Belial? or what part hath he that believeth with an infidel? 17. Wherefore, come out from among them, and be ye separate, saith the Lord, and touch not the unclean *thing*.

Eph. 5.7. Be not ye therefore partakers with them. 11. Have no fellowship with the unfruitful works of darkness, but rather reprove *them*.

2 The. 3.6. Withdraw yourselves from every brother that walketh disorderly.

1 Tim. 5.22. Neither be partaker of other men's sins.

1 Tim. 6.5. Men of corrupt minds, and destitute of the truth, supposing that gain is godliness : from such withdraw thyself.

2 Tim. 3.4. Heady, high-minded, lovers of pleasures more than lovers of God ; 5. Having a form of godliness, but denying the power thereof : from such turn away.

2 Pet. 2.7. Just Lot, vexed with the filthy conversation of the wicked : 8. (For that righteous man dwelling among them, in seeing and hearing, vexed *his* righteous soul from day to day with *their* unlawful deeds :) 18. They allure through the lusts of the flesh, *through much* wantonness, those that were clean escaped from them who live in error.

2 Jno. 10. If there come any unto you, and bring not this doctrine, receive him not into *your* house, neither bid him God speed : 11. For he that biddeth him God speed is partaker of his evil deeds.

Rev. 2.2. Thou canst not bear them which are evil : and thou hast tried them which say they are apostles, and are not, and hast found them liars.

Rev. 18.4. Come out of her, my people, that ye be not partakers of her sins, and that ye receive not of her plagues.

See CHURCH-DISCIPLINE. — MARRIAGE, IRRELIGIOUS.—MINISTERS UNFAITHFUL.

EVIL COMPANY, DANGER OF. EXAMPLES. Sodomites, Gen. 13.13. Gen. 19.9,15. Shechemites, Gen. 34.1. Moabites, Num. 25. Psa. 106.28. Delilah, Jud. 16.1-21. Rehoboam's counsellors, 1 Kin. 12.8. Manasseh, 2 Kin. 21.9. Ahaziah, 2 Chr. 20.37. 2 Chr. 22.3-5. Solomon's wives, Neh. 13.26. Amaziah, 2 Chr. 25.7-9.

EVIL-MERODACH, son of Nebuchadnezzar, and king of Babylon. His kind treatment of King Jehoiachin, 2 Kin. 25.27-30. Jer. 52.31-34.

EVIL-SPEAKING. See SPEAKING EVIL.

EXAMPLE. See LIKENESS TO CHRIST— SAINT'S EXAMPLE—EVIL COMPANY.

EXCHANGERS. See MONEY-CHANGERS.

EXCOMMUNICATION, Gen. 17.14. Ex. 12.15. Lev. 22.3. Num. 15.31. Separation of Jews from heathen, Neh. 13.1-3. Neh. 9.2. Ezr. 4.3. Ezr. 10.11. Putting out of the synagogue, Jno. 9.22,34,35. Jno. 16.2. Jno. 12.42. See CHURCH-DISCIPLINE.

EXECUTIONER, Mar. 6.27. Gen. 37.36 (*marg.*) Jer. 39.9 (*marg.*) Dan. 2.14 (*marg.*)

EXORCISM, practised by the Jews, Mat. 12.28. Sceva's sons punished in attempting, Act. 19.13-16. See DEMONS.

EYELIDS, or EYES. Painting of, Eze. 23.40.

EZEKIEL, a priest ; with the Jewish captives by the Chebar ; the time of his prophesying, Eze. 1.1-3. His wife's death, Eze. 24.18. His popularity, Eze. 33.31,32.

EZEL, STONE OF. A waymark where David and Jonathan met, 1 Sam. 20.19.

EZION-GABER, a city of Idumea, on the Red Sea, one of the encampments of the Israelites, Num. 33.35. Deu. 2.8. Solomon's navy at, 1 Kin. 9.26. Jehoshaphat's navy at, 1 Kin. 22.48.

EZRA, a priest of the line of Eleazar, Ezr. 7.1-5. A scribe, Ezr. 7.6,10,21. Neh. 12.26. Calls for a fast, Ezr. 8.21-23. Returns from Babylon with Jews, bearing a commission from Artaxerxes, Ezr. 7. Ezr. 8. Fasts, and exhorts the people to put away their heathen wives, Ezr. 9. Ezr. 10.1-17. Teaches the law, Ezr. 7.10,25. Reads the law at the feast of tabernacles ; his prayer, Neh. 8. Assists at the dedication of the wall, Neh. 12.36.

F

FAIR-HAVENS, a harbour of Crete, Act. 27.8.

FAIRS. See MARKETS.

FAITH. Gen. 15.1. Fear not, Abram : I *am* thy shield, *and* thy exceeding great reward.

Ex. 3.12. Certainly I will be with thee ; and this *shall be* a token unto thee, ye shall serve God upon this mountain.

Ex. 4.12. Now therefore go, and I will be with thy mouth, and teach thee what thou shalt say. *v.* 11.

Ex. 14.13. Moses said unto the people, Fear ye not, stand still, and see the salvation of the Lord.

Deu. 20.1. When thou goest out to battle against thine enemies, and seest horses, and chariots, *and* a people more than thou, be not afraid of them : for the Lord thy God *is* with thee, which brought thee up out of the land of Egypt. Num. 21.34. Deu. 1.21-31. Deu. 3.2,22. Deu. 7.17-21. Deu. 31.23. Jos. 10.25. Jud. 6.14-16. 2 Kin. 19.6,7. 2 Chr. 20.15,17.

Deu. 31.8. The Lord, he *it is* that doth go before thee ; he will be with thee, he will not fail thee, neither forsake thee : fear not, neither be dismayed. *v.* 6-8.

Jos. 1.9. Have not I commanded thee? Be strong, and of a good courage ; be not afraid, neither be thou dismayed : for the Lord thy God *is* with thee whithersoever thou goest. *v.* 5-9.

2 Chr. 15.7. Let not your hands be weak : for your work shall be rewarded.

2 Chr. 16.9. The eyes of the Lord run to and fro throughout the whole earth, to shew himself strong in the behalf of *them* whose heart *is* perfect toward him.

2 Chr. 20.20. Believe in the Lord your God, so shall ye be established ; believe his prophets, so shall ye prosper.

Neh. 4.14. Be not ye afraid of them : remember the Lord, *which is* great and terrible.

Job 35.14. Although thou sayest thou shalt not see him, *yet* judgment *is* before him ; therefore trust thou in him.

Psa. 4.5. Put your trust in the Lord.

Psa. 5.11. Let all those that put their trust in thee rejoice : let them ever shout for joy, because thou defendest them.

Psa. 9.9. A refuge in times of trouble. 10. And they that know thy name will put their trust in thee : for thou, Lord, hast not forsaken them that seek thee

Psa. 17.7. O thou that savest by thy right hand them which put their trust in thee from those that rise up against them.

Psa. 18.30. He is a buckler to all them that trust in him. 31. For who is God, save the Lord? or who is a rock, save our God? 2 Sam. 22.31,32.

Psa. 25.10. All the paths of the Lord are mercy and truth unto such as keep his covenant and his testimonies.

Psa. 27.14. Wait on the Lord: be of good courage, and he shall strengthen thine heart.

Psa. 31.19. How great is thy goodness, which thou hast laid up for them that fear thee; which thou hast wrought for them that trust in thee before the sons of men! 24. Be of good courage, and he shall strengthen your heart, all ye that hope in the Lord.

Psa. 32.10. He that trusteth in the Lord, mercy shall compass him about.

Psa. 33.18. The eye of the Lord is upon them that fear him, upon them that hope in his mercy; 19. To deliver their soul from death.

Psa. 34.8. O taste and see that the Lord is good: blessed is the man that trusteth in him. 22. The Lord redeemeth the soul of his servants: and none of them that trust in him shall be desolate. v. 1-8. Ps. 2.12.

Psa. 36.7. How excellent is thy lovingkindness, O God! therefore the children of men put their trust under the shadow of thy wings.

Psa. 37.3. Trust in the Lord, and do good; so shalt thou dwell in the land, and verily thou shalt be fed. 5. Commit thy way unto the Lord; trust also in him, and he shall bring it to pass. 7. Rest in the Lord, and wait patiently for him. 39. The salvation of the righteous is of the Lord: he is their strength in the time of trouble. 40. The Lord shall help them, and deliver them: he shall deliver them from the wicked, and save them, because they trust in him.

Psa. 40.4. Blessed is that man that maketh the Lord his trust.

Psa. 55.22. Cast thy burden upon the Lord, and he shall sustain thee: he shall never suffer the righteous to be moved.

Psa. 62.8. Trust in him at all times; ye people, pour out your heart before him: God is a refuge for us.

Psa. 64.10. The righteous shall be glad in the Lord, and shall trust in him.

Psa. 78.7. That they might set their hope in God.

Psa. 84.5. Blessed is the man whose strength is in thee. 12. O Lord of hosts, blessed is the man that trusteth in thee.

Psa. 91.1. He that dwelleth in the secret place of the most High shall abide under the shadow of the Almighty. 9. Because thou hast made the Lord, which is my refuge, even the most High, thy habitation; 10. There shall no evil befall thee.

Psa. 112.7. He shall not be afraid of evil tidings: his heart is fixed, trusting in the Lord. 8. His heart is established, he shall not be afraid.

Psa. 115.9. O Israel, trust thou in the Lord: he is their help and their shield. 11. Ye that fear the Lord, trust in the Lord: he is their help and their shield.

Psa. 118.8. It is better to trust in the Lord than to put confidence in man. 9. It is better to trust in the Lord than to put confidence in princes.

Psa. 125.1. They that trust in the Lord shall be as mount Zion, which cannot be removed, but abideth for ever.

Psa. 130.7. Let Israel hope in the Lord: for with the Lord there is mercy, with him is plenteous redemption. 8. And he shall redeem Israel from all his iniquities. Psa. 131.3.

Psa. 146.5. Happy is he that hath the God of Jacob for his help, whose hope is in the Lord his God.

Psa. 147.11. The Lord taketh pleasure in them that fear him, in those that hope in his mercy.

Pro. 1.33. Whoso hearkeneth unto me shall dwell safely, and shall be quiet from fear of evil.

Pro. 3.5. Trust in the Lord with all thine heart; and lean not unto thine own understanding. 6. In all thy ways acknowledge him, and he shall direct thy paths. 24. When thou liest down, thou shalt not be afraid: yea, thou shalt lie down, and thy sleep shall be sweet. 25. Be not afraid of sudden fear, neither of the desolation of the wicked, when it cometh. 26. For the Lord shall be thy confidence, and shall keep thy foot from being taken.

Pro. 14.26. In the fear of the Lord is strong confidence.

Pro. 16.3. Commit thy works unto the Lord, and thy thoughts shall be established. 20. Whoso trusteth in the Lord, happy is he.

Pro. 18.10. The name of the Lord is a strong tower: the righteous runneth into it, and is safe.

Pro. 22.19. That thy trust may be in the Lord, I have made known to thee this day.

Pro. 23.18. Thine expectation shall not be cut off.

Pro. 28.25. He that putteth his trust in the Lord shall be made fat.

Pro. 29.25. Whoso putteth his trust in the Lord shall be safe.

Pro. 30.5. He is a shield unto them that put their trust in him.

Ecc. 11.1. Cast thy bread upon the waters: for thou shalt find it after many days.

Isa. 8.13. Sanctify the Lord of hosts himself; and let him be your fear, and let him be your dread. 14. And he shall be for a sanctuary.

Isa. 10.20. The remnant of Israel shall stay upon the Lord, the Holy One of Israel, in truth.

Isa. 14.32. The Lord hath founded Zion, and the poor of his people shall trust in it.

Isa. 26.3. Thou wilt keep him in perfect peace, whose mind is stayed on thee: because he trusteth in thee. 4. Trust ye in the Lord for ever: for in the Lord Jehovah is everlasting strength. 20. Come, my people, enter thou into thy chambers, and shut thy doors about thee: hide thyself as it were for a little moment, until the indignation be overpast.

Isa. 27.5. Let him take hold of my strength, that he may make peace with me; and he shall make peace with me.

Isa. 30.15. Thus saith the Lord God, the Holy One of Israel; In returning and rest shall ye be saved; in quietness and in confidence shall be your strength.

Isa. 35.4. Be strong, fear not: behold, your God will come *with* vengeance, *even* God *with* a recompence; he will come and save you.

Isa. 41.10. Fear thou not; for I *am* with thee: be not dismayed; for I *am* thy God: I will strengthen thee; yea, I will help thee; yea, I will uphold thee with the right hand of my righteousness. 13. I the Lord thy God will hold thy right hand, saying unto thee, Fear not; I will help thee. 14. Fear not, thou worm Jacob, *and* ye men of Israel; I will help thee, saith the Lord, and thy redeemer, the Holy One of Israel.

Isa. 43.1. Thus saith the Lord that created thee, O Jacob, and he that formed thee, O Israel, Fear not: for I have redeemed thee, I have called *thee* by thy name; thou *art* mine. 2. When thou passest through the waters, I *will be* with thee; and through the rivers, they shall not overflow thee: when thou walkest through the fire, thou shalt not be burned; neither shall the flame kindle upon thee. 5. Fear not: for I *am* with thee: I will bring thy seed from the east, and gather thee from the west; 10. Know and believe me, and understand that I *am* he.

Isa. 44.2. Thus saith the Lord that made thee, and formed thee from the womb, *which* will help thee; Fear not, O Jacob, my servant; and thou, Jesurun, whom I have chosen. 8. Fear ye not, neither be afraid: have not I told thee from that time, and have declared *it?* ye *are* even my witnesses. Is there a God beside me?

Isa. 45.22. Look unto me, and be ye saved, all the ends of the earth: for I *am* God, and *there is* none else. 24. Surely, shall *one* say, In the Lord have I righteousness and strength: *even* to him shall *men* come; and all that are incensed against him shall be ashamed. 25. In the Lord shall all the seed of Israel be justified, and shall glory.

Isa. 49.15. Can a woman forget her sucking child, that she should not have compassion on the son of her womb? yea, they may forget, yet will I not forget thee.

Isa. 50.10. Who *is* among you that feareth the Lord, that obeyeth the voice of his servant, that walketh *in* darkness, and hath no light? let him trust in the name of the Lord, and stay upon his God.

Isa. 51.12. I, *even* I, *am* he that comforteth you: who *art* thou, that thou shouldest be afraid of a man *that* shall die, and of the son of man *which* shall be made *as* grass; 13. And forgettest the Lord thy maker, that hath stretched forth the heavens, and laid the foundations of the earth; and hast feared continually every day because of the fury of the oppressor, as if he were ready to destroy?

Isa. 55.3. Incline your ear, ahd come unto me: hear, and your soul shall live; and I will make an everlasting covenant with you, *even* the sure mercies of David.

Isa. 56.6. The sons of the stranger, that join themselves to the Lord, to serve him, and to love the name of the Lord, to be his servants, every one that taketh hold of my covenant; 7. Even them will I bring to my holy mountain, and make them joyful in my house of prayer: their burnt-offerings and their sacrifices *shall be* accepted.

Isa. 57.13. He that putteth his trust in me shall possess the land, and shall inherit my holy mountain.

Isa. 64.4. Neither hath the eye seen, O God, beside thee, *what* he hath prepared for him that waiteth for him. 5. Thou meetest him that rejoiceth and worketh righteousness, *those that* remember thee in thy ways: behold, thou art wroth; for we have sinned: in those is continuance, and we shall be saved.

Jer. 1.7. Say not, I *am* a child: for thou shalt go to all that I shall send thee, and whatsoever I command thee thou shalt speak. 8. Be not afraid of their faces: for I *am* with thee to deliver thee, saith the Lord. 19. They shall fight against thee; but they shall not prevail against thee; for I *am* with thee, saith the Lord, to deliver thee.

Jer. 17.7. Blessed *is* the man that trusteth in the Lord, and whose hope the Lord is. 8. For he shall be as a tree planted by the waters.

Jer. 39.18. I will surely deliver thee, and thou shalt not fall by the sword, but thy life shall be for a prey unto thee: because thou hast put thy trust in me, saith the Lord.

Jer. 42.11. Be not afraid of the king of Babylon, of whom ye are afraid; be not afraid of him, saith the Lord: for I *am* with you to save you, and to deliver you from his hand.

Jer. 49.11. Leave thy fatherless children, I will preserve *them* alive; and let thy widows trust in me.

Joel 2.21. Fear not, O land; be glad and rejoice: for the Lord will do great things.

Joel 3.16. The Lord *will be* the hope of his people, and the strength of the children of Israel.

Nah. 1.7. The Lord *is* good, a stronghold in the day of trouble; and he knoweth them that trust in him.

Hab. 2.3. Though it tarry, wait for it; because it will surely come, it will not tarry. 4. The just shall live by his faith.

Zeph. 3.16. Fear thou not: *and to* Zion, Let not thine hands be slack. 17. The Lord thy God in the midst of thee *is* mighty; he will save, he will rejoice over thee with joy; he will rest in his love, he will joy over thee with singing.

Zec. 4.10. For who hath despised the day of small things? for they shall rejoice, and shall see the plummet in the hand of Zerubbabel *with* those seven; they *are* the eyes of the Lord, which run to and fro through the whole earth.

Zec. 8.9. Let your hands be strong, ye that hear in these days these words by the mouth of the prophets.

Zec. 9.12. Turn you to the strong hold, ye prisoners of hope: even to-day do I declare *that* I will render double unto thee.

Mat. 6.25. Take no thought for your life, what ye shall eat, or what ye shall drink; nor yet for your body, what ye shall put on. 32. For your heavenly Father knoweth that ye have need of all these things. 33. But seek ye first the kingdom of God, and his righteousness; and all these things shall be added unto you.

Mat. 10.29. Are not two sparrows sold for a farthing? and one of them shall not fall on the ground without your Father. 30. But the very hairs of your head are all numbered.

31. Fear ye not therefore, ye are of more value than many sparrows. Luk. 12.6,7.

Mar. 1.15. Repent ye, and believe the gospel.

Luk. 1.45. Blessed is she that believed : for there shall be a performance of those things which were told her from the Lord.

Luk. 8.21. My mother and my brethren are these which hear the word of God, and do it. Luk. 11.27,28.

Luk. 12.32. Fear not, little flock ; for it is your Father's good pleasure to give you the kingdom.

Luk. 17.5. Lord, increase our faith.

Luk. 21.28. When these things begin to come to pass, then look up, and lift up your heads ; for your redemption draweth nigh.

Jno. 3.33. He that hath received his testimony hath set to his seal that God is true.

Act. 13.48. As many as were ordained to eternal life believed.

Act. 26.18. Inheritance among them which are sanctified by faith that is in me.

Rom. 11.20. Because of unbelief they were broken off, and thou standest by faith. 23. They also, if they abide not still in unbelief, shall be graffed in.

Rom. 15.13. The God of hope fill you with all joy and peace in believing, that ye may abound in hope.

1 Cor. 1.21. It pleased God by the foolishness of preaching to save them that believe.

1 Cor. 2.5. Your faith should not stand in the wisdom of men, but in the power of God.

Gal. 3.6. Abraham believed God, and it was accounted to him for righteousness. 7. Know ye therefore that they which are of faith, the same are the children of Abraham.

Eph. 2.8. By grace are ye saved through faith ; and that not of yourselves : it is the gift of God.

Eph. 6.16. The shield of faith, wherewith ye shall be able to quench all the fiery darts of the wicked.

Col. 1.23. Continue in the faith grounded and settled, and be not moved away from the hope of the gospel.

Col. 2.12. Buried with him in baptism, wherein also ye are risen with him through the faith of the operation of God.

1 The. 2.13. Ye received it not as the word of men, but as it is in truth, the word of God, which effectually worketh also in you that believe.

1 The. 5.8. Putting on the breastplate of faith and love.

2 The. 2.13. Salvation through sanctification of the Spirit and belief of the truth.

1 Tim. 1.5. The end of the commandment is charity out of a pure heart, and of a good conscience, and of faith unfeigned.

1 Tim. 1.19. Holding faith, and a good conscience ; which some having put away, concerning faith have made shipwreck.

1 Tim. 2.15. She shall be saved in childbearing, if they continue in faith and charity and holiness.

1 Tim. 4.10. The living God, who is the Saviour of all men, specially of those that believe.

1 Tim. 6.11. Follow after righteousness, godliness, faith. 12. Fight the good fight of faith, lay hold on eternal life, whereunto thou

art also called, and hast professed a good profession. 17. Charge them that are rich in this world, that they be not high-minded, nor trust in uncertain riches, but in the living God.

2 Tim. 4.7. I have fought a good fight, I have finished my course, I have kept the faith : 8. Henceforth there is laid up for me a crown of righteousness, which the Lord, the righteous judge, shall give me at that day : and not to me only, but unto all them also that love his appearing.

Heb. 4.3. We which have believed do enter into rest.

Heb. 6.1. The foundation of repentance from dead works, and of faith toward God. 7. The earth which drinketh in the rain that cometh oft upon it, and bringeth forth herbs meet for them by whom it is dressed, receiveth blessing from God. 12. Be not slothful, but followers of them who through faith and patience inherit the promises. 18. Who have fled for refuge to lay hold upon the hope set before us.

Heb. 10.35. Cast not away therefore your confidence, which hath great recompence of reward. 38. The just shall live by faith : but if any man draw back, my soul shall have no pleasure in him. 39. But we are not of them who draw back unto perdition ; but of them that believe to the saving of the soul.

Heb. 11.1. Faith is the substance of things hoped for, the evidence of things not seen. 2. For by it the elders obtained a good report. 4. By faith Abel offered unto God a more excellent sacrifice than Cain, by which he obtained witness that he was righteous. 5. By faith Enoch was translated that he should not see death. 6. Without faith it is impossible to please him : for he that cometh to God must believe that he is, and that he is a rewarder of them that diligently seek him.

Heb. 11.7. By faith Noah, being warned of God of things not seen as yet, moved with fear, prepared an ark to the saving of his house : by the which he condemned the world, and became heir of the righteousness which is by faith. 27. By faith he forsook Egypt, not fearing the wrath of the king : for he endured, as seeing him who is invisible. 33. Who through faith subdued kingdoms, wrought righteousness, obtained promises, stopped the mouths of lions, 34. Quenched the violence of fire, escaped the edge of the sword, out of weakness were made strong, waxed valiant in fight, turned to flight the armies of the aliens.

Heb. 12.12. Lift up the hands which hang down, and the feeble knees ; 13. And make straight paths for your feet, lest that which is lame be turned out of the way ; but let it rather be healed.

Heb. 13.5. Let your conversation be without covetousness ; and be content with such things as ye have : for he hath said, I will never leave thee, nor forsake thee. 6. So that we may boldly say, The Lord is my helper, and I will not fear what man shall do unto me.

Jas. 2.5. Hath not God chosen the poor of this world rich in faith, and heirs of the kingdom which he hath promised to them that love him? 19. Thou believest that there is one God : thou doest well.

1 Pet. 1.5. Who are kept by the power of God through faith unto salvation ready to be

revealed in the last time. 7. The trial of your faith, being much more precious than of gold that perisheth, though it be tried with fire, might be found unto praise and honour and glory at the appearing of Jesus Christ. 9. The end of your faith, *even* the salvation of *your* souls. 21. Who by him do believe in God, that raised him up from the dead, and gave him glory; that your faith and hope might be in God.

1 Pet. 4.19. Let them that suffer according to the will of God commit the keeping of their souls *to him* in well-doing, as unto a faithful Creator.

1 Pet. 5.7. Casting all your care upon him; for he careth for you.

1 Jno. 2.14. Ye are strong, and the word of God abideth in you, and ye have overcome the wicked one.

1 Jno. 3.21. Beloved, if our heart condemn us not, *then* have we confidence toward God.

1 Jno. 5.4. Whatsoever is born of God overcometh the world: and this is the victory that overcometh the world, *even* our faith.

Rev. 22.7. Blessed *is* he that keepeth the sayings of the prophecy of this book.

FAITH EXEMPLIFIED, Gen. 16.13. Thou God seest me: for she said, Have I also here looked after him that seeth me?

Gen. 24.7. The Lord God of heaven, which took me from my father's house, and from the land of my kindred, and which spake unto me, and that sware unto me, saying, Unto thy seed will I give this land. 40. The Lord, before whom I walk, will send his angel with thee, and prosper thy way.

Gen. 28.20. If God will be with me, and will keep me in this way that I go, and will give me bread to eat, and raiment to put on, 21. So that I come again to my father's house in peace ; then shall the Lord be my God.

Gen. 48.21. I die: but God shall be with you, and bring you again unto the land of your fathers. Gen. 50.24.

Gen. 49.18. I have waited for thy salvation, O Lord. 25. By the God of thy father, who shall help thee ; and by the Almighty, who shall bless thee with blessings.

Ex. 15.2. The Lord *is* my strength and song, and he is become my salvation : he *is* my God, and I will prepare him an habitation ; my father's God, and I will exalt him. 16. By the greatness of thine arm they shall be *as* still as a stone ; till thy people pass over, O Lord, till the people pass over, *which* thou hast purchased. 17. Thou shalt bring them in, and plant them in the mountain of thine inheritance. *v.* 1-19.

Ex. 18.11. Now I know that the Lord *is* greater than all gods : for in the thing wherein they dealt proudly *he was* above them.

Num. 10.29. We are journeying unto the place of which the Lord said, I will give it you : come thou with us, and we will do thee good : for the Lord hath spoken good concerning Israel.

Num. 14.8. If the Lord delight in us, then he will bring us into this land, and give it us. 9. Neither fear ye the people of the land ; for they *are* bread for us : their defence is departed from them, and the Lord *is* with us : fear them not.

Jos. 14.12. If so be the Lord *will be* with me, then I shall be able to drive them out, as the Lord said.

Ruth 2.12. A full reward be given thee of the Lord God of Israel, under whose wings thou art come to trust.

1 Sam. 14.6. It may be that the Lord will work for us : for *there* is no restraint to the Lord to save by many or by few.

1 Sam. 17.47. This assembly shall know that the Lord saveth not with sword and spear : for the battle *is* the Lord's, and he will give you into our hands.

1 Sam. 25.29. The soul of my lord shall be bound in the bundle of life with the Lord thy God.

2 Sam. 7.28. O Lord God, thou *art* that God, and thy words be true, and thou hast promised this goodness unto thy servant.

2 Sam. 15.25. Carry back the ark of God into the city : if I shall find favour in the eyes of the Lord, he will bring me again, and shew me *both* it, and his habitation.

2 Sam. 23.5. He hath made with me an everlasting covenant, ordered in all *things*, and sure.

1 Chr. 28.20. The Lord God, *even* my God, *will be* with thee ; he will not fail thee, nor forsake thee, until thou hast finished all the work.

2 Chr. 13.12. God himself *is* with us for *our* captain, and his priests with sounding trumpets.

2 Chr. 14.11. Lord, *it is* nothing with thee to help, whether with many, or with them that have no power: help us, O Lord our God ; for we rest on thee, and in thy name we go against this multitude. *v.* 15.

2 Chr. 20.12. We have no might against this great company that cometh against us ; neither know we what to do : but our eyes *are* upon thee.

2 Chr. 32.7. *There be* more with us than with him : 8. With him *is* an arm of flesh ; but with us *is* the Lord our God to help us, and to fight our battles.

Ezr. 8.22. The hand of our God *is* upon all them for good that seek him.

Neh. 1.10. These *are* thy servants and thy people, whom thou hast redeemed by thy great power, and by thy strong hand. *v.* 8-10.

Neh. 2.20. The God of heaven, he will prosper us ; therefore we his servants will arise and build.

Neh. 4.20. Our God shall fight for us.

Job 5.8. I would seek unto God, and unto God would I commit my cause : 9. Which doeth great things and unsearchable.

Job 10.12. Thou hast granted me life and favour, and thy visitation hath preserved my spirit.

Job 13.15. Though he slay me, yet will I trust in him : 16. He also *shall be* my salvation.

Job 14.15. Thou wilt have a desire to the work of thine hands.

Job. 19.25. I know *that* my redeemer liveth, and *that* he shall stand at the latter *day* upon the earth : 26. And *though* after my skin *worms* destroy this *body*, yet in my flesh shall I see God : 27. Whom I shall see for myself, and mine eyes shall behold, and not another; *though* my reins be consumed within me. 28. The root of the matter is found in me.

Job 23.6. Will he plead against me with *his* great power? No ; but he would put *strength* in me.

Psa. 3.3. Thou, O Lord, *art* a shield for me; my glory, and the lifter up of mine head. 5. I laid me down and slept; I awaked; for the Lord sustained me. 6. I will not be afraid of ten thousands of people, that have set *themselves* against me.

Psa. 4.3. The Lord hath set apart him that is godly for himself: the Lord will hear when I call unto him. 8. I will both lay me down in peace, and sleep: for thou, Lord, only makest me dwell in safety.

Psa. 6.8. The Lord hath heard the voice of my weeping. 9. The Lord hath heard my supplication; the Lord will receive my prayer.

Psa. 7.1. O Lord my God, in thee do I put my trust: 10. My defence *is* of God, which saveth the upright in heart.

Psa. 9.3. When mine enemies are turned back, they shall fall and perish at thy presence. 4. For thou hast maintained my right and my cause.

Psa. 11.1. In the Lord put I my trust: how say ye to my soul, Flee *as* a bird to your mountain?

Psa. 13.5. I have trusted in thy mercy; my heart shall rejoice in thy salvation.

Psa. 16.1. Preserve me, O God: for in thee do I put my trust. 2. O *my* soul, thou hast said unto the Lord, Thou *art* my Lord. 5. The Lord *is* the portion of mine inheritance and of my cup: thou maintainest my lot. 8. I have set the Lord always before me: because *he* is at my right hand, I shall not be moved. 11. Thou wilt shew me the path of life: in thy presence *is* fulness of joy.

Psa. 17.6. I have called upon thee, for thou wilt hear me, O God.

Psa. 18.1. I will love thee, O Lord, my strength. 2. The Lord *is* my rock, and my fortress, and my deliverer; my God, my strength, in whom I will trust; 'my buckler, and the horn of my salvation, *and* my high tower. 3. I will call upon the Lord, *who is worthy* to be praised: so shall I be saved from mine enemies. 18. They prevented me in the day of my calamity: but the Lord was my stay. 28. Thou wilt light my candle: the Lord my God will enlighten my darkness. 29. For by thee I have run through a troop; and by my God have I leaped over a wall. 2 Sam. 22.2-5.

Psa. 20.5. In the name of our God we will set up *our* banners: 6. Now know I that the Lord saveth his anointed; he will hear him from his holy heaven with the saving strength of his right hand. 7. Some *trust* in chariots, and some in horses: but we will remember the name of the Lord our God.

Psa. 21.7. The king trusteth in the Lord, and through the mercy of the most High he shall not be moved.

Psa. 22.4. Our fathers trusted in thee: they trusted, and thou didst deliver them. 5. They cried unto thee, and were delivered: they trusted in thee, and were not confounded.

Psa. 23.1. The Lord *is* my shepherd; I shall not want. *v.* 1-6.

Psa. 25.1. Unto thee, O Lord, do I lift up my soul. 2. O my God, I trust in thee: let me not be ashamed. 5. Lead me in thy truth, and teach me: for thou *art* the God of my salvation; on thee do I wait all the day. 15. Mine eyes *are* ever toward the Lord; for he shall pluck my feet out of the net. 20. O keep my soul, and deliver me: let me not be ashamed; for I put my trust in thee.

Psa. 26.1. I have trusted also in the Lord; *therefore* I shall not slide. 12. My foot standeth in an even place: in the congregations will I bless the Lord.

Psa. 27.1. The Lord *is* my light and my salvation; whom shall I fear? the Lord *is* the strength of my life; of whom shall I be afraid? 5. In the time of trouble he shall hide me in his pavilion: in the secret of his tabernacle shall he hide me; he shall set me up upon a rock. 6. And now shall mine head be lifted up above mine enemies round about me: 10. When my father and my mother forsake me, then the Lord will take me up.

Psa. 28.7. The Lord *is* my strength and my shield; my heart trusted in him, and I am helped.

Psa. 31.1. In thee, O Lord, do I put my trust; let me never be ashamed. 3. Thou *art* my rock and my fortress; therefore for thy name's 'sake lead me, and guide me. 4. Pull me out of the net that they have laid privily for me: for thou *art* my strength. 5. Into thine hand I commit my spirit: thou hast redeemed me, O Lord God of truth. 6. I trust in the Lord. 14. I trusted in thee, O Lord: I said, Thou *art* my God. 15. My times *are* in thy hand.

Psa. 32.7. Thou *art* my hiding-place; thou shalt preserve me from trouble; thou shalt compass me about with songs of deliverance.

Psa. 33.20. Our soul waiteth for the Lord, he is our help and our shield. 21. Our heart shall rejoice in him, because we have trusted in his holy name. 22. Let thy mercy, O Lord, be upon us, according as we hope in thee.

Psa. 35.10. All my bones shall say, Lord, who *is* like unto thee, which deliverest the poor from him that is too strong for him.

Psa. 38.9. Lord, all my desire *is* before thee; and my groaning is not hid from thee. 15. In thee, O Lord, do I hope: thou wilt hear, O Lord my God.

Psa. 39.7. Lord, what wait I for? my hope *is* in thee.

Psa. 40.17. I *am* poor and needy; *yet* the Lord thinketh upon me: thou *art* my help and my deliverer.

Psa. 41.12. Thou upholdest me in mine integrity, and settest me before thy face for ever.

Psa. 42.6. O my God, my soul is cast down within me: therefore will I remember thee. 8. *Yet* the Lord will command his lovingkindness in the daytime, and in the night his song *shall be* with me, *and* my prayer unto the God of my life.

Psa. 43.5. Why art thou cast down, O my soul? and why art thou disquieted within me? hope in God: for I shall yet praise him, *who* is the health of my countenance, and my God. Psa. 42.5.

Psa. 44.5. Through thee will we push down our enemies: through thy name will we tread them under that rise up against us. 8. In God we boast all the day long, and praise thy name for ever.

Psa. 46.1. God *is* our refuge and strength, a very present help in trouble. 2. Therefore will not we fear, though the earth be removed, and though the mountains be carried into the midst of the sea; 3. *Though* the waters thereof roar *and* be troubled, *though* the mountains shake with the swelling thereof. 5. God *is* in the midst of her; she shall not be moved: God shall help her, *and that* right early. 7. The Lord of hosts *is* with us; the God of Jacob *is* our refuge.

Psa. 47.3. He shall subdue the people under us, and the nations under our feet. 4. He shall choose our inheritance for us.

Psa. 48.8. As we have heard, so have we seen in the city of the Lord of hosts, in the city of our God: God will establish it for ever. 14. This God *is* our God for ever and ever: he will be our guide *even* unto death.

Psa. 52.8. I trust in the mercy of God for ever and ever.

Psa. 54.4. Behold, God *is* mine helper: the Lord *is* with them that uphold my soul.

Psa. 55.16. I will call upon God; and the Lord shall save me. 17. Evening and morning, and at noon, will I pray, and cry aloud: and he shall hear my voice.

Psa. 56.3. What time I am afraid, I will trust in thee. 4. In God I will praise his word, in God I have put my trust; I will not fear what flesh can do unto me. 8. Thou tellest my wanderings: put thou my tears into thy bottle: *are they* not in thy book? 9. When I cry *unto thee*, then shall mine enemies turn back: this I know; for God *is* for me. *v.* 11. Psa. 55.23.

Psa. 57.1. My soul trusteth in thee: yea, in the shadow of thy wings will I make my refuge, until *these* calamities be overpast. 2. I will cry unto God most high; unto God that performeth *all things* for me. 3. He shall send from heaven, and save me *from* the reproach of him that would swallow me up. God shall send forth his mercy and his truth.

Psa. 59.9. *Because of* his strength will I wait upon thee: for God *is* my defence. 10. The God of my mercy shall prevent me: God shall let me see *my desire* upon mine enemies. 17. Unto thee, O my strength, will I sing: for God *is* my defence, *and* the God of my mercy.

Psa. 60.9. Who will bring me *into* the strong city? who will lead me into Edom? 10. *Wilt* not thou, O God, *which* hadst cast us off? and *thou*, O God, *which* didst not go out with our armies? 12. Through God we shall do valiantly: for he *it is that* shall tread down our enemies. Psa. 108.10-13.

Psa. 61.2. From the end of the earth will I cry unto thee, when my heart is overwhelmed: lead me to the rock *that* is higher than I. 4. I will abide in thy tabernacle for ever: I will trust in the covert of thy wings. 6. Thou wilt prolong the king's life: *and* his years as many generations. 7. He shall abide before God for ever.

Psa. 62.1. Truly my soul waiteth upon God: from him *cometh* my salvation. 5. My soul, wait thou only upon God; for my expectation *is* from him. 6. He only *is* my rock and my salvation: *he is* my defence; I shall not be moved. 7. In God *is* my salvation and my glory: the rock of my strength, *and* my refuge, *is* in God.

Psa. 63.6. I remember thee upon my bed, *and* meditate on thee in the *night* watches. 7. Because thou hast been my help, therefore in the shadow of thy wings will I rejoice.

Psa. 66.9. Which holdeth our soul in life, and suffereth not our feet to be moved.

Psa. 67.6. God, *even* our own God, shall bless us.

Psa. 69.19. Thou hast known my reproach, and my shame, and my dishonour: mine adversaries *are* all before thee. 35. God will save Zion, and will build the cities of Judah: that they may dwell there, and have it in possession. 36. The seed also of his servants shall inherit it: and *they* that love his name shall dwell therein.

Psa. 70.5. Make haste unto me, O God: thou *art* my help and my deliverer.

Psa. 71.1. In thee, O Lord, do I put my trust: let me never be put to confusion. 3. Be thou my strong habitation, whereunto I may continually resort: thou hast given commandment to save me; for thou *art* my rock and my fortress. 5. Thou *art* my hope, O Lord God: *thou art* my trust from my youth. 6. By thee have I been holden up from the womb: 7. I am as a wonder unto many; but thou *art* my strong refuge. 14. I will hope continually, and will yet praise thee more and more.

Psa. 71.16. I will go in the strength of the Lord God: I will make mention of thy righteousness, *even* of thine only. 20. *Thou*, which hast shewed me great and sore troubles, shalt quicken me again, and shalt bring me up again from the depths of the earth. 21. Thou shalt increase my greatness, and comfort me on every side.

Psa. 73.23. I *am* continually with thee: thou hast holden *me* by my right hand. 24. Thou shalt guide me with thy counsel, and afterward receive me *to* glory. 26. My flesh and my heart faileth: *but* God *is* the strength of my heart, and my portion for ever. 28. *It is* good for me to draw near to God: I have put my trust in the Lord God.

Psa. 74.12. God *is* my King of old, working salvation in the midst of the earth.

Psa. 77.10. *I will remember* the years of the right hand of the most High. 11. I will remember the works of the Lord: surely I will remember thy wonders of old. 12. I will meditate also of all thy work, and talk of thy doings.

Psa. 86.2. O thou my God, save thy servant that trusteth in thee. 7. In the day of my trouble I will call upon thee: for thou wilt answer me.

Psa. 89.18. For the Lord *is* our defence; and the Holy One of Israel *is* our king. 26. Thou *art* my father, my God, and the rock of my salvation.

Psa. 90.1. Lord, thou hast been our dwelling-place in all generations.

Psa. 91.2. *He is* my refuge and my fortress: my God; in him will I trust.

Psa. 92.10. My horn shalt thou exalt like *the horn of* an unicorn: I shall be anointed with fresh oil. 15. The Lord *is* upright: *he is* my rock, and *there is* no unrighteousness in him.

Psa. 94.17. Unless the Lord *had been* my help, my soul had almost dwelt in silence. 18. When I said, My foot slippeth; thy mercy, O Lord, held me up. 22. The Lord is my defence; and my God *is* the rock of my refuge.

Psa. 102.13. Thou shalt arise, *and* have mercy upon Zion: for the time to favour her, yea, the set time, is come.

Psa. 115.12. The Lord hath been mindful of us: he will bless *us*; he will bless the house of Israel; he will bless the house of Aaron. 13. He will bless them that fear the Lord, *both* small and great. 14. The Lord shall increase you more and more, you and your children.

Psa. 116.7. Return unto thy rest, O my soul; for the Lord hath dealt bountifully with thee.

Psa. 118.6. The Lord *is* on my side; I will not fear: what can man do unto me? 7. The Lord taketh my part with them that help me: therefore shall I see *my desire* upon them that hate me. 10. All nations compassed me about: but in the name of the Lord will I destroy them. 14. The Lord *is* my strength and song, and is become my salvation. 17. I shall not die, but live, and declare the works of the Lord.

Psa. 119.42. I have wherewith to answer him that reproacheth me: for I trust in thy word. 43. And take not the word of truth utterly out of my mouth; for I have hoped in thy judgments. 57. *Thou art* my portion, O Lord. 74. I have hoped in thy word. 81. My soul fainteth for thy salvation: *but* I hope in thy word. 114. Thou *art* my hiding-place and my shield: I hope in thy word. 151. Thou *art* near, O Lord; and all thy commandments *are* truth. 166. Lord, I have hoped for thy salvation.

Psa. 121.2. My help *cometh* from the Lord, which made heaven and earth. Psa. 124.8.

Psa. 130.5. I wait for the Lord, my soul doth wait, and in his word do I hope. 6. My soul *waiteth* for the Lord more than they that watch for the morning.

Psa. 138.7. Though I walk in the midst of trouble, thou wilt revive me: thou shalt stretch forth thine hand against the wrath of mine enemies, and thy right hand shall save me. 8. The Lord will perfect *that which* concerneth me: thy mercy, O Lord, *endureth* for ever.

Psa. 140.6. I said unto the Lord, Thou *art* my God: hear the voice of my supplications, O Lord. 7. O God the Lord, the strength of my salvation, thou hast covered my head in the day of battle. 12. I know that the Lord will maintain the cause of the afflicted, *and* the right of the poor.

Psa. 141.8. Mine eyes *are* unto thee, O God the Lord: in thee is my trust.

Psa. 142.3. When my spirit was overwhelmed within me, then thou knewest my path. 5. Thou *art* my refuge *and* my portion in the land of the living.

Psa. 143.8. In thee do I trust: cause me to know the way wherein I should walk; for I lift up my soul unto thee. 9. I flee unto thee to hide me.

Psa. 144.2. My goodness, and my fortress; my high tower, and my deliverer; my shield, and *he* in whom I trust; who subdueth my people under me. 10. *It is he* that giveth salvation unto kings: who delivereth David his servant from the hurtful sword. Isa. 17.13,14.

Isa. 8.10. Take counsel together, and it shall come to nought; speak the word, and it shall not stand: for God *is* with us. 17. I will wait upon the Lord, that hideth his face from the house of Jacob, and I will look for him.

Isa. 12.2. Behold, God *is* my salvation; I will trust, and not be afraid: for the Lord Jehovah *is* my strength and *my* song; he also is become my salvation.

Isa. 25.9. Lo, this *is* our God; we have waited for him, and he will save us: this *is* the Lord; we have waited for him, we will be glad and rejoice in his salvation.

Isa. 26.1. We have a strong city; salvation will *God* appoint *for* walls and bulwarks. 8. In the way of thy judgments, O Lord, have we waited for thee; the desire of *our* soul *is* to thy name, and to the remembrance of thee.

Isa. 33.2. O Lord, be gracious unto us; we have waited for thee. 22. The Lord *is* our judge, the Lord *is* our lawgiver, the Lord *is* our king; he will save us.

Isa. 38.16. O Lord, by these *things men* live, and in all these *things is* the life of my spirit: so wilt thou recover me, and make me to live.

Isa. 63.16. Doubtless thou *art* our father, though Abraham be ignorant of us, and Israel acknowledge us not: thou, O Lord, *art* our father, our redeemer. 19. We are *thine*.

Isa. 64.8. Now, O Lord, thou *art* our father; we *are* the clay, and thou our potter; and we all *are* the work of thy hand.

Jer. 10.23. O Lord, I know that the way of man *is* not in himself: *it is* not in man that walketh to direct his steps.

Jer. 14.9. Thou, O Lord, *art* in the midst of us, and we are called by thy name; leave us not. 22. *Art* not thou he, O Lord our God? therefore we will wait upon thee: for thou hast made all these *things*.

Jer. 16.19. O Lord, my strength, and my fortress, and my refuge in the day of affliction.

Jer. 17.12. A glorious high throne from the beginning *is* the place of our sanctuary. 17. Thou *art* my hope in the day of evil.

Jer. 20.11. The Lord *is* with me as a mighty terrible one: therefore my persecutors shall stumble, and they shall not prevail.

Lam. 3.24. The Lord *is* my portion, saith my soul; therefore will I hope in him. *v.* 25-32.

Dan. 3.17. Our God whom we serve is able to deliver us from the burning fiery furnace, and he will deliver *us* out of thine hand, O king.

Dan. 6.16. Thy God whom thou servest continually, he will deliver thee.

Jon. 2.2. I cried by reason of mine affliction unto the Lord, and he heard me: out of the belly of hell cried I, *and* thou heardest my voice. *v.* 3-9.

Mic. 7.7. I will look unto the Lord; I will wait for the God of my salvation: my God will hear me. 8. Rejoice not against me, O mine enemy: when I fall, I shall arise; when I sit in darkness, the Lord *shall be* a light unto me. 9. I will bear the indignation of the Lord, because I have sinned against him, until he plead my cause, and execute judgment for me: he will bring me forth to the light, *and* I shall behold his righteousness. 20. Thou wilt perform the truth to Jacob, *and* the mercy to Abraham, which thou hast sworn unto our fathers from the days of old.

Hab. 3.17. Although the fig-tree shall not blossom, neither *shall* fruit *be* in the vines; the labour of the olive shall fail, and the fields shall yield no meat; the flock shall be cut off from the fold, and *there shall be* no herd in the stalls : 18. Yet I will rejoice in the Lord, I will joy in the God of my salvation. 19. The Lord God *is* my strength, and he will make my feet like hinds' *feet*, and he will make me to walk upon mine high places.

Zeph. 3.12. An afflicted and poor people, and they shall trust in the name of the Lord.

Luk. 1.38. Be it unto me according to thy word.

Act. 24.14. So worship I the God of my fathers, believing all things which are written in the law and in the prophets : 15. And have hope toward God, that there shall be a resurrection of the dead, both of the just and unjust.

Act. 27.25. ' I believe God, that it shall be even as it was told me.

Rom. 8.18. I reckon that the sufferings of this present time *are* not worthy *to be compared* with the glory which shall be revealed in us. 38. I am persuaded, that neither death, nor life, nor angels, nor principalities, nor powers, nor things present, nor things to come, 39. Nor height, nor depth, nor any other creature, shall be able to separate us from the love of God, which is in Christ Jesus our Lord.

Rom. 15.29. ↘I am sure that, when I come unto you, I shall come in the fulness of the blessing of the gospel of Christ.

2 Cor. 1.10. Who delivered us from so great a death, and doth deliver : in whom we trust that he will yet deliver *us;*

2 Cor. 4.8. *We are* troubled on every side, yet not distressed ; *we are* perplexed, but not in despair ; 9. Persecuted, but not forsaken ; cast down, but not destroyed. 13. We having the same spirit of faith, according as it is written, I believed, and therefore have I spoken ; we also believe, and therefore speak. 16. For which cause we faint not ; but though our outward man perish, yet the inward *man* is renewed day by day.

2 Cor. 4.17. Our light affliction, which is but for a moment, worketh for us a far more exceeding *and* eternal weight of glory ; 18. While we look not at the things which are seen, but at the things which are not seen.

2 Cor. 5.7. We walk by faith, not by sight.

1 Tim. 4.10. We both labour and suffer reproach, because we trust in the living God, who is the Saviour of all men, specially of those that believe.

2 Pet. 3.13. We, according to his promise, look for new heavens and a new earth, wherein dwelleth righteousness.

1 Jno. 4.16. We have known and believed the love that God hath to us. God is love.

FAITH, Examples of. Abraham, Gen. 12.1-4. Gen. 15.5,6. Gen. 22.1-10. Rom. 4.18-21. Heb. 11.8-19. Jacob, Heb. 11.21. Joseph, Gen. 50.20,24. Heb. 11.22. Jochebed, Ex. 2.2. Heb. 11.23. Pharaoh's servants, Ex. 9.20. Moses, Ex. 17.15. Heb. 11.24-29.

Caleb, Num. 13.30. Rahab, Jos. 2.9,11. Heb. 11.31. David, 1 Sam. 17.32. 1 Sam. 30.6. 1 Chr. 27.23. Act. 2.30. Heb. 11.32. Israelites, Ex. 4.31. 1 Chr. 5.20. 2 Chr. 13.18. Heb. 11.29,30. Widow of Zarephath, 1 Kin. 17.13-15. Amaziah, 2 Chr. 25.7-10. Hezekiah, 2 Kin. 18.5. Ninevites, Jon. 3.5. Joseph, Mat. 1.24. Zacharias, Luk. 1.64. Abel, &c., see Heb. 11.

FAITH in Christ. Mat. 8.13. As thou hast believed, *so* be it done unto thee.

Mat. 9.22. Daughter, be of good comfort ; thy faith hath made thee whole. 29. Then touched he their eyes, saying, According to your faith be it unto you.

Mat. 11.6. Blessed is *he*, whosoever shall not be offended in me. 28. Come unto me, all *ye* that labour and are heavy laden, and I will give you rest. 29. Take my yoke upon you, and learn of me ; for I am meek and lowly in heart : and ye shall find rest unto your souls. 30. For my yoke *is* easy, and my burden is light.

Mat. 14.27. Be of good cheer : it is I ; be not afraid. Jno. 6.20.

Mat. 15.28. Be it unto thee even as thou wilt.

Mat. 17.7. Jesus touched them, and said, Arise, and be not afraid.

Mar. 9.23. If thou canst believe, all things *are* possible to him that believeth.

Mar. 11.23. Whosoever shall say unto this mountain, Be thou removed, and be thou cast into the sea ; and shall not doubt in his heart, but shall believe that those things which he saith shall come to pass ; he shall have whatsoever he saith. 24. Therefore I say unto you, What things soever ye desire, when ye pray, believe that ye receive *them*, and ye shall have *them*. Mat. 17.20. Mat. 21.21,22.

Luk. 8.50. Fear not : believe only, and she shall be made whole. Mar. 5.36.

Luk. 17.6. If ye had faith as a grain of mustard seed, ye might say unto this sycamine tree, Be thou plucked up by the root, and be thou planted in the sea ; and it should obey you.

Luk. 18.42. Jesus said unto him, Receive thy sight : thy faith hath saved thee.

Jno. 6.29. This is the work of God, that ye believe on him whom he hath sent. 45. Every man therefore that hath heard, and hath learned of the Father, cometh unto me.

Jno. 9.35. Dost thou believe on the Son of God?

Jno. 11.40. If thou wouldest believe, thou shouldest see the glory of God.

Jno. 12.36. While ye have light, believe in the light, that ye may be the children of light.

Jno. 13.7. What I do thou knowest not now ; but thou shalt know hereafter. 20. He that receiveth whomsoever I send receiveth me ; and he that receiveth me receiveth him that sent me.

Jno. 14.1. Let not your heart be troubled : ye believe in God, believe also in me. 11. Believe me for the very works' sake. 12. He that believeth on me, the works that I do shall he do also ; and greater *works* than these shall he do ; because I go unto my Father.

Jno. 16.33. These things I have spoken unto you, that in me ye might have peace.

Jno. 18.37. Every one that is of the truth heareth my voice.

Jno. 20.27. And be not faithless, but believing. 29. Jesus saith unto him, Thomas, because thou hast seen me, thou hast believed : blessed *are* they that have not seen, and *yet* have believed.

Act. 3.16. His name, through faith in his name, hath made this man strong, whom ye see and know ; yea, the faith which is by him hath given him this perfect soundness in the presence of you all.

Act. 20.21. Testifying faith toward our Lord Jesus Christ.

Eph. 3.17. That Christ may dwell in your hearts by faith.

Eph. 4.13. Till we all come in the unity of the faith, and of the knowledge of the Son of God, unto a perfect man, unto the measure of the stature of the fulness of Christ.

Col. 2.7. Rooted and built up in him, and stablished in the faith.

2 Tim. 1.13. In faith and love which is in Christ Jesus.

2 Tim. 2.1. Be strong in the grace that is in Christ Jesus.

Heb. 4.16. Come boldly unto the throne of grace, that we may obtain mercy, and find grace to help in time of need.

Heb. 6.19. Which *hope* we have as an anchor of the soul, both sure and stedfast, and which entereth into that within the veil.

Heb. 10.22. Draw near with a true heart in full assurance of faith.

Heb. 12.2. Looking unto Jesus the author and finisher of *our* faith.

Heb. 13.7. Whose faith follow, considering the end of *their* conversation, Jesus Christ.

1 Jno. 3.23. This is his commandment, That we should believe on the name of his Son Jesus Christ.

1 Jno. 5.14. This is the confidence that we have in him, that, if we ask any thing according to his will, he heareth us.

Rev. 1.17. Fear not ; I am the first and the last.

Rev. 3.18. I counsel thee to buy of me gold tried in the fire, that thou mayest be rich ; white raiment, that thou mayest be clothed. 20. Behold, I stand at the door, and knock : if any man hear my voice, and open the door, I will come in to him, and will sup with him, and he with me.

FAITH IN CHRIST EXEMPLIFIED. Mat. 8.2. Lord, if thou wilt, thou canst make me clean.

Mat. 9.18. My daughter is even now dead : but come and lay thy hand upon her, and she shall live. 21. If I may but touch his garment, I shall be whole. Mar. 5.28. Luk. 8.48.

Mat. 9.28. Believe ye that I am able to do this? They said unto him, Yea, Lord.

Mat. 14.33. Of a truth thou art the Son of God.

Mat. 15.27. Truth, Lord : yet the dogs eat of the crumbs which fall from their masters' table. *v.* 26,28. Mar. 7.27-30.

Mat. 16.16. Thou art the Christ, the Son of the living God.

Mar. 9.24. Lord, I believe ; help thou mine unbelief. Jno. 9.38.

Luk. 5.5. Master, we have toiled all the night, and have taken nothing : nevertheless at thy word I will let down the net.

Luk. 7.6. Lord, trouble not thyself : for I am not worthy that thou shouldest enter under my roof : 7. Wherefore neither thought I myself worthy to come unto thee : but say in a word, and my servant shall be healed.

Luk. 23.42. Lord, remember me when thou comest into thy kingdom.

Jno. 1.41. We have found the Messias. 45. We have found him, of whom Moses in

the law, and the prophets, did write. 49. Thou art the Son of God ; thou art the King of Israel.

Jno. 4.29. Come, see a man, which told me all things that ever I did : is not this the Christ? 42. We have heard *him* ourselves, and know that this is indeed the Christ, the Saviour of the world.

Jno. 6.14. This is of a truth that prophet that should come into the world. 68. Lord, to whom shall we go? thou hast the words of eternal life. 69. And we believe and are sure that thou art that Christ, the Son of the living God.

Jno. 7.31. When Christ cometh, will he do more miracles than these which this *man* hath done?

Jno. 10.22. All things that John spake of this man were true.

Jno. 11.21. Lord, if thou hadst been here, my brother had not died. 22. But I know, that even now, whatsoever thou wilt ask of God, God will give *it* thee. 27. I believe that thou art the Christ, the Son of God, which should come into the world. *v.* 32.

Jno. 16.30. Now are we sure that thou knowest all things, and needest not that any man should ask thee : by this we believe that thou camest forth from God.

Jno. 20.28. Thomas answered and said unto him, My Lord and my God.

Act. 8.37. I believe that Jesus Christ is the Son of God.

Act. 11.17. God gave them the like gift as *he did* unto us, who believed on the Lord Jesus Christ.

Rom. 7.24. Wretched man that I am ! who shall deliver me from the body of this death? 25. I thank God through Jesus Christ our Lord.

Rom. 8.35. Who shall separate us from the love of Christ? *shall* tribulation, or distress, or persecution, or famine, or nakedness, or peril, or sword? 37. Nay, in all these things we are more than conquerors through him that loved us.

2 Cor. 12.9. Most gladly therefore will I rather glory in my infirmities, that the power of Christ may rest upon me. 10. Therefore I take pleasure in infirmities, in reproaches, in necessities, in persecutions, in distresses, for Christ's sake.

Gal. 2.20. I am crucified with Christ : nevertheless I live ; yet not I, but Christ liveth in me : and the life which I now live in the flesh, I live by the faith of the Son of God, who loved me, and gave himself for me.

Phil. 4.13. I can do all things through Christ which strengtheneth me.

1 Tim. 1.14. The grace of our Lord was exceeding abundant with faith and love which is in Christ Jesus.

2 Tim. 1.12. I know whom I have believed, and am persuaded that he is able to keep that which I have committed unto him against that day.

2 Tim. 4.18. The Lord shall deliver me from every evil work, and will preserve *me* unto his heavenly kingdom.

FAITH IN CHRIST, EXAMPLES OF. The wise men, Mat. 2.1,2,11. Peter, &c., Mar. 1.16-20. Luk. 5.3-11. Leper, Luk. 17.19. A woman, Mat. 9.21,22. Blind men, Mat. 9.29,30. Mat. 20.31. Mar. 10.52. Luk. 18.42.

Sick of Gennesareth, Mat. 14.36. Mar. 3.10. Mar. 6.54-56.

Peter, Act. 3.16. Act. 11.17. Friends of a paralytic, Mar. 2.4,5. A woman that was a sinner, Luk. 7.50. Philip, Jno. 1.45,46. Samaritans, Jno. 4. Act. 8.12. Nobleman, Jno. 4.50,53. Abraham, Jno. 8.56. Blind man, Jno. 9.35-38.

Mary, Luk. 10.39,42. Jno. 11.32. John, Jno. 20.8. The disciples, Jno. 2.11,22. Jno. 17.7,8. Jews at Jerusalem, Jno. 2.23. Jno. 8.30. Jno. 11.45. Jno. 12.11. Three thousand at Pentecost, Act. 2.41. Five thousand, Act. 4.4. Multitudes, Act. 5.14.

Stephen, Act. 6.8. Ethiopian eunuch, Act. 8.37. People of Lydda and Saron, Act. 9.35. People of Joppa, Act. 9.42. People of Antioch, Act. 11.21,22,24. Barnabas, Act. 11.24. Sergius Paulus, Act. 13.7,12. Cripple at Lystra, Act. 14.9.

Eunice, Lois, and Timothy, 2 Tim. 1.5. Act. 16.1. Lydia, Act. 16.14. Philippian gaoler, Act. 16.31-34. Crispus and Corinthians, Act. 18.8. 1 Cor. 15.11. Jews at Rome, Act. 28.24. Ephesians, Eph. 1.15. Colossians, Col. 1.2,4. Thessalonians, 1 The. 1.6. 1 The. 3.6-8. 2 The. 1.3,4. Philemon, Philem. 1,5. Church at Thyatira, Rev. 2.19.

FAITH IN CHRIST, SALVATION BY. Mat. 7.24. Whosoever heareth these sayings of mine, and doeth them, I will liken him unto a wise man, which built his house upon a rock: 25. And the rain descended, and the floods came, and the winds blew, and beat upon that house; and it fell not: for it was founded upon a rock. Luk. 6.46-49.

Mar. 16.16. He that believeth, and is baptized, shall be saved.

Luk. 7.50. Thy faith hath saved thee, go in peace.

Jno. 1.12. As many as received him, to them gave he power to become the sons of God, even to them that believe on his name.

Jno. 3.14. Must the Son of man be lifted up; 15. That whosoever believeth in him should not perish, but have eternal life. 16. God so loved the world, that he gave his only-begotten Son, that whosoever believeth in him should not perish, but have everlasting life. 18. He that believeth on him is not condemned. 36. He that believeth on the Son hath everlasting life. Jno. 6.47.

Jno. 5.24. He that heareth my word, and believeth on him that sent me, hath everlasting life, and shall not come into condemnation; but is passed from death unto life.

Jno. 6.35. He that cometh to me shall never hunger; and he that believeth on me shall never thirst. 51. If any man eat of this bread, he shall live for ever: and the bread that I will give is my flesh, which I will give for the life of the world. 53. Except ye eat the flesh of the Son of man, and drink his blood, ye have no life in you. 54. Whoso eateth my flesh, and drinketh my blood, hath eternal life; and I will raise him up at the last day. 56. He that eateth my flesh, and drinketh my blood, dwelleth in me, and I in him. 57. As the living Father hath sent me, and I live by the Father: so he that eateth me, even he shall live by me. v. 58.

Jno. 7.38. He that believeth on me, as the scripture hath said, out of his belly shall flow rivers of living water.

Jno. 8.12. I am the light of the world: he that followeth me shall not walk in darkness, but shall have the light of life. 51. If a man keep my saying, he shall never see death.

Jno. 10.9. I am the door: by me if any man enter in, he shall be saved, and shall go in and out, and find pasture. 27. My sheep hear my voice, and I know them, and they follow me: 28. And I give unto them eternal life.

Jno. 11.25. I am the resurrection, and the life: he that believeth in me, though he were dead, yet shall he live: 26. Whosoever liveth and believeth in me shall never die.

Jno. 12.26. If any man serve me, let him follow me; and where I am, there shall also my servant be: if any man serve me, him will my Father honour. 36. While ye have light, believe in the light, that ye may be the children of light. 44. He that believeth on me, believeth not on me, but on him that sent me. 46. I am come a light into the world, that whosoever believeth on me should not abide in darkness.

Jno. 14.6. I am the way, and the truth, and the life: no man cometh unto the Father, but by me.

Jno. 16.27. The Father himself loveth you, because ye have loved me, and have believed that I came out from God.

Jno. 20.31. These are written, that ye might believe that Jesus is the Christ, the Son of God; and that believing ye might have life through his name.

Act. 10.43. Through his name whosoever believeth in him shall receive remission of sins.

Act. 15.11. Through the grace of the Lord Jesus Christ, we shall be saved, even as they.

Act. 16.31. Believe on the Lord Jesus Christ, and thou shalt be saved, and thy house.

Act. 26.18. That they may receive forgiveness of sins, and inheritance among them which are sanctified by faith that is in me.

Rom. 10.9. If thou shalt confess with thy mouth the Lord Jesus, and shalt believe in thine heart that God hath raised him from the dead, thou shalt be saved. 13. Whosoever shall call upon the name of the Lord shall be saved. v. 10.

2 Cor. 2.15. We are unto God a sweet savour of Christ, in them that are saved, and in them that perish: 16. To the one we are the savour of death unto death; and to the other the savour of life unto life.

Gal. 2.16. A man is not justified by the works of the law, but by the faith of Jesus Christ, even we have believed in Jesus Christ, that we might be justified by the faith of Christ. 20. I am crucified with Christ: nevertheless I live; yet not I, but Christ liveth in me: and the life which I now live in the flesh I live by the faith of the Son of God.

Gal. 3.22. That the promise by faith of Jesus Christ might be given to them that believe. 29. If ye be Christ's, then are ye Abraham's seed, and heirs according to the promise.

Gal. 5.6. In Jesus Christ neither circumcision availeth any thing, nor uncircumcision; but faith which worketh by love.

Eph. 2.20. Built upon the foundation of

the apostles and prophets, Jesus Christ himself being the chief corner *stone.*

Eph. 3.12. In whom we have boldness and access with confidence by the faith of him.

Phil. 3.3. We are the circumcision, which worship God in the spirit, and rejoice in Christ Jesus, and have no confidence in the flesh. 7. What things were gain to me, those I counted loss for Christ. 8. Yea doubtless, and I count all things *but* loss for the excellency of the knowledge of Christ Jesus my Lord : for whom I have suffered the loss of all things, and do count them *but* dung, that I may win Christ. 9. And be found in him, not having mine own righteousness, which is of the law, but that which is through the faith of Christ, the righteousness which is of God by faith.

1 Tim. 1.16. In me first Jesus Christ might shew forth all long-suffering, for a pattern to them which should hereafter believe on him to life everlasting.

1 Tim. 2.11. If we be dead with *him,* we shall also live with *him :* 12. If we suffer, we shall also reign with *him.*

2 Tim. 3.15. Wise unto salvation through faith which is in Christ Jesus.

Heb. 5.9. He became the author of eternal salvation unto all them that obey him.

Heb. 7.25. He is able also to save them to the uttermost that come unto God by him.

Heb. 10.19. Boldness to enter into the holiest by the blood of Jesus.

1 Pet. 1.8. In whom, though now ye see *him* not, yet believing, ye rejoice with joy unspeakable.

1 Pet. 2.6. I lay in Sion a chief corner stone, elect, precious : and he that believeth on him shall not be confounded. 7. Unto you therefore which believe *he is* precious. Isa. 28.16.

1 Pet. 3.21. Baptism doth also now save us (not the putting away of the filth of the flesh, but the answer of a good conscience toward God,) by the resurrection of Jesus Christ.

2 Pet. 1.1. Obtained like precious faith with us through the righteousness of God and our Saviour Jesus Christ.

1 Jno. 2.23. *He that acknowledgeth the Son hath the Father also.*

1 Jno. 4.15. Whosoever shall confess that Jesus is the Son of God, God dwelleth in him, and he in God.

1 Jno. 5.4. This is the victory that overcometh the world, *even* our faith. 5. Who is he that overcometh the world, but he that believeth that Jesus is the Son of God ? 10. He that believeth on the Son of God hath the witness in himself. 13. Unto you that believe on the name of the Son of God ; that ye may know that ye have eternal life, and that ye may believe on the name of the Son of God. 20. We know that the Son of God is come, and hath given us an understanding, that we may know him that is true, and we are in him that is true, *even* in his Son Jesus Christ.

Jude 21. Looking for the mercy of our Lord Jesus Christ unto eternal life.

Rev. 7.14. Have washed their robes, and made them white in the blood of the Lamb.

See UNION TO CHRIST—CHRIST SAVIOUR.

FAITH, JUSTIFYING. See JUSTIFICATION BY FAITH. Faith in the Gospel, see WORD OF GOD LOVED. Weak Faith, see DOUBT.

FALL OF MAN. Gen. 3.6. When the woman saw that the tree *was* good for food, and that it *was* pleasant to the eyes, and a tree to be desired to make *one* wise, she took of the fruit thereof, and did eat, and gave also unto her husband with her ; and he did eat. Gen. 2.17. Gen. 3.

Job 31.33. If I covered my transgressions as Adam, by hiding mine iniquity in my bosom.

Ecc. 7.29. Lo, this only have I found, that God hath made man upright ; but they have sought out many inventions.

Isa. 43.27. Thy first father hath sinned.

Hos. 6.7. They, like men (Adam, *marg.*), have transgressed the covenant.

Rom. 5.12. By one man sin entered into the world, and death by sin ; and so death passed upon all men, for that all have sinned. 14. Death reigned from Adam to Moses, even over them that had not sinned after the similitude of Adam's transgression, who is the figure of him that was to come. 18. By the offence of one *judgment came* upon all men to condemnation. *v.* 12-21.

Rom. 8.20. The creature was made subject to vanity, not willingly, but by reason of him who hath subjected *the same.* 22. We know that the whole creation groaneth and travaileth in pain together until now.

1 Cor. 15.21. By man came death. 22. In Adam all die.

2 Cor. 11.3. The serpent beguiled Eve through his subtilty.

1 Tim. 2.13. Adam was first formed, then Eve. 14. Adam was not deceived, but the woman being deceived was in the transgression.

See MAN, NATURAL STATE OF.

FALSE CONFIDENCE, SELF-CONFIDENCE. Deu. 29.19. That he bless himself in his heart, saying, I shall have peace, though I walk in the imagination of mine heart.

1 Kin. 20.11. Let not him that girdeth on *his harness* boast himself as he that putteth it off.

2 Kin. 18.21. Thou trustest upon the staff of this bruised reed, *even* upon Egypt, on which if a man lean, it will go into his hand, and pierce it. Isa. 36.6.

Job 11.20. Their hope *shall be as* the giving up of the ghost.

Job 15.31. Let not him that is deceived trust in vanity : for vanity shall be his recompence.

Job 29.18. I said, I shall die in my nest, and I shall multiply my days as the sand.

Psa. 10.6. He hath said in his heart, I shall not be moved : for *I shall* never *be* in adversity.

Psa. 20.7. Some *trust* in chariots, and some in horses : but we will remember the name of the Lord our God. 8. They are brought down and fallen : but we are risen, and stand upright.

Psa. 30.6. In my prosperity I said, I shall never be moved.

Psa. 33.16. No king saved by the multitude of an host : a mighty man is not delivered by much strength. 17. An horse *is* a vain thing for safety : neither shall he deliver *any* by his great strength.

Psa. 36.2. He flattereth himself in his own eyes, until his iniquity be found to be hateful.

Psa. 40.4. Blessed *is* that man that maketh the Lord his trust, and respecteth not the proud.

Psa. 44.6. I will not trust in my bow, neither shall my sword save me.

Psa. 49.6. They that trust in their wealth, and boast themselves in the multitude of their riches; 7. None *of them* can by any means redeem his brother.

Psa. 52.7. Lo, *this is* the man *that* made not God his strength; but trusted in the abundance of his riches, *and* strengthened himself in his wickedness.

Psa. 60.11. Give us help from trouble: for vain *is* the help of man. Psa. 108.12.

Psa. 62.9. Men of low degree *are* vanity, *and* men of high degree *are* a lie: to be laid in the balance, they *are* altogether *lighter* than vanity.

Psa. 75.6. Promotion *cometh* neither from the east, nor from the west, nor from the south. 7. But God *is* the judge: he putteth down one, and setteth up another.

Psa. 118.8. *It is* better to trust in the Lord than to put confidence in man. *v.* 3.

Psa. 146.3. Put not your trust in princes, *nor* in the son of man, in whom *there is* no help. 4. His breath goeth forth, he returneth to his earth; in that very day his thoughts perish.

Pro. 3.5. Trust in the Lord with all thine heart; and lean not unto thine own understanding. 7. Be not wise in thine own eyes.

Pro. 11.28. He that trusteth in his riches shall fall.

Pro. 12.15. The way of a fool *is* right in his own eyes.

Pro. 14.16. A wise *man* feareth, and departeth from evil: but the fool rageth, and is confident.

Pro. 16.25. There is a way that seemeth right unto a man, but the end thereof *are* the ways of death.

Pro. 23.4. Cease from thine own wisdom.

Pro. 26.12. Seest thou a man wise in his own conceit? *there is* more hope of a fool than of him.

Pro. 28.26. He that trusteth in his own heart is a fool.

Pro. 29.26. Many seek the ruler's favour; but *every* man's judgment *cometh* from the Lord.

Isa. 2.22. Cease ye from man, whose breath *is* in his nostrils: for wherein is he to be accounted of?

Isa. 5.21. Woe unto *them that are* wise in their own eyes, and prudent in their own sight!

Isa. 8.12. Say ye not, A confederacy, to all *them to* whom this people shall say, A confederacy.

Isa. 22.11. Ye made also a ditch between the two walls for the water of the old pool: but ye have not looked unto the maker thereof, neither had respect unto him that fashioned it long ago.

Isa. 28.15. We have made a covenant with death, and with hell are we at agreement; when the overflowing scourge shall pass through, it shall not come unto us: for we have made lies our refuge, and under falsehood have we hid ourselves.

Isa. 28.18. Your covenant with death shall be disannulled, and your agreement with hell shall not stand; when the overflowing scourge shall pass through; then ye shall be trodden down by it.

Isa. 30.1. Woe to the rebellious children, saith the Lord, that take counsel, but not of me; and that cover with a covering, but not of my spirit, that they may add sin to sin: 2. That walk to go down into Egypt, and have not asked at my mouth.

Isa. 30.5. They were all ashamed of a people *that* could not profit them, nor be an help nor profit, but a shame, and also a reproach. 7. For the Egyptians shall help in vain, and to no purpose: therefore have I cried concerning this, Their strength *is* to sit still. Isa. 20.5.

Isa. 30.10. Which say to the seers, See not; and to the prophets, Prophesy not unto us right things, speak unto us smooth things, prophesy deceits. 15. In returning and rest shall ye be saved; in quietness and in confidence shall be your strength: and ye would not. 16. Ye said, No; for we will flee upon horses; therefore shall ye flee: and, We will ride upon the swift; therefore shall they that pursue you be swift.

Isa. 31.1. Woe to them that go down to Egypt for help; and stay on horses, and trust in chariots, because *they are* many; and in horsemen, because they are very strong; but they look not unto the Holy One of Israel, neither seek the Lord! 3. Now the Egyptians *are* men, and not God; and their horses flesh, and not spirit. When the Lord shall stretch out his hand, both he that helpeth shall fall, and he that is holpen shall fall down, and they all shall fail together.

Isa. 47.7. I shall be a lady for ever: *so* that thou didst not lay these *things* to thy heart. 8. *Thou that art* given to pleasures, that dwellest carelessly, that sayest in thine heart, I *am*, and none else beside me; I shall not sit *as* a widow, neither shall I know the loss of children. 10. Thou hast trusted in thy wickedness: thou hast said, None seeth me. Thy wisdom and thy knowledge, it hath perverted thee.

Isa. 56.12. To-morrow shall be as this day, *and* much more abundant.

Isa. 57.13. When thou criest, let thy companies deliver thee; but the wind shall carry them all away; vanity shall take *them*.

Jer. 2.13. They have forsaken me the fountain of living waters, *and* hewed them out cisterns, broken cisterns, that can hold no water.

Jer. 2.18. What hast thou to do in the way of Egypt, to drink the waters of Sihor? or what hast thou to do in the way of Assyria, to drink the waters of the river? 37. The Lord hath rejected thy confidences, and thou shalt not prosper in them.

Jer. 3.23. In vain *is salvation hoped for* from the hills, *and from* the multitude of mountains.

Jer. 5.17. They shall impoverish thy fenced cities, wherein thou trustedst, with the sword.

Jer. 6.14. They have healed also the hurt *of the daughter* of my people slightly, saying, Peace, peace; when *there is* no peace. Jer. 8.11.

Jer. 12.5. *If* in the land of peace, *wherein* thou trustedst, *they wearied thee*, then how wilt thou do in the swelling of Jordan?

Jer. 14.13. The prophets say unto them, Ye shall not see the sword, neither shall ye have famine; but I will give you assured peace.

Jer. 17.5. Cursed *be* the man that trusteth in man, and maketh flesh his arm, and whose heart departeth from the Lord.

Jer. 21.13. I *am* against thee, O inhabitant of the valley, *and* rock of the plain, saith the Lord; which say, Who shall come down against us? or who shall enter into our habitations?

Jer. 23.17. They say unto every one that walketh after the imagination of his own heart, No evil shall come upon you.

Jer. 48.7. Because thou hast trusted in thy works and in thy treasures, thou shalt also be taken. 11. Moab hath been at ease from his youth, and he hath settled on his lees.

Jer. 49.4. O backsliding daughter? that trusted in her treasures, *saying*, Who shall come unto me? 5. Behold, I will bring a fear upon thee; ye shall be driven out every man right forth.

Lam. 4.17. Our eyes as yet failed for our vain help: in our watching we have watched for a nation *that* could not save *us*.

Eze. 13.10. They have seduced my people, saying, Peace; and *there was* no peace; and one built up a wall, and, lo, others daubed it with untempered *morter*: 11. There shall be an overflowing shower; and ye, O great hailstones, shall fall; and a stormy wind shall rend it.

Eze. 29.6. They have been a staff of reed to the house of Israel. 7. When they took hold of thee by thy hand, thou didst break, and rend all their shoulder: and when they leaned upon thee, thou brakest, and madest all their loins to be at a stand.

Eze. 30.8. I have set a fire in Egypt, and all her helpers shall be destroyed.

Hos. 5.13. Then went Ephraim to the Assyrian, and sent to king Jareb: yet could he not heal you, nor cure you of your wound.

Hos. 7.9. Strangers have devoured his strength, and he knoweth *it* not: yea, gray hairs are here and there upon him, yet he knoweth not. 11. Ephraim also is like a silly dove without heart: they call to Egypt, they go to Assyria. *v.* 11-16.

Hos. 10.13. Ye have eaten the fruit of lies: because thou didst trust in thy way, in the multitude of thy mighty men.

Hos. 12.1. Ephraim feedeth on wind, and followeth after the east wind: he daily increaseth lies and desolation.

Hos. 14.3. Asshur shall not save us; we will not ride upon horses: neither will we say any more to the work of our hands, Ye *are* our gods.

Amos 6.1. Woe to them *that are* at ease in Zion, and trust in the mountain of Samaria. 3. Ye that put far away the evil day. *v.* 1-7.

Obad. 3. The pride of thine heart hath deceived thee, thou that dwellest in the clefts of the rock, whose habitation *is* high; that saith in his heart, Who shall bring me down to the ground?

Mic. 3.11. The priests thereof teach for hire, and the prophets thereof divine for money: yet will they lean upon the Lord, and say, *Is* not the Lord among us? none evil can come upon us.

Zeph. 1.12. I will search Jerusalem with candles, and punish the men that are settled on their lees: that say *in* their heart, The Lord will not do good, neither will he do evil.

Zeph. 2.15. This *is* the rejoicing city that

dwelt carelessly, that said in her heart, I *am*, and *there is* none beside me: how is she become a desolation.

Zec. 4.6. Not by might, nor by power, but by my spirit, saith the Lord of hosts.

Mat. 25.5. While the bridegroom tarried, they all slumbered and slept.

Mar. 10.24. How hard is it for them that trust in riches to enter into the kingdom of God!

Luk. 11.35. Take heed therefore that the light which is in thee be not darkness.

Luk. 12.19. I will say to my soul, Soul, thou hast much goods laid up for many years; take thine ease, eat, drink, *and* be merry. 20. But God said unto him, Thou fool, this night thy soul shall be required of thee.

Luk. 17.28. They did eat, they drank, they bought, they sold, they planted, they builded; 29. But the same day that Lot went out of Sodom it rained fire and brimstone from heaven, and destroyed *them* all. 30. Even thus shall it be in the day when the Son of man is revealed.

Jno. 5.45. There is *one* that accuseth you, *even* Moses, in whom ye trust.

Rom. 2.3. Thinkest thou this, O man, that judgest them which do such things, and doest the same, that thou shalt escape the judgment of God?

Rom. 12.16. Be not wise in your own conceits.

1 Cor. 3.21. Let no man glory in men.

2 Cor. 1.9. We should not trust in ourselves, but in God.

1 The. 5.3. When they shall say, Peace and safety; then sudden destruction cometh upon them, as travail upon a woman with child; and they shall not escape.

1 Tim. 6.17. Be not high-minded, nor trust in uncertain riches, but in the living God.

Jas. 4.13. Go to now, ye that say, To-day or to-morrow we will go into such a city, and continue there a year, and buy and sell, and get gain: 14. Whereas ye know not what *shall be* on the morrow. 15. For that ye *ought* to say, If the Lord will, we shall live, and do this, or that.

Rev. 18.7. She saith in her heart, I sit a queen, and am no widow, and shall see no sorrow. 8. Therefore shall her plagues come in one day.

FALSE CONFIDENCE. EXAMPLES OF: Builders of Babel, Gen. 11.4. Sennacherib, 2 Kin. 19.23. Asa, 2 Chr. 16.7-9. Hezekiah, Isa. 22.11. Jonah, Jon. 1.5. Peter, Luk. 22.33,34. Jno. 13.37,38. The disciples, Mat. 26.35. Jno. 16.31,32.

FALSEHOOD AND DECEIT. Ex. 20.16. Thou shalt not bear false witness against thy neighbour. Deu. 5.20. Mat. 19.18.

Ex. 23.1. Thou shalt not raise a false report: put not thine hand with the wicked to be an unrighteous witness.

Lev. 6.3. Or have found that which was lost, and lieth concerning it, and sweareth falsely; in any of all these that a man doeth, sinning therein.

Lev. 19.11. Neither deal falsely, neither lie one to another. 12. Ye shall not swear by my name falsely. 16. Thou shalt not go up and down *as* a tale-bearer among thy people: neither shalt thou stand against the blood of thy neighbour. Ex. 20.7.

Deu. 19.18. *If* the witness be a false witness, *and* hath testified falsely against his brother; 19. Then shall ye do unto him as he had thought to have done unto his brother.

Job 13.4. Ye *are* forgers of lies, ye *are* all physicians of no value.

Job 21.34. How then comfort ye me in vain, seeing in your answers there remaineth falsehood?

Job 27.4. My lips shall not speak wickedness, nor my tongue utter deceit.

Job 31.5. If I have walked with vanity, or if my foot hath hasted to deceit; 6. Let me be weighed in an even balance, that God may know mine integrity.

Psa. 5.6. Thou shalt destroy them that speak leasing: the Lord will abhor the bloody and deceitful man. 9. *There is* no faithfulness in their mouth; their inward part *is* very wickedness; their throat *is* an open sepulchre; they flatter with their tongue.

Psa. 10.7. His mouth is full of deceit and fraud: under his tongue *is* mischief and vanity.

Psa. 12.2. *With* flattering lips *and* with a double heart do they speak. 3. The Lord shall cut off all flattering lips.

Psa. 27.12. False witnesses are risen up against me, and such as breathe out cruelty.

Psa. 28.3. The workers of iniquity; which speak peace to their neighbours, but mischief *is* in their hearts.

Psa. 31.18. Let the lying lips be put to silence; which speak grievous things proudly and contemptuously against the righteous.

Psa. 34.13. Keep thy tongue from evil, and thy lips from speaking guile. 1 Pet. 3.10.

Psa. 35.11. False witnesses did rise up: they laid to my charge *things* that I knew not.

Psa. 36.3. The words of his mouth *are* iniquity and deceit.

Psa. 50.19. Thou givest thy mouth to evil, and thy tongue frameth deceit. 20. Thou sittest *and* speakest against thy brother; thou slanderest thine own mother's son.

Psa. 52.2. Thy tongue deviseth mischiefs; like a sharp razor, working deceitfully. 3. Thou lovest evil more than good; *and* lying rather than to speak righteousness. 4. Thou lovest all devouring words, O *thou* deceitful tongue. 5. God shall likewise destroy thee for ever.

Psa. 55.21. *The words* of his mouth were smoother than butter, but war *was* in his heart: his words were softer than oil, yet *were* they drawn swords. 23. But thou, O God, shalt bring them down into the pit of destruction: bloody and deceitful men shall not live out half their days.

Psa. 58.3. They go astray as soon as they be born, speaking lies.

Psa. 59.12. *For* the sin of their mouth *and* the words of their lips let them even be taken in their pride: and for cursing and lying *which* they speak.

Psa. 62.4. They delight in lies: they bless with their mouth, but they curse inwardly.

Psa. 63.11. The mouth of them that speak lies shall be stopped.

Psa. 101.5. Whoso privily slandereth his neighbour, him will I cut off. 7. He that worketh deceit shall not dwell within my house: he that telleth lies shall not tarry in my sight.

Psa. 109.2. The mouth of the deceitful are opened against me; they have spoken against me with a lying tongue.

Psa. 119.69. The proud have forged a lie against me. 163. I hate and abhor lying.

Psa. 120.3. What shall be done unto thee, thou false tongue? 4. Sharp arrows of the mighty, with coals of juniper.

Psa. 144.8. Whose mouth speaketh vanity; and their right hand *is* a right hand of falsehood.

Pro. 6.12. A wicked man walketh with a froward mouth. 13. He winketh with his eyes, he speaketh with his feet, he teacheth with his fingers. 16. These six *things* doth the Lord hate: 17. A lying tongue, &c.

Pro. 10.9. He that perverteth his ways shall be known. 10. He that winketh with the eye causeth sorrow. 18. He that hideth hatred *with* lying lips, and he that uttereth a slander, *is* a fool. 31. The froward tongue shall be cut out.

Pro. 11.9. An hypocrite with *his* mouth destroyeth his neighbour.

Pro. 12.17. *He that* speaketh truth sheweth forth righteousness: but a false witness deceit. 19. A lying tongue is but for a moment. 20. Deceit *is* in the heart of them that imagine evil. 22. Lying lips *are* abomination to the Lord.

Pro. 13.5. A righteous *man* hateth lying.

Pro. 14.5. A faithful witness will not lie: but a false witness will utter lies. 8. The folly of fools *is* deceit. 25. A deceitful *witness* speaketh lies.

Pro. 17.4. A wicked doer giveth heed to false lips; *and* a liar giveth ear to a naughty tongue. 7. Excellent speech becometh not a fool: much less do lying lips a prince.

Pro. 19.9. A false witness shall not be unpunished: *he that* speaketh lies shall perish. 22. A poor man *is* better than a liar. 28. An ungodly witness scorneth judgment.

Pro. 20.17. Bread of deceit *is* sweet to a man; but afterwards his mouth shall be filled with gravel.

Pro. 21.6. The getting of treasures by a lying tongue *is* a vanity tossed to and fro of them that seek death. 28. A false witness shall perish.

Pro. 24.28. Be not a witness against thy neighbour without cause; and deceive *not* with thy lips.

Pro. 25.18. A man that beareth false witness against his neighbour *is* a maul, and a sword, and a sharp arrow.

Pro. 26.18. As a mad *man* who casteth firebrands, arrows, and death, 19. So *is* the man *that* deceiveth his neighbour, and saith, Am not I in sport? 24. He that hateth dissembleth with his lips, and layeth up deceit within him: 25. When he speaketh fair, believe him not; for *there are* seven abominations in his heart. 26. *Whose* hatred is covered by deceit, his wickedness shall be shewed before the *whole* congregation. 28. A lying tongue hateth *those that are* afflicted by it.

Pro. 27.14. He that blesseth his friend with a loud voice, rising early in the morning, it shall be counted a curse to him.

Isa. 32.7. He deviseth wicked devices to destroy the poor with lying words, even when the needy speaketh right.

Isa. 57.11. Of whom hast thou been afraid

or feared, that thou hast lied, and hast not remembered me.

Isa. 59.3. Your lips have spoken lies, your tongue hath muttered perverseness. 4. None calleth for justice, nor *any* pleadeth for truth: they trust in vanity, and speak lies.

Isa. 63.8. He said, Surely they *are* my people, children *that* will not lie.

Jer. 7.28. Truth is perished, and is cut off from their mouth.

Jer. 9.3. They bend their tongues *like* their bow *for* lies: but they are not valiant for the truth. 5. They will deceive every one his neighbour, and will not speak the truth: they have taught their tongue to speak lies, *and* weary themselves to commit iniquity. 6. Thine habitation *is* in the midst of deceit; through deceit they refuse to know me, saith the Lord. 8. Their tongue *is as* an arrow shot out; it speaketh deceit: *one* speaketh peaceably to his neighbour with his mouth, but in heart he layeth his wait.

Jer. 12.6. Even thy brethren, and the house of thy father, even they have dealt treacherously with thee ; yea, they have called a multitude after thee : believe them not, though they speak fair words unto thee.

Hos. 4.1. The Lord hath a controversy with the inhabitants of the land, for *there* is no truth in the land.

Obad. 7. The men that were at peace with thee have deceived thee.

Mic. 6.12. The inhabitants thereof have spoken lies, and their tongue *is* deceitful in their mouth.

Nah. 3.1. Woe to the bloody city ! it *is* all full of lies *and* robbery.

Zec. 5.4. I will bring it forth, saith the Lord of hosts, and it shall enter into the house of the thief, and into the house of him that sweareth falsely by my name: and it shall remain in the midst of his house, and shall consume it, with the timber thereof, and the stones thereof. *v.* 15.

Zec. 8.17. Let none of you imagine evil in your hearts against his neighbour ; and love no false oath : for all these *are things* that I hate, saith the Lord.

Mal. 3.5. I will be a swift witness against false swearers.

Mat. 15.19. For out of the heart proceed evil thoughts, false witness.

Jno. 8.44. When he speaketh a lie, he speaketh of his own : for he is a liar, and the father of it.

Act. 5.3. Why hath Satan filled thine heart to lie to the Holy Ghost.

Eph. 4.25. Putting away lying, speak every man truth with his neighbour.

Col. 3.9. Lie not one to another, seeing that ye have put off the old man with his deeds.

1 Tim. 1.9. The law is not made for a righteous man, but for the lawless and disobedient. 10. For liars, for perjured persons.

1 Tim. 4.2. Speaking lies in hypocrisy.

1 Pet. 3.16. Having a good conscience ; that, whereas they speak evil of you, as of evildoers, they may be ashamed that falsely accuse your good conversation in Christ.

Rev. 21.8. All liars shall have their part in the lake which burneth with fire and brimstone. 27. And there shall in no wise enter into it any thing that *maketh* a lie.

Rev. 22.15. Without *are* dogs, and whosoever loveth and maketh a lie.

FALSEHOOD, DECEIT, AND FALSE WITNESS. EXAMPLES OF : Satan, Gen. 3.4,5. Adam and Eve, Gen. 3.12,13. Cain, Gen. 4.9. Abraham, Gen. 12.11-19. Gen. 20.2. Sarah, Gen. 18.15. Isaac, Gen. 26.6,7. Rebecca and Jacob, Gen. 27.6-24,46.

Joseph's brethren, Gen. 37.31-33. Potiphar's wife, Gen. 39.14-17. Magicians, Ex. 8.19. Pharaoh, Ex. 8.29. Aaron, Ex. 32.24. Israelites, Num. 16.13. Rahab, Jos. 2.4-6. Gibeonites, Jos. 9. Ehud, Jud. 3.20. Doeg, 1 Sam. 22.10. Saul, 1 Sam. 15.13. 1 Sam. 22.13-15.

David, 1 Sam. 21.2. 1 Sam. 27.10-12. 2 Sam. 15.34. Michal, 1 Sam. 19.14. An Amalekite, 2 Sam. 1.10 with 1 Sam. 31.1-6. Absalom, 2 Sam. 15.7-10. Ziba, 2 Sam. 16.1,2 with 2 Sam. 19.24-28. Hushai, 2 Sam. 16.16-19. Shimei, 1 Kin. 2.43. Jeroboam, 1 Kin. 14.2. The old prophet, 1 Kin. 13.11-18. Naboth's accusers, 1 Kin. 21.13. Gehazi, 2 Kin. 5.22-27. Jehu, 2 Kin. 10.18-25. Zedekiah, 2 Chr. 36.13. Eze. 16.59. Eze. 17.15-20. Samaritans, Ezr. 4. Sanballat, &c., Neh. 6. Haman, Est. 3.8. Jeremiah's enemies, Jer. 37.13,14. Jer. 38.4. Jer. 42.5-20.

Herod, Mat. 2.8. Jews, Mat. 11.18,19. Mat. 21.25-27. Christ's accusers, Mar. 14.55,56. Luk. 23.2. Jno. 18.30. Psa. 27.12. Psa. 35.11. Peter, Mar. 14.68,71. Roman soldiers, Mat. 28.13,15. Ananias and Sapphira, Act. 5.1-10. Stephen's accusers, Act. 6.11,13.

Paul's accusers, Act. 16.20. Act. 17.7. Act. 24.5. Act. 25.7. Rom. 3.8. Lysias, Act. 22.24-29 with Act. 23.27. Cretians, Tit. 1.12. See SPEAKING EVIL—HYPOCRISY AND TREACHERY. False Teachers, see TEACHERS, FALSE.

FAMILIAR SPIRITS. The divining spirit supposed to be present in the conjuror, Lev. 19.31. Lev. 20.6,27. Deu. 28.8. 1 Chr. 10.13. Isa. 8.19. Isa. 19.3. The shade of the dead evoked, Isa. 29.4. See NECROMANCY—SORCERY—DEMONS.

FAMINE. Description of, Deu. 28.53-57. Isa. 5.13. Isa. 17.11. Jer. 5.17. Jer. 14.1-6. Jer. 48.33. Lam. 1.11,19. Lam. 2.11-22. Lam. 4.4-10. Joel 1.17-20. A judgment from God, Lev. 26.19-29. Deu. 28.23,24,38-42. 1 Kin. 17.1. 2 Kin. 8.1. 1 Chr. 21.12. Psa. 105.16. Psa. 107.33,34. Isa. 3.1-8. Eze. 4.16,17. Eze. 5.16,17. Eze. 14.13. Amos 4.6-9. Amos 5.16,17. Hag. 1.10,11. Luk. 21.11. Rev. 6.5-8.

Examples: Gen. 12.10. Gen. 26.1. Gen. 41.53-57. Ruth 1.1. 2 Sam. 21.1. 1 Kin. 17. 2 Kin. 6.25-29. 2 Kin. 7.4. 2 Kin. 25.3. Jer. 52.6. Act. 11.28.

FAN. See THRESHING.

FARMS AND FARMING. See AGRICULTURE—VINEYARDS.

FARTHING. Two words are used for this, (1.) *Assarion*, about 3 farthings of our money, the tenth part of the Roman denarius, which is in value 7¾d., Mat. 10.29. Luk. 12.6. (2.) *Kodrantes*, the fourth part of an assarion, scarcely one farthing, Mat. 5.26. Mar. 12.42.

FAST, of the 7th month, Zec. 8.19. The only fast appointed by Moses. See ATONEMENT, DAY OF.

FASTING. Isa. 58.3. Wherefore have we fasted, *say they,* and thou seest not? *wherefore* have we afflicted our soul, and thou takest no knowledge? Behold, in the day of your fast ye find pleasure, and exact all your labours. 4. Behold, ye fast for strife and debate, and to smite with the fist of wickedness: ye shall not fast as *ye do this* day, to make your voice to be heard on high. 5. Is it such a fast that I have chosen? a day for a man to afflict his soul? *is it* to bow down his head as a bulrush, and to spread sackcloth and ashes *under him?* wilt thou call this a fast, and an acceptable day to the Lord?

Isa. 58.6. *Is* not this the fast that I have chosen? to loose the bands of wickedness, to undo the heavy burdens, and to let the oppressed go free, and that ye break every yoke? *v.* 7,8.

Jer. 14.12. When they fast, I will not hear their cry.

Joel 1.14. Sanctify ye a fast, call a solemn assembly, gather the elders, *and* all the inhabitants of the land, *into* the house of the Lord your God, and cry unto the Lord.

Joel 2.12. Turn ye *even* to me with all your heart, and with fasting, and with weeping, and with mourning.

Zec. 7.5. When ye fasted and mourned in the fifth and seventh *month,* even those seventy years, did ye at all fast unto me, *even* to me?

Zec. 8.19. The fast of the fourth *month,* and the fast of the fifth, and the fast of the seventh, and the fast of the tenth, shall be to the house of Judah joy and gladness, and cheerful feasts; therefore love the truth and peace.

Mat. 6.16. When ye fast, be not, as the hypocrites, of a sad countenance: for they disfigure their faces, that they may appear unto men to fast. Verily I say unto you, They have their reward. 17. But thou, when thou fastest, anoint thine head, and wash thy face; 18. That thou appear not unto men to fast, but unto thy Father which is in secret: and thy Father, which seeth in secret, shall reward thee openly.

Mat. 17.21. This kind goeth not out but by prayer and fasting.

Luk. 5.33. Why do the disciples of John fast often, and make prayers, and likewise *the disciples* of the Pharisees; but thine eat and drink? 34. And he said unto them, Can ye make the children of the bride-chamber fast while the bridegroom is with them? 35. But the days will come, when the bridegroom shall be taken away from them, and then shall they fast in those days.

1 Cor. 7.5. That ye may give yourselves to fasting and prayer.

FASTING, EXAMPLES OF: Israelites, Jud. 20.26. 1 Sam. 7.6. David, 2 Sam. 12.16,22. Psa. 35.13. Psa. 69.10. Psa. 109.24. Ahab, 1 Kin. 21.27. Jehoshaphat, 2 Chr. 20.3. Ezra, Ezr. 10.6. Nehemiah, Neh. 1.4. Jews, Ezr. 8.21-23. Neh. 9.1. Est. 4.3,16. Jer. 36.9.

Darius, Dan. 6.18. Daniel, Dan. 9.3. Dan. 10.2,3. Ninevites, Jon. 3.5-10. John's disciples, Mat. 9.14. Anna, Luk. 2.37. Pharisees, Mar. 2.18. Luk. 18.12. Cornelius, Act. 10.30. Apostles and Church, Act. 13.2,3. Act. 14.23. 2 Cor. 6.5. 2 Cor. 11.27.

For forty days by Moses, Ex. 24.18. Ex.

34.28. Deu. 9.9,18. By Elijah, 1 Kin. 19.8. Christ, Mat. 4.2. Fasting in mourning, 1 Sam. 31.13. 2 Sam. 1.12. 2 Sam. 3.35.

FAT, burnt in sacrifice; of animals, Lev. 10.15. Lev. 17.6. 1 Sam. 2.15,16. Isa. 43.24: on the day they were killed, Ex. 23.18. Of the intestines of bullocks burnt, Ex. 29.13. Lev. 1.8. Lev. 3.3-5. Lev. 4.8-10. Lev. 8.16,25,26.

Of sheep or rams, Ex. 29.22. Lev. 3.9-11. Lev. 7.3-5. Of goats, Lev. 3.14-16. Lev. 16.25. Used in sacrifice, forbidden as food, Lev. 3.16,17. Lev. 7.23. Other portions eaten, Deu. 32.14. Neh. 8.10. Offered to idols, Deu. 32.38. Illustrative, Gen. 45.18. Gen. 49.20: Psa. 81.16. Isa. 25.6.

FATHER, signifying ancestor, 2 Kin. 16.2. Mat. 3.9. Inventor or founder, Gen. 4.20,21. A title of honour, Jud. 17.10. 2 Kin. 2.12. 2 Kin. 5.13. See PARENTS.

FATHERLESS. See WIDOWS AND ORPHANS.

FATHOM (Gr. *orguia*), a measure, equal to the arms extended, 6 or 7 feet, Act. 27.28.

FAVOUR OF GOD. See GOD, FAVOUR OF.

FEAR OF GOD. Ex. 18.21. Able men, such as fear God, men of truth.

Ex. 20.20. God is come to prove you, and that his fear may be before your faces, that ye sin not.

Lev. 22.32. Neither shall ye profane my holy name; but I will be hallowed among the children of Israel.

Deu. 4.10. I will make them hear my words, that they may learn to fear me all the days that they shall live upon the earth, and *that* they may teach their children.

Deu. 5.29. O that there were such an heart in them, that they would fear me, and keep all my commandments always, that it might be well with them, and with their children for ever!

Deu. 6.2. That thou mightest fear the Lord thy God, to keep all his statutes and his commandments.

Deu. 10.12. Now, Israel, what doth the Lord thy God require of thee, but to fear the Lord thy God, to walk in all his ways, and to love him, and to serve the Lord thy God with all thy heart and with all thy soul. 20. Thou shalt fear the Lord thy God; him shalt thou serve, and to him shalt thou cleave, and swear by his name. 21. He *is* thy praise, and he *is* thy God, that hath done for thee these great and terrible things, which thine eyes have seen. Deu. 6.13. Deu. 13.4. Deu. 14.23.

Deu. 28.58. Fear this glorious and fearful name, The Lord thy God.

Jos. 4.24. That all the people of the earth might know the hand of the Lord, that it *is* mighty: that ye might fear the Lord your God for ever.

Jos. 24.14. Fear the Lord, and serve him in sincerity and in truth.

1 Sam. 2.30. Them that honour me I will honour, and they that despise me shall be lightly esteemed.

1 Sam. 12.14. If ye will fear the Lord, and serve him, and obey his voice, and not rebel against the commandment of the Lord, then shall both ye and also the king that reigneth over you continue following the Lord your

God. 24. Only fear the Lord, and serve him in truth with all your heart: for consider how great *things* he hath done for you.

2 Sam. 23.3. He that ruleth over men *must be* just, ruling in the fear of God.

1 Kin. 8.40. That they may fear thee all the days that they live in the land which thou gavest unto our fathers.

Neh. 5.9. Ought ye not to walk in the fear of our God.

2 Kin. 17.36. Him shall ye fear, and him shall ye worship. 39. The Lord your God ye shall fear; and he shall deliver you out of the hand of all your enemies. *v.* 28.

2 Chr. 19.7. Let the fear of the Lord be upon you; take heed and do *it:* for *there is* no iniquity with the Lord our God. 9. Thus shall ye do in the fear of the Lord, faithfully, and with a perfect heart.

Ezr. 10.3. Those that tremble at the commandment of our God.

Job 28.28. Behold, the fear of the Lord, that *is* wisdom; and to depart from evil *is* understanding.

Job 37.24. Men do therefore fear him: he respecteth not any *that are* wise of heart.

Psa. 2.11. Serve the Lord with fear, and rejoice with trembling.

Psa. 4.4. Stand in awe, and sin not: commune with your own heart upon your bed, and be still.

Psa. 15.4. He honoureth them that fear the Lord.

Psa. 19.9. The fear of the Lord *is* clean, enduring for ever.

Psa. 22.23. Ye that fear the Lord, praise him; all ye the seed of Jacob, glorify him; and fear him, all ye the seed of Israel. 25. I will pay my vows before them that fear him.

Psa. 25.12. What man *is* he that feareth the Lord? him shall he teach in the way *that* he shall choose. 13. His soul shall dwell at ease; and his seed shall inherit the earth. 14. The secret of the Lord *is* with them that fear him; and he will shew them his covenant.

Psa. 31.19. *Oh* how great *is* thy goodness, which thou hast laid up for them that fear thee.

Psa. 33.8. Let all the earth fear the Lord: let all the inhabitants of the world stand in awe of him. 18. The eye of the Lord *is* upon them that fear him, upon them that hope in his mercy.

Psa. 34.7. The angel of the Lord encampeth round about them that fear him, and delivereth them. 9. O fear the Lord, ye his saints: for *there is* no want to them that fear him. 11. Come, ye children, hearken unto me: I will teach you the fear of the Lord.

Psa. 46.10. Be still, and know that I *am* God: I will be exalted among the heathen.

Psa. 52.6. The righteous also shall see, and fear.

Psa. 60.4. Thou hast given a banner to them that fear thee, that it may be displayed because of the truth.

Psa. 64.9. All men shall fear, and shall declare the work of God; for they shall wisely consider of his doing.

Psa. 67.7. God shall bless us; and all the ends of the earth shall fear him.

Psa. 72.5. They shall fear thee as long as the sun and moon endure, throughout all generations.

Psa. 76.7. Thou, *even* thou, *art* to be feared. 11. Let all that be round about him bring presents unto him that ought to be feared.

Psa. 85.9. His salvation *is* nigh them that fear him; that glory may dwell in our land.

Psa. 86.11. Unite my heart to fear thy name.

Psa. 89.7. God is greatly to be feared in the assembly of the saints, and to be had in reverence of all *them that are* about him.

Psa. 90.11. Who knoweth the power of thine anger? even according to thy fear, *so is* thy wrath.

Psa. 96.4. The Lord *is* great, and greatly to be praised: he *is* to be feared above all gods. 9. Fear before him, all the earth.

Psa. 102.15. The heathen shall fear the name of the Lord, and all the kings of the earth thy glory.

Psa. 103.11. As the heaven is high above the earth, *so* great is his mercy toward them that fear him. 13. Like as a father pitieth *his* children, *so* the Lord pitieth them that fear him. 17. The mercy of the Lord *is* from everlasting to everlasting upon them that fear him.

Psa. 111.5. He hath given meat unto them that fear him. 10. The fear of the Lord *is* the beginning of wisdom. Pro. 1.7. Pro. 9.10.

Psa. 112.1. Blessed *is* the man *that* feareth the Lord, *that* delighteth greatly in his commandments.

Psa. 115.11. Ye that fear the Lord, trust in the Lord. 13. He will bless them that fear the Lord, *both* small and great.

Psa. 118.4. Let them now that fear the Lord say, that his mercy *endureth* for ever.

Psa. 119.63. I *am* a companion of all *them* that fear thee, and of them that keep thy precepts. 74. They that fear thee will be glad when they see me; because I have hoped in thy word. 79. Let those that fear thee turn unto me, and those that have known thy testimonies. Psa. 66.16.

Psa. 128.1. Blessed *is* every one that feareth the Lord; that walketh in his ways. 4. Thus shall the man be blessed that feareth the Lord.

Psa. 130.4. *There is* forgiveness with thee, that thou mayest be feared.

Psa. 135.20. Ye that fear the Lord, bless the Lord.

Psa. 145.19. He will fulfil the desire of them that fear him: he also will hear their cry, and will save them.

Psa. 147.11. The Lord taketh pleasure in them that fear him.

Pro. 2.5. Then shalt thou understand the fear of the Lord.

Pro. 3.7. Fear the Lord, and depart from evil.

Pro. 8.13. The fear of the Lord *is* to hate evil.

Pro. 10.27. The fear of the Lord prolongeth days.

Pro. 13.13. He that feareth the commandment shall be rewarded.

Pro. 14.2. He that walketh in his uprightness feareth the Lord: but *he that is* perverse in his ways despiseth him. 16. A wise *man* feareth, and departeth from evil. 26. In the fear of the Lord *is* strong confidence. 27. The fear of the Lord *is* a fountain of life, to depart from the snares of death.

Pro. 15.16. Better *is* little with the fear of the Lord than great treasure and trouble therewith. 33. The fear of the Lord *is* the instruction of wisdom.

Pro. 16.6. By the fear of the Lord *men* depart from evil.

Pro. 19.23. The fear of the Lord *tendeth* to life: and *he that hath it* shall abide satisfied; he shall not be visited with evil.

Pro. 22.4. By humility *and* the fear of the Lord *are* riches, and honour, and life.

Pro. 23.17. *Be thou* in the fear of the Lord all the day long.

Pro. 24.21. Fear thou the Lord and the king.

Pro. 28.14. Happy *is* the man that feareth alway.

Pro. 31.30. A woman *that* feareth the Lord, she shall be praised.

Ecc. 3.14. God doeth *it*, that *men* should fear before him.

Ecc. 7.18. He that feareth God shall come forth of them all.

Ecc. 8.12. I know that it shall be well with them that fear God, which fear before him.

Ecc. 12.13. Fear God, and keep his commandments: for this *is* the whole *duty* of man. Ecc. 5.7. 1 Pet. 2.17.

Isa. 8.13. Sanctify the Lord of hosts himself; and *let* him *be* your fear, and *let* him *be* your dread.

Isa. 25.3. The strong people glorify thee, the city of the terrible nations shall fear thee.

Isa. 29.13. Their fear toward me is taught by the precept of men. 23. Sanctify the Holy One of Jacob, and shall fear the God of Israel.

Isa. 33.6. The fear of the Lord *is* his treasure. 13. Hear, ye *that are* far off, what I have done; and, ye *that are* near, acknowledge my might.

Isa. 50.10. Who *is* among you that feareth the Lord? let him trust in the name of the Lord, and stay upon his God.

Isa. 59.19. So shall they fear the name of the Lord from the west, and his glory from the rising of the sun.

Isa. 60.5. Thine heart shall fear, and be enlarged.

Jer. 5.22. Fear ye not me? saith the Lord: will ye not tremble at my presence, which have placed the sand *for* the bound of the sea by a perpetual decree, that it cannot pass it.

Jer. 10.7. Who would not fear thee, O King of nations? for to thee doth it appertain: forasmuch as among all the wise *men* of the nations, and in all their kingdoms, *there is* none like unto thee.

Jer. 32.39. I will give them one heart, and one way, that they may fear me for ever, for the good of them, and of their children after them. 40. I will put my fear in their hearts, that they shall not depart from me.

Jer. 33.9. They shall fear and tremble for all the goodness and for all the prosperity that I procure unto it.

Hos. 3.5. Afterward shall the children of Israel return, and shall fear the Lord and his goodness in the latter days.

Mic. 7.16. The nations shall see and be confounded at all their might: they shall lay *their* hand upon *their* mouth, their ears shall be deaf. 17. They shall lick the dust like a serpent, they shall move out of their holes like worms of the earth: they shall be afraid of the Lord our God, and shall fear because of thee.

Zeph. 1.7. Hold thy peace at the presence of the Lord God.

Zeph. 3.7. I said, Surely thou wilt fear me, thou wilt receive instruction; so their dwelling should not be cut off.

Zech. 2.13. Be silent, O all flesh, before the Lord: for he is raised up out of his holy habitation.

Mal. 1.6. A son honoureth *his* father, and a servant his master: if then I *be* a father, where *is* mine honour? and if I *be* a master, where *is* my fear? saith the Lord of hosts unto you, O priests, that despise my name.

Mal. 3.16. They that feared the Lord spake often one to another: and the Lord hearkened, and heard *it*, and a book of remembrance was written before him for them that feared the Lord, and that thought upon his name.

Mal. 4.2. Unto you that fear my name shall the Sun of righteousness arise with healing in his wings.

Mat. 10.28. Rather fear him which is able to destroy both soul and body in hell.

Luk. 1.50. His mercy *is* on them that fear him from generation to generation.

Luk. 12.5. I will forewarn you whom ye shall fear: Fear him, which after he hath killed hath power to cast into hell; yea, I say unto you, Fear him.

Luk. 23.40. Dost not thou fear God, seeing thou art in the same condemnation?

Act. 10.35. In every nation he that feareth him, and worketh righteousness, is accepted with him.

Act. 13.16. Men of Israel, and ye that fear God. 26. Whosoever among you feareth God, to you is the word of this salvation sent.

Rom. 11.20. Be not high-minded, but fear.

2 Cor. 7.1. Perfecting holiness in the fear of God.

Eph. 5.21. Submitting yourselves one to another in the fear of God.

Eph. 6.5. Servants, be obedient to them that are *your* masters according to the flesh, with fear and trembling, in singleness of your heart, as unto Christ. 1 Pet. 2.18.

Phil. 2.12. Work out your own salvation with fear and trembling.

Col. 3.22. Not with eye-service, as menpleasers; but in singleness of heart, fearing God.

Heb. 5.7. Was heard in that he feared.

Heb. 12.28. Let us have grace, whereby we may serve God acceptably with reverence and godly fear. 29. For our God *is* a consuming fire.

1 Pet. 1.17. Pass the time of your sojourning *here* in fear.

1 Pet. 3.2. Your chaste conversation *coupled* with fear. 15. *Be* ready always to *give* an answer to every man that asketh you a reason of the hope that is in you with meekness and fear.

Rev. 11.18. Give reward unto thy servants the prophets, and to the saints, and them that fear thy name, small and great.

Rev. 14.7. Fear God, and give glory to him; for the hour of his judgment is come.

Rev. 19.5. Praise our God, all ye his servants, and ye that fear him, both small and great.

FEAR OF GOD, EXAMPLES OF: Abraham, Gen. 22.12. Jacob, Gen. 28.16,17. Joseph, Gen. 42.18. Egyptians, Ex. 1.17,21. Ex. 9.20. Obadiah, 1 Kin. 18.3,12. Jehoshaphat, 2 Chr. 20.3. Nehemiah, Neh. 5.15. Hanani, Neh. 7.2. Job, Job 1.8.

David, Psa. 5.7. Psa.119.38. Hezekiah, Jer.26.19. Jonah, Jon. 1.9. Habakkuk, Hab. 3.2. Jews, Hag. 1.12. Phinehas, Mal. 2.5. Num. 25.11-13. Women at the sepulchre, Mat. 28.8. Churches, Act. 9.31. Cornelius, Act. 10.2. Noah, Heb. 11.7. See CONVICTION OF SIN—FAITH.

FEAR OF MAN. Jos. 7.5. The hearts of the people melted, and became as water.

Pro. 28.1. The wicked flee when no man pursueth.

Pro. 29.25. The fear of man bringeth a snare.

Isa. 7.2. His heart was moved, and the heart of his people, as the trees of the wood are moved with the wind.

Mat. 10.28. Fear not them which kill the body, but are not able to kill the soul.

Luk. 12.4. Be not afraid of them that kill the body, and after that have no more that they can do.

Gal. 1.10. Do I now persuade men, or God? or do I seek to please men? for if I yet pleased men, I should not be the servant of Christ, Jer. 1.8,17.

Gal. 6.12. As many as desire to make a fair show in the flesh, they constrain you to be circumcised; only lest they should suffer persecution for the cross of Christ.

Eph. 6.6. Not with eye-service, as men-pleasers; but as the servants of Christ, doing the will of God from the heart.

2 Tim. 4.16. At my first answer no man stood with me, but all *men* forsook me.

FEAR OF MAN, EXAMPLES OF: Aaron, Ex. 32.22-24. Saul, 1 Sam. 15.24. Zedekiah, Jer. 38.19. Pilate, Mar. 15.15. Jno. 19.8. Jews, Jno. 12.42,43. Disciples, Mat. 26.56. Peter, Mat. 26.69-74. Gal. 2.12. See DOUBT—FLATTERY—LUKEWARMNESS.

FEASTS. Dinner or supper, Gen. 43.16. Pro. 15.17. Mat. 22.4. Mar. 6.21. Luk. 11.37,38. Luk. 14.12,16. Jno. 12.2. Jno. 21.12,15. Banquet of wine, Est. 5.6. Est. 7.7.

Men present at alone, Gen. 43.32-34. 1 Sam. 9.22. Est. 1.8,9. Mar. 6.21. Luk. 14.24. Men and women present at, Ex. 32.6 with v. 2,3. Dan. 5.1-3. Thanksgiving at, see PRAYER AT MEALS. Drinking wine at, 1 Sam. 25.36. 1 Kin. 20.16. Hos. 7.5. Est. 1.7,8,10. Dan. 5.1-3. Jno. 2.1-11. Music and dancing at, see DANCING—MUSIC.

Guest-chamber for, Luk. 22.11,12. Were under the direction of a governor, Jno. 2.8,9. Host stood during the meal, Gen. 18.8.

GUESTS saluted by the host, Luk. 7.45. Gen. 18.2. Gen. 19.1. Feet and hands washed, see ABLUTION. Were anointed, see ANOINTING. Were placed according to age, Gen. 43.33; and rank, 1 Sam. 9.22. Luk. 14.8-10. Reclined on couches, Amos 6.7. Luk. 7.38. Waited on by female friends, Jno. 12.2. Choice portion sent to, by the host, Gen. 43.34. 1 Sam. 9.23,24. Ate from one dish, Mat. 26.23.

Given by kings, 1 Sam. 20.5. 2 Sam. 9.10. 1 Kin. 2.7. 1 Kin. 4.22 1 Kin 18.19. Est.

1.3-8. On birthdays, Gen. 40.20. Mar. 6.21. At coronation, 1 Kin. 1.25. 1 Chr. 12.38-40. Family feasts, Gen. 31.54. Job 42.11. Job 1.4. On weaning children, Gen. 21.8.

At sheep-shearing, 1 Sam. 25.2,36. 2 Sam. 13.23. At sacrifices, Den. 12.6,7. Religious festivals, 1 Sam. 20.6,24-29. Neh. 8.10,12. Ratifying covenants, Gen. 26.30. National deliverances, Est. 8.17. Est. 9.17-19. Illustrative, Luk. 14.16. Rev. 19.9,17. See MARRIAGE—HARVEST.

FEASTS or **FESTIVALS**, called Solemn feasts, Num. 15.3. 2 Chr. 8.13. Lam. 2.6. Eze. 46.9. Set feasts, Num. 29.39. Ezr. 3.5. Appointed feasts, Isa. 1.14. Holy convocations, Lev. 23.4. The first and eighth days were counted as Sabbaths, Lev. 23.39,40. Num. 28.18,25. Num. 29.12,35. Neh. 8.1,18.

Kept with thanksgiving and joy, Lev. 23.40. Deu. 16.11-14. 2 Chr. 30.21-26. Ezr. 6.22. Neh. 8.9-12,17. Psa. 42.4. Psa. 122.4. Isa. 30.29. Zec. 8.19. With hospitality, 1 Sam. 1.4,9. Neh. 8.10. With sacrifices, blowing of trumpets, and singing, see OFFERINGS—TRUMPETS—MUSIC. Promise of protection while observing, Ex. 34.24.

Three great annual feasts (Passover, Pentecost, Tabernacles), kept by all males, Ex. 23.17. Ex. 34.23. Deu. 16.16. Psa. 42.4. Psa. 122.4. Eze. 36.38. Luk. 2.44. Jno. 4.45. Jno. 7. By strangers, Jno. 12.20. Act. 2.1-11. By women, 1 Sam. 1.3,9. Luk. 2.41. By children at 12 years old, Luk. 2.42. By Christ, Mat. 26.17-20. Luk. 22.15. Jno. 2.13,23. Jno. 5.1. Jno. 7.10. Jno. 10.22. By Paul, Act. 18.21. Act. 19.21. Act. 20.6,16. Act. 24.11,17.

FEAST OF DEDICATION OF SOLOMON'S TEMPLE, 1 Kin. 8.65. 2 Chr. 7.8-10. Held in winter; Christ taught in the temple at, Jno. 10.22-39.

————, IDOLATROUS, Ex. 32.6. 1 Kin. 12.32.

———— OF THE NEW MOON, at the beginning of each month, Num. 10.10. Num. 28.11. Silver trumpets blown by the priests at, Num. 10.10. Psa. 81.3,4. Sacrifices at, Num. 28.11-15. 1 Chr. 23.31. 2 Chr. 31.3. Ezr. 3.5. No trading allowed on, Amos 8.5.

———— OF PASSOVER, instituted to commemorate the passing over of the first-born, and deliverance from Egypt, Ex. 12.3-42. Heb. 11.28. Psa. 81.3-5. Called the Lord's Passover, Ex. 12.11,27. Feast of unleavened bread, Lev. 23.6. Luk. 22.1. Days of unleavened bread, Act. 12.3. Act 20.6.

Passover is applied to (1.) the Paschal lamb, Luk. 22.7. 1 Cor. 5.7. (2.) The Paschal meal, Mat. 26.18,19. Heb. 11.28. (3.) The Paschal festival, comprehending the seven days of unleavened bread, Luk. 2.41-43. Luk. 22.1. Jno. 2.13. Jno. 11.55.

Passover lamb, a male of the first year, without blemish, kept up from the 10th Abib to the 14th, Ex. 12.3-6. Killed in the evening of the 14th, Ex. 12.6 (see Mar. 15.34). By the head of each household, Ex. 12.3-7. At the tabernacle door, Deu. 16.5-7. By Levites, when the people were ceremonially unclean, 2 Chr. 30.17. 2 Chr. 35.3-11. Ezr. 6.20. Blood of, sprinkled, Ex. 12.7,22. 2 Chr. 30.16. A bone of, not to be broken, Ex. 12.46. Num. 9.12 (see Jno. 19.33,36). Roasted whole,

Ex. 12.8,9. 2 Chr. 35.13. Eaten with bitter herbs and unleavened bread, Ex. 12.8. Num. 9.11. Jno. 13.26. Not to be left till morning, Ex. 12.10. Ex. 23.18. Ex. 34.25. Num. 9.12. Wine used with, Mat. 26.27-29.

Leaven put away, and unleavened bread eaten 7 days, Ex. 12.8,15-20. Ex. 13.3,6. Ex. 23.15. Lev. 23.6. Num. 9.11. Num. 28.17. Deu. 16.3,4. Mar. 14.12. Luk. 22.7. Act. 12.3. 1 Cor. 5.8. Punishment for eating leaven, Ex. 12.15.

Sacrifices offered daily, Lev. 23.8. Num. 28.19-24. A sheaf of first-fruits offered on the day after the passover week, Lev. 23.10-14 with Jos. 5.10,11.

Kept by all who were circumcised, Ex. 12.43-49. Num. 9.14 ; and purified, Num. 9.6,7,13. 2 Chr. 30.3,15-19. Jno. 11.55. Kept with rejoicing, 2 Chr. 30.21,26.

On the first observance of, blood sprinkled on the doorposts, Ex. 12.7,22 ; and eaten in haste standing, Ex. 12.11.

Commenced on 14th of Abib, and lasted seven days, the first and eighth days being holy convocations, Ex. 12.18. Lev. 23.5-8. Jno. 19.31. The time of changed on special occasions, Num. 9.6-11. 2 Chr. 30.2,3,15.

Neglect of, punished, Num. 9.13. Rooms lent for, Luk. 22.11,12. A prisoner released at, by the Romans, Mat. 27.15. Luk. 23.16,17. Lord's Supper instituted at, Mat. 26.26-28. Christ crucified during, Jno. 18.28. The Sabbath occurring during the feast, called a high day, Jno. 19.31. Illustrative, 1 Cor. 5.7,8.

Kept on leaving Egypt, Ex. 12.28,50. Heb. 11.28. In the wilderness, Num. 9.3-5. On entering Canaan, Jos. 5.10,11. By Hezekiah, 2 Chr. 30.1. By Josiah, 2 Kin. 23.22,23. 2 Chr. 35.1.18. After return from captivity, Ezr. 6.19,20. By Christ, Mat. 26.17-20. Luk. 22.15. Jno. 2.13,23.

FEAST OF PENTECOST (Pentecost signifies the fiftieth). Held on the 50th day after offering the first sheaf of barley harvest, Lev. 23.15,16. Deu. 16.9 (that is, 50 days after the Passover), compare Lev. 23.10-14 with Jos. 5.10,11 ; hence called feast of weeks (that is, a week multiplied by a week, 7 times 7), Ex. 34.22. Deu. 16.10. Called feast of harvest, Ex. 23.16. Day of the first-fruits, Num. 28.26. Day of Pentecost, Act. 2.1. Act. 20.16. 1 Cor. 16.8.

First-fruits of bread offered at, Lev. 23.17. Num. 15.19,20. Sacrifices at, Lev. 23.18,19. Num. 28.27-31. Celebrated by a holy convocation, with rejoicing and thanksgiving, Lev. 23.21. Num. 28.26. Deu. 16.10,12. The law given at, on the 3d or 4th day of the 3d month (that is, 50 days from the Passover), Ex. 19.1,16. The Holy Ghost given on the 1st day of, Act. 2.

—————— OF PURIM (that is, Lots) instituted by Mordecai to commemorate the Jews' deliverance from Haman's plots, Est. 9.20-32 with Est. 3.7-15.

—————— OF TABERNACLES OF INGATHERING. Commemorative of the sojourn of Israel in the Desert, Lev. 23.43. Was held after the vintage and harvest, Deu. 16.13. Ex. 23.16. Began on the 15th of the 7th month, Lev. 23.34,39. Kept idolatrously by Jeroboam at Bethel in the 8th month, 1 Kin. 12 32.

Lasted 7 days, Num. 29.12. Deu. 16.13,15.

First and eighth days holy convocations, Lev. 23.39. Num. 29.12,35. Jno. 7.37. The people dwelt in booths 7 days, Lev. 23.40-43. Neh. 8.15,16. Neglect of this rule, Neh. 8.17.

Sacrifices offered daily on, Lev. 23.36,37. Num. 29.13-39. Celebrated with joy, Lev. 23.40. Deu. 16.14,15. The law publicly read at, every seventh or Sabbatical year, Deu. 31.10-12. Neh. 8.18. Kept at the dedication of the temple, 1 Kin. 8.2,65. After the captivity, Ezr. 3.4. Neh. 8.14-18. By Christ, Jno. 7.2,14.

FEAST OF TRUMPETS. Celebrated on the 1st day of 7th month by blowing trumpets, Lev. 23.24. Num. 29.1. Sacrifices on, Num. 29.2-6. Work forbidden on, Lev. 23.24,25.

FEET, sitting at, as disciples, Deu. 33.3. Luk. 10.39. Act. 22.3. See ABLUTION.

FELIX, a Roman governor in Judea. Paul brought before him at Cesarea, Act. 23.24-35. Act. 24. He trembles at Paul's reasoning, Act. 24.25. Keeps him bound for two years, Act. 24.26,27. Act. 25.14.

FENCE WALL, HEDGE, Gen. 49.22. Num. 22.24. Psa. 62.3. Ecc. 10.8. Song 4.12. Isa. 5.2,5. Nah. 3.17. Mat. 21.33. Of stone, Pro. 24.30,31. Mic. 7.11. Of thorns, Pro. 15.19. Hos. 2.6.

FERRET, Lev. 11.30.

FERRY-BOAT, 2 Sam. 19.18.

FESTIVALS. See FEASTS.

FESTUS, or PORCIUS FESTUS, Roman governor in Judea. Succeeds Felix, Act. 24.27. Trial of Paul by, Act. 25. Act. 26.

FETTERS, 2 Chr. 33.11. 2 Chr. 36.6. Mar. 5.4. Of brass, Jud. 16.21. 2 Kin. 25.7. Of iron, Psa. 149.8. For the feet, 2 Sam. 3.34. Psa. 105.18. See CHAINS.

FEVER, or AGUE, Lev. 26.16. Deu. 28.22. Mat. 8.14.

FIDELITY TO GOD. See DECISION—ZEAL—PERSECUTION.

FIG. In Canaan, Num. 13.23. Deu. 8.8. In Egypt, Psa. 105.33. Its leaves, Gen. 3.7. Mat. 24.32. Jno. 1.48,50. Fruit, Jud. 9.11. Hos. 9.10. 1 Sam. 25.18. Neh. 13.15. Nah. 3.12. Dried, 1 Sam. 30.12. Wild, Amos 7.14 (marg.) Jer. 29.17. Miracles connected with, Isa. 38.21. 2 Kin. 20.7. Mar. 11.12-14,20,21. Parables of, Jer. 24.2. Luk. 13.6-9. Luk. 21.29-31. Illustrative, 1 Kin. 4.25. Rev. 6.13. See SYCAMORE.

FILE, 1 Sam. 13.21.

FINES. See PUNISHMENTS.

FINGER-BREADTH, a measure, 4 equal to 3 inches, Jer. 52.21.

FIR-TREE, Psa. 104.17. Isa. 41.19. Isa. 55.13. Hos. 14.8. Wood of, used in the temple, 1 Kin. 6.15,34. In houses, Song 1.17. For ships, Eze. 27.5. For musical instruments, 2 Sam. 6.5.

FIRE. Illustrative and symbolical, Ex. 3.2 Ex. 19.18. Deu. 4.24. Eze. 1.4. Rev. 1.14. Psa. 18.8. Jer. 48.45. Mal. 3.2. Mat. 3.11. Act. 2.3. Psa. 104.4. Deu. 32.22. Isa. 33.14. Mar. 9.44. Rev. 20.9. Rev. 21.8. Jer. 23.29

Luk. 12.49.   Obad. 18.   Isa. 50.11.   Pro. 16.27.

FIRE, Sacred, Lev. 9.24 with Lev. 10 1. Jud. 6.21.   Jud. 13.19,20.   2 Chr. 7.1.   1 Kin. 18.38. See Gen. 4.4.   Gen. 15.17.

FIREBRAND.   Illustrative, Amos 4.11. Zec. 3.2.   See Lamp.

FIRE-PANS of the tabernacle and temple, Ex. 38.3.   2 Kin. 25.15.

FIRKIN (Gr. *metretes*), about 8 galls., Jno. 2.6.

FIRMAMENT, or Expanse (the air and sky), Gen. 1.6-8,14-17,20.   Psa. 19.1.   Eze. 1.22-26.

FIRST-BORN, The.   Birthright of, Gen. 25.31.   Heb. 12.16.   Gen. 27.29,35-37.   Gen. 43.33.   Gen. 48.13-18.   Gen. 49.3.   Set aside, examples of: Esau, Gen. 25.23,33.   Gen. 27.35-37.   Rom. 9.12,13.   Manasseh, Gen. 48.15-20.   Reuben, 1 Chr. 5.1,2.   Adonijah, 1 Kin. 2.15.   Hosah's son, 1 Chr. 26.10. See Inheritance.

Of Egyptians slain, Ex. 11.5.   Ex. 12.12,29. Ex. 13.15 ; and buried, Num. 33.4.   Of kings, succeeded to the throne, 2 Kin. 3.27.   2 Chr. 21.3.   Sacrificed to idols, 2 Kin. 3.27.   Mic. 6.7.   Daughters married before the younger, Gen. 29.26.

Of man and beast (males) dedicated to God to commemorate the passing over of the first-born of Israel, Ex. 13.2,12.   Ex. 22.29,30. Ex. 34.19.   Lev. 27.26.   Num. 3.13.   Num. 8.17.   Deu. 15.19.   Neh. 10.36.

Sons to be presented to God, Neh. 10.36. Luk. 2.22,23.   To be redeemed, Ex. 34.20. Num. 18.15 ; by the Levites being taken in their room, Num. 3.12,40-45.   Num. 8.16-18 ; by money, 5 shekels for each of the 273 more than the number of Levites, the price being given to the priests, Num. 3.40-50.   Num. 18.16.

Of clean animals, to be sacrificed when 7 days old as a thank-offering, Ex. 34.19. Lev. 22.27.   Lev. 27.26.   Num. 18.17.   Deu. 15.19-22.   Neh. 10.36.   Of unclean animals to be redeemed, Lev. 27.27.   Num. 18.15,16. Firstling of the ass to be redeemed with a lamb, or its neck to be broken, Ex. 13.13. Ex. 34.20.

First-born, besides its ordinary meaning, is a term of honour.   Compare Ex. 4.22.   Jer. 31.9.   Col. 1.15.   Psa. 89.27.   Heb. 1.6.   Rom. 8.29.   Rev. 1.5.   Heb. 12.23.

FIRST-FRUITS consisted of the first ripe fruits and corn, the first produce of oil and wine and fleece, Ex. 22.29.   Num. 18.12.   Deu. 18.4.   2 Chr. 31.5.   Neh. 10.35,37,39 ; the fruit of trees in the 4th year, Lev. 19.24. Required to be the best of their kind, Num. 18.12.

A sheaf presented as a wave-offering on 15th Nisan (the morrow after the Sabbath), Lev. 23.10-14.   Two wave loaves at Pentecost, Lev. 23.17.   Dough as a heave-offering, Num. 15.20.   Neh. 10.37.   Eze. 44.30.   Not to be burned, Lev. 2.12.

To be brought to God's house, Ex. 22.29. Ex. 23.19.   Ex. 34.26.   Deu. 26.2.   With confession and thanksgiving, Deu. 26.3-10.   Given to the priests, Lev. 23.20.   Num. 18.12,13. Deu. 18.3-5 ; and to prophets, 2 Kin. 4.42.

FISHES.   Clean and unclean, Lev. 11.9-12. Deu. 14.9,10.   See Leviathan — Whale. Taken with nets or drags, Ecc. 9.12.   Hab. 1.14-17.   Mat. 4.21.   Luk. 5.2-6.   Jno. 21.6-8. Hooks, Isa. 19.8.   Amos 4.2.   Mat. 17.27. Spears, Job 41.7.

Artificial pools for, Song 7.4.   Isa. 19.10. In Egypt, Num. 11.5 ; and Palestine, Neh. 13.16. Jno. 21.13.   A great fish swallows Jonah, Jon. 1.17.   Jon. 2.   Mat. 12.40.   Miracles of Christ connected with, Mat. 14.19.   Mat. 15.36. Mat. 17.27.   Luk. 5.6.   Jno. 21.6,11.

FISHERMEN, some of the apostles were, Mat. 4.18-21.   Jno. 21.2.

FITCH, or Vetch.   Isa. 28.25,27.   Eze. 4.9.

FLAG (Bulrush), Ex. 2.3,5.   Job 8.11.   Isa. 19.6.   Jon. 2.5.

FLAGON, signifying raisin cake, Hos. 3.1 (*marg.*).   2 Sam. 6.19.   Song 2.5.

FLATTERY. Job 17.5.   He that speaketh flattery to *his* friends, even the eyes of his children shall fail.

Job 32.21.   Neither let me give flattering titles unto man.   22. For I know not to give flattering titles ; *in so doing* my maker would soon take me away.

Psa. 12.2.   They speak vanity every one with his neighbour : *with* flattering lips, *and* with a double heart, do they speak.   3. The Lord shall cut off all flattering lips.   Psa. 5.9.

Psa. 49.13.   This their way *is* their folly : yet their posterity approve their sayings. 18. *Men* will praise thee, when thou doest well to thyself.   Pro. 6.24.

Pro. 7.21.   With her much fair speech she caused him to yield, with the flattering of her lips she forced him.   22. He goeth after her straightway, as an ox goeth to the slaughter.

Pro. 14.20.   The rich *hath* many friends.

Pro. 19.4.   Wealth maketh many friends. 6. Many will entreat the favour of the prince : and every man *is* a friend to him that giveth gifts.

Pro. 20.19.   Meddle not with him that flattereth with his lips.

Pro. 22.16.   He that giveth to the rich, *shall* surely *come* to want.

Pro. 24.24.   He that saith unto the wicked, Thou *art* righteous ; him shall the people curse, nations shall abhor him.

Pro. 25.26.   A righteous man falling down before the wicked *is as* a troubled fountain, and a corrupt spring.

Pro. 26.28.   A flattering mouth worketh ruin.

Pro. 28.23.   He that rebuketh a man afterwards shall find more favour than he that flattereth with the tongue.

Pro. 29.5.   A man that flattereth his neighbour spreadeth a net for his feet.

Dan. 11.21.   He shall come in peaceably, and obtain the kingdom by flatteries.   34. Many shall cleave to them with flatteries.

Luk. 6.26.   Woe unto you, when all men shall speak well of you ! for so did their fathers to the false prophets.

Gal. 1.10.   Do I seek to please men? for if I yet pleased men, I should not be the servant of Christ.

Eph. 6.6.   Not with eye-service, as men-pleasers.

1 The. 2.4.   Even so we speak, not as pleasing

men, but God, which trieth our hearts.
5. For neither at any time used we flattering
words, as ye know, nor a cloak of covetousness; God *is* witness: 6. Nor of men sought
we glory, neither of you, nor *yet* of others.

Jude 16. Their mouth speaketh great swelling *words*, having men's persons in admira-
tion because of advantage.

FLATTERY. EXAMPLES OF: Jacob, Gen.
33.10. Mephibosheth, 2 Sam. 9.8. Woman
of Tekoah, 2 Sam. 14.17. Absalom, 2 Sam.
15.2-6. Israel and Judah, 2 Sam. 19.41-43.
Ahab, 1 Kin. 20.4. False prophets, 1 Kin.
22.13. Job's friends, Job 29.5.25. Darius'
courtiers, Dan. 6.7. Herodians, Luk. 20.21.
Tyrians, Act. 12.22.

FLAX, Jud. 15.14. Grown in Egypt, Ex.
9.31. Palestine, Jos. 2.6. Made into cord,
Est. 1.6. Eze. 40.3. Woven into linen, Pro.
31.13. Isa. 19.9. Hos. 2.5,9. Illustrative,
Mat. 12.20. See LINEN.

FLEA, 1 Sam. 24.14. 1 Sam. 26.20.

FLESH, signifying the body, Gen. 2.21.
Job 19.26. Psa. 16.9. Mat. 26.41. The
mortality of the body, Gen. 6.3. 2 Chr. 32.8.
Mankind, Gen. 6.12. Num. 16.22. All living
beings, Gen. 7.15. Blood relations, Gen. 29.14.
Gen. 37.27. Illustrative, Eze. 36.26. Jno.
8.15. Rom. 7.25. Rom. 8.3. Eph. 2.3. Jno.
6.51-63.

FLESH-HOOKS belonging to the brazen
altar, Ex. 27.3. Ex. 38.3. Num. 4.14. 1 Sam.
2.13,14. Of the temple, golden, 1 Chr. 28.17.
Of brass, 2 Chr. 4.16.

FLIES, Eccl. 10.1. Plague of, in Egypt,
Ex. 8.21-31. Psa. 78.45. Psa. 105.31. Illustrative, Isa. 7.18.

FLINT, Deu. 8.15. Deu. 32.13. Psa. 114.8.
Isa. 50.7.

FLOOD, THE, history of, Gen. *c.* 6 to 8.
Job 22.16. Psa. 90.5. Mat. 24.38. Luk.
17.26,27. Heb. 11.7. 1 Pet. 3.20. 2 Pet. 2.5.
Promise it should not return, Gen. 8.20-21.
Isa. 54.9.

FLOUR. See WHEAT—BARLEY—OFFER-
ING, MEAT-OFFERING.

FLOWERS. See PLANTS.

FLUTE, Dan. 3.5,7,10,15. See ORGAN—
PIPE.

FOOD. Before the flood, Gen. 1.29. Gen.
2.9,16. Gen. 3.17-19. After the flood, Gen.
9.3. Unclean animals forbidden to the Israelites, Lev. 11. Deu. 14; and animals that
died, Ex. 22.31. Lev. 17.15. See BLOOD—
FAT. Rules regarding meat offered to idols,
Act. 15.29. 1 Cor. 10.25-33. All kinds of food
lawful, Rom. 14.14,20,21. 1 Cor. 8.8. 1 Cor.
10.30. 1 Tim. 4.3-5.

Kinds of, see ALMOND, APPLE, BARLEY,
BEAN, BREAD, BROTH, BUTTER, CHEESE,
CORN, CUCUMBER, DATE, FIG, FISHES,
HONEY, LEEKS, LENTILES, MALLOWS, MAN-
DRAKE, MANNA, MELON, MILK, MILLET,
MULBERRY, NUTS, OIL, ONION, PANNAG,
POMEGRANATE, PULSE, RAISINS, RYE, SALT,
VINEGAR, WHEAT, WINE. See also FEASTS—
PRAYER AT MEALS—GOD'S GOODNESS IN
PROVIDENCE.

FORDS. Of Jordan, Jos. 2.7. Jud. 3.28.
Jud. 12.5,6. Of Jabbok, Gen. 32.22. Of
Arnon, Isa. 16 2. Of the Euphrates, Jer. 51.32.

FOREIGNERS. See STRANGERS.

FORERUNNER, name of Christ, Heb. 6.20.

FORESTS. See PALESTINE, WOODS OF.

FORGETTING GOD. See GODLESSNESS
—BACKSLIDING—PRAYERLESSNESS.

FORGIVENESS OF ENEMIES. Ex. 23.4.
If thou meet thine enemy's ox or his ass going
astray, thou shalt surely bring it back to him
again. 5. If thou see the ass of him that
hateth thee lying under his burden, and
wouldest forbear to help him, thou shalt surely
help with him.

Pro. 19.11. The discretion of a man deferreth his anger; and *it is* his glory to pass over
a transgression.

Pro. 24.17. Rejoice not when thine enemy
falleth, and let not thine heart be glad when
he stumbleth. 29. Say not, I will do so to
him as he hath done to me: I will render to
the man according to his work.

Pro. 25.21. If thine enemy be hungry, give
him bread to eat; and if he be thirsty, give
him water to drink: 22. For thou shalt heap
coals of fire upon his head, and the Lord shall
reward thee. Rom. 12.20.

Ecc. 7.21. Take no heed unto all words
that are spoken; lest thou hear thy servant
curse thee.

Mat. 5.7. Blessed *are* the merciful: for
they shall obtain mercy. 39. Resist not evil:
but whosoever shall smite thee on thy right
cheek, turn to him the other also. 40. And
if any man will sue thee at the law, and take
away thy coat, let him have *thy* cloak also.
41. And whosoever shall compel thee to go a
mile, go with him twain.

Mat. 5.43. It hath been said, Thou shalt
love thy neighbour, and hate thine enemy.
44. But I say unto you, Love your enemies,
bless them that curse you, do good to them
that hate you, and pray for them which
despitefully use you, and persecute you;
45. That ye may be the children of your Father
which is in heaven: for he maketh his sun to
rise on the evil and on the good, and sendeth
rain on the just and on the unjust. 46. For
if ye love them which love you, what reward
have ye? do not even the publicans the same?
v. 47,48. Luk. 6.27-34.

Mat. 6.12. Forgive us our debts, as we forgive our debtors. 14. If ye forgive men their
trespasses, your heavenly Father will also forgive you: 15. But if ye forgive not men
their trespasses, neither will your Father forgive your trespasses.

Mat. 18.32. O thou wicked servant, I forgave thee all that debt, because thou desiredst
me: 33. Shouldest not thou also have had
compassion on thy fellow-servant, even as I
had pity on thee? 34. And his lord was wroth,
and delivered him to the tormentors, till he
should pay all that was due unto him. 35. So
likewise shall my heavenly Father do also unto
you, if ye from your hearts forgive not every
one his brother their trespasses.

Mar. 11.25. When ye stand praying, forgive, if ye have ought against any: that your
Father also which is in heaven may forgive
you. *v.* 26.

Luk. 6.35. Love ye your enemies, and do
good, and lend, hoping for nothing again; and
your reward shall be great, and ye shall be the
children of the Highest: for he is kind unto

the unthankful and *to* the evil. 36. Be ye therefore merciful, as your Father also is merciful. 37. Condemn not, and ye shall not be condemned : forgive, and ye shall be forgiven.

Luk. 17.3. If thy brother trespass against thee, rebuke him ; and if he repent, forgive him. 4. And if he trespass against thee seven times in a day, and seven times in a day turn again to thee, saying, I repent ; thou shalt forgive him. Mat. 18.21,22.

Rom. 12.14. Bless them which persecute you : bless, and curse not. 17. Recompense to no man evil for evil. 19. Avenge not yourselves, but *rather* give place unto wrath : for it is written, Vengeance *is* mine ; I will repay, saith the Lord. 21. Be not overcome of evil, but overcome evil with good.

1 Cor. 4.12. Being reviled, we bless ; being persecuted, we suffer it : 13. Being defamed, we entreat.

Eph. 4.32. Be ye kind one to another, tenderhearted, forgiving one another, even as God for Christ's sake hath forgiven you.

Col. 3.13. Forbearing one another, and forgiving one another, if any man have a quarrel against any : even as Christ forgave you, so also *do* ye.

Philm. 10. I beseech thee for my son Onesimus. 18. If he hath wronged thee, or oweth *thee* ought, put that on mine account.

1 Pet. 3.9. Not rendering evil for evil, or railing for railing : but contrariwise blessing ; knowing that ye are thereunto called, that ye should inherit a blessing.

FORGIVENESS OF ENEMIES. EXAMPLES OF : Joseph, Gen. 45.5-15. Gen. 50.19-21. Moses, Num. 12.1,13. David, 1 Sam. 24.10-12. 1 Sam. 26.9-23. 2 Sam. 1.14-17. 2 Sam. 2.4-6. 2 Sam. 16.9-13. 2 Sam. 19.19-23. Psa. 7.4. Solomon, 1 Kin. 1.53. See MALICE—MEEKNESS.

FORGIVENESS OF ENEMIES, PRAYER FOR. Luk. 23.34. Then said Jesus, Father, forgive them ; for they know not what they do.

Act. 7.60. He kneeled down, and cried with a loud voice, Lord, lay not this sin to their charge.

2 Tim. 4.16. All *men* forsook me : *I pray God* that it may not be laid to their charge.

FORGIVENESS OF SIN. See PARDON—GOD'S MERCY—CHRIST, PARDON FROM.

FORK, 1 Sam. 13.21.

FORMALISM. See PRIVILEGES—WORKS —SELF-RIGHTEOUSNESS.

FORNICATION. See ADULTERY.

FORT, FORTRESS, CASTLE, STRONGHOLD, TOWER. Towers and castles in cities, Jud. 8.17. 1 Chr. 11.7. 2 Chr. 26.15. Isa. 25.12. On city-walls, see JERUSALEM, TOWERS OF—CITIES. Watch-towers, 2 Kin. 9.17. Isa. 21.5. Isa. 32.14.

In the desert, 2 Chr. 26.10. Forts built in besieging a city, 2 Kin. 25.1. Eze. 17.17. Eze. 26.8 ; of wood, Deu. 20.19,20. Natural caves among rocks, Jud. 6.2. 1 Sam. 23.29. Isa. 33.16. Illustrative, Psa. 71.3. Psa. 144.2. Nah. 1.7.

FORTUNATUS, a Corinthian Christian, visits Paul at Ephesus, and returns bearing Paul's epistle, 1 Cor. 16.17,18.

FORTY. Peculiar occurrences of the number forty. 40 days' rain at the flood, Gen. 7.17.

Noah sends out the raven after 40 days, Gen. 8.6. 40 days embalming, Gen. 50.3. Manna and wandering in the wilderness 40 years, Num. 14.34. Ex. 16.35.

Moses in the Mount 40 days, Ex. 24.18. Ex. 34.28. Deu. 9.9,25. Spies searched the land 40 days, Num. 13.25. 40 stripes as a punishment, Deu. 25.3. Peace lasted 40 years, Jud. 3.11. Jud. 5.31. Jud. 8.28. Elijah fasted 40 days, 1 Kin. 19.8 ; and Christ, Mat. 4.2. 40 days' warning to Nineveh, Jon. 3.4. Symbolical, Eze. 4.6. Eze. 29.11.

FOUNDATIONS OF BUILDINGS, 1 Kin. 5.17. 1 Kin. 7.9. Ezr. 4.12. Ezr. 6.3. Jer. 51.26. Luk. 6.48,49. Act. 16.26. Illustrative, Psa. 87.1. Isa. 28.16. Isa. 48.13. Rom. 15.20. 1 Cor. 3.11. Eph. 2.20. 1 Tim. 6.19. Heb. 6.1. Rev. 21.14. See CORNER-STONE.

FOUNDING OF METALS, Jud. 17.4. Isa. 41.7 (*marg.*). Jer. 6.29. Jer. 10.9,14. See BRASS—GOLD—IRON—SILVER—FURNACE.

FOUNTAIN. Illustrative, Psa. 36.9. Jer. 2.13. Zec. 13.1. Rev. 7.17. Pro. 25.26. Jer. 6.7. Symbolical, Rev. 8.10. Rev. 16.4. See WELLS.

FOWLS. See BIRDS.

FOX, Psa. 63.10. Luk. 9.58. Samson's use of, against the Philistines, Jud. 15.4. Illustrative, Eze. 13.4. Luk. 13.32.

FRANKINCENSE, Song 4.6,14. Used in the sacred anointing oil, Ex. 30.34. Put on the shewbread, Lev. 24.7 ; and on meat-offerings, Lev. 2.1,2,15,16. Lev. 6.15. Neh. 13.9. Forbidden with meat-offering when brought as a sin-offering, Lev. 5.11 ; or jealousy-offering, Num. 5.15. Used as a perfume, Song 3.6. Translated incense, Isa. 43.23. Isa. 60.6. Isa. 66.3. Jer. 6.20.

FRAUD. See DISHONESTY.

FRIENDSHIP, Deu. 13.6. Thy friend which is as thine own soul.

Pro. 17.17. A friend loveth at all times, and a brother is born for adversity.

Pro. 18.24. A man *that hath* friends must shew himself friendly : and there is a friend *that* sticketh closer than a brother.

Pro. 25.17. Withdraw thy foot from thy neighbour's house ; lest he be weary of thee, and so hate thee.

Pro. 27.9. Ointment and perfume rejoice the heart : so *doth* the sweetness of a man's friend by hearty counsel. 10. Thine own friend, and thy father's friend, forsake not ; neither go into thy brother's house in the day of thy calamity : *for* better *is* a neighbour *that is* near than a brother far off. 17. Iron sharpeneth iron ; so a man sharpeneth the countenance of his friend. 19. As in water face answereth to face, so the heart of man to man.

Ecc. 4.9. Two *are* better than one ; because they have a good reward for their labour. 10. For if they fall, the one will lift up his fellow : but woe to him *that is* alone when he falleth ; for *he hath* not another to help him up. 11. Again, if two lie together, then they have heat : but how can one be warm *alone?* 12. And if one prevail against him, two shall withstand him ; and a threefold cord is not quickly broken.

FRIENDSHIP. EXAMPLES OF : Ruth and Naomi, Ruth 1.16,17. David and Jonathan,

1 Sam. 18.1-4. 1 Sam. 19.2-5. 1 Sam. 20.14-17. 2 Sam. 1.26. 2 Sam. 9.1-13. David and Nahash, 2 Sam. 10.2. David and Hiram, 1 Kin. 5.1. David and Hushai, 2 Sam. 16-16. Paul and Epaphroditus, Philm. 2.25,30. Paul and Titus, 2 Cor. 2.13. Paul and Timothy, 2 Tim. 1.2.

FRIENDS, FALSE. See TREACHERY.

FRINGES, the Jews commanded to make, on their garments, Deu. 22.12. A blue ribband used for, Num. 15.38-41. The Pharisees made broad, Mat. 23.5.

FROGS, plague of, in Egypt, Ex. 8.2-14. Psa. 78.45. Psa. 105.30. Symbolical, Rev. 16.13.

FRONTLETS. See PHYLACTERIES.

FRUIT. Illustrative, Pro. 8.19. Pro. 10.16. Pro. 11.30. Pro. 12.14. Psa. 132.11. Mat. 7.16. Gal. 5.22. Eph. 5.9. Heb. 13.15.

FRUIT-TREES. See PLANTS—AGRICULTURE—VINEYARDS.

FRYING-PAN, Lev. 2.7. Lev. 7.9.

FULLER (Bleacher), Mal. 3.2. Mar. 9.3.

FUNERALS. See BURIAL—MOURNING.

FURLONG (Gr. *stadios*), about the 9th of an English mile, Luk. 24.13. Jno. 11.18. Rev. 21.16.

FURNACE or OVEN, Gen. 15.17. Neh. 3.11. Of iron, 1 Kin. 8.51. Of earth, Psa. 12.6. Used for baking, Lev. 2.4. Lev. 7.9. Lev. 11.35. Lev. 26.26. Hos. 7.4. For melting silver, Eze. 22.22. Mal. 3.3; and gold, Pro. 17.3; and lead and tin, Eze. 22.20. Shadrach, &c., cast into, Dan. 3.6-26. Illustrative, Deu. 4.20. Psa. 21.9. Isa. 31.9. Lam. 5.10. Hos. 7.6,7. Mal. 4.1. Mat. 6.30. Mat. 13.42.

G

GAAL, makes himself ruler of the Shechemites, defeated by Abimelech, Jud. 9.26-41.

GAASH, a hill of Mount Ephraim, where Joshua was buried, Jos. 24.30. Jud. 2.9. 2 Sam. 23.30.

GABBATHA, or PAVEMENT, a place outside the judgment-hall, where the Jews remained during Christ's trial, and in which Pilate passed sentence on him, Jno. 19.13 with Jno. 18.28,29,38.

GABRIEL, the angel who appeared to Daniel, Dan. 8.15-18. Dan. 9.21-23. Zacharias, Luk. 1.11-19. Mary, Luk. 1.26-29.

GAD, son of Jacob and Zilpah, Gen. 30.10,11. Gen 35.26. His children, Gen. 46.16. Blessed by Jacob, Gen. 49.19.

——, TRIBE OF. Numbered at Sinai, Num. 1.14,24,25; and in the plains of Moab, Num. 26.15-18. In Jotham's days, 1 Chr. 5.11-17. Encamped south of the tabernacle, and marched under the standard of Reuben, Num. 2.10,14,16. Num. 10.18-20.
Blessing of Moses on, Deu. 33.20,21. Possessed much cattle, Num. 32.1. Inheritance east of Jordan, Num. 32. Deu. 3.12,16. Deu. 29.8. Jos. 13.8,24-28. Jos. 18.7. Jos. 22.9. 1 Chr. 5.11. Assisted the other tribes to conquer the Canaanites, Num. 32.16-32. Jos. 1.12-18. Jos. 4.12,13. Jos. 22.1-8.

Built an altar of witness called Ed, Jos. 22.10-34. Many joined David at Ziklag and Hebron, 1 Chr. 12.8-15,37,38. With the Reubenites conquered the Hagarites in the time of Saul, 1 Chr. 5.10,18-22. Conquered by Hazael, king of Syria, 2 Kin. 10.32,33. Taken captive by Assyrians, 1 Chr. 5.26. Land of, seized by the Ammonites, Jer. 49.1. For what is common to the tribes, see ISRAELITES, TRIBES OF.

GAD, David's seer, 2 Sam. 24.11. Bids David leave Adullam, 1 Sam. 22.5. Reproves David for numbering the people, 2 Sam. 24.11-14. 1 Chr. 21.9-13. Bids him build an altar on the threshing-floor of Ornan, 2 Sam. 24.18,19. 1 Chr. 21.18,19. Assists David in arranging the temple service, 2 Chr. 29.25. His writings, 1 Chr. 29.29.

GADARENES, or GERGESENES. Christ casts out a legion of devils in their country; they ask him to depart, Mar. 5.1-19. Mat. 8.28-34.

GAIUS, a Macedonian, Act. 19.29. Baptized at Corinth, 1 Cor. 1.14. Resides in Derbe, Act. 20.4. A companion of Paul, seized by the Ephesians, Act. 19.29. Accompanies Paul to Macedonia, Act. 20.4. His hospitality at Rome, Rom. 16.23. His piety, 3 Jno. 1.

GALATIA, a province of Asia Minor, 1 Pet. 1.1. The churches in, visited by Paul, Act. 16.6. Act. 18.23. Collection for the saints at Jerusalem, 1 Cor. 16.1. Paul's epistle to Galatians.

GALBANUM, a spice used in the sacred anointing oil, Ex. 30.34.

GALEED, or MIZPEH (*witness*), the heap of stones raised by Jacob and Laban as witness of their covenant, Gen. 31.47,49.

GALILEE, a district of Naphtali, Jos. 20.7. Jos. 21.32. 2 Kin. 15.29. 1 Chr. 6.76. Hiram obtains 20 cities in, 1 Kin. 9.11. Called Galilee of the nations, Isa. 9.1. Mat. 4.15.

——, in the New Testament signifies the northern of the three divisions of Palestine, Herod tetrarch of, Luk. 3.1. Mar. 6.21. Luk. 23.6,7. Christ resides in, Mat. 17.22. Mat. 19.1. Jno. 7.1,9.
Christ's teaching and miracles in, Mat. 4.23,25. Mat. 15.29-31. Mar. 1.14,28,39. Mar. 3.7. Luk. 4.14,44. Luk. 5.17. Luk. 23.5. Jno. 1.43. Jno. 4.3,43-45. Act. 10.37. See towns of BETHSAIDA, CANA, CAPERNAUM, CHORAZIN, DECAPOLIS, NAZARETH.
Disciples were chiefly from, Act. 1.11. Act. 2.7. Women from, ministered to Christ, Mat. 27.55,56. Mar. 15.41. Luk. 23.49,55. Christ appeared to his disciples in, after his resurrection, Mat. 26.32. Mat. 28.7,10,16,17. Mar. 14.28. Mar. 16.7. Jno. 21. Churches in, Act. 9.31. Dialect of, Mar. 14.70.

GALILEE, SEA OF, called the Sea of Tiberias, Jno. 21.1. Lake of Gennesareth, Luk. 5.1. Sea of Cinnereth, Num. 34.11. Jos. 13.27. Disciples called by Jesus on the shore of, Mat. 4.18-22. Jesus teaches from a ship on, Mat. 13.1,2. Miracles of Christ on, Mat. 8.24-32. Mat. 14.22-33. Mat. 17.27. Jno. 21.

GALILEAN, a term of reproach, Jno. 7.41,52. Applied to Christ, Mat. 26.69; and his disciples, Mar. 14.70. Luk. 22.59.

GALILEANS, Jewish insurgents, led by Judas, and massacred by Pilate, Luk. 13.1,2 with Act. 5.37.

GALL or **BILE,** Job 16.13. Job 20.14,25. Another word is also translated gall, it is a bitter plant, Deu. 29.18. Psa. 69.21. Mat. 27.34. Translated hemlock, Hos. 10.4. Spoken of asps. Job 20.16. Deu. 32.33. Illustrative, Act. 8.23.

GALLIO, pro-consul of Achaia, dismisses the accusation of the Jews against Paul, Act. 18.12-17.

GALLOWS, Est. 5.14. Est. 6.4. Est. 7.9,10. Est. 9.13,25. Translated tree, Jos. 8.29. Jos. 10.26. Est. 2.23.

GAMALIEL, a member of the Sanhedrim; his speech, Act. 5.33-40. Paul's teacher, Act. 22.3.

GAMES, with birds, Job 41.5. Sword-play, 2 Sam. 2.14. Allusions to, 1 Cor. 9.26. 2 Tim. 4.7. Phil. 3.14. Heb. 12.1. Fighting with wild beasts, 1 Cor. 15.32. 1 Cor. 4.9. Of children, Zec. 8.5. Mat. 11.16-17. See MUSIC—DANCING—RACE.

GAMMADIMS (brave warriors), Eze. 27.11.

GARDEN, idolatrous rites in, Isa. 1.29. Isa. 57.5. Hos. 4.13. See VINEYARD—AGRICULTURE.

GAREB, a hill near Jerusalem, Jer. 31.39.

GARLIC, a plant, Num. 11.5.

GARMENT. See DRESS.

GARNER. See BARN.

GARRISON, a camp or fortified place, 1 Sam. 14.1. 2 Sam. 23.14. Also the soldiers of the camp, 1 Sam. 13.3. 2 Sam. 8.6.

GATES OF CITIES, construction of, 2 Sam. 18.24. Deu. 3.5. Jos. 6.26. 1 Sam. 23.7. 2 Chr. 8.5. Of Iron, Act. 12.10. Of wood, Neh. 1.3. Of brass, Psa. 107.16. Isa. 45.2. Two-leaved, Isa. 45.1. Eze. 41.24. See BARS. Places of public resort, Gen. 19.1. 1 Sam. 4.18. Psa. 69.12. Pro. 1.21. Pro. 17.19,20. Act. 14.13.

Courts of Justice and Councils held at, Deu. 16.18. Deu. 21.19. Deu. 22.15. Deu. 25.7. Jos. 20.4. 2 Sam. 15.2. 1 Kin. 22.10. Jer. 38.7. Jer. 39.3. Zec. 8.16. Markets held at, Gen. 23.10,16. Gen. 34.20. Ruth 4.1. 2 Kin. 7.1,18. Proclamations at, Pro. 1.21. Pro. 8.3. Jer. 7.2.

The law read, and public worship held at, Neh. 8. Criminals punished at, Lev. 24.23. Deu. 17.5. Jer. 20.2. Act. 7.58. Heb. 13.12. Enemies' bodies exposed at, 2 Kin. 10.8; and buried at, Jos. 8.29.

Carcase of sin-offering burned outside of, Lev. 4.12. Heb. 13.11-13. Shut at sunset, Jos. 2.5,7. On the Sabbath, Neh. 13.19. Kept by porters, 2 Kin. 7.17. Neh. 13.19,22. Of Gaza, carried away by Samson, Jud. 16.2,3. Illustrative, Gen. 22.17. Mat. 16.18. Isa. 3.26. Isa. 60.11. Gate of death, Job 38.17. Psa. 9.13. Of righteousness, Psa. 118.19. Everlasting gate, Psa. 24.7. Strait gate, Mat. 7.13. Symbolical, Rev. 21.12,13,21,25. See JERUSALEM, GATES OF.

GATH, one of the 5 chief cities of the Philistines, Jos. 13.3. 1 Sam. 6.17. Amos 6.2.

Mic. 1.10. Anakim, ancient inhabitants of, Jos. 11.22. Goliath and his sons dwelt in, 1 Sam. 17.4. 1 Chr. 20.5-8. Obed-edom belonged to, 2 Sam. 6.10. The ark taken to, 1 Sam. 5.8.

David takes refuge at, with Achish the king, 1 Sam. 21.10-15. 1 Sam. 27.2-7. A band of Gittites under Ittai join David, 2 Sam. 15.18-22. 2 Sam. 18.2. Taken by David, 1 Chr. 18.1. Shimei fetches his servants from, 1 Kin. 2.39-41. Fortified by Rehoboam, 2 Chr. 11.8. Taken by Hazael, 2 Kin. 12.17. Recovered by Jehoash, 2 Kin. 13.25. Besieged by Uzziah, 2 Chr. 26.6.

GATH, or **GITTAH-HEPHER,** a city of Zebulon, Jos. 19.13. The birthplace of Jonah, 2 Kin. 14.25.

GATH-RIMMON, a city of Dan, Jos. 19.45. A Levitical city of refuge, Jos. 21.24,25. 1 Chr. 6.69.

GAZA, or **AZZAH,** one of the five chief cities of the Philistines, Jos. 13.3. Jer. 25.20. The frontier of the Canaanites, Gen. 10.19. Inhabited by the Avims, Deu. 2.23; and Anakims, Jos. 11.22. Given to Judah, Jos. 15.47. Taken by Judah, Jud. 1.18.

Samson, feats of strength, imprisonment, and destruction of himself and the people in, Jud. 16.1-3,21-30. Possessed by Solomon, 1 Kin. 4.24. Taken by Pharaoh, Jer. 47.1,5. Prophecies against, Amos 1.6,7. Zeph. 2.4. Zec. 9.5.

————, DESERT OF, Philip met and baptised the Ethiopian eunuch in, Act. 8.26-39.

GEBA. See GIBEAH.

GEBAL, Psa. 83.7. A Phenician town given to Reuben, Jos. 13.5. Stone-masons from, 1 Kin. 5.18 (marg.). Shipbuilders in, Eze. 27.9.

GEBIM, locality not known, Isa. 10.31.

GEDALIAH, Jewish governor at Mizpah, appointed by Nebuchadnezzar, 2 Kin. 25.22-24. Protects Jeremiah, Jer. 39.14. Jer. 40.5,6. Warned against Ishmael, murdered by him, Jer. 40. Jer. 41.1-10. 2 Kin. 25.25,26.

GEDEROTH, a town of Judah, Jos. 15.41. Taken by the Philistines, 2 Chr. 28.18.

GEDOR, VALLEY OF, taken by Simeonites, 1 Chr. 4.39,41.

GEHAZI, Elisha's servant. Is sent to lay Elisha's staff on a dead child, 2 Kin. 4.12,29,31. Is struck with leprosy for falsehood, 2 Kin. 5.20-27. Recounts to Joram the deeds of Elisha, 2 Kin. 8.4,5.

GEMARIAH, son of Shaphan, an officer of Jehoiakim. Opposes the burning of Jeremiah's roll, Jer. 36.10-26.

————, son of Hilkiah, sent to Babylon by Zedekiah. Carries Jeremiah's letter to the captives, Jer. 29.3.

GENEALOGIES. Cain's descendants, Gen. 4.16-22. Adam to Noah, Gen. 5. 1 Chr. 1.1-4. Noah's descendants, Gen. 10. 1 Chr. 1.4-23. Shem to Abraham, Gen. 11.10-32. 1 Chr. 1.24-28. Nahor's descendants, Gen. 22.20-24. Abraham and Keturah's descendants, Gen. 25.1-4. 1 Chr. 1.32,33.

Ishmael's descendants, Gen. 25.12-16. 1 Chr. 1.29-31. Esau's descendants, Gen. 36. 1 Chr. 1.35-54. Jacob's descendants, Gen. 35.23-26. Ex. 1.5. Ex. 6.14-27. Num. 26. 1 Chr. c. 2-9.

Pharez to David, Ruth 4.18-22. Jews who returned from captivity, Ezr. 7.1-5. Ezr. 8.1-15. Neh. c. 7.11.12.

Abraham to Christ, Mat. 1. Adam to Christ, Luk. 3.23-38. Public registers of, kept, 2 Chr. 12.15. Neh. 7.5. Tables of, lost, Neh. 7.64. See BOOKS.

GENEROSITY. See LIBERALITY—UN-SELFISHNESS—POOR, KINDNESS TO.

GENNESARETH. See GALILEE.

GENTILES. See HEATHEN—GREEKS—SALVATION—PROSELYTES.

GERAH, the 20th part of a shekel, or 12 grains, worth about three halfpence, Ex. 30.13. Lev. 27.25.

GERAR, a city of the Philistines, Gen. 10.19. Abimelech, king of; Abraham and Isaac dwelt in, Gen. 20.1. Gen. 26.6. Asa's victory at, 2 Chr. 14.13,14.

———, VALLEY OF, Gen. 26.17-22.

GERGESENES. See GADARENES.

GERIZIM, a hill in Ephraim from which the blessings were pronounced, Deu. 11.29. Deu. 27.12. Jos. 8.33. Jotham's address to the Shechemites on, Jud. 9.7. Samaritan temple on, Jno. 4.20.

GERSHOM, eldest son of Moses, Ex. 2.22. Ex. 18.3.

GERSHON, eldest son of Levi, and head of the Gershonites, Gen. 46.11. Ex. 6.16. Num. 3.17-26. 1 Chr. 6.1,16,17,20,21. See LEVITES, DIVISIONS OF.

GESHEM, the Arabian, opposes Nehemiah in building Jerusalem, Neh. 2.19. Neh. 6.1-6.

GESHUR, a district and town of Bashan. Imperfectly conquered by Reubenites, &c., Deu. 3.14. Jos. 13.2,13. 1 Chr. 2.23. Wasted by David, 1 Sam. 27.8. Talmai, king of, his daughter marries David, 2 Sam. 3.3. Absalom flees to, 2 Sam. 13.37,38. 2 Sam. 15.8.

GETHSEMANE, a garden in the valley of Jehoshaphat. Often visited by Christ, Jno. 18.1,2. Christ's agony and betrayal in, Mat. 26.36-50. Mar. 14.32-46. Luk. 22.39-49.

GEZER, GAZER, or GOB. The Canaanitish king of, defeated by Joshua, Jos. 10.33. Jos. 12.12. A Levitical city of Ephraim but imperfectly subdued, Jos. 16.3,10. Jud. 1.29. 1 Chr. 7.28. Battle with Philistines at, 1 Chr. 20.4. 2 Sam. 21.18. Invaded by David, 1 Sam. 27.8. Destroyed by Pharaoh and rebuilt by Solomon, 1 Kin. 9.15-17.

GIANTS, before the Flood, Gen. 6.4. See ANAKIM, EMIM, GOLIATH, ISHBI-BENOTH, OG, REPHAIM. ZAMZUMMIM.

GIBBETHON, a Levitical city of Dan, Jos. 19.44. Jos. 21.23. Besieged by Israel while possessed by Philistines, 1 Kin. 15.27. 1 Kin. 16.15,17.

GIBEAH, GEBA, or GABA, a priestly city of Benjamin, Jos. 18.24. Jos. 21.17. 1 Chr. 6.60. 1 Chr. 8.6. The N. boundary, 2 Kin. 23.8. Zec. 14.10. Destroyed by Israelites for the people's wickedness, Jud. 19.12-30. Jud. 20. Hos. 9.9. Hos. 10.9.

Saul's residence, 1 Sam. 10.26. 1 Sam. 15.34. 1 Sam. 22.6. 1 Sam. 26.1. Jonathan defeats

the Philistines at, 1 Sam. 14. The ark in Abinadab's house at, 2 Sam. 6.3 with 1 Sam. 7.1. Saul's sons hanged at, 2 Sam. 21.6. Rebuilt by Asa, 1 Kin. 15.22. Inhabited after captivity, Ezr. 2.26.

GIBEON, a city of the Amorites, Jos. 10. 2 2 Sam. 21.2. Joshua entrapped into a treaty with, Jos. 9. Inhabitants made hewers of wood, Jos. 9.27. Joshua defeats the Amorites near; miracle of the sun standing still, Jos. 10. Isa. 28.21.

A priestly city of Benjamin, Jos. 18.25. Jos. 21.17. The tabernacle at, and sacrifices made at, 1 Kin. 3.4. 1 Chr. 16.39. 1 Chr. 21.29. 2 Chr. 1.3,13. David defeats Philistines at, 1 Chr. 14.16. Saul's slaughter of Gibeonites punished, 2 Sam. 21.1-9.

Solomon's visions at, 1 Kin. 3.5. 1 Kin. 9.2. Joab slays Asahel at, 2 Sam. 3.30; and Amasa, 2 Sam. 20.8. Ishmael's soldiers join Johanan at, Jer. 41.11-16.

———, POOL OF, 2 Sam. 2.13. Jer. 41.12.

GIBLITES. See GEBAL.

GIDEON, JERUBBAAL, or JERUBBESHETH. An angel commissions him to deliver Israel; he asks a sign; his offering accepted; builds an altar, Jud. 6.11-24. As commanded by God, destroys Baal's altar, Jud. 6.25-32. Summons an army, Jud. 6.33-35.

Encouraged by the sign of the fleece of wool, Jud. 6.36-40. His army, by divine direction, reduced to 300; sign of the Midianite's dream; his stratagem; war-cry; defeats the Midianites, Jud. 7. Jud. 8.4,11-12,28. 1 Sam. 12.11. Blamed by the Ephraimites; he pacifies them, Jud. 8.1-3.

Destroys Succoth and Penuel, Jud. 8.4-17. Country at peace 40 years, Jud. 8.28. Refuses to be made king, Jud. 8.22,23. Makes a golden ephod, which was worshipped, Jud. 8.24-27. His wives and sons, Jud. 8.30,31. Death, v. 32. Faith, Heb. 11.32. Israelites return to idolatry after his death, Jud. 8.33-35.

GIFTS. See OFFERINGS—PRESENTS.

GIHON, the second river in Eden, and boundary of Ethiopia, Gen. 2.13.

———, two pools near Jerusalem, called the Upper and Lower Pools. Solomon proclaimed at, 1 Kin. 1.33,38,45. The waters of the Upper Pool brought into the city by Hezekiah, 2 Kin. 18.17. 2 Kin. 20.20. 2 Chr. 32.4,30. 2 Chr. 33.14. Neh. 2.13-15. Neh. 3.13-16. Isa. 7.3. Isa. 22.9-11. Isa. 36.2.

GILBOA, a hill S. of Jezreel, on which Saul was defeated by the Philistines; his death, 1 Sam. 28.4. 1 Sam. 31.1-8. 2 Sam. 1.6,21. 1 Chr. 10.1-8.

GILEAD. The whole district E. of Jordan possessed by the two and a half tribes, Deu. 34.1 with 2 Kin. 10.33. Jud. 20.1; or only a part of the district, Deu. 3.13. Jos. 13.11. See BASHAN. Originally belonging to Bashan, &c., given to Reuben, &c., Num. 32. Deu. 3.10-16. Jos. 17.1-6. Jos. 22.9.

Hagarites driven from; by Reuben, 1 Chr. 5.10,18-22. Invaded by the Ammonites, and delivered by Jephthah, Jud. 10.15-18. Jud. 11. Amos 1.13. Jephthah buried in, Jud. 12.7. Elijah a native of, 1 Kin. 17.1. Israelites retreat to, from the Philistines, 1 Sam. 13.7. Absalom's camp in, 2 Sam. 17.26.

Invaded by Hazael, 2 Kin. 10.33. Amos 1.3. By Tiglath, 2 Kin. 15.29. Fertility of, Jer. 22.6. Jer. 50.19. Famous for cattle, Num. 32.1. 1 Chr. 5.9; and spices, Gen. 37.25. Jer. 8.22. Jer. 46.11.

GILEAD, MOUNT, Jud. 7.3. Song 4.1. Song 6.5. Laban overtakes Jacob at, Gen. 31.21-25.

————, CITY OF, Hos. 6.8. Hos. 12.11.

————, grandson of Manasseh, and head of the family of Gileadites, Num. 26.29. Num. 27.1.

GILGAL, a district and town W. of Jordan, Deu. 11.30. First encampment of Israel, and head-quarters of Joshua, Jos. 4.19. Jos. 9.6. Jos. 10.6,43. Jos. 14.6. 12 stones set up at, Jos. 4.20. Israel circumcised, and passover kept at, Jos. 5.9,10.

Samuel judges at, 1 Sam. 7.16. Saul made king at, 1 Sam. 10.8. 1 Sam. 11.14,15. He offers a burnt-offering at; the loss of his kingdom predicted, 1 Sam. 13.4-15. 1 Sam. 15.6-23. Agag slain by Samuel at, 1 Sam. 15.33. David received by Judah at, after Absalom's death, 2 Sam. 19.15,40. Elisha's miracle at; the school of the prophets in, 2 Kin. 4.38-40. Idolatry at, Jud. 3.19 (marg.), Hos. 4.15. Hos. 9.15. Hos. 12.11. Amos 4.4. Amos 5.5.

GIRDLE OF LINEN, Pro. 31.24. Of leather, 2 Kin. 1.8. Mat. 3.4. Worn round the loins, Job 12.18. Isa. 5.27. By women, Isa. 3.24.

Of the high-priest, Ex. 28.4,39. Ex. 39.29. Lev. 8.7. Lev. 16.4. His embroidered girdle, Ex. 28.8,27,28. Ex. 29.5. Lev. 8.7. Of the priests, Ex. 28.40. Ex. 29.9. Lev. 8.13.

A sword-belt, 2 Sam. 20.8. 1 Sam. 18.4. 2 Kin. 3.21 (marg.). Used as a purse (Gr. Zonee), Mat. 10.9. Mar. 6.8. Illustrative, Isa. 22.21. Isa. 11.5. Eph. 6.14. Symbolical, Jer. 13.1-11. Act. 21.11. Rev. 15.6.

GIRGASHITES, descendants of Canaan, Gen. 10.16. 1 Chr. 1.14. Their land given to Israel, Gen. 15.21. Deu. 7.1. Jos. 3.10. Possessed by Israel, Jos. 24.11. Neh. 9.8.

GITTITE. See GATH.

GITTITH, an instrument of music common in Gath. Titles, Psa. 8. Psa. 81. Psa. 84.

GLASS. Symbolical, Rev. 21.18,21. Sea of, Rev. 15.2. See MIRROR.

GLEANINGS. To be left to the poor and the stranger, Lev. 19.9,10. Lev. 23.22. Deu. 24.19-22. Ruth a gleaner, Ruth 2.2,3. Illustrative, Jud. 8.2. Isa. 17.6. Jer. 49.9. Mic. 7.1.

GLEDE, Deu. 14.13. Possibly the vulture, see Lev. 11.14.

GLORIFYING GOD AND CHRIST. Job 36.3. I will fetch my knowledge from afar, and will ascribe righteousness to my Maker.

Psa. 50.15. I will deliver thee, and thou shalt glorify me.

Psa. 142.7. Bring my soul out of prison, that I may praise thy name.

Isa. 24.15. Glorify ye the Lord in the fires, even the name of the Lord God of Israel in the isles of the sea.

Mat. 5.16. Let your light so shine before men, that they may see your good works, and glorify your Father which is in heaven.

Jno. 15.8. Herein is my Father glorified, that ye bear much fruit.

Jno. 21.19. This spake he, signifying by what death he should glorify God.

Rom. 12.11. Not slothful in business; fervent in spirit; serving the Lord.

Rom. 15.6. With one mind and one mouth glorify God, even the Father of our Lord Jesus Christ.

1 Cor. 1.31. He that glorieth, let him glory in the Lord.

1 Cor. 6.19. Ye are not your own? 20. For ye are bought with a price: therefore glorify God in your body, and in your spirit, which are God's.

1 Cor. 10.31. Whether therefore ye eat, or drink, or whatsoever ye do, do all to the glory of God.

2 Cor. 8.19. This grace, which is administered by us to the glory of the same Lord.

Gal. 2.19. I through the law am dead to the law, that I might live unto God.

Eph. 6.6. As the servants of Christ, doing the will of God from the heart; 7. With good will doing service, as to the Lord, and not to men.

Phil. 1.20. Christ shall be magnified in my body, whether it be by life, or by death. 21. For to me to live is Christ.

Col. 3.23. Whatsoever ye do, do it heartily, as to the Lord, and not unto men.

2 The. 1.12. That the name of our Lord Jesus Christ may be glorified in you.

1 Tim. 5.14. Give none occasion to the adversary to speak reproachfully.

1 Tim. 6.1. Count their own masters worthy of all honour, that the name of God and his doctrine be not blasphemed.

Tit. 2.5. Good, obedient to their own husbands, that the word of God be not blasphemed. 10. Adorn the doctrine of God our Saviour in all things.

1 Pet. 2.9. Shew forth the praises of him who hath called you out of darkness into his marvellous light. 12. Whereas they speak against you as evil-doers, they may, by your good works which they shall behold, glorify God in the day of visitation. 13. Submit yourselves to every ordinance of man for the Lord's sake.

1 Pet. 4.11. If any man minister, let him do it as of the ability which God giveth: that God in all things may be glorified through Jesus Christ. 14. If ye be reproached for the name of Christ, happy are ye; for the spirit of glory and of God resteth upon you: on their part he is evil spoken of, but on your part he is glorified.

See GOD GLORIFIED BY THE CHURCH.

GLUTTONY. See SENSUALITY.

GNAT, Mat. 23.24.

GOAD, for oxen, 1 Sam. 13.21. Shamgar slays 600 men with, Jud. 3.31. Illustrative, Ecc. 12.11.

GOAT, Deu. 14.4. Kids of, much used for food, Gen. 27.9. 1 Sam. 16.20. Kid or lamb slain at the passover-feast, Ex. 12.5. 2 Chr. 35.7. Kids not to be killed till 8 days old, Lev. 22.27. Not to be seethed in the mother's milk, Ex. 23.19.

Abraham's sacrifice of, Gen. 15.9. Gideon's, Jud. 6.19. Manoah's, Jud. 13.19. Large flocks of, 1 Sam. 25.2. 2 Chr. 17.11. Led by males, Jer. 50.8. Bashan noted for, Deu. 32.14; and Gilead, Song 4.1. Song 6.5.

Wild goats, 1 Sam. 24.2. Job 39.1-4. Psa. 104.18. Hair of, tabernacle curtains of, Ex. 26.7. Ex. 35.23. Ex. 36.14. Clothing of, Num. 31.20. Bolsters of, 1 Sam. 19.13. See TENTS. Symbolical, Dan. 8.5,8,21.

SACRIFICES OF. See OFFERINGS.

GOB. See GEZER.

GOBLET. See CUP.

GOD, ANGER OF. See GOD, HIS JUSTICE— SIN, PUNISHMENT OF.

GOD CREATOR. Gen. 1.1. In the beginning God created the heaven and the earth. 2. And the Spirit of God moved upon the face of the waters. 3. And God said, Let there be light: and there was light. *v.* 1-31. Gen. 2.1-25.

Ex. 20.11. *In* six days the Lord made heaven and earth, the sea, and all that in them *is.* Psa. 146.6.

1 Sam. 2.8. The pillars of the earth *are* the Lord's, and he hath set the world upon them.

Neh. 9.6. Thou hast made heaven, the heaven of heavens, with all their host, the earth, and all *things* that *are* therein, the seas, and all *that is* therein, and thou preservest them all. 2 Kin. 19.15.

Job 9.8. Which alone spreadeth out the heavens, and treadeth upon the waves of the sea. 9. Which maketh Arcturus, Orion, and Pleiades, and the chambers of the south.

Job 12.8. Speak to the earth, and it shall teach thee; and the fishes of the sea shall declare unto thee. 9. Who knoweth not in all these that the hand of the Lord hath wrought this?

Job 26.7. He stretcheth out the north over the empty place, *and* hangeth the earth upon nothing. 13. By his spirit he hath garnished the heavens; his hand hath formed the crooked serpent. *v.* 8.

Job 28.24. Seeth under the whole heaven; 25. To make the weight for the winds; and he weigheth the waters by measure. 26. When he made a decree for the rain, and a way for the lightning of the thunder.

Job 37.16. Dost thou know the balancings of the clouds, the wondrous works of him which is perfect in knowledge? 18. Hast thou with him spread out the sky, *which is* strong, *and* as a molten looking glass?

Job 38.4. Where wast thou when I laid the foundations of the earth? declare, if thou hast understanding. 7. When the morning stars sang together, and all the sons of God shouted for joy? 8. Or *who* shut up the sea with doors, when it brake forth, *as if* it had issued out of the womb? 9. When I made the cloud the garment thereof, and thick darkness a swaddling-band for it, 10. And brake up for it my decreed *place,* and set bars and doors. *v.* 4-38.

Psa. 8.3. Thy heavens, the work of thy fingers, the moon and the stars, which thou hast ordained.

Psa. 19.1. The heavens declare the glory of God; and the firmament sheweth his handywork. 4. In them hath he set a tabernacle for the sun.

Psa. 24.1. The earth *is* the Lord's, and the fulness thereof; the world, and they that dwell therein. 2. For he hath founded it upon the seas, and established it upon the floods.

Psa. 33.6. By the word of the Lord were the heavens made; and all the host of them by the breath of his mouth. 7. He gathereth the waters of the sea together as an heap: he layeth up the depth in storehouses. 9. For he spake, and it was *done;* he commanded, and it stood fast.

Psa. 65.6. Which by his strength setteth fast the mountains; *being* girded with power.

Psa. 74.16. The day *is* thine, the night also *is* thine: thou hast prepared the light and the sun. 17. Thou hast set all the borders of the earth: thou hast made summer and winter.

Psa. 78.69. He built his sanctuary like high *palaces,* like the earth which he hath established for ever.

Psa. 89.11. The heavens *are* thine, the earth also *is* thine: as *for* the world and the fulness thereof, thou hast founded them. 12. The north and the south thou hast created them.

Psa. 90.2. Before the mountains were brought forth, or ever thou hadst formed the earth and the world, even from everlasting to everlasting, thou *art* God.

Psa. 95.4. In his hand *are* the deep places of the earth: the strength of the hills *is* his also. 5. The sea *is* his, and he made it: and his hands formed the dry *land.*

Psa. 102.25. Of old hast thou laid the foundation of the earth: and the heavens *are* the work of thy hands. Psa. 96.5.

Psa. 103.22. Bless the Lord, all his works in all places of his dominion.

Psa. 104.2. Who stretchest out the heavens like a curtain: 3. Who layeth the beams of his chambers in the waters. 5. *Who* laid the foundations of the earth, *that* it should not be removed for ever. 6. Thou coveredst it with the deep as *with* a garment: the waters stood above the mountains. 24. O Lord, how manifold are thy works! in wisdom hast thou made them all: the earth is full of thy riches. 30. Thou sendest forth thy spirit, they are created: and thou renewest the face of the earth. *v.* 31.

Psa. 119.90. Thou hast established the earth, and it abideth. 91. They continue this day according to thine ordinances: for all *are* thy servants.

Psa. 124.8. The Lord, who made heaven and earth. Psa. 134.3.

Psa. 136.5. To him that by wisdom made the heavens: 6. To him that stretched out the earth above the waters: 7. To him that made great lights: 8. The sun to rule by day: 9. The moon and stars to rule by night.

Psa. 148.5. He commanded, and they were created. 6. He hath also stablished them for ever and ever: he hath made a decree which shall not pass.

Pro. 3.19. The Lord by wisdom hath founded the earth; by understanding hath he established the heavens.

Pro. 8.26. While as yet he had not made the earth, nor the fields, nor the highest part of the dust of the world. 27. When he prepared the heavens, I *was* there: when he set a compass upon the face of the depth: 28. When he established the clouds above: when he strengthened the fountains of the deep: 29. When he gave to the sea his decree, that the waters should not pass his commandment: when he appointed the foundations of the earth.

Pro. 26.10. The great *God* that formed all *things*.

Pro. 30.4. Who hath gathered the wind in his fists? who hath bound the waters in a garment? who hath established all the ends of the earth?

Ecc. 3.11. He hath made every *thing* beautiful in his time : no man can find out the work that God maketh from the beginning to the end.

Ecc. 11.5. Thou knowest not the works of God who maketh all.

Isa. 40.12. Who hath measured the waters in the hollow of his hand, and meted out heaven with the span, and comprehended the dust of the earth in a measure, and weighed the mountains in scales, and the hills in a balance? 26. Lift up your eyes on high, and behold who hath created these *things*, that bringeth out their host by number : he calleth them all by names by the greatness of his might, for that *he is* strong in power ; not one faileth. 28. The everlasting God, the Lord, the Creator of the ends of the earth, fainteth not.

Isa. 42.5. He that created the heavens, and stretched them out ; he that spread forth the earth, and that which cometh out of it.

Isa. 44.24. I the Lord that maketh all *things*; that stretcheth forth the heavens alone ; that spreadeth abroad the earth by myself.

Isa. 45.7. I form the light, and create darkness : I make peace, and create evil : I the Lord do all these *things*. 12. I have made the earth, and created man upon it : I, *even* my hands, have stretched out the heavens, and all their host have I commanded. 18. The Lord that created the heavens ; God himself that formed the earth and made it ; he hath established it, he created it not in vain, he formed it to be inhabited.

Isa. 48.13. Mine hand also hath laid the foundation of the earth, and my right hand hath spanned the heavens : *when* I call unto them, they stand up together.

Isa. 51.13. The Lord thy maker, that hath stretched forth the heavens, and laid the foundations of the earth.

Isa. 66.2. All those things hath my hand made.

Jer. 5.22. Will ye not tremble at my presence, which have placed the sand *for* the bound of the sea by a perpetual decree, that it cannot pass it.

Jer. 10.16. He *is* the former of all *things*. Jer. 51.19.

Jer. 27.5. I have made the earth, the man and the beast that *are* upon the ground, by my great power and by my outstretched arm, and have given it unto whom it seemed meet unto me.

Jer. 31.35. The Lord, which giveth the sun for a light by day, *and* the ordinances of the moon and of the stars for a light by night.

Jer. 32.17. Thou hast made the heaven and the earth by thy great power and stretched out arm.

Jer. 33.2. The Lord the maker thereof, the Lord that formed it, to establish it.

Jer. 51.15. He hath made the earth by his power, he hath established the world by his wisdom, and hath stretched out the heaven by his understanding. 16. When he uttereth *his* voice, *there is* a multitude of waters in the heavens. Jer. 10, 12, 13.

Amos 4.13. He that formeth the mountains, and createth the wind.

Amos 5.8. *Seek him* that maketh the seven stars and Orion, and turneth the shadow of death into the morning, and maketh the day dark with night.

Amos 9.6. *It is* he that buildeth his stories in the heaven, and hath founded his troop in the earth ; he that calleth for the waters of the sea, and poureth them out upon the face of the earth : The Lord *is* his name.

Jon. 1.9. The God of heaven, which hath made the sea and the dry *land*.

Zec. 12.1. The Lord, which stretcheth forth the heavens, and layeth the foundation of the earth, and formeth the spirit of man within him.

Act. 14.15. The living God, which made heaven, and earth, and the sea, and all things that are therein. Act. 4.24.

Act. 17.24. God that made the world and all things therein, seeing that he is Lord of heaven and earth.

Rom. 4.17. God, who calleth those things which be not as though they were.

Rom. 11.36. Of him, and through him, and to him, *are* all things : to whom *be* glory for ever. Amen.

1 Cor. 8.6. To us *there is but* one God, the Father, of whom *are* all things, and we in him ; and one Lord Jesus Christ, by whom *are* all things, and we by him.

2 Cor. 4.6. God who commanded the light to shine out of darkness.

2 Cor. 5.18. All things *are* of God. 1 Cor. 11.12.

Eph. 3.9. God, who created all things by Jesus Christ.

1 Tim. 6.13. God, who quickeneth all things.

Heb. 1.2. *His* Son, whom he hath appointed heir of all things, by whom also he made the worlds.

Heb. 2.10. Him, for whom *are* all things, and by whom *are* all things.

Heb. 3.4. He that built all things *is* God.

Heb. 11.3. The worlds were framed by the word of God, so that things which are seen were not made of things which do appear.

Rev. 4.11. Thou hast created all things, and for thy pleasure they are, and were created.

Rev. 10.6. Him that liveth for ever and ever, who created heaven, and the things that therein are, and the earth, and the things that therein are, and the sea, and the things which are therein.

Rev. 14.7. Worship him that made heaven, and earth, and the sea, and the fountains of waters.

GOD CREATOR OF MAN. Gen. 1.26. God said, Let us make man in our image, after our likeness : 27. So God created man in his *own* image, in the image of God created he him ; male and female created he them. Gen. 2.7.

Gen. 3.19. Out of it wast thou taken : for dust thou *art*, and unto dust shalt thou return.

Gen. 5.1. God created man, in the likeness of God made he him ; 2. Male and female created he them ; and blessed them, and called their name Adam, in the day when they were created.

Gen. 9.6. In the image of God made he man.

Ex. 4.11. Who hath made man's mouth?

or who maketh the dumb, or deaf, or the seeing, or the blind? have not I the Lord?

Num. 16.22. O God, the God of the spirits of all flesh. Num. 27.16.

Deu. 4.32. God created man upon the earth.

Deu. 32.6. Hath he not made thee, and established thee? 15. He forsook God which made him. 18. Of the Rock *that* begat thee thou art unmindful, and hast forgotten God that formed thee.

Job 10.8. Thine hands have made me and fashioned me together round about. 9. Thou hast made me as the clay; and wilt thou bring me into dust again? 11. Thou hast clothed me with skin and flesh, and hast fenced me with bones and sinews. 12. Thou hast granted me life and favour, and thy visitation hath preserved my spirit. Psa. 119.73.

Job 12.10. In whose hand *is* the soul of every living thing, and the breath of all mankind.

Job 27.3. All the while my breath *is* in me, and the spirit of God *is* in my nostrils.

Job 31.15. Did not he that made me in the womb make him? and did not one fashion us in the womb?

Job 33.4. The Spirit of God hath made me, and the breath of the Almighty hath given me life.

Job 34.19. Nor regardeth the rich more than the poor? for they all *are* the work of his hands. Pro. 22.2.

Job 38.36. Who hath put wisdom in the inward parts? or who hath given understanding to the heart?

Psa. 24.1. The earth *is* the Lord's, and the fulness thereof; the world, and they that dwell therein.

Psa. 33.15. He fashioneth their hearts alike; he considereth all their works.

Psa. 86.9. All nations whom thou hast made shall come and worship before thee, O Lord.

Psa. 94.9. He that planted the ear, shall he not hear? he that formed the eye, shall he not see?

Psa. 95.6. Let us kneel before the Lord our maker.

Psa. 100.3. Know ye that the Lord he *is* God: *it is* he *that* hath made us, and not we ourselves; *we are* his people, and the sheep of his pasture.

Psa. 139.13. Thou hast possessed my reins: thou hast covered me in my mother's womb.

Psa. 149.2. Let Israel rejoice in him that made him.

Pro. 20.12. The hearing ear, and the seeing eye, the Lord hath made even both of them.

Ecc. 11.5. Thou knowest not the works of God who maketh all.

Ecc. 12.1. Remember now thy Creator in the days of thy youth.

Isa. 42.5. He that giveth breath unto the people upon it, and spirit to them that walk therein.

Isa. 43.1. The Lord that created thee, O Jacob, and he that formed thee, O Israel. 7. I have created him for my glory, I have formed him; yea, I have made him. 15. I *am* the Lord, your Holy One, the Creator of Israel, your King.

Isa. 44.2. The Lord that made thee, and formed thee from the womb, *which* will help thee. *v.* 24.

Isa. 45.12. I have made the earth, and

created man upon it. 18. He created it not in vain, he formed it to be inhabited.

Isa. 51.13. Forgettest the Lord thy Maker.

Isa. 64.8. Now, O Lord, thou *art* our father; we *are* the clay, and thou our potter; and we all *are* the work of thy hand.

Jer. 27.5. I have made the earth, the man and the beast that *are* upon the ground, by my great power, and by my outstretched arm, and have given it unto whom it seemed meet unto me.

Dan. 5.23. The God in whose hand thy breath *is*, and whose *are* all thy ways, hast thou not glorified.

Zec. 12.1. The Lord, which stretcheth forth the heavens, and formeth the spirit of man within him.

Mal. 2.10. Have we not all one father? hath not one God created us?

Act. 17.25. He giveth to all life, and breath, and all things; 26. And hath made of one blood all nations of men for to dwell on all the face of the earth, and hath determined the times before appointed, and the bounds of their habitation; 28. In him we live, and move, and have our being; as certain also of your own poets have said, For we are also his offspring. 29. Forasmuch then as we are the offspring of God.

1 Cor. 12.18. Now hath God set the members every one of them in the body, as it hath pleased him. 24. God hath tempered the body together, having given more abundant honour to that *part* which lacked: 25. That there should be no schism in the body.

1 Cor. 15.38. God giveth it a body as it hath pleased him, and to every seed his own body.

Heb. 12.9. The Father of Spirits.

1 Pet. 4.19. Commit the keeping of their souls *to him* in well-doing, as unto a faithful Creator.

See LIFE FROM GOD.

GOD ETERNAL AND UNCHANGEABLE. Gen. 21.33. The everlasting God. Rom. 16.26.

Ex. 3.15. The God of Abraham, the God of Isaac, and the God of Jacob, hath sent me unto you: this *is* my name for ever, and this *is* my memorial unto all generations.

Num. 23.19. God *is* not a man, that he should lie; neither the son of man, that he should repent: hath he said, and shall he not do *it?* or hath he spoken, and shall he not make it good? 20. Behold, I have received *commandment* to bless: and he hath blessed; and I cannot reverse it.

Deu. 32.40. I lift up my hand to heaven, and say, I live for ever.

Deu. 33.27. The eternal God *is thy* refuge, and underneath *are* the everlasting arms.

1 Sam. 15.29. The Strength of Israel will not lie nor repent: for he *is* not a man, that he should repent.

Job 23.13. He *is* in one *mind*, and who can turn him? and *what* his soul desireth, even *that* he doeth.

Job 36.26. Neither can the number of his years be searched out.

Psa. 33.11. The counsel of the Lord standeth for ever, the thoughts of his heart to all generations.

Psa. 55.19. God, he that abideth of old.

Psa. 90.1. Lord, thou hast been our dwelling-place in all generations. 2. Before the mountains were brought forth, or ever thou hadst formed the earth and the world, even from everlasting to everlasting, thou *art* God.

4. A thousand years in thy sight *are but* as yesterday when it is past, and *as* a watch in the night.

Psa. 92.8. Thou, Lord, *art most* high for evermore.

Psa. 93.2. Thy throne *is* established of old : thou *art* from everlasting.

Psa. 102.12. Thou, O Lord, shalt endure for ever ; and thy remembrance unto all generations. 24. Thy years *are* throughout all generations. 25. Of old hast thou laid the foundation of the earth : and the heavens *are* the work of thy hands. 26. They shall perish, but thou shalt endure : yea, all of them shall wax old like a garment : as a vesture shalt thou change them, and they shall be changed : 27. But thou *art* the same, and thy years shall have no end. Psa. 9.7.

Psa. 104.31. The glory of the Lord shall endure for ever.

Psa. 111.3. His righteousness endureth for ever.

Psa. 135.13. Thy name, O Lord, *endureth* for ever; *and* thy memorial, O Lord, throughout all generations.

Psa. 145.13. Thy kingdom *is* an everlasting kingdom, and thy dominion *endureth* throughout all generations.

Psa. 146.10. The Lord shall reign for ever, *even* thy God, O Zion, unto all generations. Ex. 15.18.

Pro. 19.21. The counsel of the Lord, that shall stand.

Ecc. 3.14. Whatsoever God doeth, it shall be for ever : nothing can be put to it, nor any thing taken from it.

Ecc. 7.13. Who can make *that* straight, which he hath made crooked ?

Isa. 26.4. In the Lord Jehovah *is* everlasting strength.

Isa. 31.2. He also *is* wise, and will bring evil, and will not call back his words.

Isa. 40.28. Hast thou not heard, *that* the everlasting God, the Lord, the Creator of the ends of the earth, fainteth not, neither is weary ?

Isa. 41.4. Who hath wrought and done *it*, calling the generations from the beginning ? I the Lord, the first, and with the last ; I *am* he.

Isa. 43.13. Yea, before the day *was* I *am* he.

Isa. 44.6. I *am* the first, and I *am* the last ; and beside me *there is* no God. Isa. 48.12.

Isa. 46.4. *Even* to *your* old age I *am* he ; and *even* to hoar hairs will I carry *you :* I have made, and I will bear.

Isa. 57.15. The high and lofty One, who inhabiteth eternity.

Isa. 59.1. The Lord's hand is not shortened, that it cannot save : neither his ear heavy, that it cannot hear.

Isa. 63.16. Thy name *is* from everlasting.

Jer. 10.10. An everlasting king.

Jer. 17.12. A glorious high throne from the beginning *is* the place of our sanctuary.

Lam. 5.19. Thou, O Lord, remainest for ever ; thy throne from generation to generation.

Hos. 13.14. Repentance shall be hid from mine eyes.

Mic. 2.7. Is the spirit of the Lord straitened ?

Hab. 1.12. *Art* thou not from everlasting, O Lord my God, mine Holy One ?

Mal. 3.6. I *am* the Lord, I change not ; therefore ye sons of Jacob are not consumed.

Rom. 1.20. The invisible things of him from the creation of the world are clearly seen, being understood by the things that are made, *even* his eternal power and Godhead. 23. The glory of the uncorruptible God.

1 Tim. 1.17. Unto the King eternal, immortal, invisible, the only wise God, *be* honour and glory for ever and ever. Amen.

1 Tim. 6.16. Who only hath immortality ; to whom *be* honour and power everlasting.

Heb. 6.17. God, willing more abundantly to shew unto the heirs of promise the immutability of his counsel, confirmed *it* by an oath : 18. That by two immutable things, in which *it was* impossible for God to lie, we might have a strong consolation.

Heb. 9.14. Christ, who through the eternal Spirit offered himself without spot to God.

Jas. 1.17. The Father of lights, with whom is no variableness, neither shadow of turning.

2 Pet. 3.8. One day *is* with the Lord as a thousand years, and a thousand years as one day.

1 Jno. 2.13. Ye have known him *that is* from the beginning.

Rev. 4.8. Holy, holy, holy, Lord God Almighty, which was, and is, and is to come. 9. Him that sat on the throne, who liveth for ever and ever. *v.* 10. Rev. 1.4. Rev. 5.14. Rev. 11.17. Rev. 15.7.

See NEXT SUBJECT.

GOD, FAITHFULNESS OF. Gen. 9.16. The bow shall be in the cloud ; and I will look upon it, that I may remember the everlasting covenant between God and every living creature of all flesh that *is* upon the earth. *v.* 15. Gen. 6.18.

Gen. 21.1. The Lord visited Sarah as he had said, and the Lord did unto Sarah as he had spoken.

Gen. 24.27. Blessed *be* the Lord God of my master Abraham, who hath not left destitute my master of his mercy and his truth.

Gen. 28.15. I will not leave thee, until I have done *that* which I have spoken to thee of.

Gen. 32.10. I am not worthy of the least of all the mercies, and of all the truth, which thou hast shewed unto thy servant.

Ex. 6.4. I have also established my covenant with them, to give them the land of Canaan. 5. I have also heard the groaning of the children of Israel, whom the Egyptians keep in bondage ; and I have remembered my covenant. Ex. 2.24.

Ex. 12.41. At the end of the four hundred and thirty years, even the selfsame day it came to pass, that all the hosts of the Lord went out from the land of Egypt.

Ex. 28.12. Aaron shall bear their names before the Lord upon his two shoulders for a memorial.

Ex. 34.6. The Lord God, abundant in goodness and truth.

Lev. 26.44. When they be in the land of their enemies, I will not cast them away, neither will I abhor them, to destroy them utterly, and to break my covenant with them : for I *am* the Lord their God. 45. But I will for their sakes remember the covenant of their ancestors.

Deu. 4.31. He will not forsake thee, neither destroy thee, nor forget the covenant of thy fathers which he sware unto them.   Jud. 2.1.

Deu. 7.8. Because the Lord loved you, and because he would keep the oath which he had sworn unto your fathers, hath the Lord brought you out with a mighty hand. 9. Know therefore that the Lord thy God, he *is* God, the faithful God, which keepeth covenant and mercy with them that love him and keep his commandments to a thousand generations. Neh. 1.5.   Dan. 9.4.

Deu. 9.5. Not for thy righteousness, or for the uprightness of thine heart, dost thou go to possess their land : but that he may perform the word which the Lord sware unto thy fathers.

Deu. 32.4. *He is* the Rock, his work *is* perfect ; for all his ways *are* judgment: a God of truth, and without iniquity ; just and right *is* he.

Jos. 23.14. Not one thing hath failed of all the good things which the Lord your God spake concerning you ; all are come to pass unto you, *and* not one thing hath failed thereof.   Jos. 21.45.

1 Sam. 12.22. The Lord will not forsake his people for his great name's sake : because it hath pleased the Lord to make you his people.

2 Sam. 7.28. O Lord God, thou *art* that God, and thy words be true, and thou hast promised this goodness unto thy servant.

2 Sam. 23.5. He hath made with me an everlasting covenant, ordered in all *things*, and sure.

1 Kin. 8.23. Who keepest covenant and mercy with thy servants that walk before thee with all their heart : 24. Who hast kept with thy servant David my father that thou promisedst him : thou spakest also with thy mouth, and hast fulfilled *it* with thine hand, as *it is* this day. 56. Blessed *be* the Lord, that hath given rest unto his people Israel, according to all that he promised : there hath not failed one word of all his good promise, which he promised by the hand of Moses. *v.* 15, 20. 2 Chr. 6.4-15.

2 Kin. 8.19. The Lord would not destroy Judah for David his servant's sake, as he promised him to give him alway a light, *and* to his children. 2 Chr. 21.7.

2 Kin. 13.23. The Lord was gracious unto them, and had compassion on them, and had respect unto them, because of his covenant with Abraham, Isaac, and Jacob, and would not destroy them, neither cast he them from his presence as yet.

1 Chr. 17.27. Thou blessest, O Lord, and *it shall be* blessed for ever.

1 Chr. 28.20. The Lord God, *even* my God, *will be* with thee ; he will not fail thee, nor forsake thee, until thou hast finished all the work for the service of the house of the Lord. Deu. 31.6.

Ezr. 9.9. Our God hath not forsaken us in our bondage, but hath extended mercy unto us.

Neh. 9.8. And hast performed thy words ; for thou *art* righteous. *v.* 32.

Psa. 18.30. *As for* God, his way *is* perfect : the word of the Lord is tried : he *is* a buckler to all those that trust in him. 2 Sam. 22.31.

Psa. 19.9. The judgments of the Lord *are* true *and* righteous altogether.

Psa. 25.10. All the paths of the Lord *are*

mercy and truth unto such as keep his covenant and his testimonies.

Psa. 31.5. Thou hast redeemed me, O Lord God of truth.

Psa. 33.4. The word of the Lord *is* right ; and all his works *are done* in truth.

Psa. 36.5. Thy faithfulness *reacheth* unto the clouds.

Psa. 37.28. The Lord loveth judgment, and forsaketh not his saints ; they are preserved for ever.

Psa. 40.10. I have declared thy faithfulness and thy salvation : I have not concealed thy loving-kindness and thy truth from the great congregation.

Psa. 57.3. God shall send forth his mercy and his truth. 10. Thy mercy *is* great unto the heavens, and thy truth unto the clouds.

Psa. 71.22. I will also praise thee with the psaltery, *even* thy truth, O my God.

Psa. 86.15. Plenteous in mercy and truth.

Psa. 89.1. With my mouth will I make known thy faithfulness to all generations. 2. Thy faithfulness shalt thou establish in the very heavens. 5. The heavens shall praise thy faithfulness also in the congregation of the saints. 8. O Lord God of hosts, who *is* a strong Lord like unto thee? or to thy faithfulness round about thee? 14. Mercy and truth shall go before thy face. 24. My faithfulness and my mercy *shall be* with him.

Psa. 89.28. My mercy will I keep for him for evermore, and my covenant shall stand fast with him. 33. My loving-kindness will I not utterly take from him, nor suffer my faithfulness to fail. 34. My covenant will I not break, nor alter the thing that is gone out of my lips. 2 Sam. 7.14,15.

Psa. 91.4. His truth *shall be thy* shield and buckler.

Psa. 92.2. To shew forth thy faithfulness every night. 15. To shew that the Lord *is* upright : *he is* my rock, and *there is* no unrighteousness in him. *v.* 14.

Psa. 94.14. The Lord will not cast off his people, neither will he forsake his inheritance.

Psa. 98.3. He hath remembered his mercy and his truth toward the house of Israel.

Psa. 100.5. His truth endureth to all generations.

Psa. 103.17. The mercy of the Lord *is* from everlasting to everlasting upon them that fear him, and his righteousness unto children's children.

Psa. 105.8. He hath remembered his covenant for ever, the word *which* he commanded to a thousand generations. 42. He remembered his holy promise, *and* Abraham his servant.

Psa. 111.5. He will ever be mindful of his covenant. 7. The works of his hands *are* verity and judgment ; all his commandments *are* sure. 8. They stand fast for ever and ever, *and are* done in truth and uprightness. 9. He sent redemption unto his people : he hath commanded his covenant for ever.

Psa. 117.2. The truth of the Lord *endureth* for ever.

Psa. 119.65. Thou hast dealt well with thy servant, O Lord, according unto thy word. 89. For ever, O Lord, thy word is settled in heaven. 90. Thy faithfulness *is* unto all generations.

Psa. 132.11. The Lord hath sworn *in* truth unto David ; he will not turn from it.

Psa. 138.2. Praise thy name for thy lovingkindness and for thy truth : for thou hast magnified thy word above all thy name.

Psa. 146.6. Which keepeth truth for ever.

Isa. 25.1. Thy counsels of old *are* faithfulness *and* truth.

Isa. 42.16. These things will I do unto them, and not forsake them.

Isa. 44.21. O Israel, thou shalt not be forgotten of me.

Isa. 49.7. The Lord that is faithful. 16. I have graven thee upon the palms of *my* hands ; thy walls *are* continually before me.

Isa. 51.6. The heavens shall vanish away like smoke, and the earth shall wax old like a garment, and they that dwell therein shall die in like manner : but my salvation shall be for ever, and my righteousness shall not be abolished. 8. The moth shall eat them up like a garment, and the worm shall eat them like wool : but my righteousness shall be for ever, and my salvation from generation to generation.

Isa. 54.9. As I have sworn that the waters of Noah should no more go over the earth ; so have I sworn that I would not be wroth with thee, nor rebuke thee. 10. For the mountains shall depart, and the hills be removed ; but my kindness shall not depart from thee, neither shall the covenant of my peace be removed, saith the Lord that hath mercy on thee.

Isa. 65.16. He who blesseth himself in the earth shall bless himself in the God of truth ; and he that sweareth in the earth shall swear by the God of truth.

Jer. 29.10. After seventy years be accomplished at Babylon I will visit you, and perform my good word toward you, in causing you to return to this place.

Jer. 31.36. If those ordinances depart from before me, saith the Lord, *then* the seed of Israel also shall cease from being a nation before me for ever. 37. If heaven above can be measured, and the foundations of the earth searched out beneath, I will also cast off all the seed of Israel for all that they have done, saith the Lord.

Jer. 32.40. I will make an everlasting covenant with them, that I will not turn away from them, to do them good.

Jer. 33.14. The days come, saith the Lord, that I will perform that good thing which I have promised unto the house of Israel. 20. If ye can break my covenant of the day, and my covenant of the night, and that there should not be day and night in their season ; 21. *Then* may also my covenant be broken with David my servant. *v.* 25, 26.

Jer. 51.5. Israel *hath* not *been* forsaken, nor Judah of his God, of the Lord of hosts ; though their land was filled with sin against the Holy One of Israel.

Lam. 3.23. Great *is* thy faithfulness.

Eze. 16.60. I will remember my covenant with thee in the days of thy youth, and I will establish unto thee an everlasting covenant. *v.* 62.

Hos. 2.19. I will betroth thee unto me for ever ; yea, I will betroth thee unto me in righteousness, and in judgment, and in lovingkindness, and in mercies. 20. I will even betroth thee unto me in faithfulness.

Mic. 7.20. Thou wilt perform the truth to Jacob, *and* the mercy to Abraham, which thou hast sworn unto our fathers from the days of old.

Hag. 2.5. *According to* the word that I covenanted with you when ye came out of Egypt, so my spirit remaineth among you.

Zech. 9.11. By the blood of thy covenant I have sent forth thy prisoners out of the pit wherein *is* no water.

Mat. 24.34. This generation shall not pass, till all these things be fulfilled. *v.* 35.

Luk. 1.54. He hath holpen his servant Israel, in remembrance of *his* mercy ; 55. As he spake to our fathers, to Abraham, and to his seed for ever. 68. He hath visited and redeemed his people, 69. And hath raised up an horn of salvation for us in the house of his servant David ; 70. As he spake by the mouth of his holy prophets. 72. To perform the mercy *promised* to our fathers, and to remember his holy covenant ; 73. The oath which he sware to our father Abraham.

Jno. 8.26. He that sent me is true.

Act. 13.32. The promise which was made unto the fathers, 33. God hath fulfilled the same unto us their children, in that he hath raised up Jesus again.

Rom. 3.3. Shall their unbelief make the faith of God without effect ? 4. God forbid : yea, let God be true, but every man a liar.

Rom. 11.2. God hath not cast away his people which he foreknew. 29. The gifts and calling of God *are* without repentance. *v.* 1.

Rom. 15.8. Jesus Christ was a minister of the circumcision for the truth of God, to confirm the promises *made* unto the fathers.

1 Cor. 1.9. God *is* faithful, by whom ye were called unto the fellowship of his Son Jesus Christ our Lord.

1 Cor. 10.13. God is faithful, who will not suffer you to be tempted above that ye are able.

2 Cor. 1.20. All the promises of God in him *are* yea, and in him Amen.

1 The. 5.24. Faithful *is* he that calleth you, who also will do *it*.

2 Tim. 2.13. If we believe not, *yet* he abideth faithful : he cannot deny himself. 19. The foundation of God standeth sure, having this seal, The Lord knoweth them that are his.

Tit. 1.2. Eternal life, which God, that cannot lie, promised before the world began.

Heb. 6.10. God *is* not unrighteous to forget your work and labour of love. 13. When God made promise to Abraham, because he could swear by no greater, he sware by himself. 18. *It was* impossible for God to lie.

Heb. 10.23. He *is* faithful that promised. 37. Yet a little while, and he that shall come will come, and will not tarry.

1 Pet. 4.19. A faithful Creator.

2 Pet. 3.9. The Lord is not slack concerning his promise, as some men count slackness.

1 Jno. 1.9. He is faithful and just to forgive us *our* sins.

Rev. 6.10. O Lord, holy and true.

Rev. 15.3. Just and true *are* thy ways, thou King of saints.

See PRAYER, PLEAS EMPLOYED—PERSEVERANCE— PROPHECY, ITS FULFILMENT— GOD ETERNAL.

GOD THE FATHER, SON, and HOLY GHOST.

Gen. 1.26. God said, Let us make man in our image, after our likeness.

Gen. 3.22. The Lord God said, Behold, the man is become as one of us.

Gen. 11.7. Go to, let us go down.

Ex. 17.7. They tempted the Lord, saying, Is the Lord among us, or not? & 1 Cor. 10.9. Neither let us tempt Christ, as some of them also tempted. & Heb. 3.7. Wherefore as the Holy Ghost saith, To-day if ye will hear his voice, 8. Harden not your hearts, as in the provocation, in the day of temptation in the wilderness: 9. When your fathers tempted me.

Isa. 6.8. Whom shall I send, and who will go for us?

Isa. 11.2. The spirit of the Lord shall rest upon him. 3. And shall make him of quick understanding in the fear of the Lord.

Isa. 42.1. My servant, whom I uphold; mine elect, *in whom* my soul delighteth; I have put my spirit upon him. Mat. 12.18.

Isa. 48.16. From the time that it was, there *am* I: and now the Lord God, and his Spirit, hath sent me.

Isa. 61.1. The Spirit of the Lord God is upon me. Luk. 4.18.

Isa. 63.9. In all their affliction he was afflicted, and the angel of his presence saved them: 10. But they rebelled, and vexed his holy Spirit.

Mat. 1.18. She was found with child of the Holy Ghost. 20. That which is conceived in her is of the Holy Ghost.

Mat. 3.11. He shall baptise you with the Holy Ghost. Mar. 1.8. Luk. 3.16.

Mat. 12.28. I cast out devils by the Spirit of God. Luk. 11.20.

Mat. 28.19. Baptizing them in the name of the Father, and of the Son, and of the Holy Ghost.

Luk. 1.35. The Holy Ghost shall come upon thee, and the power of the Highest shall overshadow thee; therefore also that holy thing, which shall be born of thee, shall be called the Son of God.

Luk. 3.22. The Holy Ghost descended in a bodily shape, like a dove, upon him; and a voice came from heaven, which said, Thou art my beloved Son; in thee I am well pleased. *v.* 21. Mat. 3.16. Mar. 1.10.

Luk. 4.1. Jesus being full of the Holy Ghost returned from Jordan, and was led by the Spirit into the wilderness. 14. Jesus returned in the power of the Spirit into Galilee. Mat. 4.1. Mar. 1.12.

Jno. 1.33. Upon whom thou shalt see the Spirit descending, and remaining on him, the same is he which baptizeth with the Holy Ghost. *v.* 32.

Jno. 3.34. He whom God hath sent speaketh the words of God: for God giveth not the Spirit by measure *unto him.*

Jno. 7.39. This spake he of the Spirit, which they that believe on him should receive: for the Holy Ghost was not yet *given;* because that Jesus was not yet glorified.

Jno. 14.26. The Holy Ghost, whom the Father will send in my name, he shall teach you all things, and bring all things to your remembrance, whatsoever I have said unto you.

Jno. 15.26. When the Comforter is come, whom I will send unto you from the Father, *even* the Spirit of truth, which proceedeth from the Father, he shall testify of me.

Jno. 16.7. If I go not away, the Comforter will not come unto you; but if I depart, I will send him unto you.

Jno. 16.13. When he, the Spirit of truth, is come, he will guide you into all truth: for he shall not speak of himself; but whatsoever he shall hear, *that* shall he speak: and he will shew you things to come. 14. He shall glorify me: for he shall receive of mine, and shall shew *it* unto you. 15. All things that the Father hath are mine: therefore said I, that he shall take of mine, and shall shew *it* unto you.

Jno. 20.22. He breathed on *them*, and saith unto them, Receive ye the Holy Ghost.

Act. 1.2. He through the Holy Ghost had given commandments unto the apostles. 4. Wait for the promise of the Father, which, *saith he*, ye have heard of me.

Act. 2.33. Having received of the Father the promise of the Holy Ghost, he hath shed forth this.

Act. 10.38. God anointed Jesus of Nazareth with the Holy Ghost and with power: for God was with him.

Rom. 1.3. His Son Jesus Christ our Lord, which was made of the seed of David according to the flesh; 4. Declared *to be* the Son of God with power, according to the spirit of holiness by the resurrection from the dead.

Rom. 8.9. If so be that the Spirit of God dwell in you. Now if any man have not the Spirit of Christ, he is none of his. 27. He that searcheth the hearts knoweth what *is* the mind of the Spirit, because he maketh intercession for the saints according to *the will of* God.

1 Cor. 2.10. The Spirit searcheth all things, yea, the deep things of God. 11. The things of God knoweth no man, but the Spirit of God.

1 Cor. 6.19. Your body is the temple of the Holy Ghost *which is* in you, which ye have of God.

1 Cor. 12.3. No man speaking by the Spirit of God calleth Jesus accursed: and *that* no man can say that Jesus is the Lord, but by the Holy Ghost.

2 Cor. 3.17. The Lord is that Spirit: and where the Spirit of the Lord is, there is liberty.

2 Cor. 5.5. God, who also hath given unto us the earnest of the Spirit. 2 Cor. 1.22.

2 Cor. 13.14. The grace of the Lord Jesus Christ, and the love of God, and the communion of the Holy Ghost.

Gal. 4.4. God sent forth his Son, made of a woman. 6. God hath sent forth the Spirit of his Son into your hearts.

Phil. 1.19. The supply of the Spirit of Jesus Christ.

2 The. 2.13. God hath from the beginning chosen you to salvation through sanctification of the Spirit and belief of the truth: 14. Whereunto he called you by our gospel, to the obtaining of the glory of our Lord Jesus Christ.

1 Tim. 3.16. God was manifest in the flesh, justified in the Spirit.

Tit. 3.4. The kindness and love of God our Saviour toward man appeared. 5. According to his mercy he saved us, by the washing of regeneration, and renewing of the Holy Ghost; 6. Which he shed on us abundantly through Jesus Christ our Saviour.

Heb. 9.14. Who through the eternal Spirit offered himself without spot to God.

1 Pet. 1.2. Elect according to the foreknowledge of God the Father, through sanctification

of the Spirit, unto obedience and sprinkling of the blood of Jesus Christ.

1 Pet. 3.18. Christ also hath once suffered for sins, the just for the unjust, that he might bring us to God, being put to death in the flesh, but quickened by the Spirit. *v.* 19.

1 Jno. 5.6. This is he that came by water and blood, *even* Jesus Christ. And it is the Spirit that beareth witness, because the Spirit is truth. 7. There are three that bear record in heaven, the Father, the Word, and the Holy Ghost: and these three are one.

Rev. 3.1. He that hath the seven Spirits of God.

Rev. 5.6. A Lamb as it had been slain, having seven horns and seven eyes, which are the seven Spirits of God sent forth into all the earth.

See CHRIST, SON OF GOD.

GOD, HIS FAVOUR AND PRESENCE WITH THE CHURCH—SAINTS' ACCESS TO, AND COMMUNION WITH GOD. Gen. 4.4. The Lord had respect unto Abel and to his offering.

Gen. 5.24. Enoch walked with God: and he *was* not; for God took him.

Gen. 6.8. Noah found grace in the eyes of the Lord. *v.* 9.

Gen. 12.2. I will bless thee, and make thy name great. Gen. 17.15,16. Gen. 25.11.

Gen. 18.33. The Lord went his way, as soon as he had left communing with Abraham. *v.* 17.

Gen. 32.28. Thy name shall be called no more Jacob, but Israel: for as a prince hast thou power with God and with men, and hast prevailed.

Gen. 46.4. I will go down with thee into Egypt.

Ex. 3.12. Certainly I will be with thee.

Ex. 20.24. In all places where I record my name I will come unto thee, and I will bless thee.

Ex. 24.2. Moses alone shall come near the Lord. Ex. 20.21.

Ex. 29.45. I will dwell among the children of Israel, and will be their God. *v.* 46.

Ex. 33.11. The Lord spake unto Moses face to face, as a man speaketh unto his friend. 17. Thou hast found grace in my sight, and I know thee by name. 22. While my glory passeth by, I will put thee in a clift of the rock, and will cover thee with my hand while I pass by: 23. And I will take away mine hand, and thou shalt see my back parts: but my face shall not be seen. *v.* 12.

Lev. 26.11. I will set my tabernacle among you: and my soul shall not abhor you. 12. And I will walk among you, and will be your God.

Num. 5.3. Their camps in the midst whereof I dwell.

Num. 6.27. They shall put my name upon the children of Israel; and I will bless them.

Num. 14.14. Thou Lord *art* among this people, that thou Lord art seen face to face, and *that* thy cloud standeth over them, and *that* thou goest before them.

Num. 23.20. I have received *commandment* to bless: and he hath blessed; and I cannot reverse it. 21. He hath not beheld iniquity in Jacob, neither hath he seen perverseness in Israel: the Lord his God *is* with him, and the shout of a king *is* among them. Num. 22.12. Num. 24.1.

Deu. 4.7. What nation *is there* so great,

who *hath* God so nigh unto them, as the Lord our God *is* in all *things that* we call upon him *for?*

Deu. 33.23. Naphtali, satisfied with favour, and full with the blessing of the Lord.

Jos. 1.5. As I was with Moses, *so* I will be with thee: I will not fail thee, nor forsake thee. 9. The Lord thy God *is* with thee whithersoever thou goest. Deu. 31.6,8.

1 Kin. 6.13. I will dwell among the children of Israel, and will not forsake my people Israel.

2 Chr. 15.2. The Lord *is* with you, while ye be with him; and if ye seek him, he will be found of you.

Job 10.12. Thou hast granted me life and favour, and thy visitation hath preserved my spirit.

Job 13.3. Surely I would speak to the Almighty, and I desire to reason with God.

Job 22.27. Thou shalt make thy prayer unto him, and he shall hear thee.

Job 23.3. Oh that I knew where I might find him! *that* I might come *even* to his seat!

Job 29.3. When his candle shined upon my head, *and when* by his light I walked *through* darkness; 4. As I was in the days of my youth, when the secret of God *was* upon my tabernacle. 5. When the Almighty *was* yet with me.

Psa. 3.8. Thy blessing *is* upon thy people.

Psa. 5.12. Thou, Lord, wilt bless the righteous; with favour wilt thou compass him as *with* a shield.

Psa. 9.11. Sing praises to the Lord, which dwelleth in Zion.

Psa. 11.7. The righteous Lord loveth righteousness; his countenance doth behold the upright.

Psa. 18.19. He delivered me, because he delighted in me. 25. With the merciful thou wilt shew thyself merciful; with an upright man thou wilt shew thyself upright. *v.* 26. 2 Sam. 22.20.

Psa. 24.4. He that hath clean hands, and a pure heart; 5. He shall receive the blessing from the Lord.

Psa. 25.14. The secret of the Lord *is* with them that fear him; and he will shew them his covenant.

Psa. 30.7. Lord, by thy favour thou hast made my mountain to stand strong.

Psa. 36.9. For with thee *is* the fountain of life: in thy light shall we see light.

Psa. 37.18. The Lord knoweth the days of the upright. 23. The steps of a *good* man are ordered by the Lord: and he delighteth in his way.

Psa. 41.11. By this I know that thou favourest me, because mine enemy doth not triumph over me. 12. And as for me, thou upholdest me in mine integrity, and settest me before thy face for ever.

Psa. 44.3. Neither did their own arm save them; but thy right hand, and thine arm, and the light of thy countenance, because thou hadst a favour unto them.

Psa. 46.7. The Lord of hosts *is* with us; the God of Jacob *is* our refuge.

Psa. 58.11. Verily there is a reward for the righteous.

Psa. 68.16. *This is* the hill *which* God desireth to dwell in; yea, the Lord will dwell *in it* for ever. 18. Thou hast received gifts tor men; yea, *for* the rebellious also, that the Lord God might dwell *among them.*

Psa. 73.28. *It is* good for me to draw near to God.

Psa. 76.1. In Judah *is* God known: his name *is* great in Israel. 2. In Salem also is his tabernacle, and his dwelling-place in Zion.

Psa. 84.11. The Lord will give grace and glory.

Psa. 87.2. The Lord loveth the gates of Zion more than all the dwellings of Jacob.

Psa. 89.17. For thou *art* the glory of their strength: and in thy favour our horn shall be exalted.

Psa. 92.10. My horn shalt thou exalt like *the horn of* an unicorn: I shall be anointed with fresh oil. **Psa. 75.10. Psa. 112.9.**

Psa. 94.19. In the multitude of my thoughts within me thy comforts delight my soul.

Psa. 102.13. The time to favour her, yea, the set time, is come.

Psa. 115.12. The Lord hath been mindful of us: he will bless *us;* he will bless the house of Israel; he will bless the house of Aaron. 13. He will bless them that fear the Lord, *both* small and great. *v.* 15.

Psa. 132.13. The Lord hath chosen Zion; he hath desired *it* for his habitation. 14. This *is* my rest for ever: here will I dwell; for I have desired it.

Psa. 139.18. When I awake, I am still with thee.

Psa. 140.13. The upright shall dwell in thy presence.

Psa. 147.11. The Lord taketh pleasure in them that fear him, in those that hope in his mercy.

Psa. 149.4. The Lord taketh pleasure in his people: he will beautify the meek with salvation.

Pro. 3.4. So shalt thou find favour and good understanding in the sight of God and man. 32. His secret *is* with the righteous. 35. The wise shall inherit glory. *v.* 23.

Pro. 8.35. Whoso findeth me findeth life, and shall obtain favour of the Lord.

Pro. 10.6. Blessings are upon the head of the just. 22. The blessing of the Lord, it maketh rich, and he addeth no sorrow with it. 24. The desire of the righteous shall be granted.

Pro. 11.27. He that diligently seeketh good procureth favour.

Pro. 12.2. A good *man* obtaineth favour of the Lord.

Pro. 14.9. Among the righteous *there is* favour.

Pro. 16.7. When a man's ways please the Lord, he maketh even his enemies to be at peace with him.

Isa. 28.5. In that day shall the Lord of hosts be for a crown of glory, and for a diadem of beauty.

Isa. 30.26. The light of the moon shall be as the light of the sun, and the light of the sun shall be sevenfold, as the light of seven days, in the day that the Lord bindeth up the breach of his people, and healeth the stroke of their wound.

Isa. 33.17. Thine eyes shall see the king in his beauty. 21. There the glorious Lord *will be* unto us a place of broad rivers *and* streams. *v.* 22.

Isa. 41.10. Fear thou not; for I *am* with

thee: be not dismayed; for I *am* thy God. **Isa. 43.5.**

Isa. 43.21. This people have I formed for myself; they shall shew forth my praise.

Isa. 54.8. With everlasting kindness will I have mercy on thee, saith the Lord thy Redeemer.

Isa. 60.10. In my favour have I had mercy on thee.

Isa. 61.9. The seed which the Lord hath blessed.

Isa. 61.6. Ye shall be named the priests of the Lord.

Jer. 15.20. I *am* with thee to save thee and to deliver thee, saith the Lord.

Lam. 3.24. The Lord *is* my portion, saith my soul; therefore will I hope in him.

Eze. 37.27. My tabernacle also shall be with them.

Eze. 39.29. Neither will I hide my face any more from them: for I have poured out my spirit upon the house of Israel.

Eze. 48.35. The name of the city from *that* day *shall be,* The Lord *is* there.

Hos. 14.4. I will love them freely: for mine anger is turned away from him.

Joel 2.27. Ye shall know that I *am* in the midst of Israel, and *that* I *am* the Lord your God, and none else: and my people shall never be ashamed. *v.* 26.

Joel 3.16. The Lord *will be* the hope of his people, and the strength of the children of Israel. 17. So shall ye know that I *am* the Lord your God dwelling in Zion, my holy mountain. *v.* 20,21.

Amos 3.2. You only have I known of all the families of the earth.

Zeph. 3.15. The king of Israel, *even* the Lord, *is* in the midst of thee: thou shalt not see evil any more. *v.* 17.

Hag. 1.13. I *am* with you, saith the Lord.

Zec. 2.5. For I, saith the Lord, will be unto her a wall of fire round about, and will be the glory in the midst of her.

Zec. 8.3. I am returned unto Zion, and will dwell in the midst of Jerusalem.

Zec. 9.16. And the Lord their God shall save them in that day as the flock of his people: for *they shall be* as the stones of a crown, lifted up as an ensign upon his land.

Luk. 1.28. Hail, *thou that art* highly favoured, the Lord *is* with thee: blessed *art* thou among women. 30. Fear not, Mary: for thou hast found favour with God. 66. The hand of the Lord was with him.

Luk. 2.52. Jesus increased in wisdom and stature, and in favour with God and man. **1 Sam. 2.26.**

Jno. 14.16. He shall give you another Comforter, that he may abide with you for ever; 17. *Even* the Spirit of truth; ye know him; for he dwelleth with you, and shall be in you. 18. I will not leave you comfortless: I will come to you. 19. Because I live, ye shall live also. 20. At that day ye shall know that I *am* in my Father, and ye in me, and I in you. 21. I will love him, and will manifest myself to him. 23. We will come unto him, and make our abode with him.

Jno. 15.15. I call you not servants; for the servant knoweth not what his lord doeth: but I have called you friends; for all things that I have heard of my Father I have made known unto you.

Act. 4.33. Great grace was upon them all.

Act. 10.35. He that feareth him, and worketh righteousness, is accepted with him.

Rom. 2.29. Whose praise *is* not of men, but of God.

1 Cor. 1.9. God *is* faithful, by whom ye were called unto the fellowship of his Son.

1 Cor. 3.21. All things are yours.

1 Cor. 6.2. The saints shall judge the world. *v.* 3.

1 Cor. 10.16. Is it not the communion of the blood of Christ? The bread which we break, is it not the communion of the body of Christ?

2 Cor. 4.15. All things are for your sakes.

2 Cor. 5.9. We labour, that, whether present or absent, we may be accepted of him.

2 Cor. 10.18. Not he that commendeth himself is approved, but whom the Lord commendeth.

Gal. 4.6. Because ye are sons, God hath sent forth the Spirit of his Son into your hearts, crying, Abba, Father.

Eph. 1.6. He hath made us accepted in the Beloved.

Eph. 2.13. Now in Christ Jesus ye who sometimes were far off are made nigh by the blood of Christ. 14. He is our peace. 18. Through him we both have access by one Spirit unto the Father. 22. In whom ye also are builded together for an habitation of God through the Spirit. *v.* 19. Eph. 2.16.

Eph. 3.12. In whom we have boldness and access with confidence by the faith of him. Rom. 5.2.

Phil. 2.1. If *there be* therefore any consolation in Christ, if any fellowship of the Spirit.

Heb. 4.16. Let us therefore come boldly unto the throne of grace, that we may obtain mercy, and find grace to help in time of need.

Heb. 10.19. Having therefore, brethren, boldness to enter into the holiest by the blood of Jesus. 22. Let us draw near with a true heart in full assurance of faith.

Heb. 11.5. Before his translation he had this testimony, that he pleased God.

Jas. 2.23. He was called the Friend of God.

1 Pet. 2.9. A chosen generation, a royal priesthood.

1 Jno. 1.3. Truly our fellowship *is* with the Father, and with his Son Jesus Christ.

1 Jno. 3.19. Hereby we know that we are of the truth, and shall assure our hearts before him.

1 Jno. 4.17. Herein is our love made perfect, that we may have boldness in the day of judgment: because as he is, so are we in this world. 18. There is no fear in love; but perfect love casteth out fear: because fear hath torment. He that feareth is not made perfect in love.

Rev. 1.6. Hath made us kings and priests unto God. Rev. 5.10.

Rev. 3.20. I will come in to him, and will sup with him, and he with me. Rev. 19.9.

Rev. 21.3. Behold, the tabernacle of God *is* with men, and he will dwell with them, and they shall be his people, and God himself shall be with them, *and be* their God.

Rev. 22.3. The throne of God and of the Lamb shall be in it; and his servants shall serve him: 4. And they shall see his face; and his name *shall be* in their foreheads.

GOD, HIS FAVOUR AND BLESSING, PRAYER FOR. Ex. 33.13. Shew me now thy way, that I may know thee, that I may find grace in thy sight: and consider that this nation *is* thy people. 15. If thy presence go not *with me*, carry us not up hence. 16. For wherein shall it be known here that I and thy people have found grace in thy sight? *is it* not in that thou goest with us? so shall we be separated, I and thy people, from all the people that *are* upon the face of the earth.

Ex. 34.9. If now I have found grace in thy sight, O Lord, let my Lord, I pray thee, go among us, (for it *is* a stiff-necked people,) and pardon our iniquity and our sin, and take us for thine inheritance.

Num. 10.36. Return, O Lord, unto the many thousands of Israel.

Deu. 26.15. Look down from thy holy habitation, from heaven, and bless thy people Israel.

Deu. 33.16. *For* the good will of him that dwelt in the bush; let the blessing come upon the head of Joseph.

2 Sam. 7.29. Let it please thee to bless the house of thy servant, that it may continue for ever before thee: for thou, O Lord God, hast spoken *it*; and with thy blessing let the house of thy servant be blessed for ever.

1 Kin. 8.57. The Lord our God be with us, as he was with our fathers: let him not leave us, nor forsake us.

1 Chr. 4.10. Oh that thou wouldest bless me indeed, and enlarge my coast, and that thine hand might be with me, and that thou wouldest keep *me* from evil, that it may not grieve me!

Neh. 5.19. Think upon me, my God, for good. Neh. 13.14,31.

Psa. 4.6. Lord, lift thou up the light of thy countenance upon us.

Psa. 17.7. Shew thy marvellous lovingkindness, O thou that savest by thy right hand.

Psa. 19.14. Let the words of my mouth, and the meditation of my heart, be acceptable in thy sight, O Lord, my strength, and my redeemer.

Psa. 27.4. One *thing* have I desired of the Lord, that will I seek after; that I may dwell in the house of the Lord all the days of my life, to behold the beauty of the Lord, and to enquire in his temple. 9. Hide not thy face *far* from me; put not thy servant away in anger.

Psa. 28.9. Save thy people, and bless thine inheritance: feed them also, and lift them up for ever.

Psa. 31.16. Make thy face to shine upon thy servant: save me for thy mercies' sake.

Psa. 35.3. Say unto my soul, I *am* thy salvation.

Psa. 36.10. O continue thy loving-kindness unto them that know thee; and thy righteousness to the upright in heart.

Psa. 40.11. Withhold not thou thy tender mercies from me, O Lord: let thy lovingkindness and thy truth continually preserve me. 17. Thou *art* my help and my deliverer; make no tarrying, O my God.

Psa. 42.1. As the hart panteth after the water brooks, so panteth my soul after thee, O God. 2. My soul thirsteth for God, for the living God: when shall I come and appear before God?

Psa. 51.8. Make me to hear joy and gladness; *that* the bones *which* thou hast broken may rejoice. 11. Cast me not away from thy presence; and take not thy Holy Spirit from me. 12. Restore unto me the joy of thy salvation; and uphold me *with thy* free Spirit.

Psa. 63.1. O God, thou *art* my God; early will I seek thee: my soul thirsteth for thee, my flesh longeth for thee in a dry and thirsty land, where no water is; 2. To see thy power and thy glory, so *as* I have seen thee in the sanctuary.

Psa. 67.1. God be merciful unto us, and bless us; *and* cause his face to shine upon us. Psa. 119.135.

Psa. 71.3. Be thou my strong habitation, whereunto I may continually resort.

Psa. 80.1. Give ear, O Shepherd of Israel, thou that leadest Joseph like a flock; thou that dwellest *between* the cherubims, shine forth. 2. Before Ephraim and Benjamin and Manasseh stir up thy strength, and come *and* save us. 3. Turn us again, O God, and cause thy face to shine; and we shall be saved.

Psa. 84.9. Behold, O God our shield, and look upon the face of thine anointed.

Psa. 85.4. Turn us, O God of our salvation, and cause thine anger toward us to cease. 6. Wilt thou not revive us again: that thy people may rejoice in thee?

Psa. 86.4. Rejoice the soul of thy servant: for unto thee, O Lord, do I lift up my soul.

Psa. 90.14. O satisfy us early with thy mercy; that we may rejoice and be glad all our days. 16. Let thy work appear unto thy servants, and thy glory unto their children. 17. And let the beauty of the Lord our God be upon us: and establish thou the work of our hands upon us; yea, the work of our hands establish thou it. *v.* 15.

Psa. 101.2. O when wilt thou come unto me?

Psa. 106.4. Remember me, O Lord, with the favour *that thou bearest unto* thy people: O visit me with thy salvation; 5. That I may see the good of thy chosen, that I may rejoice in the gladness of thy nation, that I may glory with thine inheritance.

Psa. 119.8. O forsake me not utterly. 58. I entreated thy favour with *my* whole heart. 132. Look thou upon me, and be merciful unto me, as thou usest to do unto those that love thy name.

Psa. 141.2. Let my prayer be set forth before thee *as* incense; *and* the lifting up of my hands *as* the evening sacrifice.

Psa. 143.7. Hear me speedily, O Lord: my spirit faileth: hide not thy face from me, lest I be like unto them that go down into the pit. 8. Cause me to hear thy loving-kindness in the morning; for in thee do I trust: cause me to know the way wherein I should walk; for I lift up my soul unto thee.

Jer. 14.8. O the hope of Israel, the saviour thereof in time of trouble, why shouldest thou be as a stranger in the land, and as a wayfaring man *that* turneth aside to tarry for a night?

2 Cor. 13.14. The grace of the Lord Jesus Christ, and the love of God, and the communion of the Holy Ghost, *be* with you all. Amen.

See GOD'S LOVE — SPIRITUAL PEACE — ADOPTION.

GOD GLORIFIED BY CHRIST. Isa. 49.3. Thou *art* my servant, O Israel, in whom I will be glorified.

Jno. 8.50. I seek not mine own glory: there is one that seeketh and judgeth.

Jno. 12.28. Father, glorify thy name. Then came there a voice from heaven, *saying*, I have both glorified *it*, and will glorify *it* again.

Jno. 13.31. Now is the Son of man glorified, and God is glorified in him. 32. If God be glorified in him, God shall also glorify him in himself, and shall straightway glorify him.

Jno. 14.13. Whatsoever ye shall ask in my name, that will I do, that the Father may be glorified in the Son.

Jno. 17.1. Glorify thy Son, that thy Son also may glorify thee.

Eph. 3.21. Unto him *be* glory in the church by Christ Jesus throughout all ages, world without end.

Phil. 2.11. Every tongue should confess that Jesus Christ *is* Lord, to the glory of God the Father.

GOD GLORIFIED IN THE CHURCH. Psa. 68.24. They have seen thy goings, O God; *even* the goings of my God, my King, in the sanctuary.

Psa. 102.16. When the Lord shall build up Zion, he shall appear in his glory. 21. To declare the name of the Lord in Zion, and his praise in Jerusalem; 22. When the people are gathered together, and the kingdoms, to serve the Lord.

Psa. 106.8. He saved them for his name's sake, that he might make his mighty power to be known.

Isa. 12.6. Cry out and shout, thou inhabitant of Zion: for great *is* the Holy One of Israel in the midst of thee.

Isa. 24.23. The Lord of hosts shall reign in mount Zion, and in Jerusalem, and before his ancients gloriously.

Isa. 26.15. Thou hast increased the nation: thou art glorified.

Isa. 28.5. In that day shall the Lord of hosts be for a crown of glory, and for a diadem of beauty, unto the residue of his people.

Isa. 29.23. When he seeth his children, the work of mine hands, in the midst of him, they shall sanctify my name, and sanctify the Holy One of Jacob, and shall fear the God of Israel.

Isa. 33.5. The Lord is exalted; for he dwelleth on high: he hath filled Zion with judgment and righteousness.

Isa. 35.2. They shall see the glory of the Lord, *and* the excellency of our God.

Isa. 40.5. The glory of the Lord shall be revealed, and all flesh shall see *it* together.

Isa. 43.7. Every one that is called by my name: for I have created him for my glory, I have formed him; yea, I have made him. 21. This people have I formed for myself: they shall shew forth my praise. 25. I, *even* I, *am* he that blotteth out thy transgressions for mine own sake, and will not remember thy sins.

Isa. 44.23. The Lord hath redeemed Jacob, and glorified himself in Israel.

Isa. 48.11. For mine own sake, *even* for mine own sake, will I do *it*: for how should *my name* be polluted? and I will not give my glory unto another. *v.* 9.

Isa. 49.26. All flesh shall know that I the Lord *am* thy Saviour and thy Redeemer, the mighty One of Jacob.

Isa. 52.10. The Lord hath made bare his holy arm in the eyes of all the nations; and all the ends of the earth shall see the salvation of our God.

Isa. 55.13. It shall be to the Lord for a name, for an everlasting sign *that* shall not be cut off.

Isa. 60.1. Arise, shine; for thy light is come, and the glory of the Lord is risen upon thee. 2. For, behold, the darkness shall cover the earth, and gross darkness the people : but the Lord shall arise upon thee, and his glory shall be seen upon thee. 6. They shall shew forth the praises of the Lord 19. But the Lord shall be unto thee an everlasting light, and thy God thy glory. 20. Thy sun shall no more go down ; neither shall thy moon withdraw itself : for the Lord shall be thine everlasting light, and the days of thy mourning shall be ended. 21. Thy people also *shall be* all righteous : they shall inherit the land for ever, the branch of my planting, the work of my hands, that I may be glorified.

Isa. 61.3. That they might be called trees of righteousness, the planting of the Lord, that he might be glorified.

Isa. 62.3. Thou shalt also be a crown of glory in the hand of the Lord, and a royal diadem in the hand of thy God.

Isa. 63.12. That led *them* by the right hand of Moses with his glorious arm, dividing the water before them, to make himself an everlasting name? *v.* 14.

Isa. 66.18. I will gather all nations and tongues ; and they shall come, and see my glory.

Jer. 13.11. That they might be unto me for a people, and for a name, and for a praise, and for a glory.

Jer. 33.9. It shall be to me a name of joy, a praise and an honour before all the nations of the earth, which shall hear all the good that I do unto them.

Eze. 20.14. I wrought for my name's sake, that it should not be polluted before the heathen, in whose sight I brought them out. 44. Ye shall know that I *am* the Lord, when I have wrought with you for my name's sake.

Eze. 36.22. I do not *this* for your sakes, O house of Israel, but for mine holy name's sake, which ye have profaned among the heathen, whither ye went. 23. And I will sanctify my great name, which was profaned among the heathen, which ye have profaned in the midst of them ; and the heathen shall know that I *am* the Lord, saith the Lord God, when I shall be sanctified in you before their eyes.

Luk. 2.14. Glory to God in the highest, and on earth peace.

Jno. 17.10. All mine are thine, and thine are mine ; and I am glorified in them.

Act. 15.14. God at the first did visit the Gentiles, to take out of them a people for his name.

2 Cor. 1.20. All the promises of God in him *are* yea, and in him Amen, unto the glory of God by us.

2 Cor. 4.15. All things *are* for your sakes. that the abundant grace might through the thanksgiving of many redound to the glory of God.

Eph. 1.6. To the praise of the glory of his grace, wherein he hath made us accepted in the beloved. 12. We should be to the praise of his glory, who first trusted in Christ. 14. The

redemption of the purchased possession, unto the praise of his glory.

Eph. 2.7. That in the ages to come he might shew the exceeding riches of his grace in *his* kindness toward us through Christ Jesus.

Eph. 3.10. To the intent that now unto the principalities and powers in heavenly *places* might be known by the church the manifold wisdom of God.

Phil. 1.11. The fruits of righteousness, which are by Jesus Christ, unto the glory and praise of God.

Rev. 21.10. The holy Jerusalem, descending out of heaven from God. 11. Having the glory of God. 23. The city had no need of the sun, neither of the moon, to shine in it : for the glory of God did lighten it, and the Lamb *is* the light thereof. See GLORIFYING GOD.

GOD GLORIFIED IN JUDGMENTS. See JUDGMENTS, DESIGN AND EFFECT.

GOD, HIS GLORY AND GREATNESS. EX. 3.2. The angel of the Lord appeared unto him in a flame of fire out of the midst of a bush : and he looked, and, behold, the bush burned with fire, and the bush *was* not consumed.

Ex. 19.18. Sinai was altogether on a smoke, because the Lord descended upon it in fire : and the smoke thereof ascended as the smoke of a furnace, and the whole mount quaked greatly. *v.* 16,19. Ex. 20.18,19. Deu. 4.11,12,33,36. Deu. 5.5,24,25.

Ex. 24.10. They saw the God of Israel : and *there was* under his feet as it were a paved work of a sapphire stone, and as it were the body of heaven in *his* clearness. 17. And the sight of the glory of the Lord *was* like devouring fire on the top of the mount in the eyes of the children of Israel.

Ex. 33.20. Thou canst not see my face : for there shall no man see me, and live. 22. It shall come to pass, while my glory passeth by, that I will put thee in a clift of the rock. *v.* 23.

Ex. 34.5. The Lord descended in the cloud, and stood with him there, and proclaimed the name of the Lord. 6. And the Lord passed by before him, and proclaimed, The Lord, The Lord God, merciful and gracious. *v.* 29-35. Ex. 33.18,19.

Deu. 10.17. The Lord your God *is* God of gods, and Lord of lords, a great God, a mighty, and a terrible. Deu. 7.21.

Deu. 28.58. Fear this glorious and fearful name, The Lord Thy God.

Deu. 33.2. He shined forth from mount Paran, and he came with ten thousands of saints. 26. *There is* none like unto the God of Jeshurun, *who* rideth upon the heaven in thy help, and in his excellency on the sky.

1 Kin. 19.12. After the earthquake a fire ; *but* the Lord *was* not in the fire : and after the fire a still small voice.

Job 9.32. *He is* not a man, as I *am*, *that* I should answer him, *and* we should come together in judgment. 33. Neither is there any daysman betwixt us, *that* might lay his hand upon us both.

Job 13.11. Shall not his excellency make you afraid? and his dread fall upon you?

Job 22.12. *Is* not God in the height of heaven? and behold the height of the stars, how high they are !

Job 25.3. Is there any number of his armies? and upon whom doth not his light arise?

Job 33.12. God is greater than man.

Job 35.5. Look unto the heavens, and see; and behold the clouds *which* are higher than thou. 6. If thou sinnest, what doest thou against him? or *if* thy transgressions be multiplied, what doest thou unto him? 7. If thou be righteous, what givest thou him? or what receiveth he of thine hand?

Job 37.5. God thundereth marvellously with his voice; great things doeth he, which we cannot comprehend. 22. With God *is* terrible majesty. *v.* 4.

Psa. 18.9. He bowed the heavens also, and came down: and darkness *was* under his feet. 10. And he rode upon a cherub, and did fly: yea, he did fly upon the wings of the wind. 11. He made darkness his secret place; his pavilion round about him *were* dark waters *and* thick clouds of the skies. *v.* 7-15. 2 Sam. 22.

Psa. 46.10. Be still, and know that I *am* God: I will be exalted among the heathen, I will be exalted in the earth.

Isa. 1.24. The Lord, the Lord of hosts, the mighty One of Israel.

Isa. 2.10. Enter into the rock, and hide thee in the dust, for fear of the Lord, and for the glory of his majesty.

Isa. 6.1. I saw also the Lord sitting upon a throne, high and lifted up, and his train filled the temple. 3. And one cried unto another, and said, Holy, holy, holy, *is* the Lord of hosts: the whole earth *is* full of his glory. *v.* 1-5.

Isa. 30.30. The Lord shall cause his glorious voice to be heard, and shall shew the lighting down of his arm, with the indignation of *his* anger, and *with* the flame of a devouring fire, *with* scattering, and tempest, and hailstones.

Isa. 33.10. Now will I rise, saith the Lord; now will I be exalted; now will I lift up myself.

Isa. 40.15. Behold, he taketh up the isles as a very little thing. 16. And Lebanon *is* not sufficient to burn, nor the beasts thereof sufficient for a burnt-offering. 17. All nations before him *are* as nothing; and they are counted to him less than nothing, and vanity. 18. To whom then will ye liken God? or what likeness will ye compare unto him? 22. He that sitteth upon the circle of the earth, and the inhabitants thereof *are* as grasshoppers. Isa. 46.5.

Isa. 55.9. *As* the heavens are higher than the earth, so are my ways higher than your ways, and my thoughts than your thoughts.

Isa. 57.15. Thus saith the high and lofty One that inhabiteth eternity, whose name *is* Holy; I dwell in the high and holy *place*.

Isa. 66.1. The heaven *is* my throne, and the earth *is* my footstool: where *is* the house that ye build unto me? and where *is* the place of my rest? 2. For all those *things* hath mine hand made.

Jer. 17.12. A glorious high throne from the beginning *is* the place of our sanctuary.

Eze. 1.26. Above the firmament that *was* over their heads *was* the likeness of a throne, as the appearance of a sapphire stone: and upon the likeness of the throne *was* the likeness as the appearance of a man above upon it.

28. As the appearance of the bow that is in the cloud in the day of rain, so *was* the appearance of the brightness round about. This *was* the appearance of the likeness of the glory of the Lord. *v.* 1-27. Eze. 3.23.

Eze. 43.2. The glory of the God of Israel came from the way of the east: and his voice *was* like a noise of many waters: and the earth shined with his glory.

Eze. 44.2. This gate shall be shut, it shall not be opened, and no man shall enter in by it; because the Lord, the God of Israel, hath entered in by it, therefore it shall be shut.

Dan. 7.9. The Ancient of days did sit, whose garment *was* white as snow, and the hair of his head like the pure wool: his throne *was like* the fiery flame, *and* his wheels *as* burning fire. 10. A fiery stream issued and came forth from before him: thousand thousands ministered unto him, and ten thousand times ten thousand stood before him.

Mal. 1.14. I am a great King, saith the Lord of hosts, and my name *is* dreadful among the heathen.

Act. 17.29. We ought not to think that the Godhead is like unto gold, or silver, or stone, graven by art and man's device.

Rom. 1.23. The glory of the uncorruptible God.

2 Cor. 11.31. The God and Father of our Lord Jesus Christ, which is blessed for evermore.

Eph. 1.17. The Father of glory.

Eph. 4.6. One God and Father of all, who *is* above all, and through all, and in you all.

Phil. 4.19. My God shall supply all your need according to his riches in glory by Christ Jesus.

Heb. 12.29. For our God *is* a consuming fire.

1 Jno. 1.5. God is light, and in him is no darkness at all.

Rev. 4.2. *One* sat on the throne. 3. And he that sat was to look upon like a jasper and a sardine stone: and *there was* a rainbow round about the throne, in sight like unto an emerald. *v.* 2-6.

Rev. 15.8. The temple was filled with smoke from the glory of God, and from his power.

Rev. 22.5. There shall be no night there; and they need no candle, neither light of the sun; for the Lord God giveth them light.

See CLOUD OF GLORY—MERCY-SEAT.

GOD, HIS GLORY AND GREATNESS, PRAISE OF. Ex. 15.1. I will sing unto the Lord, for he hath triumphed gloriously: the horse and his rider hath he thrown into the sea. *v.* 6, 11.

Ex. 18.11. I know that the Lord *is* greater than all gods: for in the thing wherein they dealt proudly *he was* above them.

Deu. 32.3. I will publish the name of the Lord: ascribe ye greatness unto our God. 4. *He is* the Rock, his work *is* perfect: for all his ways *are* judgment. 31. Their rock *is* not as our Rock, even our enemies themselves *being* judges.

Jud. 5.4. When thou marchedst out of the field of Edom, the earth trembled, and the heavens dropped, the clouds also dropped water. 5. The mountains melted from before the Lord, *even* that Sinai from before the Lord God of Israel.

2 Sam. 7.22. Thou art great, O Lord God: for *there* is none like thee, neither *is there any* God beside thee.

1 Kin. 8.27. But will God indeed dwell on the earth? behold, the heaven and heaven of heavens cannot contain thee; how much less this house that I have builded? 2 Chr. 6.18.

2 Chr. 2.5. Great *is* our God above all gods.

Neh. 9.5. Bless the Lord your God for ever and ever: and blessed be thy glorious name, which is exalted above all blessing and praise. 32. Our God, the great, the mighty, and the terrible God, who keepest covenant and mercy.

Neh. 1.5. Neh. 4.14.

Psa. 8.1. O Lord our Lord, how excellent *is* thy name in all the earth! who hast set thy glory above the heavens. *v.* 9.

Psa. 11.4. The Lord *is* in his holy temple, the Lord's throne *is* in heaven.

Psa. 19.1. The heavens declare the glory of God; and the firmament sheweth his handywork. *v.* 2-4.

Psa. 24.8. Who *is* this King of glory? The Lord strong and mighty, the Lord mighty in battle. 9. Lift up your heads, O ye gates; even lift *them* up, ye everlasting doors; and the King of glory shall come in. *v.* 10.

Psa. 29.2. Give unto the Lord the glory due unto his name; worship the Lord in the beauty of holiness. *v.* 3,4.

Psa. 47.2. The Lord most high *is* terrible; *he is* a great King over all the earth. 5. God is gone up with a shout, the Lord with the sound of a trumpet.

Psa. 48.1. Great *is* the Lord, and greatly to be praised in the city of our God.

Psa. 50.1. The mighty God, *even* the Lord, hath spoken, and called the earth from the rising of the sun unto the going down thereof. 2. Out of Zion, the perfection of beauty, God hath shined. 3. Our God shall come, and shall not keep silence: a fire shall devour before him, and it shall be very tempestuous round about him.

Psa. 57.11. Be thou exalted, O God, above the heavens: *let* thy glory *be* above all the earth. *v.* 5. Psa. 108.8.

Psa. 68.7. O God, when thou wentest forth before thy people, when thou didst march through the wilderness; 8. The earth shook, the heavens also dropped at the presence of God: *even* Sinai itself *was moved* at the presence of God, the God of Israel. 17. The chariots of God *are* twenty thousand, *even* thousands of angels: the Lord *is* among them, as *in* Sinai, in the holy *place.* 34. Ascribe ye strength unto God: his excellency *is* over Israel, and his strength *is* in the clouds. 35. O God, *thou art* terrible out of thy holy places: the God of Israel *is* he that giveth strength and power unto *his* people. Blessed *be* God. 2 Sam. 22. Psa. 18.7-15.

Psa. 71.19. Thy righteousness also, O God, *is* very high, who hast done great things: O God, who *is* like unto thee!

Psa. 72.18. Blessed *be* the Lord God, the God of Israel, who only doeth wondrous things. 19. And blessed *be* his glorious name for ever: and let the whole earth be filled *with* his glory; Amen, and Amen.

Psa. 76.4. Thou *art* more glorious *and* excellent than the mountains of prey.

Psa. 77.13. Thy way, O God, *is* in the sanctuary: who *is so* great a God as *our* God?

Psa. 86.8. Among the gods *there is* none like unto thee, O Lord; neither *are there any works* like unto thy works. 10. Thou *art* great, and doest wondrous things: thou *art* God alone.

Psa. 89.6. Who in the heaven can be compared unto the Lord? *who* among the sons of the mighty can be likened unto the Lord? 7. God is greatly to be feared in the assembly of the saints, and to be had in reverence of all *them that are* about him. 14. Justice and judgment *are* the habitation of thy throne: mercy and truth shall go before thy face. *v.* 8.

Psa. 92.5. O Lord, how great are thy works! *and* thy thoughts are very deep. 8. Thou, Lord, *art most* high for evermore.

Psa. 96.3. Declare his glory among the heathen, his wonders among all people. 4. The Lord is great, and greatly to be praised: he *is* to be feared above all gods. 6. Honour and majesty *are* before him: strength and beauty *are* in his sanctuary. 7. Give unto the Lord, O ye kindreds of the people, give unto the Lord glory and strength. 1 Chr. 16.24,25.

Psa. 97.2. Clouds and darkness *are* round about him: righteousness and judgment *are* the habitation of his throne. 6. The heavens declare his righteousness, and all the people see his glory. 9. Thou, Lord, *art* high above all the earth: thou art exalted far above all gods. *v.* 3-5.

Psa. 99.1. The Lord reigneth; let the people tremble: he sitteth *between* the cherubims; let the earth be moved. 2. The Lord *is* great in Zion; and he *is* high above all the people. 3. Let them praise thy great and terrible name; *for* it is holy.

Psa. 104.1. O Lord my God, thou art very great; thou art clothed with honour and majesty. 2. Who coverest *thyself* with light as *with* a garment: who stretchest out the heavens like a curtain: 3. Who layeth the beams of his chambers in the waters: who maketh the clouds his chariot: who walketh upon the wings of the wind: 31. The glory of the Lord shall endure for ever: the Lord shall rejoice in his works.

Psa. 106.2. Who can utter the mighty acts of the Lord? *who* can shew forth all his praise?

Psa. 113.4. The Lord *is* high above all nations, *and* his glory above the heavens. 5. Who *is* like unto the Lord our God, who dwelleth on high? 6. Who humbleth *himself* to behold *the things that are* in heaven, and in the earth!

Psa. 114.7. Tremble, thou earth, at the presence of the Lord, at the presence of the God of Jacob.

Psa. 135.5. I know that the Lord *is* great, and *that* our Lord *is* above all gods.

Psa. 136.2. O give thanks unto the God of gods: 3. O give thanks to the Lord of lords: for his mercy *endureth* for ever. 4. To him who alone doeth great wonders.

Psa. 138.5. They shall sing in the ways of the Lord: for great *is* the glory of the Lord.

Psa. 145.3. Great *is* the Lord, and greatly to be praised; and his greatness *is* unsearchable. 5. I will speak of the glorious honour of thy majesty, and of thy wondrous works. 10. All thy works shall praise thee, O Lord; and thy saints shall bless thee. 11. They shall speak of the glory of thy kingdom, and talk of thy power; 12. To make known to the sons of men his mighty acts, and the glorious majesty of his kingdom.

Psa. 148.13. Let them praise the name of

the Lord: for his name alone is excellent; his glory is above the earth and heaven.

Psa. 150.2. Praise him for his mighty acts: praise him according to his excellent greatness.

Isa. 6.3. Holy, holy, holy, is the Lord of hosts: the whole earth is full of his glory.

Isa. 12.4. Praise the Lord, call upon his name, declare his doings among the people, make mention that his name is exalted. 5. Sing unto the Lord; for he hath done excellent things: this is known in all the earth. 6. Cry out and shout, thou inhabitant of Zion: for great is the Holy One of Israel in the midst of thee.

Isa. 24.14. They shall lift up their voice, they shall sing for the majesty of the Lord, they shall cry aloud from the sea. 15. Wherefore glorify ye the Lord in the fires, even the name of the Lord God of Israel in the isles of the sea.

Jer. 32.18. The Great, the Mighty God, the Lord of hosts, is his name, 19. Great in counsel, and mighty in work.

Eze. 3.12. Blessed be the glory of the Lord from his place.

Dan. 4.34. I blessed the most High, and I praised and honoured him that liveth for ever, whose dominion is an everlasting dominion, and his kingdom is from generation to generation. v. 35.

Hab. 2.20. The Lord is in his holy temple: let all the earth keep silence before him.

Hab. 3.3. His glory covered the heavens, and the earth was full of his praise. 4. And his brightness was as the light; he had horns coming out of his hand: and there was the hiding of his power. 5. Before him went the pestilence, and burning coals went forth at his feet. v. 6.

Mat. 6.9. Our Father which art in heaven, hallowed be thy name. 13. Thine is the kingdom, and the power, and the glory, for ever. Amen.

Luk. 2.14. Glory to God in the highest.

Rom. 11.36. Of him, and through him, and to him, are all things: to whom be glory for ever.

1 Tim. 6.15. Who is the blessed and only Potentate, the King of kings, and Lord of lords; 16. Who only hath immortality, dwelling in the light which no man can approach unto; whom no man hath seen, nor can see: to whom be honour and power everlasting. Amen.

Jude 25. To the only wise God our Saviour, be glory and majesty, dominion and power, both now and ever.

Rev. 4.11. Thou art worthy, O Lord, to receive glory, and honour, and power: for thou hast created all things, and for thy pleasure they are and were created.

See GOD, KING—GOD, OMNIPOTENCE OF—ZEAL FOR GOD'S GLORY—GLORYFYING GOD.

GOD, GOODNESS OF. Ex. 33.19. I will make all my goodness pass before thee.

Ex. 34.6. Abundant in goodness and truth.

Deu. 30.9. The Lord will again rejoice over thee for good, as he rejoiced over thy fathers.

Psa. 8.4. What is man, that thou art mindful of him? and the son of man, that thou visitest him? Psa. 144.3.

Psa. 17.7. Thy marvellous loving-kindness.

Psa. 25.8. Good and upright is the Lord.

Psa. 33.5. The earth is full of the goodness of the Lord.

Psa. 34.8. O taste and see that the Lord is good.

Psa. 36.7. How excellent is thy loving-kindness, O God! therefore the children of men put their trust under the shadow of thy wings.

Psa. 52.1. The goodness of God endureth continually. 9. I will wait on thy name; for it is good before thy saints.

Psa. 69.16. Thy loving-kindness is good.

Psa. 100.5. The Lord is good; his mercy is everlasting.

Psa. 104.13. The earth is satisfied with the fruit of thy works.

Psa. 106.1. O give thanks unto the Lord; for he is good.

Psa. 107.8. Oh that men would praise the Lord for his goodness, and for his wonderful works to the children of men! 9. For he satisfieth the longing soul, and filleth the hungry soul with goodness. 43. Whoso is wise, and will observe these things, even they shall understand the loving-kindness of the Lord.

Psa. 119.64. The earth, O Lord, is full of thy mercy. 68. Thou art good, and doest good.

Psa. 143.10. Thy spirit is good.

Psa. 145.7. They shall abundantly utter the memory of thy great goodness. 9. The Lord is good to all: and his tender mercies are over all his works.

Jer. 9.24. I am the Lord which exercise loving-kindness, judgment, and righteousness, in the earth: for in these things I delight, saith the Lord.

Lam. 3.25. The Lord is good unto them that wait for him, to the soul that seeketh him.

Hos. 3.5. Shall fear the Lord and his goodness in the latter days.

Nah. 1.7. The Lord is good, a strong hold in the day of trouble.

Mat. 7.11. If ye then, being evil, know how to give good gifts unto your children, how much more shall your Father which is in heaven give good things to them that ask him?

Mat. 19.17. There is none good but one, that is God.

Luk. 1.53. He hath filled the hungry with good things.

Luk. 6.35. He is kind unto the unthankful and to the evil.

Rom. 2.4. The goodness of God leadeth thee to repentance.

Rom. 11.22. Toward thee, goodness, if thou continue in his goodness.

2 The. 1.11. That our God would fulfil all the good pleasure of his goodness.

Tit. 3.4. The kindness and love of God our Saviour toward man appeared.

Jas. 1.5. God, that giveth to all men liberally, and upbraideth not. 17. Every good gift and every perfect gift is from above, and cometh down from the Father of lights.

1 Jno. 4.8. God is love.

See GOD, LOVE OF.

GOD, GOODNESS OF, IN PROVIDENCE.—TEMPORAL BLESSINGS FROM GOD. Gen. 1.30. To every beast of the earth, and to every fowl of the air, and to every thing that creepeth upon the earth, wherein there is life, I have given every green herb for meat.

Gen. 5.22. Seed time and harvest, and cold

and heat, and summer and winter, and day and night shall not cease.

Gen. 9.1. God blessed Noah and his sons, and said unto them, Be fruitful, and multiply, and replenish the earth. 3. Every moving thing that liveth shall be meat for you ; even as the green herb have I given you all things. *v. 2.*

1 Sam. 2.7. The Lord maketh poor, and maketh rich : he bringeth low, and lifteth up. 8. He raiseth up the poor out of the dust, *and* lifteth up the beggar from the dunghill, to set *them* among princes, and to make them inherit the throne of glory.

1 Chr. 29.12. Both riches and honour *come* of thee, and thou reignest over all ; and in thine hand *is* power and might ; and in thine hand *it is* to make great, and to give strength unto all. 14. All things *come* of thee, and of thine own have we given thee. 16. All this store that we have prepared to build thee an house for thine holy name *cometh* of thine hand, and *is* all thine own.

Job 5.10. Who giveth rain upon the earth, and sendeth waters upon the fields.

Job 12.23. He increaseth the nations, and destroyeth them : he enlargeth the nations, and straiteneth them *again.*

Job 22.18. He filled their houses with good *things.*

Job 37.6. He saith to the snow, Be thou *on* the earth ; likewise to the small rain, and to the great rain of his strength. 10. By the breath of God frost is given : and the breadth of the waters is straitened. 13. He causeth it to come, whether for correction, or for his land, or for mercy. 17. Thy garments *are* warm, when he quieteth the earth by the south *wind.*

Job 38.25. Who hath divided a watercourse for the overflowing of waters, or a way for the lightning of thunder ; 26. To cause it to rain on the earth, *where* no man is *; on* the wilderness, wherein *there is* no man ; 27. To satisfy the desolate and waste *ground ;* and to cause the bud of the tender herb to spring forth? 41. Who provideth for the raven his food ? when his young ones cry unto God, they wander for lack of meat.

Job 39.5. The wild ass. 6. Whose house I have made the wilderness, and the barren lands his dwellings.

Psa. 36.6. O Lord, thou preservest man and beast. 7. How excellent *is* thy loving-kindness, O God ! therefore the children of men put their trust under the shadow of thy wings.

Psa. 65.8. Thou makest the outgoings of the morning and evening to rejoice. 9. Thou visitest the earth, and waterest it : thou greatly enrichest it with the river of God, *which* is full of water : thou preparest them corn, when thou hast so provided for it. 10. Thou waterest the ridges thereof abundantly : thou settlest the furrows thereof : thou makest it soft with showers : thou blessest the springing thereof. 11. Thou crownest the year with thy goodness ; and thy paths drop fatness. *v. 12,13.*

Psa. 68.6. God setteth the solitary in families : he bringeth out those which are bound with chains.

Psa. 104.14. He causeth the grass to grow for the cattle, and herb for the service of man : that he may bring forth food out of the earth ; 15. And wine *that* maketh glad the heart of man, *and* oil to make *his* face to shine,

and bread *which* strengtheneth man's heart. 27. These wait all upon thee ; that thou mayest give *them* their meat in due season. 28. *That* thou givest them they gather : thou openest thine hand, they are filled with good. *v. 1-35.*

Psa. 107.35-38. Psa. 145.15,16.

Psa. 115.16. The earth hath he given to the children of men.

Psa. 127.1. Except the Lord build the house, they labour in vain that build it : except the Lord keep the city, the watchman waketh *but* in vain. *v. 2-5.* Psa. 113.9.

Psa. 135.7. He causeth the vapours to ascend from the ends of the earth : he maketh lightnings for the rain ; he bringeth the wind out of his treasuries.

Psa. 136.25. Who giveth food to all flesh : for his mercy *endureth* for ever.

Psa. 146.7. Which giveth food to the hungry.

Psa. 147.8. Who covereth the heaven with clouds, who prepareth rain for the earth, who maketh grass to grow upon the mountains. 9. He giveth to the beast his food, *and* to the young ravens which cry.

Ecc. 2.24. A man should eat and drink, and he should make his soul enjoy good in his labour. This also I saw, that it *was* from the hand of God. Ecc. 3.13.

Ecc. 5.19. Every man also to whom God hath given riches and wealth, and hath given him power to eat thereof, and to take his portion, and to rejoice in his labour ; this *is* the gift of God.

Isa. 55.10. The rain cometh down, and the snow from heaven, and returneth not thither, but watereth the earth, and maketh it bring forth and bud, that it may give seed to the sower, and bread to the eater.

Jer. 5.24. Let us now fear the Lord our God, that giveth rain, both the former and the latter, in his season : he reserveth unto us the appointed weeks of the harvest.

Jer. 10.13. When he uttereth his voice, *there is* a multitude of waters in the heavens, and he causeth the vapours to ascend from the ends of the earth ; he maketh lightnings with rain, and bringeth forth the wind out of his treasures. Jer. 51.16.

Jer. 14.22. Are there *any* among the vanities of the Gentiles that can cause rain ? or can the heavens give showers ? *art* not thou he, O Lord our God ? therefore we will wait upon thee : for thou hast made all these *things.*

Jer. 27.6. The beasts of the field have I given him also to serve him.

Dan. 5.18. The most high gave Nebuchadnezzar thy father a kingdom, and majesty, and glory, and honour.

Hos. 2.8. She did not know that I gave her corn, and wine, and oil, and multiplied her silver and gold.

Amos 4.7. I caused it to rain upon one city.

Mat. 5.45. He maketh his sun to rise on the evil and on the good, and sendeth rain on the just and on the unjust.

Mat. 10.29. Are not two sparrows sold for a farthing ? and one of them shall not fall on the ground without your Father.

Act. 14.17. He left not himself without witness, in that he did good, and gave us rain from heaven, and fruitful seasons, filling our hearts with food and gladness.

1 Cor. 16.2. Every one of you lay by him in store, as *God* hath prospered him.

1 Tim. 6.17. The living God, who giveth us richly all things to enjoy.

GOD, GOODNESS OF, IN PROVIDENCE TO HIS PEOPLE. — TEMPORAL BLESSINGS OF SAINTS FROM GOD. Gen. 22.17. In blessing I will bless thee, and in multiplying I will multiply thy seed as the stars of the heaven, and as the sand which is upon the sea-shore ; and thy seed shall possess the gate of his enemies. Gen. 26.4,5.

Gen. 28.20. If God will be with me, and will keep me in this way that I go, and will give me bread to eat, and raiment to put on, 21. So that I come again to my father's house in peace ; then shall the Lord be my God.

Gen. 49.24. His bow abode in strength, and the arms of his hands were made strong by the hands of the mighty God of Jacob. 25. Even by the God of thy father, who shall help thee ; and by the Almighty, who shall bless thee with blessings of heaven above, blessings of the deep that lieth under, blessings of the breasts, and of the womb. v. 11, 12, 20.

Ex. 23.22. If thou shalt indeed obey his voice, and do all that I speak ; then I will be an enemy unto thine enemies, and an adversary unto thine adversaries.

Ex. 34.24. Neither shall any man desire thy land, when thou shalt go up to appear before the Lord thy God thrice in the year.

Lev. 26.4. I will give you rain in due season, and the land shall yield her increase, and the trees of the field shall yield their fruit. 5. And your threshing shall reach unto the vintage, and the vintage shall reach unto the sowing time: and ye shall eat your bread to the full, and dwell in your land safely. 6. I will give peace in the land, and ye shall lie down, and none shall make you afraid: and I will rid evil beasts out of the land, neither shall the sword go through your land. 10. And ye shall eat old store, and bring forth the old because of the new.

Deu. 1.10. The Lord your God hath multiplied you, and, behold, ye are this day as the stars of heaven for multitude.

Deu. 2.7. The Lord thy God hath blessed thee in all the works of thy hand : he knoweth thy walking through this great wilderness : these forty years the Lord thy God hath been with thee ; thou hast lacked nothing.

Deu. 4.4. Ye that did cleave unto the Lord your God are alive every one of you this day. v. 40. Num. 10.29. Deu. 6.2-25. Deu. 5.33. Deu. 12.28.

Deu. 5.29. O that there were such an heart in them, that they would fear me, and keep all my commandments always, that it might be well with them, them, and with their children for ever ! Deu. 29.9.

Deu. 7.13. He will love thee, and bless thee, and multiply thee : he will also bless the fruit of thy womb, and the fruit of thy land, thy corn, and thy wine, and thine oil, the increase of thy kine, and the flocks of thy sheep, in the land which he sware unto thy fathers to give thee. 14. Thou shalt be blessed above all people : there shall not be male or female barren among you, or among your cattle. 15. And the Lord will take away from thee all sickness, and will put none of the evil diseases of Egypt, which thou knowest, upon thee. v. 16-24. Ex. 15.26. Ex. 23.25,26.

Lev. 25.18,19. Deu. 6.2,3. Deu. 11.7,8. Deu. 13.17,18. Deu. 30.15,16,19,20.

Deu. 8.3. Man doth not live by bread only, but by every word that proceedeth out of the mouth of the Lord doth man live.

Deu. 8.18. Remember the Lord thy God : for it is he that giveth thee power to get wealth. v. 1-7.

Deu. 10.18. He loveth the stranger, in giving him food and raiment.

Deu. 11.12. A land which the Lord thy God careth for : the eyes of the Lord thy God are always upon it, from the beginning of the year even unto the end of the year. v. 13-15.

Deu. 12.7. Ye shall eat before the Lord your God, and ye shall rejoice in all that ye put your hand unto, ye and your households, wherein the Lord thy God hath blessed thee.

Deu. 15.4. Save when there shall be no poor among you ; for the Lord shall greatly bless thee in the land which the Lord thy God giveth thee for an inheritance to possess it : 5. Only if thou carefully hearken unto the voice of the Lord thy God. 6. For the Lord thy God blesseth thee, as he promised thee : and thou shalt lend unto many nations, but thou shalt not borrow ; and thou shalt reign over many nations, but they shall not reign over thee. Deu. 26.19. Deu. 28.2-13.

Deu. 29.5. I have led you forty years in the wilderness : your clothes are not waxen old upon you, and thy shoe is not waxen old upon thy foot. Deu. 8.4.

Deu. 32.13. He made him ride on the high places of the earth, that he might eat the increase of the fields ; and he made him to suck honey out of the rock, and oil out of the flinty rock ; 14. Butter of kine, and milk of sheep, with fat of lambs, and rams of the breed of Bashan, and goats, with the fat of kidneys of wheat ; and thou didst drink the pure blood of the grape. 47. It is not a vain thing for you ; because it is your life : and through this thing ye shall prolong your days in the land.

Josh. 1.8. This book of the law shall not depart out of thy mouth ; for then thou shalt make thy way prosperous, and then thou shalt have good success.

Ruth 1.6. The Lord had visited his people in giving them bread.

2 Sam. 7.8. I took thee from the sheepcote, from following the sheep, to be ruler over my people, over Israel : 9. And I was with thee whithersoever thou wentest, and have cut off all thine enemies out of thy sight, and have made thee a great name, like unto the name of the great men that are in the earth. 1 Chr. 17.7,8.

1 Kin. 2.3. That thou mayest prosper in all that thou doest, and whithersoever thou turnest thyself : 4. That the Lord may continue his word which he spake concerning me, saying, If thy children take heed to their way, to walk before me in truth with all their heart and with all their soul, there shall not fail thee (said he) a man on the throne of Israel. 1 Kin. 9.4,5. 1 Chr. 22.9,13. 2 Chr. 7.17,18. Psa. 122.12.

1 Chr. 28.8. Keep and seek for all the commandments of the Lord your God : that ye may possess this good land, and leave it for an inheritance for your children after you for ever.

2 Chr. 1.12. Wisdom and knowledge is

granted unto thee ; and I will give thee riches, and wealth, and honour, such as none of the kings have had that *have been* before thee, neither shall there any after thee have the like.

2 Chr. 30.9. If ye turn again unto the Lord, your brethren and your children *shall find* compassion before them that lead them captive, so that they shall come again into this land.

2 Chr. 31.10. Since *the people* began to bring the offerings into the house of the Lord, we have had enough to eat, and have left plenty : for the Lord hath blessed his people ; and that which is left *is* this great store.

Neh. 9.25. They took strong cities, and a fat land, and possessed houses full of all goods, wells digged, vineyards, and oliveyards, and fruit trees in abundance : so they did eat, and were filled, and became fat, and delighted themselves in thy great goodness.

Job 5.24. Thou shalt know that thy tabernacle *shall be* in peace. 25. Thou shalt know also that thy seed *shall be* great, and thine offspring as the grass of the earth. 26. Thou shalt come to *thy* grave in a full age, like as a shock of corn cometh in in his season.

Job 8.7. Though thy beginning was small, yet thy latter end should greatly increase. 20. God will not cast away a perfect *man*, 21. Till he fill thy mouth with laughing, and thy lips with rejoicing. *v.* 6.

- Job 11.17. *Thine* age shall be clearer than the noonday ; thou shalt shine forth, thou shalt be as the morning. 18. And thou shalt be secure, because there is hope : yea, thou shalt dig *about thee, and* thou shalt take thy rest in safety. 19. Also thou shalt lie down, and none shall make *thee* afraid ; yea, many shall make suit unto thee.

Job 22.24. Then shalt thou lay up gold as dust, and the *gold* of Ophir as the stones of the brooks. 25. Yea, the Almighty shall be thy defence, and thou shalt have plenty of silver. 28. Thou shalt also decree a thing, and it shall be established unto thee : and the light shall shine upon thy ways.

Job 29.5. When the Almighty *was* yet with me, *when* my children *were* about me. 19. My root *was* spread out by the waters, and the dew lay all night upon my branch. 20. My glory *was* fresh in me, and my bow was renewed in my hand.

Job 36.11. If they obey and serve *him*, they shall spend their days in prosperity, and their years in pleasures.

Psa. 21.3. Thou preventest him with the blessings of goodness : thou settest a crown of pure gold on his head. 4. He asked life of thee, *and* thou gavest *it* him, *even* length of days for ever and ever. 5. His glory *is* great in thy salvation : honour and majesty hast thou laid upon him.

Psa. 23.1. The Lord *is* my shepherd ; I shall not want. 5. Thou preparest a table before me in the presence of mine enemies : thou anointest my head with oil ; my cup runneth over.

Psa. 33.12. Blessed *is* the nation whose God *is* the Lord ; *and* the people *whom* he hath chosen for his own inheritance.

Psa. 34.9. O fear the Lord, ye his saints : for *there* is no want to them that fear him. 10. The young lions do lack, and suffer hunger : but they that seek the Lord shall not want any good *thing*.

Psa. 37.3. Trust in the Lord, and do good ; *so* 'shalt thou dwell in the land, and verily thou shalt be fed. 19. They shall not be ashamed in the evil time : and in the days of famine they shall be satisfied. 22. *Such as be* blessed of him shall inherit the earth. 25. I have been young, and *now* am old ; yet have I not seen the righteous forsaken, nor his seed begging bread. 34. Wait on the Lord, and keep his way, and he shall exalt thee to inherit the land.

Psa. 44.3. Neither did their own arm save them : but thy right hand, and thine arm, and the light of thy countenance, because thou hadst a favour unto them.

Psa. 67.6. *Then* shall the earth yield her increase ; *and* God, *even* our own God, shall bless us.

Psa. 68.9. Thou, O God, didst send a plentiful rain, whereby thou didst confirm thine inheritance, when it was weary. 10. Thy congregation hath dwelt therein : thou, O God, hast prepared of thy goodness for the poor.

Psa. 69.35. God will save Zion, and will build the cities of Judah : that they may dwell there, and have it in possession. 36. The seed also of his servants shall inherit it : and they that love his name shall dwell therein.

Psa. 72.16. There shall be an handful of corn in the earth upon the top of the mountains ; the fruit thereof shall shake like Lebanon : and *they* of the city shall flourish like grass of the earth.

Psa. 78.55. He cast out the heathen also before them, and divided them an inheritance by line, and made the tribes of Israel to dwell in their tents.

Psa. 81.16. He should have fed them also with the finest of the wheat : and with honey out of the rock should I have satisfied thee. b. 13-15.

Psa. 85.12. Yea, the Lord shall give *that which is* good ; and our land shall yield her increase.

Psa. 100.3. Know ye that the Lord he *is* God : *it* is he *that* hath made us, and not we ourselves ; *we are* his people, and the sheep of his pasture.

Psa. 103.3. Who healeth all thy diseases; 4. Who redeemeth thy life from destruction ; who crowneth thee with loving-kindness and tender mercies ; 5. Who satisfieth thy mouth with good *things ; so that* thy youth is renewed like the eagle's.

Psa. 105.24. He increased his people greatly ; and made them stronger than their enemies.

Psa. 111.5. he hath given meat unto them that fear him : he will ever be mindful of his covenant.

Psa. 128.2. Thou shalt eat the labour of thine hands : happy *shalt* thou *be*, and *it shall be* well with thee. 3. Thy wife *shall be* as a fruitful vine by the sides of thine house : thy children like olive plants round about thy table. 4. Behold, that thus shall the man be blessed that feareth the Lord. 5. The Lord shall bless thee out of Zion : and thou shalt see the good of Jerusalem all the days of thy life. 6. Yea, thou shalt see thy children's children, *and* peace upon Israel.

Psa. 144.12. That our sons *may be* as plants grown up in their youth ; *that* our daughters *may be* as corner stones, polished after the similitude of a palace : 13. *That* our garners *may be* full, affording all manner of store: *that* our sheep may bring forth thousands and ten thousands in our streets: 14. *That* our oxen *may be* strong to labour; *that there be* no breaking in, nor going out; that *there be* no complaining in our streets. 15. Happy *is that* people, that is in such a case: *yea,* happy *is that* people, whose God *is* the Lord.

Psa. 147.13. He hath strengthened the bars of thy gates; he hath blessed thy children within thee. 14. He maketh · peace *in* thy borders, *and* filleth thee with the finest of the wheat.

Pro. 2.21. The upright shall dwell in the land, and the perfect shall remain in it.

Pro. 3.1. Let thine heart keep my commandments : 2. For length of days, and long life, and peace, shall they add to thee.

Pro. 10.22. The blessing of the Lord, it maketh rich, and he addeth no sorrow with it. 27. The fear of the Lord prolongeth days.

Pro. 11.10. When it goeth well with the righteous, the city rejoiceth : 11. By the blessing of the upright the city is exalted. 31. The righteous shall be recompensed in the earth.

Pro. 13.25. The righteous eateth to the satisfying of his soul.

Pro. 14.11. The tabernacle of the upright shall flourish. 19. The evil bow before the good; and the wicked at the gates of the righteous. 34. Righteousness exalteth a nation. Ecc. 2.26.

Pro. 15.6. In the house of the righteous *is* much treasure.

Pro. 16.7. When a man's ways please the Lord, he maketh even his enemies to be at peace with him.

Pro. 28.10. The upright shall have good *things* in possession.

Ecc. 9.7. Go thy way, eat thy bread with joy, and drink thy wine with a merry heart; for God now accepteth thy works.

Isa. 1.19. If ye be willing and obedient, ye shall eat the good of the land.

Isa. 30.23. Then shall he give the rain of thy seed, that thou shalt sow the ground withal; and bread of the increase of the earth, and it shall be fat and plenteous : in that day shall thy cattle feed in large pastures. 26. Moreover the light of the moon shall be as the light of the sun, and the light of the sun shall be sevenfold, as the light of seven days, in the day that the Lord bindeth up the breach of his people, and healeth the stroke of their wound. *v.* 24,25.

Isa. 33.16. Bread shall be given him; his waters *shall be* sure.

Isa. 43.20. I give waters in the wilderness, *and* rivers in the desert, to give drink to my people, my chosen.

Isa. 48.21. They thirsted not *when* he led them through the deserts: he caused the waters to flow out of the rock for them : he clave the rock also, and the waters gushed out.

Isa. 51.2. I called him alone, and blessed him, and increased him.

Isa. 61.9. Their seed shall be known among the Gentiles, and their offspring among the people : all that see them shall acknowledge them, that they *are* the seed *which* the Lord hath blessed.

Isa. 62.9. They that have gathered it shall eat it, and praise the Lord; and they that have

brought it together shall drink it in the courts of my holiness.

Isa. 65.13. My servants shall eat, but ye shall be hungry : behold, my servants shall drink, but ye shall be thirsty. 23. They shall not labour in vain, nor bring forth for trouble; for they *are* the seed of the blessed of the Lord, and their offspring with them.

Jer. 22.15. Did not thy father eat and drink, and do judgment and justice, *and* then *it was* well with him ? 16. He judged the cause of the poor and needy; then *it was* well *with him.*

Jer. 30.19. Out of them shall proceed thanksgiving and the voice of them that make merry : and I will multiply them, and they shall not be few; I will also glorify them, and they shall not be small.

Jer. 33.11. The voice of joy, and the voice of gladness, the voice of the bridegroom, and the voice of the bride, the voice of them that shall say, Praise the Lord of hosts : for the Lord *is* good; for his mercy *endureth* for ever: *and* of them that shall bring the sacrifice of praise into the house of the Lord. For I will cause to return the captivity of the land, as at the first, saith the Lord.

Eze. 36.30. I will multiply the fruit of the tree, and the increase of the field, that ye shall receive no more reproach of famine among the heathen. 36. Then the heathen that are left round about you shall know that I the Lord build the ruined *places, and* plant that that was desolate : I the Lord have spoken *it,* and I will do *it.* 38. As the holy flock, as the flock of Jerusalem in her solemn feasts; so shall the waste cities be filled with flocks of men : and they shall know that I *am* the Lord. *v.* 28-38.

Hos. 2.21. I will hear the heavens, and they shall hear the earth; 22. And the earth shall hear the corn, and the wine, and the oil; and they shall hear Jezreel.

Joel 2.21. Fear not, O land; be glad and rejoice : for the Lord will do great things. 23. Be glad then, ye children of Zion, and rejoice in the Lord your God : for he hath given you the former rain moderately, and he will cause to come down for you the rain, the former rain, and the latter rain in the first *month.* 26. Ye shall eat in plenty, and be satisfied, and praise the name of the Lord your God, that hath dealt wondrously with you: and my people shall never be ashamed. *v.* 18-26.

Amos 9.13. The days come, saith the Lord, that the plowman shall overtake the reaper, and the treader of grapes him that soweth seed; and the mountains shall drop sweet wine, and all the hills shall melt.

Hag. 2.19. Is the seed yet in the barn ? yea, as yet the vine, and the fig tree, and the pomegranate, and the olive tree, hath not brought forth : from this day will I bless *you.*

Zec. 3.7. If thou wilt keep my charge, then thou shalt also judge my house, and shalt also keep my courts, and I will give thee places to walk among these that stand by.

Zec. 8.12. The seed *shall be* prosperous; the vine shall give her fruit, and the ground shall give her increase, and the heavens shall give their dew; and I will cause the remnant of this people to possess all these *things.*

Zec. 9.17. How great *is* his goodness, and

how great *is* his beauty ! corn shall make the young men cheerfu', and new wine the maids.

Zec. 10.1. Ask ye of the Lord rain in the time of the latter rain ; *so* the Lord shall make bright clouds, and give them showers of rain, to every one grass in the field.

Mal. 3.10. Bring ye all the tithes into the storehouse, that there may be meat in mine house, and prove me now herewith, saith the Lord of hosts, if I will not open you the windows of heaven, and pour you out a blessing, that *there shall* not *be room enough to receive it.* 12. All nations shall call you blessed : for ye shall be a delightsome land, saith the Lord of hosts. *v.* 11.

Mat. 5.5. Blessed *are* the meek : for they shall inherit the earth.

Mat. 6.26. Behold the fowls of the air : for they sow not, neither do they reap, nor gather into barns ; yet your heavenly Father feedeth them. Are ye not much better than they? 30. If God so clothe the grass of the field, which to-day is, and to-morrow is cast into the oven, *shall* he not much more *clothe* you, O ye of little faith? 31. Therefore take no thought, saying, What shall we eat? or, What shall we drink? or, Wherewithal shall we be clothed? 32. (For after all these things do the Gentiles seek :) for your heavenly Father knoweth that ye have need of all these things. 33. But seek ye first the kingdom of God, and his righteousness ; and all these things shall be added unto you.

Luk. 22.35. When I sent you without purse, and scrip, and shoes, lacked ye any thing? And they said, Nothing.

Jno. 6.31. Our fathers did eat manna in the desert ; as it is written, He gave them bread from heaven to eat.

GOD, HIS GOODNESS TO HIS PEOPLE EXEMPLIFIED. To Noah, Gen. 7.1. Abraham, Gen. 24.1. Isaac, Gen. 26.12-14,28. Joseph, Gen. 39.2,3,23. Israelites in Egypt, Ex. 11.3 ; in the wilderness, Ex. 17.1-7. Num. 11. Num. 20.10. Neh. 9.15. Psa. 78.15-30. Psa. 105. 40,41. David, 2 Sam. 5.10. 1 Chr. 14.17. Obed-Edom, 2 Sam. 6.11. Solomon, 1 Chr. 29.25. 2 Chr. 1.1. 1 Kin. 3.13. Elijah, 1 Kin. 17.2-9. 1 Kin. 19.5-8. Widow of Zarephath, 1 Kin. 17.12-16. Hezekiah, 2 Kin. 18.6,7. 2 Chr. 32.29. Asa, 2 Chr. 14.6,7. Jehoshaphat, 2 Chr. 17.3-5. 2 Chr. 20.30. Uzziah, 2 Chr. 26.5-15. Jotham, 2 Chr. 27.6. Job, Job 1.10. Job 42.10,12. Daniel, Dan. 1.9. See THANKFULNESS.

GOD HOLY. Ex.3.5. Draw not nigh hither : put off thy shoes from off thy feet, for the place whereon thou standest *is* holy ground. Jos. 5.15.

Ex. 15.11. Who *is* like unto thee, O Lord, among the gods? who *is* like thee, glorious in holiness?

Lev. 19.2. Ye shall be holy : for I the Lord your God *am* holy. Lev. 11.44. Lev. 20.26. Lev. 21.8.

Deu. 32.4. *He is* the Rock, his work *is* perfect : for all his ways *are* judgment : a God of truth and without iniquity, just and right *is* he.

Jos. 24.19. Ye cannot serve the Lord : for he *is* an holy God.

1 Sam. 2.2. *There is* none holy as the Lord.

1 Sam. 6.20. Who is able to stand before this holy Lord God?

1 Chr. 16.10. Glory ye in his holy name. Psa. 105.3.

Job 4.17. Shall mortal man be more just than God? shall a man be more pure than his maker? *v.* 18,19.

Job 6.10. I have not concealed the words of the Holy One.

Job 15.15. The heavens are not clean in his sight.

Job 25.5. Behold even to the moon, and it shineth not ; yea, the stars are not pure in his sight.

Job 34.10. Far be it from God, *that he should do* wickedness ; and *from* the Almighty, *that he should commit* iniquity.

Job 36.23. Who can say, Thou hast wrought iniquity?

Psa. 11.7. The righteous Lord loveth righteousness ; his countenance doth behold the upright.

Psa. 22.3. Thou *art* holy, O *thou* that inhabitest the praises of Israel.

Psa. 30.4. Give thanks at the remembrance of his holiness.

Psa. 33.4. The word of the Lord *is* right ; and all his works *are done* in truth. 5. He loveth righteousness and judgment.

Psa. 36.6. Thy righteousness *is* like the great mountains.

Psa. 47.8. God sitteth upon the throne of his holiness.

Psa. 48.10. Thy right hand is full of righteousness.

Psa. 60.6. God hath spoken in his holiness. Psa. 108.6.

Psa. 89.35. Once have I sworn by my holiness that I will not lie unto David.

Psa. 92.15. The Lord *is* upright : *he is* my rock, and *there is* no unrighteousness in him.

Psa. 99.3. Let them praise thy great and terrible name ; *for* it *is* holy. 5. Exalt ye the Lord our God, and worship at his footstool ; *for* he *is* holy. *v.* 9.

Psa. 111.9. Holy and reverend *is* his name.

Psa. 119.142. Thy righteousness *is* an everlasting righteousness.

Psa. 145.17. The Lord *is* righteous in all his ways, and holy in all his works.

Pro. 9.10. The knowledge of the holy *is* understanding.

Isa. 5.16. God that is holy shall be sanctified in righteousness.

Isa. 6.3. Holy, holy, holy, *is* the Lord of hosts : the whole earth *is* full of his glory.

Isa. 29.23. They shall sanctify my name, and sanctify the Holy One of Jacob. Isa. 41.14.

Isa. 45.19. I the Lord speak righteousness, I declare things that are right.

Isa. 47.4. Our redeemer, the Lord of hosts *is* his name, the Holy One of Israel.

Isa. 52.10. The Lord hath made bare his holy arm in the eyes of all the nations. Psa. 98.1.

Isa. 57.15. The high and lofty One, who inhabiteth eternity, whose name *is* holy.

Eze. 39.7. So will I make my holy name known in the midst of my people Israel ; and I will not *let them* pollute my holy name any more : and the heathen shall know that I *am* the Lord, the Holy One in Israel. *v.* 25. Eze. 36.21,22.

Hos. 11.9. I *am* God, and not man; the Holy One in the midst of thee.

Mat. 5.48. Be ye therefore perfect, even as your Father which is in heaven is perfect.

Mat. 19.17. *There is* none good but one, *that is*, God.   Mar. 10.18.   Luk. 18.19.

Luk. 1.49.   Holy *is* his name.

Jno. 17.11.   Holy Father, keep through thine own name those whom thou hast given me.

Jas. 1.13.   God cannot be tempted with evil, neither tempteth he any man.

1 Pet. 1.15.   He which hath called you is holy.

1 Jno. 1.5.   God is light, and in him is no darkness at all.

1 Jno. 2.20.   Ye have an unction from the Holy One.

Rev. 4.8.   Holy, holy, holy, Lord God Almighty, which was, and is, and is to come.

Rev. 6.10.   O Lord, holy and true.

Rev. 15.4.   Who shall not fear thee, O Lord, and glorify thy name? for *thou* only *art* holy.

See SIN, GOD SEES.—SIN, GOD HATES.—SIN SEPARATES FROM GOD.

GOD INFINITE AND UNSEARCHABLE.   Deu. 29.29.   The secret *things belong* unto the Lord our God.

Jud. 13.18.   Why askest thou thus after my name, seeing it *is* secret?   Gen. 32.29.

1 Kin. 8.12.   The Lord said that he would dwell in the thick darkness.   27.   Will God indeed dwell on the earth? behold, the heaven and heaven of heavens cannot contain thee; how much less this house that I have builded? 2 Chr. 2.6.   2 Chr. 6.1,18.

Job 5.9.   Which doeth great things and unsearchable; marvellous things without number.   Job 9.10.

Job 11.7.   Canst thou by searching find out God? canst thou find out the Almighty unto perfection?   8.   *It is* as high as heaven; what canst thou do? deeper than hell; what canst thou know?   9.   The measure thereof *is* longer than the earth, and broader than the sea.

Job 26.9.   He holdeth back the face of his throne, *and* spreadeth his cloud upon it.   14.   Lo, these *are* parts of his ways: but how little a portion is heard of him? but the thunder of his power who can understand?

Job 36.26.   Behold, God *is* great, and we know *him* not, neither can the number of his years be searched out.

Job 37.5.   Great things doeth he, which we cannot comprehend.   23.   *Touching* the Almighty, we cannot find him out.

Psa. 77.19.   Thy way *is* in the sea, and thy path in the great waters, and thy footsteps are not known.

Psa. 92.5.   O Lord, how great are thy works ! *and* thy thoughts are very deep.

Psa. 97.2.   Clouds and darkness *are* round about him.

Psa. 139.6.   *Such* knowledge *is* too wonderful for me; it is high, I cannot *attain* unto it.

Psa. 145.3.   Great *is* the Lord, and greatly to be praised; and his greatness *is* unsearchable.

Psa. 147.5.   Great *is* our Lord, and of great power: his understanding *is* infinite.

Pro. 25.2.   *It is* the glory of God to conceal a thing.

Pro. 30.4.   Who hath ascended up into heaven, or descended? who hath gathered the wind in his fists? who hath bound the waters

in a garment? who hath established all the ends of the earth? what *is* his name, and what *is* his son's name, if thou canst tell?

Ecc. 11.5.   Thou knowest not the works of God who maketh all.

Isa. 40.28.   *There is* no searching of his understanding.

Isa. 45.15.   Verily thou *art* a God that hidest thyself, O God of Israel, the Saviour.

Jer. 23.24.   Do not I fill heaven and earth?

Nah. 1.3.   The Lord *hath* his way in the whirlwind and in the storm, and the clouds *are* the dust of his feet.

Mat. 11.27.   No man knoweth the Son, but the Father; neither knoweth any man the Father, save the Son, and *he* to whomsoever the Son will reveal *him*.

Rom. 11.33.   O the depth of the riches both of the wisdom and knowledge of God ! how unsearchable *are* his judgments, and his ways past finding out !   34.   For who hath known the mind of the Lord? or who hath been his counsellor?

1 Cor. 2.10.   The Spirit searcheth all things, yea, the deep things of God.   11.   For what man knoweth the things of a man, save the spirit of man which is in him? even so the things of God knoweth no man, but the Spirit of God.

GOD INVISIBLE.   Ex. 33.20.   Thou canst not see my face: for there shall no man see me, and live.

Deu. 4.15.   Ye saw no manner of similitude on the day *that* the Lord spake unto you in Horeb out of the midst of the fire.

Job 9.11.   Lo, he goeth by me, and I see *him* not: he passeth on also, but I perceive him not.

Job 23.8.   Behold, I go forward, but he *is* not *there*; and backward, but I cannot perceive him: 9.   On the left hand, where he doth work, but I cannot behold *him*: he hideth himself on the right hand, that I cannot see *him*.

Jno. 1.18.   No man hath seen God at any time; the only-begotten Son, which is in the bosom of the Father, he hath declared *him*.

Jno. 4.24.   God is a Spirit.   See Luk. 24.39.

Jno. 6.46.   Not that any man hath seen the Father, save he which is of God, he hath seen the Father.

Rom. 1.20.   The invisible things of him from the creation of the world are clearly seen, being understood by the things that are made, *even* his eternal power and Godhead.

Col. 1.15.   The image of the invisible God.

1 Tim. 1.17.   Unto the King eternal, immortal, invisible.

1 Tim. 6.16.   Who only hath immortality, dwelling in the light which no man can approach unto; whom no man hath seen, nor can see.

1 Jno. 4.12.   No man hath seen God at any time.

GOD JEALOUS.   Ex. 20.5.   I the Lord thy God *am* a jealous God, visiting the iniquity of the fathers upon the children.   7.   The Lord will not hold him guiltless that taketh his name in vain.   Deu. 5.11.

Ex. 34.14.   Thou shalt worship no other god: for the Lord, whose name *is* Jealous, *is* a jealous God.   Deu. 6.15.

Num. 14.21.   *As* truly *as* I live, all the earth shall be filled with the glory of the Lord.

Deu. 4.24. The Lord thy God is a consuming fire, even a jealous God.

Deu. 29.20. The Lord will not spare him, but then the anger of the Lord and his jealousy shall smoke against that man.

Deu. 32.16. They provoked him to jealousy with strange gods. 21. They have moved me to jealousy with that which is not God; they have provoked me to anger with their vanities. 26. I said, I would scatter them into corners, I would make the remembrance of them to cease from among men. 27. Were it not that I feared the wrath of the enemy, lest their adversaries should behave themselves strangely, and lest they should say, Our hand is high, and the Lord hath not done all this. 1 Kin. 14.22. Psa. 78.58.

Jos. 24.19. Ye cannot serve the Lord: for he is an holy God; he is a jealous God; he will not forgive your transgressions nor your sins.

Jud. 7.2. Lest Israel vaunt themselves against me, saying, Mine own hand hath saved me. v. 3-8.

Isa. 48.11. For mine own sake, even for mine own sake, will I do it: for how should my name be polluted? and I will not give my glory unto another.

Eze. 20.22. I withdrew mine hand, and wrought for my name's sake, that it should not be polluted in the sight of the heathen, in whose sight I brought them forth. v. 9,14.

Eze. 23.25. I will set my jealousy against thee.

Eze. 36.5. Surely in the fire of my jealousy have I spoken against the residue of the heathen. 21. I had pity for mine holy name, which the house of Israel had profaned among the heathen. 22. I do not this for your sakes, O house of Israel, but for mine holy name's sake, which ye have profaned among the heathen, whither ye went. 23. And I will sanctify my great name, which was profaned among the heathen.

Eze. 38.18. My fury shall come up in my face. 19. For in my jealousy and in the fire of my wrath have I spoken.

Eze. 39.7. So will I make my holy name known in the midst of my people Israel; and I will not let them pollute my holy name any more: and the heathen shall know that I am the Lord, the Holy One in Israel. 25. And have mercy upon the whole house of Israel, and will be jealous for my holy name.

Nah. 1.2. God is jealous, and the Lord revengeth; the Lord revengeth, and is furious; the Lord will take vengeance on his adversaries.

See GOD GLORIFIED.

GOD, JUSTICE OF.—GOD A JUDGE. Gen. 15.16. The iniquity of the Amorites is not yet full.

Gen. 18.21. I will go down now, and see whether they have done altogether according to the cry of it, which is come unto me; and if not, I will know. 25. That be far from thee to do after this manner, to slay the righteous with the wicked: and that the righteous should be as the wicked, that be far from thee: Shall not the Judge of all the earth do right? v. 20.

Num. 16.22. O God, the God of the spirits of all flesh, shall one man sin, and wilt thou be wroth with all the congregation?

Deu. 10.17. A great God, a mighty, and a terrible, which regardeth not persons, nor taketh reward. 2 Sam. 14.14. Rom. 2.11.

Deu. 32.4. He is the Rock, his work is perfect: for all his ways are judgment: a God of truth and without iniquity, just and right is he. 35. To me belongeth vengeance, and recompence.

Jos. 24.19. He is an holy God; he is a jealous God; he will not forgive your transgressions nor your sins. Ex. 20.5. Ex. 34.7.

1 Sam. 2.3. The Lord is a God of knowledge, and by him actions are weighed. 10. The Lord shall judge the ends of the earth.

2 Sam. 22.26. With the merciful thou wilt shew thyself merciful, and with the upright man thou wilt shew thyself upright. 27. With the pure thou wilt shew thyself pure; and with the froward thou wilt shew thyself unsavoury. Psa. 18.25,26.

1 Kin. 8.32. Hear thou in heaven, and do, and judge thy servants, condemning the wicked, to bring his way upon his head; and justifying the righteous, to give him according to his righteousness. Jud. 9.56,57. 2 Chr. 6.22,23.

2 Chr. 19.7. There is no iniquity with the Lord our God, nor respect of persons, nor taking of gifts.

Neh. 9.33. Thou art just in all that is brought upon us; for thou hast done right, but we have done wickedly.

Job 4.17. Shall mortal man be more just than God? shall a man be more pure than his maker?

Job 8.3. Doth God pervert judgment? or doth the Almighty pervert justice?

Job 9.28. I know that thou wilt not hold me innocent.

Job 21.22. He judgeth those that are high.

Job 23.7. There the righteous might dispute with him; so should I be delivered for ever from my judge.

Job 34.10. Far be it from God, that he should do wickedness; and from the Almighty, that he should commit iniquity. 11. For the work of a man shall he render unto him, and cause every man to find according to his ways. 12. Yea, surely God will not do wickedly, neither will the Almighty pervert judgment.

Job 34.17. Wilt thou condemn him that is most just? 19. Him that accepteth not the persons of princes, nor regardeth the rich more than the poor? 23. He will not lay upon man more than right; that he should enter into judgment with God.

Job 35.14. Thou sayest thou shalt not see him, yet judgment is before him.

Job 36.19. Will he esteem thy riches? no, not gold, nor all the forces of strength.

Job 37.23. He is excellent in power, and in judgment, and in plenty of justice.

Psa. 7.9. The righteous God trieth the hearts and reins. 11. God judgeth the righteous, and God is angry with the wicked every day. v. 8. Heb. 10.30.

Psa. 9.4. Thou hast maintained my right and my cause; thou satest in the throne judging right. 7. He hath prepared his throne for judgment. 8. And he shall judge the world in righteousness, he shall minister judgment to the people in uprightness.

Psa. 11.4. His eyes behold, his eyelids try, the children of men. 5. The Lord trieth the righteous: but the wicked and him that loveth violence his soul hateth. 7. The righteous Lord loveth righteousness; his countenance doth behold the upright.

Psa. 19.9. The judgments of the Lord *are* true *and* righteous altogether.

Psa. 50.4. He shall call to the heavens from above, and to the earth, that he may judge his people. 6. The heavens shall declare his righteousness: for God *is* judge himself. Psa. 75.7.

Psa. 51.4. Against thee, thee only, have I sinned, and done *this* evil in thy sight: that thou mightest be justified when thou speakest, *and* be clear when thou judgest.

Psa. 58.11. Verily *there is* a reward for the righteous: verily he is a God that judgeth in the earth.

Psa. 62.12. Thou renderest to every man according to his work.

Psa. 67.4. Thou shalt judge the people righteously, and govern the nations upon earth.

Psa. 71.19. Thy righteousness also, O God, *is* very high, who hast done great things: O God, who *is* like unto thee!

Psa. 76.8. Thou didst cause judgment to be heard from heaven; the earth feared, and was still, 9. When God arose to judgment, to save all the meek of the earth.

Psa. 85.10. Mercy and truth are met together; righteousness and peace have kissed *each other.*

Psa. 89.14. Justice and judgment *are* the habitation of thy throne. Psa. 97.2.

Psa. 90.8. Thou hast set our iniquities before thee, our secret *sins* in the light of thy countenance. 11. Who knoweth the power of thine anger? even according to thy fear, *so is* thy wrath.

Psa. 94.1. O God, to whom vengeance belongeth, shew thyself. 2. Lift up thyself, thou judge of the earth: render a reward to the proud. 10. He that chastiseth the heathen, shall not he correct? Psa. 82.8.

Psa. 96.13. He cometh to judge the earth: he shall judge the world with righteousness, and the people with his truth. *v.* 10. 1 Chr. 16.33.

Psa. 98.2. His righteousness hath he openly shewed in the sight of the heathen. *v.* 3,9.

Psa. 99.4. The king's strength also loveth judgment; thou dost establish equity, thou executest judgment and righteousness in Jacob. 8. Thou wast a God that forgavest them, though thou tookest vengeance of their inventions.

Psa. 103.6. The Lord executeth righteousness and judgment for all that are oppressed.

Psa. 111.7. The works of his hands *are* verity and judgment.

Psa. 119.137. Righteous *art* thou, O Lord, and upright *are* thy judgments. Psa. 129.4.

Psa. 143.2. Enter not into judgment with thy servant: for in thy sight shall no man living be justified.

Psa. 145.17. The Lord *is* righteous in all his ways, and holy in all his works.

Pro. 11.31. The righteous shall be recompensed in the earth: much more the wicked and the sinner.

Pro. 17.3. The fining pot *is* for silver, and the furnace for gold: but the Lord trieth the hearts.

Pro. 24.12. Doth not he that pondereth the heart consider *it?* and he that keepeth thy soul, doth *not* he know *it?* and shall *not* he render to *every* man according to his works?

Pro. 29.13. The poor and the deceitful man meet together: the Lord lighteneth both their eyes. 26. Many seek the ruler's favour; but *every* man's judgment *cometh* from the Lord.

Ecc. 3.15. God requireth that which is past. 17. God shall judge the righteous and the wicked: for *there is* a time there for every purpose and for every work.

Ecc. 11.9. Know thou, that for all these *things* God will bring thee into judgment.

Ecc. 12.14. God shall bring every work into judgment, with every secret thing, whether *it be* good, or whether *it be* evil.

Isa. 1.27. Zion shall be redeemed with judgment, and her converts with righteousness.

Isa. 3.13. The Lord standeth up to plead, and standeth to judge the people. 14. The Lord will enter into judgment with the ancients of his people, and the princes thereof.

Isa. 10.17. The light of Israel shall be for a fire, and his Holy One for a flame: and it shall burn and devour his thorns and his briers in one day; 18. And shall consume the glory of his forest, and of his fruitful field, both soul and body.

Isa. 26.7. Thou, most upright, dost weigh the path of the just.

Isa. 28.17. Judgment also will I lay to the line, and righteousness to the plummet. 21. The Lord shall rise up as *in* mount Perazim, he shall be wroth as *in* the valley of Gibeon, that he may do his work, his strange work; and bring to pass his act, his strange act.

Isa. 30.18. The Lord *is* a God of judgment: blessed *are* all they that wait for him. 27. Behold, the name of the Lord cometh from far, burning *with* his anger, and the burden *thereof is* heavy: his lips are full of indignation, and his tongue as a devouring fire: 30. The Lord shall cause his glorious voice to be heard, and shall shew the lighting down of his arm, with the indignation of *his* anger, and *with* the flame of a devouring fire, *with* scattering, and tempest, and hailstones.

Isa. 31.2. He also *is* wise, and will bring evil, and will not call back his words: but will arise against the house of the evildoers, and against the help of them that work iniquity.

Isa. 45.21. There *is* no God else beside me; a just God and a Saviour.

Isa. 61.8. I the Lord love judgment, I hate robbery for burnt-offering; and I will direct their work in truth.

Jer. 9.24. I *am* the Lord which exercise loving-kindness, judgment, and righteousness, in the earth: for in these *things* I delight, saith the Lord.

Jer. 10.10. At his wrath the earth shall tremble, and the nations shall not be able to abide his indignation.

Jer. 11.20. O Lord of hosts, that judgest righteously, that triest the reins and the heart. Jer. 20.12.

Jer. 12.1. Righteous *art* thou, O Lord, when I plead with thee: yet let me talk with thee of *thy* judgments.

Jer. 32.19. Great in counsel, and mighty in work: for thine eyes *are* open upon all the ways of the sons of men: to give every one according to his ways, and according to the fruit of his doings.

Jer. 50.7. The Lord, the habitation of justice.

Jer. 51.10. The Lord hath brought forth our righteousness : come, and let us declare in Zion the work of the Lord our God.

Lam. 1.18. The Lord is righteous ; for I have rebelled against his commandment.

Eze. 14.23. Ye shall know that I have not done without cause all that I have done in it, saith the Lord God.

Eze. 18.25. Is not my way equal ? are not your ways unequal ? See v. 1-32. Eze. 33.11-16.

Dan. 4.37. All whose works are truth, and his ways judgment : and those that walk in pride he is able to abase.

Dan. 7.9. The thrones were cast down, and the Ancient of days did sit, whose garment was white as snow, and the hair of his head like the pure wool : his throne was like the fiery flame, and his wheels as burning fire. 10. A fiery stream issued and came forth from before him : thousand thousands ministered unto him, and ten thousand times ten thousand stood before him : the judgment was set, and the books were opened.

Dan. 9.7. O Lord, righteousness belongeth unto thee, but unto us confusion of faces. 14. The Lord watched upon the evil, and brought it upon us : for the Lord our God is righteous in all his works which he doeth.

Hos. 10.10. It is in my desire that I should chastise them.

Amos 8.7. Surely I will never forget any of their works.

Nah. 1.3. Will not at all acquit the wicked. 6. Who can stand before his indignation ? and who can abide in the fierceness of his anger ? his fury is poured out like fire, and the rocks are thrown down by him.

Zeph. 3.5. The just Lord is in the midst thereof ; he will not do iniquity : every morning doth he bring his judgment to light, he faileth not.

Mal. 3.5. I will come near to you to judgment ; and I will be a swift witness against the sorcerers, and against the adulterers, and against false swearers, and against those that oppress the hireling in his wages, the widow, and the fatherless, and that turn aside the stranger from his right, and fear not me, saith the Lord of hosts. 18. Then shall ye return, and discern between the righteous and the wicked.

Act. 17.31. He hath appointed a day, in the which he will judge the world in righteousness by that man whom he hath ordained.

Rom. 1.32. Knowing the judgment of God, that they which commit such things are worthy of death.

Rom. 2.2. We are sure that the judgment of God is according to truth. 5. Treasurest up unto thyself wrath against the day of wrath and revelation of the righteous judgment of God. 16. God shall judge the secrets of men by Jesus Christ.

Rom. 3.4. Let God be true, but every man a liar ; as it is written, That thou mightest be justified in thy sayings, and mightest overcome when thou art judged. 5. Is God unrighteous who taketh vengeance ? (I speak as a man.) 6. God forbid : for then how shall God judge the world ? 26. To declare at this time his righteousness : that he might be just, and the justifier of him which believeth in Jesus.

Rom. 9.14. Is there unrighteousness with God ? God forbid.

Rom. 11.22. Behold therefore the goodness and severity of God : on them which fell, severity ; but toward thee, goodness, if thou continue in his goodness : otherwise thou also shalt be cut off.

Eph. 6.8. Whatsoever good thing any man doeth, the same shall he receive of the Lord, whether he be bond or free. 9. Your master also is in heaven ; neither is there respect of persons with him. Col. 3.25. Act. 10.34.

2 The. 1.5. Which is a manifest token of the righteous judgment of God. 6. It is a righteous thing with God to recompense tribulation to them that trouble you.

Heb. 6.10. God is not unrighteous to forget your work and labour of love.

Heb. 12.23. God the Judge of all. 29. Our God is a consuming fire. Deu. 4.24.

1 Pet. 1.17. The Father, who without respect of persons judgeth according to every man's work.

2 Pet. 2.9. The Lord knoweth how to deliver the godly out of temptations, and to reserve the unjust unto the day of judgment to be punished.

1 Jno. 1.9. He is faithful and just to forgive us our sins.

Jude 6. The angels which kept not their first estate, but left their own habitation, he hath reserved in everlasting chains, under darkness, unto the judgment of the great day.

Rev. 6.16. Fall on us, and hide us from the face of him that sitteth on the throne, and from the wrath of the Lamb : 17. For the great day of his wrath is come ; and who shall be able to stand ?

Rev. 11.18. Thy wrath is come, and the time of the dead, that they should be judged, and that thou shouldst give reward unto thy servants the prophets, and to the saints, and them that fear thy name, small and great ; and shouldest destroy them which destroy the earth.

Rev. 15.3. Just and true are thy ways, thou King of saints.

Rev. 16.5. Thou art righteous, O Lord, which art, and wast, and shalt be, because thou hast judged thus. 6. For they have shed the blood of saints and prophets, and thou hast given them blood to drink ; for they are worthy. 7. And I heard another out of the altar say, Even so, Lord God Almighty, true and righteous are thy judgments.

Rev. 18.8. Strong is the Lord God who judgeth her.

Rev. 19.2. True and righteous are his judgments : for he hath judged the great whore, which did corrupt the earth with her fornication, and hath avenged the blood of his servants at her hand.

See SIN, PUNISHMENT—JUDGMENT, LAST—CHRIST A JUDGE.

GOD KING.—SUPREME AND UNIVERSAL PROPRIETOR. Gen. 14.19. The most high God, possessor of heaven and earth.

Gen. 24.3. The God of heaven, and the God of the earth.

Ex. 8.22. I am the Lord, in the midst of the earth.

Ex. 9.29. The earth is the Lord's. Jos. 3.11.

Ex. 15.18. The Lord shall reign for ever and ever.

Num. 27.16. The Lord, the God of the spirits of all flesh.

Deu. 2.19. I will not give thee of the land of the children of Ammon *any* possession: because I have given it unto the children of Lot *for* a possession.

Deu. 10.14. The heaven and the heaven of heavens *is* the Lord's thy God, the earth *also*, with all that therein *is*. 17. The Lord your God *is* God of gods, and Lord of lords, a great God, a mighty, and a terrible, which regardeth not persons. Ex. 19.5.

Deu. 32.8. When the Most High divided to the nations their inheritance, when he separated the sons of Adam, he set the bounds of the people according to the number of the children of Israel. 39. I, *even* I, *am* he, and *there is* no god with me: I kill, and I make alive; I wound, and I heal: neither *is there any* that can deliver out of my hand.

1 Sam. 2.6. The Lord killeth, and maketh alive: he bringeth down to the grave, and bringeth up. 7. The Lord maketh poor, and maketh rich: he bringeth low, and lifteth up. 8 He raiseth up the poor out of the dust, *and* lifteth up the beggar from the dunghill, to set *them* among princes, and to make them inherit the throne of glory: for the pillars of the earth *are* the Lord's, and he hath set the world upon them.

2 Kin. 19.15. Thou art the God, *even* thou alone, of all the kingdoms of the earth; thou hast made heaven and earth.

1 Chr. 29.11. All *that is* in the heaven and in the earth *is thine;* thine *is* the kingdom, O Lord, and thou art exalted as head above all. 12. Both riches and honour *come* of thee, and thou reignest over all; and in thine hand *is* power and might; and in thine hand *it is* to make great, and to give strength unto all.

2 Chr. 20.6. *Art* not thou God in heaven? and rulest *not* thou over all the kingdoms of the heathen? and in thine hand *is there not* power and might, so that none is able to withstand thee?

Neh. 9.6. Thou, *even* thou, *art* Lord alone: thou hast made heaven, the heaven of heavens, with all their host, the earth, and all *things* that *are* therein, the seas, and all that *is* therein, and thou preservest them all; and the host of heaven worshippeth thee.

Job 9.12. Behold, he taketh away, who can hinder him? who will say unto him, What doest thou?

Job 12.9. Who knoweth not in all these that the hand of the Lord hath wrought this? 10. In whose hand *is* the soul of every living thing, and the breath of all mankind. 16. With him *is* strength and wisdom: the deceived and the deceiver *are* his. 17. He leadeth counsellers away spoiled, and maketh the judges fools.

Job 25.2. Dominion and fear *are* with him, he maketh peace in his high places.

Job 33.13. Why dost thou strive against him? for he giveth not account of any of his matters.

Job 34.13. Who hath given him a charge over the earth? or who hath disposed the whole world? 24. He shall break in pieces mighty men without number, and set others in their stead. 33. *Should it be* according to thy mind? he will recompense it, whether thou refuse, or whether thou choose,

Job 36.23. Who hath enjoined him his way? or who can say, Thou hast wrought iniquity? *v.* 1-33.

Job 41.11. *Whatsoever is* under the whole heaven is mine.

Psa. 10.16. The Lord *is* King for ever and ever: the heathen are perished out of his land.

Psa. 22.28. The kingdom *is* the Lord's: and he *is* the governor among the nations.

Psa. 24.1. The earth *is* the Lord's, and the fulness thereof; the world, and they that dwell therein. 10. Who is this King of glory? The Lord of hosts, he *is* the King of glory. 1 Cor. 10.26.

Psa. 29.10. The Lord sitteth upon the flood; yea, the Lord sitteth King for ever.

Psa. 44.4. Thou art my King, O God: command deliverances for Jacob.

Psa. 47.2. The Lord most high *is* terrible; *he is* a great King over all the earth. 3. He shall subdue the people under us, and the nations under our feet. 7. God *is* the King of all the earth: sing ye praises with understanding. 8. God reigneth over the heathen: God sitteth upon the throne of his holiness.

Psa. 50.10. Every beast of the forest *is* mine, *and* the cattle upon a thousand hills. 11. I know all the fowls of the mountains: and the wild beasts of the field *are* mine. 12. If I were hungry, I would not tell thee: for the world *is* mine, and the fulness thereof.

Psa. 59.13. Let them know that God ruleth in Jacob unto the ends of the earth.

Psa. 65.5. O God of our salvation; *who art* the confidence of all the ends of the earth, and of them that are afar off *upon* the sea.

Psa. 66.7. He ruleth by his power for ever; his eyes behold the nations: let not the rebellious exalt themselves.

Psa. 74.12. God *is* my King of old.

Psa. 75.6. Promotion *cometh* neither from the east, nor from the west, nor from the south. 7. But God *is* the judge: he putteth down one, and setteth up another.

Psa. 76.11. Let all that be round about him bring presents unto him that ought to be feared. 12. He shall cut off the spirit of princes: *he is* terrible to the kings of the earth.

Psa. 82.1. God standeth in the congregation of the mighty; he judgeth among the gods. 8. Arise, O God, judge the earth: for thou shalt inherit all nations.

Psa. 83.18. Thou, whose name alone *is* Jehovah, *art* the most high over all the earth.

Psa. 89.11. The heavens *are* thine, the earth also *is* thine: *as for* the world and the fulness thereof, thou hast founded them. 18. The Lord *is* our defence; and the Holy One of Israel *is* our king.

Psa. 93.1. The Lord reigneth, the world also is stablished, that it cannot be moved. 2. Thy throne *is* established of old: thou *art* from everlasting.

Psa. 95.3. The Lord *is* a great God, and a great King above all gods. 4. In his hand *are* the deep places of the earth: the strength of the hills *is* his also. 5. The sea *is* his, and he made it: and his hands formed the dry land.

Psa. 96.10. Say among the heathen *that* the Lord reigneth: the world also shall be established that it shall not be moved: he shall judge the people righteously.

Psa. 97.1. The Lord reigneth; let the earth rejoice; let the multitude of isles be glad *thereof.* 2. Righteousness and judgment *are* the habitation of his throne. *v.* 5,9.

Psa. 98.6. Make a joyful noise before the Lord the King.

Psa. 99.1. The Lord reigneth; let the people tremble.

Psa. 103.19. The Lord hath prepared his throne in the heavens; and his kingdom ruleth over all.

Psa. 105.7. He *is* the Lord our God: his judgments *are* in all the earth.

Psa. 115.3. Our God *is* in the heavens: he hath done whatsoever he hath pleased. 16. The heaven, *even* the heavens, *are* the Lord's: but the earth hath he given to the children of men.

Psa. 135.5. Our Lord *is* above all gods. 6. Whatsoever the Lord pleased, *that* did he in heaven, and in earth, in the seas, and all deep places.

Psa. 145.11. They shall speak of the glory of thy kingdom, and talk of thy power; 12. To make known to the sons of men his mighty acts, and the glorious majesty of his kingdom. 13. Thy kingdom *is* an everlasting kingdom, and thy dominion *endureth* throughout all generations.

Psa. 146.10. The Lord shall reign for ever, *even* thy God, O Zion, unto all generations. Isa. 52.7.

Ecc. 9.1. The righteous, and the wise, and their works, *are* in the hand of God.

Isa. 24.23. The Lord of hosts shall reign in mount Zion, and in Jerusalem, and before his ancients gloriously.

Isa. 33.22. The Lord is our King, he will save us.

Isa. 40.22. He that sitteth upon the circle of the earth, and the inhabitants thereof *are* as grasshoppers. 23. That bringeth the princes to nothing; he maketh the judges of the earth as vanity.

Isa. 43.15. I *am* the Lord, your Holy One, the Creator of Israel, your King.

Isa. 44. 6. The Lord the King of Israel, and his redeemer the Lord of hosts.

Isa. 45.7. I form the light, and create darkness: I make peace, and create evil: I the Lord do all these *things.*

Isa. 54.5. The God of the whole earth shall he be called.

Jer. 10.10. The Lord *is* the true God, he *is* the living God, and an everlasting king: at his wrath the earth shall tremble, and the nations shall not be able to abide his indignation.

Jer. 18.6. O house of Israel, cannot I do with you as this potter? saith the Lord. Behold, as the clay *is* in the potter's hand, so *are* ye in mine hand.

Jer. 27.5. I have made the earth, the man and the beast that *are* upon the ground, by my great power and by my outstretched arm, and have given it unto whom it seemed meet unto me. 6. And now have I given all these lands into the hand of Nebuchadnezzar the king of Babylon, my servant; and the beasts of the field have I given him also to serve him. *v.* 7. Jer. 32.27,28.

Lam. 3.37. Who *is* he *that* saith, and it cometh to pass, *when* the Lord commandeth *it* not? 38. Out of the mouth of the most High proceedeth not evil and good?

Lam. 5.19. Thou, O Lord, remainest for ever; thy throne from generation to generation.

Eze. 16.50. I took them away as I saw good.

Eze. 17.24. All the trees of the field shall know that I the Lord have brought down the high tree, have exalted the low tree, have dried up the green tree, and have made the dry tree to flourish: I the Lord have spoken and have done *it.*

Eze. 18.4. All souls are mine; as the soul of the father, so also the soul of the son is mine.

Dan. 2.20. Wisdom and might are his: 21. And he changeth the times and the seasons: he removeth kings, and setteth up kings. 47. Your God *is* a God of gods, and a Lord of kings.

Dan. 4.3. His kingdom *is* an everlasting kingdom, and his dominion *is* from generation to generation. 17. The most High ruleth in the kingdom of men, and giveth it to whomsoever he will, 'and setteth up over it the basest of men. 25. Thy dwelling shall be with the beasts of the field, till thou know that the most High ruleth in the kingdom of men, and giveth it to whomsoever he will. 35. All the inhabitants of the earth *are* reputed as nothing: and he doeth according to his will in the army of heaven, and *among* the inhabitants of the earth; and none can stay his hand, or say unto him, What doest thou? 37. I Nebuchadnezzar praise and extol and honour the King of heaven, all whose works *are* truth, and his ways judgment: and those that walk in pride he is able to abase. *v.* 34.

Dan. 5.18. God gave Nebuchadnezzar thy father a kingdom. 26. Mene; God hath numbered thy kingdom, and finished it.

Dan. 6.26. He *is* the living God, and stedfast for ever, and his kingdom *that* which shall not be destroyed, and his dominion *shall be even* unto the end.

Mic. 4.7. The Lord shall reign over them in mount Zion from henceforth, even for ever. 13. I will consecrate their gain unto the Lord, and their substance unto the Lord of the whole earth.

Hag. 2.8. The silver *is* mine, and the gold *is* mine.

Mal. 1.14. I *am* a great King, saith the Lord of hosts, and my name *is* dreadful among the heathen.

Mat. 6.13. Thine is the kingdom, and the power, and the glory, for ever.

Mat. 11.25. O Father, Lord of heaven and earth.

Mat. 20.15. Is it not lawful for me to do what I will with mine own? Is thine eye evil, because I am good?

Luk. 1.53. He hath filled the hungry with good things; and the rich he hath sent empty away.

Luk. 4.27. Many lepers were in Israel in the time of Eliseus the prophet; and none of them was cleansed, saving Naaman the Syrian.

Jno. 10.29. My Father, which gave *them* me, is greater than all; and no *man* is able to pluck *them* out of my Father's hand.

Jno. 19.11. Thou couldst have no power *at all* against me, except it were given thee from above.

Act. 17.24. Seeing that he is Lord of heaven and earth, dwelleth not in temples made with hands; 25. Neither is worshipped with men's hands, as though he needed anything, seeing he giveth to all life, and breath, and all things; 26. And hath made of one blood all nations of men for to dwell on all the face of the earth, and hath determined the times before appointed, and the bounds of their habitation.

Eph. 4.6. One God and Father of all, who *is* above all, and through all, and in you all.

Heb. 1.3. The Majesty on High.

Heb. 2.10. Him, for whom *are* all things, and by whom *are* all things.

Jas. 4.12. There is one lawgiver, who is able to save and to destroy.

Rev. 4.11. Thou hast created all things, and for thy pleasure they are, and were created.

Rev. 11.4. The God of the earth. 13. The God of heaven. 17. Thou hast taken to thee thy great power, and hast reigned.

Rev. 19.6. Alleluia, for the Lord God Omnipotent reigneth.

See GOD, JUSTICE OF.—RULERS DIVINELY APPOINTED.—GOD'S PROVIDENCE OVERRULING.

GOD, LOVE OF.—SAINTS RELATION TO GOD. Gen. 17.7. I will establish my covenant between me and thee and thy seed after thee in their generations for an everlasting covenant, to be a God unto thee, and to thy seed after thee.

Ex. 3.6. I *am* the God of thy father, the God of Abraham, the God of Isaac, and the God of Jacob. Gen. 46.3.

Ex. 6.7. I will take you to me for a people, and I will be to you a God. Ex. 29.45,46.

Ex. 19.4. Ye have seen what I did unto the Egyptians, and *how* I bare you on eagles' wings, and brought you unto myself. 5. Ye shall be a peculiar treasure unto me above all people: 6. Ye shall be unto me a kingdom of priests, and an holy nation.

Lev. 20.26. Ye shall be holy unto me: for I the Lord *am* holy, and have severed you from *other* people, that ye should be mine. *v.* 24.

Lev. 22.32. I will be hallowed among the children of Israel: I *am* the Lord which hallow you, 33. That brought you out of the land of Egypt, to be your God. Lev. 11.44,45. Lev. 25.38. Num. 15.41.

Lev. 25.23. The land *is* mine; for ye *are* strangers and sojourners with me. 42. They *are* my servants, which I brought forth out of the land of Egypt: they shall not be sold as bondmen. *v.* 55.

Lev. 26.12. I will walk among you, and will be your God, and ye shall be my people.

Deu. 4.20. The Lord hath taken you, and brought you forth out of the iron furnace, *even* out of Egypt, to be unto him a people of inheritance, as *ye are* this day. 34. Hath God assayed to go *and* take him a nation from the midst of *another* nation, according to all that the Lord your God did for you in Egypt before your eyes? 37. Because he loved thy fathers, therefore he chose their seed after them. Deu. 9.29. 1 Kin. 8.51-53.

Deu. 7.7. The Lord did not set his love upon you, nor choose you, because ye were more in number than any people; for ye *were* the fewest of all people: 8. But because the Lord loved you. 13. And he will love thee, and bless thee, and multiply thee.

Deu. 10.15. The Lord had a delight in thy fathers to love them, and he chose their seed

after them, *even* you above all people, as *it is* this day.

Deu. 14.2. Thou *art* an holy people unto the Lord thy God, and the Lord hath chosen thee to be a peculiar people unto himself, above all the nations that *are* upon the earth. Deu. 7.6.

Deu. 23.5. The Lord thy God turned the curse into a blessing unto thee, because the Lord thy God loved thee.

Deu. 26.18. The Lord hath avouched thee this day to be his peculiar people, as he hath promised thee, and that *thou* shouldest keep all his commandments; 19. And to make thee high above all nations which he hath made, in praise, and in name, and in honour; and that thou mayest be an holy people unto the Lord thy God, as he hath spoken.

Deu. 27.9. Take heed, and hearken, O Israel; this day thou art become the people of the Lord thy God.

Deu. 28.9. The Lord shall establish thee an holy people unto himself, as he hath sworn unto thee, if thou shalt keep the commandments of the Lord thy God, and walk in his ways. 10. And all people of the earth shall see that thou art called by the name of the Lord. Deu. 29.13.

Deu. 32.9. The Lord's portion *is* his people; Jacob is the lot of his inheritance. 10. He found him in a desert land, and in the waste howling wilderness; he led him about, he instructed him, he kept him as the apple of his eye. 11. As an eagle stirreth up her nest, fluttereth over her young, spreadeth abroad her wings, taketh them, beareth them on her wings: 12. *So* the Lord alone did lead him.

Deu. 33.3. Yea, he loved the people; all his saints *are* in thy hand: and they sat down at thy feet; *every one* shall receive of thy words. 12. The beloved of the Lord shall dwell in safety by him; *and the LORD* shall cover him all the day long, and he shall dwell between his shoulders.

2 Sam. 7.23. What one nation in the earth *is* like thy people, *even* like Israel, whom God went to redeem for a people to himself? 24. For thou hast confirmed to thyself thy people Israel *to be* a people unto thee for ever: and thou, Lord, art become their God.

2 Sam. 12.24. He called his name Solomon: and the Lord loved him. Neh. 13.26.

2 Chr. 20.7. Abraham thy friend.

Psa. 4.3. The Lord hath set apart him that is godly for himself.

Psa. 22.30. A seed shall serve him; it shall be accounted to the Lord for a generation.

Psa. 31.19. *Oh* how great *is* thy goodness, which thou hast laid up for them that fear thee; *which* thou hast wrought for them that trust in thee before the sons of men! 21. Blessed *be* the Lord: for he hath shewed me his marvellous kindness in a strong city.

Psa. 33.12. Blessed *is* the nation whose God *is* the Lord; *and* the people *whom* he hath chosen for his own inheritance.

Psa. 42.8. The Lord will command his loving-kindness in the daytime.

Psa. 47.4. He shall choose our inheritance for us, the excellency of Jacob whom he loved.

Psa. 48.9. We have thought of thy lovingkindness, O God, in the midst of thy temple. 14. This God *is* our God for ever and ever: he will be our guide *even* unto death.

Psa. 50.5. Gather my saints together unto me; those that have made a covenant with me by sacrifice. 7. Hear, O my people, and I will speak; O Israel, and I will testify against thee: I *am* God, *even* thy God.

Psa. 63.3. Because thy loving-kindness *is* better than life, my lips shall praise thee.

Psa. 73.1. Truly God *is* good to Israel, *even* to such as are of a clean heart.

Psa. 74.2. Remember thy congregation, *which* thou hast purchased of old; the rod of thine inheritance, *which* thou hast redeemed; this mount Zion, wherein thou hast dwelt.

Psa. 78.68. Chose the tribe of Judah, the mount Zion which he loved. *v.* 61,62.

Psa. 81.13. Oh that my people had hearkened unto me, *and* Israel had walked in my ways!

Psa. 89.33. My loving-kindness will I not utterly take from him, nor suffer my faithfulness to fail.

Psa. 90.1. Lord, thou hast been our dwelling-place in all generations.

Psa. 100.3. Know ye that the Lord he *is* God: *it is* he *that* hath made us, and not we ourselves; *we are* his people, and the sheep of his pasture. Psa. 79.13. Psa. 95.7.

Psa. 103.4. Who redeemeth thy life from destruction; who crowneth thee with loving-kindness and tender mercies.

Psa. 105.6. O ye seed of Abraham his servant, ye children of Jacob his chosen.

Psa. 114.2. Judah was his sanctuary, *and* Israel his dominion.

Psa. 135.4. The Lord hath chosen Jacob unto himself, *and* Israel for his peculiar treasure.

Psa. 146.8. The Lord loveth the righteous.

Psa. 148.14. He also exalteth the horn of his people, the praise of all his saints; *even* of the children of Israel, a people near unto him.

Pro. 11.20. *Such as are* upright in *their* way *are* his delight.

Pro. 15.9. He loveth him that followeth after righteousness.

Isa. 5.7. The vineyard of the Lord of hosts *is* the house of Israel, and the men of Judah his pleasant plant.

Isa. 41.8. Thou, Israel, *art* my servant, Jacob whom I have chosen, the seed of Abraham my friend. 9. *Thou* whom I have taken from the ends of the earth, and called thee from the chief men thereof, and said unto thee, Thou *art* my servant; I have chosen thee, and not cast thee away. 10. Fear thou not; for I *am* with thee: be not dismayed; for I *am* thy God.

Isa. 43.1. Thus saith the Lord that created thee, O Jacob, and he that formed thee, O Israel, Fear not: for I have redeemed thee, I have called *thee* by thy name; thou *art* mine. 2. When thou passest through the waters, I *will be* with thee; and through the rivers, they shall not overflow thee: when thou walkest through the fire, thou shalt not be burned; neither shall the flame kindle upon thee. 3. For I *am* the Lord thy God, the Holy One of Israel, thy Saviour: I gave Egypt *for* thy ransom, Ethiopia and Seba for thee.

Isa. 43.4. Since thou wast precious in my sight, thou hast been honourable, and I have loved thee: therefore will I give men for thee, **and** people for thy life. 7. Every one that is

called by my name: for I have created him for my glory, I have formed him; yea, I have made him.

Isa. 44.1. O Jacob my servant; and Israel, whom I have chosen: 2. Thus saith the Lord that made thee, and formed thee from the womb, *which* will help thee; Fear not, O Jacob, my servant; and thou, Jesurun, whom I have chosen. 21. I have formed thee; thou *art* my servant: O Israel, thou shalt not be forgotten of me. 22. I have blotted out, as a thick cloud, thy transgressions, and, as a cloud, thy sins: return unto me; for I have redeemed thee.

Isa. 48.12. Hearken unto me, O Jacob and Israel, my called.

Isa. 49.15. Can a woman forget her sucking child, that she should not have compassion on the son of her womb? yea, they may forget, yet will I not forget thee. 16. Behold, I have graven thee upon the palms of *my* hands; thy walls *are* continually before me.

Isa. 51.16. I have covered thee in the shadow of mine hand, that I may plant the heavens, and lay the foundations of the earth, and say unto Zion, Thou *art* my people.

Isa. 54.5. Thy maker *is* thine husband; the Lord of hosts *is* his name; and thy Redeemer the Holy One of Israel. 6. The Lord hath called thee as a woman forsaken and grieved in spirit, and a wife of youth, when thou wast refused, saith thy God. 10. The mountains shall depart, and the hills be removed; but my kindness shall not depart from thee, neither shall the covenant of my peace be removed, saith the Lord that hath mercy on thee.

Isa. 62.4. Thou shalt no more be termed Forsaken; neither shall thy land any more be termed Desolate: but thou shalt be called Hephzi-bah, and thy land Beulah: for the Lord delighteth in thee, and thy land shall be married. 5. *As* the bridegroom rejoiceth over the bride, *so* shall thy God rejoice over thee.

Isa. 63.7. I will mention the loving-kindnesses of the Lord, *and* the praises of the Lord, according to all that the Lord hath bestowed on us, and the great goodness toward the house of Israel, which he hath bestowed on them according to his mercies, and according to the multitude of his loving-kindnesses. 8. For he said, Surely they *are* my people, children *that* will not lie: so he was their Saviour. 9. In all their affliction he was afflicted, and the angel of his presence saved them: in his love and in his pity he redeemed them; and he bare them, and carried them all the days of old.

Isa. 65.19. I will rejoice in Jerusalem, and joy in my people: and the voice of weeping shall be no more heard in her.

Isa. 66.13. As one whom his mother comforteth, so will I comfort you.

Jer. 3.14. Turn, O backsliding children, saith the Lord; for I am married unto you.

Jer. 10.16. The portion of Jacob *is* not like them: for he *is* the former of all *things*; and Israel *is* the rod of his inheritance: Jer. 51.19.

Jer. 12.7. I have forsaken mine house, I have left mine heritage; I have given the dearly beloved of my soul into the hand of her enemies.

Jer. 13.11. As the girdle cleaveth to the loins of a man, so have I caused to cleave unto me the whole house of Israel and the whole house of Judah, saith the Lord; that they might be unto me for a people, and for a name, and for a praise, and for a glory.

Jer. 15.16. I am called by thy name, O Lord God of hosts.

Jer. 31.3. Yea, I have loved thee with an everlasting love: therefore with loving-kindness have I drawn thee. 14. I will satiate the soul of the priests with fatness, and my people shall be satisfied with my goodness. 32. I was a husband unto them, saith the Lord.

Jer. 32.41. I will rejoice over them to do them good, and I will plant them in this land assuredly with my whole heart and with my whole soul.

Eze. 16.8. When I passed by thee, and looked upon thee, behold, thy time *was* the time of love; and I spread my skirt over thee, and covered thy nakedness: yea, I sware unto thee, and entered into a covenant with thee, saith the Lord God, and thou becamest mine. *v.* 1-14.

Eze. 34.31. Ye my flock, the flock of my pasture, *are* men, *and* I *am* your God.

Eze. 37.27. My tabernacle also shall be with them: yea, I will be their God, and they shall be my people.

Hos. 2.19. I will betroth thee unto me for ever; yea, I will betroth thee unto me in righteousness, and in judgment, and in loving-kindness, and in mercies. 20. I will even betroth thee unto me in faithfulness: and thou shalt know the Lord. 23. I will say to *them which were* not my people, Thou *art* my people; and they shall say, *Thou art* my God. 1 Pet. 2.10.

Hos. 9.10. I found Israel like grapes in the wilderness; I saw your fathers as the first-ripe in the fig tree at her first time.

Hos. 11.1. When Israel *was* a child, then I loved him, and called my son out of Egypt. 3. I taught Ephraim also to go, taking them by their arms. 4. I drew them with cords of a man, with bands of love: and I was to them as they that take off the yoke on their jaws, and I laid meat unto them.

Zeph. 3.17. The Lord thy God in the midst of thee *is* mighty; he will save, he will rejoice over thee with joy; he will rest in his love, he will joy over thee with singing.

Hag. 2.23. In that day will I take thee, O Zerubbabel, my servant, and will make thee as a signet: for I have chosen thee, saith the Lord of hosts.

Zec. 1.14. I am jealous for Jerusalem and for Zion with a great jealousy.

Zec. 2.8. He that toucheth you toucheth the apple of his eye.

Zec. 8.8. They shall be my people, and I will be their God, in truth and in righteousness. Jer. 30.22.

Zec. 13.9. I will bring the third part through the fire, and will refine them as silver is refined, and will try them as gold is tried: they shall call on my name, and I will hear them: I will say, It *is* my people: and they shall say, The Lord *is* my God.

Mal. 1.2. I have loved you, saith the Lord.

Mal. 3.16. The Lord hearkened, and heard *it,* and a book of remembrance was written before him for them that feared the Lord, and that thought upon his name. 17. They shall be mine, saith the Lord of hosts, in that day

when I make up my jewels; and I will spare them, as a man spareth his own son that serveth him.

Jno. 3.16. God so loved the world, that he gave his only-begotten Son, that whosoever believeth in him should not perish, but have everlasting life.

Jno. 14.21. He that loveth me shall be loved of my Father, and I will love him. 23. If a man love me, he will keep my words: and my Father will love him, and we will come unto him.

Jno. 16.27. The Father himself loveth you, because ye have loved me, and have believed.

Jno. 17.10. All mine are thine, and thine are mine; and I am glorified in them. 23. That the world may know that thou hast sent me, and hast loved them, as thou hast loved me. 26. That the love wherewith thou hast loved me may be in them, and I in them.

Jno. 20.17. I ascend unto my Father, and your Father; and *to* my God, and your God.

Rom. 1.7. Beloved of God, called *to be* saints: Grace to you and peace from God our Father.

Rom. 5.8. God commendeth his love toward us, in that, while we were yet sinners, Christ died for us.

Rom. 8.31. If God *be* for us, who *can be* against us? 32. He that spared not his own Son, but delivered him up for us all, how shall he not with him also freely give us all things? 39. Nor height, nor depth, nor any other creature, shall be able to separate us from the love of God, which is in Christ Jesus our Lord.

Rom. 11.28. As touching the election, *they are* beloved for the fathers' sakes.

1 Cor. 2.9. Eye hath not seen, nor ear heard, neither have entered into the heart of man, the things which God hath prepared for them that love him. Isa. 64.4.

1 Cor. 3.9. Ye are God's husbandry, *ye are* God's building.

1 Cor. 6.19. Ye are not your own. 20. For ye are bought with a price: therefore glorify God in your body, and in your spirit, which are God's. 1 Cor. 7.23.

2 Cor. 6.16. Ye are the temple of the living God; as God hath said, I will dwell in them, and walk in *them;* and I will be their God, and they shall be my people.

2 Cor. 13.14. The love of God, and the communion of the Holy Ghost, *be* with you all.

Eph. 1.3. Blessed *be* the God and Father of our Lord Jesus Christ, who hath blessed us with all spiritual blessings in heavenly *places* in Christ.

Eph. 2.4. God, who is rich in mercy, for his great love wherewith he loved us. 5. Even when we were dead in sins, hath quickened us together with Christ.

Col. 3.12. The elect of God, holy and beloved.

2 The. 2.16. God, even our Father, which hath loved us, and hath given *us* everlasting consolation and good hope through grace.

Heb. 11.16. God is not ashamed to be called their God: for he hath prepared for them a city.

Heb. 12.6. Whom the Lord loveth he chasteneth.

Jas. 1.18. Of his own will begat he us with the word of truth, that we should be a kind of first-fruits of his creatures.

1 Jno. 3.1. Behold, what manner of love the Father hath bestowed upon us.

1 Jno. 4.9. In this was manifested the love of God toward us, because that God sent his only-begotten Son into the world, that we might live through him. 10. Herein is love, not that we loved God, but that he loved us, and sent his Son *to be* the propitiation for our sins.

1 Jno. 4.12. God dwelleth in us, and his love is perfected in us. 13. Hereby know we that we dwell in him, and he in us, because he hath given us of his Spirit. 15. Whosoever shall confess that Jesus is the Son of God, God dwelleth in him, and he in God. 16. And we have known and believed the love that God hath to us. God is love; and he that dwelleth in love dwelleth in God, and God in him. 19. We love him, because he first loved us.

1 Jno. 5.19. We know that we are of God.

Jude 21. Keep yourselves in the love of God.

Rev. 3.12. Him that overcometh will I make a pillar in the temple of my God, and he shall go no more out: and I will write upon him the name of my God, and the name of the city of my God.

Rev. 14.1. With him an hundred forty *and* four thousand, having his Father's name written in their foreheads.

See GOD, FAVOUR OF.—GOD, MERCY OF.—ADOPTION.

GOD, MERCY AND LONG-SUFFERING OF.

Gen. 6.3. My spirit shall not always strive with man, for that he also *is* flesh: -yet his days shall be an hundred and twenty years.

Gen. 8.21. I will not again curse the ground any more for man's sake; for the imagination of man's heart *is* evil from his youth; neither will I again smite any more every thing living, as I have done.

Gen. 15.16. They shall come hither again: for the iniquity of the Amorites *is* not yet full.

Gen. 18.26. If I find in Sodom fifty righteous within the city, then I will spare all the place for their sakes. *v.* 27-32.

Gen. 19.16. While he lingered, the men laid hold upon his hand, and upon the hand of his wife, and upon the hand of his two daughters; the Lord being merciful unto him: and they brought him forth.

Ex. 20.6. Shewing mercy unto thousands of them that love me, and keep my commandments. 22. Ye have seen that I have talked with you from heaven. Deu. 5.10.

Ex. 22.27. When he crieth unto me, I will hear; for I *am* gracious.

Ex. 25.17. Thou shalt make a mercy-seat. Psa. 80.1. Heb. 4.16.

Ex. 32.14. The Lord repented of the evil which he thought to do unto his people. 34. Behold, mine Angel shall go before thee.

Ex. 33.19. I will make all my goodness pass before thee, and I will proclaim the name of the Lord before thee; and will be gracious to whom I will be gracious, and will shew mercy on whom I will shew mercy.

Ex. 34.6. The Lord, the Lord God, merciful and gracious, long-suffering, and abundant in goodness and truth. 7. Keeping mercy for thousands, forgiving iniquity and transgression and sin.

Lev. 26.44. I will not cast them away, neither will I abhor them, to destroy them utterly, and to break my covenant with them:

for I *am* the Lord their God. 45. But I will for their sakes remember the covenant of their ancestors. *v.* 40-43.

Num. 14.18. The Lord *is* long-suffering, and of great mercy, forgiving iniquity and transgression. 19. Pardon, I beseech thee, the iniquity of this people according unto the greatness of thy mercy, and as thou hast forgiven this people, from Egypt even until now. 20. And the Lord said, I have pardoned according to thy word.

Num. 16.48. He stood between the dead and the living; and the plague was stayed.

Num. 21.8. The Lord said unto Moses, Make thee a fiery serpent, and set it upon a pole: and it shall come to pass, that every one that is bitten, when he looketh upon it, shall live.

Deu. 4.31. The Lord thy God *is* a merciful God; he will not forsake thee, neither destroy thee, nor forget the covenant of thy fathers.

Deu. 5.29. O that there were such an heart in them, that they would fear me, and keep all my commandments always, that it might be well with them, and with their children for ever!

Deu. 7.9. Which keepeth covenant and mercy with them that love him and keep his commandments to a thousand generations.

Deu. 32.29. O that they were wise, *that* they understood this, *that* they would consider their latter end! 36. The Lord shall judge his people, and repent himself for his servants, when he seeth that *their* power is gone, and *there is* none shut up, or left. 43. And will be merciful unto his land, *and* to his people.

Jud. 2.18. The Lord was with the judge, and delivered them out of the hand of their enemies all the days of the judge: for it repented the Lord because of their groanings by reason of them that oppressed them and vexed them. Ex. 2.24,25. Jud. 3.9,15.

Jud. 10.16. His soul was grieved for the misery of Israel.

2 Sam. 12.13. The Lord also hath put away thy sin; thou shalt not die.

2 Sam. 14.14. Yet doth he devise means, that his banished be not expelled from him.

2 Sam. 24.14. Let us fall now into the hand of the Lord; for his mercies *are* great. 16. When the angel stretched out his hand upon Jerusalem to destroy it, the Lord repented him of the evil, and said to the angel that destroyed the people, It is enough; stay now thine hand.

1 Kin. 8.23. *There is* no God like thee, in heaven above, or on earth beneath, who keepest covenant and mercy with thy servants that walk before thee with all their heart.

1 Kin. 11.39. I will for this afflict the seed of David, but not for ever.

2 Kin. 13.23. The Lord was gracious unto them, and had compassion on them, and would not destroy them, neither cast he them from his presence as yet.

2 Kin. 14.26. The Lord saw the affliction of Israel, *that it was* very bitter: for *there was* not any shut up, nor any left, nor any helper for Israel. 27. And the Lord said not that he would blot out the name of Israel from under heaven: but he saved them by the hand of Jeroboam.

2 Chr. 7.14. Seek my face, and turn from

their wicked ways; then will I hear from heaven, and will forgive their sin, and will heal their land.

2 Chr. 30.9. The Lord your God *is* gracious and merciful, and will not turn away *his* face from you, if ye return unto him.

2 Chr. 36.15. The Lord God of their fathers sent to them by his messengers, rising up betimes, and sending; because he had compassion on his people, and on his dwellingplace. Jer. 7.25.

Ezr. 9.13. Thou our God hast punished us less than our iniquities *deserve*, and hast given us *such* deliverance as this. Job 11.6.

Ezr. 10.2. Yet now there is hope in Israel concerning this thing.

Neh. 1.10. These *are* thy servants and thy people, whom thou hast redeemed by thy great power, and by thy strong hand.

Neh. 9.17. Thou *art* a God ready to pardon, gracious and merciful, slow to anger, and of great kindness, and forsookest them not. 27. In the time of their trouble, when they cried unto thee, thou heardest *them* from heaven; and according to thy manifold mercies thou gavest them saviours, who saved them out of the hand of their enemies. 28. When they returned, and cried unto thee, thou heardest *them* from heaven; and many times didst thou deliver them according to thy mercies; 29. And testifiedst against them, that thou mightest bring them again unto thy law. 30. Yet many years didst thou forbear them, and testifiedst against them by thy spirit in thy prophets. 31. For thy great mercies' sake, thou didst not utterly consume them, nor forsake them; for thou *art* a gracious and merciful God. *v.* 17-20. 2 Chr. 24.19.

Job 24.12. Men groan from out of the city, and the soul of the wounded crieth out: yet God layeth not folly *to them.*

Job 33.26. He shall pray unto God, and he will be favourable unto him: and he shall see his face with joy: for he will render unto man his righteousness. *v.* 24-30.

Psa. 25.6. Remember, O Lord, thy tender mercies and thy loving-kindnesses; for they *have been* ever of old. 8. Good and upright *is* the Lord: therefore will he teach sinners in the way.

Psa. 30.5. His anger *endureth but* a moment; in his favour *is* life: weeping may endure for a night, but joy *cometh* in the morning.

Psa. 31.7. I will be glad and rejoice in thy mercy: for thou hast considered my trouble; thou hast known my soul in adversities.

Psa. 32.1. Blessed *is he whose* transgression *is* forgiven, *whose* sin *is* covered. 2. Blessed *is* the man unto whom the Lord imputeth not iniquity. 5. I will confess my transgressions unto the Lord; and thou forgavest the iniquity of my sin.

Psa. 36.5. Thy mercy, O Lord, *is* in the heavens.

Psa. 50.21. These things hast thou done, and I kept silence.

Psa. 57.10. Thy mercy *is* great unto the heavens.

Psa. 62.12. Unto thee, O Lord, *belongeth* mercy.

Psa. 65.3. Iniquities prevail against me: *as for* our transgressions, thou shalt purge them away.

Psa. 69.16. Thy loving-kindness *is* good:

turn unto me according to the multitude of thy tender mercies.

Psa. 78.38. But he, *being* full of compassion, forgave *their* iniquity, and destroyed *them* not: yea, many a time turned he his anger away, and did not stir up all his wrath. 39. For he remembered that they *were but* flesh; a wind that passeth away, and cometh not again. *v.* 4-72. Psa. 106.43-46.

Psa. 85.2. Thou hast forgiven the iniquity of thy people, thou hast covered all their sin. 3. Thou hast taken away all thy wrath: thou hast turned *thyself* from the fierceness of thine anger. 10. Mercy and truth are met together; righteousness and peace have kissed *each other.*

Psa. 86.5. Thou, Lord, *art* good, and ready to forgive; and plenteous in mercy unto all them that call upon thee. 13. Great *is* thy mercy toward me: and thou hast delivered my soul from the lowest hell. 15. Thou, O Lord, *art* a God full of compassion, and gracious, long-suffering, and plenteous in mercy and truth.

Psa. 89.2. Mercy shall be built up for ever. 14. Mercy and truth shall go before thy face. 28. My mercy will I keep for him for evermore.

Psa. 99.8. Thou answeredst them, O Lord our God: thou wast a God that forgavest them.

Psa. 100.5. The Lord *is* good; his mercy *is* everlasting.

Psa. 103.3. Who forgiveth all thine iniquities; who healeth all thy diseases. 8. The Lord *is* merciful and gracious, slow to anger, and plenteous in mercy. 9. He will not always chide: neither will he keep *his anger* for ever. 10. He hath not dealt with us after our sins; nor rewarded us according to our iniquities. 11. For as the heaven is high above the earth, so great is his mercy toward them that fear him. 12. As far as the east is from the west, so far hath he removed our transgressions from us.

Psa. 103.13. Like as a father pitieth *his* children, so the Lord pitieth them that fear him. 14. For he knoweth our frame; he remembereth that we *are* dust. 17. The mercy of the Lord *is* from everlasting to everlasting upon them that fear him, and his righteousness unto children's children.

Psa. 106.1. His mercy *endureth* for ever. Psa. 107.1. Psa. 136.3.

Psa. 108.4. Thy mercy *is* great above the heavens.

Psa. 111.4. The Lord *is* gracious and full of compassion.

Psa. 116.5. Gracious *is* the Lord, and righteous; yea, our God *is* merciful. 2 Chr. 30.9.

Psa. 117.2. His merciful kindness is great toward us.

Psa. 119.64. The earth, O Lord, is full of thy mercy. 156. Great *are* thy tender mercies, O Lord.

Psa. 130.4. *There is* forgiveness with thee, that thou mayest be feared. 7. Let Israel hope in the Lord: for with the Lord *there is* mercy, and with him *is* plenteous redemption. 8. And he shall redeem Israel from all his iniquities.

Psa. 135.14. He will repent himself concerning his servants.

Psa. 138.2. I will praise thy name for thy loving-kindness and for thy truth.

Psa. 145.8. The Lord *is* gracious, and full

of compassion; slow to anger, and of great mercy. 9. The Lord *is* good to all: and his tender mercies *are* over all his works.

Psa. 146.7. Which executeth judgment for the oppressed: which giveth food to the hungry. The Lord looseth the prisoners: 8. The Lord openeth *the eyes of* the blind: the Lord raiseth them that are bowed down.

Pro. 16.6. By mercy and truth iniquity is purged.

Pro. 28.13. Whoso confesseth and forsaketh *them* shall have mercy.

Isa. 1.5. Why should ye be stricken any more? 18. Come now, and let us reason together, saith the Lord: though your sins be as scarlet, they shall be as white as snow; though they be red like crimson, they shall be as wool.

Isa. 6.7. Lo, this hath touched thy lips; and thine iniquity is taken away, and thy sin purged.

Isa. 12.1. I will praise thee: though thou wast angry with me, thine anger is turned away, and thou comfortedst me.

Isa. 17.6. Yet gleaning grapes shall be left in it, as the shaking of an olive-tree, two *or* three berries in the top of the uppermost bough, four *or* five in the outmost fruitful branches thereof, saith the Lord God of Israel. Isa. 24.13.

Isa. 27.8. He stayeth his rough wind in the day of the east wind. *v.* 7.

Isa. 30.18. Therefore will the Lord wait, that he may be gracious unto you, and therefore will he be exalted, that he may have mercy upon you: for the Lord *is* a God of judgment: blessed *are* all they that wait for him. 19. For the people shall dwell in Zion at Jerusalem: thou shalt weep no more: he will be very gracious unto thee at the voice of thy cry; when he shall hear it, he will answer thee.

Isa. 33.24. The people that dwell therein *shall* be forgiven *their* iniquity.

Isa. 38.17. Thou hast in love to my soul *delivered it* from the pit of corruption: for thou hast cast all my sins behind thy back.

Isa. 40.2. Her iniquity is pardoned: for she hath received of the Lord's hand double for all her sins.

Isa. 43.25. I, *even* I, *am* he that blotteth out thy transgressions for mine own sake, and will not remember thy sins. *v.* 24.

Isa. 44.22. I have blotted out, as a thick cloud, thy transgressions, and, as a cloud, thy sins: return unto me; for I have redeemed thee.

Isa. 48.9. For my name's sake will I defer mine anger, and for my praise will I refrain for thee, that I cut thee not off. 11. For mine own sake, *even* for mine own sake, will I do *it*: for how should *my name* be polluted? and I will not give my glory unto another.

Isa. 49.13. Sing, O heavens; and be joyful, O earth; and break forth into singing, O mountains: for the Lord hath comforted his people, and will have mercy upon his afflicted. *v.* 14,15.

Isa. 54.7. For a small moment have I forsaken thee; but with great mercies will I gather thee. 8. In a little wrath I hid my face from thee for a moment; but with everlasting kindness will I have mercy on thee, saith the Lord thy Redeemer. 9. For this *is as* the waters of Noah unto me: for *as* I have sworn

that the waters of Noah should no more go over the earth; so have I sworn that I would not be wroth with thee, nor rebuke thee.

Isa. 55.7. Let the wicked forsake his way, and the unrighteous man his thoughts: and let him return unto the Lord, and he will have mercy upon him; and to our God, for he will abundantly pardon. 8. For my thoughts *are* not your thoughts, neither *are* your ways my ways, saith the Lord. 9. For *as* the heavens are higher than the earth, so are my ways higher than your ways, and my thoughts than your thoughts.

Isa. 57.11. Have not I held my peace even of old, and thou fearest me not? 15. I dwell in the high and holy *place*, with him also *that is* of a contrite and humble spirit, to revive the spirit of the humble, and to revive the heart of the contrite ones. 16. I will not contend for ever, neither will I be always wroth: for the spirit should fail before me, and the souls *which* I have made. 18. I have seen his ways, and will heal him: I will lead him also, and restore comforts unto him and to his mourners. 19. I create the fruit of the lips; Peace, peace to *him that is* far off, and to *him that is* near, saith the Lord; and I will heal him.

Isa. 60.10. In my wrath I smote thee, but in my favour have I had mercy on thee.

Isa. 65.2. I have spread out my hands all the day unto a rebellious people, which walketh in a way *that was* not good, after their own thoughts. 8. As the new wine is found in the cluster, and *one* saith, Destroy it not; for a blessing *is* in it: so will I do for my servants' sakes, that I may not destroy them all.

Jer. 3.12. Go and proclaim these words toward the north, and say, Return, thou backsliding Israel, saith the Lord; *and* I will not cause mine anger to fall upon you: for I *am* merciful, saith the Lord, *and* I will not keep anger for ever. 22. Return, ye backsliding children, *and* I will heal your backslidings. *v.* 1-22.

Jer. 4.27. The whole land shall be desolate; yet will I not make a full end.

Jer. 5.10. Go ye up upon her walls, and destroy; but make not a full end.

Jer. 9.24. I *am* the Lord which exercise loving-kindness, judgment, and righteousness, in the earth: for in these *things* I delight, saith the Lord.

Jer. 29.11. I know the thoughts that I think toward you, saith the Lord, thoughts of peace, and not of evil, to give you an expected end.

Jer. 30.11. I *am* with thee, saith the Lord, to save thee: though I make a full end of all nations whither I have scattered thee, yet will I not make a full end of thee: but I will correct thee in measure. Jer. 46.28.

Jer. 31.20. *Is* Ephraim my dear son? *is he* a pleasant child? for since I spake against him, I do earnestly remember him still: therefore my bowels are troubled for him; I will surely have mercy upon him, saith the Lord. 34. I will forgive their iniquity, and I will remember their sin no more. 37. If heaven above can be measured, and the foundations of the earth searched out beneath, I will also cast off all the seed of Israel for all that they have done, saith the Lord.

Jer. 32.18. Thou shewest loving-kindness unto thousands.

Jer. 33.8. I will cleanse them from all their iniquity, whereby they have sinned against me; and I will pardon all their iniquities, whereby they have sinned, and whereby they have transgressed against me. 11. The voice of them that shall say, Praise the Lord of hosts: for the Lord *is* good; for his mercy *endureth* for ever: *and* of them that shall bring the sacrifice of praise into the house of the Lord. For I will cause to return the captivity of the land, as at the first, saith the Lord.

Jer. 36.3. Return every man from his evil way; that I may forgive their iniquity and their sin. *v.* 6,7.

Jer. 50.20. The iniquity of Israel shall be sought for, and *there shall be* none; and the sins of Judah, and they shall not be found: for I will pardon them whom I reserve.

Jer. 51.5. Israel *hath* not *been* forsaken, nor Judah of his God, of the Lord of hosts; though their land was filled with sin against the Holy One of Israel.

Lam. 3.22. *It is of* the Lord's mercies that we are not consumed, because his compassions fail not. 23. *They are* new every morning: great *is* thy faithfulness. 31. The Lord will not cast off for ever: 32. But though he cause grief, yet will he have compassion according to the multitude of his mercies. 33. For he doth not afflict willingly nor grieve the children of men.

Eze. 14.22. Therein shall be left a remnant that shall be brought forth, *both* sons and daughters: behold, they shall come forth unto you, and ye shall see their way and their doings: and ye shall be comforted concerning the evil that I have brought upon Jerusalem, *even* concerning all that I have brought upon it.

Eze. 16.6. When I passed by thee, and saw thee polluted in thine own blood, I said unto thee *when thou wast* in thy blood, Live; yea, I said unto thee *when thou wast* in thy blood, Live. 42. So will I make my fury toward thee to rest, and my jealousy shall depart from thee, and I will be quiet, and will be no more angry. 63. I am pacified toward thee for all that thou hast done, saith the Lord God.

Eze. 18.23. Have I any pleasure at all that the wicked should die? saith the Lord God: *and* not that he should return from his ways, and live? 31. Cast away from you all your transgressions, whereby ye have transgressed; and make you a new heart and a new spirit: for why will ye die, O house of Israel? 32. For I have no pleasure in the death of him that dieth, saith the Lord God: wherefore turn *yourselves*, and live ye.

Eze. 20.17. Nevertheless mine eye spared them from destroying them, neither did I make an end of them in the wilderness. 42. Ye shall know that I *am* the Lord, when I shall bring you into the land of Israel, into the country *for* the which I lifted up mine hand to give it to your fathers. *v.* 11-44.

Eze. 33.11. *As* I live, saith the Lord God, I have no pleasure in the death of the wicked; but that the wicked turn from his way and live: turn ye, turn ye from your evil ways; for why will ye die, O house of Israel?

Eze. 36.25. Then will I sprinkle clean water upon you, and ye shall be clean: from all your filthiness, and from all your idols, will I cleanse you. 32. Not for your sakes do I *this*, saith the Lord God, be it known unto you.

Dan. 9.4. O Lord, the great and dreadful God, keeping the covenant and mercy to them that love him, and to them that keep his commandments. 9. To the Lord our God *belong* mercies and forgivenesses, though we have rebelled against him.

Hos. 2.14. I will allure her, and bring her into the wilderness, and speak comfortably unto her. 23. I will sow her unto me in the earth; and I will have mercy upon her that had not obtained mercy. *v.* 14-23. Rom. 9.15,18. 1 Pet. 2.10.

Hos. 11.8. How shall I give thee up, Ephraim? how shall I deliver thee, Israel? how shall I make thee as Admah? how shall I set thee as Zeboim? mine heart is turned within me, my repentings are kindled together. 9. I will not execute the fierceness of mine anger, I will not return to destroy Ephraim: for I *am* God, and not man; the Holy One in the midst of thee.

Hos. 14.4. I will heal their backsliding, I will love them freely: for mine anger is turned away from him. *v.* 1-8.

Joel 2.13. Turn unto the Lord your God: for he *is* gracious and merciful, slow to anger, and of great kindness, and repenteth him of the evil. 18. Then will the Lord be jealous for his land, and pity his people.

Joel 3.21. I will cleanse their blood *that* I have not cleansed: for the Lord dwelleth in Zion.

Amos 7.3. The Lord repented for this: It shall not be, saith the Lord.

Jonah 4.2. I knew that thou *art* a gracious God, and merciful, slow to anger, and of great kindness, and repentest thee of the evil. 11. Should not I spare Nineveh, that great city, wherein are more than sixscore thousand persons that cannot discern between their right hand and their left hand; and *also* much cattle?

Mic. 7.18. Who *is* a God like unto thee, that pardoneth iniquity, and passeth by the transgression of the remnant of his heritage? he retaineth not his anger for ever, because he delighteth *in* mercy. 19. He will turn again, he will have compassion upon us; he will subdue our iniquities; and thou wilt cast all their sins into the depths of the sea.

Nah. 1.3. The Lord *is* slow to anger, and great in power.

Zeph. 2.7. The Lord their God shall visit them, and turn away their captivity.

Zec. 1.16. I am returned to Jerusalem with mercies: my house shall be built in it. 17. The Lord shall yet comfort Zion, and shall yet choose Jerusalem.

Zec. 3.9. I will remove the iniquity of that land in one day.

Zec. 10.6. I will strengthen the house of Judah, and I will save the house of Joseph, and I will bring them again to place them; for I have mercy upon them: and they shall be as though I had not cast them off: for I *am* the Lord their God, and will hear them.

Mal. 3.6. I *am* the Lord, I change not; therefore ye sons of Jacob are not consumed.

Mat. 6.14. If ye forgive men their trespasses, your heavenly Father will also forgive you.

Mat. 12.31. All manner of sin and blasphemy shall be forgiven unto men. 32. Whosoever speaketh a word against the Son of man, it shall be forgiven him.

Mar. 3.28. All sins shall be forgiven unto the sons of men, and blasphemies wherewith soever they shall blaspheme. Luk. 12.10.

Luk. 1.50. His mercy *is* on them that fear him from generation to generation. 77. To give knowledge of salvation unto his people by the remission of their sins, 78. Through the tender mercy of our God; whereby the dayspring from on high hath visited us.

Luk. 6.36. Be ye therefore merciful, as your Father also is merciful.

Act. 3.19. Be converted, that your sins may be blotted out, when the times of refreshing shall come from the presence of the Lord.

Act. 17.30. The times of this ignorance God winked at; but now commandeth all men every where to repent.

Act. 26.18. To turn *them* from darkness to light, and *from* the power of Satan unto God, that they may receive forgiveness of sins.

Rom. 2.4. Despisest thou the riches of his goodness and forbearance and long-suffering; not knowing that the goodness of God leadeth thee to repentance? (See parable of the fig-tree, Luk. 13.6-9.)

Rom. 3.25. Whom God hath set forth *to be* a propitiation through faith in his blood, to declare his righteousness for the remission of sins that are past, through the forbearance of God.

Rom. 9.22. *What* if God, willing to shew *his* wrath, and to make his power known, endured with much long-suffering the vessels of wrath fitted to destruction: 23. That he might make known the riches of his glory on the vessels of mercy, which he had afore prepared unto glory.

Rom. 10.12. The same Lord over all is rich unto all that call upon him. 13. For whosoever shall call upon the name of the Lord shall be saved.

Rom. 11.32. God hath concluded them all in unbelief, that he might have mercy upon all.

Rom. 15.9. That the Gentiles might glorify God for *his* mercy.

1 Cor. 15.10. By the grace of God I am what I am; and his grace which *was bestowed* upon me was not in vain.

2 Cor. 1.3. Blessed *be* God, even the Father of our Lord Jesus Christ, the Father of mercies, and the God of all comfort.

2 Cor. 4.15. All things *are* for your sakes, that the abundant grace might through the thanksgiving of many redound to the glory of God.

2 Cor. 12.9. My grace is sufficient for thee: for my strength is made perfect in weakness.

Eph. 1.6. To the praise of the glory of his grace, wherein he hath made us accepted in the Beloved: 7. In whom we have redemption through his blood, the forgiveness of sins, according to the riches of his grace; 8. Wherein he hath abounded toward us in all wisdom and prudence.

Eph. 2.4. God, who is rich in mercy, for his great love wherewith he loved us, 5. Even when we were dead in sins, hath quickened us together with Christ, (by grace ye are saved;) 6. And hath raised *us* up together, and made *us* sit together in heavenly *places* in Christ Jesus. 7. That in the ages to come he might

shew the exceeding riches of his grace in *his* kindness toward us through Christ Jesus.

1 Tim. 1.13. Who was before a blasphemer, and a persecutor, and injurious: but I obtained mercy

Tit. 3.5. According to his mercy he saved us.

Heb. 8.12. I will be merciful to their unrighteousness, and their sins and their iniquities will I remember no more.

Heb. 9.22. Without shedding of blood is no remission.

Jas. 2.13. Mercy rejoiceth against judgment.

Jas. 4.8. Draw nigh to God, and he will draw nigh to you.

Jas. 5.11. The Lord is very pitiful, and of tender mercy. 15. If he have committed sins, they shall be forgiven him.

1 Pet. 1.3. According to his abundant mercy hath begotten us again unto a lively hope by the resurrection of Jesus Christ.

1 Pet. 3.20. The long-suffering of God waited in the days of Noah.

1 Pet. 5.10. The God of all grace, who hath called us unto his eternal glory by Christ Jesus.

2 Pet. 3.9. The Lord is not slack concerning his promise, as some men count slackness; but is long-suffering to us-ward, not willing that any should perish, but that all should come to repentance. 15. Account *that* the long-suffering of our Lord *is* salvation.

1 Jno. 1.9. If we confess our sins, he is faithful and just to forgive us *our* sins, and to cleanse us from all unrighteousness.

1 Jno. 5.16. If any man see his brother sin a sin *which is* not unto death, he shall ask, and he shall give him life for them that sin not unto death. 17. All unrighteousness is sin: and there is a sin not unto death.

Rev. 2.21. I gave her space to repent.

See GOD A SAVIOUR.—PARDON.—REPENTANCE.—GOD, LOVE OF.

GOD, OMNIPOTENT. Gen. 1.3. God said, Let there be light: and there was light.

Gen. 17.1. I *am* the Almighty God; walk before me, and be thou perfect.

Gen. 18.14. Is any thing too hard for the Lord?

Ex. 14.24. The Lord looked unto the host of the Egyptians through the pillar of fire and of the cloud, and troubled the host.

Ex. 15.3. The Lord *is* a man of war: the Lord *is* his name. 6. Thy right hand, O Lord, is become glorious in power: thy right hand, O Lord, hath dashed in pieces the enemy. 7. And in the greatness of thine excellency thou hast overthrown them that rose up against thee. 11. Who *is* like unto thee, O Lord, among the gods? who *is* like thee, glorious in holiness, fearful *in* praises, doing wonders? 12. Thou stretchedst out thy right hand, the earth swallowed them. *v.* 8,10.

Num. 11.23. Is the Lord's hand waxed short? thou shalt see now whether my word shall come to pass unto thee or not. Deu. 11.2.

Num. 23.20. I have received *commandment* to bless: and he hath blessed; and I cannot reverse it.

Deu. 3.24. O Lord God, thou hast begun to shew thy servant thy greatness, and thy mighty hand: for what God *is there* in heaven or in earth, that can do according to thy works, and according to thy might?

Deu. 7.21. The Lord thy God *is* among you, a mighty God and terrible.

Deu. 32.39. I kill, and I make alive; I wound, and I heal: neither *is there any* that can deliver out of my hand. Job 10.7.

Deu. 33.26. *There is* none like unto the God of Jeshurun, *who* rideth upon the heaven in thy help, and in his excellency on the sky. 27. The eternal God *is thy* refuge, and underneath *are* the everlasting arms.

Jos. 4.24. That all the people of the earth might know the hand of the Lord, that it *is* mighty.

1 Sam. 2.6. The Lord killeth, and maketh alive: he bringeth down to the grave, and bringeth up. 7. The Lord maketh poor and maketh rich: he bringeth low, and lifteth up. 10. The adversaries of the Lord shall be broken to pieces; out of heaven shall he thunder upon them. *v.* 8.

1 Sam. 14.6. *There is* no restraint to the Lord to save by many or by few.

2 Sam. 22.13. Through the brightness before him were coals of fire kindled. 16. And the channels of the sea appeared, the foundations of the world were discovered, at the rebuking of the Lord, at the blast of the breath of his nostrils. Psa. 18.

1 Chr. 29.11. Thine, O Lord, *is* the greatness, and the power, and the glory, and the victory, and the majesty. 12. In thine hand *is* power and might; and in thine hand *it is* to make great, and to give strength unto all.

2 Chr. 14.11. Lord, *it is* nothing with thee to help, whether with many, or with them that have no power.

2 Chr. 16.9. The eyes of the Lord run to and fro throughout the whole earth, to shew himself strong in the behalf of *them* whose heart *is* perfect toward him.

2 Chr. 20.6. In thine hand *is there not* power and might, so that none is able to withstand thee?

2 Chr. 25.8. God hath power to help, and to cast down. 9. The Lord is able to give thee much more than this.

Ezr. 8.22. The hand of our God *is* upon all them for good that seek him; but his power and his wrath *is* against all them that forsake him.

Neh. 1.10. Whom thou hast redeemed by thy great power, and by thy strong hand.

Job 9.4. *He is* wise in heart, and mighty in strength: who hath hardened *himself* against him, and hath prospered? 5. Which removeth the mountains, and they know not: which overturneth them in his anger. 6. Which shaketh the earth out of her place, and the pillars thereof tremble. 7. Which commandeth the sun, and it riseth not; and sealeth up the stars. 10. Which doeth great things past finding out; yea, and wonders without number. 12. He taketh away, who can hinder him? who will say unto him, What doest thou? 13. *If* God will not withdraw his anger, the proud helpers do stoop under him. 19. If *I speak* of strength, lo, *he is* strong. Job 5.9.

Job 11.10. If he cut off, and shut up, or gather together, then who can hinder him?

Job 12.14. He breaketh down, and it cannot be built again: he shutteth up a man, and there can be no opening. 16. With him *is* strength and wisdom. *v.* 15.

Job 14.20. Thou prevailest for ever against him, and he passeth: thou changest his countenance, and sendest him away.

Job 23.13. He *is* in one *mind*, and who can turn him? and *what* his soul desireth, even *that* he doeth. 14. For he performeth *the thing that is* appointed for me.

Job 26.11. The pillars of heaven tremble and are astonished at his reproof. 14. The thunder of his power who can understand? *v.* 12.

Job 34.14. If he set his heart upon man, *if* he gather unto himself his spirit and his breath; 15. All flesh shall perish together, and man shall turn again unto dust.

Job 36.5. God *is* mighty, and despiseth not *any: he is* mighty in strength and *and* wisdom. 22. Behold, God exalteth by his power. *v.* 27-33.

Job 37.23. *He is* excellent in power, and in judgment. *v.* 1-22.

Job 38.8. *Who* shut up the sea with doors, when it brake forth. 11. And said, Hitherto shalt thou come, but no further: and here shall thy proud waves be stayed? *v.* 37.

Job 40.9. Hast thou an arm like God? or canst thou thunder with a voice like him?

Job 41.10. Who then is able to stand before me? 11. Who hath prevented me, that I should repay *him?*

Job 42.2. I know that thou canst do every *thing*.

Psa. 21.13. Be thou exalted, Lord, in thine own strength: *so* will we sing and praise thy power.

Psa. 29.3. The voice of the Lord *is* upon the waters: the God of glory thundereth: the Lord *is* upon many waters. 4. The voice of the Lord *is* powerful; the voice of the Lord *is* full of majesty. 5. The voice of the Lord breaketh the cedars. *v.* 6-9.

Psa. 33.9. He spake, and it was *done*; he commanded, and it stood fast.

Psa. 46.6. The heathen raged, the kingdoms were moved: he uttered his voice, the earth melted.

Psa. 62.11. God hath spoken once; twice have I heard this; that power *belongeth* unto God.

Psa. 65.6. Which by his strength setteth fast the mountains; *being* girded with power: 7. Which stilleth the noise of the seas, the noise of their waves, and the tumult of the people.

Psa. 66.3. How terrible *art thou in* thy works! through the greatness of thy power shall thine enemies submit themselves unto thee. 7. He ruleth by his power for ever.

Psa. 68.33. Him that rideth upon the heavens of heavens, *which were* of old; lo, he doth send out his voice, *and that* a mighty voice. *v.* 34,35.

Psa. 74.13. Thou didst divide the sea by thy strength: thou breakest the heads of the dragons in the waters. 15. Thou didst cleave the fountain and the flood: thou driedst up mighty rivers.

Psa. 76.6. At thy rebuke, O God of Jacob, both the chariot and horse are cast into a dead sleep. 7. Who may stand in thy sight when once thou art angry?

Psa. 77.14. Thou *art* the God that doest wonders: thou hast declared thy strength among the people. 16. The waters saw thee, O God, the waters saw thee; they were afraid:

the depths also were troubled. 18. The voice of thy thunder *was* in the heaven : the lightnings lightened the world: the earth trembled and shook.

Psa. 78.26. He caused an east wind to blow in the heaven ; and by his power he brought in the south wind. *v.* 12-16,43-51.

Psa. 79.11. According to the greatness of thy power preserve thou those that are appointed to die.

Psa. 89.8. O Lord God of hosts, who *is* a strong Lord like unto thee? 9. Thou rulest the raging of the sea : when the waves thereof arise, thou stillest them. 13. Thou hast a mighty arm : strong is thy hand, *and* high is thy right hand.

Psa. 90.3. Thou turnest man to destruction; and sayest, Return, ye children of men.

Psa. 93.1. The Lord is clothed with strength, *wherewith* he hath girded himself. 4. The Lord on high *is* mightier than the noise of many waters, *yea*, *than* the mighty waves of the sea.

Psa. 97.3. A fire goeth before him, and burneth up his enemies round about. 4. His lightnings enlightened the world : the earth saw, and trembled. 5. The hills melted like wax at the presence of the Lord.

Psa. 98.1. He hath done marvellous things : his right hand, and his holy arm, hath gotten him the victory.

Psa. 104.7. At thy rebuke they fled; at the voice of thy thunder they hasted away. 9. Thou hast set a bound that they may not pass over ; that they turn not again to cover the earth. 29. Thou hidest thy face, they are troubled : thou takest away their breath, they die, and return to their dust. 30. Thou sendest forth thy spirit, they are created : and thou renewest the face of the earth. 32. He looketh on the earth, and it trembleth : he toucheth the hills, and they smoke. Psa. 105. Psa. 114.3-8. Psa. 135.8-12. Psa. 136.10-22.

Psa. 106.8. He saved them for his name's sake, that he might make his mighty power to be known.

Psa. 107.25. He commandeth, and raiseth the stormy wind, which lifteth up the waves thereof. 29. He maketh the storm a calm, so that the waves thereof are still.

Psa. 111.6. He hath shewed his people the power of his works.

Psa. 114.7. Tremble, thou earth, at the presence of the Lord, at the presence of the God of Jacob; 8. Which turned the rock *into* a standing water.

Psa. 115.3. Our God *is* in the heavens : he hath done whatsoever he hath pleased.

Psa. 118.16. The right hand of the Lord is exalted : the right hand of the Lord doeth valiantly.

Psa. 135.6. Whatsoever the Lord pleased, *that* did he in heaven, and in earth, in the seas, and all deep places.

Psa. 144.5. Bow thy heavens, O Lord, and come down : touch the mountains, and they shall smoke.

Psa. 145.6. *Men* shall speak of the might of thy terrible acts : and I will declare thy greatness. 16. Thou openest thine hand, and satisfiest the desire of every living thing.

Psa. 147.5. Great *is* our Lord, and of great power. 16. He giveth snow like wool : he scattereth the hoarfrost like ashes. 18. He

sendeth out his word, and melteth them : he causeth his wind to blow, *and* the waters flow.

Psa. 148.5. He commanded, and they were created. 8. Fire, and hail ; snow, and vapours; stormy wind fulfilling his word.

Pro. 21.30. *There is* no wisdom nor understanding nor counsel against the Lord.

Pro. 30.4. Who hath gathered the wind in his fists? who hath bound the waters in a garment? who hath established all the ends of the earth?

Isa. 14.24. Surely as I have thought, so shall it come to pass ; and as I have purposed, *so* shall it stand. 27. The Lord of hosts hath purposed, and who shall disannul *it?* and his hand *is* stretched out, and who shall turn it back?

Isa. 17.13. The nations shall rush like the rushing of many waters : but *God* shall rebuke them, and they shall flee far off, and shall be chased as the chaff of the mountains before the wind, and like a rolling thing before the whirlwind. Psa. 2.4,5.

Isa. 19.1. The idols of Egypt shall be moved at his presence, and the heart of Egypt shall melt in the midst of it.

Isa. 23.11. He stretched out his hand over the sea, he shook the kingdoms.

Isa. 26.4. In the Lord JEHOVAH *is* everlasting strength.

Isa. 27.4. Who would set the briers *and* thorns against me in battle? I would go through them, I would burn them together.

Isa. 31.3. When the Lord shall stretch out his hand, both he that helpeth shall fall, and he that is holpen shall fall down, and they all shall fail together.

Isa. 33.3. At the noise of the tumult the people fled ; at the lifting up of thyself the nations were scattered. 13. Ye *that are* near, acknowledge my might.

Isa. 40.12. Who hath measured the waters in the hollow of his hand, and meted out heaven with the span, and comprehended the dust of the earth in a measure, and weighed the mountains in scales, and the hills in a balance? 22. He that sitteth upon the circle of the earth, and the inhabitants thereof *are* as grasshoppers ; that stretcheth out the heavens as a curtain, and spreadeth them out as a tent to dwell in. 24. He shall also blow upon them, and they shall wither, and the whirlwind shall take them away as stubble.

Isa. 40.26. Who hath created these *things*, that bringeth out their host by number : he calleth them all by names by the greatness of his might, for that *he is* strong in power ; not one faileth. 28. Hast thou not heard, *that* the everlasting God, the Lord, the Creator of the ends of the earth, fainteth not, neither is weary?

Isa. 43.13. *There is* none that can deliver out of my hand : I will work, and who shall let it? 16. The Lord, which maketh a way in the sea, and a path in the mighty waters ; 17. Which bringeth forth the chariot and horse, the army and the power.

Isa 44.27. That saith to the deep, Be dry, and I will dry up thy rivers.

Isa. 46.10. My counsel shall stand, and I will do all my pleasure : 11. I have spoken *it*, I will also bring it to pass ; I have purposed *it*, I will also do it.

Isa. 48.13. Mine hand also hath laid the

foundation of the earth, and my right hand hath spanned the heavens: *when* I call unto them, they stand up together.

Isa. 50.2. Is my hand shortened at all, that it cannot redeem? or have I no power to deliver? behold, at my rebuke I dry up the sea, I make the rivers a wilderness. 3. I clothe the heavens with blackness, and I make sackcloth their covering.

Isa. 51.10. *Art* thou not it which hath dried the sea, the waters of the great deep; that hath made the depths of the sea a way for the ransomed to pass over? *v.* 15.

Isa. 52.10. The Lord hath made bare his holy arm in the eyes of all the nations.

Isa. 59.1. The Lord's hand is not shortened, that it cannot save.

Isa. 60.16. Thy Redeemer, the mighty One of Jacob.

Isa. 63.12. With his glorious arm, dividing the water before them, to make himself an everlasting name?

Jer. 5.22. Tremble at my presence, which have placed the sand *for* the bound of the sea by a perpetual decree, that it cannot pass it: and though the waves thereof toss themselves, yet can they not prevail; though they roar, yet can they not pass over it?

Jer. 10.6. *There is* none like unto thee, O Lord; thou *art* great, and thy name *is* great in might. 13. When he uttereth his voice, *there is* a multitude of waters in the heavens, and he causeth the vapours to ascend from the ends of the earth; he maketh lightnings with rain, and bringeth forth the wind out of his treasures.

Jer. 20.11. The Lord *is* with me as a mighty terrible one: therefore my persecutors shall stumble.

Jer. 32.17. Thou hast made the heaven and the earth by thy great power and stretched out arm, *and* there is nothing too hard for thee. 27. I *am* the Lord, the God of all flesh: is there any thing too hard for me?

Jer. 50.44. Who *is* like me? and who will appoint me the time? and who *is* that shepherd that will stand before me?

Dan. 2.20. Wisdom and might are his.

Dan. 3.17. Our God whom we serve is able to deliver us from the burning fiery furnace.

Dan. 4.35. He doeth according to his will in the army of heaven, and *among* the inhabitants of the earth: and none can stay his hand, or say unto him, What doest thou?

Dan. 6.27. He delivereth and rescueth, and he worketh signs and wonders in heaven and in earth.

Joel 2.11. The Lord shall utter his voice before his army: for his camp *is* very great: for *he is* strong that executeth his word: for the day of the Lord *is* great and very terrible; and who can abide it?

Joel 3.16. The Lord also shall roar out of Zion, and utter his voice from Jerusalem; and the heavens and the earth shall shake. Amos 1.2.

Amos 4.13. He that formeth the mountains, and createth the wind, and declareth unto man what *is* his thought, that maketh the morning darkness, and treadeth upon the high places of the earth, The Lord, The God of hosts, *is* his name.

Amos 9.5. He that toucheth the land, and it shall melt. 6. *It is* he that buildeth his stories in the heaven, and hath founded his troop in the earth; he that calleth for the waters of the sea, and poureth them out upon the face of the earth.

Mic. 1.3. The Lord cometh forth out of his place, and will come down, and tread upon the high places of the earth. 4. And the mountains shall be molten under him, and the valleys shall be cleft, as wax before the fire, *and* as the waters *that are* poured down a steep place.

Nah. 1.3. The Lord *is* great in power; the Lord *hath* his way in the whirlwind and in the storm, and the clouds *are* the dust of his feet. 4. He rebuketh the sea, and maketh it dry, and drieth up all the rivers. 5. The mountains quake at him, and the hills melt, and the earth is burned at his presence, yea, the world, and all that dwell therein. 6. Who can stand before his indignation? and who can abide in the fierceness of his anger? his fury is poured out like fire, and the rocks are thrown down by him.

Hab. 3.6. He stood, and measured the earth: he beheld, and drove asunder the nations; and the everlasting mountains were scattered, the perpetual hills did bow. 9. Thy bow was made quite naked. Thou didst cleave the earth with rivers. 10. The mountains saw thee, *and* they trembled: the overflowing of the water passed by: the deep uttered his voice, *and* lifted up his hands on high. 11. The sun *and* moon stood still in their habitation: at the light of thine arrows they went, *and* at the shining of thy glittering spear. 15. Thou didst walk through the sea with thine horses, *through* the heap of great waters.

Zec. 9.14. The Lord shall be seen over them, and his arrow shall go forth as the lightning: and the Lord God shall blow the trumpet, and shall go with whirlwinds of the south.

Mat. 6.13. Thine is the kingdom, and the power.

Mat. 10.28. Fear him which is able to destroy both soul and body in hell.

Mat. 19.26. With God all things are possible.

Mar. 10.27. Luk. 18.27.

Mat. 22.29. Ye do err, not knowing the scriptures, nor the power of God.

Mar. 14.36. Father, all things *are* possible unto thee.

Luk. 1.37. With God nothing shall be impossible. 49. He that is mighty hath done to me great things. 51. He hath shewed strength with his arm; he hath scattered the proud in the imagination of their hearts.

Luk. 11.20. If I with the finger of God cast out devils, no doubt the kingdom of God is come upon you.

Rom. 1.20. His eternal power and Godhead.

Rom. 4.21. What he had promised, he was able also to perform.

1 Cor. 6.14. God hath both raised up the Lord, and will also raise up us by his own power.

2 Cor. 13.4. Though he was crucified through weakness, yet he liveth by the power of God.

Eph. 1.19. What *is* the exceeding greatness of his power to us-ward who believe, according to the working of his mighty power, 20. Which he wrought in Christ, when he raised him from the dead.

Eph. 3.20. Him that is able to do exceeding abundantly above all that we ask or think, according to the power that worketh in us.

Heb. 12.26. Whose voice then shook the earth: but now he hath promised, saying, Yet once more I shake not the earth only, but also heaven. 29. Our God *is* a consuming fire.

Jas. 4.12. One lawgiver, who is able to save and to destroy.

1 Pet. 1.5. Kept by the power of God through faith unto salvation.

Rev. 4.11. Thou art worthy, O Lord, to receive glory, and honour, and power. Rev. 5.13.

Rev. 11.17. Thou hast taken to thee thy great power, and hast reigned.

Rev. 19.6. The Lord God omnipotent reigneth.

See GOD A KING—GOD'S GLORY—PERSE-CUTORS' PUNISHMENT—SIN PUNISHMENT.

GOD OMNIPRESENT. Gen. 28.16. Surely the Lord is in this place, and I knew *it* not.

Ex. 20.24. In all places where I record my name I will come unto thee, and I will bless thee.

Deu. 4.39. Know therefore this day, and consider *it* in thine heart, that the Lord he *is* God in heaven above, and upon the earth beneath. Jos. 2.11.

1 Kin. 8.27. Will God indeed dwell on the earth? Behold, the heaven, and heaven of heavens, cannot contain thee; how much less this house that I have builded! 2 Chr. 2.6. Act. 7.48,49.

Psa. 139.3. Thou compassest my path, and my lying down. 5. Thou hast beset me behind and before, and laid thine hand upon me. 7. Whither shall I go from thy Spirit? or whither shall I flee from thy presence? 8. If I ascend up into heaven, thou *art* there; if I make my bed in hell, behold thou *art there*. 9. *If* I take the wings of the morning, *and* dwell in the uttermost parts of the sea; 10. Even there shall thy hand lead me, and thy right hand shall hold me.

Isa. 57.15. Thus saith the high and lofty One that inhabiteth eternity, whose name *is* Holy; I dwell in the high and holy *place*, with him also *that is* of a contrite and humble spirit.

Isa. 66.1. The heaven *is* my throne, and the earth *is* my footstool: where *is* the house that ye build unto me? and where *is* the place of my rest?

Jer. 23.23. *Am* I a God at hand, saith the Lord, and not a God afar off? 24. Can any hide himself in secret places that I shall not see him? saith the Lord: do not I fill heaven and earth? saith the Lord.

Jonah 1.3. Jonah rose up to flee unto Tarshish from the presence of the Lord, and went down to Joppa; and he found a ship going to Tarshish. 4. But the Lord sent out a great wind into the sea.

Act. 17.24. God, that made the world, and all things therein, seeing that he is Lord of heaven and earth, dwelleth not in temples made with hands. 27. That they should seek the Lord, if haply they might feel after him, and find him, though he be not far from every one of us: 28. For in him we live, and move, and have our being.

1 Cor. 12.6. There are diversities of operations, but it is the same God which worketh all in all.

Eph. 1.23. Him that filleth all in all.

GOD, HIS OMNISCIENCE, FOREKNOWLEDGE, AND WISDOM. Gen. 16.13. Thou God seest me.

Ex. 3.7. I have surely seen the affliction of my people which *are* in Egypt, and have heard their cry by reason of their taskmasters; for I know their sorrows. *v.* 3,7,9,19,20. Ex. 6.1. Ex. 11.1. Ex. 14.3,4.

Num. 14.27. I have heard the murmurings of the children of Israel, which they murmur against me.

Deu. 2.7. He knoweth thy walking through this great wilderness: these forty years the Lord thy God *hath been* with thee.

Deu. 31.21. I know their imagination which they go about, even now, before I have brought them into the land which I sware.

1 Sam. 2.3. The Lord *is* a God of knowledge, and by him actions are weighed. Gen. 20.6.

1 Sam. 16.7. *The LORD seeth* not as man seeth; for man looketh on the outward appearance, but the Lord looketh on the heart.

2 Sam. 7.20. Thou, Lord God, knowest thy servant.

1 Kin. 8.39. Thou, *even* thou only, knowest the hearts of all the children of men. 2 Chr. 6.30.

2 Kin. 19.27. I know thy abode, and thy going out, and thy coming in, and thy rage against me.

1 Chr. 28.9. The Lord searcheth all hearts, and understandeth all the imaginations of the thoughts.

1 Chr. 29.17. I know also, my God, that thou triest the heart.

2 Chr. 16.9. The eyes of the Lord run to and fro throughout the whole earth, to shew himself strong in the behalf of *them* whose heart *is* perfect toward him. Zec. 4.10.

Neh. 9.10. Thou knewest that they dealt proudly against them.

Job 9.4. *He is* wise in heart, and mighty in strength.

Job 12.13. With him *is* wisdom and strength, he hath counsel and understanding. 22. He discovereth deep things out of darkness, and bringeth out to light the shadow of death. *v.* 16.

Job 21.22. Shall *any* teach God knowledge? seeing he judgeth those that are high.

Job 23.10. He knoweth the way that I take.

Job 24.1. Times are not hidden from the Almighty. 23. His eyes *are* upon their ways.

Job 26.6. Hell *is* naked before him, and destruction hath no covering.

Job 28.10. His eye seeth every precious thing. 24. He looketh to the ends of the earth, *and* seeth under the whole heaven.

Job 31.4. Doth not he see my ways, and count all my steps?

Job 34.21. His eyes *are* upon the ways of man, and he seeth all his goings. 22. There *is* no darkness, nor shadow of death, where the workers of iniquity may hide themselves. 25. He knoweth their works.

Job 36.4. He that is perfect in knowledge *is* with thee. 5. *He is* mighty in strength *and* wisdom.

Job 37.16. The wondrous works of him which is perfect in knowledge.

Job 42.2. No thought can be withholden from thee.

Psa. 1.6. The Lord knoweth the way of the righteous.

Psa. 7.9. The righteous God trieth the hearts and reins.

Psa. 11.4. His eyes behold, his eyelids try, the children of men.

Psa. 33.13. The Lord looketh from heaven; he beholdeth all the sons of men. 14. From the place of his habitation he looketh upon all the inhabitants of the earth. 15. He considereth all their works.

Psa. 37.18. The Lord knoweth the days of the upright.

Psa. 38.9. Lord, all my desire is before thee; and my groaning is not hid from thee.

Psa. 44.21. Shall not God search this out? for he knoweth the secrets of the heart.

Psa. 66.7. His eyes behold the nations.

Psa. 69.19. Thou hast known my reproach, and my shame, and my dishonour: mine adversaries are all before thee.

Psa. 92.5. Thy thoughts are very deep.

Psa. 94.9. He that planted the ear, shall he not hear? he that formed the eye, shall he not see? 10. He that teacheth man knowledge, shall not he know? 11. The Lord knoweth the thoughts of man, that they are vanity. 1 Cor. 3.20.

Psa. 103.14. He knoweth our frame; he remembereth that we are dust.

Psa. 104.24. O Lord, how manifold are thy works! in wisdom hast thou made them all: the earth is full of thy riches.

Psa. 119.168. All my ways are before thee.

Psa. 121.3. He that keepeth thee will not slumber. 4. Behold, he that keepeth Israel shall neither slumber nor sleep.

Psa. 136.5. Him that by wisdom made the heavens.

Psa. 139.1. O Lord, thou hast searched me, and known me. 2. Thou knowest my downsitting and mine uprising, thou understandest my thought afar off. 3. Thou compassest my path and my lying down, and art acquainted with all my ways. 4. For there is not a word in my tongue, but, lo, O Lord, thou knowest it altogether. 12. The darkness hideth not from thee; but the night shineth as the day: the darkness and the light are both alike to thee. 14. I will praise thee; for I am fearfully and wonderfully made. 15. My substance was not hid from thee, when I was made in secret, and curiously wrought in the lowest parts of the earth. 16. Thine eyes did see my substance, yet being unperfect; and in thy book all my members were written, which in continuance were fashioned, when as yet there was none of them. v. 1-24.

Psa. 142.3. When my spirit was overwhelmed within me, then thou knewest my path.

Psa. 147.4. He telleth the number of the stars; he calleth them all by their names. 5. Great is our Lord, and of great power: his understanding is infinite. Isa. 40.26.

Pro. 3.19. The Lord by wisdom hath founded the earth; by understanding hath he established the heavens. 20. By his knowledge the depths are broken up, and the clouds drop down the dew.

Pro. 5.21. The ways of man are before

the eyes of the Lord, and he pondereth all his goings.

Pro. 15.3. The eyes of the Lord are in every place, beholding the evil and the good. 11. Hell and destruction are before the Lord: how much more then the hearts of the children of men?

Pro. 16.2. The Lord weigheth the spirits.

Pro. 17.3. The fining pot is for silver, and the furnace for gold: but the Lord trieth the hearts.

Pro. 24.12. Doth not he that pondereth the heart consider it? and he that keepeth thy soul, doth not he know it? Pro. 21.2.

Isa. 28.29. The Lord of hosts, which is wonderful in counsel, and excellent in working.

Isa. 29.15. Woe unto them that seek deep to hide their counsel from the Lord, and their works are in the dark, and they say, Who seeth us? and who knoweth us? 16. Shall the thing framed say of him that framed it, He had no understanding?

Isa. 40.13. Who hath directed the spirit of the Lord, or being his counsellor hath taught him? 14. With whom took he counsel, and who instructed him, and taught him in the path of judgment, and taught him knowledge, and shewed to him the way of understanding? 27. Why sayest thou, O Jacob, and speakest, O Israel, My way is hid from the Lord, and my judgment is passed over from my God? 28. There is no searching of his understanding.

Isa. 41.4. Who hath wrought and done it, calling the generations from the beginning? I the Lord, the first, and with the last; I am he.

Isa. 42.9. Behold, the former things are come to pass, and new things do I declare: before they spring forth I tell you of them.

Isa. 44.7. Who, as I, shall call, and shall declare it, and set it in order for me, since I appointed the ancient people? and the things that are coming, and shall come.

Isa. 45.4. I have even called thee by thy name: I have surnamed thee, though thou hast not known me. v. 21.

Isa. 46.10. Declaring the end from the beginning, and from ancient times the things that are not yet done, saying, My counsel shall stand, and I will do all my pleasure.

Isa. 48.5. I have even from the beginning declared it to thee; before it came to pass I shewed it thee: lest thou shouldest say, Mine idol hath done them, and my graven image, and my molten image, hath commanded them. 6. Thou hast heard, see all this; and will not ye declare it? I have shewed thee new things from this time, even hidden things, and thou didst not know them. v. 3.

Isa. 66.18. I know their works and their thoughts.

Jer. 5.3. O Lord, are not thine eyes upon the truth?

Jer. 10.7. Among all the wise men of the nations, and in all their kingdoms, there is none like unto thee.

Jer. 11.20. O Lord of hosts, that judgest righteously, that triest the reins and the heart. Jer. 20.12.

Jer. 17.10. I the Lord search the heart, I try the reins, even to give every man according to his ways, and according to the fruit of his doings.

Jer. 23.24. Can any hide himself in secret

places that I shall not see him? saith the Lord. Do not I fill heaven and earth? saith the Lord.

Jer. 32.19. Great in counsel, and mighty in work: for thine eyes *are* open upon all the ways of the sons of men.

Jer. 51.15. He hath established the world by his wisdom, and hath stretched out the heaven by his understanding. Jer. 10.12.

Eze. 11.5. I know the things that come into your mind, *every one of* them.

Dan. 2.20. Wisdom and might are his. 22. He revealeth the deep and secret things: he knoweth what *is* in the darkness, and the light dwelleth with him. 28. There is a God in heaven that revealeth secrets, and maketh known to the king Nebuchadnezzar what shall be in the latter days.

Amos 4.13. He that declareth unto man what *is* his thought.

Amos 9.2. Though they dig into hell, thence shall mine hand take them; though they climb up to heaven, thence will I bring them down: 3. And though they hide themselves in the top of Carmel, I will search and take them out thence; and though they be hid from my sight in the bottom of the sea, thence will I command the serpent, and he shall bite them: 4. And though they go into captivity before their enemies, thence will I command the sword, and it shall slay them.

Mat. 6.4. Thy Father which seeth in secret. 8. Your Father knoweth what things ye have need of, before ye ask him. 32. Your heavenly Father knoweth that ye have need of all these things.

Mat. 10.29. One of them shall not fall on the ground without your Father. 30. But the very hairs of your head are all numbered.

Mat. 24.36. Of that day and hour knoweth no *man*, no, not the angels of heaven, but my Father only. Mar. 13.32.

Luk. 16.15. God knoweth your hearts.

Act. 1.24. Thou, Lord, which knowest the hearts of all *men*, shew whether of these two thou hast chosen.

Act. 15.8. God, which knoweth the hearts, bare them witness. 18. Known unto God are all his works from the beginning of the world.

Rom. 8.27. He that searcheth the hearts. 29. Whom he did foreknow, he also did predestinate.

Rom. 11.33. O the depth of the riches both of the wisdom and knowledge of God! how unsearchable *are* his judgments, and his ways past finding out! 34. For who hath known the mind of the Lord? or who hath been his counsellor?

1 Cor. 1.25. The foolishness of God is wiser than men.

1 Cor. 8.3. If any man love God, the same is known of him.

Gal. 4.9. Ye have known God, or rather are known of God.

Eph. 1.8. He hath abounded toward us in all wisdom and prudence.

Eph. 3.10. The manifold wisdom of God.

1 The. 2.4. God, which trieth our hearts.

1 Tim. 1.17. Unto the King eternal, immortal, invisible, the only wise God. Rom. 16.27. Jude 25.

2 Tim. 2.19. The Lord knoweth them that are his.

Heb. 4.13. Neither is there any creature that is not manifest in his sight: but all things *are* naked and opened unto the eyes of him with whom we have to do.

1 Pet. 1.2. Elect according to the foreknowledge of God the Father.

1 Jno. 1.5. God is light, and in him is no darkness at all.

1 Jno. 3.20. If our heart condemn us, God is greater than our heart, and knoweth all things.

See also SIN SEEN BY GOD.

GOD—ONE GOD—THE ONLY GOD—GOD ONLY TO BE WORSHIPPED. Ex. 8.10. There is none like unto the Lord our God.

Ex. 9.14. *There is* none like me in all the earth.

Ex. 15.11. Who *is* like unto thee, O Lord, among the gods? who *is* like thee, glorious in holiness, fearful *in* praises, doing wonders?

Ex. 20.3. Thou shalt have no other gods before me. Deu. 5.7.

Ex. 34.14. Thou shalt worship no other god: for the Lord, whose name *is* Jealous, *is* a jealous God.

Deu. 4.35. The Lord he *is* God; *there is* none else beside him. 39. The Lord he *is* God in heaven above, and upon the earth beneath: *there is* none else.

Deu. 6.4. Hear, O Israel: The Lord our God *is* one Lord.

Deu. 10.17. The Lord your God *is* God of gods, and Lord of lords.

Deu. 32.12. The Lord alone did lead him, and *there was* no strange god with him. 39. See now that I, *even* I, *am* he, and *there is* no god with me.

Jos. 22.22. The Lord God of gods, the Lord God of gods, he knoweth.

Jud. 13.16. If thou wilt offer a burnt-offering, thou must offer it unto the Lord.

1 Sam. 2.2. *There is* none holy as the Lord: for *there is* none beside thee: neither *is there* any rock like our God.

1 Sam. 7.3. Prepare your hearts unto the Lord, and serve him only.

2 Sam. 7.22. *There is* none like thee, neither *is there any* God beside thee.

2 Sam. 22.32. Who *is* God, save the Lord? or who *is* a rock, save our God? Psa. 18.31.

1 Kin. 8.23. Lord God of Israel, *there is* no God like thee, in heaven above, or on earth beneath. 60. That all the people of the earth may know that the Lord *is* God, *and that there is* none else. 2 Chr. 6.14.

2 Kin. 17.36. Him shall ye fear, and him shall ye worship, and to him shall ye do sacrifice.

2 Kin. 19.15. Thou art the God, *even* thou alone, of all the kingdoms of the earth; thou hast made heaven and earth. Isa. 37.16. Psa. 86.10.

Ezr. 1.3. The Lord God of Israel, he *is* the God.

Neh. 9.6. Thou, *even* thou, *art* Lord alone; and the host of heaven worshippeth thee.

Psa. 96.5. All the gods of the nations *are* idols: but the Lord made the heavens.

Isa. 40.25. To whom then will ye liken me, or shall I be equal? saith the Holy One.

Isa. 42.8. I *am* the Lord: that *is* my name: and my glory will I not give to another, neither my praise to graven images.

Isa. 43.10. I *am* he: before me there was no God formed, neither shall there be after me. 11. I, *even* I, *am* the Lord; and beside me *there* is no saviour.

Isa. 44.6. I *am* the first, and I *am* the last; and beside me *there* is no God. 8. Is there a God beside me? yea, *there* is no God; I know not *any*.

Isa. 45.5. I *am* the Lord, and *there* is none else, *there* is no God beside me: 6. That they may know from the rising of the sun, and from the west, that *there* is none beside me. I *am* the Lord, and *there* is none else. 21. *There* is no God else beside me; a just God and a Saviour; *there* is none beside me. *v.* 18.

Isa. 46.5. To whom will ye liken me, and make *me* equal, and compare me, that we may be like? 9. I *am* God, and *there* is none else; *I am* God, and *there* is none like me. Isa. 45.22.

Jer. 10.6. *There* is none like unto thee, O Lord; thou *art* great, and thy name *is* great in might. 7. Who would not fear thee, O King of nations? for to thee doth it appertain: forasmuch as among all the wise *men* of the nations, and in all their kingdoms, *there* is none like unto thee. 10. The Lord *is* the true God, he *is* the living God, and an everlasting king.

Jer. 14.22. Are there *any* among the vanities of the Gentiles that can cause rain? or can the heavens give showers? *art* not thou he, O Lord our God?

Jer. 32.27. I *am* the Lord, the God of all flesh: is there any thing too hard for me?

Hos. 13.4. Thou shalt know no god but me: for *there* is no saviour beside me.

Mal. 2.10. Have we not all one father? hath not one God created us?

Mat. 4.10. Thou shalt worship the Lord thy God, and him only shalt thou serve.

Mat. 23.9. Call no *man* your father upon the earth: for one is your Father, which is in heaven.

Mar. 12.32. Thou hast said the truth: for there is one God, and there is none other but he.

Jno. 17.3. That they might know thee the only true God.

Rom. 1.25. Who changed the truth of God into a lie, and worshipped and served the creature more than the Creator, who is blessed for ever.

Rom. 3.29. *Is he* the God of the Jews only? *is he* not also of the Gentiles? Yes, of the Gentiles also.

1 Cor. 8.4. *There* is none other God but one. 5. For though there be that are called gods, whether in heaven or in earth, (as there be gods many, and lords many.) 6. But to us *there* is *but* one God, the Father, of whom *are* all things.

Gal. 3.20. God is one.

Eph. 4.6. One God and Father of all, who *is* above all, and through all, and in you all.

Col. 2.18. Let no man beguile you of your reward in a voluntary humility and worshipping of angels.

1 The. 1.9. Ye turned to God from idols to serve the living and true God.

1 Tim. 2.5. *There* is one God, and one mediator between God and men.

Rev. 19.10. I fell at his feet to worship him. And he said unto me, See *thou do it* not: I am thy fellow-servant, and of thy brethren that have the testimony of Jesus: worship God. Rev. 22.8,9.

See IDOLATRY—WORSHIP.

GOD PROTECTOR, GUIDE, AND DELIVERER. Gen. 28.15. I *am* with thee, and will keep thee in all *places* whither thou goest, and will bring thee again into this land; for I will not leave thee, until I have done *that* which I have spoken to thee of. Gen. 31.3,13.

Ex. 6.6. I will bring you out from under the burdens of the Egyptians, and I will rid you out of their bondage, and I will redeem you with a stretched out arm, and with great judgments: 7. And I will take you to me for a people, and I will be to you a God: and ye shall know that I *am* the Lord your God, which bringeth you out from under the burdens of the Egyptians. Ex. 3.17.

Ex. 8.22. I will sever in that day the land of Goshen, in which my people dwell, that no swarms *of flies* shall be there. *v.* 13. Ex. 11.7.

Ex. 12.23. When he seeth the blood upon the lintel, and on the two side posts, the Lord will pass over the door, and will not suffer the destroyer to come in unto your houses to smite *you. v.* 13.

Ex. 13.21. The Lord went before them by day in a pillar of a cloud, to lead them the way; and by night in a pillar of fire, to give them light; to go by day and night. 22. He took not away the pillar of the cloud by day, nor the pillar of fire by night, *from* before the people.

Ex. 15.16. Fear and dread shall fall upon them; by the greatness of thine arm they shall be *as* still as a stone; till thy people pass over, O Lord, till the people pass over, *which* thou hast purchased. 17. Thou shalt bring them in, and plant them in the mountain of thine inheritance, *in* the place, O Lord, *which* thou hast made for thee to dwell in, *in* the Sanctuary, O Lord, *which* thy hands have established.

Ex. 19.4. I bare you on eagles' wings, and brought you unto myself.

Ex. 23.20. I send an Angel before thee, to keep thee in the way, and to bring thee into the place which I have prepared. *v.* 21-31.

Ex. 34.24. I will cast out the nations before thee, and enlarge thy borders: neither shall any man desire thy land, when thou shalt go up to appear before the Lord thy God thrice in the year.

Num. 10.33. The ark of the covenant of the Lord went before them in the three days' journey, to search out a resting-place for them.

Num. 23.23. Surely *there* is no enchantment against Jacob, neither *is there* any divination against Israel: according to this time it shall be said of Jacob and of Israel, What hath God wrought!

Deu. 1.31. The Lord thy God bare thee, as a man doth bear his son, in all the way that ye went.

Deu. 7.21. The Lord thy God *is* among you, a mighty God and terrible. 22. The Lord thy God will put out those nations before thee by little and little.

Deu. 9.3. The Lord thy God *is* he which goeth over before thee; *as* a consuming fire he shall destroy them, and he shall bring them down before thy face: so shalt thou drive them out, and destroy them quickly, as the Lord hath said unto thee.

Deu. 11.25. There shall no man be able to

stand before you: *for* the Lord your God shall lay the fear of you and the dread of you upon all the land that ye shall tread upon.

Deu. 23.14. The Lord thy God walketh in the midst of thy camp, to deliver thee, and to give up thine enemies before thee.

Deu. 30.4. If *any* of thine be driven out unto the outmost *parts* of heaven, from thence will the Lord thy God gather thee, and from thence will he fetch thee. 20. He *is* thy life, and the length of thy days.

Deu. 33.12. The beloved of the Lord shall dwell in safety by him; *and the LORD* shall cover him all the day long, and he shall dwell between his shoulders. 25. Thy shoes *shall be* iron and brass; and as thy days, *so shall* thy strength *be*. 26. *There is* none like unto the God of Jeshurun, *who* rideth upon the heaven in thy help, and in his excellency on the sky. 27. The eternal God *is thy* refuge, and underneath *are* the everlasting arms: and he shall thrust out the enemy from before thee; and shall say, Destroy *them*. 28. Israel then shall dwell in safety alone: the fountain of Jacob *shall be* upon a land of corn and wine; also his heavens shall drop down dew. *v.* 29.

Jos. 23.10. One man of you shall chase a thousand: for the Lord your God, he *it is* that fighteth for you, as he hath promised you.

1 Sam. 2.6. The Lord killeth, and maketh alive: he bringeth down to the grave, and bringeth up. 9. He will keep the feet of his saints, and the wicked shall be silent in darkness; for by strength shall no man prevail.

1 Sam. 9.16. That he may save my people out of the hand of the Philistines: for I have looked upon my people, because their cry is come unto me.

1 Sam. 15.29. The strength of Israel.

2 Sam. 22.28. The afflicted people thou wilt save.

2 Kin. 20.6. I will deliver thee and this city out of the hand of the king of Assyria; and I will defend this city for mine own sake, and for my servant David's sake.

2 Chr. 16.9. The eyes of the Lord run to and fro throughout the whole earth, to shew himself strong in the behalf of *them* whose heart *is* perfect toward him.

2 Chr. 20.15. Be not afraid nor dismayed by reason of this great multitude: for the battle *is* not yours, but God's. 17. Ye shall not *need* to fight in this *battle;* set yourselves, stand ye *still*, and see the salvation of the Lord with you, O Judah and Jerusalem: fear not, nor be dismayed; to-morrow go out against them: for the Lord *will be* with you. Deu. 20.1.

Job 1.10. Hast not thou made an hedge about him, and about his house, and about all that he hath on every side?

Job 5.11. To set up on high those that be low; that those which mourn may be exalted to safety. 18. He maketh sore, and bindeth up: he woundeth, and his hands make whole. 19. He shall deliver thee in six troubles: yea, in seven there shall no evil touch thee. 20. In famine he shall redeem thee from death: and in war from the power of the sword. 21. Thou shalt be hid from the scourge of the tongue: neither shalt thou be afraid of destruction when it cometh. *v.* 22-24.

Job 11.18. And thou shalt be secure, because there is hope; yea, thou shalt dig *about thee,*

and thou shalt take thy rest in safety. 19. Also thou shalt lie down, and none shall make *thee* afraid.

Job 22.25. The Almighty shall be thy defence, and thou shalt have plenty of silver.

Job 33.18. He keepeth back his soul from the pit, and his life from perishing by the sword.

Job 36.7. He withdraweth not his eyes from the righteous: but with kings *are they* on the throne; yea, he doth establish them for ever, and they are exalted. 16. Even so would he have removed thee out of the strait *into* a broad place, where *there is* no straitness; and that which should be set on thy table *should* be full of fatness.

Psa. 1.6. The Lord knoweth the way of the righteous.

Psa. 10.17. Lord, thou hast heard the desire of the humble: thou wilt prepare their heart, thou wilt cause thine ear to hear: 18. To judge the fatherless and the oppressed, that the man of the earth may no more oppress.

Psa. 12.7. Thou shalt keep them, O Lord, thou shalt preserve them from this generation for ever.

Psa. 14.5. God *is* in the generation of the righteous.

Psa. 17.7. O thou that savest by thy right hand them which put their trust *in thee* from those that rise up *against* them.

Psa. 18.27. Thou wilt save the afflicted people.

Psa. 25.8. Good and upright *is* the Lord: therefore will he teach sinners in the way. 9. The meek will he guide in judgment: and the meek will he teach his way. 12. What man *is* he that feareth the Lord? him shall he teach in the way *that* he shall choose.

Psa. 31.20. Thou shalt hide them in the secret of thy presence from the pride of man: thou shalt keep them secretly in a pavilion from the strife of tongues. 23. O love the Lord, all ye his saints: *for* the Lord preserveth the faithful.

Psa. 32.6. Surely in the floods of great waters they shall not come nigh unto him. 8. I will instruct thee and teach thee in the way which thou shalt go: I will guide thee with mine eye.

Psa. 34.15. The eyes of the Lord *are* upon the righteous, and his ears *are open* unto their cry. 17. *The righteous* cry, and the Lord heareth, and delivereth them out of all their troubles. 19. Many *are* the afflictions of the righteous: but the Lord delivereth him out of them all. 20. He keepeth all his bones: not one of them is broken. *v.* 21,22.

Psa. 37.17. The Lord upholdeth the righteous. 23. The steps of a *good* man are ordered by the Lord: and he delighteth in his way. 24. Though he fall, he shall not be utterly cast down: for the Lord upholdeth *him with* his hand. 28. The Lord loveth judgment, and forsaketh not his saints; they are preserved for ever. 32. The wicked watcheth the righteous, and seeketh to slay him. 33. The Lord will not leave him in his hand, nor condemn him when he is judged.

Psa. 41.1. The Lord will deliver him in time of trouble. 2. The Lord will preserve him, and keep him alive; *and* he shall be blessed upon the earth: and thou wilt not deliver him unto the will of his enemies.

3. The Lord will strengthen him upon the bed of languishing: thou wilt make all his bed in his sickness.

Psa. 46.5. God *is* in the midst of her; she shall not be moved: God shall help her, *and that* right early. 7. The Lord of hosts *is* with us; the God of Jacob *is* our refuge.

Psa. 48.3. God is known in her palaces for a refuge.

Psa. 50.15. Call upon me in the day of trouble: I will deliver thee, and thou shalt glorify me.

Psa. 68.6. God setteth the solitary in families: he bringeth out those which are bound with chains. 22. I will bring *my people* again from the depths of the sea.

Psa. 72.14. He shall redeem their soul from deceit and violence: and precious shall their blood be in his sight.

Psa. 78.69. He built his sanctuary like high *palaces*, like the earth which he hath established for ever.

Psa. 80.1. O Shepherd of Israel, thou that leadest Joseph like a flock.

Psa. 84.11. The Lord God *is* a sun and shield: the Lord will give grace and glory.

Psa. 87.5. The Highest himself shall establish her.

Psa. 91.1. He that dwelleth in the secret place of the most High shall abide under the shadow of the Almighty. 3. Surely he shall deliver thee from the snare of the fowler, *and* from the noisome pestilence. 4. He shall cover thee with his feathers, and under his wings shalt thou trust: his truth *shall be thy* shield and buckler. A thousand shall fall at thy side, and ten thousand at thy right hand; *but* it shall not come nigh thee.

Psa. 91.9. Because thou hast made the Lord, *which is* my refuge, *even* the most High, thy habitation; 10. There shall no evil befal thee, neither shall any plague come nigh thy dwelling. 14. Because he hath set his love upon me, therefore will I deliver him: I will set him on high, because he hath known my name. 15. He shall call upon me, and I will answer him: I *will be* with him in trouble; I will deliver him, and honour him. *v.* 1-16.

Psa. 94.13. That thou mayest give him rest from the days of adversity.

Psa. 97.10. He preserveth the souls of his saints; he delivereth them out of the hand of the wicked.

Psa. 102.19. From heaven did the Lord behold the earth; 20. To hear the groaning of the prisoner; to loose those that are appointed to death.

Psa. 103.3. Who healeth all thy diseases; 4. Who redeemeth thy life from destruction. 6. The Lord executeth righteousness and judgment for all that are oppressed.

Psa. 107.9. He satisfieth the longing soul, and filleth the hungry soul with goodness. 10. Such as sit in darkness and in the shadow of death, *being* bound in affliction and iron.

Psa. 112.4. Unto the upright there ariseth light in the darkness.

Psa. 121.3. He will not suffer thy foot to be moved: he that keepeth thee will not slumber. 4. Behold, he that keepeth Israel shall neither slumber nor sleep. 7. The Lord shall preserve thee from all evil: he shall preserve thy soul. 8. The Lord shall preserve thy going out and thy coming in from this time forth, and even for evermore. *v.* 5,6.

Psa. 125.1. They that trust in the Lord *shall be* as mount Zion, *which* cannot be removed, *but* abideth for ever. 2. *As* the mountains *are* round about Jerusalem, so the Lord *is* round about his people from henceforth, even for ever. 3. For the rod of the wicked shall not rest upon the lot of the righteous.

Psa. 127.1. Except the Lord build the house, they labour in vain that build it: except the Lord keep the city, the watchman waketh *but* in vain.

Psa. 145.14. The Lord upholdeth all that fall, and raiseth up all *those that be* bowed down. 19. He will fulfil the desire of them that fear him: he also will hear their cry, and will save them. 20. The Lord preserveth all them that love him.

Psa. 146.7. The Lord looseth the prisoners. 8. The Lord openeth *the eyes of* the blind: the Lord raiseth them that are bowed down.

Psa. 147.2. The Lord doth build up Jerusalem: he gathereth together the outcasts of Israel. 3. He healeth the broken in heart, and bindeth up their wounds.

Pro. 2.7. *He is* a buckler to them that walk uprightly. 8. He keepeth the paths of judgment, and preserveth the way of his saints.

Pro. 3.6. In all thy ways acknowledge him, and he shall direct thy paths. 23. Then shalt thou walk in thy way safely, and thy foot shall not stumble. 24. When thou liest down, thou shalt not be afraid: yea, thou shalt lie down, and thy sleep shall be sweet.

Pro. 10.3. The Lord will not suffer the soul of the righteous to famish. 30. The righteous shall never be removed.

Pro. 11.8. The righteous is delivered out of trouble.

Pro. 12.3. The root of the righteous shall not be moved. 21. There shall no evil happen to the just. *v.* 13.

Pro. 14.26. In the fear of the Lord *is* strong confidence: and his children shall have a place of refuge.

Pro. 15.19. The way of the righteous *is* made plain.

Pro. 16.9. A man's heart deviseth his way: but the Lord directeth his steps. 33. The lot is cast into the lap; but the whole disposing thereof *is* of the Lord.

Pro. 19.23. The fear of the Lord *tendeth* to life: and *he that hath it* shall abide satisfied; he shall not be visited with evil.

Pro. 20.24. Man's goings *are* of the Lord.

Pro. 21.31. The horse is prepared against the day of battle: but safety *is* of the Lord.

Pro. 24.16. A just *man* falleth seven times, and riseth up again.

Isa. 4.5. The Lord will create upon every dwelling-place of mount Zion, and upon her assemblies, a cloud and smoke by day, and the shining of a flaming fire by night: for upon all the glory *shall be* a defence. 6. And there shall be a tabernacle for a shadow in the daytime from the heat, and for a place of refuge, and for a covert from storm and from rain.

Isa. 10.27. His burden shall be taken away from off thy shoulder, and his yoke from off thy neck.

Isa. 14.3. The Lord shall give thee rest from thy sorrow, and from thy fear, and from the hard bondage wherein thou wast made to serve.

Isa. 26.7. Thou, most upright, dost weigh the path of the just.

Isa. 27.3. I the Lord do keep it; I will water it every moment : lest *any* hurt it, I will keep it night and day.

Isa. 30.21. Thine ears shall hear a word behind thee, saying, This *is* the way, walk ye in it, when ye turn to the right hand, and when ye turn to the left. 26. The light of the moon shall be as the light of the sun, and the light of the sun shall be sevenfold, as the light of seven days, in the day that the Lord bindeth up the breach of his people, and healeth the stroke of their wound.

Isa. 31.5. As birds flying, so will the Lord of hosts defend Jerusalem ; defending also he will deliver *it*; *and* passing over he will preserve *it*. 9. His princes shall be afraid of the ensign, saith the Lord, whose fire *is* in Zion, and his furnace in Jerusalem. *v.* 4.

Isa. 32.2. A man shall be as an hiding-place from the wind, and a covert from the tempest ; as rivers of water in a dry place, as the shadow of a great rock in a weary land. 18. My people shall dwell in a peaceable habitation, and in sure dwellings, and in quiet resting places.

Isa. 33.16. He shall dwell on high: his place of defence *shall be* the munitions of rocks. 20. Thine eyes shall see Jerusalem a quiet habitation, a tabernacle *that* shall not be taken down ; not one of the stakes thereof shall ever be removed, neither shall any of the cords thereof be broken.

Isa. 35.9. No lion shall be there, nor *any* ravenous beast shall go up thereon, it shall not be found there ; but the redeemed shall walk *there*.

Isa. 37.32. Out of Jerusalem shall go forth a remnant, and they that escape out of mount Zion : the zeal of the Lord of hosts shall do this. 35. I will defend this city to save it for mine own sake, and for my servant David's sake.

Isa. 40.11. He shall feed his flock like a shepherd : he shall gather the lambs with his arm, and carry *them* in his bosom, *and* shall gently lead those that are with young. 29. He giveth power to the faint ; and to *them that have* no might he increaseth strength. 31. They that wait upon the Lord shall renew *their* strength ; they shall mount up with wings as eagles ; they shall run, and not be weary ; *and* they shall walk, and not faint.

Isa. 42.13. The Lord shall go forth as a mighty man, he shall stir up jealousy like a man of war : he shall cry, yea, roar ; he shall prevail against his enemies. 16. I will bring the blind by a way *that* they knew not ; I will lead them in paths *that* they have not known : I will make darkness light before them, and crooked things straight. These things will I do unto them, and not forsake them.

Isa. 43.2. When thou· passest through the waters, I *will* be with thee ; and through the rivers, they shall not overflow thee : when thou walkest through the fire, thou shalt not be burned ; neither shall the flame kindle upon thee.

Isa. 45.2. I will go before thee, and make the crooked places straight : I will break in pieces the gates of brass, and cut in sunder the bars of iron. *v.* 4.

Isa. 46.4. And *even* to *your* old age I *am* he ; and *even* to hoar hairs will I carry *you:* I have made, and I will bear ; even I will carry, and will deliver *you. v.* 3.

Isa. 48.17. I *am* the Lord thy God, which teacheth thee to profit, which leadeth thee by the way *that* thou shouldest go.

Isa. 49.9. They shall feed in the ways, and their pastures *shall be* in all high places. 10. They shall not hunger nor thirst ; neither shall the heat nor sun smite them: for he that hath mercy on them shall lead them, even by the springs of water shall he guide them. 17. Thy children shall make haste ; thy destroyers and they that made thee waste shall go forth of thee. 25. Even the captives of the mighty shall be taken away, and the prey of the terrible shall be delivered : for I will contend with him that contendeth with thee, and I will save thy children.

Isa. 51.9. Awake, awake, put on strength, O arm of the Lord ; awake, as in the ancient days, in the generations of old. 10. *Art* thou not it which hath dried the sea, the waters of the great deep ; that hath made the depths of the sea a way for the ransomed to pass over?

Isa. 51.22. Thus saith thy Lord the Lord, and thy God *that* pleadeth the cause of his people, Behold, I have taken out of thine hand the cup of trembling, *even* the dregs of the cup of my fury ; thou shalt no more drink it again.

Isa. 52.12. Ye shall not go out with haste, nor go by flight : for the Lord will go before you ; and the God of Israel *will be* your rereward.

Isa. 54.14. In righteousness shalt thou be established : thou shalt be far from oppression ; for thou shalt not fear : and from terror ; for it shall not come near thee. 15. Behold, they shall surely gather together, *but* not by me : whosoever shall gather together against thee shall fall for thy sake. 17. No weapon that is formed against thee shall prosper ; and every tongue *that* shall rise against thee in judgment thou shalt condemn. This *is* the heritage of the servants of the Lord, and their righteousness *is* of me, saith the Lord.

Isa. 57.14. Cast ye up, cast ye up, prepare the way, take up the stumbling-block out of the way of my people.

Isa. 58.11. The Lord shall guide thee continually, and satisfy thy soul in drought, and make fat thy bones : and thou shalt be like a watered garden, and like a spring of water, whose waters fail not.

Isa. 59.19. When the enemy shall come in like a flood, the Spirit of the Lord shall lift up a standard against them.

Isa. 63.9. In all their affliction he was afflicted, and the angel of his presence saved them : in his love and in his pity he redeemed them ; and he bare them, and carried them all the days of old.

Jer. 2.3. Israel *was* holiness unto the Lord, *and* the first-fruits of his increase : all that devour him shall offend ; evil shall come upon them, saith the Lord. 6. The Lord that brought us up out of the land of Egypt, that led us through the wilderness ; through a land of deserts, and of pits ; through a land of drought, and of the shadow of death ; through a land that no man passed through, and where no man dwelt? 20. For of old time I have broken thy yoke, and burst thy bands.

Jer. 3.4. My father, thou *art* the guide of my youth.

Jer. 11.4. The day *that* I brought them forth out of the land of Egypt, from the iron furnace.

Jer. 30.7. It *is* even the time of Jacob's trouble; but he shall be saved out of it. 8. I will break his yoke from off thy neck, and will burst thy bonds, and strangers shall no more serve themselves of him. 11. I *am* with thee, saith the Lord, to save thee: though I make a full end of all nations whither I have scattered thee, yet will I not make a full end of thee. *v.* 17.

Jer. 31.9. They shall come with weeping, and with supplications will I lead them : I will cause them to walk by the rivers of waters in a straight way, wherein they shall not stumble: for I am a father to Israel, and Ephraim *is* my firstborn. 10. He that scattered Israel will gather him, and keep him, as a shepherd *doth* his flock. 28. Like as I have watched over them, to pluck up, and to break down, and to throw down, and to destroy, and to afflict ; so will I watch over them, to build, and to plant, saith the Lord.

Eze. 9.4. Set a mark upon the foreheads of the men that sigh and that cry for all the abominations that be done in the midst thereof. 6. But come not near any man upon whom *is* the mark; and begin at my sanctuary.

Eze. 11.16. Although I have scattered them among the countries, yet will I be to them as a little sanctuary in the countries where they shall come.

Eze. 34.11. Behold, I, *even* I, will both search my sheep, and seek them out. 12. As a shepherd seeketh out his flock in the day that he is among his sheep *that are* scattered ; so will I seek out my sheep, and will deliver them out of all places where they have been scattered in the cloudy and dark day. 15. I will feed my flock, and I will cause them to lie down, saith the Lord God. 16. I will seek that which was lost, and bring again that which was driven away, and will bind up *that which was* broken, and will strengthen that which was sick. *v.* 13,14.

Dan. 3.27. Upon whose bodies the fire had no power, nor was an hair of their head singed, neither were their coats changed, nor the smell of fire had passed on them. 18. Blessed *be* the God of Shadrach, Meshach, and Abednego, who hath sent his angel, and delivered his servants that trusted in him.

Dan. 12.1. Shall Michael stand up, the great prince which standeth for the children of thy people : and at that time thy people shall be delivered, every one that shall be found written in the book.

Hos. 2.18. Will I make a covenant for them with the beasts of the field, and with the fowls of heaven, and *with* the creeping things of the ground : and I will break the bow and the sword and the battle out of the earth, and will make them to lie down safely.

Hos. 13.10. I will be thy king: where *is any other* that may save thee in all thy cities?

Joel 2.18. Then will the Lord be jealous for his land, and pity his people.

Amos 5.9. That strengtheneth the spoiled

against the strong, so that the spoiled shall come against the fortress.

Amos 9.9. I will sift the house of Israel among all nations, like as *corn* is sifted in a sieve, yet shall not the least grain fall upon the earth.

Mic. 2.13. Their king shall pass before them, and the Lord on the head of them.

Nah. 1.12. Though I have afflicted thee, I will afflict thee no more.

Zeph. 3.13. They shall feed and lie down, and none shall make *them* afraid. 15. The Lord hath taken away thy judgments, he hath cast out thine enemy: the king of Israel, *even* the Lord, *is* in the midst of thee: thou shalt not see evil any more. 17. The Lord thy God, in the midst of thee *is* mighty ; he will save, he will rejoice over thee with joy ; he will rest in his love, he will joy over thee with singing. 19. I will undo all that afflict thee: and I will save her that halteth, and gather her that was driven out ; and I will get them praise and fame in every land where they have been put to shame. *v.* 20.

Zec. 2.5. I, saith the Lord, will be unto her a wall of fire round about, and will be the glory in the midst of her. 8. He that toucheth you toucheth the apple of his eye.

Zec. 4.6. Not by might, nor by power, but by my Spirit, saith the Lord of hosts. 7. Who *art* thou, O great mountain ? before Zerubbabel *thou shalt become* a plain: and he shall bring forth the head-stone *thereof with* shoutings, *crying*, Grace, grace, unto it. 10. Who hath despised the day of small things ? for they shall rejoice, and shall see the plummet in the hand of Zerubbabel *with* those seven ; they *are* the eyes of the Lord, which run to and fro through the whole earth.

Zec. 9.8. I will encamp about mine house because of the army, because of him that passeth by, and because of him that returneth: and no oppressor shall pass through them any more: for now have I seen with mine eyes. 14. The Lord shall be seen over them, and his arrow shall go forth as the lightning: and the Lord God shall blow the trumpet, and shall go with whirlwinds of the south. 15. The Lord of hosts shall defend them. 16. The Lord their God shall save them in that day as the flock of his people: for *they shall be as* the stones of a crown, lifted up as an ensign upon his land.

Zec. 12.8. Shall the Lord defend the inhabitants of Jerusalem ; and he that is feeble among them at that day shall be as David ; and the house of David *shall be* as God, as the angel of the Lord before them.

Mat. 10.29. Are not two sparrows sold for a farthing ? and one of them shall not fall on the ground without your Father. 30. But the very hairs of your head are all numbered. 31. Fear ye not therefore, ye are of more value than many sparrows. Luk. 12.6,7.

Mat. 24.22. For the elect's sake those days shall be shortened. 31. He shall send his angels with a great sound of a trumpet, and they shall gather together his elect from the four winds, from one end of heaven to the other. Mar. 13.20.

Luk. 18.7. Shall not God avenge his own elect, which cry day and night unto him, though he bear long with them ? 8. I tell you that he will avenge them speedily.

Luk. 21.18. There shall not an hair of your head perish.

Act. 17.28. In him we live, and move, and have our being.

Rom. 8.28. We know that all things work together for good to them that love God.

1 Cor. 10.13. God is faithful, who will not suffer you to be tempted above that ye are able; but will with the temptation also make a way to escape, that ye may be able to bear it.

2 The. 3.3. The Lord is faithful, who shall stablish you, and keep you from evil.

Heb. 1.14. Are they not all ministering spirits, sent forth to minister for them who shall be heirs of salvation?

1 Pet. 3.12. The eyes of the Lord are over the righteous, and his ears are open unto their prayers. 13. Who is he that will harm you, if ye be followers of that which is good?

2 Pet. 2.9. The Lord knoweth how to deliver the godly out of temptations.

Rev. 3.10. I also will keep thee from the hour of temptation, which shall come upon all the world, to try them that dwell upon the earth.

Rev. 7.3. Hurt not the earth, neither the sea, nor the trees, till we have sealed the servants of our God in their foreheads.

Rev. 12.6. The woman fled into the wilderness, where she hath a place prepared of God, that they should feed her there.

GOD PROTECTOR, &c.—HIS CARE EXEMPLIFIED: To Noah, Gen. 6.18. Gen. 7. Gen. 8.1-19. Abraham and Sarah, Gen. 12.17. Gen. 20.3. Lot, Gen. 19. Hagar, Gen. 21.17-19. Jacob, Gen. 31.24,29. Gen. 33.3-10. Gen. 35.5. Joseph, Gen. 39.2,21.

Moses, Ex. 2. Israelites in Egypt, Ex. 1.9-12. Ex. 2.23-25. Ex. 3.7-9. Ex. 9.4-7. Ex. 10.23. Ex. 12.13. Deliverance from Egypt, Ex. 13.3,17-22. Ex. 14. Ex. 19.4. Lev. 26.13. In the wilderness, Ex. 40.36-38. Num. 9.17-23. Num. 10.33. Num. 22.12. Num. 23.8. Deu. 1.31. Deu. 23.5.

Joshua's victories, Jos. c. 6 to 11. Jos. 24.11-13. Israelites under the Judges, Jud. 3.9,15-31. Jud. 4.15-24. Jud. 8.28. Jud. 11.32. 1 Sam. 7.10. Dav'd, 2 Sam. 7. 2 Sam. 8.14. 1 Chr. 11.13,14. Ahab, 1 Kin. 20. Samaria, 2 Kin. 7.18. Jehoahaz, 2 Kin. 13.2-5. Jeroboam II., 2 Kin. 14.26,27. Rehoboam, 2 Chr. 12.2-12., Abijah, 2 Chr. 13.4-18. Asa, 2 Chr. 14.11-14. Jehoshaphat, 2 Chr. 17.10. 2 Chr. 20.

Hezekiah, 2 Kin. 19. Manasseh, 2 Chr. 33.12,13. Jews, Ezr. 5. Ezr. 6. Neh. 4.7-15. Est. 8.8-17. Est. 9. Eze. 9.4,6. Job, Job 1.9-12. Job 2.6. Jeremiah and Baruch, Jer. 36.26. Daniel, &c., Dan. 2.18-23. Dan. 3.27. Dan. 6. Jonah, Jonah 1.17. Wise men, Mat. 2.12. Jesus and his parents, Mat. 2.13,19-22. Peter, Act. 12.3-17. Paul and Silas, Act. 16.26-39. Paul, Act. 27.24. Act. 28.5,6.

See AFFLICTION, COMFORT IN.—FAITH.—GOD SAVIOUR.—POOR, GOD'S CARE OF.—GOD, FAVOUR OF.

GOD, HIS PROVIDENCE MISUNDERSTOOD—HIS PROVIDENCE MYSTERIOUS. Job 10.15. If I be wicked, woe unto me; and if I be righteous, yet will I not lift up my head. I am full of confusion.

Job 12.6. The tabernacle of robbers prosper, and they that provoke God are secure; into whose hand God bringeth abundantly.

Job 17.8. Upright men shall be astonied at this.

Job 21.7. Wherefore do the wicked live, become old, yea, are mighty in power?

Job 24.1. Why, seeing times are not hidden from the Almighty, do they that know him, not see his days? v. 1-12.

Job 33.13. Why dost thou strive against him? for he giveth not account of any of his matters.

Psa. 10.5. Thy judgments are far above out of his sight.

Psa. 73.2. As for me, my feet were almost gone; my steps had well nigh slipped. 3. For I was envious at the foolish, when I saw the prosperity of the wicked. 13. Verily I have cleansed my heart in vain, and washed my hands in innocency. 14. For all the day long have I been plagued, and chastened every morning. 15. If I say, I will speak thus; behold, I should offend against the generation of thy children. 16. When I thought to know this, it was too painful for me; 17. Until I went into the sanctuary of God: then understood I their end. v. 4,5,12.

Psa. 89.47. Wherefore hast thou made all men in vain?

Pro. 28.5. Evil men understand not judgment.

Ecc. 7.15. A just man that perisheth in his righteousness, and there is a wicked man that prolongeth his life in his wickedness.

Ecc. 8.14. There be just men, unto whom it happeneth according to the work of the wicked; again, there be wicked men, to whom it happeneth according to the work of the righteous. v. 12-17.

Ecc. 9.2. All things come alike to all: there is one event to the righteous, and to the wicked; to the good and to the clean, and to the unclean; to him that sacrificeth, and to him that sacrificeth not: as is the good, so is the sinner; and he that sweareth, as he that feareth an oath. 11. The race is not to the swift, nor the battle to the strong, neither yet bread to the wise, nor yet riches to men of understanding, nor yet favour to men of skill; but time and chance happeneth to them all.

Jer. 12.1. Righteous art thou, O Lord, when I plead with thee: yet let me talk with thee of thy judgments: Wherefore doth the way of the wicked prosper? wherefore are all they happy that deal very treacherously? 2. Thou hast planted them, yea, they have taken root: they grow, yea, they bring forth fruit: thou art near in their mouth, and far from their reins.

Jer. 50.7. Their adversaries said, We offend not, because they have sinned against the Lord.

Dan. 12.10. None of the wicked shall understand.

Hab. 1.2. O Lord, how long shall I cry, and thou wilt not hear! even cry out unto thee of violence, and thou wilt not save! 3. Why dost thou shew me iniquity, and cause me to behold grievance? 11. Then shall his mind change, and he shall pass over, and offend, imputing this his power unto his god. 13. Wherefore lookest thou upon them that deal treacherously, and holdest thy tongue when the wicked devoureth the man that is more righteous than he? 14. And makest men as the fishes of the sea, as the creeping things, that have no ruler over them?

Mic. 4.12. They know not the thoughts of

the Lord, neither understand they his counsel: for he shall gather them as the sheaves into the floor.

Mal. 3.14. Ye have said, It *is* vain to serve God: and what profit *is it* that we have kept his ordinance, and that we have walked mournfully before the Lord of hosts? 15. And now we call the proud happy; yea, they that work wickedness are set up; yea, *they that* tempt God are even delivered.

See MAN'S IGNORANCE—SPIRITUAL BLINDNESS.

GOD, HIS PROVIDENCE OVERRULING. Gen. 50.20. As for you, ye thought evil against me; *but* God meant it unto good, to bring to pass, as *it is* this day, to save much people alive. Gen. 45.5-7. Psa. 105.17.

Ex. 14.4. I will harden Pharaoh's heart, that he shall follow after them; and I will be honoured upon Pharaoh.

Num. 23.7. Balak the king of Moab hath brought me, *saying*, Come, curse me Jacob, and come, defy Israel. 8. How shall I curse, whom God hath not cursed? or how shall I defy, *whom* the Lord hath not defied? 23. Surely *there is* no enchantment against Jacob, neither *is there* any divination against Israel: according to this time it shall be said of Jacob and of Israel, What hath God wrought! *v.*1-30. Num. 22.12-18. Num. 24.10-13.

Deu. 2.30. Sihon would not let us pass by him: for the Lord thy God hardened his spirit, and made his heart obstinate, that he might deliver him into thy hand, as *appeareth* this day. Jos. 11.20.

Deu. 23.5. The Lord thy God would not hearken unto Balaam; but the Lord thy God turnéd the curse into a blessing unto thee, because the Lord thy God loved thee.

Jud. 9.23. God sent an evil spirit between Abimelech and the men of Shechem. 24. That the cruelty *done* to the threescore and ten sons of Jerubbaal might come, and their blood be laid upon Abimelech their brother, which slew them; and upon the men of Shechem, which aided him in the killing of his brethren.

2 Sam. 17.14. The Lord had appointed to defeat the good counsel of Ahithophel, to the intent that the Lord might bring evil upon Absalom.

1 Kin. 12.15. The king hearkened not unto the people; for the cause was from the Lord, that he might perform his saying, which the Lord spake by Ahijah the Shilonite unto Jeroboam. 1 Kin. 11.14-40. 2 Chr. 10.15.

1 Chr. 5.26. The God of Israel stirred up the spirit of Pul, and the spirit of Tilgath, and he carried them away.

2 Chr. 36.22. That the word of the Lord *spoken* by the mouth of Jeremiah might be accomplished, the Lord stirred up the spirit of Cyrus king of Persia. Ezr. 1.1.

Ezr. 5.5. The eye of their God was upon the elders of the Jews, that they could not cause them to cease, till the matter came to Darius.

Ezr. 6.22. The Lord had made them joyful, and turned the heart of the king of Assyria unto them, to strengthen their hands in the work of the house of God.

Neh. 6.16. They were much cast down in their own eyes: for they perceived that this work was wrought of our God.

Est. 7.10. So they hanged Haman on the gallows that he had prepared for Mordecai. Est. 6.1-12. Est. 9.25.

Est. 9.1. In the day that the enemies of the Jews hoped to have power over them, (though it was turned to the contrary, that the Jews had rule over them that hated them.)

Job 5.12. He disappointeth the devices of the crafty, so that their hands cannot perform *their* enterprise. 13. He taketh the wise in their own craftiness: and the counsel of the froward is carried headlong. Isa. 8.9,10.

Psa. 17.13. Deliver my soul from the wicked, *which is* thy sword: 14. From men *which are* thy hand, O Lord.

Psa. 75.7. He putteth down one, and setteth up another.

Psa. 76.10. Surely the wrath of man shall praise thee: the remainder of wrath shalt thou restrain.

Pro. 13.22. The wealth of the sinner *is* laid up for the just.

Pro. 14.19. The evil bow before the good; and the wicked at the gates of the righteous.

Pro. 16.7. When a man's ways please the Lord, he maketh even his enemies to be at peace with him.

Pro. 16.33. The lot is cast into the lap; but the whole disposing thereof *is* of the Lord.

Pro. 19.21. *There are* many devices in a man's heart; nevertheless the counsel of the Lord, that shall stand.

Pro. 21.1. The king's heart *is* in the hand of the Lord, *as* the rivers of water: he turneth it whithersoever he will. 18. The wicked *shall be* a ransom for the righteous, and the transgressor for the upright.

Pro. 28.8. He that by usury and unjust gain increaseth his substance, he shall gather it for him that will pity the poor.

Ecc. 2.26. To the sinner he giveth travail, to gather and to heap up, that he may give to *him that* is good before God.

Ecc. 3.1. To every *thing there is* a season, and a time to every purpose under the heaven. 10. I have seen the travail, which God hath given to the sons of men to be exercised in it.

Isa. 10.5. O Assyrian, the rod of mine anger, and the staff in their hand is mine indignation. 6. I will send him against an hypocritical nation, and against the people of my wrath will I give him a charge. 7. Howbeit he meaneth not so, neither doth his heart think so; but *it is* in his heart to destroy and cut off nations not a few.

Isa. 13.3. I have commanded my sanctified ones, I have also called my mighty ones for mine anger, *even* them that rejoice in my highness. 4. The Lord of hosts mustereth the host of the battle. 5. They come from a far country, from the end of heaven, *even* the Lord, and the weapons of his indignation, to destroy the whole land.

Isa. 41.2. Who raised up the righteous *man* from the east, called him to his foot, gave the nations before him, and made *him* rule over kings? he gave *them* as the dust to his sword, *and* as driven stubble to his bow. 4. Who hath wrought and done *it*, calling the generations from the beginning? I the Lord, the first, and with the last; I *am* he.

Isa. 43.14. For your sake I have sent to Babylon, and have brought down all their nobles, and the Chaldeans, whose cry *is* in the ships.

Isa. 44.28. That saith of Cyrus, *He is* my shepherd, and shall perform all my pleasure: even saying to Jerusalem, Thou shalt be built ; and to the temple, Thy foundation shall be laid.

Isa. 45.5. I girded thee, though thou hast not known me. 13. I have raised him up in righteousness, and I will direct all his ways : he shall build my city, and he shall let go my captives, not for price nor reward, saith the Lord of hosts. *v.* 1-5.

Isa. 48.14. The Lord hath loved him : he will do his pleasure on Babylon, and his arm *shall be on* the Chaldeans. 15. I, *even* I, have spoken ; yea, I have called him : I have brought him, and he shall make his way prosperous.

Isa. 54.16. I have created the smith that bloweth the coals in the fire, and that bringeth forth an instrument for his work ; and I have created the waster to destroy. 17. No weapon that is formed against thee shall prosper ; and every tongue *that* shall rise against thee in judgment thou shalt condemn.

Jer. 51.20. Thou *art* my battle ax *and* weapons of war : for with thee will I break in pieces the nations, and with thee will I destroy kingdoms ; 21. And with thee will I break in pieces the horse and his rider ; and with thee will I break in pieces the chariot and his rider.

Jer. 52.3. Through the anger of the Lord it came to pass in Jerusalem and Judah, till he had cast them out from his presence, that Zedekiah rebelled against the king of Babylon.

Eze. 21.26. Remove the diadem, and take off the crown : this *shall* not *be* the same : exalt *him that is* low, and abase *him that is* high. 27. I will overturn, overturn, overturn, it : and it shall be no *more*, until he come whose right it is ; and I will give it *him.*

Eze. 29.19. I will give the land of Egypt unto Nebuchadrezzar king of Babylon ; and he shall take her multitude, and take her spoil, and take her prey ; and it shall be the wages for his army. 20. I have given him the land of Egypt *for* his labour wherewith he served against it, because they wrought for me, saith the Lord God.

Dan. 11.27. Both these kings' hearts *shall be* to do mischief, and they shall speak lies at one table ; but it shall not prosper : for yet the end *shall be* at the time appointed.

Act. 3.17. I wot that through ignorance ye did *it*, as *did* also your rulers. 18. But those things, which God before had shewed by the mouth of all his prophets, that Christ should suffer, he hath so fulfilled.

Rom. 1.10. Making request, if by any means now at length I might have a prosperous journey by the will of God to come unto you.

Rom. 8.28. All things work together for good to them that love God, to them who are the called according to *his* purpose.

1 Cor. 4.19. I will come to you shortly, if the Lord will.

1 Cor. 16.7. I trust to tarry a while with you, if the Lord permit.

Phil. 1.12. The things *which happened* unto me have fallen out rather unto the furtherance of the gospel.

Philm. 15. Perhaps he therefore departed for a season, that thou shouldest receive him for ever.

Jas. 4.15. Ye *ought* to say, If the Lord will, we shall live, and do this, or that.

Rev. 17.17. God hath put in their hearts to fulfil his will, and to agree, and give their kingdom unto the beast, until the words of God shall be fulfilled.

See GOD KING—PREDESTINATION—AFFLIC-TION FROM GOD—WAR FROM GOD.—GOD, GOODNESS OF, IN PROVIDENCE.

GOD A SAVIOUR. Ex. 15.2. The Lord *is* my strength and song, and he is become my salvation.

Deu. 32.15. The Rock of his salvation. 31. Their rock *is* not as our Rock. 39. I kill, and I make alive ; I wound, and I heal.

Deu. 33.29. Happy *art* thou, O Israel : who *is* like unto thee, O people saved by the Lord, the shield of thy help, and who *is* the sword of thy excellency ! *v.* 25-29.

Job 33.24. He is gracious unto him, and saith, Deliver him from going down to the pit : I have found a ransom. 27. *If any* say, I have sinned, and perverted *that which was* right, and it profited me not ; 28. He will deliver his soul from going into the pit, and his life shall see the light. 29. Lo, all these *things* worketh God oftentimes with man, 30. To bring back his soul from the pit, to be enlightened with the light of the living.

Psa. 3.8. Salvation *belongeth* unto the Lord : thy blessing *is* upon thy people.

Psa. 18.30. He *is* a buckler to all those that trust in him. 31. For who *is* God save the Lord ? or who *is* a rock save our God ? 1 Sam. 2.2.

Psa. 25.5. Thou *art* the God of my salvation ; on thee do I wait all the day.

Psa. 27.1. The Lord *is* my light and my salvation ; whom shall I fear ? the Lord *is* the strength of my life ; of whom shall I be afraid ?

Psa. 28.8. The Lord *is* their strength, and he *is* the saving strength of his anointed.

Psa. 31.5. Into thine hand I commit my spirit : thou hast redeemed me, O Lord God of truth.

Psa. 33.18. The eye of the Lord *is* upon them that fear him, upon them that hope in his mercy ; 19. To deliver their soul from death.

Psa. 34.22. The Lord redeemeth the soul of his servants : and none of them that trust in him shall be desolate.

Psa. 36.9. With thee *is* the fountain of life : in thy light shall we see light.

Psa. 37.39. The salvation of the righteous *is* of the Lord : he *is* their strength in the time of trouble. 40. The Lord shall help them, and deliver them : he shall deliver them from the wicked, and save them, because they trust in him.

Psa. 50.23. To him that ordereth *his* conversation *aright* will I shew the salvation of God.

Psa. 62.1. Truly my soul waiteth upon God : from him *cometh* my salvation. 6. He only *is* my rock and my salvation : *he is* my defence ; I shall not be moved. 7. In God *is* my salvation and my glory : the rock of my strength, *and* my refuge, *is* in God. *v.* 2.

Psa. 65.5. O God of our salvation ; *who art* the confidence of all the ends of the earth, and of them that are afar off *upon* the sea.

Psa. 68.19. *Who* daily loadeth us *with benefits, even* the God of our salvation. 20. *He that is* our God is the God of salvation ; and unto God the Lord *belong* the issues from death.

Psa. 71.16. I will go in the strength of the Lord God: I will make mention of thy righteousness, *even* of thine only.

Psa. 74.12. God *is* my King of old, working salvation in the midst of the earth.

Psa. 76.9. When God arose to judgment, to save all the meek of the earth.

Psa. 85.9. His salvation *is* nigh them that fear him; that glory may dwell in our land.

Psa. 96.2. Shew forth his salvation from day to day.

Psa. 98.2. The Lord hath made known his salvation: his righteousness hath he openly shewed in the sight of the heathen. 3. He hath remembered his mercy and his truth toward the house of Israel: all the ends of the earth have seen the salvation of our God.

Psa. 111.9. He sent redemption unto his people: he hath commanded his covenant for ever.

Psa. 118.27. God *is* the Lord, which hath shewed us light.

Psa. 121.7. The Lord shall preserve thee from all evil: he shall preserve thy soul.

Psa. 133.3. There the Lord commanded the blessing, *even* life for evermore.

Psa. 149.4. The Lord taketh pleasure in his people: he will beautify the meek with salvation.

Isa. 12.2. Behold, God *is* my salvation; I will trust, and not be afraid: for the Lord JEHOVAH *is* my strength an *my* song; he also is become my salvation.

Isa. 25.4. Thou hast been a strength to the poor, a strength to the needy in his distress, a refuge from the storm, a shadow from the heat, when the blast of the terrible ones *is* as a storm *against* the wall. 9. Lo, this *is* our God; we have waited for him, and he will save us: this *is* the Lord; we have waited for him, we will be glad and rejoice in his salvation.

Isa. 35.4. Your God will come *with* vengeance, *even* God *with* a recompence; he will come and save you.

Isa. 41.14. Fear not, thou worm Jacob, *and* ye men of Israel; I will help thee, saith the Lord, and thy redeemer, the Holy One of Israel. Isa. 48.17.

Isa. 43.3. I *am* the Lord thy God, the Holy One of Israel, thy Saviour: I gave Egypt *for* thy ransom. 11. I, *even* I, *am* the Lord; and beside me *there is* no saviour. 12. I have declared, and have saved, and I have shewed, when *there was* no strange *god* among you. *v. 14.*

Isa. 44.22. Return unto me, for I have redeemed thee. 23. Break forth into singing, ye mountains, O forest, and every tree therein: for the Lord hath redeemed Jacob, and glorified himself in Israel. 24. Thus saith the Lord, thy redeemer, and he that formed thee from the womb. *v. 6.*

Isa. 45.15. Verily thou *art* a God that hidest thyself, O God of Israel, the Saviour. 17. Israel shall be saved in the Lord with an everlasting salvation: ye shall not be ashamed nor confounded world without end. 21. *There is* no God else beside me; a just God and a Saviour; *there is* none beside me. 22. Look unto me, and be ye saved, all the ends of the earth: for I *am* God, and *there is* none else.

Isa. 46.12. Hearken unto me, ye stout-

hearted, that *are* far from righteousness: 13. I bring near my righteousness; it shall not be far off, and my salvation shall not tarry: and I will place salvation in Zion for Israel my glory.

Isa. 47.4. *As for* our redeemer, the Lord of hosts *is* his name, the Holy One of Israel.

Isa. 49.25. I will save thy children.

Isa. 50.2. Is my hand shortened at all, that it cannot redeem? or have I no power to deliver?

Isa. 52.3. Ye have sold yourselves for nought; and ye shall be redeemed without money. 9. The Lord hath comforted his people, he hath redeemed Jerusalem. 10. The Lord hath made bare his holy arm in the eyes of all the nations; and all the ends of the earth shall see the salvation of our God.

Isa. 60.16. Thou shalt know that I the Lord *am* thy Saviour and thy Redeemer, the mighty One of Jacob.

Isa. 63.8. He said, Surely they *are* my people, children *that* will not lie: so he was their Saviour.

Jer. 3.23. In vain *is salvation hoped for* from the hills, *and from* the multitude of mountains: truly in the Lord our God *is* the salvation of Israel.

Jer. 8.22. *Is there* no balm in Gilead; *is there* no physician there? why then is not the health of the daughter of my people recovered?

Jer. 14.8. O the hope of Israel, the saviour thereof in time of trouble, why shouldest thou be as a stranger in the land.

Jer. 30.17. I will restore health unto thee, and I will heal thee of thy wounds, saith the Lord, because they called thee an Outcast, *saying*, This *is* Zion, whom no man seeketh after.

Jer. 33.6. I will bring it health and cure, and I will cure them, and will reveal unto them the abundance of peace and truth.

Jer. 50.34. Their Redeemer *is* strong; the Lord of hosts *is* his name: he shall throughly plead their cause.

Eze. 37.23. I will save them out of all their dwelling-places, wherein they have sinned, and will cleanse them: so shall they be my people, and I will be their God.

Hos. 1.7. I will have mercy upon the house of Judah, and will save them by the Lord their God.

Hos. 13.4. Thou shalt know no god but me: for *there is* no saviour beside me. 9. O Israel, thou hast destroyed thyself; but in me *is* thine help.

Joel 3.16. The Lord *will be* the hope of his people, and the strength of the children of Israel.

Jonah 2.9. Salvation *is* of the Lord.

Zec. 9.11. By the blood of thy covenant I have sent forth thy prisoners out of the pit wherein *is* no water. 12. Turn you to the strong hold, ye prisoners of hope: even to day do I declare *that* I will render double unto thee. 16. The Lord their God shall save them in that day as the flock of his people: for *they shall be as* the stones of a crown, lifted up as an ensign upon his land.

Luk. 1.68. Blessed *be* the Lord God of Israel, for he hath visited and redeemed his people.

Jno. 3.16. God so loved the world, that he

gave his only-begotten Son, that whosoever believeth in him should not perish, but have everlasting life. 17. For God sent not his Son into the world to condemn the world ; but that the world through him might be saved.

Jno. 6.39. This is the Father's will which hath sent me, that of all which he hath given me I should lose nothing, but should raise it up again at the last day.

Rom. 1.16. I am not ashamed of the gospel of Christ : for it is the power of God unto salvation to every one that believeth.

Rom. 6.23. The gift of God is eternal life through Jesus Christ our Lord.

Rom. 8.30. Whom he did predestinate, them he also called : and whom he called, them he also justified : and whom he justified, them he also glorified. 31. What shall we then say to these things ? If God be for us, who can be against us ? 32. He that spared not his own Son, but delivered him up for us all, how shall he not with him also freely give us all things ?

1 Cor. 1.18. Unto us which are saved it is the power of God.

2 Cor. 5.18. All things are of God, who hath reconciled us to himself by Jesus Christ, and hath given to us the ministry of reconciliation.

Eph. 1.3. Blessed be the God and Father of our Lord Jesus Christ, who hath blessed us with all spiritual blessings in heavenly places in Christ. 5. Having predestinated us unto the adoption of children by Jesus Christ to himself, according to the good pleasure of his will.

1 The. 5.9. God hath not appointed us to wrath, but to obtain salvation by our Lord Jesus Christ.

2 The. 2.16. God, even our Father, which hath loved us, and hath given us everlasting consolation and good hope through grace, 17. Comfort your hearts, and stablish you in every good word and work.

1 Tim. 2.3. God our Saviour ; 4. Who will have all men to be saved, and to come unto the knowledge of the truth.

1 Tim. 4.10. We trust in the living God, who is the Saviour of all men, specially of those that believe.

2 Tim. 1.9. Who hath saved us, and called us with an holy calling, not according to our works, but according to his own purpose and grace, which was given us in Christ Jesus before the world began.

Tit. 1.2. Eternal life, which God, that cannot lie, promised before the world began.

Tit. 2.11. The grace of God that bringeth salvation hath appeared to all men.

Tit. 3.4. After that the kindness and love of God our Saviour toward man appeared, 5. Not by works of righteousness which we have done, but according to his mercy he saved us.

1 Pet. 1.5. Kept by the power of God through faith unto salvation.

1 Jno. 4.9. In this was manifested the love of God toward us, because that God sent his only-begotten Son into the world, that we might live through him. 10. Herein is love, not that we loved God, but that he loved us, and sent his Son to be the propitiation for our sins.

1 Jno. 5.11. God hath given to us eternal life, and this life is in his Son.

Rev. 7.10. Salvation to our God which sitteth upon the throne, and unto the Lamb.

Rev. 19.1. Salvation, and glory, and honour, and power, unto the Lord our God.

See GOD PROTECTOR—GOD'S MERCY.

GOD, SOVEREIGNTY OF. See PREDESTINATION.—GOD, PROVIDENCE OF.

GOD SELF-EXISTENT. Ex. 3.14. I AM THAT I AM : and he said, Thus shalt thou say unto the children of Israel, I AM hath sent me unto you.

Job 22.2. Can a man be profitable unto God, as he that is wise may be profitable unto himself ? 3. Is it any pleasure to the Almighty, that thou art righteous ? or is it gain to him, that thou makest thy ways perfect ?

Job 35.6. If thou sinnest, what doest thou against him ? or if thy transgressions be multiplied, what doest thou unto him ? 7. If thou be righteous, what givest thou him ? or what receiveth he of thine hand ? 8. Thy wickedness may hurt a man as thou art ; and thy righteousness may profit the son of man.

Jer. 10.10. He is the living God.

Jno. 5.26. The Father hath life in himself.

Act. 17.24. Seeing that he is Lord of heaven and earth, dwelleth not in temples made with hands ; 25. Neither is worshipped with men's hands, as though he needed any thing, seeing he giveth to all life, and breath, and all things.

See GOD ETERNAL.

GOD A SPIRIT. Jno. 4.24. God is a Spirit : and they that worship him must worship him in spirit and in truth.

Act. 17.29. As we are the offspring of God, we ought not to think that the Godhead is like unto gold, or silver, or stone, graven by art and man's device. See GOD INVISIBLE, HOLY SPIRIT

GOD UNCHANGEABLE. See GOD ETERNAL.

GODS, HEATHEN. See IDOLATRY.

GODLESSNESS. HATRED OF GOD. Gen. 25.34. Thus Esau despised his birthright. Heb. 12.16.

Deu. 7.10. He will not be slack to him that hateth him, he will repay him to his face.

Deu. 32.15. He forsook God which made him, and lightly esteemed the Rock of his salvation.

1 Sam. 2.30. They that despise me shall be lightly esteemed.

Job 8.11. Can the flag grow without water ? 12. Whilst it is yet in his greenness, and not cut down, it withereth before any other herb. 13. So are the paths of all that forget God.

Job 35.10. None saith, Where is God my maker, who giveth songs in the night.

Psa. 2.2. The rulers take counsel together, against the Lord, and against his anointed. 4. He that sitteth in the heavens shall laugh : the Lord shall have them in derision.

Psa. 9.17. The wicked shall be turned into hell, and all the nations that forget God.

Psa. 10.4. The wicked, through the pride of his countenance, will not seek after God : God is not in all his thoughts.

Psa. 14.2. The Lord looked down from heaven upon the children of men, to see if there were any that did understand, and seek God. 3. They are all gone aside. Psa. 53.2,3. Rom. 3.11,18.

Psa. 28.5. Because they regard not the

works of the Lord, nor the operation of his hands, he shall destroy them, and not build them up. Isa. 5.12.

Psa. 36.1. The transgression of the wicked saith within my heart, *that there is* no fear of God before his eyes.

Psa. 50.22. Consider this, ye that forget God, lest I tear *you* in pieces, and *there be* none to deliver.

Psa. 52.7. Lo, *this is* the man *that* made not God his strength ; but trusted in the abundance of his riches, *and* strengthened himself in his wickedness.

Psa. 53.4. Have the workers of iniquity no knowledge? who eat up my people *as* they eat bread : they have not called upon God.

Psa. 54.3. They have not set God before them.

Psa. 55.19. They have no changes, therefore they fear not God.

Psa. 86.14. The assemblies of violent *men* have sought after my soul ; and have not set thee before them.

Pro. 14.2. *He that is* perverse in his ways despiseth Him.

Isa. 1.3. The ox knoweth his owner, and the ass his master's crib : *but* Israel doth not know, my people doth not consider.

Isa. 17.10. Because thou hast forgotten the God of thy salvation, and hast not been mindful of the Rock of thy strength, therefore shalt thou plant pleasant plants, and shalt set it with strange slips.

Isa. 22.11. Ye have not looked unto the maker thereof, neither had respect unto him that fashioned it long ago.

Isa. 30.11. Cause the Holy One of Israel to cease from before us.

Isa. 31.1. But they look not unto the Holy One of Israel, neither seek the Lord !

Jer. 2.32. Can a maid forget her ornaments, *or* a bride her attire? yet my people have forgotten me days without number.

Dan. 5.23. The God in whose hand thy breath *is*, and whose *are* all thy ways, hast thou not glorified.

Hos. 7.2. They consider not in their hearts *that* I remember all their wickedness.

Mal. 2.17. Ye have wearied the Lord with your words. Yet ye say, Wherein have we wearied *him*? When ye say, Every one that doeth evil *is* good in the sight of the Lord, and he delighteth in them ; or, Where *is* the God of judgment?

Mal. 3.8. Will a man rob God? Yet ye have robbed me. But ye say, Wherein have we robbed thee?

Jno. 5.42. I know you, that ye have not the love of God in you. 44. Ye receive honour one of another, and seek not the honour that *cometh* from God only.

Jno. 15.23. He that hateth me, hateth my Father also. 24. But now have they both seen and hated both me and my Father. 25. They hated me without a cause.

Rom. 1.21. When they knew God, they glorified *him* not as God, neither were thankful. 28. As they did not like to retain God in *their* knowledge, God gave them over to a reprobate mind.

Rom. 8.7. The carnal mind is enmity against God.

Eph. 4.18. Being alienated from the life of God through the ignorance that is in them, because of the blindness of their heart.

Col. 1.21. You, that were sometime alienated and enemies in *your* mind by wicked works.

Heb. 10.27. Fiery indignation, which shall devour the adversaries.

Jas. 4.4. Know ye not that the friendship of the world is enmity with God? whosoever therefore will be a friend of the world is the enemy of God.

See PRAYERLESSNESS — IMPENITENCE — UNBELIEF.

GOG, MAGOG, Eze. 38. Eze. 39. Rev. 20.8.

GOLAN, a town in Bashan, given to Manasseh, a Levitical city of refuge, Deu. 4.43. Jos. 20.8. Jos. 21.27. 1 Chr. 6.71.

GOLD. Brought from Havilah, Gen. 2.11,12. From Ophir, 1 Kin. 10.11. 1 Chr. 29.4. Tarshish, 1 Kin. 22.48. Parvaim, 2 Chr. 3.6. Sheba, Psa. 72.15. Uphaz, Jer. 10.9. Pure gold, Job 28.19. Fine, Job 31.24. Song 5.11. Beaten, 2 Chr. 9.15. Wrought, Psa. 45.13.

Made into wire, Ex. 39.3. Molten and refined, Pro. 17.3. Pro. 27.21. Zec. 13.9. Mal. 3.3. Gold-dust, Job 28.6. Wedge of, Jos. 7.21. Isa. 13.12. Money of, Ex. 25.39. 1 Chr. 21.25. Bed of, Est. 1.6. Abundance of, in Solomon's time, 1 Kin. 10.2,14,21,25.

Articles made of, see CROWN, CHAINS, CUPS, IDOLS, JEWELS, PRIESTS' GARMENTS, RINGS, SCEPTRE, SHIELDS, TEMPLE, VESSELS AND FURNITURE of. Apples of, Pro. 25.11. Illustrative, Ecc. 12.6. Jer. 51.7. Lam. 4.1. 1 Cor. 3.12. Symbolical, Dan. 2.32-45. Rev. 21.18,21.

GOLDEN CANDLESTICK. See CANDLESTICK.

GOLDSMITH, 2 Chr. 2.7,14. Neh. 3.31,32. Isa. 40.19. Isa. 46.6.

GOLGOTHA. See CALVARY.

GOLIATH OF GATH, a giant slain by David, 1 Sam. 17. 1 Sam. 21.9. 1 Sam. 22.10. His sons, &c., 2 Sam. 21.15-22. 1 Chr. 20.4-8.

GOMER, son of Japheth, Gen. 10.2,3. 1 Chr. 1.5,6. People descended from him, Eze. 38.6.

GOMORRAH, one of the cities of the plain, Gen. 10.19. Gen. 13.10. King of, defeated by Chedorlaomer, Gen. 14.2,8-11. Destroyed with Sodom for wickedness, Gen. 18.20. Gen. 19.24-28. Deu. 29.23. Deu. 32.32. Isa. 1.9,10. Isa. 13.19. Jer. 23.14. Jer. 49.18. Jer. 50.40. Amos 4.11. Zeph. 2.9. Mat. 10.15. Mar. 6.11. Rom. 9.29. 2 Pet. 2.6. Jude 7.

GOOD WORKS. See HOLINESS—OBEDIENCE.—WORKS, INSUFFICIENCY OF.

GOPHER-WOOD (cypress?), the ark made of, Gen. 6.14.

GOSHEN, a district in Egypt assigned to the Israelites, Gen. 45.10. Gen. 46.28. Gen. 47. Exempted from plagues, Ex. 8.22. Ex. 9.26.

————, a town and district of Judah, Jos. 10.41. Jos. 11.16. Jos. 15.51.

GOSPEL DISPENSATION. See CHURCH, PROPHECIES OF.

GOSPEL (Gr. *euangellion*), EXCELLENCE OF. Psa. 89.15. Blessed *is* the people that know the joyful sound.

Isa. 2.5. Come ye, and let us walk in the light of the Lord.

Isa. 9.2. The people that walked in darkness have seen a great light: they that dwell in the land of the shadow of death, upon them hath the light shined.

Isa. 25.7. He will destroy in this mountain the face of the covering cast over all people, and the vail that is spread over all nations.

Isa. 29.18. In that day shall the deaf hear the words of the book, and the eyes of the blind shall see out of obscurity, and out of darkness.

Isa. 29.24. They also that erred in spirit shall come to understanding, and they that murmured shall learn doctrine.

Isa. 32.3. The eyes of them that see shall not be dim, and the ears of them that hear shall hearken.

Isa. 35.5. The eyes of the blind shall be opened, and the ears of the deaf shall be unstopped.

Isa. 46.13. I bring near my righteousness; it shall not be far off, and my salvation shall not tarry: and I will place salvation in Zion for Israel my glory.

Isa. 51.4. I will make my judgment to rest for a light of the people.

Isa. 52.7. How beautiful upon the mountains are the feet of him that bringeth good tidings, that publisheth peace; that bringeth good tidings of good, that publisheth salvation; that saith unto Zion, Thy God reigneth!

Eze. 47.8. These waters issue out toward the east country, and go down into the desert, and go into the sea: *which being* brought forth into the sea, the waters shall be healed. 12. By the river upon the bank thereof, on this side and on that side, shall grow all trees for meat, whose leaf shall not fade, neither shall the fruit thereof be consumed: it shall bring forth new fruit according to his months, because their waters they issued out of the sanctuary: and the fruit thereof shall be for meat, and the leaf thereof for medicine. *v.* 1-12.

Mat. 13.44. The kingdom of heaven is like unto treasure hid in a field; the which when a man hath found, he hideth, and for joy thereof goeth and selleth all that he hath, and buyeth that field. 45. Again, the kingdom of heaven is like unto a merchant man, seeking goodly pearls: 46. Who, when he had found one pearl of great price, went and sold all that he had, and bought it.

Luk. 1.78. The dayspring from on high hath visited us, 79. To give light to them that sit in darkness and *in* the shadow of death, to guide our feet into the way of peace.

Luk. 2.34. This *child* is set for the fall and rising again of many in Israel.

Luk. 17.20. The kingdom of God cometh not with observation: 21. Neither shall they say, Lo here! or, lo there! for, behold, the kingdom of God is within you.

Jno. 1.17. Grace and truth came by Jesus Christ.

Jno. 4.14. Whosoever drinketh of the water that I shall give him shall never thirst; but the water that I shall give him shall be in him a well of water springing up into everlasting life.

Jno. 8.32. Ye shall know the truth, and the truth shall make you free.

Jno. 12.35. Yet a little while is the light with you. Walk while ye have the light, lest darkness come upon you. 50. I know that his commandment is life everlasting.

Jno. 18.36. My kingdom is not of this world: if my kingdom were of this world, then would my servants fight, that I should not be delivered to the Jews: but now is my kingdom not from hence.

Act. 2.11. We do hear them speak in our tongues the wonderful works of God.

Act. 5.20. Go, stand and speak in the temple to the people all the words of this life.

Act. 13.32. We declare unto you glad tidings, how that the promise which was made unto the fathers, 33. God hath fulfilled the same unto us their children, in that he hath raised up Jesus.

Act. 16.17. The servants of the most high God, which shew unto us the way of salvation.

Act. 20.24. The ministry, which I have received of the Lord Jesus, to testify the gospel of the grace of God. 32. The word of his grace, which is able to build you up, and to give you an inheritance among all them which are sanctified.

Rom. 1.16. It is the power of God unto salvation to every one that believeth; to the Jew first, and also to the Greek. 17. For therein is the righteousness of God revealed from faith to faith: as it is written, The just shall live by faith.

Rom. 10.17. Faith *cometh* by hearing, and hearing by the word of God.

Rom. 15.29. The fulness of the blessing of the gospel of Christ.

Rom. 16.25. Him that is of power to stablish you according to my gospel, and the preaching of Jesus Christ, (according to the revelation of the mystery, which was kept secret since the world began, 26. But now is made manifest, and by the scriptures of the prophets, according to the commandment of the everlasting God, made known to all nations for the obedience of faith.)

1 Cor. 1.18. The preaching of the cross is to them that perish foolishness; but unto us which are saved it is the power of God. 21. It pleased God by the foolishness of preaching to save them that believe. 24. Unto them which are called, both Jews and Greeks, Christ the power of God, and the wisdom of God. 25. Because the foolishness of God is wiser than men; and the weakness of God is stronger than men.

1 Cor. 2.6. We speak wisdom among them that are perfect: yet not the wisdom of this world, nor of the princes of this world, that come to nought: 7. But we speak the wisdom of God in a mystery, *even* the hidden *wisdom*, which God ordained before the world unto our glory. 9. Eye hath not seen, nor ear heard, neither have entered into the heart of man, the things which God hath prepared for them that love him.

1 Cor. 4.20. The kingdom of God *is* not in word, but in power.

1 Cor. 15.1. I declare unto you the gospel which I preached unto you, which also ye have received, and wherein ye stand; 2. By which also ye are saved, if ye keep in memory what I preached unto you, unless ye have believed in vain.

2 Cor. 3.6. The letter killeth, but the spirit giveth life.

2 Cor. 3.18. We all, with open face beholding as in a glass the glory of the Lord, are changed into the same image from glory to glory, *even* as by the Spirit of the Lord.

2 Cor. 4.4. Lest the light of the glorious gospel of Christ, who is the image of God, should shine unto them. 7. This treasure.

2 Cor. 9.15. Thanks *be* unto God for his unspeakable gift.

2 Cor. 10.4. The weapons of our warfare *are* not carnal, but mighty through God to the pulling down of strong holds; 5. Casting down imaginations, and every high thing that exalteth itself against the knowledge of God, and bringing into captivity every thought to the obedience of Christ.

Eph. 1.13. Ye heard the word of truth, the gospel of your salvation.

Eph. 3.8. The unsearchable riches of Christ. 10. The manifold wisdom of God.

Eph. 5.13. Whatsoever doth make manifest is light.

Eph. 6.15. The gospel of peace.

Col. 1.5. The hope which is laid up for you in heaven, whereof ye heard before in the word of the truth of the gospel.

2 The. 1.10. He shall come to be glorified in his saints, and to be admired in all them that believe (because our testimony among you was believed) in that day.

2 The. 2.10. The love of the truth, that they might be saved. 14. He called you by our gospel, to the obtaining of the glory of our Lord Jesus Christ.

1 Tim. 1.11. The glorious gospel of the blessed God.

1 Tim. 2.4. Who will have all men to be saved, and to come unto the knowledge of the truth.

1 Tim. 3.16. Great is the mystery of godliness: God was manifest in the flesh, justified in the Spirit, seen of angels, preached unto the Gentiles, believed on in the world.

1 Tim. 4.6. Nourished up in the words of faith and of good doctrine, whereunto thou hast attained.

2 Tim. 1.10. Hath brought life and immortality to light through the gospel.

Heb. 5.13. The word of righteousness.

Heb. 6.1. Leaving the principles of the doctrine of Christ, let us go on unto perfection.

Heb. 7.19. The law made nothing perfect, but the bringing in of a better hope *did*; by the which we draw nigh unto God.

Heb. 12.22. Ye are come unto mount Sion, and unto the city of the living God.

Jas. 1.18. Of his own will begat he us with the word of truth. 21. The ingrafted word, which is able to save your souls. 25. Whoso looketh into the perfect law of liberty, and continueth *therein*, he being not a forgetful hearer, but a doer of the work, this man shall be blessed in his deed.

1 Pet. 1.23. Being born again, not of corruptible seed, but of incorruptible, by the word of God, which liveth and abideth for ever.

1 Pet. 4.6. For this cause was the gospel preached also to them that are dead, that they might be judged according to men in the flesh, but live according to God in the spirit.

1 Pet. 5.12. This is the true grace of God wherein ye stand.

2 Pet. 1.19. A more sure word of prophecy;

whereunto ye do well that ye take heed, as unto a light that shineth in a dark place, until the day dawn, and the day-star arise in your hearts.

2 Pet. 2.2. The way of truth. 21. The way of righteousness . . . the holy commandment.

1 Jno. 2.8. The darkness is past, and the true light now shineth.

See LAW MOSAIC, CHARACTER OF.—SANCTIFICATION BY THE WORD.

GOSPEL FROM GOD. Jno. 7.17. If any man will do his will, he shall know of the doctrine, whether it be of God.

Jno. 17.7. All things whatsoever thou hast given me are of thee. 8. For I have given unto them the words which thou gavest me; and they have received *them*, and have known surely that I came out from thee, and they have believed that thou didst send me. Jno. 13.20.

Act. 10.36. The word which *God* sent unto the children of Israel, preaching peace by Jesus Christ.

1 Cor. 1.18. Unto us which are saved it is the power of God. 21. It pleased God by the foolishness of preaching to save them that believe.

1 Cor. 2.4. My preaching *was* not with enticing words of man's wisdom, but in demonstration of the Spirit and of power. 5. That your faith should not stand in the wisdom of men, but in the power of God. 6. We speak wisdom among them that are perfect: yet not the wisdom of this world, nor of the princes of this world, that come to nought: 7. But we speak the wisdom of God in a mystery, *even* the hidden *wisdom*, which God ordained before the world unto our glory.

Eph. 3.9. The mystery, which from the beginning of the world hath been hid in God.

Col. 1.26. The mystery which hath been hid from ages and from generations, but now is made manifest to his saints.

1 The. 2.13. The word of God which ye heard of us, ye received *it* not *as* the word of men, but as it is in truth, the word of God.

1 Tim. 1.11. The glorious gospel of the blessed God. Rom. 1.1.

1 Pet. 1.25. The word of the Lord endureth for ever. And this is the word which by the gospel is preached unto you. Isa. 40.8.

1 Pet. 5.12. This is the true grace of God.

1 Jno. 4.6. We are of God: he that knoweth God heareth us; he that is not of God heareth not us.

Jude 3. The faith which was once delivered unto the saints.

See WORD OF GOD.

GOSPEL TO BE PREACHED. See MINISTERS—ZEAL—SALVATION—LIBERALITY.

——— TO BE RECEIVED. See WORD OF GOD.—WORSHIP.

———, SUCCESS OF. See CHURCH, PROPHECIES OF.—WORD OF GOD LOVED.—IDOLATRY, EXTINCTION OF.

———, TRUTH OF. Jno. 21.24. We know that his testimony is true.

Act. 5.38. If this counsel or this work be of men, it will come to nought: 39. But if it be of God, ye cannot overthrow it; lest haply ye be found even to fight against God.

Act. 10.39. And we are witnesses of all things which he did both in the land of the Jews, and in Jerusalem. 40. Him God raised up the third day, and shewed him openly; 41. Not to all the people, but unto witnesses chosen before of God, *even* to us, who did eat and drink with him after he rose from the dead.

Act. 26.25. I am not mad, most noble Festus; but speak forth the words of truth and soberness.

2 Cor. 1.19. The Son of God, Jesus Christ, who was preached among you by us, was not yea and nay, but in him was yea.

2 Pet. 1.16. We have not followed cunningly devised fables, when we made known unto you the power and coming of our Lord Jesus Christ, but were eyewitnesses of his majesty.

See WORD OF GOD.—GOSPEL, EXCELLENCE OF.—MIRACLES, DESIGN OF.

GOURD, a climbing-plant which sheltered Jonah, Jonah 4.6-10. Wild gourd, a kind of cucumber, poisonous, 2 Kin. 4.39.

GOVERNMENT. See RULERS.

GOZAN, a river of Media. Israelites taken captive to, by Tiglath, 1 Chr. 5.26; and Shalmanezer, 2 Kin. 17.6. 2 Kin. 18.11. 2 Kin. 19.12.

GRACE. Signifying beauty, Jas. 1.11. Favour, Gen. 6.8. Ruth 2.2. Luk. 2.40. Jno. 1.16. Act. 4.33. The gospel considered as favour, Gal. 1.6. Tit. 2.11. Spiritual influence, Col. 3.16. Col. 4.6. Phil. 1.7. See under such titles as REGENERATION.—GOD, FAVOUR OF.

Growth in grace, see DECISION—SANCTIFICATION—SPIRITUAL DILIGENCE.

GRAFTING. See INGRAFTING.

GRAPE. See VINE—VINEYARDS—WINE.

GRASS, Num. 22.4. 1 Kin. 18.5. Pro. 27.25. Isa. 37.27. Illustrative, Isa. 40.6,7. Jas. 1.10.

GRASSHOPPER. See LOCUST.

GRATE, Ex. 27.4,5. Ex. 38.4,5.

GRATITUDE TO GOD. See THANKFULNESS.

———— TO MAN. Examples of: Jethro, Ex. 2.20. Joshua, Jos. 6.22-25. Naomi, Ruth 1.8. Ruth 2.19,20. Israelites, 1 Sam. 14.45. Saul, 1 Sam. 15.6. 1 Sam. 24.16-19. Gileadites, 1 Sam. 31.11-13 with 1 Sam. 11. David, 2 Sam. 10.2. 1 Kin. 2.7. Solomon, 1 Kin. 2.26. Elisha, 2 Kin. 4.13. Naaman, 2 Kin. 5.15,16. Paul, 2 Tim. 1.16-18. See INGRATITUDE.

GRAVES. See BURIAL-PLACES.

GRAVING. See ENGRAVING.

GREAT SEA. See MEDITERRANEAN.

GREAVES, armour for the legs worn by Goliath, 1 Sam. 17.6.

GREECE, Act. 20.2. Provinces of, see ACHAIA, DALMATIA, ILLYRICUM, MACEDONIA, with their cities. Other cities, ATHENS, NICOPOLIS. Prophecies of, Dan. 2.39. Dan. c. 7, & 8, & 11. Zec. 9.13. See JAVAN. Gods of, see DIANA, JUPITER, MERCURY.

GRECIANS (Gr. *Hellenistes*), or Hellenists—that is, Jews or proselytes who spoke Greek, Act. 6.1. Act. 11.20. Opposition of, to the gospel, Act. 6.9-14. Act. 9.29.

GREEK (Gr. *Hellen*). An inhabitant of Greece, or a Greek in language and customs, Jno. 12.20. Act. 16.1. Act. 18.17. Mar. 7.26. Translated Gentile, Jno. 7.35. Rom. 2.9,10. Rom. 3.9. 1 Cor. 10.32. 1 Cor. 12.13. It has the same meaning though translated *Greek*, Rom. 10.12. Gal. 3.28. Col. 3.11. Comp. Rom. 1.16 with Rom. 2.9.

GREYHOUND (*marg.* a horse), Pro. 30.31.

GRINDING. See MILLS.

GROVES. Abraham planted, Gen. 21.33. Forbidden, Deu. 16.21. Isa. 1.29. Isa. 17.8. Isa. 27.9. Mic. 5.14. Planted by Israelites for idolatrous uses, Jud. 3.7. 1 Kin. 14.15,23. 1 Kin. 15.13. 1 Kin. 18.19. 2 Kin. 13.6. 2 Kin. 17.10,16. 2 Kin. 21.3-7. 2 Chr. 24.18. Jer. 17.2.

To be destroyed, Ex. 34.13. Deu. 7.5. Deu. 12.3. Jud. 6.25. Destroyed by Gideon, Jud. 6.28. By Hezekiah, 2 Kin. 18.4. By Josiah, 2 Kin. 23.14. By Asa, 2 Chr. 14.3. By Jehoshaphat, 2 Chr. 17.6. 2 Chr. 19.3.

GUARDS. See KING'S OFFICERS—EXECUTIONERS—WATCHMEN—CHERETHITES—PELETHITES.

GUEST. See FEASTS—HOSPITALITY.

GUIDANCE. See WISDOM, PRAYER FOR—GOD PROTECTOR.

GUR-BAAL, a town of Arabia. People of, defeated by Uzziah, 2 Chr. 26.7.

H

HABAKKUK, a prophet of Judah, Hab. 1.1.

HABERGEON, a garment on which the breastplate was fastened, Ex. 28.32. Ex. 39.23. See BREASTPLATE.

HABOR AND HALAH, towns in Media, to which the 10 tribes were taken by Shalmanezer, 2 Kin. 17.6. 2 Kin. 18.11. And by Tiglath, 1 Chr. 5.26.

HACHILAH, a hill of Ziph, the hiding-place of David, 1 Sam. 23.19. 1 Sam. 26.1,3.

HADAD, a king of Edom, defeats the Midianites, Gen. 36.35. 1 Chr. 1.46.

————, an Edomite of the seed-royal, flees to Egypt from David; returns and wars against Solomon, 1 Kin. 11.14-22,25.

HADADEZER, king of Zobah, in Syria, conquered by David, 2 Sam. 8.3-12. 2 Sam. 10.15-19. 1 Kin. 11.24. 1 Chr. 18.3-10. 1 Chr. 19.6-19.

HADADRIMMON. See MEGIDDO.

HADRACH, a district near Damascus, Zec. 9.1.

HAGAR, an Egyptian handmaid of Sarah, becomes Abraham's wife, Gen. 16.1-3. Despises her mistress; harshly used; flees to the wilderness; the angel of the Lord bids her return; Ishmael born, Gen. 16.4-15. Gen. 25.12.

Sarah causes Abraham to send her away; an angel directs her to a well, and promises prosperity to her son, Gen. 21. Story of, allegorized, Gal. 4.22-31.

HAGARENES, a tribe of Ishmaelites, Psa. 83.6. Conquered by Reubenites, &c., 1 Chr. 5.10-22.

HAGGAI the prophet, encourages the Jews

to rebuild the temple, Ezr. 5.1. Ezr. 6.14. Time of his prophecy, Hag. 1.1. Hag. 2.1,10,20.

HAGGITH, David's wife, and mother of Adonijah, 2 Sam. 3.4. 1 Kin. 1.5,6. 1 Chr. 3.2.

HAIL, Job 38.22. Hag. 2.17. Plague of, Ex. 9.18-29. Illustrative, Isa. 28.2. Rev. 8.7. Rev. 11.19. Rev. 16.21.

HAIR. Worn long and plaited, by women, Isa. 3.24. Luk. 7.38. 1 Cor. 11.15. 1 Tim. 2.9. 1 Pet. 3.3. Rev. 9.8. Worn long by Absalom, 2 Sam. 14.26. Men condemned for having long hair, 1 Cor. 11.14. See MOURNING — LEPROSY — NAZARITE — BALDNESS — BARBER—CAUL—TIRE.

HALAH. See HABOR.

HALAK, a mountain near Seir, Jos. 12.7.

HALLELUJAH, OR ALLELUIA, Rev. 19.1. In the O. T. always translated, Praise ye the Lord, as Psa. 106.1. Psa. 113.1.

HALLOWED THINGS. See DEDICATION.

HAM, Noah's younger son, Gen. 5.32 with Gen. 9.18,24. 1 Chr. 1.4. Mocks his father; prophecy against him, Gen. 9.22-25. His descendents, Gen. 10.6-20. 1 Chr. 1.8-16.

——, name of Egypt, Psa. 78.51. Psa. 105.23,27. Psa. 106.22.

HAMAN, an Agagite or Amalekite, Est. 3.1 with 1 Sam. 15.8. His pride; plot against the Jews; defeated by Esther and Mordecai; he is hanged, Est. c. 3 to 9.

HAMATH, a small kingdom south of Damascus, north boundary of Palestine, Num. 34.8. Jos. 13.5. 1 Kin. 8.65. 2 Kin. 14.25. Eze. 47.16. People of, Canaanites, Gen. 10.18. Its prosperity, Amos 6.2. Toi, king of, sends presents to David, 2 Sam. 8.9,10. 1 Chr. 18.3,9,10.

Conquered by Jeroboam II., 2 Kin. 14.25,28. By the Assyrians, 2 Kin. 18.34. 2 Kin. 19.13. By the Chaldeans, 2 Kin. 25.20,21. Inhabitants from, colonize Samaria, 2 Kin. 17.24. Ashima, a goddess of, 2 Kin. 17.30. Israelites in captivity at, Isa. 11.11. Prophecy against, Jer. 49.23.

HAMMER, 1 Kin. 6.7. Isa. 41.7. Illustrative, Jer. 23.29. Jer. 50.23.

HAMON-GOG (multitude of Gog), Eze. 39.11,15 (marg.). See GOG.

HAMOR, the father of Shechem; his intercourse with Jacob and family; is murdered by Simeon and Levi, Gen. 33.19. Gen. 34. Gen. 49.6.

HANAMEEL, sells land to Jeremiah, his cousin, as predicted, Jer. 32.6-12.

HANANEEL, a tower in Jerusalem, Neh. 3.1. Neh. 12.39. Jer. 31.38. Zec. 14.10.

HANANI, brother of Nehemiah, and governor of Jerusalem, Neh. 1.2. Neh. 7.2.

——, a prophet, imprisoned by Asa for prophesying against him, 2 Chr. 16.7.

HANANIAH, a false prophet; opposition of, to Jeremiah; death of, as predicted, Jer. 28.

HAND. Signifies power, Gen. 9.2; help, 2 Kin. 15.9; he himself, Act. 4.28. Right hand signifies honour, Psa. 110.1; might, Ex. 15.6. High hand signifies great power, Psa. 89.13. Left-handed signifies ambi-dexter (two right hands), Jud. 3.15. Lifting up the hand against one signifies to rebel, 2 Sam. 20.21.

Pouring water on, signifies service, 2 Kin. 3.11. Washing of, a declaration of innocence, Deu. 21.6,7. Mat. 27.24. Kissing, an act of adoration, Job 31.27. Leaning upon, a sign of friendship, 2 Kin. 7.2. Lifting up, mode of taking an oath, Gen. 14.22; and of blessing, Lev. 9.22. Stretching out, in supplication, Psa. 88.9; in invitation, Isa. 65.2.

Laying on of, Gen. 48.14. Num. 8.10. Mat. 19.15. Mar. 6.5. Mar. 8.23. Mar. 16.18. Luk. 4.40. Act. 6.6. Act. 8.17. Act. 9.17. Act. 13.3. Act. 19.6. 1 Tim. 5.22. Laying on of, by witnesses, upon the head of the accused, Deu. 13.9. By the offerer upon the sacrifice, Lev. 1.4.

HANDBREADTH, a measure, 1 Kin. 7.26. Psa. 39.5. Isa. 48.13. Translated span, Lam. 2.20.

HANDKERCHIEF, or NAPKIN, Eze. 13.18,21. Luk. 19.20. Jno. 11.44. Jno. 20.7. Act. 19.12.

HANGING, a mode of capital punishment practised by Egyptians, Gen. 40.19,22. By Israelites, Jos. 8.29. 2 Sam. 4.12. By Persians, Est. 7.10. The body of the person hanged counted accursed, and to be buried the same day, Deu. 21.22,23. Gal. 3.13.

HANGINGS. See CURTAINS.

HANNAH. Her son Samuel given in answer to prayer, 1 Sam. 1.1-21. She dedicates him to God, 1 Sam. 1.22-28. 1 Sam. 2.18,19. Her song of thanksgiving, 1 Sam. 2.1-10.

HANUN, son of Nahash, king of the Ammonites. His treatment of David's messengers, and punishment, 2 Sam. 10. 1 Chr. 19.

HAPPINESS. See SPIRITUAL PEACE—CONTENTMENT.

HARA, a place in Media, to which the Israelites were taken captive, 1 Chr. 5.26.

HARAN, brother of Abraham, and father of Lot, Gen. 11.27,28.

——, or CHARRAN, a place in Mesopotamia or Padan-aram. Terah dies at, Gen. 11.32. Abraham dwells at, Gen. 11.31. Gen. 12.4,5. Act. 7.4. Jacob resides with Laban in, Gen. 27.43. Gen. 28.7. Gen. 29. Gen. 31.18. Conquered by the Assyrians, 2 Kin. 19.12. Merchants of, Eze. 27.23. Idolatry in, Jos. 24.14. Isa. 37.12.

HARE, Lev. 11.6. Deu. 14.7.

HARETH, a forest in Judah, to which David fled from Saul, 1 Sam. 22.5.

HARNESS. See BREASTPLATE.

HAROD, a well east of Jordan, near which Joshua defeated Midian, Jud. 7.1.

HAROSHETH of the Gentiles, the abode of Sisera, Jud. 4.2,13,16.

HARP. Invented by Jubal, Gen. 4.21. Used by prophets, 1 Sam. 10.5. By David, 2 Sam. 6.5,14-16. 1 Chr. 13.8. 1 Chr. 15.16-29. Levites appointed by David and Solomon to play on, for the temple service, 1 Chr. 16.5,37. 1 Chr. 25.1-7. 2 Chr. 5.12,13.

Used on Jehoshaphat's triumph, 2 Chr. 20.27,28. On the day of atonement, 2 Chr. 29.25. At the dedication of the wall, Neh. 12.27,36.

Played with the hand by David, 1 Sam.

16.16,23. Made by Solomon of Almug, 1 Kin.
10.12. 2 Chr. 9.11. Musical notes of, 1 Cor.
14.7.

Used at entertainments, Gen. 31.27. Job
21.12. Job 30.31. Isa. 5.12. Isa. 24.8. Isa.
30.32. Eze. 26.13. Rev. 18.22. In the streets,
Isa. 23.16.

Used in praise, Psa. 33.2. Psa. 43.4. Psa.
49.4. Psa. 57.8. Psa. 71.22. Psa. 81.2. Psa.
92.3. Psa. 98.5. Psa. 108.2. Psa. 137.2,3.
Psa. 147.7. Psa. 149.3. Psa. 150.3. Symbolical, Rev. 5.8. Rev. 14.2. Rev. 15.2.

Called a stringed instrument, used in praise,
Psa. 150.4. Isa. 38.20. Hab. 3.19. Eze.
33.32. Same as Neginoth, titles of, Psalms
4.6.54.55.61.67.76.

Called an instrument of ten strings, used in
praise, Psa. 33.2,3. Psa. 92.3. Psa. 144.9.

Called a three-stringed instrument, played
by women, 1 Sam. 18.6 (*marg.*). See PSALTERY
—SACKBUT—MUSIC.

HARROW OF IRON, 2 Sam. 12.31. 1 Chr.
20.3.

HART. See DEER.

HARVEST. Of barley earlier than wheat,
Ex. 9.31,32. Jos. 3.15. Ruth 1.22. Ruth
2.23. 2 Sam. 21.9. Of wheat at Pentecost,
Ex. 34.22. Lev. 23.15-17. Vintage after
wheat harvest, Lev. 26.5. Rain rare during,
Pro. 26.1. Isa. 18.4. 1 Sam. 12.17.

Sabbath kept in, Ex. 34.21. Celebrated with
feasting, Jud. 9.27. Ruth 3.2-7. Psa. 126.5.
Isa. 9.3. Isa. 16.10. Jer. 48.32,33. Promises
of, Gen. 8.22. Jer. 5.24. Joel 2.23,24. Illustrative, Job 24.6. Jer. 8.20. Mat. 9.37. Mat.
13.39. Rev. 14.15. Feast of tabernacles at the
close of, see FEAST OF TABERNACLES. See
FIRST-FRUITS—REAPING—GLEANING.

HAT. See DRESS, HEAD-DRESS.

HATRED. See MALICE. Hatred of Christ,
see CHRIST'S SUFFERINGS. Of God, see GOD-
LESSNESS. Of Saints, see SAINTS HATED—PER-
SECUTION. Of Sin, see SIN HATED—ZEAL
AGAINST SIN.

HAVILAH, a son of Cush, Gen. 10.7. A
son of Joktan, Gen. 10.29.

————, a district east of Palestine, Gen.
25.18. 1 Sam. 15.7.

————, a country in the east, famous for
gold, Gen. 2.11,12.

HAVOTH-JAIR, TOWNS OF. See JAIR.

HAWK AND NIGHT-HAWK, Lev. 11.16.
Deu. 14.15.

HAY or GRASS, Pro. 27.25. Isa. 15.6. See
GRASS.

HAZAEL, king of Syria, Elijah commanded
to anoint him king, 1 Kin. 19.15. Sent by
Benhadad to inquire of Elisha, who predicts
his reign and cruelty, 2 Kin. 8.8-13. Murders
Benhadad and succeeds him, 2 Kin. 8.14,15.
Defeats Ahaziah and Joram at Ramoth-Gilead,
2 Kin. 8.28,29. 2 Kin. 9.14. 2 Chr. 22.5,6.

Takes Gath; invades Judah; subsidized by
Jehoash, 2 Kin. 12.17,18. Defeats and oppresses Israel in the reign of Jehu, 2 Kin.
10.32,33. Amos 1.3; and of Jehoahaz, 2 Kin.
13.3,22. Death of, 2 Kin. 13.24.

HAZEL-TREE, Gen. 30.37.

HAZEZON-TAMAR. See ENGEDI.

HAZOR. Jabin, king of, conquered by

Joshua, Jos. 11.1-14. Jabin II. oppresses
Israel; is conquered by Deborah and Barak,
Jud. 4. The town rebuilt by Solomon, 1 Kin.
9.15. Taken by Tiglath, 2 Kin. 15.29. Re-
peopled after the captivity, Neh. 11.33. Prophecy against, Jer. 49.28-33.

HEAD-BANDS, Isa. 3.20.

HEART, hardness of. See IMPENITENCE—
MAN'S NATURAL STATE—SINNERS, DESCRIP-
TION OF. Renewal of, see REGENERATION.

HEARTH, Isa. 30.14. Jer. 36.22,23. Baking on, Gen. 18.6.

HEATH, Jer. 17.6. Jer. 48.6.

HEATHEN. The Hebrew word in the
singular is applied to the Israelites, and translated people or nation, Ex. 32.10. Jos. 5.6.
Isa. 42.6. In the *plural*, it signifies foreign
nations, and is rendered Gentiles, and nations,
Gen. 10.5; Heathen, Lev. 25.44. The Greek
word, *ethnos*, is translated nation, Mat. 21.43;
nations, Mat. 24.9; Gentiles, Mat. 4.15;
heathen, Act. 4.25.

Lev. 18.24. In all these the nations are
defiled which I cast out before you: 25. And
the land is defiled: therefore I do visit the
iniquity thereof upon it, and the land itself
vomiteth out her inhabitants. *v.* 1-30.

Deu. 12.31. Every abomination to the Lord,
which he hateth, have they done unto their
gods; for even their sons and their daughters
they have burnt in the fire.

Ezr. 9.11. It is an unclean land with the
filthiness of the people of the lands, with their
abominations, which have filled it from one
end to another with their uncleanness.

Psa. 74.20. The dark places of the earth
are full of the habitations of cruelty.

Isa. 25.7. The covering cast over all people,
and the vail that is spread over all nations.

Isa. 60.2. Darkness shall cover the earth,
and gross darkness the people.

Jer. 10.2. Learn not the way of the heathen,
and be not dismayed at the signs of heaven;
for the heathen are dismayed at them. 3. For
the customs of the people *are* vain.

Mat. 6.7. When ye pray, use not vain
repetitions, as the heathen *do:* for they think
that they shall be heard for their much speaking. 31. What shall we eat? or, What shall
we drink? or, Wherewithal shall we be
clothed? 32. After all these things do the
Gentiles seek.

Act. 14.16. Who in times past suffered all
nations to walk in their own ways.

Rom. 2.12. As many as have sinned without
law shall also perish without law. 14. When
the Gentiles, which have not the law, do by
nature the things contained in the law, these,
having not the law, are a law unto themselves:
15. Which shew the work of the law written
in their hearts, their conscience also bearing
witness.

1 Cor. 10.20. They sacrifice to devils, and
not to God.

1 Cor. 12.2. Ye were Gentiles, carried away
unto these dumb idols, even as ye were led.

Gal. 2.15. Sinners of the Gentiles.

Eph. 2.12. At that time ye were without
Christ, being aliens from the commonwealth
of Israel, and strangers from the covenants of
promise, having no hope, and without God in
the world.

Eph. 4.17. Walk not as other Gentiles walk,

in the vanity of their mind; 18. Having the understanding darkened, being alienated from the life of God through the ignorance that is in them, because of the blindness of their heart; 19. Who, being past feeling, have given themselves over unto lasciviousness, to work all uncleanness with greediness.

Eph. 5.12. It is a shame even to speak of those things which are done of them in secret. Rom. 1.21-32.

1 The. 4.5. Gentiles which know not God.

1 Pet. 4.3. Wrought the will of the Gentiles, when we walked in lasciviousness, lusts, excess of wine, revellings, banquetings, and abominable idolatries: 4. Wherein they think it strange that ye run not with *them* to the same excess of riot, speaking evil of *you*.

See IDOLATRY.

HEATHEN, CONVERSION OF. See CHURCH, PROPHECIES OF.

HEAVE-OFFERING. See OFFERING.

HEAVEN—SAINTS FINAL REWARD. Deu. 26.15. Look down from thy holy habitation, from heaven.

1 Kin. 8.27. Behold, the heaven and heaven of heavens cannot contain thee. 30. Hear thou in heaven thy dwelling-place.

1 Kin. 22.19. I saw the Lord sitting on his throne, and all the host of heaven standing by him on his right hand and on his left.

1 Chr. 16.27. Glory and honour *are* in his presence; strength and gladness *are* in his place.

Psa. 11.4. The Lord *is* in his holy temple, the Lord's throne *is* in heaven.

Psa. 16.11. In thy presence *is* fulness of joy; at thy right hand *there are* pleasures for evermore.

Psa. 17.15. As for me, I will behold thy face in righteousness: I shall be satisfied, when I awake, with thy likeness.

Psa. 23.6. I will dwell in the house of the Lord for ever.

Psa. 24.3. Who shall ascend into the hill of the Lord? or who shall stand in his holy place? 7. Lift up your heads, O ye gates; and be ye lift up, ye everlasting doors; and the King of glory shall come in.

Psa. 37.18. Their inheritance shall be for ever. 28. The Lord forsaketh not his saints; they are preserved for ever.

Psa. 73.24. Thou shalt guide me with thy counsel, and afterward receive me *to* glory.

Psa. 115.16. The heaven, *even* the heavens, *are* the Lord's.

Pro. 3.35. The wise shall inherit glory.

Pro. 10.25. The righteous *is* an everlasting foundation.

Isa. 25.8. He will swallow up death in victory; and the Lord God will wipe away tears from off all faces; and the rebuke of his people shall he take away from off all the earth.

Isa. 33.17. Thine eyes shall see the king in his beauty: they shall behold the land that is very far off.

Isa. 51.11. The redeemed of the Lord shall return, and come with singing unto Zion; and everlasting joy *shall be* upon their head: they shall obtain gladness and joy; *and* sorrow and mourning shall flee away. Isa. 30.19. Isa. 35.10. Isa. 65.18,19.

Isa. 57.15. The high and lofty One that

inhabiteth eternity, whose name *is* Holy; I dwell in the high and holy *place*.

Isa. 63.15. Look down from heaven, and behold from the habitation of thy holiness and of thy glory.

Isa. 66.1. The heaven *is* my throne, and the earth *is* my footstool.

Dan. 12.3. They that be wise shall shine as the brightness of the firmament; and they that turn many to righteousness as the stars for ever and ever.

Mal. 3.17. They shall be mine, saith the Lord of hosts, in that day when I make up my jewels; and I will spare them, as a man spareth his own son that serveth him.

Mat. 5.8. Blessed *are* the pure in heart: for they shall see God. 12. Rejoice, and be exceeding glad: for great *is* your reward in heaven.

Mat. 6.20. Lay up for yourselves treasures in heaven, where neither moth nor rust doth corrupt, and where thieves do not break through nor steal. Luk. 12.33.

Mat. 8.11. Many shall come from the east and west, and shall sit down with Abraham, and Isaac, and Jacob, in the kingdom of heaven.

Mat. 13.30. Gather the wheat into my barn. 43. Then shall the righteous shine forth as the sun in the kingdom of their Father. 49. At the end of the world: the angels shall come forth, and sever the wicked from among the just. Mat. 3.12.

Mat. 18.10. In heaven their angels do always behold the face of my Father which is in heaven.

Mat. 22.30. In the resurrection they neither marry, nor are given in marriage, but are as the angels of God in heaven.

Mat. 25.34. Then shall the King say unto them on his right hand, Come, ye blessed of my Father, inherit the kingdom prepared for you from the foundation of the world. 46. But the righteous into life eternal.

Luk. 10.20. Rather rejoice, because your names are written in heaven.

Luk. 12.32. Fear not, little flock; for it is your Father's good pleasure to give you the kingdom.

Luk. 15.7. Joy shall be in heaven over one sinner that repenteth.

Luk. 16.22. The beggar died, and was carried by the angels into Abraham's bosom.

Luk. 20.36. Neither can they die any more: for they are equal unto the angels; and are the children of God, being the children of the resurrection.

Luk. 22.29. I appoint unto you a kingdom, as my Father hath appointed unto me; 30. That ye may eat and drink at my table in my kingdom, and sit on thrones judging the twelve tribes of Israel.

Luk. 23.43. Verily I say unto thee, To-day shalt thou be with me in paradise.

Jno. 5.29. They that have done good, unto the resurrection of life.

Jno. 10.28. I give unto them eternal life; and they shall never perish, neither shall any *man* pluck them out of my hand.

Jno. 12.26. Where I am, there shall also my servant be: if any man serve me, him will *my* Father honour.

Jno. 13.36. Whither I go, thou canst not follow me now; but thou shalt follow me afterwards.

Jno. 14.2. In my Father's house are many mansions : if it were not so, I would have told you. I go to prepare a place for you. 3. If I go and prepare a place for you, I will come again, and receive you unto myself ; that where I am, there ye may be also.

Jno. 17.22. And the glory which thou gavest me I have given them. 24. Father, I will that they also, whom thou hast given me, be with me where I am ; that they may behold my glory.

Act. 7.55. He, being full of the Holy Ghost, looked up stedfastly into heaven, and saw the glory of God, and Jesus standing on the right hand of God. v. 56.

Rom. 2.7. To them who by patient continuance in well doing seek for glory and honour and immortality, eternal life : 10. Glory, honour, and peace, to every man that worketh good.

Rom. 5.17. They which receive abundance of grace and of the gift of righteousness shall reign in life by one, Jesus Christ.

Rom. 6.23. The gift of God is eternal life through Jesus Christ our Lord.

Rom. 8.17. If children, then heirs ; heirs of God, and joint-heirs with Christ ; if so be that we suffer with him, that we may be also glorified together. 18. For I reckon that the sufferings of this present time are not worthy to be compared with the glory which shall be revealed in us. 21. The creature itself also shall be delivered from the bondage of corruption into the glorious liberty of the children of God.

1 Cor. 1.8. Who shall also confirm you unto the end, that ye may be blameless in the day of our Lord Jesus Christ.

1 Cor. 2.9. Eye hath not seen, nor ear heard, neither have entered into the heart of man, the things which God hath prepared for them that love him. Isa. 64.4.

1 Cor. 9.25. They do it to obtain a corruptible crown ; but we an incorruptible.

1 Cor. 13.10. When that which is perfect is come, then that which is in part shall be done away. 12. Now we see through a glass, darkly ; but then face to face : now I know in part ; but then shall I know even as also I am known.

1 Cor. 15.41. There is one glory of the sun, and another glory of the moon, and another glory of the stars : for one star differeth from another star in glory. 42. So also is the resurrection of the dead. 50. Flesh and blood cannot inherit the kingdom of God ; neither doth corruption inherit incorruption.

2 Cor. 4.17. A far more exceeding and eternal weight of glory. 18. The things which are not seen are eternal.

2 Cor. 5.1. A building of God, an house not made with hands, eternal in the heavens. 4. For we that are in this tabernacle do groan, being burdened : not for that we would be unclothed, but clothed upon, that mortality might be swallowed up of life. 7. We walk by faith, not by sight. v. 2 8.

2 Cor. 12.4. He was caught up into paradise, and heard unspeakable words, which it is not lawful for a man to utter.

Eph. 1.18. That ye may know what is the hope of his calling, and what the riches of the glory of his inheritance in the saints.

Col. 1.5. The hope which is laid up for you

in heaven. 12. Partakers of the inheritance of the saints in light.

Col. 3.4. When Christ, who is our life, shall appear, then shall ye also appear with him in glory.

1 The. 2.12. Walk worthy of God, who hath called you unto his kingdom and glory.

1 The. 4.17. We which are alive and remain shall be caught up together with them in the clouds, to meet the Lord in the air : and so shall we ever be with the Lord.

2 The. 1.7. To you who are troubled rest with us, when the Lord Jesus shall be revealed from heaven with his mighty angels.

2 The. 2.14. He called you by our gospel, to the obtaining of the glory of our Lord Jesus Christ.

2 Tim. 2.10. That they may also obtain the salvation which is in Christ Jesus with eternal glory. 11. It is a faithful saying : For if we be dead with him, we shall also live with him : 12. If we suffer, we shall also reign with him.

2 Tim. 4.8. There is laid up for me a crown of righteousness, which the Lord, the righteous judge, shall give me at that day : and not to me only, but unto all them also that love his appearing.

Heb. 4.9. There remaineth therefore a rest to the people of God.

Heb. 8.2. The true tabernacle, which the Lord pitched, and not man.

Heb. 9.8. The way into the holiest of all was not yet made manifest. 11. A greater and more perfect tabernacle, not made with hands, that is to say, not of this building.

Heb. 10.34. Ye have in heaven a better and an enduring substance.

Heb. 11.10. He looked for a city which hath foundations, whose builder and maker is God. 16. A better country, that is, an heavenly . . . he hath prepared for them a city.

Heb. 12.22. Ye are come unto mount Sion, and unto the city of the living God, the heavenly Jerusalem, and to an innumerable company of angels. 23. To the general assembly and church of the first-born, which are written in heaven, and to God the Judge of all, and to the spirits of just men made perfect. 24. And to Jesus the mediator of the new covenant. 28. We receiving a kingdom which cannot be moved.

Heb. 13.14. Here have we no continuing city, but we seek one to come.

Jas. 1.12. He shall receive the crown of life, which the Lord hath promised to them that love him.

Jas. 2.5. Heirs of the kingdom which he hath promised to them that love him ?

1 Pet. 1.4. An inheritance incorruptible, and undefiled, and that fadeth not away, reserved in heaven for you. 13. Hope to the end for the grace that is to be brought unto you at the revelation of Jesus Christ.

1 Pet. 5.1. A partaker of the glory that shall be revealed. 4. When the chief Shepherd shall appear, ye shall receive a crown of glory that fadeth not away. 10. Who hath called us unto his eternal glory by Christ Jesus.

2 Pet. 1.11. An entrance shall be ministered unto you abundantly into the everlasting kingdom of our Lord and Saviour Jesus Christ.

2 Pet. 3.13. We, according to his promise, look for new heavens and a new earth, wherein dwelleth righteousness.

1 Jno. 2.17. He that doeth the will of God abideth for ever.

1 Jno. 3.2. It doth not yet appear what we shall be: but we know that, when he shall appear, we shall be like him; for we shall see him as he is.

Rev. 2.7. To him that overcometh will I give to eat of the tree of life, which is in the midst of the paradise of God. 10. Be thou faithful unto death, and I will give thee a crown of life. 17. To him that overcometh will I give to eat of the hidden manna, and will give him a white stone, and in the stone a new name written, which no man knoweth saving he that receiveth it. 26. To him will I give power over the nations. 28. And I will give him the morning-star. *v.* 27.

Rev. 3.4. They shall walk with me in white: for they are worthy. 5. He that overcometh, the same shall be clothed in white raiment; and I will not blot out his name out of the book of life, but I will confess his name before my Father, and before his angels. 12. Him that overcometh will I make a pillar in the temple of my God, and he shall go no more out: and I will write upon him the name of my God, and the name of the city of my God, *which is* new Jerusalem, which cometh down out of heaven from my God: and *I will write upon him* my new name.

Rev. 3.21. To him that overcometh will I grant to sit with me in my throne, even as I also overcame, and am set down with my Father in his throne. Luk. 12.8.

Rev. 4.4. Round about the throne *were* four and twenty seats: and upon the seats I saw four and twenty elders sitting, clothed in white raiment; and they had on their heads crowns of gold.

Rev. 5.9. They sung a new song, saying, Thou art worthy to take the book, and to open the seals thereof: for thou wast slain, and hast redeemed us to God by thy blood out of every kindred, and tongue, and people, and nation.

Rev. 6.11. White robes were given unto every one of them; and it was said unto them, that they should rest.

Rev. 7.9. Lo, a great multitude, which no man could number, of all nations, and kindreds, and people, and tongues, stood before the throne, and before the Lamb, clothed with white robes, and palms in their hands.

Rev. 7.13. What are these which are arrayed in white robes? and whence came they? 14. These are they which came out of great tribulation, and have washed their robes, and made them white in the blood of the Lamb. 15. Therefore are they before the throne of God, and serve him day and night in his temple: and he that sitteth on the throne shall dwell among them. 16. They shall hunger no more, neither thirst any more; neither shall the sun light on them, nor any heat. 17. For the Lamb which is in the midst of the throne shall feed them, and shall lead them unto living fountains of waters: and God shall wipe away all tears from their eyes. Isa. 49.9,10.

Rev. 11.18. That thou shouldest give reward unto thy servants the prophets, and to the saints, and them that fear thy name, small and great.

Rev. 14.1. A Lamb stood on the mount Sion, and with him an hundred forty *and* four thousand, having his Father's name written in their foreheads. 2. And I heard a voice from heaven, as the voice of many waters, and as the voice of a great thunder: and I heard the voice of harpers harping with their harps: 3. And they sung as it were a new song before the throne, and before the four beasts, and the elders: and no man could learn that song but the hundred *and* forty *and* four thousand, which were redeemed from the earth.

Rev. 14.4. These were redeemed from among men, *being* the first-fruits unto God and to the Lamb. 5. And in their mouth was found no guile: for they are without fault before the throne of God.

Rev. 15.2. I saw as it were a sea of glass mingled with fire: and them that had gotten the victory over the beast, and over his image, and over his mark, *and* over the number of his name, stand on the sea of glass, having the harps of God.

Rev. 21.1. I saw a new heaven and a new earth: for the first heaven and the first earth were passed away; and there was no more sea. 2. And I John saw the holy city, new Jerusalem, coming down from God out of heaven, prepared as a bride adorned for her husband. 3. And I heard a great voice out of heaven saying, Behold, the tabernacle of God *is* with men, and he will dwell with them, and they shall be his people, and God himself shall be with them, *and be* their God. 4. And God shall wipe away all tears from their eyes; and there shall be no more death, neither sorrow, nor crying, neither shall there be any more pain: for the former things are passed away. 5. And he that sat upon the throne said, Behold, I make all things new.

Rev. 21.9. Come hither, I will shew thee the bride, the Lamb's wife. 10. And he carried me away in the spirit to a great and high mountain, and shewed me that great city, the holy Jerusalem, descending out of heaven from God.

Rev. 21.11. Having the glory of God: and her light *was* like unto a stone most precious, even like a jasper stone, clear as crystal. 18. The building of the wall of it was *of* jasper: and the city *was* pure gold, like unto clear glass. 19. And the foundations of the wall of the city *were* garnished with all manner of precious stones. 21. And the twelve gates *were* twelve pearls; every several gate was of one pearl: and the street of the city *was* pure gold, as it were transparent glass.

Rev. 21.22. And I saw no temple therein: for the Lord God Almighty and the Lamb are the temple of it. 23. And the city had no need of the sun, neither of the moon, to shine in it: for the glory of God did lighten it, and the Lamb *is* the light thereof. 24. And the nations of them which are saved shall walk in the light of it: and the kings of the earth do bring their glory and honour into it.

Rev. 21.25. And the gates of it shall not be shut at all by day: for there shall be no night there. 27. There shall in no wise enter into it any thing that defileth, neither *whatsoever* worketh abomination, or *maketh* a lie: but they which are written in the Lamb's book of life.

Rev. 22.1. He shewed me a pure river of water of life, clear as crystal, proceeding out of the throne of God and of the Lamb. 2. In the midst of the street of it, and on either side of the river, *was there* the tree of life, which bare twelve *manner of* fruits, *and* yielded her fruit every month : and the leaves of the tree *were* for the healing of the nations. 3. And there shall be no more curse : but the throne of God and of the Lamb s̄hall be in it ; and his servants shall serve him.

Rev. 22.4. And they shall see his face ; and his name *shall be* in their foreheads. 5. And there shall be no night there ; and they need no candle, neither light of the sun ; for the Lord God giveth them light : and they shall reign for ever and ever.

See PRAISE IN HEAVEN.

HEAVEN. The sky and region of the air, dew, clouds, and rain, Gen. 1.1,8,9. Gen. 7.11. Gen. 19.24. Deu. 1.10. Deu. 28.12. Isa. 51.6. Mal. 3.10.

———— OF HEAVENS, or THIRD HEAVEN, 2 Chr. 2.6. Psa. 68.33. Psa. 115.16. 2 Cor. 12.2. Eph. 4.10. Heb. 7.26.

HEAVENLY-MINDEDNESS. See SPIRITUAL DILIGENCE.

HEBER THE KENITE, descended from Hobab, Jud. 4.11,17.

HEBREW, a name given to Abraham, Gen. 14.13 (see Gen. 11.16). To Joseph, Gen. 39.14. To people of Canaan, Gen. 40.15. To Israelites, Ex. 2.6. Deu. 15.12. Jonah 1.9. To Jews of Palestine, Act. 6.1. To strict Jews, 2 Cor. 11.22. Phil. 3.5. See ISRAELITES.

———— , the language of the Jews, Act. 21.40. Act. 22.2. Act. 26.14. Jno. 5.2. Inscription on the cross written in, Jno. 19.20. Called the Jews' language, 1 Kin. 18.26. Partially lost during the captivity, Neh. 8.8. Corrupted after the restoration, Neh. 13.24.

HEBRON, built 7 years before Zoan in Egypt ; the Anakim in, Num. 13.22. Named Kirjath-arba, Gen. 23.2 ; and Arba, Gen. 35.27. Jos. 15.13. Abraham, Isaac, and Jacob dwell near, see MAMRE. Sarah dies at, Gen. 23.2. Hoham, king of, slain by Joshua at Makkedah, Jos. 10.3-39. Anakims in, destroyed by Joshua, Jos. 11.21 ; and by Caleb, who takes the city, Jos. 14.6-15. Jud. 1.10,20. A priestly city of refuge, Jos. 20.7. Jos. 21.11,13. Samson brings the gates of Gaza to, Jud. 16.3.

David reigns at, 2 Sam. 2.1-11. 2 Sam. 3. Abner buried at, 2 Sam. 3.32. Murderers of Ishbosheth hanged at, 2 Sam. 4.12. David anointed king of all Israel at, 2 Sam. 5.1-5. Absalom's rebellion at, 2 Sam. 15.9,10. Fortified by Rehoboam, 2 Chr. 11.10. Re-peopled after the captivity, Neh. 11.25. Pool of, 2 Sam. 4.12.

HEDGE. See FENCE.

HEGAI, chamberlain of Ahasuerus, his kindness to Esther, Est. 2.8,9.

HEIFER, offered in sacrifice, Gen. 15.9. 1 Sam. 16.2 ; as an atonement for a town in cases of murder, Deu. 21.1-9. Used in ploughing, Jud. 14.18 ; and treading out corn, Hos. 10.11. Illustrative, Hos. 4.16. Hos. 10.11.

———— , RED, offering of, Num. 19.2-10. Heb. 9.13.

HEIR. See INHERITANCE.

HELBON, in Syria, wine of, exported, Eze. 27.18.

HELKATH-HAZZURIM (the field of strong men), in Gibeon, where Joab and Abner fought, 2 Sam. 2.16.

HELL. (1.) Heb. *Sheol,* the under world, translated the grave, Gen. 37.35. Gen. 42.38, &c. ; the pit, Num. 16.30. Job 17.16. (2.) Gr. *Hades,* the abode of the dead, Act. 2.27,31 ; the place of punishment, Luk. 16.23 ; translated grave, 1 Cor. 15.55. (3.) Gr. *Gehenna,* the place of punishment, Mat. 5.22. Mat. 10.28. Mat. 18.9. Mat. 23.15,33. Luk. 12.5. Jas. 3.6. (4.) Gr. *Tartarus,* place of punishment, 2 Pet. 2.4.

Psa. 9.17. The wicked shall be turned into hell, *and* all the nations that forget God.

Pro. 15.24. The way of life is above to the wise, that he may depart from hell beneath.

Isa. 30.33. Tophet *is* ordained of old ; yea, for the king it is prepared ; he hath made *it* deep *and* large : the pile thereof *is* fire and much wood ; the breath of the Lord, like a stream of brimstone, doth kindle it.

Isa. 33.14. Who among us shall dwell with the devouring fire ? who among us shall dwell with everlasting burnings?

Mat. 3.12. He will burn up the chaff with unquenchable fire.

Mat. 7.13. Wide *is* the gate, and broad *is* the way, that leadeth to destruction, and many there be which go in thereat. *v.* 14.

Mat. 10.28. Rather fear him which is able to destroy both soul and body in hell.

Mat. 13.42. Shall cast them into a furnace of fire : there shall be wailing and gnashing of teeth. *v.* 50.

Mat. 22.13. Cast *him* into outer darkness ; there shall be weeping and gnashing of teeth.

Mat. 25.41. Then shall he say also unto them on the left hand, Depart from me, ye cursed, into everlasting fire, prepared for the devil and his angels. 46. These shall go away into everlasting punishment.

Mar. 9.43. It is better for thee to enter into life maimed, than having two hands to go into hell, into the fire that never shall be quenched : 44. Where their worm dieth not, and the fire is not quenched. Mat. 5.29. Mat. 18.8,9.

Luk. 16.23. In hell he lift up his eyes, being in torments, and seeth Abraham afar off, and Lazarus in his bosom. 24. And he cried and said, Father Abraham, have mercy on me, and send Lazarus, that he may dip the tip of his finger in water, and cool my tongue ; for I am tormented in this flame. 26. Between us and you there is a great gulf fixed : so that they which would pass from hence to you cannot ; neither can they pass to us, that *would come* from thence. Act. 1.25.

2 The. 1.9. Who shall be punished with everlasting destruction from the presence of the Lord, and from the glory of his power.

2. Pet. 2.4. If God spared not the angels that sinned, but cast *them* down to hell, and delivered *them* into chains of darkness, to be reserved unto judgment.

Jude 6. The angels which kept not their first estate, but left their own habitation, he hath reserved in everlasting chains under darkness unto the judgment of the great day.

Rev. 9.1. To him was given the key of the bottomless pit. 2. And he opened the bottomless pit ; and there arose a smoke out of the pit, as the smoke of a great furnace ; and the sun and the air were darkened by reason of the smoke of the pit. Rev. 11.7.

Rev. 14.10. Shall drink of the wine of the wrath of God, which is poured out without mixture into the cup of his indignation ; and he shall be tormented with fire and brimstone in the presence of the holy angels, and in the presence of the Lamb : 11. The smoke of their torment ascendeth up for ever and ever : and they have no rest day nor night.

Rev. 19.20. These both were cast alive into a lake of fire burning with brimstone.

Rev. 20.10. The devil that deceived them was cast into the lake of fire and brimstone, where the beast and the false prophet *are*, and shall be tormented day and night for ever and ever. 15. Whosoever was not found written in the book of life was cast into the lake of fire.

Rev. 21.8. Shall have their part in the lake which burneth with fire and brimstone ; which is the second death. Rev. 2.11.

See SIN, PUNISHMENT OF.—JUDGMENT.

HELM, or RUDDER, Act. 27.40. Jas. 3.4.

HELMET of brass, 1 Sam. 17.5,38. 2 Chr. 26.14. Jer. 46.4. Illustrative, Isa. 59.17. Eph. 6.17. 1 The. 5.8.

HELP. See AFFLICTION, PRAYER IN.—GOD PROTECTOR.

HELPS, 1 Cor. 12.28. Compare Act. 6.1-6. Rom. 16.1.

HEMAN, of the tribe of Judah, his wisdom, 1 Kin. 4.31. 1 Chr. 2.6. Author of Psa. 88.

————, a Levite, and one of the 3 masters of the temple music, 1 Chr. 6.33. 1 Chr. 15.17. 1 Chr. 16.42. Called the king's seer, 1 Chr. 25.5. His sons and daughters temple-singers, 1 Chr. 25.5,6.

HEMLOCK, a poisonous plant, Hos. 10.4. Amos 6.12.

HEN. Illustrative, Mat. 23.37. Luk. 13.34.

HEPHZI-BAH (my delight is in her), a name of Judah, Isa. 62.4.

HERALD, Dan. 3.4. Deu. 20.10.

HERBS. See PLANTS.

HERESY, a sect or party. Translated sect, Act. 5.17. Act. 15.5. Act. 24.5, (verse 14, translated *heresy*, is the same word), Act. 26.5. Act. 28.22. Translated heresies, and signifying dissension, 1 Cor. 11.19. Gal. 5.20. 2 Pet. 2.1. Heretic, a factious person, Tit. 3.10. For heresy in the modern use of the word, see MINISTERS, FALSE TEACHERS.

HERES, a hill near Aijalon, Jud. 1.35.

HERMOGENES, a disciple who forsook Paul, 2 Tim. 1.15.

HERMON, a mountain of the Lebanon range. Called Sirion, Deu. 3.8,9. Psa. 29.6. Zion, Deu. 4.48. Psa. 133.3. Shenir, Deu. 3.9. 1 Chr. 5.23. Song 4.8.

HEROD I. called the Great, king of Judea, sends the wise men to Bethlehem ; slays the children of Bethlehem ; his death, Mat. 2. His sons were Archelaus, Aristobulus (not named in Scripture), Philip, Herod II. His grandson, Herod III., son of Aristobulus. His great-grandson Agrippa, son of Herod III. His granddaughter Herodias, daughter of Aristobulus ; her daughter was Salome.

HEROD II., son of Herod I., tetrarch of Galilee, Luk. 3.1. Luk. 23.7. Marries his brother's wife, Mat. 14.3,4. Mar. 6.17-19. Hears John preach ; beheads him in prison, Mar. 6.16-28. Mat. 14.3-11. Desires to see Jesus, Mat. 14.1,2. Mar. 6.14. Luk. 9.7,9. Luk. 23.8. His cruelty, Luk. 13.31,32. Christ brought before, Luk. 23.6-12,15. Act. 4.27.

———— **III.**, son of Aristobulus, and grandson of Herod I., kills James ; imprisons Peter ; his blasphemy and sudden death, Act. 12.1-23.

HERODIANS, a sect of the Jews ; their opposition to Jesus, Mat. 22.16. Mar. 3.6. Mar. 12.13.

HERODIAS, wife of Philip and concubine of his brother Herod, instigates the murder of John the Baptist, Mat. 14.3-12. Mar. 6.17-28. Luk. 3.19.

HERODION, a disciple at Rome, and a kinsman of Paul, Rom. 16.11.

HERON, Lev. 11.19. Deu. 14.18.

HESHBON, the chief city of Sihon, king of the Amorites, taken by the Israelites, Num. 21.25-35. Deu. 1.4. Built by Reuben, Num. 32.37. Given to Gad ; made a Levitical city, Jos. 21.38,39. Fish-pools of, Song 7.4. Prophecy of, as belonging to Moab, Isa. 16.8. Jer. 48.2,34,35 ; and Ammon, Jer. 49.1-3.

HETH. See HITTITES.

HEZEKIAH, 12th king of Judah (reign, 29 years), son and successor of Ahaz, 2 Kin. 16.20. 2 Kin. 18.1,2. 1 Chr. 3.13. 2 Chr. 29.1. Mat. 1.9. Purifies and repairs the temple ; restores its worship ; offers sacrifices, 2 Chr. 29. Keeps the passover, 2 Chr. 30.

Destroys idols, 2 Kin. 18.4. 2 Chr. 31.1. 2 Chr. 33.3. His regulations concerning the priests, Levites, tithes, and offerings, 2 Chr. 31.2-21. His piety and prosperity, 2 Kin. 18.3,5-7. 2 Chr. 29.2. 2 Chr. 31.20,21. 2 Chr. 32.32. Conquers the Philistines ; frees himself from tribute to Sennacherib, 2 Kin. 18.7,8.

Invaded by Sennacherib ; cuts off the supply of water, and fortifies Jerusalem ; pays him tribute, 2 Kin. 18.13-16. 2 Chr. 32.1-8. Jerusalem besieged by Tartan, Rabshakeh, &c. ; their blasphemy ; attempt to excite the Jews to revolt against Hezekiah, 2 Kin. 18.13-37. 2 Chr. 32.9-19. Isa. 36.

He sends to ask Isaiah's prayers ; receives a blasphemous letter from Sennacherib ; prays for deliverance ; is encouraged by Isaiah ; Assyrian army destroyed, 2 Kin. 19. 2 Chr. 32.20-22. Isa. 37. His sickness ; message from Isaiah ; prayer ; miracle of the shadow receding 10 degrees ; his recovery, 2 Kin. 20.1-11. 2 Chr. 32.24. Isa. 38.1-8.21,22.

His psalm of thanksgiving, Isa. 38.9-20. Receives ambassadors from Babylon ; shews them his treasures ; is rebuked by Isaiah ; his repentance, 2 Kin. 20.12-19. 2 Chr. 32.25,26,31. Isa. 39. His riches and prosperity, 2 Kin. 17.7. 2 Chr. 32.27-30. Makes a conduit in Jerusalem. See GIHON.

Conquest of Amalekites, &c., in his reign, by Simeon, 1 Chr. 4.39-43. Proverbs of Solomon, copied by his scribes, Pro. 25.1. His prayer on Micah's prophecy, Jer. 26.19. His death and burial, 2 Kin. 20.21. 2 Chr. 32.33. Prophecies respecting, 2 Kin. 19.20-34. 2 Kin. 20.5,6,16-18. Isa. 38.5-8. Isa. 39.5-7. Jer. 26.18,19.

HIDDEKEL, the 3d river of Eden, Gen. 2.14. Daniel's vision in Persia by, Dan. 10.4.

HIEL THE BETHELITE, rebuilds Jericho; his son's death as predicted, 1 Kin. 16.34 with Jos. 6.26.

HIERAPOLIS, a city of Phrygia, a church in, Col. 4.13.

HIGGAION (meditation), a musical term, use of not known, Psa. 9.16.

HIGH PLACES. Used for the worship of God, by Abraham, Gen. 12.8. Gen. 22.2,13 ; Jacob, Gen. 31.54 ; Samuel, 1 Sam. 9.12 ; David, 2 Sam. 24.25 ; Solomon, 1 Kin. 3.2,4. 2 Chr. 1.3 ; Elijah, 1 Kin. 18.30,38 ; Judah, 2 Chr. 33.17.

Used for idolatry, Num. 22.41. 1 Kin. 11.7. 1 Kin. 12.31. 1 Kin. 14.23. 1 Kin. 15.14. 1 Kin. 22.43. 2 Kin. 17.9,29. Jer. 7.31. Eze. 16.24,25.

To be destroyed, Lev. 26.30. Num. 33.52. Destroyed by Asa, 2 Chr. 14.3 ; Jehoshaphat, 2 Chr. 17.6 ; Hezekiah, 2 Kin. 18.4 ; Josiah, 2 Kin. 23.8. See TOPHET.

HIGH-PRIEST. See PRIEST.

HILKIAH, high-priest, assists Josiah in his reformations, and in repairing the temple, 2 Kin. c. 22 & 23. 1 Chr. 6.13. 2 Chr. 34. Finds the book of the law, 2 Kin. 22.8.

HIN, the 6th part of a bath or 1½ gal., Ex. 29.40. Num. 28.14.

HIND. See DEER.

HINNOM. See JEHOSHAPHAT, VALLEY OF.

HIRAM, or HURAM, king of Tyre, aids David in building his house, 2 Sam. 5.11. 1 Kin. 5.1. 1 Chr. 14.1. 2 Chr. 2.3. Aids Solomon in building the temple, 1 Kin. 5. 2 Chr. 2. Dissatisfied with cities given in payment, 1 Kin. 9.11-13. Sends gold ; his ships trade with Solomon's, 1 Kin. 9.14,26-28. 1 Kin. 10.11.

————, an artificer from Tyre, who superintended the building of the temple, 1 Kin. 7.13-51. 2 Chr. 2.13,14.

HITTITES, one of the 7 nations of Canaan descended from Heth, Canaan's son, Gen. 10.15. Gen. 23.10. Abraham purchases a field from, Gen. 23. Esau's wives from, Gen. 26.34. Gen. 36.2.

Their territory, Gen. 23.17-20. Num. 13.29. Jos. 1.4. Jud. 1.26. Given to the Israelites, Ex. 3.8. Deu. 7.1. Jos. 1.4. Conquered by Joshua, Jos. 9.1,2. Jos. c. 10-12. Jos. 24.11. Imperfectly conquered, Jud. 3.5. Intermarriages with Israelites, Jud. 3.6,7. Ezr. 9.1. With Solomon, 1 Kin. 11.1.

Were tributary to Solomon, 1 Kin. 9.20,21. 2 Chr. 8.7,8. Had kings in their reign, 1 Kin. 10.29. 2 Chr. 1.17 ; and Joram's, 2 Kin. 7.6. Uriah and Abimelech, David's captains, Hittites, 1 Sam. 26.6. 2 Sam. 11.3. 2 Sam. 23.39.

HIVITES, one of the 7 nations descended from Canaan, Gen. 10.17. 1 Chr. 1.15. Shechemites belonged to, Gen. 34.2 ; and Gibeonites, Jos. 9.7. Jos. 11.19. Esau's wives from, Gen. 26.34. Gen. 36.2. Their territory, Jos. 11.3. Jud.3.3. 2 Sam. 24.7. Given to the Israelites, Ex. 23,23,28. Deu. 20.17. Conquered by Joshua, Jos. 9.1. Jos. 12.8. Jos. 24.11. Imperfectly conquered, Jud. 3.5. Tributary to Solomon, 1 Kin. 9.20. 2 Chr. 8.7.

HOBAB, brother-in-law of Moses, visits him in the wilderness, Num. 10.29. Jud. 4.11. Compare Jethro.

HOBAH. See ZOBAH.

HOLINESS—SIN TO BE FORSAKEN. Gen. 17.1. I am the Almighty God ; walk before me, and be thou perfect.

Gen. 35.2. Put away the strange gods that are among you, and be clean, and change your garments.

Ex. 19.6. Ye shall be unto me a kingdom of priests, and an holy nation.

Ex. 22.31. Ye shall be holy men unto me.

Ex. 39.30. The holy crown of pure gold, and wrote upon it, HOLINESS TO THE LORD.

Lev. 11.44. I am the Lord your God: ye shall therefore sanctify yourselves, and ye shall be holy ; for I am holy: neither shall ye defile yourselves. v. 15. Lev. 19.2. Lev. 20.7.

Deu. 13.17. There shall cleave nought of the cursed thing to thine hand.

Deu. 14.2. Thou art an holy people unto the Lord thy God, and the Lord hath chosen thee to be a peculiar people unto himself. Deu. 26.19.

Jos. 7.12. Neither will I be with you any more, except ye destroy the accursed from among you. 13. Up, sanctify the people, and say, Sanctify yourselves against to-morrow: for thus saith the Lord God of Israel, There is an accursed thing in the midst of thee, O Israel: thou canst not stand before thine enemies, until ye take away the accursed thing from among you.

Job 5.24. Thou shalt visit thy habitation, and shalt not sin.

Job 28.28. To depart from evil is understanding.

Job 36.21. Take heed, regard not iniquity.

Psa. 4.4. Stand in awe, and sin not.

Psa. 24.3. Who shall ascend into the hill of the Lord? or who shall stand in his holy place? 4. He that hath clean hands, and a pure heart ; who hath not lifted up his soul unto vanity, nor sworn deceitfully. 5. He shall receive the blessing from the Lord, and righteousness from the God of his salvation. Psa. 15.1-5.

Psa. 32.2. Blessed is the man unto whom the Lord imputeth not iniquity, and in whose spirit there is no guile.

Psa. 37.27. Depart from evil, and do good ; and dwell for evermore.

Psa. 68.13. Though ye have lien among the pots, yet shall ye be as the wings of a dove covered with silver, and her feathers with yellow gold.

Psa. 73.1. Truly God is good to Israel, even to such as are of a clean heart.

Psa. 85.13. Righteousness shall go before him ; and shall set us in the way of his steps.

Psa. 94.15. Judgment shall return unto righteousness : and all the upright in heart shall follow it.

Psa. 97.10. Ye that love the Lord, hate evil : he preserveth the souls of his saints.

Psa. 119.1. Blessed are the undefiled in the way, who walk in the law of the Lord. 2. Blessed are they that keep his testimonies, and that seek him with the whole heart. 3. They also do no iniquity ; they walk in his ways.

Pro. 11.23. The desire of the righteous is only good.

Pro. 12.5. The thoughts of the righteous *are* right.

Pro. 16.17. The highway of the upright *is* to depart from evil : he that keepeth his way preserveth his soul.

Pro. 21.8. *As for* the pure, his work *is* right. 15. *It is* joy to the just to do judgment. 29. *As for* the upright, he directeth his way.

Pro. 22.1. A *good* name *is* rather to be chosen than great riches, *and* loving favour rather than silver and gold. Ecc. 7.1.

Isa. 4.3. *He that* remaineth in Jerusalem, shall be called holy, *even* every one that is written among the living in Jerusalem.

Isa. 26.2. Open ye the gates, that the righteous nation which keepeth the truth may enter in.

Isa. 32.17. The work of righteousness shall be peace ; and the effect of righteousness quietness and assurance for ever.

Isa. 35.8. It shall be called The way of holiness ; the unclean shall not pass over it.

Isa. 51.7. Ye that know righteousness, the people in whose heart *is* my law.

Isa. 52.1. Awake, awake ; put on thy strength, O Zion ; put on thy beautiful garments, O Jerusalem, the holy city : for henceforth there shall no more come into thee the uncircumcised and the unclean. 11. Depart ye, go ye out from thence, touch no unclean *thing ;* go ye out of the midst of her ; be ye clean, that bear the vessels of the Lord.

Isa. 57.2. They shall rest in their beds, *each one* walking *in* his uprightness.

Isa. 60.1. Arise, shine ; for thy light is come, and the glory of the Lord is risen upon thee. 21. Thy people also *shall be* all righteous.

Isa. 61.3. That they might be called Trees of righteousness, The planting of the Lord, that he might be glorified. 11. So the Lord God will cause righteousness and praise to spring forth before all the nations.

Amos 3.3. Can two walk together, except they be agreed ?

Zeph. 2.3. Seek ye the Lord, all ye meek of the earth, which have wrought his judgment ; seek righteousness, seek meekness.

Zec. 8.3. Jerusalem shall be called a city of truth ; and the mountain of the Lord of hosts the holy mountain. 19. Love the truth and peace.

Zec. 14.20. Upon the bells of the horses, HOLINESS UNTO THE LORD ; and the pots in the Lord's house shall be like the bowls before the altar. 21. Yea, every pot in Jerusalem and in Judah shall be holiness unto the Lord of hosts : and there shall be no more the Canaanite in the house of the Lord of hosts.

Mat. 5.8. Blessed *are* the pure in heart : for they shall see God. 29. If thy right eye offend thee, pluck it out, and cast *it* from thee : 30. If thy right hand offend thee, cut it off, and cast *it* from thee ; for it is profitable for thee that one of thy members should perish, and not *that* thy whole body should be cast into hell.

Mat. 10.16. Be ye therefore wise as serpents, and harmless as doves.

Luk. 1.74. Might serve him without fear, 75. In holiness and righteousness before him, all the days of our life.

Luk. 6.45. A good man out of the good

treasure of his heart bringeth forth that which is good ; for of the abundance of the heart his mouth speaketh.

Jno. 1.47. Behold an Israelite indeed, in whom is no guile !

Jno. 5.14. Sin no more.

Jno. 10.4. The sheep follow him : for they know his voice. 5. And a stranger will they not follow, but will flee from him.

Jno. 15.19. If ye were of the world, the world would love his own : but because ye are not of the world, but I have chosen you out of the world, therefore the world hateth you.

Jno. 17.23. I in them, and thou in me, that they may be made perfect in one.

Rom. 6.2. How shall we, that are dead to sin, live any longer therein ? 4. We are buried with him by baptism into death : that like as Christ was raised up from the dead by the glory of the Father, even so we also should walk in newness of life. 11. Reckon ye also yourselves to be dead indeed unto sin, but alive unto God through Jesus Christ our Lord. 12. Let not sin therefore reign in your mortal body, that ye should obey it in the lusts thereof.

Rom. 6.13. Neither yield ye your members as instruments of unrighteousness unto sin : but yield yourselves unto God, as those that are alive from the dead, and your members *as* instruments of righteousness unto God. 14. For sin shall not have dominion over you : for ye are not under the law, but under grace. 19. As ye have yielded your members servants to uncleanness and to iniquity unto iniquity ; even so now yield your members servants to righteousness unto holiness. 22. Being made free from sin, and become servants to God, ye have your fruit unto holiness, and the end everlasting life. *v.* 1-23.

Rom. 7.4. We should bring forth fruit unto God. 6. We are delivered from the law, that being dead wherein we were held ; that we should serve in newness of spirit, and not *in* the oldness of the letter. *v.* 1-6.

Rom. 8.1. No condemnation to them which are in Christ Jesus, who walk not after the flesh, but after the Spirit. 4. That the righteousness of the law might be fulfilled in us, who walk not after the flesh, but after the Spirit. 12. Brethren, we are debtors, not to the flesh, to live after the flesh. *v.* 1-14.

Rom. 12.1. I beseech you therefore, brethren, by the mercies of God, that ye present your bodies a living sacrifice, holy, acceptable unto God, *which is* your reasonable service. 2. And be not conformed to this world : but be ye transformed by the renewing of your mind, that ye may prove what *is* that good, and acceptable, and perfect, will of God. 9. Abhor that which is evil ; cleave to that which is good.

Rom. 13.12. The night is far spent, the day is at hand : let us therefore cast off the works of darkness, and let us put on the armour of light. 13. Let us walk honestly as in the day. 14. Put ye on the Lord Jesus Christ, and make no provision for the flesh, to *fulfil* the lusts *thereof.*

Rom. 14.17. The kingdom of God is not meat and drink ; but righteousness, and peace, and joy in the Holy Ghost.

Rom. 16.19. I would have you wise unto that which is good, and simple concerning evil.

1 Cor. 3.16. Know ye not that ye are the temple of God, and *that* the Spirit of God dwelleth in you? 17. If any man defile the temple of God, him shall God destroy; for the temple of God is holy, which *temple* ye are.

1 Cor. 5.7. Purge out therefore the old leaven, that ye may be a new lump, as ye are unleavened.

1 Cor. 6.12. All things are lawful unto me, but all things are not expedient: all things are lawful for me, but I will not be brought under the power of any. 13. The body *is* not for fornication, but for the Lord, and the Lord for the body. 19. What? know ye not that your body is the temple of the Holy Ghost *which is* in you, which ye have of God, and ye are not your own? 20. For ye are bought with a price: therefore glorify God in your body, and in your spirit, which are God's.

1 Cor. 7.23. Ye are bought with a price; be not ye the servants of men.

1 Cor. 8.12. When ye sin so against the brethren, and wound their weak conscience, ye sin against Christ.

1 Cor. 10.21. Ye cannot drink the cup of the Lord, and the cup of devils: ye cannot be partakers of the Lord's table, and of the table of devils. 31. Whether therefore ye eat, or drink, or whatsoever ye do, do all to the glory of God. 32. Give none offence, neither to the Jews, nor to the Gentiles, nor to the church of God.

1 Cor. 12.31. Covet earnestly the best gifts.

1 Cor. 15.34. Awake to righteousness, and sin not.

2 Cor. 6.14. Be ye not unequally yoked together with unbelievers: for what fellowship hath righteousness with unrighteousness? and what communion hath light with darkness? 15. And what concord hath Christ with Belial? or what part hath he that believeth with an infidel? 16. And what agreement hath the temple of God with idols? for ye are the temple of the living God. 17. Wherefore come out from among them, and be ye separate, saith the Lord, and touch not the unclean *thing*; and I will receive you.

2 Cor. 7.1. Let us cleanse ourselves from all filthiness of the flesh and spirit, perfecting holiness in the fear of God.

2 Cor. 10.3. Though we walk in the flesh, we do not war after the flesh. 5. Casting down imaginations, and every high thing that exalteth itself against the knowledge of God, and bringing into captivity every thought to the obedience of Christ.

2 Cor. 11.2. I have espoused you to one husband, that I may present *you as* a chaste virgin to Christ.

2 Cor. 13.7. I pray to God that ye do no evil; not that we should appear approved, but that ye should do that which is honest. 8. We can do nothing against the truth, but for the truth.

Gal. 2.17. If, while we seek to be justified by Christ, we ourselves also are found sinners, *is* therefore Christ the minister of sin? God forbid.

Gal. 5.22. The fruit of the Spirit is love, joy, peace, long-suffering, gentleness, goodness, faith, 23. Meekness, temperance: against such there is no law. 24. And they that are Christ's have crucified the flesh with the affec-

tions and lusts. 25. If we live in the Spirit, let us also walk in the Spirit.

Gal. 6.15. In Christ Jesus neither circumcision availeth any thing, nor uncircumcision, but a new creature.

Eph. 1.4. He hath chosen us in him before the foundation of the world, that we should be holy and without blame before him in love. 13. Ye were sealed with that Holy Spirit of promise. 14. Which is the earnest of our inheritance.

Eph. 2.21. In whom all the building fitly framed together groweth unto an holy temple in the Lord: 22. In whom ye also are builded together for an habitation of God through the Spirit.

Eph. 4.20. Ye have not so learned Christ; 21. If so be that ye have heard him, and have been taught by him, as the truth is in Jesus: 22. That ye put off concerning the former conversation the old man, which is corrupt according to the deceitful lusts; 23. And be renewed in the spirit of your mind; 24. And that ye put on the new man, which after God is created in righteousness and true holiness.

Eph. 5.1. Be ye therefore followers of God, as dear children; 3. But fornication, and all uncleanness, or covetousness, let it not be once named among you, as becometh saints; 8. Ye were sometimes darkness, but now *are ye* light in the Lord: walk as children of light: 9. For the fruit of the Spirit *is* in all goodness and righteousness and truth. 10. Proving what is acceptable unto the Lord. 11. Have no fellowship with the unfruitful works of darkness, but rather reprove *them*.

Phil. 1.10. Be sincere and without offence till the day of Christ; 11. Being filled with the fruits of righteousness, which are by Jesus Christ, unto the glory and praise of God.

Phil. 2.15. Be blameless and harmless, the sons of God, without rebuke, in the midst of a crooked and perverse nation, among whom ye shine as lights in the world.

Phil. 4.8. Whatsoever things are true, whatsoever things *are* honest, whatsoever things *are* just, whatsoever things *are* pure, whatsoever things *are* lovely, whatsoever things *are* of good report; if *there be* any virtue, and if *there be* any praise, think on these things.

Col. 1.22. To present you holy and unblameable and unreproveable in his sight.

Col. 3.5. Mortify therefore your members which are upon the earth. 9. Ye have put off the old man with his deeds; 10. And have put on the new *man*, which is renewed in knowledge after the image of him that created him. 12. The elect of God, holy and beloved.

1 The. 2.12. Walk worthy of God, who hath called you unto his kingdom and glory.

1 The. 4.3. This is the will of God, *even* your sanctification. 7. God hath not called us unto uncleanness, but unto holiness.

1 The. 5.5. Ye are all the children of light, and the children of the day: we are not of the night, nor of darkness. 22. Abstain from all appearance of evil.

2 The. 2.13. God hath from the beginning chosen you to salvation through sanctification of the Spirit.

1 Tim. 1.5. The end of the commandment is charity out of a pure heart, and *of* a good conscience, and *of* faith unfeigned.

1 Tim. 4.8. Godliness is profitable unto all

things, having promise of the life that now is, and of that which is to come. 12. Be thou an example of the believers, in word, in conversation, in charity, in spirit, in faith, in purity.

1 Tim. 5.22. Neither be partaker of other men's sins: keep thyself pure.

1 Tim. 6.6. Godliness with contentment is great gain. 11. O man of God, flee these things; and follow after righteousness, godliness, faith, love, patience, meekness. 12. Fight the good fight of faith, lay hold on eternal life, whereunto thou art also called, and hast professed a good profession before many witnesses.

2 Tim. 2.19. Let every one that nameth the name of Christ depart from iniquity. 21. If a man therefore purge himself from these, he shall be a vessel unto honour, sanctified, and meet for the master's use, *and* prepared unto every good work. 22. Flee also youthful lusts: but follow righteousness, faith, charity, peace, with them that call on the Lord out of a pure heart. *v.* 16,17.

Tit. 1.15. Unto the pure all things *are* pure.

Tit. 2.10. Adorn the doctrine of God our Saviour in all things.

Heb. 10.22. Having our hearts sprinkled from an evil conscience, and our bodies washed with pure water.

Heb. 12.1. Lay aside every weight, and the sin which doth so easily beset *us*, and let us run with patience the race that is set before us. 14. Follow peace with all *men*, and holiness, without which no man shall see the Lord. 15. Looking diligently lest any man fail of the grace of God; lest any root of bitterness springing up trouble *you*, and thereby many be defiled.

Heb. 13.9. *It is* a good thing that the heart be established with grace.

Jas. 1.21. Lay apart all filthiness and superfluity of naughtiness 27. To keep himself unspotted from the world.

Jas. 3.17. The wisdom that is from above is first pure, then peaceable, gentle, *and* easy to be intreated, full of mercy and good fruits, without partiality, and without hypocrisy.

Jas. 4.4. Whosoever therefore will be a friend of the world is the enemy of God.

1 Pet. 1.14. As obedient children, not fashioning yourselves according to the former lusts in your ignorance: 15. But as he which hath called you is holy, so be ye holy in all manner of conversatior; 16. Because it is written, Be ye holy; for I am holy.

1 Pet. 2.1. Laying aside all malice, and all guile, and hypocrisies, and envies, and all evil speakings. 5. Ye also, as lively stones, are built up a spiritual house, an holy priesthood, to offer up spiritual sacrifices, acceptable to God by Jesus Christ. 9. Ye *are* a chosen generation, a royal priesthood, an holy nation, a peculiar people; that ye should shew forth the praises of him who hath called you out of darkness into his marvellous light.

1 Pet. 2.11. I beseech *you* as strangers and pilgrims, abstain from fleshly lusts, which war against the soul; 12. Having your conversation honest among the Gentiles: that, whereas they speak against you as evildoers, they may by *your* good works, which they shall behold, glorify God in the day of visitation. 24. Who his own self bare our sins in his own body on

the tree, that we, being dead to sins, should live unto righteousness.

1 Pet. 3.11. Let him eschew evil, and do good. Psa. 34.14.

1 Pet. 4.1. Arm yourselves likewise with the same mind: for he that hath suffered in the flesh hath ceased from sin; 2. That he no longer should live the rest of *his* time in the flesh to the lusts of men, but to the will of God. 6. That they might be judged according to men in the flesh, but live according to God in the spirit. 7. The end of all things is at hand: be ye therefore sober, and watch unto prayer.

2 Pet. 1.5. Giving all diligence, add to your faith virtue; and to virtue knowledge; 6. And to knowledge temperance; and to temperance patience; and to patience godliness; 7. And to godliness brotherly kindness; and to brotherly kindness charity. 8. For if these things be in you, and abound, they make *you that ye shall* neither *be* barren nor unfruitful in the knowledge of our Lord Jesus Christ.

2 Pet. 3.11. *Seeing* then *that* all these things shall be dissolved, what manner *of persons* ought ye to be in *all* holy conversation and godliness, 12. Looking for and hasting unto the coming of the day of God. 14. Seeing that ye look for such things, be diligent that ye may be found of him in peace, without spot, and blameless.

1 Jno. 1.6. If we say that we have fellowship with him, and walk in darkness, we lie, and do not the truth: 7. But if we walk in the light, as he is in the light, we have fellowship one with another.

1 Jno. 2.1. My little children, these things write I unto you, that ye sin not. 29. Every one that doeth righteousness is born of him.

1 Jno. 3.6. Whosoever abideth in him sinneth not: whosoever sinneth hath not seen him, neither known him. 9. Whosoever is born of God doth not commit sin; for his seed remaineth in him: and he cannot sin, because he is born of God. 10. In this the children of God are manifest, and the children of the devil: whosoever doeth not righteousness is not of God, neither he that loveth not his brother. *v.* 7,8.

1 Jno. 5.4. Whatsoever is born of God overcometh the world: and this is the victory that overcometh the world, *even* our faith. 5. Who is he that overcometh the world, but he that believeth that Jesus is the Son of God? 18. Whosoever is born of God sinneth not; but he that is begotten of God keepeth himself, and that wicked one toucheth him not. 21. Little children, keep yourselves from idols.

2 Jno. 4. I found of thy children walking in truth, as we have received a commandment from the Father.

3 Jno. 11. Follow not that which is evil, but that which is good. He that doeth good is of God: but he that doeth evil hath not seen God.

Rev. 18.4. Come out of her, my people, that ye be not partakers of her sins.

Rev. 19.8. To her was granted that she should be arrayed in fine linen, clean and white: for the fine linen is the righteousness of saints.

See DECISION—OBEDIENCE—SANCTIFICATION—SPIRITUAL DILIGENCE—SIN HATED—WORSHIP, REVERENCE IN—LIKENESS TO GOD.

HOLY DAY. See FEASTS—SABBATH.

HOLY PLACE. See TABERNACLE—TEMPLE.

HOLY SPIRIT, HIS ATTRIBUTES, &c. Gen. 1.2. And the Spirit of God moved upon the face of the waters.

Gen. 6.3. My Spirit shall not always strive with man.

Neh. 9.20. Thy good Spirit.

Job 33.4. The Spirit of God hath made me, and the breath of the Almighty hath given me life.

Psa. 51.12. Thy free Spirit.

Psa. 139.7. Whither shall I go from thy Spirit? or whither shall I flee from thy presence?

Isa. 40.13. Who hath directed the Spirit of the Lord, or being his counsellor hath taught him?

Mic. 2.7. Is the Spirit of the Lord straitened? are these his doings?

Zec. 4.6. Not by might, nor by power, but by my Spirit, saith the Lord of hosts. v. 1-7.

Mat. 28.19. Baptizing them in the name of the Father, and of the Son, and of the Holy Ghost.

Luk. 1.35. The Holy Ghost shall come upon thee, and the power of the Highest shall overshadow thee ; therefore also that holy thing, which shall be born of thee, shall be called the Son of God.

Jno. 6.63. It is the Spirit that quickeneth.

Jno. 14.17. The Spirit of truth. 1 Jno. 5.6.

Act. 5.3. Why hath Satan filled thine heart to lie to the Holy Ghost? 4. Thou hast not lied unto men, but unto God.

Rom. 15.30. The love of the Spirit.

1 Cor. 2.10. God hath revealed them unto us by his Spirit : for the Spirit searcheth all things, yea, the deep things of God. 11. For what man knoweth the things of a man, save the spirit of man which is in him? even so the things of God knoweth no man, but the Spirit of God.

1 Cor. 12.11. All these worketh that one and the selfsame Spirit, dividing to every man severally as he will.

2 Cor. 13.14. The grace of the Lord Jesus Christ, and the love of God, and the communion of the Holy Ghost, be with you all.

Heb. 9.14. The eternal Spirit.

Heb. 10.29. The Spirit of grace.

1 Pet. 3.18. Christ being put to death in the flesh, but quickened by the Spirit.

1 Pet. 4.14. The Spirit of glory and of God resteth upon you.

Rev. 4.5. Seven lamps of fire burning before the throne, which are the seven Spirits of God. Rev. 1.4.

Rev. 5.6. The seven Spirits of God sent forth into all the earth.

Rev. 11.11. The Spirit of life from God.

See GOD THE FATHER, SON, AND HOLY GHOST.

HOLY SPIRIT, MIRACULOUS INFLUENCES OF. Joel 2.28,29. Mat. 12.28. Luk. 1.35. Act. 1.5,8. Act. 2.2-4. Act. 8.15-17. Act. 10.44,46. Act. 11.15. Act. 19.2-6. Rom. 15.19. 1 Cor. 12.9-11. Gal. 3.5. Heb. 2.4.

HOLY SPIRIT, PRAYER FOR. Psa 51.11. Take not thy Holy Spirit from me. 12. Uphold me with Thy free Spirit.

Song 4.16. Awake, O north wind ; and come, thou south ; blow upon my garden, that the spices thereof may flow out.

Eze. 37.9. Come from the four winds, O breath, and breathe upon these slain, that they may live.

Luk. 11.13. If ye then, being evil, know how to give good gifts unto your children : how much more shall your heavenly Father give the Holy Spirit to them that ask him?

Act. 4.31. When they had prayed, the place was shaken where they were assembled together ; and they were all filled with the Holy Ghost. Act. 1.14. Act. 2.1.

Eph. 3.16. That he would grant you, according to the riches of his glory, to be strengthened with might by his Spirit in the inner man.

HOLY SPIRIT, SINS AGAINST. Isa. 63.10. They rebelled, and vexed his Holy Spirit : therefore he was turned to be their enemy.

Mat. 12.31. But the blasphemy against the Holy Ghost shall not be forgiven unto men. 32. And whosoever speaketh a word against the Son of man, it shall be forgiven him : but whosoever speaketh against the Holy Ghost, it shall not be forgiven him, neither in this world, neither in the world to come. Luk. 12.10.

Mar. 3.29. But he that shall blaspheme against the Holy Ghost hath never forgiveness, but is in danger of eternal damnation. 1 Jno. 5.16.

Act. 7.51. Ye do always resist the Holy Ghost : as your fathers did, so do ye.

Act. 8.18. He offered them money. 19. Saying, Give me also this power, that on whomsoever I lay hands, he may receive the Holy Ghost. 20. But Peter said unto him, Thy money perish with thee, because thou hast thought that the gift of God may be purchased with money.

Eph. 4.30. Grieve not the Holy Spirit of God.

1 The. 5.19. Quench not the Spirit.

Heb. 10.29. Of how much sorer punishment, suppose ye, shall he be thought worthy, who hath done despite unto the Spirit of grace.

Rev. 2.7. He that hath an ear, let him hear what the Spirit saith unto the churches. v. 11,22.

HOLY SPIRIT, HIS WORK AND INFLUENCES. Gen. 6.3. My Spirit shall not always strive with man.

Num. 27.18. A man in whom is the Spirit. Gen. 41.38. Ex. 31.3. Ex. 35.31.

Isa. 32.15. Until the Spirit be poured upon us from on high, and the wilderness be a fruitful field, and the fruitful field be counted for a forest. v. 17.

Isa. 44.3. I will pour water upon him that is thirsty, and floods upon the dry ground ; I will pour my Spirit upon thy seed, and my blessing upon thine offspring : 4. And they shall spring up as among the grass, as willows by the water-courses.

Isa. 59.19. When the enemy shall come in like a flood, the Spirit of the Lord shall lift up a standard against him. 21. My Spirit that is upon thee, and my words which I have put in thy mouth, shall not depart out of thy mouth, nor out of the mouth of thy seed.

Isa. 63.11. Where is he that put his holy Spirit within him? 14. The Spirit of the Lord caused him to rest.

Eze. 39.29. Neither will I hide my face any more from them : for I have poured out my Spirit upon the house of Israel.

Joel 2.28. I will pour out my Spirit upon all flesh; 29. Also upon the servants and upon the handmaids in those days will I pour out my Spirit.

Hag. 2.5. *According to* the word that I covenanted with you when ye came out of Egypt, so my Spirit remaineth among you.

Zec. 4.6. Not by might, nor by power, but by my Spirit, saith the Lord of hosts.

Zec. 12.10. I will pour upon the house of David, and upon the inhabitants of Jerusalem, the Spirit of grace and of supplications: and they shall look upon me whom they have pierced, and they shall mourn.

Mat. 3.11. I indeed baptise you with water unto repentance: but he shall baptise you with the Holy Ghost, and *with* fire. Jno. 1.33. Act. 11.16.

Jno. 4.14. Whosoever drinketh of the water that I shall give him shall never thirst; but the water that I shall give him shall be in him a well of water springing up into everlasting life.

Jno. 7.38. He that believeth on me, as the scripture hath said, out of his belly shall flow rivers of living water. 39. (But this spake he of the Spirit, which they that believe on him should receive: for the Holy Ghost was not yet *given;* because that Jesus was not yet glorified.)

Jno. 14.16. I will pray the Father, and he shall give you another Comforter, that he may abide with you for ever; 17. *Even* the Spirit of truth; whom the world cannot receive, because it seeth him not, neither knoweth him: but ye know him; for he dwelleth with you, and shall be in you.

Jno. 15.26. When the Comforter is come, whom I will send unto you from the Father, *even* the Spirit of truth, which proceedeth from the Father, he shall testify of me.

Jno. 16.7. It is expedient for you that I go away: for if I go not away, the Comforter will not come unto you; but if I depart, I will send him unto you. 8. When he is come, he will reprove the world of sin, and of righteousness, and of judgment. *v.* 9-11.

Jno. 20.22. He breathed on *them*, and saith unto them, Receive ye the Holy Ghost.

Act. 2.38. Repent, and be baptized every one of you in the name of Jesus Christ for the remission of sins, and ye shall receive the gift of the Holy Ghost.

Act. 3.19. That your sins may be blotted out, when the times of refreshing shall come from the presence of the Lord.

Act. 5.32. We are his witnesses of these things; and *so is* also the Holy Ghost, whom God hath given to them that obey him.

Act. 6.5. They chose Stephen, a man full of faith and of the Holy Ghost.

Act. 9.31. Walking in the fear of the Lord, and in the comfort of the Holy Ghost, were multiplied.

Act. 10.44. The Holy Ghost fell on all them which heard the word. 45. And they of the circumcision which believed were astonished, as many as came with Peter, because that on the Gentiles also was poured out the gift of the Holy Ghost. 47. Can any man forbid water, that these should not be baptized, which have received the Holy Ghost as well as we? Act. 11.17.

Act. 11.24. He was a good man, and full of the Holy Ghost.

Act. 13.52. The disciples were filled with joy, and with the Holy Ghost.

Act. 15.8. God, which knoweth the hearts, bare them witness, giving them the Holy Ghost, even as *he did* unto us.

Act. 20.28. The flock over the which the Holy Ghost hath made you overseers.

Rom. 5.5. The love of God is shed abroad in our hearts by the Holy Ghost, which is given unto us.

Rom. 8.4. That the righteousness of the law might be fulfilled in us, who walk not after the flesh, but after the Spirit. 11. If the Spirit of him that raised up Jesus from the dead dwell in you, he that raised up Christ from the dead shall also quicken your mortal bodies by his Spirit that dwelleth in you. 14. As many as are led by the Spirit of God, they are the sons of God. 23. Not only *they*, but ourselves also, which have the first-fruits of the Spirit.

Rom. 8.26. The Spirit also helpeth our infirmities: for we know not what we should pray for as we ought: but the Spirit itself maketh intercession for us with groanings which cannot be uttered. 27. And he that searcheth the hearts knoweth what *is* the mind of the Spirit, because he maketh intercession for the saints according to *the will of* God. *v.* 1-27.

Rom. 14.17. Joy in the Holy Ghost.

Rom. 15.13. That ye may abound in hope, through the power of the Holy Ghost.

1 Cor. 2.4. Not with enticing words of man's wisdom, but in demonstration of the Spirit and of power.

1 Cor. 3.16. Know ye not that ye are the temple of God, and *that* the Spirit of God dwelleth in you? 1 Cor. 6.19.

1 Cor. 12.4. Now there are diversities of gifts, but the same Spirit. 7. The manifestation of the Spirit is given to every man to profit withal. 9. To another faith by the same Spirit. 11. All these worketh that one and the selfsame Spirit, dividing to every man severally as he will.

2 Cor. 1.22. Who hath also sealed us, and given the earnest of the Spirit in our hearts. 2 Cor. 5.5.

2 Cor. 3.6. Able ministers of the new testament; not of the letter, but of the Spirit: for the letter killeth, but the Spirit giveth life. 8. How shall not the ministration of the Spirit be rather glorious? 17. Where the Spirit of the Lord *is*, there *is* liberty.

2 Cor. 4.13. We having the same Spirit of faith.

2 Cor. 6.4. Approving ourselves as the ministers of God. 6. By pureness, by the Holy Ghost.

Gal. 3.2. Received ye the Spirit by the works of the law, or by the hearing of faith? 3. Are ye so foolish? having begun in the Spirit, are ye now made perfect by the flesh? 14. That we might receive the promise of the Spirit through faith.

Gal. 4.6. Because ye are sons, God hath sent forth the Spirit of his Son into your hearts, crying, Abba, Father.

Gal. 5.5. We through the Spirit wait for the hope of righteousness by faith. 16. Walk in the Spirit, and ye shall not fulfil the lust of the flesh, 17. For the flesh lusteth against the Spirit, and the Spirit against the flesh: and these are contrary the one to the other: so that ye cannot do the things that ye would. 18. But if ye be led of the Spirit, ye are not under the law. 25. If we live in the Spirit, let us also walk in the Spirit.

Gal. 6.8. He that soweth to the Spirit shall of the Spirit reap life everlasting.

Eph. 1.13. After that ye believed, ye were sealed with that holy Spirit of promise, 14. Which is the earnest of our inheritance until the redemption of the purchased possession, unto the praise of his glory.

Eph. 2.18. Through him we both have access by one Spirit unto the Father. 22. In whom ye also are builded together for an habitation of God through the Spirit.

Eph. 4.3. Endeavouring to keep the unity of the Spirit in the bond of peace. 4. *There is* one body, and one Spirit, even as ye are called in one hope of your calling. 30. The holy Spirit of God, whereby ye are sealed unto the day of redemption.

Eph. 5.9. The fruit of the Spirit *is* in all goodness and righteousness and truth. 18. Be filled with the Spirit.

Eph. 6.18. Praying always with all prayer and supplication in the Spirit.

Phil. 1.19. This shall turn to my salvation through your prayer, and the supply of the Spirit of Jesus Christ.

Phil. 2.1. If any fellowship of the Spirit.

Col. 1.8. Who also declared unto us your love in the Spirit.

1 The. 1.5. Our gospel came not unto you in word only, but also in power, and in the Holy Ghost. 6. Having received the word in much affliction, with joy of the Holy Ghost.

2 Tim. 1.7. God hath not given us the spirit of fear ; but of power, and of love, and of a sound mind. 14. That good thing which was committed unto thee keep by the Holy Ghost which dwelleth in us.

Heb. 6.4. Those who were once enlightened, and have tasted of the heavenly gift, and were made partakers of the Holy Ghost,

1 Pet. 4.14. Happy *are ye ;* for the Spirit of glory and of God resteth upon you.

1 Jno. 3.24. We know that he abideth in us, by the Spirit which he hath given us.

1 Jno. 4.2. Hereby know ye the Spirit of God : Every spirit that confesseth that Jesus Christ is come in the flesh is of God. 13. Hereby know we that we dwell in him, and he in us, because he hath given us of his Spirit.

1 Jno. 5.6. It is the Spirit that beareth witness, because the Spirit is truth. 7. For 'here are three that bear record in heaven, the Father, the Word, and the Holy Ghost : and these three are one. 8. And there are three that bear witness in earth, the Spirit, and the water, and the blood : and these three agree in one.

Jude 20. Building up yourselves on your most holy faith, praying in the Holy Ghost.

Rev. 1.4. Grace *be* unto you, and peace, from the seven Spirits which are before his throne.

Rev. 22.17. The Spirit and the bride say, Come.

See REGENERATION FROM THE HOLY SPIRIT —WISDOM.

HOMER, the largest dry measure, equal to 10 baths or 90 galls., Eze. 45.11,14. Num. 11.32. Isa. 5.10.

HONESTY. See INTEGRITY.

HONEY. Used for food, Ex. 16.31. 2 Sam. 17.29. Pro. 25.27. Song 4.11. Isa. 7.15. Mat. 3.4. Luk. 24.42. Forbidden to be offered with sacrifices, Lev. 2.11. Found in rocks, Deu. 32.13. Psa. 81.16 ; and woods, 1 Sam. 14.25. Samson finds, Jud. 14.8. Abounded in Canaan, Gen. 43.11. Ex. 3.8. Lev. 20.24. Deu. 8.8 ; in Egypt, Num. 16.13 ; in Assyria, 2 Kin. 18.32. Exported from Canaan, Eze. 27.17. Proverb connected with, Jud. 14.18.

HOOD, Isa. 3.23.

HOPE, Psa. 31.24. Be of good courage, and he shall strengthen your heart, all ye that hope in the Lord.

Psa. 33.18. The eye of the Lord *is* upon them that fear him, upon them that hope in his mercy ; 22. Let thy mercy, O Lord, be upon us, according as we hope in thee.

Psa. 38.15. In thee, O Lord, do I hope : thou wilt hear, O Lord my God.

Psa. 39.7. Now, Lord, what wait I for? my hope *is* in thee.

Psa. 43.5. Why art thou cast down, O my soul? and why art thou disquieted within me? hope in God : for I shall yet praise him, *who is* the health of my countenance, and my God.

Psa. 71.5. Thou *art* my hope, O Lord God: *thou art* my trust from my youth. 14. I will hope continually, and will yet praise thee more and more.

Psa. 78.7. That they might set their hope in God.

Psa. 119.74. They that fear thee will be glad when they see me ; because I have hoped in thy word. 81. My soul fainteth for thy salvation : *but* I hope in thy word. 116. Let me not be ashamed of my hope. 166. Lord, I have hoped for thy salvation.

Psa. 130.7. Let Israel hope in the Lord : for with the Lord *there is* mercy.

Psa. 146.5. Happy *is he* that *hath* the God of Jacob for his help, whose hope *is* in the Lord his God.

Pro. 10.28. The hope of the righteous *shall be* gladness.

Pro. 13.12. Hope deferred maketh the heart sick : but *when* the desire cometh, *it is* a tree of life.

Pro. 14.32. The righteous hath hope in his death.

Jer. 17.7. Blessed *is* the man that trusteth in the Lord, and whose hope the Lord is.

Lam. 3.21. This I recall to my mind, therefore have I hope. 24. The Lord *is* my portion, saith my soul ; therefore will I hope in him. 26. *It is* good that *a man* should both hope and quietly wait for the salvation of the Lord.

Hos. 2.15. I will give her the valley of Achor for a door of hope.

Joel 3.16. The Lord *will be* the hope of his people, and the strength of the children of Israel.

Act. 24.15. And have hope toward God, which they themselves also allow, that there shall be a resurrection of the dead.

Act. 26.6. I stand and am judged for the hope of the promise made of God unto our fathers : 7. Unto which *promise* our twelve tribes, instantly serving *God* day and night, hope to come : for which hope's sake, king Agrippa, I am accused of the Jews.

Act. 28.20. For the hope of Israel I am bound with this chain.

Rom. 5.2. By whom also we have access by faith into this grace wherein we stand, and rejoice in hope of the glory of God. 4. Experience, hope: 5. And hope maketh not ashamed; because the love of God is shed abroad in our hearts by the Holy Ghost which is given unto us.

Rom. 8.24. We are saved by hope: but hope that is seen is not hope: for what a man seeth, why doth he yet hope for? 25. But if we hope for that we see not, *then* do we with patience wait for *it*.

Rom. 12.12. Rejoicing in hope.

Rom. 15.4. That we, through patience and comfort of the scriptures, might have hope. 13. The God of hope fill you with all joy and peace in believing, that ye may abound in hope, through the power of the Holy Ghost.

1 Cor. 13.13. Now abideth faith, hope, charity, these three.

1 Cor. 15.19. If in this life only we have hope in Christ, we are of all men most miserable.

2 Cor. 3.12. Seeing then that we have such hope, we use great plainness of speech.

Gal. 5.5. We through the Spirit wait for the hope of righteousness by faith.

Eph. 1.18. That ye may know what is the hope of his calling.

Eph. 4.4. Ye are called in one hope of your calling.

Phil. 1.20. According to my earnest expectation and *my* hope, that in nothing I shall be ashamed, but *that* with all boldness, as always, *so* now also Christ shall be magnified in my body, whether *it be* by life, or by death.

Col. 1.5. The hope which is laid up for you in heaven. 23. *Be* not moved away from the hope of the gospel. 27. Christ in you, the hope of glory.

1 The. 1.3. Remembering without ceasing your work of faith, and labour of love, and patience of hope in our Lord Jesus Christ.

1 The. 5.8. For an helmet, the hope of salvation. Eph. 6.17.

2 The. 2.16. Our Father, which hath loved us, and hath given *us* everlasting consolation, and good hope through grace.

1 Tim. 1.1. Lord Jesus Christ, *which is* our hope.

Tit. 1.2. In hope of eternal life, which God, that cannot lie, promised before the world began.

Tit. 2.13. Looking for that blessed hope, and the glorious appearing of the great God and our Saviour Jesus Christ.

Tit. 3.7. That being justified by his grace, we should be made heirs according to the hope of eternal life.

Heb. 3.6. Whose house are we, if we hold fast the confidence and the rejoicing of the hope firm unto the end.

Heb. 6.11. Shew the same diligence to the full assurance of hope unto the end. 18. Who have fled for refuge to lay hold upon the hope set before us: 19. Which *hope* we have as an anchor of the soul, both sure and stedfast, and which entereth into that within the veil.

Heb. 11.1. Faith is the substance of things hoped for, the evidence of things not seen.

1 Pet. 1.3. According to his abundant mercy, hath begotten us again unto a lively hope, by

the resurrection of Jesus Christ. 13. Gird up the loins of your mind, be sober, and hope to the end for the grace that is to be brought unto you at the revelation of Jesus Christ. 21. That your faith and hope might be in God.

1 Pet. 3.15. *Be* ready always to *give* an answer to every man that asketh you a reason of the hope that is in you with meekness and fear.

1 Jno. 3.3. Every man that hath this hope in him purifieth himself, even as he is pure.

See FAITH EXEMPLIFIED.

HOPHNI AND PHINEHAS, sons of Eli, covetousness and vices of, 1 Sam. 2.12-36. 1 Sam. 3.11-14. Death of, in battle, 1 Sam. 4.4,11,17.

HOR, one of the mountains of Seir, Gen. 14.6. Num. 21.4. Num. 33.37. A southern boundary of the Israelites, Num. 34.7,8. Aaron's death and burial on, Num. 20.22-29. Num. 33.38,39. Deu. 32.50.

HOREB. See SINAI.

HORITES, original inhabitants of Idumea, Deu. 2.12,22. Gen. 36.20-30. 1 Chr. 1.38-42. Invaded by Chedorlaomer, Gen. 14.6. Dispossessed by the Edomites, Deu. 2.12,23.

HORMAH. Israelites defeated at, by Amalekites, Num. 14.45. Deu. 1.44. They defeat king Arad at, Num. 21.1-3. Taken by Judah and Simeon, Jud. 1.17. Jos. 12.14. Given to Simeon, Jos. 19.4. 1 Chr. 4.30. Within the bounds of Judah. Jos. 15.30. 1 Sam. 30.30.

HORN. Used as a vessel, 1 Sam. 16.1. 1 Kin. 1.39. Illustrative of power and prosperity, 1 Kin. 22.11. Psa. 92.10. Psa. 132.17. Symbolical, Dan. 7.7-24. Dan. 8.3-9,20. Hab. 3.4. Zec. 1.18-21. Rev. 5.6. Rev. 12.3. Rev. 13.1,11. Rev. 17.3-16. See TRUMPET.

HORNET or WASP, Ex. 23.28. Deu. 7.20. Jos. 24.12.

HORSE. Used in war for cavalry, Ex. 15.21. 1 Kin. 22.4. 2 Kin. 7.10. 2 Kin. 18.23. Job 39.19-25. Psa. 33.17. Pro. 21.31. Isa. 5.28. Jer. 4.13. Jer. 8.16. Jer. 12.5. Act. 23.23,32. In chariots, see CHARIOTS. Used for riding, 2 Kin. 9.18,19. Est. 6.8-11. Ecc. 10.7. Isa. 30.16. In agriculture, Isa. 28.28.

Bells of, Zec. 14.20. Harness of, Jer. 46.4. Used in Egypt, Gen. 47.17. Ex. 9.3. Ex. 14.9. The Jews forbidden to multiply, Deu. 17.16. Rebuked for multiplying, Isa. 2.7. Isa. 31.1. Eze. 17.15. Hos. 14.3. Brought from Egypt by Solomon, 1 Kin. 10.28,29. 2 Chr. 9.25,28. Brought from Babylon by the Jews, Ezr. 2.66. Neh. 7.68. Symbolical, Zec. 1.8. Rev. 6.2-8. Rev. 9.17. Rev. 19.11-21.

See BIT—BRIDLE—WHIP.

HORSELEECH, Pro. 30.15.

HOSANNA (Heb. *save now*), Mat. 21.9,15. Mar. 11.9,10. Jno. 12.13.

HOSEA, prophecies in the reign of Uzziah, &c., Hos. 1.1.

HOSEN (a tunic or under-garment), Dan. 3.21.

HOSHEA, 19th and last king of Israel (reigns 7 years), son of Elah, slays Pekah and succeeds him; his evil reign, 2 Kin. 15.30. 2 Kin. 17.1,2. Pays tribute to the king of Egypt, and offends the king of Assyria; Samaria besieged and the people taken captive, 2 Kin. 17.3-23. 2 Kin. 18.9-12. Hos. 10.3,7.

HOSPITALITY, DUTIES TO STRANGERS. Ex. 22.21. Ex. 23.9. Lev. 19.10,33,34. Lev. 24.22. Deu. 10.18,19. Deu. 24.17,18. Deu. 26.12,13. Deu. 27.19. Isa. 58.7. Luk. 14.12-14. Rom. 12.13. 1 Tim. 3.2. 1 Tim. 5.10. Tit. 1.8. Heb. 13.2. 1 Pet. 4.9. 3 Jno. 5-8.

HOSPITALITY, EXAMPLES OF: Melchizedek, Gen. 14.18 Abraham, Gen. 18.3. Lot, Gen. 19.1. Laban, Gen. 24.31. Jethro, Ex. 2.20. The old man of Gibeah, Jud. 19.16-21. The widow of Zarephath, 1 Kin. 17.10. The Shunamite, 2 Kin. 4.8. Elisha, 2 Kin. 6.22. Israelites, 1 Chr. 12.39. Job, Job 31.32. Lydia, Act. 16.15. Publius, Melitans, Act. 28.2. Gaius, 3 Jno. 5-8.

See FEASTS—STRANGERS—INHOSPITALITY.

HOSTAGES, taken by Jehoash from Judah, 2 Kin. 14.14. 2 Chr. 25.24.

HOURS, Dan. 4.33. Dan. 5.5. Of the day, reckoned from sunrise to sunset, 12 in number, Jno. 11.9. Mat. 20.3-12. Mat. 27.45,46. Mar. 15.25,33,34. Jno. 1.39. Jno. 4.6,52. Act. 2.15. Act. 3.1. Act. 10.3,9. Of the night, Act. 23.23. Symbolical, Rev. 8.1. Rev. 9.15.

HOUSE. Built of bricks, stone, and timber, and plastered, Lev. 14.40-45. Song 1.17. Isa. 9.10. Gen. 11.3. Ex. 1.11-14; of earth, Eze. 8.8. Eze. 12.5. Built on town-walls, Jos. 2.15. Of several stories, Act. 20.9. Had flat roofs, see BATTLEMENT.

Had porches, Jud. 3.23. 1 Kin. 7.6,7; and courts, Est. 1.5. Chambers in, Gen. 43.30. Summer parlour of, Jud. 3.20; or loft, 1 Kin. 17.19. Inner chamber, 1 Kin. 22.25. Little chamber, 2 Kin. 4.10. Upper chamber, 2 Kin. 1.2. 2 Kin. 23.12. 2 Sam. 18.33. Act. 1.13. Act. 9.37. Act. 20.8. Guest-chamber, Mar. 14.14.

Were painted and inlaid, Jer. 22.14. Eze. 8.10,12. Fires in, Isa. 30.14. Jer. 36.22,23. Chimneys of, Hos. 13.3. Texts of scripture on, Deu. 6.9. Supplied with water, see WELLS. Leprosy found in, Lev. 14.34-53. Laws regarding the sale and mortgage of, Lev. 25.29-33. Neh. 5.3. Dedicated, Deu. 20.5. Psa. 30 (title).

Illustrative, 2 Sam. 7.18. 2 Kin. 20.1. Job 30.23. 2 Cor. 5.1. 1 Tim. 3.15. Heb. 3.2. Jno. 14.2.

See CEILING, CORNER-STONE, DOOR, FOUNDATION, IVORY, ROOF, WINDOW.

Furniture of, see BED, BENCH, COFFER, CURTAINS, LAMP, PILLOW, STOOLS, TABLES, IMPLEMENTS, VESSELS.

HULDAH, a prophetess. Her predictions concerning Josiah, 2 Kin. 22.14-20. 2 Chr. 34.22-28.

HUMILIATION. See REPENTANCE—FASTING.

HUMILITY, Deu. 9.7. Forget not, how thou provokedst the Lord thy God to wrath in the wilderness.

Deu. 15.15. Remember that thou wast a bondman in the land of Egypt.

Job 22.29. When *men* are cast down, then thou shalt say, *There is* lifting up; and he shall save the humble person.

Job 25.5. Behold even to the moon, and it shineth not; yea, the stars are not pure in his sight. 6. How much less man, *that is* a worm? and the son of man, *which is* a worm?

Psa. 9.12. He forgetteth not the cry of the humble.

Psa. 10.17. Lord, thou hast heard the desire of the humble: thou wilt prepare their heart, thou wilt cause thine ear to hear.

Psa. 22.26. The meek shall eat and be satisfied.

Psa. 25.9. The meek will he guide in judgment: and the meek will he teach his way.

Psa. 37.11. The meek shall inherit the earth; and shall delight themselves in the abundance of peace.

Psa. 138.6. Though the Lord *be* high, yet hath he respect unto the lowly.

Psa. 147.6. The Lord lifteth up the meek.

Psa. 149.4. He will beautify the meek with salvation.

Pro. 3.34. He giveth grace unto the lowly.

Pro. 10.8. The wise in heart will receive commandments.

Pro. 11.2. With the lowly *is* wisdom.

Pro. 12.15. He that hearkeneth unto counsel *is* wise.

Pro. 13.10. With the well advised *is* wisdom.

Pro. 15.33. Before honour *is* humility. Pro. 18.12.

Pro. 16.19. Better *it is to be* of an humble spirit with the lowly, than to divide the spoil with the proud.

Pro. 22.4. By humility *and* the fear of the Lord *are* riches, and honour, and life.

Pro. 27.2. Let another man praise thee, and not thine own mouth; a stranger, and not thine own lips.

Pro. 29.23. Honour shall uphold the humble in spirit.

Pro. 30.32. If thou hast done foolishly in lifting up thyself, or if thou hast thought evil, *lay* thine hand upon thy mouth.

Ecc. 5.2. Be not rash with thy mouth, and let not thine heart be hasty to utter *any* thing before God: for God *is* in heaven, and thou upon earth: therefore let thy words be few.

Isa. 29.19. The meek also shall increase *their* joy in the Lord, and the poor among men shall rejoice in the Holy One of Israel.

Isa. 41.14. Fear not, thou worm Jacob.

Isa. 51.1. Look unto the rock *whence* ye are hewn, and to the hole of the pit *whence* ye are digged. Deu. 32.7.

Isa. 57.15. I dwell in the high and holy *place*, with him also *that is* of a contrite and humble spirit, to revive the spirit of the humble, and to revive the heart of the contrite ones.

Isa. 66.2. To this *man* will I look, *even* to *him that is* poor and of a contrite spirit, and trembleth at my word.

Jer. 45.5. Seekest thou great things for thyself? seek *them* not.

· Eze. 16.63. Remember, and be confounded, and never open thy mouth any more because of thy shame, when I am pacified toward thee for all that thou hast done, saith the Lord God.

Hos. 13.1. When Ephraim spake trembling, he exalted himself in Israel.

Mic. 6.8. Walk humbly with thy God.

Zeph. 3.11. I will take away out of the midst of thee them that rejoice in thy pride, and thou shalt no more be haughty because of my holy mountain. 12. I will also leave in the midst of thee an afflicted and poor people, and they shall trust in the name of the Lord.

Mat. 5.3. Blessed *are* the poor in spirit: for their's is the kingdom of heaven. Luk. 6.20.

Mat. 11.29. Take my yoke upon you, and learn of me; for I am meek and lowly in heart: and ye shall find rest unto your souls.

Mat. 18.2. Jesus called a little child unto him, and set him in the midst of them, 3. And said, Verily I say unto you, Except ye be converted, and become as little children, ye shall not enter into the kingdom of heaven. 4. Whosoever therefore shall humble himself as this little child, the same is greatest in the kingdom of heaven. Mar. 9.33-37. Luk. 9.46-48.

Mat. 20.26. Whosoever will be great among you, let him be your minister; 27. And whosoever will be chief among you, let him be your servant. Mar. 10.43,44. Luk. 22.26.

Luk. 1.52. He hath exalted them of low degree.

Luk. 10.21. Thou hast hid these things from the wise and prudent, and hast revealed them unto babes.

Luk. 14.10. When thou art bidden, go and sit down in the lowest room; that when he that bade thee cometh, he may say unto thee, Friend, Go up higher. v. 11. Pro. 25.6,7.

Luk. 17.10. When ye shall have done all those things which are commanded you, say, We are unprofitable servants: we have done that which was our duty to do.

Luk. 18.13. The publican, standing afar off, would not lift up so much as his eyes unto heaven, but smote upon his breast, saying, God be merciful to me a sinner. 14. I tell you, this man went down to his house justified rather than the other: for every one that exalteth himself shall be abased; and he that humbleth himself shall be exalted. Mat. 23.12.

Jno. 13.14. If I then, your Lord and Master, have washed your feet; ye also ought to wash one another's feet. 15. For I have given you an example, that ye should do as I have done to you. 16. Verily, verily, I say unto you, The servant is not greater than his lord; neither he that is sent greater than he that sent him.

Rom. 12.3. Not to think of himself more highly than he ought to think; but to think soberly. 10. In honour preferring one another. 16. Mind not high things, but condescend to men of low estate. Be not wise in your own conceits.

1 Cor. 1.28. Base things of the world, and things which are despised, hath God chosen, yea, and things which are not, to bring to nought things that are: 29. That no flesh should glory in his presence.

1 Cor. 3.18. If any man among you seemeth to be wise in this world, let him become a fool, that he may be wise.

1 Cor. 10.12. Let him that thinketh he standeth take heed lest he fall.

1 Cor. 13.4. Charity vaunteth not itself, is not puffed up.

Gal. 5.26. Let us not be desirous of vainglory.

Eph. 4.2. With all lowliness and meekness, with long-suffering, forbearing one another in love.

Eph. 5.21. Submitting yourselves one to another in the fear of God.

Phil. 2.3. Let nothing be done through strife or vainglory; but in lowliness of mind let each esteem other better than themselves.

Col. 3.12. Put on therefore, as the elect of God, holy and beloved, humbleness of mind, meekness.

Jas. 1.19. Let every man be swift to hear, slow to speak, slow to wrath.

Jas. 3.1. Be not many masters, knowing that we shall receive the greater condemnation.

Jas. 4.7. Submit yourselves therefore to God. v. 6,10.

1 Pet. 5.5. Ye younger, submit yourselves unto the elder. Yea, all of you be subject one to another, and be clothed with humility: for God resisteth the proud, and giveth grace to the humble. 6. Humble yourselves therefore under the mighty hand of God, that he may exalt you in due time.

HUMILITY EXEMPLIFIED: Gen. 18.27. Behold now, I have taken upon me to speak unto the Lord, which am but dust and ashes. v. 32.

Gen. 32.10. I am not worthy of the least of all the mercies, and of all the truth, which thou hast shewed unto thy servant.

Ex. 3.11. Who am I, that I should go unto Pharaoh, and that I should bring forth the children of Israel out of Egypt?

Ex. 4.10. O my Lord, I am not eloquent, neither heretofore, nor since thou hast spoken unto thy servant: but I am slow of speech, and of a slow tongue.

2 Sam. 7.18. Who am I, O Lord God? and what is my house, that thou hast brought me hitherto? 19. And this was yet a small thing in thy sight, O Lord God; but thou hast spoken also of thy servant's house for a great while to come. And is this the manner of man, O Lord God? 1 Chr. 17.17.

1 Kin. 3.7. I am but a little child: I know not how to go out or come in. 2 Chr. 1.10.

1 Chr. 29.14. Who am I, and what is my people, that we should be able to offer so willingly after this sort? for all things come of thee, and of thine own have we given thee.

2 Chr. 2.6. Who am I then, that I should build him an house?

Ezr. 9.13. Thou our God hast punished us less than our iniquities deserve.

Job 9.14. How much less shall I answer him, and choose out my words to reason with him? 15. Whom, though I were righteous, yet would I not answer, but I would make supplication to my judge. Job 10.15.

Job 33.6. I also am formed out of the clay.

Job 40.4. Behold, I am vile; what shall I answer thee? I will lay mine hand upon my mouth. 5. Once have I spoken; but I will not answer: yea, twice; but I will proceed no further.

Job 42.4. Hear, I beseech thee, and I will speak. 5. I have heard of thee by the hearing of the ear: but now mine eye seeth thee. 6. Wherefore I abhor myself, and repent in dust and ashes.

Psa. 8.3. When I consider thy heavens, 4. What is man, that thou art mindful of him? and the son of man, that thou visitest him? Job 7.17,18. Psa. 144.3,4.

Psa. 73.22. So foolish was I, and ignorant: I was as a beast before thee.

Psa. 131.1. Lord, my heart is not haughty, nor mine eyes lofty: neither do I exercise myself in great matters, or in things too high for me. 2. Surely I have behaved and quieted myself, as a child that is weaned of his mother: my soul is even as a weaned child.

Psa. 141.5. Let the righteous smite me ; *it shall be* a kindness : and let him reprove me ; *it shall be* an excellent oil, *which* shall not break my head.

Pro. 30.2. Surely I *am* more brutish than *any* man, and have not the understanding of a man. 3. I neither learned wisdom, nor have the knowledge of the holy.

Isa. 6.5. Woe *is* me ! for I am undone : because I *am* a man of unclean lips, and I dwell in the midst of a people of unclean lips : for mine eyes have seen the King, the Lord of hosts.

Isa. 38.15. I shall go softly all my years in the bitterness of my soul.

Jer. 1.6. Ah, Lord God ! behold, I cannot speak : for I *am* a child.

Dan. 2.30. This secret is not revealed to me for *any* wisdom that I have more than any living. Gen. 41.16. Act. 3.12.

Mat. 3.14. John forbad him, saying, I have need to be baptized of thee, and comest thou to me ?

Mat. 15.27. Truth, Lord : yet the dogs eat of the crumbs which fall from their masters' table.

Luk. 7.6. Lord, trouble not thyself : for I am not worthy that thou shouldest enter under my roof : 7. Wherefore neither thought I myself worthy to come unto thee : but say in a word, and my servant shall be healed. Mat. 8.8.

Jno. 1.27. He it is, who coming after me is preferred before me, whose shoe's latchet I am not worthy to unloose.

Jno. 3.29. He that hath the bride is the bridegroom : but the friend of the bridegroom, which standeth and heareth him, rejoiceth greatly because of the bridegroom's voice : this my joy therefore is fulfilled. 30. He must increase, but I *must* decrease.

Rom. 7.18. I know that in me (that is, in my flesh,) dwelleth no good thing.

1 Cor. 15.10. By the grace of God I am what I am : I laboured more abundantly than they all : yet not I, but the grace of God which was with me.

2 Cor. 3.5. Not that we are sufficient of ourselves to think any thing as of ourselves ; but our sufficiency *is* of God.

2 Cor. 12.7. There was given to me a thorn in the flesh, the messenger of Satan to buffet me, lest I should be exalted above measure.

Eph. 3.8. Unto me, who am less than the least of all saints, is this grace given.

Phil. 3.12. Not as though I had already attained, either were already perfect. 13. Brethren, I count not myself to have apprehended.

Phil. 4.12. I know both how to be abased, and I know how to abound.

1 Tim. 1.15. Christ Jesus came into the world to save sinners ; of whom I am chief. 1 Cor. 15.9.

Rev. 4.10. The four and twenty elders fall down before him that sat on the throne, and worship him that liveth for ever and ever, and cast their crowns before the throne.

HUMILITY, EXAMPLES OF : Moses, Ex. 18.24. Gideon, Jud. 6.15. Ruth, Ruth 2.10. Saul, 1 Sam. 9.21. David, 1 Sam. 18.18-23. Elihu, Job 32.4-7. Elizabeth, Luk. 1.43. Cornelius, Act. 10.33. Paul, Rom. 1.12. Rom. 16.7. Peter, Luk. 5.8. 1 Pet. 5.1. John, Rev. 1.9. See CHRIST'S MEEKNESS—REPENTANCE.

HUNTING, Lev. 17.13. Job 38.39. Pro. 12.27. Of deer, &c., Gen. 27.3,5,33. The lion, Job 10.16. Nimrod a great hunter, Gen. 10.9 ; also Ishmael, Gen. 21.20 ; and Esau, Gen. 25.27. Gen. 27.30.

HUR. Upholds the hands of Moses, Ex. 17.10. Joint-judge with Aaron, Ex. 24.14. ——, a king of Midian, Num. 31.8. Jos. 13.21.

HUSBANDMAN. Illustrative, Jno. 15.1. 1 Cor. 3.9. See AGRICULTURE.

HUSBANDS. Duties of, Gen. 2.18,23,24. Gen. 24.67. Gen. 29.20. Deu. 24.5. 1 Sam. 1.8. Pro. 5.18,19. Ecc. 9.9. Mal. 2.14,15. 1 Cor. 7.14,16. 1 Cor. 11.3. Eph. 5.23-33. Col. 3.19. 1 Tim. 5.8. 1 Pet. 3.7. See MARRIAGE.

HUSHAI. David's companion ; his opposition to Ahithophel, 2 Sam. 15.32-37. 2 Sam. 16.16-19. 2 Sam. 17. 1 Chr. 27.33.

HUSK, Num. 6.4. A scrip, 2 Kin. 4.42 (*marg.*). A carob pod, Luk. 15.16.

HUZZAB (*marg.*, that which was established). A name of Babylon, Nah. 2.7.

HYMENIUS, a false teacher denounced by Paul, 1 Tim. 1.20. 2 Tim. 2.17.

HYMN. See PSALMS—PRAISE.

HYPOCRISY. Job 8.13. The hypocrite's hope shall perish : 14. Whose hope shall be cut off, and whose trust *shall* be a spider's web. 15. He shall lean upon his house, but it shall not stand : he shall hold it fast, but it shall not endure. *v.* 16-19.

Job 13.9. As one man mocketh another, do ye *so* mock him ? 16. An hypocrite shall not come before him.

Job 15.31. Let not him that is deceived trust in vanity : for vanity shall be his recompence. 33. He shall shake off his unripe grape as the vine, and shall cast off his flower as the olive. 34. For the congregation of hypocrites *shall* be desolate.

Job 20.5. The joy of the hypocrite *but* for a moment.

Job 27.8. What *is* the hope of the hypocrite, though he hath gained, when God taketh away his soul ? 9. Will God hear his cry when trouble cometh upon him ? 10. Will he delight himself in the Almighty ? will he always call upon God ?

Job 31.33. If I covered my transgressions as Adam, by hiding mine iniquity in my bosom.

Job 34.30. That the hypocrite reign not, lest the people be ensnared.

Job 36.13. The hypocrites in heart heap up wrath : they cry not when he bindeth them. 14. They die in youth, and their life *is* among the unclean.

Psa. 50.16. Unto the wicked God saith, What hast thou to do to declare my statutes, or *that* thou shouldest take my covenant in thy mouth ? 17. Seeing thou hatest instruction, and castest my words behind thee.

Psa. 78.36. They did flatter him with their mouth, and they lied unto him with their tongues. 37. For their heart was not right with him, neither were they stedfast in his covenant.

Pro. 21.27. The sacrifice of the wicked *is* abomination : how much more, *when* he bringeth it with a wicked mind ?

Isa. 1.13. Bring no more vain oblations : incense is an abomination unto me ; the new moons and sabbaths, the calling of assemblies, I cannot away with ; *it is* iniquity, even the solemn meeting. 15. And when ye spread forth your hands, I will hide mine eyes from you : yea, when ye make many prayers, I will not hear: your hands are full of blood. *v.* 11-14. Isa. 66.3-5.

Isa. 9.17. The Lord shall have no joy in their young men, neither shall have mercy on their fatherless and widows : for every one *is* an hypocrite and an evildoer, and every mouth speaketh folly.

Isa. 10.6. I will send him against an hypocritical nation, and against the people of my wrath will I give him a charge.

Isa. 29.13. This people draw near *me* with their mouth, and with their lips do honour me, but have removed their heart far from me, and their fear toward me is taught by the precept of men. 15. Woe unto them that seek deep to hide their counsel from the Lord, and their works are in the dark, and they say, Who seeth us? and who knoweth us? 16. Surely your turning of things upside down shall be esteemed as the potter's clay.

Isa. 32.5. The vile person shall be no more called liberal, nor the churl said *to be* bountiful. 6. His heart will work iniquity, to practise hypocrisy, and to utter error against the Lord. Isa. 33.14. The sinners in Zion are afraid ; fearfulness hath surprised the hypocrites.

Isa. 48.1. Which swear by the name of the Lord, and make mention of the God of Israel, *but* not in truth, nor in righteousness. 2. For they call themselves of the holy city, and stay themselves upon the God of Israel.

Isa. 58.2. They seek me daily, and delight to know my ways, as a nation that did righteousness, and forsook not the ordinance of their God : they ask of me the ordinances of justice ; they take delight in approaching to God. 3. Wherefore have we fasted, *say they,* and thou seest not? *wherefore* have we afflicted our soul, and thou takest no knowledge? Behold, in the day of your fast ye find pleasure, and exact all your labours.

Isa. 58.4. Behold, ye fast for strife and debate, and to smite with the fist of wickedness : ye shall not fast as *ye do this* day, to make your voice to be heard on high. 5. Is it such a fast that I have chosen? a day for a man to afflict his soul? *is it* to bow down his head as a bulrush, and to spread sackcloth and ashes *under him?* wilt thou call this a fast, and an acceptable day to the Lord?

Isa. 61.8. I hate robbery for burnt-offering.

Jer. 3.10. Her treacherous sister Judah hath not turned unto me with her whole heart, but feignedly, saith the Lord. *v.* 11.

Jer. 5.2. Though they say, The Lord liveth ; surely they swear falsely.

Jer. 6.20. To what purpose cometh there to me incense from Sheba, and the sweet cane from a far country? your burnt-offerings *are* not acceptable, nor your sacrifices sweet unto me.

Jer. 7.8. Ye trust in lying words, that cannot profit. 9. Will ye steal, murder, and commit adultery, and swear falsely, and burn incense unto Baal, and walk after other gods whom ye know not ; 10. And come and stand before me in this house, which is called by my name, and say, We are delivered to do all these abominations?

Jer. 12.2. Thou *art* near in their mouth, and far from their reins.

Jer. 42.20. Ye dissembled in your hearts, when ye sent me unto the Lord your God, saying, Pray for us unto the Lord our God : and according unto all that the Lord our God shall say, so declare unto us, and we will do *it. v.* 21,22.

Eze. 14.7. Every one which separateth himself from me, and setteth up his idols in his heart, and putteth the stumblingblock of his iniquity before his face, and cometh to a prophet to enquire of him concerning me ; I the Lord will answer him by myself : 8. And I will set my face against that man, and will make him a sign and a proverb, and I will cut him off from the midst of my people ; and ye shall know that I *am* the Lord. *v.* 4.

Eze. 20.39. Go ye, serve ye every one his idols, and hereafter *also,* if ye will not hearken unto me : but pollute ye my holy name no more with your gifts, and with your idols. Eze. 5.11. Hos. 8.13. Hos. 9.4.

Eze. 33.30. The children of thy people still are talking against thee by the walls and in the doors of the houses, and speak one to another, every one to his brother, saying, Come, I pray you, and hear what is the word that cometh forth from the Lord. 31. And they come unto thee as the people cometh, and they sit before thee *as* my people, and they hear thy words, but they will not do them : for with their mouth they shew much love, *but* their heart goeth after their covetousness. 32. And, lo, thou *art* unto them as a very lovely song of one that hath a pleasant voice, and can play well on an instrument : for they hear thy words, but they do them not.

Hos. 6.4. O Judah, what shall I do unto thee? for your goodness *is* as a morning cloud, and as the early dew it goeth away.

Hos. 7.14. They have not cried unto me with their heart, when they howled upon their beds : 16. They return, *but* not to the most High : they are like a deceitful bow.

Hos. 8.2. Israel shall cry unto me, My God, we know thee. 3. Israel hath cast off *the thing that is* good : the enemy shall pursue him.

Hos. 10.1. Israel *is* an empty vine, he bringeth forth fruit unto himself. 4. They have spoken words, swearing falsely in making a covenant.

Hos. 11.12. Ephraim compasseth me about with lies, and the house of Israel with deceit :

Amos 5.21. I hate, I despise your feast days, and I will not smell in your solemn assemblies. 23. Take thou away from me the noise of thy songs ; for I will not hear the melody of thy viols. 24. But let judgment run down as waters, and righteousness as a mighty stream. *v.* 22,25-27.

Mic. 3.11. The priests thereof teach for hire, and the prophets thereof divine for money : yet will they lean upon the Lord, and say, *Is* not the Lord among us?

Zec. 7.5. When ye fasted and mourned in the fifth and seventh *month,* even those seventy years, did ye at all fast unto me, *even* to me? 6. And when ye did eat, and when ye did drink, did not ye eat *for yourselves,* and drink *for yourselves?*

Mal. 1.6. If I *be* a master, where *is* my fear? saith the Lord of hosts unto you, O priests, that despise my name. And ye say,

Wherein have we despised thy name? 7. Ye offer polluted bread upon mine altar; and ye say, Wherein have we polluted thee? In that ye say, The table of the Lord *is* contemptible. 8. And if ye offer the blind for sacrifice, *is it* not evil? and if ye offer the lame and sick, *is it* not evil? offer it now unto thy governor; will he be pleased with thee, or accept thy person? saith the Lord of hosts.

Mal. 1.13. Ye said also, Behold, what a weariness *is it!* and ye have snuffed at it, saith the Lord of hosts; and ye brought *that which was* torn, and the lame, and the sick; thus ye brought an offering: should I accept this of your hand? saith the Lord. 14. But cursed *be* the deceiver, which hath in his flock a male, and voweth, and sacrificeth unto the Lord a corrupt thing. *v.* 9-12.

Mal. 2.13. This have ye done again, covering the altar of the Lord with tears, with weeping, and with crying out, insomuch that he regardeth not the offering any more, or receiveth *it* with good will at your hand.

Mal. 3.14. Ye have said, It *is* vain to serve God; and what profit *is it* that we have kept his ordinance, and that we have walked mournfully before the Lord of hosts?

Mat. 3.7. O generation of vipers, who hath warned you to flee from the wrath to come? 8. Bring forth therefore fruits meet for repentance.

Mat. 6.1. Do not your alms before men, to be seen of them: otherwise ye have no reward of your Father which is in heaven. 2. Therefore when thou doest *thine* alms, do not sound a trumpet before thee, as the hypocrites do in the synagogues and in the streets, that they may have glory of men. 5. When thou prayest, thou shalt not be as the hypocrites *are:* for they love to pray standing in the synagogues and in the corners of the streets, that they may be seen of men.

Mat. 6.16. When ye fast, be not as the hypocrites, of a sad countenance: for they disfigure their faces, that they may appear unto men to fast. Verily I say unto you, They have their reward.

Mat. 7.5. Thou hypocrite, first cast out the beam out of thine own eye; and then shalt thou see clearly to cast out the mote out of thy brother's eye. 21. Not every one that saith unto me, Lord, Lord, shall enter into the kingdom of heaven; but he that doeth the will of my Father which is in heaven. 22. Many will say to me in that day, Lord, Lord, have we not prophesied in thy name? and in thy name have cast out devils? and in thy name done many wonderful works? 23. And then will I profess unto them, I never knew you: depart from me, ye that work iniquity. Luk. 13.26,27.

Mat. 16.3. O *ye* hypocrites, ye can discern the face of the sky; but can ye not *discern* the signs of the times? Luk. 12.54-56.

Mat. 21.30. He answered and said, I *go,* sir: and went not.

Mat. 22.12. Friend, how camest thou in hither not having a wedding-garment? And he was speechless? 13. Then said the king to the servants, Bind him hand and foot, and take him away, and cast *him* into outer darkness. 18. Jesus perceived their wickedness, and said, Why tempt ye me, *ye* hypocrites?

Mat. 23.3. They say, and do not. 4. For they bind heavy burdens and grievous to be borne, and lay *them* on men's shoulders; but they *themselves* will not move them with one of their fingers.

Mat. 23.5. All their works they do for to be seen of men: they make broad their phylacteries, and enlarge the borders of their garments. 24. *Ye* blind guides, which strain at a gnat, and swallow a camel. 25. Woe unto you, scribes and Pharisees, hypocrites! for ye make clean the outside of the cup and of the platter, but within they are full of extortion and excess. 26. *Thou* blind Pharisee, cleanse first that *which is* within the cup and platter, that the outside of them may be clean also. *v.* 13-36.

Mat. 24.50. The lord of that servant shall come in a day when he looketh not for *him,* and in an hour that he is not aware of, 51. And shall cut him asunder, and appoint *him* his portion with the hypocrites: there shall be weeping and gnashing of teeth.

Mat. 25.3. They that *were* foolish took their lamps, and took no oil with them.

Mar. 7.7. Howbeit in vain do they worship me, teaching *for* doctrines the commandments of men. 8. For laying aside the commandment of God, ye hold the tradition of men, *as* the washing of pots and cups: and many other such like things ye do. Mat. 15.7-9.

Luk. 6.46. Why call ye me Lord, Lord, and do not the things which I say?

Luk. 8.18. Whosoever hath not, from him shall be taken even that which he seemeth to have.

Luk. 11.42. But woe unto you, Pharisees! for ye tithe mint and rue and all manner of herbs, and pass over judgment and the love of God: these ought ye to have done, and not to leave the other undone. 44. Woe unto you, scribes and Pharisees, hypocrites! for ye are as graves which appear not, and the men that walk over *them* are not aware *of them.* 52. Woe unto you, lawyers! for ye have taken away the key of knowledge: ye entered not in yourselves, and them that were entering in ye hindered. *v.* 39-52.

Luk. 12.1. Beware ye of the leaven of the Pharisees, which is hypocrisy. 2. For there is nothing covered, that shall not be revealed; neither hid, that shall not be known. Mat. 16.6,12. Mar. 8.15.

Luk. 14.34. Salt *is* good: but if the salt have lost his savour, wherewith shall it be seasoned? *v.* 35. Mar. 9.50.

Luk. 16.15. Ye are they which justify yourselves before men; but God knoweth your hearts: for that which is highly esteemed among men is abomination in the sight of God.

Luk. 20.46. Beware of the scribes, which desire to walk in long robes, and love greetings in the markets, and the highest seats in the synagogues, and the chief rooms at feasts; 47. Which devour widows' houses, and for a shew make long prayers: the same shall receive greater damnation. Mat 23.40. Mar. 12.38-40.

Jno. 6.26. Ye seek me, not because ye saw the miracles, but because ye did eat of the loaves, and were filled. 70. Have not I chosen you twelve, and one of you is a devil?

Jno. 7.19. Did not Moses give you the law, and *yet* none of you keepeth the law? Why go ye about to kill me?

Jno. 15.2. Every branch in me that beareth not fruit he taketh away. 6. If a man abide not in me, he is cast forth as a branch, and is withered ; and men gather them, and cast *them* into the fire, and they are burned.

Rom. 1.18. The wrath of God is revealed from heaven against all ungodliness and unrighteousness of men, who hold the truth in unrighteousness.

Rom. 2.13. Not the hearers of the law *are* just before God, but the doers of the law shall be justified. 21. Thou therefore which teachest another, teachest thou not thyself? thou that preachest a man should not steal, dost thou steal? 23. Thou that makest thy boast of the law, through breaking the law dishonourest thou God? 24. For the name of God is blasphemed among the Gentiles through you. *v.* 22.

2 Cor. 5.12. Them which glory in appearance, and not in heart.

Gal. 6.3. If a man think himself to be something, when he is nothing, he deceiveth himself.

Phil. 3.2. Beware of dogs, beware of evil workers, beware of the concision. 18. Many walk, of whom I have told you often, and now tell you even weeping, *that they are* the enemies of the cross of Christ : 19. Whose end *is* destruction.

1 Tim. 4.2. Speaking lies in hypocrisy ; having their conscience seared with a hot iron.

2 Tim. 3.5. Having a form of godliness, but denying the power thereof. 13. Evil men and seducers shall wax worse and worse, deceiving, and being deceived.

Tit. 1.16. They profess that they know God ; but in works they deny *him*, being abominable and disobedient, and unto every good work reprobate.

Heb. 6.4. Those who were once enlightened, and have tasted of the heavenly gift, and were made partakers of the Holy Ghost, 5. And have tasted the good word of God, and the powers of the world to come.

Jas. 1.8. A double-minded man *is* unstable in all his ways. 22. Be ye doers of the word, and not hearers only, deceiving your own selves. 23. For if any be a hearer of the word, and not a doer, he is like unto a man beholding his natural face in a glass : 24. For he beholdeth himself, and goeth his way, and straightway forgetteth what manner of man he was. 26. If any man among you seem to be religious, and bridleth not his tongue, but deceiveth his own heart, this man's religion *is* vain.

1 Pet. 2.1. Laying aside all hypocrisies. 16. As free, and not using *your* liberty for a cloke of maliciousness, but as the servants of God.

2 Pet. 2.2. Many shall follow their pernicious ways ; by reason of whom the way of truth shall be evil spoken of. 3. Through covetousness shall they with feigned words make merchandise of you : whose judgment now of a long time lingereth not, and their damnation slumbereth not. 17. These are wells without water, clouds that are carried with a tempest ; to whom the mist of darkness is reserved for ever.

1 Jno. 1.6. If we say that we have fellowship with him, and walk in darkness, we lie, and do not the truth.

1 Jno. 2.4. He that saith, I know him, and keepeth not his commandments, is a liar, and the truth is not in him. 9. He that saith he is in the light, and hateth his brother, is in darkness even until now. 19. They went out from us, but they were not of us ; for if they had been of us, they would *no doubt* have continued with us : but *they went out*, that they might be made manifest that they were not all of us.

1 Jno. 4.20. If a man say, I love God, and hateth his brother, he is a liar : for he that loveth not his brother whom he hath seen, how can he love God whom he hath not seen?

Jude 12. These are spots in your feasts of charity, when they feast with you, feeding themselves without fear : clouds *they are* without water, carried about of winds ; trees whose fruit withereth, without fruit, twice dead, plucked up by the roots ; 13. Raging waves of the sea, foaming out their own shame ; wandering stars, to whom is reserved the blackness of darkness for ever.

Rev. 2.9. *I know* the blasphemy of them which say they are Jews, and are not, but *are* the synagogue of Satan. Rev. 3.9.

Rev. 3.1. I know thy works, that thou hast a name that thou livest, and art dead.

See FALSE CONFIDENCE—SELF-RIGHTEOUSNESS—SIN SEPARATES FROM GOD—MINISTERS, FALSE—BACKSLIDING—PHARISEES.

HYPOCRISY, EXAMPLES OF : Jacob, Gen. 27.20. Pharaoh, Ex. 8.28,29. Ex. 9.27,28. Ex. 10.8-11,24. Balaam, Num. 23.10. Jude 11. Saul, 1 Sam. 15.13-15. Absalom, 2 Sam. 15.7. Hazael, 2 Kin. 8.12,13. Jehu, 2 Kin. 10.16,31. Samaritans, Ezr. 4.2. Johanan, Jer. 42.1-12,20,22. Herod, Mat. 2.8. Judas, Mat. 26.25,48. Jno. 12.5,6. High-priest, Mat. 26.65. Mat. 27.6. Pilate, Mat. 27.24. The Jews, Jno. 9.24. Jno. 11.46. Chief-priests, Jno. 18.28. Ananias and Sapphira, Act. 5.1-10. Simon Magus, Act. 8.18-23.

HYPOCRISY, TREACHERY, UNKINDNESS. 1 Chr. 12.17. If *ye be come* to betray me to mine enemies, seeing *there is* no wrong in mine hands, the God of our fathers look *thereon*, and rebuke *it*.

Job 6.15. My brethren have dealt deceitfully as a brook, *and* as the stream of brooks they pass away. 27. Yea, ye overwhelm the fatherless, and ye dig *a pit* for your friend.

Job 12.4. I am *as* one mocked of his neighbour, who calleth upon God, and he answereth him : the just upright *man is* laughed to scorn. 5. He that is ready to slip with *his* feet *is as* a lamp despised in the thought of him that is at ease.

Job 13.5. O that ye would altogether hold your peace ! and it should be your wisdom.

Job 16.4. I also could speak as ye *do* : if your soul were in my soul's stead, I could heap up words against you, and shake mine head at you. 20. My friends scorn me : *but* mine eye poureth out *tears* unto God.

Job 17.2. *Are there* not mockers with me? and doth not mine eye continue in their provocation? 6. He hath made me also a byword of the people ; and aforetime I was as a tabret.

Job 19.3. These ten times have ye reproached me : ye are not ashamed *that* ye make yourselves strange to me. 17. My breath is strange to my wife, though I intreated for the children's *sake* of mine own body. 19. All my inward friends abhorred me : and they whom I loved are turned against me. 21. Have pity upon me, have pity upon me, O ye my friends; for the hand of God hath touched me. 28. Ye should say, Why persecute we him, seeing the root of the matter is found in me? *v.* 1-28.

Job 21.34. How then comfort ye me in vain, seeing in your answers there remaineth falsehood?

Job 30.1. *They that are* younger than I have me in derision. 14. They came *upon me* as a wide breaking in *of waters:* in the desolation they rolled themselves *upon me. v.* 1-14.

Psa. 12.2. *With* flattering lips *and* with a double heart do they speak. 3. The Lord shall cut off all flattering lips.

Psa. 28.3. Which speak peace to their neighbours, but mischief *is* in their hearts.

Psa. 31.11. I was a reproach among all mine enemies, but especially among my neighbours, and a fear to mine acquaintance: they that did see me without fled from me. 12. I am forgotten as a dead man out of mind: I am like a broken vessel.

Psa. 38.11. My lovers and my friends stand aloof from my sore; and my kinsmen stand afar off.

Psa. 41.9. Yea, mine own familiar friend, in whom I trusted, which did eat of my bread, hath lifted up *his* heel against me.

Psa. 55.12. *It was* not an enemy *that* reproached me; then I could have borne *it:* neither *was* it he that hated me *that* did magnify *himself* against me; then I would have hid myself from him: 13. But *it was* thou, a man mine equal, my guide, and mine acquaintance. 20. He hath put forth his hands against such as be at peace with him: he hath broken his covenant. 21. *The words* of his mouth were smoother than butter, but war *was* in his heart: his words were softer than oil, yet *were* they drawn swords. 23. Thou, O God, shalt bring them down into the pit of destruction: bloody and deceitful men shall not live out half their days.

Psa. 62.4. They only consult to cast *him* down from his excellency: they delight in lies: they bless with their mouth, but they curse inwardly.

Psa. 69.20. Reproach hath broken my heart; and I am full of heaviness: and I looked *for* some to take pity, but *there was* none; and for comforters, but I found none.

Psa. 142.4. I looked on *my* right hand, and beheld, but *there was* no man that would know me: refuge failed me; no man cared for my soul.

Pro. 3.29. Devise not evil against thy neighbour, seeing he dwelleth securely by thee.

Pro. 23.7. As he thinketh in his heart, so *is* he: Eat and drink, saith he to thee; but his heart *is* not with thee. 8. The morsel *which* thou hast eaten shalt thou vomit up, and lose thy sweet words.

Pro. 25.19. Confidence in an unfaithful man in time of trouble *is like* a broken tooth, and a foot out of joint. 20. *As* he that taketh away a garment in cold weather, *and as* vinegar upon nitre, so *is* he that singeth songs to an heavy heart.

Pro. 26.23. Burning lips and a wicked heart *are like* a potsherd covered with silver dross. 24. He that hateth dissembleth with his lips, and layeth up deceit within him; 25. When he speaketh fair, believe him not; for *there*

are seven abominations in his heart. 26. *Whose* hatred is covered by deceit, his wickedness shall be shewed before the *whole* congregation.

Pro. 27.5. Open rebuke *is* better than secret love. 6. Faithful *are* the wounds of a friend; but the kisses of an enemy *are* deceitful. 10. Better *is* a neighbour *that is* near than a brother far off. 14. He that blesseth his friend with a loud voice, rising early in the morning, it shall be counted a curse to him.

Ecc. 10.8. He that diggeth a pit shall fall into it; and whoso breaketh an hedge, a serpent shall bite him.

Isa. 33.1. When thou shalt make an end to deal treacherously, they shall deal treacherously with thee.

Jer. 9.4. Take ye heed every one of his neighbour, and trust ye not in any brother: for every brother will utterly supplant, and every neighbour will walk with slanders. 8. Their tongue *is as* an arrow shot out; it speaketh deceit: *one* speaketh peaceably to his neighbour with his mouth, but in heart he layeth his wait.

Jer. 12.6. Even thy brethren, and the house of thy father, even they have dealt treacherously with thee; yea, they have called a multitude after thee: believe them not, though they speak fair words unto thee.

Lam. 1.2. Among all her lovers she hath none to comfort her: all her friends have dealt treacherously with her; they are become her enemies.

Eze. 29.7. When they took hold of thee by thy hand, thou didst break, and rend all their shoulder; and when they leaned upon thee thou brakest, and madest all their loins to be at a stand.

Obad. 7. The men that were at peace with thee have deceived thee, *and* prevailed against thee; *they that eat* thy bread have laid a wound under thee.

Mic. 7.5. Trust ye not in a friend, put ye not confidence in a guide: keep the doors of thy mouth from her that lieth in thy bosom.

Zec. 13.6. What *are* these wounds in thine hands? Then he shall answer, *Those* with which I was wounded *in* the house of my friends.

Luk. 21.16. Ye shall be betrayed both by parents, and brethren, and kinsfolks, and friends; and *some* of you shall they cause to be put to death.

HYPOCRISY AND TREACHERY, EXAMPLES OF: Simeon, Gen. 34.13. Jael, Jud. 4.18. Shechemites, Jud. 9.23. Philistines, Jud. 14.20. Saul, 1 Sam. 18.17. 1 Sam. 25.44. David, 2 Sam. 11.6-17. Absalom, 2 Sam. 13.23-29. Ahithophel, 2 Sam. 15.31.

Hushai, 2 Sam. 15.34. 2 Sam. 16.16-19. Benhadad, 1 Kin. 20.18. Tilgath, 2 Chr. 28.20. Jews, Jer. 34.12-22. Zedekiah, Eze. 17.15-19. Tyrians, Amos 1.9,10. Judas, Mat. 26.47-50.

See FALSEHOOD — FLATTERY — MALICE — POOR, UNKINDNESS TO.

HYSSOP, 1 Kin. 4.33. Used in sprinkling the blood at the first passover, Ex. 12.22. In the cleansing of lepers, Lev. 14.4,6,51,52. Heb. 9.19. In preparing the water of separation, Num. 19.6. A sponge with vinegar presented to Christ on, Jno. 19.29. Illustrative, Psa. 51.7.

I

IBZAN of Bethlehem, a judge of Israel, Jud. 12.8-10.

ICE, Job 6.16. Job 38.29. Psa. 147.17.

ICHABOD (no glory), son of Phinehas, 1 Sam. 4.21. 1 Sam. 14.3.

ICONIUM, a town of Lycaonia, in Asia Minor. Paul visits, Act. 13.51. Is persecuted at, Act. 14.1-7. 2 Tim. 3.11. Jews from, stone Paul at Lystra, Act. 14.19. He returns to the church in, Act. 14.21,22. Act. 16.2.

IDDO, a prophet. His writings, 2 Chr. 9.29. 2 Chr. 12.15. 2 Chr. 13.22.

——, a prophet, grandfather of the prophet Zechariah, Zec. 1.1.

IDLENESS. Pro. 6.6. Go to the ant, thou sluggard; consider her ways, and be wise. 9. How long wilt thou sleep, O sluggard? when wilt thou arise out of thy sleep? 10. Yet a little sleep, a little slumber, a little folding of the hands to sleep: 11. So shall thy poverty come as one that travelleth, and thy want as an armed man. Pro. 24.33.

Pro. 10.4. He becometh poor that dealeth *with* a slack hand. 5. He that sleepeth in harvest *is* a son that causeth shame. 26. As vinegar to the teeth, and as smoke to the eyes, so *is* the sluggard to them that send him.

Pro. 12.9. *He that is* despised, and hath a servant, *is* better than he that honoureth himself, and lacketh bread. 24. The slothful shall be under tribute. 27. The slothful *man* roasteth not that which he took in hunting.

Pro. 13.4. The soul of the sluggard desireth, and *hath* nothing.

Pro. 14.23. The talk of the lips *tendeth* only to penury.

Pro. 15.19. The way of the slothful *man is* as an hedge of thorns.

Pro. 18.9. He also that is slothful in his work is brother to him that is a great waster.

Pro. 19.15. Slothfulness casteth into a deep sleep; and an idle soul shall suffer hunger.

Pro. 20.4. The sluggard will not plow by reason of the cold; *therefore* shall he beg in harvest, and *have* nothing. 13. Love not sleep, lest thou come to poverty.

Pro. 21.25. The desire of the slothful killeth him; for his hands refuse to labour. 26. He coveteth greedily all the day long.

Pro. 23.21. Drowsiness shall clothe *a man* with rags.

Pro. 24.30. I went by the field of the slothful, and by the vineyard of the man void of understanding; 31. And, lo, it was all grown over with thorns, *and* nettles had covered the face thereof, and the stone wall thereof was broken down.

Pro. 26.13. The slothful *man* saith, There *is* a lion in the way; a lion *is* in the streets. 14. *As* the door turneth upon his hinges, so *doth* the slothful upon his bed. 15. The slothful hideth his hand in *his* bosom; it grieveth him to bring it again to his mouth. 16. The sluggard *is* wiser in his own conceit than seven men that can render a reason. Pro. 22.13. Pro. 19.24.

Ecc. 10.18. By much slothfulness the build-

ing decayeth; and through idleness of the hands the house droppeth through.

Isa. 56.10. His watchmen *are* blind : sleeping, lying down, loving to slumber.

Eze. 16.49. This was the iniquity of thy sister Sodom, pride, fulness of bread, and abundance of idleness was in her and in her daughters.

Act. 17.21. All the Athenians and strangers which were there spent their time in nothing else, but either to tell, or to hear some new thing.

1 Tim. 5.13. Withal they learn *to be* idle, wandering about from house to house; and not only idle, but tattlers also and busybodies.

2 The. 3.10. That if any would not work, neither should he eat. 11. For we hear that there are some which walk among you disorderly, working not at all, but are busybodies. See INDUSTRY.

IDOLATRY. Gen. 35.2. Put away the strange gods that *are* among you.

Ex. 20.3. Thou shalt have no other gods before me. 4. Thou shalt not make unto thee any graven image, or any likeness *of any thing* that *is* in heaven above, or that *is* in the earth beneath, or that *is* in the water under the earth : 5. Thou shalt not bow down thyself to them, nor serve them : for I the Lord thy God *am* a jealous God. 23. Ye shall not make with me gods of silver, neither shall ye make unto you gods of gold. Deu. 5.7-9.

Ex. 23.13. Make no mention of the name of other gods, neither let it be heard out of thy mouth. 1 Cor. 10.7.

Lev. 26.1. Make you no idols nor graven image, neither rear you up a standing image, neither shall ye set up *any* image of stone in your land, to bow down unto it : for I *am* the Lord your God. 30. I will destroy your high places, and cut down your images, and cast your carcases upon the carcases of your idols, and my soul shall abhor you. Deu. 16.21,22.

Deu. 4.15. Take ye therefore good heed unto yourselves ; for ye saw no manner of similitude on the day *that* the Lord spake unto you in Horeb out of the midst of the fire : 16. Lest ye corrupt *yourselves*, and make you a graven image, the similitude of any figure, the likeness of male or female. 19. Lest thou when thou seest the sun, and the moon, and the stars, *even* all the host of heaven, shouldest be driven to worship them, and serve them, which the Lord thy God hath divided unto all nations under the whole heaven. *v.* 15-23. Deu. 4.25-28. Deu. 11.16,17,28. Deu. 28.15-68. Deu. 30.17,18. Deu. 31.16-21,29. Deu. 32.15-26. 1 Kin. 9.6-9.

Deu. 27.15. Cursed *be* the man that maketh *any* graven or molten image, an abomination unto the Lord, the work of the hands of the craftsman, and putteth *it* in a secret *place*. Ex. 34.17. Lev. 19.4.

Job 31.26. If I beheld the sun when it shined, or the moon walking *in* brightness; 27. And my heart hath been secretly enticed, or my mouth hath kissed my hand : 28. This *also were* an iniquity to be *punished by* the judge : for I should have denied the God *that is* above.

Psa. 16.4. Their sorrows shall be multiplied *that* hasten *after* another *god*.

Psa. 44.20. If we have forgotten the name of our God, or stretched out our hands to a strange god; 21. Shall not God search this out?

Psa. 59.8. Thou shalt have all the heathen in derision.

Psa. 79.6. Pour out thy wrath upon the heathen that have not known thee.

Psa. 81.9. There shall no strange god be in thee; neither shalt thou worship any strange god.

Psa. 97.7. Confounded be all they that serve graven images, that boast themselves of idols.

Isa. 42.17. They shall be turned back, they shall be greatly ashamed, that trust in graven images, that say to the molten images, Ye *are* our gods. Isa. 45.16.

Joel 3.12. Let the heathen be wakened, and come up to the valley of Jehoshaphat: for there will I sit to judge all the heathen round about.

Jonah 2.8. They that observe lying vanities forsake their own mercy.

Mic. 4.5. All people will walk every one in the name of his god.

Mic. 5.15. I will execute vengeance in anger and fury upon the heathen, such as they have not heard.

Hab. 1.16. They sacrifice unto their net, and burn incense unto their drag.

Act. 15.29. That ye abstain from meats offered to idols. v. 20. 1 Cor. 8.1-13.

Act. 17.16. He saw the city wholly given to idolatry.

Rom. 1.25. Who changed the truth of God into a lie, and worshipped and served the creature more than the Creator.

1 Cor. 6.10. Idolators shall not inherit the kingdom of God.

1 Cor. 10.14. My dearly beloved, flee from idolatry. 20. They sacrifice to devils, and not to God: and I would not that ye should have fellowship with devils. v. 21,22.

1 Jno. 5.21. Little children, keep yourselves from idols.

Rev. 21.8. Idolators shall have their part in the lake which burneth with fire and brimstone: which is the second death. Rev. 22.15.

IDOLATRY, Examples of: Abraham's ancestors, Jos. 24.2. Laban, Gen. 31.19,30. Jacob's household, Gen. 35.2-4. Egyptians, Num. 33.4. Deu. 29.17. Isa. 19.3. Chaldeans, Jer. 50.38. Nah. 1.14. Hab. 1.16. Nebuchadnezzar, Dan. 3. Belshazzar, Dan. 5.1-5. Samaritans, 2 Kin. 17.29-41. Mariners, Jonah 1.5. Athenians, Act. 17.16,23-29.

IDOLATRY of the Israelites. In Egypt and the wilderness, Ex. 32. Num. 25.1-9. Deu. 9.12-21. Jos. 24.14,23. Psa. 106.19,28. Amos 5.25,26. Act. 7.40-43. 1 Cor. 10.7.

Under the Judges, Jud. 2. Jud. 3.5-12. Jud. 4.1-3. Jud. 5.8. Jud. 6.1-10. Jud. 8.27. Jud. 9.27. Jud. 10.6-16. Jud. 13.1. Jud. 17.5. Jud. 18.17-31.

Under the Kings. Solomon, 1 Kin. 9.6-9. 1 Kin. 11. Neh. 13.26. Jeroboam, 1 Kin. 12.28-33. 1 Kin. 13. 1 Kin. 15.29. 1 Kin. 14.9-16. 2 Chr. 11.15. Rehoboam, 1 Kin. 14.22-25. 2 Chr. 12.1-8. Abijam, 1 Kin.15.3. Nadab, 1 Kin. 15.26. Baasha, 1 Kin. 15.34. 1 Kin. 16.1-7,11-13.

Zimri, 1 Kin. 16.19. Omri, 1 Kin. 16.25,26. Ahab, 1 Kin. 16.30-33. 1 Kin. 18.18-40. 1 Kin. 19.1,18. 1 Kin. 21.20-29. Ahaziah, 1 Kin. 22.52,53. 1 Kin. 1.2-4,16. 2 Chr. 20.35. Je-

horam, 2 Kin. 3.3,13,14. Jehoram (Judah), 2 Kin. 8.18. 2 Chr. 21.6,11-19.

Ahaziah, 2 Kin. 8.27. 2 Chr. 22.3,4. 2 Chr. 24.7. Jehu, 2 Kin. 10.29,31. Joash, 2 Kin. 12.3. 2 Chr. 24.17-24. Jehoahaz, 2 Kin. 13.2-7. Jehoash, 2 Kin. 13.11. Amaziah, 2 Kin. 14.3,4. 2 Chr. 25.2,14-16,20,27. Jeroboam II., 2 Kin. 14.24. Uzziah, 2 Kin. 15.4.

Zachariah, Menahem, Pekahiah, Pekah, 2 Kin. 15.9,18,24,28,29. Jotham, 2 Kin. 15.35. 2 Chr. 27.2. Ahaz, 2 Kin. 16.3,4,10-16. 2 Kin. 18.4. 2 Chr. 28.2-6,19-25. 2 Chr. 29.6-9,19. 2 Chr. 30.6-9. 2 Chr. 31.1. Hoshea, 2 Kin. 17.6-23. 2 Kin. 18.9-12.

Manasseh, 2 Kin. 21.1-16. 2 Kin. 24.2,3. 2 Chr. 33.1-11. Amon, 2 Kin. 21.20-22. 2 Kin. 22.16-20. 2 Kin. 23.4-27. 2 Chr. 33.22,23. 2 Chr. 34. Jehoahaz, 2 Kin. 23.32. Jehoiakim, 2 Kin. 23.37. 2 Chr. 36.5,8. Jehoiachin, 2 Kin. 24.9. Zedekiah, 2 Kin. 24.19,20. 2 Chr. 36.12-21.

Warnings and punishment, Neh. 9.27-37. Psa. 78.58-64. Psa. 106.34-42. Isa. 1.29-31. Isa. 2.6-22. Isa. 30.22. Isa. 57.3-13. Isa. 65.3,4. Jer. 1.15,16. Jer. 3.1-11. Jer. 5.1-17. Jer. 7. Jer. 8.1,2,19. Jer. 13.9-27. Jer. 16. Jer. 17.1-6. Jer. 18.13-15. Jer. 19. Jer. 32.35. Jer. 44. Eze. 6. Eze. 7.19. Eze. 8.5-18. Eze. 9. Eze. 14.1-14. Eze. 16. Eze. 20. Eze. 22.4. Eze. 23. Eze. 44.10-12. Hos. 1.2. Hos. 4.12-19. Hos. 5.1-3. Hos. 8.5-14. Hos. 9.10. Hos. 10. Hos. 11.2. Hos. 12.11-14. Hos. 13.1-4. Hos. 14.8. Amos 3.14. Amos 4.4,5. Amos 5.5. Mic. 1.1-9. Mic. 5.12-14. Mic. 6.16. Zeph. 1. Mal. 2.11-13.

See Idolatrous Offerings—Idolatry, objects of—Backsliding.

IDOLATRY, Extinction of, predicted. Ex. 12.12. Against all the gods of Egypt will I execute judgment. Num. 33.4.

Isa. 2.18. The idols he shall utterly abolish. 20. A man shall cast his idols of silver, and his idols of gold, which they made *each one* for himself to worship, to the moles and to the bats. Isa. 31.7.

Isa. 17.7. At that day shall a man look to his Maker, and his eyes shall have respect to the Holy One of Israel. 8. And he shall not look to the altars, the work of his hands, neither shall respect *that* which his fingers have made, either the groves, or the images.

Isa. 27.9. When he maketh all the stones of the altar as chalkstones that are beaten in sunder, the groves and images shall not stand up.

Jer. 10.11. The gods that have not made the heavens and the earth, *even* they shall perish from the earth. 15. They *are* vanity, *and* the work of errors: in the time of their visitation they shall perish.

Jer. 51.44. I will punish Bel in Babylon. 47. I will do judgment upon the graven images of Babylon. v. 52. Isa. 21.9.

Zeph. 2.11. The Lord *will be* terrible unto them: for he will famish all the gods of the earth.

Zec. 13.2. I will cut off the names of the idols out of the land, and they shall no more be remembered: and also I will cause the prophets and the unclean spirit to pass out of the land.

See Church, Prophecies of.

IDOLATRY, Folly of. 1 Kin. 18.27. Elijah

mocked them, and said, Cry aloud : for he *is* a god ; either he is talking, or he is pursuing, or he is in a journey, *or* peradventure he sleepeth, and must be awaked. Jud. 6.31. 1 Sam. 5.3,4.

2 Chr. 25.15. Why hast thou sought after the gods of the people, which could not deliver their own people out of thine hand? 2 Kin. 3.13. Isa. 36.18. Isa. 16.12. 1 Sam. 12.21.

Psa. 115.4. Their idols *are* silver and gold, the work of men's hands. 5. They have mouths, but they speak not : eyes have they, but they see not. 8. They that make them are like unto them ; *so is* every one that trusteth in them. Psa. 96.5. Psa. 135.15-18. Isa. 2.8.

Isa. 41.23. Shew the things that are to come hereafter, that we may know that ye *are* gods : yea, do good, or do evil, that we may be dismayed, and behold *it* together. 24. Behold, ye *are* of nothing, and your work of nought : an abomination *is he that* chooseth you. *v.* 26-29. Isa. 43.9.

Isa. 44.19. None considereth in his heart, neither *is there* knowledge nor understanding to say, I have burned part of it in the fire ; yea, also I have baked bread upon the coals thereof ; I have roasted flesh, and eaten *it* : and shall I make the residue thereof an abomination? shall I fall down to the stock of a tree? *v.* 9-20. Isa. 40.19,20.

Isa. 45.20. They have no knowledge that set up the wood of their graven image, and pray unto a god *that* cannot save.

Isa. 46.1. Bel boweth down, Nebo stoopeth, their idols were upon the beasts, and upon the cattle : your carriages *were* heavy loaden ; *they are* a burden to the weary *beast.* 2. They stoop, they bow down together ; they could not deliver the burden, but themselves are gone into captivity.

Isa. 46.6. They lavish gold out of the bag, and weigh silver in the balance, *and* hire a goldsmith ; and he maketh it a god : they fall down, yea, they worship. 7. They bear him upon the shoulder, they carry him, and set him in his place, and he standeth : from his place shall he not remove : yea, *one* shall cry unto him, yet can he not answer, nor save him out *of* his trouble.

Isa. 47.13. Thou art wearied in the multitude of thy counsels. Let now the astrologers, the star-gazers, the monthly prognosticators, stand up, and save thee from *these things* that shall come upon thee. 14. Behold, they shall be as stubble ; the fire shall burn them ; they shall not deliver themselves from the power of the flame : *there shall* not be a coal to warm at, *nor* fire to sit before it. *v.* 12-15. 2 Kin. 19.18. Isa. 37.19. Zec. 10.2.

Isa. 57.13. When thou criest, let thy companies deliver thee ; but the wind shall carry them all away ; vanity shall take *them.*

Jer. 2.28. Where *are* thy gods that thou hast made thee? let them arise, if they can save thee in the time of thy trouble : for *according to* the number of thy cities are thy gods, O Judah. Deu. 32.37,38. Jud. 10.14. Jer. 11.12.

Jer. 10.5. They *are* upright as the palm tree, but speak not : they must needs be borne, because they cannot go. Be not afraid of them ; for they cannot do evil, neither also *is it* in them to do good. *v.* 3-16. Jer. 48.13. Jer. 51.17. Hab. 2.18,19.

Jer. 14.22. Are there *any* among the vanities of the Gentiles that can cause rain?

Jer. 16.19 Our fathers have inherited lies, vanity, and *things* wherein *there* is no profit. 20. Shall a man make gods unto himself, and they *are* no gods?

Hos. 8.5. Thy calf, O Samaria, hath cast *thee* off ; 6. The workmen made it ; therefore it *is* not God : but the calf of Samaria shall be broken in pieces. Ex. 32.20. Psa. 106.20.

Act. 14.15. Turn from these vanities unto the living God.

Act. 17.22. In all things ye are too superstitious. 23. For as I passed by, and beheld your devotions, I found an altar with this inscription, TO THE UNKNOWN GOD. 29. We ought not to think that the Godhead is like unto gold, or silver, or stone, graven by art and man's device.

Rom. 1.23. Changed the glory of the uncorruptible God into an image made like to corruptible man, and to birds, and four-footed beasts, and creeping things.

1 Cor. 8.4. We know that an idol *is* nothing in the world. *v.* 5.

1 Cor. 12.2. Ye were Gentiles, carried away unto these dumb idols, even as ye were led.

Gal. 4.8. When ye knew not God, ye did service unto them which by nature are no gods.

Rev. 9.20. Repented not of the works of their hands, that they should not worship devils, and idols of gold, and silver, and brass, and stone, and of wood : which neither can see, nor hear, nor walk. Deu. 4.28. Dan. 5.23.

IDOLATRY. IDOLATROUS CANAANITES to be destroyed, Deu. 7.2-5,16. Deu. 20.16-18. Their example to be avoided, Ex. 23.31-33. Ex. 34.12-16. Lev. 18.3,27-30. Lev. 20.23. Num. 33.52. Deu. 6.14. Deu. 12.29-31. Deu. 18.9-14. Deu. 29.16-18. Deu. 31.16-18. Jos. 23.7-16. Jud. 2.1-3. Jud. 6.10. 2 Kin. 17.35.

——. IDOLATROUS OFFERINGS AND WORSHIP. Burnt-offerings of animals, Ex. 32.6. 1 Kin. 18.26. Act. 14.13.

Burnt-offerings of children (forbidden, see Lev. 18.21. Lev. 20.1-5). By Canaanites, Deu. 12.31. King of Moab, 2 Kin. 3.27. To Moloch, by Israelites, 2 Kin. 16.3. 2 Chr. 28.3. 2 Kin. 21.6. 2 Kin. 23.10. Isa. 57.5. Jer. 7.31. Jer. 32.35. Eze. 16.20,21. Eze. 20.26,31. Eze. 23.37,39. To demons, Psa. 106.37,38 ; and to Baal, Jer.19.5,6.

Drink-offerings, Isa. 57.6. Isa. 65.11. Jer. 7.18. Jer. 19.13. Jer. 32.29. Jer. 44.17,19,25. Eze. 20.28. Of wine, Deu. 32.38. Of blood, Psa. 16.4. Zec. 9.7. Meat-offerings, Isa. 57.6. Jer. 7.18. Jer. 44.17. Eze. 16.19. Peace-offerings, Ex. 32.6.

Incense burned on altars, 1 Kin. 12.33. 2 Chr. 30.14. 2 Chr. 34.25. Jer. 11.12,17. Jer. 48.35. Eze. 16.18. Eze. 23.41. On brick altars, Isa. 65.3. Prayers to idols, Jud. 10.14. Isa. 44.17. Isa. 45.20. Isa. 46.7. Jonah 1.5. Praise, Jud. 16.24. Dan. 5.4.

Singing and dancing, Ex. 32.18,19. Music, Dan. 3.5-7. Cutting the flesh, 1 Kin. 18.28. Jer. 41.5. Kissing, Hos. 13.2. Job 31.27. Bowing, 1 Kin. 19.18. 2 Kin. 5.18. Tithes and gifts offered, 2 Kin. 23.11. Dan. 11.38. Amos 4.4,5. Feasting and licentious practices, Ex. 32.25. Num. 25.1-3. 1 Cor. 10.7,8. Festivals, 1 Kin. 12.32. Dan. 3.2,3.

See ALTARS, IDOLATROUS—GROVES—HIGH

PLACES—GARDENS—MOUNTAINS—PRIESTS, IDOLATROUS — ROOFS — TEMPLES, IDOLATROUS.

IDOLATRY. IDOLS TO BE DESTROYED, Ex. 23.24. Ex. 34.13. Num. 33.52. Deu. 7.5,25,26. Deu. 12.2,3. Jud. 2.2. Destroyed by Jacob, Gen. 35.2-4. Moses, Ex. 32.19,20. Gideon, Jud. 6.28-32. David, 2 Sam. 5.21. Jehu, 2 Kin. 10.26-28. Jehoiada, 2 Kin. 11.18. Hezekiah, 2 Kin. 18.3-6. Josiah, 2 Kin. 23.4-20. Asa, 2 Chr. 14.3-5. 2 Chr. 15.8-16. Jehoshaphat, 2 Chr. 17.6. 2 Chr. 19.3. Jews, 2 Chr. 30.14. Manasseh, 2 Chr. 33.15.

———, OBJECTS OF. Angels, Col. 2.18. Animals, Rom. 1.23. Gods of Egypt, Ex. 12.12. Golden calf, Ex. 32.4. Brazen serpent, 2 Kin. 18.4. Net and drag, Hab. 1.16. Unknown god, Act. 17.23. God of forces, Dan. 11.38. Men, Act.14.8-18. The dead, see NECROMANCY.
IMAGES. Graven and molten, Ex. 20.4. Ex. 32.4,20. Deu. 4.23. Isa. 44.9-12. Hab. 2.18. Standing, Lev. 26.1. 1 Sam. 5.3. Isa. 46.7. Made of gold, silver, or brass, Psa. 135.15. Isa. 46.6. Dan. 3.1. Rev. 9.20. Of wood, Deu. 4.28. 2 Kin. 19.18. Isa. 44.13-19; and adorned with gold and silver, Isa. 40.19,20. Jer. 10.3-5. Of stone, Lev. 26.1. Jer. 2.27. Act. 17.29. Adorned with garments, Jer. 10.9. Eze. 16.18.
Pictures, Num. 33.52. Isa. 2.16. Pictures on walls, Eze. 8.10. Ear-rings, Gen. 35.4, see SHRINE. Golden ephod, see TERAPHIM.

See CALVES OF JEROBOAM— DEMONS— MOON — STARS — SUN — ADRAMMELECH — ASHIMA—ASHTAROTH—BAAL—BAAL-BERITH —BAAL-PEOR— BAALZEBUB— BEL—CASTOR AND POLLUX — CHEMOSH — CHIUN—DAGON —DIANA—JUPITER—MALCHAM— MERCURY —MERODACH—MOLOCH—NEBO—NERGAL— NIBHAZ—NISROCH—QUEEN OF HEAVEN— RIMMON — SUCCOTH-BENOTH — TAMMUZ — TARTAK.

———, PUNISHED WITH DEATH, Ex. 22.20. Lev. 20.2-5. Num. 25.4,5. Deu. 13.6-15. Deu. 17.2-7. See Jud. 6.31.

IDUMEA. See EDOMITES.

IGNORANCE. See MAN'S IGNORANCE— SPIRITUAL BLINDNESS—APOSTLES' IMPERFECT KNOWLEDGE—GOD'S PROVIDENCE MISUNDERSTOOD.

ILLYRICUM, or DALMATIA, a country north-west of Macedonia; Paul preaches at, Rom. 15.19. Titus sent to, 2 Tim. 4.10.

IMAGES. See IDOLATRY, OBJECTS OF.

IMMANUEL (God with us), a name of Christ, Mat. 1.23. Isa. 7.14.

IMMORTALITY. See SOUL OF MAN IMMORTAL.

IMPENITENCE. Lev. 23.29. Whatsoever soul it be that shall not be afflicted in that same day, he shall be cut off from among his people.
Lev. 26.21. If ye walk contrary unto me, and will not hearken unto me; I will bring seven times more plagues upon you according to your sins. v. 22-24.
Deu. 29.19. I shall have peace, though I walk in the imagination of mine heart.
1 Sam. 15.23. Stubbornness is as iniquity and idolatry.

Job 9.4. Who hath hardened himself against him, and hath prospered?
Job 24.13. They are of those that rebel against the light; they know not the ways thereof, nor abide in the paths thereof.
Job 33.14. God speaketh once, yea twice, yet man perceiveth it not.
Psa. 7.12. If he turn not, he will whet his sword; he hath bent his bow, and made it ready. v. 13.
Psa. 32.9. Be ye not as the horse, or as the mule, which have no understanding.
Psa. 50.17. Thou hatest instruction, and castest my words behind thee. 21. These things hast thou done, and I kept silence; but I will reprove thee, and set them in order before thine eyes.
Psa. 58.4. Like the deaf adder that stoppeth her ear; 5. Which will not hearken to the voice of charmers, charming never so wisely.
Psa. 68.21. God shall wound the head of his enemies, and the hairy scalp of such an one as goeth on still in his trespasses.
Psa. 78.8. A stubborn and rebellious generation; a generation that set not their heart aright, and whose spirit was not stedfast with God.
Psa. 81.11. My people would not hearken to my voice; and Israel would none of me. 12. So I gave them up unto their own hearts' lust: and they walked in their own counsels.
Psa. 82.5. They know not, neither will they understand; they walk on in darkness.
Psa. 95.8. Harden not your heart, as in the provocation, and as in the day of temptation in the wilderness.
Psa. 107.11. They rebelled against the words of God, and contemned the counsel of the most High: 12. Therefore he brought down their heart with labour; they fell down, and there was none to help.
Pro. 1.24. Because I have called, and ye refused; I have stretched out my hand, and no man regarded; 25. But ye have set at nought all my counsel, and would none of my reproof: 26. I also will laugh at your calamity; I will mock when your fear cometh. 28. Then shall they call upon me, but I will not answer; they shall seek me early, but they shall not find me: 29. For that they hated knowledge, and did not choose the fear of the Lord: 30. They would none of my counsel: they despised all my reproof. 31. Therefore shall they eat of the fruit of their own way, and be filled with their own devices. v. 27.
Pro. 11.3. The perverseness of transgressors shall destroy them.
Pro. 15.10. He that hateth reproof shall die. 32. He that refuseth instruction despiseth his own soul.
Pro. 19.16. He that despiseth his way shall die.
Pro. 26.11. As a dog returneth to his vomit, so a fool returneth to his folly.
Pro. 28.13. He that covereth his sins shall not prosper. 14. He that hardeneth his heart shall fall into mischief. Pro. 21.29.
Pro. 29.1. He, that being often reproved hardeneth his neck, shall suddenly be destroyed, and that without remedy.
Ecc. 8.11. Because sentence against an evil work is not executed speedily, therefore the heart of the sons of men is fully set in them to do evil.

Isa. 26.10. Let favour be shewed to the wicked, *yet* will he not learn righteousness: in the land of uprightness will he deal unjustly, and will not behold the majesty of the Lord.

Isa. 32.9. Rise up, ye women that are at ease; hear my voice, ye careless daughters; give ear unto my speech. 10. Many days and years shall ye be troubled, ye careless women.

Isa. 42.24. They would not walk in his ways, neither were they obedient unto his law. 25. Therefore he hath poured upon him the fury of his anger, and the strength of battle: and it hath set him on fire round about, yet he knew not; and it burned him, yet he laid *it* not to heart. *v.* 18-23.

Isa. 46.12. Hearken unto me, ye stouthearted, that *are* far from righteousness: 13. I bring near my righteousness.

Isa. 48.4. I knew that thou *art* obstinate, and thy neck *is* an iron sinew, and thy brow brass. 8. Yea, thou heardest not; yea, thou knewest not; yea, from that time *that* thine ear was not opened: for I knew that thou wouldest deal very treacherously, and wast called a transgressor from the womb.

Isa. 57.11. Of whom hast thou been afraid or feared, that thou hast lied, and hast not remembered me, nor laid *it* to thy heart? have not I held my peace even of old, and thou fearest me not?

Isa. 65.12. Because when I called, ye did not answer; when I spake, ye did not hear; but did evil before mine eyes, and did choose *that* wherein I delighted not. 15. Ye shall leave your name for a curse unto my chosen: for the Lord God shall slay thee. Isa. 66.4.

Jer. 3.10. And yet for all this her treacherous sister Judah hath not turned unto me with her whole heart, but feignedly, saith the Lord. *v.* 7-9.

Jer. 5.21. Hear now this, O foolish people, and without understanding; which have eyes, and see not; which have ears, and hear not: 22. Fear ye not me? saith the Lord: will ye not tremble at my presence. 23. This people hath a revolting and a rebellious heart; they are revolted and gone.

Jer. 6.10. To whom shall I speak, and give warning, that they may hear? behold, their ear *is* uncircumcised, and they cannot hearken: behold, the word of the Lord is unto them a reproach; they have no delight in it. 16. Stand ye in the ways, and see, and ask for the old paths, where *is* the good way, and walk therein, and ye shall find rest for your souls. But they said, We will not walk *therein.* 17. I set watchmen over you, *saying,* Hearken to the sound of the trumpet. But they said, We will not hearken.

Jer. 6.19. Hear, O earth: behold, I will bring evil upon this people, *even* the fruit of their thoughts, because they have not hearkened unto my words, nor to my law, but rejected it.

Jer. 7.13. I spake unto you, rising up early and speaking, but ye heard not; and I called you, but ye answered not; 14. Therefore will I do unto *this* house, which is called by my name, wherein ye trust, and unto the place which I gave to you and to your fathers, as I have done to Shiloh. 24. But they hearkened not, nor inclined their ear, but walked in the counsels *and* in the imagination of their

evil heart, and went backward, and not forward.

Jer. 7.28. But thou shalt say unto them, This *is* a nation that obeyeth not the voice of the Lord their God, nor receiveth correction: truth is perished, and is cut off from their mouth. *v.* 13-34. Jer. 11.8. Jer. 25.4. Jer. 26.4-6. Jer. 32.33. Jer. 35.14-17. Zec. 1.4.

Jer. 8.5. Why *then* is this people of Jerusalem slidden back by a perpetual backsliding? they hold fast deceit, they refuse to return. 6. I hearkened and heard, *but* they spake not aright: no man repented him of his wickedness, saying, What have I done? every one turned to his course, as the horse rusheth into the battle. 7. Yea, the stork in the heaven knoweth her appointed times; and the turtle and the crane and the swallow observe the time of their coming; but my people know not the judgment of the Lord.

Jer. 8.20. The harvest is past, the summer is ended, and we are not saved. *v.* 4-22.

Jer. 12.11. The whole land is made desolate, because no man layeth *it* to heart.

Jer. 13.17. If ye will not hear it, my soul shall weep in secret places for *your* pride; and mine eye shall weep sore, and run down with tears, because the Lord's flock is carried away captive. 27. Woe unto thee, O Jerusalem! wilt thou not be made clean? when *shall it* once *be? v.* 15. Jer. 19.15.

Jer. 14.10. Thus have they loved to wander, they have not refrained their feet, therefore the Lord doth not accept them; he will now remember their iniquity, and visit their sins. *v.* 1-16.

Jer. 15.6. Thou hast forsaken me, saith the Lord, thou art gone backward: therefore will I stretch out my hand against thee, and destroy thee; I am weary with repenting. 7. I will destroy my people, *since* they return not from their ways.

Jer. 16.12. Ye have done worse than your fathers; for, behold, ye walk every one after the imagination of his evil heart, that they may not hearken unto me. Jer. 44.10.

Jer. 17.23. They obeyed not, neither inclined their ear, but made their neck stiff, that they might not hear, nor receive instruction.

Jer. 18.12. They said, There is no hope: but we will walk after our own devices, and we will every one do the imagination of his evil heart. Jer. 2.25.

Jer. 22.21. I spake unto thee in thy prosperity; *but* thou saidst, I will not hear. This *hath been* thy manner from thy youth, that thou obeyedst not my voice.

Jer. 44.16. *As for* the word that thou hast spoken unto us in the name of the Lord, we will not hearken unto thee. 17. But we will certainly do whatsoever thing goeth forth out of our own mouth, to burn incense unto the queen of heaven, as we have done, we, and our fathers: for *then* had we plenty of victuals, and were well, and saw no evil.

Eze. 2.5. They, whether they will hear, or whether they will forbear, (for they *are* a rebellious house,) yet shall know that there hath been a prophet among them.

Eze. 3.5. For thou *art* not sent to a people of a strange speech and of an hard language, *but* to the house of Israel. 6. Surely, had I sent thee to them, they would have hearkened unto thee. 7. But the house of Israel will not hearken unto thee; for they will not hearken unto me: for all the house of Israel *are* impudent and hardhearted. 19. If thou warn the wicked, and he turn not from his wickedness, nor from his wicked way, he shall die in his iniquity. 26. I will make thy tongue cleave to the roof of thy mouth, that thou shalt be dumb, and shalt not be to them a reprover: for they *are* a rebellious house. *v.* 1-11. Eze. 2.4. Eze. 33.9.

Eze. 12.2. Thou dwellest in the midst of a rebellious house, which have eyes to see, and see not; they have ears to hear, and hear not: for they *are* a rebellious house.

Eze. 20.21. The children rebelled against me: they walked not in my statutes, neither kept my. judgments to do them, which *if* a man do, he shall even live in them; they polluted my sabbaths: then I said, I would pour out my fury upon them.

Eze. 33.4. Whosoever heareth the sound of the trumpet, and taketh not warning; if the sword come, and take him away, his blood shall be upon his own head. 5. He heard the sound of the trumpet, and took not warning; his blood shall be upon him.

Hos. 4.17. Ephraim *is* joined to idols: let him alone.

Hos. 5.4. They will not frame their doings to turn unto their God: for the spirit of whoredoms *is* in the midst of them, and they have not known the Lord.

Hos. 7.13. Woe unto them! for they have fled from me: destruction unto them! because they have transgressed against me: though I have redeemed them, yet they have spoken lies against me. 15. Though I have bound *and* strengthened their arms, yet do they imagine mischief against me.

Hos. 11.2. *As* they called them, so they went from them: they sacrificed unto Baalim, and burned incense to graven images. 7. My people are bent to backsliding from me: though they called them to the most High, none at all would exalt *him*.

Zec. 7.11. They refused to hearken, and pulled away the shoulder, and stopped their ears, that they should not hear. 12. Yea, they made their hearts as an adamant stone, lest they should h ar the law, and the words which the Lord of hosts hath sent in his spirit by the former prophets: therefore came a great wrath from the Lord of hosts. 13. Therefore it is come to pass, *that* as he cried, and they would not hear; so they cried, and I would not hear, saith the Lord of hosts. *v.* 4-14.

Mal. 2.2. If ye will not hear, and if ye will not lay *it* to heart, to give glory unto my name, saith the Lord of hosts, I will even send a curse upon you, and I will curse your blessings: yea, I have cursed them already, because ye do not lay *it* to heart. 17. Ye have wearied the Lord with your words. Yet ye say, Wherein have we wearied *him?* When ye say, Every one that doeth evil *is* good in the sight of the Lord, and he delighteth in them; or, Where *is* the God of judgment?

Mal. 4.6. He shall turn the heart of the fathers to the children, and the heart of the children to their fathers, lest I come and smite the earth with a curse.

Mat. 11.21. Woe unto thee, Chorazin! woe unto thee, Bethsaida! for if the mighty works, which were done in you, had been done in Tyre and Sidon, they would have repented long ago in sackcloth and ashes. *v.* 20-24. Mat. 12.42,44.

Mat. 23.37. How often would I have gathered thy children together, even as a hen gathereth her chickens under *her* wings, and ye would not! 38. Behold, your house is left unto you desolate. Luk. 13.34.

Mat. 24.38. Marrying and giving in marriage, until the day that Noe entered into the ark, 39. And knew not until the flood came, and took them all away: so shall also the coming of the Son of man be. 48. If that evil servant shall say in his heart, My lord delayeth his coming. 50. The lord of that servant shall come in a day when he looketh not, 51. And shall cut him asunder.

Mat. 27.4. They said, What *is that* to us? see thou *to that.* 25. Then answered all the people, and said, His blood *be* on us, and on our children.

Mar. 3.5. He looked round about on them with anger, being grieved for the hardness of their hearts.

Act. 17.51. Ye stiff-necked and uncircumcised in heart and ears, ye do always resist the Holy Ghost: as your fathers *did*, so *do* ye.

Rom. 2.4. Despisest thou the riches of his goodness and forbearance and long-suffering; not knowing that the goodness of God leadeth thee to repentance? 5. After thy hardness and impenitent heart treasurest up unto thyself wrath against the day of wrath and revelation of the righteous judgment of God.

Rev. 2.5. Remember therefore from whence thou art fallen, and repent, and do the first works; or else I will come unto thee quickly, and will remove thy candlestick out of his place, except thou repent. 16. Repent; or else I will come unto thee quickly, and will fight against them with the sword of my mouth. 21. I gave her space to repent of her fornication; and she repented not. 22. Behold I will cast her into a bed, and them that commit adultery with her into great tribulation, except they repent of their deeds.

Rev. 3.3. Remember therefore how thou hast received and heard, and hold fast, and repent. If therefore thou shalt not watch, I will come on thee as a thief, and thou shalt not know what hour I will come upon thee.

IMPENITENCE, EXAMPLES OF: Pharaoh, Ex. 4.21. Ex.5.2. Ex.7.13,16. Ex. 8.15,19,31. Ex. 9.7,12,30,34. Ex. 10.20,27. Ex. 11.9,10. Ex. 14.5-9. Israelites, Num. 14.22,23. Deu. 9.7-24. Den. 31.27. Jud. 2.17,19. 1 Sam. 8.7,8. 2 Kin. 17.14. 2 Chr. 24.19. 2 Chr. 36.16,17. Neh. 9.16,17,29,30. Jer. 36.31. Eli's sons, 1 Sam. 2.25. Amaziah, 2 Chr. 25.16. Manasseh, 2 Chr. 33.10. Amon, 2 Chr. 33.23. Zedekiah, 2 Chr. 36.12,13. Jer. 37.2. Jehoiakim and his servants, Jer. 36.22-24. Belshazzar, Dan. 5.22,23.

See AFFLICTION, IMPENITENCE IN—SPIRITUAL BLINDNESS—BACKSLIDING—INFIDELITY—UNBELIEF.

IMPLEMENTS AND TOOLS. See ANVIL, AWL, AXE, BALANCES, BELLOWS, BESOM, DISTAFF, FILE, FORK, GOAD, HAMMER, HARROW, KNIFE, MATTOCK, MAUL, MILL, MORTAR, NAIL, PEN, PLANE, PLOUGH, PLUMMET, PRUNING-HOOK, RAZOR, SAW, SHOVEL, SICKLE, SIEVE, SNUFFERS, SPINDLE,

SPOONS, TONGS, WEAVER'S BEAM, SHUTTLE. See also ARTS—MANUFACTURES.

INCENSE, composition of, Ex. 30.34-38. Made by the priests, 1 Chr. 9.30. Kept sacred, Ex. 30.34-38. Common, not to be offered, Ex. 30.9. None but priests might offer, Num. 16.40. Deu. 33.10. 1 Sam. 2.28. 1 Chr. 23.13. 2 Chr. 29.11. A portion of, placed before the testimony, Ex. 30.36.

Offered with sacred fire only in censers, Lev. 16.12. Num. 16.17,46. Every morning and evening, Ex. 30.7,8. 2 Chr. 13.11. On the golden altar, Ex. 30.1-7. Ex. 40.5,27. 2 Chr. 2.4. 2 Chr. 32.12. Before the mercy-seat on the day of atonement, Lev. 16.12,13. As an atonement, Num. 16.46,47. Prayer at the time of offering, Luk. 1.10.

Nadab and Abihu killed for offering with strange fire, Lev. 10.1,2. Korah, &c., killed for offering, Num. 16.16-35. Uzziah smitten with leprosy for offering, 2 Chr. 26.16-21. Brought by the wise men to Christ, Mat. 2.11. Illustrative, Psa. 141.2. Mal. 1.11. Symbolical, Rev. 5.8. Rev. 8.3,4.

See FRANKINCENSE—ALTAR OF INCENSE—IDOLATROUS OFFERINGS.

INDECISION. See LUKEWARMNESS—FEAR OF MAN.

INDIA, Ahasuerus' kingdom extended to, Est. 1.1. Est. 8.9.

INDUSTRY AND ECONOMY. Gen. 2.15. God took the man, and put him into the garden of Eden to dress it and to keep it.

Pro. 10.4. The hand of the diligent maketh rich. 5. He that gathereth in summer *is* a wise son.

Pro. 12.11. He that tilleth his land shall be satisfied with bread. 24. The hand of the diligent shall bear rule. 27. The substance of a diligent man *is* precious.

Pro. 13.4. The soul of the diligent shall be made fat. 11. He that gathereth by labour shall increase. 23. Much food *is in* the tillage of the poor.

Pro. 14.4. Where no oxen *are,* the crib *is* clean : but much increase *is* by the strength of the ox. 23. In all labour there is profit.

Pro. 16.26. He that laboureth laboureth for himself ; for his mouth craveth it of him.

Pro. 20.13. Love not sleep, lest thou come to poverty ; open thine eyes, *and* thou shalt be satisfied with bread.

Pro. 21.5. The thoughts of the diligent *tend* only to plenteousness ; but of every one *that is* hasty only to want.

Pro. 22.29. Seest thou a man diligent in his business ? he shall stand before kings ; he shall not stand before mean *men.*

Pro. 27.23. Be thou diligent to know the state of thy flocks, *and* look well to thy herds. *v.* 23-27.

Pro. 28.19. He that tilleth his land shall have plenty of bread.

Pro. 30.25. The ants *are* a people not strong, yet they prepare their meat in the summer ; 26. The conies *are but* a feeble folk, yet make they their houses in the rocks. *v.* 27,28.

Pro. 31.27. She looketh well to the ways of her household, and eateth not the bread of idleness. *v.* 13-27.

Ecc. 9.10. Whatsoever thy hand findeth to do, do *it* with thy might ; for *there is* no work,

nor device, nor knowledge, nor wisdom, in the grave, whither thou goest.

Ecc. 11.4. He that observeth the wind shall not sow ; and he that regardeth the clouds shall not reap. 6. In the morning sow thy seed, and in the evening withhold not thine hand : for thou knowest not whether shall prosper, either this or that, or whether they both *shall be* alike good.

Jno. 6.12. Gather up the fragments that remain, that nothing be lost.

Rom. 12.11. Not slothful in business ; fervent in spirit ; serving the Lord.

Eph. 4.28. Let him that stole steal no more : but rather let him labour, working with *his* hands the thing which is good, that he may have to give to him that needeth.

1 The. 4.11. Study to be quiet, and to do your own business, and to work with your own hands, as we commanded you ; 12. That ye may walk honestly toward them that are without, and *that* ye may have lack of nothing.

2 The. 3.12. Now them that are such we command and exhort by our Lord Jesus Christ, that with quietness they work, and eat their own bread.

See IDLENESS.

INFIDELITY, PRESUMPTION, SCOFFING. Gen. 3.1. Yea, hath God said, Ye shall not eat of every tree of the garden ? *v.* 4.

Ex. 5.2. Who *is* the Lord, that I should obey his voice to let Israel go ?

Ex. 14.11. Because *there were* no graves in Egypt, hast thou taken us away to die in the wilderness ? *v.* 12. Ex. 16.3,7. Num. 14.27-34. Num. 16.41. Num. 21.5.

Ex. 17.7. They tempted the Lord, saying, Is the Lord among us, or not ?

Num. 15.30. The soul that doeth *ought* presumptuously, (*whether he be* born in the land, or a stranger,) the same reproacheth the Lord ; and that soul shall be cut off from among his people. *v.* 31.

Deu. 29.19. When he heareth the words of this curse, that he bless himself in his heart, saying, I shall have peace, though I walk in the imagination of mine heart, to add drunkenness to thirst : 20. The Lord will not spare him, but then the anger of the Lord and his jealousy shall smoke against that man, and all the curses that are written in this book shall lie upon him, and the Lord shall blot out his name from under heaven. *v.* 21.

Deu. 32.15. Jeshurun waxed fat, and kicked : thou art waxen fat, thou art grown thick, thou art covered *with fatness ;* then he forsook God *which* made him, and lightly esteemed the Rock of his salvation.

1 Kin. 20.28. The Syrians have said, The Lord *is* God of the hills, but he *is* not God of the valleys.

1 Kin. 22.24. Zedekiah went near, and smote Micaiah on the cheek, and said, Which way went the Spirit of the Lord from me to speak unto thee ?

2 Kin. 2.23. There came forth little children out of the city, and mocked him, and said unto him, Go up, thou bald-head ; go up, thou bald-head. *v.* 24.

2 Chr. 30.6. Turn again unto the Lord God. 10. But they laughed them to scorn, and mocked them.

2 Chr. 32.15. How much less shall your God deliver you out of mine hand ? *v.* 16-19.

2 Chr. 36.16. They mocked the messengers of God, and despised his words, and misused his prophets, until the wrath of the Lord arose against his people, till *there was* no remedy.

Job 15.25. He stretcheth out his hand against God, and strengtheneth himself against the Almighty. 26. He runneth upon him, *even* on *his* neck, upon the thick bosses of his bucklers.

Job 21.14. They say unto God, Depart from us ; for we desire not the knowledge of thy ways. 15. What *is* the Almighty, that we should serve him ? and what profit should we have, if we pray unto him ?

Job 22.13. Thou sayest, How doth God know ? can he judge through the dark cloud ? 14. Thick clouds *are* a covering to him, that he seeth not ; and he walketh in the circuit of heaven. 17. Which said unto God, Depart from us : and what can the Almighty do for them ?

Job 34.7. *Who* drinketh up scorning like water. 9. For he hath said, It profiteth a man nothing that he should delight himself with God. 17. Wilt thou condemn him that is most just. 18. *Is it fit* to say to a king, *Thou art* wicked ? *and* to princes, *Ye are* ungodly ? 19. *How much less to him* that accepteth not the persons of princes, nor regardeth the rich more than the poor ? for they all *are* the work of his hands. 33. *Should it be* according to thy mind ? he will recompense it, whether thou refuse, or whether thou choose.

Job 35.3. Thou saidst, What advantage will it be unto thee ? *and*, What profit shall I have, *if I be cleansed* from my sin ?

Job 36.23. Who hath enjoined him his way ? or who can say, Thou hast wrought iniquity ?

Psa. 1.1. The seat of the scornful.

Psa. 3.2. Many *there be* which say of my soul, *There is* no help for him in God.

Psa. 4.6. Who will shew us *any* good ?

Psa. 10.11. He hath said in his heart, God hath forgotten : he hideth his face ; he will never see *it*. 13. Wherefore doth the wicked contemn God ? he hath said in his heart, Thou wilt not require *it*.

Psa. 12.3. The Lord shall cut off all flattering lips, *and* the tongue that speaketh proud things : 4. Who have said, With our tongue will we prevail ; our lips *are* our own : who *is* lord over us ?

Psa. 14.1. The fool hath said in his heart, *There is* no God. 6. Ye have shamed the counsel of the poor, because the Lord *is* his refuge. Psa. 53.1.

Psa. 42.3. They continually say unto me, Where *is* thy God ?

Psa. 50.21. These *things* hast thou done, and I kept silence ; thou thoughtest that I was altogether *such an one* as thyself.

Psa. 59.7. Swords *are* in their lips : for who, *say they,* doth hear ?

Psa. 64.5. They commune of laying snares privily ; they say, Who shall see them ?

Psa. 73.11. They say, How doth God know ? and is there knowledge in the most High ?

Psa. 78.19. Yea, they spake against God ; they said, Can God furnish a table in the wilderness ? *v.* 20-22. Psa. 107.11,12.

Psa. 94.7. They say, the Lord shall not see, neither shall the God of Jacob regard *it.* 8. Understand, ye brutish among the people :

and *ye* fools, when will ye be wise ? 9. He that planted the ear, shall he not hear ?

Psa. 106.24. They despised the pleasant land, they believed not his word. *v.* 25,26.

Pro. 1.22. How long, ye simple ones, will ye love simplicity ? and the scorners delight in their scorning, and fools hate knowledge ?

Pro. 3.34. Surely he scorneth the scorners.

Pro. 9.12. If thou be wise, thou shalt be wise for thyself : but *if* thou scornest, thou alone shalt bear it.

Pro. 14.6. A scorner seeketh wisdom, and *findeth it* not. 9. Fools make a mock at sin.

Pro. 19.29. Judgments are prepared for scorners.

Pro. 24.9. The scorner *is* an abomination to men.

Isa. 3.8. Their tongue and their doings *are* against the Lord, to provoke the eyes of his glory.

Isa. 5.18. Woe unto them, 19. That say, Let him make speed, *and* hasten his work, that we may see *it :* and let the counsel of the Holy One of Israel draw nigh and come, that we may know *it !* 24. As the fire devoureth the stubble, and the flame consumeth the chaff, *so* their root shall be as rottenness, and their blossom shall go up as dust : because they have cast away the law of the Lord of hosts, and despised the word of the Holy One of Israel. 25. Therefore is the anger of the Lord kindled against his people.

Isa. 10.15. Shall the axe boast itself against him that heweth therewith ? *or* shall the saw magnify itself against him that shaketh it ? as if the rod should shake *itself* against them that lift it up, *or* as if the staff should lift up *itself, as if it were* no wood.

Isa. 28.9. Whom shall he teach knowledge ? and whom shall he make to understand doctrine ? *them that are* weaned from the milk, *and* drawn from the breasts. 10. For precept *must be* upon precept, precept upon precept ; line upon line, line upon line ; here a little, *and* there a little. 14. Hear the word of the Lord, ye scornful men. 15. Ye have said, We have made a covenant with death, and with hell are we at agreement. 17. The hail shall sweep away the refuge of lies, and the waters shall overflow the hiding-place. 18. And your covenant with death shall be disannulled, and your agreement with hell shall not stand ; when the overflowing scourge shall pass through ; then ye shall be trodden down by it. 22. Be ye not mockers, lest your bands be made strong. *v.* 11-29.

Isa. 29.15. Woe unto them that seek deep to hide their counsel from the Lord, and their works are in the dark, and they say, Who seeth us ? and who knoweth us ? 16. Surely your turning of things upside down shall be esteemed as the potter's clay : for shall the work say of him that made it, He made me not ? or shall the thing framed say of him that framed it, He had no understanding ? 20. The scorner is consumed, and all that watch for iniquity are cut off.

Isa 45.9. Woe unto him that striveth with his Maker ! *Let* the potsherd *strive* with the potsherds of the earth. Shall the clay say to him that fashioneth it, What makest thou ? or thy work, He hath no hands ? 10. Woe unto him that saith unto *his* father, What begettest thou? or to the woman, What hast thou brought forth?

Isa. 47.10. Thou hast trusted in thy wickedness: thou hast said, None seeth me. Thy wisdom and thy knowledge, it hath perverted thee; and thou hast said in thine heart, I *am*, and none else beside me. 11. Therefore shall evil come upon thee; thou shalt not know from whence it riseth: and mischief shall fall upon thee; thou shalt not be able to put it off: and desolation shall come upon thee suddenly, *which* thou shalt not know.

Isa. 57.4. Against whom do ye sport yourselves? against whom make ye a wide mouth, *and* draw out the tongue?

Jer. 5.12. They have belied the Lord, and said, *It is* not he; neither shall evil come upon us; neither shall we see sword nor famine. 14. Wherefore thus saith the Lord God of hosts, Because ye speak this word, behold, I will make my words in thy mouth fire, and this people wood, and it shall devour them.

Jer. 17.15. They say unto me, Where *is* the word of the Lord? let it come now. Jer. 43.2.

Jer. 48.42. Moab shall be destroyed from *being* a people, because he hath magnified *himself* against the Lord. *v.* 26.

Jer. 50.24. Thou art found, and also caught, because thou hast striven against the Lord. 29. According to all that she hath done, do unto her: for she hath been proud against the Lord.

Lam. 1.7. The adversaries saw her, *and* did mock at her sabbaths.

Eze. 9.9. The city full of perverseness: for they say, The Lord hath forsaken the earth, and the Lord seeth not. 10. And as for me also, mine eye shall not spare, neither will I have pity, *but* I will recompense their way upon their head. Eze. 8.12.

Eze. 12.22. What *is* that proverb *that* ye have in the land of Israel, The days are prolonged, and every vision faileth? Eze. 11.3.

Eze. 18.2. What mean ye, that ye use this proverb concerning the land of Israel, saying, The fathers have eaten sour grapes, and the children's teeth are set on edge? 29. Yet saith the house of Israel, The way of the Lord is not equal. O house of Israel, are not my ways equal? are not your ways unequal? Eze. 33.17.

Eze. 20.49. Ah Lord God! they say of me, Doth he not speak parables?

Eze. 33.30. Thy people still are talking against thee by the walls and in the doors of the houses, and speak one to another, every one to his brother, saying, Come, I pray you, and hear what is the word that cometh forth from the Lord.

Dan. 3.15. Who *is* that God that shall deliver you out of my hands?

Dan. 8.25. He shall magnify *himself* in his heart: he shall also stand up against the Prince of princes; but he shall be broken without hand. *v.*10. Dan.7.25. Dan.11.36,37.

Hos. 7.5. He stretched out his hand with scorners. 13. Woe unto them! for they have fled from me: though I have redeemed them, yet they have spoken lies against me. 15. Though I have bound *and* strengthened their arms, yet do they imagine mischief against me.

Amos 5.18. Woe unto you that desire the day of the Lord! to what end *is* it for you? the day of the Lord *is* darkness, and not light.

Amos 7.16. Thou sayest, Prophesy not against Israel, and drop not *thy word* against the house of Isaac. 17. Therefore thus saith the Lord, Thou shalt die in a polluted land.

Mic. 7.10. Shame shall cover her which said unto me, Where is the Lord thy God?

Zeph. 1.12. I will search Jerusalem with candles, and punish the men that are settled on their lees: that say in their heart, The Lord will not do good, neither will he do evil.

Mal. 3.13. Your words have been stout against me, saith the Lord. Yet ye say, What have we spoken *so much* against thee? 14. Ye have said, It *is* vain to serve God.

Mat. 12.24. When the Pharisees heard *it*, they said, This *fellow* doth not cast out devils, but by Beelzebub the prince of the devils. Mar. 3.22. Luk. 11.15. Luk. 16.14.

Luk. 4.23. Physician, heal thyself.

Luk. 19.14. His citizens hated him, and sent a message after him, saying, We will not have this *man* to reign over us. 27. Those mine enemies, which would not that I should reign over them, bring hither, and slay *them* before me.

Jno. 18.38. Pilate saith unto him, What is truth?

Act. 2.13. Others mocking said, These men are full of new wine.

Act. 13.45. When the Jews saw the multitudes, they were filled with envy, and spake against those things which were spoken by Paul, contradicting and blaspheming.

Act. 17.18. Some said, What will this babbler say? other some, He seemeth to be a setter forth of strange gods. 32. When they heard of the resurrection of the dead, some mocked.

Act. 23.8. The Sadducees say that there is no resurrection, neither angel, nor spirit. Mat. 22.23.

Act. 25.19. Had certain questions against him of their own superstition, and of one Jesus, which was dead, whom Paul affirmed to be alive.

Rom. 9.20. Nay but, O man, who art thou that repliest against God? Shall the thing formed say to him that formed *it*, Why hast thou made me thus? 21. Hath not the potter power over the clay, of the same lump to make one vessel unto honour, and another unto dishonour? Rom. 3.5.

Heb. 10.29. Of how much sorer punishment, suppose ye, shall he be thought worthy, who hath trodden under foot the Son of God, and hath counted the blood of the covenant, wherewith he was sanctified, an unholy thing, and hath done despite unto the Spirit of grace?

2 Pet. 2.1. There shall be false teachers among you, who privily shall bring in damnable heresies, even denying the Lord that bought them, and bring upon themselves swift destruction.

2 Pet. 3.3. There shall come in the last days scoffers, walking after their own lusts, 4. And saying, Where is the promise of his coming? *v.* 5.

Jude 4. There are certain men crept in unawares, who were before of old ordained to this condemnation, ungodly men, turning the grace of our God into lasciviousness, and denying the only Lord God, and our Lord Jesus Christ. 15. To execute judgment upon all, and to convince all of all their hard *speeches* which ungodly sinners have spoken against him. 18. They told you there should be mockers in the last time, who should walk after their own ungodly lusts. *v.* 19.

See BLASPHEMY — UNBELIEF — WORD OF GOD REJECTED—SADDUCEES—CHRIST, SUFFERINGS OF—IMPENITENCE.

INGATHERING, FEAST OF. See FEAST OF TABERNACLES.

INGRAFTING. Illustrative, Rom. 11.17-24.

INGRATITUDE TO GOD—UNTHANKFULNESS. Num. 16.9. *Seemeth it but* a small thing unto you, that the God of Israel hath separated you from the congregation of Israel, to bring you near to himself?

Deu. 8.12. Lest, *when* thou hast eaten and art full, 13. And all that thou hast is multiplied ; 14. Then thine heart be lifted up, and thou forget the Lord thy God, which brought thee forth out of the land of Egypt, from the house of bondage. *v.* 11-18. Deu. 6.11,12.

Deu. 28.47. Because thou servedst not the Lord thy God with joyfulness, and with gladness of heart, for the abundance of all *things ;* 48. Therefore shalt thou serve thine enemies which the Lord shall send against thee, in hunger, and in thirst, and in nakedness, and in want of all *things*.

Deu. 32.6. Do ye thus requite the Lord, O foolish people and unwise? *is* not he thy father *that* hath bought thee? hath he not made thee, and established thee? 15. But Jeshurun waxed fat, and kicked : thou art waxen fat, thou art grown thick, thou art covered *with fatness ;* then he forsook God *which* made him, and lightly esteemed the Rock of his salvation. 18. Of the Rock *that* begat thee thou art unmindful, and hast forgotten God that formed thee. *v.* 13.

Jud. 2.10. There arose another generation after them, which knew not the Lord, nor yet the works which he had done for Israel.

Jud. 10.11. *Did* not *I deliver you* from the Egyptians, and from the Amorites? 13. Yet ye have forsaken me, and served other gods : wherefore I will deliver you no more. 14. Go and cry unto the gods which ye have chosen ; let them deliver you in the time of your tribulation. Deu. 31.20. Jud. 8.34. Neh. 9.25-28,35. Psa. 106.7,21. Jer. 2.6,7.

1 Sam. 10.19. Ye have this day rejected your God, who himself saved you out of all your adversities and your tribulations.

1 Sam. 15.17. When thou *wast* little in thine own sight, *wast* thou not *made* the head of the tribes of Israel. 19. Wherefore then didst thou not obey the voice of the Lord.

2 Sam. 12.7. I delivered thee out of the hand of Saul ; 8. And I gave thee the house of Israel and of Judah ; and if *that had been* too little, I would moreover have given unto thee such and such things. 9. Wherefore hast thou despised the commandment of the Lord, to do evil in his sight? 1 Kin. 16.2,3. 2 Chr. 12.1.

2 Chr. 26.16. When he was strong, his heart was lifted up to *his* destruction.

2 Chr. 32.25. Hezekiah rendered not again according to the benefit *done* unto him ; for his heart was lifted up : therefore there was wrath upon him, and upon Judah and Jerusalem.

Psa. 78.16. He brought streams also out of the rock, and caused waters to run down like

rivers. 17. They sinned yet more against him by provoking the most High in the wilderness. *v.* 10-64.

Isa. 1.2. I have nourished and brought up children, and they have rebelled against me.

Jer. 2.17. Hast thou not procured this unto thyself, in that thou hast forsaken the Lord thy God, when he led thee by the way? 31. Have I been a wilderness unto Israel? a land of darkness? Wherefore say my people, We are lords ; we will come no more unto thee?

Jer. 5.7. Thy children have forsaken me, and sworn by *them that are* no gods : when I had fed them to the full, they then committed adultery. 9. Shall I not visit for these *things ?* saith the Lord : and shall not my soul be avenged on such a nation as this? 24. Neither say they in their heart, Let us now fear the Lord our God, that giveth rain, both the former and the latter, in his season : he reserveth unto us the appointed weeks of the harvest.

Eze. 16.17. Thou hast also taken thy fair jewels of my gold and of my silver, which I had given thee, and madest to thyself images of men. *v.* 17-22.

Dan. 5.18. The most high God gave Nebuchadnezzar thy father a kingdom, and majesty, and glory, and honour ; 20. But when his heart was lifted up, and his mind hardened in pride, he was deposed from his kingly throne, and they took his glory from him : 21. And he was driven from the sons of men ; till he knew that the most high God ruled in the kingdom of men, and *that* he appointeth over it whomsoever he will.

Hos. 2.8. She did not know that I gave her corn, and wine, and oil, and multiplied her silver and gold, *which* they prepared for Baal. 9. Therefore will I return, and take away my corn.

Hos. 4.7. As they were increased, so they sinned against me : *therefore* will I change their glory into shame.

Hos. 7.15. Though I have bound *and* strengthened their arms, yet do they imagine mischief against me.

Hos. 11.3. I taught Ephraim also to go, taking them by their arms ; but they knew not that I healed them. *v.* 1,2.

Hos. 13.5. I did know thee in the wilderness, in the land of great drought. 6. According to their pasture, so were they filled ; they were filled, and their heart was exalted ; therefore have they forgotten me. 7. Therefore I will be unto them as a lion : as a leopard by the way will I observe *them. v.* 8.

Amos 3.2. You only have I known of all the families of the earth : therefore I will punish you for all your iniquities. *v.* 1.

Mic. 6.3. O my people, what have I done unto thee? and wherein have I wearied thee? testify against me. 4. For I brought thee up out of the land of Egypt.

Luk. 17.17. Were there not ten cleansed? but where *are* the nine? 18. There are not found that returned to give glory to God, save this stranger.

Jno. 1.11. He came unto his own, and his own received him not.

Rom. 1.21. When they knew God, they glorified *him* not as God, neither were thankful.

2 Tim. 3.2. Men shall be lovers of their own selves, unthankful.

See GODLESSNESS—BACKSLIDING.

INGRATITUDE TO MAN. Pro. 17.13. 2 Tim. 3.2. Examples of: Laban, Gen 31. Pharaoh's butler, Gen. 40.23. Israelites, Ex. 16.3. Ex. 17.2-4. Num. 16.12-14. Jud. 8.35. Shechemites, Jud. 9.17,18. Men of Keilah, 1 Sam. 23.5-12. Saul, 1 Sam. 24. Nabal, 1 Sam. 25.21. David's companions, Psa. 35.11-16. Psa. 38.20. Psa. 41.9. Psa. 109.4,5. Citizens, Ecc. 9.14-16. Joash, 2 Chr. 24.22. Jeremiah's enemies, Jer. 18.20.

See SELFISHNESS—HYPOCRISY & TREACHERY.

INHERITANCE. Of the tribes to be kept separate, Num. 36.7-9. 1 Kin. 21.3. Of the eldest son, a double share of the property, Den. 21.17. Gen. 27.37,40. 1 Chr. 5.1. Luk. 15.31. Not to be set aside, Deu. 21.15,16. See FIRST-BORN. When a man died childless, the son of his widow by his brother inherited, Gen. 38.7-11. Deu. 25.5-10. Ruth 4.1-17. Mat. 22.24-26.

Of younger sons, Gen. 37.36-40. 2 Chr. 21.3. Luk. 15.12. Of the sons of concubines, Gen. 21.10. Gen. 25.6. Gen. 48.19-22. Of daughters, Job 42.15. When there were no sons, Num. 27.4-8. An heiress not to marry out of her tribe, Num. 36.6-8. 1 Chr. 23.22.

By the next of kin, Num. 27.9-11. Property divided before the father's death, Gen. 24.36. Gen. 25.5,6. Luk. 15.12. Wills made in writing, Gal. 3.15 (marg.). Heb. 9.16,17. Verbally, Gen. 49.1. 1 Kin. 2.1.

See LAND—JUBILEE. Also, the separate tribes, as JUDAH, EPHRAIM.

INHOSPITALITY, EXAMPLES OF: Edom, Num. 20.18-21. Sihon, Num. 21.22,23. Ammonites and Moabites, Deu. 23.3-6. Men of Gibeah, Jud. 19.15. Nabal, 1 Sam. 25.10-17. Samaritans, Luk. 9.53. See HOSPITALITY.

INJUSTICE. See DISHONESTY—RULERS, TYRANNY OF—POOR, OPPRESSORS OF.

INK, Jer. 36.18. 2 Cor. 3.3. 2 Jno. 12.

INKHORN, Eze. 9.2,3,11.

INN, or LODGING-PLACE, Gen. 42.27. Gen. 43.21. Ex. 4.24. Jos. 4.3,8. 2 Kin. 19.23. Isa. 10.29. Jer. 9.2. Luk. 2.7. Luk. 10.34. Translated guest-chamber, Mar. 14.14. Luk. 22.11.

INSECTS AND WORMS. Clean and unclean, Lev. 11.21-25. Deu. 14.19. Names of, see ANT, BEE, BEETLE, CANKERWORM, CATERPILLAR, FLEA, FLIES, GNAT, HORNET, HORSELEECH, LICE, LOCUST, MOTH, PALMERWORM, SPIDER, WORM.

INSPIRATION. See APOSTLES—PROPHETS—WORD OF GOD—GOSPEL FROM GOD —LAW, MOSAIC, FROM GOD.

INSTRUCTION, SPIRITUAL. See WISDOM — SPIRITUAL BLESSINGS — SPIRITUAL DESTITUTION.

INSURRECTION. See SUBJECTS, TREASON OF.

INTEGRITY, HONESTY, CONSCIENTIOUSNESS. Gen. 18.19. Keep the way of the Lord, to do justice and judgment.

Ex. 18.21. Able men, such as fear God, men of truth, hating covetousness.

Deu. 16.20. That which is altogether just shalt thou follow, that thou mayest live.

Job 13.15. I will maintain mine own ways before him. 18. I have ordered my cause : I know that I shall be justified. Job 10.7.

Job 16.17. Not for any injustice in mine hands : also my prayer is pure.

Job 27.6. My righteousness I hold fast, and will not let it go: my heart shall not reproach me so long as I live.

Job 29.14. I put on righteousness, and it clothed me : my judgment was as a robe and a diadem.

Job 31.5. If I have walked with vanity, or if my foot hath hasted to deceit ; 6. Let me be weighed in an even balance, that God may know mine integrity. v. 1-40.

Psa. 7.3. O Lord my God, if I have done this ; if there be iniquity in my hands ; 4. If I have rewarded evil unto him that was at peace with me ; (yea, I have delivered him that without cause is mine enemy :) 5. Let the enemy persecute my soul, and take it ; 8. Judge me, O Lord, according to my righteousness, and according to mine integrity that is in me.

Psa. 15.2. He that walketh uprightly, and worketh righteousness, and speaketh the truth in his heart. 4. He that sweareth to his own hurt, and changeth not. 5. He that putteth not out his money to usury, nor taketh reward against the innocent. He that doeth these things shall never be moved.

Psa. 17.3. Thou hast proved mine heart ; thou hast visited me in the night ; thou hast tried me, and shalt find nothing ; I am purposed that my mouth shall not transgress.

Psa. 18.20. The Lord rewarded me according to my righteousness ; according to the cleanness of my hands hath he recompensed me. 2 Sam. 22.21.

Psa. 26.1. Judge me, O Lord ; for I have walked in mine integrity : I have trusted also in the Lord ; therefore I shall not slide. 2. Examine me, O Lord, and prove me ; try my reins and my heart.

Psa. 69.4. I restored that which I took not away.

Psa. 73.15. If I say, I will speak thus ; behold, I should offend against the generation of thy children.

Psa. 119.121. I have done judgment and justice.

Pro. 2.9. Understand righteousness, and judgment, and equity ; yea, every good path. Pro. 1.3.

Pro. 3.3. Let not mercy and truth forsake thee : bind them about thy neck ; write them upon the table of thine heart : 4. So shalt thou find favour and good understanding in the sight of God and man.

Pro. 4.25. Let thine eyes look right on, and let thine eyelids look straight before thee. 26. Ponder the path of thy feet, and let all thy ways be established. 27. Turn not to the right hand nor to the left : remove thy foot from evil.

Pro. 10.9. He that walketh uprightly walketh surely.

Pro. 11.3. The integrity of the upright shall guide them. 5. The righteousness of the perfect shall direct his way.

Pro. 12.22. They that deal truly are his delight.

Pro. 14.30. A sound heart *is* the life of the flesh.

Pro. 15.21. A man of understanding walketh uprightly.

Pro. 16.11. A just weight and balance *are* the Lord's: all the weights of the bag *are* his work. Lev. 19.35,36. Deu. 25.13-16. Pro. 11.1. Pro. 20.10,23. Eze. 45.10.

Pro. 19.1. Better *is* the poor than walketh in his integrity, than *he that is* perverse in his lips, and is a fool. Pro. 28.6.

Pro. 20.7. The just *man* walketh in his integrity : his children *are* blessed after him.

Pro. 21.3. To do justice and judgment *is* more acceptable to the Lord than sacrifice. 15. *It is* joy to the just to do judgment.

Pro. 22.11. He that loveth pureness of heart, *for* the grace of his lips the king *shall be* his friend.

Pro. 28.20. A faithful man shall abound with blessings.

Isa. 26.7. The way of the just *is* uprightness : thou, most upright, dost weigh the path of the just.

Isa. 33.15. He that walketh righteously, and speaketh uprightly ; he that despiseth the gain of oppressions, that shaketh his hands from holding of bribes, that stoppeth his ears from hearing of blood, and shutteth his eyes from seeing evil ; 16. He shall dwell on high : his place of defence *shall be* the munitions of rocks : bread shall be given him ; his waters *shall be* sure.

Isa. 56.1. Keep ye judgment, and do justice.

Jer. 7.5. If ye throughly amend your ways and your doings ; if ye throughly execute judgment between a man and his neighbour. 7. Then will I cause you to dwell in this place.

Eze. 18.5. If a man be just, and do that which is lawful and right. 7. And hath not oppressed any, *but* hath restored to the debtor his pledge, hath spoiled none by violence, hath given his bread to the hungry, and hath covered the naked with a garment ; 8. He *that* hath not given forth upon usury, neither hath taken any increase, *that* hath withdrawn his hand from iniquity, hath executed true judgment between man and man, 9. Hath walked in my statutes, and hath kept my judgments, to deal truly ; he *is* just, he shall surely live, saith the Lord God.

Mic. 6.8. What doth the Lord require of thee but to do justly ?

Zec. 7.9. Execute true judgment.

Mal. 2.6. The law of truth was in his mouth, and iniquity was not found in his lips : he walked with me in peace and equity.

Luk. 3.13. Exact no more than that which is appointed you. 14. Do violence to no man, neither accuse *any* falsely ; and be content with your wages.

Luk. 6.31. As ye would that men should do to you, do ye also to them likewise.

Luk. 11.42. Woe unto you, Pharisees ! for ye tithe mint and rue and all manner of herbs, and pass over judgment and the love of God : these ought ye to have done, and not to leave the other undone.

Act. 24.16. Herein do I exercise myself, to have always a conscience void of offence toward God, and *toward* men. Act. 23.1.

Rom. 9.1. I say the truth in Christ, I lie not, my conscience also bearing me witness in the Holy Ghost.

Rom. 13.5. Ye must needs be subject, not only for wrath, but also for conscience' sake.

Rom. 14.5. One man esteemeth one day above another : another esteemeth every day *alike.* Let every man be fully persuaded in his own mind. 14. To him that esteemeth any thing to be unclean, to him *it is* unclean. 22. Hast thou faith ? have *it* to thyself before God. Happy *is* he that condemneth not himself in that thing which he alloweth. 23. And he that doubteth is damned if he eat, because *he eateth* not of faith : for whatsoever *is* not of faith is sin.

2 Cor. 4.2. Have renounced the hidden things of dishonesty, not walking in craftiness, nor handling the word of God deceitfully ; but by manifestation of the truth commending ourselves to every man's conscience in the sight of God. 2 Cor. 5.11.

2 Cor. 7.2. We have wronged no man, we have corrupted no man, we have defrauded no man.

2 Cor. 8.21. Providing for honest things, not only in the sight of the Lord, but also in the sight of men.

Phil. 4.8. Brethren, whatsoever things are true, whatsoever things *are* honest, whatsoever things *are* just, think on these things.

Col. 3.22. Not with eye-service as menpleasers ; but in singleness of heart, fearing God : 23. And whatsoever ye do, do *it* heartily, as to the Lord, and not unto men. Eph. 6.6.

1 The. 2.4. As we were allowed of God to be put in trust with the gospel, even so we speak ; not as pleasing men, but God, which trieth our hearts.

1 Tim. 1.5. The end of the commandment is charity, out of a pure heart, and *of* a good conscience.

1 Tim. 3.9. Holding the mystery of the faith in a pure conscience.

Tit. 1.8. A lover of good men, sober, just, holy.

Heb. 13.18. We trust we have a good conscience, in all things willing to live honestly.

1 Pet. 2.12. Having your conversation honest among the Gentiles.

1 Pet. 3.16. Having a good conscience ; that, whereas they speak evil of you, as of evil doers, they may be ashamed that falsely accuse your good conversation in Christ.

INTEGRITY, HONESTY, CONSCIENTIOUSNESS, EXAMPLES OF : Pharaoh, Gen. 12.18. Abimelech, Gen. 26.9-11. Jacob, Gen. 31.39. Joseph, Gen. 39.9. Gen. 40.15. Joseph's brethren, Gen. 43.15-22. Gen. 44.7-16. Egyptians, Ex. 1.17-21. Moses, Num. 16.15. Samuel, 1 Sam. 12.4. David, 1 Sam. 24.5. 1 Sam. 25.15. 1 Sam. 29.6.

Workmen, 2 Kin. 12.15. 2 Kin. 22.7. Zebulun, 1 Chr. 12.33. Joab, 1 Chr. 21.6. Priests, Ezr. 8.24-30. Nehemiah, Neh. 5.15. Jonadab's descendants, Jer. 35.14. Daniel, Dan. 1.8. Dan. 6.4. Joseph, Mat. 1.19. Zaccheus, Luk. 19.8. Nathaniel, Jno. 1.47. Nicodemus, Jno. 7.51. Joseph, Luk. 23.51. Peter, Act. 10.14.

See DISHONESTY.

INTERPRETERS OF LANGUAGES, Gen. 42.23. 2 Chr. 32.31 (*marg.*). Neh. 8.8. In the Christian church, 1 Cor. 12.10,30. 1 Cor. 14.5,13,26-28. Illustrative, Job 33.23. Of dreams, Gen. 40.8. Gen. 41.16. Dan. 2.18-30.

IRIJAH, accuses Jeremiah, and gets him imprisoned, Jer. 37.13-15.

IRON. Ore of, Deu. 8.9. Job 28.2. Melted, Eze. 22.20. See FURNACE, STEEL. In Canaan, Deu. 8.9. In Tarshish, Eze. 27.12. Tubal-cain, an artificer of, Gen. 4.22. 100,000 talents of, used in the temple, 1 Chr. 29.7. Shekel of, 1 Sam. 17.7.

Articles made of, see ARMOUR, AXE, BARS, BED, CHARIOTS, FETTERS, FURNACE, GATES, HARROWS, HINGES, IDOLS, NAILS, PAN, PEN, PILLAR, PLOUGHSHARES, SCEPTRE, THRESHING INSTRUMENTS, TOOLS, WEAPONS, YOKES.

Miracle connected with, 2 Kin. 6.5,6. Illustrative, Pro. 27.17. Symbolical, Dan. 2.33-45. Dan. 4.15. Dan. 7.7,19.

IRRIGATION, Deu. 11.10. Pro. 21.1. Isa. 58.11. See WELLS.

ISAAC (Laughter), son of Abraham and Sarah, Gen. 17.19. Gen. 21.1-6. Jos. 24.3. 1 Chr. 1.28. Mat. 1.2. Gal. 4.28. Heb. 11.11. Offered up by Abraham, Gen. 22.1-19. Heb. 11.17. Jas. 2.21. Marriage to Rebecca, Gen. 24. Gen. 25.20. Inheritance, Gen. 25.5. Gen. 24.36.

Dwells at Lahai-roi, Gen. 24.62. Gen. 25.11. Buries his father, Gen. 25.9. Birth of Esau and Jacob, Gen. 25.19-26. Jos. 24.4. His partiality for Esau, Gen. 25.28 ; grief at his marriage to Canaanites, Gen. 26.35. Dwells at Gerar ; his falsehood about Rebekah, Gen. 26.1-11.

His wealth, Gen. 26.13,14. Disputes with Philistines about the wells, Gen. 26.17-23. Dwells at Beersheba, and builds an altar ; his covenant with Abimelech, Gen. 26.23-33. His blindness when old ; blesses Jacob and Esau, Gen. 27.1-40. Heb. 11.20. Sends Jacob from Beersheba to Padan-aram, Gen. 28. His death ; buried by Jacob and Esau in the cave of Machpelah, Gen. 35.27-29. Gen. 49.31.

His piety and prayerfulness, Gen. 24.63. Gen. 25.21. Gen. 26.25. Mat. 8.11. Luk. 13.28. Prophecies and promises respecting, Gen. 17.16-21. Gen. 18.10-14. Gen. 21.12. Gen. 26.2-5,24. Ex. 32.13. 1 Chr. 16.16. Rom. 9.7.

ISAIAH, son of Amos ; time of his prophesying, Isa. 1.1. Isa. 6.1. Isa. 7.1. Isa. 20.1. Isa. 36.1. Isa. 38.1. Isa. 39.1. His wife and family, Isa. 7.3. Isa. 8.3. Prophesies to Ahaz, offering him a sign, Isa. 7.3-17. Wears sackcloth ; commanded to walk barefoot, &c., Isa. 20.2,3.

His prophecy on Sennacherib's invasion ; 2 Kin. 19. Isa. 37. Sennacherib's army destroyed at his prayer, 2 Chr 32.20,21. 2 Kin. 19.4. Predicts Hezekiah's recovery, 2 Kin. 20.4-11. Isa. 38.3-8 ; and miracle of the returning shadow, 2 Kin. 20.8-11. Isa. 38.7,8. Prophesies against Hezekiah, 2 Kin. 20.14-18. Isa. 39.3-7. Writes the history of Uzziah and Hezekiah, 2 Chr. 26.22. 2 Chr. 32.32.

ISHBI-BENOB, a Philistine giant, slain by Abishai when fighting with David, 2 Sam. 21.15-17.

ISH-BOSHETH, son of Saul, 2 Sam. 2.8. Called Esh-baal, 1 Chr. 8.33. Made king over the 10 tribes by Abner, 2 Sam. 2.8-10. Abner quarrels with, and deserts him, 2 Sam. 3.6-13. He restores Michal to David, 2 Sam. 3.14-16. Murdered by his servants ; his murderer slain by David, 2 Sam. 4.1-12.

ISHI (my husband), a symbolical name, Hos. 2.16.

ISHMAEL (God shall hear), son of Abraham and Hagar, Gen. 16.11,15,16. 1 Chr. 1.28. Abraham's prayer for, Gen. 17.18. Circumcision of, Gen. 17.23-26. Mocks Isaac, and is sent away with his mother by Abraham ; dwells in the wilderness and becomes an archer ; marries an Egyptian, Gen. 21.9-21.

Present at Abraham's funeral, Gen. 25.9. Descendants of, Gen. 25.12-18. 1 Chr. 1.29-31. His daughter marries Esau, Gen. 28.9. Gen. 36.2,3. His death, Gen. 25.17,18. Prophecies respecting, Gen. 16.11,12. Gen. 17.20. Gen. 21.13,18.

————, son of Nethaniah, murders Gedaliah at the instigation of the king of Ammon, and carries some of the Jews captive to the Ammonites, Jer. 40.8-16. Jer. 41. 2 Kin. 25.23-25.

ISHMAELITES, travelling merchants to whom Joseph was sold, Gen. 37.25-36. Gen. 39.1. Also called Midianites, Gen. 37.28,36. Jud. 8.24,26. Fought against Israel, Psa. 83.6. See ARABIANS, DUMAH, HAGARENES, MIDIANITES, NEBAIOTH.

ISHTOB, 2 Sam. 10.6,8. See TOB.

ISLANDS, signifying dry land, Isa. 42.15. Country, Isa. 20.6 (marg.). Region beyond the sea, Jer. 25-22 (marg.). Names of, see CHIOS, CHITTIM, CLAUDA, COOS, CRETE, CYPRUS, ELISHAH, LESBOS, MELITA, PATMOS, RHODES, SAMOS, SAMOTHRACE, SICILY.

ISLES OF THE GENTILES are the islands of the Mediterranean above named, Gen. 10.5. Zeph. 2.11.

ISRAEL. See JACOB.

————, LAND OF. See PALESTINE.

ISRAEL, TRIBES OF. Descended from Jacob's 12 sons, Gen. 49.28. Act. 26.7. Manasseh and Ephraim reckoned among, instead of Joseph and Levi, Gen. 48.5. Jos. 14.4. See ASHER, BENJAMIN, DAN, EPHRAIM, GAD, ISSACHAR, JOSEPH, JUDAH, LEVI, MANASSEH, NAPHTALI, REUBEN, SIMEON, ZEBULUN.

Prophecies of, Gen. 48.19. Gen. 49. Deu. 33. Names of, worn on the high-priest's breastplate, Ex. 28.21. Ex. 39.14.

Half of the tribes—Simeon, Levi, Judah, Issachar, Joseph, and Benjamin—stood on mount Gerizim to pronounce the blessing ; while Reuben, Gad, Asher, Zebulun, Dan, and Naphtali, stood on mount Ebal to say Amen to the curses of the law, Deu. 27.11-26. Jos. 8.33-35.

Divided into families, each having a chief, Num. 25.14. Num. 26. Num. 36.1. Jos. 7.14. 1 Chr. c. 4-8. All inheritances were to remain in the tribe and family to which they were given, Num. 36 with 1 Chr. 23.22. 1 Kin. 21.3.

Princes, captains, or elders of, Num. 10.4. Num. 27.2. Num. 31.13. Num. 32.2. Deu. 29.10. Deu. 31.28. Jos. 9.15-21. Jos. 22.13,14. Ezr. 1.8 ; with Moses and Aaron numbered the people, Num. 1.1-18. Their offerings, Num. 7. Were sent to spy Canaan, Num. 13.1-16. Laid up their rods before the ark, Num. 17. Set up the stones of Gilgal, Jos. 4. With Joshua and Eleazar, divided Palestine, Num. 34.17-29. Jos. 14.1. Names of, in the time of Moses, Num. 2. Num. 10.14-27. 1 Chr.

2 10 ; in the time of David, 1 Chr. 27.16-22 ; of Solomon, 1 Kin. 4.7-18.

Number of, on arriving in Egypt, Gen. 46.8-27. Ex. 1.5. Deu. 10.22. Act. 7.14. At the Exodus, Ex. 12.37. At Sinai, Num. 1.46. In the plain of Moab, Num. 26. When numbered by David, 2 Sam. 24.1-9. 1 Chr. 21.5,6. 1 Chr. 27.24. At the return from captivity, Ezr. 2.64. Neh. 7.66,67.

Half a shekel to be given for each person as an atonement when numbered, Ex. 30.11-16. For the maintenance of the tabernacle, Ex. 38.24-31.

Number of, sealed by an angel in vision, *Dan* omitted, Rev. 7.1-8. Names of, on the gates of the New Jerusalem, Rev. 21.12.

ISRAELITES, ENEMIES OF, PUNISHED-See PERSECUTORS PUNISHED.

ISRAELITES, HISTORY OF. (From Abraham to the settlement in Goshen, B.C. 2056-1706. From the settlement in Goshen to the Exodus, B.C. 1706-1491.) They settle in Goshen, Gen. c. 46 & 47. Ex. 1.1-6. Act. 7.14.

Multiply in Egypt, Ex. 1.7-20. Psa. 105.24. Act. 7.17. Pharaoh's cruelty and oppression, Ex. 1.8-22. Ex. 2.11. Ex. 5. Act. 7.18-21. They build Pithom and Rameses, Ex. 1.11. God promises deliverance, Ex. 2.23-25.

Moses sent to them, Psa. 78. Psa. 105-107. Psa. 136. Act. 7. See MOSES. Murmur against Moses, Ex. 5.20,21. Ex. 14.10-12. Exempt from the plagues of Egypt, Ex. 8.22,23. Ex. 9.4-6,26. Ex. 10.23. Ex. 11.7. Ex. 12.13. Keep the first passover, Ex. 12.1-28,50. Obtain jewels from the Egyptians, Ex. 11.2,3. Ex. 12.35,36. Psa. 105.37. Depart from Rameses, Ex. 12.31-42. Ex. 13.3,4. Ex. 14.

Sojourn in Egypt 430 years, from Abraham, B.C. 1913 to B.C. 1491, Gen. 15.13. Ex. 12.40,41. Act. 7.6. Gal. 3.17. Idolatry of, in, Eze. 20.6-9. Eze. 23.8.

Leave Egypt ; number of, Ex. 12.37. None feeble, Psa. 105.37. Accompanied by a mixed multitude, Ex. 12.38. Num. 11.4. Their herds and flocks, Ex. 10.9,24. Ex. 12.38. Ex. 34.3. Num. 11.22.

Led by the angel of the Lord, Ex. 23.20-23. Ex. 32.34. Ex. 33.2,14. Psa. 78.51-54. Isa. 63.11-14. See CLOUD OF GLORY. Order of marching and encamping, Num. 2. Num. 10.14-28.

March from Rameses to Succoth, Etham, Pi-hahiroth, Ex. 12.37. Ex. 13.20. Ex. 14.2. Num. 33.5-7.

Passage of the Red Sea ; destruction of Pharaoh, Ex. 14. Deu. 11.4. Psa. 78. Psa. 105-107. Psa. 136. Song of Moses and Miriam, Ex. 15.1-20.

March 3 days through the wilderness of Shur to Marah, Ex. 15.23. Num. 33.8. Murmur at the bitter water ; it is sweetened, Ex. 15.24,25.

March to Elim, Ex. 15.27. Num. 33.9. To the Red Sea, Num. 33.10. To—

Desert of Sin, Ex. 16.1. Num. 33.11. Murmur for bread, Ex. 16.2,3. Manna sent, Ex. 16.4-36. Quails sent, Ex. 16.13.

March to Dophkah, Alush, Num. 33.12-14. Ex. 17.1. To—

Rephidim ; murmur for water, Ex. 17.2,3. Water brought from the rock at Massah or Meribah, Ex. 17.5-7. Amalekites defeated, Ex. 17.8. Deu. 25.17,18.

March to desert of Sinai in the 3d month, Num. 33.15. Ex. 18.5. Ex. 19.1. Have

judges and captains appointed, Ex. 18.25. Deu. 1.9-17. Receive the law at Sinai, see SINAI. Terror at the giving of the law, Ex. 19.16,17. Num. 17.12,13. Heb. 12.18-21. Elders go up the mount, Ex. 24.1,9-11. Covenant with the Lord, Ex. 19.3-9. Ex. 24.3-8. Make a golden calf, Ex. 32. Deu. 9. 7-21. 3000 slain by the Levites, Ex. 32.28. Plagued on account of the calf, Ex. 32.35. Mourn on God refusing to lead them, Ex. 33. 4-6. Tabernacle of Moses pitched without the camp, Ex. 33.9,10. Contributions for the tabernacle, Ex. 35.21-29. Ex. 36.3-7. Num. 7. Make the tabernacle, Ex. 35.30-35. Ex. c. 36-40. Second passover kept, Num. 9. 1-5. Numbering of the people, Num. 1.1-46 Ex. 38.25,26.

March to Taberah ; murmuring punished by fire, Num. 11.1-3. Deu. 9.22.

March to Kibroth-hattaavah, Num. 11.34. Num. 33.16. 70 elders appointed, Num. 11.16,17,24-30. Murmuring for flesh, Num. 11.4-9. Psa. 78.18. Quails sent, Num. 11.18-23,31,32. Psa. 78.26-29. Punished by plague, Num. 11.33,34. Psa. 78.30,31.

March to Hazeroth, Num. 11.35. Num. 33.17. To—

Kadesh, in the desert of Paran, or Zin, Num. 12.16. Num. 13.26. Num. 33.36. Deu. 1.2,19. Spies sent to Canaan, Num. 13. Num. 32.8. Deu. 1.22,25. Jos. 14.7. Discouraged and rebel at their report, Num. 14. Deu. 1.26-35. Deu. 9.23. Spies die of plague, Num. 14.37. Israel defeated by Amalek at Hormah, Num. 14.40-45. Deu. 1.41-44. Dwell at Kadesh, Deu. 1.46.

Turn back from Kadesh and wander for 38 years by the Red Sea, Num. 14.25-34. Deu. 1.40. Deu. 2.14. Stations visited by them, Rithmah to Ezion-Geber, Num. 33.18-36. All but two died from 20 years old, Num. 14.28-30. Deu. 2.14. Return to—

Kadesh, Num. 20.1. Num. 33.36. Jud. 11.16,17. Sabbath - breaker stoned, Num. 15.32-36. Rebellion of Korah, Num. 16. Deu. 11.6. 14,000 die of plague, Num. 16.41-50. Miriam's death, Num. 20.1. Murmur for water at Meribah, see MERIBAH. Refused a passage by Edom, Num. 20.14-21.

March from Kadesh to Beeroth and Mount Hor, or Mosera ; Aaron's death, Num. 20.22,29. Num. 33.37. Deu. 10.6. Defeat king Arad, Num. 21.

March to Zalmonah and Punon, Num. 33.41,42. Num. 21.6. Deu. 2.8. Murmur, bitten by serpents, healed on looking to the brazen serpent, Num. 21.4-9.

March to Oboth, to the mountains of Abarim or Pisgah, Num. 21.10-20. Num. 33.43-47. Deu. 2.13-24. Defeat the Amorites, Num. 21.21-31. Deu. 2.26-37.

March by Bashan to the plains of Moab, opposite Jericho, Num. 21.33. Num. 22.1. Num. 33.48,49. Defeat Og, king of Bashan, Num. 21.33-35. Deu. 3.1-17. Balak sends for Balaam to curse them, Num. c. 22-24. Deu. 23.3,4. Corrupted by the Moabites, Num. 25. The plague stayed by Phinehas, Num. 25.5-18. Conquest of Midian, Num. 31. Numbering of the people, Num. 26. Covenant with the Lord, Deu. 29. Death of Moses ; mourning for him, Deu. 34.

Their provision in the wilderness, Deu. 8.4. Deu. 29.5,6. Neh. 9.21. Circumcision omitted,

Jos. 5.5,7. Piety of those who entered Canaan, Jos. 23.8. Jer. 2.2,3. Jud. 2.7-10.

Joshua appointed to succeed Moses, Num. 27.18-23. Deu. 31.23. See JOSHUA.

ISRAELITES, HISTORY OF, UNDER THE JUDGES (B.C. 1451-1095), 450 years, Act. 13.20. Conquest of Palestine under Joshua (B.C. 1451-1427), see JOSHUA, JERICHO, AI, GIBEON.

Conquests of Judah ; partial success of different tribes, Jud. 1. Rebuked by an angel at Bochim ; repentance, Jud. 2.1-5. Worship idols ; punishment, Jud. 2.10-23. History of the Levite, and slaughter of the Benjamites, Jud. c. 19-21 (B.C. 1425-1406).

Idolatry of, and punishment, Jud. 3.5-7. 8 years' bondage to king of Mesopotamia ; delivered by Othniel ; 40 years' peace, Jud. 3.8-11 (B.C. 1402-1354).

18 years' bondage to Moab ; delivered by Ehud ; 80 years' peace, Jud. 3.12-30 (B.C. 1354-1256). Delivered from Philistines by Shamgar, Jud. 3.31.

20 years' bondage to Jabin ; delivered by Deborah and Barak ; 40 years' peace, Jud. c. 4 & 5 (B.C. 1316-1256).

Ruth's history (B.C. 1322-1312), but compare Ruth 4.18-21 with Mat. 1.5.

7 years' bondage to Midian ; reproved by a prophet ; delivered by Gideon, Jud. c. 6 & 7. Jud. 8.1-28. Gideon's ephod worshipped, Jud. 8.26,27. His refusal to be king, Jud. 8.22,23. 40 years' peace, Jud. 8.28 (B.C. 1256-1209).

Idolatry renewed, Jud. 8.33,34. Abimelech's usurpation ; civil wars, Jud. 9 (B.C. 1209-1206).

Tola and Jair Judges, Jud. 10.1-5 (B.C. 1206-1161).

Idolatry ; 18 years' bondage to the Philistines and Ammonites ; reproved by God ; their repentance, Jud. 10. Delivered by Jephthah, Jud. 11. His defeat of the Ephraimites, Jud. 12.1-7. Peace 6 years, Jud. 12.7 (B.C. 1161-1137).

Ibzan Judge 7 years, Elon 10, Abdon 8, Jud. 12.8-15 (B.C. 1137-1112).

Idolatry ; 40 years' bondage to Philistines (B.C. 1161-1120), Jud. 13.1. Eli, high-priest ; the ark taken, 1 Sam. 4 (B.C. 1141), see ARK. Samson's victories ; Judge for 20 years (B.C. 1140-1120), Jud. c. 13-16.

Samuel Judge, B.C. 1120-1095. See SAMUEL.

ISRAELITES, HISTORY OF, UNDER THE KINGS. (See details under the names of the respective kings). Saul, 1st king, 40 years ; Samuel, prophet, B.C. 1095-1056. David, 2d king, 40 years ; Nathan and Gad, prophets, B.C. 1056-1015. Solomon, 3d king, 40 years ; Ahijah, prophet, B.C. 1015-975. On Rehoboam's accession (B.C. 975) the 12 tribes were divided into two kingdoms—Judah and Benjamin forming the kingdom of Judah, and the remaining 10 tribes the kingdom of Israel.

JUDAH.	B.C.	ISRAEL.	B.C.
1. Rehoboam king 17 years. Shemaiah prophet,	975-958	1. Jeroboam king 22 years,	975-954
2. Abijah, or Abijam, king 3 years,	958-955	2. Nadab, son of Jeroboam, king about 2 years,	954-953
3. Asa king 41 years. Azariah, Hanani, prophets,	955-914	3. Baasha, a captain, king 24 years. Jehu prophet,	953-930
		4. Elah, a captain, king 2 years,	930-929
		5. Zimri, a captain, king 7 days.	
		6. Omri, a captain, king 12 years,	929-918
4. Jehoshaphat king 25 years. His son Jehoram associated with him. Jehu prophet.	914-889	7. Ahab, son of Omri, king 22 years. Elijah, Elisha, Micaiah, prophets,	918-897
		8. Amaziah, son of Ahab, king 2 years,	898-896
5. Jehoram king 4 years. Ahaziah, his son, associated with him.	889-885	9. Jehoram, son of Ahab, king 12 years,	896-884
6. Ahaziah king 1 year,	885-884	10. Jehu, a captain, king 28 years,	884-856
Athaliah's usurpation 6 years. Jehoiada the priest.	884-878	11. Jehoahaz, son of Jehu, king 17 years,	856-839
7. Joash, or Jehoash, king 40 years. Zechariah prophet,	878-839	12. Jehoash, son of Jehoahaz, king 16 years. Elisha's death,	839-825
8. Amaziah king 29 years,	839-810	13. Jeroboam II., son of Jehoash, king 41 years. Jonah, Hosea, Amos, prophets,	825-784
9. Uzziah, or Azariah, king 52 years. Jotham regent. Joel, Isaiah, prophets,	810-758	Interregnum 11 years, 2 Kin. 14.23 with 2 Kin. 15.8,	784-773
		14. Zachariah, son of Jeroboam, king 6 months,	773
		15. Shallum, a captain, king 1 month,	772
		16. Menahem, a captain, king 10 years,	772-762
		17. Pekahiah, son of Menahem, king 2 years,	761-759
10. Jotham king 16 years. Micah prophet,	758-742	18. Pekah, a captain, king 20 years,	759-738
11. Ahaz king 16 years. Isaiah, Oded, Obadiah, prophets,	742-726	Interregnum 9 years, 2 Kin. 15.30 with 2 Kin. 17.1,	738-730
		19. Hoshea, a captain, king 9 years. The 10 tribes carried captive to Assyria. Colonists brought to	
12. Hezekiah king 29 years,	726-698	Samaria, see SAMARIA,	730-721

ISRAELITES. HISTORY OF KINGS OF
JUDAH CONTINUED TO THE CAPTIVITY, B.C.
726-588.

12. Hezekiah king 29 years. Isaiah, Nahum, prophets, . . .	B.C. 726-698
13. Manasseh king 55 years, . .	698-643
14. Amon king 2 years, . . .	643-641
15. Josiah king 31 years. Jeremiah, Huldah, Zephaniah, Habakkuk, prophets, ...	641-610
16. Jehoahaz, Josiah's son, king 3 months, ...	610
17. Jehoiakim, Josiah's son, king 11 years. Daniel prophet, . .	610-599
FIRST CAPTIVITY (606).	
18. Jehoiachin, or Jeconiah, Jehoiakim's son, king 3 months, .	599
SECOND CAPTIVITY (599).	
19. Zedekiah, or Mattaniah, Josiah's son, king 11 years. Jeremiah, Ezekiel, prophets, . .	599-588
FINAL CAPTIVITY (588).	

Seraiah, &c., massacred by Nebuchadnezzar
at Riblah, 2 Kin. 25.18-21. Jer. 52.24-27.

Some of the poor left to till the land, Jer.
52.16. 2 Kin. 25.12,22; and soldiers who
had escaped, 2 Kin. 25.23. Jer. 39.10. Jer.
40.7.

Gedaliah appointed governor; slain by Ishmael, 2 Kin. 25.22-25. Jer. 40. Jer. 41. Ishmael attempts to take the people to the
Ammonites; is intercepted by Johanan, Jer.
41.11-18; who takes them to Egypt; Jeremiah
forced to accompany them, Jer. c. 42 to 44.
2 Kin. 25.26 (588).

ISRAELITES, HISTORY OF, IN CAPTIVITY (Psa. 137).

Daniel, Shadrach, &c., under Nebuchadnezzar, B.C. 606-563. Under Belshazzar, B.C.
556. Under Darius, B.C. 538. Under Cyrus,
B.C. 536. See DANIEL, SHADRACH.

Ezekiel with the captives by the river Chebar
in Chaldea, B.C. 595-574. See EZEKIEL.

Esther, Mordecai, and the Jews, under Ahasuerus, B.C. 521-495. See Book of Esther.

Ezra under Artaxerxes, B.C. 457-445. See
EZRA.

Nehemiah under Artaxerxes, B.C. 446-434.
See NEHEMIAH.

ISRAELITES, HISTORY OF, AFTER THE
CAPTIVITY.

Jeremiah's predictions that the captivity
should be 70 years, Jer. 25.11,12. Jer.
29.10-14. 2 Chr. 36.21. Ezr. 1.1. Dan. 9.2;
date from the year B.C. 606, 4 years after
Josiah's death, Jer. 25.3 with 2 Kin. 22.1 &
Dan. 1.1,2; being the first captivity, 2 Kin.
24.1. 2 Chr. 36.6,7. Dan. 1.1,2. Cyrus'
decree to build the temple was issued, B.C. 536,
70 years afterwards, 2 Chr. 36.22,23. Ezr.
1.1-4. (See CYRUS.)

The temple was destroyed B.C. 588, 2 Kin.
25.8-21. Jer. 52.12-30. Jer. 39.8-10. The
second temple finished, B.C. 575, Ezr. 6.14-22,
70 years afterwards.

Cyrus' decree to rebuild the temple, 2 Chr.
36.22,23. Ezr. 1.1-4. Restores the vessels of
the temple, Ezr. 1.5-11. Return of the Jews
under Zerubbabel, in number 49,972, Neh.
7.5-67. Ezr. 1.5,6. Ezr. 2. Psa. 87. Psa. 107.
Psa. 85. Psa. 126. An altar erected; the feast
of tabernacles observed, Ezr. 3.1-7.

Foundation of the second temple by Zerubbabel and Joshua, and its dedication (B.C.

535-515), see TEMPLE. Haggai and Zechariah,
prophets.

Ezra returns with 1754 Jews to Jerusalem,
and considerable sums of money, Ezr. c. 7 & 8.
His exertions to reform the Jews (B.C. 457-
445), see EZRA. Nehemiah appointed governor; the building of the wall; reformation
of the Jews (B.C. 445-434), see NEHEMIAH.
Malachi, the last of the prophets (B.C.
397).

The history of the Jews, as contained in the
New Testament, from B.C. 5 to A.D. 63, will
be found under the names HEROD I. (B.C. 5),
ARCHELAUS (B.C. 3), HEROD II. (A.D. 32),
PILATE (A.D. 33), HEROD III. (A.D. 41), FELIX
(A.D. 60), FESTUS (A.D. 60), AGRIPPA (A.D. 60),
JERUSALEM.

ISRAELITES, IDOLATRY OF. See IDOLATRY.

——, LOVE OF THEIR COUNTRY. See
CHURCH AND COUNTRY, LOVE OF.

ISRAELITES. PROPHECIES OF CAPTIVITY,
WAR, AND JUDGMENT, Gen. 15.13,14. Lev.
26.14-39. Deu. 28.15-68. Deu. 31.16-21. Isa.
10.1-6. Jer. 5.1-19. Jer. 32.28-36. Eze. 6.
Eze. 7. Eze. 20.45-49. Eze. 21. Eze. 23.
Eze. 38.8-23. Eze. 39.1-22. Hos. 3.3-5. Hos.
5. Joel 1. Mic. 1. Mic. 2.1-11. Mic. 6.

——. PROPHECIES OF PROSPERITY, CONVERSION, AND RESTORATION, Gen. 15.13,14.
Gen. 18.18. Gen. 48.21. Gen. 49. Ex. 3.7-22.
Ex. 6.1-8. Ex. 11.1. Ex. 12.25. Ex. 23.22-31.
Lev. 26.3-13,44,45. Num. 23.9-24. Num.
24.5-19. Deu. 30.3-10. Deu. 33. 2 Sam.
7.10. Isa. 6.13. Isa. 10.20-27. Isa. 11.11-16.
Isa. 14.1-8. Isa. 27. Isa. 30.27-33. Isa.
32.15-20. Isa. 43. Isa. 45.11-25. Isa. 48.
Isa. 54. Isa. 65.8-10. Jer. 3.12-25. Jer. 15.11.
Jer. 16.14,15. Jer. 23.1-8. Jer. 29.1-14.
Jer. 30. Jer. 31. Jer. 46.27,28. Jer. 50.4-8,
19,20,33,34. Eze. 6.8,9. Eze. 11.14-20. Eze.
20.33-44. Eze. 28.25,26. Eze. 29.21. Eze.
34.11-31. Eze. 36. Eze. 37. Eze. 39.23-29.
Eze. 43.7-12. Hos. 1.10,11. Amos 9.8-15.
Obad. 17-21. Mic. 2.12,13. Mic. 4.6-8. Mic.
5.6-15. Mic. 7.10-12. Zeph. 3.10-20. Zec.
6.9-17. Zec.10.3-12.

—— (THE 10 TRIBES). PROPHECIES:
By Elijah; of drought, 1 Kin. 17.1; and Benhadad's defeat, 1 Kin. 20.13-28. By Elisha; of
relief from famine, 2 Kin. 7.1,2,17. 7 years'
famine, 2 Kin. 8.1.

—— (THE 10 TRIBES). PROPHECIES OF
CAPTIVITY, WAR, AND JUDGMENT, 1 Kin.
14.15,16. Isa. 7.8. Isa. 8.4-7. Isa. 9.8-21.
Isa. 17.3-11. Isa. 28.1-8. Hos. 1.1-9. Hos.
2.1-13. Hos. c. 4, 8, 9, & 10. Hos. 11.5,6.
Hos. 12.7-14. Hos. 13. Amos 2.6-16. Amos
c. 3 to 9.

—— (THE 10 TRIBES). PROPHECIES OF
RESTORATION, Hos. 2.14-23. Hos. 11.9-11.
Hos. 13.13,14. Hos. 14.8.

——. (JUDAH—THE JEWS). PROPHECIES: By Jahaziel to Jehoshaphat, 2 Chr.
20.14-17. By Isaiah, of deliverance from Rezin,
Isa. 7.1-19; of Sennacherib's invasion, Isa.
7.17-25. Isa. 29.1-8. Isa. 31.4-9. Isa. 33.2-19.
Isa. 37.21-32. Of dearth, in the days of Claudius, Act. 11.27-28. Of their rejection of
Christ, Isa. 8.14,15. Isa. 49.5,7. Isa. 52.14.
Isa. 53.1-3. Zec. 11. Zec. 13. Mat. 21.33.
Mat. 22.1.

ISRAELITES. (JUDAH—THE JEWS). PROPHECIES OF CAPTIVITY, WAR, & JUDGMENT. Deu. 28.49-57. 2 Kin. 20.17,18. 2 Kin. 21.12-15. 2 Kin. 22.16,17. 2 Kin. 23.26,27. Isa. 1.1-24. Isa. 3. Isa. 4.1. Isa. 5. Isa. 6.9-13. Isa. 7.17-25. Isa. 8.14-22. Isa. 9. Isa. 10.12. Isa. 22.1-14. Isa. 28.14-22. Isa. 29.1-10. Isa. 30.1-17. Isa. 31.1-3. Isa. 32.9-14. Jer. 1.11-16. Jer. 4.5-31. Jer. 6. Jer. 7.8-34. Jer. 8. Jer. 9.9-26. Jer. 10.17-22. Jer. 11.9-23. Jer. 13.9-27. Jer. 14.14-18. Jer. 15.1-14. Jer. 16. Jer. 17.1-4. Jer. 18.15-17. Jer. 19. Jer. 20.5. Jer. 21.4-7. Jer. 25.8-38. Jer. c. 28,34, & 37. Jer. 38.1-3. Jer. 42.13-22. Jer. c. 43, 44, & 45. Eze. 4. Eze. 5. Eze. 11.7-12. Eze. c. 12, 15, 16, 17, & 19. Eze. 22.13-22. Eze. 23.22-35. Eze. 24. Eze. 33.21-29. Dan. 9.26,27. Joel 2.1-17. Amos 2.4,5. Mic. 3. Mic. 4.8-10. Hab. 1.6-11. Zeph. 1. Zec. 11. Zec. 14.1-3. Mal. 4.1. Mat. 21.33,34. Mat. 23.35-38. Mat. 24.2,14-42. Mar. 13.1-13. Luk. 13.34,35. Luk. 19.43,44. Luk. 21.5-25. Luk. 23.28-31. Rev. 1.7.

———, (JUDAH — THE JEWS). PROPHECIES OF PROSPERITY, CONVERSION, AND RESTORATION, Isa. 1.25-27. Isa. 2.1-5. Isa. 4.2-6. Isa. 25. Isa. 26.1,2,12-19. Isa. 29.18-24. Isa. 30.18-26. Isa. 32.15-20. Isa. 33.13-24. Isa. 35. Isa. 37.31,32. Isa. 40.2,9. Isa. 41.27. Isa. 44. Isa. 49.13-23. Isa. 51. Isa. 52.1-12. Isa. 60. Isa. 61.4-9. Isa. 62. Isa. 66.5-22. Jer. 3.14-18. Jer. 12.14-16. Jer. 24.1-7. Jer. 29.1-14. Jer. 32.36-44. Jer. 33. Jer. 44.28. Eze. 14.22,23. Eze. 16.60-63. Dan. 11.30-45. Dan. 12.1. Joel 3. Zeph. 2.7. Zec. 1.14-21. Zec. 2. Zec. 8. Zec. 12.5-14. Zec. 13. Zec. 14.3-21. Mal. 3.4. Rom. 11. 2 Cor. 3.16.

———, SYMBOLICAL NAMES OF. See JESHURUN, JEZREEL, LO-AMMI, LO-RUHAIM.

ISSACHAR, son of Jacob and Leah, Gen. 30.18. Ex. 1.3. 1 Chr. 2.1. Blessed by Jacob, Gen. 49.14,15. His children, Gen. 46.13. 1 Chr. 7.1.

———, TRIBE OF. Numbered at Sinai, Num. 1.28,29. Num. 2.6; and on the plains of Moab, Num. 26.25. Blessed by Moses, Deu. 33.18,19. Marched and encamped under the standard of Judah, east of the tabernacle, Num. 2.3,5. Num. 10.14,15. Inheritance of, Jos. 19.17-23. Manasseh had towns in, Jos. 17.10,11.

Assisted Deborah and Barak, Jud. 5.15. Number of soldiers in David's reign, 1 Chr. 7.2,5. Experienced men of, joined David, 1 Chr. 12.39,40. Kept Hezekiah's passover, 2 Chr. 30.18. For things common to all the tribes, see ISRAELITES, TRIBES OF.

ITALIAN BAND. Roman soldiers, Act. 10,1.

ITALY, TOWNS OF. See APPII FORUM, PUTEOLI, RHEGIUM, ROME, THREE TAVERNS.

ITHAMAR, 4th son of Aaron. Ex. 6.23. Ex. 28.1. 1 Chr. 6.3. Chief of the Gershonites and Merarites, Num. 4.28,33. Num. 7.8. Treasurer of the offerings for the tabernacle, Ex. 38.21. Forbidden to mourn for Nadab and Abihu, Lev. 10.6-20. His descendants, 1 Chr. 24.1-19. The high-priesthood in his family from Eli to Abiathar. See ELI, ABIATHAR.

ITTAI, the Gittite, one of David's captains, 2 Sam. 23.29. 1 Chr. 11.31. Fidelity to David when fleeing from Absalom, 2 Sam. 15.19-22. Heads a division of the army against Absalom, 2 Sam. 18.2,5.

ITUREA, a country north-east of Jordan (see 1 Chr. 1.31. 1 Chr. 5.19), of which Philip was tetrarch, Luk. 3.1.

IVORY, Song 5.14. Song 7.4. Eze. 27.15. Brought from Tarshish, 1 Kin. 10.22. 2 Chr. 9.21. Chittim, Eze. 27.6. Ivory palaces, 1 Kin. 22.39. Psa. 45.8. Amos 3.15. Throne of, 1 Kin. 10.18. 2 Chr. 9.17. Benches of, Eze. 27.6. Beds of, Amos 6.4.

J

JAAZANIAH, a wicked ruler in Jerusalem. Ezekiel prophesies against him, Eze. 11.1-13.

JABAL, son of Lamech, originator of the nomade (shepherd) life, Gen. 4.20.

JABBOK, a brook, the south boundary of the Reubenites, Num. 21.24. Deu. 2.37. Deu. 3.16. Jos. 12.2. Jud. 11.13,22. Jacob wrestles with the angel at, Gen. 32.22-32.

JABESH-GILEAD, a town of Manasseh, east of Jordan, sacked by Israelites for not joining in the war against Benjamin, Jud. 21.8-12. Besieged by Nahash, and relieved by Saul, 1 Sam. 11.1-11. People of, bury Saul, 1 Sam. 31.11-13. 2 Sam. 2.4-7. 2 Sam. 21.12. 1 Chr. 10.11,12.

JABEZ, his prayer for a blessing answered, 1 Chr. 4.9,10.

JABIN I., king of Hazor, in Canaan, defeated by Joshua, Jos. 11.

——— **II.** oppresses the Israelites; defeated by Barak, Jud. 4. Psa. 83.9.

JABNEEL, or JABNEH, a city of the Philistines, Jos. 15.11. Taken by Uzziah, 2 Chr. 26.6.

JACHIN AND BOAZ, two brazen pillars of the temple, 1 Kin. 7.21. 2 Chr. 3.17.

JACINTH, a precious stone, Rev. 9.17. Rev. 21.20.

JACOB (supplanter), son of Isaac and Rebekah, Gen. 25.26. Jos. 24.4. Mat. 1.2. Luk. 3.34. Act. 7.8. His birth in answer to Isaac's prayer, Gen. 25.19-26. Hos. 12.2. Rom. 9.10-13. His character and occupation, Gen. 25.27.

Buys the birthright from Esau, Gen. 25.29-34. Heb. 12.16. Obtains the blessing from Isaac by deception, Gen. 27.1-29. Heb. 11.20. Esau seeks to slay him, Gen. 27.41-46. Goes to Padan-aram, Gen. 28.1-5. His dream and vow at Bethel, Gen. 28.10-22.

Residence in Haran, Gen. 29. Gen. 30. Hos. 12.12. Married to Leah, Rachel, Zilpah, and Bilhah, Gen. 29.21-30. His experiments with the flocks, Gen. 30.25-42. Ill-treated by Laban, Gen. 31.1-8,38-41. Leaves Haran secretly; is pursued by Laban; their covenant at Mizpeh, Gen. 31.

Angels meet him at Mahanaim, Gen. 32.1,2. His prayer in fear of Esau, Gen. 32.9-12. Sends presents to propitiate him, Gen. 32.3-23. Wrestles with the angel at Penuel; his name changed to Israel (a prince of God), Gen. 32.24-32. 2 Kin. 17.34. Hos. 12.3,4.

Meets Esau, Gen. 32. Gen. 33. Journeys to Succoth, and to Sharon, Gen. 33.17,18.

Buys a field at Shechem, and builds an altar, Gen. 33.19,20. His daughter, Dinah, defiled at Shechem, Gen. 34. Goes to Bethel ; builds an altar, Gen. 35.1-15.

God renews the change of his name, Gen. 35.9-13. He sets up a pillar there, Gen. 35.14,15. Birth of Benjamin ; Rachel's death and burial, Gen. 35.16-20. Gen. 48.7. Returns to his father at Mamre, Gen. 35.27. With Esau buries Isaac, Gen. 35.28,29.

His love for Joseph and grief at his loss, Gen. 37. Sends his sons to Egypt to buy corn, Gen. 42.1,2. Gen. 43.1-14. Act. 7.12. His love for Benjamin, Gen. 42.4,36-38. Gen. 43.14. Gen. 44.27-34. Hears of Joseph, Gen. 45.25-28.

Offers sacrifices at Beersheba ; goes to Egypt by God's command, Gen. 46.1-7. 1 Sam. 12.8. Psa. 105.23. Act. 7.14,15. Meets Joseph, Gen. 46.28-34. Is presented to Pharaoh, and blesses him, Gen. 47.1-10. Dwells in Goshen, Gen. 47.11,12,27.

Joseph swears to bury him in Canaan, Gen. 47.30. Gen. 50.5. Adopts and blesses Ephraim and Manasseh, Gen. 48. Heb. 11.21. Gives land taken from the Amorites to Joseph, Gen. 48.22. Jno. 4.5. Blesses his sons, Gen. 49. His age, Gen. 47.28 ; and death, Gen. 49.29-33.

Embalmed in Egypt, and buried at Mach- pelah, Gen. 50.1-13. His children and descend- ants, Gen. 29.31-35. Gen. 30.1-24. Gen. 35.18-26. Gen. 46.8-27. Ex. 1.1-5. 1 Chr. c. 2 to 9.

Prophecies and promises to himself and his seed, Gen. 25.23. Gen. 27.28,29. Gen. 28.10-15. Gen.31.3,11. Gen. 32.28,29. Gen. '35.9-13. Gen. 46.3. Deu. 1.8. Psa. 105.6,10. Rom. 9.13.

JACOB, name given to the Israelites, Num. 23.7,10,21. Num. 24.17. Deu. 32.9. Psa. 47.4. Isa. 41.8,14. Mal. 1.2. House of Jacob, Ex. 19.3. Isa. 2.5. Isa. 29.22.

————, **WELL OF,** near Shechem, or Sy- char, Christ's conversation with Samaritan woman at, Jno. 4.5-38.

JAEL, wife of Heber the Kenite. Slays Sisera, Jud. 4.17-22. Jud. 5.24-27.

JAHAZ, a town of Moab, Isa. 15.4. Jer. 48.34. Sihon defeated at, Num. 21.23. Deu. 2.32. Jud. 11.20.

JAHAZIEL, a prophet, who predicted to Jehoshaphat the defeat of the Moabites, &c., 2 Chr. 20.14-25.

JAIR, a man of Manasseh. His 23 cities in Gilead called Havoth-jair, Num. 32.41. Deu. 3.14. Jos. 13.30. 1 Kin. 4.13. 1 Chr. 2.22,23.

————, a Judge of Israel. His 30 sons dwell in 30 cities called Havoth-jair, Jud. 10.3-5.

JAIRUS, a ruler of the synagogue, whose daughter Jesus restored to life, Mat. 9.18,23-26. Mar. 5.22-43. Luk. 8.41-56.

JAMES, an apostle. Called son of Alpheus, Mat. 10.3. Mar. 3.18. Luk. 6.15. Act. 1.13. Act. 12.17. Brother of the Lord, Mat. 13.55. Mat. 6.3. Gal. 1.19 with Gal. 2.9,12. Son of Mary, Mat. 27.56. Mar. 16.1. Luk. 24.10. Brother of Jude, Luk. 6.16. Jude 1. Called James the less, Mar. 15.40.

Sees Jesus after his resurrection, 1 Cor. 15.7. Receives Paul, Gal. 1.19. Gal. 2.9. Addresses the council at Jerusalem, Act. 15.13-21. Dis- ciples come from him to Antioch, Gal. 2.12.

Paul narrates to him his successes, Act. 21.18,19. Epistle written by, Jas. 1.1.

JAMES, an apostle, the son of Zebedee, Mat. 4.21 ; and Salome, Mat. 27.66 with Mar. 15.40 & Mar. 16.1. A fisherman, Luk. 5.10. Jno. 21.2,3. His call, Mat. 4.21,22. Mar. 1.19,20 ; and apostleship, Mat. 10.2. Mar. 3.17. Luk. 6.14. Act. 1.13.

Named Boanerges, Mar. 3.17. Was present at the draught of fishes, Luk. 5.10. At the restoration of Peter's wife's mother, Mar. 1.29. At the raising of Jairus' daughter, Mar. 5.37. Luk. 8.51. At the transfiguration, Mat. 17.1. Mar. 9.2. Luk. 9.28. With Christ in Geth- semane, Mat. 26.37. Mar. 14.33. Reproved for ambition, Mat. 20.20-23. Mar. 10.35-41. Asks Jesus about his coming, Mar. 13.3. Wishes to call down fire, Luk. 9.54. Sees Jesus after his resurrection, Jno. 21.2. 1 Cor. 15.7. Put to death by Herod, Act. 12.2.

JANNES AND JAMBRES, magicians who opposed Moses, 2 Tim. 3.8. Ex. 7.11.

JAPHETH, Noah's eldest son, Gen. 10.21. Gen. 5.32. Gen. 6.10. Gen. 9.18. Preserved in the ark, Gen. 7.13. Gen. 9.18. His filial conduct ; blessed by Noah, Gen. 9.23,27. His descendants, Gen. 10.2-5. 1 Chr. 1.5-7.

JAREB, KING (hostile king). A reference to Assyria, Hos. 5.13. Hos. 10.6.

JARHA, an Egyptian bondman, who mar- ried Sheshan's daughter, 1 Chr. 2.34,35.

JASHER, BOOK OF, Jos. 10.13. 2 Sam. 1.18.

JASHOBEAM THE HACHMONITE, one of David's chief captains, supposed to be the same as Adino, 1 Chr. 27.2 with 2 Sam. 23,8-17 & 1 Chr. 11.11-19.

JASON, a disciple at Thessalonica, assaulted by Jews, Act. 17.5-7. Paul's kinsman, Rom. 16.21.

JASPER, a precious stone, Ex.28.20. Ex. 39.13. Eze. 28.13. Rev. 4.3. Rev. 21.11,18,19.

JAVAN, son of Japheth ; his descendants, Gen. 10.2,4. 1 Chr. 1.5,7. Isa. 66.19. Mer- chants of, Eze. 27.13,19. Javan, translated Greece, Dan. 8.21. Dan. 10.20. Dan. 11.2. Zec. 9.13.

JAVELIN. See DART.

JAZER, a city of Gilead, taken from the Amorites by Gad, Num. 21.32. Num. 32.1,3,35. Jos. 13.25. A Levitical city of refuge, Jos. 21.39.

————, SEA OF, Jer. 48.32, see 2 Sam. 24.5.

JEALOUSY. Jealousy-offering, Num. 5.11-31. Image of jealousy, Eze. 8.3,14. See ENVY, JEALOUSY.

JEBUSITES, one of the 7 nations of Canaan, Deu. 7.1. Descended from Canaan, Gen. 10.16. 1 Chr. 1.14. Territory of, Num. 13.29. Jos. 11.3. Jos. 15.8,63. Jos. 18.16. Jud. 1.21. Land of, given to Israel, Gen. 15.21. Ex. 3.8,17. Ex. 23.23.

Were to be extirpated, Deu. 20.17. Defeated by Joshua, Jos. 9.1. Jos. c. 10 to 12. Jos. 24.11. Adonizedek, king of Jebus, or Jerusa- lem, slain by Joshua, Jos. 10. See Jos. 18.28. Jud. 19.10. 1 Chr. 11.4. Conquered by David ; Jerusalem taken, 2 Sam. 5.6-9.

Araunah, a Jebusite, 2 Sam. 24.16-24. Tri- butary to Solomon, 1 Kin. 9.20. Inter-

married with Israelites, Jud. 3.5,6. Ezr.
9.12.

JECONIAH. See JEHOIACHIN.

JEDUTHUN, one of the 3 chief temple
musicians, 1 Chr. 16.41. 1 Chr. 25.1. Called
Ethan, 1 Chr. 6.44. 1 Chr. 15.17. His name
affixed to Psa. 39, 62, & 77.

JEGAR-SAHADUTHA (heap of witness),
name given by Laban to Galeed, Gen. 31.47.

JEHOAHAZ, 6th king of Judah. See
AHAZIAH.

——, or SHALLUM, 16th king of Judah
(3 months' reign), fourth son of Josiah, anointed
his successor, 2 Kin. 23.30,31. 1 Chr. 3.15.
2 Chr. 36.1. Jer. 22.11. His evil reign, 2 Kin.
23.32. Deposed by Pharaoh-necho, and taken
captive to Egypt, 2 Kin. 23.33-35. 2 Chr.
36.3,4. Prophecy of his captivity and death
in Egypt, Jer. 22.10,11.

——, 11th king of Israel (17 years' reign),
son and successor of Jehu, 2 Kin. 10.35. 2 Kin.
13.1 Conquered and oppressed by the Syrians
for his sins; delivered in answer to prayer,
2 Kin. 13.2-7. His death, 2 Kin. 13.8,9.

JEHOASH, or JOASH, 12th king of Israel
(16 years' reign), son and successor of Jehoahaz;
his evil reign; visits Elisha at his death; receives a sign of success; defeats Syrians three
times, 2 Kin. 13.10-25. His parable in reply
to Amaziah's challenge; defeats him, 2 Kin.
13.12. 2 Kin. 14.8-15. 2 Chr. 25.17-24. His
death, 2 Kin. 13.13. 2 Kin. 14.16.

——, king of Judah. See JOASH.

JEHOIACHIN, JECONIAH, or CONIAH,
18th king of Judah (3 months' reign), son and
successor of Jehoiakim, 2 Kin. 24.6,8. 2 Chr.
36.8,9. Called Jeconiah, 1 Chr. 3.16. Jer.
24.1. Coniah, Jer. 22.24. Jer. 37.1. His evil
reign, 2 Kin. 24.9. 2 Chr. 36.9.

Taken to Babylon by Nebuchadnezzar, with
numerous captives (this the 2d captivity B.C.
599), 2 Kin. 24.10-16. 2 Chr. 36.10. Est. 2.6.
Jer. 27.20. Jer. 29.1,2. Eze. 1.2. Captivity
relieved by Evil-merodach after 37 years, 2 Kin.
25.27-30. Jer. 52.31-34. His children, 1 Chr.
3.17,18. Mat. 1.12. Prophecy respecting,
Jer. 22.24-30. False prophecy, Jer. 28.4.

JEHOIADA, high-priest, recovers the
throne of Judah for Joash; causes Athaliah
to be put to death, 2 Kin. 11. 2 Chr. 23.
Assists Joash in repairing the temple, 2 Kin.
12.4-16. 2 Chr. 24.4-14. Good influence on
Joash, 2 Kin. 12.2. 2 Chr. 24.2,16,22. Death
and honourable burial, 2 Chr. 24.15,16.

JEHOIAKIM, or ELIAKIM, 17th king of
Judah (11 years' reign), second son of Josiah,
1 Chr. 3.15. Mat. 1.11. Made king by Pharaoh
in the room of his brother Jehoahaz, and his
name changed from Eliakim, 2 Kin. 23.34-36.
2 Chr. 36.4. His evil reign, 2 Kin. 23.37.
2 Chr. 36.5,8. Jer. 22.13-18.

Sends to Egypt for the prophet Urijah; slays
him, Jer. 26.22. Burns Jeremiah's roll, Jer.
36. Becomes tributary to Babylon when Nebuchadnezzar conquered Pharaoh, 2 Kin. 24.1,7,
see Jer. 46.2. Invasion by Nebuchadnezzar
on his rebellion; Jerusalem taken; he is imprisoned; captives taken to Babylon (this the
beginning of the captivity, B.C. 606), 2 Kin.
24.1-4. 2 Chr. 36.6,7. Dan. 1.1,2. His death
predicted, Jer. 22.18,19.

JEHONADAB. See JONADAB.

JEHORAM, 5th king of Judah (8 years'
reign), son of Jehoshaphat, reigns jointly with,
and succeeds him, 1 Kin. 22.50. 2 Kin. 8.16.
1 Chr. 3.11. 2 Chr. 21.5. Mat. 1.8. Marries
Athaliah; her evil influence; his sins, 2 Kin.
8.18,19. 2 Chr. 21.6-13.

Murders his brethren, 2 Chr. 21.4,13. Revolt of Edom, 2 Kin. 8.20-22. 2 Chr. 21.8-10.
Invasion by Philistines and Arabians; his
sons slain, 2 Chr. 21.16,17. His death, 2 Chr.
21.18-20. 2 Kin. 8.24. Prophecy against,
2 Chr. 21.12-15.

——, king of Israel. See JORAM.

JEHOSHAPHAT, 4th king of Judah (25
years' reign), succeeds Asa his father, 1 Kin.
15.24. 1 Kin. 22.41. 1 Chr. 3.10. 2 Chr. 17.1.
Mat. 1.8. Fortifies his kingdom against Israel,
2 Chr. 17.2. His reformation, and appointment
of Levites to teach and judge the people, 1 Kin.
22.46. 2 Chr. 17.7-9. 2 Chr. 19.3-11.

His tributaries and his officers, 2 Chr.
17.11-19. Joins Ahab in war with Syria;
Micaiah predicts defeat if he goes to Ramoth-
Gilead, 1 Kin. 22. 2 Chr. 18. Jehu rebukes
him for alliance with Ahab, 2 Chr. 19.2. Ammon, Moab, &c., invade Judah, and are defeated at Jehoshaphat's prayer, 2 Chr. 20.

Ships, of destroyed; the prophet Eliezer rebukes his alliance with Ahaziah, 2 Chr. 20.35-38.
1 Kin. 22.48,49. Joins Jehoram in his war
with Moab; the Moabites defeated, according
to Elisha's prediction, 2 Kin. 3. Dedicates
spoils, 2 Kin. 12.18.

Death, 1 Kin. 22.42,50. 2 Chr. 21.1. Piety
and prosperity, 1 Kin. 22.43-46. 2. Chr. c.
17, 19, & 20. 2 Chr. 22.9. Legacies to his
children, 2 Chr. 21.2,3.

——, VALLEY OF, Joel 3.2,12. Called
Valley of Decision, Joel 3.14. See TOPHET.

JEHOSHEBA, daughter of Jehoram, and
wife of Jehoiada, preserves Joash from Athaliah, 2 Kin. 11.2. 2 Chr. 22.11.

JEHOVAH-JIREH (the Lord will provide),
the place where Abraham offered Isaac, Gen.
22.14.

—— **NISSI** (the Lord my banner), an
altar built on the defeat of Amalek, Ex. 17.15.

—— **SHALOM** (the Lord send peace),
an altar built by Gideon, Jud. 6.24.

JEHOZABAD, a servant of king Joash,
conspires against, and murders him, 2 Kin.
12.20,21. 2 Chr. 24.26.

JEHOZADAK, or JOZADAK, son of Seraiah,
a high-priest, taken captive by Nebuchadnezzar, 1 Chr. 6.14,15. Father of Joshua the high-
priest. See JOSHUA.

JEHU, 10th king of Israel (28 years' reign),
son of Nimshi, anointed king by God's
command, 1 Kin. 19.16. 2 Kin. 9.1-14. Slays
Ahaziah, Joram, and Jezebel, at Jezreel, 2 Kin.
9.14-37. 2 Chr. 22.8,9. Slays the family of
Ahab and Ahaziah, 2 Kin. 10.1-17. Slays
Baal's priests, and destroys his images, 2 Kin.
10.18-28.

Defeated by Hazael, 2 Kin. 10.32,33. Sins
and death, 2 Kin. 10.29,31,35. Prophecies respecting, 1 Kin. 19.17. 2 Kin. 10.30. 2 Kin.
15.12. Hos. 1.4.

JEHU, son of Hanani, prophesies against
Baasha, 1 Kin. 16.1-4. Rebukes Jehoshaphat
for his alliance with Ahab, 2 Chr. 19.2.

JEPHTHAH, son of Gilead, illegitimate; disinherited; his valour, Jud. 11.1-3. Delivers Israel from the Ammonites; his vow; treatment of his daughter in accordance with his vow, Jud. 11. The Ephraimites quarrel with him, and are defeated, Jud. 12.1-7. His faith, Heb. 11.32.

JEREMIAH, son of Hilkiah the priest, born at Anathoth, Jer. 1.1. Called to prophesy when young, Jer. 1.4-19. Time of prophesying, Jer. 3.6. Jer. 21.1. Jer. 25.1. Jer. 26.1. Jer. 28.1. Jer. 32.1. Jer. 34.1. Persecuted, Jer. 15.10,15. Jer. 17.15-18. Jer. 18.18-23. Jer. 26.8,16; by the men of Anathoth, Jer. 11.21; by Pashur, Jer. 20; by Zedekiah, Jer. 32. Jer. 33.1. Jer. 37.11-21. Jer. 38.

Protected by Ahikam, Jer. 26.24; and Ebedmelech, Jer. 38.7-15. His prophecies written by Baruch, Jer. 36.1-7,32. Jer. 45.1; read by the princes and burnt by Jehoiakim, Jer. 36.8-32; given to Seraiah to be read at Babylon, Jer. 51.59-64. Zedekiah inquires of God by him, Jer. 21.1,2. Jer. 37.3. Jer. 38.14; and Johanan, Jer. 42.1-6.

His prayers asked by Zedekiah, Jer. 37.3. Forbidden to marry, Jer. 16.2. Writes to the captives in Babylon, Jer. 29. Buys a field in Anathoth, Jer. 32.7-12. His lamentations for Josiah, 2 Chr. 35.25. Lam. 4.20; and over Jerusalem, Jer. 4.19. Jer. 8.18,21. Jer. 9.1. Jer. 10.19. Book of Lamentation.

Released by Nebuzar-adan at Nebuchadnezzar's command, Jer. 39.11-14. Jer. 40.1. Dwells with Gedaliah at Mizpah, Jer. 40.6. Carried to Egypt by Johanan, Jer. 43.1-7. Prophetic influence on, Jer. 6.10. Jer. 20.9. His prayers, Jer. 14.7. Jer. 32.17-25. Despondency, Jer. 12.1-3. Jer. 20.14-18. Book of Lamentations. Love to God's word, Jer. 15.16.

JERICHO, a city on the Jordan, Num. 22.1. Num. 26.3. Deu. 34.1. Called the City of Palm-trees, Deu. 34.3. Two spies sent to, received by Rahab, Jos. 2. Heb. 11.31. Joshua sees the 'captain of the Lord's host' near, Jos. 5.13-15. Besieged by Joshua, encompassed by priests, &c., 7 days, fall of its walls, destroyed as a devoted city, Jos. 6. Jos. 24.11.

Given to Benjamin, Jos. 18.12,21. The boundary of Ephraim, Jos. 16.1. The Kenites dwelt at, Jud. 1.16. Taken by Eglon, king of Moab, Jud. 3.13. David's ambassadors at, 2 Sam. 10.5. Rebuilt by Hiel; his son's death according to prophecy, 1 Kin. 16.34. Jos. 6.26. A school of the prophets at, 2 Kin. 2.4,5,15,18. Pekah brings the captives of Judah to, 2 Chr. 28.15. Christ cures two blind men near, Mat. 20.29-34. Mar. 10.46. Luk. 18.35; and visits Zaccheus at, Luk. 19.1-10.

———, PLAIN OF, between Jericho and the Jordan, down to the Dead Sea; Zedekiah captured in, 2 Kin. 25.5.

———, WATERS OF, Jos. 16.1. Healed by Elisha, 2 Kin. 2.18-22.

JEROBOAM, 1st king of the ten tribes of Israel (22 years' reign), son of Nebat, Solomon's servant; Ahijah predicts that he would be king, 1 Kin. 11.29-39. 1 Kin. 14.5-16. 1 Kin. 15.29,30. 2 Chr. 9.29. 2 Chr. 10.15. Flees to Egypt on Solomon seeking his life, 1 Kin. 11.26-40. Is brought back by Israel; presents a petition to Rehoboam which is rejected;

made king of the 10 tribes, 1 Kin. 12.1-24. 2 Chr. 10.

Sets up calves at Dan and Bethel; ordains a feast in the 8th month; banishes the Levites; makes priests of the lowest of the people, 1 Kin. 12.25-33. 1 Kin. 13.33,34. 1 Kin. 14.9,16. 1 Kin. 16.2,26,31. 2 Chr. 11.14. 2 Chr. 13.8,9. His hand withered when burning incense and opposing a prophet, 1 Kin. 13.1-10. His child dies for his idolatry according to Ahijah's prediction, 1 Kin. 14.1-18.

Wars with Rehoboam, 1 Kin. 14.30. 1 Kin. 15.6. 2 Chr. 11.1-4. 2 Chr. 12.15. Defeated by Abijah, 2 Chr. 13.3-20. Death, 1 Kin. 14.20. 2 Chr. 13.20. Genealogies written in his reign, 1 Chr. 5.17.

JEROBOAM II., 13th king of Israel (41 years' reign), son and successor of Jehoash, 2 Kin. 14.16,23. His sins, 2 Kin. 14.24. Conquers Hamath, Damascus, &c., 2 Kin. 14.25-28. Death, 2 Kin. 14.29. Prophecy against, Amos 7.7-13.

JERUBBAAL. See GIDEON.

JERUSALEM, called Jebus, Jos. 18.28. Jud. 19.10. Zion, 1 Kin. 8.1. City of David, 2 Sam. 5.7. Salem, Gen. 14.18. Psa. 76.2. Ariel, Isa. 29.1. City of God, Psa. 46.4. City of the Great King, Psa. 48.2. City of Judah, 2 Chr. 25.28. Holy City, Neh. 11.1-18. City of Solemnities, Isa. 33.20.

Chosen and loved by God, 1 Kin. 15.4. 2 Kin. 19.34. 2 Chr. 6.6. 2 Chr. 32.19. Ezr. 7.15. The chief priests dwelt at, 1 Chr. 9.34. Jno. 18.15. The feasts kept at, Deu. 16.16. Eze. 36.38. Luk. 2.41. Jno. 12.20. Act. 18.21. The tribes worshipped at, Psa. 122.3-5. Jno. 4.20. Prayer made towards, 1 Kin. 8.38. Dan. 6.10. Loved by the Jews, Psa. 122.6. Psa. 137.6. Isa. 62.1,7. See CHURCH, LOVE OF. The Jews swore by, Mat. 5.35.

Symbolical, Gal. 4.25,26. Heb. 12.22. New Jerusalem, Rev. 3.12. Rev. 21. Prophecies respecting Jerusalem. See ISRAELITES (JUDAH—THE JEWS).

———, DESCRIPTION OF. Situation and appearance, Psa. 122.3. Psa. 125.2. Song 6.4. Mic. 4.8.

GATES OF. Old gate, fish gate, sheep gate, prison gate, Neh. 12.39. Gate of Ephraim, 2 Chr. 25.23. Gate of Benjamin, Jer. 37.13. Of Joshua, 2 Kin. 23.8. Corner gate, 2 Kin. 14.13. Valley gate, Neh. 3.13. Dung gate, Neh. 12.31. Gate of the fountain, Neh. 3.15. Water gate, Neh. 3.26. Horse gate, Neh. 3.28. King's gate, 1 Chr. 9.18. Shallecheth, 1 Chr. 26.16. High gate, 2 Chr. 23.20. East gate, Neh. 3.29. Miphkad, Neh. 3.31. Middle gate, Jer. 39.3. First gate, Zec. 14.10.

TOWERS OF. See MILLO, MEAH, HANANEEL, SILOAM, OPHEL.

BUILDINGS. High-priest's palace, Jno.18.15. Castle, Act. 21.34. Stairs, Neh. 3.15. See TEMPLE, GABBATHA, PRETORIUM.

STREETS. East Street, 2 Chr. 29.4. Street of the house of God, Ezr. 10.9. Water Gate, Neh. 8.1. Ephraim Gate, Neh. 8.16. Bakers' Street, Jer. 37.21.

PLACES IN AND AROUND. Moriah, 2 Chr.3.1. Christ's sepulchre, Jno. 19.41. See COLLEGE, CALVARY—OLIVES, MT.—GAREB, GETHSEMANE—JEHOSHAPHAT, VALLEY OF—TOPHET, ACELDAMA, MAKTESH.

POOLS, FOUNTAINS, AND BROOKS. Bethesda,

Jno. 5.2. See CEDRON, EN-ROGEL, GIHON, SILOAM.

JERUSALEM, HISTORICAL NOTICES OF. Melchizedek, king of, Gen. 14.18. King of, slain by Joshua, Jos. 10.5-33. Allotted to Benjamin, Jos. 18.28. Taken by Judah, Jud. 1.8. Jointly possessed by Judah, Benjamin, and the Jebusites, Jos. 15.63. Jud. 1.21.

David brings Goliath's head to, 1 Sam. 17.54. Takes Mount Zion from the Jebusites; fortifies and makes it the capital, 2 Sam. 5.5-9. Brings the ark to, 2 Sam. 6.12. Builds an altar in, 2 Sam. 24.25.

Fortified by Solomon, the wall built, 1 Kin. 3.1. 1 Kin. 9.15. The temple built, see TEMPLE. Pillaged by Shishak, 1 Kin. 14.25,26. 2 Chr. 12.9. Pillaged; the wall broken down by Jehoash, 2 Kin. 14.13. 2 Chr. 25.23,24. Uzziah fortifies, 2 Chr. 26.9; and Jotham, 2 Chr. 27.3. Besieged in vain by Pekah and Rezin, 2 Kin. 16.5.

Supplied with water by Hezekiah, see GIHON. Besieged in vain by Sennacherib, 2 Kin. 18.17. 2 Kin. 19. 2 Chr. 32. Fortified by Manasseh, 2 Chr. 33.14. Captured by Nebuchadnezzar; 18,000 captives taken, 2 Kin. 24.10-16. Taken a second time, and destroyed, 2 Kin. 25. 2 Chr. 36.17-21. Jer. 39 (B.C. 588).

Rebuilt and fortified by Nehemiah, on the return from captivity (B.C. 445), Neh. c. 2 to 6. Dedication of the wall, Neh. 12.27-43. Inhabitants of, chosen by lot, Neh. 11.1-4, see EZRA, NEHEMIAH. Temple rebuilt, see TEMPLE.

Herod I. resided at, Mat. 2.3. Visit of the wise men, Mat. 2.1. Pontius Pilate chief governor in, Mat. 27.2. Luk. 23. Fall of the tower of Siloam in, Luk. 13.4. Wickedness of, Luk. 13.33,34.

Christ goes up to the feasts, Jno. 5.1. Jno. 7.1-14. His triumphal entry into, Mat. 21.1-11. Weeps over, Luk. 13.34. His last visit to, see CHRIST, LIFE OF, Parts 7, 8, 9. See TEMPLE, HISTORICAL NOTICES OF.

Christ's miracles at, Jno. 2.23. Jno. 3.2. Jno. 4.25. Jno. 5.1-9. Jno. 9. Discourses at, Mat. c. 21 to 25. Jno. 5.10-47. Jno. 7.14-53. Jno. c. 8 to 10 ; c. 12 to 17.

Gospel first preached at, Luk. 24.47. Act. 2.14. The disciples commanded to remain at, till the descent of the Holy Ghost, Act. 1.4. Meet for prayer in an upper room, Act. 1.12-14. Elect Matthias as an apostle, Act. 1.15-26. Descent of the Holy Ghost at Pentecost, Act. 2.1-36. Conversion of 3000, and daily additions to the church, Act. 2.37-47.

Miracle of Peter and John ; Peter's discourse, Act. 3. Peter and John imprisoned, and released ; thanksgiving of the church, Act. 4.1-30. Disciples filled with the Holy Ghost, Act. 4.31. Barnabas, &c., sell property, and have all things in common, Act. 2.44,45. Act. 4.32-37. Ananias and Sapphira's falsehood and death, Act. 5.1-11. Miracles of the apostles ; increase of the church, Act. 5.12-16.

Apostles imprisoned ; delivered by an angel ; brought before the council ; Gamaliel's address ; their preaching, Act. 5.17-42. Increase of the church ; disputes between Grecians and Hebrews ; disciples appointed to distribute the funds, Act. 6.1-7.

Stephen's disputes in the synagogue ; accusation before the council ; defence and death, Act. 6.8-15. Act. 7. Persecution by Saul ;

dispersion of disciples, who preach to the Jews of Phenice, Antioch, and Cyprus, Act. 8.1-4. Act. 11.19-21. The apostles remain in Jerusalem, Act. 8.14.

Jewish Christians blame Peter for his intercourse with Gentiles ; his defence, Act. 11.1-18. Persecution by Herod ; James killed ; Peter delivered in answer to prayers of the church ; progress of the gospel, Act. 12.1-17,24. Collections for the poor saints in, by Gentile churches, Act. 11.29,30. Rom. 15.25,26. 1 Cor. 16.1-3. Decree of council at, in reference to circumcision, &c., Act. 15.1-29.

Paul taught by Gamaliel in, Act. 22.3. His visits to, Act. 9.26-28. Act. 11.29,30. Act. 15.2-6. Gal. 2.1-7. A great tumult ; he is taken to Cesarea, Act. c. 21 & 22.

JESHIMON (a wilderness), Num. 21.20. Num. 23.28. 1 Sam. 23.19. 1 Sam. 26.1.

JESHURUN, a poetical name for the Israelites, Deu. 32.15. Deu. 33.5,26. Isa. 44.2.

JESSE, son of Obed, and father of David, Ruth 4.17,22. Mat. 1.5,6. Visited by Samuel ; David anointed, 1 Sam. 16.1-13. Sends David with a present to Saul, 1 Sam. 16.19-23. Sends David to his brethren in the army, 1 Sam. 17.17,18. Takes refuge from Saul with the king of Moab, 1 Sam. 22.3. His descendants, 1 Chr. 2.13.

JESTING, FOOLISH, forbidden, Eph. 5.4. See Mat. 12.36.

JESUS (Saviour), Mat. 1.21 (marg.). Phil. 2.10. See CHRIST.

———, signifying Joshua, Act. 7.45. Heb 4.8.

———, surnamed Justus, a fellow-labourer with Paul, Col. 4.11.

JETHRO, a priest or prince of Midian, and father-in-law of Moses, Ex. 2.16-21. Ex. 3.1. Ex. 4.18. Called Reuel, or Raguel, Ex. 2.18. Num. 10.29. Brings Moses' wife to him in the wilderness ; his counsel, Ex. 18.

JEWELS of silver and gold, Ex. 3.22. Eze. 16.17. Ex. 35.22. Num. 31.50,51. Precious stones set in gold, Song 5.14. Ex. 28.11. Ornaments for the head of women, 2 Kin. 9.30. Isa. 3.18,20. Song 1.10. Eze. 16.12 ; of men, Eze. 23.42. Illustrative, Pro. 20.15. Mal. 3.17. See BRACELETS, CHAINS, RINGS, SEALS, TABLETS, PRECIOUS STONES, PEARLS.

JEWS. See SABBATH, JEWISH MISCONCEPTIONS—CHRIST, JEWISH VIEWS OF—PHARISEES, SADDUCEES, HERODIANS—ISRAELITES, HISTORY OF—ISRAELITES, PROPHECIES OF. For language of, see HEBREW. For enemies of, punished, see PERSECUTORS PUNISHED.

JEZEBEL, daughter of Ethbaal, and wife of Ahab, 1 Kin. 16.31. Her idolatry, 1 Kin. 18.19. 2 Kin. 3.2,13. 2 Kin. 9.22. Persecutes the prophets, 1 Kin. 18.4,13. 2 Kin. 9.7 ; and Elijah, 1 Kin. 19.1-3. Causes the murder of Naboth, 1 Kin. 21.5-16. Prophecies of her death, 1 Kin. 21.17-23. 2 Kin. 9.7-10. Her reception of Jehu, 2 Kin. 9.30,31. Death of, 2 Kin. 9.32-37.

Symbolical name, Rev. 2.20.

JEZREEL, a town of Issachar, Jos. 19.18. 2 Sam. 2.9. Ahab's residence, 1 Kin. 18.45,46. 1 Kin. 21.1. Naboth's vineyard in, 1 Kin. 21.1-16. Joram's residence, 2 Kin. 8.29. Joram and Ahaziah slain by Jehu at, 2 Kin.

9.15-26. Jezebel's death at, 2 Kin. 9.30-37. Ahab's kinsmen and friends slain at, by Jehu, 2 Kin. 10.11. Prophecy of, Hos. 1.4,5,11.

JEZREEL, VALLEY OF, Jos. 17.16. Gideon defeats the Midianites in, Jud. 6.33. Battle of the Philistines near a fountain in, 1 Sam. 29.1,11. 2 Sam. 4.4.

———, a name for Israel, Hos. 2.22.

JOAB, son of Zeruiah, David's sister, 1 Chr. 2.16. Captain of the host, under David, 2 Sam. 8.16. 2 Sam. 20.23. 1 Chr. 11.6. 1 Chr. 18.15. 1 Chr. 27.34. Dedicates spoils, 1 Chr. 26.28. Defeats Abner, 2 Sam. 2.13-32. Murders Abner, 2 Sam. 3.22-30. 1 Kin. 2.5. Defeats the Jebusites, 1 Chr. 11.6. Exterminates the Edomites, 1 Kin. 11.16. Psa. 60 (*title*). Defeats the Ammonites, 2 Sam. 10.7-14. 1 Chr. 19.6-15. Besieges and takes Rabbah, 2 Sam. 11. 2 Sam. 12.26,27. 1 Chr. 20.

Brings Absalom back through the help of the widow of Tekoah, 2 Sam. 14.1-24. His field burned by Absalom, 2 Sam. 14.30-33. Defeats and slays Absalom, 2 Sam. 18. Reproves David's lamentation for Absalom, 2 Sam. 19.1-8. Amasa made chief captain instead of, 2 Sam. 19.13. 2 Sam. 17.25. Murders Amasa, 2 Sam. 20.8-13. 1 Kin. 2.5. Defeats Sheba, 2 Sam. 20.16-22. Dissuades David from numbering Israel, 2 Sam. 24.3. 1 Chr. 21.3. Numbers Israel, 2 Sam. 24.4-9. 1 Chr. 21.4,5. 1 Chr. 27.23,24. Supports Adonijah, 1 Kin. 1.7. 1 Kin. 2.28. Put to death by Solomon, 1 Kin. 2.28-34.

JOANNA, wife of Chuza, Herod's steward, ministers to Jesus, Luk. 8.3. Visits the sepulchre, Luk. 24.10.

JOASH, father of Gideon, who destroys his altar; he ridicules Baal, Jud. 6.25-31.

JOASH, or JEHOASH, 7th king of Judah (40 years' reign), son of Ahaziah; saved from Athaliah by Jehosheba, his aunt, 2 Kin. 11.1-3. 2 Chr. 22.11,12. Made king by Jehoiada, 2 Kin. 11.17-21. 2 Chr. 23. Repairs the temple, 2 Kin. 12.4-16. 2 Chr. 24.4-14,27.

His character in Jehoiada's life, 2 Kin. 12.2. 2 Chr. 24.2. His idolatry after Jehoiada's death, 2 Chr. 24.17,18. Propitiates Hazael with a bribe, 2 Kin. 12.17,18. Murders Zechariah, son of Jehoiada, 2 Chr. 24.20-22. Mat. 23.35. Is punished by invasion of Syrians, 2 Chr. 24.23,24. His diseases, 2 Chr. 24.25. Slain by his servants, 2 Kin. 12.20. 2 Chr. 24.25. Prophecy respecting, 2 Chr. 24.19,20.

———, king of Israel. See JEHOASH.

JOB, of the land of Uz; his prosperity, Job 1.1-3; his piety, Job 1.1,8. Job 2.3. Eze. 14.14,20. His sacrifices for his children, Job 1.5. His affliction, Job 1.13-19. Job 2.7,10. Resignation, Job 1.20,22. Job 2.10. Jas. 5.11.

Visited by 3 friends, Job 2.11-13. His despondency; speeches to them, Job c. 3, 6, 7, 9, 10, 12-14, 16, 17, 19, 21, 23, 24, 26-31. The Lord answers him, Job c. 38 to 41. His confession to God, Job 40.3-5. Job 42.1-6. Prays for his friends; his prosperity; children; age and death, Job 42.7-17.

JOCHEBED, mother of Moses; puts him in an ark; nurses him for Pharaoh's daughter, Ex. 2.1-9. Ex. 6.20. Act. 7.20,21. Heb. 11.23.

JOEL, son of Pethuel, a prophet, Joel 1.1. Act. 2.16.

JOHANAN, a Jewish captain, warns Gedaliah of Ishmael's plot, Jer. 40.9-16. 2 Kin. 25.22-24. Defeats Ishmael, Jer. 41.11-15. Asks Jeremiah's prayers; disregards his prophecy; takes Jeremiah to Egypt, Jer. 42. Jer. 43.1-7.

JOHN THE BAPTIST. Birth foretold by an angel, Luk. 1.11-17. Son of Zacharias and Elisabeth, Luk. 1.5,6. Birth in the hill-country of Judah, Luk. 1.39,58. Circumcision; his name given, Luk. 1.59-63. *v.* 13.

Life in the desert, Luk. 1.80. Dress and food, Mat. 3.4. Mar. 1.6. Abstemiousness, Mat. 11.18. Luk. 1.15. Luk. 7.33. Personal character, Mat. 11.7-18. Luk. 1.80. Luk. 7.24-33.

Commences his ministry; his inspiration; nature of his preaching, Mat. 3.1-3. Mar. 1.4. Luk. 3.2,3. Jno. 1.6-8. Rebukes the Pharisees, &c., Mat. 3.7-12. Luk. 3.7-18. The Jews imagine him to be the Christ, Luk. 3.15. Send priests to him, Jno. 1.19-27.

His popularity, Mat. 3.5. Mat. 14.5. Mat. 21.32,36. Mar. 1.5. Mar. 11.32. Luk. 3.7,15. Luk. 7.24. Luk. 20.6. Jno. 5.35. His testimony to Jesus, Mat. 3.11,12. Mat. 1.7,8. Luk. 3.16,17. Jno. 1.15,26-36. Jno. 3.26-36. Jno. 5.32,33. Jno. 10.41. Act. 13.25.

His baptism with water unto repentance, of multitudes from Jerusalem, &c., Mat. 3.5-10. Mar. 1.4,5. Luk. 3.3-14. Luk. 7.29. Jno. 4.1. Act. 1.5. Act. 10.37. Act. 11.16. Act. 13.24. Act. 18.25. Act. 19.3,4. Baptizes in Jordan, Mar. 1.5; at Bethabara, Jno. 1.28; and Ænon, Jno. 3.23.

Divinely instructed to baptize, Jno. 1.33, see Mat. 21.25. Mar. 11.30. Luk. 20.4. Design of his baptism, Jno. 1.25-31. He predicts the baptism by the Holy Spirit, Mat. 3.11. Mar. 1.8. Luk. 3.16. Jno. 1.26,27,33. Act. 1.5. Act. 11.16. He baptizes Jesus, Mat. 3.13-16. Mar. 1.9-11. Luk. 3.21,22. Jno. 1.32.

Christ bears testimony to John, Mat. 11.7-19. Luk. 7.24-33. Jno. 5.32-35; and declares him to be Elijah, Mat. 11.13,14. Mat. 17.12,13. Mat. 21.32. Mar. 9.13. See Isa. 40.3-5. Mal. 3.1. Mal. 4.5,6.

Worked no miracles, Jno. 10.41. His disciples fasted, Luk. 5.33. Taught by him to pray, Luk. 11.1. Dispute with the Jews about purifying, Jno. 3.25. Tell him of Christ's miracles, Mat. 11.2. Luk. 7.18. Andrew one of his disciples, Jno. 1.35-40.

Herod favours him; he rebukes Herod; is imprisoned; while in prison, sends two disciples to Jesus; beheaded at the instigation of Herodias; his disciples bury him, Mat. 14.3-12. Mar. 6.17-29. Luk. 3.19,20. Mat. 4.12. Mat. 11.2-6. Luk. 7.19-23. Herod imagines he had risen again, Mat. 14.1,2. Mat. 16.14. Mar. 6.14,16. Luk. 9.19.

JOHN THE APOSTLE, son of Zebedee and Salome, Mat. 27.56 with Mar. 15.40 and Mar. 16.1. A fisherman, Luk. 5.10. Jno. 21.2,3. His call, Mat. 4.21,22. Mar. 1.19,20. An apostle, Mat. 10.2. Mar. 3.17. Luk. 6.14. Act. 1.13.

Called Boanerges, Mar. 3.17. Is called the disciple whom Jesus loved, Jno. 13.23, Jno. 21.20. Present at the cure of Peter's wife's mother, Mar. 1.29. At the raising of Jairus' daughter, Mar. 5.37. Luk. 8.51. At the miraculous draught of fishes, Luk. 5.10. At the transfiguration, Mat. 17.1. Mar. 9.2. Luk. 9.28.

With Christ in Gethsemane, Mat. 26.37. Mar. 14.33. Luk. 22.39. Rebuked for forbidding one to work miracles, Mar. 9.38. Luk. 9.49. For wishing to call fire from heaven, Luk. 9.54. For ambition, Mar. 10.35-41. Asks about the coming of Christ, Mar. 13.3.

Sent by Jesus to prepare the passover, Luk. 22.8. Leaned on his breast at supper; asks Jesus who should betray him, Jno. 13.23,24,25. Jno. 21.20. Follows Jesus; is known to the high-priest, Jno. 18.15,16. Jesus commends his mother to his care; Mary taken home by him, Jno. 19.26,27.

Reaches the sepulchre before Peter; his faith, Jno. 20.2-8. The miraculous draught of fishes; he recognises Jesus, Jno. 21.1-7. Christ's words regarding him misunderstood, Jno. 21.21-23. Miracle with Peter in the temple, Act. 3.1-11.

Imprisoned and brought before the sanhedrim, Act. 4.1-19. Sent by the church to Samaria, Act. 8.14-17. Receives Paul, Gal. 2.1,9. Visits the churches, 2 Jno. 12. 3 Jno. 14. Banished to Patmos, Rev. 1.9.

JOHN MARK. See MARK.

JOKSHAN, son of Abraham and Keturah, father of Sheba and Dedan, Gen. 25.2,3. 1 Chr. 1.32. Portioned by Abraham and sent to the east country, Gen. 25.6.

JOKTHEEL (subdued of God), a name imposed by Amaziah upon Selah, the capital of Edom, on his conquering it, 2 Kin. 14.7.

JONADAB, David's nephew, his evil counsel to Amnon, 2 Sam. 13.3-5. Comforts David, 2 Sam. 13.32-35.

————, the son of Rechab, accompanies Jehu when destroying Baal's priests, 2 Kin. 10.15-23. Commands his sons to drink no wine; prophecy of his posterity, Jer. 35. 6-8,16-19.

JONAH, son of Amittai, of Gath-hepher, in Zebulon; prophecy by, 2 Kin. 14.25. Is sent to Nineveh; flees to Tarshish; overtaken by a storm; cast into the sea, and swallowed by a fish, Jonah 1. Is delivered from the fish, in answer to his prayer, Jonah 2. Mat. 12.40. Preaches to the Ninevites, who repent, Jonah 3. Mat. 12.41. Is displeased at God sparing the Ninevites, and is reproved by the gourd withering, Jonah 4.

JONATHAN, a Levite, son of Gershom, becomes an idolatrous priest to Micah, and afterwards to the Danites, Jud. 17.7-13 with Jud. 18. His descendants priests of Dan, Jud. 18. 30.

————, son of Saul, 1 Sam. 14.49. Defeats the Philistines in Gibeah, 1 Sam. 13.3,16. Surprises the Philistines in Michmash; his faith; endangered by Saul's oath, 1 Sam. 14. His friendship and affection for David, 1 Sam. 18.1-4. 1 Sam. 19.1-7. 1 Sam. 20. His covenant with David, 1 Sam. 18.3. 1 Sam. 20. 12-17,42. 1 Sam. 23.16-18. Slain by the Philistines, 1 Sam. 31.2,6-13. 1 Chr. 10.2. 2 Sam. 21.12-14. His body fastened to the wall of Bethshan, and buried by men of Jabesh-Gilead;

David's lament for him, 2 Sam. 1.12,17-27. His son Mephibosheth, 2 Sam. 4.4. 1 Chr. 8.34.

JONATHAN, son of Abiathar, left by David in Jerusalem as a spy, 2 Sam. 15.27. 2 Sam. 17.17-22. Brings news to Adonijah of Solomon being made king, 1 Kin. 1.42-48.

————, David's nephew, slays a giant, 1 Chr. 20.6,7. 2 Sam. 21.21.

JONATH-ELEM-RECHOKIM (literally, the dove—silent—abroad), an enigmatical allusion by David to his exile in Gath (Title), Psa. 56, see Psa. 38.13,14. Psa. 74.19.

JOPPA, or **JAPHO** (modern Jaffa), a seaport in Dan, Jos. 19.46. Cedar for the temple brought to, 2 Chr. 2.16. Ezr. 3.7. Jonah took shipping from, Jonah 1.3. Peter raises Dorcas in, Act. 9.36-43. His vision of unclean beasts in, Act. 10.9-18.

JORAM, or **JEHORAM,** 9th king of Israel (12 years' reign), son of Ahab, brother and successor of Ahaziah, 2 Kin. 1.17. 2 Kin. 3.1. His idolatry, 2 Kin. 3.2,3. Moabites rebel against, 2 Kin. 1.1. 2 Kin. 3.4,5. With Jehoshaphat defeats them, according to Elisha's prediction, 2 Kin. 3. Receives a letter from Benhadad by Naaman, 2 Kin. 5.6. Invaded by Benhadad; saves his army by Elisha's information; Syrians struck blind, led to Samaria, and dismissed by Elisha's command, 2 Kin. 6.8-23. Samaria besieged; he threatens Elisha's life because of the famine, 2 Kin. 6.24-33. Siege and famine relieved as predicted by Elisha, 2 Kin. 7. Restores the Shunamite's land on Gehazi's information, 2 Kin. 8.4-6. War with Hazael; wounded at Ramoth-Gilead, 2 Kin. 8.28,29. 2 Chr. 22.5,6. Slain by Jehu, 2 Kin. 9.14-26.

JORDAN, RIVER OF, Job. 40.23. Boundary between Reuben, Gad, Manasseh, and the rest of the tribes, Jos. 22.25. Flows into the Dead Sea, Jos. 15.5. Overflowed its banks, Jer. 12.5; at harvest-time, Jos. 3.15; in the 1st month, 1 Chr. 12.15. Lions on its banks, Jer. 49.19. Fords of, Jos. 2.7; taken by the army of Ehud, Jud. 3.28; of Gideon, Jud.7.24; of Gileadites, Jud. 12.5,6.

Crossed by Jacob, Gen. 32.10. By Gideon, Jud. 8.4. By Ammonites, Jud. 10.9. By Abner, 2 Sam. 2.29. By David, 2 Sam. 17.22. 2 Sam 19.15,31. 1 Chr. 19.17. By Absalom, 2 Sam. 17.24. Miraculously by Israelites, Jos. c. 3 & 4. Jos. 5.1. Psa. 114.3. By Elijah, 2 Kin. 2.6-8. By Elisha, 2 Kin. 2.14. Naaman's leprosy cured by washing in, 2 Kin. 5.10,14. Iron made to swim in, 2 Kin. 6.2-7. John baptizes in, Mat. 3.6. Mar. 1.5. Christ was baptized in, Mat. 3.13. Mar. 1.9.

————, PLAIN OF, Lot dwelt in, Gen. 13.10-12. Cities in, see SODOM, GOMORRHA, ADMAH, ZEBOIM. Israelites pitched in, Num. 22.1. Were numbered in, Num. 26.3,63. Addressed by Moses in, Deu. 1.1. Temple vessels cast in, by Solomon, 1 Kin. 7.46. 2 Chr. 4.17.

JOSEPH, son of Jacob and Rachel, Gen. 30.24. His father's love, Gen. 33.2. Gen. 37.3,4,35. Gen. 48.22. 1 Chr. 5.2. Jno. 4.5. His brothers' hatred; his dreams; their selling his brethren, who sell him to the Ishmaelites; taken to Egypt, Gen. 37. Psa. 105.17. Act. 7.9. Is advanced by Potiphar, but through his mistress cast into prison; advanced in the

Interprets dreams, Gen. 39. Gen. 40. Psa. 105.18.

Interprets Pharaoh's dreams and becomes chief ruler, Gen. 40. Psa. 105.19-22. His marriage and sons, Gen. 41.45-52. His provision for the famine, Gen. 41.48-57. Gen. 47.13-26. His treatment of his brethren, Gen. c. 42 to 45. Meets with his father, Gen. 46.28-34. Maintains his father and brethren, Gen. 47.1-12. Act. 7.14,15. Promises to bury his father in Canaan, Gen. 47.29-31.

Brings his sons for his father's blessing, Gen. 48. Heb. 11.21. His father's blessing, Gen. 49.22-26. Mourning for, and burial of, his father, Gen. 50.1-14. Forgives his brethren, Gen. 50.15-21. Swears his brethren to take his body to Canaan, Gen. 50.24,25. Heb. 11.22. His death and embalming, Gen. 50.22-26. His body taken by the Israelites to Canaan, and buried in Machpelah, Ex. 13.19. Jos. 24.32. Act. 7.16.

JOSEPH, a carpenter, husband of Mary, Mat. 13.55. Mar. 6.3. Mat. 1.18-25. Luk. 1.27. His genealogy, Mat.1.1-16. Luk.3.23-38. Visited by an angel, Mat. 1.20-23. Goes to Bethlehem, Luk. 2.4,16. Presents Jesus in the temple, Luk. 2,22-33. Warned by an angel, flees to Egypt, Mat. 2.13-15. Commanded by an angel to return; dwells in Nazareth, Mat. 2.19-23. Searches for Jesus in the temple, Luk. 2.41-51. His character, Mat. 1.19. Luk. 2.41.

———— OF ARIMATHEA, a rich man, a councillor, begs Christ's body, and buries it in his own new tomb, Luk. 23.50-56. Mat. 27.57-60. Mar. 15.42-47. Jno. 19.38-42.

————, or BARSABAS, surnamed Justus, the lot taken between him and Matthias for the apostleship, Act. 1.23-26.

JOSES, one of Jesus' brethren, his mother's name Mary, Mat. 13.55. Mat. 27.56.

See BARNABAS.

JOSHUA, son of Nun, Num. 13.8. 1 Chr. 7.27. Moses' servant, Ex. 24.13. Ex. 32.17. Ex. 33.11. Defeats Amalekites, Ex. 17.13. His jealousy for Moses rebuked, Num. 11.28. Moses changes his name from Oshea to Jehoshua, Num. 13.16. Is one of the 12 spies; encourages the Israelites, and has a promise of entering Canaan for his fidelity, Num. 13.8. Num. 14.6-10,30,38. Num. 32.12. Deu. 1.38. Appointed Moses' successor, Num. 27.18-23. Deu. 31.23. Deu. 34.9. Is a prophet and judge, Deu. 34.9. Jos. 1.1-9. Jos. 3.7. Jos. 8.8. Jos. 10.8.

Sends spies to Jericho, Jos. 2. Miraculous passage of the Jordan; the ark carried by priests; 12 stones set up, Jos. c. 3 & 4. Circumcises the Israelites; the passover kept; manna ceases, Jos. 5.2-9. Meets the Captain of the Lord's host, Jos. 5.13. Conquest of Canaan, Jos. c. 6 to 12. Act. 7.45. Heb. 4.8. See JERICHO, AI, GIBEON, ACHAN. His prophecy against the rebuilder of Jericho, Jos.6.26. 1 Kin. 16.34. Prayer on Israel's defeat at Ai, Jos. 7.6-9. Reads the law on Ebal and Gerizim, Jos. 8.30-35.

Divides the land, Jos. c. 13 to 21. (See the separate tribes.) Exhortation to Israel, Jos. c. 23 & 24. Writes the law in a book, Jos. 24.26. His death and burial, Jos. 24.29. Jud. 2.8,9. His influence on Israel, Jos. 24.31. Jud. 2.7. His miracles; fall of Jericho's walls,

Jos. 6. Sun and moon stand still, Jos.10.12,13, Hab. 3.11.

JOSHUA THE BETHSHEMITE, in whose field the cart with the ark rested, 1 Sam. 6.14,18.

————, or JESHUA, high-priest, returns from Babylon, Ezr. 2.2. Assists to build the temple, Ezr. 3. Ezr. 5.2. Hag. 1.1,12-14. Hag. 2.2. Withstands the Samaritans, Ezr. 4.3. Symbolical prophecies respecting, Zec. 3. Zec. 6.9-15.

JOSIAH, 15th king of Judah (31 years' reign), son and successor of Amon, 2 Kin. 21.24,26. 2 Kin. 22.1. 1 Chr. 3.14. 2 Chr. 33.25. 2 Chr. 34.1. Mat. 1.10. His early piety, 2 Kin. 22.2. 2 Chr. 34.2,3. Destroys idolatry; repairs the temple; humbles himself on reading the law; sends to Huldah, 2 Kin. 22. 2 Chr. 34.1-28.

Reads the law publicly; makes a covenant with God; destroys idols; defiles the altar at Bethel, as predicted, 2 Kin. 23.1-20. 2 Chr. 34.29-33. Keeps the passover; extirpates wizards, &c.; his piety, 2 Kin. 23.21-25. 2 Chr. 35.1-19,26.

Defeated by Pharaoh-Necho; slain at Megiddo, 2 Kin. 23.29,30. 2 Chr. 35.20-24, see Zec. 12.11, Lament of Jeremiah for, 2 Chr. 35.25. Prophets in his reign, Jer.1.2. Jer. 25.3. Zeph. 1.1. Prophecy respecting, 1 Kin. 13.1-3.

JOT (Heb. *yod*, Gr. *iota*, Eng. *i*), the smallest letter in the alphabet, Mat. 5.18.

JOTHAM, Gideon's youngest son, escapes when his brothers are slaughtered by Abimelech; rebukes the Shechemites in a parable; dwells in Beer, Jud. 9.5-21.

————, 10th king of Judah (16 years' reign), judges in his father Uzziah's lifetime, 2 Kin. 15.5. 2 Chr. 26.21. Succeeds to the throne, 2 Kin. 15.32. 1 Chr. 3.12. 2 Chr. 26.23. 2 Chr. 27.1. Mat. 1.9. Repairs the temple, 2 Kin. 15.35. 2 Chr. 27.3.

Builds cities and forts, 2 Chr. 27.3,4. His piety and prosperity, 2 Kin. 15.34. 2 Chr. 27.2,6. Conquers Ammonites, 2 Chr. 27.5. Rezin and Pekah invade Judah unsuccessfully, 2 Kin. 15.37. His death, 2 Kin. 15.38. 2 Chr. 27.9.

JOY. SPIRITUAL JOY, see SPIRITUAL PEACE. JOY OF SINNERS, see WORLDLINESS.

JOZACHAR, a servant of king Joash, murders him, 2 Kin. 12.20,21. Called Zabad, 2 Chr. 24.26.

JUBAL, son of Lamech, the inventor of the harp and organ, Gen. 4.21.

JUBILEE, called Year of Liberty, Eze. 46.17. Acceptable year of the Lord, Isa. 61.2. Held every 50th year, commencing on the day of atonement; proclaimed by trumpets, Lev. 25.8-10. Redemption of all property sold or mortgaged, except dwelling-houses, Lev. 25. 10-16,23-34. Lev. 27.17-24. Num. 36.4. No field-labour on, Lev. 25.11,12. Servants released on, Lev. 25.40,41,54.

JUDAH, son of Jacob and Leah, Gen. 35.23. Sells Joseph, Gen. 37.26. His marriage and children, Gen. 38.1-5. Gen. 46.12. Num. 26.19,20. 1 Chr. 2.3,4. 1 Chr. 4.1. His fornication, Gen. 38.12-30. Becomes surety for Benjamin, Gen. 43.3-9. Pleads before Joseph,

Gen. 44.14-34. Sent by Jacob to Joseph, Gen. 46.28. Jacob's blessing on, Gen. 49.8-12.

JUDAH, TRIBE OF. Numbered in Sinai, Num. 1.26,27. Num. 2.4; and in the plain of Moab, Num. 26.22. Encamped east of the tabernacle; and led the first division, Num. 2.3,9. Num. 10.14. Blessing of Moses on, Deu. 33.7.

Their inheritance, Jos. 15. Jos. 18.5. Jos. 19.9. Led the wars against Canaan and Benjamin, Jud. 1.1-20. Jud. 20.18. The number of, in Saul's army, 1 Sam. 11.8. David reigns over for 7 years, 2 Sam. 2.11. 2 Sam. 5.5. Their reception of David after Absalom's rebellion, 2 Sam. 19.11-15,41-43. 2 Sam. 20.1,2.

Number of, in David's reign, 2 Sam. 24.9. The ruler of Israel chosen from, 1 Chr. 5.2. 1 Chr. 28.4. Psa. 60.7. Temple built in their inheritance, 1 Kin. 8.1. Psa. 78.68,69. Psa. 114.2. Form a separate kingdom under Rehoboam, see ISRAELITES, HISTORY OF, page 255. For things common to the tribes, see ISRAEL, TRIBES OF.

JUDAS OF DAMASCUS, a Jew with whom Paul lodged, Act. 9.11.

—— THE GALILEAN, his insurrection and death, Act. 5.37. See Luk. 13.1.

JUDAS ISCARIOT, an apostle, Mat. 10.4. Mar. 3.19. Luk. 6.16. Act. 1.17. Christ describes his character, Jno. 6.70. Purse-bearer; his dishonesty, Jno. 12.6. Jno. 13.29. Complains of Mary anointing Christ, Jno. 12.4,5. Christ predicts he should betray him, Mat. 26.21-25. Mar. 14.18-21. Luk. 22.21-23. Offers to betray Christ, Mat. 26.14-16. Mar. 14.10,11. Luk. 22.3-6. Jno. 13.2. Betrays Christ, Mat. 26.47-50. Mar. 14.43-45. Luk. 22.47,48. Jno. 13.30. Jno. 18.2-5. Act. 1.16,25. His remorse and suicide, Mat. 27.3-5. Act. 1.18. Prophecy respecting, Act. 1.16,20 with Psa. 41.9. Psa. 109.8.

JUDAS, or JUDE, surnamed Barsabas, a prophet sent by the apostles to Antioch with Paul; his exhortation, Act. 15.22-32.

JUDE, or JUDAS, an apostle, called Lebbeus, surnamed Thaddeus, Mat. 10.3. Mar. 3.18. Called Judas, or Jude, the brother of James, Luk. 6.16. Act. 1.13. Jude 1. Brother of the Lord, Mat. 13.55. Mar. 6.3. His question to Jesus, Jno. 14.22. His epistle, Jude 1.

JUDEA. See PALESTINE.

——, HILL-COUNTRY OF, south of Jerusalem, Jos. 20.7. Jos. 21.11. Deu. 1.20. Luk. 1.39,65.

——, WILDERNESS OF, north of the Dead Sea, Mat. 3.1. Mat. 4.1. Luk. 3.3. Jos. 15.61.

JUDGES, DUTIES OF. See RULERS—JUSTICE, ADMINISTRATION OF.

—— OF ISRAEL. See ISRAELITES, HISTORY OF, UNDER THE JUDGES.

JUDGMENT, ACCORDING TO PRIVILEGE AND WORKS. Gen. 4.7. If thou doest well, shalt thou not be accepted? and if thou doest not well, sin lieth at the door.

Job 34.11. For the work of a man shall he render unto him, and cause every man to find according to his ways.

Pro. 11.31. The righteous shall be recompensed in the earth; much more the wicked and the sinner.

Pro. 12.14. The recompence of a man's hands shall be rendered unto him.

Pro. 24.12. Doth not he that pondereth the heart consider it? and he that keepeth thy soul, doth not he know it? and shall not he render to every man according to his works? Psa. 62.12. 2 Tim. 4.14.

Isa. 3.10. Say ye to the righteous, that it shall be well with him: for they shall eat the fruit of their doings.

Isa. 5.15. The mean man shall be brought down, and the mighty man shall be humbled.

Isa. 24.2. It shall be, as with the people, so with the priest; as with the servant, so with his master; as with the maid, so with her mistress; as with the buyer, so with the seller; as with the lender, so with the borrower; as with the taker of usury, so with the giver of usury to him.

Isa. 59.18. According to their deeds, accordingly he will repay, fury to his adversaries, recompence to his enemies; to the islands he will repay recompence.

Jer. 17.10. I the Lord search the heart, I try the reins, even to give every man according to his ways, and according to the fruit of his doings.

Jer. 32.19. Thine eyes are open upon all the ways of the sons of men: to give every one according to his ways, and according to the fruit of his doings.

Eze. 7.3. I will judge thee according to thy ways, and will recompence upon thee all thine abominations. 27. I will do unto them after their way, and according to their deserts will I judge them; and they shall know that I am the Lord.

Eze. 9.6. Slay utterly old and young, both maids, and little children, and women: but come not near any man upon whom is the mark; and begin at my sanctuary.

Eze. 16.59. I will even deal with thee as thou hast done.

Eze. 18.20. The soul that sinneth, it shall die. The son shall not bear the iniquity of the father, neither shall the father bear the iniquity of the son: the righteousness of the righteous shall be upon him, and the wickedness of the wicked shall be upon him. 30. I will judge you, O house of Israel, every one according to his ways, saith the Lord God. Repent, and turn yourselves from all your transgressions; so iniquity shall not be your ruin. v. 1-30.

Eze. 33.20. Ye say, The way of the Lord is not equal. O ye house of Israel, I will judge you every one after his ways.

Eze. 39.24. According to their uncleanness and according to their transgressions have I done unto them, and hid my face from them.

Hos. 4.9. There shall be, like people, like priest: and I will punish them for their ways, and reward them their doings. Hos. 12.2.

Amos 3.2. You only have I known of all the families of the earth: therefore I will punish you for all your iniquities,

Zec. 1.6. Like as the Lord of hosts thought to do unto us, according to our ways, and according to our doings, so hath he dealt with us.

Mat. 10.14. Whosoever shall not receive you, nor hear your words, when ye depart out of that house or city, shake off the dust of your feet. 15. It shall be more tolerable for the land of Sodom and Gomorrha in the day of judgment, than for that city. Mat. 11.24. Mar. 6.11. Luk. 9.5. Luk. 10.12-15.

Mat. 12.37. By thy words thou shalt be justified, and by thy words thou shalt be condemned.

Mar. 14.21. The Son of man indeed goeth, as it is written of him : but woe to that man by whom the Son of man is betrayed ! good were it for that man if he had never been born.

Luk. 11.49. I will send them prophets and apostles, and *some* of them they shall slay and persecute : 50. That the blood of all the prophets, which was shed from the foundation of the world, may be required of this generation. *v.* 51.

Luk. 12.47. That servant, which knew his lord's will, and prepared not *himself*, neither did according to his will, shall be beaten with many *stripes*. 48. But he that knew not, and did commit things worthy of stripes, shall be beaten with few *stripes*. For unto whomsoever much is given, of him shall be much required : and to whom men have committed much, of him they will ask the more. (See Parable of the Vineyard, Isa. 5.1-6. Of the Husbandman, Isa. 28.24-28. Of the Wicked Husbandmen, Mat. 21.33-36. Of the Talents, Mat. 25.14-30.)

Jno. 3.19. This is the condemnation, that light is come into the world, and men loved darkness rather than light, because their deeds were evil.

Jno. 5.45. Do not think that I will accuse you to the Father : there is *one* that accuseth you, *even* Moses, in whom ye trust.

Jno. 9.41. If ye were blind, ye should have no sin : but now ye say, We see ; therefore your sin remaineth.

Jno. 12.48. He that rejecteth me, and receiveth not my words, hath one that judgeth him : the word that I have spoken, the same shall judge him in the last day.

Jno. 15.22. If I had not come and spoken unto them, they had not had sin : but now they have no cloke for their sin. 24. If I had not done among them the works which none other man did, they had not had sin : but now have they both seen and hated both me and my Father.

Rom. 2.9. Tribulation and anguish, upon every soul of man that doeth evil, of the Jew first, and also of the Gentile. 10. Glory, honour, and peace, to every man that worketh good, to the Jew first, and also to the Gentile : 11. For there is no respect of persons with God. 12. As many as have sinned without law shall also perish without law : and as many as have sinned in the law shall be judged by the law. 27. Shall not uncircumcision which is by nature, if it fulfil the law, judge thee, who by the letter and circumcision dost transgress the law ?

1 Cor. 3.8. Every man shall receive his own reward according to his own labour. 13. Every man's work shall be made manifest : for the day shall declare it, because it shall be revealed by fire ; and the fire shall try every man's work of what sort it is. 14. If any man's work abide which he hath built thereupon, he shall receive a reward. 15. If any man's work shall be burned, he shall suffer loss : but he himself shall be saved ; yet so as by fire. *v.* 12.

2 Cor. 2.16. To the one *we are* the savour

of death unto death ; and to the other the savour of life unto life.

2 Cor. 11.15. Whose end shall be according to their works.

Gal. 6.5. Every man shall bear his own burden. 7. Be not deceived ; God is not mocked ; for whatsoever a man soweth, that shall he also reap. 8. For he that soweth to his flesh shall of the flesh reap corruption ; but he that soweth to the Spirit shall of the Spirit reap life everlasting.

Eph. 6.8. Whatsoever good thing any man doeth, the same shall he receive of the Lord, whether *he be* bond or free.

Col. 3.25. He that doeth wrong shall receive for the wrong which he hath done : and there is no respect of persons.

1 Tim. 1.13. I obtained mercy, because I did it ignorantly in unbelief.

Heb. 2.2. If the word spoken by angels was stedfast, and every transgression and disobedience received a just recompence of reward ; 3. How shall we escape, if we neglect so great salvation ?

Heb. 10.26. If we sin wilfully after that we have received the knowledge of the truth, there remaineth no more sacrifice for sins. 29. Of how much sorer punishment, suppose ye, shall he be thought worthy, who hath trodden under foot the Son of God, and hath counted the blood of the covenant, wherewith he was sanctified, an unholy thing, and hath done despite unto the Spirit of grace ?

Heb. 12.25. If they escaped not who refused him that spake on earth, much more *shall not* we *escape*, if we turn away from him that *speaketh* from heaven.

Jas. 2.12. So speak ye, and so do, as they that shall be judged by the law of liberty. 13. He shall have judgment without mercy, that hath shewed no mercy.

1 Pet. 1.17. The Father, who without respect of persons judgeth according to every man's work.

2 Pet. 2.21. It had been better for them not to have known the way of righteousness, than, after they have known *it*, to turn from the holy commandment delivered unto them.

Rev. 2.23. I will give unto every one of you according to your works.

See SIN, FRUITS OF.

JUDGMENT - DAY — THE LAST DAY. Job 21.30. The wicked is reserved to the day of destruction ? they shall be brought forth to the day of wrath.

Psa. 102.26. They shall perish, but thou shalt endure : yea, all of them shall wax old like a garment ; as a vesture shalt thou change them, and they shall be changed.

Ecc. 3.17. God shall judge the righteous and the wicked : for *there is* a time there for every purpose, and for every work.

Ecc. 11.9. Walk in the ways of thine heart, and in the sight of thine eyes : but know thou, that for all these *things* God will bring thee into judgment.

Ecc. 12.14. God shall bring every work into judgment, with every secret thing, whether *it be* good, or whether *it be* evil.

Isa. 34.4. And all the host of heaven shall be dissolved, and the heavens shall be rolled together as a scroll ; and all their host shall fall down, as the leaf falleth off from the vine, and as a falling *fig* from the fig-tree.

Isa. 13.9-14. Isa. 24.18-20. Isa. 65.17. Joel 2.10,31.

Isa. 51.6. The heavens shall vanish away like smoke, and the earth shall wax old like a garment.

Dan. 7.9. I beheld till the thrones were cast down, and the Ancient of days did sit, whose garment *was* white as snow, and the hair of his head like the pure wool : his throne *was like* the fiery flame, *and* his wheels *as* burning fire. 10. A fiery stream issued and came forth from before him : thousand thousands ministered unto him, and ten thousand times ten thousand stood before him : the judgment was set, and the books were opened.

Joel 3.15. The sun and the moon shall be darkened, and the stars shall withdraw their shining. 16. The Lord also shall roar out of Zion, and utter his voice from Jerusalem ; and the heavens and the earth shall shake : but the Lord *will be* the hope of his people, and the strength of the children of Israel.

Mat. 7.22. Many will say to me in that day, Lord, Lord, have we not prophesied in thy name ? and in thy name have we not cast out devils ? and in thy name done many wonderful works ? 23. And then will I profess unto them, I never knew you : depart from me, ye that work iniquity.

Mat. 11.22. It shall be more tolerable for Tyre and Sidon at the day of judgment, than for you. Mat. 10.15.

Mat. 12.36. Every idle word that men shall speak, they shall give account thereof in the day of judgment. 37. For by thy words thou shalt be justified, and by thy words thou shalt be condemned. 41. The men of Nineveh shall rise in judgment with this generation, and shall condemn it : because they repented at the preaching of Jonas ; and, behold, a greater than Jonas *is* here. *v.* 42. Luk. 11.31,32.

Mat. 13.30. In the time of harvest I will say to the reapers, Gather ye together first the tares, and bind them in bundles to burn them : but gather the wheat into my barn. 40. As therefore the tares are gathered and burned in the fire ; so shall it be in the end of this world. 41. The Son of man shall send forth his angels, and they shall gather out of his kingdom all things that offend, and them which do iniquity; 42. And shall cast them into a furnace of fire : there shall be wailing and gnashing of teeth. 43. Then shall the righteous shine forth as the sun in the kingdom of their Father. *v.* 48-50.

Mat. 16.27. The Son of man shall come in the glory of his Father with his angels ; and then he shall reward every man according to his works. Mar. 8.38.

Mat 22.13. Then said the king to the servants, Bind him hand and foot, and take him away, and cast *him* into outer darkness ; there shall be weeping and gnashing of teeth. *v.* 11-13.

Mat. 24.29. Immediately after the tribulation of those days shall the sun be darkened, and the moon shall not give her light, and the stars shall fall from heaven, and the powers of the heavens shall be shaken : 30. And then shall appear the sign of the Son of man in heaven ; and then shall all the tribes of the earth mourn, and they shall see the Son of man coming in the clouds of heaven with power and great glory. 31. And he shall send his angels with a great sound of a trumpet, and they shall gather together his elect from the four winds, from one end of heaven to the other. 35. Heaven and earth shall pass away, but my words shall not pass away.

Mat. 25.31. When the Son of man shall come in his glory, and all the holy angels with him, then shall he sit upon the throne of his glory : 32. And before him shall be gathered all nations : and he shall separate them one from another, as a shepherd divideth *his* sheep from the goats : 33. And he shall set the sheep on his right hand, but the goats on the left.

Luk. 12.2. There is nothing covered, that shall not be revealed ; neither hid, that shall not be known.

Jno. 12.48. He that rejecteth me, and receiveth not my words, hath one that judgeth him : the word that I have spoken, the same shall judge him in the last day.

Act. 17.31. He hath appointed a day, in the which he will judge the world in righteousness by *that* man whom he hath ordained.

Act. 24.25. As he reasoned of righteousness, temperance, and judgment to come, Felix trembled.

Rom. 2.5. After thy hardness and impenitent heart treasurest up unto thyself wrath against the day of wrath and revelation of the righteous judgment of God ; 6. Who will render to every man according to his deeds : 16. In the day when God shall judge the secrets of men by Jesus Christ according to my gospel.

Rom. 14.10. We shall all stand before the judgment-seat of Christ. 11. *As* I live, saith the Lord, every knee shall bow to me, and every tongue shall confess to God. 12. So then every one of us shall give account of himself to God.

1 Cor. 3.13. Every man's work shall be made manifest : for the day shall declare it, because it shall be revealed by fire ; and the fire shall try every man's work of what sort it is.

1 Cor. 4.5. Judge nothing before the time, until the Lord come, who both will bring to light the hidden things of darkness, and will make manifest the counsels of the hearts : and then shall every man have praise of God.

1 Cor. 6.2. Do ye not know that the saints shall judge the world? and if the world shall be judged by you, are ye unworthy to judge the smallest matters? 3. Know ye not that we shall judge angels?

2 Cor. 5.10. We must all appear before the judgment-seat of Christ ; that every one may receive the things *done in his* body, according to that he hath done, whether *it be* good or bad.

2 The. 1.7. To you who are troubled rest with us, when the Lord Jesus shall be revealed from heaven with his mighty angels, 8. In flaming fire taking vengeance on them that know not God, and that obey not the gospel.

2 Tim. 4.1. The Lord Jesus Christ, who shall judge the quick and the dead at his appearing and his kingdom. 8. There is laid up for me a crown of righteousness, which the Lord, the righteous judge, shall give me at that day : and not to me only, but unto all them also that love his appearing.

Heb. 6.2. The doctrine of eternal judgment.

Heb. 9.27. It is appointed unto men once to die, but after this the judgment.

Heb. 10.27. A certain fearful looking for of judgment and fiery indignation, which shall devour the adversaries.

1 Pet. 4.5. Who shall give account to him that is ready to judge the quick and the dead. 7. The end of all things is at hand: be ye therefore sober, and watch unto prayer.

2 Pet. 2.4. God spared not the angels that sinned, but cast *them* down to hell, and delivered *them* into chains of darkness, to be reserved unto judgment. 9. The Lord knoweth how to reserve the unjust unto the day of judgment to be punished.

2 Pet. 3.7. The heavens and the earth, which are now, by the same word are kept in store, reserved unto fire against the day of judgment and perdition of ungodly men. 10. The day of the Lord will come as a thief in the night; in the which the heavens shall pass away with a great noise, and the elements shall melt with fervent heat, the earth also and the works that are therein shall be burned up. 11. *Seeing* then *that* all these things shall be dissolved, what manner *of persons* ought ye to be. 12. Looking for and hasting unto the coming of the day of God, wherein the heavens being on fire shall be dissolved, and the elements shall melt with fervent heat?

1 Jno. 4.17. That we may have boldness in the day of judgment.

Jude 6. The angels which kept not their first estate, but left their own habitation, he hath reserved in everlasting chains under darkness unto the judgment of the great day. 14. Behold, the Lord cometh with ten thousands of his saints, 15. To execute judgment upon all, and to convince all that are ungodly among them of all their ungodly deeds which they have ungodly committed, and of all their hard *speeches* which ungodly sinners have spoken against him. 24. Him that is able to present *you* faultless before the presence of his glory with exceeding joy.

Rev. 1.7. Behold, he cometh with clouds; and every eye shall see him, and they *also* which pierced him: and all kindreds of the earth shall wail because of him.

Rev. 6.15. The kings of the earth, and the great men, and the rich men, and the chief captains, and the mighty men, and every bondman, and every freeman, hid themselves in the dens and in the rocks of the mountains; 16. And said to the mountains and rocks, Fall on us, and hide us from the face of him that sitteth on the throne, and from the wrath of the Lamb: 17. For the great day of his wrath is come; and who shall be able to stand?

Rev. 11.18. The nations were angry, and thy wrath is come, and the time of the dead, that they should be judged, and that thou shouldest give reward unto thy servants the prophets, and to the saints, and them that fear thy name, small and great; and shouldest destroy them which destroy the earth.

Rev. 20.11. I saw a great white throne, and him that sat on it, from whose face the earth and the heaven fled away; and there was found no place for them. 12. And I saw the dead, small and great, stand before God; and the books were opened: and another book was opened, which is *the book* of life: and the dead were judged out of those things which were written in the books, according to their works. 13. And the sea gave up the dead which were in it; and death and hell delivered up the dead which were in them: and they were judged every man according to their works. 14. And death and hell were cast into the lake of fire. This is the second death. 15. And whosoever was not found written in the book of life was cast into the lake of fire.

Rev. 22.12. Behold, I come quickly; and my reward *is* with me, to give every man according as his work shall be.

See GOD JUDGE, CHRIST JUDGE—CHRIST, SECOND COMING OF—RESURRECTION.

JUDGMENT-HALL. See PRETORIUM.

JUDGMENT-SEAT. Mat. 27.19. Act. 18.12. Act. 25.10; of Christ, Rom. 14.10.

JUDGMENTS, DESIGN AND EFFECT OF, Ex. 7.3-5. Ex. 9.14,16. Ex. 10.1-4. Ex. 11.9. Ex. 14.17,18,31. Ex. 15.6,7. Ex. 16.14-16. Ex. 18.11. Ex. 34.10. Lev. 10.3. Num. 14.21-23. Deu. 28.46. Deu. 29.22-28. Neh. 9.10. Job 22.19. Psa. 9.16,20. Psa. 46.8-10. Psa. 59.13. Psa. 64.9. Psa. 76.10. Psa. 83.16-18. Psa. 97.8. Psa. 119.119,120. Psa. 141.6. Pro. 16.4. Isa. 2.17-21. Isa. 5.16. Isa. 25.2,3. Isa. 5².6. Isa. 64.2. Jer. 22.8,9. Eze. 5.15. Eze. 6.7,10. Eze. 28.22. Eze. 32.10. Eze. 33.33. Eze. 38.22,23. Eze. 39.6,7,21-23. Dan. 4.17. Hab. 3.16. Mal. 1.5. Rom. 9.17,22. 1 Cor. 10.6,11. 1 Pet. 4.17,18. Rev. 11.13. Rev. 15.4.

See AFFLICTION, ITS BENEFITS.

—————— FROM GOD. See FAMINE, PESTILENCE, WAR.

JULIUS, a centurion who had charge of Paul; his kindness, Act. 27. Act. 28.16.

JUNIA (Gr. *Junias*), a kinsman of Paul, and a disciple, Rom. 16.7.

JUNIPER (a kind of broom), a tree affording shelter to Elijah, 1 Kin. 19.4,5. Used for fuel, Psa. 120.4. Roots in famine used as food, Job 30.4.

JUPITER (Gr. *Zeus*), a heathen god, worshipped at Lycaonia; Barnabas supposed to be, Act. 14.11-13.

JUSTICE, ADMINISTRATION OF. At the tabernacle, Num. 27.2. Parties pleaded their own cause, Ex. 18.13. 2 Sam. 15.2. 1 Kin. 3.16-28. Mat. 26.62. Act. 26.1. Accusers and accused required to appear, Act. 25.16. Investigation of crime instituted, Est. 2.21-23. Advocates employed, Act. 24.1. Torture employed, Act. 22.24.

See WITNESSES, APPEAL, KINGS, RULERS—PRIEST, HIGH-PRIEST, JUDICIAL AUTHORITY OF—PUNISHMENTS.

—————— COMMANDED. See INTEGRITY—POOR, JUSTICE TO—RULERS.

JUSTIFICATION BY FAITH. Gen. 15.6. He believed in the Lord; and he counted it to him for righteousness. Rom. 4.3.

Psa. 32.2. Blessed *is* the man unto whom the Lord imputeth not iniquity. Rom. 4.6.

Psa. 71.16. I will go in the strength of the Lord God: I will make mention of thy righteousness, *even* of thine only.

Psa. 89.16. In thy name shall they rejoice all the day: and in thy righteousness shall they be exalted.

Isa. 42.21. The Lord is well pleased for his righteousness' sake; he will magnify the law, and make *it* honourable.

Isa. 45.24. In the Lord have I righteousness

and strength: even to him shall men come. 25. In the Lord shall all the seed of Israel be justified, and shall glory.

Isa. 46.12. Hearken unto me, ye stouthearted, that are far from righteousness: 13. I bring near my righteousness; it shall not be far off, and my salvation shall not tarry: and I will place salvation in Zion for Israel my glory.

Isa. 50.8. He is near that justifieth me; who will contend with me? let us stand together: who is mine adversary? let him come near to me.

Isa. 51.5. My righteousness is near; my salvation is gone forth, and mine arms shall judge the people; the isles shall wait upon me, and on mine arm shall they trust. 6. The heavens shall vanish away like smoke, and the earth shall wax old like a garment, and they that dwell therein shall die in like manner: but my salvation shall be for ever, and my righteousness shall not be abolished.

Isa. 53.11. By his knowledge shall my righteous servant justify many; for he shall bear their iniquities.

Isa. 54.17. This is the heritage of the servants of the Lord, and their righteousness is of me, saith the Lord.

Isa. 56.1. My salvation is near to come, and my righteousness to be revealed.

Isa. 61.10. My soul shall be joyful in my God: for he hath clothed me with the garments of salvation, he hath covered me with the robe of righteousness, as a bridegroom decketh himself with ornaments, and as a bride adorneth herself with her jewels.

Jer. 23.6. In his days Judah shall be saved, and Israel shall dwell safely: and this is his name whereby he shall be called, THE LORD OUR RIGHTEOUSNESS.

Zec. 3.4. Take away the filthy garments from him. And unto him he said, Behold, I have caused thine iniquity to pass from thee, and I will clothe thee with change of raiment.

Jno. 5.24. He that heareth my word, and believeth on him that sent me, hath everlasting life, and shall not come into condemnation; but is passed from death unto life.

Act. 13.39. By him all that believe are justified from all things, from which ye could not be justified by the law of Moses.

Rom. 1.16. For I am not ashamed of the gospel of Christ; for it is the power of God unto salvation to every one that believeth; to the Jew first, and also to the Greek. 17. For therein is the righteousness of God revealed from faith to faith: as it is written, The just shall live by faith.

Rom. 3.21. The righteousness of God without the law is manifested, being witnessed by the law and the prophets; 22. Even the righteousness of God which is by faith of Jesus Christ unto all and upon all them that believe: for there is no difference. 24. Being justified freely by his grace through the redemption that is in Christ Jesus: 25. Whom God hath set forth to be a propitiation through faith in his blood, to declare his righteousness for the remission of sins that are past, through the forbearance of God; 26. To declare at this time his righteousness: that he might be just, and the justifier of him which believeth in Jesus.

Rom. 3.28. A man is justified by faith without the deeds of the law. 30. It is one God, which shall justify the circumcision by faith, and uncircumcision through faith.

Rom. 4.13. The promise, that he should be the heir of the world, was not to Abraham, or to his seed, through the law, but through the righteousness of faith. 16. It is of faith, that it might be by grace; to the end the promise might be sure to all the seed; not to that only which is of the law, but to that also which is of the faith of Abraham; who is the father of us all. 20. He staggered not at the promise of God through unbelief; but was strong in faith, giving glory to God; 21. And being fully persuaded that, what he had promised, he was able also to perform. 22. And therefore it was imputed to him for righteousness. 24. To whom it shall be imputed, if we believe on him that raised up Jesus our Lord from the dead; 25. Who was delivered for our offences, and was raised again for our justification. v. 2-12.

Rom. 5.1. Being justified by faith, we have peace with God through our Lord Jesus Christ: 9. Being now justified by his blood, we shall be saved from wrath through him. 11. We also joy in God through our Lord Jesus Christ, by whom we have now received the atonement. 16. The free gift is of many offences unto justification. 17. For if by one man's offence death reigned by one; much more they which receive abundance of grace, and of the gift of righteousness, shall reign in life by one, Jesus Christ.

Rom. 5.18. Therefore, as by the offence of one judgment came upon all men to condemnation; even so by the righteousness of one the free gift came upon all men unto justification of life. 21. That as sin hath reigned unto death, even so might grace reign through righteousness unto eternal life by Jesus Christ our Lord. v. 12-21.

Rom. 7.4. Ye also are become dead to the law by the body of Christ; that ye should be married to another, even to him who is raised from the dead, that we should bring forth fruit unto God. v. 1-25.

Rom. 8.1. There is therefore now no condemnation to them which are in Christ Jesus, who walk not after the flesh, but after the Spirit. 30. Whom he called, them he also justified; and whom he justified, them he also glorified. 31. What shall we then say to these things? If God be for us, who can be against us? 33. Who shall lay any thing to the charge of God's elect? It is God that justifieth. 34. Who is he that condemneth? It is Christ that died, yea rather, that is risen again.

Rom. 9.30. The Gentiles, which followed not after righteousness, have attained to righteousness, even the righteousness which is of faith. 31. Israel, which followed after the law of righteousness, hath not attained to the law of righteousness. 32. Wherefore? Because they sought it not by faith, but as it were by the works of the law.

Rom. 10.4. Christ is the end of the law for righteousness to every one that believeth. 6. The righteousness which is of faith speaketh on this wise, 8. The word is nigh thee, even in thy mouth, and in thy heart: that is, the word of faith, which we preach; 9. That if thou shalt confess with thy mouth the Lord Jesus, and shalt believe in thine heart that God hath raised him from the dead, thou shalt be saved. 10. For with the heart man believ-eth unto righteousness ; and with the mouth confession is made unto salvation. 11. For the scripture saith, Whosoever believeth on him shall not be ashamed. *v.* 1-21.

1 Cor. 1.30. Christ, who of God is made unto us wisdom and righteousness.

1 Cor. 6.11. Ye are justified in the name of the Lord Jesus, and by the Spirit of our God.

2 Cor. 5.19. God was in Christ, reconciling the world unto himself, not imputing their tres-passes unto them ; and hath committed unto us the word of reconciliation. 21. He hath made him *to be* sin for us, who knew no sin ; that we might be made the righteousness of God in him.

Gal. 2.16. A man is not justified by the works of the law, but by the faith of Jesus Christ, even we have believed in Jesus Christ, that we might be justified by the faith of Christ, and not by the works of the law : for by the works of the law shall no flesh be jus-tified. *v.* 14-21.

Gal. 3.8. The scripture, foreseeing that God would justify the heathen through faith, 9. They which be of faith are blessed with faithful Abraham. 21. If there had been a law given which could have given life, verily righteousness should have been by the law. 22. But the scripture hath concluded all under sin, that the promise by faith of Jesus Christ might be given to them that believe. 24. The law was our schoolmaster *to bring us* unto Christ, that we might be justified by faith. Gal. 4.21-31.

Gal. 5.4. Christ is become of no effect unto you, whosoever of you are justified by the law ; ye are fallen from grace. 5. For we through the Spirit wait for the hope of righteousness by faith. 6. For in Jesus Christ neither cir-cumcision availeth any thing, nor uncircum-cision ; but faith which worketh by love.

Eph. 6.14. Having on the breastplate of righteousness.

Phil. 3.9. Be found in him, not having mine own righteousness, which is of the law, but that which is through the faith of Christ, the righteousness which is of God by faith.

Col. 2.14. Blotting out the handwriting of ordinances that was against us, which was contrary to us, and took it out of the way, nailing it to his cross.

Tit. 3.7. Being justified by his grace, we should be made heirs according to the hope of eternal life.

Heb. 11.4. By faith Abel offered unto God a more excellent sacrifice than Cain, by which he obtained witness that he was righteous, God testifying of his gifts. 7. By faith Noah, being warned of God of things not seen as yet, moved with fear, prepared an ark to the saving of his house ; by the which he condemned the world, and became heir of the righteousness which is by faith.

Jas. 2.20. Faith without works is dead. 21. Was not Abraham our father justified by works, when he had offered Isaac his son upon the altar ? 22. Seest thou how faith wrought with his works, and by works was faith made perfect ? 23. And the scripture was fulfilled which saith, Abraham believed God, and it was imputed unto him for righteousness : and he was called the Friend of God. 26. For as

the body without the spirit is dead, so faith without works is dead also.

See FAITH. SALVATION—WORKS, INSUFFI-CIENCY OF.

JUSTUS, a disciple at Corinth with whom Paul lodged, Act. 18.7.

K

KADESH, or KADESH-BARNEA, in the desert of Paran, Num. 13.26 ; of Zin, Num. 20.1. Num. 33.36. Inhabited by Amorites ; sacked by Chedorlaomer, Gen. 14.7. Well of Beer-lahai-roi near, Gen. 16.14. Abraham dwells near, Gen. 20.1. Israelites encamp by, twice, see ISRAELITES, HISTORY OF, page 255. Formed the south boundary of Israel, Num. 34.4 ; of Judah, Jos. 15.3. Joshua defeats the Canaanites in, Jos. 10.41.

KADMONITES, their land promised to Abraham's posterity, Gen. 15.19.

KANAH, a small river, the boundary be-tween Ephraim and Manasseh, Jos. 16.8. Jos. 17.9.

KEDAR, son of Ishmael, Gen. 25.13. 1 Chr. 1.29 ; and name of an Arabian tribe, Psa. 120.5. Black tents of, Song 1.5. Merchandise of, Eze. 27.21. Idolatry of, Jer. 2.10. Prophecies of, Isa. 21.16,17. Isa. 42.11. Isa. 60.7. Jer. 49.28.

KEDEMOTH, a Levitical city of Reuben, near the Arnon, Jos. 13.18. Jos. 21.37. 1 Chr. 6.79. Wilderness of, an encampment of the Israelites, Deu. 2.26.

KEDESH, a city of Naphtali, Jos. 19.37. Jos. 12.22. A Levitical city of refuge, Jos. 20.7. Jos. 21.32. 1 Chr. 6.76. Barak lived and assembled his army at, Jud. 4.6,9. Heber the Kenite lived at, Jud. 4.11. Taken by Tiglath, 2 Kin. 15.29.

———, a city of Judah, Jos. 15.23.

KEDRON. See CEDRON.

KEILAH, a city of Judah, Jos. 15.44. Besieged by the Philistines and relieved by David, 1 Sam. 23.1-6. Saul seeks David in, 1 Sam. 23.7-13.

KENITES, their land given to Abraham, Gen. 15.19. Prophecy of, by Balaam, Num. 24.21-23.

———, descendants of Hobab, the father-in-law of Moses, lived among the Israelites, Jud. 1.16. Jud. 4.11,17. (Hobab is called a Midianite, Num. 10.29, see JETHRO.) Dwell among the Amalekites ; spared by Saul, 1 Sam. 15.6. Dwell among the Israelites, 1 Chr. 2.55. David sends presents to, 1 Sam. 30.29.

KENIZZITES, their land promised to Abraham, Gen. 15.19.

KERIOTH, a city of Judah, Jos. 15.25. Possessed by Moab, Jer. 48.24,41. Amos 2.2.

KETURAH, Abraham's second wife ; her descendants, Gen. 25.1-4.

KEY, Jud. 3.25. Laying of, upon the shoulders, a symbol of authority, Isa. 22.22 ; also having the keys, Mat. 16.19. Rev. 1.18. Rev. 3.7. Rev. 9.1. Rev. 20.1. Illustrative, Luk. 11.52.

KIBROTH-HATTAAVAH, quails sent to the Israelites at ; a plague at, Num. 11.31-35. Num. 33.16,17. Deu. 9.22.

KINDNESS. See Love.

KINGDOM of Christ. See Church, prophecies of—Christ king.

KINGS. Titles of, 1 Sam. 24.8. Ezr. 7.12. Dan. 2.37. Eze. 26.7. See Cesar.

Subjects bowed before, Gen. 41.43. 2 Sam. 9.6. 1 Kin. 1.16,23,31. Mat. 27.29. In Persia, appeared only when called ; golden sceptre held out to, Est. 4.11. Salutations to, 1 Sam. 25.41. 2 Sam. 9.8. 2 Sam. 14.17,20. 2 Sam. 19.27,28. 1 Kin. 1.47. Job 34.18. Dan. 2.4. Act. 12.22. Royal apparel, 1 Kin. 22.30. Mat. 6.29, see Crown, Sceptre, Seal. Bracelets, 2 Sam. 1.10. Courtiers richly dressed, Gen. 41.14. Est. 4.2. Est. 5.1. Luk. 7.25. Leaned on courtier's hand, 2 Kin. 5.18. 2 Kin. 7.17.

Had state horses, mules, and asses, Jud. 5.10. Jud. 12.14. 1 Kin. 1.33. Est. 6.8. Attendants stood in the royal presence, 1 Kin. 10.8. 1 Kin. 12.6. Shield borne before, 1 Kin. 14.28.

Revenues obtained by confiscations, 2 Sam. 16.4. 1 Kin. 21.16. Voluntary presents, 1 Sam. 10.27. 1 Sam. 16.20. 1 Kin. 10.2. 1 Chr. 12.40. Mat. 2.11. Commerce, 1 Kin. 10.15,28. 1 Kin. 22.48. Spoils of war, 2 Sam. 12.30. 1 Chr. 26.27. 2 Chr. 24.23. Royal estates, 1 Chr. 27.25-31. 2 Chr. 26.10. 2 Chr. 32.29. Royalty of lands in Egypt, Gen. 47.23-26. See Tribute.

Officers of prince, chief-ruler or counsellor, Gen. 41.40. 1 Kin. 4.5. 1 Chr. 27.33. 2 Chr. 19.11. 2 Chr. 28.7. Est. 10.3. Overseer of the household, 1 Kin. 4.6. 2 Chr. 28.7 ; of tribute, 1 Kin. 12.18 ; of royal farms, &c., 1 Chr. 27.26-31 ; of wardrobe, 2 Kin. 22.14 ; of stores, 1 Chr. 27.25. Purveyors for royal table, 1 Kin. 4.7-19. Posts, 2 Chr. 30.6,10. Est. 8.10. Runners, 1 Kin. 1.5. Watchmen, 2 Sam. 13.34. 2 Sam. 18.24. 2 Kin. 9.17-20. Guards, 2 Kin. 11.5-8. 2 Sam. 8.18. 2 Sam. 15.18. 2 Sam. 20.23. 1 Chr. 11.25. Porters, 2 Sam. 18.26. 2 Kin. 7.11.

See Captain, Scribe, Recorder, Treasurer, Magicians, Armour-bearer, Baker, Butler, Chamberlain, Chancellor, Counsellor, Ambassador, Deputy.

Authority absolute, Dan. 5.18,19. Controlled by counsellors, Dan. 6.6-16. Est. 1.18-22.

Appointed officers of state to ride in state, Gen. 41.43. Est. 6.8-11 ; to wear a gold chain, Gen. 41.42. Dan. 5.29 ; and royal apparel, Est. 8.15. Est. 6.8. Dan. 5.7 ; and the king's signet, Gen. 41.42. Est. 3.10. Est. 8.2.

Decrees of, sealed, Est. 8.8,10, see Proclamations. Records of, kept in royal treasury, Ezr. 5.17. Ezr. 6.1. Est. 6.1. Est. 10.2. History of, written, see Books. Royal storehouses and cities, Gen. 41.35. Ex. 1.11. 1 Kin. 9.19. 2 Chr. 32.27.

KINGS of Israel, chosen by God, Deu. 17.15. 1 Sam. 9.16,17. 1 Sam. 16.12. 1 Chr. 22.10. Hos. 13.11. By lot, 1 Sam. 10.20,21. Not to be foreigners, Deu. 17.15. Hereditary in David's line, 2 Sam. 7.12-16. Psa. 89.35-37. Successor named by king, 1 Kin. 1.17,20. 2 Chr. 11.22,23.

Anointed, see Anointing. Crowned, 1 Kin. 1.33. 2 Kin. 11.12. Enthroned, 1 Kin. 1.35. 2 Chr. 23.20. Kissed, 1 Sam. 10.1. Psa. 2.12. Rode in state, 1 Kin. 1.33. Proclamation of, made with trumpets, 2 Sam. 15.10. 1 Kin. 1.34. 2 Kin. 9.13.

Coronation of, celebrated by sacrifices, 1 Sam. 11.15 ; by feasting and music, 1 Kin. 1.9,40,41. 1 Chr. 12.39,40 ; by acclamations, 1 Sam. 10.24. 1 Kin. 1.25,39. 2 Kin. 11.12 ; by oath of allegiance, 2 Kin. 11.4.

Required to govern by law, 1 Sam. 10.25. 2 Sam. 5.3. Deu. 17.18. 2 Kin. 11.12,17. 2 Chr. 23.11. Had the power of life and death, 1 Sam. 22.17,18. 2 Sam. 1.15. 2 Sam. 4.12. 1 Kin. 2.23-31. Forbidden to multiply wives, &c., Deu. 17.16,17, see Polygamy.

Judged at the gate, 2 Sam. 15.2, see Throne. Connection of, with public worship, see David, Solomon, Hezekiah, Josiah. Duties of, see Rulers.

KINGS of Israel and Judah. See Israelites' history.

KING'S DALE, Gen. 14.17. 2 Sam. 18.18.

KIR, a country to which Tiglath carried the Damascenes, 2 Kin. 16.9. Prophecies of, Isa. 22.6. Amos 1.5. Amos 9.7.

KIR-HERES, or Kir-Hareseth, a city of Moab, captured by Jehoram, 2 Kin. 3.25. Prophecies of, Isa. 15.1. Isa. 16.7,11. Jer. 48. 31,36.

KIRJATHAIM, a town east of Jordan, belonging to the Emims, Gen. 14.5. Rebuilt by the Reubenites, Num. 32.37. Jos. 13.19. Prophecies against, when possessed by the Moabites, Jer. 48.1,23. Eze. 25.9.

————, a Levitical city of Naphtali, 1 Chr. 6.76.

KIRJATH-ARBA. See Hebron.

KIRJATH-HUZOTH, a city of Moab to which Balak brought Balaam, Num. 22.39.

KIRJATH-JEARIM, or Baalah (city of the wood), a city belonging to the Gibeonites, Jos. 9.17. Given to Judah, Jos. 15.9,60. Jos. 18.14. The ark remains 20 years in, 1 Sam. 6.21. 1 Sam. 7.1,2. 1 Chr. 13.5,6. 2 Chr. 1.4. See Psa. 132.6. Inhabited after the captivity, Ezr. 2.25. Neh. 7.29. Urijah the prophet from, Jer. 26.20.

KIRJATH-SANNAH, or Sepher. See Debir.

KISH, son of Ner, and father of Saul, 1 Sam. 9.1. 1 Sam. 14.51.

KISHON, a river falling into the sea north of Carmel ; Sisera's army destroyed in, Jud. 4.7,13. Jud. 5.21. Psa. 83.9. Elijah slays Baal's prophets at, 1 Kin. 18.40.

KISS, a mode of salutation on meeting, Gen. 27.26,27. Gen. 29.11. Gen. 48.10. Gen. 50.1. Ex. 18.7 ; on parting, Gen. 31.55. Ruth 1.14. 2 Sam. 19.39. Act. 20.37 ; on reconciliation, Gen. 33.4. 2 Sam. 14.33. Luk. 15.20. A mark of homage, Psa. 2.12. 1 Sam. 10.1. Pro. 24.26 ; of honour, Pro. 24.26. Kissing the feet, Luk. 7.38 ; the ground, Psa. 72.9. Isa. 49.23. Mic. 7.17. A holy kiss, Rom. 16.16. 1 The. 5.26. A kiss of love, 1 Pet. 5.14. A treacherous kiss, Pro. 27.6. 2 Sam. 20.9. Luk. 22.48. Idolatrous, Job 31.27. Hos. 13.2.

KITE, Lev. 11.14. Deu. 14.13. Translated vulture, Job 28.7.

KNEADING - TROUGH, Ex. 8.3. Ex. 12.34. Translated store, Deu. 28.5,17.

KNIFE, Gen. 22.6. 1 Kin. 18.28. Ezr. 1.9.

Of flint, Jos. 5.2 (marg.). A penknife (the knife of a writer), Jer. 36.23.

KNOWLEDGE. See WISDOM, SELF-EXAMINATION.

KOA (a prince?), Eze. 23.23.

KOHATH, second son of Levi, Gen. 46.11. Ex. 6.16. His posterity, Ex. 6.18. Num. 3.19,27. See LEVITES, DIVISIONS OF.

KORAH, grandson of Kohath, and cousin of Moses, Ex. 6.18,20,21. His rebellion ; destroyed by an earthquake, Num. 16. Num. 26.9,10. Deu. 11.6. Psa. 106.17. Jude 11. His children spared, Num. 26.11.

KORHITES, sons of Korah, Ex. 6.24. Num. 26.58. A family of singers, 2 Chr. 20.19. Psa. 42.44-49 (title).

L

LABAN, son of Bethuel, and brother of Rebekah, Gen. 22.23. Gen. 24.29. Gen. 25.20. His reception of Abraham's servant, Gen. 24.29-60 ; and of Jacob, Gen. 29.12-15. Jacob marries his daughters, Gen. 29.16-30. His illtreatment of Jacob, Gen. 29.23,27. Gen. 30.27-43. Gen. 31. Pursues Jacob, and makes a covenant with him, Gen. 31.22-55.

LACHISH, a town of Judah, Jos. 15.39. Taken by Joshua, Jos. 10. Fortified by Rehoboam, 2 Chr. 11.9. Amaziah murdered at, 2 Kin. 14.19. Besieged by Sennacherib, 2 Chr. 32.9. 2 Kin. 18.13-17. 2 Kin. 19.8 ; and by Nebuchadnezzar, Jer. 34.7. Prophecy against, Mic. 1.13.

LADDER, vision of, by Jacob, Gen. 28.12.

LAHAI-ROI. See BEER-LAHAI-ROI.

LAISH. See DAN.

LAKES. See SEAS.

LAMA SABACHTHANI (why hast thou forsaken me?), Mat. 27.46. Mar. 15.34. See Psa. 22.1.

LAMECH, his polygamy, Gen. 4.18-24.

———, son of Methusaleh, and father of Noah, Gen. 5.28.

LAMENESS disqualified for the priesthood, Lev. 21.18. Miraculous cures of, Mat. 11.5. Mat. 15.30. Mat. 21.14. Act. 3.2. Act. 8.7. Act. 14.8. Kindness to the lame, Job 29.15. Luk. 14.21. Illustrative, Pro. 26.7. Isa. 33.23. Isa. 35.6. Mar. 9.45. Heb. 12.13. In animals, disqualified for sacrifice, Deu. 15.21. Mal. 1.8,13.

LAMP. 1. (Heb. *lappeed*), Gen. 15.17. Jud. 7.20. Translated torch, or fire-brand, Jud. 15.4. Nah. 2.4. Zec. 12.6 ; burning lamp, Job 41.19. Illustrative, Isa. 62.1. 2. (Heb. *naar*), Ex. 25.37. 1 Sam. 3.3. Translated candle, Jer. 25.10. Zeph. 1.12. Illustrative, Job 18.6. Psa. 119.105.
3. (Gr. *lampas*), Mat. 25.4. Translated torch, Jno. 18.3 ; light, Act. 20.8. Symbolic, Rev. 4.5. Rev. 8.10. 4. (Gr. *luknos*), translated candle, Mat. 5.15. Rev. 22.5. Illustrative, Mat. 6.22. 2 Pet. 1.19. Rev. 21.23.

LAMP-STAND, or CANDLESTICK, Mar. 4.21. Of silver in the temple, 1 Chr. 28.15. See CANDLESTICK, GOLDEN.

LANCE, LANCET. See SPEAR.

LAND, laws regarding its redemption at the Jubilee, Lev. 25.23-33. Lev. 27.17-24. By repurchase, Lev. 25.24-31. Lev. 27.19,20. Jer. 32.7,8. By marrying deceased brother's wife, Ruth 4.3-5. Price of land regulated by Jubilee Year, Lev. 25.15,16. Lev. 27.18. Witnesses present at buying or selling, Gen. 23.10-16. Ruth 4.9. A written agreement, signed, sealed, and witnessed, Jer. 32.9-14. The shoe loosed, Deu. 25.9. Ruth 4.7,8. Psa. 60.8. Mortgages of, Neh. 5.1-4. Land of Egyptians bought by Pharaoh, Gen. 47.20-26.
See INHERITANCE.

LANDMARKS, removal of, prohibited, Deu. 19.14. Deu. 27.17. Pro. 22.28. Job 24.2.

LANGUAGE, one universal, Gen. 11.1,6. Confusion of, at Babel, Gen. 11.1-9. Gen. 10.5,20,31.

LANGUAGES, Ashdod, Neh. 13.24. Chaldee, Dan. 1.4. Egyptian, &c., Act. 2.10. Psa. 114.1. Greek, Luk. 23.38. Act. 21.37. Latin, Luk. 23.38. Act. 2.10. Lycaonian, Act.14.11. Parthian, &c., Act. 2.9-11. Syriac, 2 Kin. 18.26. Ezr. 4.7. Dan. 2.4, see HEBREW. Dialects, Ephraimite, Jud. 12.5,6. Galilean, Mar. 14.70. See INTERPRETERS.

LANTERN, Jno. 18.3, see LAMP.

LAODICEA, a town in Phrygia, Paul's anxiety for the church in, Col. 2.1. Zeal of Epaphras for, Col. 4.13. Paul's epistle to be read in, Col. 4.15,16. Epistle to ; lukewarmness of, Rev. 1.11. Rev. 3.14-22.

LAPWING, Lev. 11.19. Deu. 14.18.

LASEA, a city of Crete, Act. 27.8.

LAST-DAY. See JUDGMENT — CHRIST, SECOND COMING OF.

LATIN, the Roman language, Luk. 23.38. Act. 2.10.

LATTICE. See WINDOW.

LAVER OF BRASS, made of the women's mirrors, Ex. 38.8. Placed in the court between the tabernacle and the brazen altar, for the priests to wash their hands and feet in before service, Ex. 30.18-20. Ex. 39.39. Ex. 40. 7,12,30-32. Was anointed with oil, Ex. 30.28. Lev. 8.11. A brazen sea and 10 lavers made by Solomon for the temple, 2 Chr. 4.2-14. 1 Kin. 7.23-26,30. Jer. 52.17,20. Removed by Ahaz, 2 Kin. 16.17. Carried to Babylon, 2 Kin. 25.13,16. Symbolical, a sea of glass, Rev. 4.6 with 1 Kin. 7.23.

LAW OF GOD, EXCELLENCE OF. Luk. 16.17. It is easier for heaven and earth to pass, than one title of the law to fail.
Rom. 7.12. The law *is* holy, and the commandment holy, and just, and good. 14. We know that the law is spiritual.
Rom. 13.10. Love worketh no ill to his neighbour : therefore love *is* the fulfilling of the law.
1 Tim. 1.5. The end of the commandment is charity, out of a pure heart, and *of* a good conscience, and *of* faith unfeigned. 8. The law *is* good, if a man use it lawfully.
Jas. 1.25. The perfect law of liberty.
1 Jno. 5.3. This is the love of God, that we keep his commandments ; and his commandments are not grievous.
See WORD OF GOD, EXCELLENCE OF.

LAW, MOSAIC, contained in Ex. *c.* 12, 13, 20 to 40, Leviticus, Numbers, Deuteronomy,

Hebrews. Given in Egypt, Ex. c. 12 & 13; at Sinai, see SINAI; at Paran, Num. 13.3. Num. 15.1. Deu. 1.1. Deu. 33.2. Hab. 3.3; at Shittim, in the plains of Moab, Num. 25.1. Num. 26. Num. 35; by the hands of angels, Act. 7.53. Gal. 3.19. Heb. 2.2. Deu. 33.2. Psa. 68.17.

Re-issued, with additions, by Moses in the plains of Moab, Deu. c. 1 to 34. Written on tables, see TABLES OF STONE: in a book, and laid up in the side of the ark, Deu. 31.9,26. 2 Kin. 22.8; on stones at Mount Ebal, Deu. 27.2-8. Jos. 8.32.

Read and taught by parents to their children, Deu. 4.10. Deu. 6.7. Deu. 11.19; by priests and Levites publicly, Lev. 10.11. Deu. 33.10. 2 Chr. 35.3; at Ebal and Gerizim, Deu. 27.12-26. Jos. 8.33-35; in the sabbatical year at the feast of tabernacles, Deu. 31.10-13; in the reign of Jehoshaphat, 2 Chr. 17.9; by Ezra, Neh. 8.1-18. Ezr. 7.6,10; in the synagogue, Luk. 4.21. Act. 13.15,27. Act. 15.21.

Kings to write out and govern by, Deu. 17.18-20. 2 Kin. 11.12.

See PRIESTS, OFFERINGS, LEVITES, THEFT, &c.

LAW, MOSAIC, CHARACTER OF. TEMPORARY. RELATION OF THE LAW AND GOSPEL. Deu. 4.8. What nation *is there* so great, that hath statutes and judgments *so* righteous as all this law, which I set before you this day?

Deu. 33.2. From his right hand *went* a fiery law for them.

Neh. 9.13. Gavest them right judgments, and true laws, good statutes and commandments.

Psa. 76.1. In Judah *is* God known; his name *is* great in Israel.

Psa. 78.5. He established a testimony in Jacob, and appointed a law in Israel, which he commanded our fathers, that they should make them known to their children. 7. That they might set their hope in God, and not forget the works of God, but keep his commandments.

Jer. 3.16. In those days, saith the Lord, they shall say no more, The ark of the covenant of the Lord: neither shall it come to mind: neither shall they remember it; neither shall they visit *it*.

Eze. 20.11. I gave them my statutes, and shewed them my judgments, which *if* a man do, he shall even live in them. *v.* 25.

Dan. 9.27. He shall confirm the covenant with many for one week: and in the midst of the week he shall cause the sacrifice and the oblation to cease. *v.* 24-27.

Hos. 8.12. I have written to him the great things of my law.

Mat. 5.17. Think not that I am come to destroy the law, or the prophets: I am not come to destroy, but to fulfil. *v.* 18.

Mat. 19.8. Moses because of the hardness of your hearts suffered you to put away your wives.

Luk. 10.24. Many prophets and kings have desired to see those things which ye see, and have not seen *them*; and to hear those things which ye hear, and have not heard *them*.

Luk. 16.16. The law and the prophets *were* until John.

Jno. 1.17. The law was given by Moses, *but* grace and truth came by Jesus Christ.

Jno. 4.21. The hour cometh, when ye shall neither in this mountain, nor yet at Jerusalem, worship the Father.

Jno. 8.35. The servant abideth not in the house for ever: *but* the Son abideth ever.

Act. 3.25. The covenant which God made with our fathers.

Act. 10.28. Ye know how that it is an unlawful thing for a man that is a Jew to keep company, or come unto one of another nation; but God hath shewed me that I should not call any man common or unclean. *v.* 9-28.

Act. 13.39. By him all that believe are justified from all things, from which ye could not be justified by the law of Moses.

Act. 15.10. Why tempt ye God, to put a yoke upon the neck of the disciples, which neither our fathers nor we were able to bear?

Act. 24.14. After the way which they call heresy, so worship I the God of my fathers, believing all things which are written in the law and in the prophets.

Rom. 3.1. What advantage then hath the Jew? or what profit *is there* of circumcision? 2. Much every way: chiefly, because that unto them were committed the oracles of God.

Rom. 7.10. The commandment, which *was* ordained to life, I found *to be* unto death. 16. If then I do that which I would not, I consent unto the law that *it is* good.

Rom. 8.3. What the law could not do, in that it was weak through the flesh, God sending his own Son in the likeness of sinful flesh, and for sin condemned sin in the flesh.

Rom. 9.4. To whom *pertaineth* the adoption.

2 Cor. 3.7. If the ministration of death, written *and* engraven in stones, was glorious, so that the children of Israel could not stedfastly behold the face of Moses for the glory of his countenance; which *glory* was *to* be done away: 8. How shall not the ministration of the spirit be rather glorious? 9. For *if* the ministration of condemnation *be* glory, much more doth the ministration of righteousness exceed in glory. 10. For even that which was made glorious had no glory in this respect, by reason of the glory that excelleth. 11. For if that which is done away *was* glorious, much more that which remaineth *is* glorious.

2 Cor. 3.12. Seeing then that we have such hope, we use great plainness of speech: 13. And not as Moses, *which* put a vail over his face, that the children of Israel could not stedfastly look to the end of that which is abolished: 14. But their minds were blinded: for until this day remaineth the same vail untaken away in the reading of the old testament; which *vail* is done away in Christ.

Gal. 2.14. If thou, being a Jew, livest after the manner of Gentiles, and not as do the Jews, why compellest thou the Gentiles to live as do the Jews?

Gal. 3.19. Wherefore then *serveth* the law? It was added because of transgressions, till the seed should come to whom the promise was made. 21. *Is* the law then against the promises of God? God forbid: for if there had been a law given which could have given life, verily righteousness should have been by the law. 23. Before faith came, we were kept under the law, shut up unto the faith which should afterwards be revealed. 24. Wherefore the law was our schoolmaster *to bring us* unto Christ, that we might be justified by faith. 25. But after that faith is come, we are no longer under a schoolmaster.

Gal. 4.3. We, when we were children, were

in bondage under the elements of the world : 4. But when the fulness of the time was come, God sent forth his Son, made of a woman, made under the law, 5. To redeem them that were under the law, that we might receive the adoption of sons. 9. Now, after that ye have known God, or rather are known of God, how turn ye again to the weak and beggarly elements, whereunto ye desire again to be in bondage? 10. Ye observe days, and months, and times, and years. *v.* 1-12, 21-31.

Eph. 2.15. Having abolished in his flesh the enmity, *even* the law of commandments *contained* in ordinances.

Col. 2.14. Blotting out the handwriting of ordinances that was against us, which was contrary to us, and took it out of the way, nailing it to his cross. 16. Let no man therefore judge you in meat, or in drink, or in respect of an holy-day, or of the new moon, or of the sabbath *days :* 17. Which are a shadow of things to come ; but the body *is* of Christ. 20. If ye be dead with Christ from the rudiments of the world, why, as though living in the world, are ye subject to ordinances, 21. Touch not ; taste not ; handle not ; 22. Which all are to perish with the using.

Heb. 7.18. There is verily a disannulling of the commandment going before for the weakness and unprofitableness thereof. 19. The law made nothing perfect, but the bringing in of a better hope *did ;* by the which we draw nigh unto God. *v.* 1-28.

Heb. 8.4. There are priests that offer gifts according to the law : 5. Who serve unto the example and shadow of heavenly things, as Moses was admonished of God when he was about to make the tabernacle : for, See, saith he, *that* thou make all things according to the pattern shewed to thee in the mount. 6. He is the mediator of a better covenant, which was established upon better promises. 7. For if that first *covenant* had been faultless, then should no place have been sought for the second. 8. For finding fault with them, he saith, Behold, the days come, saith the Lord, when I will make a new covenant. 13. In that he saith, A new *covenant*, he hath made the first old. Now that which decayeth and waxeth old *is* ready to vanish away. *v.* 9-12.

Heb. 9.8. The Holy Ghost this signifying, that the way into the holiest of all was not yet made manifest, while as the first tabernacle was yet standing : 9. Which *was* a figure for the time then present, in which were offered both gifts and sacrifices, that could not make him that did the service perfect, as pertaining to the conscience ; 10. *Which stood* only in meats and drinks, and divers washings, and carnal ordinances, imposed *on them* until the time of reformation. 23. *It was* therefore necessary that the patterns of things in the heavens should be purified with these ; but the heavenly things themselves with better sacrifices than these.

Heb. 10 1. The law having a shadow of good things to come, *and* not the very image of the things, can never with those sacrifices which they offered year by year continually make the comers thereunto perfect. 2. For then would they not have ceased to be offered ? because that the worshippers once purged should have had no more conscience of sins. 3. But in those *sacrifices there* is a remem-

brance again *made* of sins every year. 4. For *it is* not possible that the blood of bulls and of goats should take away sins. *v.* 1-18.

Heb. 11.40. God having provided some better thing for us, that they without us should not be made perfect.

Heb. 12.18. Ye are not come unto the mount that might be touched, and that burned with fire, nor unto blackness, and darkness, and tempest, 19. And the sound of a trumpet, and the voice of words. 27. This *word*, Yet once more, signifieth the removing of those things that are shaken, as of things that are made, that those things which cannot be shaken may remain.

See WORKS, JUSTIFICATION.

LAW, MOSAIC, FROM GOD, Ex. 19.16-24. Ex. 20.1-17. Ex. 24.12-18. Ex. 31.18. Ex. 32.15,16. Ex. 34.1-4,28. Lev. 26.46. Num. 36.13. Deu. 4.10-13,36. Deu. 5.1-22. Deu. 9.10. Deu. 10.1-5. Deu. 33.2-4. 1 Kin. 8.9. Neh. 9.14. Psa. 78.5. Psa. 103.7. Mal. 4.4. Act. 7.53. Gal. 3.19. Heb. 9.18-21.

LAWYER. See SCRIBES.

LAZARUS OF BETHANY, brother of Martha and Mary ; Christ's love to him ; his sickness, death, and resurrection, Jno. 11. At supper with Christ in Bethany ; visited by the Jews ; his life plotted against, Jno. 12.1,2,9-11,17,18.

——, parable of, Luk. 16.19-31.

LEAD, Ex. 15.10. Used for inscriptions, Job 19.24. Traffic in, Eze. 27.12. Leadfounder, Jer. 6.29. Eze. 22.18,20.

LEAGUE. See ALLIANCE.

LEAH, daughter of Laban, marries Jacob ; her children, Gen. 29.16,17,23-35. Gen. 30. 9-21. Gen. 31.4-16. Gen. 33.2,7. Ruth 4.11.

LEARNING. See WISDOM.

LEASING (falsehood), Psa. 4.2.

LEATHER, used for girdles, 2 Kin. 1.8. Mat. 3.4. Usually translated skin, Gen. 3.21. Mar. 1.6 ; or hide, Lev. 8.17.

LEAVEN. For bread, Ex. 12.34,39. Hos. 7.4. Mat. 13.33. 1 Cor. 5.6. Used with the peace-offering of thanksgiving, Lev. 7.13. Amos 4.5. With the wave loaves of first-fruits, Lev. 23.15-17. Num. 15.19-21. Forbidden with meat-offerings, Lev. 2.11. Lev. 6.17. Lev. 10.12. Ex. 23.18. Ex. 34.25. And at the passover, see PASSOVER. Illustrative, Mat. 13.33. Luk. 13.21. Mat. 16.6-12. Luk. 12.1. 1 Cor. 5.6-8. Gal. 5.9.

LEBANON, MOUNT, the north boundary of Palestine, Deu. 1.7. Deu. 3.25. Deu. 11.24. Jos. 1.4. Jos. 9.1. Snows of, Jer. 18.14. Streams of, Song 4.15. Cedars of, see CEDAR. Fir and algum trees of, 2 Kin. 19.23. 2 Chr. 2.8. Flowers of, Nah. 1.4. Cattle of, Isa. 40.16. Thunder-storm on, Psa. 29. Inhabited by Hivites, Jud. 3.3. House of the forest of, 1 Kin. 7.2-5. Valley of, Jos. 11.17. Jos. 12.7. Tower of, Song 7.4.

LEBBEUS. See JUDE.

LEEKS, Num. 11.5. Translated grass, 1 Kin. 18.5 ; herb, Job 8.12 ; hay, Pro. 27.25.

LEES, the crust and dregs of wine, Isa. 25.6. Psa. 75.8. Jer. 48.11. Zeph. 1.12.

LEGION (a division of the Roman army, consisting of 6000 men), Mat. 26.53. Mar. 5.9,15.

LEHI. See RAMATH-LEHI.

LEMUEL, an unknown king, Pro. 31.1,4.

LENTILE, a leguminous plant, used for food, Gen. 25.34. 2 Sam. 17.28. 2 Sam. 23.11. Eze. 4.9.

LEOPARD, Song 4.8. Isa. 11.6. Jer. 5.6. Jer. 13.23. Hos. 13.7. Hab. 1.8. Symbolical, Dan. 7.6.

LEPROSY, Lev. 13. Inflicted as a punishment on Miriam, Num. 12.10 ; on Gehazi, 2 Kin. 5.27 ; on Uzziah, 2 Chr. 26.20,21. Cured miraculously, Num. 12.13,14 ; by Elijah, 2 Kin. 5.8-14 ; by Christ and his disciples, Mat. 8.3. Mat. 10.8. Luk. 5.13. Luk. 17.13,14. Hereditary, 2 Sam. 3.29. 2 Kin. 5.27.

Lepers were examined by the priest, Lev. 13. Deu. 24.8. Mat. 8.4. Luk. 17.14. Were excluded from the priesthood, Lev. 22.2-4 ; and from public worship, 2 Chr. 26.21. Dwelt alone, Lev. 13.46. Num. 5.2. Num. 12.14. 2 Kin. 15.5. Were commanded to rend their clothes, and cry 'unclean,' Lev. 13.45. Luk. 17.12.

Purification of, when pronounced by the priest to be cured ; sacrifices ; a living bird let loose ; the leper washed, shaved all his hair, was sprinkled and anointed with blood and oil, Lev. 14. Houses and garments affected with ; laws regarding, Lev. 13.49-59. Lev. 14.35-53.

LESHEM. See DAN.

LETTERS, Ezr. 4.11-22. Act. 15.23-29. Act. 23.25-30. 2 The. 3.17. Sealed, 1 Kin. 21.8. Est. 3.12.

See SALUTATIONS, POSTS.

LEVI, son of Jacob and Leah, Gen. 29.34. Gen. 35.23. 1 Chr. 2.1. Massacres the Shechemites, Gen. 34.25-31. Jacob's last words to, Gen. 49.5-7. His children and descendants, Gen. 46.11. Ex. 6.16-27. Num. 3.17. 1 Chr. 6. 1 Chr. 24.20-30. His death, Ex. 6.16.

LEVI THE PUBLICAN. See MATTHEW.

LEVIATHAN, Job 3.8 (marg.) ; supposed to be a crocodile, Job 41 ; a serpent, Isa. 27.1. Psa. 104.26. Illustrative, Psa. 74.14.

LEVITES. The descendants of Levi ; chosen by God, Num. 3.6-13. Num. 16.9. Deu. 10.8. 1 Chr. 15.2 ; as a reward for their zeal, Ex. 32.26-28. Deu. 33.9,10. Mal. 2.4,5. Taken instead of the first-born of Israel, Num. 3.12,41-45. Num. 8.14,16-18. Num. 18.6. Cattle of, taken instead of the firstlings of Israel, Num. 3.41,45.

Consecration of, by purification, Num. 8. 6,7,21. By sacrifices, Num. 8.8,12. By imposition of the elders' hands, and being presented to God as an offering by the high-priest for the people, Num. 8.9-20. Punishment of, for encroaching on the priestly office, Num. 4.19,20. Num. 16.1-35,40. Num. 18.3.

Governed by chiefs, 2 Chr. 35.9. Ezr. 8.29. Neh. 11.22. Entered upon their service at 25 years of age, Num. 8.24 ; at 20 years, after David's time, 1 Chr. 23.24,27. Ezr. 3.8 ; upon full service at 30 years, Num. 4.3,30,47. 1 Chr. 23.3. Superannuated at 50 years, Num. 4.47. Num. 8.25,26.

Marched in the centre of Israel, Num. 2.17. Encamped round the tabernacle, Num. 1.50-53. Num. 3.23,35. Lodged round the temple while in attendance, 1 Chr. 9.27,33. At liberty to reside and minister at the temple instead of in their cities ; provision for, Deu. 18.6-8.

Name Levite used for a particular class, Ezr. 10.23,24. Neh. 7.1,73. Illustrative, Isa. 66.21. Prophecies of, Jer. 33.18. Eze. 44.10-14. Mal. 3.3.

LEVITES, DUTIES OF. Ministered to the priests, and assisted them in the service of the tabernacle, Num. 3.6-9. Num. 8.19. Num. 18.2-6,23. Deu. 10.8. 1 Chr. 6.48. 1 Chr. 23.4,28,31. Killed the sacrifices on extraordinary occasions, 2 Chr. 29.34. 2 Chr. 35.11. Ezr. 6.20,21.

Carried and pitched the tabernacle, Num. 1.50,51. Carried the ark, 1 Chr. 15.2. Kept the charge of the tabernacle and its vessels, Num. 1.50. Num. c. 3 & 4. Num. 8.22-26. Num. 18.3. 1 Chr. 9.28,29. 1 Chr. 23.32. Ezr. 8.24-34. Kept the sacred oil, flour, wine, and spices, 1 Chr. 9.29. Kept the tithes and dedicated things, 1 Chr. 9.26. 1 Chr. 26.20-28. 1 Chr. 29.8. 2 Chr. 31.11-19. Neh. 12.44. Neh. 13.12,13. Prepared the shewbread, unleavened bread, and things baked in pans, 1 Chr. 23.29.

Taught the people, Deu. 33.10. 2 Chr.17.8,9. 2 Chr. 30.22. 2 Chr. 35.3. Neh. 8.7-13. Mal. 2.6,7. Acted as scribes, see SCRIBES. Collected money for the temple, 2 Chr. 24.5,11. 2 Chr. 34.9. Ezr. 8.29,30,33. Superintended repairs of temple, 2 Chr. 34.12,13. Ezr. 3.8,9. Servants of, see NETHINIMS.

Divided by David into 4 classes—overseers of the temple, officers or judges, porters, and singers, 1 Chr. 23.4-6; by divine command, 1 Chr. 28.12,13,21. 2 Chr. 8.14. Chiefs of the 4 classes dwelt at Jerusalem after captivity, 1 Chr. 9.26,34. Subdivided into 24 courses, being sons of Laadan, 3 ; of Shimei, 7 ; of Gershom, 1 ; of Eliezer, 1 ; of Izhar, 1 ; of Hebron, 4 ; of Uzziel, 2 ; of Malhi, 2 ; of Mushi, 3, 1 Chr. 23.7-23, see 1 Chr. 24.20-31.

Overseers, 24,000, 1 Chr. 23.4.   2 Chr. 34.12.

Officers and judges, 6000, 1 Chr. 23.4. 1 Chr. 26.29-32. 2 Chr.19.8-11. 2 Chr. 34.13. Neh. 11.16. Deu. 16.18. Regulated weights and measures, 1 Chr. 23.29 with Ex. 30.13.

Porters or warders, 1 Chr. 9.17-32. 2 Chr. 23.4. 2 Chr. 34.13. 2 Chr. 35.15. Neh. 12.25. 4000 of, 1 Chr. 23.5.

Porters, 24 courses : sons of Shelemiah, 7 ; of Obed-edom (omitting Shemaiah), 7 ; of Shemaiah, 6 ; of Hosah, 4 ; 1 Chr. 26.1-12. 24 each day at the gates of the temple, 1 Chr. 26.13-19. Cast lots for their different stations, 1 Chr. 24.31. 1 Chr. 25.8-31. 1 Chr. 26.13-18. Neh. 10.34.

Singers conducted the temple music, see MUSIC, SACRED. 4000 of, 1 Chr. 23.5. Provision for, Neh. 12.47. Neh. 13.5 ; by Artaxerxes, Neh. 11.23. Chambers of, Eze. 40.44. Villages of, near Jerusalem, Neh. 12.29. Return from captivity, Ezr. 2.41,65. Ezr. 7.7. Neh. 7.1,67. Neh. 11.22. Their covenant, Neh. 10.28.

LEVITES, DUTIES OF, AND DIVISION INTO THREE CLASSES.

	KOHATHITES.	MERARITES.	GERSHONITES.
Families of the Kohathites, Merarites, and Gershonites—	Ex. 6.18,20-25. Num. 3.19,27-30. 1 Chr. 6.1-15,18. 1 Chr. 23.12-20.	Ex. 6.19. Num. 3. 20,33-35. 1 Chr. 6. 19,29,30. 1 Chr. 23. 21-23.	Ex. 6.17. Num. 3. 18,21-24. 1 Chr. 6. 17,20-28. 1 Chr. 23. 7-11.
Pitched by the tabernacle—	South, Num. 3.29.	North, Num. 3.35.	West, Num. 3.23.
Had charge of—	The ark, table, candlestick, altars, vessels, and vail; carried them on their shoulders, Num. 3.31. Num. 4.4-15,18-20. Num. 10.21. Num. 7.9. Also the shewbread and things made in pans, 1 Chr. 9.31,32.	The boards, bars, pillars, and sockets of tabernacle, Num. 3. 36,37. Num. 4.31-33. Num. 10.17. Had 4 waggons and 8 oxen for their use, Num. 7.8.	The tabernacle, tent, coverings, hangings, cords, Num. 3.25,26. Num. 4.23-26. Num. 10.17. Had 2 waggons and 4 oxen for their use, Num. 7.7.
Divided into courses—	1 Chr. 23.6.	1 Chr. 23.6.	1 Chr. 23.6.
Porters—	1 Chr. 9.17-32. 1 Chr. 26.1-5,14,15,19.	1 Chr. 26.10-12, 16,19.	.
Singers in 24 courses. See MUSIC, SACRED.	1 Chr. 6.33-38. 2 Chr. 20.19.	1 Chr. 6.44-47. 1 Chr. 15.17.	1 Chr. 6.39-43.
Officers and judges of—	1 Chr. 26.6-9,29-32.		
Treasurers—	1 Chr. 26.23-26.	.	1 Chr. 26.21,22.
Overseers—	2 Chr. 34.12.	.	.
Aided in purifying the temple—	2 Chr. 29.12-19.	2 Chr. 29.12-19.	2 Chr. 29.12-19.
Soldiers under David—	1 Chr. 12.6.		
Chiefs of—	Num. 3.30. 1 Chr.15.5.	Num. 3.35. 1 Chr. 15.6.	Num. 3.24. 1 Chr. 15.7.
Governed by—	High-priest's eldest son, Num. 3.32. 1 Chr. 9.20.	High-priest's second son, Num. 4.33.	High-priest's second son, Num. 4.28.
Number of, from a month old—	8600, Num. 3.28.	6200, Num. 3.34.	7500, Num. 3.22.
——— from 30 years old—	2750, Num. 4.36.	3200, Num. 4.44.	2630, Num. 4.40.
——— that brought up the ark—	112, 1 Chr. 15.5,8-10.	220, 1 Chr. 15.6.	130, 1 Chr. 15.7.
——— that returned with Ezra—	.	38, Ezr. 8.19.	128, Ezr. 2.41.
Cities of, in—	Ephraim, Dan, and Manasseh W., Jos. 21.5,20-26. 1 Chr. 6.61.	Reuben, Gad, Zebulon, Jos. 21.7,34-40. 1 Chr. 6.63,77-81.	Issachar, Asher, Naphtali, Manasseh E., Jos.21.6,27-33. 1 Chr. 6.62.

LEVITES, EMOLUMENTS OF. Levites had no inheritance; to be maintained by the nation, Num. 18.20,24. Num. 26.62. Deu. 10.9. Deu. 12.12,18,19. Deu. 14.27-29. Deu. 16.11-14. Deu. 26.11-13. Jos. 13.33. Jos. 14.3. Jos. 18.7. Neh. 12.44,47; from a month old, 2 Chr. 31.16-18.

Forty-eight cities, with suburbs, given to, 6 of which were cities of refuge, and 13 belonged to the priests, Num. 35.2-8. Jos. 14.4. Jos. 21. 1 Chr. 6.54-81. 1 Chr. 13.2. 2 Chr. 23.2. Their cities redeemable at any time; fields of, not to be sold, Lev. 25.32-34.

Tithes, see TITHES. Gave a tenth of the tithes to the high-priest as a heave-offering, Num. 18.26-28. Neh. 10.38,39. Portions of the offerings and sacrifices, Deu. 18.1-8. Jos. 13.14. Offered a heave-offering out of every gift made to them, the remainder their own, Num. 18.29-32. Neh. 12.47. A hundredth part of the spoils taken in war, Num. 31.30,42-47.

LEVITES, HISTORICAL NOTICES OF. Numbered separately from a month old, Num. 1.47-49. Num. 2.33. Num. 3.14-39. Num. 26.57-62; and from 30 years old, Num. 4.2,3. 1 Chr. 23.3-5. Not numbered by Joab, 1 Chr. 21.6.

Zeal against worshippers of golden calf, Ex. 32.26-29. Mal. 2.4,5. Pronounce the blessings on Mount Ebal, Deu. 27.12. Jos. 8.33. Meet David to make him king; number of, 1 Chr. 12.26-28. Bring the ark to Jerusalem, 1 Chr. 15.26,27; and into the temple, 2 Chr. 5.4,5. Their offerings, 1 Chr. 15.26. 2 Chr. 5.4,5.

Cast out by Jeroboam; come to Judah and Jerusalem, 2 Chr. 11.13-17. 2 Chr. 13.9,10. Guard king Joash, 2 Kin. 11.7-11. 2 Chr. 23.7. Delay in joining Ezra, Ezr. 8.15. Return with him, Ezr. 2.40-70. Ezr. 7.7. Ezr. 8.16-19,29,30.

Their offerings for the second temple, Ezr. 1.5,6.

Families and number returned from captivity, that dwelt in Jerusalem, 1 Chr. 9.14-34. Neh. 11.18. Artaxerxes frees from tribute, Ezr. 7.24. Reproved for having idolatrous wives, Ezr. 9.1,2. Covenant to put them away, Ezr. 10.5,23.

Aid in building wall of Jerusalem, Neh. 3.17. Return with Zerubbabel; number of, Neh. 7.43,73. Neh. 12. Put their names and seals to covenant of Israel with God, Neh. 9.38. Neh. 10.9,28. Defrauded of their tithes; desert their duty; brought back by Nehemiah, Neh. 13.10-13,30,31. Sent to John from Jerusalem, Jno. 1.19.

LIARS. See FALSEHOOD.

LIBERALITY AND ZEAL. Ex. 22.29. Thou shalt not delay *to offer* the first of thy ripe fruits, and of thy liquors: the firstborn of thy sons shalt thou give unto me. 30. Likewise shalt thou do with thine oxen, *and* with thy sheep. Ex. 32.19.

Ex. 23.15. None shall appear before me empty. Ex. 34.20.

Ex. 25.2. Speak unto the children of Israel, that they bring me an offering: of every man that giveth it willingly with his heart ye shall take my offering. 8. And let them make me a sanctuary; that I may dwell among them.

Ex. 35.10. Every wise hearted among you shall come, and make all that the Lord hath commanded. *v.* 5.

Lev. 19.5. If ye offer a sacrifice of peace-offerings unto the Lord, ye shall offer it at your own will. Lev. 22.29. Num. 35.8.

Deu. 16.10. Keep the feast of weeks unto the Lord thy God with a tribute of a freewill offering of thine hand, which thou shalt give *unto the Lord thy God,* according as the Lord thy God hath blessed thee. 17. Every man *shall give* as he is able, according to the blessing of the Lord thy God which he hath given thee.

1 Chr. 22.19. Arise therefore, and build ye the sanctuary of the Lord God.

1 Chr. 28.10. The Lord hath chosen thee to build an house for the sanctuary: be strong, and de .c. 20. He will not fail thee, nor forsake thee, until thou hast finished all the work for the service of the house of the Lord. *v.* 18.

1 Chr. 29.5. Who *then* is willing to consecrate his service this day unto the Lord?

2 Chr. 15.7. Be ye strong therefore, and let not your hands be weak: for your work shall be rewarded.

Ezr. 1.2. He hath charged me to build him an house at Jerusalem. 3. Who *is there* among you of all his people? The Lord his God *be* with him, and let him go up. 4. Let the men of his place help him with silver, and with gold, and with goods, and with beasts, beside the freewill-offering for the house of God that *is* in Jerusalem.

Pro. 3.9. Honour the Lord with thy substance, and with the firstfruits of all thine increase: 10. So shall thy barns be filled with plenty, and thy presses shall burst out with new wine.

Pro. 11.24. There is that scattereth, and yet increaseth. 25. The liberal soul shall be made fat: and he that watereth shall be watered also himself.

Pro. 13.7. *There is* that maketh himself poor, yet *hath* great riches.

Pro. 14.22. Mercy and truth *shall be* to them that devise good.

Pro. 21.26. The righteous giveth and spareth not.

Pro. 22.9. He that hath a bountiful eye shall be blessed.

Ecc. 11.1. Cast thy bread upon the waters: for thou shalt find it after many days. 2. Give a portion to seven and also to eight.

Isa. 32.8. The liberal deviseth liberal things; and by liberal things shall he stand.

Isa. 60.7. All the flocks of Kedar shall be gathered together unto thee, the rams of Nebaioth shall minister unto thee: they shall come up with acceptance on mine altar, and I will glorify the house of my glory. 9. Surely the isles shall wait for me, and the ships of Tarshish first, to bring thy sons from far, their silver and their gold with them, unto the name of the Lord thy God. 17. For brass I will bring gold, and for iron I will bring silver, and for wood brass, and for stones iron.

Hag. 1.8. Go up to the mountain, and bring wood, and build the house; and I will take pleasure in it, and I will be glorified, saith the Lord.

Hag. 2.18. *Even* from the day that the foundation of the Lord's temple was laid, consider *it.* 19. Is the seed yet in the barn? yea, as yet the vine, and the fig tree, and the pomegranate, and the olive tree, hath not brought forth: from this day will I bless *you.*

Mal. 3.10. Bring ye all the tithes into the store-house, that there may be meat in mine house, and prove me now herewith, saith the Lord of hosts, if I will not open you the windows of heaven, and pour you out a blessing, that *there shall not be room enough to receive it.* 11. And I will rebuke the devourer for your sakes. 12. And all nations shall call you blessed: for ye shall be a delightsome land, saith the Lord of hosts.

Luk. 6.38. Give, and it shall be given unto you; good measure, pressed down, and shaken together, and running over, shall men give into your bosom. For with the same measure that ye mete withal it shall be measured to you again. Mat. 5.42.

Luk. 16.9. Make to yourselves friends of the mammon of unrighteousness; that, when ye fail, they may receive you into everlasting habitations.

Act. 20.35. Remember the words of the Lord Jesus, how he said, It is more blessed to give than to receive.

Rom. 12.8. He that giveth, *let him do it* with simplicity.

1 Cor. 16.1. Concerning the collection for the saints, as I have given order to the churches of Galatia, even so do ye. 2. Upon the first *day* of the week let every one of you lay by him in store, as *God* hath prospered him, that there be no gatherings when I come.

2 Cor. 8.7. As ye abound in every *thing, see* that ye abound in this grace also. 9. Ye know the grace of our Lord Jesus Christ, that, though he was rich, yet for your sakes he became poor, that ye through his poverty might be rich. 11. Now therefore perform the doing *of it;* that as *there was* a readiness to will, so *there may be* a performance also out of that which ye have. 12. If there be first a willing mind,

it is accepted according to that a man hath, *and* not according to that he hath not. 13. *I mean* not that other men be eased, and ye burdened: 14. But by an equality, *that* now at this time your abundance *may be a supply* for their want, that their abundance also may be *a supply* for your want : that there may be equality. 24. Shew ye to them, and before the churches, the proof of your love, and of our boasting on your behalf. *v.* 8,15.

2 Cor. 9.6. He which soweth sparingly shall reap also sparingly ; and he which soweth bountifully shall reap also bountifully. 7. Every man according as he purposeth in his heart, *so let him give;* not grudgingly, or of necessity : for God loveth a cheerful giver. 8. God *is* able to make all grace abound toward you ; that ye, always having all sufficiency in all *things,* may abound to every good work. 10. He that ministereth seed to the sower both minister bread for *your* food, and multiply your seed sown, and increase the fruits of your righteousness ; 11. Being enriched in every thing to all bountifulness, which causeth through us thanksgiving to God. 12. The administration of this service not only supplieth the want of the saints, but is abundant also by many thanksgivings unto God. *v.* 13.

Eph. 4.28. Let him labour, working with *his* hands the thing which is good, that he may have to give to him that needeth.

1 Tim. 6.18. That they do good, that they be rich in good works, ready to distribute, willing to communicate ; 19. Laying up in store for themselves a good foundation against the time to come.

Philm. 14. Thy benefit should not be as it were of necessity, but willingly.

Heb. 13.16. To do good and to communicate forget not : for with such sacrifices God is well pleased.

See MINISTERS, MAINTENANCE OF—RICHES, RIGHT USE OF—FIRST-FRUITS, TITHES—POOR, KINDNESS TO—LOVE, COVETOUSNESS.

LIBERALITY AND ZEAL, EXAMPLES OF : Jacob, Gen. 28.22. Israelites at the erection of the tabernacle, Ex. 35.21-29. Ex. 36.3-7. Ex. 38.8. Num. 7. Num. 31.48-54. Jos.18.1. Reubenites, Jos. 22.24-29. David, 2 Sam. 7.2. 1 Chr. 17.1. 2 Sam. 8.11. 1 Kin. 7.51. 1 Kin. 8.17,18. 1 Chr. 21.24. 1 Chr. 22. 1 Chr. 26.26. 1 Chr. 28.2. 1 Chr. 29.2-5,17. Psa. 132.1-5.

Israelites' offerings for the temple, 1 Chr. 29.6-9,16,17. Samuel, &c., 1 Chr. 26.27,28. Solomon, 1 Kin. 4.29. 1 Kin. 5.4,5. 2 Chr. 2.1-6. 1 Kin. 6. 1 Kin. 7.51. 1 Kin. 8.13. Asa and Abijam, 1 Kin. 15.15. Jehoshaphat, &c., 2 Kin. 12.18. Joash and his people, 2 Kin. 12.4-14. 2 Chr. 24.4-14. Hezekiah, 2 Chr. 29. 2 Chr. 30.1-12. 2 Chr. 31.1-10,21. Manasseh, 2 Chr. 33.16. Josiah, 2 Kin.22 3-6. 2 Kin. 23.21,22. 2 Chr. 34.8-13. 2 Chr. 35.1-19. Jews after the captivity, Ezr. 1.5,6. Ezr. 2.68,69. Ezr. 3.2-9. Ezr. 5.2-6. Ezr. 6.14-22. Ezr. 8.25-35. Neh. 4.6. Neh. 6.3. Neh. 7.70-72. Neh. 10.32-39. Neh. 13.12,31. Hag. 1.12-14. Hag. 2.18,19. Cyrus, Ezr. 1.2-4,7-11. Ezr. 3.7. Ezr. 5.13-15. Ezr. 6.3. Darius, Ezr. 6.7-12. Artaxerxes, Ezr. 7.13-27. Ezr. 8.24-36. Centurion, Luk. 7.4,5. Mary Magdalene, &c., Luk. 8.2,3. Poor widow, Luk. 21.2-4. Christians in Jerusalem, Act. 2.44, 45. Act. 4.32-37 ; in Antioch, Act. 11.29 ; at Philippi, Phil. 4.18 ; Corinth, 2 Cor. 8.19. 2 Cor. 9.13 ; Macedonia, 2 Cor. 8.1-4.

LIBERTINES (freedmen), synagogue of, in Jerusalem ; dispute with Stephen, Act. 6.9.

LIBERTY, CHRISTIAN. Psa. 119.45. I will walk at liberty : for I seek thy precepts.

Jno. 8.32. Ye shall know the truth, and the truth shall make you free. 36. If the Son therefore shall make you free, ye shall be free indeed.

Rom. 6.1. Shall we continue in sin, that grace may abound ? 2. God forbid. 15. Shall we sin, because we are not under the law, but under grace ? God forbid.

Rom. 7.6. We are delivered from the law, that being dead wherein we were held ; that we should serve in newness of spirit, and not *in* the oldness of the letter.

Rom. 8.2. The law of the Spirit of life in Christ Jesus hath made me free from the law of sin and death. 15. Ye have not received the spirit of bondage again to fear. 21. The glorious liberty of the children of God.

Rom. 14.6. He that regardeth the day, regardeth *it* unto the Lord ; and he that regardeth not the day, to the Lord he doth not regard *it.* He that eateth, eateth to the Lord, for he giveth God thanks ; and he that eateth not, to the Lord he eateth not, and giveth God thanks.

1 Cor. 7.22. He that is called in the Lord, *being* a servant, is the Lord's freeman : likewise also he that is called, *being* free, is Christ's servant.

1 Cor. 8.8. Meat commendeth us not to God : for neither, if we eat, are we the better ; neither, if we eat not, are we the worse. 9. But take heed lest by any means this liberty of your's become a stumbling-block to them that are weak. *v.* 1-13.

1 Cor. 9.4. Have we not power to eat and to drink ? 5. Have we not power to lead about a sister, a wife, as well as other apostles, and *as* the brethren of the Lord, and Cephas ? 6. Or I only and Barnabas, have not we power to forbear working ? 19. Though I be free from all *men,* yet have I made myself servant unto all, that I might gain the more.

1 Cor. 10.23. All things are lawful for me, but all things are not expedient : all things are lawful for me, but all things edify not. 29. Conscience, I say, not thine own, but of the other : for why is my liberty judged of another *man's* conscience ? 30. For if I by grace be a partaker, why am I evil spoken of for that for which I give thanks ?

2 Cor. 3.17. Where the Spirit of the Lord *is,* there is liberty.

Gal. 2.3. Neither Titus, who was with me, being a Greek, was compelled to be circumcised : 4. And that because of false brethren unawares brought in, who came in privily to spy out our liberty which we have in Christ Jesus, that they might bring us into bondage : 5. To whom we gave place by subjection, no, not for an hour ; that the truth of the gospel might continue with you. Act. 15.24-29.

Gal. 4.3. We, when we were children, were in bondage under the elements of the world : 4. But when the fulness of the time was come, God sent forth his Son, made of a woman, made under the law, 5. To redeem them that were under the law, that we might receive the adoption of sons. 7. Thou art no more a servant, but a son; and if a son, then an heir of God through Christ. 26. Jerusalem which is above is free, which is the mother of us all. 31. We are not children of the bondwoman, but of the free.

Gal. 5.1. Stand fast therefore in the liberty wherewith Christ hath made us free, and be not entangled again with the yoke of bondage. 13. Brethren, ye have been called unto liberty; only *use* not liberty for an occasion to the flesh, but by love serve one another. 18. If ye be led of the Spirit, ye are not under the law.

Col. 2.20. If ye be dead with Christ from the rudiments of the world, why, as though living in the world, are ye subject to ordinances.

2 Tim. 1.7. God hath not given us the spirit of fear; but of power, and of love, and of a sound mind.

Jas. 1.25. The perfect law of liberty.

1 Pet. 2.16. As free, and not using *your* liberty for a cloke of maliciousness, but as the servants of God.

1 Jno. 4.18. There is no fear in love: but perfect love casteth out fear: because fear hath torment. He that feareth is not made perfect in love.

See BIGOTRY—LAW, MOSAIC.

LIBNAH, a Canaanitish city, taken by Joshua, Jos. 10.29,30,39. A Levitical city of Judah, Jos. 15.42. Jos. 21.13. Revolted against Jehoram, 2 Kin. 8.22. 2 Chr. 21.10. Besieged by Sennacherib, 2 Kin. 19.8,35. Isa. 37.36.

LIBYA, a country west of Egypt, peopled by Lubims, associated with Egyptians and Ethiopians, 2 Chr. 12.3. 2 Chr. 16.8. Jer. 46.9. Eze. 38.5. Nah. 3.9. Libyans at Jerusalem on the day of Pentecost, Act. 2.10. Prophecy of, Eze. 30.5. Town of, see CYRENE.

LICE, plague of, Ex. 8.16-19. Psa. 105.31.

LICENTIOUSNESS. See ADULTERY—SENSUALITY.

LIFE ETERNAL. See SOUL, IMMORTALITY OF.

LIFE, FRAILTY OF. Gen. 47.9. The days of the years of my pilgrimage *are* an hundred and thirty years: few and evil have the days of the years of my life been.

1 Sam. 20.3. *There is* but a step between me and death.

2 Sam. 14.14. We must needs die, and *are* as water spilt on the ground, which cannot be gathered up again.

1 Chr. 29.15. We *are* strangers before thee, and sojourners, as *were* all our fathers: our days on the earth *are* as a shadow, and *there is* none abiding.

Job 4.19. Them that dwell in houses of clay, whose foundation *is* in the dust, *which* are crushed before the moth? 20. They are destroyed from morning to evening: they perish for ever without any regarding *it.* 21. Doth not their excellency *which is* in them go away? they die, even without wisdom.

Job 7.6. My days are swifter than a weaver's shuttle, and are spent without hope. 7. O remember that my life *is* wind. *v.* 17.

Job 8.9. We *are but* of yesterday, and know nothing, because our days upon earth *are* a shadow.

Job 9.25. Now my days are swifter than a post: they flee away, they see no good. 26. They are passed away as the swift ships: as the eagle *that* hasteth to the prey.

Job 10.9. Remember, I beseech thee, that thou hast made me as the clay; and wilt thou bring me into dust again? 20. *Are* not my days few? cease *then, and* let me alone, that I may take comfort a little.

Job 13.12. Your remembrances *are* like unto ashes, your bodies to bodies of clay. 25. Wilt thou break a leaf driven to and fro? and wilt thou pursue the dry stubble? 28. He, as a rotten thing, consumeth, as a garment that is moth eaten. Gen. 18.27.

Job 14.1. Man *that is* born of a woman *is* of few days, and full of trouble. 2. He cometh forth like a flower, and is cut down: he fleeth also as a shadow, and continueth not.

Psa. 22.29. None can keep alive his own soul.

Psa. 39.5. Thou hast made my days *as* an handbreadth; and mine age *is* as nothing before thee: verily every man at his best state *is* altogether vanity. 6. Surely every man walketh in a vain shew: surely they are disquieted in vain: he heapeth up *riches,* and knoweth not who shall gather them.

Psa. 39.11. When thou with rebukes dost correct man for iniquity, thou makest his beauty to consume away like a moth: surely every man *is* vanity.

Psa. 78.39. He remembered that they *were but* flesh; a wind that passeth away, and cometh not again.

Psa. 89.47. Remember how short my time is: wherefore hast thou made all men in vain?

Psa. 90.3. Thou turnest man to destruction; and sayest, Return, ye children of men. 5. Thou carriest them away as with a flood; they are *as* a sleep in the morning; *they are* like grass *which* groweth up; 6. In the morning it flourisheth, and groweth up; in the evening it is cut down, and withereth. 9. All our days are passed away in thy wrath: we spend our years as a tale *that is told.* 10. The days of our years *are* threescore years and ten; and if by reason of strength *they be* fourscore years, yet *is* their strength labour and sorrow; for it is soon cut off, and we fly away.

Psa. 102.11. My days *are* like a shadow that declineth; and I am withered like grass.

Psa. 103.14. He knoweth our frame; he remembereth that we *are* dust. 15. *As for* man, his days *are* as grass: as a flower of the field, so he flourisheth. 16. For the wind passeth over it, and it is gone; and the place thereof shall know it no more.

Psa. 144.4. Man is like to vanity: his days *are* as a shadow that passeth away. *v.* 3.

Psa. 146.4. His breath goeth forth, he returneth to his earth; in that very day his thoughts perish.

Pro. 27.1. Boast not thyself of to-morrow; for thou knowest not what a day may bring forth.

Ecc. 6.12. Who knoweth what *is* good for man in *this* life, all the days of his vain life which he spendeth as a shadow?

Isa. 2.22. Cease ye from man, whose breath *is* in his nostrils: for wherein is he to be accounted of?

Isa. 38.12. Mine age is departed, and is removed from me as a shepherd's tent: I have cut off like a weaver my life: he will cut me off with pining sickness: from day *even* to night wilt thou make an end of me.

Isa. 40.6. All flesh *is* grass, and all the goodliness thereof *is* as the flower of the field: 7. The grass withereth, the flower fadeth: because the spirit of the Lord bloweth upon it: surely the people *is* grass. 24. He shall also blow upon them, and they shall wither, and the whirlwind shall take them away as stubble. 1 Pet. 1.24.

Isa. 50.9. Lo, they all shall wax old as a garment; the moth shall eat them up.

Isa. 51.8. The moth shall eat them up like a garment, and the worm shall eat them like wool. 12. Who *art* thou, that thou shouldest be afraid of a man *that* shall die, and of the son of man *which* shall be made *as* grass?

Isa. 64.6. We all do fade as a leaf.

Jas. 4.14. Ye know not what *shall be* on the morrow. For what *is* your life? It is even a vapcur, that appeareth for a little time, and then vanisheth away.

See DEATH.

LIFE FROM GOD. Gen. 2.7. The Lord God formed man *of* the dust of the ground, and breathed into his nostrils the breath of life; and man became a living soul.

Deu. 8.3. Man doth not live by bread only, but by every *word* that proceedeth out of the mouth of the Lord doth man live.

Deu. 30.20. He *is* thy life, and the length of thy days.

1 Sam. 2.6. The Lord killeth, and maketh alive: he bringeth down to the grave, and bringeth up.

Psa. 30.3. O Lord, thou hast brought up my soul from the grave: thou hast kept me alive, that I should not go down to the pit.

Psa. 68.20. Unto God the Lord *belong* the issues from death.

Psa. 104.30. Thou sendest forth thy spirit, they are created: and thou renewest the face of the earth.

Ecc. 12.7. The spirit shall return unto God who gave it.

Isa. 38.16. O Lord, by these *things men* live, and in all these *things is* the life of my spirit: so wilt thou recover me, and make me to live. 17. Thou hast in love to my soul *delivered it* from the pit of corruption.

Rom. 4.17. God, who quickeneth the dead, and calleth those things which be not as though they were.

1 Tim. 6.13. God, who quickeneth all things.

See GOD, CREATOR OF MAN.

LIGHT, illustrative, Isa. 8.20. Isa. 58.8. Mat. 4.16. Psa. 119.105. 2 Pet. 1.19. Luk. 16.8. Mat. 5.14,16. Jno. 5.35. Eph. 5.8. 1 Kin. 11.36. Psa. 27.1. 1 Jno. 1.5. Luk. 2.32. Jno. 1.9. Jno. 8.12.

LIGHTNING. See THUNDER.

LIGURE, a gem, Ex. 28.19. Ex. 39.12.

LIKENESS TO GOD AND CHRIST. CHRIST OUR EXAMPLE. Gen. 1.26. God said, Let us make man in our image, after our likeness. *v.* 27. Gen. 5.1.

Psa. 17.15. I shall be satisfied, when I awake, with thy likeness.

Mat. 5.48. Be ye therefore perfect, even as your Father which is in heaven is perfect.

Mat. 11.29. Take my yoke upon you, and

learn of me; for I am meek and lowly in heart; and ye shall find rest unto your souls.

Jno. 10.4. He goeth before them, and the sheep follow him: for they know his voice.

Jno. 13.15. I have given you an example, that ye should do as I have done to you. *v.* 14-16,34.

Jno. 17.14. The world hath hated them, because they are not of the world, even as I am not of the world. 18. As thou hast sent me into the world, even so have I also sent them into the world. 21. That they all may be one; as thou, Father, *art* in me, and I in thee, that they also may be one in us: that the world may believe that thou hast sent me 22. And the glory which thou gavest me I have given them; that they may be one, even as we are one.

Rom. 8.29. Whom he did foreknow, he also did predestinate *to be* conformed to the image of his Son.

Rom. 13.14. Put ye on the Lord Jesus Christ.

Rom. 15.2. Let every one of us please *his* neighbour for *his* good to edification. 3. For even Christ pleased not himself. 5. The God of patience and consolation grant you to be like-minded one toward another according to Christ Jesus.

2 Cor. 3.18. We all, with open face beholding as in a glass the glory of the Lord, are changed into the same image from glory to glory, *even* as by the Spirit of the Lord.

2 Cor. 4.10. Always bearing about in the body the dying of the Lord Jesus, that the life also of Jesus might be made manifest in our body.

Gal. 3.27. As many of you as have been baptized into Christ, have put on Christ.

Gal. 4.19. My little children, of whom I travail in birth again until Christ be formed in you.

Eph. 3.19. That ye might be filled with all the fulness of God.

Eph. 4.13. Till we all come in the unity of the faith, and of the knowledge of the Son of God, unto a perfect man, unto the measure of the stature of the fulness of Christ. 15. May grow up into him in all things, which is the head, *even* Christ. 24. Put on the new man, which after God is created in righteousness and true holiness. *v.* 32.

Phil. 2.5. Let this mind be in you, which was also in Christ Jesus.

Col. 3.10. Put on the new *man,* which is renewed in knowledge after the image of him that created him. 11. Christ is all, and in all.

1 The. 1.6. Ye became followers of us, and of the Lord, having received the word in much affliction, with joy of the Holy Ghost.

Heb. 3.1. Holy brethren, partakers of the heavenly calling, consider the Apostle and High-Priest of our profession, Christ Jesus.

Heb. 12.2. Looking unto Jesus the author and finisher of *our* faith; who for the joy that was set before him endured the cross, despising the shame, and is set down at the right hand of the throne of God. 3. Consider him that endured such contradiction of sinners against himself, lest ye be wearied and faint in your minds. *v.* 4.

1 Pet. 1.15. As he which hath called you is holy, so be ye holy in all manner of conversation. *v.* 16. Lev. 11.44,45.

1 Pet. 2.21. Christ also suffered for us, leaving us an example, that ye should follow his steps. v. 22,23. Eph. 5.2.

1 Jno. 2.6. He that saith he abideth in him ought himself also so to walk, even as he walked.

1 Jno. 3.1. The world knoweth us not, because it knew him not. 2. Beloved, now are we the sons of God : and it doth not yet appear what we shall be ; but we know that when he shall appear, we shall be like him ; for we shall see him as he is. 3. Every man that hath this hope in Him purifieth himself, even as He is pure. v. 7,16.

1 Jno. 4.17. Herein is our love made perfect, that we may have boldness in the day of judgment : because as he is, so are we in this world. v. 11,18.

Rev. 14.4. These are they which follow the Lamb whithersoever he goeth.

LILY, Song 2.1,2. Hos. 14.5. Mat. 6.28-30. Red lily, Song 5.13. Artificial flower-work of, 1 Kin. 7.19,22,26. 2 Chr. 4. Musical instrument named from (Heb. *Shoshannim*), *titles*, Psa. 45. Psa. 69. Psa. 80 ; and Persian king's palace (Chal. *Shushan*), Dan. 8.2.

LIME, Isa. 33.12. Amos 2.1. Translated plaster, Deu. 27.2,4.

LINEN, manufacture of, 1 Chr. 4.21. By women, Pro. 31.24. Brought from Egypt, Eze. 27.7. 1 Kin. 10.28 ; and from Syria, Eze. 27.16. Tabernacle curtains made of, Ex. 26.1. Hangings of, Ex. 27.9. Priests' garments of, Ex. 28-8,15,39-42. Lev. 6.10. Lev. 16. 4,23,32.

Garments of, worn by men, Gen. 41.42. Est. 8.15. Luk. 16.19 ; by women, Isa. 3.23. Eze. 16.10,13. Girdles made of, Jer. 13.1. Mar. 14.51,52. Bed-clothes of, Pro. 7.16. Forbidden to be woven with wool, Lev. 19.19. Deu. 22.11. Christ's body wrapped in, Mar. 15.46. Jno. 20.5. Translated silk, Pro. 31.22. Gen. 41.42 (*marg.*). Illustrative, Rev. 19.8,14. Symbolical, Eze. 9.2. Dan. 10.5. Rev. 15.6.

LION, courage, strength, fierceness of, Gen. 49.9. Deu. 33.20. Job 4.10. Job 28.8. Psa. 7.2. Psa. 22.13. Pro. 20.2. Pro. 30.30. Isa. 38.13. Joel 1.6. Mic. 5.8. Nah. 2.12. Cunning, Psa. 17.12. Haunts of, Jer. 4.7. Jer. 25.38. Jer. 49.19. Carvings of, 1 Kin. 7.29,36. 1 Kin. 10.19,20.

A lion slain by Samson, Jud. 14.5-8. David, 1 Sam. 17.34. Benaiah, 2 Sam. 23.20. Prophet slain by, 1 Kin. 13.24-28. Man slain by, 1 Kin. 20.36. Samaritans killed by, 2 Kin. 17.25,26. Daniel in den of, Dan. 6. Riddle about, Jud. 14.14,18. Proverb, Ecc. 9.4. Parable, Eze. 19.1-9. Illustrative, Isa. 11.7. Isa. 35.9. 2 Tim. 4.17. 1 Pet. 5.8. Symbol of Judah, Gen. 49.9. Rev. 5.5. Of Jerusalem, Isa. 29.1 (*marg.*). Symbolical, Eze. 1.10. Eze. 10.14. Dan. 7.4. Rev. 4.7. Rev. 9.8,17. Rev. 13.2.

LITTER, Isa. 66.20. Translated waggon, Num. 7.3.

LIVER, Ex. 29.13,22. Wound in, mortal, Pro. 7.23. Lam. 2.11. Superstitions connected with, Eze. 21.21.

LIVING FOR GOD. See GLORIFYING GOD, SPIRITUAL DILIGENCE, DECISION.

LIZARD, Lev. 11.30.

LO-AMMI (not my people), a name given to Hosea's son, typical of Israel, Hos. 1.9. See Hos. 2.23.

LOCK, Neh. 3.13,14. Song 5.5.

LOCUST, Lev. 11.22 (often translated grasshopper, as Jud. 6.5, &c.) Number of, Nah. 3.15. Devastation of, Deu. 28.38. 1 Kin. 8.37. 2 Chr. 7.13. Joel 1.4. Habits of, Pro. 30.27. Isa. 33.4. Used for food, Mat. 3.4. Plague of, Ex. 10.1-19. Symbolical, Rev. 9.3-11.

LOD. See LYDDA.

LODGE. See BOOTH.

LOG, the smallest liquid measure, 12th of a hin, about 1 pint, Lev. 14.10,12,15,24.

LOIS, Timothy's grandmother, 2 Tim. 1.5.

LOOKING - GLASS, 2 Cor. 3.18. Jas. 1.23,24. 1 Cor. 13.12. 2 Cor. 3.18. Of brass, Ex. 38.8. Molten, Job 37.18.

LORD'S DAY. See SABBATH.

LORD'S SUPPER. Mat. 26.26-28. Mar. 14.22-24. Luke 22.19,20. John 13.1-4. Act. 2.42,46. Act. 20.7. 1 Cor. 5.7,8. 1 Cor. 10.16,17,21,22. 1 Cor. 11.17-34. 2 Pet. 2.13.

LO-RUHAMAH (unpitied), name of Hosea's daughter, typical of Israel, Hos. 1.6-8.

LOT, son of Haran, and nephew of Abraham ; leaves Ur, and comes to Haran with Abraham, Gen. 11.27,31. Leaves Haran for Canaan, Gen. 12.5. Returns from Egypt, Gen. 13.1. Strife between his and Abraham's herdsmen ; parts with Abraham and dwells in Sodom, Gen. 13.5-13. 2 Pet. 2.7. Taken captive ; rescued by Abraham, Gen. 14.12,16. Warned by angels ; rescued from Sodom ; his wife looks back, and is destroyed, Gen. 19. Luk. 17.28-32. His drunkenness and incest ; his descendants, Gen. 19.30-38. Deu. 2.9,19. Psa. 83.8. See AMMONITES, MOABITES.

LOT, THE. Pro. 16.33. Pro. 18.18. Isa. 34.17. Joel 3.3. Used to choose the scapegoat, Lev. 16.8-10. The inheritance of the tribes in Palestine, Num. 26.55. Jos. 15. Jos. 18.10. Jos. 19.51. Jos. 21. 1 Chr. 6.61,65. A king, 1 Sam. 10.20,21. The service of the priests and Levites, 1 Chr. 24.5-31. 1 Chr. 26.13. Neh. 10.34. Luk. 1.9. The inhabitants of Jerusalem after the captivity, Neh. 11.1. An apostle, Act. 1.26. Christ's garments, Psa. 22.18. Mat. 27.35.

Used to discover Achan's trespass, Jos. 7. 14-18. Jonathan's violation of Saul's oath, 1 Sam. 14.41,42. When to destroy the Jews ; by Haman, Est. 3.7. Est. 9.24. Jonah's sin, Jon. 1.7.

———, signifying property or inheritance, Jud. 1.3. Psa. 16.5. Dan. 12.13.

LOTS, FEAST OF. See FEAST OF PURIM.

LOVE TO GOD AND CHRIST. Ex. 20.6. Shewing mercy unto thousands of them that love me, and keep my commandments. Deu. 5.10.

Deu. 7.9. The faithful God, which keepeth covenant and mercy with them that love him and keep his commandments to a thousand generations.

Deu. 10.12. What doth the Lord thy God require of thee, but to fear the Lord thy God, to walk in all his ways, and to love him, and to serve the Lord thy God with all thy heart and with all thy soul ?

Deu. 13.3. The Lord your God proveth you, to know whether ye love the Lord your God with all your heart, and with all your soul.

Deu. 30.6. The Lord thy God will circumcise thine heart, and the heart of thy seed, to love the Lord thy God with all thine heart, and with all thy soul that thou mayest live. *v.* 16,20.

Jos. 22.5. Take diligent heed to love the Lord your God, and to walk in all his ways, and to keep his commandments, and to cleave unto him, and to serve him with all your heart and with all your soul. Deu. 11.1,13,22.

Jos. 23.11. Take good heed therefore unto yourselves, that ye love the Lord your God.

Psa. 31.23. O love the Lord, all ye his saints: *for* the Lord preserveth the faithful.

Psa. 37.4. Delight thyself also in the Lord; and he shall give thee the desires of thine heart.

Psa. 45.10. Forget also thine own people, and thy father's house; 11. So shall the king greatly desire thy beauty: for he *is* thy Lord; and worship thou him. (See Song of Solomon.)

Psa. 69.36. They that love his name shall dwell therein.

Psa. 91.14. Because he hath set his love upon me, therefore will I deliver him: I will set him on high, because he hath known my name.

Psa. 97.10. Ye that love the Lord, hate evil.

Psa. 145.20. The Lord preserveth all those that love him.

Pro. 8.17. I love them that love me; and those that seek me early shall find me.

Pro. 23.26. My son, give me thine heart, and let thine eyes observe my ways.

Isa. 56.6. The sons of the stranger, that join themselves to the Lord, to serve him, and to love the name of the Lord, to be his servants. 7. Even them will I bring to my holy mountain, and make them joyful in my house of prayer.

Mat. 10.37. He that loveth father or mother more than me is not worthy of me: and he that loveth son or daughter more than me is not worthy of me.

Mat. 25.34. Come, ye blessed of my Father, inherit the kingdom prepared for you from the foundation of the world; 35. For I was an hungred, and ye gave me meat. 40. Verily I say unto you, Inasmuch as ye have done *it* unto one of the least of these my brethren, ye have done *it* unto me. *v.* 36.

Mar. 9.41. Whosoever shall give you a cup of water to drink in my name, because ye belong to Christ, verily I say unto you, he shall not lose his reward.

Mar. 12.29. Jesus answered him, The first of all the commandments *is*, Hear, O Israel; The Lord our God is one Lord: 30. And thou shalt love the Lord thy God with all thy heart, and with all thy soul, and with all thy mind, and with all thy strength: this *is* the first commandment. 33. To love him with all the heart, and with all the understanding, and with all the soul, and with all the strength, and to love *his* neighbour as himself, is more than all whole burnt-offerings and sacrifices. Deu. 6.5. Mat. 22.37.

Luk. 11.42. Ye tithe mint and rue, and all manner of herbs, and pass over judgment and the love of God: these ought ye to have done, and not to leave the other undone.

Jno. 8.42. If God were your Father, ye would love me.

Jno. 14.15. If ye love me, keep my commandments. 21. He that hath my commandments, and keepeth them, he it is that loveth me: and he that loveth me shall be loved of my Father, and I will love him, and will manifest myself to him. 23. If a man love me, he will keep my words: and my Father will love him, and we will come unto him, and make our abode with him.

Jno. 15.9. As the Father hath loved me, so have I loved you; continue ye in my love.

Jno. 17.26. That the love wherewith thou hast loved me may be in them, and I in them.

Rom. 5.5. The love of God is shed abroad in our hearts by the Holy Ghost which is given unto us.

Rom. 8.28. We know that all things work together for good to them that love God.

1 Cor. 8.3. If any man love God, the same is known of him.

1 Cor. 13.1. Though I speak with the tongues of men and of angels, and have not charity, I am become *as* sounding brass, or a tinkling cymbal. 13. Now abideth faith, hope, charity, these three; but the greatest of these *is* charity. *v.* 2,3.

1 Cor. 14.1. Follow after charity.

1 Cor. 16.22. If any man love not the Lord Jesus Christ, let him be Anathema Maranatha.

2 Cor. 5.14. The love of Christ constraineth us; because we thus judge, that if one died for all, then were all dead: 15. And *that* he died for all, that they which live should not henceforth live unto themselves, but unto him which died for them and rose again.

Gal. 5.6. In Jesus Christ neither circumcision availeth any thing, nor uncircumcision; but faith which worketh by love. 22. The fruit of the Spirit is love.

Eph. 3.17. That Christ may dwell in your hearts by faith; that ye, being rooted and grounded in love, 18. May be able to comprehend with all saints what *is* the breadth, and length, and depth, and height; 19. And to know the love of Christ, which passeth knowledge, that ye might be filled with all the fulness of God.

Eph. 4.15. Speaking the truth in love, may grow up into him in all things, which is the head, *even* Christ.

Eph. 6.24. Grace *be* with all them that love our Lord Jesus Christ in sincerity.

Phil. 1.9. I pray, that your love may abound yet more and more in knowledge and *in* all judgment.

2 The. 3.5. The Lord direct your hearts into the love of God, and into the patient waiting for Christ.

2 Tim. 1.7. God hath not given us the spirit of fear; but of power, and of love, and of a sound mind. 13. Hold fast the form of sound words, in faith and love which is in Christ Jesus.

2 Tim. 4.8. There is laid up for me a crown of righteousness . . . and not to me only, but unto all them also that love his appearing.

Jas. 1.12. He shall receive the crown of life, which the Lord hath promised to them that love him.

Jas. 2.5. Heirs of the kingdom which he hath promised to them that love him.

1 Pet. 1.8. Whom having not seen, ye love: in whom, though now ye see *him* not, yet believing, ye rejoice with joy unspeakable and full of glory.

1 Pet. 2.7. Unto you therefore which believe *he is* precious.

1 Jno. 2.5. Whoso keepeth his word, in him verily is the love of God perfected: hereby know we that we are in him. 15. If any man love the world, the love of the Father is not in him.

1 Jno. 3.17. Whoso hath this world's good, and seeth his brother have need, and shutteth up his bowels *of compassion* from him, how dwelleth the love of God in him? 18. Let us not love in word, neither in tongue; but in deed and in truth.

1 Jno. 4.12. God dwelleth in us, and his love is perfected in us. 16. We have known and believed the love that God hath to us. God is love; and he that dwelleth in love dwelleth in God, and God in him. 17. Herein is our love made perfect. 18. There is no fear in love; but perfect love casteth out fear: because fear hath torment. He that feareth is not made perfect in love. 19. We love him, because he first loved us. 20. If a man say, I love God, and hateth his brother, he is a liar: for he that loveth not his brother whom he hath seen, how can he love God whom he hath not seen?

1 Jno. 5.1. Every one that loveth him that begat loveth him also that is begotten of him. 2. By this we know that we love the children of God, when we love God, and keep his commandments. 3. For this is the love of God, that we keep his commandments.

2 Jno. 6. This is love, that we walk after his commandments.

Jude 21. Keep yourselves in the love of God.

Rev. 2.4. I have *somewhat* against thee, because thou hast left thy first love. Rev. 3.15.

Love to God AND CHRIST, EXAMPLES OF:
Solomon, 1 Kin. 3.3. Mary of Bethany, Mat. 26.6-13. Jno. 12.3-8. Luk. 10.39. Peter, Mat. 17.4. Jno. 13.37. Jno. 18.10. Jno. 20.3-6. Jno. 21.7. Thomas, Jno. 11.16. The disciples, Mar. 16.10. Luk. 24.17-41. Jno. 20.20. Mary Magdalene, &c., Mat. 27.55,56,61. Mat. 28.1-9. Luk. 8.2,3. Luk. 23.55,56. Luk. 24.1-10. Jno. 20.1,2,11-18. A man, Mar. 5.18. Joseph, Mat. 27.57-60. Nicodemus, Jno. 19.39,40. Women of Jerusalem, Luk. 23.27.

Love to God AND CHRIST EXEMPLIFIED.
Psa. 18.1. I will love thee, O Lord, my strength.

Psa. 63.6. I remember thee upon my bed, *and* meditate on thee in the *night* watches.

Psa. 73.25. Whom have I in heaven *but thee?* and *there* is none upon earth *that* I desire beside thee. 26. My flesh and my heart faileth: *but* God *is* the strength of my heart, and my portion for ever.

Psa. 116.1. I love the Lord, because he hath heard my voice *and* my supplications.

Jer. 2.2. I remember thee, the kindness of thy youth, the love of thine espousals, when thou wentest after me in the wilderness, in a land *that was* not sown. 3. Israel *was* holiness unto the Lord, *and* the firstfruits of his increase.

Luk. 2.29. Lord, now lettest thou thy servant depart in peace, according to thy word: 30. For mine eyes have seen thy salvation.

Luk. 7.47. Her sins, which are many, are forgiven; for she loved much: but to whom little is forgiven, *the same* loveth little.

Jno. 16.27. The Father himself loveth you, because ye have loved me.

Jno. 21.17. Lord, thou knowest all things; thou knowest that I love thee.

Act. 21.13. I am ready not to be bound only, but also to die at Jerusalem for the name of the Lord Jesus.

2 Cor. 5.8. We are confident, *I say*, and willing rather to be absent from the body, and to be present with the Lord. *v. 6.*

Gal. 6.14. God forbid that I should glory, save in the cross of our Lord Jesus Christ, by whom the world is crucified unto me, and I unto the world.

Phil. 1.23. Having a desire to depart, and to be with Christ; which is far better: *v.* 20,21.

Phil. 3.7. What things were gain to me, those I counted loss for Christ. 8. Yea doubtless, and I count all things *but* loss for the excellency of the knowledge of Christ Jesus my Lord: for whom I have suffered the loss of all things, and do count them *but* dung, that I may win Christ.

Philm. 5. Hearing of thy love and faith, which thou hast toward the Lord Jesus.

Heb. 6.10. God *is* not unrighteous, to forget your work and labour of love, which ye have shewed toward his name.

See DECISION, SPIRITUAL DILIGENCE, WORSHIP LOVED.

LOVE, KINDNESS, SYMPATHY. Lev. 19.18. Thou shalt love thy neighbour as thyself: I *am* the Lord. 34. *But* the stranger that dwelleth with you shall be unto you as one born among you, and thou shalt love him as thyself; for ye were strangers in the land of Egypt.

Num. 24.9. Blessed *is* he that blesseth thee.

Deu. 22.1. Thou shalt not see thy brother's ox or his sheep go astray, and hide thyself from them: thou shalt in any case bring them again unto thy brother. *v.* 2-4.

Deu. 23.15. Thou shalt not deliver unto his master the servant which is escaped from his master unto thee. 16. He shall dwell with thee, *even* among you, in that place which he shall choose in one of thy gates, where it liketh him best: thou shalt not oppress him.

Job 6.14. To him that is afflicted pity *should be shewed* from his friend.

Job 16.5. I would strengthen you with my mouth, and the moving of my lips should assuage *your grief.*

Job 19.28. Ye should say, Why persecute we him, seeing the root of the matter is found in me?

Job 22.29. When *men* are cast down, then thou shalt say, *There is* lifting up; and he shall save the humble person.

Psa. 15.4. He honoureth them that fear the Lord.

Psa. 35.27. Let them shout for joy, and be glad, that favour my righteous cause: yea, let them say continually, Let the Lord be magnified, which hath pleasure in the prosperity of his servant.

Psa. 54.4. The Lord *is* with them that uphold my soul.

Psa. 112.4. *He is* gracious, and full of compassion, and righteous. 5. A good man sheweth favour, and lendeth.

Psa. 119.74. They that fear thee will be glad when they see me ; because I have hoped in thy word. 79. Let those that fear thee turn unto me.

Psa. 133.1. Behold, how good and how pleasant *it is* for brethren to dwell together in unity ! *v.* 2, 3.

Psa. 142.7. The righteous shall compass me about; for thou shalt deal bountifully with me.

Pro. 3.3. Let not mercy and truth forsake thee : bind them about thy neck ; write them upon the table of thine heart : 4. So shalt thou find favour and good understanding in the sight of God and man.

Pro. 10.12. Love covereth all sins.

Pro. 11.17. The merciful man doeth good to his own soul.

Pro. 12.25. Heaviness in the heart of man maketh it stoop ; but a good word maketh it glad.

Pro. 15.17. Better *is* a dinner of herbs where love is, than a stalled ox and hatred therewith.

Pro. 17.9. He that covereth a transgression seeketh love. 17. A friend loveth at all times, and a brother is born for adversity.

Pro. 19.22. The desire of a man *is* his kindness.

Pro. 29.10. The bloodthirsty hate the upright : but the just seek his soul.

Pro. 31.26. In her tongue *is* the law of kindness.

Song 8.6. Love *is* strong as death ; jealousy *is* cruel as the grave ; the coals thereof *are* coals of fire, *which hath* a most vehement flame. 7. Many waters cannot quench love, neither can the floods drown it : if a man would give all the substance of his house for love, it would utterly be contemned.

Isa. 11.13. Ephraim shall not envy Judah, and Judah shall not vex Ephraim.

Zec. 7.9. Shew mercy and compassions every man to his brother.

Mal. 2.10. Have we not all one father ? hath not one God created us ? why do we deal treacherously every man against his brother ?

Mat. 5.41. Whosoever shall compel thee to go a mile, go with him twain. 42. Give to him that asketh thee, and from him that would borrow of thee turn not thou away.

Mat. 10.41. He that receiveth a prophet in the name of a prophet shall receive a prophet's reward ; and he that receiveth a righteous man in the name of a righteous man shall receive a righteous man's reward. 42. And whosoever shall give to drink unto one of these little ones a cup of cold *water* only in the name of a disciple, verily I say unto you, He shall in no wise lose his reward.

Mat. 25.34. Come, ye blessed of my Father, inherit the kingdom prepared for you from the foundation of the world : 35. For I was an hungred, and ye gave me meat. 40. And the King shall answer and say unto them, Verily I say unto you, Inasmuch as ye have done *it* unto one of the least of these my brethren, ye have done *it* unto me. *v.* 34-40.

Mar. 9.41. Whosoever shall give you a cup of water to drink in my name, because ye belong to Christ, verily I say unto you, he shall not lose his reward.

Mar. 12.31. Thou shalt love thy neighbour as thyself. There is none other commandment greater than these. 33. And to love *his* neighbour as himself, is more than all whole burntofferings and sacrifices. Mat. 22.39.

Luk. 6.31. As ye would that men should do to you, do ye also to them likewise. 32. If ye love them which love you, what thank have ye ? for sinners also love those that love them. 33. And if ye do good to them which do good to you, what thank have ye ? for sinners also do even the same. 34. And if ye lend *to them* of whom ye hope to receive, what thank have ye ? for sinners also lend to sinners, to receive as much again. 35. But love ye your enemies, and do good, and lend, hoping for nothing again ; and your reward shall be great, and ye shall be the children of the Highest : for he is kind unto the unthankful and *to* the evil. Mat. 7.12.

Luk. 10.36. Which now of these three, thinkest thou, was neighbour unto him that fell among the thieves ? 37. And he said, He that shewed mercy on him. Then said Jesus unto him, Go, and do thou likewise. *v.* 30-37.

Jno. 13.14. If I then, *your* Lord and Master, have washed your feet, ye also ought to wash one another's feet. 15. I have given you an example, that ye should do as I have done to you. 34. A new commandment I give unto you, That ye love one another ; as I have loved you, that ye also love one another. 35. By this shall all *men* know that ye are my disciples, if ye have love one to another.

Jno. 15.17. These things I command you, that ye love one another. *v.* 12.

Rom. 12.9. *Let* love be without dissimulation. 10. *Be* kindly affectioned one to another with brotherly love ; in honour preferring one another. 15. Rejoice with them that do rejoice, and weep with them that weep. 16. *Be* of the same mind one toward another. Mind not high things, but condescend to men of low estate.

Rom. 13.8. Owe no man anything, but to love one another : for he that loveth another hath fulfilled the law. 9. If *there* be any other commandment, it is briefly comprehended in this saying, namely, Thou shalt love thy neighbour as thyself. 10. Love worketh no ill to his neighbour : therefore love *is* the fulfilling of the law.

Rom. 14.19. Follow after the things which make for peace, and things wherewith one may edify another. 21. *It is* good neither to eat flesh, nor to drink wine, nor *any thing* whereby thy brother stumbleth, or is offended, or is made weak.

Rom. 15.1. We then that are strong ought to bear the infirmities of the weak, and not to please ourselves. 2. Let every one of us please *his* neighbour for *his* good to edification. 5. The God of patience and consolation grant you to be likeminded one toward another according to Christ Jesus. 7. Receive ye one another, as Christ also received us to the glory of God.

Rom. 16.2. Receive her in the Lord, as becometh saints, and assist her in whatsoever business she hath need of you : for she hath been a succourer of many, and of myself also.

1 Cor. 8.1. Knowledge puffeth up; but charity edifieth.

1 Cor. 10.24. Let no man seek his own, but every man another's *wealth*.

1 Cor. 12.26. Whether one member suffer, all the members suffer with it; or one member be honoured, all the members rejoice with it.

1 Cor. 13.1. Though I speak with the tongues of men and of angels, and have not charity, I am become *as* sounding brass, or a tinkling cymbal. 3. Though I bestow all my goods to feed *the poor*, and though I give my body to be burned, and have not charity, it profiteth me nothing. 4. Charity suffereth long, *and* is kind ; charity envieth not ; charity vaunteth not itself, is not puffed up, 5. Doth not behave itself unseemly, seeketh not her own, is not easily provoked, thinketh no evil ; 6. Rejoiceth not in iniquity, but rejoiceth in the truth ; 7. Beareth all things, believeth all things, hopeth all things, endureth all things.

1 Cor. 13.8. Charity never faileth: but whether *there be* prophecies, they shall fail ; whether *there be* tongues, they shall cease ; whether *there be* knowledge, it shall vanish away. 13. Now abideth faith, hope, charity, these three ; but the greatest of these *is* charity.

1 Cor. 14.1. Follow after charity.

1 Cor. 16.14. Let all your things be done with charity.

Gal. 5.13. By love serve one another. 14. For all the law is fulfilled in one word, *even* in this ; Thou shalt love thy neighbour as thyself. 22. The fruit of the Spirit is love, . . . goodness.

Gal. 6.1. If a man be overtaken in a fault, ye which are spiritual, restore such an one in the spirit of meekness ; considering thyself, lest thou also be tempted. 2. Bear ye one another's burdens, and so fulfil the law of Christ. 10. As we have therefore opportunity, let us do good unto all *men*, especially unto them who are of the household of faith.

Eph. 4.2. With all lowliness and meekness, with long-suffering, forbearing one another in love. 32 Be ye kind one to another, tender-hearted, forgiving one another, even as God for Christ's sake hath forgiven you.

Eph. 5.2. Walk in love, as Christ also hath loved us, and hath given himself for us an offering and a sacrifice to God for a sweet-smelling savour.

Phil. 1.9. I pray, that your love may abound yet more and more in knowledge and *in* all judgment.

Phil. 2.2. Fulfil ye my joy, that ye be like-minded, having the same love, *being* of one accord, of one mind. 4. Look not every man on his own things, but every man also on the things of others.

Phil. 4.2. I beseech Euodias, and beseech Syntyche, that they be of the same mind in the Lord. 3. I entreat thee also, true yoke-fellow, help those women which laboured with me in the gospel.

Col. 2.2. That their hearts might be comforted, being knit together in love.

Col. 3.12. Put on therefore, as the elect of God, holy and beloved, bowels of mercies, kindness, humbleness of mind, meekness, long-suffering ; 14. Above all these things *put on* charity, which is the bond of perfectness.

1 The. 3.12. The Lord make you to increase and abound in love one toward another, and toward all *men*, even as we *do* toward you.

1 The. 4.9. As touching brotherly love ye need not that I write unto you : for ye yourselves are taught of God to love one another. 10. And indeed ye do it toward all the brethren which are in all Macedonia : but we beseech you, brethren, that ye increase more and more ; 18. Comfort one another with these words.

1 The. 5.8. Putting on the breastplate of faith and love. 11. Comfort yourselves together, and edify one another, even as also ye do. 14. Comfort the feeble-minded, support the weak, be patient toward all.

1 Tim. 1.5. The end of the commandment is charity out of a pure heart, and *of* a good conscience, and *of* faith unfeigned. 14. The grace of our Lord was exceeding abundant with faith and love which is in Christ Jesus.

1 Tim. 5.10. Well reported of for good works ; if she have lodged strangers, if she have washed the saints' feet, if she have relieved the afflicted, if she have diligently followed every good work.

1 Tim. 6.2. They that have believing masters, let them not despise *them*, because they are brethren ; but rather do *them* service, because they are faithful and beloved, partakers of the benefit. 11. Follow after righteousness, godliness, faith, love, patience, meekness.

2 Tim. 1.8. Be not thou therefore ashamed of the testimony of our Lord, nor of me his prisoner.

Tit. 3.15. Greet them that love us in the faith.

Philm. 12. Receive him, that is, mine own bowels. 16. Not now as a servant, but above a servant, a brother beloved, specially to me, but how much more unto thee, both in the flesh, and in the Lord ? 20. Yea, brother, let me have joy of thee in the Lord : refresh my bowels in the Lord. 21. Having confidence in thy obedience I wrote unto thee, knowing that thou wilt also do more than I say.

Heb. 5.2. Who can have compassion on the ignorant, and on them that are out of the way ; for that he himself also is compassed with infirmity.

Heb. 10.24. Let us consider one another to provoke unto love and to good works.

Heb. 13.1. Let brotherly love continue. 3. Remember them that are in bonds, as bound with them ; *and* them which suffer adversity, as being yourselves also in the body.

Jas. 1.27. Pure religion and undefiled before God and the Father is this, To visit the fatherless and widows in their affliction.

Jas. 2.8. If ye fulfil the royal law according to the scripture, Thou shalt love thy neighbour as thyself, ye do well.

1 Pet. 1.22. Ye have purified your souls in obeying the truth through the Spirit unto unfeigned love of the brethren, see *that ye* love one another with a pure heart fervently.

1 Pet. 2.17. Honour all *men*. Love the brotherhood.

1 Pet. 3.8. *Be ye* all of one mind, having compassion one of another, love as brethren, *be* pitiful, *be* courteous. v. 9.

1 Pet. 4.8. Have fervent charity among yourselves : for charity shall cover the multitude of sins.

2 Pet. 1.7. Add . . . to godliness, brotherly kindness; and to brotherly kindness, charity.

1 Jno. 2.10. He that loveth his brother abideth in the light, and there is none occasion of stumbling in him.

1 Jno. 3.11. This is the message that ye heard from the beginning, that we should love one another.   14. We know that we have passed from death unto life, because we love the brethren. He that loveth not *his* brother abideth in death. 16. Hereby perceive we the love *of God*, because he laid down his life for us: and we ought to lay down *our* lives for the brethren. 17. But whoso hath this world's good, and seeth his brother have need, and shutteth up his bowels *of compassion* from him, how dwelleth the love of God in him? 18. My little children, let us not love in word, neither in tongue; but in deed and in truth. 23. Love one another, as he gave us commandment. *v.* 19.

1 Jno. 4.7. Let us love one another: for love is of God; and every one that loveth is born of God, and knoweth God. 11. If God so loved us, we ought also to love one another. 12. If we love one another, God dwelleth in us, and his love is perfected in us. 20. If a man say, I love God, and hateth his brother, he is a liar: for he that loveth not his brother whom he hath seen, how can he love God whom he hath not seen? 21. And this commandment have we from him, That he who loveth God love his brother also.

1 Jno. 5.1. Every one that loveth him that begat loveth him also that is begotten of him. 2. By this we know that we love the children of God, when we love God, and keep his commandments.

2 Jno. 5. Not as though I wrote a new commandment unto thee, but that which we had from the beginning, that we love one another.

Jude 22. Of some have compassion, making a difference.

LOVE, KINDNESS, &c., EXAMPLES OF: Abraham, Gen. 14.14-16. Jacob, Gen. 29.10. Reuben, Gen. 37.21,22. Joseph, Gen. 43.30-34. Gen. 45.1-5. Gen. 50.19-24. Pharaoh, Gen. 45.16-20. Gen. 47.5,6. Pharaoh's daughter, Ex. 2.6-10. Moses, Ex. 2.17. Num. 10.29-32. Jethro, Ex. 18.9. Reubenites, Jos. 1.12-15. Jos. 22.1-6. Rahab, Jos. 2.6-16. Israelites, Jud. 21.2,3. 2 Chr. 28.9-15. Naomi, Ruth, and Boaz, Ruth, c. 1, 2, 3. Samuel, 1 Sam. 15.30,31. David's servants, 2 Sam. 12.17-19. David's subjects, 2 Sam. 15.30. 2 Sam. 17.27,29. Obadiah, 1 Kin. 18.4. Elisha, 2 Kin. 8.1. Evil-merodach, 2 Kin. 25.28-30. Jehoshabeath, 2 Chr. 22.11. Nehemiah, Neh. 5.10-15. Mordecai, Est. 2.7. Job's friends, Job 2.11-13. Job 42.11. Ahikam, Jer. 26.24. Ebed-melech, Jer. 38.7-13. Nebuchadnezzar, Jer. 39.11,12. Dan. 1.3-20. Nebuzaradan, Jer. 40.1-5. Bartimeus' friends, Mar. 10.49. Jews, Jno. 11.19,33. Centurion, Luk. 7.2-6. John, Jno. 19.27. Philippian gaoler, Act. 16.33,34. Felix, Act. 24.23. Julius, Act. 27.3,43. Roman Christians, Act. 28.15. Titus, 2 Cor. 7.6.

LOVE, KINDNESS, &c., EXEMPLIFIED. Job 30.25. Did not I weep for him that was in trouble? was *not* my soul grieved for the poor? Psa. 35.13. When they were sick, my clothing *was* sackcloth: I humbled my soul with fasting; and my prayer returned into mine own bosom. 14. I behaved myself as though *he had been* my friend *or* brother: I bowed down heavily, as one that mourneth *for his* mother.

Act. 2.46. They, continuing daily with one accord in the temple, and breaking bread from house to house, did eat their meat with gladness and singleness of heart. *v.* 44,45.

Act. 4.32. The multitude of them that believed were of one heart and of one soul: neither said any *of them* that ought of the things which he possessed was his own; but they had all things common. *v.* 34-37.

Phil. 2.22. As a son with the father, he hath served with me in the gospel. 25. Epaphroditus, my brother, and companion in labour, and fellowsoldier, but your messenger, and he that ministered to my wants. 26. For he longed after you all, and was full of heaviness, because that ye had heard that he had been sick.

Phil. 4.21. The brethren which are with me greet you. , 22. All the saints salute you, chiefly they that are of Cæsar's household.

Col. 1.4. We heard of your faith in Christ Jesus, and of the love *which ye have* to all the saints. 8. Who also declared unto us your love in the Spirit. Eph. 1.15.

1 The. 1.3. Remembering without ceasing your work of faith, and labour of love.

1 The. 3.6. Brought us good tidings of your faith and charity, and that ye have good remembrance of us always, desiring greatly to see us.

1 The. 4.9. Ye yourselves are taught of God to love one another.

2 The. 1.3. The charity of every one of you all toward each other aboundeth.

2 Tim. 1.16. The Lord give mercy unto the house of Onesiphorus; 'for he oft refreshed me, and was not ashamed of my chain. 17. But, when he was in Rome, he sought me out very diligently, and found *me*. 18. The Lord grant unto him that he may find mercy of the Lord in that day: and in how many things he ministered unto me at Ephesus, thou knowest very well.

Philm. 5. Hearing of thy love and faith, which thou hast toward the Lord Jesus, and toward all saints. 7. We have great joy and consolation in thy love, because the bowels of the saints are refreshed by thee, brother.

Heb. 6.10. God *is* not unrighteous to forget your work and labour of love, which ye have shewed toward his name, in that ye have ministered to the saints, and do minister.

Heb. 10.33. Ye became companions of them that were so used. 34. For ye had compassion of me in my bonds.

2 Jno. 1. The elder unto the elect lady and her children, whom I love in the truth; and not I only, but also all they that have known the truth. 3. Grace be with you, mercy, *and* peace, from God the Father, and from the Lord Jesus Christ, the Son of the Father, in truth and love. 4. I rejoiced greatly that I found of thy children walking in truth. 12. I trust to come unto you, and speak face to face, that our joy may be full.

3 Jno. 1. The elder unto the well-beloved Gaius, whom I love in the truth. 3. I rejoiced greatly, when the brethren came and testified of the truth that is in thee, even as thou walkest in the truth. 4. I have no greater joy than

to hear that my children walk in truth. 5. Beloved, thou doest faithfully whatsoever thou doest to the brethren, and to strangers; 6. Which have born witness of thy charity before the church: whom if thou bring forward on their journey after a godly sort, thou shalt do well. 8. We therefore ought to receive such, that we might be fellow-helpers to the truth.

Rev. 2.19. I know thy works, and charity.

LOVE, EXEMPLIFIED BY PAUL. HIS ZEAL.

Act. 20.26. I take you to record this day, that I am pure from the blood of all men. 27. For I have not shunned to declare unto you all the counsel of God. 31. Watch, and remember, that by the space of three years I ceased not to warn every one night and day with tears.

Rom. 1.12. That I may be comforted together with you by the mutual faith both of you and me.

Rom. 9.3. I could wish that myself were accursed from Christ for my brethren, my kinsmen according to the flesh. v. 1,2.

Rom. 15.14. I myself also am persuaded of you, my brethren, that ye also are full of goodness, filled with all knowledge, able also to admonish one another. 15. Nevertheless, brethren, I have written the more boldly unto you in some sort, as putting you in mind, because of the grace that is given to me of God. 24. I trust to see you in my journey, and to be brought on my way thitherward by you, if first I be somewhat filled with your company. 32. That I may come unto you with joy by the will of God, and may with you be refreshed.

Rom. 16.8. Greet Amplias my beloved in the Lord. 19. Your obedience is come abroad unto all men. I am glad therefore on your behalf. v. 1-16. Col. 4.7.

1 Cor. 1.4. I thank my God always on your behalf, for the grace of God which is given you by Jesus Christ.

1 Cor. 4.14. I write not these things to shame you, but as my beloved sons I warn you. 15. For though ye have ten thousand instructers in Christ, yet have ye not many fathers: for in Christ Jesus I have begotten you through the gospel. 16. Wherefore I beseech you, be ye followers of me.

1 Cor. 8.13. If meat make my brother to offend, I will eat no flesh while the world standeth, lest I make my brother to offend.

2 Cor. 1.4. Who comforteth us in all our tribulation, that we may be able to comfort them which are in any trouble, by the comfort wherewith we ourselves are comforted of God. 5. For as the sufferings of Christ abound in us, so our consolation also aboundeth by Christ. 6. And whether we be afflicted, it is for your consolation and salvation, which is effectual in the enduring of the same sufferings which we also suffer: or whether we be comforted, it is for your consolation and salvation. 14. Ye have acknowledged us in part, that we are your rejoicing, even as ye also are our's in the day of the Lord Jesus. v. 23,24.

2 Cor. 2.4. Out of much affliction and anguish of heart I wrote unto you with many tears; not that ye should be grieved, but that ye might know the love which I have more abundantly unto you. v. 1-17.

2 Cor. 3.2. Ye are our epistle written in our hearts, known and read of all men.

2 Cor. 4.5. Ourselves your servants for Jesus' sake.

2 Cor. 6.4. In all things approving ourselves as the ministers of God. 6. By long-suffering, by kindness, by the Holy Ghost, by love unfeigned. 11. O ye Corinthians, our mouth is open unto you, our heart is enlarged. 12. Ye are not straitened in us, but ye are straitened in your own bowels. 13. Now for a recompence (I speak as unto my children,) be ye also enlarged.

2 Cor. 7.3. I have said before, that ye are in our hearts to die and live with you. 4. Great is my boldness of speech toward you, great is my glorying of you. 7. He told us your earnest desire, your mourning, your fervent mind toward me; so that I rejoiced the more. 12. Though I wrote unto you, I did it not for his cause that had done the wrong, nor for his cause that suffered wrong, but that our care for you in the sight of God might appear unto you.

2 Cor. 11.2. I am jealous over you with godly jealousy: for I have espoused you to one husband, that I may present you as a chaste virgin to Christ.

2 Cor. 12.14. The third time I am ready to come to you; and I will not be burdensome to you: for I seek not yours, but you: for the children ought not to lay up for the parents, but the parents for the children. 15. I will very gladly spend and be spent for you; though the more abundantly I love you, the less I be loved. 16. I did not burden you: nevertheless, being crafty, I caught you with guile. 19. We do all things, dearly beloved, for your edifying. 21. And lest, when I come again, my God will humble me among you, and that I shall bewail many which have sinned already.

2 Cor. 13.9. We are glad, when we are weak, and ye are strong: and this also we wish, even your perfection.

Gal. 4.11. I am afraid of you, lest I have bestowed upon you labour in vain. 12. Brethren, I beseech you, be as I am; for I am as ye are: ye have not injured me at all. 19. My little children, of whom I travail in birth again until Christ be formed in you, 20. I desire to be present with you now, and to change my voice; for I stand in doubt of you. v. 11-20.

Eph. 3.13. I desire that ye faint not at my tribulations for you, which is your glory.

Eph. 6.22. Whom I have sent unto you for the same purpose, that ye might know our affairs, and that he might comfort your hearts. v. 24.

Phil. 1.3. I thank my God upon every remembrance of you. 7. I have you in my heart; inasmuch as both in my bonds, and in the defence and confirmation of the gospel, ye all are partakers of my grace. 8. For God is my record, how greatly I long after you all in the bowels of Jesus Christ. 24. To abide in the flesh is more needful for you. 25. And having this confidence, I know that I shall abide and continue with you all for your furtherance and joy of faith; 26. That your rejoicing may be more abundant in Jesus Christ for me by my coming to you again.

Phil. 2.19. I trust in the Lord Jesus to send Timotheus shortly unto you, that I also may be of good comfort, when I know your state.

Phil. 3.18. Many walk, of whom I have told you often, and now tell you even weeping, *that they are* the enemies of the cross of Christ.

Phil. 4.1. My brethren dearly beloved and longed for, my joy and crown, so stand fast in the Lord, *my* dearly beloved.

Col. 1.3. We give thanks to God and the Father of our Lord Jesus Christ, praying always for you, 4. Since we heard of your faith in Christ Jesus, and of the love *which ye have* to all the saints. 24. Who now rejoice in my sufferings for you, and fill up that which is behind of the afflictions of Christ in my flesh for his body's sake, which is the church. 28. Whom we preach, warning every man, and teaching every man in all wisdom; that we may present every man perfect in Christ Jesus.

Col. 2.1. I would that ye knew what great conflict I have for you, and *for* them at Laodicea, and *for* as many as have not seen my face in the flesh. 5. Though I be absent in the flesh, yet am I with you in the spirit, joying and beholding your order, and the stedfastness of your faith in Christ.

1 The. 1.3. Remembering without ceasing your work of faith, and labour of love, and patience of hope in our Lord Jesus Christ, in the sight of God and our Father; 4. Knowing, brethren beloved, your election of God.

1 The. 2.7. We were gentle among you, even as a nurse cherisheth her children. 8. Being affectionately desirous of you, we were willing to have imparted unto you, not the gospel of God only, but also our own souls, because ye were dear unto us. 11. Ye know how we exhorted and comforted and charged every one of you, as a father *doth* his children.

1 The. 2.17. We, brethren, being taken from you for a short time in presence, not in heart, endeavoured the more abundantly to see your face with great desire. 19. What *is* our hope, or joy, or crown of rejoicing? *Are* not even ye in the presence of our Lord Jesus Christ at his coming? 20. For ye are our glory and joy.

1 The. 3.5. I sent to know your faith, lest by some means the tempter have tempted you, and our labour be in vain. 7. Brethren, we were comforted over you in all our affliction and distress by your faith : 8. For now we live, if ye stand fast in the Lord. 9. For what thanks can we render to God again for you, for all the joy wherewith we joy for your sakes before our God. 10. Night and day praying exceedingly that we might see your face, and might perfect that which is lacking in your faith? 12. Abound in love one toward another, and toward all *men*, even as we *do* toward you.

2 The. 1.4. We ourselves glory in you in the churches of God for your patience and faith in all your persecutions and tribulations that ye endure.

2 Tim. 1.4. Greatly desiring to see thee, being mindful of thy tears, that I may be filled with joy.

2 Tim. 2.10. I endure all things for the elect's sakes, that they may also obtain the salvation which is in Christ Jesus with eternal glory.

Philm. 8. Though I might be much bold in Christ to enjoin thee that which is convenient. 9. Yet for love's sake I rather beseech *thee*,

being such an one as Paul the aged, and now also a prisoner of Jesus Christ. 17. If thou count me therefore a partner, receive him as myself. 18. If he hath wronged thee, or oweth *thee* ought, put that on mine account ; 19. I Paul have written *it* with mine own hand, I will repay *it*.

Heb. 6.9. Beloved, we are persuaded better things of you, and things that accompany salvation, though we thus speak.

Heb. 13.22. I beseech you, brethren, suffer the word of exhortation : for I have written a letter unto you in few words.

See CHURCH, LOVE OF—CHURCH, DUTY TO MINISTERS — UNION — FRIENDSHIP — HOSPITALITY — POOR, KINDNESS TO — LIBERALITY.

LOYALTY. See SUBJECTS.

LUBIM. See LIBYA.

LUCIFER (day-star), applied to Nebuchadnezzar, Isa. 14.12. It occurs nowhere else.

LUCIUS OF CYRENE, a Christian teacher in Antioch, Act. 13.1. Rom. 16.21.

LUD AND LUDIM. See LYDIANS.

LUKE, author of a gospel and The Acts of the Apostles, Luk. 1.1-4. Act. 1.1,2. A physician, Col. 4.14. A companion and fellow-labourer of Paul, Act. 16.10. Act. 20.5,6,13-15. Act. 21.1-18. Act. c. 27 & 28. 2 Tim. 4.11. Philm. 24.

LUKEWARMNESS AND INDECISION. Gen. 49.4. Unstable as water, thou shalt not excel.

Jud. 5.16. Why abodest thou among the sheepfolds, to hear the bleatings of the flocks? For the divisions of Reuben *there were* great searchings of heart. 23. Curse ye Meroz, said the angel of the Lord, curse ye bitterly the inhabitants thereof ; because they came not to the help of the Lord, to the help of the Lord against the mighty. *v.* 17.

1 Kin. 18.21. How long halt ye between two opinions? if the Lord *be* God, follow him : but if Baal, *then* follow him.

Psa. 78.8. A generation *that* set not their heart aright, and whose spirit was not stedfast with God. 57. But turned back, and dealt unfaithfully like their fathers: they were turned aside like a deceitful bow. *v.* 37.

Psa. 106.12. Then believed they his words; they sang his praise. 13. They soon forgat his works ; they waited not for his counsel.

Pro. 17.24. The eyes of a fool *are* in the ends of the earth.

Isa. 43.22. But thou hast not called upon me, O Jacob; but thou hast been weary of me, O Israel. *v.* 23,24.

Jer. 9.3. They are not valiant for the truth upon the earth.

Jer. 48.10. Cursed *be* he that doeth the work of the Lord deceitfully.

Eze. 13.5. Ye have not gone up into the gaps, neither made up the hedge for the house of Israel to stand in the battle in the day of the Lord.

Eze. 16.30. How weak is thine heart, saith the Lord God, seeing thou doest all these *things*.

Hos. 6.4. O Ephraim, what shall I do unto thee? O Judah, what shall I do unto thee? for your goodness *is* as a morning cloud, and as the early dew it goeth away.

Hos. 10.2. Their heart is divided; now shall they be found faulty.

Zeph. 1.5. I will cut off them that worship *and* that swear by the Lord, and that swear by Malcham.

Hag. 1.2. This people say, The time is not come, the time that the Lord's house should be built. *v.* 4-11. Hag. 2.15,16.

Mal. 3.8. Ye have robbed me. But ye say, Wherein have we robbed thee?

Mat. 6.24. No man can serve two masters: for either he will hate the one, and love the other; or else he will hold to the one, and despise the other. Ye cannot serve God and mammon.

Mat. 13.5. Some fell upon stony places, where they had not much earth: and forthwith they sprung up, because they had no deepness of earth: 6. And when the sun was up, they were scorched; and because they had no root, they withered away.

Mat. 26.41. The spirit indeed *is* willing, but the flesh *is* weak.

Luk. 9.62. No man, having put his hand to the plough, and looking back, is fit for the kingdom of God.

Luk. 17.32. Remember Lot's wife. 33. Whosoever shall seek to save his life shall lose it.

Jno. 5.35. Ye were wiliing for a season to rejoice in his light.

Act. 26.28. Agrippa said unto Paul, Almost thou persuadest me to be a Christian.

Gal. 1.6. I marvel that ye are so soon removed from him that called you into the grace of Christ unto another gospel.

Eph. 4.14. Be no more children, tossed to and fro, and carried about with every wind of doctrine, by the sleight of men, *and* cunning craftiness, whereby they lie in wait to deceive.

Heb. 13.9. Be not carried about with divers and strange doctrines. For *it is* a good thing that the heart be established with grace.

Jas. 1.6. ~ He that wavereth is like a wave of the sea driven with the wind and tossed. 8. A double-minded man *is* unstable in all his ways.

Jas. 4.17. To him that knoweth to do good, and doeth *it* not, to him it is sin.

Rev. 2.4. I have *somewhat* against thee, because thou hast left thy first love.

Rev. 3.2. Strengthen the things which remain, that are ready to die: for I have not found thy works perfect before God. 15. I know thy works, that thou art neither cold nor hot: I would thou wert cold or hot. 16. So then because thou art lukewarm, and neither cold nor hot, I will spue thee out of my mouth.

LUKEWARMNESS AND INDECISION, EX-AMPLES OF: Solomon, 1 Kin. 3.3. Israelites, Ex. 32 with Ex. 24.7. 1 Kin. 22.43. 2 Kin. 12.3. 2 Chr. 20.33. 2 Chr. 33.17. Asa, 1 Kin. 15.14. Jehoram, 2 Kin. 3.2,3. Naaman, 2 Kin. 5.17,18. Jehu, 2 Kin. 10.16-31. Samaritans, 2 Kin. 17.41. Levites, 2 Chr. 24.5. Amaziah and Joash, 2 Kin. 14.3,4. 2 Chr. 25.2. Jews, Neh. 3.5. Neh. 13.11. Christ's hearers, Jno. 6.66. Jno. 12.42. Mark, Act. 15.38. Felix, Act. 24.25.

See DOUBT, WATCHFULNESS, WORLDLI-NESS, BACKSLIDING.

LUNACY. See MADNESS.

LUZ. See BETHEL.

LYBIA. See LIBYA.

LYCAONIA, a province of Asia Minor, Act. 14.6. Towns of, visited by Paul, see DERBE. ICONIUM, LYSTRA.

LYCIA, a province in the south-west of Asia Minor, Act. 27.5. Towns of, visited by Paul, see MYRA, PATARA.

LYDDA or LOD, inhabited by Benjamites, 1 Chr. 8.12. Ezr. 2.33. Neh. 11.35. A church at; Eneas cured at, by Peter; Dorcas raised to life, Act. 9.32-43.

LYDIA of Thyatira, her conversion; baptism of herself and household at Philippi; entertainment of Paul, Act. 16.14,15,40.

———, a province in the west of Asia Minor (not named in Scripture), peopled (it is supposed) by descendants of Lud, Gen. 10.22. Towns of, see PHILADELPHIA, SARDIS, THYATIRA.

LYDIANS, or LUDIM, a people of Africa, sprung from Ludim, Gen. 10.13. Fought with bows and arrows, Isa. 66.19. Jer. 46.9. Eze. 27.10. Eze. 30.5.

LYSANIAS, tetrarch of Abilene, Luk. 3.1.

LYSIAS. See CLAUDIUS LYSIAS.

LYSTRA, a city of Lycaonia, to which Paul and Barnabas fled from Iconium; Paul heals a cripple at; the people offer divine honours to him and Barnabas; persecution at, Act. 14.6-19. 2 Tim. 3.11. Church at, revisited by Paul, Act. 14.21-23. Act. 16.1,2.

M

MAACAH, king of Gath, and father of Achish, 1 Kin. 2.39.

———, daughter of Talmai, king of Geshur, David's wife, and mother of Absalom, 2 Sam. 3.3. 1 Chr. 3.2.

———, daughter of Absalom, wife of Rehoboam, and mother of Abijah, 1 Kin. 15.2,10 (*marg.*). 2 Chr. 11.20,21. Called Michaiah, daughter of Uriel, 2 Chr. 13.2. Her idols destroyed by her grandson Asa, 2 Chr. 15.16.

———, a district of Syria inhabited by a remnant of Canaanites, Jos. 13.11,13. Deu. 3.14. Jos. 12.5. King of, assists the Ammonites against David, 2 Sam. 10.6,8. 1 Chr. 19.6,7.

MACEDONIA, a province of Greece; Paul's vision respecting, Act. 16.9-12; and visits to, Act. 16.9-12. Act. 20.1,3. 2 Cor. 2.13. 2 Cor. 7.5. 1 Tim. 1.3. See also towns of AMPHI-POLIS, APOLLONIA, BEREA, NEAPOLIS, PHI-LIPPI, THESSALONICA. Paul's purpose to visit, Act. 19.21. 1 Cor. 16.5. 2 Cor. 1.16. Churches in, 2 Cor. 9.2,4. 1 The. 1.7. 1 The. 4.10. Liberality of, to the saints of Jerusalem, Rom. 15.26. 2 Cor. 8.1-5; and to Paul, 2 Cor. 11.9. Timothy and Erastus sent to, by Paul, Act. 19.22. Gaius and Aristarchus, men of, Act. 19.29. Act. 27.2. Prophecies of, see GREECE.

MACHIR, son of Manasseh, Gen. 50.23. Father of Gilead, Num. 26.29. Num. 36.1. Jud. 5.14. Gilead and Bashan, given to, Num. 32.39,40. Deu. 3.15. Jos. 13.31. Jos. 17.1.

MACHPELAH, a cave near Hebron, bought by Abraham from Ephron the Hittite, the burial-place of Sarah and Abraham, Gen. 23. Gen. 25.9. Of Isaac, Rebekah, and Leah, Gen. 49.31. Of Jacob, Gen. 50.13 ; but see Act. 7.16.

MADAI, son of Japheth, Gen. 10.2. 1 Chr. 1.5 ; everywhere else translated Medes. See PERSIA.

MADNESS, Deu. 28.28. Pro. 26.18. Zec. 12.4. Feigned by David, 1 Sam. 21.15. Cured by Christ, Mat. 4.24. Mat. 17.15. Christ charged with, Jno. 10.20 ; and Paul, Act. 26.24.

MAGDALA, a town near the sea of Galilee, visited by Christ, Mat. 15.39.

MAGI, translated WISE MEN, guided by a star to Jerusalem; interview with Herod; guided by a star to Jesus ; worship him ; present gifts ; warned in a dream to return home by a new way, Mat. 2.1-12.

MAGICIANS, counsellors of kings, Gen. 41.8,24. Ex. 7.11,22. Dan. 1.20. Dan 2.10,27. Dan. 4.7. Dan. 5.11. See SORCERY.

MAGISTRATES. See RULERS—JUSTICE, ADMINISTRATION OF.

MAGOG, son of Japheth, Gen. 10.2. 1 Chr. 1.5. Prophecy against, Eze. 38.2. Eze. 39.6. Symbolical, Rev. 20.8.

MAGOR-MISSABIB (fear round about), Jer. 20.3.

MAHALATH, a guitar or lute, (*title*) Psa. 53. Mahalath Leannoth, to sing to a lute, (*title*) Psa. 88.

MAHANAIM (two hosts), a place east of Jordan, so named by Jacob when met by angels, Gen. 32.2. A town of Gad, Jos. 13.26,30. A Levitical city, Jos. 21.38. Ish-bosheth reigns at, 2 Sam. 2.8-12. David comes to, when fleeing from Absalom, 2 Sam. 17.27-29. 1 Kin. 2.8.

MAHANEH-DAN (camp of Dan), Jud. 18.12. Jud. 13.25.

MAHER-SHALAL-HASH-BAZ, son of Isaiah, prophecy respecting, Isa. 8.1-4.

MAHLON, son of Elimelech and Naomi, and husband of Ruth, Ruth 1.2. Ruth 4.10.

MAIL, COAT OF, worn by Goliath, 1 Sam. 17.5. See BREASTPLATE.

MAKKEDAH, a royal city of the Canaanites, taken by Joshua, Jos. 10.28. Jos. 12.16. Given to Judah, Jos. 15.41.

————, cave of, 5 Canaanitish kings take refuge in, and are slain by Joshua, Jos. 10. 10,16-27.

MAKTESH, supposed to be a part of Jerusalem, occupied by merchants, Zeph. 1.11.

MALACHI, the last of the Old Testament prophets, Mal. 1.1.

MALCHAM OR MOLOCH, a god worshipped by the Jews, Zeph. 1.5. See MOLOCH.

MALCHUS, servant of Caiaphas; his ear cut off by Peter; cured by Christ, Jno. 18.10. Mat. 26.51. Mar. 14.47. Luk. 22.50,51.

MALEFACTORS, two crucified with Christ, Luk. 23.32-39. Mat. 27.38,44.

MALICE, HATRED, REVENGE, CRUELTY. Lev. 19.14. Thou shalt not curse the deaf, nor put a stumblingblock before the blind, but shalt fear thy God. 17. Thou shalt not hate thy brother in thine heart: thou shalt in any wise rebuke thy neighbour, and not suffer sin

upon him. 18. Thou shalt not avenge nor bear any grudge against the children of thy people ; but thou shalt love thy neighbour as thyself. Deu. 27.18.

Deu. 32.33. Their wine *is* the poison of dragons, and the cruel venom of asps.

Job 5.12. He disappointed the devices of the crafty, so that their hands cannot perform *their* enterprise. *v.* 13.

Job 24.2. *Some* remove the landmarks; they violently take away flocks, and feed there*of.* 3. They drive away the ass of the fatherless, they take the widow's ox for a pledge. 4. They turn the needy out of the way. *v.* 5.

Job 31.29. If I rejoiced at the destruction of him that hated me, or lifted up myself when evil found him : 30. Neither have I suffered my mouth to sin by wishing a curse to his soul. 2 Kin. 6.21,22.

Psa. 4.2. O ye sons of men, how long *will* ye turn my glory into shame ?

Psa. 7.14. He travaileth with iniquity, and hath conceived mischief, and brought forth falsehood. 15. He made a pit, and digged it, and is fallen into the ditch *which* he made. 16. His mischief shall return upon his own head, and his violent dealing shall come down upon his own pate. Job 15.35.

Psa. 10.7. His mouth is full of cursing and deceit and fraud: under his tongue *is* mischief and vanity. 9. He lieth in wait secretly as a lion in his den : he lieth in wait to catch the poor : he doth catch the poor, when he draweth him into his net. 14. Thou hast seen *it* ; for thou beholdest mischief and spite, to requite *it* with thy hand. *v.* 2-15.

Psa. 21.11. They intended evil against thee : they imagined a mischievous device, *which* they are not able *to perform.*

Psa. 22.7. All they that see me laugh me to scorn : they shoot out the lip, they shake the head, *saying*, 8. He trusted on the Lord *that* he would deliver him: let him deliver him, seeing he delighted in him.

Psa. 35.15. In mine adversity they rejoiced, and gathered themselves together: *yea,* the abjects gathered themselves together against me, and I knew *it* not ; they did tear *me*, and ceased not : 16. With hypocritical mockers in feasts, they gnashed upon me with their teeth. 20. They speak not peace: but they devise deceitful matters against *them that are* quiet in the land. 21. Yea, they opened their mouth wide against me, *and* said, Aha, aha, our eye hath seen *it*.

Psa. 38.16. When my foot slippeth, they magnify *themselves* against me. 19. Mine enemies *are* lively, *and* they are strong : and they that hate me wrongfully are multiplied.

Psa. 41.5. Mine enemies speak evil of me, When shall he die, and his name perish? 6. And if he come to see *me*, he speaketh vanity : his heart gathereth iniquity to itself ; *when* he goeth abroad, he telleth *it*. 7. All that hate me whisper together against me : against me do they devise my hurt. *v.* 8.

Psa. 55.10. Day and night they go about it upon the walls thereof: mischief also and sorrow *are* in the midst of it. 11. Wickedness *is* in the midst thereof: deceit and guile depart not from her streets.

Psa. 56.5. Every day they wrest my words : and their thoughts *are* against me for evil. 6. They gather themselves together, they hide themselves, they mark my steps, when they wait for my soul.

Psa. 57.4. My soul *is* among lions: *and* I lie *even among* them that are set on fire, *even* the sons of men, whose teeth *are* spears and arrows, and their tongue a sharp sword. 6. They have prepared a net for my steps; my soul is bowed down: they have digged a pit before me, into the midst whereof they are fallen *themselves.*

Psa. 59.3. Lo, they lie in wait for my soul : the mighty are gathered against me; not *for* my transgression, nor *for* my sin, O Lord. 4. They run and prepare themselves without *my* fault. *v.* 6,7.

Psa. 62.3. How long will ye imagine mischief against a man? ye shall be slain all of you : as a bowing wall *shall ye be, and as a* tottering fence.

Psa. 64.3. Who whet their tongue like a sword, *and* bend *their bows to shoot* their arrows, *even* bitter words : 4. That they may shoot in secret at the perfect : suddenly do they shoot at him, and fear not. 5. They encourage themselves *in* an evil matter : they commune of laying snares privily ; they say, Who shall see them? 6. They search out iniquities ; they accomplish a diligent search : both the inward *thought* of every one *of them,* and the heart, *is* deep. Psa. 140.2,3,5.

Psa. 69.4. They that hate me without a cause are more than the hairs of mine head : they that would destroy me, *being* mine enemies wrongfully, are mighty. 10. When I wept, *and chastened* my soul with fasting, that was to my reproach. 11. I made sackcloth also my garment ; and I became a proverb to them. 12. They that sit in the gate speak against me ; and I *was* the song of the drunkards. 26. They persecute *him* whom thou hast smitten ; and they talk to the grief of those whom thou hast wounded.

Psa. 70.2. Let them be turned backward, and put to confusion, that desire my hurt. 3. Let them be turned back for a reward of their shame that say, Aha, aha.

Psa. 71.10. Mine enemies speak against me ; and they that lay wait for my soul take counsel together, 11. Saying, God hath forsaken him : persecute and take him ; for *there is* none to deliver *him. v.* 13,24.

Psa. 74.20. The dark places of the earth are full of the habitations of cruelty.

Psa. 86.14. O God, the proud are risen against me, and the assemblies of violent *men* have sought after my soul ; and have not set thee before them.

Psa. 102.8. Mine enemies reproach me all the day ; *and* they that are mad against me are sworn against me.

Psa. 109.17. As he loved cursing, so let it come unto him : as he delighted not in blessing, so let it be far from him. 18. As he clothed himself with cursing like as with his garment, so let it come into his bowels like water, and like oil into his bones. *v.* 16-25.

Psa. 119.150. They draw nigh that follow after mischief : they are far from thy law. *v.* 78.

Pro. 4.16. They sleep not, except they have done mischief ; and their sleep is taken away, unless they cause *some* to fall. 17. For they eat the bread of wickedness, and drink the wine of violence.

Pro. 6.14. Frowardness *is* in his heart, he deviseth mischief continually ; he soweth discord. 15. Therefore shall his calamity come suddenly ; suddenly shall he be broken without remedy. 18. An heart that deviseth wicked imaginations, feet that be swift in running to mischief. *v.* 16.

Pro. 10.11. Violence covereth the mouth of the wicked. 12. Hatred stirreth up strifes.

Pro. 11.17. *He that is* cruel troubleth his own flesh.

Pro. 12.10. **The tender mercies of the** wicked *are* cruel.

Pro. 14.17. A man of wicked devices is hated. 22. Do they not err that devise evil?

Pro. 15.17. Better *is* a dinner of herbs where love is, than a stalled ox and hatred therewith.

Pro. 16.30. He shutteth his eyes to devise froward things : moving his lips he bringeth evil to pass.

Pro. 17.5. Whoso mocketh the poor reproacheth his Maker : *and* he that is glad at calamities shall not be unpunished.

Pro. 20.22. Say not thou, I will recompense evil ; *but* wait on the Lord, and he shall save thee.

Pro. 21.10. The soul of the wicked desireth evil : his neighbour findeth no favour in his eyes.

Pro. 24.8. He that deviseth to do evil shall be called a mischievous person. 17. Rejoice not when thine enemy falleth, and let not thine heart be glad when he stumbleth : 18. Lest the Lord see *it,* and it displease him. 29. Say not, I will do so to him as he hath done to me : I will render to the man according to his work.

Pro. 26.2. As the bird by wandering, so the curse causeless shall not come. 27. Whoso diggeth a pit shall fall therein : and he that rolleth a stone, it will return upon him.

Pro. 28.10. Whoso causeth the righteous to go astray in an evil way, he shall fall himself into his own pit.

Pro. 30.14. *There is* a generation, whose teeth *are as* swords, and their jaw teeth *as* knives, to devour the poor from off the earth, and the needy from *among* men.

Isa. 29.20. All that watch for iniquity are cut off : 21. That make a man an offender for a word, and lay a snare for him that reproveth in the gate, and turn aside the just for a thing of nought.

Isa. 32.6. The vile person will speak villany, and his heart will work iniquity, to practise hypocrisy, and to utter error against the Lord, to make empty the soul of the hungry, and he will cause the drink of the thirsty to fail. 7. He deviseth wicked devices to destroy the poor with lying words, even when the needy speaketh right.

Isa. 59.5. They hatch cockatrice' eggs, and weave the spider's web : he that eateth of their eggs dieth, and that which is crushed breaketh out into a viper. 6. Their webs shall not become garments, neither shall they cover themselves with their works : their works *are* works of iniquity, and the act of violence *is* in their hands. *v.* 7.

Jer. 20.10. I heard the defaming of many, fear on every side. Report, *say they,* and we will report it. All my familiars watched for my halting, *saying,* Peradventure he will be enticed, and we shall prevail against him, and we shall take our revenge on him.

Lam. 4.3. Even the sea monsters draw out the breast, they give suck to their young ones: the daughter of my people *is become* cruel, like the ostriches in the wilderness. 4. The tongue of the sucking child cleaveth to the roof of his mouth for thirst: the young children ask bread, *and* no man breaketh *it* unto them.

Eze. 18.18. Because he cruelly oppressed, spoiled his brother by violence, and did *that* which *is* not good among his people, lo, even he shall die in his iniquity.

Eze. 25.3. Because thou saidst, Aha, against my sanctuary, when it was profaned. 6. Because thou hast clapped *thine* hands, and stamped with the feet, and rejoiced in heart with all thy despite against the land of Israel; 7. Behold, therefore I will stretch out mine hand upon thee, and will deliver thee for a spoil to the heathen.

Eze. 25.15. Because the Philistines have dealt by revenge, *and* have taken vengeance with a despiteful heart, to destroy *it* for the old hatred. 17. I will execute great vengeance upon them with furious rebukes.

Eze. 26.2. Because that Tyrus hath said against Jerusalem, Aha, she is broken *that was* the gates of the people: she is turned unto me: I shall be replenished, *now* she is laid waste: 3. Behold, I *am* against thee, O Tyrus.

Amos 1.11. I will not turn away *the punishment* thereof; because he did pursue his brother with the sword, and did cast off all pity, and his anger did tear perpetually, and he kept his wrath for ever.

Mic. 2.1. Woe to them that devise iniquity, and work evil upon their beds! when the morning is light, they practise it, because it is in the power of their hand.

Zec. 8.17. Let none of you imagine evil in your hearts against his neighbour; for all these *are things* that I hate. Zec. 7.10.

Mat. 5.38. Ye have heard that it hath been said, An eye for an eye, and a tooth for a tooth: 39. But I say unto you, That ye resist not evil: but whosoever shall smite thee on thy right cheek, turn to him the other also. *v.* 40,41. Luk. 6.29.

Mat. 6.15. If ye forgive not men their trespasses, neither will your Father forgive your trespasses.

Mat. 18.33. Shouldest not thou also have had compassion on thy fellow-servant, even as I had pity on thee? 34. And his lord was wroth, and delivered him to the tormentors, till he should pay all that was due unto him.

Mat. 26 52. Put up again thy sword into his place: for all they that take the sword shall perish with the sword.

Jno. 8.44. Ye are of *your* father the devil, and the lusts of your father ye will do: he was a murderer from the beginning.

Jno. 18.23. If I have spoken evil, bear witness of the evil: but if well, why smitest thou me?

Rom. 12.19. Avenge not yourselves, but *rather* give place unto wrath: for it is written, Vengeance *is* mine; I will repay, saith the Lord.

1 Cor. 14.20. In malice be ye children.

Gal. 5.19. The works of the flesh are manifest. 20. Hatred, variance, emulations, wrath,

21. Envyings, of the which I tell you before, as I have also told *you* in time past, that they which do such things shall not inherit the kingdom of God.

Eph. 4.31. Let all bitterness, and wrath, and anger, and clamour, and evil speaking, be put away from you, with all malice.

Phil. 1.15. Some indeed preach Christ even of envy and strife; and some also of good will: 16. The one preach Christ of contention, not sincerely, supposing to add affliction to my bonds.

Col. 3.8. Put off all these; anger, wrath, malice.

1 The. 5.15. See that none render evil for evil unto any *man*.

Tit. 3.3. We ourselves also were sometimes living in malice and envy, hateful, *and* hating one another.

Jas. 2.13. He shall have judgment without mercy, that hath shewed no mercy.

1 Pet. 2.1. Laying aside all malice, and all guile.

1 Pet. 3.9. Not rendering evil for evil, or railing for railing.

1 Jno. 2.9. He that saith he is in the light, and hateth his brother, is in darkness even until now. 11. He that hateth his brother is in darkness, and walketh in darkness, and knoweth not whither he goeth, because that darkness hath blinded his eyes.

1 Jno. 3.10. Whosoever doeth not righteousness is not of God, neither he that loveth not his brother. 14. He that loveth not *his* brother abideth in death. 15. Whosoever hateth his brother is a murderer: and ye know that no murderer hath eternal life abiding in him.

1 Jno. 4.20. If a man say, I love God, and hateth his brother, he is a liar: for he that loveth not his brother whom he hath seen, how can he love God whom he hath not seen?

3 Jno. 10. His deeds which he doeth, prating against us with malicious words: and not content therewith, neither doth he himself receive the brethren, and forbiddeth them that would, and casteth *them* out of the church.

MALICE, HATRED, REVENGE, CRUELTY, EXAMPLES OF: Ishmael, Gen. 21.9. Sarah, Gen. 21.10. Esau, Gen. 27.41. Joseph's brethren, Gen. 37. Gen. 42.21. Potiphar's wife, Gen. 39.14-20. Ammonites, Deu. 23.1-5. Adonibezek, Jud. 1.7. Samson, Jud. 15.3-11. Philistines, Jud. 16.21. Saul, 1 Sam.18. 1 Sam. 19. 1 Sam. 20.30-33. 1 Sam. 22.6-18. 1 Sam. 23.7-23. 1 Sam.24.14-17. 1 Sam. 26.18. David, 1 Sam. 25.21-34. Shimei, 2 Sam. 16.5-8. Ahithophel, 2 Sam. 17.1-3. Jezebel, 1 Kin. 19.1,2. Ahaziah, 2 Kin. 1. Jehoram, 2 Kin. 6.31. Samaritans, &c., Ezr. 4. Neh. 2.10. Neh. 4. Neh. 6. Haman, Est. 3.5-15. Est. 5.9-14. Jeremiah's enemies, Jer. 26.8-11. Jer. 38. Nebuchadnezzar, Jer. 52.11. Daniel's enemies, Dan. 6.4-9. Edomites, Obad. 10-16. Herodias, Mar. 6.24-28. Herod, Luk. 23.11. James & John, Luk. 9.54. Peter, Jno. 18.10. Jews, Act. 23.12. Act. 25.3. Soldiers, Act. 27.42.

See PHARISEES — CHRIST'S sufferings — PERSECUTION — MURDER — POOR, OPPRESSION OF — HYPOCRISY AND TREACHERY — SPEAKING EVIL — STRIFE — ANGER — FORGIVENESS — LOVE.

MALLOWS, a plant eaten by the poor, Job 30.4.

MAMMON (that in which one trusts), a name for the world or riches, Mat. 6.24. Luk. 16.9,11,13.

MAMRE, THE AMORITE, a confederate of Abraham, Gen. 14.13,24.

——, PLAIN OF. Abraham dwells in, near Hebron, Gen. 13.18. Gen. 18.1; also Isaac, Gen. 35.27. See MACHPELAH.

MAN, CREATED IN THE IMAGE OF GOD—ALL MEN EQUAL, Gen. 1.27. Gen. 9.6. Ex. 30.15. Job 31.15. Psa. 33.14,15. Pro. 22.2. Ecc. 7.29. Mal. 2.10. Act. 17.26,29. 1 Cor. 11.7. Jas. 3.9. See GOD, CREATOR OF MAN—LIFE—SOUL—DEATH—LIKENESS TO GOD.

——, HIS DOMINION OVER CREATION, Gen. 1.26,28. Gen. 2.19,20. Gen. 9.2,3. Job 35.11. Psa. 8.5-8. Ecc. 5.9. Jer. 27.6. Jer. 28.14. Dan. 2.38. Jas. 3.7.

——, HIS IGNORANCE, Job 8.9. We *are but of* yesterday, and know nothing, because our days upon earth *are* a shadow.

Job 11.7. Canst thou by searching find out God? canst thou find out the Almighty unto perfection? 8. *It is* as high as heaven; what canst thou do? deeper than hell; what canst thou know? 12. Vain man would be wise, though man be born *like* a wild ass's colt.

Job 28.12. Where shall wisdom be found? and where *is* the place of understanding? 13. Man knoweth not the price thereof; neither is it found in the land of the living. 20. Whence then cometh wisdom? and where *is* the place of understanding? 21. Seeing it is hid from the eyes of all living.

Job 36.26. God *is* great, and we know *him* not, neither can the number of his years be searched out. 29. Can *any* understand the spreadings of the clouds, *or* the noise of his tabernacle?

Job 37.5. God thundereth marvellously with his voice: great things doeth he, which we cannot comprehend. 15. Dost thou know when God disposed them, and caused the light of his cloud to shine? 16. Dost thou know the balancings of the clouds, the wondrous works of him which is perfect in knowledge? 19. Teach us what we shall say unto him; *for* we cannot order *our speech* by reason of darkness. 20. The Almighty, we cannot find him out. Job *c.* 38 & 39.

Psa. 139.6. *Such* knowledge *is* too wonderful for me; it is high, I cannot *attain* unto it.

Pro. 27.1. Thou knowest not what a day may bring forth.

Pro. 30.4. Who hath ascended up into heaven, or descended? who hath gathered the wind in his fists? who hath bound the waters in a garment? who hath established all the ends of the earth? what *is* his name, and what *is* his son's name, if thou canst tell?

Ecc. 3.11. No man can find out the work that God maketh from the beginning to the end.

Ecc. 7.23. I said, I will be wise; but it *was* far from me. 24. That which is far off, and exceeding deep, who can find it out?

Ecc. 8.6. The misery of man *is* great upon him. 7. For he knoweth not that which shall be: for who can tell him when it shall be?

17. I beheld all the work of God, that a man cannot find out the work that is done under the sun: because though a man labour to seek *it* out, yet he shall not find *it;* yea, further, though a wise *man* think to know *it,* yet shall he not be able to find *it.*

Ecc. 9.12. Man also knoweth not his time.

Ecc. 11.5. As thou knowest not what *is* the way of the spirit, *nor* how the bones *do grow* in the womb of her that is with child: even so thou knowest not the works of God who maketh all.

Jno. 13.7. What I do thou knowest not now; but thou shalt know hereafter.

Act. 1.7. It is not for you to know the times or the seasons, which the Father hath put in his own power.

1 Cor. 13.9. We know in part, and we prophesy in part. 12. Now we see through a glass, darkly; but then face to face: now I know in part.

Rev. 5.2. Who is worthy to open the book, and to loose the seals thereof? 3. And no man in heaven, nor in earth, neither under the earth, was able to open the book, neither to look thereon.

See SPIRITUAL BLINDNESS—GOD'S PROVIDENCE MISUNDERSTOOD.

MAN, NATURAL STATE OF. SIN UNIVERSAL. Gen. 6.5. God saw that the wickedness of man *was* great in the earth, and *that* every imagination of the thoughts of his heart *was* only evil continually. 12. God looked upon the earth, and, behold, it was corrupt; for all flesh had corrupted his way upon the earth. *v.* 11.

Gen. 8.21. The imagination of man's heart *is* evil from his youth.

Job 4.17. Shall mortal man be more just than God? shall a man be more pure than his maker? 18. Behold, he put no trust in his servants; and his angels he charged with folly: 19. How much less *in* them that dwell in houses of clay.

Job 9.2. How should man be just with God? 3. If he will contend with him, he cannot answer him one of a thousand. 20. If I justify myself, mine own mouth shall condemn me: *if I say,* I *am* perfect, it shall also prove me perverse. 29. *If* I be wicked, why then labour I in vain? 30. If I wash myself with snow water, and make my hands never so clean; 31. Yet shalt thou plunge me in the ditch, and mine own clothes shall abhor me.

Job 11.12. Vain man would be wise, though man be born *like* a wild ass's colt.

Job 14.4. Who can bring a clean *thing* out of an unclean? not one.

Job 15.14. What *is* man, that he should be clean? and *he which is* born of a woman, that he should be righteous? 15. Behold, he putteth no trust in his saints; yea, the heavens are not clean in his sight. 16. How much more abominable and filthy *is* man, which drinketh iniquity like water?

Job 25.4. How then can man be justified with God? or how can he be clean *that is* born of a woman? 5. Behold even to the moon, and it shineth not; yea, the stars are not pure in his sight. 6. How much less man, *that is* a worm?

Psa. 14.2. The Lord looked down from heaven upon the children of men, to see if there were any that did understand, *and* seek

God. 3. They are all gone aside, they are all together become filthy: there is none that doeth good, no, not one. v. 1.

Psa. 51.5. Behold, I was shapen in iniquity; and in sin did my mother conceive me.

Psa. 58.2. In heart ye work wickedness. 3. The wicked are estranged from the womb: they go astray as soon as they be born, speaking lies. 4. Their poison is like the poison of a serpent: they are like the deaf adder that stoppeth her ear; 5. Which will not hearken to the voice of charmers, charming never so wisely.

Psa. 94.11. The Lord knoweth the thoughts of man, that they are vanity.

Psa. 119.96. I have seen an end of all perfection.

Psa. 130.3. If thou, Lord, shouldest mark iniquities, O Lord, who shall stand?

Psa. 143.2. In thy sight shall no man living be justified.

Pro. 10.20. The heart of the wicked is little worth.

Pro. 20.9. Who can say, I have made my heart clean, I am pure from my sin?

Pro. 21.8. The way of man is froward and strange.

Ecc. 7.20. There is not a just man upon earth, that doeth good, and sinneth not. 29. God hath made man upright; but they have sought out many inventions. 2 Chr. 6.36.

Ecc. 9.3. The heart of the sons of men is full of evil, and madness is in their heart while they live.

Isa. 1.5. The whole head is sick, and the whole heart faint. v. 6.

Isa. 42.7. To open the blind eyes, to bring out the prisoners from the prison, and them that sit in darkness out of the prison house.

Isa. 43.8. The blind people that have eyes, and the deaf that have ears.

Isa. 48.8. Yea, thou heardest not; yea, thou knewest not; yea, from that time that thine ear was not opened: for I knew that thou wouldest deal very treacherously, and wast called a transgressor from the womb.

Isa. 53.6. All we like sheep have gone astray; we have turned every one to his own way.

Isa. 64.6. We are all as an unclean thing, and all our righteousnesses are as filthy rags; and we all do fade as a leaf; and our iniquities, like the wind, have taken us away.

Jer. 2.22. Though thou wash thee with nitre, and take thee much soap, yet thine iniquity is marked before me, saith the Lord God.

Jer. 13.23. Can the Ethiopian change his skin, or the leopard his spots? then may ye also do good, that are accustomed to do evil.

Jer. 16.12. Ye walk every one after the imagination of his evil heart, that they may not hearken unto me.

Jer. 17.9. The heart is deceitful above all things, and desperately wicked: who can know it?

Eze. 16.6. When I passed by thee, and saw thee polluted in thine own blood, I said unto thee when thou wast in thy blood, Live. Eze. 37.1-3.

Eze. 36.25. From all your filthiness, and from all your idols, will I cleanse you. 26. A new heart also will I give you, and a new spirit will I put within you; and I will take away

the stony heart out of your flesh, and I will give you an heart of flesh.

Hos. 6.7. They like men have transgressed the covenant: there have they dealt treacherously against me.

Mat. 12.34. O generation of vipers, how can ye, being evil, speak good things? for out of the abundance of the heart the mouth speaketh. 35. A good man out of the good treasure of the heart bringeth forth good things: and an evil man out of the evil treasure bringeth forth evil things.

Mat. 15.19. Out of the heart proceed evil thoughts, murders, adulteries, fornications, thefts, false witness, blasphemies. Mar. 7. 21-23.

Luk. 1.79. To give light to them that sit in darkness and in the shadow of death.

Jno. 3.19. This is the condemnation, that light is come into the world, and men loved darkness rather than light, because their deeds were evil.

Jno. 8.23. Ye are from beneath; I am from above; ye are of this world.

Jno. 14.17. The Spirit of truth; whom the world cannot receive, because it seeth him not, neither knoweth him.

Act. 8.23. Thou art in the gall of bitterness, and in the bond of iniquity.

Rom. 2.1. Thou art inexcusable, O man, whosoever thou art that judgest: for wherein thou judgest another, thou condemnest thyself; for thou that judgest doest the same things.

Rom. 3.9. Are we better than they? No, in no wise: for we have before proved both Jews and Gentiles, that they are all under sin; 19. That every mouth may be stopped, and all the world may become guilty before God. 23. All have sinned, and come short of the glory of God.

Rom. 5.12. Death passed upon all men, for that all have sinned: 13. For until the law sin was in the world: but sin is not imputed when there is no law. 14. Nevertheless death reigned from Adam to Moses, even over them that had not sinned after the similitude of Adam's transgression.

Rom. 6.6. Our old man is crucified with him, that the body of sin might be destroyed, that henceforth we should not serve sin. 19. Ye have yielded your members servants to uncleanness and to iniquity unto iniquity; 20. When ye were the servants of sin, ye were free from righteousness. v. 17.

Rom. 7.5. When we were in the flesh, the motions of sins, which were by the law, did work in our members to bring forth fruit unto death. 11. Sin, taking occasion by the commandment, deceived me, and by it slew me. 13. Sin, that it might appear sin, working death in me by that which is good; that sin by the commandment might become exceeding sinful. 14. I am carnal, sold under sin. 15. For that which I do I allow not: for what I would, that do I not; but what I hate, that do I. 18. I know that in me (that is, in my flesh,) dwelleth no good thing: for to will is present with me; but how to perform that which is good I find not. 19. For the good that I would I do not: but the evil which I would not, that I do. 20. Now if I do that I would not, it is no more I that do it, but sin that dwelleth in me. 21. I find then a law, that, when I would do good, evil is present with me. 23. I see another law in my members, warring against the law of my mind, and bringing me into captivity to the law of sin which is in my members. 25. With the mind I myself serve the law of God; but with the flesh the law of sin.

Rom. 8.5. They that are after the flesh do mind the things of the flesh. 6. To be carnally minded *is* death. 7. The carnal mind *is* enmity against God: for it is not subject to the law of God, neither indeed can be. 8. So then they that are in the flesh cannot please God.

Rom. 8.13. If ye live after the flesh, ye shall die: but if ye through the Spirit do mortify the deeds of the body, ye shall live.

Rom. 11.17. Thou, being a wild olive-tree.

1 Cor. 2.14. The natural man receiveth not the things of the Spirit of God: for they are foolishness unto him: neither can he know *them*, because they are spiritually discerned.

1 Cor. 3.3. Ye are yet carnal: for whereas *there is* among you envying, and strife, and divisions, are ye not carnal, and walk as men?

1 Cor. 5.9. Not to company with fornicators: 10. Yet not altogether with the fornicators of this world, or with the covetous, or extortioners, or with idolaters; for then must ye needs go out of the world.

2 Cor. 5.14. If one died for all, then were all dead.

Gal. 3.10. As many as are of the works of the law are under the curse. 11. No man is justified by the law in the sight of God. 22. The scripture hath concluded all under sin.

Gal. 5.17. The flesh lusteth against the Spirit, and the Spirit against the flesh: and these are contrary the one to the other: so that ye cannot do the things that ye would. 19. The works of the flesh are manifest, which are *these;* Adultery fornication, uncleanness, lasciviousness, 20. Idolatry, witchcraft, hatred, variance, emulations, wrath, strife, seditions, heresies, 21. Envyings, murders, drunkenness, revellings, and such like.

Eph. 2.1. You *hath he quickened*, who were dead in trespasses and sins; 2. Wherein in time past ye walked according to the course of this world, according to the prince of the power of the air, the spirit that now worketh in the children of disobedience. 3. Among whom also we all had our conversation in times past in the lusts of our flesh, fulfilling the desires of the flesh and of the mind; and were by nature the children of wrath, even as others.

Eph. 2.12. At that time ye were without Christ, being aliens from the commonwealth of Israel, and strangers from the covenants of promise, having no hope, and without God in the world. *v.* 11.

Eph. 4.17. Walk not as other Gentiles walk, in the vanity of their mind, 18. Having the understanding darkened, being alienated from the life of God through the ignorance that is in them, because of the blindness of their heart: 19. Who being past feeling have given themselves over unto lasciviousness, to work all uncleanness with greediness. 22. Put off concerning the former conversation the old man, which is corrupt according to the deceitful lusts.

Eph. 5.8. Ye were sometimes darkness. 14. Awake thou that sleepest, and arise from the dead.

Col. 1.13. Who hath delivered us from the power of darkness. 21. You, that were sometime alienated and enemies in *your* mind by wicked works.

Col. 2.13. You being dead in your sins and the uncircumcision of your flesh.

Col. 3.5. Mortify therefore your members which are upon the earth; fornication, uncleanness, inordinate affection, evil concupiscence, and covetousness, which is idolatry: 7. In the which ye also walked sometime, when ye lived in them.

2 Tim. 2.26. *That* they may recover themselves out of the snare of the devil, who are taken captive by him at his will.

Tit. 3.3. We ourselves also were sometimes foolish, disobedient, deceived, serving divers lusts and pleasures, living in malice and envy, hateful, *and* hating one another.

Jas. 3.2. In many things we offend all.

Jas. 4.5. The spirit that dwelleth in us lusteth to envy.

1 Pet. 1.18. Your vain conversation *received* by tradition from your fathers.

1 Pet. 2.9. Who hath called you out of darkness. 25. Ye were as sheep going astray.

1 Pet. 3.19. Spirits in prison.

2 Pet. 1.4. Having escaped the corruption that is in the world through lust.

1 Jno. 1.8. If we say that we have no sin, we deceive ourselves, and the truth is not in us. 10. If we say that we have not sinned, we make him a liar, and his word is not in us.

1 Jno. 2.16. All that *is* in the world, the lust of the flesh, and the lust of the eyes, and the pride of life, is not of the Father, but is of the world.

1 Jno. 3.10. In this the children of God are manifest, and the children of the devil: whosoever doeth not righteousness is not of God, neither he that loveth not his brother.

1 Jno. 5.19. The whole world lieth in wickedness.

Rev. 3.17. Thou sayest, I am rich, and increased with goods, and have need of nothing; and knowest not that thou art wretched, and miserable, and poor, and blind, and naked.

See FALL, THE—SIN—SINNERS—SPIRITUAL BLINDNESS—REGENERATION.

MAN, TRUST IN. See FALSE CONFIDENCE.

———, WORSHIP OF, FORBIDDEN. See GOD THE ONLY GOD.

MAN OF SIN, 2 The. 2.3. See APOSTACY OF THE LAST DAYS.

MANAEN, a Christian teacher in Antioch, Herod's foster-brother, Act. 13.1 (*marg.*).

MANASSEH, second son of Joseph, adopted by Jacob, Gen. 41.51. Gen. 46.20. Gen. 48.5. Jos. 14.4. Blessed by Jacob, Gen. 48.13-20. His children, Gen. 50.23. Jos. 17.1-3. 1 Chr. 7.14-19.

———, TRIBE OF, numbered at Sinai, Num. 1.34,35; and in the plains of Moab, Num. 26.29-34. Marched and encamped under the standard of Ephraim, west of tabernacle, Num. 2.18,20. Num. 10.22,23. Blessing of Moses on, Deu. 33.13-17. With Reuben and Gad aid the other tribes to conquer Canaan, Deu. 3.18-20. Jos. 1.12-15. Jos. 4.12,13. Built the altar of witness, Jos. 22. Inheritance of, east of Jordan, Num. 32.33,39-42.

Num. 34.14,15. Deu. 3.14,15. Jos. 12.6. Jos. 13.7,29-31. West of Jordan, Jos. 16.9. Jos. 17.1-11. Did not drive out all the Canaanites, Jud. 1.27. Aid Gideon against the Midianites, Jud. 6.35. Jud. 7.23. Some of, join David at Ziklag, 1 Chr. 12.19,31. Join in Hezekiah's Passover, 2 Chr. 15.9. Return from captivity, 1 Chr. 9.3. For things common to the tribes, see ISRAELITES, TRIBES OF.

MANASSEH, 13th king of Judah (55 years' reign) ; son and successor of Hezekiah ; his idolatry and persecutions, 2 Kin. 21.1-17. 2 Kin. 24.4. 2 Chr. 33.1-9,19. Prophecies against him, 2 Kin. 21.10-16. 2 Chr. 33.10. Jer. 15.4. Taken captive to Babylon; his repentance and restoration, 2 Chr. 33.11-19. Builds walls and forts ; destroys idols and repairs the temple, 2 Chr. 33.14-16. His death, 2 Kin. 21.18. 2 Chr. 33.20.

MANDRAKE, a plant used for food, Gen. 30.14-16. Odorous, Song 7.13.

MANEH, Eze. 45.12. Translated pounds ; equal to 100 shekels (about 4 oz.), 1 Kin. 10.17 with 2 Chr. 9.16.

MANGER or CRIB, Job. 39.9. Pro. 14.4. Isa. 1.3. Jesus laid in, Luk. 2.7,12,16. Translated stall, Luk. 13.15.

MANNA, given to Israelites in the wilderness ; mode of gathering it ; double supply of, on 6th day, Ex. 16.4-31. Num. 11.7,8. Deu. 8.3,16. Neh. 9.20. Psa. 78.24. Jno. 6.31,49,58. A pot of, laid up in the ark, Ex. 16.33. Heb. 9.4. Israelites murmur at, Num. 11.6-10. Supply of, continued 40 years ; ceased on entering Canaan, Ex. 16.35. Jos. 5.12. Illustrative, Jno. 6.48-51. Rev. 2.17.

MANNERS AND CUSTOMS. See such heads as FEASTS, MARRIAGE, TRAVELLING, &c.

MANOAH, father of Samson, whose birth was predicted to him by an angel ; his prayer and offering, Jud. 13. Obtains a wife for Samson, Jud. 14.1-11.

MANSLAUGHTER, Ex. 21.13. Num. 35. 22,23. Deu. 19.5.

MANSLAYERS might be slain by the next of kin to the deceased, Num. 35.19,27. Might escape by fleeing to a city of refuge, Num. 35.15. Jos. 20.4. See Pro. 28.17. Were tried, Num. 35.12,24. Must remain in the city of refuge till the high-priest's death, Num. 35.25,28. An ox goring a man, to be killed, Ex. 21.28-32. See MURDER.

MANTLE. See DRESS.

MANUFACTURES. See ARTS.

MAON, a town of Judah near South Carmel, Jos. 15.55. Nabal's abode, 1 Sam. 25.2. Maonites oppress Israel, Jud. 10.12 ; called Mehunims, defeated by Uzziah, 2 Chr. 26.7.

——, wilderness of, David escapes to, 1 Sam. 23.24,25.

MARAH (bitter, see Ruth 1.20) ; in the wilderness of Shur ; its bitter waters sweetened by Moses, Ex. 15.23-25. Num. 33.8.

MARANATHA (the Lord will come), 1 Cor. 16.22.

MARBLE, 1 Chr. 29.2. Est. 1.6. Song 5.15. Rev. 18.12.

MARESHAH, a city of Judah, Jos. 15.44. Fortified by Rehoboam, 2 Chr. 11.8. Asa defeats the Ethiopians near, 2 Chr. 14.9,10. Eliezer the prophet's birthplace, 2 Chr. 20.37. Prophecy of, Mic. 1.15.

MARINER. See SHIPS.

MARK or MARCUS (John Mark), son of Mary, a disciple. accompanies Paul and Barnabas, Act. 12.12,25. Act. 13.5. Leaves them at Perga, Act. 13.13. Act. 15.38. Paul refuses to take him to Syria, &c. ; he goes with Barnabas his kinsman, Act. 15.37,39. Col. 4.10. A companion of Peter, 1 Pet. 5.13. With Paul in his imprisonment at Rome, Col. 4.10,11. 2 Tim. 4.11. Philm. 24.

MARKET or FAIR. Of the Tyrians, Eze. 27.13-25 ; of sheep, &c., in the temple, Jno. 2.14,15. Mat. 21.12. Luk. 19.45.

MARKET-PLACE, hiring in, Mat. 20.3. Place of resort, Mat. 23.7. Mar. 7.4. Luk. 7.32. Paul brought before judges in, at Philippi, Act. 16.19 ; preached in, at Athens, Act. 17.17. Held at gates, Gen. 23.10,16. Gen. 34.20. Ruth 4.1. 2 Kin. 7.1,18.

MARRIAGE. Parents contracted for their children, Gen. 21.21. Gen. 34.6-8. Jud. 1.12. Jud. 14.2. 1 Sam. 17.25. Might refuse their consent, Ex. 22.17. Consulted the parties, Gen. 24.57,58. Gen. 34.8. 1 Sam. 18.20.

Presents given by the suitor to the father and family of the bride, Gen. 24.53. Gen. 34.12. Deu. 22.29. Hos. 3.2. Or services, Gen. 29.18. Jos. 15.16. 1 Sam. 17.25. 1 Sam. 18.25.

Manner of asking in marriage, Gen. 34.6,11. Jud. 14.2,10. 1 Sam. 25.40. See BETROTHAL.

Solemnized by a feast, lasting some days, Gen. 29.22. Jud. 14.12. Jno. 2.1-5. Est. 2.18. Mat. 22.11,12. Guests provided with garments, Mat. 22.11,12. A benediction at the close, Gen. 24.60. Ruth 4.11,12. Psa. 45.16,17. At the gate before witnesses, Ruth 4.1,10,11.

The bride richly dressed and adorned with jewels, Psa. 45.13,14. Isa. 49.18. Jer. 2.32. Rev. 21.2. Received presents, Gen. 24.53. Psa. 45.12. Attended by female companions, Psa. 45.9. Had a handmaid given by her father, Gen. 24.59. Gen. 29.24,29. Was conducted in procession to the bridegroom's house, Gen. 29.23. Psa. 45.14,15. Mat. 25.1-6.

The bridegroom adorned with jewels, Isa. 61.10. Crowned, Song 3.11. Accompanied by friends, Jud. 14.11. Jno. 3.29. Exempted from going to war for a year, Deu. 24.5.

The eldest sister married first, Gen. 29.26. The Jews' opinion of celibacy, Jud. 11.38. Isa. 4.1. Jer. 16.9. Christ's miracle at a marriage, Jno. 2.1-11.

With a deceased brother's widow, Gen. 38. 8,11. Deu. 25.5-10. Ruth 4.5. Mat. 22.24. Of priests, Lev. 21.7,13-15. Of an heiress, Num. 36.8. Of ministers, Mat. 8.14. 1 Cor. 9.5. 1 Tim. 3.2,12. Act. 21.8,9. Of widows, Rom. 7.2,3. 1 Cor. 7.39. 1 Tim. 5.14.

Marriage forbidden within certain degrees of affinity, Lev. 18.6-18. Lev. 20.11-21. Deu. 22.30.

Illustrative, Isa. 54.5. Isa. 62.4,5. Jer. 3.14. Hos. 2.19,20. Mat. 22.2. Mat. 25.10. Eph. 5.30-32. Rev. 19.7.

Divinely instituted and indissoluble, Gen. 1.27,28. Gen. 2.18-25. Mal. 2.13-16. Mat.

5.31,32. Mat. 19.3-9. Mar. 10.6. Luk. 16.18.
Rom. 7.2,3. 1 Cor. 7.1-16,25-40. 1 Tim. 4.1,3.
1 Tim. 5.14. Heb. 13.4.

See DIVORCE, POLYGAMY, ADULTERY,
HUSBANDS, WOMEN.

MARRIAGE, IRRELIGIOUS AND IDOLA-
TROUS FORBIDDEN, Gen. 24.3. Gen. 28.1.
Ex. 34.16. Deu. 7.3,4. Jos. 23.12,13. Ezr.
9.12. Neh. 13.26,27. Mal. 2.11,12. 1 Cor.
7.39. 2 Cor. 6.14.

EXAMPLES OF: Sons of God, Gen. 6.2-5.
Esau, Gen. 26.34. Israelites, Jud. 3.6-8. Samson, Jud. 14.1-16. Solomon, 1 Kin. 3.1.
1 Kin. 11.1-4. Ahab, 1 Kin. 16.31. Jews,
Ezr. 9.1-12. Ezr. 10. Neh. 13.25-27. Mal.
2.11-13.

MARS-HILL. A hill in Athens on which
the council of Areopagus was held. (The Greek
word *Areopagus, v.* 19, is the same translated
Mars-hill, *v.* 22.) Paul's address on, Act.
17.19-32.

MARTHA OF BETHANY, sister of Mary &
Lazarus, Jno. 11.1. Entertains Jesus; is admonished by him, Luk. 10.38-42. Loved by
Jesus, Jno. 11.5. Her brother Lazarus' death
and resurrection, Jno. 11.1-46. Serves Jesus
at supper, Jno.12.2.

MARTYRS. See PERSECUTION.

MARY, THE MOTHER OF JESUS, Mat. 13.55.
Mar. 6.3. Jno. 6.42. Her lineage, Mat. 1.1-16.
Luk. 3.23-38. Espoused to Joseph, Mat. 1.18.
Luk. 1.27. The angel Gabriel sent to announce
to her that Christ should be born of her, Luk.
1.26,28-38. Visits Elizabeth for 3 months;
Elizabeth's salutation, Luke 1.39-46. Her
thanksgiving, Luk. 1.46-55. Goes to Bethlehem ; birth of Jesus, Luk. 2.4-7. Mat. 1.18-25.
Mat. 2.1. Visited by shepherds, Luk. 2.16-19 ;
and by the wise men, Mat. 2.11. Presents
Jesus in the temple ; Simeon's prophecy ; her
sacrifice of purification, Luk. 2.22-39.

Flees to Egypt; returns to Nazareth, Mat.
2.14,20-23. Luk. 2.39. Goes to the feast and
seeks Jesus; her question to Jesus, and his
answer, Luk. 2.41-49. Marvels at what she
hears of Jesus, Luk. 2.19,33,48-51. Is present
with Jesus at his first miracle; accompanies
him to Capernaum, Jno. 2.1-10. Desires to
see him when preaching, Mat. 12.46. Mar.
3.31. Luk. 8.19. Stands by the cross ; Jesus
commends her to John, who takes her to his
home, Jno. 19.25-27. Is with the disciples in
the upper room, Act. 1.14.

—— OF BETHANY, sister of Lazarus and
Martha ; her piety, Luk. 10.39,42. Loved by
Jesus, Jno. 11.1,5. Her brother Lazarus' death
and resurrection, Jno. 11.1-46. Anoints the
feet of Jesus, Mat. 26.7-13. Mar. 14.3-9. Jno.
11.2. Jno. 12.3-7.

MARY MAGDALENE. Jesus casts seven
devils out of her ; ministers to Christ, Mar.
16.9. Luk. 8.2,3. Beholds Christ's crucifixion,
Mat. 27.56. Mar. 15.40. Jno. 19.25. Watches
the sepulchre, Mat. 27.61. Mar. 15.47. Luk.
23.55,56. Visits the sepulchre with spices;
addressed by an angel, Mat. 28.1-7. Mar. 16.
1-7. Luk. 24.1-8. Jno. 20.1,11-13. Met by
Jesus ; his message to the disciples ; goes to
announce Christ's resurrection, Mat. 28.8-10.
Mar. 16.8-11. Luk. 24.9-11,22. Jno. 20.14-18.

——, mother of James the Less ; wife
of Cleophas, and sister of the mother of Jesus,

Jno. 19.25. Mother of James and Joses, Mat.
27.56. Mar. 15.40. Present at the crucifixion,
Mat. 27.56. Mar. 15.40. Jno. 19.25. Watches
the sepulchre, Mat. 27.61. Mar. 15.47. Visits
the sepulchre with spices, Mat. 28.1. Mar.
16.1. Tells the disciples of Christ's resurrection,
Luk. 24.10.

MARY, mother of John Mark, Act. 12.12.

——, a Roman disciple, who laboured
for Paul, Rom. 16.6.

MASCHIL (instruction), a title of Psalms
32, 42, 44, 45, 52, 53, 54, 74, 88, 89, 142.

MASON, 1 Kin. 5.18. 2 Kin. 12.12. 2 Kin.
22.6. 1 Chr. 14.1. Ezr. 3.7.

MASSAH. See MERIBAH.

MASTERS. Lev. 25.43. Thou shalt not
rule over him with rigour ; but shalt fear thy
God.

Deu. 5.14. The Sabbath of the Lord thy
God : *in it* thou shalt not do any work, thou,
nor thy son, nor thy daughter, nor thy manservant, nor thy maidservant, nor thine ox,
nor thine ass, nor any of thy cattle, nor thy
stranger that *is* within thy gates ; that thy
manservant and thy maidservant may rest as
well as thou.

Deu. 24.14. Thou shalt not oppress an hired
servant *that is* poor and needy, *whether he be*
of thy brethren, or of thy strangers that *are* in
thy land within thy gates : 15. At his day
thou shalt give *him* his hire, neither shall the
sun go down upon it ; for he *is* poor, and
setteth his heart upon it : lest he cry against
thee unto the Lord, and it be sin unto thee.
Lev. 19.13.

Job 31.13. If I did despise the cause of my
manservant or of my maidservant, when they
contended with me ; 14. What then shall I
do when God riseth up? and when he visiteth,
what shall I answer him? 15. Did not he that
made me in the womb make him?

Psa. 101.6. He that walketh in a perfect
way, he shall serve me. *v.* 7.

Pro. 29.21. He that delicately bringeth up
his servant from a child shall have him become
his son at the length.

Jer. 22.13. Woe unto him that useth his
neighbour's service without wages, and giveth
him not for his work.

Mal. 3.5. I will be a swift witness against
those that oppress the hireling in *his* wages.

Luk. 10.7. The labourer is worthy of his hire.

Eph. 6.9. Ye masters, do the same things
unto them, forbearing threatening : knowing
that your Master also is in heaven ; neither is
there respect of persons with him.

Col. 4.1. Masters, give unto *your* servants
that which is just and equal ; knowing that ye
also have a Master in heaven.

Philm. 15. Receive him for ever ; 16. Not
now as a servant, but above a servant, a
brother beloved, specially to me, but how
much more unto thee, both in the flesh, and in
the Lord?

Jas. 5.4. Behold, the hire of the labourers
who have reaped down your fields, which is of
you kept back by fraud, crieth : and the cries
of them which have reaped are entered into
the ears of the Lord of sabaoth.

——, BAD, EXAMPLES OF. Sarah, Gen.
16.6. Laban, Gen. 31.7. Potiphar's wife, Gen.
39.7-20. Amalekite, 1 Sam. 30.13.

MASTERS, GOOD, EXAMPLES OF. Abraham, Gen. 18.19. Centurion, Luk. 7.2.
See SERVANTS.

MATTANIAH. See ZEDEKIAH.

MATTHEW, or LEVI, a publican, the son of Alpheus; his call to follow Christ; makes a feast for Jesus, Mat. 9.9,10. Mar. 2.14,15. Luk. 5.27-29. An apostle, Mat. 10.3. Mar. 3.18. Luk. 6.15. Act. 1.13.

MATTHIAS, an apostle chosen in place of Judas, Act. 1.23-26.

MATTOCK, an edge tool, 1 Sam. 13.20,21. Used for digging, Isa. 7.25. Another word translated mattock in 2 Chr. 34.6.

MAUL, Pro. 25.18.

MAZZAROTH (lodgings or stations of the sun), Job 38.32 (marg., 12 signs).

MEAH, a tower in Jerusalem, Neh. 3.1. Neh. 12.39.

MEAL. See BREAD—BARLEY.

MEALS. See FEASTS—PRAYER BEFORE MEALS.

MEASURE. (1.) Heb. Cor; Gr. Koros; 10 ephahs, 90 galls.; corn and oil measured by, Gen. 18.6. 1 Sam. 25.18. 1 Kin. 4.22. 1 Kin. 5.11. 1 Kin. 18.32. 2 Kin. 7.1. 2 Chr. 2.10. 2 Chr. 27.5. Luk. 16.7. Illustrative, Isa. 40.12. (2.) Gr. Batos; Heb. Bath; about 9 galls., Luk. 16.6.
(3.) Gr. Saton; Heb. Seah; ⅓ of an ephah, about 1½ peck, or 3 galls., Mat. 13.33. Luk. 13.21. (4.) Gr. Choenix, about 1 quart, Rev. 6.6. (5.) Gr. Metron, a general term like our word measure, Mat. 7.2. Rev. 21.17.

MEASURES. Of capacity, see BATH, CAB, FIRKIN, HIN, HOMER, LOG, MEASURE, OMER. Of length and distance, see ACRE, CUBIT, DAY'S JOURNEY, FATHOM, FINGER-BREADTH, FURLONG, HANDBREADTH, REED, SPAN, MILE, SABBATH-DAY'S JOURNEY, SILVERLING.

————, required to be just, Lev. 19.35,36. Deu. 25.14,15. Pro. 20.10. Eze. 45.10. Amos 8.5. Mic. 6.10.

MEASURING-ROD, or LINE, Jer. 31.39. Eze. 40.3,5. Eze. 42.15-19. Zec. 2.1.

MEAT-OFFERING. See OFFERING.

MEDAD AND ELDAD prophesy in the camp of Israel, Num. 11.26-28.

MEDEBA, a town of Moab, Num. 21.30. Isa. 15.2. Given to Reuben, Jos. 13.9,16. Joab defeats the Ammonites at, 1 Chr. 19.7-15.

MEDES. See MADAI—PERSIA.

MEDICINE. See DISEASES, TREATMENT OF.

MEDITERRANEAN SEA (this name not in Scripture), called the Great Sea, Num. 34.6,7. Jos. 1.4. Jos. 9.1. Jos. 15.12,47. Jos. 23.4. Eze. 47.10,15,20. Eze. 48.28. The sea of the Philistines, Ex. 23.31; of Joppa, Ezr. 3.7. The sea, Jos. 15.4,46. Act. 17.14. The hinder sea, Zec. 14.8. The utmost sea, Deu. 11.24. Joel 2.20. Isles of, see CHIOS, CLAUDA, COOS, CRETE, CYPRUS, LESBOS, MELITA, PATMOS, RHODES, SAMOS, SAMOTHRACE.

MEEKNESS, PATIENCE. Pro. 12.20. To the counsellors of peace is joy.
Pro. 14.29. He that is slow to wrath is of great understanding.

Pro. 15.1. A soft answer turneth away wrath. 18. He that is slow to anger appeaseth strife.

Pro. 16.32. He that is slow to anger is better than the mighty; and he that ruleth his spirit than he that taketh a city.

Pro. 17.1. Better is a dry morsel, and quietness therewith, than an house full of sacrifices with strife.

Pro. 19.11. The discretion of a man deferreth his anger; and it is his glory to pass over a transgression.

Pro. 20.3. It is an honour for a man to cease from strife.

Pro. 25.15. By long forbearing is a prince persuaded, and a soft tongue breaketh the bone.

Pro. 29.8. Wise men turn away wrath.

Ecc. 7.8. The patient in spirit is better than the proud in spirit.

Ecc. 10.4. If the spirit of the ruler rise up against thee, leave not thy place; for yielding pacifieth great offences.

Lam. 3.28. He sitteth alone and keepeth silence, because he hath borne it upon him. 29. He putteth his mouth in the dust; if so be there may be hope. 30. He giveth his cheek to him that smiteth him: he is filled full with reproach.

Amos 3.3. Can two walk together, except they be agreed?

Zeph. 2.3. Seek ye the Lord, all ye meek of the earth, which have wrought his judgment; seek righteousness, seek meekness.

Mat. 5.5. Blessed are the meek: for they shall inherit the earth. 9. Blessed are the peacemakers: for they shall be called the children of God.

Mat. 11.29. Take my yoke upon you, and learn of me; for I am meek and lowly in heart: and ye shall find rest unto your souls.

Mar. 9.50. Have peace one with another.

Rom. 12.18. If it be possible, as much as lieth in you, live peaceably with all men.

Rom. 14.19. Follow after the things which make for peace, and things wherewith one may edify another.

1 Cor. 7.15. God hath called us to peace.

1 Cor. 10.32. Give none offence, neither to the Jews, nor to the Gentiles, nor to the church of God.

1 Cor. 11.19. There must be also heresies among you, that they which are approved may be made manifest among you.

1 Cor. 13.4. Charity suffereth long, and is kind; charity envieth not; charity vaunteth not itself, is not puffed up. 5. Doth not behave itself unseemly, seeketh not her own, is not easily provoked, thinketh no evil. 7. Beareth all things, believeth all things, hopeth all things, endureth all things.

2 Cor. 13.11. Be perfect, be of good comfort, be of one mind, live in peace; and the God of love and peace shall be with you.

Gal. 5.22. The fruit of the Spirit is love, joy, peace, long-suffering, gentleness, goodness, faith. 23. Meekness, temperance: against such there is no law. 26. Let us not be desirous of vain glory, provoking one another, envying one another.

Gal. 6.1. If a man be overtaken in a fault, ye which are spiritual, restore such an one in the spirit of meekness; considering thyself, lest thou also be tempted.

Eph. 4.2. With all lowliness and meekness, with long-suffering, forbearing one another in love.

Phil. 2.14. Do all things without murmurings and disputings : 15. That ye may be blameless and harmless, the sons of God, without rebuke.

Col. 3.12. Put on therefore, as the elect of God, holy and beloved, bowels of mercies, kindness, humbleness of mind, meekness, long-suffering ; 13. Forbearing one another, and forgiving one another.

1 The. 4.11. Study to be quiet, and to do your own business.

1 The. 5.14. Be patient toward all *men*.

2 The. 3.5. The Lord direct your hearts into the love of God, and into the patient waiting for Christ.

1 Tim. 3.2. A bishop then must be blameless. 3. Patient, not a brawler.

1 Tim. 6.11. Follow after patience, meekness.

2 Tim. 2.24. The servant of the Lord must not strive ; but be gentle unto all *men*, apt to teach, patient, 25. In meekness instructing those that oppose themselves.

Tit. 2.2. That the aged men be sound in the faith, in charity, in patience. 9. *Exhort* servants to be obedient unto their own masters, *and* to please *them* well in all *things;* not answering again.

Tit. 3.2. To speak evil of no man, to be no brawlers, *but* gentle, shewing all meekness unto all men.

Heb. 10.36. Ye have need of patience, that, after ye have done the will of God, ye might receive the promise.

Heb. 12.14. Follow peace with all *men*.

Jas. 1.4. Let patience have *her* perfect work, that ye may be perfect and entire, wanting nothing.

Jas. 3.13. Who *is* a wise man, and endued with knowledge among you? let him shew out of a good conversation his works with meekness of wisdom. 17. The wisdom that is from above is first pure, then peaceable, gentle, *and* easy to be entreated, full of mercy and good fruits, without partiality, and without hypocrisy. 18. And the fruit of righteousness is sown in peace of them that make peace.

1 Pet. 2.18. Servants, *be* subject to *your* masters with all fear ; not only to the good and gentle, but also to the froward. 19. For this *is* thank-worthy, if a man for conscience toward God endure grief, suffering wrongfully. 20. For what glory *is* it, if, when ye be buffeted for your faults, ye shall take it patiently ? but if, when ye do well, and suffer *for it,* ye take it patiently, this *is* acceptable with God. 21. For even hereunto were ye called ; because Christ also suffered for us, leaving us an example, that ye should follow his steps : 23. Who, when he was reviled, reviled not again ; when he suffered, he threatened not ; but committed *himself* to him that judgeth righteously.

1 Pet. 3.4. That which is not corruptible, *even the ornament* of a meek and quiet spirit, which is in the sight of God of great price. 11. Let him eschew evil, and do good ; let him seek peace, and ensue it. 15. *Be* ready always to *give* an answer to every man that asketh you a reason of the hope that is in you with meekness and fear. Psa. 34.14.

2 Pet. 1.5. Add to your faith, patience.

MEEKNESS, PATIENCE, EXAMPLES OF : Abraham, Gen. 13.8. Isaac, Gen. 26.20-22. Moses, Ex. 2.13. Ex. 15.24. Ex. 16.7,8. Ex. 17.2. Num. 12.3. Num. 16.4-11. Gideon, Jud. 8.2,3. Hannah, 1 Sam. 1.13-16. Saul, 1 Sam 10.27. David, 1 Sam. 17.29. 2 Sam. 16.9-14. Psa. 38.13,14. Psa. 120.5-7. Paul, Act. 21.20-26. 1 The. 2.7. Job, Jas. 5.11. The angel, Jud. 9.

See FORGIVENESS, HUMILITY, PERSECUTION, CHRIST'S MEEKNESS, ANGER, STRIFE.

MEGIDDO, a town of Manasseh in Issachar, Jos. 17.11. 1 Chr. 7.29. King of, conquered by Joshua, Jos. 12.21. Inhabitants of, not driven out, Jud. 1.27. Fortified by Solomon, 1 Kin. 9.15. 1 Kin. 4.12. Ahaziah flees to, when wounded ; and dies at, 2 Kin. 9.27.

————, VALLEY AND WATERS OF. Sisera, &c., defeated at, by Barak, Jud. 5.19. Josiah slain at, 2 Kin. 23.29,30. 2 Chr. 35.22. Zec. 12.11.

MELCHIZEDEK, king of Salem ; his priesthood ; blesses Abraham, and receives tithes from him, Gen. 14.18-20. Psa. 110.4. Heb. 5.6,10,11. Heb. 6.20. Heb. 7.1-21.

MELITA (now Malta), an island in the Mediterranean, to which Paul escaped when shipwrecked ; his treatment by Publius and the inhabitants, and his miracles, Act. 28.1-10.

MELON, a fruit grown in Egypt, Num. 11.5.

MELZAR, the steward, intrusted with the care of Daniel, &c., Dan. 1.11-16.

MEMPHIS (the capital of Lower Egypt), Hos. 9.6. Called Noph ; Jews dwelt in during the captivity, Jer. 44.1. Prophecies of, Isa. 19.13. Jer. 2.16. Jer. 46.14,19. Eze. 30.13,16.

MENAHEM, 16th king of Israel (10 years' reign) ; slays Shallum and succeeds him ; his cruelty and sins ; bribes the king of Assyria ; his death, 2 Kin. 15.13-22.

MENE (to number), Dan. 5.25,26.

MEPHIBOSHETH, son of Jonathan, 2 Sam. 4.4. Called Merib-baal, 1 Chr. 8.34. 1 Chr. 9.40. His lameness, 2 Sam. 4.4. David's kindness to him, 2 Sam. 9. 2 Sam. 21.7. Remains in Jerusalem during Absalom's rebellion, 2 Sam. 16.1-4. Blamed by David ; his defence, 2 Sam. 19.24-30. His inheritance divided with Ziba, 2 Sam. 16.4. 2 Sam. 19.29.

MERAB, Saul's eldest daughter, promised to David ; married to Adriel, 1 Sam. 18.17,19. Her sons delivered up to the Gibeonites, 2 Sam. 21.8,9 (*marg.*).

MERARI, son of Levi, and head of the Merarites, Gen. 46.11. Ex. 6.16. Num. 3.17,33-35. 1 Chr. 6.1,19. See LEVITES, DIVISIONS OF.

MERATHAIM, a name of Babylon, Jer. 50.21.

MERCHANT. See COMMERCE.

MERCURY (Gr. *Hermes*), a god worshipped in Lycaonia ; Paul supposed to be, Act. 14.12.

MERCY. See PARDON—FORGIVENESS—LOVE—GOD'S MERCY.

MERCY-SEAT, of gold 2½ cubits long, and 1½ cubits broad, placed upon the Ark of the

Covenant between the cherubim, Ex. 25.17-22. Ex. 26.34. Ex. 30.6. Ex. 31.7. Ex. 35.12. Ex. 37.6-9. Ex. 39.35. Ex. 40.20. 1 Kin. 8.7. 1 Chr. 28.11. Heb. 9.5. Sprinkled with the blood of sin-offerings on the day of atonement, Lev. 16.14,15. God's presence manifested in the cloud upon, Ex. 25.22. Ex. 30.6,36. Lev. 16.2. Num. 7.89. Num. 17.4. 1 Sam. 4.4. 2 Sam. 6.2. 2 Kin. 19.15. 1 Chr. 13.6. Psa. 80.1. Psa. 99.1. Isa. 37.16. Heb. 4.16. See ARK, CHERUBIM.

MERIBAH (strife), a place in the desert of Sin, where water was brought from the rock; called Massah, Ex. 17.1-7. Deu. 33.8.

————, or MERIBAH KADESH, a fountain produced for Israel in the desert of Zin; Moses and Aaron punished for their sin at, Num. 20.12,13,24. Num. 27.14. Deu. 32.51. Psa. 81.7. Psa. 106.32. Eze. 47.19. Eze. 48.28.

MERODACH, a Babylonian idol, Jer. 50.2.

MERODACH-BALADAN king of Babylon, sends an embassy to Hezekiah, 2 Kin. 20.12. Isa. 39.1.

MEROM, WATERS OF (the upper lake of the Jordan); Joshua's victory over Canaanite kings near, Jos. 11.5-7.

MEROZ, a place in the north of Palestine; people of, rebuked for not aiding Barak, Jud. 5.23.

MESHA, the boundary of the descendants of Joktan, Gen. 10.30.

————, king of Moab, pays tribute of lambs, &c., to Ahab; revolts after Ahab's death, 2 Kin. 1.1. 2 Kin. 3.4,5.

MESHACH or **MISHAEL**. See SHADRACH.

MESHECH, a country bordering on Armenia, Eze. 39.1 with Gen. 10.2. 1 Chr. 1.5. Eze. 32.26. Eze. 38.2,3. Merchants of, Eze. 27.13. It signifies barbarians in Psa. 120.5.

MESOPOTAMIA (Mesopotamia is Greek, signifying between the rivers. The Hebrew is Aram-naharaim; that is, Aram of the 2 rivers, Psa. 60 (title); also Padan-Aram; that is, the plain of Aram), a country between the Euphrates and Tigris northwards; residence of Bethuel, Abram, Laban, and Jacob, Gen. 24. Gen. 25.20. Gen. 28.2-7. Gen. 31.18. Gen. 33.18. Gen. 46.15. Gen. 48.7. Act. 7.2; see Gen. 11.28-31. Balaam belonged to, Deu. 23.4. Chushan, king of, subdues Israel; defeated by Othniel, Jud. 3.8-10. People of, defeated by David, Psa. 60 (title). Aid the Ammonites, 1 Chr. 19.6. Present at Pentecost, Act. 2.9. Towns of, see CARCHEMISH, HARAN, NAHOR, REZEPH, TEL-ABIB, UR. River of, see CHEBAR.

MESSIAH. See CHRIST THE MESSIAH.

METALS. See BRASS, GOLD, IRON, LEAD, SILVER, TIN. Working in, see BEATENWORK, FURNACE, REFINER, SMITH.

METHEG-AMMAH (the bridle of Ammah; that is, Gath, which was in Ammah), captured by David from the Philistines, 2 Sam. 8.1; see 1 Chr. 18.1. See GATH.

METHUSELAH, his life and death, Gen. 5.21-27. 1 Chr. 1.3.

MICAH, a man of Mount Ephraim; robs his mother, and makes images, which are stolen by the Danites, Jud. c. 17 & 18.

MICAH THE MORASTHITE, time of his prophesying, Jer. 26.18,19. Mic. 1.1.

MICAIAH, a prophet, imprisoned by Ahab for predicting his death, 1 Kin. 22.8-28. 2 Chr. 18.4-27.

MICHAEL THE ARCHANGEL, his succour of the Jews, Dan. 10.13.21. Dan. 12.1. Contention with the devil, Jude 9; see Zec. 3.2. Rev. 12.7.

MICHAIAH, reports to the princes Jeremiah's prophecy, Jer. 36.11-13.

MICHAL, youngest daughter of Saul, married to David, 1 Sam. 18.20-28. Saves David's life, 1 Sam. 19.12-17. Given by Saul to Phalti, 1 Sam. 25.44. David demands her restoration, 2 Sam. 3.13-16. Despises David for dancing before the ark; dies childless, 2 Sam. 6.16,20-23. 1 Chr. 15.29.

MICHMASH, a town of Benjamin, 1 Sam. 13.5. Re-inhabited after the captivity, Neh. 11.31. Ezr. 2.27.

————, PASS OF, Isa. 10.28,29. Jonathan conquers the Philistines in, 1 Sam. 13.2-23. 1 Sam. 14.5,31.

MICHTAM (mystery), title Psa. 16.56-60.

MIDIANITES, descended from Midian, son of Abraham and Keturah, Gen. 25.1,2,4. 1 Chr. 1.32,33. Their territory, Ex. 2.15. Ex. 3.1. 1 Kin. 11.18. Called Ishmaelites; their trade, Gen. 37.25-36. Their camels, &c., Num. 31.32-39. Jud. 8.21-26. Isa. 60.6. Moses marries a daughter of Jethro, priest of Midian, Ex. 2.16,21. Ex. 3. Ex. 4.19. Ex. 18.1. Num. 10.29. Join Moab in calling Balaam, Num. 22.4. Seduce Israel to idolatry, &c., Num. 25. Israel commanded to destroy, Num. 25.17. Israel destroys five kings of, Num. 31.1-20. Jos. 13.21. Gideon delivers Israel from, and slays their kings Zebah and Zalmunna, Jud. c. 6 to 8. Psa. 83.9. Isa. 9.4. Isa. 10.26; and two princes, Oreb and Zeeb, Jud. 7.25. Psa. 83.11. Idol of, See BAALPEOR. Prophecies of, Isa. 60.6. Hab. 3.7. See EPHAH.

MIDWIVES, Gen. 35.17. Piety of, in Egypt, Ex. 1.15-21.

MIGDOL, a town of Egypt on the borders of the Red Sea; Israel encamped between it and the sea, Ex. 14.2. Num. 33.7. See Eze. 29.10 (marg.). Eze. 30.6 (marg.). Jews dwell in, during the captivity, Jer. 44.1. Prophecy against, Jer. 46.14.

MIGRON, a town between Ai and Michmash, Isa. 10.28. Saul encamps at, 1 Sam. 14.2. See MICHMASH, PASS OF.

MILCOM. See MOLECH.

MILE, a Roman measure of 1000 paces or 1611 yards (the English mile is 1760 yards), Mat. 5.41.

MILETUS (a city and seaport of Ionia, 36 miles south of Ephesus), Paul meets the elders of Ephesus at; his address, Act. 20.15-38. Trophimus left at, by Paul, 2 Tim. 4.20.

MILK, used as food, Gen. 18.8. Jud. 4.19. Song 5.1. Eze. 25.4; of goats, Pro. 27.27; of sheep, Deu. 32.14. Isa. 7.21,22; of camels, Gen. 32.15; of cows, Deu. 32.14. 1 Sam. 6. 7,10. A kid was not to be seethed in its mother's milk, Ex. 23.19. Deu. 14.21. Illustrative, Ex. 33.3. Isa. 60.16. Joel 3.18. Isa. 55.1. Heb. 5.12,13. 1 Pet. 2.2. See BUTTER, CHEESE.

MILL, Jer. 25.10. Mat. 18.6. Formed of two stones, Deu. 24.6. Job 41.24. Isa. 47.2. Women employed at, Ex. 11.5. Mat. 24.41; and captives, Jud. 16.21. Lam. 5.13. Manna ground in, Num. 11.8. Abimelech killed by a piece of millstone, Jud. 9.53. A millstone not to be taken in pledge, Deu. 24.6.

MILLENNIUM (1000 years), prophecy of, Rev. 20.1-7. See CHURCH, PROPHECIES OF.

MILLET, a small grain, Eze. 4.9.

MILLO, TOWER OF, part of the fortifications of Jerusalem built by David and Solomon, 2 Sam. 5.9. 1 Kin. 9.15,24. 1 Kin. 11.27. 1 Chr. 11.8. 2 Chr. 32.5. Joash slain at, 2 Kin. 12.20.

————, a fortress in Shechem, Jud. 9.6,20.

MINERALS. See ADAMANT, ALABASTER, BRIMSTONE, CHALK, COAL, CORAL, FLINT, LIME, MARBLE, METALS, NITRE, PITCH, SALT, SLIME, STONE.

MINISTERS, PROPHETS, PRIESTS, APOSTLES, AND TEACHERS; DUTIES AND CHARACTER OF. Lev. 10.11. Teach the children of Israel all the statutes which the Lord hath spoken. *v.* 8-11.

Lev. 21.6. They shall be holy unto their God, and not profane the name of their God : for the offerings of the Lord made by fire, *and* the bread of their God, they do offer: therefore they shall be holy. 2 Chr. 29.11.

1 Sam. 2.35. I will raise me up a faithful priest, *that* shall do according to *that* which *is* in mine heart and in my mind.

Isa. 32.20. Blessed *are* ye that sow beside all waters.

Isa. 40.2. Speak ye comfortably to Jerusalem, and cry unto her, that her warfare is accomplished, that her iniquity is pardoned. 9. O Zion, that bringest good tidings, get thee up into the high mountain ; O Jerusalem, that bringest good tidings, lift up thy voice with strength ; lift *it* up, be not afraid ; say unto the cities of Judah, Behold your God ! 11. Depart ye, depart ye, go ye out from thence, touch no unclean *thing* ; go ye out of the midst of her ; be ye clean, that bear the vessels of the Lord. Nah. 1.15.

Isa. 58.1. Cry aloud, spare not, lift up thy voice like a trumpet, and shew my people their transgression, and the house of Jacob their sins.

Isa. 62.6. I have set watchmen upon thy walls, O Jerusalem, *which* shall never hold their peace day nor night : ye that make mention of the Lord, keep not silence, 7. And give him no rest, till he establish, and till he make Jerusalem a praise in the earth.

Jer. 1.7. Say not, I *am* a child : for thou shalt go to all that I shall send thee, and whatsoever I command thee thou shalt speak. 8. Be not afraid of their faces : for I *am* with thee, to deliver thee, saith the Lord. 17. Gird up thy loins, and arise, and speak unto them all that I command thee : be not dismayed at their faces, lest I confound thee before them. 18. For, behold, I have made thee this day a defenced city, and an iron pillar, and brasen walls against the whole land, against the kings of Judah, against the princes thereof, against the priests thereof, and against the people of the land. 19. And they shall fight against thee : but they shall not prevail against thee ; for I *am* with thee, saith the Lord, to deliver thee. Jer. 15.20,21.

Jer. 3.15. I will give you pastors according to mine heart, which shall feed you with knowledge and understanding.

Jer. 6.27. I have set thee *for* a tower *and a* fortress among my people, that thou mayest know and try their way.

Jer. 15.19. Thus saith the Lord, If thou return, then will I bring thee again, *and* thou shalt stand before me : and if thou take forth the precious from the vile, thou shalt be as my mouth : let them return unto thee ; but return not thou unto them.

Jer. 23.4. I will set up shepherds over them which shall feed them : and they shall fear no more, nor be dismayed, neither shall they be lacking, saith the Lord. 22. If they had stood in my counsel, and had caused my people to hear my words, then they should have turned them from their evil way, and from the evil of their doings. 28. The prophet that hath a dream, let him tell a dream ; and he that hath my word, let him speak my word faithfully.

Jer. 26.2. Stand in the court of the Lord's house, and speak unto all the cities of Judah, which come to worship in the Lord's house, all the words that I command thee to speak unto them ; diminish not a word.

Eze. 2.6. Be not afraid of them, neither be afraid of their words, though briers and thorns *be* with thee, and thou dost dwell among scorpions : be not afraid of their words, nor be dismayed at their looks, though they *be* a rebellious house. 7. And thou shalt speak my words unto them, whether they will hear, or whether they will forbear : for they *are* most rebellious. 8. But thou, son of man, hear what I say unto thee ; Be not thou rebellious like that rebellious house : open thy mouth, and eat that I give thee.

Eze. 3.8. Behold, I have made thy face strong against their faces, and thy forehead strong against their foreheads. 9. As an adamant harder than flint have I made thy forehead : fear them not, neither be dismayed at their looks, though they *be* a rebellious house. 10. Son of man, all my words that I shall speak unto thee receive in thine heart, and hear with thine ears. 27. When I speak with thee, I will open thy mouth, and thou shalt say unto them, Thus saith the Lord God ; He that heareth, let him hear ; and he that forbeareth, let him forbear : for they *are* a rebellious house. *v.* 1-11,17-27.

Eze. 6.11. Thus saith the Lord God ; Smite with thine hand, and stamp with thy foot, and say, Alas for all the evil abominations of the house of Israel !

Eze. 33.7. I have set thee a watchman unto the house of Israel ; therefore thou shalt hear the word at my mouth, and warn them from me. 8. When I say unto the wicked, O wicked *man*, thou shalt surely die ; if thou dost not speak to warn the wicked from his way, that wicked *man* shall die in his iniquity ; but his blood will I require at thine hand. 9. Nevertheless, if thou warn the wicked of his way to turn from it ; if he do not turn from his way, he shall die in his iniquity ; but thou hast delivered thy soul. *v.* 1-9.

Eze. 34.2. Thus saith the Lord God unto the shepherds, Woe *be* to the shepherds of Israel that do feed themselves! should not the shepherds feed the flocks? *v.* 1-31.

Eze. 37.4. Again he said unto me, Prophesy upon these bones, and say unto them, O ye dry bones, hear the word of the Lord. 9. Then said he unto me, Prophesy unto the wind, prophesy, son of man, and say to the wind, Thus saith the Lord God ; Come from the four winds, O breath, and breathe upon these slain, that they may live.

Mal. 2.6. The law of truth was in his mouth, and iniquity was not found in his lips : he walked with me in peace and equity, and did turn many away from iniquity. 7. For the priest's lips should keep knowledge, and they should seek the law at his mouth : for he *is* the messenger of the Lord of hosts.

Mat. 5.19. Whosoever therefore shall break one of these least commandments, and shall teach men so, he shall be called the least in the kingdom of heaven : but whosoever shall do and teach *them*, the same shall be called great in the kingdom of heaven.

Mat. 7.6. Give not that which is holy unto the dogs, neither cast ye your pearls before swine, lest they trample them under their feet, and turn again and rend you.

Mat. 10.11. Into whatsoever city or town ye shall enter, enquire who in it is worthy ; and there abide till ye go thence. 12. And when ye come into an house, salute it. 13. And if the house be worthy, let your peace come upon it ; but if it be not worthy, let your peace return to you. 16. Behold, I send you forth as sheep in the midst of wolves : be ye therefore wise as serpents, and harmless as doves.

Mat. 10.25. It is enough for the disciple that he be as his master, and the servant as his lord. If they have called the master of the house Beelzebub, how much more *shall they call* them of his household ? 27. What I tell you in darkness, *that* speak ye in light : and what ye hear in the ear, *that* preach ye upon the housetops. 28. And fear not them which kill the body, but are not able to kill the soul : but rather fear him which is able to destroy both soul and body in hell.

Mat. 13.52. Every scribe *which is* instructed unto the kingdom of heaven is like unto a man *that is* an householder, which bringeth forth out of his treasure *things* new and old.

Mat. 20.25. Ye know that the princes of the Gentiles exercise dominion over them, and they that are great exercise authority upon them. 26. But it shall not be so among you : but whosoever will be great among you, let him be your minister ; 27. And whosoever will be chief among you, let him be your servant : 28. Even as the Son of man came not to be ministered unto, but to minister, and to give his life a ransom for many.

Mat. 23.8. Be not ye called Rabbi : for one is your Master, *even* Christ ; and all ye are brethren. 9. And call no *man* your father upon the earth : for one is your Father, which is in heaven. 10. Neither be ye called masters : for one is your Master, *even* Christ. 11. But he that is greatest among you shall be your servant.

Mat. 28.19. Go ye therefore, and teach all nations, baptising them in the name of the Father, and of the Son, and of the Holy Ghost.

20. Teaching them to observe all things whatsoever I have commanded you : and, lo, I am with you alway, *even* unto the end of the world. Amen.

Mar. 16.15. He said unto them, Go ye into all the world, and preach the gospel to every creature.

Luk. 6.40. The disciple is not above his master ; but every one that is perfect shall be as his master.

Luk. 10.4. Carry neither purse, nor scrip, nor shoes : and salute no man by the way. 7. In the same house remain, eating and drinking such things as they give : for the labourer is worthy of his hire. Go not from house to house. *v.* 1-16.

Luk. 12.42. Who then is that faithful and wise steward, whom *his* lord shall make ruler over his household, to give *them their* portion of meat in due season ? 43. Blessed *is* that servant, whom his Lord when he cometh shall find so doing. 44. Of a truth I say unto you, that he will make him ruler over all that he hath. Mat. 24.45.

Luk. 22.26. But ye *shall* not be so : but he that is greatest among you, let him be as the younger ; and he that is chief, as he that doth serve. 27. For whether *is* greater, he that sitteth at meat, or he that serveth? *is* not he that sitteth at meat? but I am among you as he that serveth. *v.* 24-28.

Jno. 3.27. A man can receive nothing, except it be given him from heaven.

Jno. 4.36. He that reapeth receiveth wages, and gathereth fruit unto life eternal : that both he that soweth and he that reapeth may rejoice together. 37. And herein is that saying true, One soweth and another reapeth. 38. I sent you to reap that whereon ye bestowed no labour : other men laboured, and ye are entered into their labours.

Jno. 10.2. He that entereth in by the door is the shepherd of the sheep. 3. To him the porter openeth ; and the sheep hear his voice : and he calleth his own sheep by name, and leadeth them out. 4. And when he putteth forth his own sheep, he goeth before them, and the sheep follow him : for they know his voice. 5. And a stranger will they not follow, but will flee from him : for they know not the voice of strangers.

Jno. 13.13. Ye call me Master and Lord : and ye say well ; for *so* I am. 14. If I then, *your* Lord and Master, have washed your feet, ye also ought to wash one another's feet. 15. For I have given you an example, that ye should do as I have done to you. 16. Verily, verily, I say unto you, The servant is not greater than his lord ; neither he that is sent greater than he that sent him. 17. If ye know these things, happy are ye if ye do them.

Jno. 15.20. Remember the word that I said unto you, The servant is not greater than his lord. If they have persecuted me, they will also persecute you ; if they have kept my saying, they will keep yours also. 21. But all these things will they do unto you for my name's sake, because they know not him that sent me.

Jno. 17.18. As thou hast sent me into the world, even so have I also sent them into the world. 20. Neither pray I for these alone, but for them also which shall believe on me through their word.

Act. 5.20. Go, stand and speak in the temple to the people all the words of this life.

Act. 18.9. Be not afraid, but speak, and hold not thy peace: 10. For I am with thee, and no man shall set on thee to hurt thee: for I have much people in this city.

Act. 20.28. Take heed therefore unto yourselves, and to all the flock, over the which the Holy Ghost hath made you overseers, to feed the church of God, which he hath purchased with his own blood.

Rom. 2.21. Thou therefore which teachest another, teachest thou not thyself? thou that preachest a man should not steal, dost thou steal? 22. Thou that sayest a man should not commit adultery, dost thou commit adultery? thou that abhorrest idols, dost thou commit sacrilege? 23. Thou that makest thy boast of the law, through breaking the law dishonourest thou God?

Rom. 10.14. How shall they believe in him of whom they have not heard? and how shall they hear without a preacher? 15. And how shall they preach, except they be sent? as it is written, How beautiful are the feet of them that preach the gospel of peace, and bring glad tidings of good things! Isa. 52.7.

Rom. 12.6. Having then gifts differing according to the grace that is given to us, whether prophecy, *let us prophesy* according to the proportion of faith; 7. Or ministry, *let us wait on our* ministering; or he that teacheth, on teaching; 8. Or he that exhorteth, on exhortation: he that giveth, *let him do it* with simplicity; he that ruleth, with diligence; he that sheweth mercy, with cheerfulness. *v.* 3-5.

Rom. 15.17. I have therefore whereof I may glory through Jesus Christ in those things which pertain to God. 29. I am sure that, when I come unto you, I shall come in the fulness of the blessing of the gospel of Christ.

1 Cor. 3.5. Who then is Paul, and who *is* Apollos, but ministers by whom ye believed, even as the Lord gave to every man? 6. I have planted, Apollos watered; but God gave the increase. 7. So then neither is he that planteth any thing, neither he that watereth; but God that giveth the increase. 8. Now he that planteth and he that watereth are one: and every man shall receive his own reward according to his own labour.

1 Cor. 4.2. Moreover it is required in stewards, that a man be found faithful. *v.* 1.

1 Cor. 9.10. That he that ploweth should plow in hope; and that he that thresheth in hope should be partaker of his hope.

2 Cor. 2.14. Thanks *be* unto God, which always causeth us to triumph in Christ, and maketh manifest the savour of his knowledge by us in every place. 15. We are unto God a sweet savour of Christ, in them that are saved, and in them that perish: 16. To the one *we are* the savour of death unto death; and to the other the savour of life unto life: and who *is* sufficient for these things?

2 Cor. 4.7. We have this treasure in earthen vessels, that the excellency of the power may be of God, and not of us.

2 Cor. 8.23. *They are* the messengers of the churches, *and* the glory of Christ.

Eph. 4.11. He gave some, apostles; and some, prophets; and some, evangelists; and some, pastors and teachers; 12. For the perfecting of the saints, for the work of the ministry, for the edifying of the body of Christ.

Col. 4.17. Take heed to the ministry which thou hast received in the Lord, that thou fulfil it.

1 The. 5.12. Know them which labour among you, and are over you in the Lord, and admonish you.

1 Tim. 1.3. Charge some that they teach no other doctrine. 4. Neither give heed to fables and endless genealogies, which minister questions, rather than godly edifying which is in faith: *so do.*

1 Tim. 1.18. War a good warfare; 19. Holding faith, and a good conscience; which some having put away concerning faith have made shipwreck.

1 Tim. 3.1. This *is* a true saying, If a man desire the office of a bishop, he desireth a good work. 2. A bishop then must be blameless, the husband of one wife, vigilant, sober, of good behaviour, given to hospitality, apt to teach; 3. Not given to wine, no striker, not greedy of filthy lucre; but patient, not a brawler, not covetous; 4. One that ruleth well his own house, having his children in subjection with all gravity; 5. (For if a man know not how to rule his own house, how shall he take care of the church of God?) 6. Not a novice, lest being lifted up with pride he fall into the condemnation of the devil. 7. Moreover he must have a good report of them which are without; lest he fall into reproach and the snare of the devil. 15. If I tarry long, that thou mayest know how thou oughtest to behave thyself in the house of God.

1 Tim. 4.6. If thou put the brethren in remembrance of these things, thou shalt be a good minister of Jesus Christ, nourished up in the words of faith and of good doctrine, whereunto thou hast attained. 7. But refuse profane and old wives' fables, and exercise thyself *rather* unto godliness. 12. Be thou an example of the believers, in word, in conversation, in charity, in spirit, in faith, in purity. 13. Till I come, give attendance to reading, to exhortation, to doctrine. 14. Neglect not the gift that is in thee, which was given thee by prophecy, with the laying on of the hands of the presbytery. 15. Meditate upon these things; give thyself wholly to them; that thy profiting may appear to all. 16. Take heed unto thyself, and unto the doctrine; continue in them: for in doing this thou shalt both save thyself, and them that hear thee.

1 Tim. 5.17. Let the elders that rule well be counted worthy of double honour, especially they who labour in the word and doctrine. 21. I charge *thee* before God, and the Lord Jesus Christ, and the elect angels, that thou observe these things without preferring one before another, doing nothing by partiality.

1 Tim. 6.11. O man of God, flee these things; and follow after righteousness, godliness, faith, love, patience, meekness. 13. I give thee charge in the sight of God, who quickeneth all things, and *before* Christ Jesus, who before Pontius Pilate witnessed a good confession; 14. That thou keep *this* commandment without spot, unrebukeable, until the appearing of our Lord Jesus Christ. 20. O Timothy, keep that which is committed to thy trust, avoiding profane *and* vain babblings, and oppositions of science falsely so called:

21. Which some professing have erred concerning the faith.

2 Tim. 1.6. I put thee in remembrance that thou stir up the gift of God, which is in thee by the putting on of my hands. 13. Hold fast the form of sound words, which thou hast heard of me, in faith and love which is in Christ Jesus. 14. That good thing which was committed unto thee keep by the Holy Ghost which dwelleth in us.

2 Tim. 2.1. My son, be strong in the grace that is in Christ Jesus. 2. The things that thou hast heard of me among many witnesses, the same commit thou to faithful men, who shall be able to teach others also. 3. Endure hardness, as a good soldier of Jesus Christ. 4. No man that warreth entangleth himself with the affairs of *this* life; that he may please him who hath chosen him to be a soldier. 5. If a man also strive for masteries, *yet* is he not crowned, except he strive lawfully. 6. The husbandman that laboureth must be first partaker of the fruits. 7. Consider what I say; and the Lord give thee understanding in all things.

2 Tim. 2.14. Of these things put *them* in remembrance, charging *them* before the Lord that they strive not about words to no profit, *but* to the subverting of the hearers. 15. Study to shew thyself approved unto God, a workman that needeth not to be ashamed, rightly dividing the word of truth. 16. Shun profane *and* vain babblings: for they will increase unto more ungodliness. 20. In a great house there are not only vessels of gold and of silver, but also of wood and of earth; and some to honour, and some to dishonour. 21. If a man therefore purge himself from these, he shall be a vessel unto honour, sanctified, and meet for the master's use, *and* prepared unto every good work. (See *v.* 16,17.)

2 Tim. 2.23. Foolish and unlearned questions avoid, knowing that they do gender strifes. 24. And the servant of the Lord must not strive; but be gentle unto all *men*, apt to teach, patient, 25. In meekness instructing those that oppose themselves; if God peradventure will give them repentance to the acknowledging of the truth; 26. And *that* they may recover themselves out of the snare of the devil, who are taken captive by him at his will.

2 Tim. 3.14. Continue thou in the things which thou hast learned and hast been assured of, knowing of whom thou hast learned *them*; 16. All scripture *is* given by inspiration of God, and *is* profitable for doctrine, for reproof, for correction, for instruction in righteousness: 17. That the man of God may be perfect, throughly furnished unto all good works.

2 Tim. 4.1. I charge *thee* therefore before God, and the Lord Jesus Christ, who shall judge the quick and the dead at his appearing and his kingdom; 2. Preach the word; be instant in season, out of season; reprove, rebuke, exhort with all longsuffering and doctrine. 5. Watch thou in all things, endure afflictions, do the work of an evangelist, make full proof of thy ministry.

Tit. 1.5. For this cause left I thee in Crete, that thou shouldest set in order the things that are wanting, and ordain elders in every city, as I had appointed thee: 6. If any be blameless, the husband of one wife, having faithful children not accused of riot or unruly. 7. For a bishop must be blameless, as the steward of God; not self-willed, not soon angry, not given to wine, no striker, not given to filthy lucre; 8. But a lover of hospitality, a lover of good men, sober, just, holy, temperate; 9. Holding fast the faithful word as he hath been taught, that he may be able by sound doctrine both to exhort and to convince the gainsayers. 13. Rebuke them sharply, that they may be sound in the faith; 14. Not giving heed to Jewish fables, and commandments of men, that turn from the truth.

Tit. 2.1. Speak thou the things which become sound doctrine. 7. In all things shewing thyself a pattern of good works: in doctrine *shewing* uncorruptness, gravity, sincerity, 8. Sound speech, that connot be condemned; that he that is of the contrary part may be ashamed, having no evil thing to say of you. 15. Speak, and exhort, and rebuke with all authority. Let no man despise thee.

Tit. 3.8. *This is* a faithful saying, and these things I will that thou affirm constantly, that they which have believed in God might be careful to maintain good works. These things are good and profitable unto men. 9. Avoid foolish questions, and genealogies, and contentions, and strivings about the law; for they are unprofitable and vain. (See Epistles to Timothy, and Titus, in full.)

Heb. 5.12. Ye have need that one teach you again which *be* the first principles of the oracles of God; and are become such as have need of milk, and not of strong meat. 13. For every one that useth milk *is* unskilful in the word of righteousness: for he is a babe. *v.* 14.

Heb. 13.7. Remember them which have the rule over you, who have spoken unto you the word of God: whose faith follow, considering the end of *their* conversation: 8. Jesus Christ the same yesterday, and to day, and for ever. 17. Obey them that have the rule over you, and submit yourselves: for they watch for your souls, as they that must give account, that they may do it with joy, and not with grief: for that *is* unprofitable for you.

Jas. 3.1. My brethren, be not many masters, knowing that we shall receive the greater condemnation. 13. Who *is* a wise man and endued with knowledge among you? let him shew out of a good conversation his works with meekness of wisdom. *v.* 3,17,18.

1 Pet. 4.10. As every man hath received the gift, *even so* minister the same one to another, as good stewards of the manifold grace of God. 11. If any man speak, *let him speak* as the oracles of God; if any man minister, *let him do it* as of the ability which God giveth: that God in all things may be glorified through Jesus Christ.

1 Pet. 5.1. The elders which are among you I exhort, who am also an elder. 2. Feed the flock of God which is among you, taking the oversight *thereof*, not by constraint, but willingly; not for filthy lucre, but of a ready mind; 3. Neither as being lords over *God's* heritage, but being ensamples to the flock. 4. And when the chief Shepherd shall appear, ye shall receive a crown of glory that fadeth not away

See APOSTLES — CHURCH-GOVERNMENT — ANGELS OF THE CHURCHES — BISHOP — ELDER — DEACON — EVANGELIST — HELPS — ORDINATION.

MINISTERS, Good. See Zeal—Love exemplified by Paul—Prayer, intercessory.

MINISTERS, Maintenance of. Mat. 10. 9,10. Mar. 6.8. Luk. 9.3. Luk. 10.7. Act. 18.3. Act. 20.33,34. Rom. 15.27. 1 Cor. 4. 12. 1 Cor. 9.6-18. 2 Cor. 11.7-12. 2 Cor. 12.13,17,18. Gal. 6.6. Phil. 4.10,14-18. 1 The. 2.6,9. 2 The. 3.8,9. 1 Tim. 5.18.

See Priests—Levites, emoluments of —Church, duty to ministers.

MINISTERS, Marriage of. Mat. 8.14. 1 Cor. 9.5. 1 Tim. 3.2,12. Act. 21.8,9.

MINISTERS, Prayer for, enjoined. Mat. 9.38. Pray ye therefore the Lord of the harvest, that he will send forth labourers into his harvest. Luk. 10.2.

Rom. 15.30. I beseech you, brethren, for the Lord Jesus Christ's sake, and for the love of the Spirit, that ye strive together with me in *your* prayers to God for me ; 31. That I may be delivered from them that do not believe in Judea ; and that my service which *I have* for Jerusalem may be accepted of the saints ; 32. That I may come unto you with joy by the will of God, and may with you be refreshed.

2 Cor. 1.11. Ye also helping together by prayer for us, that for the gift *bestowed* upon us by the means of many persons, thanks may be given by many on our behalf.

Eph. 6.19. For me, that utterance may be given unto me, that I may open my mouth boldly, to make known the mystery of the gospel, 20. For which I am an ambassador in bonds : that therein I may speak boldly, as I ought to speak.

Phil. 1.19. I know that this shall turn to my salvation through your prayer, and the supply of the Spirit of Jesus Christ.

Col. 4.3. Praying also for us, that God would open unto us a door of utterance, to speak the mystery of Christ, for which I am also in bonds : 4. That I may make it manifest, as I ought to speak.

2 The. 3.1. Brethren, pray for us, that the word of the Lord may have *free* course, and be glorified, even as *it is* with you : 2. And that we may be delivered from unreasonable and wicked men : for all *men* have not faith. 1 The. 5.25.

Philm. 22. I trust that through your prayers I shall be given unto you.

Heb. 13.18. Pray for us : for we trust we have a good conscience, in all things willing to live honestly. 19. But I beseech *you* the rather to do this, that I may be restored to you the sooner.

MINISTERS, Prayer for, exemplified. Jos. 1.17. Only the Lord thy God be with thee, as he was with Moses.

2 Chr. 6.41. Let thy priests, O Lord God, be clothed with salvation, and let thy saints rejoice in goodness.

Psa. 132.9. Let thy priests be clothed with righteousness.

Act. 1.24. They prayed, and said, Thou, Lord, which knowest the hearts of all *men*, shew whether of these two thou hast chosen.

Act. 4.29. Now, Lord, behold their threatenings : and grant unto thy servants, that with all boldness they may speak thy word.

Act. 6.6. When they had prayed, they laid *their* hands on them.

Act. 12.5. Prayer was made without ceasing of the church unto God for him.

Act. 14.23. When they had ordained them elders in every church, and had prayed with fasting, they commended them to the Lord.

MINISTERS, Unfaithful—False Teachers, Prophets, and Priests—Heresy. Deu. 18.20. The prophet, which shall presume to speak a word in my name, which I have not commanded him to speak, or that shall speak in the name of other gods, even that prophet shall die. 22. When a prophet speaketh in the name of the Lord, if the thing follow not, nor come to pass, that *is* the thing which the Lord hath not spoken, *but* the prophet hath spoken it presumptuously : thou shalt not be afraid of him. Deu. 13.3,5.

Pro. 19.27. Cease, my son, to hear the instruction *that causeth* to err from the words of knowledge.

Isa. 3.12. They which lead thee cause *thee* to err, and destroy the way of thy paths.

Isa. 5.20. Woe unto them that call evil good, and good evil ; that put darkness for light, and light for darkness ; that put bitter for sweet, and sweet for bitter !

Isa. 8.20. To the law and to the testimony : if they speak not according to this word, *it is* because *there is* no light in them.

Isa. 9.14. The Lord will cut off from Israel head and tail, branch and rush, in one day. 15. The ancient and honourable, he *is* the head ; and the prophet that teacheth lies, he *is* the tail. 16. For the leaders of this people cause *them* to err ; and *they that are* led of them *are* destroyed.

Isa. 28.7. The priest and the prophet have erred through strong drink, they are swallowed up of wine, they are out of the way through strong drink ; they err in vision, they stumble *in* judgment.

Isa. 29.10. The Lord hath poured out upon you the spirit of deep sleep, and hath closed your eyes : the prophets and your rulers, the seers hath he covered. 11. And the vision of all is become unto you as the words of a book that is sealed.

Isa. 30.10. Which say to the seers, See not ; and to the prophets, Prophesy not unto us right things, speak unto us smooth things, prophesy deceits.

Isa. 43.27. Thy teachers have transgressed against me. 28. Therefore I have profaned the princes of the sanctuary, and have given Jacob to the curse.

Isa. 44.20. He feedeth on ashes : a deceived heart hath turned him aside, that he cannot deliver his soul, nor say, *Is there* not a lie in my right hand ?

Isa. 56.10. His watchmen *are* blind : they are all ignorant, they *are* all dumb dogs, they cannot bark ; sleeping, lying down, loving to slumber. 11. Yea, *they are* greedy dogs *which* can never have enough, and they *are* shepherds *that* cannot understand : they all look to their own way, every one for his gain, from his quarter. 12. Come ye, *say they*, I will fetch wine, and we will fill ourselves with strong drink.

Jer. 2.8. The priests said not, Where *is* the Lord ? and they that handle the law knew me not : the pastors also transgressed against me, and the prophets prophesied by Baal, and walked after *things that* do not profit.

Jer. 5.30. A wonderful and horrible thing is committed in the land; 31. The prophets prophesy falsely, and the priests bear rule by their means; and my people love *to have it* so. *v.* 13,14.

Jer. 6.13. From the prophet even unto the priest every one dealeth falsely. 14. They have healed also the hurt *of the daughter* of my people slightly, saying, Peace, peace; when *there is* no peace. Jer. 8.10,11.

Jer. 10.21. The pastors are become brutish, and have not sought the Lord: therefore they shall not prosper, and all their flocks shall be scattered.

Jer. 12.10. Many pastors have destroyed my vineyard, they have trodden my portion under foot, they have made my pleasant portion a desolate wilderness.

Jer. 13.20. Where *is* the flock *that* was given thee, thy beautiful flock?

Jer. 14.14. The prophets prophesy lies in my name: I sent them not, neither have I commanded them, neither spake unto them: they prophesy unto you a false vision and divination, and a thing of nought, and the deceit of their heart. *v.* 13-16. Isa. 23.21.

Jer. 23.1. Woe be unto the pastors that destroy and scatter the sheep of my pasture! saith the Lord. 2. Therefore thus saith the Lord God of Israel against the pastors that feed my people; Ye have scattered my flock, and driven them away, and have not visited them: behold, I will visit upon you the evil of your doings. 11. Both prophet and priest are profane; yea, in my house have I found their wickedness, saith the Lord. 15. Behold, I will feed them with wormwood, and make them drink the water of gall: for from the prophets of Jerusalem is profaneness gone forth into all the land.

Jer. 23.17. They say still unto them that despise me, The Lord hath said, Ye shall have peace; and they say unto every one that walketh after the imagination of his own heart, No evil shall come upon you. 31. Behold, I *am* against the prophets, saith the Lord, that use their tongues, and say, He saith. 32. That prophesy false dreams, saith the Lord, and do tell them, and cause my people to err by their lies, and by their lightness. 36. The burden of the Lord shall ye mention no more: for every man's word shall be his burden; for ye have perverted the words of the living God. *v.* 25-39. Jer. 27.9-18.

Jer. 50.6. My people hath been lost sheep: their shepherds have caused them to go astray, they have turned them away *on* the mountains: they have gone from mountain to hill, they have forgotten their resting-place.

Lam. 2.14. Thy prophets have seen vain and foolish things for thee: and they have not discovered thine iniquity, to turn away thy captivity.

Eze. 13.5. Ye have not gone up into the gaps, neither made up the hedge for the house of Israel to stand in the battle in the day of the Lord. 10. They have seduced my people, saying, Peace; and *there was* no peace; and one built up a wall, and, lo, others daubed it with untempered *mortar*: 11. Say unto them which daub *it* with untempered *mortar*, that it shall fall. 18. Will ye hunt the souls of my people, and will ye save the souls alive *that come* unto you?

Eze. 13.19. Will ye pollute me among my people for handfuls of barley and for pieces of bread, to slay the souls that should not die, and to save the souls alive that should not live, by your lying to my people? 22. With lies ye have made the heart of the righteous sad, whom I have not made sad; and strengthened the hands of the wicked, that he should not return from his wicked way, by promising him life. *v.* 1-23.

Eze. 14.9. If the prophet be deceived when he hath spoken a thing, I the Lord have deceived that prophet, and I will stretch out my hand upon him, and will destroy him from the midst of my people Israel. 10. They shall bear the punishment of their iniquity: the punishment of the prophet shall be even as the punishment of him that seeketh *unto him.*

Eze. 22.25. A conspiracy of her prophets in the midst thereof, like a roaring lion ravening the prey; they have devoured souls; they have taken the treasure and precious things; they have made her many widows in the midst thereof. 26. Her priests have violated my law, and have profaned mine holy things: they have put no difference between the holy and profane, neither have they shewed *difference* between the unclean and the clean, and have hid their eyes from my sabbaths, and I am profaned among them. *v.* 27-31.

Eze. 34.2. Woe *be* to the shepherds of Israel that do feed themselves! should not the shepherds feed the flocks? 3. Ye eat the fat, and ye clothe you with the wool, ye kill them that are fed: *but* ye feed not the flock. 4. The diseased have ye not strengthened, neither have ye healed that which was sick, neither have ye bound up *that which was* broken, neither have ye brought again that which was driven away, neither have ye sought that which was lost: but with force and with cruelty have ye ruled them.

Eze. 34.6. My flock was scattered upon all the face of the earth, and none did search or seek *after them.* 10. Behold, I *am* against the shepherds; and I will require my flock at their hand, and cause them to cease from feeding the flock; neither shall the shepherds feed themselves any more: for I will deliver my flock from their mouth, that they may not be meat for them. *v.* 1-31.

Eze. 44.8. Ye have not kept the charge of mine holy things: but ye have set keepers of my charge in my sanctuary for yourselves. 10. The Levites that are gone away far from me, they shall even bear their iniquity.

Hos. 4.6. My people are destroyed for lack of knowledge: because thou hast rejected knowledge, I will also reject thee, that thou shalt be no priest to me: seeing thou hast forgotten the law of thy God, I will also forget thy children. 8. They eat up the sin of my people, and they set their heart on their iniquity. 9. And there shall be, like people, like priest: and I will punish them for their ways, and reward them their doings. *v.* 10-13.

Hos. 6.9. As troops of robbers wait for a man, *so* the company of priests murder in the way by consent: for they commit lewdness.

Hos. 9.8. The watchman of Ephraim *was* with my God: *but* the prophet *is* a snare of a fowler in all his ways, *and* hatred in the house of his God. *v.* 7. Hos. 5.1.

Mic. 2.11. If a man walking in the spirit

and falsehood do lie, *saying*, I will prophesy unto thee of wine and of strong drink; he shall even be the prophet of this people.

Mic. 3.5. The prophets that make my people err, that bite with their teeth, and cry, Peace; and he that putteth not into their mouths, they even prepare war against him. 6. Therefore night *shall be* unto you, that ye shall not have a vision; and it shall be dark unto you, that ye shall not divine; and the sun shall go down over the prophets, and the day shall be dark over them. 7. Then shall the seers be ashamed, and the diviners confounded: yea, they shall all cover their lips; for *there is* no answer of God. 11. The priests thereof teach for hire, and the prophets thereof divine for money: yet will they lean upon the Lord, and say, *Is* not the Lord among us? none evil can come upon us.

Zeph. 3.4. Her prophets *are* light *and* treacherous persons: her priests have polluted the sanctuary, they have done violence to the law.

Zec. 10.3. Mine anger was kindled against the shepherds, and I punished the goats: for the Lord of hosts hath visited his flock the house of Judah.

Zec. 11.16. Lo, I will raise up a shepherd in the land, *which* shall not visit those that be cut off, neither shall seek the young one, nor heal that that is broken, nor feed that that standeth still: but he shall eat the flesh of the fat, and tear their claws in pieces. 17. Woe to the idol shepherd that leaveth the flock! the sword *shall be* upon his arm, and upon his right eye: his arm shall be clean dried up, and his right eye shall be utterly darkened.

Zec. 13.2. I will cause the prophets and the unclean spirit to pass out of the land. 3. When any shall yet prophesy, then his father and his mother that begat him shall say unto him, Thou shalt not live: for thou speakest lies in the name of the Lord: and his father and his mother that begat him shall thrust him through when he prophesieth. 4. And it shall come to pass in that day, *that* the prophets shall be ashamed every one of his vision, when he hath prophesied; neither shall they wear a rough garment to deceive: 5. But he shall say, I *am* no prophet.

Mal. 1.6. If I *be* a master, where *is* my fear? saith the Lord of hosts unto you, O priests, that despise my name. And ye say, Wherein have we despised thy name? *v*. 7-10.

Mal. 2.8. Ye are departed out of the way; ye have caused many to stumble at the law; ye have corrupted the covenant of Levi, saith the Lord of hosts. 9. Therefore have I also made you contemptible and base before all the people, according as ye have not kept my ways, but have been partial in the law. *v*. 1-3.

Mat. 5.19. Whosoever therefore shall break one of these least commandments, and shall teach men so, he shall be called the least in the kingdom of heaven.

Mat. 7.15. Beware of false prophets, which come to you in sheep's clothing, but inwardly they are ravening wolves. 22. Many will say to me in that day, Lord, Lord, have we not prophesied in thy name? and in thy name have cast out devils? and in thy name done many wonderful works? 23. And then will I profess unto them, I never knew you: depart from me, ye that work iniquity.

Mat. 15.9. In vain they do worship me, teaching *for* doctrines the commandments of men. 13. Every plant, which my heavenly Father hath not planted, shall be rooted up. 14. They be blind leaders of the blind. And if the blind lead the blind, both shall fall into the ditch. Luk. 6.39.

Mat. 23.3. All therefore whatsoever they bid you observe, *that* observe and do; but do not ye after their works: for they say, and do not. 4. For they bind heavy burdens and grievous to be borne, and lay *them* on men's shoulders; but they *themselves* will not move them with one of their fingers. 13. Woe unto you, scribes and Pharisees, hypocrites! for ye shut up the kingdom of heaven against men: for ye neither go in *yourselves*, neither suffer ye them that are entering to go in.

Mat. 24.4. Take heed that no man deceive you. 5. For many shall come in my name, saying, I am Christ; and shall deceive many. 24. There shall arise false Christs, and false prophets, and shall shew great signs and wonders; insomuch that, if *it were* possible, they shall deceive the very elect. *v*. 11,26, 48-51.

Luk. 11.35. Take heed therefore that the light which is in thee be not darkness. 52. Ye have taken away the key of knowledge: ye entered not in yourselves, and them that were entering in ye hindered. *v*. 46-51.

Luk. 12.45. If that servant say in his heart, My lord delayeth his coming; and shall begin to beat the men-servants and maidens, and to eat and drink, and to be drunken; 46. The lord of that servant will come in a day when he looketh not for *him*, and at an hour when he is not aware, and will cut him in sunder and will appoint him his portion with the unbelievers.

Jno. 3.10. Art thou a master of Israel, and knowest not these things?

Jno. 5.43. If another shall come in his own name, him ye will receive.

Jno. 10.1. He that entereth not by the door into the sheepfold, but climbeth up some other way, the same is a thief and a robber. 5. A stranger will they not follow, but will flee from him: for they know not the voice of strangers. 8. All that ever came before me are thieves and robbers: but the sheep did not hear them. 10. The thief cometh not, but for to steal, and to kill, and to destroy. 12. He that is an hireling, and not the shepherd, whose own the sheep are not, seeth the wolf coming, and leaveth the sheep, and fleeth: and the wolf catcheth them, and scattereth the sheep. 13. The hireling fleeth, because he is an hireling, and careth not for the sheep.

Act. 20.29. After my departing shall grievous wolves enter in among you, not sparing the flock. 30. Also of your own selves shall men arise, speaking perverse things, to draw away disciples after them.

Rom. 2.19. Art confident that thou thyself art a guide of the blind, a light of them which are in darkness. 20. An instructor of the foolish, a teacher of babes, which hast the form of knowledge and of the truth in the law. 21. Thou therefore which teachest another, teachest thou not thyself? thou that preachest a man should not steal, dost thou steal? *v*. 22.

Rom. 3.8. Some affirm that we say, Let us

do evil, that good may come, whose damnation is just.

Rom. 16.17. Mark them which cause divisions and offences contrary to the doctrine which ye have learned; and avoid them. 18. For they that are such serve not our Lord Jesus Christ, but their own belly; and by good words and fair speeches deceive the hearts of the simple.

1 Cor. 1.12. Every one of you saith, I am of Paul; and I of Apollos; and I of Cephas; and I of Christ. 13. Is Christ divided? was Paul crucified for you? or were ye baptized in the name of Paul?

1 Cor. 3.10. Let every man take heed how he buildeth thereupon. 11. For other foundation can no man lay than that is laid, which is Jesus Christ. 2i. Therefore let no man glory in men. *v.* 1-4.

1 Cor. 11.18. I hear that there be divisions among you; and I partly believe it. 19. For there must be also heresies among you, that they which are approved may be made manifest among you.

2 Cor. 2.17. We are not as many, which corrupt the word of God.

2 Cor. 11.3. I fear, lest by any means, as the serpent beguiled Eve through his subtilty, so your minds should be corrupted from the simplicity that is in Christ. 4. For if he that cometh preacheth another Jesus, whom we have not preached, or *if* ye receive another spirit, which ye have not received, or another gospel, which ye have not accepted, ye might well bear with *him.* 13. Such *are* false apostles, deceitful workers, transforming themselves into the apostles of Christ. 14. And no marvel; for Satan himself is transformed into an angel of light. 15. Therefore *it is* no great thing if his ministers also be transformed as the ministers of righteousness; whose end shall be according to their works. *v.* 1-33.

Gal. 1.6. I marvel that ye are so soon removed from him that called you into the grace of Christ unto another gospel: 7. Which is not another; but there be some that trouble you, and would pervert the gospel of Christ. 8. But though we, or an angel from heaven, preach any other gospel unto you than that which we have preached unto you, let him be accursed.

Gal. 2.4. False brethren unawares brought in, who came in privily to spy out our liberty which we have in Christ Jesus, that they might bring us into bondage.

Gal. 5.10. He that troubleth you shall bear his judgment, whosoever he be.

Eph. 4.14. Be no more children, tossed to and fro, and carried about with every wind of doctrine, by the sleight of men, *and* cunning craftiness, whereby they lie in wait to deceive.

Phil. 1.15. Some indeed preach Christ even of envy and strife; and some also of good will: 16. The one preach Christ of contention, not sincerely, supposing to add affliction to my bonds.

Phil. 3.2. Beware of dogs, beware of evil workers, beware of the concision.

Col. 2.4. This I say, lest any man should beguile you with enticing words. 8. Beware lest any man spoil you through philosophy and vain deceit, after the tradition of men, after the rudiments of the world, and not after Christ. 18. Let no man beguile you of your

reward in a voluntary humility and worshipping of angels, intruding into those things which he hath not seen, vainly puffed up by his fleshly mind.

1 Tim. 1.3. Charge some that they teach no other doctrine, 4. Neither give heed to fables and endless genealogies, which minister questions, rather than godly edifying which is in faith: *so do.* 6. From which some having swerved, have turned aside unto vain jangling; 7. Desiring to be teachers of the law; understanding neither what they say, nor whereof they affirm. 19. Holding faith and a good conscience; which some having put away concerning faith have made shipwreck.

1 Tim. 4.1. In the latter times some shall depart from the faith, giving heed to seducing spirits, and doctrines of devils; 2. Speaking lies in hypocrisy; having their conscience seared with a hot iron; 3. Forbidding to marry, *and commanding* to abstain from meats. 7. Refuse profane and old wives' fables, and exercise thyself *rather* unto godliness.

1 Tim. 6.3. If any man teach otherwise, and consent not to wholesome words, *even* the words of our Lord Jesus Christ, and to the doctrine which is according to godliness; 4. He is proud, knowing nothing, but doting about questions and strifes of words, whereof cometh envy, strife, railings, evil surmisings, 5. Perverse disputings of men of corrupt minds, and destitute of the truth, supposing that gain is godliness: from such withdraw thyself. 20. Keep that which is committed to thy trust, avoiding profane *and* vain babblings, and oppositions of science falsely so called: 21. Which some professing have erred concerning the faith.

2 Tim. 2.14. Strive not about words to no profit, *but* to the subverting of the hearers. 16. Shun profane *and* vain babblings: for they will increase unto more ungodliness. 17. And their word will eat as doth a canker: of whom is Hymenæus and Philetus; 18. Who concerning the truth have erred, saying that the resurrection is past already; and overthrow the faith of some.

2 Tim 3.6. Of this sort are they which creep into houses, and lead captive silly women laden with sins, led away with divers lusts, 8. As Jannes and Jambres withstood Moses, so do these also resist the truth: men of corrupt minds, reprobate concerning the faith. 9. But they shall proceed no further: for their folly shall be ~manifest unto all *men*, as their's also was. 13. Evil men and seducers shall wax worse and worse, deceiving, and being deceived. 2 Tim 4.3.

Tit. 1.10. Many unruly and vain talkers and deceivers, specially they of the circumcision: 11. Whose mouths must be stopped, who subvert whole houses, teaching things which they ought not, for filthy lucre's sake. 14. Giving heed to Jewish fables, and commandments of men, that turn from the truth.

Tit. 3.10. An heretick after the first and second admonition reject; 11. Knowing that he that is such is subverted, and sinneth, being condemned of himself.

Heb. 13.9. Be not carried about with divers and strange doctrines.

2 Pet. 2.1. There were false prophets also among the people, even as there shall be false

teachers among you, who privily shall bring in damnable heresies, even denying the Lord that bought them, and bring upon themselves swift destruction. 2. Many shall follow their pernicious ways; by reason of whom the way of truth shall be evil spoken of. 3. Through covetousness shall they with feigned words make merchandise of you: whose judgment now of a long time lingereth not, and their damnation slumbereth not.

2 Pet. 2.14. A heart they have, exercised with covetous practices; cursed children: 15. Which have forsaken the right way, and are gone astray, following the way of Balaam *the son* of Bosor, who loved the wages of unrighteousness; 16. But was rebuked for his iniquity: 17. These are wells without water, clouds that are carried with a tempest; to whom the mist of darkness is reserved for ever. 18. When they speak great swelling *words* of vanity, they allure through the lusts of the flesh, *through much* wantonness, those that were clean escaped from them who live in error. 19. While they promise them liberty, they themselves are the servants of corruption. *v.* 1-22.

2 Pet. 3.16. Things hard to be understood, which they that are unlearned and unstable wrest, as *they do* also the other scriptures, unto their own destruction.

1 Jno. 2.18. As ye have heard that antichrist shall come, even now are there many antichrists; whereby we know that it is the last time. 26. These *things* have I written unto you concerning them that seduce you.

1 Jno. 4.1. Beloved, believe not every spirit, but try the spirits whether they are of God: because many false prophets are gone out into the world. 2. Hereby know ye the Spirit of God: Every spirit that confesseth that Jesus Christ is come in the flesh is of God: 3. And every spirit that confesseth not that Jesus Christ is come in the flesh is not of God: and this is that *spirit* of antichrist, whereof ye have heard that it should come; and even now already is it in the world.

1 Jno. 4.5. They are of the world: therefore speak they of the world, and the world heareth them.

2 Jno. 7. Many deceivers are entered into the world, who confess not that Jesus Christ is come in the flesh. This is a deceiver and an antichrist. 10. If there come any unto you, and bring not this doctrine, receive him not into *your* house, neither bid him God speed: 11. For he that biddeth him God speed is partaker of his evil deeds.

3 Jno. 10. I will remember his deeds which he doeth, prating against us with malicious words: and not content therewith, neither doth he himself receive the brethren, and forbiddeth them that would, and casteth *them* out of the church.

Jude 4. There are certain men crept in unawares, who were before of old ordained to this condemnation, ungodly men, turning the grace of our God into lasciviousness, and denying the only Lord God, and our Lord Jesus Christ. 11. Woe unto them! for they have gone in the way of Cain, and ran greedily after the error of Balaam for reward, and perished in the gainsaying of Core.

Rev. 2.2. How thou canst not bear them which are evil: and thou hast tried them which say they are apostles, and are not, and hast found them liars. 14. Thou hast there them that hold the doctrine of Balaam, who taught Balac to cast a stumblingblock before the children of Israel, to eat things sacrificed unto idols, and to commit fornication. 15. So hast thou also them that hold the doctrine of the Nicolaitanes, which thing I hate.

Rev. 2.20. Thou sufferest that woman Jezebel, which calleth herself a prophetess, to teach and to seduce my servants to commit fornication, and to eat things sacrificed unto idols. 21. And I gave her space to repent of her fornication; and she repented not. 22. Behold, I will cast her into a bed, and them that commit adultery with her into great tribulation, except they repent of their deeds. 23. And I will kill her children with death.

See Ahab, Alexander, Amaziah, Balaam, Caiaphas, Demas, Diotrephes, Eli's sons, Elymas, Hananiah, Hymeneus, Jezebel, Jonathan, Judas, Korah, Nadab, Nicolaitanes, Noadiah, Philetus, Shemaiah, Zedekiah. See also Pharisees, —Priests, idolatrous—Scribes—Backsliding.

MINNI, a province of Armenia, Jer. 51.27.

MINNITH, a town of the Ammonites, Jud. 11.33. Eze. 27.17.

MINSTREL. See Music—Mourning.

MINT, Mat. 23.23. Luk. 11.42.

MIRACLES, Design of. To witness of God, Ex. 3.20. Ex. 7.5,17. Ex. 8.10,22. Ex. 9.16,29. Ex. 10.1,2,16,17. Ex. 11.1,7-9. Ex. 12.12. Ex. 14.4,17,18,25,31. Ex. 16.6,12. Deu. 4.33-35. Jos. 2.11. Jos. 3.10,11. Jos. 4.24. Jos. 5.1. Jud. 2.7. 1 Sam. 6.6. 1 Sam. 12.17,18. 1 Kin. 18.37,39. 2 Kin. 5.15. 2 Chr. 7.3. Dan. 2.47. Dan. 3.28,29. Jonah 1.16. Luk. 5.26. Luk. 18.43. Jno. 9.3. Jno. 11. 4,40. Act. 4.22.

To witness to Christ as the Messiah, Mat. 9.6. Mat. 11.2-6 with Isa. 35.5,6. Mat. 12. 23-30. Mat. 13.54. Mat. 14.33. Mat. 15.31. Mat. 27.54. Mar. 2.12. Mar. 3.23-27. Mar. 6.2. Mar. 7.37. Luk. 5.23-26. Luk. 7.16. Luk. 11.17-23. Luk. 18.43. Jno. 2.11,18-23. Jno. 3.2. Jno. 4.45,48,53. Jno. 5.20,36. Jno. 6.14,30,31. Jno. 7.31. Jno. 9.4,16,17,30-33. Jno. 10.21,25,32,37-42. Jno. 11.4,15,37,40-45. Jno. 12.10,11,18,30,42. Jno. 14.10,11. Jno. 15.24. Jno. 20.30,31. Act. 2.22.

To witness to the inspiration of prophets, Ex. 4.5-9. Ex. 14.31. Ex. 19.9. Num. 16. 5-7,28-40. Num. 17.5,10. Jos. 4.14. 1 Kin. 17.24. 1 Kin. 18.36.

To witness to the apostles, and to the truth of the Gospel, Mar. 16.17-20. Act. 1.8. Act. 2. Act. 3.1-16. Act. 4.10,16-22,33. Act. 5. 11-14. Act. 8.6-8. Act. 9.33-35,42. Act. 13. 12. Act. 14.3,11-18. Rom. 15.18,19. 1 Cor. 1.6,7. 1 Cor. 14.22. Heb. 2.4.

MIRACLES. Miraculous Judgments, Blessings, and Events. The flood, Gen. c. 7 & 8. Confusion of tongues, Gen. 11.7-9. Sodomites' blindness, Gen. 19.11. Destruction of Sodom, &c., Gen. 19. Aaron's rod becomes a serpent, Ex. 7.10,12. Pillar of cloud, Ex. 13. 20,21.

Destruction of Nadab, &c., Lev. 10.1,2; of Israelites at Taberah, Num. 11.1. Aaron's rod blossoms, Num. 17.8 Balaam's ass speaking, Num. 22.23-30. Manna and quails sent,

Ex. 16.12-15. Num. 11.31. Manna preserved on the Sabbath, Ex. 16.23,24; and for generations, Ex. 16.32-34.

Passage of Jordan, Jos. 3.11-17. Fall of Jericho, Jos. 6.20. Amorites defeated, Jos. 10.11. Sun and moon stand still, Jos. 10.12-14. Gideon's fleece, Jud. 6.37-40. Samson supplied with water, Jud. 15.19. His feats of strength, Jud. 15.14-16. Jud. 16.1-14. Fall of Dagon, 1 Sam. 5.3,4. Bethshemites smitten, 1 Sam. 6.19. Thunder, &c., in answer to Samuel's prayer, 1 Sam. 12.16-18. Plague stopped at David's prayer, 1 Chr. 21.26. Jeroboam's hand withered, 1 Kin. 13.3-6. Appearance of water as blood, 2 Kin. 3.20-22. Panic of Syrians, 2 Kin. 7.6,7. Elijah's and Elisha's miracles. See ELIJAH—ELISHA.

Destruction of Sennacherib's army, 2 Kin. 19.35. Isa. 37.36. Return of the shadow on the sun-dial, 2 Kin. 20.9-11. Hezekiah's cure, Isa. 38.21. Deliverance of Shadrach, &c., Dan. 3.23-27; and of Daniel, Dan. 6.22. The sea calmed on Jonah being cast into it, Jonah 1.15. Jonah in the fish, Jonah 1.17. Jonah 2.10. His gourd, Jonah 4.6,7.

Sacrifices consumed by fire from heaven; of Aaron, Lev. 9.24; of Gideon, Jud. 6.21; of Manoah, Jud. 13.19,20; of Solomon, 2 Chr. 7.1; of Elijah, 1 Kin. 18.38.

Star at Christ's birth, Mat. 2.1,2,9. Darkness and earthquake at Christ's death, Mat. 27.45,51-53. Earthquake at Christ's resurrection, Mat. 28.2. Mar. 16.4. Zacharias' dumbness and cure, Luk. 1.20,64. The pool of Siloam troubled by an angel, Jno. 5.4.

The sick cured, and evil spirits cast out; by the seventy, Luk. 10.17-20; by the apostles, Mar. 6.13. Act. 2.43. Act. 5.12. Stephen, Act. 6.8. Philip, Act. 8.7,13.

See CHRIST, MIRACLES OF.

MIRACLES OF MOSES. The burning-bush, Ex. 3.2. Moses' rod changed to a serpent, Ex. 4.2-4. His hand made leprous and cured, Ex. 4.6,7. Plagues of Egypt, Ex. c. 7 to 12. Passage of the Red Sea, Ex. 14.21-29. The waters of Marah sweetened, Ex. 15.25. Water brought from the rock in Horeb, Ex. 17.5,6; and at Meribah, Num. 20.11. Victory over Amalek, Ex. 17.11. Forty days' fast, Ex. 34.28. Shining of Moses' face, Ex. 34.29-35. Miriam's leprosy healed, Num. 12.10-15. Korah, &c., destroyed, Num. 16.31-35. Israelites healed by brazen serpent, Num. 21.9.

MIRACLES OF PETER. Peter cures the sick, Act. 5.15,16. Cures Eneas, Act. 9.34. Raises Dorcas, Act. 9.40. Ananias' and Sapphira's death, Act. 5.5,10. Peter and John cure a lame man, Act. 3.2-11. Peter, &c., delivered from prison, Act. 5.19-23. Act. 12.6-11.

MIRACLES OF PAUL. Paul strikes Elymas with blindness, Act. 13.11. Heals a cripple, Act. 14.10. Casts out evil spirits, and cures sick, Act. 16.18. Act. 19.11,12. Act. 28.8,9. Raises Eutychus to life, Act. 20.9-12. Shakes off a viper, Act. 28.5. Paul cured of blindness, Act. 9.3-6,17,18. Paul and Silas released from prison, Act. 16.26.

MIRACLES. MIRACULOUS GIFTS. 2 Kin. 2.9. Elisha said, I pray thee, let a double portion of thy spirit be upon me. 10. And he said, Thou hast asked a hard thing: *nevertheless*, if thou see me *when I am* taken from thee, it shall be so unto thee; but if not, it shall not be *so*. v. 12.

Luk. 10.20. In this rejoice not, that the spirits are subject unto you; but rather rejoice, because your names are written in heaven.

Act. 8.20. Thy money perish with thee, because thou hast thought that the gift of God may be purchased with money.

1 Cor. 13.2. Though I have *the gift of* prophecy, and understand all mysteries, and all knowledge; and though I have all faith, so that I could remove mountains, and have not charity, I am nothing. 8. Charity never faileth: but whether *there be* prophecies, they shall fail; whether *there be* tongues, they shall cease; whether *there be* knowledge, it shall vanish away. v. 9,10.

1 Cor. 14.1. Desire spiritual *gifts*, but rather that ye may prophesy. 12. As ye are zealous of spiritual *gifts*, seek that ye may excel to the edifying of the church. 18. I thank my God, I speak with tongues more than ye all. 22. Tongues are for a sign, not to them that believe, but to them that believe not: but prophesying *serveth* not for them that believe not, but for them which believe. 39. Covet to prophesy, and forbid not to speak with tongues. v. 1-39.

Jas. 5.14. Is any sick among you? let him call for the elders of the church; and let them pray over him, anointing him with oil in the name of the Lord: 15. And the prayer of faith shall save the sick, and the Lord shall raise him up; and if he have committed sins, they shall be forgiven him.

Rev. 11.6. These have power to shut heaven, that it rain not in the days of their prophecy: and have power over waters to turn them to blood, and to smite the earth with all plagues, as often as they will.

See PROPHECY—TONGUES—HOLY SPIRIT, MIRACULOUS INFLUENCES OF.

MIRACLES PERFORMED IN CHRIST'S NAME. By the seventy, Luk. 10.17-20; by Christ's disciples, Mar. 9.39. Jno. 14.12; by the apostles, Act. 3.6,12,13,16. Act. 4.10,30. Act. 9.34,35. Act. 16.18. See HOLY SPIRIT, MIRACULOUS INFLUENCES OF.

————, UNBELIEF IN. Pharaoh, Ex. c. 7 to 11. Israelites, Num. 14.11,22. Deu. 29.2-4. Psa. 78.32. Psa. 106.7. Pharisees and Jews, Mat. 9.34. Jno. 9.24,29. Jno. 10.20,21. Jno. 11.46. Jno. 12.37. Jno. 15.24. Act. 2.12,13. Men of Capernaum, &c., Mat. 11.20-24. Christ's brethren, Jno. 7.4,5.

MIRIAM, sister of Moses, Num. 26.59. Her care of Moses when in the ark, Ex. 2.4-8. A prophetess; her song of triumph, Ex. 15.20,21. Mic. 6.4. Her jealousy of Moses; punished with leprosy; her cure, Num. 12. Deu. 24.9. Death of, Num. 20.1.

MISREPHOTH-MAIM, place near Sidon, Joshua's victory at, Jos. 11.8. Jos. 13.6.

MISSIONS. See ZEAL—MINISTERS.

MIST, the ground watered by, at creation, Gen. 2.6. Illustrative, 2 Pet. 2.17.

MITE, half a *kodrantes;* that is, less than half a farthing, Mar. 12.42. Luk. 12.59. Luk. 21.2. See FARTHING.

MITRE, Ex. 28.4,36-39. Ex. 39.28-31.

MITYLENE, a town in the isle of Lesbos, visited by Paul, Act. 20.14.

MIZAR (a little hill), Psa. 42.6.

MIZPAH, or MIZPEH (watch-tower), named by Laban from the heap of stones set up at, Gen. 31.23,49. A city of Gilead, Jud. 11.29. Hos. 5.1. The armies of Israel and Ammonites encamped in, Jud. 10.17. Jud. 11.11,29. Jephthah dwelt in, Jud. 11.34.

————, a city of Benjamin, Jos. 18.26. Israelites convened at, Jud. 20.1,3. Jud. 21.1. 1 Sam. 7.5-7,12. 1 Sam. 10.17. Samuel judges at, 1 Sam. 7.16. Fortified by Asa, 1 Kin. 15.22. 2 Chr. 16.6. Gedaliah, the Chaldean governor, resides at, 2 Kin. 25.23,25. Jer. 40.6-15. Jer. 41.1-14. Inhabited after the captivity, Neh. 3.7,15,19.

————, a town in the plains of Judah, Jos. 15.38. Supposed to be the same as the watch-tower in 2 Chr. 20.24.

————, a town of Moab, to which David brought his parents, 1 Sam. 22.3.

————, VALLEY OF, in the region of Lebanon, Jos. 11.3,8.

MIZRAIM, son of Ham; his descendants, Gen. 10.6,13,14. 1 Chr. 1.8,11,12. A name of Egypt, see EGYPT.

MNASON OF CYPRUS, an old disciple with whom Paul lodged, Act. 21.16.

MOABITES, descended from Lot's son, Moab, Gen. 19.37. Called people of Chemosh, Num. 21.29. Rulers of, 1 Chr. 4.22. Their territory, Num. 21.10-30. Deu. 2.8-19. Jud. 11.18. Refuse Israel passage, Jud. 11.17. Balak, king of, sends for Balaam, Num. c. 22 to 24. Jos. 24.9,10. Mic. 6.5. Entice Israel to idolatry, &c., Num. 25.1-3.

Israel forbidden to make war on, Deu. 2.9. Jud. 11.15; or to make league with, Deu. 23.6; or to admit to the congregation, Deu. 3.3,4. Intermarriages with, Ruth 1.4. 1 Chr. 11.1. 1 Chr. 8.8. Ezr. 9.1,2. Neh. 13.23. Eglon, king of, subdues Israel; is slain by Ehud, Jud. 3.12-30. 1 Sam. 12.9; defeated by Saul, 1 Sam. 14.47.

Enmity to Israel, Psa. 83.6.8. Gave an asylum to David's parents, 1 Sam. 22.3,4. Conquered by David, and become tributary, 2 Sam. 8.2. 2 Sam. 23.20. 1 Chr. 11.22. 1 Chr. 18.2,11. Psa. 60.8. Mesha, king of, tributary to Ahab, 2 Kin. 1.1. 2 Kin. 3.4; revolts from Jehoram, and is defeated by him; sacrifices his son, 2 Kin. 3.5-27.

Invade Israel in the reign of Jehoash, 2 Kin. 13.20. Invade Judah with the Ammonites; and defeated by Jehoshaphat, 2 Chr. 20. Invade Judah in the reign of Jehoiakim, 2 Kin. 24.2. Jews among, during the captivity, Jer. 40.11.

Idols of, see BAAL-PEOR, CHEMOSH. Mountains of, see NEBO, PEOR, PISGAH. River of, see ARNON. Towns of, Isa. 15. Jer. 48. See AR or AREOPOLIS, DIBON, ELEALAH, ENEGLAIM, HESHBON, KIRJATH-HUZOTH, KIR-MOAB.

Prophecies of, Ex. 15.15. Num. 24.17. Isa. 11.14. Isa. 15. Isa. 16. Isa. 25.10-12. Jer. 9.25,26. Jer. 25.21. Jer. 27.1-11. Jer. 48. Eze. 25.8-11. Dan. 11.41. Amos 2.1-3. Zeph. 2.8-11.

MOAB, PLAINS OF, south of Ar or Arnon; Israelites pitch in, Deu. 2.18,24. Jud. 11.18,22. Num. 22.1. Num. 33.48; are numbered in, Num. 26.3,63. The law given in, Num. 36.13.

Deu. 1.5. Covenant in, Deu. 29.1. Allotment of tribes given in, Jos. 13.32.

MOCKING. See INFIDELITY.

MOLE, Lev. 11.30. Isa. 2.20.

MOLECH, MOLOCH, or MILCOLM, a god of the Ammonites, Act. 7.43. Solomon built a high place for, 1 Kin. 11.7. Children passed through the fire to, 2 Kin. 23.10. Jer. 32.35. 2 Kin. 16.3. 2 Kin. 21.6. 2 Chr. 28.3. Isa. 57.5. Jer. 7.31. Eze. 16.20,21. Eze. 20.26,31. Eze. 23.37,39. See Lev. 18.21. Lev. 20.2-5.

Josiah destroys the high place of, 2 Kin. 23.10. Supposed to be the same as Malcham, Zeph. 1.5; and (as Melech means *king*) the king of the Ammonites, Jer. 49.1 (*marg.*). Amos 1.15; and the same as Baal, Jer. 32.35 with Jer. 19.5,6.

MONEY, weighed, Gen. 23.16. Gen. 43.21. Job 28.15. Jer. 32.10. Zec. 11.12. Cesar's image on, Mat. 22.20,21. Metals used in, see BRASS, GOLD, SILVER. Coins of, see DARIC, DRAM, FARTHING, MITE, PENNY, PIECE OF SILVER, SHEKEL, TALENT.

See COVETOUSNESS, LIBERALITY, RICHES, USURY.

MONEY-CHANGERS; their traffic in the temple, Mat. 21.12. Mar. 11.15. Jno. 2.15, see Gen. 23.16.

MONTH, Gen. 7.11. Gen. 8.4. Began with the new moon, Num. 10.10 with Num. 28.11. 1 Sam. 20.5,18,24,27. Twelve in the year, 1 Chr. 27.1-15. See 1st Month, ABIB; 2, ZIF; 3, SIVAN; 6, ELUL; 7, ETHANIM; 8, BUL; 9, CHISLEU; 10, TEBETH; 11, SEBAT; 12, ADAR. The 4th and 5th months are not referred to by name in scripture.

MONUMENTS. See BURIAL-PLACES—PILLARS.

MOON, Gen. 1.16. Job 31.26. Psa. 8.3. Psa. 136.9. Ecc. 12.2. Song 6.10. Jer. 31.35. 1 Cor. 15.41. Its influences, Deu. 33.14. Psa. 121.6. Months regulated by, Psa. 104.19. Joseph's dream concerning, Gen. 37.9. Joshua commands it to stand still, Jos. 10.12,13. Hab. 3.11. Worship of, forbidden, Deu. 4.19. Deu. 17.3. Worshipped, 2 Kin. 23.5. Job 31.26,27. Jer. 8.2. Worshipped as queen of heaven, Jer. 7.18. Jer. 44.17-19,25. Darkening of, illustrative, Job 25.5. Isa. 13.10. Isa. 24.23. Eze. 32.7. Joel 2.10,31. Joel 3.15. Mat. 24. 29. Luk. 21.25. Rev. 6.12. Rev. 8.12. Shining of, illustrative, Isa. 30.26. Isa. 60.19. Rev. 21.23. Symbolical, Rev. 12.1.

————, NEW, FEAST OF. See FEASTS.

MORAL LAW. See LAW OF GOD.

MORDECAI, a captive Jew; his parentage; educates his cousin Esther; reveals a conspiracy against the king, Est. 2. Est. 6. 1-3. Refuses submission to Haman, who plots his death, and that of the Jews, Est. 3. Est. 5.9-14. His mourning; induces Esther to petition the king, Est. 4. Led in state by Haman, Est. 6. Made chief-minister; plans for the Jews safety, Est. c. 8 to 10. Institutes the feast of Purim, Est. 9.20-32.

MOREH, PLAIN OF, near Shechem; Abraham dwelt in, Gen. 12.6. Gilgal near, Deu. 11.30.

————, HILL OF. Gideon's defeat of the Midianites near, Jud. 7.1.

MORIAH, a hill on which Abraham offered Isaac, Gen. 22.2.   The Temple built on, 2 Chr. 3.1.

MORTAR, Ex. 1.14. Slime used for, at Babel, Gen. 11.3. Trodden, Nah. 3.14. Isa. 41.25. Used for plaster, Lev. 14.42,45. Untempered, Eze. 13.10-15. Eze. 22.28.

———, Pro. 27.22.   Manna pounded in, Num. 11.8.

MORTIFY, signifies to put to death, Rom. 8.13. Col. 3.5. So rendered, Mat. 10.21. Rom. 4.19, &c.

MOSAIC Law. See LAW, MOSAIC.

MOSES (drawn out), son of Amram and Jochebed, of the tribe of Levi ; his birth, Ex. 2.1-4. Ex. 6.20. Act. 7.20. Heb. 11.23. Found in an ark on the river brink, and adopted by Pharaoh's daughter, Ex. 2.5-10. Act. 7.21. His learning, Act. 7.22.

Refuses to be called the son of Pharaoh's daughter, Heb. 11.24-26. Slays an Egyptian, and separates two Israelites, Ex. 2.11-14. Act. 7.23-28. Flees to Midian ; marries Jethro's daughter ; his family, Ex. 2.15-22. 1 Chr. 23. 14-17. Act. 7.29. Num. 12.1. His children uncircumcised ; God seeks to slay him, Ex. 4.24-26. Keeps Jethro's flock ; sees the burning-bush ; sent by God to announce deliverance to Israel ; signs given to him ; the rod becomes a serpent, Ex. 3. Ex. 4.1-17. Act. 7.30-36.

Returns to Egypt ; meets with Aaron ; his miracles before Israel, Ex. 4.18-31. Pleads his inability ; Aaron made his spokesman, Ex. 3.11. Ex. 4.1,10-16. Ex. 6.12,30. Ex. 7.1,2. His despondency, Ex. 5.22,23.

His appearances before Pharaoh, and miracles, Ex. c. 5 to 10. Ex. 12.31. 80 years old at this time, Ex. 7.7. Withstood by magicians, Ex. 7.11,22. Ex. 8.7,18.   2 Tim. 3.8.   His reputation in Egypt, Ex. 11.3.

Leads the Israelites out of Egypt (see p. 254) ; takes the bones of Joseph with him, Ex. 13.19. Hos. 12.13. Crosses the Red Sea ; the sea divided, Ex. 14. His song, Ex. 15.1-19. Heals the waters of Marah, Ex. 15.23-26. Water brought from the rock in Horeb, Ex. 17.5,6.

His hands held up while Joshua defeats Amalek, Ex. 17.9-12. Builds altars, Ex. 17.15. Ex. 24.4. Jethro brings his family to him, Ex. 18.1-12. His mode of judging Israel ; appoints judges by Jethro's advice, Ex. 18. 13,25. Deu. 1.9-17.

Ascends Mount Sinai to God ; the giving of the law, Ex. 19.3-19,20. Ex. 20.21. Ex. 24. Ex. 34. Deu. 5.31. Deu. 9.9. Deu. 10.10. Heb. 11.21. See LAW, MOSAIC. Fasts 40 days, Ex. 24.18. Deu. 9.9.   Fasts a second time, Ex. 34.28. Deu. 10.10.

Breaks the tables and destroys the golden calf ; rebukes Aaron, Ex. 32.19-24. Deu. 9.17,21. 3000 idolaters slain by his command, Ex. 32.25-29. Makes 2 new tables, Ex. 34.4. Deu. 10.1,2. God reveals his glory to him, Ex. 33.18,23. Ex. 34.4-7. His face shines ; he puts on a vail, Ex. 34.29-35. 2 Cor. 3.7,13. Sets up the Tabernacle, see TABERNACLE. Reproves Aaron's sons for neglecting the sin-offering, Lev. 10.16-20. Solicits Hobab to accompany Israel, Num. 10.29-32. Doubts God's promise to provide flesh, Num. 11.21-23. Aaron and Miriam's jealousy of him ; her leprosy removed on his prayer, Num. 12. Rebellion of Korah, &c., Num. 16. His sin

at Meribah ; water given on striking the rock, Num. 20.1-12. Psa. 106.32,33. Erects the serpent of brass, Num. 21.9. Jno. 3.14. Appoints Joshua his successor ; his charge, Num. 27.22,23. Deu. 31.7,8,14,23. Deu. 34.9. Reproves Israel for sparing Midian, Num. 31.14-17. His vigour when 120 years old, Deu. 31.2. Deu. 34.7.

Not allowed to enter Canaan for his sin at Meribah ; views Canaan from Pisgah : his death and burial ; Israel mourns for, Num. 27.12-14. Deu. 1.37. Deu. 3.25-27. Deu. 32.49-52. Deu. 34.1-8.

A prophet, Ex. 3.10. Ex. 4.5,11,12. Ex. 6.13. Ex. 7.2. Ex. 19.9. Ex. 33.11. Lev. 27.34. Num. 11.17. Num. 12.7,8. Num. 36.13. Deu. 1.3. Deu. 5.31. Deu. 18.15,18. Deu. 34.10,12. Hos. 12.13. Mar. 7.9,10. Act. 7.37,38. See PROPHETS, INSPIRATION OF.

Israelites murmur against him, Ex. 5.20,21. Ex. 14.11,12. Ex. 16.2,3. Ex. 17.2,3. Num. 14.2-4. Num. 16.41. Num. 20.2-5. Num. 21.4-6. Deu. 1.12,26-28. Replies to Israel's murmurs, Ex. 14.13,14. Ex. 16.6-9. Num. 1.29-31.

His prayers : Prayer for Pharaoh, Ex. 8.12,30. Ex. 9.33. Ex. 10.18 ; for Israel, Ex. 15.25. Ex. 17.4. Ex. 32.11-13,30-32. Ex. 34.9. Num. 11.2. Num. 14.5,13-20. Num. 16.45,46. Num. 20.6. Num. 21.7. Deu. 9.25-29. Psa. 106.23 ; for Miriam, Num. 12.13 ; for Aaron, Deu. 9.20 ; for God's presence, Ex. 33.12-23 ; for a successor, Num. 27.16 ; to be allowed to enter Canaan, Deu. 3.23-25.

His piety, Jer. 15.1. Heb. 3.2,5. Heb. 11. 24-26. His meekness, Num. 12.3. Ex. 14.13,14. His anger and complaints against Israel, Ex. 5.22,23. Ex. 6.12. Ex. 32.19. Num. 11.10-15. Num. 16.15. Num. 20.10. Num. 31.14. His magnanimity when Eldad and Medad prophesied, Num. 11.29 ; when God said he would make of Moses a great nation, Ex. 32.10. Num. 14.12,13.

He and his family encamped before the tabernacle, Num. 3.38. The ram of consecration belonged to him, Ex. 29.26. Lev. 8.29. Blesses the people, Lev. 9.23. Num. 10.35,36. Deu. 1.11 ; before his death, Deu. 33.

His writings, Ex. 17.14. Ex. 24.14. Num. 33.2. Deu. 1.1. Deu. 4.44. Deu. 5.1. Deu. 31.9,19,22,24. Deu. 32. Psa. 90 (title). Luk. 20.37. Rev. 15.3. Appears with Elijah on the Mount of Transfiguration, Mat. 17.3,4. Mar. 9.4,5. Luk. 9.30. His miracles. See MIRACLES. See ISRAELITES, p. 254.

MOTH, Job 4.19. Job 27.18. Psa. 39.11. Garments eaten by, Job 13.28. Isa. 50.9. Hos. 5.12. Mat. 6.19,20. Jas. 5.2.

MOUNTAINS, ROCKS, AND HILLS. Used for divine worship, Gen. 22.2. Ex. 3.12. 1 Sam. 10.5. Mic. 4.1,2 ; for idolatrous worship, Deu. 12.2. 1 Kin. 14.23. Jer. 3.6. Hos. 4.13. Beacons set up on, Isa. 13.2. Isa. 18.3. Isa. 30.17.

Christ's temptation on, Mat. 4.8 ; sermon on, Mat. 5.1 ; he chooses apostles on, Mar. 3.13,14. His prayers on, Mat. 14.23. Luk. 6.12. Luk. 9.28. Miracles on, Mat. 15.29,30. Jno. 6.3. Transfiguration on, Mar. 9.2. Meeting with disciples on, Mat. 28.16.

Burning mountains, Jer. 51.25. Nah. 1.5,6. Rev. 8.8. Ex. 19.18. Illustrative, Mic. 4.2. Zec. 4.7. Mat. 21.21. 1 Cor. 13.2. Symbolical, Gal. 4.24,25. Rev. 8.8. Rev. 17.9.

See ABANA, ABARIM, ARARAT, HALAK, NEBO, PEOR, PISGAH, SEIR, SEPHAR, SINAI, ROCK—PALESTINE, MOUNTAINS OF.

MOURNING. Rending the garments, Gen. 37.29,34. Gen. 44.13. Num. 14.6. Jud. 11.35. 2 Sam. 1.2,11. 2 Sam. 3.31. 2 Sam. 13.19,31. 2 Sam. 15.32. 2 Kin. 2.12. 2 Kin. 5.8. 2 Kin. 6.30. 2 Kin. 11.14. 2 Kin. 19.1. 2 Kin. 22.11,19. Ezr. 9.3,5. Job 1.20. Job 2.12. Jer. 41.5. Mat. 26.65. Act. 14.14. Illustrative, Joel 2.13.

Wearing mourning-dress, Gen. 38.14. 2 Sam. 14.2. See SACKCLOTH. Cutting or plucking off the hair and beard, Ezr. 9.3. Jer. 7.29. See BALDNESS. Uncovering the head, Lev. 10.6. Lev. 13.45. Lev. 21.10. Num. 5.18. Covering the head and face, 2 Sam. 15.30. 2 Sam. 19.4. Est. 6.12. Jer. 14.3,4 ; and the upper lip, Lev. 13.45. Eze. 24.17,22. Mic. 3.7 (*marg.*). Lying on the ground, 2 Sam. 12.16. 2 Sam. 13.31. See ASHES.

Laying aside ornaments, Ex. 33.4,6. Neglecting the person, 2 Sam. 14.2. 2 Sam. 19.24. Cutting the flesh forbidden, Lev. 19.28. Lev. 21.5. Deu. 14.1. Practised, Jer. 16.6. Jer. 41.5. Jer. 47.5. Jer. 48.37. Walking barefoot, 2 Sam. 15.30. Isa. 20.2. Laying the hand on the head, 2 Sam. 13.19. Jer. 2.37. Loud cries and lamentations, Ex. 12.30. 1 Sam. 30.4. Jer. 22.18. Fasting, 1 Sam. 31. 13. 2 Sam. 1.12. 2 Sam. 3.35. Cup of consolation given, Jer. 16.7.

Lasted many days, Gen. 50.3,10. Deu. 34.8. Job 2.13. Caused ceremonial defilement, Num. 19.11-16. Num. 31.19. Lev. 21.1. Prevented offerings from being accepted, Deu. 26.14. Hos. 9.4. Of priests only, for next of kin, Lev. 21.1-11. See Lev. 10.6.

Hired mourners or minstrels employed, 2 Chr. 35.25. Ecc. 12.5. Jer. 9.17. Amos 5.16. Mat. 9.23. Laments or dirges, 2 Sam. 1.17-27. 2 Sam. 3.33,34. 2 Sam. 18.33. 2 Kin. 2.12. 2 Chr. 35.25.

MOUSE, forbidden to be eaten, Lev. 11.29. Eaten by idolaters, Isa. 66.17. Images of, sent by the Philistines with the ark, 1 Sam. 6.4,5,11,18.

MOWING OF GRASS, Psa. 72.6. Psa. 90.6. Psa. 129.7. Amos 7.1.

MUFFLER, a thin spangled veil, Isa. 3.19.

MULBERRY-TREE (a kind of poplar), 2 Sam. 5.23,24. Psa. 84.6 (*marg.*).

MULE, Psa. 32.9. Used for riding, 2 Sam. 13.29. 2 Sam. 18.9. Est. 8.10,14. Isa. 66.20. For carrying burdens, 2 Kin. 5.17. 1 Chr. 12.40. In war, Zec. 14.15. Brought in tribute, 1 Kin. 10.25. Number brought from Babylon, Ezr. 2.66. Neh. 7.68. Trade in, by Tyrians, Eze. 27.14. The word translated mule in Gen. 36.24, probably signifies warm springs.

MURDER. Gen. 4.10. What hast thou done? the voice of thy brother's blood crieth unto me from the ground. 11. And now *art* thou cursed from the earth, which hath opened her mouth to receive thy brother's blood from thy hand. *v.* 12.

Gen. 9.5. Surely your blood of your lives will I require ; at the hand of every beast will I require it, and at the hand of man ; at the hand of every man's brother will I require the life of man. 6. Whoso sheddeth man's blood,

by man shall his blood be shed : for in the image of God made he man.

Gen. 49.7. Cursed *be* their anger, for *it was* fierce ; and their wrath, for it was cruel : I will divide them in Jacob, and scatter them in Israel.

Ex. 20.13. Thou shalt not kill. Deu. 5.17. Mat. 5.21. Rom. 13.9.

Deu. 27.24. Cursed *be* he that smiteth his neighbour secretly. 25. Cursed *be* he that taketh reward to slay an innocent person. And all the people shall say, Amen.

1 Kin. 21.19. Hast thou killed, and also taken possession? Thus saith the Lord, In the place where dogs licked the blood of Naboth shall dogs lick thy blood, even thine.

2 Chr. 24.22. When he died, he said, The Lord look upon *it*, and require *it*.

Job 24.14. The murderer rising with the light killeth the poor and needy, and in the night is as a thief. *v.* 1-25.

Psa. 5.6. The Lord will abhor the bloody and deceitful man.

Psa. 9.12. When he maketh inquisition for blood, he remembereth them.

Psa. 10.8. In the secret places doth he murder the innocent.

Psa. 26.9. Gather not my soul with sinners, nor my life with bloody men : 10. In whose hands *is* mischief.

Psa. 37.32. The wicked watcheth the righteous and seeketh to slay him.

Psa. 38.12. They also that seek after my life lay snares *for me.*

Psa. 55.23. Thou, O God, shalt bring them down into the pit of destruction : bloody and deceitful men shall not live out half their days.

Psa. 94.6. They slay the widow and the stranger, and murder the fatherless.

Pro. 1.11. They say, Come with us, let us lay wait for blood, let us lurk privily for the innocent without cause : 12. Let us swallow them up alive as the grave ; and whole, as those that go down into the pit. 16. Their feet run to evil, and make haste to shed blood. Isa. 59.7.

Pro. 6.16. Seven *are* an abomination unto him. 17. Hands that shed innocent blood.

Pro. 12.6. The words of the wicked *are* to lie in wait for blood.

Isa. 26.21. The earth also shall disclose her blood, and shall no more cover her slain.

Jer. 2.34. In thy skirts is found the blood of the souls of the poor innocents : I have not found it by secret search, but upon all these. Jer. 19.4.

Jer. 7.9. Will ye murder, 10. And come and stand before me in this house, which is called by my name, and say, We are delivered to do all these abominations?

Eze. 22.9. In thee are men that carry tales to shed blood.

Eze. 35.6. *As* I live, saith the Lord God, I will prepare thee unto blood, and blood shall pursue thee : sith thou hast not hated blood, even blood shall pursue thee.

Hos. 1.4. I will avenge the blood of Jezreel upon the house of Jehu.

Hos. 4.1. The Lord hath a controversy with the inhabitants of the land, because *there is* no truth, nor mercy. 2. They break out, and blood toucheth blood. 3. Therefore shall the land mourn.

Hab. 2.10. Thou hast consulted shame to

thy house by cutting off many people, and hast sinned *against* thy soul. 12. Woe to him that buildeth a town with blood.

Mat. 15.19. Out of the heart proceed evil thoughts, murders.

Gal. 5.19. The works of the flesh are manifest. 21. Murders, and such like: of the which I tell you before, as I have also told *you* in time past, that they which do such things shall not inherit the kingdom of God.

1 Pet. 4.15. Let none of you suffer as a murderer.

1 Jno. 3.15. Ye know that no murderer hath eternal life abiding in him. *v.* 12.

Rev. 9.21. Neither repented they of their murders.

Rev. 21.8. Murderers shall have their part in the lake which burneth with fire and brimstone: which is the second death.

Rev. 22.15. Without *are* murderers.

MURDER, EXAMPLES OF: Cain, Gen. 4.8. Lamech, Gen. 4.23,24. Simeon and Levi, Gen. 34.25-31. Pharaoh, Ex. 1.22. Ehud, Jud. 3.16-23. Jael, Jud. 4.21. Abimelech, Jud. 9.5,18,56. An Amalekite, 2 Sam. 1.16. Abner, 2 Sam. 2.18-24. Joab, 2 Sam. 3.24-27. 2 Sam. 20.9,10. 1 Kin. 2.5. Rechab and Baanah, 2 Sam. 4.5-8. David, 2 Sam. 11.14-17. 2 Sam. 12.9. Psa. 51.14. Absalom, 2 Sam. 13.22-29. Ahab and Jezebel, 1 Kin. 21.10-24. 2 Kin. 6.32. Hazael, 2 Kin. 8.12,15. Jehu, 2 Kin. 9.24-37. 2 Kin. 10.1-14. Athaliah, 2 Kin. 11.1. Menahem, 2 Kin. 15.16. Manasseh, 2 Kin. 21.16. Jehoram, 2 Chr. 21.4. Joash, 2 Chr. 24.21. Amaziah's soldiers, 2 Chr. 25.12. Nebuchadnezzar, Jer. 39.6. Ishmael, Jer. 41.1-7. Ammonites, Amos 1. 13-15. Herod I., Mat. 2.16. Herod II., Mar. 6.27. Barabbas, Mar. 15.7. Act. 3.14. Sanhedrim and Pilate, Mat. 26. Mat. 27. Sanhedrim, Act. 7.54-60. Herod III., Act. 12.2,19.

See PERSECUTION — MALICE — SUBJECTS, TREASON OF.

MURDER, PUNISHMENT OF. Death, Gen. 9.5,6. Ex. 21.12. Num. 35.16. To be inflicted by the next of kin, Num. 35.19,21. See 2 Sam. 21.1-7. Not to be commuted, Num. 35.32. Murderers had no protection in the cities of refuge, Deu. 19.11,12; or from altars, Ex. 21.14. 1 Kin. 2.28-33. Mode of clearing those suspected of, Deu. 21.3-9. See Mat. 27.24. Imputed to the nearest city, when the murderer was unknown, Deu. 21.1-8.

MURDER, PUNISHMENT OF. EXAMPLES OF: Murderers of Saul, 2 Sam. 1.15,16; of Ish-bosheth, 2 Sam. 4.11,12. Joab, 1 Kin. 2.31-34. Haman, Est. 7.10.

——— SUICIDE FORBIDDEN, Ex. 20. 13. Act. 16.27,28. EXAMPLES OF: Saul and his armour-bearer, 1 Sam. 31.4,5. Zimri, 1 Kin. 16.18. Ahithophel, 2 Sam. 17.23. Judas, Mat. 27.5.

MURMURING AND DISCONTENT. Ex. 16.8. The Lord heareth your murmurings which ye murmur against him : and what *are* we ? your murmurings *are* not against us, but against the Lord. Num. 16.12.

Job 15.11. *Are* the consolations of God small with thee? is there any secret thing with thee? 12. Why doth thine heart carry thee away ? and what do thy eyes wink at, 13. That thou turnest thy spirit against God, and lettest *such* words go out of thy mouth?

Job 33.12. *In* this thou art not just : I will answer thee, that God is greater than man. 13. Why dost thou strive against him? for he giveth not account of any of his matters.

Job 34.37. He addeth rebellion unto his sin, he clappeth *his hands* among us, and multiplieth his words against God.

Psa. 37.1. Fret not thyself because of evildoers, neither be thou envious against the workers of iniquity.

Pro. 19.3. The foolishness of man perverteth his way : and his heart fretteth against the Lord.

Ecc. 7.10. Say not thou, What is *the cause* that the former days were better than these? for thou dost not enquire wisely concerning this.

Lam. 3.39. Wherefore doth á living man complain, a man for the punishment of his sins ?

1 Cor. 10.10. Neither murmur ye, as some of them also murmured, and were destroyed of the destroyer.

Phil. 2.14. Do all things without murmurings and disputings.

Jude 16. These are murmurers, complainers, walking after their own lusts ; and their mouth speaketh great swelling *words*.

MURMURING, EXAMPLES OF: Cain, Gen. 4.13,14. Rachel, Gen. 30.1. Moses, Ex. 5. 22,23. Num. 11.11-15. Israelites, Ex. 5.21. Ex. 14.11,12. Ex. 15.23,24. Ex. 16.2,3. Ex. 17.2. Num. 11.1-10,33. Num. 14. Num. 16. 41. Num. 20.2-5. Num. 21.5,6. Deu. 1. 27,28. Psa. 106.24-26. Korah, &c., Num. 16. 8-11. Job, c. 3, 6, 7, 9, 10, 13, 19, 23, 30. David, 2 Sam. 6.8. Psa. 116.10,11. Asaph, Psa. 73.3. Elijah, 1 Kin. 19.4,10. Solomon, Ecc. 2.17,18. Hezekiah, Isa. 38.10-18. Jeremiah, Jer. 20.14-18. Lam. 3. Jonah, Jonah 4.

See DOUBT — ENVY — CONTENTMENT — RESIGNATION — INGRATITUDE.

MUSIC, INSTRUMENTS OF. Invented by Jubal, Gen. 4.21. By David, 1 Chr. 23.5. 2 Chr. 7.6. 2 Chr. 29.26. Amos 6.5. Made by Solomon, 1 Kin. 10.12. 2 Chr. 9.11. Ecc. 2.8. By Tyrians, Eze. 28.13.

See BELLS, CYMBAL, DULCIMER, FLUTE, GITTITH, HARP, MAHALATH, NEGINOTH, ORGAN, PIPE, PSALTERY, SACKBUT, TIMBREL, TRUMPET.

MUSIC, SACRED—SINGING. Singing in course, Ezr. 3.11. In 2 companies in courses, Neh. 12.31,32. One singer answering another, Ex. 15.20,21. Jud. 5.1,12. 1 Sam. 18.7. Psa. 24.7,9 with *v.* 8,10. Ward against ward, Neh. 12.24. Answer of the congregation, Ezr. 3.11. Men and women together, Jud. 5.1. Ex. 15.1-21. In harmony, 2 Chr. 5.13. In octaves or with bass (*marg.*). 1 Chr. 15.21. Psa. 6 & 12 (*titles*). (Sheminith or octave.) Standing, 2 Chr. 5.12. 1 Chr. 6.33 (*marg.*), *v.* 39,44. Illustrative, Job 38.7. Isa. 35.10. Isa. 55.12. Hos. 2.15. See PRAISE.

MUSIC, SACRED—SINGING AND INSTRUMENTAL MUSIC. In sacred processions, Ex. 15.1,20,21. 2 Sam. 6.5,14-16. 1 Chr. 13.8. 1 Chr. 15.16-29; singers going first, Psa. 68.25. At the tabernacle in Gibeon, 1 Chr. 16.39-42. 1 Chr. 6.31,32. Before the ark in Jerusalem, 1 Chr. 16.4-6,37,38. 1 Chr. 6.31. With sacrifices at the feasts, 2 Chr. 15.14. 2 Chr. 23.18. 2 Chr. 29.25-28. Isa. 30.29. Silver trumpets only used in the time of Moses, Num. 10.2,10; and at the jubilee, Lev. 25.8-10.

In the Temple, arrangements made by David, Gad, and Nathan, by divine command, 2 Chr. 29.25-30. 2 Chr. 5.12,13. 2 Chr. 7.6. 2 Chr. 8.14. 2 Chr. 23.18. Ezr. 3.10,11. Neh. 12.24,46. By David and his captains, 1 Chr. 25.1-7. By David and the Levites, 1 Chr. 15.16-24. 2 Chr. 35.15. By Hezekiah, 2 Chr. 31.2.

4000 Levites appointed by David, 1 Chr. 23.5. Divided into 24 courses of 12 each, for which lots were cast, 1 Chr. 25.1-31. 1 Chr. 16.4-6,41,42. 2 Chr. 5.12,13. 2 Chr. 31.2. Were dressed in white, 2 Chr. 5.12. See Rev. 7.9,10. Priests appointed, who used trumpets only, see TRUMPET.

Levites divided into 3 bands; stood at the east end of the altar, 2 Chr. 5.12,13. Heman, a Kohathite, stood in the middle with his sons and daughters with trumpets, 1 Chr. 6.33-44. 1 Chr. 25.4-7. Jeduthan or Ethan, a Merarite, on Heman's left, with his sons, having harps, 1 Chr. 6.44-47. 1 Chr. 25.3. Asaph, a Gershonite, on Heman's right, and his sons, with cymbals, 1 Chr. 16.5. 1 Chr. 6.39-43. 1 Chr. 25.1,2. 2 Chr. 35.15. Ezr. 3.10,11. Chenaniah, the master of the song, 1 Chr. 15.27. Other leaders, 1 Chr. 16.4-6. Hab. 3.19. Neh. 12.42.

Levite musicians were devoted to the temple service, 1 Chr. 9.33. Neh. 12.45. Officiated daily, 1 Chr. 23.30. 2 Chr. 30.21. Taught music, 1 Chr. 23.13. 1 Chr. 25.6-8. Officiated in bringing up the ark, 1 Chr. 15.27; at the dedication of the wall, Neh. 12.27-29.

MUSIC—SINGING. By females, Ex. 15. 20,21. Jud. 5.1,12. 1 Sam. 18.7. 1 Chr. 25. 5. 2 Sam. 19.35. Ecc. 2.8. Ezr. 2.65. Neh. 7.67; and males, 2 Sam. 19.35. Ecc. 2.8. 2 Chr. 35.15. At entertainments, Pro. 25.20. Amos 8.10. On digging a well, Num. 21.17. At harvest, Isa. 16.10.

MUSIC — SINGING AND INSTRUMENTAL MUSIC. In war and triumphs, Ex. 15.1,20,21. Jud. 11.34. 1 Sam. 18.6. 2 Chr. 20.19-28. See TRUMPET. In idolatrous worship, Dan. 3. 5-15. At proclamation of kings, 1 Kin. 1.40. 2 Kin. 9.13. 2 Kin. 11.14. 2 Chr. 23.13.

At dedication of the wall of Jerusalem, Neh. 12.35-41. At entertainments, &c., Gen. 31.27. Job 21.12. Job 30.31. Isa. 5.12. Isa. 14.11. Isa. 24.8. Isa. 30.32. Jer. 31.4. Eze. 33.32. Eze. 26.13. Amos 6.5. Mat. 11.17. Rev. 18. 22. With dancing, see DANCING. In the streets, Isa. 23.16. At funerals, Mat 9.23. 2 Chr. 35.25.

MUSTARD-TREE, a large tree bearing a small seed; illustrative, Mat. 13.31,32. Luk. 13.19. Mat. 17.20.

MUTH-LABBEN (death to the son), supposed to be an air to which Psa. 9 was to be sung.

MYRA, a seaport of Lycia, in Asia Minor; visited by Paul, Act. 27.5,6.

MYRRH, (1) an odorous gum. Used in the holy anointing oil, Ex. 30.23; as a perfume, and in anointing the person, Est. 2.12. Psa. 45.8. Pro. 7.17. Song 3.6. Song 5.5,13. Grown in Palestine, Song 4.6,14. Song 5.1. Presented to Christ by the wise men, Mat. 2. 11. Wine mingled with; refused by Christ,

Mar. 15.23. Brought by Nicodemus to embalm Christ, Jno. 19.39.

(2) Another substance, taken to Egypt from Palestine by Ishmaelites, Gen. 37.25; and Jacob's sons, Gen. 43.11.

MYRTLE, Neh. 8.15. Isa. 41.19. Isa. 55. 13. Zec. 1.8.

MYSIA, a province of Asia Minor, visited by Paul, &c., Act. 16.7,8. Towns of, see Assos —PERGAMOS.

N

NAAMAN, chief captain of Benhadad; cured by Elisha of leprosy, 2 Kin. 5. Luk. 4.27.

NABAL, his conduct to David; drunkenness and death, 1 Sam. 25.

NABOTH THE JEZREELITE, murdered by Ahab and Jezebel; his vineyard taken possession of, 1 Kin.21.1-24. His murder punished, 2 Kin. 9.21-36.

NACHON'S THRESHING-FLOOR, near Jerusalem, called by David Perez-uzza, where Uzzah was slain for putting his hand to the ark of God, 2 Sam. 6.6,7. Called the threshing-floor of Chidon, 1 Chr. 13.9.

NADAB, Aaron's eldest son, Ex. 6.23. Goes up to the mount, Ex. 24.9. Consecrated to the priesthood, Ex. 28.1. Offers strange fire, and is consumed, Lev. 10.1,2. Num. 3.4. Num. 26.61.

———, son of Jeroboam, 2d king of Israel; his wickedness; after 2 years' reign, slain by Baasha, while besieging Gibbethon, 1 Kin. 14.20. 1 Kin. 15.25-31.

NAHASH, supposed to be the same as Jesse, 2 Sam. 17.25 with 1 Chr. 2.13-16.

———, king of the Ammonites, besieges Jabesh-gilead; is defeated by Saul, 1 Sam. 11. His kindness to David, 2 Sam. 10.2. His death, 1 Chr. 19.1,2.

NAHOR, Abraham's grandfather, Gen. 11. 24-26. 1 Chr. 1.26.

———, Abraham's brother; his marriage and children, Gen. 11.27,29. Gen. 22.20-24. Gen 24.15. A city in Mesopotamia, called after him, Gen. 24.10. His piety, Gen. 31.53.

NAHUM THE PROPHET, a native of Elkosh; supposed by some to be in Galilee; by others in Assyria, Nah. 1.1.

NAIL of wood, Jud. 4.21. Ezr. 9.8. Isa. 22.23,25. Zec. 10.4. Translated pin, Ex. 27.19. Jud. 16.14. Stake, Isa. 33.20. Isa. 54.2. Nail of iron, 1 Chr. 22.3. Of gold, 2 Chr. 3.9.

NAIN, in Galilee, a town where Jesus raised a widow's son, Luk. 7.11-17.

NAIOTH, in Ramah; Samuel dwells at; a school of the prophets in; David flees to; Saul and his messengers prophesy in, 1 Sam. 19.18-24.

NAKED. The word often means undress, 1 Sam. 19.24. 2 Sam. 6.14 with v. 20. Isa. 20.2. Jno. 21.7.

NAMES. Given to persons, with a prophetical significance, as Seth (appointed), Gen. 4.25. Noah (rest), Gen. 5.29. Jesus (saviour), Mat. 1.21.

Given from circumstances connected with their birth or history; as Eve (living), Gen. 3.20. Peleg (division), Gen. 10.25. Isaac (laughter), Gen. 21.3,6. Jacob (supplanter), Gen. 27.36. Reuben (a son), &c., Gen. 29.32-35. Gen. 30.6-24. Gen. 35.18. Moses (drawn out), Ex. 2.10. Solomon (peace), 1 Chr. 22.9. Manasseh (forgetting); Ephraim (fruitful), Gen. 41.51,52. Gershom (a stranger), Ex. 2.22. Eliezer (my God a help), Ex. 18.4. Ichabod (no glory), 1 Sam. 4.21. Jabez (sorrowful), 1 Chr. 4.9. Beriah (calamity), 1 Chr. 7.23. Mahar-shalal-hash-baz (make speed to spoil), Isa. 8.3.

Changed, as Abram to Abraham, Gen. 17.5. Sarai to Sarah, Gen. 17.15. Jacob to Israel, Gen. 32.28. Joseph to Zaphnath-paaneah, Gen. 41.45. Gideon to Jerubbaal, Jud. 6.32. Daniel to Belteshazzar, &c., Dan. 1.7. Simon to Peter, Mat. 16.18. Saul to Paul, Act. 13.9.

Given to children from those of ancestors, as Nahor, Gen. 11.25 with v. 26. Caleb, 1 Chr. 2.19 with v. 50. Maachah, 2 Chr. 11.20 with 2 Sam. 3.3. Azariah, 1 Chr. 6.9 with v. 10,13. John, Luk. 1.61.

Given to places from their owners, Psa. 49.11; as Enoch, Gen. 4.17. Havoth-jair, Num. 32.41,42. Dan, Jud. 18.29. Samaria, 1 Kin. 16.24.

Of places, from events connected with them, as Babel (confusion), Gen. 11.9. Beersheba (well of the oath), Gen. 21.31. Bethel (house of God), Gen. 28.19. Beer-lahai-roi (the well of him that liveth and seeth me), Gen. 16.14. Jehovah-jireh (the Lord will provide), Gen. 22.14. Zoar (little), Gen. 19.22. Peniel (the face of God), Gen. 32.30. Allon-bachuth (the oak of weeping), Gen. 35.8.

Abel-mizraim (mourning of the Egyptians), Gen. 50.11. Marah (bitterness), Ex. 15.23. Meribah (strife) ; Massah (temptation), Ex. 17. 7. Jehovah-nissi (the Lord my banner), Ex. 17.15. Taberah (burning), Num. 11.3. Kibroth-hattaavah (graves of lust), Num. 11. 34. Eshcol (cluster of grapes), Num. 13.24. Achor (trouble), Jos. 7.26. Ed (witness), Jos. 22.34. Bochim (weepers), Jud. 2.5. Enhakkore (well of prayer), Jud. 15.19. Ebenezer (stone of help), 1 Sam. 7.12.

Baal-perazim (plain of breaches), 2 Sam. 5. 20. Perez-uzzah (breach of Uzzah), 2 Sam. 6.8. Jachin (he shall establish) ; Boaz (strength), 1 Kin. 7.21. Cabul (displeasing), 1 Kin. 9.13. Aceldama (field of blood), Act. 1.19.

NAOMI, wife of Elimelech, returns from Moab to Bethlehem, with her daughter-in-law Ruth ; instructs Ruth how to conduct herself to Boaz ; sells her inheritance to Boaz, Ruth c. 1 to 4.

NAPHTALI, son of Jacob and Bilhah, Gen. 30.7,8. Gen. 35.25. Ex. 1.4. Blessed by Jacob, Gen. 49.21. His sons, Gen. 46.24. 1 Chr. 7.13.

————, TRIBE OF, numbered at Sinai, Num. 1.42,43 ; and in the plains of Moab, Num. 26.48-50. Marched and encamped under the standard of Dan, north of the tabernacle, Num. 2.25,29. Num. 10.25,27. Blessing of Moses on, Deu. 33.23. Their inheritance, Jos. 19.32-39 ; not fully possessed, Jud. 1.33.

Aid Deborah and Barak, Jud. 4.6,10. Jud. 5.18 ; and Gideon, Jud. 6.35. Jud.7.23. Aid in bringing up the ark, Psa. 68.27. Number

of, in David's army, 1 Chr. 12.34,40. Invaded by Benhadad, 1 Kin. 15.20. 2 Chr. 16.4. Taken captive by Tiglath, 2 Kin. 15.29. Isa. 9.1. For things common to the tribes, see ISRAELITES, TRIBES OF.

NATHAN THE PROPHET, commissioned to prevent David from building the temple, 2 Sam. 7.1-17. 1 Chr. 17.1-15. His parable and rebuke of David, 2 Sam. 12.1-15. Psa. 51 (title). Names Solomon Jedediah (beloved of Jehovah), 2 Sam. 12.25. Acquaints Bathsheba and David with Adonijah's usurpation, 1 Kin. 1.10-14,22-27. With Zadok, anoints Solomon king, 1 Kin. 1.32-45. His chronicles, 1 Chr. 29.29. 2 Chr. 9.29. Regulation of the temple service, 2 Chr. 29.25. His children's honours, 1 Kin. 4.5. Representative of the family of the prophets, Zec. 12.12.

NATHANAEL (BARTHOLOMEW ?) from Cana, Jno. 21.2. Brought by Philip to Jesus ; his character and faith, Jno. 1.45-51. Sees Jesus after his resurrection, Jno. 21.2.

NATIONAL Afflictions. See JUDGMENTS, FAMINE, PESTILENCE, WAR. National peace, see PEACE. National sins, see SINS, NATIONAL. National sacrifices, see OFFERINGS.

NATIONS, dispersion of, Gen. 10. Gen. 11.1-9. Deu. 32.8.

NAZARENE, applied to Christ, Mat. 2.23. (Nazareth signifies twig, compare Isa. 11.1. Zec. 3.8.) Applied to Christians, Act. 24.5.

NAZARETH, a town of Galilee, the residence of Joseph and Mary, Luk. 1.26,27,56. Luk. 2.4. Residence of Jesus, after returning from Egypt, Mat. 2.23. Luk. 2.39,51. Mat. 4.13. Mar. 1.9. The people of, seek to cast him from the brow of a hill, Luk. 4.16-30. Its bad repute, Jno. 1.46.

NAZARITE Vow (the word signifies separation) ; its nature, Num. 6.1-8. Lam. 4.7. Amos 2.11,12. Broken by defilement ; required to be resumed ; sacrifices of purification necessary, Num. 6.9-12. Offerings and ceremonies on completing the vow, Num. 6.13-21. Act. 18.18. Act. 21.24-27.

EXAMPLES : Samson, Jud. 13.5,7. Jud. 16.17. Samuel, 1 Sam. 1.11,28. Rechabites, Jer. 35. John the Baptist, Luk. 1.15. Luk. 7.33. Paul, &c., Act. 8.18. Act. 21.23-26.

NEAPOLIS, a city of Macedonia, visited by Paul, Act. 16.11.

NEBAIOTH, first-born of Ishmael, Gen. 25.13. 1 Chr. 1.29. Name of a pastoral tribe ; conversion of, predicted, Isa. 60.7.

NEBO, a Babylonian idol, Isa. 46.1. Compounded in the name Nebuchadnezzar, &c.

————, MOUNT, in Moab ; Pisgah, one of the hills of ; Moses views Canaan from, and dies, Deu. 32.49,50. Deu. 34.1.

————, a district and town in Moab, possessed by Reubenites, Num. 32.3,38. 1 Chr. 5.8. Prophecies against, Isa. 15.2. Jer. 48. 1,22.

————, a town in Judah, Neh. 7.33.

NEBUCHADNEZZAR, or NEBUCHADREZZAR, king of Babylon ; called Lucifer, Isa. 14.12. Invades Judah ; makes Jehoiakim tributary, 2 Kin. 24.1. Carries him to Babylon, 2 Chr. 36.5-7. Dan. 1.1,2. Takes Jerusalem,

and carries Jehoiachin captive, 2 Kin. 24.10-16.
2 Chr. 36.10.

Makes Zedekiah king, 2 Kin. 24.17. 2 Chr.
36.10. Takes him and the Jews captive, 2 Kin.
25. Jer. 39. 1 Chr. 6.15. Ezr. 1.7. Ezr.
2.1. Ezr. 5.12. Mat. 1.11,17. Conquers
Pharaoh, 2 Kin. 24.7. Jer. 46.2. Kind treatment of Jeremiah, Jer. 39.11-14. Invades
Tyre, Eze. 29.18.

His great power, Isa. 14.4-14. Jer. 50.23.
Eze. 26. Dan. 5.18,19. His dreams interpreted by Daniel, Dan. c. 2 & 4. Makes a
golden image; casts the 3 Hebrews into a furnace, Dan. 3. Loses his reason; loses and is
restored to his throne; acknowledges God,
Dan. 4. Prophecies against, see BABYLON.

NEBUZARADAN, a Babylonian captive,
destroys Jerusalem, and takes the people captive, 2 Kin. 25.8-21. Jer. 52.12-30. Leaves a
governor, Jer. 43.6. Kind treatment of Jeremiah, Jer. 39.9-13. Jer. 40.1-5.

NECHO. See PHARAOH-NECHO.

NECROMANCY (enquiring of the dead)
forbidden, Deu. 18.11. Deu. 26.14. Isa. 8.19.
EXAMPLES OF: Psa. 106.28. The witch of
Endor, 1 Sam. 28.

NEEDLEWORK. See EMBROIDERY.

NEGINOTH (stringed instruments), Psa.
4, 61, 67, 76 (titles). Hab. 3.19.

NEHEMIAH, his parentage, Neh. 1.1.
Neh. 7.2. Cup-bearer to Artaxerxes, Neh. 2.1.
Mourns and prays for Jerusalem, Neh. 1.
Petitions the king, and is sent by him as gover-
nor to Jerusalem, Neh. 2.1-8. His resistance
to Sanballat, &c., Neh. 2.9-11,19,20. Neh. 4.
Neh. 6.

Repairs the wall of Jerusalem, Neh. 2.12-18.
Neh. 3. Neh. 4. Neh. 6.15,16. Reproves
the sins of the Jews, Neh. 5.1-13. His conduct
as governor, Neh. 5.14-19. Neh. 7.1-5. Neh.
8.9. Signs and seals a covenant with God,
Neh. 9.38. Neh. 10.1.

Returns to Jerusalem after 12 years' absence,
Neh. 13.6,7. His zeal for the Sabbath, and
reproof of the sins of the Jews, Neh. 13.7-31.

NEHILOTH (destinies or fortunes), Psa.
v. (title), referring to the subject of the Psalm.

NEHUSHTAN (a piece of brass), the name
given by Hezekiah to the brazen serpent, when
he destroyed it on account of its being worshipped, 2 Kin. 18.4.

NEPHTOAH, a stream bordering Judah,
Jos. 15.9. Jos. 18.15.

NER, father of Abner, and Saul's uncle,
1 Sam. 14.50; or grandfather, 1 Chr. 8.33.
1 Chr. 9.36,39.

NERGAL, an idol worshipped by the Cuth-
ites in Samaria, 2 Kin. 17.30.

NET. See FISHES.

NETHINIMS, servants of the Levites,
appointed by David, Ezr. 8.20. Return from
the captivity, 1 Chr. 9.2. Ezr. 2.43,58,70.
Ezr. 7.7,24. Ezr. 8.17. Neh. 3.26,31. Neh.
7.46,60,73. Neh. 10.28. Neh. 11.3,21.

NETTLES, Isa. 34.13. Hos. 9.6. Job
30.7. Pro. 24.31. Zeph. 2.9.

NIBHAZ, an idol worshipped by the Avites
in Samaria, 2 Kin. 17.31.

NICANOR, one of the seven deacons, Act.
6.5.

NICODEMUS, a Pharisee and ruler of the
Jews; his conversation with Jesus by night,
Jno. 3.1-21. Defends him in the Sanhedrim,
Jno. 7.50-52. Brings spices to anoint his
body, Jno. 19.39.

NICOLAITANES, Rev. 2.6,15.

NICOLAS, a proselyte of Antioch, one of
the seven deacons, Act. 6.5,6.

NICOPOLIS, a city of Thrace ; Paul resides
in, Tit. 3.12.

NIGHT, divided into first or evening watch,
Lam. 2.19; second, or middle, or midnight
watch, Jud. 7.19. Luk. 12.38; third, or early,
or morning watch, Ex. 14.24. 1 Sam. 11.11.
Luk. 12.38. Jno. 18.28.

By the Romans into 4 watches, Mat. 14.25.
Mar. 13.35; into hours, Act. 23.23. Illus-
trative, Isa. 15.1. Isa. 21.11,12. Jno. 9.4.
Rom. 13.12. 1 Thes. 5.5. Rev. 21.25.

NIGHTHAWK (owl?), Lev. 11.16. Deu.
14.15.

NILE (this name does not occur in Scripture), called THE RIVER, being the principal
river of Egypt, Isa. 11.15. Isa. 19.5-10. Eze.
29.4. Amos 8.8. Called Sihor, Isa. 23.3.
Jer. 2.18, see SIHOR. Not the same as the
river of Egypt, see RIVER OF EGYPT.

NIMRIM, a stream near Beth-nimrah, in
Gad, Isa. 15.6. Jer. 48.34 with Num. 32.
3,36.

NIMROD, son of Cush, and grandson
of Ham; his greatness; conquests; builds
Babel, &c., Gen. 10.8-10. 1 Chr. 1.10. Mic.
5.6.

NINEVEH, the capital of Assyria; built
by Asshur, Gen. 10.11,12. Its greatness, Jonah
4.11. Nah. 3.16,17. Sennacherib assassinated in, 2 Kin. 19.36,37. Isa. 37.37,38. Jonah
sent to; the king and people repent, Jonah c.
1 to 4. Luk. 11.30-32. Prophecies against, Nah.
c. 1 to 3. Zeph. 2.13-15.

NISAN, 1st Month. See ABIB.

NISROCH, an Assyrian idol; Sennacherib
assassinated while worshipping, 2 Kin. 19.36,37.
Isa. 37.37,38.

NITRE (a carbonate of soda; what is
usually called nitre or saltpetre, is a nitrate
of potash), Pro. 25.20. Jer. 2.22.

NO (Thebes), a city of Upper Egypt; prophecies against, Jer. 46.25. Eze. 30.14-16.
Its greatness and ruin, Nah. 3.8.

NOADIAH, a false prophetess who opposed
Nehemiah in rebuilding Jerusalem, Neh. 6.14.

NOAH, son of Lamech, Gen. 5.28,29. His
character, Gen. 6.8,9. Eze. 14.14,20. 2 Pet.
2.5. Builds the ark by God's command, Gen.
6.14-22. Heb. 11.7. 1 Pet. 3.20. Enters the
ark, Gen. 7. Mat. 24.38. Luk. 17.27. Leaves
the ark ; offers sacrifice, and is blessed by God,
Gen. 8. Gen. 9.1-17.

His children, Gen. 5.32. Gen. 6.10. Gen.
7.13. Is intoxicated, Gen. 9.20-24. Curses
Canaan; blesses Shem and Japhet, Gen.
9.25-27. His death, Gen. 9.28,29.

NOB, a city of the priests, 1 Sam. 22.19.
Near Jerusalem, Isa. 10.32. Belonging to
Benjamin, Neh. 11.31,32. The tabernacle at,
in Saul's time ; David flees to ; Ahimelech in,
1 Sam. 21.1-6. Destroyed by Doeg, 1 Sam.
22.9,11,19.

NOBLES. See RULERS.

NOBLEMAN OF CAPERNAUM; his son cured by Jesus, Jno. 4.46-53.

NOD (wandering), Cain dwelt in, Gen. 4.16.

NOPH (Memphis), the capital of Egypt, Jer. 2.16. Jews in, Jer. 44.1. Prophecies against, Isa. 19.13. Jer. 46.14-19. Eze. 30.13-16.

NOSE JEWELS. See RINGS.

NOVICE (newly planted), a neophyte, or new convert, 1 Tim. 3.6.

NUMBER OF THE BEAST, 666, Rev. 13. 17,18. In Hebrew, Greek, and Latin, the *letters*, as I., V., X., &c. were used for our figures 1, 5, 10, &c. The number of the beast is the sum of all the letters of a name counted as figures, which must amount to 666.

NUTS, Gen. 43.11. Song 6.11.

NYMPHAS, a Christian in Colosse; a church in his house, Col. 4.15.

O

OAK, 1st (Heb. *Alah* or *Elah,* as 1 Sam. 17.2,19. 1 Sam. 21.9. Isa. 1.30). Jacob hides his family gods under, Gen. 35.4. Joshua places the stone with the law inscribed beside, Jos. 24.26. An angel appears to Gideon under, Jud. 6.11,19. Absalom caught in, 2 Sam. 18. 9,14. The prophet of Judah found sitting under, 1 Kin. 13.14. Saul's bones buried under, 1 Chr. 10.12. Idols set up under, Eze. 6.13. Translated teil, Isa. 6.13; elm or terebinth, Hos. 4.13.

2d (Heb. *Alon*), Isa. 6.13. Isa. 44.14. Amos 2.9. Bashan noted for, Isa. 2.13. Eze. 27.6. Zec. 11.2. Deborah buried under, Gen. 35.8. Idolatry practised under, Hos. 4.13.

OAR, Isa. 33.21. Eze. 27.29. Of oak, Eze. 27.6.

OATHS. In witness-bearing, Ex. 22.11. Lev. 6.3-5. Num. 5.19,21. 1 Kin. 8.31. Mat. 26.63. Heb. 6.16. In covenants, Gen. 14.22. Gen. 21.23. Gen. 24.2,3. Gen. 25.33. Gen. 26.28-31. Gen. 31.53. Gen. 47.29-31. Gen. 50.25. Jos. 2.14. Jos. 9.15-20. Jos. 14.9. Jud. 11.10. Jud. 21.5. Ruth 1.17. Ruth 3. 13. 1 Sam. 14.24. 1 Sam. 19.6. 1 Sam. 20. 13-17. 1 Sam. 24.21,22. 1 Sam. 28.10. 2 Sam. 3.35. 2 Sam. 21.7. 1 Kin. 1.29,30. 1 Kin. 12.23. 2 Kin. 2.2. 2 Kin. 6.31. Ezr. 10.5,19. Neh. 5.13. Jer. 38.16. Jer. 40.9. Mat. 14.9. Act. 23.12-15. Heb. 6.17.

In appeals to God, Gen. 42.15,16. 1 Sam. 1.26. 1 Sam. 3.17. 1 Sam. 20.3. 2 Cor. 1.23. 2 Cor. 11.31. Gal. 1.20. 1 The. 2.5. 1 The. 5.27.

Of allegiance, 2 Kin. 11.4. 1 Chr. 29.24 (*marg.*), Ecc. 8.2. Eze. 17.12-19.

Idolatrous swearing forbidden and exemplified, Jos. 23.7. 1 Kin. 19.2. Jer. 12.16. Amos 8.14. Zeph. 1.5.

OATHS, FALSE. See FALSEHOOD—INTEGRITY.

OATHS, FORMS OF. God, or the Lord, do so to me, and more also, Ruth 1.2. 2 Sam. 3.35. 1 Kin. 2.23. 2 Kin. 6.31. God do so to thee, and more also, 1 Sam. 3.17. As the Lord liveth, Jud. 8.19. Ruth 3.13. 1 Sam. 19.6. 1 Sam. 28.10. 1 Kin. 1.29.

As the Lord liveth, and as thy soul liveth,

1 Sam. 20.3. 2 Kin. 2.2. As the Lord liveth that made us this soul, Jer. 38.16. As thy soul liveth, 1 Sam. 1.26. The Lord be witness between us, Jud. 11.10. Our life for yours, Jos. 2.14.

Let the Lord require it at the hand of David's enemies, 1 Sam. 20.16. I swear by the Lord, 2 Sam. 19.7. 1 Kin. 2.42. God is witness, 1 The. 2.5. I call God for a record, 2 Cor. 1. 23. Before God I lie not, Gal. 1.20. God knoweth that I lie not, 2 Cor. 11.31.

By the fear of Isaac, Gen. 31.53. By the life of Pharaoh, Gen. 42.15. I adjure thee by the living God, Mat. 26.63. I shook my lap and said, so God shake out every man from his house, Neh. 5.13.

I have lift up mine hand unto the Lord, Gen. 14.22. Put thy hand under my thigh, . . . and swear, Gen. 24.2,3. And they gave their hands, Ezr. 10.19. See ANATHEMA—BLASPHEMY.

OBADIAH, governor of Ahab's household; his piety; protects 100 prophets from Jezebel; sent by Elijah to fetch Ahab, 1 Kin. 18.3-16.

————, THE PROPHET, Obad. 1.

OBED-EDOM, a Gittite; the ark rests with him 3 months; his house is blessed, 2 Sam. 6.10-12. 1 Chr. 13.13-14.

————, a porter, 1 Chr. 15.18. 1 Chr. 16.38; and musician, 1 Chr. 15.21. 1 Chr. 16.5; and door-keeper, 1 Chr. 15.24; with his sons, 1 Chr. 16.38. 1 Chr. 26.4-8,15.

————, a treasurer, 2 Chr. 25.24.

OBEDIENCE AND GOOD WORKS, Gen. 17.9. Keep my covenant therefore, thou, and thy seed after thee.

Gen. 18.19. He will command his children and his household after him, and they shall keep the way of the Lord, to do justice and judgment; that the Lord may bring upon Abraham that which he hath spoken of him.

Ex. 14.15. Wherefore criest thou unto me? speak unto the children of Israel, that they go forward.

Ex. 19.5. If ye will obey my voice indeed, and keep my covenant, then ye shall be a peculiar treasure unto me above all people.

Ex. 23.22. If thou shalt indeed obey his voice, and do all that I speak; then I will be an enemy unto thine enemies. Deu. 7.9.

Lev. 19.36. I *am* the Lord your God, which brought you out of the land of Egypt. 37. Therefore shall ye observe all my statutes, and all my judgments, and do them. *v.* 19.

Lev. 20.8. Ye shall keep my statutes, and do them: I *am* the Lord which sanctify you. 22. Keep all my statutes, and all my judgments, and do them: that the land, whither I bring you to dwell therein, spue you not out. Lev. 22.31. Deu. 5.1,32.

Num. 15.39. Remember all the commandments of the Lord, and do them; and that ye seek not after your own heart and your own eyes. *v.* 40.

Deu. 4.1. Hearken, O Israel, unto the statutes and unto the judgments, which I teach you, for to do *them,* that ye may live, and go in and possess the land. 2. Ye shall not add unto the word which I command you, neither shall ye diminish *ought* from it, that ye may keep the commandments of the Lord your God which I command you.

Deu. 4.6. Keep therefore and do *them;* for this *is* your wisdom and your understanding in the sight of the nations, which shall hear all these statutes, and say, Surely this great nation *is* a wise and understanding people. Deu. 12.1,32.

Deu. 10.12. What doth the Lord thy God require of thee, but to fear the Lord thy God, to walk in all his ways, and to love him, and to serve the Lord thy God with all thy heart and with all thy soul. 13. To keep the commandments of the Lord, and his statutes, which I command thee this day for thy good? *v.* 20. Deu. 8.6.

Deu. 11.1. Love the Lord thy God, and keep his charge, and his statutes, and his judgments, and his commandments, alway. 22. If ye shall diligently keep all these commandments which I command you, to do them, to love the Lord your God, to walk in all his ways, and to cleave unto him; 23. Then will the Lord drive out all these nations from before you. 26. I set before you this day a blessing and a curse; 27. A blessing, if ye obey the commandments of the Lord your God, which I command you this day. *v.* 32.

Deu. 26.16. This day the Lord thy God hath commanded thee to do these statutes and judgments: thou shalt therefore keep and do them with all thine heart, and with all thy soul.

Deu. 27.9. Take heed, and hearken, O Israel; this day thou art become the people of the Lord thy God. 10. Thou shalt therefore obey the voice of the Lord thy God, and do his commandments and his statutes, which I command thee this day. 26. Cursed *be* he that confirmeth not *all* the words of this law to do them. *v.* 1.

Deu. 32.46. Set your hearts unto all the words which I testify among you this day, which ye shall command your children to observe to do, all the words of this law. 2 Kin. 17.37.

Jos. 22.5. Take diligent heed to do the commandment and the law, which Moses the servant of the Lord charged you, to love the Lord your God, and to walk in all his ways, and to keep his commandments, and to cleave unto him, and to serve him with all your heart and with all your soul Deu. 13.4.

Jos. 23.6. Be ye therefore very courageous to keep and to do all that is written in the book of the law of Moses, that ye turn not aside therefrom *to* the right hand or *to* the left. Deu. 28.14.

Jos. 24.14. Fear the Lord, and serve him in sincerity and in truth: and put away the gods which your fathers served, and serve ye the Lord. 15. If it seem evil unto you to serve the Lord, choose you this day whom ye will serve.

1 Sam. 12.20. Turn not aside from following the Lord, but serve the Lord with all your heart.

1 Sam. 15.22. Hath the Lord *as great* delight in burnt-offerings and sacrifices, as in obeying the voice of the Lord? Behold, to obey *is* better than sacrifice, *and* to hearken than the fat of rams. 24. Only fear the Lord, and serve him in truth with all your heart: for consider how great *things* he hath done for you.

1 Kin. 8.61. Let your heart therefore be perfect with the Lord our God, to walk in his statutes, and to keep his commandments.

2 Kin. 21.8. Neither will I make the feet of Israel move any more out of the land which I gave their fathers; only if they will observe to do according to all that I have commanded them.

1 Chr. 16.15. Be ye mindful always of his covenant; the word *which* he commanded to a thousand generations.

1 Chr. 28.7. I will establish his kingdom for ever, if he be constant to do my commandments and my judgments. 9. Know thou the God of thy father, and serve him with a perfect heart and with a willing mind: for the Lord searcheth all hearts, and understandeth all the imaginations of the thoughts: if thou seek him, he will be found of thee; but if thou forsake him, he will cast thee off for ever. *v.* 10. 1 Kin. 6.12,13.

1 Chr. 29.5. Who *then* is willing to consecrate his service this day unto the Lord?

Ezr. 7.23. Whatsoever is commanded by the God of heaven, let it be diligently done.

Neh. 1.5. The great and terrible God, that keepeth covenant and mercy for them that love him and observe his commandments. Ex. 20.6. Deu. 5.10.

Neh. 5.9. It *is* not good that ye do: ought ye not to walk in the fear of our God because of the reproach of the heathen our enemies?

Job 22.22. Receive, I pray thee, the law from his mouth, and lay up his words in thine heart.

Psa. 2.11. Serve the Lord with fear, and rejoice with trembling. 12. Kiss the Son, lest he be angry, and ye perish *from* the way, when his wrath is kindled but a little.

Psa. 19.11. By them is thy servant warned: *and* in keeping of them *there is* great reward.

Psa. 25.10. All the paths of the Lord *are* mercy and truth unto such as keep his covenant and his testimonies.

Psa. 50.23. To him that ordereth *his* conversation *aright* will I shew the salvation of God.

Psa. 76.11. Vow, and pay unto the Lord your God.

Psa. 103.17. The mercy of the Lord *is* from everlasting to everlasting upon them that fear him, and his righteousness unto children's children. 18. To such as keep his covenant, and to those that remember his commandments to do them.

Psa. 106.3. Blessed *are* they that keep judgment, *and* he that doeth righteousness at all times.

Psa. 111.10. A good understanding have all they that do *his commandments*.

Psa. 112.1. Blessed *is* the man *that* feareth the Lord, *that* delighteth greatly in his commandments.

Psa. 119.2. Blessed *are* they that keep his testimonies, *and that* seek him with the whole heart. 4. Thou hast commanded *us* to keep thy precepts diligently. 6. Then shall I not be ashamed, when I have respect unto all thy commandments.

Psa. 128.1. Blessed *is* every one that feareth the Lord; that walketh in his ways.

Pro. 2.20. Walk in the way of good *men*, and keep the paths of the righteous.

Pro. 4.12. When thou goest, thy steps shall

not be straitened; and when thou runnest, thou shalt not stumble. 13. Take fast hold of instruction; let *her* not go: keep her; for she *is* thy life. 20. My son, attend to my words; incline thine ear unto my sayings. 21. Let them not depart from thine eyes; keep them in the midst of thine heart. 22. For they *are* life unto those that find them, and health to all their flesh.

Pro. 7.2. Keep my commandments, and live; and my law as the apple of thine eye.

Pro. 10.2. Righteousness delivereth from death. 9. He that walketh uprightly walketh surely. 16. The labour of the righteous *tendeth* to life. 17. He *is in* the way of life that keepeth instruction.

Pro. 11.3. The integrity of the upright shall guide them. 6. The righteousness of the upright shall deliver them. 18. To him that soweth righteousness *shall be* a sure reward. 19. Righteousness *tendeth* to life. 30. The fruit of the righteous *is* a tree of life. *v.* 4.

Pro. 12.28. In the way of righteousness *is* life; and *in* the pathway *thereof there is* no death.

Pro. 13.6. Righteousness keepeth *him that is* upright in the way. 13. He that feareth the commandment shall be rewarded. 21. To the righteous good shall be repayed.

Pro. 14.2. He that walketh in his uprightness feareth the Lord.

Pro. 19.16. He that keepeth the commandment keepeth his own soul.

Pro. 21.3. To do justice and judgment *is* more acceptable to the Lord than sacrifice. 21. He that followeth after righteousness and mercy findeth life, righteousness, and honour.

Pro. 28.18. Whoso walketh uprightly shall be saved.

Pro. 29.18. He that keepeth the law, happy *is* he.

Ecc. 8.5. Whoso keepeth the commandment shall feel no evil thing.

Ecc. 12.13. Fear God, and keep his commandments: for this *is* the whole *duty* of man.

Isa. 3.10. Say ye to the righteous, that *it shall be* well *with him*: for they shall eat the fruit of their doings. Isa. 5.1-4.

Isa. 32.16. Then judgment shall dwell in the wilderness, and righteousness remain in the fruitful field. 17. And the work of righteousness shall be peace; and the effect of righteousness quietness and assurance for ever.

Isa. 48.18. O that thou hadst hearkened to my commandments! then had thy peace been as a river, and thy righteousness as the waves of the sea.

Isa. 56.1. Keep ye judgment, and do justice: for my salvation *is* near to come, and my righteousness to be revealed. 2. Blessed *is* the man *that* doeth this, and the son of man *that* layeth hold on it; that keepeth the sabbath from polluting it, and keepeth his hand from doing any evil.

Isa. 58.6. *Is* not this the fast that I have chosen? to loose the bands of wickedness, to undo the heavy burdens, and to let the oppressed go free, and that ye break every yoke? 8. Then shall thy light break forth as the morning, and thine health shall spring forth speedily: and thy righteousness shall go before thee; the glory of the Lord shall be thy rereward.

Isa. 64.4. Neither hath the eye seen, O God, beside thee, *what* he hath prepared for him that waiteth for him. 5. Thou meetest him that rejoiceth and worketh righteousness, *those that* remember thee in thy ways: in those is continuance, and we shall be saved.

Jer. 6.16. Ask for the old paths, where *is* the good way, and walk therein, and ye shall find rest for your souls.

Jer. 7.5. If ye throughly amend your ways and your doings; if ye throughly execute judgment between a man and his neighbour; 6. *If* ye oppress not the stranger, the fatherless, and the widow, and shed not innocent blood in this place, neither walk after other gods to your hurt: 7. Then will I cause you to dwell in this place. 23. Obey my voice, and I will be your God, and ye shall be my people: and walk ye in all the ways that I have commanded you, that it may be well unto you.

Jer. 11.7. I earnestly protested unto your fathers in the day *that* I brought them up out of the land of Egypt, *even* unto this day, rising early and protesting, saying, Obey my voice. *v.* 4. Eze. 11.20.

Eze. 2.8. Hear what I say unto thee; Be not thou rebellious like that rebellious house: open thy mouth, and eat that I give thee.

Eze. 3.21. If thou warn the righteous *man,* that the righteous sin not, and he doth not sin, he shall surely live, because he is warned.

Eze. 18.21. If the wicked will turn from all his sins that he hath committed, and keep all my statutes, and do that which is lawful and right, he shall surely live, he shall not die. 22. In his righteousness that he hath done he sha¹¹ live. 23. Have I any pleasure at all that th wicked should die? saith the Lord God: *an* not that he should return from his ways, an live? *v.* 1-9,14-30.

Eze. 20.11. I gave them my statutes, an shewed them my judgments, which *if* a ma do, he shall even live in them. 19. Walk i my statutes, and keep my judgments, and d them. Lev. 18.4,5. Neh. 9.29.

Hos. 6.6. I desired mercy, and not sacri fice; and the knowledge of God more thar burnt-offerings.

Hos. 10.12. Sow to yourselves in righteousness, reap in mercy; break up your fallow ground: for *it is* time to seek the Lord, till he come and rain righteousness upon you.

Hos. 12.6. Turn thou to thy God: keep mercy and judgment, and wait on thy God continually.

Hos. 14.9. The ways of the Lord *are* right, and the just shall walk in them.

Amos 5.14. Seek good, and not evil, that ye may live: and so the Lord, the God of hosts, shall be with you, as ye have spoken. 15. Hate the evil, and love the good, and establish judgment in the gate: it may be that the Lord God of hosts will be gracious. 24. Let judgment run down as waters, and righteousness as a mighty stream.

Mic. 2.7. Do not my words do good to him that walketh uprightly?

Mic. 6.8. He hath shewed thee, O man, what *is* good; and what doth the Lord require of thee, but to do justly, and to love mercy, and to walk humbly with thy God?

Zeph. 3.7. I said, Surely thou wilt fear me, thou wilt receive instruction; so their dwelling should not be cut off.

Mal. 1.6. A son honoureth *his* father, and a servant his master: if then I *be* a father, where *is* mine honour? and if I *be* a master, where *is* my fear? saith the Lord of hosts unto you, O priests, that despise my name.

Mal. 4.4. Remember ye the law of Moses my servant, which I commanded unto him in Horeb for all Israel, *with* the statutes and judgments.

Mat. 3.8. Bring forth therefore fruits meet for repentance. 15. Thus it becometh us to fulfil all righteousness.

Mat. 5.16. Let your light so shine before men, that they may see your good works, and glorify your Father which is in heaven. 19. Whosoever therefore shall break one of these least commandments, and shall teach men so, he shall be called the least in the kingdom of heaven: but whosoever shall do and teach *them,* the same shall be called great in the kingdom of heaven.

Mat. 6.4. Thy Father which seeth in secret himself shall reward thee openly.

Mat. 7.12. All things whatsoever ye would that men should do to you, do ye even so to them: for this is the law and the prophets. 17. Every good tree bringeth forth good fruit. 21. Not every one that saith unto me, Lord, Lord, shall enter into the kingdom of heaven; but he that doeth the will of my Father which is in heaven. *v.* 24,25.

Mat. 11.29. Take my yoke upon you, and learn of me; for I am meek and lowly in heart: and ye shall find rest unto your souls. 30. For my yoke *is* easy, and my burden is light.

Mat. 13.23. But he that received seed into the good ground is he that heareth the word, and understandeth *it*; which also beareth fruit, and bringeth forth, some an hundredfold, some sixty, some thirty. *v.* 8. Mar. 4.20.

Mat. 19.17. If thou wilt enter into life, keep the commandments.

Mat. 22.21. Render therefore unto Cesar the things which are Cesar's; and unto God the things that are God's. 37. Thou shalt love the Lord thy God with all thy heart, and with all thy soul, and with all thy mind. 38. This is the first and great commandment. 39. And the second *is* like unto it, Thou shalt love thy neighbour as thyself. 40. On these two commandments hang all the law and the prophets. Mar. 12.17,39. Luk. 20.25.

Mat. 23.3. Whatsoever they bid you observe, *that* observe and do; but do not ye after their works: for they say, and do not. 23. Ye pay tithe of mint and anise and cummin, and have omitted the weightier *matters* of the law, judgment, mercy, and faith: these ought ye to have done, and not to leave the other undone.

Mat. 25.21. Well done, *thou* good and faithful servant: thou hast been faithful over a few things, I will make thee ruler over many things: enter thou into the joy of thy lord.

Mar. 3.35. Whosoever shall do the will of God, the same is my brother, and my sister, and mother. Luk. 8.15,19-21. Mat. 12.7,50.

Luk. 6.46. Why call ye me, Lord, Lord, and do not the things which I say? 47. Whosoever cometh to me, and heareth my sayings, and doeth them, I will shew you to whom he is like: 48. He is like a man which built an house, and digged deep, and laid the foundation on a rock: and when the flood arose, the stream beat vehemently upon that house, and could not shake it: for it was founded upon a rock. *v.* 31.

Luk. 12.37. Blessed *are* those servants, whom the lord when he cometh shall find watching: verily I say unto you, that he shall gird himself, and make them to sit down to meat, and will come forth and serve them. *v.* 38.

Jno. 3.21. He that doeth truth cometh to the light, that his deeds may be made manifest, that they are wrought in God.

Jno. 10.27. My sheep hear my voice, and I know them, and they follow me.

Jno. 12.26. If any man serve me, let him follow me; and where I am, there shall also my servant be: if any man serve me, him will *my* Father honour.

Jno. 13.17. If ye know these things, happy are ye if ye do them.

Jno. 14.15. If ye love me, keep my commandments. 21. He that hath my commandments, and keepeth them, he it is that loveth me. 23. If a man love me, he will keep my words: and my Father will love him, and we will come unto him, and make our abode with him.

Jno. 15.8. Herein is my Father glorified, that ye bear much fruit; so shall ye be my disciples. 10. If ye keep my commandments, ye shall abide in my love; even as I have kept my Father's commandments, and abide in his love. 14. Ye are my friends, if ye do whatsoever I command you. 16. I have chosen you, and ordained you, that ye should go and bring forth fruit, and *that* your fruit should remain.

Act. 5.29. We ought to obey God rather than men.

Act. 10.35. In every nation he that feareth him, and worketh righteousness, is accepted with him.

Rom. 2.7. To them who, by patient continuance in well-doing, seek for glory, and honour, and immortality, eternal life; 10. Glory, honour, and peace, to every man that worketh good, to the Jew first, and also to the Gentile. 13. Not the hearers of the law *are* just before God, but the doers of the law shall be justified.

Rom. 3.31. Do we then make void the law through faith? God forbid: yea, we establish the law.

Rom. 6.16. To whom ye yield yourselves servants to obey, his servants ye are to whom ye obey; whether of sin unto death, or of obedience unto righteousness.

Rom. 10.5. Moses describeth the righteousness which is of the law, That the man which doeth those things shall live by them.

Rom. 12.11. Not slothful in business; fervent in spirit; serving the Lord. 17. Provide things honest in the sight of all men. *v.* 3-8.

Rom. 14.18. He that in these things serveth Christ *is* acceptable to God, and approved of men.

1 Cor. 7.19. Circumcision is nothing, and uncircumcision is nothing, but the keeping of the commandments of God.

1 Cor. 15.58. Be ye stedfast, unmoveable, always abounding in the work of the Lord, forasmuch as ye know that your labour is not in vain in the Lord.

Gal. 3.10. Cursed *is* every one that continueth not in all things which are written in the book of the law to do them. 12. The man that doeth them shall live in them.

Gal. 5.3. I testify again to every man that is circumcised, that he is a debtor to do the whole law.

Gal. 6.8. He that soweth to the Spirit, shall of the Spirit reap life everlasting. 9. And let us not be weary in well-doing: for in due season we shall reap, if we faint not.

Eph. 2.10. We are his workmanship, created in Christ Jesus unto good works, which God hath before ordained that we should walk in them.

Eph. 4.1. Walk worthy of the vocation wherewith ye are called. 17. Henceforth walk not as other Gentiles walk, in the vanity of their mind.

Eph. 6.6. As the servants of Christ, doing the will of God from the heart ; 7. With good will doing service, as to the Lord, and not to men : 8. Whatsoever good thing any man doeth, the same shall he receive of the Lord, whether *he be* bond or free.

Phil. 1.27. Let your conversation be as it becometh the gospel of Christ.

Phil. 4.9. Those things, which ye have both learned, and received, and heard, and seen in me, do : and the God of peace shall be with you. 17. I desire fruit that may abound to your account.

Col. 1.6. Which is come unto you, as *it is* in all the world ; and bringeth forth fruit, as *it doth* also in you, since the day ye heard *of it*, and knew the grace of God in truth. 10. Walk worthy of the Lord unto all pleasing, being fruitful in every good work, and increasing in the knowledge of God.

Col. 3.24. Of the Lord ye shall receive the reward of the inheritance: for ye serve the Lord Christ.

1 The. 4.1. We beseech you, brethren, and exhort *you* by the Lord Jesus, that as ye have received of us how ye ought to walk and to please God, *so* ye would abound more and more.

1 The. 5.15. Ever follow that which is good, both among yourselves, and to all *men*.

2 The. 3.4. We have confidence in the Lord touching you, that ye both do and will do the things which we command you.

1 Tim. 2.2. Lead a quiet and peaceable life in all godliness and honesty. 3. For this *is* good and acceptable in the sight of God our Saviour. 10. But (which becometh women professing godliness) with good works. 15. Continue in faith and charity and holiness with sobriety.

1 Tim. 5.25. The good works *of some* are manifest beforehand ; and they that are otherwise cannot be hid.

1 Tim. 6.14. Keep *this* commandment without spot, unrebukeable, until the appearing of our Lord Jesus Christ. 18. That they do good, that they be rich in good works.

2 Tim. 2.5. If a man also strive for masteries, *yet* is he not crowned, except he strive lawfully. *v.* 6,7.

Tit. 2.12. Denying ungodliness and worldly lusts, we should live soberly, righteously, and godly, in this present world. 14. That he might redeem us from all iniquity, and purify unto himself a peculiar people, zealous of good works.

Tit. 3.8. *This is* a faithful saying, and these

things I will that thou affirm constantly, that they which have believed in God might be careful to maintain good works. These things are good and profitable unto men. 14. Let our's also learn to maintain good works for necessary uses, that they be not unfruitful.

Heb. 13.16. To do good and to communicate forget not : for with such sacrifices God is well pleased.

Jas. 1.22. Be ye doers of the word, and not hearers only, deceiving your own selves. 23. For if any be a hearer of the word, and not a doer, he is like unto a man beholding his natural face in a glass : 24. For he beholdeth himself, and goeth his way, and straightway forgetteth what manner of man he was. 25. But whoso looketh into the perfect law of liberty, and continueth *therein*, he being not a forgetful hearer, but a doer of the work, this man shall be blessed in his deed.

Jas. 2.10. Whosoever shall keep the whole law, and yet offend in one *point*, he is guilty of all. 11. For he that said, Do not commit adultery, said also, Do not kill. Now if thou commit no adultery, yet if thou kill, thou art become a transgressor of the law. 12. So speak ye, and so do, as they that shall be judged by the law of liberty.

Jas. 2.14. What *doth it* profit, my brethren, though a man say he hath faith, and have not works? can faith save him? 18. A man may say, Thou hast faith, and I have works : shew me thy faith without thy works, and I will shew thee my faith by my works. 26. For as the body without the spirit is dead, so faith without works is dead also. *v.* 14-26.

Jas. 3.13. Shew out of a good conversation his works with meekness of wisdom.

Jas. 4.7. Submit yourselves therefore to God.

1 Pet. 2.5. Offer up spiritual sacrifices, acceptable to God by Jesus Christ. 12. Having your conversation honest among the Gentiles : that, whereas they speak against you as evildoers, they may by *your* good works, which they shall behold, glorify God in the day of visitation. 15. So is the will of God, that with well doing ye may put to silence the ignorance of foolish men. 25. Ye were as sheep going astray ; but are now returned unto the Shepherd and Bishop of your souls.

1 Pet. 3.11. Let him eschew evil, and do good ; let him seek peace, and ensue it. 15. Sanctify the Lord God in your hearts : and *be* ready always to *give* an answer to every man that asketh you a reason of the hope that is in you with meekness and fear : 16. Having a good conscience ; that, whereas they speak evil of you, as of evil-doers, they may be ashamed that falsely accuse your good conversation in Christ.

1 Pet. 4.19. Let them that suffer according to the will of God, commit the keeping of their souls *to him* in well doing, as unto a faithful Creator.

2 Pet. 1.5. Giving all diligence, add to your faith virtue ; and to virtue knowledge ; 6. And to knowledge temperance ; and to temperance patience ; and to patience godliness ; 7. And to godliness brotherly kindness ; and to brotherly kindness charity. 8. For if these things be in you, and abound, they make *you that ye shall* neither *be* barren nor unfruitful in the knowledge of our Lord Jesus Christ.

1 Jno. 2.3. Hereby we do know that we know him, if we keep his commandments. 4. He that saith, I know him, and keepeth not his commandments, is a liar, and the truth is not in him. 5. But whoso keepeth his word, in him verily is the love of God perfected: hereby know we that we are in him. 6. He that saith he abideth in him ought himself also so to walk, even as he walked. 17. He that doeth the will of God abideth for ever.

1 Jno. 3.4. Sin is the transgression of the law. 22. Whatsoever we ask, we receive of him, because we keep his commandments, and do those things that are pleasing in his sight. 24. He that keepeth his commandments dwelleth in him, and he in him.

1 Jno. 5.3. This is the love of God, that we keep his commandments: and his commandments are not grievous.

2 Jno. 6. This is love, that we walk after his commandments. This is the commandment, That, as ye have heard from the beginning, ye should walk in it.

Rev. 12.17. Which keep the commandments of God, and have the testimony of Jesus Christ.

Rev. 14.13. Blessed *are* the dead which die in the Lord from henceforth: Yea, saith the Spirit, that they may rest from their labours; and their works do follow them.

Rev. 22.7. Blessed *is* he that keepeth the sayings of the prophecy of this book. 14. Blessed *are* they that do his commandments, that they may have right to the tree of life, and may enter in through the gates into the city.

See HOLINESS.

OBEDIENCE, EXAMPLES OF: Noah, Gen. 6. 9,22. Gen. 7.5. Heb. 11.7. Abraham, Gen. 12.1-4. Gen. 17.23. Gen. 21.4. Gen. 22.12. Neh. 9.8. Act. 7.3,8. Heb. 11.8-17. Jacob, Gen. 35.1,7. Moses and Aaron, Ex. 7.6. Ex. 40.16,21,23,32. Israelites, Ex. 12.28. Ex. 39. 42,43. Num. 9.20,21. Jud. 2.7. Psa. 99.7. Caleb, Deu. 1.36. Joshua, Jos. 10.40. Jos. 11.15. Reubenites, Jos. 22.2,3. Gideon, Jud. 6.25-28. David, 1 Sam. 18.14. 1 Sam. 25.28. 1 Kin. 11.6,34. 1 Kin. 15.5. 2 Chr. 29.2. Act. 13.22. Elisha, 1 Kin. 19.19-21. Hezekiah, 2 Kin. 18.6. 2 Chr. 31.20-21. Josiah, 2 Kin. 22.2. 2 Kin. 23.24,25. Asa, 2 Chr. 14.2. Jehoshaphat, 2 Chr. 17.3-6. 2 Chr. 20.32. 2 Chr. 22.9. Jehoiada, 2 Chr. 24.16. Uzziah, 2 Chr. 26.4,5. Jotham, 2 Chr. 27.2. Levites, 2 Chr. 29.34. Jews, 2 Chr. 34.33. Ezr. 3.1-6. Neh. 13.1-3. Ezra, Ezr. 7.10. Hanani, Neh. 7.2. Job, Job 1.8. Jonah, Jonah 3.3. John the Baptist, Mat. 3.15. Apostles, Mat. 4.18-22. Mat. 9.9. Joseph and Mary, Mat. 2.14,21. Luk. 2.21,39. Zacharias, Luk. 1.6. Simeon, Luk. 2.25. Joseph, Luk. 23.50. Nathanael, Jno. 1.47. Cornelius, Act. 10.2. Paul, Act. 23.1. Act. 26.4,5. 2 Tim. 1.3.

OBEDIENCE AND **GOOD WORKS EXEMPLIFIED**. Gen. 6.9. Noah was a just man, *and* perfect in his generations, *and* Noah walked with God.

Num. 9.23. At the commandment of the Lord they rested in their tents, and at the commandment of the Lord they journeyed: they kept the charge of the Lord, at the commandment of the Lord by the hand of Moses.

Num. 14.24. But my servant Caleb, because he had another spirit with him, and hath followed me fully, him will I bring into the land whereinto he went; and his seed shall possess it.

2 Kin. 18.6. For he clave to the Lord, *and* departed not from following him, but kept his commandments.

2 Kin. 20.3. O Lord, remember now how I have walked before thee in truth, and with a perfect heart, and have done *that which is* good in thy sight.

2 Chr. 24.16. He had done good in Israel, both toward God, and toward his house.

2 Chr. 31.20. Thus did Hezekiah throughout all Judah, and wrought *that which was* good, and right, and truth, before the Lord his God. 21. And in every work that he began in the service of the house of God, and in the law, and in the commandments, to seek his God, he did *it* with all his heart, and prospered.

Ezr. 7.10. Ezra had prepared his heart to seek the law of the Lord, and to do *it*.

Neh. 7.2. He *was* a faithful man, and feared God above many.

Job 1.8. Hast thou considered my servant Job, that *there is* none like him in the earth, a perfect and an upright man, one that feareth God, and escheweth evil?

Psa. 17.3. Thou hast proved mine heart; thou hast visited *me* in the night; thou hast tried me, *and* shalt find nothing; I am purposed *that* my mouth shall not transgress.

Psa. 26.3. Thy lovingkindness *is* before mine eyes: and I have walked in thy truth. 6. I will wash mine hands in innocency: so will I compass thine altar, O Lord.

Psa. 99.7. He spake unto them in the cloudy pillar: they kept his testimonies, and the ordinance *that* he gave them.

Psa. 101.2. I will behave myself wisely in a perfect way. O when wilt thou come unto me? I will walk within my house with a perfect heart. 3. I will set no wicked thing before mine eyes: I hate the work of them that turn aside; *it* shall not cleave to me.

Psa. 119.30. I have chosen the way of truth: thy judgments have I laid *before* me. 31. I have stuck unto thy testimonies: O Lord, put me not to shame. 45. I will walk at liberty: for I seek thy precepts. 55. I have remembered thy name, O Lord, in the night, and have kept thy law. 56. This I had, because I kept thy precepts. 59. I thought on my ways, and turned my feet unto thy testimonies. 60. I made haste, and delayed not to keep thy commandments.

Psa. 119.101. I have refrained my feet from every evil way, that I might keep thy word. 102. I have not departed from thy judgments: for thou hast taught me. 112. I have inclined mine heart to perform thy statutes alway, *even unto* the end. 166. Lord, I have hoped for thy salvation, and done thy commandments. 167. My soul hath kept thy testimonies; and I love them exceedingly. 168. I have kept thy precepts and thy testimonies: for all my ways *are* before thee.

Mat. 9.9. He saith unto him, Follow me. And he arose, and followed him.

Luk. 1.6. They were both righteous before God, walking in all the commandments and ordinances of the Lord blameless.

Luk. 2.25. The same man *was* just and devout, waiting for the consolation of Israel: and the Holy Ghost was upon him.

Luk. 23.50. *He was* a good man, and a just.

Jno. 1.47. And saith of him, Behold an Israelite indeed, in whom is no guile !

Act. 10.2. *A* devout *man*, and one that feared God with all his house, which gave much alms to the people, and prayed to God alway.

Act. 23.1. Men *and* brethren, I have lived in all good conscience before God until this day.

Act. 24.16. Herein do I exercise myself, to have always a conscience void of offence toward God, and *toward* men.

Rom. 6.17. Ye have obeyed from the heart that form of doctrine which was delivered you.

2 Cor. 1.12. Our rejoicing is this, the testimony of our conscience, that in simplicity and godly sincerity, not with fleshly wisdom, but by the grace of God, we have had our conversation in the world, and more abundantly to you-ward.

2 Cor. 6.3. Giving no offence in any thing, that the ministry be not blamed : 4. But in all *things* approving ourselves as the ministers of God, in much patience, in afflictions, in necessities, in distresses.

Phil. 3.12. I follow after, if that I may apprehend that for which also I am apprehended of Christ Jesus. 13. Brethren, I count not myself to have apprehended : but *this* one thing *I do*, forgetting those things which are behind, and reaching forth unto those things which are before. 14. I press toward the mark for the prize of the high calling of God in Christ Jesus.

1 The. 1.9. Ye turned to God, from idols to serve the living and true God.

1 The. 2.10. Ye *are* witnesses, and God *also*, how holily, and justly, and unblameably, we behaved ourselves among you that believe.

2 Tim. 1.3. I thank God, whom I serve from *my* forefathers with pure conscience.

Rev. 2.19. I know thy works, and charity, and service, and faith, and thy patience, and thy works ; and the last *to be* more than the first.

Rev. 3.4. Thou hast a few names even in Sardis which have not defiled their garments ; and they shall walk with me in white : for they are worthy.

Rev. 14.4. These are they which were not defiled with women ; for they are virgins. These are they which follow the Lamb whithersoever he goeth. These were redeemed from among men, *being* the firstfruits unto God and to the Lamb. 5. And in their mouth was found no guile : for they are without fault before the throne of God.

See DECISION—INTEGRITY—SAINTS, CHARACTER OF—SANCTIFICATION—SPIRITUAL DILIGENCE.

OBEDIENCE, TEMPORAL REWARD. See GOD'S GOODNESS IN PROVIDING FOR HIS PEOPLE.

————— TO PARENTS. See CHILDREN.

————— TO RULERS. See SUBJECTS.

OBLATION, an offering. See OFFERINGS.

OBSERVER OF TIMES. See SORCERY.

ODED, a prophet who commanded Pekah to release the captives of Judah, 2 Chr. 28.9-13. For another Oded, see AZARIAH.

OFFERINGS were of two classes ; bloody, such as burnt-offerings ; and unbloody, such as meat and drink offerings. The different kinds, with the manner and occasions in which they were offered, will be found in alphabetical order below. For the offerings at the feasts, see FEASTS.

OFFERINGS, BLOODY SACRIFICES. Of divine appointment, Gen. 3.21 with Gen. 1.29 and Gen. 9.3. Gen. 4.4,5 with Heb. 11.4. Gen. 15.9. Gen. 35.1. Job 42.8. Psa. 4.5. (See the different OFFERINGS.) Consumed by fire from heaven, see FIRE, SACRED. Cessation of, prophesied, Dan. 9.27. Hos. 3.4. Heb. 7.18,19,27. Heb. 9.10,12. Heb. 10.10,14. To be offered to God only, Ex. 22.20. Jud. 13.16. To devils, forbidden, Lev. 17.7.

Offerers to be purified, Ex. 19.10,14. 1 Sam. 16.5. To offer willingly, Lev. 1.3. Lev. 19.5. Lev. 22.19,29.

All animals to be without blemish, Lev. 1.3,10. Lev. 22.19-24. Deu. 15.21. Deu. 17.1. Mal. 1.8,14 ; and young, Ex. 12.5. Lev. 9.3. Animals offered, sheep or goats, by Abel, Gen. 4.4. Every clean beast and fowl, by Noah, Gen. 8.20. Under the Levitical law, sheep, rams, lambs, goats, kids, bulls, cows, calves, doves, sparrows. See BURNT-OFFERING — PEACE-OFFERING — SIN-OFFERING — HEIFER—DOVE—SPARROW

Animals bound to the horns of altar, Psa. 118.27. Offerings salted, Lev. 2.13. Eze. 43.24. Mar. 9.49 Fat always burned, see FAT. Blood poured out at the altar, Deu. 12.27. Mode of offering the different sacrifices, see OFFERINGS, MODE OF OFFERING. Priest's portion of, see PRIEST'S EMOLUMENTS.

No leaven used with, Ex. 23.18. Ex. 34.25 ; except in thanksgiving, Lev. 7.13. Amos 4.5. Blessed before being eaten of, 1 Sam. 9.13. Accompanied with confession, Lev. 16.21.

Offered at the door of the tabernacle, Lev. 1.3. Lev. 3.2. Lev. 17.4,8,9. At a place divinely appointed, Deu. 12.6,11,14,27. At the temple, 2 Chr. 7.12. 1 Kin. 8.62. 1 Kin. 12.27. On altars, see ALTAR. Accompanied with music and singing, see MUSIC, SACRED.

Of Abel, Gen. 4.3-5. Abraham, Gen. 15. 9-11,17. Jacob, Gen. 31.54. Gen. 46.1. At giving of the law, Ex. 24.5. By Jethro, Ex. 18.12. Elkanah, 1 Sam. 1.21. 1 Sam. 2.19. Samuel, 1 Sam. 9.12,13. Hezekiah, 2 Chr. 29.31. By Philistines, 1 Sam. 6.15, see BURNT-OFFERING, p. 325.

At Bochim, Jud. 2.5. Ophrah, Jud. 6.26. On a rock, Jud. 13.19. At Mizpeh, 1 Sam. 7.9 ; Ramah, 1 Sam. 7.17 ; Gilgal, 1 Sam. 10.8. 1 Sam. 11.15 ; Bethlehem, 1 Sam. 16. 3,5. 1 Sam. 20.6,29 ; Giloh, 2 Sam. 15.12 ; the threshing-floor of Araunah, 1 Chr. 21.18,26; Gibeon, 2 Chr. 1,3 ; Carmel, 1 Kin. 18.38. Various high places, 1 Kin. 3.2.

Not accepted, Cain, Gen. 4 3-5 ; Nadab, Lev. 10.1,2. See OFFERINGS, INSUFFICIENCY OF. Abused by Eli's sons, 1 Sam. 2.13,29.

Were offered as thanksgivings, see THANK-OFFERING. In acknowledgment of sin, Heb. 10.3. Ratified covenants, Gen. 8.20-22. Gen. 15.8-18. Gen. 31.54. Ex. 24.5-8. Psa. 50.5. Heb. 9.19,20.

Were expiatory, or an atonement for sin, Lev. 1.4. Lev. 4. Lev. 5.10. Lev. 6.2,7. Lev.

17.11. Num. 15.24-26. 1 Sam. 3.14. 1 Sam. 26.19. Job 1.5. Job 42.8. Eze. 45.15. Heb. 9.13. Heb. 10.3. Heb. 13.11. Emblematic of Christ, Psa. 40.6-8 with Heb. 10.5. Isa. 53.6,11,12 with Lev. 16.21. 1 Cor. 5.7. 2 Cor. 5.21. Eph. 5.2. Heb. 10.1,11,12 and Heb. 13.11-13. Illustrative, Psa. 51.17. Jer. 33.11. Rom. 12.1. Phil. 4.18. Heb. 13.15.

OFFERINGS. BURNT-OFFERING, or HOLO-CAUST (see OFFERINGS, MODE OF). Trumpets blown over, Num. 10.10; with singing, &c., 2 Chr. 23.18. 2 Chr. 29.27,28. Accompanied with meat and drink-offerings, Num. 15.3-16. Ashes of, carried without the camp to a clean place, Lev. 4.12. Lev. 6.10,11. Num. 19.9. Skin belonged to the priests, Lev. 7.8.

Daily Burnt-offering: a lamb morning and evening, Ex. 29.38-42. Num. 28.1-8. On Sabbath doubled, Num. 28.9,10. Prayer at, Act. 3.1. Prophecy of its abolition, Dan. 11.31.

At the new-moon, 2 bulls, 1 ram, 7 lambs, Num. 28.11-15. Daily during passover-week, 2 bulls, 1 ram, 7 lambs, Num. 28.19-24. Daily during feast of trumpets, 1 bull, 1 ram, 7 lambs, Num. 29.1-6. Daily during feast of tabernacles, beginning with 13 bulls, 2 rams, 14 lambs, on the first day, number lessening each day, Lev. 23.36,37. Num. 29.13-40.

With the sheaf of first-fruits, a he-lamb, Lev. 23.12. On the day of first-fruits, 2 young bulls, 1 ram, 7 lambs, Num. 28.26-31. At Pentecost, 1 bull, 2 rams, 7 lambs, Lev. 23.18; or 2 bulls, Num. 28.27. On Day of Atonement, a ram for the high-priest, Lev. 16.3,24; a ram for the congregation, Lev. 16.5,24; and 1 bull, 1 ram, 7 lambs, Num. 29.8. At consecration of priests, 2 rams, Ex. 29.15-25. Lev. 8.18-28; and 1 ram, Lev. 9.1-14; of Levites, 1 bull, Num. 8.8-12. For the congregation, 1 calf, 1 lamb, Lev. 9.3,4,15-21. For private persons, a bull or ram, or pigeon, Lev. 1.3,11,15.

For sins of ignorance, 1 young bull, Num. 15.24,25. Trespass-offering, for one who hears swearing, &c., a turtle-dove or young pigeon, Lev. 5.7-10. For purification of women, 1 lamb or pigeon, Lev. 12.6,8. For lepers, 1 lamb or pigeon, Lev. 14.10,21,22,31. For defilement, 1 pigeon, Lev. 15.15,30. For Nazarites' defilement, 1 pigeon, Num. 6.11. On expiry of vow, 1 lamb, Num. 6.14,16. At all festivals, 1 Chr. 23.31. 2 Chr. 2.4. 2 Chr. 31.3.

By Noah, of clean beasts and fowls, Gen. 8. 20. Abraham, a ram, Gen. 22.13. Jethro, Ex. 18.12. At the giving of the law, Ex. 24.5. By Moses, Ex. 40.29. Princes of Israel, Num. 7.15-89; Balak, Num. 23.3,6,15,17; Joshua, Jos. 8.31; Gideon, Jud. 6.26; Manoah, Jud. 13.16,19,23; Israel, Jud. 20.26. Jud. 21.4. 1 Sam. 6.14,15; Samuel, 1 Sam. 7.9,10; Saul, 1 Sam. 13.9; David, 2 Sam. 6.17,18. 2 Sam. 24.25. At Solomon's coronation, 1 Chr. 29.21. By Solomon, 1 Kin. 3.4. 1 Chr. 16.40. 1 Kin. 3.15. 1 Kin. 9.25. At dedication of temple, 1 Kin. 8.64. By Elijah, 1 Kin. 18.33-38. By Ahaz, 2 Kin. 16.13,15. In Jehoiada's days, 2 Chr. 24.14. By Hezekiah, 2 Chr. 29.24,27. 2 Chr. 30.15; Judah, 2 Chr. 29.31-35; Josiah, 2 Chr. 35.12-14; Joshua, Ezr. 3.2-6; Jews, Ezr. 8.35; Job, Job 1.5; Job's friends, Job 42.8. See IDOLATROUS OFFERINGS p. 243.

OFFERINGS. DRINK-OFFERING. Of wine, was offered with all sacrifices, Lev. 23.13.18.

Num. 6.17. Num. 15.24. Num. 28.5-15,24-31. Num. 29.6-11,18-40. Ezr. 7.17.

With a burnt-offering of a lamb, consisted of ¼ hin of wine; of a ram, ⅓ hin; of a bullock, ½ hin, Ex. 29.40,41. Num. 15.4-12. Num. 28.7,14,15. With the first-fruits, ½ hin, Lev. 23.13. Poured out unto the Lord, in the holy place, Num. 28.7. Not to be offered on incense-altar, Ex. 30.9.

Offered by Jacob, Gen. 35.14. Ahaz, 2 Kin. 16.13. At Solomon's coronation, 1 Chr. 29.21. By Hezekiah, 2 Chr. 29.35. See IDOLATRY, p. 243.

OFFERINGS OF FIRST-FRUITS. See FIRST-FRUITS.

————. HEAVE-OFFERING. Heaved up by the priest; that is, consecrated by elevating it, Ex. 29.27.

Consisted of the right shoulder of peace-offerings, at consecration of priests, Ex. 29. 27,28. Lev. 7.32,34; and on expiry of Nazarite vows, Num. 6.20. In thanksgivings, consisted of bread leavened and unleavened, Lev. 7.12-14. In first-fruits, consisted of first-fruits of the threshing-floor, and a cake of the first dough, Num. 15.19-21. Neh. 10.37.

A tithe of the tithes offered by the Levites, as a heave-offering, Num. 18.25-30. Neh. 10.38; and part of spoils taken in war, Num. 31.29,41. Tithes so called, Num. 18.24. Heave-offering, called a wave-offering, Lev. 10.15. Given to the priests, Ex. 29.28. Lev. 7.14,34. Lev. 10. 15. Num. 18.8-19. Eze. 44.30. To be eaten in a clean place, Lev. 10.14. Num. 18.10. To be brought to the temple, Deu. 12.6,11,17,18.

————, HUMAN OFFERINGS forbidden, Lev. 18.21. Lev. 20.2-5. Deu. 12.31. Isa. 57.5. Isa. 66.3. See IDOLATRY, p. 243.

————, IDOLATROUS. See IDOLATRY, p. 243.

OFFERINGS, INSUFFICIENCY OF. 1 Sam. 15.22. Hath the Lord *as great* delight in burnt-offerings and sacrifices, as in obeying the voice of the Lord? Behold, to obey *is* better than sacrifice, *and* to hearken than the fat of rams.

Psa. 40.6. Sacrifice and offering thou didst not desire; mine ears hast thou opened: burnt-offering and sin-offering hast thou not required.

Psa. 50.8. I will not reprove thee for thy sacrifices, or thy burnt-offerings, *to have been* continually before me. 9. I will take no bullock out of thy house, *nor* he-goats out of thy folds: 10. For every beast of the forest *is* mine, *and* the cattle upon a thousand hills. 11. I know all the fowls of the mountains; and the wild beasts of the field *are* mine. 12. If I were hungry, I would not tell thee: for the world *is* mine, and the fulness thereof. 13. Will I eat the flesh of bulls, or drink the blood of goats? 14. Offer unto God thanksgiving; and pay thy vows unto the most High.

Psa. 51.16. For thou desirest not sacrifice, else would I give *it*; thou delightest not in burnt-offering. 17. The sacrifices of God *are* a broken spirit: a broken and a contrite heart, O God, thou wilt not despise.

Pro. 21.3. To do justice and judgment *is* more acceptable to the Lord than sacrifice. 27. The sacrifice of the wicked *is* abomination: how much more *when* he bringeth it with a wicked mind?

Isa. 1.11. To what purpose *is* the multitude of your sacrifices unto me? saith the Lord : I am full of the burnt-offerings of rams, and the fat of fed beasts ; and I delight not in the blood of bullocks, or of lambs, or of he-goats. 13. Bring no more vain oblations : incense is an abomination unto me ; the new-moons and sabbaths, the calling of assemblies, I cannot away with ; *it is* iniquity, even the solemn meeting. 14. Your new-moons and your appointed feasts my soul hateth : they are a trouble unto me ; I am weary to bear *them.*

Isa. 40.16. Lebanon *is* not sufficient to burn, nor the beasts thereof sufficient for a burnt-offering.

Isa. 66.3. He that killeth an ox, *is as if* he slew a man ; he that sacrificeth a lamb, *as if* he cut off a dog's neck ; he that offereth an oblation, *as if he offered* swine's blood ; he that burneth incense, *as if* he blessed an idol : yea, they have chosen their own ways, and their soul delighteth in their abominations.

Jer. 6.20. To what purpose cometh there to me incense from Sheba, and the sweet cane from a far country ? your burnt-offerings *are* not acceptable, nor your sacrifices sweet unto me.

Jer. 7.21. Put your burnt-offerings unto your sacrifices, and eat flesh. 22. For I speak not unto your fathers, nor commanded them in the day that I brought them out of the land of Egypt, concerning burnt-offerings or sacrifices : 23. But this thing commanded I them, saying, Obey my voice, and I will be your God.

Jer. 14.12. When they fast, I will not hear their cry ; and when they offer burnt-offering and an oblation, I will not accept them : but I will consume them by the sword, and by the famine, and by the pestilence.

Hos. 6.6. I desired mercy, and not sacrifice ; and the knowled e of God more than burnt-offerings.

Hos. 8.13. They sacrifice flesh *for* the sacrifices of mine offerings, and eat *it ; but* the Lord accepteth them not : now will he remember their iniquity.

Amos 5.21. I hate, I despise your feast-days, and I will not smell in your solemn assemblies. 22. Though ye offer me burnt-offerings, and your meat-offerings, I will not accept *them ;* neither will I regard the peace-offerings of your fat beasts. 23. Take thou away from me the noise of thy songs ; for I will not hear the melody of thy viols. 24. But let judgment run down as waters, and righteousness as a mighty stream. Hos. 9.4.

Mic. 6.6. Wherewith shall I come before the Lord, *and* bow myself before the high God? shall I come before him with burnt-offerings, with calves of a year old? 7. Will the Lord be pleased with thousands of rams, *or* with ten thousands of rivers of oil? shall I give my first-born *for* my transgression, the fruit of my body *for* the sin of my soul? 8. He hath shewed thee, O man, what *is* good : and what doth the Lord require of thee, but to do justly, and to love mercy, and to walk humbly with thy God?

Mar. 12.33. To love him with all the heart, and with all the understanding, and with all the soul, and with all the strength, and to love *his* neighbour as himself, is more than all whole burnt-offerings and sacrifices.

Heb. 9.9. In which were offered both gifts and sacrifices, that could not make him that did the service perfect, as pertaining to the conscience.

Heb. 10.1. For the law having a shadow of good things to come, *and* not the very image of the things, can never with those sacrifices, which they offered year by year continually, make the comers thereunto perfect : 2. For then would they not have ceased to be offered? because that the worshippers once purged should have had no more conscience of sins. 3. But in those *sacrifices there is* a remembrance again *made* of sins every year. 4. For *it is* not possible that the blood of bulls and of goats should take away sins. 5. Wherefore, when he cometh into the world, he saith, Sacrifice and offering thou wouldest not, but a body hast thou prepared me.

Heb. 10.6. In burnt-offerings and *sacrifices* for sin thou hast had no pleasure : 7. Then said I, Lo, I come (in the volume of the book it is written of me) to do thy will, O God. 8. Above, when he said, Sacrifice, and offering, and burnt-offerings, and *offering* for sin, thou wouldest not, neither hadst pleasure *therein ;* (which are offered by the law ;) 9. Then said he, Lo, I come to do thy will, O God. He taketh away the first, that he may establish the second. 10. By the which will we are sanctified, through the offering of the body of Jesus Christ once *for all.* 11. And every priest standeth daily ministering, and offering oftentimes the same sacrifices, which can never take away sins. See Law, **mosaic, character of.**

OFFERINGS. Meat-offering. Of flour, corn, bread. (The original is often translated present, Gen. 32.13,18. Gen. 43.11 ; and is used of the first offering mentioned in scripture, Gen. 4.3-5.)

When offered with a lamb, consisted of 1-10th of flour, 1-4th hin beaten oil, Ex. 29.40. With a ram, 2-10ths flour, 1-3d hin oil, Num. 15.6. With a bullock, 3-10ths flour, half a hin oil. Num. 15.9.

Unbaked voluntary meat-offerings : consisted of fine flour, with oil and frankincense, a handful burnt on the altar with the incense, the rest the priest's, Lev. 2.1-3.

When baked in an oven, pan, or frying-pan ; consisted of cakes or wafers of fine flour, with oil and salt ; part burnt on the altar, the rest the priest's, Lev. 2.4-11. Lev. 5.13. Lev. 7.9,10,37. Lev. 9.17. Num. 4.16. Num. 18.9. 1 Chr. 23.29. Eze. 44.29. For the priests wholly burnt, Lev. 6.19-33.

Offered with all sacrifices, Num. 15.3-16. Num. 28.5. With sheaf of first-fruits, Lev. 23.13. At new-moons, Num. 28.12,13. Passover, Num. 28.20,21. Feast of trumpets, Num. 29.3,4. Fast-day of 7th month ; and feast of tabernacles, Num. 29.14. On Sabbaths, Num. 28.9.

Burnt, morning and evening, with the continual burnt-offering, Ex. 29.40,41. Ex. 40.29. Num. 15.4. Num. 28.5. 2 Kin. 3.20. 2 Kin. 16.15. Neh. 10.33.

At Pentecost, 2 wave-loaves of 2-10ths flour, with leaven, Lev. 23.16,17. Of first-fruits, consisted of green ears of corn dried by the fire, with oil, frankincense, and salt, Lev. 2. 12-16. For cleansing of lepers consisted of 3-10ths flour, with oil ; if poor,1-10th, Lev.14. 10,20,21,31. As an offering of jealousy, 1-10th ephah barley-meal, without oil or frank-incense, Num. 5.15,18,25,26. As a sin-offering by the poor, without oil or frankincense, Lev. 5.11,12. By a Nazarite on fulfilling his vows, Num. 6.15,17. On consecration of Levites, Num. 8.8. For sins of ignorance, Num. 15.24.

Not to be offered on altar of incense, Ex. 30.9. Not made with leaven or honey, Lev. 2.11; exception, Lev. 23.16,17. Priest's portion eaten in the holy place, with unleavened bread, Lev. 2.3. Lev. 6.14-18. Lev. 10.12,13. Lev. 44.29. Num. 18.9,10.

Chambers for, Neh. 12.44. Neh. 13.5,9. Eze. 42.13.

Offered by Aaron, at the consecration of himself and sons, Ex. 29.2,23. Lev. 8.26. Lev. 9.4,5. By princes of Israel, Num. 7.13-87. Manoah, Jud. 13.19,23. Solomon, 1 Kin. 8.64. Not given to the Levites, Neh. 13.9,10. Neglected, Joel 1.9,13.

See IDOLATRY, p. 243.

OFFERINGS. MODE OF OFFERING. (There were three modes in which bloody sacrifices were offered, technically called Sin-offering, Burnt-offering, Peace-offering. A comparison of the Tables below will shew the difference between these three modes of offering sacrifices; and that they varied according as the animal was from the herd, or flock, or a bird. The *occasions* on which these offerings were made, will be found under the heads BURNT-OFFERING, SIN-OFFERING, PEACE-OFFERING, TRESPASS-OFFERING.)

OFFERINGS OF THE HERD—CATTLE.

SIN-OFFERINGS.	BURNT-OFFERINGS.	PEACE-OFFERINGS.
Brought before the tabernacle, Ex. 29.10.	Brought before the tabernacle, Lev. 1.3.	Brought before the tabernacle, Lev. 3.2.
Offerer put his hand on the head of, Ex. 29.10; the elders for the congregation, Lev. 4.15.	Offerer put his hand on the head of, Lev. 1.4.	Offerer put his hand on the head of, Lev. 3.2.
Killed at the tabernacle door by Moses for Aaron, Ex. 29. 11. By the priest, Lev.16.15; aided by Levites, 2 Chr. 29.34.	Killed at the door of the tabernacle by offerer, Lev. 1.5.	Killed at the door of the tabernacle by offerer, Lev. 3.2.
Blood in certain cases put by the priest on the horns of altar of burnt-offering with the finger, Ex. 29.12. Lev. 4.25,30,34. Lev. 8.15.		
Blood poured out by the priest beside the bottom of the altar, Ex. 29.12. Lev. 4.7. Lev. 8.15.	Blood sprinkled round about upon the altar by the priest, Lev. 1.5.	Blood sprinkled round about upon the altar by the priest, Lev. 3.2.
Blood, in certain cases, put by the priest on the horns of altar of incense, and sprinkled 7 times before the vail, Lev. 4.6,7,16-18.		
Blood on the Day of Atonement sprinkled on the mercy-seat, and before the mercy-seat eastward 7 times, and on the incense-altar, Lev. 16.14,18,19.		
Burnt *on the altar* by the priest; viz., fat covering the inwards, caul above the liver, 2 kidneys and fat upon them, Ex. 29.13. Lev. 8.16. Lev. 4.8,10,19,20.	Burnt by the priest on the altar, after being flayed and cut in pieces; the priest laid the parts; viz., the head and fat, on the wood, washed the inwards and legs, and burned all, Lev. 1.6-9.	Burnt upon the altar by the priest; viz., fat covering the inwards, caul above the liver, 2 kidneys and fat upon them, Lev. 3.3-5.
Burnt *without the camp* by the priest whenever the blood was presented in the holy place; viz., flesh, skin, head, legs, inwards, and dung, Ex. 29.14. Lev. 8.17. Lev. 4.7-12,17-21. Lev. 6.30.		
Eaten by the priests in the holy place when the blood had not been presented in the holy place, Lev. 6.25-29. Num. 18,9,10. Eze. 44.29.		The rest of the Peace-offering eaten. See HEAVE-OFFERING, WAVE-OFFERING.

OFFERINGS. MODE OF OFFERING—*continued.*

OFFERINGS OF THE FLOCK—SHEEP AND GOATS.

SIN-OFFERINGS.	BURNT-OFFERINGS.	PEACE-OFFERINGS.
Offerer put his hands on the head of, Lev. 4.24,29,33.	Offerer put his hands on the head of, Ex. 29.15. Lev. 8.18. Lev. 1.4.	Offerer put his hands on the head of, Lev. 3.8,13.
Killed by offerer at the door of the tabernacle, Lev. 4.24,29,33; by Moses for Aaron, Ex. 29.16. Lev. 8.19.	Killed by offerer at the door of the tabernacle, Lev. 17.8,9. Lev. 9.5,12; by Moses for Aaron, Ex. 29.16. Lev. 8.19. Killed on the north side of the altar, Lev. 1.11.	Killed by offerer at the door of the tabernacle, Lev. 3.8. Lev. 3.13.
Blood put by the priest on the horns of altar of burnt-offering with the finger, Lev. 4.25,30,34.	Blood sprinkled round about upon the altar by priests, Ex. 29.16. Lev. 8.19. Lev. 1.11.	Blood sprinkled by the priest round about upon the altar, Lev. 3.8,13.
Blood poured out by the priest beside the bottom of the altar, Lev. 4.25,30,34.		
Blood on the Day of Atonement sprinkled on the mercy-seat, and before the mercy-seat, 7 times ; put on the horns of incense-altar, and sprinkled on it 7 times, Lev. 16.15,18,19.		
Burnt on the altar by the priest ; viz., fat covering the inwards, caul above the liver, 2 kidneys and fat upon them, Lev. 4.26,31,35 with Lev. 3.14-16.	Burnt on the altar by the priest, after being cut in pieces, inwards and legs washed, Ex. 29.17,18. Lev. 1.10-13. Lev. 8.20,21,28.	Burnt on the altar by the priest ; viz., fat covering the inwards, caul above the liver, 2 kidneys, and fat upon them—of a goat, Lev. 3.14-16; also the rump of a lamb, Lev. 3.9-11.
Eaten by the priests in the holy place when the blood had not been presented in the holy place, Lev. 6.25-29. Num. 18.9,10. Eze. 44.29. See Lev. 10.17-19.		The rest of the Peace-offering eaten. See HEAVE-OFFERING, WAVE-OFFERING. (The ram of consecration was a Peace-offering with some peculiarities in the mode of sacrifice, Ex. 29.19-28,31-34. Lev. 8.22-32.)

OFFERINGS OF TURTLE-DOVES OR YOUNG PIGEONS.

SIN-OFFERINGS.	BURNT-OFFERINGS.
	Brought to the altar by the priest, Lev. 1.15.
Head wrung off by the priest, Lev. 5.8.	Head wrung off and burnt by the priest, Lev. 1.15.
Blood sprinkled by the priest upon the side of the altar, Lev. 5.9.	
Blood wrung out by the priest at the bottom of the altar, Lev. 5.9.	Blood wrung out by the priest at the side of the altar, Lev. 1.15.
	Crop and feathers plucked off by the priest and cast on the east side of the altar among the ashes, Lev. 1.16.
	Cleft with the wings by the priest, but not divided, and burnt on the altar, Lev. 1.17.
Burnt by the priest before the burnt-offering, Lev. 5.8.	Burnt by the priest after the sin-offering, Lev. 5.10.

OFFERINGS. Paschal Lamb. See Feast, passover.

———, Peace-offering. Mode of offering, see Offerings, mode of.

At consecration of priests, one ram, called ram of consecration, Ex. 29.19-22,31. For Aaron and his sons, 1 bull, 1 ram, Lev. 9.4. For the congregation, 1 bull, 1 ram, Lev. 9. 3,4,15-21. For a private person, 1 bull, or 1 lamb, or 1 goat, Lev. 3.1-13. At Pentecost, 2 lambs, Lev. 23.19. Offered at all the festivals, Num. 10.10. On expiry of Nazarite's vow, Num. 6.14.

Of thanksgiving, and freewill-offerings, see Thanksgiving-offering — Voluntary-offering. Meat and drink offerings with, Num. 15.8-15. Trumpets blown over, Num. 10.10. Parts of, eaten, see Wave-offering —Heave-offering. Defiled persons not to eat, Lev. 7.20,21.

At giving of the law, Ex. 24.5. By the princes, Num. 7.17-88. By Joshua, Jos. 8.31. By Israel, Jud. 20.26. Jud. 21.4. At Saul's coronation, 1 Sam. 11.15. By David, 2 Sam. 6.17,18. 2 Sam. 24.25. Solomon, 1 Kin. 3.15. 1 Kin. 8.63,64. 1 Kin. 9.25. Ahaz, 2 Kin. 16.13. Hezekiah, 2 Chr. 29.35. 2 Chr. 30.22. Manasseh, 2 Chr. 33.16. Before the golden calf, Ex. 32.6.

———. Red Heifer. See Heifer, red.

———. Scape Goat. See Scape Goat.

OFFERINGS. Sin-offering. (See Offerings, mode of.) A kid at new-moon, Num. 28.15 ; and daily during passover, feast of trumpets, and tabernacles, Num. 28.22-24. Num. 29.5,6,16-38. A kid at Pentecost, Lev. 23.19. Num. 28.30. On Day of Atonement, a young bull for the priest ; a goat for the people, Lev. 16.3-19,25-28. Num. 29.11. Atonement made with the blood of sin-offering upon the horns of the altar of incense yearly, Ex. 30.10. Lev. 16.18. At consecration of priests, 1 bull, Lev. 8.2,14. Ex. 29.10 ; of altar, 1 bull for 7 days, Ex. 29.36,37.

For sins of ignorance. For a priest, 1 bull, Lev. 4.3,4. For the people, 1 bull, Lev. 4.13-21 ; or a kid, Num. 15.24. For a ruler, 1 male kid, Lev. 4.22-26. For one of the people, a female kid or lamb, Lev. 4.27,35. Num. 15.27. As a trespass-offering, Lev. 5.1-19. Lev. 6.1-7, see Trespass-offering. For priests, 1 calf, Lev. 9.1-14. At consecration of Levites, 1 young bull, Num. 8.8,12. For the congregation, 1 kid, Lev. 9.3,4,15-21. For purification of women, a dove, Lev. 12.6-8. For lepers' purification, 1 lamb or dove, Lev. 14.19,22,31 ; or flour, if poor, Lev. 5.11-13. For defilement, 1 dove, Lev. 15.15,30. For Nazarite's defilement, 1 dove, Num. 6.10,11. On expiry of vow, a ewe-lamb, Num. 6.14,16.

Vessels in which it was sodden, if earthen, broken ; if brass, scoured, Lev. 6.28.

By the princes, Num. 7.16-87 ; Hezekiah, 2 Chr. 29.21-24 ; Jews, Ezr. 8.35.

OFFERINGS. Thanksgiving-offering. A peace-offering with a meat-offering, leavened and unleavened, eaten by the offerer on the same day, Lev. 7.11-15. Lev. 22.29, see Deu. 12.11,12. 1 Sam. 9.12,13. Called a sacrifice of praise or thanksgiving, Psa. 116.17. Jer. 33.11. Amos 4.5. Offered by Judah, 2 Chr.

29.31. Manasseh, 2 Chr. 33.16. At dedication of wall, Neh. 12.27.

OFFERINGS. Trespass-offering. Offered for one who hears swearing without revealing it, or who touches uncleanness, or who is guilty in relation to an oath—a female lamb or kid as a sin-offering ; or two turtle-doves or young pigeons, one as a sin-offering, one a burnt-offering ; or an ephah of fine flour as a sin-offering, Lev. 5.1-14.

For sinning through ignorance in holy things —a ram valued by the priest, with a fifth additional, Lev. 5.14-16. Lev. 6.4,5, see 2 Kin. 12.16. For sinning unwittingly, or for falsehood—a ram valued by the priest, Lev. 5.17-19. Lev. 6.1-7.

For lepers—one he-lamb, a sin-offering ; another as burnt-offering ; or one lamb a peace-offering, and 2 doves, one a sin, the other a burnt-offering, Lev. 14.10-22. For criminal connection with a bondmaid—a ram, Lev. 19. 21,22. For idolatrous marriages, Ezr. 10.19. For a Nazarite defiled—a lamb of 1st year, Num. 6.12.

Portion of, eaten by the priest, Lev. 7.6,7. Lev. 14.13. Num. 18.9,10. Trespass-offering of the Philistines in sending back the ark, 1 Sam. 6.3,8,17,18.

OFFERINGS. Voluntary-offering, either of the cattle or flock, must be perfect, Lev. 22.17-25. A peace-offering, eaten on the day of offering, or next day, Lev. 7.11-18. To be accompanied with meat and drink offerings, Num. 15.1-16. At Feast of Weeks, as God had blessed the offerer, Deu. 16.10. When vowed, must be paid, Deu. 23.23.

OFFERINGS. Wave-offering, waved by the priest ; that is, consecrated by waving it, Ex. 29.24. Lev. 8.27.

Consisted at consecration of priests of the fat of a ram, rump, fat covering inwards, caul above liver, two kidneys, with the fat, right shoulder of ram, with 1 loaf bread, 1 cake oiled bread, 1 wafer of unleavened bread ; all waved before the Lord, and burnt on the altar of burnt-offering, Ex. 29.22-25. Lev. 8. 25-29. Lev. 9.19,20. The breast to be waved ; it belonged to the priest, Ex. 29.26-28. To be brought by the offerer, the fat with the breast waved, the fat burned, Lev. 7.29-31. Lev. 10. 14,15. Lev. 9.20,21.

For lepers, a he-lamb, and a log of oil, Lev. 14.12,21,24. A sheaf of first-fruits, waved on the morrow after the Sabbath, Lev. 23.10,11. At Pentecost, 2 wave-loves of 2-10ths fine flour leavened, with the sacrifices, Lev. 23. 17-20. On expiry of Nazarite's vow, the sodden left shoulder of a ram, with one leavened, and one unleavened cake, Num. 6. 19,20. The jealousy-offering, Num. 5.25.

The breast, &c., belonged to the priest, Ex. 29.26-28. Lev. 7.31,34. Lev. 8.29. Lev. 9. 21. Lev. 23.20. Num. 18.11,18. To be eaten in a clean place, Lev. 10.14,15. Levites offered before the Lord as a wave-offering, Num. 8.11 (marg.), 13,15,21.

———. Wood-offering, wood for the altar, Neh. 10.34. Neh. 13.31.

OG, king of Bashan, Num. 21.33. A giant ; his iron bedstead, 9 cubits long, preserved in Rabbath, Deu. 3.11. Jos. 13.12. Defeated by Moses, and his kingdom given to Manasseh, &c. Num. 32.33. Deu. 1.4. Deu. 3.1-13.

Deu. 4.47. Deu. 29.7. Deu. 31.4. Jos. 2.10. Jos. 9.10. Jos. 12.4. Jos. 13.12,30,31. 1 Kin. 4.19. Neh. 9.22. Psa. 135.11. Psa. 136.20.

OIL of OLIVES. Mode of making, see OLIVE-TREE. Abundant in Palestine, Deu. 7.13. Deu. 8.8. Deu. 11.14. Deu. 32.13. Deu. 33.24. 2 Kin. 18,32. Jer. 31.12. Hos. 2.8,22. Joel 2.19,24. Stores of, Neh. 5.11. Jer. 40.10. Jer. 41.8. Rev. 6.6. Royal storehouses of, 1 Chr. 27.28. 2 Chr. 11.11. 2 Chr. 32.28. Scarcity of, threatened, Deu. 28.40,51. Joel 1.10. Hag. 1.11. Merchandize of, Eze. 27. 17. Hos. 12.1. Luk. 16.6. Rev. 18.13.

Given as payment, 1 Kin. 5.11. 2 Chr. 2.10,15. Ezr. 3.7. Used in food, Num. 11.8. 1 Kin. 17.12-16. 1 Chr. 12.40. Eze. 16.13,19. Hos. 2.5,8; for anointing, see ANOINTING; for lamps, Mat. 25.3,4,8; for the sacred lamp, Ex. 25.6. Ex. 27.20. Ex. 35.8,14,28. Ex. 39.37. Lev. 24.2. Num. 4.9,16. To sprinkle and anoint a leper at his cleansing, Lev. 14. 12-29. In offerings, see MEAT-OFFERING, p. 326.

Tithes of, offered, Deu. 12.17. Deu. 14.23. Neh. 10.39, see FIRST-FRUITS. Levites had charge of, 1 Chr. 9.29. Poured on a pillar by Jacob, Gen. 28.18. Gen. 35.14.

OIL, SACRED, or holy anointing oil. An ointment made by the priests, according to divine direction, Ex. 25.6. Ex. 30.23-25. Ex. 31.11. Ex. 35.8,15,28. Ex. 37.29. Ex. 39.38. Num. 4.16. 1 Chr. 9.30. Punishment for profaning, Ex. 30.31-33. Used for idols, Eze. 23.41. See ANOINTING, SACRED.

OIL-TREE. See OLIVE-TREE.

OINTMENT, a composition of oil and perfumes, of great value, 2 Kin. 20.13. Est. 2.12. Ecc. 7.1. Ecc. 10.1. Song 1.3. Song 4.10. Amos 6.6. Mar. 14.3-5. Jno. 12.3-5. See ANOINTING.

OLD AGE. Job 5.26. Thou shalt come to *thy* grave in a full age, like as a shock of corn cometh in in his season. Gen. 15.15. Gen. 25.8. 1 Chr. 29.28.

Job 11.17. *Thine* age shall be clearer than the noonday; thou shalt shine forth, thou shalt be as the morning. Job 42.12.

Job 32.7. Days should speak, and multitude of years should teach wisdom. 9. Great men are not *always* wise: neither do the aged understand judgment. Job 12.12.

Psa. 71.9. Cast me not off in the time of old age; forsake me not when my strength faileth. 18. Now also when I am old and grey-headed, O God, forsake me not; until I have shewed thy strength unto *this* generation, *and* thy power to every one *that* is to come.

Psa. 90.10. The days of our years *are* threescore years and ten; and if by reason of strength *they* be fourscore years, yet *is* their strength labour and sorrow; for it is soon cut off, and we fly away. Gen. 47.9. Ecc. 6.3.

Psa. 92.14. They shall still bring forth fruit in old age; they shall be fat and flourishing. Psa. 148.12. Old men, and children: 13. Let them praise the name of the Lord.

Pro. 16.31. The hoary head *is* a crown of glory, *if* it be found in the way of righteousness. Pro. 17.6. Pro. 20.29.

Ecc. 12.1. While the evil days come not, nor the years draw nigh, when thou shalt say, I have no pleasure in them; 2. While the

sun, or the light, or the moon, or the stars, be not darkened. *v.* 1-6. Gen. 27.2. Deu. 34.7. 2 Sam. 19.35.

Isa. 46.4. *Even* to *your* old age I *am* he; and *even* to hoar hairs will I carry *you*: I have made, and I will bear; even I will carry, and will deliver *you*.

Tit. 2.2. That the aged men be sober, grave, temperate, sound in faith, in charity, in patience. 3. The aged women likewise, that *they be* in behaviour as becometh holiness, not false accusers, not given to much wine, teachers of good things. Philm. 9. Luk. 2.37.

OLIVE-TREE. Cultivated in Palestine, Ex. 23.11. Deu. 6.11. Deu. 8.8. Jos. 24.13. 1 Chr. 27.28; and Assyria, 2 Kin. 18.32. Its beauty, Jer. 11.16. Hos. 14.6. Flowering of, Job 15.33. Beaten to remove the fruit, Deu. 24.20. Isa. 17.6. Isa. 24.13. Fruit beaten to extract the oil, Ex. 27.20; also pressed, Joel 2.24; Hag. 2.16; or trodden, Mic. 6.15. Wood of, 1 Kin. 6.23,31-33. Dove plucked a twig from, Gen. 8.11. Booths of, Neh. 8.15. Parable of, Jud. 9.8. Illustrative, Psa. 52.8. Psa. 128.3. Jer. 11.16. Rom. 11.17,24. Symbolical, Zec. 4.3-12. Rev. 11.4.

See OIL, OLIVE. Olive-yard, see VINE-YARD.

OLIVES, MOUNT OF, or OLIVET, east of Jerusalem, Eze. 11.23. Olive-trees on, Neh. 8.15. David flees from Absalom by, 2 Sam. 15.30. Christ enters Jerusalem from. Mat. 21.1. Mar. 11.1. Luk. 19.29,37. Teaches from, Mat. 24.3. Mar. 13.3. Retires to, Luk. 21.37. Jno. 8.1. Retires to, from the passover-feast, Luk. 22.39. Mat. 26.30. Mar. 14.26, see GETHSEMANE. Ascends from, Act. 1.12. Prophecy of, Zec. 14.4. Eze. 11.23. Called Mount of Corruption, from idolatry practised on, by Solomon, 2 Kin. 23.13 (*marg.*), 1 Kin. 11.7.

OMEGA, the last letter of the Greek alphabet, poetically used for 'the last;' applied to Christ, Rev. 1.8,11. Rev. 21.6. Rev. 22.13.

OMER, 10th of an ephah, about seven pints, Ex. 16.36. An omer of manna gathered for every Israelite; 2 on the 6th day, Ex. 16.16-18, 22. An omer of, laid up in the ark, Ex. 16. 32-33.

OMRI, 8th king of Israel (12 years' reign), made king when Elah was slain by Zimri; defeats Zimri, Tibni, &c., 1 Kin. 16.16-23. Founds Samaria, 1 Kin. 16.24. His idolatry and death, 1 Kin. 16.25-28. Mic. 6.16.

ON (sun), a city of Egypt, supposed to be Heliopolis (city of the sun), Gen. 41.45,50. Gen. 46.20. Beth-shemesh (house of the sun), supposed to be the same, Jer. 43.13.

————, a Reubenite, a conspirator with Korah against Moses, Num. 16.1.

ONAN, son of Judah, Gen. 38.4-9. Gen. 46.12. Num. 26.19. 1 Chr. 2.3.

ONESIMUS, a runaway slave; converted by Paul, who returns him to his master with a letter interceding for him, Philm. Col. 4.9.

ONESIPHORUS, his kindness to Paul, 2 Tim. 1.16-18. 2 Tim. 4.19.

ONION, Num. 11.5.

ONO, a city of Benjamin, in the valley of Charashim, 1 Chr. 8.12. Neh. 6.2. Neh. 11.35.

ONYCHA, the shell of a species of mussel, which emits a musky odour in burning, Ex. 30.34.

ONYX, a precious stone, Job 28.16. Found in Havilah, Gen. 2.12. Two of, set in the high-priest's ephod, graven with the names of the 12 tribes, Ex. 28.9-12. Ex. 39.6. Set in his breastplate, Ex. 28.20. Ex. 39.13. Brought by Israelites to Moses, Ex. 25.7. Ex. 35.9. Worn by Tyrians, Eze. 28.13.

OPHEL, a wall, tower, and suburb of Jerusalem, 2 Chr. 27.3. 2 Chr. 33.14. Neh. 3. 26,27. Neh. 11.21.

OPHIR, son of Joktan, a descendant of Shem, Gen. 10.29. 1 Chr. 1.23.

——, a gold country, Job 22.24. Job 28.16. Psa. 45.9. Gold brought from, by Solomon, 1 Kin. 9.28. 1 Chr. 29.4. 2 Chr. 8.18. 2 Chr. 9.10 ; and Hiram, with precious stones and almug-trees, 1 Kin. 10.11. Jehoshaphat's ships sail for, 1 Kin. 22.48. Gold of, sold in wedges, Isa. 13.12. See UPHAZ.

OPHRAH, a town of Benjamin, Jos. 18.23. Gideon visited by an angel in, Jud. 6.11 ; builds an altar in, Jud. 6.24. His ephod worshipped in, Jud. 8.27. He is buried in, Jud. 8.32. Abimelech slays his brethren in, Jud. 9.5. The Philistines plunder, 1 Sam. 13.17.

OPPRESSION. See RULERS, TYRRANICAL —POOR, UNKINDNESS TO—MASTERS.

ORACLE, a name of the most holy place, 1 Kin. 6.5. Psa. 28.2. A name of the Scriptures, Act. 7.38. Rom. 3.2. Heb. 5.12. 1 Pet. 4.11.

ORATOR, an advocate or pleader, Act. 24.1. Isa. 3.3.

ORDINATION. 1. (Gr. *kathistemi*), of elders, Tit. 1.5. Elsewhere translated, to make, Mat. 24.47 ; to appoint, Act. 6.3. 2. (Gr. *kcirotones*), Act. 14.23. Translated choose, 2 Cor. 8.19. See PRIESTS—LEVITES—CHURCH-GOVERNMENT.

OREB, a Midianitish prince, slain on the rock Oreb by the Ephraimites, Jud. 7.25. Jud. 8.3. Psa. 83.11. Isa. 10.26.

ORGAN, a pipe or reed, invented by Jubal, Gen. 4.21. Used in entertainments, Job 21.12. Job 30.31 ; in praise, Psa. 150.4. See FLUTE —PIPE.

ORIGINAL SIN. See MAN'S NATURAL STATE—FALL, THE—SINNERS, CHARACTER OF.

ORION, Job 9.9. Job 38.31. Amos 5.8. Translated constellations, Isa. 13.10.

ORNAMENTS. See DRESS—JEWELS.

ORNAN. See ARAUNAH.

ORPAH, wife of Mahlon, leaves Naomi and returns to Moab, Ruth 1.1-14.

ORPHANS. See WIDOWS.

OSPREY, a kind of eagle or hawk, Lev. 11.13. Deu. 14.12.

OSSIFRAGE, a large eagle, Lev. 11.13. Deu. 14.12.

OSTRICH, Job 39.13-18. Lam. 4.3. Isa. 13.21 (*marg.*). Isa. 34.13 (*marg.*). Isa. 43.20 (*marg.*).

OTHNIEL, a judge of Israel, conquers Kirjath-sepher, and receives Caleb's daughter, Jos.

15.16-20. Jud. 1.13,14. 1 Chr. 4.13. Delivers Israel from Chushan, and judges Israel 40 years, Jud. 3.9,10.

OUCHES, sockets in which precious stones are set, Ex. 28.11.

OVEN. See FURNACE.

OVERSEER (Gr. *Episkopos*), Act. 20.28. Translated bishop, Phil. 1.1. 1 Tim. 3.2. Tit. 1.7. 1 Pet. 2.25.

OWL, different words are so translated, (1.) Lev. 11.17. Deu. 14.16. Psa. 102.6. (2.) Deu. 14.15. (3.) Lev. 11.16. Deu. 14.15. Job 30.29. Isa. 34.11. Isa. 34.13. Isa. 43.20. Jer. 50.39. Mic. 1.8. (4.) Great owl, Lev. 11.17. Deu. 14.16. Isa. 34.11. (5.) Great owl, Isa. 34.15. (6.) Screech owl (*marg.*), night-monster), Isa. 34.14.

OX. See BULL.

P

PADAN-ARAM. See MESOPOTAMIA.

PAINTING. Of the face, 2 Kin. 9.30 (*marg.* eyes), Jer. 4.30. Of the eyes, Eze. 23.40. Of rooms, Jer. 22.14. See PICTURES.

PALACES, 1 Kin. 21.1. 2 Kin. 15.25. Ezr. 6.2. Jer. 49.27. Amos 1.12. Amos 2.2. Amos 3.9. Nah. 2.6. At Jerusalem, of David, 2 Sam. 7.2 ; of Solomon, 1 Kin. 7.1-12. At Babylon, Dan. 4.29. Dan. 5.5. Dan. 6.18. At Shushan, Neh. 1.1. Est. 1.2. Est. 7.7. Dan. 8.2.

Of ivory, 1 Kin. 22.39. Psa. 45.8. A garden-house, 2 Kin. 9.27. Summer-house, Amos 3.15. Winter-house, Jer. 36.22. Palace contained the royal treasures and decrees, 1 Kin. 15.18. Ezr. 6.2.

PALESTINE, called Canaan, Gen. 11.31; Palestina, Ex. 15.14 ; land of Israel, 1 Sam. 13.19 ; of the Hebrews, Gen. 40.15 ; of the Jews, Act. 10.39 ; of promise, Heb. 11.9 Holy land, Zec. 2.12. Pleasant land, Dan. 8.9. Glorious land, Dan. 11.16. The Lord's land, Hos. 9.3. Immanuel's land, Isa. 8.8. Beulah and Hephzibah, Isa. 62.4.

Boundaries of, Jos. 15.1. Jos. c. 16 to 19 ; in Solomon's time, 1 Kin. 4.21,24. 2 Chr. 9. 26 ; as predicted, Gen. 15.18. Ex. 23.31. Num. 34. Deu. 11.24. Jos. 1.3,4.

Divided among the 12 tribes, Jos. c. 14-19. Into 12 provinces by Solomon, 1 Kin. 4.7-19. Into 2 kingdoms, Judah & Israel, 1 Kin. 11. 35,36. 1 Kin. 12.16-21. Roman provinces of, Luk. 3.1. Jno. 4.4. Provinces and districts of, see ABILENE, GALILEE, GILEAD, ITUREA, JUDEA, SAMARIA, TRACHONITIS.

Description of, Gen. 13.10. Deu. 8.7-10. Deu. 11.10-12.

——, CAVES OF. See ADULLAM, EN-GEDI, MACHPELAH, MAKKEDAH.

PALESTINE, CITIES, TOWNS, AND DIS-TRICTS OF, Num. 32. Jos. c. 12 to 21. Jud. 1. 1 Kin. 4. 2 Kin. 15.29. 1 Chr. c. 4 to 8. 1 Chr. 11.26-47. 2 Chr. 8.2-6. 2 Chr. 11.6-10. Ezr. 2. Neh. 3.7-19. Neh. 11.21-36. See ABEL, ABEL-MEHOLAH, ABEL-MIZRAIM, ACCHO, ACHZIB, ADAM, ADMAH, AI, ANTI-PATRIS, APHEK, ARAD, ARIMATHEA, AROER, ARUMAH, ASHTAROTH, AZEKAH, BAAL-GAD, BAAL-HAMON, BAAL-HAZOR, BAAL-HERMON. BAAL-MEON, BAAL-PERAZIM,

BAAL-SHALISHA, BAAL-TAMAR, BAHURIM, BEEROTH, BEERSHEBA, BETHABARA, BETHANY, BETH-ARBEL, BETH-AVEN, BETHEL, BETH-HORON, BETHLEHEM, BETHPHAGE, BETHSAIDA, BETHSHAN, BEZEK, BOCHIM, CABUL, CANA, CAPERNAUM, CARMEL, CESAREA, CESAREA PHILIPPI, CHORAZIN, CINNEROTH, DALMANUTHA, DAN, DECAPOLIS, DOR, DOTHAN, EDREI, ELKOSH, EMMAUS, ENDOR, EN-GEDI, ENON, EPHRAIM, ESHTAOL, GADARENES, GEBIM, GEDEROTH, GESHUR, GILEAD, GILGAL, GOMORRAH, GOSHEN, HAVOTH-JAIR, HELKATH-HAZZURIM, JABESH-GILEAD, JEHOVAH-JIREH, JERICHO, JERUSALEM, JOPPA, KEILAH, KERIOTH, KIRJATH-AIM, KIRJATH-JEARIM, LACHISH, LYDDA.

MAGDALA, MAKKEDAH, MAON, MARESHAH, MEGIDDO, MEROZ, MICHMASH, MIGRON, MILLO, MISREPHOTH, MIZPEH, NAIN, NAIOTH, NAZARETH, NEBO, ONO, OPHRAH, PENIEL, PEREZ-UZZAH, PIRATHON, RAMAH, RAMATHAIM, RAMATH-LEHI, RIBLAH, RIMMON, SALIM, SALT, SAMARIA, SHAALBIM, SHALIM, SHALISHA, SHAMIR, SHARON, SHILOH, SHOCHOH, SHUNEM, SHUR, SUCCOTH, TADMOR, TAPPUAH, TEKOAH, TELEM, THEBEZ, TIBERIAS, TIMNATH, TIPHSAH, TIRZAH, ZARETAN, ZEBOIM, ZIKLAG, ZIPH, ZOAR, ZORAH. See also MOABITES—PHILISTINES, TOWNS OF.

Levitical cities, Jos. 21. 1 Chr. 6.54-81. See AJALON, ANATHOTH, BETHSHEMESH, DEBIR, GEZER, GIBBETHON, GATH-RIMMON, GIBEAH, GIBEON, HESHBON, JAZER, KEDEMOTH, LIBNAH, MAHANAIM, NOB, REHOB, TAANACH, TABOR; with the cities of refuge, BEZOR, GOLAN, HEBRON, KEDESH-NAPHTALI, RAMOTH-GILEAD, SHECHEM.

PALESTINE, DESERTS OF. See BEERSHEBA, BETH-AVEN, EN-GEDI, GAZA, JESHIMON, JUDEA, KEDEMOTH, MAON, TEKOAH, ZIPH.

———, MOUNTAINS, HILLS, AND ROCKS OF. See ABEL, AMMAR, BAAL-PERAZIM, BASHAN, BETHEL, BETHER, BETH-HACCEREM, CARMEL, EBAL, EPHRAIM, GAASH, GAREB, GERIZIM, GILBOA, GILEAD, HACHILAH, HERES, HERMON, JUDEA, LEBANON, MIZAR, MOREH, MORIAH, OLIVES, OREB, RIMMON, SAMARIA, SENEH, TABOR, ZALMON, ZEMARIM, ZION, ZIZ.

———, RIVERS AND BROOKS OF. See BESOR, CEDRON, CHERITH, EGYPT, JABBOK, JORDAN, KANAH, KISHON, NEPHTOAH, NIMRIM.

———, SEAS AND LAKES OF. See DEAD SEA, GALILEE, JAZER, MEDITERRANEAN, MEROM.

———, TOWERS OF. See EDAR, LEBANON, JERUSALEM, TOWERS IN.

———, VALLEYS AND PLAINS OF. See ACHOR, AJALON, AVEN, BACA, BERACHAH, CHARASHIM, ELAH, ESHCOL, GEDOR, GERAR, JEHOSHAPHAT, JERICHO, JEZREEL, JORDAN, LEBANON, MAMRE, MEGIDDO, MIZPEH, MOAB, MOREH, REPHAIM, SALT, SHAVEH, SHITTIM, SIDDIM, SOREK, SUCCOTH, TABOR, ZEPHATHAH.

———, WELLS AND FOUNTAINS OF. See BEER-LAHAI-ROI, BEERSHEBA, BETHESDA, BETHLEHEM, ENON, ENROGEL, GIBEON, GIHON, HAROD, HEBRON, JACOB, JERICHO, JEZREEL, MEGIDDO, REHOBOTH, SILOAM, SITNAH.

PALESTINE, WOODS AND FORESTS OF. See EPHRAIM, HARETH.

PALM-TREE. Song 7.7,8. Jer. 10.5. Joel 1.12. 70 at Elim, Ex. 15.27. Deborah judged under, Jud. 4.5. Jericho the city of, Deu. 34.3. Booths made of, Lev. 23.40. Neh. 8.15. Carvings of. in the temple, 1 Kin. 6.29,32,35. 2 Chr. 3.5. Eze. 40.16. Eze. 41.18. Branches carried in procession, Jno. 12.13. Illustrative, Psa. 92.12. Rev. 7.9.

PALMER-WORM, a kind of locust, Joel 1.4. Joel 2.25. Amos 4.9.

PALSY cured by Jesus, Mat. 4.24. Mat. 8.6,13. Mat. 9.2,6; by Philip, Act. 8.7; Peter, Act. 9.33,34.

PAMPHYLIA, a province in the south of Asia Minor. Strangers from, at Jerusalem, Act. 2.10. Paul visits, Act. 13.13. Act. 14.24. Act. 27.5. Towns of, see PERGA, ATTALIA.

PANNAG (sweet cake), Eze. 17.27.

PAPER, 2 Jno. 12. Paper reeds, Isa. 19.7. See BOOKS—PARCHMENT.

PAPHOS, a city of Cyprus on the west: Paul visits; Elymas struck blind; Sergius Paulus converted at, Act. 13.6-12.

PARABLES. Jotham's parable of the trees, Jud. 9.8-15. The poor man's ewe-lamb, 2 Sam. 12.1-6. Parable by the woman of Tekoah, 2 Sam. 14.5-12. By a prophet to Ahab, 1 Kin. 20.39-42. Of the thistle and cedar, 2 Kin. 14.9. A vine from Egypt, Psa. 80.8-16. Wisdom personified, Pro. 8. Pro. 9. The vineyard, Isa. 5.1-7. The husbandman, Isa. 28.23-29. Bottles filled with wine, Jer. 13. 12-14. A vine branch, Eze. 15. Two eagles and a vine, Eze. 17. Lions' whelps, Eze. 19. 1-9. A wasted vine, Eze. 19.10-14. Aholah, and Aholibah, Eze. 23. Holy flesh, Hag. 2. 11-14. See CHRIST, PARABLES OF—RIDDLE —SYMBOLS.

PARADISE, or THE GARDEN OF EDEN, Gen. 2.8-14. Isa. 51.3. Eze. 28.13. Eze. 31. 9,16,18. Eze. 36.35. Joel 2.3. Adam and Eve placed in, Gen. 2.8,15,16; and driven from, Gen. 3.23. Guarded by cherubim, Gen. 3.24. Name of heaven, Luk. 23.43. 2 Cor. 12.4, see v. 2. Rev. 2.7, see Rev. 22.1,2.

PARAN, a desert extending from the south of Judah to Sinai, Num. 10.12. Num. 13.26. Ishmael dwells in, Gen. 21.21. Israelites send the spies from, Num. 12.16. Receive the law a second time in, Deu. 1.1. Deu. 33.2. Hab. 3.3. David dwells in, 1 Sam. 25.1. Hadad flees to, 1 Kin. 11.18.

PARCEL, Gen. 33.19. Jno. 4.5. Translated field, 2 Sam. 14.30; piece, 2 Sam. 23.11; portion, 2 Kin. 9.21; plat, 2 Kin. 9.26.

PARCHMENTS, of Paul, 2 Tim. 4.13. See BOOKS—PAPER.

PARDON. See GOD'S MERCY—GOD SAVIOUR — SALVATION — REPENTANCE — JUSTIFICATION.

PARDON THROUGH CHRIST. Mat. 1.21. Thou shalt call his name JESUS: for he shall save his people from their sins.

Luk. 24.47. That repentance and remission

of sins should be preached in his name among all nations, beginning at Jerusalem.

Act. 2.38. Repent, and be baptized every one of you in the name of Jesus Christ for the remission of sins.

Act. 10.36. *God* sent unto the children of Israel, preaching peace by Jesus Christ: (he is Lord of all.) 43. Through his name whosoever believeth in him shall receive remission of sins.

Act. 13.38. Through this man is preached unto you the forgiveness of sins: 39. And by him all that believe are justified from all things, from which ye could not be justified by the law of Moses.

Act. 26.18. To turn *them* from darkness to light, and *from* the power of Satan unto God, that they may receive forgiveness of sins, and inheritance among them which are sanctified by faith that is in me.

Eph. 4.32. God for Christ's sake hath forgiven you.

Col. 2.13. You, being dead in your sins and the uncircumcision of your flesh, hath he quickened together with him, having forgiven you all trespasses.

1 Jno. 2.12. Your sins are forgiven you for his name's sake.

See CHRIST'S DEATH, ITS DESIGN—CHRIST, PARDON FROM—CHRIST SAVIOUR.

PARDON AND SALVATION. PRAYER FOR.
Ex. 32.31. Oh! this people have sinned a great sin, and have made them gods of gold. 32. Yet now, if thou wilt forgive their sin.

Ex. 34.9. If now I have found grace in thy sight, O Lord, let my Lord, I pray thee, go among us; for it *is* a stiffnecked people; and pardon our iniquity and our sin, and take us for thine inheritance.

Num. 14.19. Pardon, I beseech thee, the iniquity of this people, according unto the greatness of thy mercy, and as thou hast forgiven this people from Egypt even until now. 20. And the Lord said, I have pardoned according to thy word.

2 Sam. 24.10. I have sinned greatly in that I have done: and now, I beseech thee, O Lord, take away the iniquity of thy servant; for I have done very foolishly.

1 Kin. 8.38. What prayer and supplication soever be *made* by any man, *or* by all thy people Israel, which shall know every man the plague of his own heart, and spread forth his hands towards this house: 39. Then hear thou in heaven thy dwelling-place, and forgive, and do, and give to every man according to his ways, whose heart thou knowest; (for thou, *even* thou only, knowest the hearts of all the children of men.)

1 Kin. 8.47. *Yet* if they shall bethink themselves in the land whither they were carried captives, and repent, and make supplication unto thee in the land of them that carried them captives, saying, We have sinned, and have done perversely, we have committed wickedness; 48. And *so* return unto thee with all their heart, and with all their soul, in the land of their enemies, which led them away captive, and pray unto thee toward their land, which thou gavest unto their fathers, the city which thou hast chosen, and the house which I have built for thy name. 49. Then hear thou their prayer and their supplication in heaven

thy dwelling-place, and maintain their cause, 50. And forgive thy people that have sinned against thee, and all their transgressions wherein they have transgressed against thee. *v.* 30-50.

2 Chr. 30.18. The good Lord pardon every one 19. *That* prepareth his heart to seek God, the Lord God of his fathers.

Neh. 13.22. Spare me according to the greatness of thy mercy.

Psa. 6.2. Have mercy upon me, O Lord; for I *am* weak: O Lord, heal me; for my bones are vexed. 4. Return, O Lord, deliver my soul: Oh save me for thy mercies' sake.

Psa. 14.7. Oh that the salvation of Israel *were come* out of Zion!

Psa. 19.12. Who can understand *his* errors? cleanse thou me from secret *faults.*

Psa. 25.5. Lead me in thy truth, and teach me: for thou *art* the God of my salvation; on thee do I wait all the day. 6. Remember, O Lord, thy tender mercies, and thy loving-kindnesses; for they *have been* ever of old. 7. Remember not the sins of my youth, nor my transgressions: according to thy mercy remember thou me for thy goodness' sake, O Lord. 11. For thy name's sake, O Lord, pardon mine iniquity; for it *is* great. 18. Look upon mine affliction and my pain; and forgive all my sins.

Psa. 26.11. Redeem me, and be merciful unto me.

Psa. 27.7. Hear, O Lord, *when* I cry with my voice: have mercy also upon me, and answer me.

Psa. 28.9. Save thy people, and bless thine inheritance: feed them also, and lift them up for ever.

Psa. 30.10. Hear, O Lord, and have mercy upon me: Lord, be thou my helper.

Psa. 31.16. Make thy face to shine upon thy servant: save me for thy mercies' sake.

Psa. 33.22. Let thy mercy, O Lord, be upon us, according as we hope in thee.

Psa. 35.3. Say unto my soul, I *am* thy salvation.

Psa. 38.22. Make haste to help me, O Lord my salvation.

Psa. 39.8. Deliver me from all my transgressions: make me not the reproach of the foolish.

Psa. 40.11. Withhold not thou thy tender mercies from me, O Lord: let thy loving-kindness and thy truth continually preserve me.

Psa. 41.4. Lord, be merciful unto me: heal my soul; for I have sinned against thee. 10. But thou, O Lord, be merciful unto me, and raise me up.

Psa. 44.26. Arise for our help, and redeem us, for thy mercies' sake.

Psa. 51.1. Have mercy upon me, O God, according to thy loving kindness: according unto the multitude of thy tender mercies blot out my transgressions. 2. Wash me throughly from mine iniquity, and cleanse me from my sin. 3. For I acknowledge my transgressions: and my sin *is* ever before me. 7. Purge me with hyssop, and I shall be clean: wash me, and I shall be whiter than snow. 8. Make me to hear joy and gladness; *that* the bones *which* thou hast broken may rejoice. 9. Hide thy face from my sins, and blot out all mine iniquities. 14. Deliver me from bloodguiltiness, O God, thou God of my salvation: *and* my tongue shall sing aloud of thy righteousness.

Psa. 69.29. I *am* poor and sorrowful : let thy salvation, O God, set me up on high.

Psa. 71.2. Deliver me in thy righteousness, and cause me to escape : incline thine ear unto me, and save me.

Psa. 79.8. O remember not against us former iniquities : let thy tender mercies speedily prevent us : for we are brought very low. 9. Help us, O God of our salvation, for the glory of thy name : and deliver us, and purge away our sins, for thy name's sake.

Psa. 80.2. Stir up thy strength, and come *and* save us. 3. Turn us again, O God, and cause thy face to shine ; and we shall be saved. 4. O Lord God of hosts, how long wilt thou be angry against the prayer of thy people ?

Psa. 85.4. Turn us, O God of our salvation, and cause thine anger toward us to cease. 7. Shew us thy mercy, O Lord, and grant us thy salvation.

Psa. 86.2. O thou my God, save thy servant that trusteth in thee. 3. Be merciful unto me, O Lord : for I cry unto thee daily. 16. O turn unto me, and have mercy upon me ; give thy strength unto thy servant, and save the son of thine handmaid.

Psa. 90.13. Return, O Lord, how long? and let it repent thee concerning thy servants. 14. O satisfy us early with thy mercy ; that we may rejoice and be glad all our days.

Psa. 118.25. Save now, I beseech thee, O Lord : O Lord, I beseech thee, send now prosperity.

Psa. 119.41. Let thy mercies come also unto me, O Lord, *even* thy salvation, according to thy word. 58. I entreated thy favour with *my* whole heart : be merciful unto me according to thy word. 77. Let thy tender mercies come unto me, that I may live. 94. I *am* thine, save me ; for I have sought thy precepts. 124. Deal with thy servant according unto thy mercy. 132. Look thou upon me, and be merciful unto me, as thou usest to do unto those that love thy name.

Psa. 119.146. I cried unto thee ; save me, and I shall keep thy testimonies. 174. I have longed for thy salvation, O Lord ; and thy law *is* my delight. 175. Let my soul live, and it shall praise thee ; and let thy judgments help me. 176. I have gone astray like a lost sheep ; seek thy servant ; for I do not forget thy commandments.

Psa. 123.3. Have mercy upon us, O Lord, have mercy upon us.

Psa. 138.8. Thy mercy, O Lord, *endureth* for ever : forsake not the works of thine own hands.

Psa. 143.1. Hear my prayer, O Lord, give ear to my supplications : in thy faithfulness answer me, *and* in thy righteousness. 2. And enter not into judgment with thy servant ; for in thy sight shall no man living be justified.

Isa. 64.9. Be not wroth very sore, O Lord, neither remember iniquity for ever : behold, see, we beseech thee, we *are* all thy people.

Jer. 14.7. O Lord, though our iniquities testify against us, do thou *it* for thy name's sake : for our backslidings are many ; we have sinned against thee. 21. Do not abhor *us*, for thy name's sake, do not disgrace the throne of thy glory : remember, break not thy covenant with us. *v.* 20.

Jer. 17.14. Heal me, O Lord, and I shall be healed ; save me, and I shall be saved : for thou *art* my praise.

Dan. 9.18. O my God, incline thine ear, and hear ; open thine eyes, and behold our desolations, and the city which is called by thy name : for we do not present our supplications before thee for our righteousnesses, but for thy great mercies. 19. O Lord, hear ; O Lord, forgive ; O Lord, hearken and do ; defer not, for thine own sake, O my God : for thy city and thy people are called by thy name. *v.* 15-17.

Hos. 14.2. Say unto him, Take away all iniquity, and receive *us* graciously : so will we render the calves of our lips.

Amos 7.2. O Lord God, forgive, I beseech thee : by whom shall Jacob arise? for he *is* small.

Hab. 3.2. O Lord, revive thy work in the midst of the years, in the midst of the years make known ; in wrath remember mercy.

Mat. 6.12. Forgive our debts as we forgive our debtors.

Luk. 18.13. The publican, standing afar off, would not lift up so much as *his* eyes unto heaven, but smote upon his breast, saying, God be merciful to me a sinner.

Luk. 23.42. He said unto Jesus, Lord, remember me when thou comest into thy kingdom. 43. And Jesus said unto him, Verily I say unto thee, To day shalt thou be with me in paradise.

Jno. 6.34. Lord, evermore give us this bread.

2 Tim. 1.18. The Lord grant unto him that he may find mercy of the Lord in that day.

See SPIRITUAL BLESSINGS, PRAYER FOR— REPENTANCE.

PARENTS. Gen. 18.19. I know him, that he will command his children and his household after him, and they shall keep the way of the Lord.

Ex. 13.14. When thy son asketh thee in time to come, saying, What *is* this? thou shalt say unto him, By strength of hand the Lord brought us out from Egypt, from the house of bondage. *v.* 8. Ex. 10.2. Ex. 12. 26,27. Jos. 4.6,7,21-24.

Ex. 20.10. The sabbath of the Lord thy God : *in it* thou shalt not do any work, thou, nor thy son, nor thy daughter.

Lev. 23.3. It *is* the sabbath of the Lord in all your dwellings.

Deu. 4.9. Keep thy soul diligently, lest thou forget the things which thine eyes have seen : but teach them thy sons, and thy sons' sons ; 10. I will make them hear my words, that they may learn to fear me all the days that they shall live upon the earth, and *that* they may teach their children.

Deu. 6.7. Thou shalt teach them diligently unto thy children, and shalt talk of them when thou sittest in thine house, and when thou walkest by the way, and when thou liest down, and when thou risest up. *v.* 20-25. Deu. 11.19.

Deu. 31.12. Gather the people together, men, and women, and children, and thy stranger that *is* within thy gates, that they may hear, and that they may learn, and fear the Lord your God, and observe to do all the words of this law : 13. And *that* their children, which have not known *any thing*, may hear, and learn to fear the Lord your God.

Deu. 32.46. Set your hearts unto all the words which I testify among you this day, which ye shall command your children to observe to do, all the words of this law.

Psa. 78.5. A law in Israel, which he commanded our fathers, that they should make them known to their children: 6. That the generation to come might know them, even the children which should be born; who should arise and declare them to their children.

Psa. 103.13. Like as a father pitieth his children, so the Lord pitieth them that fear him.

Pro. 3.12. Whom the Lord loveth he correcteth; even as a father the son in whom he delighteth.

Pro. 13.22. A good man leaveth an inheritance to his children's children. 24. He that spareth his rod hateth his son: but he that loveth him chasteneth him betimes.

Pro. 19.18. Chasten thy son while there is hope, and let not thy soul spare for his crying.

Pro. 22.6. Train up a child in the way he should go: and when he is old, he will not depart from it. 15. Foolishness is bound in the heart of a child; but the rod of correction shall drive it far from him.

Pro. 23.13. Withhold not correction from the child: for if thou beatest him with the rod, he shall not die. 14. Thou shalt beat him with the rod, and shalt deliver his soul from hell.

Pro. 29.15. The rod and reproof give wisdom: but a child left to himself bringeth his mother to shame. 17. Correct thy son, and he shall give thee rest; yea, he shall give delight unto thy soul.

Pro. 31.28. Her children arise up, and call her blessed.

Isa. 38.19. The father to the children shall make known thy truth.

Isa. 49.15. Can a woman forget her sucking child, that she should not have compassion on the son of her womb?

Isa. 66.13. As one whom his mother comforteth, so will I comfort you.

Jer. 31.1. Will I be the God of all the families of Israel, and they shall be my people?

Jer. 49.11. Leave thy fatherless children, I will preserve them alive.

Joel 1.3. Tell ye your children of it, and let your children tell their children, and their children another generation.

Mal. 4.6. He shall turn the heart of the fathers to the children, lest I come and smite the earth with a curse.

Mat. 10.37. He that loveth son or daughter more than me is not worthy of me.

Luk. 11.11. If a son shall ask bread of any of you that is a father, will he give him a stone? 13. Ye then, being evil, know how to give good gifts unto your children.

2 Cor. 12.14. The children ought not to lay up for the parents, but the parents for the children.

Eph. 6.4. Fathers, provoke not your children to wrath: but bring them up in the nurture and admonition of the Lord.

Col. 3.21. Fathers, provoke not your children to anger, lest they be discouraged.

1 The: 2.11. Ye know how we exhorted and comforted and charged every one of you, as a father doth his children.

1 Tim. 3.4. One that ruleth well his own house, having his children in subjection with all gravity; 12. Let the deacons be the hus-

bands of one wife, ruling their children and their own houses well.

1 Tim. 5.8. If any provide not for his own, and specially for those of his own house, he hath denied the faith, and is worse than an infidel.

Tit. 2.4. Teach the young women to be sober, to love their husbands, to love their children.

Heb. 12.7. What son is he whom the father chasteneth not?

See CHILDREN.

PARENTS' AFFECTION, EXAMPLES OF:
1 Kin. 3.16-28. Hagar, Gen. 21.16. Rebekah, Gen. 27.46. Jacob, Gen. 32.11. Gen. 33.5. Gen. 42.4. Gen. 43.14. Gen. 44.22,30. Gen. 45.28. Gen. 46.30. Jochebed, Ex. 2. Naomi, Ruth 1.8,9. Hannah, 1 Sam. 2.19. David, 2 Sam. 12.16,17. 2 Sam. 18.5,32,33. Bathsheba, Prov. 4.3. Rizpah, 2 Sam. 21.10. Mary, Mat. 12.46. Luk. 2.48. Jno. 2.5. Jno. 19.25. Jairus, Mar. 5.23. Father of demoniac, Mar. 9.24. Nobleman, Jno. 4.49.

———, INDULGENT, EXAMPLES OF: Isaac and Rebekah, Gen. 25.28. Gen. 27.6-17. Jacob, Gen. 37.3,4. Micah's mother, Jud. 17.3. Eli, 1 Sam. 2.27-36. 1 Sam. 3.13,14. David, 1 Kin. 1.6.

———, PIETY AND WATCHFULNESS, EXAMPLES OF: Abraham, Gen. 18.19. Gen. 24.2-4. Isaac, Gen. 28.1,2; see Gen. 27.46. Reubenites, Jos. 22.24-28. Israelites, Jos. 8.35. Psa. 44.1. Psa. 78.2-4. Jews, 2 Chr. 20.13. Ezr. 10.1. Neh. 10.30. Neh. 12.43. Joshua, Jos. 24.15. Manoah, Jud. 13.8,12. Hannah, 1 Sam. 1.27,28. Eli, 1 Sam. 2.23,24. David, 1 Kin. 2.1-3. 1 Chr. 22.11-13. 1 Chr. 28.9. Pro. 4.4. Mother of Lemuel, Pro. 31.1. Solomon, Pro. 4.10,11. Mary, Luk. 2.19,51. Mothers in Jerusalem, Luk. 18.15. Lois and Eunice, 2 Tim. 1.5. 2 Tim. 3.15. Moses' parents, Heb. 11.23.

———, PRAYERS AND BLESSINGS OF, EXAMPLES OF: Abraham, Gen. 17.18. Isaac, Gen. 27.28,29,39,40. Gen. 28.3,4. Jacob, Gen. 48.15-20. Gen. 49. Hannah, 1 Sam. 1.27. David, 2 Sam. 7.25-29. 1 Chr. 17.16-27. 2 Sam. 12.16. 1 Chr. 22.12. 1 Chr. 29.19. Job, Job 1.5.

PARENTS, WARNINGS TO. Ex. 20.5. Visiting the iniquity of the fathers upon the children unto the third and fourth generation of them that hate me.

Isa. 14.20. The seed of evildoers shall never be renowned. 21. Prepare slaughter for his children for the iniquity of their fathers; that they do not rise, nor possess the land, nor fill the face of the world with cities.

Jer. 9.14. Have walked after the imagination of their own heart, and after Baalim, which their fathers taught them.

Jer. 10.25. Pour out thy fury upon the heathen that know thee not, and upon the families that call not on thy name.

Lam. 5.7. Our fathers have sinned, and are not; and we have borne their iniquities.

Eze. 16.44. As is the mother, so is her daughter. 45. Thou art thy mother's daughter, that loatheth her husband and her children; and thou art the sister of thy sisters, which loathed their husbands and their children.

Eze. 20.18. Walk ye not in the statutes of

your fathers, neither observe their judgments, nor defile yourselves with their idols.

Amos 2.4. Their lies caused them to err, after the which their fathers have walked.

See SIN, HEREDITARY CONSEQUENCES OF.

PARENTS, WICKED, EXAMPLES OF: Saul, 1 Sam. 20.32,33. Rehoboam, 1 Kin. 15.3. Maacah, 1 Kin. 15.13. Ahab and Jezebel, 1 Kin. 22.52. King of Moab, 2 Kin. 3.27. A mother in Jerusalem, 1 Kin. 3.20,26; in Samaria, 2 Kin. 6.28,29. Manasseh, 2 Kin. 21.6. Jehoiakim, 2 Kin. 24.9. Athaliah, 2 Chr. 22.2,3,10. Herodias, Mat. 14.8.

PARMENAS, one of the seven deacons, Act. 6.5.

PARTHIANS in Jerusalem at Pentecost, Act. 2.9.

PARTRIDGE, 1 Sam. 26.20. Jer. 17.11.

PARVAIM, a gold country, 2 Chr. 3.6.

PASHUR, chief-governor of the temple, imprisons Jeremiah, who names him Magor-missabib (fear round about), and predicts his death in Babylon, Jer. 20.1-6.

——, son of Melchiah, visits Jeremiah, Jer. 21.1. Procures his imprisonment, Jer. 38.1-6.

PASSION, signifies suffering, and is applied to Christ's death in, Act. 1.3.

PASSOVER, FEAST OF. See FEASTS.

PASTOR (Gr. *poimen*), Eph. 4.11. Generally translated shepherd, Jno. 10.2. Heb. 13.20. 1 Pet. 2.25.

PATARA, a port of Lycia in Asia Minor; Paul visits, Act. 21.1.

PATHROS (Upper Egypt, see Gen. 10.14). Jewish captives in, Isa. 11.11. Jer. 44.1,15. Eze. 29.14. Prophecy against, Eze. 30.14.

PATIENCE. See MEEKNESS — RESIGNATION—PERSECUTION.

PATMOS, an isle in the Ægean sea, John banished to, Rev. 1.9.

PATRIARCHAL GOVERNMENT. See RULERS.

PATRIOTISM. See CHURCH AND COUNTRY, LOVE OF.

PAUL. Called Saul and Paul, Act. 13.9. Of the tribe of Benjamin, Phil. 3.5. A Hebrew of the Hebrews, 2 Cor. 11.22. Phil. 3.5. A Pharisee, and son of a Pharisee, Act. 22.3. Act. 23.6. Act. 26.5. Phil. 3.5. Gal. 1.14.

Born at Tarsus, Act. 9.11. Act. 21.39. Act. 22.3. Circumcised, Phil. 3.5. A Roman citizen by birth, Act. 16.37. Act. 22.25-28. Taught by Gamaliel at Jerusalem, Act. 22.3. Act. 26.4. A tent-maker, Act. 18.3. Act. 20.34. 1 Cor. 4.12. 1 Thes. 2.9. 2 Thes. 3.8.

His part in Stephen's death, Act. 7.58. Act. 8.1. Act. 22.20. His persecution of the Christians; journey to Damascus; his vision of Christ, and blindness, Act. 8.1-4. Act. 9.1-9,13,14,21. Act. 22.4-11,19. Act. 26.9-15. Gal. 1.13. 1 Tim. 1.13. 1 Cor. 9.1. 1 Cor. 15.8.

His vision of Ananias, who visits him and restores his sight, Act. 9.12,17,18. Act. 22.13. His baptism, Act. 22.16. His call to be an apostle, Act. 9.6,15,16. Act. 22.14-21. Act. 26.16-18. See APOSTLES, p. 24-26. Preaches at Damascus, Act. 9.19-22,27. Act. 26.20.

His journey into Arabia; returns to Damascus,

Gal. 1.17. Escapes from Damascus, Act. 9.23-25. 2 Cor. 11.31-33. Goes to Jerusalem; brought by Barnabas to the apostles, Act. 9.26-28. Gal. 1.18,19. Disputes with the Grecians, Act. 9.29. His vision; he is commanded to go to the Gentiles, Act. 22.17-21.

Persecuted; goes to Syria and Cilicia, Act. 9.29,30. Act. 22.18,21. Gal. 1.21-24. With Barnabas, goes to Antioch, Act. 11.25,26. They carry the contributions of the church at Antioch to Jerusalem, Act. 11.29,30. Return to Antioch, Act. 12.25.

Are sent by the Holy Ghost to the Gentiles, Act. 13.2,3. Go to Seleucia, Cyprus, Salamis, Paphos, Act. 13.4-6. Conversion of Sergius Paulus; Elymas struck blind, Act. 13.6-12.

They go to Perga and Antioch in Pisidia; Paul's sermon to the Jews; they are expelled from the synagogue; preach to the Gentiles, Act. 13.13-48. 2 Tim. 3.11.

Come to Iconium; their success, miracles, and persecutions, Act. 13.51,52. Act. 14.1-5. 2 Tim. 3.11.

Come to Lystra; Paul heals a lame man; worship offered them; Paul's address; Paul stoned; recovers from apparent death, Act. 14. 6-20. 2 Cor. 11.25. 2 Tim. 3.11.

They come to Derbe; return to Lystra, Iconium, and Antioch; exhort the disciples and ordain elders, Act. 14.20-23. Pass through Pisidia, Pamphylia, Perga, and Attalia, Act. 14.24,25.

Return to Antioch; report to the church the success of their mission, Act. 14.26-28. Dispute respecting circumcision, Act. 15.1,2,5. Gal. 1.7. Gal. 2.4,5.

Are sent by the church at Antioch to the Apostles, &c., at Jerusalem; their address, Act. 15.2-6,12. Gal. 2.1-7. Public recognition of their mission to the Gentiles, and Paul's apostleship, Act. 15.22-26. Gal. 2.7-10.

They return to Antioch with the letter of the church, Act. 15.22-31. Paul rebukes Peter for separating from the Gentiles at Antioch, Gal. 2.11-16. See 2 Pet. 3.15. His dispute and separation from Barnabas on account of Mark, Act. 15.37-39. See Act. 13.5,13.

Revisits the churches of Syria and Cilicia with Silas, Act. 15.36,40,41. Act. 16.4,5. Comes to Derbe and Lystra; circumcises Timothy; takes him for his companion, Act. 16.1-3. Passes through Phrygia, Galatia, and Mysia, Act. 16.6,7. Gal. 4.13-15. Forbidden by the Holy Ghost to preach in Asia and Bithynia, Act. 16.6,7.

Comes to Troas; vision of a Macedonian, Act. 16.8-10. Is joined by Luke, who writes the history, Act. 16.10,11.

Sails to Samothracia and Neapolis; comes to Philippi; conversion of Lydia; casts out a demon from a female slave, Act. 16.11-18. Paul and Silas scourged and imprisoned; the prison doors opened by an earthquake; conversion of jailer; Paul refuses to depart secretly; they are released by the magistrates, Act. 16.19-40. 2 Cor. 6.5. 2 Cor. 11.25. 1 The. 2.2.

Passes through Amphipolis and Apollonia to Thessalonica; his preaching, success, and persecution, Act. 17.1-9. 1 The. 1. 1 The. 2. 2 The. 1.1-4. 2 The. 3.8-10.

Escapes to Berea; preaching, success, and persecution, Act. 17.10-13.

Paul sails to Athens; sends for Silas and Timothy, Act. 17.14,15. Sends Timothy to Thessalonica, 1 The. 3.1-5. His reflections at Athens; disputes with Jews and Greeks; his sermon at Mars Hill; effects of his preaching, Act. 17.16-34.

Visits Corinth; abode with Aquila, &c.; is rejoined by Silas and Timothy, Act. 18.1-5. 1 The. 3.6. His address to the Jews; success among the Gentiles, Act. 18.4-8,11. 1 Cor. 1. Encouraged by a vision, Act. 18.9,10. The Jews bring Paul before Gallio, Act. 18.12-17.

Leaves Corinth with Aquila, &c.; termination of his vow at Cenchreas, Act. 18.18. Visits Ephesus for a short time on his way to Jerusalem, Act. 18.19-21. Visits Cesarea, Antioch, Galatia, and Phrygia, Act. 18.22,23.

Comes to Ephesus; baptizes 12 of John's disciples; his preaching for 3 years, and miracles; magicians' books burned; his success, Act. 19.1-20. 1 Cor. 16.8,9. Probably pays a second visit to Corinth, see 2 Cor. 2.1. 2 Cor. 12.14. 2 Cor. 13.1,2. 2 Cor. 12.21. Purposes to visit Macedonia and Corinth, before going to Jerusalem at Pentecost, and afterwards Rome and Spain, Act. 19.21. Act. 20.16. Rom. 1.10-15. Rom. 15.22-29. 1 Cor. 16.5-8. Directs collections to be made for the brethren at Jerusalem, 1 Cor. 16.1-4. Gal. 2.10. Sends Timothy and Erastus to Macedonia, &c., Act. 19.22. 1 Cor. 4.17. Persecution raised at Ephesus by Demetrius, Act. 19. 23-41. 2 Tim. 4.14. 2 Cor. 1.8.

Paul quits Ephesus, Act. 20.1. Leaves Timothy at Ephesus, 1 Tim. 1.3. Comes to Troas; waits for Titus; his preaching; success; comes to Macedonia and Philippi, 2 Cor. 2.12,13. Act. 20.1,2.

Meets with Titus, who brings intelligence from Corinth, 2 Cor. 7.5-7,13-15. Sends Titus, &c., back to Corinth, to continue the collection for the saints, 2 Cor. 8.6,16-24. 2 Cor. 9. Journeys to Illyricum, Rom. 15.19,20.

Visits Greece and Corinth to receive the collection, Act. 20.2,3. See Rom. 16.1,23 with 1 Cor. 1.14. The Jews plot against him; instead of sailing to Syria, he returns by Macedonia, Act. 20.3-5.

Comes to Philippi at the passover, and joins his companions at Troas; celebrates the Lord's Supper on the 1st day of the week, and preaches; restores Eutychus to life, Act. 20.4-12. 2 Tim. 4.13.

Goes on foot to Assos; meets Luke, &c.; sails to Mitylene, Chios, Samos, Trogyllium, and Miletus; sends for the elders of Ephesus; his address, prayer, and farewell, Act. 20.13-38.

Sails to Coos, Rhodes, Patara, and Tyre; brethren dissuade Paul from going to Jerusalem; prayer and farewell, Act. 21.1-6. Comes to Ptolemais and Cesarea; dwells with Philip; Agabus' prophecy; Paul's determination to go to Jerusalem, Act. 21.7-15.

Arrives at Jerusalem, with the offerings of the churches; his reception, 2 Cor. 8.19,20. Rom. 15.25-31; narrates his labours to the apostles and elders, Act. 21.16-19. By the advice of the brethren he purifies himself, and bears the expenses of 4 Nazarites, Act. 21. 20-27.

Paul falsely accused by the Jews; beaten by the mob; apprehended by soldiers under Lysias, Act. 21.27-40. His address to the people who clamour for his life, Act. 22.

Claims his privilege as a Roman; escapes scourging, Act. 22.24-30. Pleads before the sanhedrim; his rebuke to Ananias when smitten; dissension among his accusers, Act. 23.1-10. Is encouraged by a vision, Act. 23.11.

His nephew informs Lysias of the Jews' vow to kill Paul, who is sent to Felix at Cesarea, Act. 23.12-35. Accused by Tertullus; his defence; he preaches; Felix trembles; keeps Paul a prisoner for 2 years, till succeeded by Festus, Act. 24. The Jews request that Paul may be brought to Jerusalem, intending to kill him; Festus examines him at Cesarea; Paul appeals to Cesar; is brought before Agrippa, Act. 25. His speech; Festus declares him mad; he and Agrippa pronounce him innocent, Act. 26.

He sails for Italy, passing Sidon, Cyprus, Crete, &c.; predicts shipwreck; his vision of an angel; wrecked on Melita, Act. 27. Kindness of the barbarians; shakes a viper from his hand; heals many sick, Act. 28.1-10. Sails from Melita by Syracuse, &c.; met at Appiiforum by brethren; arrives at Rome; his address to the Jews, Act. 28.11-29. Continues 2 years in custody at Rome; preaches successfully in his lodging, Act. 28.16,30,31. Eph. 6.20. Phil. 1.12-14. Phil. 4.22. Col. 4.18. 2 Tim. 1.8. Philm. 9,10.

His companions and fellow-prisoners in Rome, Act. 27.2. Phil. 2.19-23,25. Col. 1.7. Col. 4.10,14. Philm. 23,24. Epaphroditus is sent by the Philippians to minister to him, Phil. 2.25-30. Phil. 4.18.

Is supposed to have been acquitted at Rome, Philm. 22; and to have visited, as he promised, Macedonia, Phil. 2.23,24; and Spain, Rom. 15.28. He visits Ephesus and Macedonia, 1 Tim. 1.3; and Crete, Tit. 1.5; Miletus, Corinth, 2 Tim. 4.20; Nicopolis, Tit. 3.12; Rome, 2 Tim. 4.16,17. His imprisonment; he is chained, 2 Tim. 1.8,16. 2 Tim. 2.9. His first trial, 2 Tim. 4.16,17. Luke and Onesiphorus, his companions, 2 Tim. 4.11. 2 Tim. 1.16,17. His faith in prospect of death, 2 Tim. 4.6-8,18.

See APOSTLES—MIRACLES—LOVE OF PAUL —PERSECUTION OF PAUL—ZEAL OF PAUL— PRAYER, INTERCESSORY, OF PAUL—MINISTERS.

PAVEMENT. See GABBATHA.

PAVILION. See TENT.

PEACE, NATIONAL. Promises of, Lev. 26.6. 1 Kin. 2.33. 2 Kin. 20.19. 1 Chr. 22.9. Psa. 29.11. Psa. 46.9. Psa. 72.3,7. Psa. 128.6. Pro. 16.7. Isa. 2.4. Isa. 14.4-7. Isa. 60.17,18. Isa. 65.25. Jer. 30.10. Jer. 50.34. Eze. 34. 25-28. Hos. 2.18. Mic. 4.3,4. Zec. 1.11. Zec. 3.10. Zec. 8.4,5. Zec. 9.10. Zec. 14.11. Prayer for, Jer. 29.7. 1 Tim. 2.1,2. Given by God, Jos. 21.44. 1 Chr. 22.18. 1 Chr. 23.25. Psa. 147.13,14. Ecc. 3.8. Isa. 45.7. Examples of peace, Jos. 14.15. Jud. 3.11,30. 1 Kin. 4.24,25. See WAR.

PEACE-MAKERS. See MEEKNESS.

PEACE, SPIRITUAL. See `SPIRITUAL PEACE.

PEACOCKS, Job 39.13. Brought from Tarshish to Solomon, 1 Kin. 10.22. 2 Chr. 9.21.

PEARL, Job 28.18. Value of, Mat. 13. 45,46. Rev. 17.4. Rev. 18.12,16. Ornaments of, 1 Tim. 2.9. Illustrative, Mat. 7.6. Symbolical, Rev. 21.21.

PEKAH, son of Remaliah, and 18th king of Israel (20 years' reign), conspires against Pekahiah, and succeeds him, 2 Kin. 15.25,27. With Rezin, wars against Judah ; takes many captives, 2 Kin. 15.37. 2 Kin. 16.5. 2 Chr. 28.5-15. Isa. 7.1. Ahaz, king of Judah, sends for Tiglath, who carries part of Israel captive to Assyria, 2 Kin. 15.29 with 2 Kin. 16.7. 1 Chr.'5.26. Isa. 9.1. Pekah's wicked reign, 2 Kin. 15.27,28. Murdered by Hoshea, 2 Kin. 15.30. Prophecies against, Isa. 7.1-16. Isa. 8.4-10.

PEKAHIAH, son of Menahem, and 17th king of Israel (2 years' reign), succeeds his father ; his wicked reign ; murdered by Pekah, 2 Kin. 15.22-26.

PEKOD, a name of Babylon, Jer. 50.21. Eze. 23.23.

PELATIAH, death of, at Ezekiel's prophecy, Eze. 11.1,13.

PELEG (division), the earth was divided in his days, Gen. 10.25. Gen. 11.16-19. 1 Chr. 1.19,25.

PELETHITES, part of David's guard, 1 Kin. 1.38. 2 Sam. 8.18. 2 Sam. 20.7,23. 1 Chr. 18.17. Faithful in Absalom's rebellion, 2 Sam. 15.18.

PELICAN, Lev. 11.18. Deu. 14.17. Psa. 102.6. Translated cormorant, Isa. 34.11. Zeph. 2.14.

PEN. (1.) Isa. 8.1 ; translated graving-tool, Ex. 32.4. (2.) Psa. 45.1. Jer. 8.8. Of iron, Job 19.24. Jer. 17.1. (3.) 3 Jno. 13.

PENKNIFE, Jer. 36.23.

PENIEL or **PENUEL**, east of Jordan, Jacob wrestles with the angel in, Gen. 32.24-31.

———, a fortified town ; its tower destroyed by Gideon, Jud. 8.8,17. Built by Jeroboam, 1 Kin. 12.25.

PENITENCE. See REPENTANCE.

PENNY (Gr. *denarion*), about 7½d., Mat. 18.28. Mar. 6.37. Mar. 14.5. Luk. 7.41. Luk. 10.35. Cesar's image on, Mat. 22.19-21. A day's wages, Mat. 20.2. A measure (1 quart) of wheat, or 3 measures (3 quarts) of barley, sold for a penny, Rev. 6.6.

PENTECOST. See FEAST OF PENTECOST.

PEOR, a mountain of Moab ; Balak builds altars for Balaam on, Num. 23.28-30. See BAAL-PEOR.

PERAZIM. See BAAL-PERAZIM.

PERES (to divide), Dan. 5.28. See UPHARZIN.

PEREZ-UZZAH (breach of Uzzah), name given to the place where Uzzah was killed for touching the ark, 2 Sam. 6.8. 1 Chr. 13.11.

PERFUMES, Pro. 27.9. Song 3.6. Isa. 57.9. Beds perfumed with myrrh, Pro. 7.17. See INCENSE—SPICES—OINTMENT.

PERGA, a town of Pamphylia, in Asia Minor ; Mark leaves Paul at, Act. 13.13. Paul preaches at, Act. 14.25.

PERGAMOS, a town of Mysia ; an epistle written to the church of, Rev. 1.11. Rev. 2. 12-17.

PERIZZITES, one of the 7 Canaanitish nations, Deu. 7.1. Inhabited Canaan in the time of Abraham, Gen. 13.7 ; of Jacob, Gen. 34.30. Their territory, Jos. 11.3. Jos. 17.15.

Their land promised to Abraham's posterity, Gen. 15.20. Ex. 3.8. Ex. 23.23. Jos. 3.10. Neh. 9.8. Israel commanded to destroy, Deu. 20.17. Defeated by Joshua, Jos. 9.1,2. Jos. 11.3. Jos. 12.8. Jos. 24.11 ; by Judah, Jud. 1.4,5. Israelites intermarried with, Jud. 3.5-7. Ezr. 9.1. Tributary to Solomon, 1 Kin. 9.20. 2 Chr. 8.7.

PERJURY. See FALSEHOOD.

PERSECUTION. SAINTS DUTY IN PERSECUTION. Gen. 49.23. The archers have sorely grieved him, and shot *at him*, and hated him.

Psa. 11.2. They make ready their arrow upon the string, that they may privily shoot at the upright in heart.

Psa. 37.32. The wicked watcheth the righteous, and seeketh to slay him.

Psa. 44.15. The shame of my face hath covered me, 16. For the voice of him that reproacheth and blasphemeth. 17. All this is come upon us ; yet have we not forgotten thee, neither have we dealt falsely in thy covenant. 18. Our heart is not turned back, neither have our steps declined from thy way. 22. Yea, for thy sake are we killed all the day long ; we are counted as sheep for the slaughter.

Psa. 74.7. They have cast fire into thy sanctuary, they have defiled *by casting down* the dwelling-place of thy name to the ground. 8. They said in their hearts, Let us destroy them together : they have burned up all the synagogues of God in the land.

Psa. 94.5. They break in pieces thy people, O Lord, and afflict thine heritage.

Psa. 119.51. The proud have had me greatly in derision : *yet* have I not declined from thy law. 61. The bands of the wicked have robbed me : *but* I have not forgotten thy law. 69. The proud have forged a lie against me : *but* I will keep thy precepts with *my* whole heart. 85. The proud have digged pits for me, which *are* not after thy law. 86. They persecute me wrongfully ; help thou me.

Psa. 119.87. They had almost consumed me upon earth ; but I forsook not thy precepts. 95. The wicked have waited for me to destroy me : *but* I will consider thy testimonies. 157. Many *are* my persecutors and mine enemies ; *yet* do I not decline from thy testimonies. 161. Princes have persecuted me without a cause : but my heart standeth in awe of thy word.

Isa. 59.15. Yea, truth faileth ; and he *that* departeth from evil maketh himself a prey : and the Lord saw *it*, and it displeased him.

Jer. 2.30. Your own sword hath devoured your prophets, like a destroying lion.

Jer. 11.19. I *was* like a lamb *or* an ox *that* is brought to the slaughter ; and I knew not that they had devised devices against me, *saying*, Let us destroy the tree with the fruit thereof, and let us cut him off from the land of the living, that his name may be no more remembered.

Jer. 15.10. I have neither lent on usury, nor men have lent to me on usury ; *yet* every one of them doth curse me.

Jer. 18.18. Then said they, Come, and let us devise devices against Jeremiah. Come, and let us smite him with the tongue, and let us not give heed to any of his words.

Jer. 20.7. I am in derision daily, every one mocketh me. 8. For since I spake, I cried out, I cried violence and spoil; because the word of the Lord was made a reproach unto me, and a derision, daily.

Jer. 26.12. The Lord sent me to prophesy against this house and against this city all the words that ye have heard. 14. As for me, behold, I *am* in your hand: do with me as seemeth good and meet unto you.

Jer. 50.7. All that found them hath devoured them: and their adversaries said, We offend not.

Dan. 3.16. We *are* not careful to answer thee in this matter. 17. If it be *so*, our God whom we serve is able to deliver us from the burning fiery furnace, and he will deliver *us* out of thine hand, O king. 18. But if not, be it known unto thee, O king, that we will not serve thy gods, nor worship the golden image which thou hast set up.

Dan. 6.10. When Daniel knew that the writing was signed, he went into his house; and his windows being open in his chamber toward Jerusalem, he kneeled upon his knees three times a day, and prayed, and gave thanks before his God, as he did aforetime.

Hab. 1.13. The wicked devoureth *the man that is* more righteous than he.

Mat. 10.16. I send you forth as sheep in the midst of wolves: be ye therefore wise as serpents, and harmless as doves. 22. And ye shall be hated of all *men* for my name's sake: but he that endureth to the end shall be saved. 23. But when they persecute you in this city, flee ye into another. 28. Fear not them which kill the body, but are not able to kill the soul: but rather fear him which is able to destroy both soul and body in hell. *v.* 16-39.

Mat. 11.6. Blessed is *he*, whosoever shall not be offended in me. Luk. 7.23.

Mar. 13.11. When they shall lead *you*, and deliver you up, take no thought beforehand what ye shall speak, neither do ye premeditate: but whatsoever shall be given you in that hour, that speak ye: for it is not ye that speak, but the Holy Ghost.

Luk. 6.22. Blessed are ye, when men shall hate you, and when they shall separate you *from their company*, and shall reproach *you*, and cast out your name as evil, for the Son of man's sake. 23. Rejoice ye in that day, and leap for joy: for, behold, your reward *is* great in heaven: for in the like manner did their fathers unto the prophets.

Luk. 17.33. Whosoever shall seek to save his life shall lose it; and whosoever shall lose his life shall preserve it. Mar. 8.35.

Luk. 21.19. In your patience possess ye your souls.

Jno. 12.25. He that loveth his life shall lose it; and he that hateth his life in this world shall keep it unto life eternal.

Jno. 16.1. These things have I spoken unto you, that ye should not be offended.

Act. 4.19. Peter and John answered and said unto them, Whether it be right in the sight of God to hearken unto you more than unto God, judge ye. 20. For we cannot but speak the things which we have seen and heard.

Act. 5.29. We ought to obey God rather than men. 40. When they had called the apostles, and beaten *them*, they commanded that they should not speak in the name of Jesus, and let them go. 41. And they departed

from the presence of the council, rejoicing that they were counted worthy to suffer shame for his name. 42. And daily in the temple, and in every house, they ceased not to teach and preach Jesus Christ.

Act. 7.52. Which of the prophets have not your fathers persecuted? and they have slain them which shewed before of the coming of the Just One; of whom ye have been now the betrayers and murderers.

Act. 8.4. They that were scattered abroad went every where preaching the word.

Rom. 8.17. If so be that we suffer with *him*, that we may be also glorified together.

1 Cor. 13.3. Though I give my body to be burned, and have not charity, it profiteth me nothing.

Gal. 4.29. As then he that was born after the flesh persecuted him *that was born* after the Spirit, even so *it is* now.

Phil. 1.14. Many of the brethren in the Lord, waxing confident by my bonds, are much more bold to speak the word without fear. 28. In nothing terrified by your adversaries: which is to them an evident token of perdition, but to you of salvation, and that of God. 29. Unto you it is given in the behalf of Christ, not only to believe on him, but also to suffer for his sake.

2 The. 1.4. We ourselves glory in you in the churches of God for your patience and faith in all your persecutions and tribulations that ye endure.

2 Tim. 1.8. Be not thou therefore ashamed of the testimony of our Lord, nor of me his prisoner: but be thou partaker of the afflictions of the gospel according to the power of God.

2 Tim. 2.12. If we suffer, we shall also reign with *him*: if we deny *him*, he also will deny us.

Heb. 10.32. Call to remembrance the former days, in which, after ye were illuminated, ye endured a great fight of afflictions; 33. Partly, whilst ye were made a gazing-stock both by reproaches and afflictions; and partly, whilst ye became companions of them that were so used. 34. Ye had compassion of me in my bonds, and took joyfully the spoiling of your goods, knowing in yourselves that ye have in heaven a better and an enduring substance.

Heb. 11.25. Choosing rather to suffer affliction with the people of God, than to enjoy the pleasures of sin for a season; 26. Esteeming the reproach of Christ greater riches than the treasures in Egypt: for he had respect unto the recompence of the reward. 27. By faith he forsook Egypt, not fearing the wrath of the king: for he endured, as seeing him who is invisible.

Heb. 11.33. Who through faith stopped the mouths of lions. 34. Quenched the violence of fire, escaped the edge of the sword, out of weakness were made strong. 35. Others were tortured, not accepting deliverance; that they might obtain a better resurrection: 36. And others had trial of *cruel* mockings and scourgings, yea, moreover of bonds and imprisonment: 37. They were stoned, they were sawn asunder, were tempted, were slain with the sword: they wandered about in sheepskins and goatskins; being destitute, afflicted, tormented; 38. (Of whom the world was not worthy:) they wandered in deserts, and in mountains, and *in* dens and caves of the earth.

Heb. 12.3. Consider him that endured such contradiction of sinners against himself, lest ye be wearied and faint in your minds. 4. Ye have not yet resisted unto blood, striving against sin.

Heb. 13.13. Let us go forth therefore unto him without the camp, bearing his reproach.

Jas. 2.6. Do not rich men oppress you, and draw you before the judgment seats?

Jas. 5.6. Ye have condemned *and* killed the just; *and* he doth not resist you.

Jas. 5.10. Take, my brethren, the prophets, who have spoken in the name of the Lord, for an example of suffering affliction, and of patience.

1 Pet. 3.14. If ye suffer for righteousness' sake, happy *are ye*: and be not afraid of their terror, neither be troubled; 17. *It is* better, if the will of God be so, that ye suffer for well doing, than for evil doing.

1 Pet. 4.12. Beloved, think it not strange concerning the fiery trial which is to try you, as though some strange thing happened unto you: 13. But rejoice, inasmuch as ye are partakers of Christ's sufferings; that, when his glory shall be revealed, ye may be glad also with exceeding joy. 14. If ye be reproached for the name of Christ, happy *are ye*; for the spirit of glory and of God resteth upon you: on their part he is evil spoken of, but on your part he is glorified. 16. If *any man suffer* as a Christian, let him not be ashamed; but let him glorify God on this behalf. 19. Let them that suffer according to the will of God commit the keeping of their souls *to him* in well doing, as unto a faithful Creator.

Rev. 2.3. Hast borne, and hast patience, and for my name's sake hast laboured, and hast not fainted. 10. Be thou faithful unto death, and I will give thee a crown of life. 13. I know thy works, and where thou dwellest, *even* where Satan's seat *is*: and thou holdest fast my name, and hast not denied my faith, even in those days wh͏̄erein Antipas *was* my faithful martyr, who was slain among you, where Satan dwelleth.

Rev. 12.11. They overcame him by the blood of the Lamb, and by the word of their testimony; and they loved not their lives unto the death.

Rev. 20.4. *I saw* the souls of them that were beheaded for the witness of Jesus, and for the word of God, and which had not worshipped the beast, neither his image, neither had received *his* mark upon their foreheads, or in their hands; and they lived and reigned with Christ a thousand years.

See SAINTS HATED—MALICE.

PERSECUTION, EXAMPLES OF: Of Moses, Ex. 2.15. Ex. 17.4. Elijah, 1 Kin. 18.10. 1 Kin. 19.2. 2 Kin. 1.9. Micaiah, 1 Kin. 22. 26. Elisha, 2 Kin. 6.31. Hanani, 2 Chr. 16. 10. Zachariah, 2 Chr. 24.21. Mat. 23.35. Jeremiah, Jer. 15.10,15. Jer. 17.15-18. Jer. 18.18-23. Jer. 26. Jer. 32.2. Jer. 33.1. Jer. 36.26. Jer. 37. Jer. 38.1-6. Urijah, Jer. 26.23. Jews, Ezr. 4. Neh. 4. John, Mat. 14.3-12. Simon, Mar. 15.21. Disciples, Jno. 9.22,34. Lazarus, Jno. 12.10. Apostles, Act. 4.3-18. Act. 5.18-42. Act. 12.1-19. Rev. 1.9 (see next subject). Stephen, Act. 6.9-15.

Act. 7. The church, Act. 8.1. Act. 9.1-14. Timothy, Heb. 13.23. Antipas, Rev. 2.13.

See CHRIST'S SUFFERINGS—BARNABAS—PERSECUTION PUNISHED.

PERSECUTION OF PAUL. Act. 9.16. I will shew him how great things he must suffer for my name's sake.

Act. 16.25. At midnight Paul and Silas prayed, and sang praises unto God: and the prisoners heard them. *v.* 2-24.

Act. 20.22. I go bound in the spirit unto Jerusalem, not knowing the things that shall befall me there: 23. Save that the Holy Ghost witnesseth in every city, saying that bonds and afflictions abide me. 24. But none of these things move me: neither count I my life dear unto myself, so that I might finish my course with joy, and the ministry which I have received of the Lord Jesus, to testify the gospel of the grace of God.

Act. 21.13. What mean ye to weep and to break mine heart? for I am ready not to be bound only, but also to die at Jerusalem for the name of the Lord Jesus.

Rom. 8.35. Who shall separate us from the love of Christ? *shall* tribulation, or distress, or persecution, or famine, or nakedness, or peril, or sword? 36. As it is written, For thy sake we are killed all the day long; we are accounted as sheep for the slaughter. 37. Nay, in all these things we are more than conquerors through him that loved us.

1 Cor. 4.9. I think that God hath set forth us the apostles last, as it were appointed to death: for we are made a spectacle unto the world, and to angels, and to men. 11. Even unto this present hour we both hunger, and thirst, and are naked, and are buffeted, and have no certain dwelling-place. 12. And labour, working with our own hands: being reviled, we bless; being persecuted, we suffer it: 13. Being defamed, we entreat: we are made as the filth of the world, *and are* the offscouring of all things unto this day.

2 Cor. 1.8. Our trouble which came to us in Asia, that we were pressed out of measure, above strength, insomuch that we despaired even of life: 9. But we had the sentence of death in ourselves, that we should not trust in ourselves, but in God which raiseth the dead; 10. Who delivered us from so great a death, and doth deliver: in whom we trust that he will yet deliver *us*.

2 Cor. 4.8. *We are* troubled on every side, yet not distressed; *we are* perplexed, but not in despair; 9. Persecuted, but not forsaken; cast down, but not destroyed; 10. Always bearing about in the body the dying of the Lord Jesus, that the life also of Jesus might be made manifest in our body. 11. For we which live are alway delivered unto death for Jesus' sake, that the life also of Jesus might be made manifest in our mortal flesh. 12. So then death worketh in us, but life in you.

2 Cor. 6.4. In all *things* approving ourselves as the ministers of God, in much patience, in afflictions, in necessities, in distresses, 5. In stripes, in imprisonments, in tumults, in labours, in watchings, in fastings; 8. By honour and dishonour, by evil repoit and good report: as deceivers, and *yet* true.

2 Cor. 11.23. In labours more abundant, in stripes above measure, in prisons more frequent, in deaths oft. 24. Of **the Jews five**

times received I forty *stripes* save one. 25. Thrice was I beaten with rods, once was I stoned, thrice I suffered shipwreck, a night and a day I have been in the deep; 26. *In* journeyings often, *in* perils of waters, *in* perils of robbers, *in* perils by *mine own* countrymen, *in* perils by the heathen, *in* perils in the city, *in* perils in the wilderness, *in* perils in the sea, *in* perils among false brethren; 27. In weariness and painfulness, in watchings often, in hunger and thirst, in fastings often, in cold and nakedness. *v.* 28-33.

2 Cor. 12.10. I take pleasure in infirmities, in reproaches, in necessities, in persecutions, in distresses for Christ's sake: for when I am weak, then am I strong.

Gal. 5.11. I, brethren, if I yet preach circumcision, why do I yet suffer persecution? then is the offence of the cross ceased.

Gal. 6.17. I bear in my body the marks of the Lord Jesus.

Phil. 1.30. Having the same conflict which ye saw in me, and now hear *to be* in me.

Phil. 2.17. If I be offered upon the sacrifice and service of your faith, I joy, and rejoice with you all. 18. For the same cause also do ye joy, and rejoice with me.

Col. 1.24. Who now rejoice in my sufferings for you, and fill up that which is behind of the afflictions of Christ in my flesh for his body's sake, which is the church.

1 The. 2.2. Even after that we had suffered before, and were shamefully entreated, as ye know, at Philippi, we were bold in our God to speak unto you the gospel of God with much contention. 15. Who both killed the Lord Jesus, and their own prophets, and have persecuted us.

2 Tim. 1.12. For the which cause I also suffer these things: nevertheless I am not ashamed.

2 Tim. 2.9. I suffer trouble, as an evil doer, *even* unto bonds; but the word of God is not bound. 10. I endure all things for the elect's sakes, that they may also obtain the salvation which is in Christ Jesus with eternal glory.

2 Tim. 4.16. At my first answer no man stood with me, but all *men* forsook me: *I pray God* that it may not be laid to their charge. 17. Notwithstanding the Lord stood with me, and strengthened me; that by me the preaching might be fully known, and *that* all the Gentiles might hear: and I was delivered out of the mouth of the lion.

At Damascus, Act. 9.23-25. 2 Cor. 11.32. At Jerusalem, Act. 9.29. Act. 21.27-40. Act. 22.22-30. Act. *c.* 23 to 25. Act. 26.6,7,21. At Antioch, Iconium, and Lystra, Act. 13.45-51. Act. 14. 2 Tim. 3.11. At Philippi, Act. 16. 19-39. At Thessalonica, and Berea, Act. 17. 5-9,13. At Corinth, Act. 18.6-17. At Ephesus, Act. 19.14-41. 1 Cor. 15.32. In Greece, Act. 20.3. At Rome, Act. 23.11. Act. 28.16-30. Eph. 3.1. Eph. 4.1. Eph. 6.20. Phil. 1. 7,12-16. Col. 4.3,10,18. 2 Tim. 1.8,12. 2 Tim. 2.9. 2 Tim. 4.16,17. Philm. 1.9,10,23. Heb. 13.19. See ZEAL OF PAUL.

PERSECUTION, PRAYER IN. See AFFLICTION.

PERSECUTION PREDICTED. Isa. 26.20. Come, my people, enter thou into thy chambers, and shut thy doors about thee: hide thyself as it were for a little moment, until the indignation be overpast.

Eze. 3.25. Behold, they shall put bands upon thee, and shall bind thee with them, and thou shalt not go out among them.

Dan. 7.21. I beheld, and the same horn made war with the saints, and prevailed against them. 25. He shall speak *great* words against the most High, and shall wear out the saints of the most High, and think to change times and laws: and they shall be given into his hand until a time and times and the dividing of time.

Mat. 10.16. I send you forth as sheep in the midst of wolves. 17. But beware of men: for they will deliver you up to the councils, and they will scourge you in their synagogues; 18. And ye shall be brought before governors and kings for my sake, for a testimony against them and the Gentiles. 21. And the brother shall deliver up the brother to death, and the father the child: and the children shall rise up against *their* parents, and cause them to be put to death. 22. And ye shall be hated of all *men* for my name's sake. 34. I came not to send peace, but a sword. 36. A man's foes *shall be* they of his own household. *v.* 35.

Mar. 10.30. Luk. 21.12-18.

Mat. 20.23. Ye shall drink indeed of my cup, and be baptized with the baptism that I am baptized with.

Mat. 24.10. Then shall many be offended, and shall betray one another, and shall hate one another.

Luk. 12.49. I am come to send fire on the earth; and what will I, if it be already kindled? *v.* 11,12.

Luk. 22.36. But now, he that hath a purse, let him take *it*, and likewise *his* scrip: and he that hath no sword, let him sell his garment, and buy one.

Jno. 15.20. The servant is not greater than his lord. If they have persecuted me, they will also persecute you; if they have kept my saying, they will keep yours also. 21. But all these things will they do unto you for my name's sake.

Jno. 16.2. They shall put you out of the synagogues: yea, the time cometh, that whosoever killeth you will think that he doeth God service. *v.* 1-4.

Jno. 21.19. This spake he, signifying by what death he should glorify God. *v.* 18.

Act. 14.22. Exhorting them to continue in the faith, and that we must through much tribulation enter into the kingdom of God.

Act. 23.11. The Lord stood by him, and said, Be of good cheer, Paul; for as thou hast testified of me in Jerusalem, so must thou bear witness also at Rome.

2 Tim. 3.12. All that will live godly in Christ Jesus shall suffer persecution.

Rev. 2.10. Fear none of those things which thou shalt suffer: behold, the devil shall cast *some* of you into prison, that ye may be tried; and ye shall have tribulation ten days.

Rev. 3.10. The hour of temptation, which shall come upon all the world, to try them that dwell upon the earth.

Rev. 6.11. It was said unto them, that they should rest yet for a little season, until their fellow-servants also and their brethren, that should be killed as they *were*, should be fulfilled.

Rev. 12.17. The dragon was wroth with the woman, and went to make war with the remnant of her seed, which keep the commandments of God, and have the testimony of Jesus Christ. *v.* 1-17. Rev. 11.7-10. Rev. 13.7.

Rev. 17.6. I saw the woman drunken with the blood of the saints, and with the blood of the martyrs of Jesus.

PERSECUTION, WARNINGS AGAINST. ENEMIES OF THE CHURCH AND OF ISRAEL PUNISHED. Gen. 12.3. Num. 24.9. Deu. 28.7. Deu. 30.7. Deu. 32.42,43. Jos. 21.44. Psa. 2.1-5,9. Psa. 6.10. Psa. 7.11-13. Psa. 14.4. Psa. 17.10-13. Psa. 27.2. Psa. 31.18. Psa. 34.21. Psa. 35.4-8,26. Psa. 37.12-15. Psa. 40.14,15. Psa. 54.5,7. Psa. 59.10,15. Psa. 62.3. Psa. 63.9,10. Psa. 64.7,8. Psa. 69.22-23. Psa. 78.65,66. Psa. 83. Psa. 94.23. Psa. 105.14. Psa. 109. Psa. 129. Psa. 137. Psa. 140.8-11. Isa. 8.9,10. Isa. 25.5. Isa. 29.7,8. Isa. 34. Isa. 41.11-16. Isa. 51.7,8,22,23. Isa. 54.15,17. Isa. 59.19. Isa.66.5,6. Jer. 10.25. Jer. 12.14. Jer. 30.16. Jer. 46.28. Lam. 3.59-66. Lam. 4.13-16. Mic. 4.11-13. Mic. 5.8,9. Mic. 7.10-17. Nah. 1. Hab. 3.7-15. Zeph. 3.15,19. Zec. 1.15,21. Zec. 2.8,9. Zec. 12.2-9. Zec. 14.3,12. Mat. 18.6,10. Mat. 21.33-41. Mat. 22.6,7. Mat. 23.34-38. Mat. 26.52. Luk. 9.54-56. Luk. 13.31-35. Luk. 18.7,8. Phil. 1.28. 1 The. 2.15,16. 2 The. 1.6. Heb. 10.13. Rev. 3.9. Rev. 11.5. Rev. 13.10. Rev. 16.5-7,19. Rev. 18.6,20-24. Rev. 19.2,19-21. Rev. 20.9.

Pharaoh, Gen. 15.13,14. Ex. c. 1,4,5,7 to 11,14. Ex. 15.4-12. Neh. 9.11. Amalekites, Deu. 25.17-19. Jeroboam, 1 Kin. 13.4. Ahab and Jezebel, 1 Kin. 18.4. 1 Kin. 19.2,14. 1 Kin. 22.26. 2 Kin. 9.7-10. Jews, 2 Chr. 36.16. Neh. 9.26,27. Haman, Est. 3. Est. 7.4-10. Est. 9.1. Sennacherib, Isa. 30.31. Isa. 37.

Nebuchadnezzar, &c., Jer. 25.12. Jer. 50. 10,11. Jer. 51.24,49. Edom, Egypt, &c., Eze. 25. Eze. 28.24. Eze. c. 35 & 36 & 38. Joel 3.19. Amos 1.11,12. Obad. 1-20. Zeph. 2.8-10.

Enemies of Jeremiah, Jer. 11.19-23. Jer. 20.1-12; of Shadrach, &c., Dan. 3.22; of Daniel, Dan. 6.24; of Amos, Amos 7.12-17.

See GOD PROTECTOR.

PERSEVERANCE OF SAINTS. Job 17.9. The righteous also shall hold on his way, and he that hath clean hands shall be stronger and stronger.

Psa. 37.24. Though he fall, he shall not be utterly cast down: for the Lord upholdeth *him with* his hand. 28. The Lord loveth judgment, and forsaketh not his saints; they are preserved for ever.

Psa. 73.24. Thou shalt guide me with thy counsel, and afterward receive me *to* glory.

Psa. 138.8. The Lord will perfect *that which* concerneth me.

Pro. 4.18. The path of the just *is* as the shining light, that shineth more and more unto the perfect day.

Isa. 43.7. Every one that is called by my name: for I have created him for my glory, I have formed him; yea, I have made him.

Isa. 45.17. Israel shall be saved in the Lord with an everlasting salvation: ye shall not be ashamed nor confounded world without end.

Isa. 51.6. The heavens shall vanish away like smoke, and the earth shall wax old like a garment, and they that dwell therein shall die in like manner: but my salvation shall be for ever, and my righteousness shall not be abolished. *v.* 8.

Isa. 55.3. I will make an everlasting covenant with you, *even* the sure mercies of David.

Jer. 32.40. I will make an everlasting covenant with them, that I will not turn away from them, to do them good; but I will put my fear in their hearts, that they shall not depart from me.

Mat. 24.24. If *it were* possible, they shall deceive the very elect.

Luk. 10.42. Mary hath chosen that good part, which shall not be taken away from her.

Luk. 22.31. Satan hath desired *to have* you, that he may sift *you* as wheat: 32. But I have prayed for thee, that thy faith fail not.

Jno. 6.37. All that the father giveth me shall come to me; and him that cometh to me I will in no wise cast out. 39. This is the Father's will which hath sent me, that of all which he hath given me I should lose nothing, but should raise it up again at the last day. 40. And this is the will of him that sent me, that every one which seeth the Son, and believeth on him, may have everlasting life: and I will raise him up at the last day.

Jno. 10.28. I give unto them eternal life; and they shall never perish, neither shall any *man* pluck them out of my hand. 29. My Father, which gave *them* me, is greater than all; and no *man* is able to pluck *them* out of my Father's hand.

Rom. 8.30. Whom he did predestinate, them he also called: and whom he called, them he also justified: and whom he justified, them he also glorified. 33. Who shall lay any thing to the charge of God's elect? *It is* God that justifieth. 34. Who *is* he that condemneth? *It is* Christ that died, yea rather, that is risen again, who is even at the right hand of God, who also maketh intercession for us. 35. Who shall separate us from the love of Christ? *shall* tribulation, or distress, or persecution, or famine, or nakedness, or peril, or sword? 37. Nay, in all these things we are more than conquerors through him that loved us. 38. For I am persuaded, that neither death, nor life, nor angels, nor principalities, nor powers, nor things present, nor things to come, 39. Nor height, nor depth, nor any other creature, shall be able to separate us from the love of God, which is in Christ Jesus our Lord.

Rom. 11.29. The gifts and calling of God *are* without repentance.

1 Cor. 1.8. Who shall also confirm you unto the end, *that ye may be* blameless in the day of our Lord Jesus Christ. 9. God *is* faithful, by whom ye were called unto the fellowship of his Son Jesus Christ our Lord.

2 Cor. 1.21. He which stablisheth us with you in Christ, and hath anointed us, *is* God. 22. Who hath also sealed us, and given the earnest of the Spirit in our hearts.

Phil. 1.6. Being confident of this very thing, that he which hath begun a good work in you will perform *it* until the day of Jesus Christ.

Phil. 4.3. Whose names *are* in the book of life.

Col. 1.5. The hope which is laid up for you in heaven.

1 The. 5.9. God hath not appointed us to wrath, but to obtain salvation by our Lord Jesus Christ. 10. Who died for us, that

whether we wake or sleep, we should live together with him. 24. Faithful *is* the that calleth you, who also will do *it*. *v*. 23.

2 Tim. 1.12. I know whom I have believed, and am persuaded that he is able to keep that which I have committed unto him against that day.

2 Tim. 4.18. The Lord shall deliver me from every evil work, and will preserve *me* unto his heavenly kingdom.

Heb. 6.17. God willing, more abundantly to shew unto the heirs of promise the immutability of his counsel, confirmed *it* by an oath : 18. That by two immutable things, in which *it was* impossible for God to lie, we might have a strong consolation, who have fled for refuge to lay hold upon the hope set before us.

Heb. 12.23. The general assembly and church of the first-born, which are written in heaven.

1 Pet. 1.4. An inheritance incorruptible, and undefiled, and that fadeth not away, reserved in heaven for you, 5. Who are kept by the power of God through faith unto salvation ready to be revealed in the last time.

1 Jno. 2.19. They went out from us, but they were not of us ; for if they had been of us, they would *no doubt* have continued with us : but *they went out*, that they might be made manifest that they were not all of us. 27. The anointing which ye have received of him abideth in you, and ye need not that any man teach you : but as the same anointing teacheth you of all things, and is truth, and is no lie, and even as it hath taught you, ye shall abide in him.

2 Jno. 2. The truth's sake, which dwelleth in us, and shall be with us for ever. 9. Whosoever transgresseth, and abideth not in the doctrine of Christ, hath not God. He that abideth in the doctrine of Christ, he hath both the Father and the Son.

Rev. 22.4. They shall see his face ; and his name *shall be* in their foreheads. 11. He that is righteous, let him be righteous still : and he that is holy, let him be holy still.

See GOD, FAITHFULNESS OF.

PERSEVERANCE ENJOINED. See DE-CISION—SPIRITUAL DILIGENCE.

PERSIA AND MEDIA. Peopled by descendants of Elam, son of Shem, see ELAM-ITES ; and by descendants of Madai, son of Japheth, see MADAI. Boundaries of ; provinces of, Est. 1.1. Dan. 6.1. Dan. 8.2. Decrees of, unchangeable, Dan. 6.8,12. Est. 8.8.

Treatment of the Jews by its kings, see DARIUS THE MEDIAN, CYRUS, ARTAXERXES I., DARIUS II., ARTAXERXES II., DARIUS THE PERSIAN, AHASUERUS. Towns of, see ACHMETHA, SHUSHAN. River of, see ULAI. Prophecies of, Jer. 49.34-39. Jer. 51.11-64. Eze. 32.24,25. Dan. 2.21-39. Dan. 5.28. Dan. 7. Dan. 8. Dan. 11.1-4.

PERSIS, a Roman disciple, commended for zeal, Rom. 16.12.

PESTILENCE. Sent from God on the Egyptians, Ex. 12.29. Ex. 15.26. Psa. 78.50. Israelites at Kibroth, Num. 11.33,34. The ten spies, Num. 14.37. Israelites on the rebellion of Korah, Num. 16.45-49. At Shittim, Num. 25.3,4,8. Psa. 106.29. On the Philistines, 1 Sam. 5.9-12. Israel, in David's reign,

2 Sam. 24.15. 1 Chr. 21.12-14. Sennacherib's army, 2 Kin. 19.35. Jews, Amos 4.10 ; at the siege of Jerusalem, Jer. 32.24.

Predicted as a judgment from God, Ex. 9.15. Lev. 26.16-25. Num. 14.12. Deu. 28.21-35. Deu. 29.22. 2 Sam. 24.13. 2 Chr. 7.13. 2 Chr. 21.14-19. Jer. 14.12. Jer. 21.6-9. Jer. 24.10. Jer. 27.8,13. Jer. 29.17,18. Jer. 32.36. Jer. 34.17. Jer. 38.2. Jer. 42.17,22. Jer. 44.13. Eze. 5.12,17. Eze. 6.11,12. Eze. 7.15. Eze. 14.19-21. Eze. 24.16. Eze. 28.23. Eze. 33.27. Eze. 38.22. Hab. 3.5. Zec. 14.12-18. Mat. 24.7. Luk. 21.11. Rev. 6.8. Rev. 16.2.

Miraculously stayed, Num. 16.47,48. Num. 25.8. 1 Chr. 21.22-27. Promises of protection from, Ex. 12.13. Ex. 15.26. Ex. 30.12. Psa. 91.3,6. Jer. 21.7.

PETER, his original name Simon, son of Jonas, changed to Cephas (*Heb*.) or Peter, (*Greek*), both signifying a stone, Jno. 1.42. Mar. 3.16. Mat. 16.16-19. A fisherman of Bethsaida, in Galilee, Mat. 4.18. Luk. 5.1-7. Jno. 1.44. Brought to Jesus by his brother Andrew, Jno. 1.40,41.

His call by Christ ; a miraculous draught, Mat. 4.18-20. Mar. 1.16-18. Luk. 5.1-11. His wife's mother healed by Jesus, Mat. 8.14. Mar. 1.29,30. Luk. 4.38. Finds Jesus and says, 'All men seek for Thee,' Mar. 1.36,37. Chosen an apostle, Mat. 10.2. Mat. 16.18,19. Mar. 3.16. Luk. 6.14. Act. 1.13.

Asks an explanation of a parable, Luk. 12.41. Complains of the people crowding Jesus, Luk. 8.45. Witnesses the raising of Jairus' daughter, Mar. 5.37. Luk. 8.51. Walks on the water to meet Jesus ; his faith fails, Mat. 14.28-31. Asks an explanation of the discourse respecting meats, Mat. 15.15.

His confession of Christ, Mat. 16.16-19. Mar. 8.29. Luk. 9.20. Jno. 6.68,69. Rebuked for dissuading Christ from suffering, Mat. 16. 22,23. Mar. 8.32,33. Witnesses the transfiguration, Mat. 17.1-4. Mar. 9.2-6. Luk. 9. 28-33. 2 Pet. 1.16-18. Finds the tribute-money in the fish's mouth, Mat. 17.24-27.

Asks how often he should forgive, Mat. 18.21. Declares that he has left all for Christ, Mat. 19.27. Mar. 10.28. Luk. 18.28. Shews Jesus the withered fig-tree, Mar. 11.21. Inquires about Christ's coming, Mar. 13.3,4. Is sent with John to prepare the passover, Luk. 22.8.

Is unwilling that Christ should wash his feet, Jno. 13.6-11. Beckons to John to ask who should betray Christ, Jno. 13.24. Christ foretells his fall ; Peter declares his fidelity, Mat. 26.33-35. Mar. 14.29-31. Luk. 22. 31-34. Jno. 13.36-38. Is with Jesus in Gethsemane ; reproved for his unwatchfulness, Mat. 26.36-46. Mar. 14.33-42. Luk. 22.40-46.

Cuts off the ear of Malchus, Jno. 18. 10,11,26. Mat. 26.51-54. Mar. 14.47. Luk. 22.50,51. Follows Christ afar off, Mat. 26.58. Mar. 14.54. Luk. 22.54. Jno. 18.15. Is brought by John into the high-priest's palace, Jno. 18.16. Denies Christ 3 times ; his repentance, Mat. 26.69-75. Mar. 14.66-72. Luk. 22.55-62. Jno. 18.17,18,25-27.

Visits the sepulchre with John, Luk. 24.12. Jno. 20.2-6. Christ sends him a message, Mar. 16.7. Appears to him, Luk. 24.34. 1 Cor. 15.5. Appears to him at the sea of Tiberias ; a miraculous draught ; inquires if he loved him, and foretells his death ; commands him to feed his sheep ; reproves his curiosity respecting John, Jno. 21.1-23. 2 Pet. 1.14.

Is present at the prayer-meeting in Jerusalem ; recommends the election of an apostle, Act. 1.13-22. His address at Pentecost, Act. 2.14-40. Cures a lame man ; addresses the people, Act. 3. Brought before the Sanhedrim ; his defence, Act. 4.1-22. Death of Ananias and Sapphira, Act. 5.1-11.

His miracles, Act. 5.12-16. Imprisoned with the twelve ; his defence ; is scourged, and released, Act. 5.17-42. Is sent by the apostles to Samaria ; denounces Simon Magus ; returns to Jerusalem, Act. 8.14-25. Receives Paul, Gal. 1.18. Gal. 2.9. Preaches in different places ; comes to Lydda ; cures Eneas ; his success, Act. 9.32-34.

Comes to Joppa ; raises Dorcas, Act. 9. 36-43 While praying at Joppa, has a vision of clean and unclean beasts, Act. 10.9-16. Act. 11.1-17. Visits Cornelius in Cesarea ; baptises him and many other Gentiles, Act. 10.17-48. At Jerusalem, defends his receiving the Gentiles, Act. 11.1-18.

Imprisoned by Herod, and released by an angel, Act. 12.3-19. Visits Antioch, and is blamed by Paul for withdrawing from the Gentiles, Gal. 2.11-16, see 2 Pet. 3.15. Is called the apostle of the circumcision, Gal. 2. 7-9. Was married, Mat. 8.14. 1 Cor. 9.5.

Bears testimony to Paul's inspiration, 2 Pet. 3.15,16. A party in Corinth call themselves by his name, 1 Cor. 1.12. His miracles, see MIRACLES, p. 310.

See APOSTLES—MINISTERS.

PETRA. See SELA.

PHALTIEL, Michal's second husband, 1 Sam. 25.44. 2 Sam. 3.15.

PHARAOH I. king of Egypt (B.C. 1920) ; his treatment of Abraham, Gen. 12.14-20.

PHARAOH II. (B.C. 1715), imprisons his butler and baker, Gen. 40.1-3,20-23. His dreams interpreted by Joseph ; makes Joseph chief-ruler, Gen. 41. Buys Egyptians' land, &c., Gen. 47.14-26. Invites Jacob and his family to settle in Egypt ; his subsequent kindness to them, Gen. 45.16-20. Gen. 47.1-11. Gen. 50.4-6.

PHARAOH III. (B.C. 1635), of a new dynasty ; enslaves Israel, and destroys their male children, Ex. 1.8-22. His oppression, Ex. 2.11. His daughter adopts Moses, Ex. 2.5-10.

PHARAOH IV. (B.C. 1531), seeks to slay Moses, Ex. 2.15. His death, Ex. 2.23.

PHARAOH V. (B.C. 1491), his interviews with Moses and Aaron, Ex. 5.1-4. Ex. 7.10. Ex. 8.1,25. Ex. 9.1,13,27. Ex. 10.3,8,16,24. Ex. 12.31. Increased oppression of Israel, Ex. 5.5-23. Miracles of Moses before him, Ex. c. 7 to 14. His impenitence, Ex. 7.13,22. Ex. 8.15,19,32. Ex. 9.7,12,34. Ex. 10.20. Ex. 11.10. Ex. 14. Asks Moses' intercession, Ex. 8.8,25. Ex. 9.27. Ex. 10.16. Dismisses Israel, Ex. 12.31. Pursues Israel, and is drowned, Ex. 14.5-31. Ex. 15.19, see RED SEA.

PHARAOH VI. (B.C. 1040), gives an asylum to Hadad in David's reign, 1 Kin. 11.17-22. His daughter married to Solomon (B.C. 1014),

1 Kin. 3.1. Her marriage-portion, 1 Kin. 9. 15,16.

PHARAOH VII. (B.C. 710), contemporary with Hezekiah, 2 Kin. 18.21.

PHARAOH-NECHO (B.C. 610), invades Assyria ; defeats Josiah, who is slain at Megiddo, 2 Kin. 23.29,30. 2 Chr. 35.20-24. Deposes Jehoahaz ; makes Jehoiakim king, 2 Kin. 23.33-35. 2 Chr. 36.3,4. Defeated by Nebuchadnezzar, 2 Kin. 24.7. Jer. 46.2. Attacks the Philistines, Jer. 47.1.

PHARAOH-HOPHRA (B.C. 590), aids Zedekiah, and affords an asylum to the Jews, Jer. 37.4-7. Jer. 44. Eze. 17.15-17. Prophecy of his captivity in Babylon, Jer. 44. 30. Jer. 46.25,26. Eze. 29. Eze. 30.21-26.

PHARISEES. Believed in the resurrection, Act. 23.6,8 ; in the old Testament, Act. 22.3. Act. 26.5. Phil. 3.5 ; and in tradition, Mat. 15.1-20. Mar. 7.1-15. Gal. 1.14. Hypocrisy of, Mat. 3.7-10. Mat. 6.2-5,16. Mat. 15.7-9. Mat. 16.12. Luk. 12.1. Mat. 23.3-5,14. Luk. 11.44.

Pride and self-righteousness of, Mat. 9.11-13. Mat. 21.45. Mat. 23.5-12. Luk. 16.15. Luk. 18. 11,14. Covetousness of, Mat. 23.14. Luk. 16.14. Strict outward observance of the law, Mat. 12.2-7. Mat. 23.23-28.

Secret wickedness of, Mat. 5.20. Mat. 16. 1,4. Mat. 23.14,23-28. Luk. 11.39-42. Jno. 8.7,9. Fasted often, Mat. 9.14. Luk. 18.12. Their zeal in proselytizing, Mat. 23.15. Act. 22.3. Were false teachers, Mat. 15.9,14. Mat. 16.11,12. Mat. 23.16-24.

Were rulers, Mat. 23.2,3. Act. 5.34. Act. 23.6. Their disciples, Mat. 22.16. Luk. 5.33. Act. 22.3. Were respected for their learning, Jno. 7.48. Act. 5.34. Rejected John, Luk. 7.30. See Mat. 3.7. Their unbelief in Christ, Mat. 12.38,39. Mat. 15.12. Mat. 16.1. Mat. 21.45. Luk. 14.1. Luk. 16.14. Jno. 7.48.

Tempted Christ with questions, Mat. 19.3. Mat. 22.15-22. Hated and slandered him, Mat. 9.34. Mat. 12.10. Luk. 5.21. Luk. 6.7. Luk. 7.34,39. Luk. 14.1. Luk. 15.2. Jno. 8.13. Jno.9.16,24,29. Persecuted Christ and his disciples, Mat. 23.29-35. Jno. 4.1-3. Act. 8.3. Act. 9.1, see CHRIST'S SUFFERINGS.

Some of, invited Christ to their houses, Luk. 7.36. Luk. 11.37. Luk. 14.1 ; and became his disciples, Jno. 3.1. Act. 15.5. Act. 22.3. See CHRIST, JEWS' RECEPTION OF—SABBATH, JEWISH MISCONCEPTIONS OF.

PHARPAR, a river of Damascus, 2 Kin. 5.12.

PHEBE (Gr. *diaconos*), a servant of the church at Cenchrea, commended for her charity, Rom. 16.1,2.

PHENICE, a city on the south-east of Crete, Act. 27.12-14.

PHENICIA, or PHENICE. Inhabitants descended from Canaan, Gen. 10.15,17,18. Called Zidonians, Jud. 18.7. Eze. 32.30. For their commerce, relations with the Jews, Elijah's miracle among, Christ's miracles among, and their relation to the Romans, see TYRE, SIDON, SAREPTA. Gospel preached in, Mar. 3.8. Act. 11.19. Paul visits the churches in, Act. 15.3. Act. 21.2-4. Act. 27.3. Towns of, see ACCHO, SAREPTA, SIDON, TYRE. Idols of, see BAAL, BAALZEBUB, CHIUN.

PHILADELPHIA, a city of Asia Minor; epistle addressed to, Rev. 1.11. Rev. 3.7.

PHILEMON, a Christian, whose slave had absconded; Paul's letter to, Philm. 1-25.

PHILETUS, a false teacher, 2 Tim. 2.17,18.

PHILIP THE APOSTLE, of Bethsaida; his call by Christ; brings Nathanael to Jesus, Jno. 1.43-45. An apostle, Mat. 10.3. Mar. 3.18. Luk. 6.14. Act. 1.13. Christ's question to him before feeding the 5000, Jno. 6.5-7. Brings Greeks to Jesus, Jno. 12.20-22. Question to Jesus at the last supper, Jno. 14.8,9.

PHILIP THE EVANGELIST, chosen one of the seven deacons, Act. 6.5. Sent to Samaria; his success, Act. 8.5-12. Teaches and baptises the eunuch; comes to Cesarea, and dwells there, Act. 8.26-40. Act. 21.8. His four daughters prophesy, Act. 21.9.

PHILIP, son of Herod I., tetrarch of Iturea and Trachonitis, Luk. 3.1. Herod II.'s adultery with his wife, Mat. 14.3. Mar. 6.17. Luk. 3.19.

PHILIPPI, a city of Macedonia, and a Roman colony; Lydia's conversion under Paul in; Paul casts out a spirit of divination; is imprisoned with Silas; an earthquake; the jailer's conversion; Paul asserts his rights as a citizen, Act. 16.12-40. 1 The. 2.2. Paul visits, Act. 20.1-6. Liberality of the church at, Phil. 4.10-18. Visited by Epaphroditus, Phil. 2.25. Epistle to the church of.

PHILISTINES, descended from Casluhim, Gen. 10.14. 1 Chr. 1.12; and Caphtorim, Jer. 47.4. Amos 9.7. Termed Cherethites, 1 Sam. 30.14,16. Eze. 25.16. Zeph. 2.5. Territory of, Ex. 13.17. Ex. 23.31. Deu. 2.23. Jos. 13.3. Jos. 15.47. Lords of, Jos. 13.3. Jud. 3.3. Jud. 16.5,30. 1 Sam. 5.8,11. 1 Sam. 6.4,12. 1 Sam. 7.7. 1 Sam. 29.2,6,7. Kings of, see ABIMELECH—ACHISH. Abimelech's covenant with Abraham, Gen. 21.22-32; with Isaac, Gen. 26.

Slaughter the children of Ephraim, 1 Chr. 7.21. After the Israelites' conquest of Palestine, remained in the land, Jud. 3.3,4. Defeated by Shamgar, Jud. 3.31. Jud. 10.11. Oppress Israel, Jud. 10.7. Israel in their power 40 years, and delivered by Samson, Jud. c. 13 to 16. 1 Sam. 12.9,11. Defeat Israel under Hophni; take the ark; are plagued, and restore it, 1 Sam. c. 4 to 6. Defeated by Israel under Samuel, 1 Sam. 7.

Oppress Israel, and are defeated by Saul and Jonathan, 1 Sam. 9.16. 1 Sam. 13. 1 Sam. 14. Goliath slain by David, and their army defeated, 1 Sam. 17. Defeated by David under Saul, 1 Sam. 18.27,30. 1 Sam. 19.8. 1 Sam. 23.1-5. Invade Israel, 1 Sam. 23.27. David takes refuge with king Achish, 1 Sam. 27. Psa. 56 (title). Defeated by Amalekites, 1 Sam. 30.14,16. Invade Israel, 1 Sam. 29. 1 Chr. 12.19. Defeat and slay Saul and Jonathan, 1 Sam. 31. 1 Chr. 10.1.

Defeated in David's reign, 2 Sam. 5.17-25. 2 Sam. 8.1. 2 Sam. 21.15-22. 2 Sam. 23.9-16. 1 Chr. 14.8-17. 1 Chr. 18.1. 1 Chr. 20.4-8. 2 Chr. 9.26.

Tributary to Jehoshaphat, 2 Chr. 17.11. Invade Judah in Jehoram's reign, 2 Chr. 21.16. Defeated by Uzziah, 2 Chr. 26.6,7. Invade Judah in Ahaz's reign, 2 Chr. 28.18. Defeated by Hezekiah, 2 Kin. 18.8.

Gath taken by the Syrians, 2 Kin. 12.17. Philistines defeated by the Assyrians, Isa. 20.1. Gaza taken by Pharaoh, Jer. 47.1. Jews intermarried with, Neh. 13.23.

Soothsayers of, Isa. 2.6. Language of, Neh. 13.24. Idols of, see ASHTAROTH, BEEL-ZEBUB, DAGON. Towns of, see GERAR, GIBBETHON, METHEG-AMMA, JABNEEL. The 5 lordships of, see ASHDOD, ASKELON, EKRON, GATH, GAZA. Prophecies of, Psa. 87.4. Isa. 9.11,12. Isa. 11.14. Isa. 14.29-31. Jer. 25.17-20. Jer. 47. Eze. 16.27. Eze. 25.15-17. Amos 1.6-8. Amos 3.9. Obad. 19. Zeph. 2.4-7. Zeph. 9. 5-7. See CAPHTORIM, CASLUHIM, CHERETHITES, PELETHITES.

PHILOSOPHERS. See EPICUREANS—STOICS.

PHILOSOPHY, the Jewish or Rabbinical theology, Col. 2.8 with v. 16. 1 Tim. 6.20.

PHINEHAS, high-priest, Eleazar's son, Ex. 6.25. 1 Chr. 6.4,50. Slays Zimri; is promised an everlasting priesthood, Num. 25.7-15. Psa. 106.30. Ruler of the Kohathites, 1 Chr. 9.19,20. Carries the trumpets to the war against Midian, Num. 31.6. Heads the deputation to the Reubenites, &c., Jos. 22.13-32. His property in Ephraim, Jos. 24.33. Inquires of the Lord, Jud. 20.28.

————, son of Eli, wickedness of; his death predicted, 1 Sam. 1.3. 1 Sam. 2. 13-17,22-25,34. 1 Sam. 3.11-14. Carries the ark against the Philistines; is slain, 1 Sam. 4.4,11,17. His wife's death, 1 Sam. 4.19-22.

PHRYGIA, an inland province of Asia Minor; strangers from, at Jerusalem during Pentecost, Act. 2.10. Paul visits, Act. 16.6. Act. 18.23. Towns of, see COLOSSE, HIERAPOLIS, LAODICEA.

PHUT. See LIBYA.

PHYGELLUS AND HERMOGENES, Asiatic disciples who forsook Paul, 2 Tim. 1.15.

PHYLACTERY (a safeguard), or FRONTLET (a band), worn across the brow or on the arm, inscribed with texts, Mat. 23.5. Ex. 13. 9,16. Deu. 6.8. Deu. 11.18.

PHYSICIAN, 2 Chr. 16.12. Luk. 8.43. Embalmed, Gen. 50.2. Proverbs respecting, Mar. 2.17. Luk. 4.23. Illustrative, Job 13.4. Jer. 8.22. Luk. 5.31. Luke a physician, Col. 4.14. See DISEASES.

PICTURE, figure or image, Lev. 26.1 (marg.), Num. 33.52. Pro. 25.11. Isa. 2.16.

PIECE OF SILVER, 1. (Heb. Kesitah), about 4 shekels (?), Gen. 33.19. Jos. 24.32. Job 42.11. 2. (Gr. drachme), equal to a Roman penny or 7½d., Luk. 15.8,9.

PIETY. See such subjects as HOLINESS—SPIRITUAL DILIGENCE — PRAYERFULNESS, &c. CHILDREN, GOOD.

PIGEON. See DOVE.

PI-HAHIROTH, an encampment of the Israelites, Ex. 14.2. Num. 33.7.

PILATE, PONTIUS, Roman governor of Judea, Luk. 3.1. Slays the Galileans, Luk. 13.1. Tries and condemns Jesus, Mat. 27. Mar. 15. Luk. 23. Jno. 18.28-40. Jno. 19. Act. 3.13. Act. 4.27. Act. 13.28. 1 Tim. 6.13.

PILLAR OF SALT, Lot's wife changed to, Gen. 19.26. Pillar of cloud, see CLOUD OF GLORY.

PILLARS AND MEMORIAL STONES, set up by Jacob, Gen. 28.18,22. Gen. 31.13,45-51. Gen. 35.14; by Moses, Ex. 24.4; by Joshua at Gilgal, Jos. 4.3-9. On Mount Ebal, Deu. 27.2-4. Jos. 8.32; and in Shechem, Jos. 24. 26,27. Jud. 9.6. By Reuben and Gad, near Jordan, Jos. 22.26-34; by Samuel, 1 Sam. 7. 12; by Absalom, 2 Sam. 18.18. Stone of Bohan, Jos. 15.6. Jos. 18.17; of Ezel, 1 Sam. 20.19; of Gibeon, 2 Sam. 20.8; of Zoheleth, 1 Kin. 1.9. Idolatrous, to be destroyed, Deu. 12.3.

PILLOW or BOLSTER, Gen. 28.11,18. 1 Sam. 26.7,11,16. 1 Kin. 19.6. Eze. 13.18,20. Mar. 4.38. Of goat's hair, 1 Sam. 19.13,16.

PILOT, Eze. 27.8,27-29. Translated shipmaster (the master-pilot), Jonah 1.6.

PIN. See NAIL.

PINE-TREE, Isa. 41.19. Isa. 60.13. Booths of, Neh. 8.15.

PIPE, a musical wind instrument, Jer. 48.36. 1 Cor. 14.7. Used by prophets, 1 Sam. 10.5. At the coronation of Adonijah, 1 Kin. 1.40. At entertainments, Isa. 5.12. Mat. 11.17. By the people in praise, Isa. 30.29. Sound of, 1 Cor. 14.7. Jer. 48.36. Pipers, Rev. 18.22. Translated minstrels, Mat. 9.23. See FLUTE—ORGAN.

PIRATHON, a town in Ephraim; Abdon buried in, Jud. 12.13-15. 1 Chr. 11.31.

PISGAH, a hill of the chain of Abarim, in Moab, Num. 21.20. Deu. 3.17. Deu. 4.49. Jos. 12.3 (marg.). Balak builds 7 altars on, for Balaam, Num. 23.14. Moses views the promised land from, and dies on, Deu. 3.27. Deu. 34.1-7.

PISIDIA, a district of Asia Minor; Paul preaches in, Act. 14.24. See ANTIOCH OF PISIDIA.

PISON, one of the 4 rivers of Eden, Gen. 2.11.

PIT, BOTTOMLESS (Gr. abyss), Rev. 9. 1,2,11. Rev. 11.7. Rev. 17.8. Rev. 20.1,3.

PITCH, Isa. 34.9. Ark of Noah painted with, Gen. 6.14; of Moses, Ex. 2.3. See SLIME.

PITCHER, Mar. 14.13. Carried on the shoulder, Gen. 24.18,45,46. Of earth, Lam. 4. 2. Gideon's stratagem with, Jud. 7.10-20. Translated barrel, 1 Kin. 17.12. 1 Kin. 18.33. Illustrative, Ecc. 12.6.

PITHOM, a treasure city in Egypt, built by the Israelites, Ex. 1.11.

PLAGUES OF EGYPT, Psa. 105. The river becomes blood, Ex. 7.14-25. The frogs, Ex. 8.1-15. Lice, Ex. 8.16-19. Flies, Ex. 8. 20. On cattle, &c., Ex. 9.1-7. Of boils and blains, Ex. 9.8-12. Hail, Ex. 9.18-34. Locusts, Ex. 10.1-20. Darkness, Ex. 10.21-23. Death of the first-born, Ex. 11.4-7. Ex. 12.29,30. Egyptians drowned in the Red Sea. Ex. 14. See PESTILENCE.

PLAIN. See VALLEYS.

PLANE, chisel or carving tool, Isa 44.13.

PLANET. See STAR.

PLANTS AND TREES. See ALGUM, ALMOND, ALOE, ANISE, APPLE, ASH, BALM, BARLEY, BAY, BEAN, BOX, BRAMBLE, BULRUSH, CAMPHIRE, CANE, CASSIA, CEDAR, CHESTNUT, CINNAMON, COCKLE, CORIANDER, CORN, CUCUMBER, CUMMIN, CYPRESS, DATE, EBONY, ELM, FIG, FIR, FITCH, FLAG, FLAX, FRANKINCENSE, GALBANUM, GALL, GARLIC, GOPHER, GOURD, GRASS, HAZEL, HEATH, HEMLOCK, HUSK, HYSSOP, JUNIPER, LEEKS, LENTILE, LILY, MALLOW, MANDRAKE, MELON, MILLET, MINT, MULBERRY, MUSTARD, MYRRH, MYRTLE, NETTLE, NUT, OAK, OLIVE, ONION, PALM, PINE, POMEGRANATE, POPLAR, REED, ROSE, RUE, RYE, SAFFRON, SHITTIM, SPIKENARD, STACTE, SYCAMINE, SYCAMORE, TARE, TEIL, THISTLE, THORN, THYME, VINE, WHEAT, WILLOW, WORMWOOD.

PLEASURES, WORLDLY. See WORLDLINESS.

PLEDGES, Gen. 38.17-20. See CREDITORS —HOSTAGES.

PLEIADES (a cluster), a group of stars, Job 9.9. Job 38.31. Translated 7 stars, Amos 5.8.

PLOUGH and PLOUGHING, Isa. 28.24. Isa. 61.5. With oxen, 1 Kin. 19.19. Job 1.14. With an ox and ass together forbidden, Deu. 22.10. Illustrative, Jud. 14.18. Psa. 129.3. Hos. 10.13. Pro. 21.4. See EARING.

PLUMMET or PLUMB-LINE, made of lead or tin, Zec. 4.10 (marg.). Used by masons, Amos 7.7,8. Illustrative, Isa. 28.17. 2 Kin. 21.13.

POETS, HEATHEN, quotation from (Aratus of Cilicia), Act. 17.28. (Epimenides of Crete), Tit. 1.12. See SONGS.

POLITENESS. See SALUTATIONS.

POLLUX. See CASTOR.

POLYGAMY, forbidden, Deu. 17.16,17. (Lev. 18.18?). Mal. 2.15. Mat. 19.4,5. Mar. 10.2-8. 1 Tim. 3.2,12.

Practised, Job 27.15. By Lamech, Gen. 4.19. Abraham, Gen. 16. Esau, Gen. 26.34. Gen. 28.9. Jacob, Gen. 29.30. Ashur, 1 Chr. 4.5. Gideon, Jud. 8.30. Elkanah, 1 Sam. 1.2. David, 2 Sam. 3.2-5. Solomon, 1 Kin. 11.1-8. Rehoboam, 2 Chr. 11.18-23. Abijah, 2 Chr. 13.21. Jehoram, 2 Chr. 21.14. Joash, 2 Chr. 24.3. Ahab, 2 Kin. 10.1. Jehoiachin, 2 Kin. 24.15. Belshazzar, Dan. 5.2, see 1 Chr. c. 2 to 8. Law respecting the first-born, Deu. 21.15-17. See MARRIAGE.

POMEGRANATE, a kind of apple, Song 4.3. Song 6.7. Wine made from, Song 8.2. Cultivated in Palestine, Song 4.13. Deu. 8.8. Joel 1.12. 1 Sam. 14.2. Spies brought fruit of, Num. 13.23. Saul under at Migron, 1 Sam. 14.2. Ornaments of, on the ephod, Ex. 28. 33,34. Ex. 39.24; and on the pillars of the temple, 1 Kin. 7.18,20,42. Jer. 52.22,23.

PONTUS, the north-east province of Asia Minor; strangers from, in Jerusalem at Pentecost, Act. 2.9. Peter addresses his epistle to the strangers in, 1 Pet. 1.1.

POOLS. See WELLS.

POOR, THE. Job. 30.3. For want and famine they were solitary; fleeing into the wilderness in former time desolate and waste, 4. Who cut up mallows by the bushes, and juniper roots for their meat. 5. They were driven forth from among men (they cried after them as after a thief;) 6. To dwell in the cliffs of the valleys, *in* caves of the earth, and *in* the rocks. *v.* 7,8. Pro. 31.6,7.

Pro. 10.15. The destruction of the poor *is* their poverty.

Pro. 13.7. *There is* that maketh himself poor, yet *hath* great riches. 23. Much food *is in* the tillage of the poor.

Pro. 18.23. The poor useth entreaties : but the rich answereth roughly.

Pro. 19.1. Better *is* the poor that walketh in his integrity, than *he that is* perverse in his lips, and is a fool. 22. a poor man *is* better than a liar.

Pro. 22.7. The rich ruleth over the poor, and the borrower *is* servant to the lender.

Pro. 28.6. Better *is* the poor that walketh in his uprightness, than *he that is* perverse in *his* ways, though he *be* rich. 11. The rich man *is* wise in his own conceit ; but the poor that hath understanding searcheth him out.

Pro. 30.8. Give me neither poverty nor riches ; feed me with food convenient for me. 9. Lest I be poor, and steal, and take the name of my God *in vain.*

Ecc. 4.13. Better *is* a poor and a wise child than an old and foolish king, who will no more be admonished.

Ecc. 5.12. The sleep of a labouring man *is* sweet, whether he eat little or much. *v.* 9-12.

Ecc. 6.8. For what hath the wise more than the fool ? what hath the poor that knoweth to walk before the living ?

Ecc. 9.15. There was found in it a poor wise man, and he by his wisdom delivered the city ; yet no man remembered that same poor man. 16. Then said I, Wisdom *is* better than strength: nevertheless the poor man's wisdom *is* despised, and his words are not heard.

Jer. 5.3. They have made their faces harder than a rock ; they have refused to return. 4. Therefore I said, Surely these *are* poor ; they are foolish : for they know not the way of the Lord, *nor* the judgment of their God.

Luk. 9.58. Foxes have holes, and birds of the air *have* nests ; but the Son of man hath not where to lay *his* head.

2 Cor. 6.10. As poor, yet making many rich ; as having nothing, and *yet* possessing all things.

POOR, God's Care of. Job 5.15. He saveth the poor from the sword, from their mouth, and from the hand of the mighty. 16. So the poor hath hope, and iniquity stoppeth her mouth.

Job 31.15. Did not he that made me in the womb make him ? and did not one fashion us in the womb ?

Job 34.19. *Him* that accepteth not the persons of princes, nor regardeth the rich more than the poor ; for they all *are* the work of his hands. 28. They cause the cry of the poor to come unto him, and he heareth the cry of the afflicted.

Job 36.6. He preserveth not the life of the wicked : but giveth right to the poor. 15. He delivereth the poor in his affliction, and openeth their ears in oppression.

Psa. 9.18. The needy shall not alway be forgotten : the expectation of the poor shall *not* perish for ever.

Psa. 10.14. Thou hast seen *it* ; for thou beholdest mischief and spite, to requite *it* with thy hand : the poor committeth himself unto thee.

Psa. 12.5. For the oppression of the poor, for the sighing of the needy, now will I arise, saith the Lord ; I will set *him* in safety *from him that* puffeth at him.

Psa. 14.6. Ye have shamed the counsel of the poor, because the Lord *is* his refuge.

Psa. 34.6. This poor man cried, and the Lord heard *him*, and saved him out of all his troubles.

Psa. 35.10. Lord, who *is* like unto thee, which deliverest the poor from him that is too strong for him, yea, the poor and the needy from him that spoileth him ?

Psa. 68.10. Thou, O God, hast prepared of thy goodness for the poor.

Psa. 69.33. The Lord heareth the poor, and despiseth not his prisoners.

Psa. 72.2. He shall judge thy people with righteousness, and thy poor with judgment. 4. He shall judge the poor of the people, he shall save the children of the needy, and shall break in pieces the oppressor. 12. He shall deliver the needy when he crieth ; the poor also, and *him* that hath no helper. 13. He shall spare the poor and needy, and shall save the souls of the needy.

Psa. 74.21. O let not the oppressed return ashamed : let the poor and needy praise thy name.

Psa. 102.17. He will regard the prayer of the destitute, and not despise their prayer.

Psa. 107.9. He satisfieth the longing soul, and filleth the hungry soul with goodness. 36. There he maketh the hungry to dwell, that they may prepare a city for habitation. 41. Yet setteth he the poor on high from affliction, and maketh *him* families like a flock.

Psa. 109.31. He shall stand at the right hand of the poor, to save *him* from those that condemn his soul.

Psa. 113.7. He raiseth up the poor out of the dust, *and* lifteth the needy out of the dunghill ; 8. That he may set *him* with princes, *even* with the princes of his people. 1 Sam. 2.7,8.

Psa. 132.15. I will abundantly bless her provision : I will satisfy her poor with bread.

Psa. 140.12. I know that the Lord will maintain the cause of the afflicted, *and* the right of the poor.

Psa. 146.7. Which executeth judgment for the oppressed ; which giveth food to the hungry.

Pro. 22.2. The rich and poor meet together : the Lord *is* the maker of them all. 22. Rob not the poor, because he *is* poor ; neither oppress the afflicted in the gate : 23. For the Lord will plead their cause, and spoil the soul of those that spoiled them.

Pro. 29.13. The poor and the deceitful man meet together ; the Lord lighteneth both their eyes.

Ecc. 5.8. If thou seest the oppression of the poor, and violent perverting of judgment and justice in a province, marvel not at the matter : for *he that is* higher than the highest regardeth ; and *there be* higher than they.

Isa. 11.4. With righteousness shall he judge the poor, and reprove with equity for the meek of the earth.

Isa. 14.30. The firstborn of the poor shall feed, and the needy shall lie down in safety. 32. The Lord hath founded Zion, and the poor of his people shall trust in it.

Isa. 25.4. Thou hast been a strength to the poor, a strength to the needy in his distress, a refuge from the storm, a shadow from the heat, when the blast of the terrible ones *is* as a storm *against* the wall.

Isa. 29.19. The poor among men shall rejoice in the Holy One of Israel.

Isa. 41.17. *When* the poor and needy seek water, and *there* is none, *and* their tongue faileth for thirst, I the Lord will hear them, *I* the God of Israel will not forsake them.

Jer. 20.13. Praise ye the Lord: for he hath delivered the soul of the poor from the hand of evildoers.

Zeph. 3.12. I will also leave in the midst of thee an afflicted and poor people, and they shall trust in the name of the Lord.

Zec. 11.7. I will feed the flock of slaughter, *even* you, O poor of the flock. **11.** So the poor of the flock that waited upon me knew that it *was* the word of the Lord.

Mat. 11.5. The poor have the gospel preached to them.

Mar. 12.43. This poor widow hath cast more in than all they which have cast into the treasury: **44.** For all *they* did cast in of their abundance; but she of her want did cast in all that she had, *even* all her living.

Luk. 4.18. The Spirit of the Lord *is* upon me, because he hath anointed me to preach the gospel to the poor.

Luk. 16.22. The beggar died, and was carried by the angels into Abraham's bosom.

Jas. 2.5. Hath not God chosen the poor of this world rich in faith, and heirs of the kingdom which he hath promised to them that love him?

See GOD PROTECTOR—GOD'S GOODNESS—CONTENTMENT—AFFLICTION.

POOR, JUSTICE TO. Ex. 23.3. Neither shalt thou countenance a poor man in his cause. **6.** Thou shalt not wrest the judgment of thy poor in his cause.

Lev. 19.15. Ye shall do no unrighteousness in judgment; thou shalt not respect the person of the poor, nor honour the person of the mighty: *but* in righteousness shalt thou judge thy neighbour.

Psa. 82.3. Defend the poor and fatherless: do justice to the afflicted and needy. **4.** Deliver the poor and needy: rid *them* out of the hand of the wicked.

Pro. 29.14. The king that faithfully judgeth the poor, his throne shall be established for ever.

Pro. 31.9. Open thy mouth, judge righteously, and plead the cause of the poor and needy.

Isa. 1.17. Seek judgment, relieve the oppressed, judge the fatherless, plead for the widow.

Isa. 16.3. Execute judgment; make thy shadow as the night in the midst of the noonday; hide the outcasts; bewray not him that wandereth. **4.** Let mine outcasts dwell with thee, Moab; be thou a cover to them from the face of the spoiler.

Jer. 22.16. He judged the cause of the poor and needy: then *it was* well *with him: was* not this to know me? saith the Lord.

See POOR, NEGLECT OF—RULERS.

POOR, KINDNESS TO, ENJOINED—ALMS-GIVING. Deu. 15.7. If there be among you a poor man of one of thy brethren, within any of thy gates, in thy land which the Lord thy God giveth thee, thou shalt not harden thine heart, nor shut thine hand, from thy poor brother; **8.** But thou shalt open thine hand wide unto him, and shalt surely lend him sufficient for his need, *in that* which he wanteth. **10.** Thou shalt surely give him, and thine heart shall not be grieved when thou givest unto him: because that for this thing the Lord thy God shall bless thee in all thy works, and in all that thou puttest thine hand unto. **11.** For the poor shall never cease out of the land: therefore I command thee, saying, Thou shalt open thine hand wide unto thy brother, to thy poor, and to thy needy, in thy land. *v.* 9.

Job 29.11. When the ear heard *me*, then it blessed me; and when the eye saw *me*, it gave witness to me: **12.** Because I delivered the poor that cried, and the fatherless, and *him that had* none to help him. **13.** The blessing of him that was ready to perish came upon me: and I caused the widow's heart to sing for joy. **15.** I was eyes to the blind, and feet *was* I to the lame. **16.** I *was* a father to the poor: and the cause *which* I knew not I searched out.

Job 30.25. Did not I weep for him that was in trouble? was *not* my soul grieved for the poor?

Job 31.16. If I have withheld the poor from *their* desire, or have caused the eyes of the widow to fail; **17.** Or have eaten my morsel myself alone, and the fatherless hath not eaten thereof; **18.** (For from my youth he was brought up with me, as *with* a father, and I have guided her from my mother's womb;) **19.** If I have seen any perish for want of clothing, or any poor without covering; **20.** If his loins have not blessed me, and *if* he were *not* warmed with the fleece of my sheep. **22.** *Then* let mine arm fall from my shoulder blade, and mine arm be broken from the bone. *v.* 21,38-40.

Psa. 37.21. The righteous sheweth mercy, and giveth. **26.** *He is* ever merciful, and lendeth; and his seed *is* blessed.

Psa. 41.1. Blessed *is* he that considereth the poor: the Lord will deliver him in time of trouble. **2.** The Lord will preserve him, and keep him alive; *and* he shall be blessed upon the earth: and thou wilt not deliver him unto the will of his enemies. **3.** The Lord will strengthen him upon the bed of languishing: thou wilt make all his bed in his sickness.

Psa. 112.4. *He is* gracious, and full of compassion, and righteous. **5.** A good man sheweth favour, and lendeth. **9.** He hath dispersed, he hath given to the poor; his righteousness endureth for ever; his horn shall be exalted with honour.

Pro. 14.21. He that hath mercy on the poor, happy *is* he. **31.** He that honoureth him hath mercy on the poor.

Pro. 19.17. He that hath pity upon the poor lendeth unto the Lord; and that which he hath given will he pay him again.

Pro. 22.9. He that hath a bountiful eye shall be blessed; for he giveth of his bread to the poor.

Pro. 28.8. He that by usury and unjust gain increaseth his substance, he shall gather it for him that will pity the poor. **27.** He that giveth unto the poor shall not lack.

Pro. 29.7. The righteous considereth the cause of the poor.

Pro. 31.20. She stretcheth out her hand to the poor; yea, she reacheth forth her hands to the needy.

Isa. 58.7. *Is it* not to deal thy bread to the hungry, and that thou bring the poor that are cast out to thy house? when thou seest the naked, that thou cover him; and that thou hide not thyself from thine own flesh? 10. *If* thou draw out thy soul to the hungry, and satisfy the afflicted soul; then shall thy light rise in obscurity, and thy darkness *be* as the noon day.

Eze. 18.7. Hath not oppressed any, hath given his bread to the hungry, and hath covered the naked with a garment. *v.* 16,17.

Dan. 4.27. Break off thy sins by righteousness, and thine iniquities by shewing mercy to the poor; if it may be a lengthening of thy tranquillity.

Mat. 5.42. Give to him that asketh thee, and from him that would borrow of thee turn not thou away. *v.* 46.

Mat. 6.1. Take heed that ye do not your alms before men, to be seen of them: otherwise ye have no reward of your Father which is in heaven. 3. But when thou doest alms, let not thy left hand know what thy right hand doeth: 4. That thine alms may be in secret: and thy Father which seeth in secret himself shall reward thee openly. *v.* 2.

Mat. 25.35. I was an hungered, and ye gave me meat: I was thirsty, and ye gave me drink: I was a stranger, and ye took me in: 36. Naked, and ye clothed me: I was sick, and ye visited me: I was in prison, and ye came unto me. *v.* 3.

Mar. 14.7. Ye have the poor with you always, and whensoever ye will ye may do them good.

Luk. 3.11. He that hath two coats, let him impart to him that hath none; and he that hath meat, let him do likewise.

Luk. 6.35. Do good, and lend, hoping for nothing again; and your reward shall be great, and ye shall be the children of the Highest: for he is kind unto the unthankful and *to* the evil. *v.* 30-34. [Parable of the good Samaritan, Luk. 10.30-37.]

Luk. 11.41. Rather give alms of such things as ye have; and, behold, all things are clean unto you.

Luk. 12.33. Sell that ye have, and give alms; provide yourselves bags which wax not old, a treasure in the heavens that faileth not, where no thief approacheth, neither moth corrupteth.

Luk. 14.12. When thou makest a dinner or a supper, call not thy friends, nor thy brethren, neither thy kinsmen, nor *thy* rich neighbours; lest they also bid thee again, and a recompence be made thee. 13. But when thou makest a feast, call the poor, the maimed, the lame, the blind: 14. And thou shalt be blessed; for they cannot recompense thee: for thou shalt be recompensed at the resurrection of the just.

Luk. 18.22. Yet lackest thou one thing: sell all that thou hast, and distribute unto the poor, and thou shalt have treasure in heaven: and come, follow me. Mat. 19.21. Mar. 10.2.

Act. 20.35. That so labouring ye ought to support the weak, and to remember the words of the Lord Jesus, how he said, It is more blessed to give than to receive.

Rom. 12.8. He that sheweth mercy, with cheerfulness. 13. Distributing to the necessity of saints; given to hospitality.

1 Cor. 13.3. Though I bestow all my goods to feed *the poor*, and have not charity, it profiteth me nothing.

1 Cor. 16.1. Concerning the collection for the saints, as I have given order to the churches of Galatia, even so do ye. 2. Upon the first *day* of the week let every one of you lay by him in store, as *God* hath prospered him, that there be no gatherings when I come.

2 Cor. 9.5. I thought it necessary to exhort the brethren, that they would go before unto you, and make up beforehand your bounty, whereof ye had notice before, that the same might be ready, as *a matter of* bounty, and not as *of* covetousness. *v.* 1-15.

Gal. 2.10. *They would* that we should remember the poor; the same which I also was forward to do.

Gal. 6.10. As we have therefore opportunity, let us do good unto all *men*, especially unto them who are of the household of faith.

Eph. 4.28. Let him labour, working with *his* hands the thing which is good, that he may have to give to him that needeth.

1 Tim. 5.10. Well reported of for good works; if she have washed the saints' feet, if she have relieved the afflicted. 16. If any man or woman that believeth have widows, let them relieve them, and let not the church be charged; that it may relieve them that are widows indeed.

Heb. 13.3. Remember them that are in bonds, as bound with them; *and* them which suffer adversity, as being yourselves also in the body.

Jas. 1.27. Pure religion and undefiled before God and the Father is this, To visit the fatherless and widows in their affliction.

POOR, KINDNESS TO, EXAMPLES OF: Boaz, Ruth 2.16. Jews, Est. 9.22. Temanites, Isa. 21.14. Nebuzaradan, Jer. 39.10. Zaccheus, Luk. 19.8. Christian churches, Act. 6.1. Act. 11.29. Rom. 15.25,26. 2 Cor. 8.1-4. Dorcas, Act. 9.36. Cornelius, Act. 10.2,4.

See LIBERALITY.

POOR, LAWS REGARDING. Gleanings to be left for, see GLEANINGS. Portions of tithes and sacrifices to be given to, Deu. 14.29. Neh. 8.10. Usury forbidden to be taken from, Ex. 22.25. Lev. 25.36. Pledges to be returned, see CREDITORS. Hired servants' treatment, Deu. 24.14,15. See SERVANTS. Privileges at the Sabbatical year and Jubilee, Ex. 23.11. Lev. 25.25-28,39,40. Deu. 15.9. Their sacrifices, Lev. 5.7-11. Lev. 14.21. Atonement-money, half a shekel, Ex. 30.15.

POOR, NEGLECT AND OPPRESSION OF, WARNING AGAINST. Job 20.19. Because he hath oppressed *and* hath forsaken the poor; *because* he hath violently taken away an house which he builded not; 20. Surely he shall not feel quietness in his belly, he shall not save of that which he desired.

Job 22.6. Thou hast taken a pledge from thy brother for nought, and stripped the naked of their clothing. 7. Thou hast not given water to the weary to drink, and thou hast withholden bread from the hungry. 9. Thou hast sent widows away empty, and the arms of the fatherless have been broken. 10. Therefore snares *are* round about thee, and sudden fear troubleth thee; 11. Or darkness, *that* thou canst not see; and abundance of waters cover thee.

Job 24.4. They turn the needy out of the way: the poor of the earth hide themselves together. 7. They cause the naked to lodge without clothing, that *they have* no covering in the cold; 8. They are wet with the showers of the mountains, and embrace the rock for want of a shelter; 9. They pluck the fatherless from the breast, and take a pledge of the poor; 10. They cause *him* to go naked without clothing, and they take away the sheaf *from* the hungry.

Psa. 10.2. The wicked in *his* pride doth persecute the poor: let them be taken in the devices that they have imagined. 8. His eyes are privily set against the poor. 9. He lieth in wait to catch the poor: he doth catch the poor, when he draweth him into his net. 10. He croucheth, *and* humbleth himself, that the poor may fall by his strong ones.

Psa. 37.14. The wicked have drawn out the sword, and have bent their bow, to cast down the poor and needy.

Psa. 109.16. Because that he remembered not to shew mercy, but persecuted the poor and needy man, that he might even slay the broken in heart.

Pro. 14.20. The poor is hated even of his own neighbour.

Pro. 17.5. Whoso mocketh the poor reproacheth his Maker: *and* he that is glad at calamities shall not be unpunished.

Pro. 19.4. The poor is separated from his neighbour. 7. All the brethren of the poor do hate him: how much more do his friends go far from him? he pursueth *them with* words, *yet* they *are* wanting to him.

Pro. 21.13. Whoso stoppeth his ears at the cry of the poor, he also shall cry himself, but shall not be heard.

Pro. 22.16. He that oppresseth the poor to increase his *riches, and* he that giveth to the rich, *shall* surely *come* to want.

Pro. 28.3. A poor man that oppresseth the poor *is like* a sweeping rain, which leaveth no food. 15. *As* a roaring lion, and a ranging bear; *so is* a wicked ruler over the poor people. *v.* 27.

Pro. 29.7. The righteous considereth the cause of the poor: *but* the wicked regardeth not to know *it.*

Pro. 30.14. *There is* a generation whose teeth *are as* swords, and their jaw-teeth *as* knives, to devour the poor from off the earth, and the needy from *among* men.

Isa. 3.14. The Lord will enter into judgment with the ancients of his people, and the princes thereof: for ye have eaten up the vineyard; the spoil of the poor *is* in your houses. 15. What mean ye *that* ye beat my people to pieces, and grind the faces of the poor? saith the Lord God of hosts.

Isa. 10.1. Woe unto them that decree unrighteous decrees, and that write grievousness *which* they have prescribed; 2. To turn aside the needy from judgment, and to take away the right from the poor of my people, that widows may be their prey, and *that* they may rob the fatherless!

Isa. 32.6. The vile person will speak villany, and his heart will work iniquity, to make empty the soul of the hungry; and he will

cause the drink of the thirsty to fail. 7. He deviseth wicked devices to destroy the poor with lying words, even when the needy speaketh right.

Eze. 16.49. This was the iniquity of thy sister Sodom, pride, neither did she strengthen the hand of the poor and needy.

Eze. 18.12. Hath oppressed the poor and needy, hath spoiled by violence, hath not restored the pledge.

Eze. 22.29. The people of the land have used oppression, and exercised robbery, and have vexed the poor and needy; yea, they have oppressed the stranger wrongfully.

Amos 2.6. For three transgressions of Israel, and for four, I will not turn away *the punishment* thereof; because they sold the righteous for silver, and the poor for a pair of shoes; 7. That pant after the dust of the earth on the head of the poor, and turn aside the way of the meek. 8. And they lay *themselves* down upon clothes laid to pledge by every altar.

Amos 4.1. Hear this word, ye which oppress the poor, which crush the needy, which say to their masters, Bring, and let us drink. 2. The Lord God hath sworn by his holiness, that, lo, the days shall come upon you, that he will take you away with hooks.

Amos 5.11. As your treading *is* upon the poor, and ye take from him burdens of wheat: ye have built houses of hewn stone, but ye shall not dwell in them; ye have planted pleasant vineyards, but ye shall not drink wine of them. 12. For I know your manifold transgressions and your mighty sins: they turn aside the poor in the gate *from their right.*

Amos 8.4. Hear this, O ye that swallow up the needy, even to make the poor of the land to fail. 6. That we may buy the poor for silver, and the needy for a pair of shoes.

Hab. 3.14. Their rejoicing *was* as to devour the poor secretly.

Zec. 7.10. Oppress not the widow, nor the fatherless, the stranger, nor the poor.

Mat. 25.42. I was an hungred, and ye gave me no meat: I was thirsty, and ye gave me no drink. 45. Then shall he answer them, saying, Verily I say unto you, Inasmuch as ye did *it* not to one of the least of these, ye did *it* not to me.

Luk. 16.20. There was a certain beggar named Lazarus, which was laid at his gate, full of sores, 21. And desiring to be fed with the crumbs which fell from the rich man's table: moreover, the dogs came and licked his sores.

Jno. 12.6. This he said, not that he cared for the poor; but because he was a thief.

Jas. 2.2. If there come in also a poor man in vile raiment; 3. And ye have respect to him that weareth the gay clothing, and say unto him, Sit thou here in a good place; and say to the poor, Stand thou there, or sit here under my footstool; 4. Are ye not then partial in yourselves. 6. Ye have despised the poor. 15. If a brother or sister be naked, and destitute of daily food, 16. And one of you say unto them, Depart in peace, be *ye* warmed and filled; notwithstanding ye give them not those things which are needful to the body; what *doth it* profit?

1 Jno. 3.17. Whoso hath this world's good,

and seeth his brother have need, and shutteth up his bowels *of compassion* from him, how dwelleth the love of God in him? 18. My little children, let us not love in word, neither in tongue; but in deed and in truth. 19. And hereby we know that we are of the truth, and shall assure our hearts before him.

See RULERS.

POPLAR, Gen. 30.37. Idolatrous sacrifices under, Hos. 4.13.

PORCH. See HOUSE—TEMPLE-PORCH.

PORTERS. See LEVITES.

POSTS (runners), Job 9.25. Jer. 51.31; of Hezekiah, 2 Chr. 30.6,10; Ahasuerus, Est. 3. 13,15. Rode on horseback, mules, and camels, Est. 8.10,14.

POTIPHAR, captain of Pharaoh's guard; buys Joseph; imprisons him, Gen. 39.

POTIPHERA, prince or priest of On; father of Joseph's wife, Gen. 41.45.

POTSHERD, a fragment of earthenware, Job 2.8. Isa. 45.9.

POTTAGE. See BROTH.

POTTER, 1 Chr. 4.23. Working of the clay, Isa. 41.25. Turning vessels, Jer. 18.3,4. Field of, bought with Judas' money, Mat. 27. 7-10. Zec. 11.13. Illustrative, Isa. 64.8. Rom. 9.21. Potter's clay symbolical, Dan. 2.41.

POUND. 1. (Heb. *maneh*), 100 shekels, abo^t 4 lbs., 1 Kin. 10.17 with 2 Chr. 9.15,16; but only 15 shekels in Eze. 45.12. 2. (Gr. *mina*), about £3, 10s., Luk. 19.13. 3. (Gr. *litra*), about 12 oz., Jno. 12.3. Jno. 19.39.

PRAISE. Standing, 1 Chr. 6.33 (*marg.*), 39,44. 1 Chr. 23.30. 2 Chr. 5.12. 2 Chr. 7.6. 2 Chr. 20.19. Neh. 9.5. Psa. 135.2,3. See MUSIC, SACRED—WORSHIP.

PRAISE. Ex. 15.2. He *is* my God, and I will prepare him an habitation; my father's God, and I will exalt him. *v.* 1.

Deu. 10.21. He *is* thy praise, and he *is* thy God, that hath done for thee these great and terrible things.

Jud. 5.3. Hear, O ye kings; give ear, O ye princes; I, *even* I, will sing unto the Lord; I will sing *praise* to the Lord God of Israel.

2 Sam. 22.4. I will call on the Lord, *who is* worthy to be praised. Psa. 18.3.

1 Chr. 16.31. Let the heavens be glad, and let the earth rejoice: and let *men* say among the nations, The Lord reigneth. 33. Then shall the trees of the wood sing out at the presence of the Lord. 36. Blessed *be* the Lord God of Israel for ever and ever. And all the people said, Amen, and praised the Lord. 1 Chr. 29.20. 2 Chr. 7.3. Neh. 8.6.

1 Chr. 23.30. Stand every morning to thank and praise the Lord, and likewise at even.

Job 36.24. Remember that thou magnify his work, which men behold.

Psa. 7.17. I will praise the Lord according to his righteousness: and will sing praise to the name of the Lord most high.

Psa. 8.2. Out of the mouth of babes and sucklings hast thou ordained strength because of thine enemies, that thou mightest still the enemy and the avenger.

Psa. 9.11. Sing praises to the Lord, which

dwelleth in Zion: declare among the people his doings.

Psa. 22.22. I will declare thy name unto my brethren: in the midst of the congregation will I praise thee. 23. Ye that fear the Lord, praise him; all ye the seed of Jacob, glorify him; and fear him, all ye the seed of Israel. 25. My praise *shall be* of thee in the great congregation.

Psa. 26.12. In the congregations will I bless the Lord.

Psa. 30.4. Sing unto the Lord, O ye saints of his, and give thanks at the remembrance of his holiness. Psa. 97.12.

Psa. 33.1. Rejoice in the Lord, O ye righteous: *for* praise is comely for the upright. 2. Praise the Lord with harp: sing unto him with the psaltery *and* an instrument of ten strings. 3. Sing unto him a new song; play skilfully with a loud noise.

Psa. 34.1. I will bless the Lord at all times: his praise *shall* continually *be* in my mouth. 2. My soul shall make her boast in the Lord. 3. O magnify the Lord with me, and let us exalt his name together.

Psa. 35.28. My tongue shall speak of thy righteousness *and* of thy praise all the day long. *v.* 18.

Psa. 41.13. Blessed *be* the Lord God of Israel from everlasting, and to everlasting. Amen, and Amen.

Psa. 42.4. I went with them to the house of God, with the voice of joy and praise, with a multitude that kept holy day.

Psa. 43.3. O send out thy light and thy truth: let them lead me; let them bring me unto thy holy hill, and to thy tabernacles. 4. Then will I go unto the altar of God, unto God my exceeding joy: yea, upon the harp will I praise thee, O God my God.

Psa. 47.1. O clap your hands, all ye people; shout unto God with the voice of triumph. 6. Sing praises to God, sing praises: sing praises unto our King, sing praises. 7. For God *is* the King of all the earth: sing ye praises with understanding.

Psa. 50.23. Whoso offereth praise glorifieth me.

Psa. 51.14. O God, thou God of my salvation: my tongue shall sing aloud of thy righteousness. 15. O Lord, open thou my lips; and my mouth shall shew forth thy praise.

Psa. 52.9. I will praise thee for ever, because thou hast done *it:* and I will wait on thy name; for *it is* good before thy saints.

Psa. 56.10. In God will I praise *his* word: in the Lord will I praise *his* word.

Psa. 57.7. My heart is fixed, O God, my heart is fixed: I will sing and give praise. 8. Awake up, my glory; awake, psaltery and harp: I *myself* will awake early. 9. I will praise thee, O Lord, among the people: I will sing unto thee among the nations. Psa. 108. 1-3.

Psa. 61.8. So will I sing praise unto thy name for ever, that I may daily perform my vows.

Psa. 63.3. Because thy lovingkindness *is* better than life, my lips shall praise thee. 4. Thus will I bless thee while I live: I will lift up my hands in thy name. 5. My soul shall be satisfied as *with* marrow and fatness; and my mouth shall praise *thee* with joyful lips:

6. When I remember thee upon my bed, *and* meditate on thee in the *night* watches.

Psa. 65.1. Praise waiteth for thee, O God, in Sion : and unto thee shall the vow be performed.

Psa. 66.1. Make a joyful noise unto God, all ye lands : 2. Sing forth the honour of his name : make his praise glorious. 8. O bless our God, ye people, and make the voice of his praise to be heard.

Psa. 67.3. Let the people praise thee, O God ; let all the people praise thee. 4. O let the nations be glad and sing for joy.

Psa. 68.4. Sing unto God, sing praises to his name : extol him that rideth upon the heavens by his name JAH, and rejoice before him. 26. Bless ye God in the congregations, *even* the Lord, from the fountain of Israel. *v.* 32-34.

Psa. 69.30. I will praise the name of God with a song, and will magnify him with thanksgiving. 31. *This* also shall please the Lord better than an ox. 34. Let the heaven and earth praise him, the seas, and every thing that moveth therein.

Psa. 70.4. Let all those that seek thee rejoice and be glad in thee : and let such as love thy salvation say continually, Let God be magnified. Psa. 40.16.

Psa. 71.8. Let my mouth be filled *with* thy praise *and with* thy honour all the day. 14. I will hope continually, and will yet praise thee more and more. 15. My mouth shall shew forth thy righteousness *and* thy salvation all the day ; for I know not the numbers *thereof*. 22. I will also praise thee with the psaltery, *even* thy truth, O my God : unto thee will I sing with the harp, O thou Holy One of Israel.

Psa. 75.1. Unto thee, O God, do we give thanks, *unto thee* do we give thanks : for *that* thy name is near thy wondrous works declare. 9. I will declare for ever ; I will sing praises to the God of Jacob.

Psa. 79.13. We thy people and sheep of thy pasture will give thee thanks for ever : we will shew forth thy praise to all generations.

Psa. 81.1. Sing aloud unto God our strength : make a joyful noise unto the God of Jacob. 2. Take a psalm, and bring hither the timbrel.

Psa. 84.4. Blessed *are* they that dwell in thy house : they will be still praising thee.

Psa. 86.12. I will praise thee, O Lord my God, with all my heart : and I will glorify thy name for evermore.

Psa. 87.7. As well the singers as the players on instruments *shall be there*.

Psa. 89.52. Blessed *be* the Lord for evermore. Amen, and Amen.

Psa. 92.1. *It is a good thing* to give thanks unto the Lord, and to sing praises unto thy name, O most High : 2. To shew forth thy lovingkindness in the morning, and thy faithfulness every night.

Psa. 95.1. O come, let us sing unto the Lord : let us make a joyful noise to the rock of our salvation. 2. Let us come before his presence with thanksgiving, and make a joyful noise unto him with psalms. 6. O come, let us worship and bow down : let us kneel before the Lord our maker. 7. For he *is* our God ; and we *are* the people of his pasture, and the sheep of his hand.

Psa. 96.1. O sing unto the Lord a new song : sing unto the Lord, all the earth. 2. Sing unto the Lord, bless his name ; shew forth his salvation from day to day. 7. Give unto the Lord, O ye kindreds of the people, give unto the Lord glory and strength. 8. Give unto the Lord the glory due *unto* his name : bring an offering, and come into his courts. 9. O worship the Lord in the beauty of holiness : fear before him, all the earth.

Psa. 98.4. Make a joyful noise unto the Lord, all the earth : make a loud noise, and rejoice, and sing praise. 5. Sing unto the Lord with the harp ; with the harp, and the voice of a psalm. 6. With trumpets and sound of cornet make a joyful noise before the Lord, the King.

Psa. 99.3. Let them praise thy great and terrible name ; *for* it *is* holy. 5. Exalt ye the Lord our God, and worship at his footstool ; *for* he *is* holy. *v.* 9.

Psa. 100.1. Make a joyful noise unto the Lord, all ye lands. 2. Serve the Lord with gladness : come before his presence with singing. 4. Enter into his gates with thanksgiving, *and* into his courts with praise : be thankful unto him, *and* bless his name.

Psa. 101.1. I will sing of mercy and judgment : unto thee, O Lord, will I sing.

Psa. 103.22. Bless the Lord, all his works in all places of his dominion : bless the Lord, O my soul. *v.* 20.

Psa. 104.33. I will sing unto the Lord as long as I live : I will sing praise to my God while I have my being. 34. My meditation of him shall be sweet : I will be glad in the Lord.

Psa. 105.1. O give thanks unto the Lord ; call upon his name : make known his deeds among the people. 2. Sing unto him, sing psalms unto him : talk ye of all his wondrous works. 3. Glory ye in his holy name : let the heart of them rejoice that seek the Lord.

Psa. 106.1. Praise ye the Lord. O give thanks unto the Lord ; for *he is* good : for his mercy *endureth* for ever. 48. Blessed *be* the Lord God of Israel from everlasting to everlasting : and let all the people say, Amen. Praise ye the Lord.

Psa. 107.32. Let them exalt him also in the congregation of the people, and praise him in the assembly of the elders. *v.* 1.

Psa. 109.30. I will greatly praise the Lord with my mouth ; yea, I will praise him among the multitude.

Psa. 111.1. Praise ye the Lord. I will praise the Lord with *my* whole heart, in the assembly of the upright, and *in* the congregation. 10. His praise endureth for ever.

Psa. 115.18. We will bless the Lord from this time forth and for evermore. Praise the Lord.

Psa. 116.13. I will take the cup of salvation, and call upon the name of the Lord. 18. Now in the presence of all his people, 19. In the courts of the Lord's house, in the midst of thee, O Jerusalem. Praise ye the Lord.

Psa. 117.1. O praise the Lord, all ye nations : praise him, all ye people. 2. For his merciful kindness is great toward us : and the truth of the Lord *endureth* for ever. Praise ye the Lord.

Psa. 118.15. The voice of rejoicing and salvation *is* in the tabernacles of the righteous.

28. Thou art my God, and I will praise thee: thou art my God, I will exalt thee. v. 29.

Psa. 119.7. I will praise thee with uprightness of heart, when I shall have learned thy righteous judgments. 62. At midnight I will rise to give thanks unto thee because of thy righteous judgments. 108. Accept, I beseech thee, the freewill-offerings of my mouth, O Lord, and teach me thy judgments. 164. Seven times a day do I praise thee because of thy righteous judgments. 171. My lips shall utter praise, when thou hast taught me thy statutes. 172. My tongue shall speak of thy word: for all thy commandments are righteousness.

Psa. 134.1. Behold, bless ye the Lord, all ye servants of the Lord, which by night stand in the house of the Lord. 2. Lift up your hands in the sanctuary, and bless the Lord. Psa. 113.1; 2.

Psa. 135.1. Praise ye the name of the Lord; praise him, O ye servants of the Lord. 2. Ye that stand in the house of the Lord, in the courts of the house of our God, 3. Praise the Lord; for the Lord is good: sing praises unto his name; for it is pleasant. 19. Bless the Lord, O house of Israel: bless the Lord, O house of Aaron: 20. Bless the Lord, O house of Levi: ye that fear the Lord, bless the Lord. 21. Blessed be the Lord out of Zion, which dwelleth at Jerusalem. Praise ye the Lord.

Psa. 136.2. O give thanks unto the God of gods: for his mercy endureth for ever. v. 1-26.

Psa. 138.1. I will praise thee with my whole heart: before the gods will I sing praise unto thee. 2. I will worship toward thy holy temple, and praise thy name for thy lovingkindness and for thy truth.

Psa. 140.13. Surely the righteous shall give thanks unto thy name: the upright shall dwell in thy presence.

Psa. 144.9. I will sing a new song unto thee, O God: upon a psaltery and an instrument of ten strings will I sing praises unto thee.

Psa. 145.1. I will extol thee, my God, O king; and I will bless thy name for ever and ever. 2. Every day will I bless thee; and I will praise thy name for ever and ever. 21. My mouth shall speak the praise of the Lord: and let all flesh bless his holy name for ever and ever.

Psa. 146.1. Praise ye the Lord. Praise the Lord, O my soul. 2. While I live will I praise the Lord: I will sing praises unto my God while I have any being.

Psa. 147.1. Praise ye the Lord: for it is good to sing praises unto our God; for it is pleasant; and praise is comely. 7. Sing unto the Lord with thanksgiving; sing praise upon the harp unto our God. 12. Praise the Lord, O Jerusalem; praise thy God, O Zion.

Psa. 148.1. Praise ye the Lord from the heavens: praise him in the heights. 2. Praise ye him, all his angels: all his hosts. 3. Sun and moon: all ye stars of light. 4. Ye heavens of heavens, and ye waters that be above the heavens. 5. Let them praise the name of the Lord: for he commanded, and they were created. 11. Kings of the earth, and all people; princes, and all judges of the earth: 12. Both young men, and maidens; old men, and children: 13. Let them praise the name of the Lord: for his name alone is

excellent; his glory is above the earth and heaven. v. 1-14.

Psa. 149.1. Sing unto the Lord a new song, and his praise in the congregation of saints. 2. Let Israel rejoice in him that made him: let the children of Zion be joyful in their King. 3. Let them praise his name in the dance: let them sing praises unto him with the timbrel and harp. 5. Let the saints be joyful in glory: let them sing aloud upon their beds. 6. Let the high praises of God be in their mouth. Psa. 150.

Isa. 12.1. Thou shalt say, O Lord, I will praise thee: though thou wast angry with me, thine anger is turned away, and thou comfortedst me. v. 1-6.

Isa. 24.16. From the uttermost part of the earth have we heard songs, even glory to the righteous.

Isa. 35.10. The ransomed of the Lord shall return, and come to Zion with songs and everlasting joy upon their heads.

Isa. 38.19. The living, the living, he shall praise thee, as I do this day.

Isa. 42.10. Sing unto the Lord a new song, and his praise from the end of the earth, ye that go down to the sea, and all that is therein; the isles, and the inhabitants thereof. 11. Let the wilderness and the cities thereof lift up their voice, the villages that Kedar doth inhabit: let the inhabitants of the rock sing, let them shout from the top of the mountains. 12. Let them give glory unto the Lord, and declare his praise in the islands.

Isa. 43.21. This people have I formed for myself; they shall shew forth my praise.

Isa. 51.3. He will make her wilderness like Eden, joy and gladness shall be found therein, thanksgiving, and the voice of melody.

Isa. 52.8. Thy watchmen shall lift up the voice; with the voice together shall they sing.

Isa. 61.3. To appoint unto them that mourn in Zion, to give unto them the garment of praise for the spirit of heaviness.

Jer. 31.7. Sing with gladness for Jacob, and shout among the chief of the nations: publish ye, praise ye, and say, O Lord, save thy people.

Jer. 33.11. The voice of joy, and the voice of gladness, the voice of them that shall say, Praise the Lord of hosts: for the Lord is good; for his mercy endureth for ever: and of them that shall bring the sacrifice of praise into the house of the Lord.

Dan. 2.20. Blessed be the name of God for ever and ever: for wisdom and might are his. 23. I thank thee, and praise thee, O thou God of my fathers.

Dan. 4.37. I Nebuchadnezzar praise and extol and honour the King of heaven, all whose works are truth, and his ways judgment.

Jonah 2.9. I will sacrifice unto thee with the voice of thanksgiving; I will pay that that I have vowed.

Mat. 26.30. When they had sung an hymn, they went out into the mount of Olives. Mar. 14.20.

Luk. 1.46. Mary said, My soul doth magnify the Lord. 47. And my spirit hath rejoiced in God my Saviour. 68. Blessed be the Lord God of Israel; for he hath visited and redeemed his people, 69. And hath raised up an horn of salvation for us in the house of his servant David.

Luk. 2.20. The shepherds returned, glorifying and praising God for all the things that they had heard and seen.

Luk. 19.37. The whole multitude of the disciples began to rejoice and praise God with a loud voice for all the mighty works that they had seen; 38. Saying, Blessed *be* the King that cometh in the name of the Lord; peace in heaven, and glory in the highest.

Luk. 24.53. Were continually in the temple, praising and blessing God.

Act. 2.46. Did eat their meat with gladness and singleness of heart, 47. Praising God.

Act. 4.24. They lifted up their voice to God with one accord, and said, Lord, thou *art* God, which hast made heaven, and earth, and the sea, and all that in them is.

Act. 16.25. At midnight Paul and Silas prayed, and sang praises unto God: and the prisoners heard them.

Rom. 11.36. Of him, and through him, and to him, *are* all things: to whom *be* glory for ever. Amen.

Rom. 16.27. To God only wise, *be* glory through Jesus Christ for ever. Amen.

1 Cor. 14.15. I will sing with the spirit, and I will sing with the understanding also.

1 Cor. 15.57. Thanks *be* to God, which giveth us the victory through our Lord Jesus Christ.

Eph. 1.3. Blessed *be* the God and Father of our Lord Jesus Christ, who hath blessed us with all spiritual blessings in heavenly *places* in Christ.

Eph. 3.20. Now unto him that is able to do exceeding abundantly above all that we ask or think, according to the power that worketh in us, 21. Unto him *be* glory in the church by Christ Jesus throughout all ages, world without end. Amen.

Eph. 5.19. Speaking to yourselves in psalms and hymns and spiritual songs, singing and making melody in your heart to the Lord. Col. 3.16.

Phil. 4.20. Unto God and our Father *be* glory for ever and ever. Amen. Gal. 1.5.

1 Tim. 1.17. Unto the King eternal, immortal, invisible, the only wise God, *be* honour and glory for ever and ever. Amen.

Heb. 13.15. By him therefore let us offer the sacrifice of praise to God continually, that is, the fruit of *our* lips giving thanks to his name.

Jas. 5.13. Is any merry? let him sing psalms.

1 Pet. 1.3. Blessed *be* the God and Father of our Lord Jesus Christ, which, according to his abundant mercy, hath begotten us again unto a lively hope, by the resurrection of Jesus Christ from the dead.

1 Pet. 2.9. Shew forth the praises of him who hath called you out of darkness into his marvellous light.

1 Pet. 5.11. To him *be* glory and dominion for ever and ever. Amen. 2 Pet. 3.18.

Rev. 14.7. Fear God, and give glory to him; worship him that made heaven, and earth, and the sea, and the fountains of waters.

Rev. 15.4. Who shall not fear thee, O Lord, and glorify thy name? for *thou* only *art* holy:

for all nations shall come and worship before thee.

Rev. 19.5. Praise our God, all ye his servants, and ye that fear him, both small and great.

See GOD'S GLORY, PRAISE OF—SPIRITUAL PEACE—THANKFULNESS.

PRAISE IN CHRIST'S NAME, Eph. 5.20. Heb. 13.15.   1 Pet. 2.5.

PRAISE IN HEAVEN, AND BY ANGELS. Neh. 9.6. The host of heaven worshippeth thee.

Job. 38.7. The morning-stars sang together, and all the sons of God shouted for joy.

Psa. 24.7. Lift up your heads, O ye gates; and be ye lift up, ye everlasting doors; and the King of glory shall come in. 8. Who *is* this King of glory? The Lord strong and mighty, the Lord mighty in battle. *v.* 9,10.

Psa. 103.20. Bless the Lord, ye his angels, that excel in strength, that do his commandments, hearkening unto the voice of his word. 21. Bless ye the Lord, all *ye* his hosts; *ye* ministers of his, that do his pleasure.

Psa. 148.2. Praise ye him, all his angels: praise ye him, all his hosts.

Isa. 6.3. One cried unto another, and said, Holy, holy, holy, *is* the Lord of hosts; the whole earth *is* full of his glory.

Eze. 3.12. Then the spirit took me up, and I heard behind me a voice of a great rushing, *saying*, Blessed *be* the glory of the Lord from his place.

Luk. 2.13. Suddenly there was with the angel a multitude of the heavenly host, praising God, and saying, 14. Glory to God in the highest, and on earth peace, good will toward men.

Rev. 1.6. Hath made us kings and priests unto God and his Father; to him *be* glory and dominion for ever and ever.

Rev. 4.8. They rest not day and night, saying, Holy, holy, holy, Lord God Almighty, which was, and is, and is to come. 9. And when those beasts give glory and honour and thanks to him that sat on the throne, who liveth for ever and ever, 10. The four and twenty elders fall down before him that sat on the throne, and worship him that liveth for ever and ever, and cast their crowns before the throne, saying, 11. Thou art worthy, O Lord, to receive glory and honour and power: for thou hast created all things, and for thy pleasure they are, and were created.

Rev. 5.9. They sung a new song, saying, Thou art worthy to take the book, and to open the seals thereof: for thou wast slain, and hast redeemed us to God by thy blood out of every kindred, and tongue, and people, and nation; 10. And hast made us unto our God kings and priests: and we shall reign on the earth. 11. I beheld, and I heard the voice of many angels round about the throne and the beasts and the elders: 12. Saying with a loud voice, Worthy is the Lamb that was slain to receive power, and riches,· and wisdom, and strength, and honour, and glory, and blessing. 13. And every creature which is in heaven, and on the earth, and under the earth, and such as are in the sea, and all that are in them, heard I saying, Blessing, and honour, and glory, and power, *be* unto him that sitteth upon the throne, and unto the Lamb for ever and ever. 14. And the four beasts said, Amen.

Rev. 7.10. Cried with a loud voice, saying, Salvation to our God which sitteth upon the throne, and unto the Lamb. 11. And all the angels stood round about the throne, and *about* the elders and the four beasts, and fell before the throne on their faces, and worshipped God. 12. Saying, Amen: Blessing, and glory, and wisdom, and thanksgiving, and honour, and power, and might, *be* unto our God for ever and ever. Amen.

Rev. 11.16. The four and twenty elders, which sat before God on their seats, fell upon their faces, and worshipped God, 17. Saying, We give thee thanks, O Lord God Almighty, which art, and wast, and art to come; because thou hast taken to thee thy great power, and hast reigned.

Rev. 14.2. I heard a voice from heaven, as the voice of many waters, and as the voice of a great thunder: and I heard the voice of harpers harping with their harps: 3. And they sung as it were a new song before the throne, and before the four beasts, and the elders: and no man could learn that song but the hundred *and* forty *and* four thousand, which were redeemed from the earth.

Rev. 15.3. They sing the song of Moses the servant of God, and the song of the Lamb, saying, Great and marvellous *are* thy works, Lord God Almighty; just and true *are* thy ways, thou King of saints. 4. Who shall not fear thee, O Lord, and glorify thy name? for *thou* only *art* holy: for all nations shall come and worship before thee; for thy judgments are made manifest.

Rev. 19.1. I heard a great voice of much people in heaven, saying, Alleluia; Salvation, and glory, and honour, and power, unto the Lord our God. 3. And again they said, Alleluia. 4. And the four and twenty elders and the four beasts fell down and worshipped God that sat on the throne, saying, Amen; Alleluia. 5. And a voice came out of the throne, saying, Praise our God, all ye his servants, and ye that fear him, both small and great. 6. And I heard as it were the voice of a great multitude, and as the voice of many waters, and as the voice of mighty thunderings, saying, Alleluia: for the Lord God omnipotent reigneth. 7. Let us be glad and rejoice, and give honour to him: for the marriage of the Lamb is come, and his wife hath made herself ready.

PRAYER. [Prayer, in connection with the following objects, will be found under the heads: AFFLICTION—GOD'S FAVOUR—HOLY SPIRIT—MINISTERS—PARDON—SPIRITUAL BLESSINGS—TEMPORAL BLESSINGS—TEMPTATION—WISDOM.]

Kneeling in, 1 Kin. 8.54. 2 Chr. 6.13. Ezr. 9.5. Psa. 95.6. Isa. 45.23. Dan. 6.10. Luk. 22.41. Act. 7.60. Act. 9.40. Act. 20. 36. Act. 21.5. Eph. 3.14. Phil. 2.10.

Bowing, and falling on the face, Gen. 24. 26,52. Ex. 4.31. Ex. 12.27. Num. 16.22,45. Num. 20.6. Jos. 5.14. Jos. 7.6. 1 Chr. 21. 16. 2 Chr. 20.18. Eze. 9.8. Mat. 26.39. Mar. 14.35. See Isa. 6.2. Rev. 11.16.

Spreading out the hands, 1 Kin. 8.22,38,54. Ezr. 9.5. Neh. 8.6. Psa. 28.2. Psa. 63.4. Psa. 88.9. Psa. 134.2. Psa. 141.2. Isa. 1.15. Lam. 3.41. 1 Tim. 2.8.

Standing, 1 Sam. 1.26. 1 Kin. 8.14,55. 2 Chr. 20.9. Neh. 9.2,4. Mar. 11.25. Luk. 18.11,13.

PRAYER, ANSWER PROMISED TO PRAYER —PRAYER ENJOINED. EX. 22.23. If thou afflict them in any wise, and they cry at all unto me, I will surely hear their cry. 27. When he crieth unto me, I will hear; for I *am* gracious.

Deu. 4.7. What nation *is there so* great, who *hath* God so nigh unto them, as the Lord our God *is* in all *things that* we call upon him *for?* 29. But if from thence thou shalt seek the Lord thy God, thou shalt find *him,* if thou seek him with all thy heart and with all thy soul.

1 Kin. 3.5. God said, Ask what I shall give thee. 2 Chr. 1.7.

1 Chr. 16.11. Seek the Lord and his strength, seek his face continually. 35. Say ye, Save us, O God of our salvation, and gather us together, and deliver us from the heathen, that we may give thanks to thy holy name, *and* glory in thy praise.

1 Chr. 28.9. If thou seek him, he will be found of thee; but if thou forsake him, he will cast thee off for ever.

2 Chr. 7.14. If my people, which are called by my name, shall humble themselves, and pray, and seek my face, and turn from their wicked ways; then will I hear from heaven, and will forgive their sin, and will heal their land. 15. Now mine eyes shall be open, and mine ears attent unto the prayer *that is made* in this place. 1 Kin. 8.22-53. 2 Chr. 6.

Job 8.5. If thou wouldest seek unto God betimes, and make thy supplication to the Almighty; 6. If thou *wert* pure and upright; surely now he would awake for thee.

Job 12.4. Who calleth upon God, and he answereth him.

Job 22.27. Thou shalt make thy prayer unto him, and he shall hear thee, and thou shalt pay thy vows.

Job 33.26. He shall pray unto God, and he will be favourable unto him: and he shall see his face with joy.

Job 34.28. They cause the cry of the poor to come unto him, and he heareth the cry of the afflicted.

Psa. 9.12. He forgetteth not the cry of the humble.

Psa. 10.17. Lord, thou hast heard the desire of the humble: thou wilt prepare their heart, thou wilt cause thine ear to hear.

Psa. 18.3. I will call upon the Lord, *who is* worthy to be praised: so shall I be saved from mine enemies.

Psa. 32.6. For this shall every one that is godly pray unto thee in a time when thou mayest be found: surely in the floods of great waters they shall not come nigh unto him.

Psa. 34.15. The eyes of the Lord *are* upon the righteous, and his ears *are open* unto their cry. 17. *The righteous* cry, and the Lord heareth, and delivereth them out of all their troubles.

Psa. 37.4. Delight thyself also in the Lord; and he shall give thee the desires of thine heart. 5. Commit thy way unto the Lord; trust also in him; and he shall bring *it* to pass.

Psa. 38.15. In thee, O Lord, do I hope: thou wilt hear, O Lord my God.

Psa. 50.15. Call upon me in the day of

trouble : 1 will deliver thee, and thou shalt glorify me.

Psa. 55.16.　As for me, I will call upon God; and the Lord shall save me.　17. Evening, and morning, and at noon, will I pray, and cry aloud : and he shall hear my voice.

Psa. 56.9.　When I cry *unto thee*, then shall mine enemies turn back : this I know ; for God *is* for me.

Psa. 62.8.　Ye people, pour out your heart before him.

Psa. 65.2.　O thou that hearest prayer, unto thee shall all flesh come.　5. *By* terrible things in righteousness wilt thou answer us, O God of our salvation ; *who art* the confidence of all the ends of the earth, and of them that are afar off *upon* the sea.

Psa. 69.33.　The Lord heareth the poor, and despiseth not his prisoners.

Psa. 81.10.　Open thy mouth wide, and I will fill it.

Psa. 86.5.　Thou, Lord, *art* good, and ready to forgive ; and plenteous in mercy unto all them that call upon thee.　7. In the day of my trouble I will call upon thee : for thou wilt answer me.

Psa. 91.15.　He shall call upon me, and I will answer him : I *will be* with him in trouble ; I will deliver him, and honour him.

Psa. 102.17.　He will regard the prayer of the destitute, and not despise their prayer. 18. This shall be written for the generation to come : and the people which shall be created shall praise the Lord.

Psa. 145.18.　The Lord *is* nigh unto all them that call upon him, to all that call upon him in truth.　19. He will fulfil the desire of them that fear him : he also will hear their cry, and will save them.

Pro. 2.3.　If thou criest after knowledge, *and* liftest up thy voice for understanding. 5. Then shalt thou understand the fear of the Lord, and find the knowledge of God.

Pro. 15.8.　The sacrifice of the wicked *is* an abomination to the Lord : but the prayer of the upright *is* his delight.　29. He heareth the prayer of the righteous.

Pro. 16.1.　The preparations of the heart in man, and the answer of the tongue, *is* from the Lord.　3. Commit thy works unto the Lord, and thy thoughts shall be established.

Ecc. 5.2.　Be not rash with thy mouth, and let not thine heart be hasty to utter *any* thing before God : for God *is* in heaven, and thou upon earth : therefore let thy words be few.

Isa. 19.20.　They shall cry unto the Lord because of the oppressors, and he shall send them a saviour, and a great one, and he shall deliver them.

Isa. 30.19.　He will be very gracious unto thee at the voice of thy cry ; when he shall hear it, he will answer thee.

Isa. 45.19.　I said not unto the seed of Jacob, Seek ye me in vain.

Isa. 55.6.　Seek ye the Lord while he may be found, call ye upon him while he is near.

Isa. 58.9.　Then shalt thou call, and the Lord shall answer ; thou shalt cry, and he shall say, Here I *am.*

Isa. 65.24.　It shall come to pass, that before they call, I will answer ; and while they are yet speaking, I will hear.

Jer. 29.12.　Then shall ye call upon me, and ye shall go and pray unto me, and I will

hearken unto you.　13. And ye shall seek me, and find *me,* when ye shall search for me with all your heart.

Jer. 31.9.　They shall come with weeping, and with supplications will I lead them.

Jer. 33.3.　Call unto me, and I will answer thee, and shew thee great and mighty things, which thou knowest not.

Lam. 2.19.　Arise, cry out in the night : in the beginning of the watches pour out thine heart like water before the face of the Lord : lift up thy hands toward him for the life of thy young children, that faint for hunger in the top of every street.

Lam. 3.41.　Let us lift up our heart with *our* hands unto God in the heavens.

Eze. 36.37.　Thus saith the Lord God ; I will yet *for* this be enquired of by the house of Israel, to do *it* for them.

Hos. 14.2.　Take with you words, and turn to the Lord : say unto him, Take away all iniquity, and receive *us* graciously : so will we render the calves of our lips.

Joel 2.32.　Whosoever shall call on the name of the Lord shall be delivered.

Zeph. 2.3.　Seek ye the Lord, all ye meek of the earth, which have wrought his judgment ; seek righteousness, seek meekness : it may be ye shall be hid in the day of the Lord's anger.

Zec. 8.21.　The inhabitants of one *city* shall go to another, saying, Let us go speedily to pray before the Lord, and to seek the Lord of hosts : I will go also.

Zec. 10.1.　Ask ye of the Lord rain in the time of the latter rain ; *so* the Lord shall make bright clouds, and give them showers of rain, to every one grass in the field.　6. They shall be as though I had not cast them off : for I *am* the Lord their God, and will hear them.

Zec. 12.10.　I will pour upon the house of David, and upon the inhabitants of Jerusalem, the spirit of grace and of supplications.

Zec. 13.9.　They shall call on my name, and I will hear them : I will say, It *is* my people : and they shall say, The Lord *is* my God.

Mat. 6.5.　When thou prayest, thou shalt not be as the hypocrites *are* : for they love to pray standing in the synagogues and in the corners of the streets, that they may be seen of men.　Verily I say unto you, They have their reward.　6. But thou, when thou prayest, enter into thy closet ; and, when thou hast shut thy door, pray to thy Father which is in secret ; and thy Father, which seeth in secret, shall reward thee openly.　7. But when ye pray, use not vain repetitions, as the heathen *do* : for they think that they shall be heard for their much speaking.　8. Be not ye therefore like unto them : for your Father knoweth what things ye have need of before ye ask him. 9. After this manner therefore pray ye : Our Father which art in heaven, Hallowed be thy name.　*v.* 9-13.

Mat. 7.7.　Ask, and it shall be given you ; seek, and ye shall find ; knock, and it shall be opened unto you :　8. For every one that asketh receiveth ; and he that seeketh findeth ; and to him that knocketh it shall be opened. 11. If ye then, being evil, know how to give good gifts unto your children, how much more shall your Father which is in heaven give good things to them that ask him?　*v.* 9,10.

Mat. 17.21.　This kind goeth not out but by prayer and fasting.

Mat. 18.19. If two of you shall agree on earth as touching any thing that they shall ask, it shall be done for them of my Father which is in heaven. 20. For where two or three are gathered together in my name, there am I in the midst of them.

Mat. 21.22. All things, whatsoever ye shall ask in prayer, believing, ye shall receive.

Mat. 24.20. Pray ye that your flight be not in the winter, neither on the sabbath.

Mar. 11.24. What things soever ye desire, when ye pray, believe that ye receive *them*, and ye shall have *them*. 25. When ye stand praying, forgive, if ye have ought against any; that your Father also which is in heaven may forgive you your trespasses.

Mar. 13.33. Take ye heed, watch and pray: for ye know not when the time is.

Mar. 14.38. Watch ye and pray, lest ye enter unto temptation. The spirit truly *is* ready, but the flesh *is* weak. Mat. 26.41. Luk. 22.46.

Luk. 11.13. If ye then, being evil, know how to give good gifts unto your children: how much more shall *your* heavenly Father give the Holy Spirit to them that ask him? *v.* 5-12.

Luk. 18.1. Men ought always *to* pray, and not to faint. 7. Shall not God avenge his own elect, which cry day and night unto him, though he bear long with them? 8. I tell you that he will avenge them speedily. *v.* 1-5.

Luk. 21.36. Watch ye therefore, and pray always, that ye may be accounted worthy to escape all these things that shall come to pass, and to stand before the Son of man.

Jno. 4.10. If thou knewest the gift of God, and who it is that saith to thee, Give me to drink; thou wouldest have asked of him, and he would have given thee living water. 23. The hour cometh, and now is, when the true worshippers shall worship the Father in spirit and in truth: for the Father seeketh such to worship him. 24. God *is* a Spirit: and they that worship him must worship *him* in spirit and in truth.

Jno. 9.31. We know that God heareth not sinners: but if any man be a worshipper of God, and doeth his will, him he heareth.

Jno. 14.13. Whatsoever ye shall ask in my name, that will I do, that the Father may be glorified in the Son. 14. If ye shall ask any thing in my name, I will do *it*.

Jno. 15.7. If ye abide in me, and my words abide in you, ye shall ask what ye will, and it shall be done unto you. *v.* 16.

Jno. 16.23. Whatsoever ye shall ask the Father in my name, he will give *it* you. 24. Hitherto have ye asked nothing in my name: ask, and ye shall receive, that your joy may be full. 26. Ye shall ask in my name: and I say not unto you, that I will pray the Father for you: 27. For the Father himself loveth you, because ye have loved me, and have believed that I came out from God.

Act. 8.22. Repent therefore of this thy wickedness, and pray God, if perhaps the thought of thine heart may be forgiven thee.

Act. 22.16. Arise, and be baptized, and wash away thy sins, calling on the name of the Lord.

Rom. 8.26. The Spirit also helpeth our infirmities: for we know not what we should pray for as we ought; but the Spirit itself maketh intercession for us with groanings which cannot be uttered. *v.* 27.

Rom. 10.12. The same Lord over all is rich unto all that call upon him. 13. For whosoever shall call upon the name of the Lord shall be saved.

Rom. 12.12. Continuing instant in prayer.

Eph. 2.18. Through him we both have access by one Spirit unto the Father.

Eph. 3.20. Him that is able to do exceeding abundantly above all that we ask or think, according to the power that worketh in us.

Eph. 6.18. Praying always with all prayer and supplication in the Spirit, and watching thereunto with all perseverance and supplication for all saints.

Phil. 4.6. Be careful for nothing; but in every thing by prayer and supplication with thanksgiving let your requests be made known unto God.

Col. 4.2. Continue in prayer, and watch in the same with thanksgiving.

1 The. 5.17. Pray without ceasing.

1 Tim. 2.8. I will therefore that men pray every where, lifting up holy hands, without wrath and doubting.

Heb. 4.16. Come boldly unto the throne of grace, that we may obtain mercy, and find grace to help in time of need.

Heb. 10.22. Draw near with a true heart, in full assurance of faith, having our hearts sprinkled from an evil conscience, and our bodies washed with pure water.

Heb. 11.6. Without faith *it is* impossible to please *him:* for he that cometh to God must believe that he is, and *that* he is a rewarder of them that diligently seek him.

Jas. 1.5. If any of you lack wisdom, let him ask of God, that giveth to all *men* liberally, and upbraideth not; and it shall be given him. 6. But let him ask in faith, nothing wavering. For he that wavereth is like a wave of the sea driven with the wind and tossed. 7. For let not that man think that he shall receive any thing of the Lord.

Jas. 4.2. Ye have not, because ye ask not. 3. Ye ask, and receive not, because ye ask amiss, that ye may consume *it* upon your lusts. 8. Draw nigh to God, and he will draw nigh to you.

Jas. 5.13. Is any among you afflicted? let him pray.

1 Pet. 1.17. If ye call on the Father, who without respect of persons judgeth according to every man's work, pass the time of your sojourning *here* in fear.

1 Pet. 3.7. Giving honour unto the wife, as being heirs together of the grace of life; that your prayers be not hindered. *v.* 12.

1 Pet. 4.7. The end of all things is at hand: be ye therefore sober, and watch unto prayer.

1 Jno. 3.22. Whatsoever we ask, we receive of him, because we keep his commandments, and do those things that are pleasing in his sight.

1 Jno. 5.14. This is the confidence that we have in him, that, if we ask any thing according to his will, he heareth us: 15. And if we know that he hear us, whatsoever we ask, we know that we have the petitions that we desired of him.

Jude 20. But ye, beloved, building up

yourselves on your most holy faith, praying in the Holy Ghost.

Rev. 5.8. Having every one of them golden vials full of odours, which are the prayers of saints.

Rev. 8.3. Another angel came and stood at the altar, having a golden censer; and there was given unto him much incense, that he should offer *it* with the prayers of all saints upon the golden altar which was before the throne. 4. And the smoke of the incense, *which came* with the prayers of the saints, ascended up before God out of the angel's hand.

See WORSHIP ENJOINED.

PRAYER ANSWERED. Psa. 3.4. I cried unto the Lord with my voice, and he heard me out of his holy hill.

Psa. 4.1. Thou hast enlarged me *when I was* in distress; have mercy upon me, and hear my prayer.

Psa. 6.8. The Lord hath heard the voice of my weeping. 9. The Lord hath heard my supplication; the Lord will receive my prayer.

Psa. 18.6. In my distress I called upon the Lord, and cried unto my God: he heard my voice out of his temple, and my cry came before him, *even* into his ears. Psa. 120.1.

Psa. 21.2. Thou hast given him his heart's desire, and hast not withholden the request of his lips. 4. He asked life of thee, *and* thou gavest *it* him, *even* length of days for ever and ever.

Psa. 22.4. Our fathers trusted in thee: they trusted, and thou didst deliver them. 5. They cried unto thee, and were delivered: they trusted in thee, and were not confounded. 24. He hath not despised nor abhorred the affliction of the afflicted; neither hath he hid his face from him; but when he cried unto him, he heard.

Psa. 28.6. Blessed *be* the Lord, because he hath heard the voice of my supplications.

Psa. 30.2. O Lord my God, I cried unto thee, and thou hast healed me. 3. O Lord, thou hast brought up my soul from the grave: thou hast kept me alive, that I should not go down to the pit.

Psa. 31.22. I said in my haste, I am cut off from before thine eyes: nevertheless thou heardest the voice of my supplications when I cried unto thee.

Psa. 34:4. I sought the Lord, and he heard me, and delivered me from all my fears. 5. They looked unto him, and were lightened: and their faces were not ashamed. 6. This poor man cried, and the Lord heard *him*, and saved him out of all his troubles.

Psa. 40.1. I waited patiently for the Lord; and he inclined unto me, and heard my cry.

Psa. 66.19. Verily God hath heard *me*; he hath attended to the voice of my prayer. 20. Blessed *be* God, which hath not turned away my prayer, nor his mercy from me.

Psa. 77.1. I cried unto God with my voice, *even* unto God with my voice; and he gave ear unto me. 2. In the day of my trouble I sought the Lord.

Psa. 81.7. Thou calledst in trouble, and I delivered thee; I answered thee in the secret place of thunder.

Psa. 99.6. Moses, and Aaron, and Samuel called upon the Lord, and he answered them.

Psa. 106.44. He regarded their affliction, when he heard their cry.

Psa. 107.6. They cried unto the Lord in their trouble, *and* he delivered them out of their distresses. 7. And he led them forth by the right way, that they might go to a city of habitation. *v.* 13-20.

Psa. 116.1. I love the Lord, because he hath heard my voice *and* my supplications. 2. Because he hath inclined his ear unto me, therefore will I call upon *him* as long as I live.

Psa. 118.5. I called upon the Lord in distress: the Lord answered me, *and set me* in a large place. 21. I will praise thee: for thou hast heard me, and art become my salvation.

Psa. 119.26. I have declared my ways, and thou heardest me.

Psa. 138.3. In the day when I cried thou answeredst me, *and* strengthenedst me *with* strength in my soul.

Lam. 3.57. Thou drewest near in the day *that* I called upon thee: thou saidst, Fear not. 58. O Lord, thou hast pleaded the causes of my soul; thou hast redeemed my life.

Hos. 12.3. By his strength he had power with God: 4. Yea, he had power over the angel, and prevailed: he wept, and made supplication unto him: he found him *in* Beth-el, and there he spake with us.

Jonah 2.2. I cried by reason of mine affliction unto the Lord, and he heard me; out of the belly of hell cried I, *and* thou heardest my voice. 7. When my soul fainted within me I remembered the Lord: and my prayer came in unto thee, into thine holy temple.

Luk. 23.42. Lord, remember me when thou comest into thy kingdom. 43. And Jesus said unto him, Verily I say unto thee, To-day shalt thou be with me in paradise.

Act. 4.31. When they had prayed, the place was shaken where they were assembled together; and they were all filled with the Holy Ghost.

2 Cor. 12.8. For this thing I besought the Lord thrice, that it might depart from me. 9. And he said unto me, My grace is sufficient for thee; for my strength is made perfect in weakness.

Jas. 5.16. The effectual fervent prayer of a righteous man availeth much. 17. Elias was a man subject to like passions as we are, and he prayed earnestly that it might not rain: and it rained not on the earth by the space of three years and six months. 18. And he prayed again, and the heaven gave rain, and the earth brought forth her fruit.

PRAYER ANSWERED, EXAMPLES OF: Abraham, Gen. 15. Lot, Gen. 19.20,21. Abraham's servant, Gen. 24.12-21. Isaac, Gen. 25.21. Jacob, Gen. 32. Moses, Ex. 14.15,16. Ex. 15.25. Ex. 17.4-6. Num. 11.11-17. Israelites, Ex. 2.23-25. Ex. 14.10. Jud. 3.9,15. Jud. 4.3,23. Jud. 6.7-14. Jud. 10.10,15,16. 1 Sam. 12.10,11. 2 Chr. 15.4,15. Neh. 9.27. Psa. 106.15. Gideon, Jud. 6.36-40. Manoah, Jud. 13.8,9. Samson, Jud. 15.18,19. Jud. 16.28-30. Hannah, 1 Sam. 1.10-17. David, 1 Sam. 23.10-12. Solomon, 1 Kin. 3.1-13. 1 Kin. 9.2,3. Jabez, 1 Chr. 4.10. Abijah's army, 2 Chr. 13.14-18. Asa, 2 Chr. 14.11-15. 2 Chr. 15.15. Elijah, 1 Kin. 18.36-38. Elisha, 2 Kin. 6.18,20. Jehoshaphat, 2 Chr. 18.31. 2 Chr. 20.6-27. Jehoahaz, 2 Kin. 13.4. Levites, 2 Chr. 30.27, Hezekiah and Isaiah, 2 Kin.

19.14-20. 2 Chr. 32.20,21,24. 2 Kin. 20.1-6, 10,11. Manasseh, 2 Chr. 33.13,19. Reubenites, &c., 1 Chr. 5.20. Jews, Ezr. 8.21,23. Zec. 7.1-4. Daniel, Dan. 9.20-23. Dan. 10.12. Zacharias, Luk. 1.13. Ananias, Act. 10.4.

See ENQUIRING OF GOD—PRAYER, INTERCESSORY.

PRAYER, ANSWERS TO, DENIED. See SIN SEPARATES FROM GOD—HYPOCRISY.

―――― IN CHRIST'S NAME, Mat. 18.20. Jno. 14.13,14. Jno. 15.16. Jno. 16.23-26. Eph. 2.18. Eph. 5.20. Col. 3.17. 1 Pet. 2.5. See CHRIST HIGH-PRIEST.

―――― BY DIVINE AID. Job 37.19. Teach us what we shall say unto him ; *for* we cannot order *our speech* by reason of darkness.

Zec. 12.10. I will pour upon the house of David, and upon the inhabitants of Jerusalem, the spirit of grace and of supplications.

Luk. 11.1. Lord, teach us to pray.

Rom. 8.26. The Spirit also helpeth our infirmities ; for we know not what we should pray for as we ought : but the Spirit itself maketh intercession for us with groanings which cannot be uttered. 27. And he that searcheth the hearts knoweth what *is* the mind of the Spirit, because he maketh intercession for the saints according to *the will of* God.

Eph. 2.18. Through him we both have access by one Spirit, unto the Father.

Eph. 6.18. Praying always with all prayer and supplication in the Spirit.

Jude 20. Praying in the Holy Ghost.

See CHRIST HIGH-PRIEST.

―――― TO GOD ONLY. See GOD THE ONLY GOD.

PRAYER, INTERCESSORY, ENJOINED. Num. 6.23. Speak unto Aaron and unto his sons, saying, On this wise ye shall bless the children of Israel, saying unto them, 24. The Lord bless thee, and keep thee : 25. The Lord make his face shine upon thee, and be gracious unto thee : 26. The Lord lift up his countenance upon thee, and give thee peace.

1 Sam. 12.23. As for me, God forbid that I should sin against the Lord in ceasing to pray for you.

Job 42.8. My servant Job shall pray for you : for him will I accept : lest I deal with you *after your* folly, in that ye have not spoken of me *the thing which is* right, like my servant Job. 10. The Lord turned the captivity of Job, when he prayed for his friends : also the Lord gave Job twice as much as he had before.

Psa. 122.6. Pray for the peace of Jerusalem : they shall prosper that love thee.

Isa. 62.6. I have set watchmen upon thy walls, O Jerusalem, *which* shall never hold their peace day nor night : ye that make mention of the Lord, keep not silence, 7. And give him no rest, till he establish, and till he make Jerusalem a praise in the earth.

Jer. 29.7. Seek the peace of the city whither I have caused you to be carried away captives, and pray unto the Lord for it.

Joel 2.17. Let the priests, the ministers of the Lord, weep between the porch and the altar, and let them say, Spare thy people, O Lord, and give not thine heritage to reproach.

Mat. 5.44. Pray for them which despitefully use you, and persecute you.

Eph. 6.18. Praying always with all prayer and supplication in the Spirit, and watching

thereunto with all perseverance and supplication for all saints.

1 Tim. 2.1. I exhort therefore, that, first of all, supplications, prayers, intercessions, *and* giving of thanks, be made for all men ; 2. For kings, and *for* all that are in authority.

Jas. 5.14. Is any sick among you ? let him call for the elders of the church ; and let them pray over him, anointing him with oil in the name of the Lord : 15. And the prayer of faith shall save the sick, and the Lord shall raise him up ; and if he have committed sins, they shall be forgiven him. 16. Pray one for another, that ye may be healed. The effectual fervent prayer of a righteous man availeth much.

1 Jno. 5.16. If any man see his brother sin a sin *which is* not unto death, he shall ask, and he shall give him life for them that sin not unto death.

See MINISTERS, PRAYER FOR.

PRAYER, INTERCESSORY, EXAMPLES OF : Jacob, Gen. 47.7. Gen. 49. Moses, Num. 16. 20-22. Deu. 1.11. Deu. 33.6-17. Naomi, Ruth 1.8,9. David, 2 Sam. 12.16. Joab, 2 Sam. 24.3. Benaiah, 1 Kin. 1.37. Ezra, Ezr. 9. 3-15. Nehemiah, Neh. 1.4-9. Job, Job 1.5. Job. 42.10. See PARENTS' PRAYERS.

―――――, EXAMPLES OF INTERCESSORY PRAYER ANSWERED : Abraham, Gen. 17. 18,20. Gen. 18.23-32. Gen. 20.7,17,18. Moses for Pharaoh, Ex. 8.12,13,30,31. Ex. 9.33. Ex. 10.18,19 ; for Israelites, Ex. 17.11,13. Ex. 32.11-14,31-34. Ex. 33.15-17. Num. 11.2. Num. 14.13-20. Num. 21.7,8. Deu. 9.18,19,25. Deu. 10.10. Psa. 106.23 ; for Miriam, Num. 12.13 ; and for Aaron, Deu. 9.20. Samuel, 1 Sam. 7.5-12. Solomon, 1 Kin. 8. 2 Chr. 6. 2 Chr. 7.12-16. A prophet, 1 Kin. 13.6. Elijah, 1 Kin. 17.20-23. Elisha, 2 Kin. 4.33-36. Isaiah, 2 Kin. 19. Jeremiah, Jer. 42.2-10. Shadrach, Dan. 2. 17-23. Peter, Act. 9.40. The church, Act. 12.5-12. Paul, Act. 28.8.

PRAYER, INTERCESSORY, EXEMPLIFIED. Gen. 48.16. The angel which redeemed me from all evil, bless the lads ; and let my name be named on them, and the name of my fathers Abraham and Isaac ; and let them grow into a multitude in the midst of the earth. *v.* 15-20.

Ex. 32.31. Moses returned unto the Lord, and said, Oh, this people have sinned a great sin, and have made them gods of gold. 32. Yet now, if thou wilt forgive their sin— ; and if not, blot me, I pray thee, out of thy book which thou hast written.

Ex. 34.9. If now I have found grace in thy sight, O Lord, let my Lord, I pray thee, go among us ; for it *is* a stiffnecked people ; and pardon our iniquity and our sin, and take us for thine inheritance.

Num. 10.35. Rise up, Lord, and let thine enemies be scattered ; and let them that hate thee flee before thee. 36. Return, O Lord, unto the many thousands of Israel.

Num. 27.16. Let the Lord, the God of the spirits of all flesh, set a man over the congregation, 17. Which may go out before them, and which may go in before them, and which may lead them out, and which may bring them in.

Jos. 7.8. O Lord, what shall I say, when Israel

turneth their backs before their enemies! 9. For the Canaanites and all the inhabitants of the land shall hear *of it*, and shall environ us round, and cut off our name from the earth: and what wilt thou do unto thy great name? *v. 7-26.*

Jud. 5.31. *Let* them love him *be* as the sun when he goeth forth in his might.

Ruth 2.12. The Lord recompense thy work, and a full reward be given thee of the Lord God of Israel, under whose wings thou art come to trust.

1 Sam. 1.17. Go in peace: and the God of Israel grant *thee* thy petition that thou hast asked of him.

2 Sam. 24.17. Lo, I have sinned, and I have done wickedly: but these sheep, what have they done? let thine hand, I pray thee, be against me, and against my father's house.

1 Kin. 8.29. That thine eyes may be open toward this house night and day, *even* toward the place of which thou hast said, My name shall be there: that thou mayest hearken unto the prayer which thy servant shall make toward this place. 38. What prayer and supplications soever be *made* by any man, *or* by all thy people Israel, which shall know every man the plague of his own heart, and spread forth his hands toward this house: 39. Then hear thou in heaven thy dwelling-place, and forgive, and do, and give to every man according to his ways, whose heart thou knowest; (for thou, *even* thou only, knowest the hearts of all the children of men.)

1 Kin. 8.44. If thy people go out to battle against their enemy, whithersoever thou shalt send them, and shall pray unto the Lord toward the city which thou hast chosen, and *toward* the house that I have built for thy name: 45. Then hear thou in heaven their prayer and their supplication, and maintain their cause.

1 Chr. 29.18. O Lord God of Abraham, Isaac, and of Israel, our fathers, keep this for ever in the imagination of the thoughts of the heart of thy people, and prepare their heart unto thee: 19. Give unto Solomon my son a perfect heart, to keep thy commandments, thy testimonies, and thy statutes, and to do all *these things*, and to build the palace, *for* the which I have made provision.

2 Chr. 6.40. Now, my God, let, I beseech thee, thine eyes be open, and *let* thine ears *be* attent unto the prayer *that is made* in this place. 41. Now therefore arise, O Lord God, into thy resting-place, thou, and the ark of thy strength.

2 Chr. 30.18. The good Lord pardon every one 19. *That* prepareth his heart to seek God, the Lord God of his fathers, though *he be* not *cleansed* according to the purification of the sanctuary.

Psa. 7.9. Oh let the wickedness of the wicked come to an end; but establish the just.

Psa. 12.1. Help, Lord; for the godly man ceaseth; for the faithful fail from among the children of men.

Psa. 20.1. The Lord hear thee in the day of trouble; the name of the God of Jacob defend thee; 2. Send thee help from the sanctuary, and strengthen thee out of Zion; 3. Remember all thy offerings, and accept thy burnt sacrifice. 4. Grant thee according to thine own heart, and fulfil all thy counsel.

Psa. 25.22. Redeem Israel, O God, out of all his troubles.

Psa. 28.9. Save thy people, and bless thine inheritance: feed them also, and lift them up for ever.

Psa. 36.10. O continue thy lovingkindness unto them that know thee; and thy righteousness to the upright in heart.

Psa. 51.18. Do good in thy good pleasure unto Zion: build thou the walls of Jerusalem.

Psa. 80.1. O thou that dwellest *between* the cherubims, shine forth. 2. Before Ephraim and Benjamin and Manasseh stir up thy strength, and come *and* save us. 14. Return, we beseech thee, O God of hosts: look down from heaven, and behold, and visit this vine; 15. And the vineyard which thy right hand hath planted, and the branch *that* thou madest strong for thyself. 19. Turn us again, O Lord God of hosts, cause thy face to shine; and we shall be saved.

Psa. 122.7. Peace be within thy walls, *and* prosperity within thy palaces. 8. For my brethren and companions' sakes, I will now say, Peace *be* within thee.

Psa. 125.4. Do good, O Lord, unto *those that be* good, and to *them that are* upright in their hearts.

Psa. 132.9. Let thy priests be clothed with righteousness; and let thy saints shout for joy. 10. For thy servant David's sake turn not away the face of thine anointed. *v. 8.*

Psa. 134.3. The Lord that made heaven and earth bless thee out of Zion.

Psa. 141.5. For yet my prayer also *shall be* in their calamities.

Isa. 62.1. For Zion's sake will I not hold my peace, and for Jerusalem's sake I will not rest, until the righteousness thereof go forth as brightness, and the salvation thereof as a lamp *that* burneth.

Jer. 18.20. Remember that I stood before thee to speak good for them, *and* to turn away thy wrath from them.

Eze. 9.8. Ah Lord God! wilt thou destroy all the residue of Israel in thy pouring out of thy fury upon Jerusalem? Eze. 11.13.

Dan. 9.17. Now therefore, O our God, hear the prayer of thy servant, and his supplications, and cause thy face to shine upon thy sanctuary that is desolate, for the Lord's sake. 19. O Lord, hear; O Lord, forgive; O Lord, hearken and do; defer not, for thine own sake, O my God: for thy city and thy people are called by thy name. *v. 1-19.*

Mic. 7.14. Feed thy people with thy rod, the flock of thine heritage, which dwell solitary in the wood, in the midst of Carmel: let them feed *in* Bashan and Gilead, as in the days of old.

Mat. 6.10. Thy kingdom come. Thy will be done in earth, as *it is* in heaven.

Act. 7.60. Lord, lay not this sin to their charge.

Act. 8.15. Who, when they were come down, prayed for them, that they might receive the Holy Ghost.

2 Cor. 9.14. By their prayer for you, which long after you for the exceeding grace of God in you.

1 Pet. 5.10. The God of all grace, who hath called us unto his eternal glory by Christ Jesus, after that ye have suffered a while, make you perfect, stablish, strengthen, settle *you*.

PRAYER, INTERCESSORY, EXEMPLIFIED BY PAUL. Rom. 1.9. Without ceasing I make mention of you always in my prayers.

Rom. 10.1. Brethren, my heart's desire and prayer to God for Israel is, that they might be saved.

1 Cor. 1.3. Grace *be* unto you, and peace, from God our Father, and *from* the Lord Jesus Christ. Gal. 1.3.

2 Cor. 9.10. He that ministereth seed to the sower both minister bread for *your* food, and multiply your seed sown, and increase the fruits of your righteousness.

2 Cor. 13.7. Now I pray to God that ye do no evil.

Gal. 6.16. As many as walk according to this rule, peace *be* on them, and mercy, and upon the Israel of God.

Eph. 1.16. I cease not to give thanks for you, making mention of you in my prayers; 17. That the God of our Lord Jesus Christ, the Father of glory, may give unto you the spirit of wisdom and revelation in the knowledge of him : 18. The eyes of your understanding being enlightened ; that ye may know what is the hope of his calling, and what the riches of the glory of his inheritance in the saints, 19. And what *is* the exceeding greatness of his power to us-ward who believe, according to the working of his mighty power. 1 The. 1.2.

Eph. 3.14. For this cause I bow my knees unto the Father of our Lord Jesus Christ, 15. Of whom the whole family in heaven and earth is named, 16. That he would grant you, according to the riches of his glory, to be strengthened with might by his Spirit in the inner man ; 17. That Christ may dwell in your hearts by faith ; that ye, being rooted and grounded in love, 18. May be able to comprehend with all saints what *is* the breadth, and length, and depth, and height ; 19. And to know the love of Christ, which passeth knowledge, that ye might be filled with all the fulness of God.

Phil. 1.3. I thank my God upon every remembrance of you, 4. Always in every prayer of mine for you all making request with joy, 5. For your fellowship in the gospel from the first day until now. 9. This I pray, that your love may abound yet more and more in knowledge and *in* all judgment. *v.* 10.

Col. 1.3. We give thanks to God and the Father of our Lord Jesus Christ, praying always for you. 9. Since the day we heard *it*, do not cease to pray for you, and to desire that ye might be filled with the knowledge of his will in all wisdom and spiritual understanding.

Col. 2.1. For I would that ye knew what great conflict I have for you, and *for* them of Laodicea, and *for* as many as have not seen my face in the flesh. 2. That their hearts might be comforted, being knit together in love, and unto all riches of the full assurance of understanding, to the acknowledgment of the mystery of God, and of the Father, and of Christ. Col. 4.12.

1 The. 3.10. Night and day praying exceedingly that we might see your face, and might perfect that which is lacking in your faith ? 12. The Lord make you to increase and abound in love one toward another, and toward all *men*, even as we *do* toward you : 13. To the end he may stablish your hearts unblameable in holiness before God, even our Father, at the coming of our Lord Jesus Christ with all his saints. 2 Tim. 1.3.

1 The. 5.23. The very God of peace sanctify you wholly ; and *I pray God* your whole spirit and soul and body be preserved blameless unto the coming of our Lord Jesus Christ.

2 The. 1.11. We pray always for you, that our God would count you worthy of *this* calling, and fulfil all the good pleasure of *his* goodness, and the work of faith with power.

2 The. 2.16. Now our Lord Jesus Christ himself, and God, even our Father, which hath loved us, and hath given *us* everlasting consolation and good hope through grace, 17. Comfort *your* hearts, and stablish you in every good word and work.

2 The. 3.5. The Lord direct your hearts into the love of God, and into the patient waiting for Christ. 16. The Lord of peace himself give you peace always by all means. The Lord *be* with you all.

2 Tim. 1.18. The Lord grant unto him that he may find mercy of the Lord in that day.

2 Tim. 2.7. The Lord give thee understanding in all things.

2 Tim. 4.16. At my first answer no man stood with me, but all *men* forsook me : *I pray God* that it may not be laid to their charge. *v.* 16.

Philm. 6. That the communication of thy faith may become effectual by the acknowledging of every good thing which is in you in Christ Jesus. *v.* 4,5.

Heb. 13.20. The God of peace, 21. Make you perfect in every good work to do his will, working in you that which is wellpleasing in his sight, through Jesus Christ.

See CHRIST'S PRAYERS.

PRAYER, INTERCESSORY, SOLICITED. Of Moses, by Pharaoh, Ex. 8.8,28. Ex. 9.28. Ex. 10.17. Ex. 12,32; and by Israelites, Num. 21.7. Of Samuel, by Israel, 1 Sam. 12.19. Of a prophet, by Jeroboam, 1 Kin. 13.6. Of Isaiah, by Hezekiah, 2 Kin. 19.1-4. Of Jeremiah, by Zedekiah, Jer. 37.3; and by Johanan, &c., Jer. 42.1-6. Of Shadrach, &c., by Daniel, Dan. 2.17,18. Of the Jews, by Darius, Ezr. 6.10. Of Paul, by Simon Magus, Act. 8.24. Of the Churches, by Paul, Rom. 15.30-32. 2 Cor. 1.11. Eph. 6.19,20. Col. 4.3. 1 The. 5.25. 2 The. 3.1. Heb. 13.18.

——— AT MEALS. 1 Sam. 9.13. The people will not eat until he come, because he doth bless the sacrifice ; *and* afterwards they eat that be bidden.

Mat. 14.19. Looking up to heaven, he blessed and brake.

Mar. 8.6. He took the seven loaves and gave thanks. 7. And they had a few small fishes : and he blessed and commanded to set them also before *them*. Mat. 15.36. Mar. 6.41. Luk. 9.16. Jno. 6.11,23.

Act. 27.35. He took bread, and gave thanks to God in presence of them all.

Rom. 14.6. He that eateth, eateth to the Lord, for he giveth God thanks.

1 Cor. 10.30. If I by grace be a partaker, why am I evil spoken of for that for which I give thanks?

1 Cor. 11.24. When he had given thanks,

he brake *it*, and said, Take, eat. Mat. 26.26,27. Mar. 14.22,23. Luk. 22.19.

1 Tim. 4.3. Meats, which God hath created to be received with thanksgiving of them which believe and know the truth. 4. For every creature of God *is* good, and nothing to be refused, if it be received with thanksgiving: 5. For it is sanctified by the word of God and prayer.

PRAYER, Pleas employed in. Gen. 18.24. Peradventure there be fifty righteous within the city: wilt thou also destroy and not spare the place for the fifty righteous that *are* therein? 25. That be far from thee to do after this manner, to slay the righteous with the wicked: and that the righteous should be as the wicked, that be far from thee: Shall not the Judge of all the earth do right?

Gen. 32.9. O God of my father Abraham, and God of my father Isaac, the Lord which saidst unto me, Return unto thy country, and to thy kindred, and I will deal well with thee. 11. Deliver me, I pray thee, from the hand of my brother, from the hand of Esau: for I fear him, lest he will come and smite me, *and* the mother with the children. 12. And thou saidst, I will surely do thee good, and make thy seed as the sand of the sea, which cannot be numbered for multitude.

Ex. 32.11. Lord, why doth thy wrath wax hot against thy people, which thou hast brought forth out of the land of Egypt with great power, and with a mighty hand? 12. Wherefore should the Egyptians speak, and say, For mischief did he bring them out, to slay them in the mountains, and to consume them from the face of the earth? Turn from thy fierce wrath, and repent of this evil against thy people. 13. Remember Abraham, Isaac, and Israel, thy servants, to whom thou swearest by thine own self, and saidst unto them, I will multiply your seed as the stars of heaven, and all this land that I have spoken of will I give unto your seed, and they shall inherit *it* for ever.

Ex. 33.13. I pray thee, if I have found grace in thy sight, shew me now thy way, that I may know thee, that I may find grace in thy sight: and consider that this nation *is* thy people.

Num. 14.13. Moses said unto the Lord, Then the Egyptians shall hear *it*, (for thou broughtest up this people in thy might from among them;) 14. And they will tell *it* to the inhabitants of this land: 15. Now *if* thou shalt kill *all* this people as one man, then the nations which have heard the fame of thee will speak, saying, 16. Because the Lord was not able to bring this people into the land which he sware unto them, therefore he hath slain them in the wilderness. 17. I beseech thee, let the power of my Lord be great, according as thou hast spoken, saying, 18. The Lord *is* longsuffering, and of great mercy, forgiving iniquity and transgression. Deu. 9.26-29.

Num. 16.22. O God, the God of the spirits of all flesh, shall one man sin, and wilt thou be wroth with all the congregation?

Deu. 3.24. O Lord God, thou hast begun to shew thy servant thy greatness, and thy mighty hand: for what God *is there* in heaven or in earth that can do according to thy works, and according to thy might? 25. I pray thee,

let me go over and see the good land that *is* beyond Jordan.

Jos. 7.8. O Lord, what shall I say, when Israel turneth their backs before their enemies! 9. For the Canaanites and all the inhabitants of the land shall hear *of it*, and shall environ us round, and cut off our name from the earth: and what wilt thou do unto thy great name?

2 Sam. 7.25. And now, O Lord God, the word that thou hast spoken concerning thy servant, and concerning his house, establish *it* for ever, and do as thou hast said. 26. And let thy name be magnified for ever. 27. And thou, O Lord of hosts, God of Israel, hast revealed to thy servant, saying, I will build thee an house; therefore hath thy servant found in his heart to pray this prayer unto thee. 28. And now, O Lord God, thou *art* that God, and thy words be true, and thou hast promised this goodness unto thy servant: 29. Therefore now let it please thee to bless the house of thy servant.

1 Kin. 8.25. Lord God of Israel, keep with thy servant David my father that thou promisedst him. 26. Let thy word, I pray thee, be verified, which thou spakest unto thy servant David my father.

1 Kin. 18.36. Let it be known this day that thou *art* God in Israel, and *that* I *am* thy servant, and *that* I have done all these things at thy word. 37. Hear me, O Lord, hear me, that this people may know that thou *art* the Lord God, and *that* thou hast turned their heart back again.

2 Kin. 19.16. Hear the words of Sennacherib, which hath sent him to reproach the living God. 19. Now therefore, O Lord our God, I beseech thee, save thou us out of his hand, that all the kingdoms of the earth may know that thou *art* the Lord God, *even* thou only. 1 Kin. 8.59,60.

2 Chr. 14.11. Help us, O Lord our God; for we rest on thee, and in thy name we go against this multitude. O Lord, thou *art* our God; let not man prevail against thee.

Psa. 4.1. Thou hast enlarged me *when I was* in distress; have mercy upon me, and hear my prayer.

Psa. 9.19. Arise, O Lord; let not man prevail: let the heathen be judged in thy sight. 20. Put them in fear, O Lord: *that* the nations may know themselves *to be but* men.

Psa. 27.9. Put not thy servant away in anger: thou hast been my help; leave me not, neither forsake me, O God of my salvation.

Psa. 31.3. Thou *art* my rock and my fortress; therefore for thy name's sake lead me, and guide me.

Psa. 38.16. *Hear me*, lest *otherwise* they should rejoice over me.

Psa. 69.6. Let not them that wait on thee, O Lord God of hosts, be ashamed for my sake: let not those that seek thee be confounded for my sake, O God of Israel. 13. O God, in the multitude of thy mercy hear me, in the truth of thy salvation. 16. For thy loving-kindness *is* good: turn unto me according to the multitude of thy tender mercies.

Psa. 71.18. Now also when I am old and grey-headed, O God, forsake me not; until I have shewed thy strength unto *this* generation, *and* thy power to every one *that* is to come.

Psa. 74.10. O God, how long shall the adversary reproach? shall the enemy blaspheme thy name for ever? 11. Why withdrawest thou thy hand, even thy right hand? pluck *it* out of thy bosom. 18. Remember this, *that* the enemy hath reproached, O Lord, and *that* the foolish people have blasphemed thy name. 20. Have respect unto the covenant: for the dark places of the earth are full of the habitations of cruelty. 21. O let not the oppressed return ashamed: let the poor and needy praise thy name. 22. Arise, O God, plead thine own cause: remember how the foolish man reproacheth thee daily. 23. Forget not the voice of thine enemies: the tumult of those that rise up against thee increaseth continually. Psa. 79.10,12. Psa. 83.1,2.

Psa. 86.17. Shew me a token for good; that they which hate me may see *it*, and be ashamed: because thou, Lord, hast holpen me, and comforted me.

Psa. 89.49. Lord, where *are* thy former loving-kindnesses, *which* thou swarest unto David in thy truth?

Psa. 106.47. Save us, O Lord our God, and gather us from among the heathen, to give thanks unto thy holy name, *and* to triumph in thy praise.

Psa. 109.21. But do thou for me, O God the Lord, for thy name's sake: because thy mercy *is* good, deliver thou me. 26. O save me according to thy mercy: 27. That they may know that this *is* thy hand; *that* thou, Lord, hast done it.

Psa. 115.1. Not unto us, O Lord, not unto us, but unto thy name give glory, for thy mercy, *and* for thy truth's sake. 2. Wherefore should the heathen say, Where *is* now their God?

Psa. 119.38. Stablish thy word unto thy servant, who *is* devoted to thy fear. 49. Remember the word unto thy servant, upon which thou hast caused me to hope. 88. Quicken me after thy loving-kindness. 116. Uphold me according unto thy word, that I may live: and let me not be ashamed of my hope. 124. Deal with thy servant according unto thy mercy. 149. Hear my voice according unto thy loving-kindness.

Psa. 132.10. For thy servant David's sake turn not away the face of thine anointed.

Psa. 143.11. Quicken me, O Lord, for thy name's sake: for thy righteousness' sake bring my soul out of trouble.

Isa. 63.17. Return for thy servants' sake, the tribes of thine inheritance.

Lam. 3.56. Thou hast heard my voice: hide not thine ear at my breathing, at my cry.

Joel 2.17. Spare thy people, O Lord, and give not thine heritage to reproach, that the heathen should rule over them: wherefore should they say among the people, Where *is* their God?

See PARDON, PRAYER FOR—PRAYER IN CHRIST'S NAME.

PRAYER, PUBLIC AND SOCIAL. See WORSHIP.

PRAYERFULNESS — EARNESTNESS IN PRAYER. Gen. 18.32. Oh let not the Lord be angry, and I will speak yet but this once: Peradventure ten shall be found there. *v. 23-32.*

Gen. 32.26. He said, I will not let thee go, except thou bless me.

Ex. 32.32. Yet now, if thou wilt forgive their sin—; and if not, blot me, I pray thee, out of thy book which thou hast written.

Deu. 9.25. Thus I fell down before the Lord forty days and forty nights, as I fell down *at the first;* because the Lord had said he would destroy you.

Jud. 6.39. Let not thine anger be hot against me, and I will speak but this once: let me prove, I pray thee, but this once with the fleece.

Jud. 16.28. Samson called unto the Lord, and said, O Lord God, remember me, I pray thee, and strengthen me, I pray thee, only this once, O God.

1 Sam. 1.10. She *was* in bitterness of soul, and prayed unto the Lord, and wept sore.

1 Sam. 12.23. As for me, God forbid that I should sin against the Lord in ceasing to pray for you.

Ezr. 9.5. At the evening sacrifice I arose up from my heaviness; and having rent my garment and my mantle, I fell upon my knees, and spread out my hands unto the Lord my God.

Neh. 1.6. Let thine ear now be attentive, and thine eyes open, that thou mayest hear the prayer of thy servant, which I pray before thee now, day and night. 1 Kin. 8.28,52.

Neh. 2.4. Then the king said unto me, For what dost thou make request? So I prayed to the God of heaven.

Psa. 5.1. Give ear to my words, O Lord, consider my meditation. 2. Hearken unto the voice of my cry, my King, and my God: for unto thee will I pray. 3. My voice shalt thou hear in the morning, O Lord; in the morning will I direct *my prayer* unto thee, and will look up.

Psa. 17.1. Hear the right, O Lord, attend unto my cry, give ear unto my prayer, *that goeth* not out of feigned lips. 6. I have called upon thee, for thou wilt hear me, O God: incline thine ear unto me, *and hear* my speech.

Psa. 19.14. Let the words of my mouth, and the meditation of my heart, be acceptable in thy sight, O Lord, my strength, and my redeemer.

Psa. 20.9. Save, Lord: let the king hear us when we call.

Psa. 22.2. O my God, I cry in the daytime, but thou hearest not; and in the night season, and am not silent. 19. But be not thou far from me, O Lord: O my strength, haste thee to help me.

Psa. 27.7. Hear, O Lord, *when* I cry with my voice: have mercy also upon me, and answer me. *v. 8.*

Psa. 28.1. Unto thee will I cry, O Lord my rock; be not silent to me: lest, *if* thou be silent to me, I become like them that go down into the pit. 2. Hear the voice of my supplications, when I cry unto thee, when I lift up my hands toward thy holy oracle.

Psa. 35.22. *This* thou hast seen, O Lord: keep not silence: O Lord, be not far from me. 23. Stir up thyself, and awake to my judgment, *even* unto my cause, my God and my Lord.

Psa. 38.9. Lord, all my desire *is* before thee; and my groaning is not hid from thee.

Psa. 39.12. Hear my prayer, O Lord, and give ear unto my cry; hold not thy peace at my tears.

Psa. 42.8. In the night his song *shall be* with me, *and* my prayer unto the God of my life.

Psa. 55.1. Give ear to my prayer, O God; and hide not thyself from my supplication. 2. Attend unto me, and hear me: I mourn in my complaint, and make a noise. 16. As for me, I will call upon God; and the Lord shall save me. 17. Evening, and morning, and at noon, will I pray, and cry aloud: and he shall hear my voice.

Psa. 57.2. I will cry unto God most high; unto God that performeth *all things* for me.

Psa. 61.2. From the end of the earth will I cry unto thee, when my heart is overwhelmed.

Psa. 73.28. *It is* good for me to draw near to God.

Psa. 84.8. O Lord God of hosts, hear my prayer: give ear, O God of Jacob.

Psa. 86.3. Be merciful unto me, O Lord: for I cry unto thee daily. 6. Give ear, O Lord, unto my prayer; and attend to the voice of my supplications. Psa. 54.2.

Psa. 88.1. O Lord God of my salvation, I have cried day *and* night before thee: 2. Let my prayer come before thee: incline thine ear unto my cry. 9. Lord, I have called daily upon thee, I have stretched out my hands unto thee. 13. Unto thee have I cried, O Lord; and in the morning shall my prayer prevent thee.

Psa. 102.1. Hear my prayer, O Lord, and let my cry come unto thee. 2. Hide not thy face from me in the day *when* I am in trouble; incline thine ear unto me: in the day *when* I call answer me speedily.

Psa. 109.4. I *give myself unto* prayer.

Psa. 116.2. Because he hath inclined his ear unto me, therefore will I call upon *him* as long as I live.

Psa. 119.58. I entreated thy favour with *my* whole heart. 145. I cry with *my* whole heart; hear me, O Lord. 147. I prevented the dawning of the morning, and cried.

Psa. 130.1. Out of the depths have I cried unto thee, O Lord. 2. Lord, hear my voice: let thine ears be attentive to the voice of my supplications.

Psa. 141.1. Lord, I cry unto thee: make haste unto me; give ear unto my voice, when I cry unto thee. 2. Let my prayer be set forth before thee *as* incense; *and* the lifting up of my hands *as* the evening sacrifice.

Psa. 142.1. I cried unto the Lord with my voice: with my voice unto the Lord did I make my supplication. 2. I poured out my complaint before him; I shewed before him my trouble.

Isa. 62.1. For Zion's sake will I not hold my peace, and for Jerusalem's sake I will not rest, until the righteousness thereof go forth as brightness, and the salvation thereof as a lamp *that* burneth.

Isa. 64.12. Wilt thou refrain thyself for these *things*, O Lord? wilt thou hold thy peace, and afflict us very sore?

Dan. 6.10. He kneeled upon his knees three times a day, and prayed, and gave thanks before his God, as he did aforetime.

Dan. 9.3. I set my face unto the Lord God, to seek by prayer and supplications, with fasting, and sackcloth, and ashes.

Hos. 12.3. By his strength he had power with God. 4. Yea, he had power over the angel, and prevailed; he wept, and made supplication unto him.

Jonah 1.14. They cried unto the Lord, and said, We beseech thee, O Lord, we beseech thee, let us not perish for this man's life.

Mat. 15.23. He answered her not a word. And his disciples came and besought him, saying, Send her away; for she crieth after us. 25. Then came she and worshipped him, saying, Lord, help me.

Mat. 20.31. The multitude rebuked them, because they should hold their peace: but they cried the more, saying, Have mercy on us, O Lord, *thou* son of David.

Luk. 2.37. She *was* a widow of about fourscore and four years, which departed not from the temple, but served *God* with fastings and prayers night and day. 1 Tim. 5.5.

Luk. 18.7. Shall not God avenge his own elect, which cry day and night unto him?

Jno. 4.49. The nobleman saith unto him, Sir, come down ere my child die.

Act. 6.4. We will give ourselves continually to prayer.

Act. 9.11. Behold, he prayeth.

Act. 10.2. A devout *man*, and one that . . . . . prayed to God alway. 9. Peter went up upon the housetop to pray about the sixth hour.

Act. 12.5. Prayer was made without ceasing of the church unto God for him.

Rom. 1.9. God is my witness, that without ceasing I make mention of you always in my prayers.

Rom. 8.26. With groanings which cannot be uttered.

1 Cor. 14.15. I will pray with the spirit, and I will pray with the understanding also.

2 Cor. 12.8. For this thing I besought the Lord thrice, that it might depart from me.

Eph. 1.16. I cease not to give thanks for you, making mention of you in my prayers.

Col. 1.9. For this cause we also, since the day we heard *it*, do not cease to pray for you.

1 The. 3.10. Night and day praying exceedingly.

2 Tim. 1.3. Without ceasing I have remembrance of thee in my prayers night and day.

See CHRIST, PRAYERS OF — WORSHIP LOVED.

PRAYERLESSNESS. Jos. 9.14. The men took of their victuals, and asked not *counsel* at the mouth of the Lord.

Job 15.4. Yea, thou castest off fear, and restrainest prayer before God.

Job 21.14. They say unto God, Depart from us; for we desire not the knowledge of thy ways. 15. What is the Almighty, that we should serve him? and what profit should we have, if we pray unto him? Job 27.10.

Psa. 14.4. Have all the workers of iniquity no knowledge? who eat up my people *as* they eat bread, and call not upon the Lord. Psa. 53.4.

Isa. 43.22. Thou hast not called upon me, O Jacob; but thou hast been weary of me, O Israel.

Isa. 64.7. *There is* none that calleth upon thy name, that stirreth up himself to take hold of thee.

Jer. 10.21. The pastors are become brutish, and have not sought the Lord: therefore they shall not prosper, and all their flocks shall be scattered. 25. Pour out thy fury upon the heathen that know thee not, and upon the families that call not on thy name. Psa. 79.6.

Hos. 7.7. *There is* none among them that calleth unto me.

Jonah 1.6. What meanest thou, O sleeper? arise, call upon thy God.

Zeph. 1.4. I will cut off . . . . 6. Them that are turned back from the Lord; and *those* that have not sought the Lord, nor enquired for him.

Jas. 4.2. Ye have not, because ye ask not. See GODLESSNESS.

PREACHING. See ZEAL—MINISTERS.

PRECIOUS STONES. Used in the high-priest's breast-plate and ephod, Ex. 28.9-21. Ex. 39.6-14. Offered for the tabernacle, Ex. 35.27; and temple, 1 Chr. 29.2,6. Engraved, Ex. 28.9-11. Zec. 3.9. Brought from Sheba, 1 Kin. 10.2. Eze. 27.22; from Ophir, 1 Kin. 10.11.

See JEWELS: ADAMANT, AGATE, AME-THYST, BERYL, CARBUNCLE, CHALCEDONY, CHRYSOLITE, CHRYSOPHRASUS, CORAL, CRYSTAL, DIAMOND, EMERALD, JACINTH, JASPER, LIGURE, ONYX, PEARL, RUBY, SAPPHIRE, SARDINE or SARDIUS, SARDONYX, TOPAZ.

PREDESTINATION—ELECTION. Gen. 21.12. In Isaac shall thy seed be called.

Ex. 9.16. For this *cause* have I raised thee up, for to shew in thee my power; and that my name may be declared throughout all the earth.

Ex. 33.19. And will be gracious to whom I will be gracious, and will shew mercy on whom I will shew mercy.

Deu. 10.15. The Lord had a delight in thy fathers to love them, and he chose their seed after them. Deu. 4.37. Deu. 7.7,8.

Deu. 32.8. When the Most High divided to the nations their inheritance, when he separated the sons of Adam, he set the bounds of the people according to the number of the children of Israel.

Jos. 11.20. It was of the Lord to harden their hearts, that they should come against Israel in battle, that he might destroy them.

1 Sam. 12.22. It hath pleased the Lord to make you his people.

2 Chr. 6.6. I have chosen Jerusalem, that my name might be there; and have chosen David to be over my people Israel.

Psa. 33.12. Blessed *is* the people *whom* he hath chosen for his own inheritance.

Psa. 65.4. Blessed *is the man whom* thou choosest, and causest to approach *unto thee.*

Psa. 78.68. But chose the tribe of Judah, the mount Zion which he loved.

Psa. 135.4. The Lord hath chosen Jacob unto himself, *and* Israel for his peculiar treasure.

Isa. 44.1. Hear, O Jacob, my servant; and Israel, whom I have chosen: 2. Thus saith the Lord that made thee, and formed thee from the womb, *which* will help thee; Fear not, O Jacob, my servant; and thou, Jesurun, whom I have chosen. 7. Who, as I, shall call, and shall declare it, and set it in order for me, since I appointed the ancient people? and the things that are coming, and shall come.

Jer. 1.5. Before I formed thee in the belly I knew thee; and before thou camest forth out of the womb I sanctified thee, *and* I ordained thee a prophet.

Mat. 11.25. Thou hast hid these things from the wise and prudent, and hast revealed them unto babes. 26. Even so, Father: for so it seemed good in thy sight.

Mat. 20.23. To sit on my right hand, and on my left, is not mine to give, but for whom it is prepared of my Father.

Mat. 25.34. Come, ye blessed of my Father, inherit the kingdom prepared for you from the foundation of the world.

Mar. 13.20. For the elect's sake, whom he hath chosen, he hath shortened the days.

Luk. 10.20. Rather rejoice, because your names are written in heaven. *v.* 21.

Luk. 22.22. The Son of man goeth, as it was determined: but woe unto that man by whom he is betrayed. Mat. 26.24. Mar. 14.21.

Jno. 6.37. All that the Father giveth me shall come to me; and him that cometh to me I will in no wise cast out. 39. And this is the Father's will which hath sent me, that of all which he hath given me I should lose nothing, but should raise it up again at the last day.

Jno. 13.18. I speak not of you all: I know whom I have chosen: but that the scripture may be fulfilled.

Jno. 15.16. Ye have not chosen me, but I have chosen you, and ordained you.

Jno. 17.2. Thou hast given him power over all flesh, that he should give eternal life to as many as thou hast given him. 6. I have manifested thy name unto the men which thou gavest me out of the world: thine they were, and thou gavest them me. 9. I pray not for the world, but for them which thou hast given me; for they are thine.

Jno. 21.23. If I will that he tarry till I come, what *is that* to thee?

Act. 1.7. It is not for you to know the times or the seasons, which the Father hath put in his own power.

Act. 2.23. Him, being delivered by the determinate counsel and foreknowledge of God, ye have taken, and by wicked hands have crucified and slain.

Act. 3.18. Those things, which God before had shewed by the mouth of all his prophets, that Christ should suffer, he hath so fulfilled.

Act. 4.28. For to do whatsoever thy hand and thy counsel determined before to be done.

Act. 13.48. As many as were ordained to eternal life believed.

Act. 17.26. And hath determined the times before appointed, and the bounds of their habitation.

Act. 22.14. The God of our fathers hath chosen thee, that thou shouldest know his will.

Rom. 8.28. Them who are the called according to *his* purpose. 29. For whom he did foreknow, he also did predestinate *to be* conformed to the image of his Son. 30. Moreover whom he did predestinate, them he also called: and whom he called, them he also justified: and whom he justified, them he also glorified.

Rom. 9.11. For *the children* being not yet born, neither having done any good or evil, that the purpose of God according to election might stand, not of works, but of him that calleth. 18. Therefore hath he mercy on whom he will *have mercy*, and whom he will he hardeneth. *v.* 7-33. Mal. 1.2,3.

Rom. 11.5. At this present time also there is a remnant according to the election of grace. 7. Israel hath not obtained that which he seeketh for: but the election hath obtained it, and the rest were blinded.

1 Cor. 2.7. The hidden *wisdom*, which God ordained before the world unto our glory.

Gal. 1.15. It pleased God, who separated me from my mother's womb, and called *me* by his grace.

Eph. 1.4. He hath chosen us in him before the foundation of the world, that we should be holy and without blame before him in love: 5. Having predestinated us unto the adoption of children by Jesus Christ to himself, according to the good pleasure of his will. 9. Having made known unto us the mystery of his will, according to his good pleasure which he hath purposed in himself. 11. In whom also we have obtained an inheritance, being predestinated according to the purpose of him who worketh all things after the counsel of his own will.

Eph. 3.11. The eternal purpose which he purposed in Christ Jesus our Lord.

1 The. 1.4. Knowing, brethren beloved, your election of God.

1 The. 2.12. Walk worthy of God, who hath called you unto his kingdom and glory.

2 The. 2.13. God hath from the beginning chosen you to salvation through sanctification of the Spirit and belief of the truth.

2 Tim. 1.9. Who hath saved us, and called *us* with an holy calling, not according to our works, but according to his own purpose and grace, which was given us in Christ Jesus before the world began.

Tit. 1.2. Eternal life, which God, that cannot lie, promised before the world began.

Jas. 1.18. Of his own will begat he us with the word of truth, that we should be a kind of first-fruits of his creatures.

1 Pet. 1.2. Elect according to the foreknowledge of God the Father, through sanctification of the Spirit, unto obedience and sprinkling of the blood of Jesus Christ. 20. Who verily was foreordained before the foundation of the world, but was manifest in these last times for you.

2 Pet. 1.10. Give diligence to make your calling and election sure.

Rev. 13.8. All that dwell upon the earth shall worship him, whose names are not written in the book of life of the Lamb slain, from the foundation of the world.

See GOD'S PROVIDENCE OVERRULING— PROPHECY, FULFILMENT OF.

PREPARATION-DAY, the day before the Sabbath, Mat. 27.62. Mar. 15.42. Luk. 23.54. Jno. 19.14,31,42.

PRESBYTERY (Gr. *Presbuterion*), 1 Tim. 4.14. Translated elders, Luk. 22.66. Act. 22.5. See ELDERS.

PRESENCE OF GOD. See GOD, FAVOUR OF — GOD PROTECTOR — WORSHIP ENJOINED.

PRESENTS. Given to prophets, 1 Sam. 9.7. 2 Kin. 4.42. To Judges, see BRIBERY. To persons of rank, Gen. 43.11. 1 Sam. 17.18.

By subjects to kings, 2 Sam. 17.27-29, see TRIBUTE. By kings to their subjects, 2 Sam. 6.19. By kings to each other, 1 Kin. 10.10. 1 Kin. 15.18,19. By relations, Gen. 43.34.

Given at marriages, Gen. 24.53. Psa. 45.12. Est. 2.18. On restoration to health, 2 Kin. 20.12. Job 42.10,11. On parting from friends, Gen. 45.22,23. At public rejoicings, Est. 9.19. To confirm covenants, Gen. 21.28-30. 1 Sam. 18.3,4. To propitiate favour, Gen. 32.20. Pro. 21.14. To reward service, Dan. 5.7.

Consisted of cattle and horses, Gen. 32.14,15. Food, Gen. 43.11,34. 1 Kin. 14.3. Garments, weapons, and armour, Jud. 14.12. 1 Sam. 18.4. 2 Kin. 5.5. Dan. 5.7. Est. 6.8. Gold and silver, 1 Kin. 10.25. Jewels, Gen. 24. 22,53. Land, Gen. 48.22. Money, Job 42.11. Servants, Gen. 20.14. Spices, 1 Kin. 10.2.

Receiving of, a proof of good-will, 1 Sam. 25.35. Mal. 1.8.

PRESUMPTION. See INFIDELITY— PRIDE—UNBELIEF—WORSHIP, PRESUMPTION IN.

PRETORIUM, the open court before the palace, Mar. 15.16. Translated common hall, Mat. 27.27; judgment-hall, Jno. 18.28,33. Jno. 19.9. It is the palace itself in Act. 23. 35. Phil. 1.13.

PRIDE—AMBITION—VANITY—PRESUMPTION. Ex. 18.11. Now I know that the Lord *is* greater than all gods: for in the thing wherein they dealt proudly *he was* above them.

Lev. 26.19. I will break the pride of your power; and I will make your heaven as iron, and your earth as brass.

Deu. 8.13. Lest when all that thou hast is multiplied; 14. Then thine heart be lifted up, and thou forget the Lord thy God. 17. And thou say in thine heart, My power and the might of *mine* hand hath gotten me this wealth.

1 Sam. 2.3. Talk no more so exceeding proudly; let *not* arrogancy come out of your mouth: for the Lord *is* a God of knowledge, and by him actions are weighed. 4. The bows of the mighty men *are* broken, and they that stumbled are girded with strength. 5. *They that were* full have hired out themselves for bread.

1 Kin. 20.11. Let not him that girdeth on *his* harness boast himself as he that putteth it off.

2 Kin. 14.9. The thistle that *was* in Lebanon sent to the cedar that *was* in Lebanon, saying, Give thy daughter to my son to wife: and there passed by a wild beast that *was* in Lebanon, and trode down the thistle. Jud. 9.8-15. 2 Chr. 25.18,19.

Job 11.12. Vain man would be wise, though man be born *like* a wild ass's colt.

Job 12.2. No doubt but ye *are* the people, and wisdom shall die with you. *v.* 3.

Job 13.5. O that ye would altogether hold your peace! and it should be your wisdom. *v.* 1,2.

Job 15.7. Art thou the first man *that* was born or wast thou made before the hills? 8. Hast thou heard the secret of God? and dost thou restrain wisdom to thyself? 9. What knowest thou, that we know not? *what* understandest thou, which *is* not in us? 12. Why doth thine heart carry thee away? and what do thy eyes wink at, 13. That thou turnest thy spirit against God, and lettest *such* words go out of thy mouth?

Job 18.3. Wherefore are we counted as beasts, *and* reputed vile in your sight? 4. Shall the earth be forsaken for thee? and shall the rock be removed out of his place? *v.* 2.

Job 21.31. Who shall declare his way to his face? and who shall repay him *what* he hath done? 32. Yet shall he be brought to the grave, and shall remain in the tomb.

Job 32.9. Great men are not *always* wise: neither do the aged understand judgment. 12. *There was* none of you that convinced Job, *or* that answered his words: 13. Lest ye should say, We have found out wisdom: God thrusteth him down, not man.

Job 37.24. He respecteth not any *that are* wise of heart.

Psa. 9.20. Put them in fear, O Lord: *that* the nations may know themselves *to be but* men.

Psa. 10.2. The wicked in *his* pride doth persecute the poor. 3. The wicked boasteth of his heart's desire. 4. The wicked, through the pride of his countenance, will not seek *after God:* God is not in all his thoughts. 5. *As for* all his enemies, he puffeth at them. 6. He hath said in his heart, I shall not be moved: for *I shall* never be in adversity.

Psa. 12.3. The Lord shall cut off the tongue that speaketh proud things: 4. Who have said, With our tongue will we prevail; our lips *are* our own: who *is* lord over us?

Psa. 18.27. Thou wilt save the afflicted people; but wilt bring down high looks.

Psa. 31.23. The Lord preserveth the faithful, and plentifully rewardeth the proud doer.

Psa. 49.11. Their inward thought *is, that* their houses *shall continue* for ever, *and* their dwelling-places to all generations: they call *their* lands after their own names.

Psa. 52.7. *This is* the man *that* made not God his strength; but trusted in the abundance of his riches, *and* strengthened himself in his wickedness.

Psa. 73.6. Pride compasseth them about as a chain; violence covereth them *as a* garment. 8. They are corrupt, and speak wickedly *concerning* oppression: they speak loftily. 9. They set their mouth against the heavens, and their tongue walketh through the earth.

Psa. 75.5. Lift not up your horn on high: speak *not with* a stiff neck. 6. For promotion *cometh* neither from the east, nor from the west, nor from the south.

Psa. 101.5. Him that hath an high look and a proud heart will not I suffer.

Psa. 119.21. Thou hast rebuked the proud *that are* cursed, which do err from thy commandments. 69. The proud have forged a lie against me. 70. Their heart is as fat as grease.

Psa. 138.6. The proud he knoweth afar off.

Pro. 3.34. Surely he scorneth the scorners.

Pro. 6.16. An abomination unto him: 17. A proud look.

Pro. 8.13. Pride, and arrogancy, ... do I hate.

Pro. 10.17. He that refuseth reproof erreth.

Pro. 11.2. *When* pride cometh, then cometh shame. 12. He that is void of wisdom despiseth his neighbour.

Pro. 12.9. *He that is* despised, and hath a servant, *is* better than he that honoureth himself, and lacketh bread. 15. The way of a fool *is* right in his own eyes.

Pro. 13.10. Only by pride cometh contention. 18. Poverty and shame *shall be to* him that refuseth instruction.

Pro. 14.21. He that despiseth his neighbour sinneth.

Pro. 15.5. A fool despiseth his father's instruction. 10. Correction *is* grievous unto him that forsaketh the way: *and* he that hateth reproof shall die. 12. A scorner loveth not one that reproveth him: neither will he go unto the wise. 25. The Lord will destroy the house of the proud. 32. He that refuseth instruction despiseth his own soul.

Pro. 16.5. Every one *that is* proud in heart *is* an abomination to the Lord: *though* hand join in hand, he shall not be unpunished. 18. Pride *goeth* before destruction, and an haughty spirit before a fall. 19. Better *it is to be* of an humble spirit with the lowly, than to divide the spoil with the proud.

Pro. 17.19. He that exalteth his gate seeketh destruction.

Pro. 18.11. The rich man's wealth *is* his strong city, and as an high wall in his own conceit. 12. Before destruction the heart of man is haughty. 13. He that answereth a matter before he heareth *it,* it *is* folly and shame unto him.

Pro. 20.6. Most men will proclaim every one his own goodness.

Pro. 21.4. An high look, and a proud heart, *is* sin. 24. Proud *and* haughty scorner *is* his name, who dealeth in proud wrath.

Pro. 25.6. Put not forth thyself in the presence of the king, and stand not in the place of great *men.* 7. For better *it is* that it be said unto thee, Come up hither; than that thou shouldest be put lower in the presence of the prince. 14. Whoso boasteth himself of a false gift *is like* clouds and wind without rain. 27. *For men* to search their own glory *is not* glory.

Pro. 26.5. Answer a fool according to his folly, lest he be wise in his own conceit. 12. Seest thou a man wise in his own conceit? *there is* more hope of a fool than of him. 16. The sluggard *is* wiser in his own conceit than seven men that can render a reason.

Pro. 27.2. Let another man praise thee, and not thine own mouth; a stranger, and not thine own lips.

Pro. 28.11. The rich man *is* wise in his own conceit; but the poor that hath understanding searcheth him out. 25. He that is of a proud heart stirreth up strife.

Pro. 29.8. Scornful men bring a city into a snare. 23. A man's pride shall bring him low.

Pro. 30.12. *There is* a generation *that are* pure in their own eyes, and *yet* is not washed from their filthiness. 13. *There is* a generation, O how lofty are their eyes! and their eyelids are lifted up.

Isa. 2.11. The lofty looks of man shall be humbled, and the haughtiness of men shall be bowed down, and the Lord alone shall be exalted in that day. 12. For the day of the Lord of hosts *shall be* upon every *one that is* proud and lofty, and upon every *one that is* lifted up; and he shall be brought low.

Isa. 3.16. Because the daughters of Zion are haughty, and walk with stretched-forth necks, and wanton eyes, walking, and mincing *as* they go, and making a tinkling with their feet. *v.* 16-26.

Isa. 5.8. Woe unto them that join house to house, *that* lay field to field, till *there be* no place, that they may be placed alone in the midst of the earth! 15. The mighty man shall be humbled, and the eyes of the lofty shall be humbled.

Isa. 9.9. All the people shall know, *even* Ephraim, and the inhabitants of Samaria, that say in the pride and stoutness of heart, 10. The bricks are fallen down, but we will build with hewn stones; the sycamores are cut down, but we will change *them into* cedars.

Isa. 10.7. *It is* in his heart to destroy and cut off nations not a few. 8. For he saith, *Are* not my princes altogether kings? 12. I will punish the fruit of the stout heart of the king of Assyria, and the glory of his high looks. 13. He saith, By the strength of my hand I have done *it*, and by my wisdom. 14. And my hand hath found, as a nest, the riches of the people: and as one gathereth eggs *that are* left, have I gathered all the earth; and there was none that moved the wing, or opened the mouth, or peeped. 15. Shall the axe boast itself against him that heweth therewith? 16. Therefore shall the Lord, the Lord of hosts, send among his fat ones leanness. *v.* 7-33.

Isa. 13.11. I will cause the arrogancy of the proud to cease, and will lay low the haughtiness of the terrible.

Isa. 14.12. How art thou fallen from heaven, O Lucifer, son of the morning! *how* art thou cut down to the ground, which didst weaken the nations! 16. *Is* this the man that made the earth to tremble, that did shake kingdoms. *v.* 4-27.

Isa. 22.16. What hast thou here? and whom hast thou here, that thou hast hewed thee out a sepulchre here, *as* he that heweth him out a sepulchre on high, *and* that graveth an habitation for himself in a rock? 19. And I will drive thee from thy station, and from thy state shall he pull thee down. *v.* 17,18.

Isa. 23.7. *Is* this your joyous *city*, whose antiquity *is* of ancient days? her own feet shall carry her afar off to sojourn. 9. The Lord of hosts hath purposed it, to stain the pride of all glory, *and* to bring into contempt all the honourable of the earth.

Isa. 24.4. The world languisheth *and* fadeth away, the haughty people of the earth do languish. 21. The Lord shall punish the host of the high ones *that are* on high, and the kings of the earth upon the earth.

Isa. 26.5. He bringeth down them that dwell on high; the lofty city, he layeth it low; he layeth it low, *even* to the ground; he bringeth it *even* to the dust.

Isa. 28.3. The crown of pride, the drunkards of Ephraim, shall be trodden under feet.

Isa. 37.29. Because thy rage against me, and thy tumult, is come up into mine ears, therefore will I put my hook in thy nose, and my bridle in thy lips, and I will turn thee back by the way by which thou camest. *v.* 1-38.

Isa. 44.25. That turneth wise *men* backward, and maketh their knowledge foolish.

Isa. 47.7. Thou saidst, I shall be a lady for ever. 8. I *am*, and none else beside me; I shall not sit *as* a widow, neither shall I know the loss *of* children: 9. But these two *things* shall come to thee in a moment in one day, the loss of children, and widowhood. *v.* 1-11.

Jer. 4.30. Though thou rentest thy face with painting, in vain shalt thou make thyself fair; *thy* lovers will despise thee, they will seek thy life.

Jer. 9.23. Let not the wise *man* glory in his wisdom, neither let the mighty *man* glory in his might, let not the rich *man* glory in his riches.

Jer. 13.9. After this manner will I mar the pride of Judah, and the great pride of Jerusalem. 15. Hear ye, and give ear; be not proud: for the Lord hath spoken. 17. But if ye will not hear it, my soul shall weep in secret places for *your* pride; and mine eye shall weep sore, and run down with tears, because the Lord's flock is carried away captive.

Jer. 48.7. Because thou hast trusted in thy works and in thy treasures, thou shalt also be taken. 14. How say ye, We *are* mighty and strong men for the war? 15. Moab is spoiled, and gone up *out of* her cities. 29. We have heard the pride of Moab, (he is exceeding proud) his loftiness, and his arrogancy, and his pride, and the haughtiness of his heart. Isa. 16.6,7.

Jer. 49.4. Wherefore gloriest thou in the valleys, thy flowing valley, O backsliding daughter? that trusted in her treasures, *saying*, Who shall come unto me? *v.* 16.

Jer. 50.31. I am against thee, *O thou* most proud, saith the Lord God of hosts: for thy day is come, the time *that* I will visit thee.

Eze. 16.56. Thy sister Sodom was not mentioned by thy mouth in the day of thy pride.

Eze. 28.2. Because thine heart *is* lifted up, and thou hast said, I *am* a God, I sit *in* the seat of God, in the midst of the seas; yet thou *art* a man, and not God, though thou set thine heart as the heart of God. 9. But thou *shalt be* a man, and no God, in the hand of him that slayeth thee. 17. Thine heart was lifted up because of thy beauty; thou hast corrupted thy wisdom by reason of thy brightness: I will cast thee to the ground, I will lay thee before kings, that they may behold thee. *v.* 3.

Eze. 30.6. The pride of her power shall come down.

Eze. 31.10. Because thou hast lifted up thyself in height, and he hath shot up his top among the thick boughs, and his heart is lifted up in his height; 11. I have therefore delivered him into the hand of the mighty one of the heathen. *v.* 12-14.

Dan. 4.37. Those that walk in pride he is able to abase.

Dan. 11.45. He shall plant the tabernacles of his palace between the seas in the glorious holy mountain; yet he shall come to his end, and none shall help him.

Hos. 5.5. The pride of Israel doth testify to his face: therefore shall Israel and Ephraim fall in their iniquity. Hos. 7.10.

Hos. 10.11. Ephraim *is as* an heifer *that is* taught, *and* loveth to tread out *the corn;* but I passed over upon her fair neck: I will make Ephraim to ride; Judah shall plow, *and* Jacob shall break his clods.

Obad. 3. The pride of thine heart hath deceived thee, thou that dwellest in the clefts of the rock, whose habitation *is* high; that saith in his heart, Who shall bring me down to the ground? 4. Though thou exalt *thyself* as the eagle, and though thou set thy nest among the stars, thence will I bring thee down, saith the Lord.

Nah. 3.19. *There is* no healing of thy bruise; thy wound is grievous: all that hear the bruit of thee shall clap their hands over thee. *v.* 8.

Hab. 2.4. His soul *which* is lifted up is not upright in him: but the just shall live by his faith. 5. *He is* a proud man, neither keepeth at home, who enlargeth his desire as hell, and *is* as death, and cannot be satisfied, but gathereth unto him all nations, and heapeth unto him all people. 9. Woe to him that coveteth an evil covetousness to his house, that he may set his nest on high, that he may be delivered from the power of evil!

Zeph. 2.10. This shall they have for their pride, because they have reproached and magnified *themselves* against the people of the Lord of hosts. 15. This *is* the rejoicing city that dwelt carelessly, that said in her heart, I *am*, and *there is* none beside me: how is she become a desolation, a place for beasts to lie down in! every one that passeth by her shall hiss, *and* wag his hand.

Zeph. 3.11. I will take away out of the midst of thee them that rejoice in thy pride, and thou shalt no more be haughty because of my holy mountain.

Mal. 4.1. Behold, the day cometh that shall burn as an oven; and all the proud, yea, and all that do wickedly, shall be stubble.

Mat. 23.8. Be not ye called Rabbi: for one is your Master, *even* Christ; and all ye are brethren. 10. Neither be ye called masters: for one is your Master, *even* Christ. 11. But he that is greatest among you shall be your servant. 12. And whosoever shall exalt himself shall be abased. *v.* 6,7. Mat. 20.26,27. Mar. 10.43. Luk. 18.14.

Mar. 7.21. Out of the heart of men proceed evil thoughts, pride.

Mar. 9.35. If any man desire to be first, *the same* shall be last of all, and servant of all.

Mar. 12.38. Beware of the scribes, which love to go in long clothing, and *love* salutations in the market-places, 39. And the chief seats in the synagogues, and the uppermost rooms at feasts.

Luk. 1.51. He hath scattered the proud in the imagination of their hearts. 52. He hath put down the mighty from *their* seats.

Luk. 14.8. When thou art bidden of any *man* to a wedding, sit not down in the highest room; lest a more honourable man than thou be bidden of him; 9. And he that bade thee and him come and say to thee, Give this man place; and thou begin with shame to take the lowest room.

Rom. 1.22. Professing themselves to be wise, they became fools. 29. Being filled with all unrighteousness; 30. Proud, boasters.

Rom. 11.20. Be not high-minded, but fear: 21. For if God spared not the natural branches, *take heed* lest he also spare not thee.

Rom. 12.3. I say, through the grace given unto me, to every man that is among you, not to think *of himself* more highly than he ought to think; but to think soberly, according as God hath dealt to every man the measure of faith. 16. Mind not high things, but con-

descend to men of low estate. Be not wise in your own conceits.

1 Cor. 1.29.   That no flesh should glory in his presence.

1 Cor. 3.18.   Let no man deceive himself. If any man among you seemeth to be wise in this world, let him become a fool, that he may be wise.

1 Cor. 4.6. Learn in us not to think *of men* above that which is written, that no one of you be puffed up for one against another. 7. For who maketh thee to differ *from another?* and what hast thou that thou didst not receive? now if thou didst receive *it*, why dost thou glory, as if thou hadst not received *it?* 8. Now ye are full, now ye are rich, ye have reigned as kings without us: and I would to God ye did reign, that we also might reign with you. 10. We *are* fools for Christ's sake. but *ye are* wise in Christ; we *are* weak, but ye *are* strong; ye *are* honourable, but we *are* despised.

1 Cor. 5.2. Ye are puffed up, and have not rather mourned, that he that hath done this deed might be taken away from among you. 6. Your glorying *is* not good. Know ye not that a little leaven leaveneth the whole lump?

1 Cor. 8.1.   Knowledge puffeth up, but charity edifieth. 2. If any man think that he knoweth any thing, he knoweth nothing yet as he ought to know.

1 Cor. 10.12. Wherefore let him that thinketh he standeth take heed lest he fall.

1 Cor. 14.38. If any man be ignorant, let him be ignorant.

2 Cor. 10.5.   Casting down imaginations, and every high thing that exalteth itself against the knowledge of God, and bringing into captivity every thought to the obedience of Christ. 12. We dare not make ourselves of the number, or compare ourselves with some that commend themselves: but they measuring themselves by themselves, and comparing themselves among themselves, are not wise. 18. Not he that commendeth himself is approved, but whom the Lord commendeth.

Gal. 6.3. If a man think himself to be something, when he is nothing, he deceiveth himself.

Eph. 4.17. Walk not as other Gentiles walk, in the vanity of their mind.

Phil. 2.3.   Let nothing *be done* through strife or vainglory; but in lowliness of mind let each esteem other better than themselves.

1 Tim. 2.9. That women adorn themselves in modest apparel, with shamefacedness and sobriety; not with broided hair, or gold, or pearls, or costly array.

1 Tim. 3.6. Not a novice, lest being lifted up with pride he fell into the condemnation of the devil.

1 Tim. 6.3. If any man teach otherwise, and consent not to wholesome words, 4. He is proud, knowing nothing. 17. Charge them that are rich in this world, that they be not highminded.

2 Tim. 3.2. Men shall be lovers of their own selves, boasters, proud; 4. Heady, highminded.

Jas. 3.1. My brethren, be not many masters, knowing that we shall receive the greater condemnation.

Jas. 4.6. God resisteth the proud, but giveth grace unto the humble.

1 Pet. 5.3. Neither as being lords over God's heritage, but being ensamples to the flock. v. 5.

1 Jno. 2.16. All that is in the world, the lust of the flesh, and the lust of the eyes, and the pride of life, is not of the Father, but is of the world.

3 Jno. 9. Diotrephes, who loveth to have the pre-eminence among them, receiveth us not.

Rev. 3.17. Thou sayest, I am rich, and increased with goods, and have need of nothing; and knowest not that thou art wretched, and miserable, and poor, and blind, and naked.

Rev. 18.7. How much she hath glorified herself, and lived deliciously, so much torment and sorrow give her: for she saith in her heart, I sit a queen, and am no widow, and shall see no sorrow. v. 8.

PRIDE, AMBITION, VANITY, EXAMPLES OF: Eve, Gen. 3.5,6. Builders of Babel, Gen. 11.4. Hagar, Gen. 16.4. Pharaoh, Ex. 5.2. Ex. 15.9,10. Neh. 9.10. Miriam and Aaron, Num. 12.2-10. Korah, &c., Num. 16.3. Abimelech, Jud. 9.1. Goliath, 1 Sam. 17.42-44. Absalom, 2 Sam. 15.4. 2 Sam. 18.18. Ahithophel, 2 Sam. 17.23. David, 2 Sam. 24.2. Adonijah, 1 Kin. 1.5. Benhadad, 1 Kin. 20.3,10. Naaman, 2 Kin. 5.11-13. Amaziah, 2 Kin. 14.8. Sennacherib, 2 Kin. 18.19-35. 2 Kin. 19. 2 Chr. 32.10-19. Hezekiah, 2 Kin. 20.13. 2 Chr. 32.31. Uzziah, 2 Chr. 26.16-19. Haman, Est. 3.5. Est. 5.11,13. Est. 6.6. Est. 7.10. Azariah, &c., Jer. 43.2. Nebuchadnezzar, Dan. 4.30-34. Dan. 5.20. Belshazzar, Dan. 5.22. The Jews, Mat. 13.55-57. Jno. 7.49. Peter, Mat. 16.22,23. Jno.13.8. James & John, Mar. 10.35. The disciples, Mar. 9.34. Pharisee, Luk. 18.11. Herod, Act. 12.21-23. See SELF-RIGHTEOUSNESS—FALSE CONFIDENCE.

PRIEST (Heb. cohen; Gr. hierus). Melchizedek is the first styled priest, Gen. 14. 18. Jethro is called priest or prince (marg.), of Midian, Ex. 2.16. Priests are mentioned before the giving of the law, Ex. 19.22,24, see OFFERINGS. In the New Testament the word is applied exclusively to the Levitical priesthood. It is figuratively applied to the Israelites, Ex. 19.6. Isa. 61.6; and to Christians, 1 Pet. 2.9. Rev. 1.6. Rev. 5.10. Rev. 20.6.

PRIEST. THE HIGH-PRIEST. Aaron of the tribe of Levi the first high-priest; descent in his family divinely appointed, Ex. 28.1. Ex. 29.29. Num. 3.10. Num. 16.40. 1 Chr. 23. 13. Heb. 5.4. Heb. 7.11; through Phinehas, Num. 25.12,13. Abiathar, of the line of Ithamar and Eli, deposed by Solomon; Zadok, of the line of Phinehas, made high-priest, 1 Kin. 2.27,35.

Chronological list of those mentioned in scripture, see AARON, ELEAZAR, PHINEHAS. Of the line of Ithamar, ELI, AHITUB, AHIMELECH, ABIATHAR. Of the line of Phinehas, ZADOK, AHIMAAZ, AZARIAH or AMARIAH, JEHOIADA, ZECHARIAH, AZARIAH, AZARIAH or AMARIAH, URIJAH, HILKIAH, AZARIAH, SERAIAH, JEHOZADAK, JOSHUA.

Under the Romans irregular, Jno. 11.49,51. Act. 4.6. Act. 23.2,5. See CAIAPHAS, ANNAS, ANANIAS.

A second priest under the high-priest, Num. 3.32. Num. 4.16. Num. 31.6. 1 Chr. 9.20. 2 Sam. 15.24. 2 Kin. 25.18. Luk. 3.2.

Without blemish, Lev. 21.16-23. Holy to the Lord, Num. 17.1-11. Lev. 21.10-12,15. A prophet, Jno. 11.49-52. Marriage-laws regarding, Lev. 21.13-15. Forbidden to mourn for the dead, Lev. 21.10-12. At his death, the man-slayer might return home, Num. 35.25. Jos. 20.6.

Consecration of, by sacrifices, washing with water, putting on the priestly garments, anointing, sprinkling with blood and oil, Ex. 29. Ex. 28.40-43. Ex. 40.12-16,30-32. Lev. c. 8 & 9. Lev. 6.20-23. Services at consecration, lasted 7 days, Lev. 8.33.

DRESS OF. Holy garments for glory and beauty, made by men taught of God, Ex. 28. 2-4. Ex. 36.1. Ex. 39.1. The different parts are as follows:—

The ephod, a scarf of fine twined linen, embroidered with gold thread, blue, purple, and scarlet, having two shoulder-pieces joined at the edges, Ex. 39.2-4. Ex. 28.4-7. Two onyx stones set in gold, engraved with the names of the 12 tribes, put on the shoulders of the ephod, Ex. 28.9-12. Ex. 39.6,7.

Breastplate of judgment of the same materials and workmanship as the ephod: doubled, about 9 inches square; set with 12 stones in 4 rows, engraven with the names of the tribes: placed above the girdle, and fastened to the shoulder-pieces of the ephod by gold chains, and a lace of blue passing through 4 gold rings in the corners of the breastplate, Ex. 28.13-29. Ex. 39.8-21.

Urim and Thummim, put in the breastplate, Ex. 28.30. Lev. 8.8. Wanting after the captivity, Ezr. 2.63. See URIM.

Girdle of the ephod, of the same materials and workmanship as the ephod, Ex. 28.4,8,39. Ex. 39.5,29.

Robe of the ephod (worn underneath the ephod, and reaching to the feet), of blue, a hole in the top of it, the hem of the skirt embroidered with pomegranates of blue, purple, scarlet and twined linen, and hung with gold bells, to sound when the priest went into the holy place, Ex. 28.4,31-35. Ex. 39.22-26.

Embroidered coat of linen (worn underneath the ephod), Ex. 28.4,39. Ex. 39.27. Lev. 16.4.

Breeches of linen, Lev. 16.4. Ex. 28.42.

Mitre, a cap of fine linen, having fastened to it by a lace of blue, a plate of gold, called the holy crown of pure gold, with the inscription, "Holiness to the Lord," indicating that the high-priest bore the iniquity of the offerings, Ex. 28.4,36-39. Ex. 39.28,30,31.

Put on at consecration; worn 7 days, Ex. 29.30. Ex. 40.13. Lev. 8.7-9.35; and on the Day of Atonement, Lev. 16.4,32. To be kept in the tabernacle, Lev. 16.23. Descended to successive high-priests, Ex. 29.29. Lev. 16.32. Num. 20.26-28.

DUTIES OF. To inquire by Urim and Thummim, see URIM. To bless the people, Lev. 9.22,23. Num. 6.23. Deu. 10.8. Deu. 21.5. 1 Chr. 23.13. To mediate and make intercession, Ex. 28.12,29,30,38. Num. 16.46. Num. 18.1, see Heb. 2.17,18. To offer gifts and sacrifices, Heb. 5.1. Heb. 8.3. To appoint the priests to their offices, 1 Sam. 2.36. To consecrate Levites, Num. 8.11-21. To take charge of the sacred treasury, 2 Kin. 12.10. 2 Kin. 22.4. 2 Chr. 24.6-14. 2 Chr. 34.9. To light the holy lamps, Ex. 27.21. Ex. 30.8.

Lev. 24.3,4. Num. 8.3. To burn incense, Ex. 30.7,8. 1 Sam. 2.28. 1 Chr. 23.13. To place shew-bread on the table every sabbath, Lev. 24.8. To offer for his own sins of ignorance, Lev. 4.3-12.

DUTIES ON THE DAY OF ATONEMENT. To make atonement for himself and his house, the people, the tabernacle &c., Lev. 16. 30-34. The high-priest washed himself, and put on the holy garments, v. 4. Cast lots for the scape-goat, v. 5,7,8.

Entered the holy of holies to burn incense before the mercy-seat, Lev. 16.12,13. Offered a young bullock for a sin-offering, for himself and his house, v. 3,6,11. Heb. 5.3. Entered the holy of holies, and sprinkled the blood of his sin-offering on the mercy-seat, Lev.16.14,27. Heb. 9.7. Offered a goat for the sin-offering of the people, Lev. 16.8,9,15,27. Entered the holy of holies a third time with the blood of the people's sin-offering, to make an atonement for the most holy place, the tabernacle, &c., v. 15-17,30. Heb. 9.7. Entered the holy of holies alone, Heb. 9.7. No person permitted, while he was there, to be in the tabernacle, Lev. 16.17,

Made an atonement with the blood of the bullock and goat, for the altar of incense, Lev. 16.18,19. Ex. 30.10. Heb. 9.22,23. Confessed the sins of the people upon the head of the scape-goat, and sent it away to the wilderness, Lev. 16.10,20-22. Washed himself and changed his garments, v. 23,24. Offered 2 rams as burnt-offerings, one for himself, the other for the people, v. 3,5,24.

JUDICIAL AUTHORITY, Deu. 17.8-13. 1 Sam. 4.18. Hos. 4.4. As president, Mat. 26.3,57-62. Act. 5.21-28. Act. 23.1-5. To number the people, Num. 1.3. To superintend the choice of a ruler, Num. 27.19. To encourage the people to battle, Deu. 20.2-4. To distribute the spoils in war, Num. 31. 21,26.

EMOLUMENTS. The same as those of the priests, see PRIESTS' EMOLUMENTS. Portion of spoils taken in war, Num. 31. 26-29.

INFERIORITY TO CHRIST, Heb. 5.2,3. Heb. 7.5-12,23-28. Heb. 8.4-13. Heb. 9.7-28. Heb. 10.1-14.

See CHRIST HIGH-PRIEST.

PRIESTS, DIVINELY APPOINTED. Of Aaron's line, Ex. 27.20,21. Ex. 28.1-4. Ex. 29.9,44. Ex. 40.15. Num. 3.10. Num. 16.40. Num. 18.7. Num. 25.13. 1 Chr. 23.13. Were holy unto the Lord, Lev. 21.6,8. Lev. 22.9,16. Isa. 52.11.

Without blemish, Lev. 21.17-23. Required to prove their genealogy, Ezr. 2.62. Neh. 7. 64. Forbidden to mourn, except for near relations, Lev. 21.1-6; or to drink wine on entering the tabernacle, Lev. 10.8-11. Eze. 44.21; or to eat what died of itself, or was torn, Lev. 22.8; or to officiate when ceremonially unclean, Lev. 22.2-9.

Marriage-laws regarding, Lev. 21.7-15. Who of their household might eat holy things, Lev. 22.10-12.

Divided by David into 24 courses, 1 Chr. 24.1-19. 1 Chr. 28.13,21. 2 Chr. 8.14. 2 Chr. 31.2. 2 Chr. 35.4,5. Ezr. 2.36-39. Neh. 13. 30. Chosen by lot, Luk. 1.9. Heads of, called elders or chiefs, see ELDERS OF THE PRIESTS.

Consecration of, by sacrifices, washing with water, putting on the priestly garments, anointing with oil, sprinkling with blood and oil, Ex. 29. Ex. 28.40-43. Ex. 40.12-16,30-32. Lev. c. 8 & 9; the services lasting 7 days, Ex. 29.30,35. Punishment for usurping the office of, Num. 3.10. Num. 16. Num. 18.7. 2 Chr. 26.18.

DRESS OF, Ex. 28.40-43. Ex. 39,27-29. Lev. 6.10. See EPHOD.

DUTIES OF. To offer sacrifices, Lev. c. 1 to 6. 1 Chr. 16.40. 2 Chr. 13.11. 2 Chr. 29.34. 2 Chr. 35.11-14. Ezr. 6.20. Heb. 10.11, see OFFERINGS, MODE OF. To wash before, Ex. 30.18-21. 2 Chr. 4.6. To offer the first-fruits, Lev. 23.10,11. Deu. 26.3,4. To bless the people, Num. 6.22-27. 2 Chr. 30.27. Teach the law, Lev. 10.11. Deu. 31.9-13. Deu. 33.10. Jer. 2.8. Mal. 2.7. Prepare and burn incense, see INCENSE. Light the holy lamps, Ex. 27.20,21. 2 Chr. 13.11. Lev. 24.3,4. Keep the sacred fire always burning, Lev. 6.12,13. Keep the charge of the sanctuary, Num. 18. 1,5,7. Cover the holy things of the sanctuary, Num. 4.5-15. Carry the ark, see ARK. Blow the trumpets for calling assemblies, and in battle, see TRUMPETS—TRUMPET, SILVER. Examine lepers, see LEPROSY. Purify the unclean, Lev. 15.31, see DEFILEMENT. Value things devoted, Lev. 27.8,12. Officiate in the holy place, Heb. 9.6. To act as magistrates, Num. 5.14-31. Deu. 17.8-13. Deu. 19.17. Deu. 21.5. 2 Chr. 19.8.

EMOLUMENTS. Tithes of the tithes, see TITHES. First-fruits, see FIRST-FRUITS. Firstlings of beasts, or substitutes of, Num. 18.17,18. Neh. 10.36. Redemption-money of first-born, Num. 3.46-51. Num. 18.15,16. Things devoted, Num. 5.9,10. Lev. 27.21. Num. 18.14. Fines, Num. 5.8. Lev. 5.16. Lev. 22.14. The shew-bread, see SHEW-BREAD. Cities of the priests, 13 in number, Jos. 21. 4,13-19. 1 Chr. 6.57-66. Neh. 11.3-20. Portions of sacrifices and offerings, Ex. 29.27-34. Lev. 2.3,10. Lev. 6.15-18,26. Lev. 7.6-10,31-34. Lev. 10.12-14. Num. 6.19-20. Num. 18.8-19. Deu. 18.3-5. Regulations by Hezekiah, 2 Chr. 31.4-19. Exempted from tribute by Artaxerxes, Ezr. 7.24.

PRIESTS, HISTORICAL NOTICES OF. Eleazar, Aaron's eldest son, was chief of the Kohathites, Num.4.16-20. Ithamar, his second son, of the Gershonites and Merarites, Num. 4.21-33. Num. 7.8.

Carried the ark through Jordan, Jos. 3. Jos. 4.15-18. To Mount Gerizim, Jos. 8.33. To the tabernacle, 1 Chr. 15.14,24; and temple, 1 Kin. 8.3,4. 2 Chr. 5.5-7.

Blew trumpets at the fall of Jericho, Jos. 6. At dedication of the temple, 2 Chr. 5.12. 2 Chr. 7.6. In Abijah's war, 2 Chr. 13.12-14. See TRUMPET.

Slaughter of, by Saul, 1 Sam. 22.11-19. Resort to Rehoboam, 2 Chr. 11.13. Prevent Uzziah from offering incense, 2 Chr. 26.17. Cleanse the temple, 2 Chr. 29.4,16.

Transgressions of, 2 Chr. 36.14 (see MINISTERS, UNFAITHFUL). Persecute Jeremiah, Jer. 26.11. Taken to Babylon, Jer. 29.1. Return from Babylon, Ezr. 1.5. Ezr. 2.36-39, 61,70. Ezr. 3.8. Ezr. 7.7. Ezr. 8.24-30. Neh. 7.39-42,63-73. Neh. 10.1-8. Neh. 12.1-7. Genealogy of some lost, Neh. 7.64,65.

Transgressions after the return; their reform,

Ezr. 9.1,2.   Ezr. 10.5,18,19.   Neh. 5.12.   Neh. 10.28.   Build the wall of Jerusalem, Neh. 3.1,22,28.   Erect the altar, Ezr. 3.2.

Send to John the Baptist, Jno. 1.19.   Opposition to Christ, see CHRIST'S SUFFERINGS. To the apostles, Act. 4.1.   Act. 5.4.   Converts to Christianity, Act. 6.7.

PRIESTS, IDOLATROUS.   Of On, Gen. 41. 45,50.   Gen. 46,20.   Land of, in Egypt, not sold, Gen. 47.22,26.   Micah's son, Jud. 17.5. Jonathan, his posterity priests till the captivity, Jud. 17.7-13.   Jud. 18.30.   Of Dagon, 1 Sam. 5.5.   1 Sam. 6.2.   Appointed by Jeroboam of the lowest of the people, 1 Kin. 12.31,32.   1 Kin. 13.2,33.   2 Chr. 11.15.   2 Chr. 13.9.   Amaziah a priest, Amos 7.10.   Of Baal; their sacrifice on Carmel ; slain by Elijah, 1 Kin. 18.19-40 ; slain by Jehu, 2 Kin. 10. 11,18-27.   Mattan slain, 2 Kin. 11.18.   Of Chemarim (idolatrous), 2 Kin. 23.5.   Zeph. 1.4. Samaritan priest sent back by the king of Assyria, 2 Kin. 17.27,28.   Of the lowest of the people, 1 Kin. 17.32.   Slain by Josiah, 2 Kin. 23.20.   Of Jupiter at Lystra, Act. 14.13.

PRINCES OF THE TRIBES.   See ISRAEL, TRIBES OF.

PRISCILLA.   See AQUILA.

PRISON, Gen. 42.16-19.   Lev. 24.12. Num. 15.34.   Ezr. 7.26.   Jer. 52.11.   Luk. 23.19.   Act. 4.3.   Act. 12.4,5.   Used for debtors, Mat. 18.30.   Mat. 5.26.

State-prison, Gen. 39.20.   Common prison, Act. 5.18.   Inner prison, Act. 16.24.   Dungeon or pit, Jer. 38.6.   Zec. 9.11.

Court of the palace, Jer. 32.2.   House of the king's scribe, Jer. 37.15.   House of captain of guard, Gen. 40.3.

PRISONERS.   Kept to hard labour, Jud. 16.21.   Fed on bread and water, 1 Kin. 22.27. Chained, Act. 12.6, see FETTERS—CHAINS. Clothed in prison garments, 2 Kin. 25.29. Placed in stocks, see STOCKS.   Visited by friends, Mat. 11.2.   Mat. 25.36.   Act. 24.23.

See JUSTICE, ADMINISTRATION OF—PUNISHMENTS.

PRIVILEGES, INSUFFICIENCY OF, TO SALVATION.   Jer. 7.4.   Trust ye not in lying words, saying, The temple of the Lord, The temple of the Lord, The temple of the Lord, are these.

Jer. 8.8.   How do ye say, We are wise, and the law of the Lord is with us? Lo, certainly in vain made he it ; the pen of the scribes is in vain.

Mat. 3.9.   Think not to say within yourselves, We have Abraham to our father : for I say unto you, that God is able of these stones to raise up children unto Abraham.   Luk. 3.8.

Mat. 7.22.   Many will say to me in that day, Lord, Lord, have we not prophesied in thy name? and in thy name have cast out devils ? and in thy name done many wonderful works ? 23. And then will I profess unto them, I never knew you : depart from me, ye that work iniquity.   Mat. 7.18-20.

Mat. 19.30.   But many that are first shall be last ; and the last shall be first.   [Parable of the householder and the labourers, Mat. 20. 1-16.]

Mar. 2.27.   The sabbath was made for man, and not man for the sabbath.

Luk. 13.26.   Then shall ye begin to say, We have eaten and drunk in thy presence, and

thou hast taught in our streets.   27. But he shall say, I tell you, I know you not whence ye are.   v. 30.

Rom. 2.25.   Circumcision verily profiteth, if thou keep the law : but if thou be a breaker of the law, thy circumcision is made uncircumcision.   28. He is not a Jew, which is one outwardly ; neither is that circumcision, which is outward in the flesh : 29. But he is a Jew, which is one inwardly ; and circumcision is that of the heart, in the spirit, and not in the letter ; whose praise is not of men, but of God.   v. 17-29.

Rom. 9.6.   They are not all Israel, which are of Israel.   31. Israel, which followed after the law of righteousness, hath not attained to the law of righteousness.

1 Cor. 7.19.   Circumcision is nothing, and uncircumcision is nothing, but the keeping of the commandments of God.   v. 18.   1 Cor. 10.1-10.

2 Cor. 5.16.   Henceforth know we no man after the flesh : yea, though we have known Christ after the flesh, yet now henceforth know we him no more.

Gal. 5.6.   In Jesus Christ neither circumcision availeth any thing, nor uncircumcision ; but faith which worketh by love.

Gal. 6.15.   In Christ Jesus neither circumcision availeth any thing, nor uncircumcision, but a new creature.

Phil. 3.3.   We are the circumcision, which worship God in the Spirit, and rejoice in Christ Jesus, and have no confidence in the flesh.   7. But what things were gain to me, those I counted loss for Christ.   v. 4-6.

Col. 2.23.   Which things have indeed a shew of wisdom in will worship, and humility, and neglecting of the body ; not in any honour to the satisfying of the flesh.

1 Tim. 4.8.   Bodily exercise profiteth little. Heb. 13.9.   It is a good thing that the heart be established with grace ; not with meats, which have not profited them that have been occupied therein.

See FALSE CONFIDENCE — HYPOCRISY — SELF - RIGHTEOUSNESS — JUSTIFICATION — WORKS.

PRIVILEGES REMOVED.   See SPIRITUAL DESTITUTION.

PRIZE, ILLUSTRATIVE, 1 Cor. 9.24.   Phil. 3.14.

PROCHORUS, one of the seven deacons, Act. 6.5.

PROCLAMATIONS.   Made by king's letters, 2 Chr. 30.1-10.   Ezr. 1.1-4.   Est. 1.22. Est. 8.10-14.   By a herald, Dan. 5.29.   Est. 6.9.   Illustrative, Isa. 40.3,9.

PROFESSION OF FAITH.   See DECISION. False profession, see HYPOCRISY — BACK-SLIDING.

PROGNOSTICATORS.   Publishers of monthly prophetic almanacs, Isa. 47.13.

PROMISES, 2 Cor. 1.20.   Heb. 6.17.   2 Pet. 1.4.   See ADOPTION—AFFLICTION—CHRIST'S DEATH, DESIGN OF—CHRIST HIGH-PRIEST—CHRIST'S LOVE—CHRIST SAVIOUR—COVENANT—DECISION—FAITH—FEAR OF GOD—GOD'S FAITHFULNESS—GOD'S FAVOUR—GOD'S GOODNESS—GOD'S LOVE—GOD'S MERCY—GOD PROTECTOR—GOD SAVIOUR—HOLY SPIRIT'S INFLUENCES—JUSTIFICATION—OBEDIENCE—

PARDON — PEACE,　NATIONAL — POOR —
PRAYER — REPENTANCE — REGENERATION —
SAINTS, CHILDREN OF — SALVATION — SANC-
TIFICATION — SPIRITUAL PEACE — SPIRITUAL
DILIGENCE — WISDOM — WIDOWS — WORSHIP.

PROPHECIES. Of Christ, see CHRIST,
PROPHECIES OF. Of the gospel dispensation
and kingdom of Christ, see CHURCH, PROPHE-
CIES OF. Of the temple, see TEMPLE. Of
countries and persons, will be found under
their various names; as ISRAELITES, BABY-
LON, DAVID, &c.

Of countries not named, Isa. 16.4,5. Isa.
17.12-14. Isa. 18. Isa. 24. Isa. 25.2-5. Isa.
27.1. Isa. 33.1-12. Isa. 41.1-7,25. Dan. 11.
5-45.

PROPHECY, ITS CERTAIN FULFILMENT.
Num. 11.23. Is the Lord's hand waxed short?
thou shalt see now whether my word shall
come to pass unto thee or not.

Isa. 34.16. Seek ye out of the book of the
Lord, and read: no one of these shall fail,
none shall want her mate: for my mouth it
hath commanded, and his spirit it hath gathered
them.

Isa. 40.8. The grass withereth, the flower
fadeth; but the word of our God shall stand
for ever.

Isa. 44.26. That confirmeth the word of his
servant, and performeth the counsel of his
messengers.

Jer. 4.28. Because I have spoken it, I have
purposed it, and will not repent, neither will I
turn back from it.

Jer. 37.9. Deceive not yourselves, saying,
The Chaldeans shall surely depart from us:
for they shall not depart. 10. For though ye
had smitten the whole army of the Chaldeans
that fight against you, and there remained but
wounded men among them, yet should they
rise up every man in his tent, and burn this
city with fire.

Jer. 44.28. All the remnant of Judah, that
are gone into the land of Egypt to sojourn
there, shall know whose words shall stand,
mine, or their's.

Jer. 51.53. Though Babylon should mount
up to heaven, and though she should fortify
the height of her strength, yet from me shall
spoilers come unto her, saith the Lord. 56.
For the Lord God of recompences shall surely
require.

Eze. 12.25. I am the Lord: I will speak,
and the word that I shall speak shall come to
pass; it shall be no more prolonged: for in
your days, O rebellious house, will I say the
word, and will perform it, saith the Lord God.

Dan. 9.12. He hath confirmed his words,
which he spake against us, and against our
judges that judged us, by bringing upon us
a great evil. 13. As it is written in the law of
Moses, all this evil is come upon us.

Hab. 2.3. The vision is yet for an appointed
time, but at the end it shall speak, and not
lie: though it tarry, wait for it; because it
will surely come, it will not tarry.

Mat. 5.18. Verily I say unto you, Till
heaven and earth pass, one jot or one tittle
shall in no wise pass from the law, till all be
fulfilled.

Mat. 24.35. Heaven and earth shall pass
away, but my words shall not pass away.
Mar. 13.31.

Mat. 26.24. The Son of man goeth as it is
written of him. 53. Thinkest thou that I
cannot now pray to my Father, and he shall
presently give me more than twelve legions of
angels? 54. But how then shall the scriptures
be fulfilled, that thus it must be? v. 56.

Mar. 14.49. I was daily with you in the
temple teaching, and ye took me not: but the
scriptures must be fulfilled.

Luk. 1.20. Thou shalt be dumb, and not able
to speak, until the day that these things shall
be performed, because thou believest not my
words, which shall be fulfilled in their season.

Luk. 21.22. These be the days of vengeance,
that all things which are written may be fulfilled. v. 33.

Luk. 24.44. All things must be fulfilled,
which were written in the law of Moses, and
in the prophets, and in the psalms, concerning
me. v. 25. Luk. 18.31.

Jno. 10.35. The scripture cannot be broken.

Act. 3.18. Those things, which God before
had shewed by the mouth of all his prophets,
that Christ should suffer, he hath so fulfilled.

Act. 13.27. Because they knew him not, nor
yet the voices of the prophets which are read
every sabbath-day, they have fulfilled them in
condemning him. 29. When they had fulfilled
all that was written of him, they took him
down from the tree.

Rom. 9.6. Not as though the word of God
hath taken none effect.

See GOD, FAITHFULNESS OF.

PROPHECY, ITS DESIGN AND VALUE.
2. Chr. 20.20. Believe in the Lord your God,
so shall ye be established; believe his prophets,
so shall ye prosper.

Isa. 48.5. I have even from the beginning
declared it to thee; before it came to pass I
shewed it thee: lest thou shouldest say, Mine
idol hath done them. 7. They are created
now, and not from the beginning; even before
the day when thou heardest them not; lest
thou shouldest say, Behold, I knew them.
v. 3,4.

Dan. 9.2. I Daniel understood by books the
number of the years, whereof the word of the
Lord came to Jeremiah the prophet, that he
would accomplish seventy years in the desolations of Jerusalem.

Jno. 2.22. When therefore he was risen
from the dead, his disciples remembered that
he had said this unto them; and they believed
the scripture, and the word which Jesus had
said.

Jno. 14.29. Now I have told you before it
come to pass, that, when it is come to pass,
ye might believe.

Jno. 16.4. These things have I told you,
that when the time shall come, ye may remember that I told you of them.

1 Cor. 14.24. If all prophesy, and there
come in one that believeth not, or one unlearned, he is convinced of all, he is judged of
all: 25. And thus are the secrets of his heart
made manifest; and so falling down on his
face he will worship God, and report that God
is in you of a truth. v. 1-33.

1 The. 5.20. Despise not prophesyings.

1 Pet. 1.10. Of which salvation the prophets
have enquired and searched diligently, who
prophesied of the grace that should come unto
you: 11. Searching what, or what manner of
time the Spirit of Christ which was in them

did signify, when it testified beforehand the sufferings of Christ, and the glory that should follow. *v.* 12.

2 Pet. 1.19. We have also a more sure word of prophecy; whereunto ye do well that ye take heed, as unto a light that shineth in a dark place, until the day dawn, and the day-star arise in your hearts: 20. Knowing this first, that no prophecy of the scripture is of any private interpretation.

Rev. 1.3. Blessed *is* he that readeth, and they that hear the words of this prophecy, and keep those things which are written therein: for the time *is* at hand. Rev. 22.7.

See PROPHETS, INSPIRATION OF—WORD OF GOD.

PROPHETESS. See MIRIAM, DEBORAH, HULDAH, ANNA, PHILIP'S DAUGHTERS.

PROPHETIC DREAMS. See DREAMS—VISIONS.

—————— AND SYMBOLICAL PERIODS AND NUMBERS. 390 days, 40 days, Eze. 4.4-6. 2300 days, Dan. 8.14. 70 weeks, 7 weeks, 62 weeks, 1 week, Dan. 9.24-27. Time, times and a half, Dan. 12.7. Rev. 12.14. 1290 days, Dan. 12.11. 1335 days, Dan. 12.12. An hour, day, month, and year, Rev. 9.15. 42 months, Rev. 11.2. Rev. 13.5. 1260 days, Rev. 11.3. Number of the beast 666, Rev. 13.18. 1000 years, Rev. 20.2-7. See DAY—SYMBOLS.

PROPHETS. Were anointed, 1 Kin. 19. 16. Schools of, 1 Kin. 20.35. 2 Kin. 2.3-15. 2 Kin. 4.1,38. 2 Kin. 9.1. Prophesied with music, 1 Sam. 10.5. 2 Kin. 3.15. Were married, 2 Kin. 4.1. Isa. 8.2,3. Eze. 24.18. Their dress, food, and mode of life, 2 Kin. 1.8. 2 Kin. 4.10. Zec. 13.4. Mat. 3.4. Luk. 1.80. Presents offered to, 1 Sam. 9.7,8. 1 Kin. 14.3. 2 Kin. 4.42. Refused, Num. 22.18. 2 Kin. 5. 5,16. Were historians, 1 Chr. 29.29. 2 Chr. 9.29. 2 Chr. 12.15. Were attached to the king's household, 2 Sam. 24.11. 2 Chr. 29.25. 2 Chr. 35.15. Their servants, 1 Kin. 19.21. 2 Kin. 3.11. 2 Kin. 4.12. Miracles of, see MIRACLES, p. 310.

CHRONOLOGICAL LIST OF. See ENOCH, NOAH, ABRAHAM, ISAAC, JACOB, JOSEPH, MOSES, ELDAD, MEDAD, BALAAM, JOSHUA, SAMUEL, DAVID, NATHAN, ASAPH, GAD, SHEMAIAH, AHIJAH, IDDO, ELIJAH, ELISHA, MICAIAH, ZECHARIAH THE HIGH-PRIEST, JEHU, ELIEZER, JAHAZIEL, ZECHARIAH, JONAH, JOEL, AMOS, HOSEA, ISAIAH, ODED, AZARIAH, HANANI, MICAH, NAHUM, ZEPHANIAH, JEREMIAH, URIJAH, HABAK-KUK, DANIEL, OBADIAH, EZEKIEL, HAGGAI, ZECHARIAH, MALACHI, ZACHARIAS, SIMEON, JOHN THE BAPTIST.

PROPHETS WHOSE NAMES ARE NOT MENTIONED. Prophet sent to reprove Israel for idolatry, Jud. 6.8. Prophet sent to predict judgments on Eli's house, 1 Sam. 2.27. Prophet of Judah, prophesies against Jeroboam's altar; paralyses the king's hand, and restores it; is slain by a lion for disobedience, 1 Kin. 13. Old prophet of Bethel, seduces the prophet of Judah to disobey God's command, 1 Kin. 13.11-32. 100 prophets hid in a cave, 1 Kin. 18.4. A prophet warns Ahab, 1 Kin. 20.35-42.

PROPHETS IN THE CHRISTIAN CHURCH, Act. 11.27. Act. 13.1. 1 Cor. 12.28. 1 Cor.

14.29-32. Eph. 4.11. Rev. 11.10. See APOSTLES, AGABUS, JUDAS OR JUDE, SILAS.
PROPHETS, FALSE. See MINISTERS, UNFAITHFUL—PRIESTS, IDOLATROUS.

PROPHETS, INSPIRATION OF. Gen. 41. 16. Joseph answered Pharaoh, saying, *It is* not in me: God shall give Pharaoh an answer of peace. *v.* 38. Gen. 40.8.

Ex. 3.14. Thus shalt thou say unto the children of Israel, I AM hath sent me unto you. *v.* 10-16.

Ex. 4.5. That they may believe that the Lord God of their fathers hath appeared unto thee. 15. Thou shalt speak unto him, and put words in his mouth: and I will be with thy mouth, and with his mouth, and will teach you what ye shall do. 27. The Lord said to Aaron, Go into the wilderness to meet Moses. *v.* 12,19.

Ex. 6.13. The Lord spake unto Moses and unto Aaron, and gave them a charge unto the children of Israel. *v.* 29. Ex. 7.2.

Ex. 19.3. Moses went up unto God, and the Lord called unto him out of the mountain, saying, Thus shalt thou say to the house of Jacob. 9. The Lord said unto Moses, Lo, I come unto thee in a thick cloud, that the people may hear when I speak with thee, and believe thee for ever. 19. When the voice of the trumpet sounded long, and waxed louder and louder, Moses spake, and God answered him by a voice.

Ex. 24.16. The seventh day he called unto Moses out of the midst of the cloud.

Ex. 33.11. The Lord spake unto Moses face to face, as a man speaketh unto his friend. *v.* 9.

Num. 7.89. When Moses was gone into the tabernacle of the congregation to speak with him, then he heard the voice of one speaking unto him from off the mercy-seat. Ex. 25.22. Lev. 1.1. Num. 1.1.

Num. 9.8. Moses said unto them, Stand still, and I will hear what the Lord will command concerning you.

Num. 12.6. If there be a prophet among you, *I* the Lord will make myself known unto him in a vision, *and* will speak unto him in a dream. 8. With him will I speak mouth to mouth, even apparently, and not in dark speeches; and the similitude of the Lord shall he behold.

Num. 16.28. Moses said, Hereby ye shall know that the Lord hath sent me to do all these works; for *I have* not *done them* of mine own mind. 29. If these men die the common death of all men, or if they be visited after the visitation of all men; *then* the Lord hath not sent me.

Num. 22.18. If Balak would give me his house full of silver and gold, I cannot go beyond the word of the Lord my God, to do less or more. 38. And Balaam said unto Balak, Lo, I am come unto thee: have I now any power at all to say any thing? the word that God putteth in my mouth, that shall I speak.

Num. 23.12. Must I not take heed to speak that which the Lord hath put in my mouth? 20. Behold, I have received *commandment* to bless: and he hath blessed; and I cannot reverse it. 26. Told not I thee, saying, All that the Lord speaketh, that I must do? *v.* 5.

Num. 24.15. Balaam the son of Beor hath said, and the man whose eyes are open hath said: 16. He hath said, which heard the words of God, and knew the knowledge of the most High, *which* saw the vision of the Almighty, falling *into a trance*, but having his eyes open.

Deu. 5.5. I stood between the Lord and you at that time, to shew you the word of the Lord. 31. But as for thee, stand thou here by me, and I will speak unto thee all the commandments, and the statutes, and the judgments, which thou shalt teach them.

Deu. 34.9. Joshua the son of Nun was full of the spirit of wisdom; for Moses had laid his hands upon him. 10. There arose not a prophet since in Israel like unto Moses, whom the Lord knew face to face.

Jos. 3.7. This day will I begin to magnify thee in the sight of all Israel, that they may know that, as I was with Moses, *so* I will be with thee.

1 Sam. 3.1. The word of the Lord was precious in those days; *there was* no open vision. 7. Samuel did not yet know the Lord, neither was the word of the Lord yet revealed unto him. 19. Samuel grew, and the Lord was with him, and did let none of his words fall to the ground. 20. And all Israel from Dan even to Beer-sheba knew that Samuel *was* established *to be* a prophet of the Lord. 21. And the Lord appeared again in Shiloh: for the Lord revealed himself to Samuel in Shiloh by the word of the Lord. *v.* 4-10.

1 Sam. 9.6. *There is* in this city a man of God, and *he is* an honourable man; all that he saith cometh surely to pass. 15. The Lord had told Samuel in his ear a day before Saul came. *v.* 16-20.

2 Sam. 7.4. And it came to pass that night, that the word of the Lord came unto Nathan. *v.* 3-7. 2 Sam. 12.1.

1 Kin. 13.20. The word of the Lord came unto the prophet that brought him back.

1 Kin. 14.5. The Lord said unto Ahijah, Behold, the wife of Jeroboam cometh to ask a thing of thee.

1 Kin. 17.1. Elijah the Tishbite, said unto Ahab, *As* the Lord God of Israel liveth, before whom I stand, there shall not be dew nor rain these years, but according to my word. 24. By this I know that thou *art* a man of God, *and* that the word of the Lord in thy mouth *is* truth.

1 Kin. 18.36. Elijah the prophet came near, and said, Lord God, let it be known this day that thou *art* God in Israel, and *that* I *am* thy servant, and *that* I have done all these things at thy word. *v.* 46.

1 Kin. 22.14. What the Lord saith unto me, that will I speak. 28. If thou return at all in peace, the Lord hath not spoken by me. And he said, Hearken, O people, every one of you. 2 Chr. 18.27.

2 Kin. 1.12. If I *be* a man of God, let fire come down from heaven, and consume thee and thy fifty.

2 Kin. 3.11. Here *is* Elisha. 12. The word of the Lord is with him. 15. When the minstrel played, the hand of the Lord came upon him.

2 Kin. 4.27. The man of God said, Let her alone; for her soul *is* vexed within her: and the Lord hath hid *it* from me, and hath not told me.

2 Kin. 5.8. Wherefore hast thou rent thy clothes? let him come now to me, and he shall know that there is a prophet in Israel. 26. Went not mine heart *with thee*, when the man turned again from his chariot to meet thee?

2 Kin. 6.12. Elisha, the prophet that *is* in Israel, telleth the king of Israel the words that thou speakest in thy bedchamber. 17. Elisha prayed, and said, Lord, I pray thee, open his eyes, that he may see. 32. Ere the messenger came to him, he said to the elders, See ye how this son of a murderer hath sent to take away mine head? *v.* 9-11.

2 Kin. 10.10. There shall fall unto the earth nothing of the word of the Lord, which the Lord spake concerning the house of Ahab: for the Lord hath done *that* which he spake by his servant Elijah.

1 Chr. 21.18. The angel of the Lord commanded Gad to say to David, that David should go up, and set up an altar unto the Lord.

1 Chr. 28.19. The Lord made me understand in writing by *his* hand upon me, *even* all the works of this pattern. Ex. 25.9. Ex. 26. 30. 2 Chr. 8.14.

2 Chr. 26.5. Zechariah had understanding in the visions of God.

2 Chr. 33.18. The words of the seers that spake to him in the name of the Lord God of Israel. Ezr. 5.1,2.

2 Chr. 36.12. He humbled not himself before Jeremiah the prophet *speaking* from the mouth of the Lord. *v.* 15.

Job 32.8. *There is* a spirit in man: and the inspiration of the Almighty giveth them understanding.

Job 33.14. God speaketh once, yea twice, *yet man* perceiveth it not 15. In a dream, in a vision of the night, when deep sleep falleth upon men, in slumberings upon the bed; 16. Then he openeth the ears of men, and sealeth their instruction.

Psa. 103.7. He made known his ways unto Moses, his acts unto the children of Israel.

Isa. 6.1. I saw also the Lord sitting upon a throne. 8. I heard the voice of the Lord, saying, Whom shall I send, and who will go for us? Then said I, Here *am* I; send me. 9. And he said, Go, and tell this people. *v.* 1-7.

Isa. 8.11. The Lord spake thus to me with a strong hand, and instructed me.

Isa. 44.26. That confirmeth the word of his servant, and performeth the counsel of his messengers.

Jer. 1.4. Then the word of the Lord came unto me, saying, 5. Before I formed thee in the belly I knew thee; and before thou camest forth out of the womb I sanctified thee, *and* I ordained thee a prophet unto the nations. 7. The Lord said unto me, Say not, I *am* a child: for thou shalt go to all that I shall send thee, and whatsoever I command thee thou shalt speak. 9. Then the Lord put forth his hand, and touched my mouth. And the Lord said unto me, Behold, I have put my words in thy mouth. 10. See, I have this day set thee over the nations and over the kingdoms, to root out, and to pull down, and to destroy, and to throw down, to build, and to plant.

Jer. 7.25. Since the day that your fathers came forth out of the land of Egypt unto this day I have even sent unto you all my servants the prophets, daily rising up early and sending *them.* Jer. 25.3.

Jer. 11.18. The Lord hath given me knowledge *of it,* and I know *it:* then thou shewedst me their doings.

Jer. 20.9. I said, I will not make mention of him, nor speak any more in his name. But *his word* was in mine heart as a burning fire shut up in my bones, and I was weary with forbearing, and I could not *stay.*

Jer. 23.9. All my bones shake ; I am like a drunken man, and like a man whom wine hath overcome, because of the Lord, and because of the words of his holiness.

Jer. 26.2. Speak unto all the cities of Judah, which come to worship in the Lord's house, all the words that I command thee to speak unto them ; diminish not a word.

Jer. 42.4. Whatsoever thing the Lord will answer you, I will declare *it* unto you ; I will keep nothing back from you. 7. After ten days, the word of the Lord came unto Jeremiah.

Eze. 1.1. The heavens were opened, and I saw visions of God. 3. The word of the Lord came expressly unto Ezekiel ; and the hand of the Lord was there upon him. *v.* 26-28.

Eze. 3.10. All my words that I shall speak unto thee receive in thine heart, and hear with thine ears. 11. And go, get thee to them of the captivity, unto the children of thy people, and speak unto them, and tell them, Thus saith the Lord God ; whether they will hear, or whether they will forbear. 27. But when I speak with thee, I will open thy mouth.

Eze. 8.3. He put forth the form of an hand, and took me by a lock of mine head ; and the spirit lifted me up between the earth and the heaven, and brought me in the visions of God to Jerusalem.

Eze. 33.22. The hand of the Lord was upon me in the evening, afore he that was escaped came ; and had opened my mouth, until he came to me in the morning ; and my mouth was opened, and I was no more dumb.

Eze. 40.2. The hand of the Lord was upon me, and brought me thither.

Dan. 1.17. God gave them knowledge and skill in all learning and wisdom : and Daniel had understanding in all visions and dreams.

Dan. 2.19. Then was the secret revealed unto Daniel in a night-vision.

Dan. 7.16. I came near unto one of them that stood by, and asked him the truth of all this. So he told me, and made me know the interpretation of the things.

Dan. 8.16. I heard a man's voice, between *the banks of* Ulai, which called, and said, Gabriel, make this *man* to understand the vision. 27. I was astonished at the vision, but none understood *it.* *v.* 15-19.

Dan. 9.22. And he informed *me,* and talked with me, and said, O Daniel, I am now come forth to give thee skill and understanding.

Dan. 10.7. And I Daniel alone saw the vision : for the men that were with me saw not the vision. 8. Therefore I was left alone, and saw this great vision, and there remained no strength in me. 9. Yet heard I the voice of his words : and when I heard the voice of his words, then was I in a deep sleep on my face, and my face toward the ground. *v.* 1-21.

Hos. 12.10. I have also spoken by the

prophets, and I have multiplied visions, and used similitudes, by the ministry of the prophets.

Amos 3.7. Surely the Lord God will do nothing, but he revealeth his secret unto his servants the prophets. 8. The lion hath roared, who will not fear ? the Lord God hath spoken, who can but prophesy ?

Amos 7.14. I *was* no prophet, neither *was* I a prophet's son ; but I *was* an herdman, and a gatherer of sycomore-fruit : 15. And the Lord took me as I followed the flock, and the Lord said unto me, Go, prophesy unto my people Israel.

Jonah 3.1. The word of the Lord came unto Jonah the second time, saying, 2. Arise, go unto Nineveh, that great city, and preach unto it the preaching that I bid thee.

Hab. 3.2. O Lord, I have heard thy speech, *and* was afraid. 16. When I heard, my belly trembled ; my lips quivered at the voice : rottenness entered into my bones, and I trembled in myself.

Hag. 1.13. Then spake Haggai the Lord's messenger in the Lord's message unto the people.

Zec. 2.4. Run, speak to this young man, saying, Jerusalem shall be inhabited. 9. Ye shall know that the Lord of hosts hath sent me.

Luk. 1.70. He spake by the mouth of his holy prophets, which have been since the world began.

Luk. 3.3. The word of God came unto John the son of Zacharias in the wilderness.

Jno. 1.6. There was a man sent from God, whose name *was* John.

Act. 3.18. Those things, which God before had shewed by the mouth of all his prophets, that Christ should suffer.

Act. 21.9. The same man had four daughters, virgins, which did prophesy.

1 Cor. 14.32. The spirits of the prophets are subject to the prophets.

Heb. 1.1. God, who at sundry times and in divers manners spake in time past unto the fathers by the prophets.

Heb. 3.5. Moses verily *was* faithful in all his house, as a servant, for a testimony of those things which were to be spoken after.

Jas. 5.10. The prophets, who have spoken in the name of the Lord.

Jude 14. Enoch also, the seventh from Adam, prophesied of these, saying, Behold, the Lord cometh with ten thousands of his saints.

Rev. 10.7. He hath declared to his servants, the prophets.

Rev. 22.6. The Lord God of the holy prophets sent his angel to shew unto his servants the things which must shortly be done. 8. I John saw these things, and heard *them.* The angel which shewed me these things.

PROPHETS, INSPIRATION OF, BY THE HOLY SPIRIT. EX. 35.31. He hath filled him with the spirit of God, in wisdom, in understanding, and in knowledge, and in all manner of workmanship.

Num. 11.25. The Lord came down in a cloud, and spake unto him, and took of the spirit that *was* upon him, and gave *it* unto the seventy elders : and it came to pass, *that,* when the spirit rested upon them, they prophesied, and did not cease. *v.* 17,26.

Num. 24.2. The spirit of God came upon him. 3. And he took up his parable and said, Balaam hath said, and the man whose eyes are open hath said. *v.* 4.

Jud. 6.34. The Spirit of the Lord came upon Gideon, and he blew a trumpet. Jud. 11.29. 1 Chr. 12.18.

Jud. 13.25. The Spirit of the Lord began to move him at times in the camp of Dan. Jud. 14.6,19.

1 Sam. 10.6. The Spirit of the Lord will come upon thee, and thou shalt prophesy with them, and shalt be turned into another man. *v.* 7,10.

1 Sam. 16.13. The Spirit of the Lord came upon David from that day forward.

1 Sam. 19.20. The Spirit of God was upon the messengers of Saul, and they also prophesied. 23. The Spirit of God was upon him also, and he went on, and prophesied, until he came to Naioth in Ramah. *v.* 24.

2 Sam. 23.2. The Spirit of the Lord spake by me, and his word *was* in my tongue. 3. The God of Israel said, the Rock of Israel spake to me. *v.* 1. Act. 2.30.

2 Kin. 2.9. Elisha said, I pray thee, let a double portion of thy spirit be upon me. 15. The spirit of Elijah doth rest on Elisha.

1 Chr. 28.11. David gave to Solomon, 12. The pattern of all that he had by the Spirit.

2 Chr. 20.14. Upon Jahaziel came the Spirit of the Lord in the midst of the congregation. 2 Chr. 15.1. 2 Chr. 24.20.

Neh. 9.30. Many years didst thou forbear them, and testifiedst against them by thy spirit in thy prophets.

Isa. 63.11. Where *is* he that put his holy Spirit within him ?

Eze. 1.20. Whithersoever the spirit was to go, they went, thither *was their* spirit to go ; and the wheels were lifted up over against them : for the spirit of the living creature *was* in the wheels.

Eze. 2.1. I will speak unto thee. 2. And the spirit entered into me when he spake unto me. 4. I do send thee unto them ; and thou shalt say unto them, Thus saith the Lord God. 5. And they shall know that there hath been a prophet among them.

Eze. 3.12. The spirit took me up, and I heard behind me a voice of a great rushing, *saying*, Blessed *be* the glory of the Lord from his place. 14. So the spirit lifted me up, and took me away, and I went in bitterness, in the heat of my spirit ; but the hand of the Lord was strong upon me. 22. The hand of the Lord was there upon me ; and he said unto me, Arise, go forth into the plain, and I will there talk with thee. 24. Then the spirit entered into me, and set me upon my feet, and spake with me.

Eze. 11.1. The spirit lifted me up, and brought me unto the east gate of the Lord's house. 5. And the Spirit of the Lord fell upon me, and said unto me, Speak ; Thus saith the Lord. 24. Afterwards the spirit took me up, and brought me in a vision by the Spirit of God into Chaldea, to them of the captivity.

Eze. 37.1. The hand of the Lord was upon me, and carried me out in the spirit of the Lord, and set me down in the midst of the valley which *was* full of bones.

Eze. 43.5. So the spirit took me up, and brought me into the inner court ; and, behold, the glory of the Lord filled the house. 6. And

I heard *him* speaking unto me out of the house ; and the man stood by me.

Joel 2.28. It shall come to pass afterward, *that* I will pour out my spirit upon all flesh ; and your sons and your daughters shall prophesy, your old men shall dream dreams, your young men shall see visions : 29. And also upon the servants and upon the handmaids in those days will I pour out my spirit.

Mic. 3.8. Truly I am full of power by the spirit of the Lord, and of judgment, and of might, to declare unto Jacob his transgression, and to Israel his sin.

Mar. 12.36. David himself said by the Holy Ghost.

Luk. 1.15. He shall be filled with the Holy Ghost, even from his mother's womb. 41. Elisabeth was filled with the Holy Ghost. 67. His father Zacharias was filled with the Holy Ghost, and prophesied.

Luk. 2.25. And the Holy Ghost was upon him. 26. And it was revealed unto him by the Holy Ghost, that he should not see death, before he had seen the Lord's Christ. 27. And he came by the Spirit into the temple.

Act. 2.2. Suddenly there came a sound from heaven as of a rushing mighty wind, and it filled all the house where they were sitting. 3. And there appeared unto them cloven tongues like as of fire, and it sat upon each of them. 4. And they were all filled with the Holy Ghost, and began to speak with other tongues, as the Spirit gave them utterance.

Act. 7.55. He, being full of the Holy Ghost, looked up steadfastly into heaven, and saw the glory of God, and Jesus standing on the right hand of God. *v.* 56.

Act. 8.29. The Spirit said unto Philip, Go near, and join thyself to this chariot. 39. The Spirit of the Lord caught away Philip, that the eunuch saw him no more.

Act. 11.28. Agabus, signified by the spirit that there should be great dearth.

Act. 21.4. Disciples, who said to Paul through the Spirit, that he should not go up to Jerusalem. 11. Thus saith the Holy Ghost, So shall the Jews at Jerusalem bind the man that owneth this girdle.

1 Cor. 12.8. To one is given by the Spirit the word of wisdom ; to another the word of knowledge by the same Spirit ; 9. To another faith by the same Spirit ; to another the gifts of healing by the same Spirit ; 10. To another the working of miracles ; to another prophecy ; to another discerning of spirits ; to another *divers* kinds of tongues ; to another the interpretation of tongues. *v.* 3.

2 Pet. 1.21. The prophecy came not in old time by the will of man : but holy men of God spake *as they were* moved by the Holy Ghost.

Rev. 2.7. He that hath an ear, let him hear what the Spirit saith unto the churches.

Rev. 14.13. I heard a voice from heaven saying unto me, Write, Blessed *are* the dead which die in the Lord from henceforth : Yea, saith the Spirit, that they may rest from their labours.

See APOSTLES' INSPIRATION — WORD OF GOD, INSPIRATION OF—HOLY SPIRIT, MIRACULOUS INFLUENCES OF — MIRACULOUS GIFTS—VISIONS.

PROPITIATION. 1. (Gr. *hilasmos*), 1 Jno. 2.2. 1 Jno. 4.10. 2. (Gr. *hilasterion*),

Rom. 3.25.   Translated mercy-seat, Heb. 9.5.

PROSELYTES. To Judaism were circumcised, Ex. 12.48. Act. 16.3. See Gen. 17.13. Worshipped with the Jews, Deu. 31.12. 1 Kin. 8.41-43. Isa. 56.3-6. Eph. 2.14. Rev. 11.2. Offered sacrifices, Lev. 17.8. Num. 15.14-16. Shared in religious feasts, Ex. 12.48. Deu. 14.29. Deu. 16.11,14. 2 Chr. 30.25. Had the benefit of the refuge cities, Num. 35.15. Jos. 20.9. Might have Hebrew servants, Lev. 25. 47,48. Were required to obey the law of Moses, Ex. 12.19,43-49. Ex. 20.10. Ex. 23.12. Lev. 16.29. Lev. 17.8-15. Lev. 18.26. Lev. 20.2. Lev. 22.18. Lev. 24.16,22. Lev. 25.47. Num. 9.14. Num. 15.14-16,26-30. Num. 19.10. Deu. 5.14.

Ammonites not allowed to enter the congregation until the 10th generation, Deu. 23.3; nor Edomites and Egyptians until the 3d, Deu. 23.7,8. Pharisees' zeal to make proselytes, Mat. 23.15.

EXAMPLES OF: Jos. 8.33. Est. 8.17. Act. 2.10. Ruth, Ruth 2.11. The centurion, Luk. 7.5. Greeks, Jno. 12.20. Women, Act. 13.50.

EXAMPLES OF GREEK PROSELYTES (called also devout, or worshippers), WHO BECAME CHRISTIANS: Nicolas of Antioch, Act. 6.5. The eunuch, Act. 8.27. Cornelius, Act. 10. Greeks at Antioch, Act. 13.43. Lydia, Act. 16.14. Greeks, Act. 17.4,17. Justus, Act. 18.7. See STRANGERS.

PROSPERITY, TEMPORAL. See GOD'S GOODNESS—TEMPORAL PROSPERITY—RICHES FROM GOD—GOD'S PROVIDENCE MISUNDERSTOOD.

PROVERBS, or SAYINGS, Jud. 14.12. 1 Sam. 10.12. 1 Sam. 24.13,14. 2 Sam. 3.8. 2 Sam. 20.18. 1 Kin. 4.32. 1 Kin. 20.11. Job 12.11. Pro. 25.25. Pro. 30.18,19. Eze. 18.2. Luk. 4.23.

PROVIDENCE. See GOD'S PROVIDENCE —GOD'S GOODNESS.

PRUDENCE. Job 34.3. The ear trieth words, as the mouth tasteth meat. 4. Let us choose to us judgment: let us know among ourselves what is good.

Psa. 39.1. I said, I will take heed to my ways, that I sin not with my tongue; I will keep my mouth with a bridle, while the wicked is before me.

Psa. 112.5. He will guide his affairs with discretion.

Pro. 6.1. If thou be surety for thy friend, if thou hast stricken thy hand with a stranger, 2. Thou art snared with the words of thy mouth.

Pro. 11.15. He that is surety for a stranger shall smart for it: and he that hateth suretiship is sure. 29. The fool shall be servant to the wise of heart.

Pro. 12.8. A man shall be commended according to his wisdom. 16. A fool's wrath is presently known: but a prudent man covereth shame. 23. A prudent man concealeth knowledge: but the heart of fools proclaimeth foolishness.

Pro. 14.8. The wisdom of the prudent is to understand his way. 15. The simple believeth every word: but the prudent man looketh well to his going. 16. A wise man feareth, and departeth from evil: but the fool rageth, and is confident. 18. The simple inherit folly: but the prudent are crowned with knowledge.

Pro. 15.5. He that regardeth reproof is prudent. 22. Without counsel purposes are disappointed: but in the multitude of counsellers they are established.

Pro. 16.20. He that handleth a matter wisely shall find good.

Pro. 17.2. A wise servant shall have rule over a son that causeth shame, and shall have part of the inheritance among the brethren. 18. A man void of understanding striketh hands, and becometh surety in the presence of his friend.

Pro. 18.16. A man's gift maketh room for him, and bringeth him before great men.

Pro. 20.5. Counsel in the heart of man is like deep water; but a man of understanding will draw it out. 16. Take his garment that is surety for a stranger. 18. Every purpose is established by counsel: and with good advice make war.

Pro. 21.5. The thoughts of the diligent tend only to plenteousness; but of every one that is hasty only to want. 20. There is treasure to be desired and oil in the dwelling of the wise; but a foolish man spendeth it up.

Pro. 22.3. A prudent man foreseeth the evil, and hideth himself: but the simple pass on, and are punished. 7. The rich ruleth over the poor, and the borrower is servant to the lender. 26. Be not thou one of them that strike hands, or of them that are sureties for debts. 27. If thou hast nothing to pay, why should he take away thy bed from under thee? Pro. 27.12.

Pro. 23.1. When thou sittest to eat with a ruler, consider diligently what is before thee: 2. And put a knife to thy throat, if thou be a man given to appetite. 3. Be not desirous of his dainties: for they are deceitful meat. 9. Speak not in the ears of a fool: for he will despise the wisdom of thy words.

Pro. 24.6. By wise counsel thou shalt make thy war: and in multitude of counsellers there is safety. 27. Prepare thy work without, and make it fit for thyself in the field; and afterwards build thine house.

Pro. 25.8. Go not forth hastily to strive, lest thou know not what to do in the end thereof, when thy neighbour hath put thee to shame. 9. Debate thy cause with thy neighbour himself; and discover not a secret to another: 10. Lest he that heareth it put thee to shame, and thine infamy turn not away.

Pro. 26.4. Answer not a fool according to his folly, lest thou also be like unto him. 5. Answer a fool according to his folly, lest he be wise in his own conceit.

Pro. 29.11. A fool uttereth all his mind: but a wise man keepeth in till afterwards.

Ecc. 8.3. Be not hasty to go out of his sight: stand not in an evil thing; for he doeth whatsoever pleaseth him.

Ecc. 10.1. Dead flies cause the ointment of the apothecary to send forth a stinking savour: so doth a little folly him that is in reputation for wisdom and honour. 10. If the iron be blunt, and he do not whet the edge, then must he put to more strength: but wisdom is profitable to direct.

Amos 5.13. The prudent shall keep silence in that time; for it is an evil time.

Mat. 7.6. Give not that which is holy unto the dogs, neither cast ye your pearls before swine, lest they trample them under their feet, and turn again and rend you.

Luk. 14.28. Which of you, intending to build a tower, sitteth not down first and counteth the cost, whether he have *sufficient* to finish *it?* 29. Lest haply, after he hath laid the foundation, and is not able to finish *it*, all that behold *it* begin to mock him, 30. Saying, This man began to build, and was not able to finish. *v.* 31,32.

Rom. 14.16. Let not then your good be evil spoken of.

Col. 4.5. Walk in wisdom toward them that are without, redeeming the time.

PRUDENCE, EXAMPLES OF: Jacob, Gen. 32.7-21. Joseph, Gen. 41.33-57. Jethro, Ex. 18.17-23. Saul, 1 Sam. 10.16. David, 1 Sam. 17.39. 1 Sam. 18.5-30. 2 Sam. 15.33-37. Abigail, 1 Sam. 25,18-31. Achish, 1 Sam. 29. Jehoram, 2 Kin. 7.12,13. Nehemiah, Neh. 2.12-16. Neh. 4.13-23. Gamaliel, Act. 5. 34-39. Paul, Act. 16.3. Act. 23.6. 2 Cor. 8.20. Town-clerk of Ephesus, Act. 19.36-40. Rehoboam's counsellors, 1 Kin. 12.7.
See WATCHFULNESS—WISDOM.

PRUNING-HOOKS or KNIVES, Isa. 2.4. Isa. 18.5. Joel 3.10. Pruning, Lev. 25.3,4. Isa. 5.6. Illustrative, Jno. 15.2.

PSALMS. Miscellaneous, Ex. 15. Num. 10.35,36. Deu. 31.22 with Deu. 32. Jud. 5. 1 Sam. 2.1-10. 2 Sam. 22. 1 Chr. 16. 1 Chr. 29.10-17. Isa. 12. Isa. 25. Isa. 26. Luk. 1. 46-79. Luk. 2.29-32. Written by David, &c., for the temple singing, 2 Sam. 23.1. 1 Chr. 16.7. Psa. 88 (title), &c.

Titles, &c. of, see AIJELETH-SHACHAR, ALA-MOTH, AL-TASCHITH, DEGREES, GITTITH, HIGGAION, JEDUTHUN, JERIATH - ELEM-RECHOKIM, LEANNOTH, MAHALATH, MAS-CHIL, MICHTAM, MUTH-LABBAN, NEGINOTH, NEHILOTH, SELAH, SHEMINITH, SHIGGAION, SHUSHAN.

PSALTERY, a kind of harp. Used by prophets, 1 Sam. 10.5. With singing, in bringing up the ark, by David, 2 Sam. 6.5. 1 Chr. 13. 8. 1 Chr. 15.16,20,28; and Solomon, 2 Chr. 5.12,13. Jeiel, appointed to play on, 1 Chr. 16.5; and Heman's sons and daughters, 1 Chr. 25.1,5,6. Made by Solomon of almug, 1 Kin. 10.12. 2 Chr. 9.11. Used at Jehoshaphat's triumph, 2 Chr. 20.28. In the temple, 2 Chr. 29.25. At the dedication of the wall, Neh. 12.27. In idolatrous worship, Dan. 3. 5,7,10,15. Employed in praise, Psa. 33.2. Psa. 57.8. Psa. 71.22. Psa. 81.2. Psa. 92.3. Psa. 108.2. Psa. 144.9. Psa. 150.3. Amos 5.23. In feasts, &c., translated viol, Isa. 5. 12. Isa. 14.11. Amos 5.23. Amos 6.5. See HARP—SACKBUT.

PTOLEMAIS. See ACCHO.

PUBLICANS. Two grades of.— Chief publican; that is, a commissioner, as Zaccheus, Luk. 19.2. Collector of taxes, as Matthew, Mat. 10.3. Luk. 5.27. Held in disrepute, Mat. 5. 46,47. Mat. 9.11. Mat. 11.19. Mat. 18.17. Mat. 21.31. Luk. 18.11. Baptized by John, Mat. 21.31,32. Luk. 3.12. Luk. 7.29. Received Christ, Mat. 21.32. Luk. 5.29,30. Luk. 7.29,34. Luk. 15.1. Parable of, Luk. 18.10-14.

PUBLIUS, a proprietor in Malta, whose father Paul healed, Act. 28.7,8.

PUL, king of Assyria, enforces tribute of Menahem, 2 Kin. 15.19. Carries the Israelites captive, 1 Chr. 5.26.

———, a people and region in Africa, Isa. 66.19.

PULSE (vegetables), Dan. 1.12,16.

PUNISHMENT OF THE WICKED. See HELL—SIN, PUNISHMENT OF—SIN, ITS FRUITS—JUDGMENT.

PUNISHMENTS. Burning, Lev. 20.14. Lev. 21.9. Gen. 38.24. Dan. 3.6. Cutting, and sawing in pieces, Dan. 2.5. Heb. 11.37. Exposing to wild beasts, Dan. 6.16.24. 1 Cor. 15.32. Drowning, Mat. 18.6. Slaying with the sword, Ex. 32.27,28. 1 Kin. 2.25,34,46. Act. 12.2. Beheading, 2 Kin. 10.6. Mar. 6.16,27. Throwing from a rock, 2 Chr. 25.12. Mutilation and torture, Jud. 1.5-7. Jud. 16.21. 1 Sam. 31.10. 2 Sam. 4.12. Isa. 50.6. Lam. 5.12. Eze. 23.25. Mat. 26.67. Mat. 27.26-30. Act. 22.24,29 (marg.), Act. 23.2,3.

FINES, Ex. 21.22,30,32,36. Deu. 22.18,19,29. Punishment like the offence (lex talionis), Ex. 21.23-25. Lev. 24.17-22. Deu. 19.19-21. Restitution, Ex. 21.33-36. Ex. 22.1-14. Lev. 6.4,5. Num. 5.7.
See BEHEADING, CRUCIFIXION, GALLOWS, HANGING, STONING, SCOURGING, BANISH-MENT, PRISONS, STOCKS, CHAINS, FETTERS.

CAPITAL PUNISHMENT, for manstealing, Ex. 21.16. Treason, 1 Kin. 2.25. Rebellion against parents, Lev. 20.9. Deu. 21.18-21. See also MURDER, ADULTERY, IDOLATRY, SORCERY, BLASPHEMY, SABBATH-BREAKING.

EXECUTED BY THE WITNESSES, Deu. 13.9. Deu. 17.7. Act. 7.5,8. By the congregation, Num. 15.35,36. Deu. 13.9. Jews under the Romans could not inflict, Jno. 18.31. The body buried the same day, Deu. 21.23. Children not to suffer for parents' crimes, Deu. 24.16, see Est. 9.14. Dan. 6.24.

PURIFICATION, by bathing, and washing the clothes, Lev. 14.8,9. Lev. 15.5-13. Lev. 16.26,28. Lev. 17.15,16. Num. 19. 7-10,19; in running water, Lev. 15.13. Washing the hands, Deu. 21.6. Mat. 27.24. Hands and feet, Ex. 30.18-21. Ex. 40.31, see Heb. 6.2. Heb. 9.10.

By sprinkling with blood, and water, Ex. 24.5-8. Lev. 14.6,7. Heb. 9.19. With water of separation, from the ashes of the red heifer, Num. 19.9,13,17-21. Num. 31.23. Heb. 9.13. By spices (Medo-Persian), Est. 2.12.

Of priests at consecration, Ex 29.4. Ex. 40.12. Lev. 8.6. Before sacrifice or ministering, Ex. 30.18-21. Ex. 40.30-32. Lev. 22.3. Of the high-priest on Day of Atonement, Lev. 16.4,24. Of Levites at consecration, Num. 8.5-7,21.

Of Nazarites, Num. 6.9-21. Act. 21.24,26. Of persons, and things ceremonially unclean, see DEFILEMENT. Of an accused person as proof of innocence, Deu. 21.1-9. Mat. 27.24. Before worship, Gen. 35.2. Ex. 19.10-14 with 1 Sam. 16.5. Jno. 11.55. Of burnt-offerings, Lev. 1.9,13. Lev. 9.14. 2 Chr. 4.6. Neglect of, punished, Lev. 7.20. Lev. 15.31. Lev. 17.16. Num. 19.13,20. Superstitious views of, Mat. 15.2. Mar. 7.2-5,8,9. Luk. 11. 38. Illustrative, Psa. 26.6. Psa. 51.7. Eze. 36.25. Heb. 10.22.
See ABLUTION—DEFILEMENT.

PURIM. See FEAST OF PURIM.

PURSE or **BAG.** For money, Pro. 1.14. Pro. 7.20. Isa. 46.6. Luk. 10.4. Luk. 12. 33. Luk. 22.35,36. When sealed, contained a fixed sum of money, 2 Kin. 5.23. 2 Kin. 12.10 with Job 14.17. For containing weights, Deu. 25.13. Pro. 16.11. Mic. 6.11. Called a scrip, 1 Sam. 17.40. Mat. 10.10. Luk. 10.4. (Gr. *zonee*), a girdle, translated purse, Mat. 10.9. Mar. 6.8.

PUT. See LIBYA.

PUTEOLI, a seaport of Italy; Paul remained 8 days at, on his way to Rome, Act. 28.13,14.

PYGARG (*marg.* dishon or bison), supposed to be a gazelle, Deu. 14.5.

Q

QUAILS (a kind of grouse). Miraculous supply of, at Sin, Ex. 16.13. At Kibroth-Hattaavah, Num. 11.31,32. Psa. 105.40.

QUARRELS. See STRIFE.

QUATERNION of SOLDIERS, a detachment of 4 men, Act. 12.4.

QUEEN, a female sovereign, see SHEBA, QUEEN OF—CANDACE—ATHALIA. The chief wife of the king, 1 Kin. 11.19. Est. 1.9. Est. 2.4. Neh. 2.6*.* Psa. 45.9. Jer. 29.2. The king's mother, 1 Kin. 15.13. Kings' wives, Song 6.8,9. Crown of, Est. 1.11. Est. 2.17. Attendants of, Est. 1.9. Psa. 45.14. Illustrative, Rev. 18.7.

—— OF HEAVEN (the moon), worshipped, Jer. 7.18. Jer. 4.4,17-19,25.

QUIVER. See ARROW.

R

RAAMAH, a town; site of unknown, Eze. 27.22. Gen. 10.7. 1 Chr. 1.9.

RAAMSES. See RAMESES.

RABBAH, or RABBATH, capital of Ammon, Jos. 13.25. Og's bedstead preserved at, Deu. 3.11. Siege and capture of, by Joab, 2 Sam. 11.1. 2 Sam. 12.26-31. 1 Chr. 20.1-3. Repossessed by the Ammonites; prophecies against, Jer. 49.2,3. Eze. 21.20. Eze. 25.5. Amos 1.14.

RABBATH-MOAB. See AR.

RABBI, or RABBONI, a title of honour, applied to teachers of the law, Mat. 23.7. Applied to Christ, Jno. 1.38,49. Jno. 3.2. Jno. 6.25; and translated master, Jno. 20.16. Mat. 26.25,49. Mar. 9.5. Mar. 11.21. Mar. 14.45. Jno. 4.31. Jno. 9.2. Jno. 11.8. Translated lord, Mar. 10.51. Applied to John the Baptist, Jno. 3.26. Forbidden to the apostles, Mat. 23.8.

RABSHAKEH, a general sent by Sennacherib against Hezekiah; his blasphemy, 2 Kin. 18.17-36. 2 Kin. 19.4,8. Isa. 36.2-22. Isa. 37.4,8.

RACA (worthless), Mat. 5.22.

RACE, Psa. 19.5. Ecc. 9.11. 1 Cor. 9.24. Illustrative, Heb. 12.1,2. Gal. 5.7. Phil. 2.16.

RACHEL, daughter of Laban, meets Jacob, Gen. 29.5-12. Loved by Jacob; married to him, Gen. 29.16-30. Gen. 33.2. Her contention with Leah and Jacob; gives Jacob her maid, Gen. 30.1-8. Her children, Joseph and Benjamin, Gen. 30.22-24. Gen. 35.16-18,24. Concurs in Jacob's flight; steals her father's images, Gen. 31.4,14-19,34. Her death, burial, and sepulchre, Gen. 35.18-20. Gen. 48.7. 1 Sam. 10.2.

RAGUEL. See JETHRO.

RAHAB of Jericho, receives the spies, Jos. 2. Jas. 2.25. Saved in the destruction of Jericho, Jos. 6.17-25. Heb. 11.31. See Mat. 1.5.

RAHAB. See EGYPT.

RAIMENT. See DRESS.

RAIN. None at creation, Gen. 2.5,6. Continued 40 days at the flood, Gen. 7.12. Miracles of Moses connected with—Ex. 9.33,34. Of Samuel, 1 Sam. 12.17,18. Of Elijah, 1 Kin. 18. Abundance of, Ezr. 10.9,13. Rare in harvest, Pro. 26.1. 1 Sam. 12.17,18; and in Egypt, Zec. 14.18. Ex. 9.33,34. Deu. 11.10; and in northerly winds, Pro. 25.23. Promised, Deu. 11.11,14. Eze. 34.26. Joel 2.23. Zec. 10.1. Withheld in judgment, Deu. 11.17. Deu. 28.24. 1 Kin. 8.35. 2 Chr. 7.13. Amos 4.7. Zec. 14.17. Small and great rain, Deu. 32.2. Job 37.6. First, or former and latter rain, Deu. 11.14. Job 29.23. Pro. 16.15. Jer. 3.3. Jer. 5.24. Hos. 6.3. See DROUGHT.

RAINBOW, appointed as a sign, Gen. 9. 8-16. Eze. 1.28. Symbolical, Rev. 4.3. Rev. 10.1.

RAISINS, an ordinary article of diet, 1 Sam. 25.18. 1 Sam. 30.12. 2 Sam. 16.1. 1 Chr. 12.40.

RAM. See SHEEP—OFFERINGS. Ram's-horn, trumpets of, Jos. 6.4-13. Translated trumpet, Ex. 19.13. Ram's skin, coverings of, dyed red for the tabernacle, Ex. 26.14. Ex. 39.34.

RAMAH or RAMATH of Benjamin, Jos. 18.25. Jer. 31.15; near Gibeah, Jud. 19. 13. Ezr. 2.26. Neh. 7.30. Neh. 11.33. Isa. 10.29. Hos. 5.8. Fortified by Baasha, and destroyed by Asa, 1 Kin. 15.17-22. 2 Chr. 16. 1-6. Jeremiah in chains at, Jer. 40.1.

—— or RAMATHAIM-ZOPHIM, in Mount Ephraim, Jud. 4.5. Residence of Elkanah, 1 Sam. 1.1,19. 1 Sam. 2.11; of Samuel, 1 Sam. 7.17. 1 Sam. 15.34. 1 Sam. 16.13. Elders of Israel ask a king at, 1 Sam. 8.4. David flees to Samuel at, 1 Sam. 19.18. Samuel buried at, 1 Sam. 28.3.

—— of Simeon, Jos. 19.8. 1 Sam. 30.27. Of Asher, Jos. 19.29. Of Naphtali, Jos. 19.36.

RAMATHAIM-ZOPHAIM, in Mount Ephraim, residence of Elkanah, 1 Sam. 1.1.

RAMATH-LEHI (the lifting up of the jaw-bone), the place where Samson slew the Philistines with the jaw-bone of an ass, Jud. 15.17.

RAMESES or RAAMSES, a district in Egypt, inhabited by the Israelites, Gen. 47.11. A treasure city built by them, Ex. 1.11; from which they departed at the Exodus, Ex. 12. 37. Num. 33.3-5.

RAMOTH-GILEAD or RAMOTH MIZPEH, in Gad, a Levitical city of refuge, Deu. 4.43.

Jos. 20.8.   1 Chr. 6.73.   In the hands of the Syrians; Ahab slain at, 1 Kin. 22.3,34. Joram wounded at, 2 Kin. 8.28.   2 Kin. 9.14,15. Jehu anointed king at, 2 Kin. 9.1-4.

RANSOM. In money, Ex. 21.30.   Ex. 30. 12.   Isa. 45.13.   Illustrative, Pro. 21.18.   Isa. 43.3.   Isa. 52.3.   Mat. 20.28, see Job 33.24. Psa. 49.7.

RASOR, Num. 6.5.   Psa. 52.2.   Isa. 7.20. Eze. 5.1.   Translated penknife, Jer. 36.23.

RAVEN, Lev. 11.15.   Deu. 14.14.   Song 5.11.   Psa. 147.9.   Isa. 34.11.   Luk. 12.24. Sent out by Noah, Gen. 8.7.   Elijah fed by, 1 Kin. 17.4-6.

REAPING, 1 Sam. 6.13.   2 Kin. 4.18. Psa. 129.7.   Isa. 17.5.   Only the heads of corn cut, Job 24.24, see Ex. 5.12.   Jer. 9.22.   See GLEANINGS.

REBEKAH, daughter of Bethuel; her reception of Abraham's servant, Gen. 24.15-28. Married to Isaac, Gen. 24.51-67.   Gen. 25.20. Enquires of the Lord, Gen. 25.22,23.   Birth of Esau and Jacob, Gen. 25.21-26.   Rom. 9.10. Partiality for Jacob, Gen. 25.28.   With Isaac visits Abimelech, Gen. 26.7-11.   Persuades Jacob to deceive his father, and obtain the blessing, Gen. 27.5-17.   Sends Jacob to Laban, Gen. 27.42-46.   Dissatisfied with Esau's wives, Gen. 26.35.   Gen. 27.46.   Her death and burial, Gen. 49.31.

REBELLION AGAINST GOD. See IMPENITENCE, GODLESSNESS, INFIDELITY. Against rulers, see SUBJECTS.

RECHAB, one of Saul's captains; murders Ishbosheth, and is executed by David, 2 Sam. 4.

RECHABITES, descended from the Kenites, 1 Chr. 2.55.   Jonadab, the son of Rechab, meets Jehu, 2 Kin. 10.15,16,23.   Their vow of abstinence, and its fulfilment rewarded, Jer. 35.

RECONCILIATION WITH GOD. See JUSTIFICATION, PARDON, GOD'S FAVOUR.

RECORDER, the king's historian, 2 Sam. 8.16.   2 Sam. 20.24.   1 Kin. 4.3.   2 Kin. 18. 18,37.   2 Chr. 34.8.

RECORDS. See BOOKS—GENEALOGIES.

RED SEA, called Egyptian Sea, Isa. 11.15. Promised boundary of Palestine, Ex. 23.31. Israelites' passage of, and Pharaoh's destruction in, Ex. 14.   Ex. 15.   Num. 33.8.   Deu. 11.4.   Jos. 2.10.   Jos. 4.23.   Jos. 24.6,7.   Jud. 11.16.   2 Sam. 22.16.   Neh. 9.9-11.   Psa. 66.6. Psa. 74.13.   Psa. 78.13,53.   Psa. 106.7-9,22. Psa. 114.3,5.   Psa. 136.13-15.   Isa. 10.26. Isa. 43.16,17.   Isa. 50.2.   Isa. 51.9,10,15.   Isa. 63.11.   Act. 7.36.   1 Cor. 10.1,2.   Heb. 11.29. Encampments by, Ex. 14.2.   Num. 14.25. Num. 21.4.   Num. 33.8-10.   Deu. 1.40.   Deu. 2.1.   Locusts from, Ex. 10.12-19.   Quails from, Num. 11.31.   Solomon's ships on, 1 Kin. 9.26. 1 Kin. 10.22.   2 Chr. 8.17,18.

——, Wilderness of, Ex. 13.18.

REDEMPTION. See GOD SAVIOUR— CHRIST SAVIOUR—CHRIST'S DEATH, DESIGN OF—PARDON—REGENERATION—SALVATION.

—— of persons or property, Lev. 27.2-8, see LAND—JUBILEE.   Of the first-born, see FIRST-BORN.   Of tithes, see TITHES.

REED, or **CANE,** 1 Kin. 14.15.   Job 40.21. Isa. 19.6,7.   Isa. 35.7.   Put into Christ's hands as a sceptre, Mat. 27.29.   Christ smitten with, Mat. 27.30.   The spunge put on, Mat. 27.48. Translated pen, 3 Jno. 13.   Illustrative, 2 Kin. 18.21.   Isa. 42.3.   Eze. 29.6.   Mat. 11.7.

——, a measuring-rod, Eze. 40.3-8.   Rev. 11.1.   Rev. 21.15,16.   Of 6 cubits, or 9 feet, Eze. 41.8.

REFINING of silver.   Illustrative, Mal. 3.2,3.   Isa. 1.25.   Isa. 48.10.   Jer. 9.7.   Zec. 13.9.   See FURNACE—SILVER.

REGENERATION AND CONVERSION, NATURE AND NECESSITY OF. FROM GOD AND CHRIST. Deu. 30.6.   The Lord thy God will circumcise thine heart, and the heart of thy seed, to love the Lord thy God with all thine heart, and with all thy soul, that thou mayest live. Deu. 29.4.

1 Kin. 8.58.   That he may incline our hearts unto him, to walk in all his ways, and to keep his commandments, and his statutes, and his judgments.

Psa. 36.9.   With thee is the fountain of life: in thy light shall we see light.

Psa. 65.3.   Iniquities prevail against me: as for our transgressions, thou shalt purge them away.

Psa. 68.18.   Thou hast received gifts for men; yea, for the rebellious also, that the Lord God might dwell among them.

Psa. 87.7.   All my springs are in thee.

Psa. 110.3.   Thy people shall be willing in the day of thy power, in the beauties of holiness.

Pro. 14.27.   The fear of the Lord is a fountain of life, to depart from the snares of death.   Pro. 4.23.   Pro. 12.28.

Pro. 16.1.   The preparations of the heart in man, and the answer of the tongue, is from the Lord.

Isa. 1.25.   I will turn my hand upon thee, and purely purge away thy dross, and take away all thy tin.

Isa. 12.3.   With joy shall ye draw water out of the wells of salvation.

Isa. 26.12.   Lord, thou wilt ordain peace for us; for thou also hast wrought all our works in us.

Isa. 32.3.   The eyes of them that see shall not be dim, and the ears of them that hear shall hearken.   4. The heart also of the rash shall understand knowledge, and the tongue of the stammerers shall be ready to speak plainly.

Isa. 35.5.   The eyes of the blind shall be opened, and the ears of the deaf shall be unstopped.   6. Then shall the lame man leap as an hart, and the tongue of the dumb sing: for in the wilderness shall waters break out.

Isa. 42.16.   I will bring the blind by a way that they knew not; I will lead them in paths that they have not known: I will make darkness light before them, and crooked things straight.

Isa. 44.3.   I will pour water upon him that is thirsty, and floods upon the dry ground; I will pour my Spirit upon thy seed, and my blessing upon thine offspring: 4. And they shall spring up as among the grass, as willows by the water-courses.   5. One shall say, I am the Lord's; and another shall call himself by the name of Jacob; and another shall subscribe *with* his hand unto the Lord, and surname *himself* by the name of Israel.

Isa. 49.9. That thou mayest say to the prisoners, Go forth; to them that *are* in darkness, Shew yourselves.

Isa. 55.2. Hearken diligently unto me, and eat ye *that which is* good, and let your soul delight itself in fatness.

Isa. 61.3. That they might be called Trees of righteousness, The planting of the Lord, that he might be glorified.

Jer. 3.17. Neither shall they walk any more after the imagination of their evil heart.

Jer. 13.23. Can the Ethiopian change his skin, or the leopard his spots? *then* may ye also do good, that are accustomed to do evil.

Jer. 17.13. The Lord, the fountain of living waters. Jer. 2.13.

Jer. 24.7. I will give them an heart to know me, that I *am* the Lord: and they shall be my people, and I will be their God: for they shall return unto me with their whole heart. 2 Chr. 33.13.

Jer. 31.3. Yea, I have loved thee with an everlasting love: therefore with lovingkindness have I drawn thee. 33. I will put my law in their inward parts, and write it in their hearts; and will be their God, and they shall be my people.

Jer. 32.38. They shall be my people, and I will be their God: 39. And I will give them one heart, and one way, that they may fear me for ever, for the good of them, and of their children after them: 40. And I will make an everlasting covenant with them, that I will not turn away from them, to do them good; but I will put my fear in their hearts, that they shall not depart from me.

Jer. 33.6. I will bring it health and cure, and I will cure them, and will reveal unto them the abundance of peace and truth.

Eze. 11.19. I will give them one heart, and I will put a new spirit within you; and I will take the stony heart out of their flesh, and will give them an heart of flesh: 20. That they may walk in my statutes, and keep mine ordinances, and do them: and they shall be my people, and I will be their God.

Eze. 36.29. I will also save you from all your uncleannesses.

Hos. 11.4. I drew them with cords of a man, with bands of love.

Hos. 14.8. I have heard *him*, and observed him: I *am* like a green fir-tree: from me *is* thy fruit found.

Zec. 12.10. I will pour upon the house of David, and upon the inhabitants of Jerusalem, the spirit of grace and of supplications; and they shall look upon me whom they have pierced, and they shall mourn.

Mat. 12.33. Either make the tree good, and his fruit good; or else make the tree corrupt, and his fruit corrupt: for the tree is known by *his* fruit. 34. O generation of vipers, how can ye, being evil, speak good things? for out of the abundance of the heart the mouth speaketh. 35. A good man out of the good treasure of the heart bringeth forth good things: and an evil man out of the evil treasure bringeth forth evil things.

Mat. 13.33. The kingdom of heaven is like unto leaven, which a woman took and hid in three measures of meal, till the whole was leavened.

Mat. 18.3. Except ye be converted, and become as little children, ye shall not enter into the kingdom of heaven.

Luk. 1.16. Many of the children of Israel shall he turn to the Lord their God. 17. And he shall go before him in the spirit and power of Elias, to turn the hearts of the fathers to the children, and the disobedient to the wisdom of the just; to make ready a people prepared for the Lord.

Jno. 1.4. In him was life; and the life was the light of men. 13. Which were born, not of blood, nor of the will of the flesh, nor of the will of man, but of God. 16. Of his fulness have all we received, and grace for grace. 33. He who baptizeth with the Holy Ghost.

Jno. 3.27. A man can receive nothing, except it be given him from heaven.

Jno. 4.10. If thou knewest the gift of God, and who it is that saith to thee, Give me to drink; thou wouldest have asked of him, and he would have given thee living water. 14. Whosoever drinketh of the water that I shall give him shall never thirst; but the water that I shall give him shall be in him a well of water springing up into everlasting life.

Jno. 5.24. He that heareth my word, and believeth on him that sent me, hath everlasting life, and shall not come into condemnation; but is passed from death unto life.

Jno. 6.44. No man can come to me, except the Father which hath sent me draw him. 45. They shall be all taught of God. Every man therefore that hath heard, and hath learned of the Father, cometh unto me. 57. As the living Father hath sent me, and I live by the Father: so he that eateth me, even he shall live by me. 65. No man can come unto me, except it were given unto him of my Father. *v.* 37.

Jno. 3.12. I am the light of the world: he that followeth me shall not walk in darkness, but shall have the light of life. 32. Ye shall know the truth, and the truth shall make you free. 36. If the Son therefore shall make you free, ye shall be free indeed.

Jno. 10.9. I am the door: by me if any man enter in, he shall be saved, and shall go in and out, and find pasture. 10. I am come that they might have life, and that they might have *it* more abundantly.

Jno. 13.8. Jesus answered him, If I wash thee not, thou hast no part with me.

Jno. 15.1. I am the true vine, and my Father is the husbandman. 3. Now ye are clean through the word which I have spoken unto you.

Jno. 17.2. Thou hast given him power over all flesh, that he should give eternal life to as many as thou hast given him.

Act. 2.47. The Lord added to the church daily such as should be saved.

Act. 3.26. God, having raised up his Son Jesus, sent him to bless you, in turning away every one of you from his iniquities.

Act. 11.17. God gave them the like gift as *he did* unto us, who believed on the Lord Jesus Christ; what was I, that I could withstand God? 21. The hand of the Lord was with them: and a great number believed, and turned unto the Lord.

Act. 15.9.   Put no difference between us and them, purifying their hearts by faith.

Act. 16.14.   A certain woman named Lydia, whose heart the Lord opened, that she attended unto the things which were spoken of Paul.

Act. 21.19.   He declared particularly what things God had wrought among the Gentiles by his ministry.

Act. 26.18.   To open their eyes, *and* to turn *them* from darkness to light, and *from* the power of Satan unto God, that they may receive forgiveness of sins, and inheritance among them which are sanctified by faith that is in me.

Rom. 2.28.   He is not a Jew, which is one outwardly; neither *is that* circumcision, which is outward in the flesh: 29. But he *is* a Jew, which is one inwardly; and circumcision *is that* of the heart, in the spirit, *and* not in the letter; whose praise *is* not of men, but of God.

Rom. 6.8.   If we be dead with Christ, we believe that we shall also live with him. 11. Reckon ye also yourselves to be dead indeed unto sin, but alive unto God through Jesus Christ our Lord. 13. Yield yourselves unto God, as those that are alive from the dead. 18. Being then made free from sin, ye became the servants of righteousness.

Rom. 7.6.   Now we are delivered from the law, that being dead wherein we were held; that we should serve in newness of spirit, and not *in* the oldness of the letter. 24. O wretched man that I am! who shall deliver me from the body of this death? 25. I thank God, through Jesus Christ our Lord. *v.* 7-25.

Rom. 8.3.   What the law could not do, in that it was weak through the flesh, God sending his own Son in the likeness of sinful flesh, and for sin, condemned sin in the flesh. 8. They that are in the flesh cannot please God. 30. Whom he did predestinate, them he also called; and whom he called, them he also justified; and whom he justified, them he also glorified. *v.* 31-34.

Rom. 9.23.   Vessels of mercy, which he had afore prepared unto glory.

Rom. 12.2.   Be not conformed to this world: but be ye transformed by the renewing of your mind, that ye may prove what *is* that good, and acceptable, and perfect, will of God.

Rom. 15.18.   I will not dare to speak of any of those things which Christ hath not wrought by me, to make the Gentiles obedient, by word and deed.

1 Cor. 1.9.   God *is* faithful, by whom ye were called unto the fellowship of his Son Jesus Christ our Lord. 24. Unto them which are called, both Jews and Greeks, Christ the power of God, and the wisdom of God. 30. Of him are ye in Christ Jesus, who of God is made unto us wisdom, and righteousness, and sanctification, and redemption.

1 Cor. 2.12.   We have received, not the spirit of the world, but the spirit which is of God; that we might know the things that are freely given to us of God. 14. The natural man receiveth not the things of the Spirit of God: for they are foolishness unto him: neither can he know *them*, because they are spiritually discerned. 15. He that is spiritual judgeth all things, yet he himself is judged of no man. 16. For who hath known the mind of the Lord, that he may instruct him? But we have the mind of Christ.

1 Cor. 3.6.   I have planted, Apollos watered; but God gave the increase. 7. So then neither is he that planteth any thing, neither he that watereth; but God that giveth the increase. 9. Ye are God's husbandry, *ye are* God's building.

1 Cor. 7.17.   As God hath distributed to every man, as the Lord hath called every one, so let him walk. 24. Let every man, wherein he is called, therein abide with God.

1 Cor. 9.1.   Are not ye my work in the Lord? 2. The seal of mine apostleship are ye in the Lord.

1 Cor. 12.6.   There are diversities of operations, but it is the same God which worketh all in all.

1 Cor. 15.10.   By the grace of God I am what I am.

2 Cor. 4.6.   God, who commanded the light to shine out of darkness, hath shined in our hearts, to *give* the light of the knowledge of the glory of God in the face of Jesus Christ.

2 Cor. 5.5.   He that hath wrought us for the self-same thing *is* God, who also hath given unto us the earnest of the Spirit. 17. If any man *be* in Christ, *he is* a new creature: old things are passed away; behold, all things are become new.

2 Cor. 10.4.   The weapons of our warfare *are* not carnal, but mighty through God, to the pulling down of strong holds. *v.* 5.

Gal. 6.15.   In Christ Jesus neither circumcision availeth any thing, nor uncircumcision, but a new creature.

Eph. 1.2.   Grace *be* to you, and peace, from God our Father, and *from* the Lord Jesus Christ. 3. Blessed *be* the God and Father of our Lord Jesus Christ, who hath blessed us with all spiritual blessings in heavenly *places* in Christ.

Eph. 2.1.   You *hath he quickened*, who were dead in trespasses and sins. 5. Even when we were dead in sins, hath quickened us together with Christ; (by grace ye are saved;) 6. And hath raised *us* up together, and made us sit together in heavenly *places* in Christ Jesus. 8. By grace are ye saved through faith; and that not of yourselves: *it is* the gift of God. 10. We are his workmanship, created in Christ Jesus unto good works.

Eph. 4.7.   Unto every one of us is given grace according to the measure of the gift of Christ. 8. Wherefore he saith, When he ascended up on high, he led captivity captive, and gave gifts unto men. 16. From whom the whole body fitly joined together and compacted by that which every joint supplieth, according to the effectual working in the measure of every part, maketh increase of the body unto the edifying of itself in love. 21. If so be that ye have heard him, and have been taught by him, as the truth is in Jesus: 22. That ye put off concerning the former conversation the old man, which is corrupt according to the deceitful lusts; 23. And be renewed in the spirit of your mind; 24. And that ye put on the new man, which after God is created in righteousness and true holiness.

Eph. 5.14.   Awake thou that sleepest, and arise from the dead, and Christ shall give thee light.

Phil. 1.6.   He which hath begun a good work in you will perform *it* until the day of Jesus Christ.

Phil. 2.13. It is God which worketh in you both to will and to do of *his* good pleasure.

Phil. 3.12. I follow after, if that I may apprehend that for which also I am apprehended of Christ Jesus. 14. The prize of the high calling of God in Christ Jesus.

Col. 1.12. Giving thanks unto the Father, which hath made us meet to be partakers of the inheritance of the saints in light. 13. Who hath delivered us from the power of darkness, and hath translated *us* into the kingdom of his dear Son.

Col. 2.11. In whom also ye are circumcised with the circumcision made without hands, in putting off the body of the sins of the flesh by the circumcision of Christ: 12. Buried with him in baptism, wherein also ye are risen with *him* through the faith of the operation of God, who hath raised him from the dead. 13. And you, being dead in your sins and the uncircumcision of your flesh, hath he quickened together with him, having forgiven you all trespasses.

Col. 3.9. Ye have put off the old man with his deeds ; 10. And have put on the new *man*, which is renewed in knowledge after the image of him that created him.

1 The. 5.24. Faithful *is* he that calleth you, who also will do *it*.

2 Tim. 2.25. If God peradventure will give them repentance to the acknowledging of the truth.

Jas. 1.18. Of his own will begat he us with the word of truth, that we should be a kind of firstfruits of his creatures.

Jas. 4.6. He giveth more grace. Wherefore he saith, God resisteth the proud, but giveth grace unto the humble.

Jas. 5.19. If any of you do err from the truth, and one convert him ; 20. Let him know, that he which converteth the sinner from the error of his way shall save a soul from death, and shall hide a multitude of sins.

1 Pet. 1.3. Blessed *be* the God and Father of our Lord Jesus Christ, which according to his abundant mercy hath begotten us again unto a lively hope by the resurrection of Jesus Christ from the dead. 23. Being born again, not of corruptible seed, but of incorruptible, by the word of God, which liveth and abideth for ever.

1 Pet. 2.3. If so be ye have tasted that the Lord *is* gracious. 9. Shew forth the praises of him who hath called you out of darkness into his marvellous light.

2 Pet. 1.3. His divine power hath given unto us all things that *pertain* unto life and godliness, through the knowledge of him that hath called us to glory and virtue : 4. Whereby are given unto us exceeding great and precious promises ; that by these ye might be partakers of the divine nature.

1 Jno. 2.27. The anointing, which ye have received of him, abideth in you ; and ye need not that any man teach you : but as the same anointing teacheth you of all things, and is truth, and is no lie, and even as it hath taught you, ye shall abide in him. 29. If ye know that he is righteous, ye know that every one that doeth righteousness is born of him.

1 Jno. 3.9. Whosoever is born of God doth not commit sin ; for his seed remaineth in him : and he cannot sin, because he is born of God.

Rev. 14.3. No man could learn that song but the hundred *and* forty *and* four thousand, which were redeemed from the earth.

Rev. 22.1. He shewed me a pure river of water of life, clear as crystal, proceeding out of the throne of God and of the Lamb. 2. In the midst of the street of it, and on either side of the river, *was there* the tree of life, which bare twelve *manner of* fruits, *and* yielded her fruit every month : and the leaves of the tree *were* for the healing of the nations.

See MAN'S NATURAL STATE—SANCTIFICATION.

REGENERATION, CONVERSION, AND SANCTIFICATION, NATURE AND NECESSITY OF. BY THE HOLY SPIRIT. Isa. 4.4. When the Lord shall have washed away the filth of the daughters of Zion, and shall have purged the blood of Jerusalem from the midst thereof, by the spirit of judgment, and by the spirit of burning.

Eze. 36.26. A new heart also will I give you, and a new spirit will I put within you ; and I will take away the stony heart out of your flesh, and I will give you an heart of flesh. 27. And I will put my Spirit within you, and cause you to walk in my statutes, and ye shall keep my judgments, and do *them*.

Eze. 11.19.

Eze. 37.9. Say to the wind, Thus saith the Lord God, Come from the four winds, O breath, and breathe upon these slain, that they may live. 14. And shall put my Spirit in you, and ye shall live. *v.* 1-14.

Jno. 3.3. Except a man be born again, he cannot see the kingdom of God. 5. Except a man be born of water and *of* the Spirit, he cannot enter into the kingdom of God. 6. That which is born of the flesh is flesh ; and that which is born of the Spirit is spirit. 8. The wind bloweth where it listeth, and thou hearest the sound thereof, but canst not tell whence it cometh, and whither it goeth : so is every one that is born of the Spirit.

Jno. 6.63. It is the Spirit that quickeneth ; the flesh profiteth nothing : the words that I speak unto you, *they* are spirit, and *they* are life.

Rom. 8.2. The law of the Spirit of life in Christ Jesus hath made me free from the law of sin and death. 5. They that are after the Spirit do mind the things of the Spirit. 9. Ye are not in the flesh, but in the Spirit, if so be that the Spirit of God dwell in you. Now if any man have not the Spirit of Christ, he is none of his. 13. If ye through the Spirit do mortify the deeds of the body, ye shall live. 15. Ye have received the Spirit of adoption, whereby we cry, Abba, Father. 16. The Spirit itself beareth witness with our spirit, that we are the children of God.

Rom. 15.16. The offering up of the Gentiles might be acceptable, being sanctified by the Holy Ghost.

1 Cor. 6.11. But ye are washed, but ye are sanctified, but ye are justified in the name of the Lord Jesus, and by the Spirit of our God.

1 Cor. 12.3. No man can say that Jesus is the Lord, but by the Holy Ghost. 13. By one Spirit are we all baptized into one body, whether *we be* Jews or Gentiles, whether *we be* bond or free ; and have been all made to drink into one Spirit.

2 Cor. 3.3. *Ye are* manifestly declared to be the epistle of Christ ministered by us, written not with ink, but with the Spirit of the living God; not in tables of stone, but in fleshy tables of the heart. 18. We all, with open face beholding as in a glass the glory of the Lord, are changed into the same image from glory to glory, *even* as by the Spirit of the Lord.

Gal. 4.29. As then he that was born after the flesh persecuted him *that was born* after the Spirit, even so *it is* now.

Gal. 5.22. The fruit of the Spirit is love, joy, peace, long-suffering, gentleness, goodness, faith. 23. Meekness, temperance: against such there is no law.

1 The. 1.5. Our gospel came not unto you in word only, but also in power, and in the Holy Ghost, and in much assurance.

2 The. 2.13. God hath from the beginning chosen you to salvation through sanctification of the Spirit, and belief of the truth.

Tit. 3.5. According to his mercy he saved us, by the washing of regeneration, and renewing of the Holy Ghost; 6. Which he shed on us abundantly through Jesus Christ our Saviour.

1 Pet. 1.2. Elect according to the foreknowledge of God the Father through sanctification of the Spirit, unto obedience and sprinkling of the blood of Jesus Christ. 22. Ye have purified your souls in obeying the truth through the Spirit.

See HOLY SPIRIT'S INFLUENCES.

REGENERATION, &c., BY THE SCRIPTURES. See WORD OF GOD SANCTIFYING.

REHOB, or BETH-REHOB, a town in the north of Palestine, Num. 13.21. Jud. 18.28. Given to Asher, Jos. 19.28,30. A Levitical city, Jos. 21.31. 1 Chr. 6.75. Canaanites in, Jud. 1.31.

———, a Syrian city, 2 Sam. 10.6,8 with 2 Sam. 8.3,12.

REHOBOAM, 4th king of the 12 tribes, and 1st king of Judah (17 years' reign), son of Solomon and Naamah, an Ammonitess, 1 Kin. 14.21,31. 1 Chr. 3.10. 2 Chr. 12.13. Mat. 1.7. Succeeds his father; crowned king at the age of 41, 1 Kin. 11.43. 1 Kin. 12.1. 1 Kin. 14.21. 2 Chr. 9.31. 2 Chr. 10.1. 2 Chr. 12.13.

Refuses to lessen the taxation, 1 Kin. 12.1-15. 2 Chr. 10. Rebellion of Jeroboam & Israel; the collector of taxes stoned, 1 Kin. 12.16-20. 2 Chr. 10.16-19. 2 Chr. 13.7. Reigns over Judah and Benjamin, 1 Kin. 12.17. 1 Kin. 14.21. 2 Chr. 10.17.

Prevented by Shemaiah from fighting against Jeroboam, 1 Kin. 12.23. 2 Chr. 11.1-4. Builds cities of defence; receives Levites; his prosperity, 2 Chr. 11.5-17. Wives and family; provision for them, 2 Chr. 11.18-23.

His backsliding; Shishak's invasion; great treasures carried off, 1 Kin. 14.25,26. 2 Chr. 12.1-11,14. His shields and guards, 1 Kin. 14.27,28. 2 Chr. 12.10,11. His repentance on Shemaiah's warning, 2 Chr. 12.5-12. Wars with Jeroboam, 1 Kin. 14.30. 1 Kin. 15.6. 2 Chr. 12.15. Death and burial, 1 Kin. 14.21,31. 2 Chr. 12.13,16.

REHOBOTH (room), one of Isaac's wells, Gen. 26.22.

REHUM, the chancellor, writes to Artaxerxes, accusing the Jews, and stops the building of the temple, Ezr. 4.8-24.

REINS, used in the modern figurative sense of the word heart, Job 16.13.

REMORSE. See CONVICTION OF SIN.

REMPHAN. See CHIUN.

RENDING OF GARMENTS. See MOURNING.

REPENTANCE. CONFESSION OF SIN ENJOINED. Ex. 33.5. I will come up into the midst of thee in a moment, and consume thee: therefore now put off thy ornaments from thee, that I may know what to do unto thee.

Lev. 16.21. Aaron shall lay both his hands upon the head of the live goat, and confess over him all the iniquities of the children of Israel, and all their transgressions in all their sins, putting them upon the head of the goat, and shall send *him* away by the hand of a fit man into the wilderness.

Lev. 26.40. If they shall confess their iniquity, and the iniquity of their fathers, with their trespass which they trespassed against me, and that also they have walked contrary unto me; 41. And *that* I also have walked contrary unto them, and have brought them into the land of their enemies; if then their uncircumcised hearts be humbled, and they then accept of the punishment of their iniquity: 42. Then will I remember my covenant; and I will remember the land.

Num. 5.6. When a man or woman shall commit any sin that men commit, to do a trespass against the Lord, and that person be guilty; 7. Then they shall confess their sin which they have done. Lev. 5.5.

Deu. 4.29. If from thence thou shalt seek the Lord thy God, thou shalt find *him*, if thou seek him with all thy heart and with all thy soul. *v.* 30,31.

Deu. 30.2. And shalt return unto the Lord thy God, and shalt obey his voice according to all that I command thee this day, thou and thy children, with all thine heart, and with all thy soul; 3. That then the Lord thy God will turn thy captivity, and have compassion upon thee. 9. For the Lord will again rejoice over thee for good, as he rejoiced over thy fathers. *v.* 8,10.

Deu. 32.29. O that they were wise, *that* they understood this, *that* they would consider their latter end!

Jos. 7.19. Give, I pray thee, glory to the Lord God of Israel, and make confession unto him.

1 Sam. 7.3. If ye do return unto the Lord with all your hearts, *then* put away the strange gods and Ashtaroth from among you, and prepare your hearts unto the Lord, and serve him only: and he will deliver you.

1 Sam. 12.20. Fear not: ye have done all this wickedness: yet turn not aside from following the Lord, but serve the Lord with all your heart.

2 Chr. 7.14. If my people, which are called by my name, shall humble themselves, and pray, and seek my face, and turn from their wicked ways; then will I hear from heaven, and will forgive their sin, and will heal their land. 1 Kin. 8.46-50. 2 Chr. 6.36.

2 Chr. 30.6. Turn again unto the Lord God and he will return to the remnant of you. 9. For the Lord your God *is* gracious and

merciful, and will not turn away *his* face from you, if ye return unto him. *v.* 7, 8.

Ezr. 10.11. Make confession unto the Lord God of your fathers, and do his pleasure: and separate yourselves from the people of the land.

Neh. 1.9. *If* ye turn unto me, and keep my commandments, and do them; though there were of you cast out unto the uttermost part of the heaven, *yet* will I gather them from thence, and will bring them unto the place that I have chosen to set my name there.

Job 11.13. If thou prepare thine heart, and stretch out thine hands toward him; 14. If iniquity *be* in thine hand, put it far away, and let not wickedness dwell in thy tabernacles. 15. For then shalt thou lift up thy face without spot; yea, thou shalt be stedfast, and shalt not fear.

Job 22.23. If thou return to the Almighty, thou shalt be built up, thou shalt put away iniquity far from thy tabernacles.

Job 33.27. He looketh upon men, and *if any* say, I have sinned, and perverted *that which was* right, and it profited me not; 28. He will deliver his soul from going into the pit, and his life shall see the light.

Job 34.31. Surely it is meet to be said unto God, I have borne *chastisement,* I will not offend *any more.* 32. *That which* I see not teach thou me: if I have done iniquity, I will do no more.

Job 36.10. He openeth also their ear to discipline, and commandeth that they return from iniquity.

Psa. 22.27. All the ends of the world shall remember, and turn unto the Lord.

Psa. 34.14. Depart from evil, and do good; seek peace, and pursue it. 18. The Lord *is* nigh unto them that are of a broken heart; and saveth such as be of a contrite spirit.

Psa. 51.17. The sacrifices of God *are* a broken spirit: a broken and a contrite heart, O God, thou wilt not despise.

Psa. 95.7. To day if ye will hear his voice, 8. Harden not your heart, as in the provocation, *and* as *in* the day of temptation in the wilderness.

Psa. 147.3. He healeth the broken in heart, and bindeth up their wounds.

Pro. 1.22. How long, ye simple ones, will ye love simplicity? and the scorners delight in their scorning, and fools hate knowledge? 23. Turn you at my reproof: behold, I will pour out my spirit unto you, I will make known my words unto you.

Pro. 9.6. Forsake the foolish, and live; and go in the way of understanding.

Pro. 28.13. He that covereth his sins shall not prosper; but whoso confesseth and forsaketh *them* shall have mercy.

Isa. 1.16. Wash you, make you clean; put away the evil of your doings from before mine eyes; cease to do evil; 17. Learn to do well; seek judgment, relieve the oppressed, judge the fatherless, plead for the widow.

Isa. 10.21. The remnant shall return, *even* the remnant of Jacob, unto the mighty God.

Isa. 22.12. In that day did the Lord God of hosts call to weeping, and to mourning, and to baldness, and to girding with sackcloth.

Isa. 31.6. Turn ye unto *him from* whom the children of Israel have deeply revolted.

Isa. 44.22. I have blotted out, as a thick cloud, thy transgressions, and, as a cloud, thy sins: return unto me; for I have redeemed thee.

Isa. 46.8. Remember this, and shew yourselves men: bring *it* again to mind, O ye transgressors.

Isa. 55.6. Seek ye the Lord while he may be found, call ye upon him while he is near: 7. Let the wicked forsake his way, and the unrighteous man his thoughts: and let him return unto the Lord, and he will have mercy upon him; and to our God, for he will abundantly pardon.

Isa. 57.15. I dwell in the high and holy *place,* with him also *that is* of a contrite and humble spirit, to revive the spirit of the humble, and to revive the heart of the contrite ones.

Isa. 59.20. The Redeemer shall come to Zion, and unto them that turn from transgression in Jacob, saith the Lord.

Isa. 61.1. He hath sent me to bind up the broken-hearted, to proclaim liberty to the captives, and the opening of the prison to *them that are* bound; 2. To proclaim the acceptable year of the Lord; to comfort all that mourn.

Isa. 66.2. To this *man* will I look, *even* to *him that is* poor and of a contrite spirit, and trembleth at my word.

Jer. 3.4. Wilt thou not from this time cry unto me, My father, thou *art* the guide of my youth? 12. Return, thou backsliding Israel, saith the Lord; *and* I will not cause mine anger to fall upon you: for I *am* merciful, saith the Lord, *and* I will not keep *anger* for ever. 13. Only acknowledge thine iniquity. 14. Turn, O backsliding children, saith the Lord; for I am married unto you: and I will take you one of a city, and two of a family, and I will bring you to Zion. 19. I said, How shall I put thee among the children, and give thee a pleasant land, a goodly heritage of the hosts of nations? and I said, Thou shalt call me, My father; and shalt not turn away from me.

Jer. 4.1. If thou wilt return, O Israel, saith the Lord, return unto me: and if thou wilt put away thine abominations out of my sight, then shalt thou not remove. 3. Break up your fallow ground, and sow not among thorns. 4. Circumcise yourselves to the Lord, and take away the foreskins of your heart, ye men of Judah and inhabitants of Jerusalem: lest my fury come forth like fire, and burn that none can quench *it,* because of the evil of your doings. 14. O Jerusalem, wash thine heart from wickedness, that thou mayest be saved. How long shall thy vain thoughts lodge within thee? Deu. 10.16.

Jer. 6.8. Be thou instructed, O Jerusalem, lest my soul depart from thee; lest I make thee desolate, a land not inhabited. 16. Stand ye in the ways, and see, and ask for the old paths, where *is* the good way, and walk therein, and ye shall find rest for your souls.

Jer. 7.5. For if ye throughly amend your ways and your doings. 7. Then will I cause you to dwell in this place.

Jer. 13.15. Hear ye, and give ear; be not proud: for the Lord hath spoken. 16. Give glory to the Lord your God, before he cause darkness, and before your feet stumble upon the dark mountains, and, while ye look for light, he turn it into the shadow of death, *and* make *it* gross darkness. *v.* 17.

Jer. 18.8. If that nation, against whom I have pronounced, turn from their evil, I will repent of the evil that I thought to do unto them. 11. Thus saith the Lord; Behold, I frame evil against you, and devise a device against you: return ye now every one from his evil way, and make your ways and your doings good.

Jer. 22.3.   Execute ye judgment and righteousness. 4. For if ye do this thing indeed, then shall there enter in by the gates of this house kings sitting upon the throne of David.

Jer. 24.7. I will give them an heart to know me, that I *am* the Lord: and they shall be my people, and I will be their God: for they shall return unto me with their whole heart.

Jer. 25.5. Turn ye again now every one from his evil way, and from the evil of your doings, and dwell in the land that the Lord hath given unto you. 6. Provoke me not to anger with the works of your hands; and I will do you no hurt. Jer. 35.15.

Jer. 26.3. If so be they will hearken, and turn every man from his evil way, that I may repent me of the evil, which I purpose to do unto them because of the evil of their doings. *v.* 13.

Jer. 31.9. They shall come with weeping, and with supplications will I lead them: I will cause them to walk by the rivers of waters in a straight way, wherein they shall not stumble: for I am a father to Israel, and Ephraim *is* my firstborn.

Jer. 36.3. It may be that the house of Judah will hear all the evil which I purpose to do unto them; that they may return every man from his evil way; that I may forgive their iniquity and their sin. *v.* 6,7.

Jer. 50.4. In those days, and in that time, saith the Lord, the children of Israel shall come, they and the children of Judah together, going and weeping: they shall go, and seek the Lord their God. 5. They shall ask the way to Zion with their faces thitherward, *saying,* Come, and let us join ourselves to the Lord in a perpetual covenant *that* shall not be forgotten.

Eze. 7.16. They shall be on the mountains like doves of the valleys, all of them mourning, every one for his iniquity. *v.* 27.

Eze. 9.4. Set a mark upon the foreheads of the men that sigh and that cry for all the abominations that be done in the midst thereof.

Eze. 11.18. They shall take away all the detestable things thereof and all the abominations thereof from thence. 19. And I will give them one heart, and I will put a new spirit within you; and I will take the stony heart out of their flesh, and will give them an heart of flesh: 20. That they may walk in my statutes, and keep mine ordinances, and do them: and they shall be my people, and I will be their God.

Eze. 12.3. It may be they will consider, though they *be* a rebellious house.

Eze. 14.6. Repent, and turn *yourselves* from your idols; and turn away your faces from all your abominations.

Eze. 16.61. Then thou shalt remember thy

ways, and be ashamed, when thou shalt receive thy sisters, thine elder and thy younger: and I will give them unto thee for daughters, but not by thy covenant. 62. And I will establish my covenant with thee; and thou shalt know that I *am* the Lord: 63. That thou mayest remember, and be confounded, and never open thy mouth any more because of thy shame, when I am pacified toward thee for all that thou hast done, saith the Lord God.

Eze. 18.21. If the wicked will turn from all his sins that he hath committed, and keep all my statutes, and do that which is lawful and right, he shall surely live, he shall not die. 22. All his transgressions that he hath committed, they shall not be mentioned unto him: in his righteousness that he hath done he shall live. 23. Have I any pleasure at all that the wicked should die? saith the Lord God: *and* not that he should return from his ways, and live? 30. Repent, and turn *yourselves* from all your transgressions; so iniquity shall not be your ruin. 31. Cast away from you all your transgressions, whereby ye have transgressed; and make you a new heart and a new spirit: for why will ye die, O house of Israel? *v.* 27,28,32.

Eze. 20.43. There shall ye remember your ways, and all your doings, wherein ye have been defiled; and ye shall loathe yourselves in your own sight for all your evils that ye have committed. Eze. 36.31.

Eze. 33.10. Thus ye speak, saying, If our transgressions and our sins *be* upon us, and we pine away in them, how should we then live? 11. Say unto them, *As* I live, saith the Lord God, I have no pleasure in the death of the wicked; but that the wicked turn from his way and live: turn ye, turn ye from your evil ways; for why will ye die, O house of Israel? 12. As for the wickedness of the wicked, he shall not fall thereby in the day that he turneth from his wickedness. *v.* 14-16,19.

Eze. 37.23. Neither shall they defile themselves any more with their idols, nor with their detestable things, nor with any of their transgressions: but I will save them out of all their dwelling-places, wherein they have sinned, and will cleanse them: so shall they be my people, and I will be their God. 24. And David my servant *shall be* king over them; and they all shall have one shepherd: they shall also walk in my judgments, and observe my statutes, and do them.

Eze. 43.9. Now let them put away their whoredom, and the carcases of their kings, far from me, and I will dwell in the midst of them for ever. 10. Son of man, shew the house to the house of Israel, that they may be ashamed of their iniquities.

Dan. 4.27. Break off thy sins by righteousness, and thine iniquities by shewing mercy to the poor; if it may be a lengthening of thy tranquillity.

Hos. 2.7. Then shall she say, I will go and return to my first husband; for then *was it* better with me than now.

Hos. 3.5. Afterwards shall the children of Israel return, and seek the Lord their God, and David their king; and shall fear the Lord and his goodness in the latter days.

Hos. 5.15. I will go *and* return to my place till they acknowledge their offence, and seek my face.

Hos. 10.12. Sow to yourselves in righteousness, reap in mercy; break up your fallow ground: for *it is* time to seek the Lord, till he come and rain righteousness upon you.

Hos. 12.6. Turn thou to thy God: keep mercy and judgment, and wait on thy God continually.

Hos. 14.1. O Israel, return unto the Lord thy God; for thou hast fallen by thine iniquity. 2. Take with you words, and turn to the Lord : say unto him, Take away all iniquity, and receive *us* graciously: so will we render the calves of our lips.

Joel 1.14. Sanctify ye a fast, call a solemn assembly, gather the elders *and* all the inhabitants of the land *into* the house of the Lord your God, and cry unto the Lord.

Joel 2.12. Turn ye *even* to me with all your heart, and with fasting, and with weeping, and with mourning: 13. And rend your heart, and not your garments, and turn unto the Lord your God : for he *is* gracious and merciful, slow to anger, and of great kindness, and repenteth him of the evil. 15. Blow the trumpet in Zion, sanctify a fast, call a solemn assembly: 16. Gather the people, sanctify the congregation, assemble the elders, gather the children, and those that suck the breasts: let the bridegroom go forth of his chamber, and the bride out of her closet. 17. Let the priests, the ministers of the Lord, weep between the porch and the altar, and let them say, Spare thy people, O Lord. 18. Then will the Lord be jealous for his land, and pity his people.

Amos 4.12. Thus will I do unto thee, O Israel: *and* because I will do this unto thee, prepare to meet thy God, O Israel.

Amos 5.6. Seek the Lord, and ye shall live; lest he break out like fire. 14. Seek good, and not evil, that ye may live: and so the Lord, the God of hosts, shall be with you, as ye have spoken. 15. Hate the evil, and love the good, and establish judgment in the gate: it may be that the Lord God of hosts will be gracious.

Jonah 3.8. Let man and beast be covered with sackcloth, and cry mightily unto God: yea, let them turn every one from his evil way, and from the violence that *is* in their hands. 9. Who can tell *if* God will turn and repent, and turn away from his fierce anger, that we perish not?

Zeph. 2.1. Gather together, O nation not desired; 2. Before the decree bring forth, *before* the day pass as the chaff, before the fierce anger of the Lord come upon you, before the day of the Lord's anger come upon you. 3. Seek ye the Lord, all ye meek of the earth, which have wrought his judgment; seek righteousness, seek meekness: it may be ye shall be hid in the day of the Lord's anger.

Hag. 1.7. Thus saith the Lord of hosts; Consider your ways.

Zec. 1.3. Turn ye unto me, saith the Lord of hosts, and I will turn unto you, saith the Lord of hosts.

Zec. 12.10. I will pour upon the house of David, and upon the inhabitants of Jerusalem, the spirit of grace and of supplications: and they shall look upon me whom they have pierced, and they shall mourn for him, as one mourneth for *his* only *son*, and shall be in bitterness for him, as one that is in bitterness for *his* firstborn. 11. In that day shall there be a great mourning in Jerusalem, as the mourning of Hadadrimmon in the valley of Megiddon. 12. And the land shall mourn, every family apart.

Mal. 3.7. Return unto me, and I will return unto you, saith the Lord of hosts.

Mat. 3.7. O generation of vipers, who hath warned you to flee from the wrath to come? 8. Bring forth therefore fruits meet for repentance. *v. 2.*

Mat. 4.17. Jesus began to preach, and to say, Repent : for the kingdom of heaven is at hand.

Mat. 5.4. Blessed *are* they that mourn : for they shall be comforted. Luk. 6.21.

Mar. 1.4. John did baptize in the wilderness, and preach the baptism of repentance for the remission of sins. 15. The time is fulfilled, and the kingdom of God is at hand; repent ye, and believe the gospel. Luk. 3.3.

Mar. 2.17. They that are whole have no need of the physician, but they that are sick : I came not to call the righteous, but sinners to repentance.

Mar. 6.12. They went out, and preached that men should repent.

Luk. 13.3. Except ye repent, ye shall all likewise perish.

Luk. 15.7. Joy shall be in heaven over one sinner that repenteth, more than over ninety and nine just persons, which need no repentance. *v. 1-10.*

Luk. 18.13. The publican, standing afar off, would not lift up so much as *his* eyes unto heaven, but smote upon his breast, saying, God be merciful to me a sinner. 14. I tell you, This man went down to his house justified *rather* than the other: for every one that exalteth himself shall be abased; and he that humbleth himself shall be exalted. *v. 10-14.*

Luk. 24.47. Repentance and remission of sins should be preached in his name among all nations, beginning at Jerusalem.

Act. 2.38. Peter said unto them, Repent, and be baptized every one of you in the name of Jesus Christ for the remission of sins, and ye shall receive the gift of the Holy Ghost. 40. With many other words did he testify and exhort, saying, Save yourselves from this untoward generation.

Act. 3.19. Repent ye therefore, and be converted, that your sins may be blotted out when the times of refreshing shall come from the presence of the Lord. 26. Unto you first, God, having raised up his Son Jesus, sent him to bless you, in turning away every one of you from his iniquities.

Act. 5.31. Him hath God exalted with his right hand *to be* a Prince and a Saviour, for to give repentance to Israel, and forgiveness of sins.

Act. 8.22. Repent therefore of this thy wickedness, and pray God, if perhaps the thought of thine heart may be forgiven thee.

Act. 17.30. The times of this ignorance God winked at; but now commandeth all men every where to repent.

Act. 20.21. Testifying both to the Jews, and also to the Greeks, repentance toward God.

Act. 26.20. That they should repent and turn to God, and do works meet for repentance.

Rom. 2.4. The goodness of God leadeth thee to repentance.

Rom. 11.23. They also, if they abide not still in unbelief, shall be graffed in: for God is able to graff them in again.

Rom. 14.11. *As* I live, saith the Lord, every knee shall bow to me, and every tongue shall confess to God.

Eph. 5.14. Awake thou that sleepest, and arise from the dead, and Christ shall give thee light.

2 Tim. 2.25. Instructing those that oppose themselves; if God peradventure will give them repentance to the acknowledging of the truth.

Heb. 6.1. The foundation of repentance from dead works.

Jas. 4.8. Draw nigh to God, and he will draw nigh to you. Cleanse *your* hands, *ye* sinners; and purify *your* hearts, *ye* double minded. 9. Be afflicted, and mourn, and weep: let your laughter be turned to mourning, and *your* joy to heaviness. 10. Humble yourselves in the sight of the Lord, and he shall lift you up.

1 Jno. 1.9. If we confess our sins, he is faithful and just to forgive us *our* sins, and to cleanse us from all unrighteousness.

Rev. 2.5. Remember therefore from whence thou art fallen, and repent, and do the first works; or else I will come unto thee quickly, and will remove thy candlestick out of his place, except thou repent. 16. Repent; or else I will come unto thee quickly, and will fight against them with the sword of my mouth.

Rev. 3.2. Be watchful, and strengthen the things which remain, that are ready to die: for I have not found thy works perfect before God. 3. Remember therefore how thou hast received and heard, and hold fast, and repent. See GOD'S MERCY.

REPENTANCE. CONFESSION OF SIN, EXAMPLES OF: Joseph's brethren, Gen. 42.21. Aaron, Num. 12.11. Balaam, Num. 22.31,34. Israelites, Ex. 33.4. Num. 21.7. Jud. 2.4,5. Jud. 10.15,16. 1 Sam. 7.4,6. 2 Chr. 15.4. 2 Chr. 28.13. 2 Chr. 30.11. Psa. 78.34. Saul, 1 Sam. 15.24. David, 2 Sam. 12.13. Ahab, 1 Kin. 21.27-29. Josiah, 2 Kin. 22.11,19,20. Rehoboam, 2 Chr. 12.6,7,12. Hezekiah, 2 Chr. 32.26. Manasseh, 2 Chr. 33.12,13. Jews, Ezr. 6.21. Ezr. 10.1-3,6,9. Neh. 5.1-13. Neh. 8.9. Neh. 9.2,3. Hag. 1.12. Mat. 3.6. A son, Mat. 21.29. Peter, Mar. 14.72. A woman, Luk. 7.37,38. Ephesians, Act. 19.18,19. Romans, Rom. 6.21.

REPENTANCE. CONFESSION OF SIN EXEMPLIFIED. 2 Sam. 24.10. David's heart smote him after that he had numbered the people. And David said unto the Lord, I have sinned greatly in that I have done: and now, I beseech thee, O Lord, take away the iniquity of thy servant; for I have done very foolishly. *v*. 17. 1 Chr. 21.17.

2 Chr. 29.6. Our fathers have trespassed, and done *that which was* evil in the eyes of the Lord our God, and have forsaken him, and have turned away their faces from the habitation of the Lord, and turned *their* backs. 8. Wherefore the wrath of the Lord was upon Judah and Jerusalem.

Ezr. 9.4. Then were assembled unto me every one that trembled at the words of the God of Israel, because of the transgression of those that had been carried away. 6. O my God, I am ashamed and blush to lift up my face to thee, my God: for our iniquities are increased over *our* head, and our trespass is grown up unto the heavens. 10. Now, O our God, what shall we say after this? for we have forsaken thy commandments. 13. After all that is come upon us for our evil deeds, and for our great trespass, seeing that thou our God hast punished us less than our iniquities *deserve*, and hast given us *such* deliverance as this: 14. Should we again break thy commandments, and join in affinity with the people of these abominations? wouldest not thou be angry with us till thou hadst consumed *us*, so that *there should be* no remnant nor escaping?

Neh. 1.6. Let thine ear now be attentive, and thine eyes open, that thou mayest hear the prayer of thy servant, which I pray before thee now, day and night, for the children of Israel thy servants, and confess the sins of the children of Israel, which we have sinned against thee: both I and my father's house have sinned. 7. We have dealt very corruptly against thee, and have not kept the commandments, nor the statutes, nor the judgments, which thou commandedst thy servant Moses.

Neh. 9.33. Thou *art* just in all that is brought upon us; for thou hast done right, but we have done wickedly. 35. For they have not served thee in their kingdom, and in thy great goodness that thou gavest them, and in the large and fat land which thou gavest before them, neither turned they from their wicked works. *v*. 2,3,16-37.

Job 7.20. I have sinned; what shall I do unto thee, O thou preserver of men?

Job 9.20. If I justify myself, mine own mouth shall condemn me: *if I say* I *am* perfect, it shall also prove me perverse.

Job 13.23. How many *are* mine iniquities and sins? make me to know my transgression and my sin.

Job 40.4. Behold, I am vile; what shall I answer thee? I will lay mine hand upon my mouth.

Job 42.5. I have heard of thee by the hearing of the ear: but now mine eye seeth thee. 6. Wherefore I abhor *myself*, and repent in dust and ashes.

Psa. 32.5. I acknowledged my sin unto thee, and mine iniquity have I not hid. I said, I will confess my transgressions unto the Lord; and thou forgavest the iniquity of my sin.

Psa. 38.3. *There is* no soundness in my flesh because of thine anger; neither *is there any* rest in my bones because of my sin. 4. For mine iniquities are gone over mine head: as an heavy burden they are too heavy for me. 5. My wounds stink *and* are corrupt because of my foolishness. 18. I will declare mine iniquity; I will be sorry for my sin.

Psa. 40.12. Innumerable evils have compassed me about: mine iniquities have taken hold upon me, so that I am not able to look up; they are more than the hairs of mine head: therefore my heart faileth me.

Psa. 41.4. Lord, be merciful unto me: heal my soul; for I have sinned against thee.

Psa. 51.3. I acknowledge my transgressions: and my sin *is* ever before me. 4. Against thee, thee only, have I sinned, and done *this* evil in thy sight: that thou mightest be justified when thou speakest, *and* be clear when thou judgest.

Psa. 65.3. Iniquities prevail against me: *as for* our transgressions, thou shalt purge them away.

Psa. 69.5. O God, thou knowest my foolishness; and my sins are not hid from thee. 10. I wept, *and chastened* my soul with fasting.

Psa. 73.21. My heart was grieved, and I was pricked in my reins. 22. So foolish *was* I, and ignorant.

Psa. 106.6. We have sinned with our fathers, we have committed iniquity, we have done wickedly.

Psa. 119.59. I thought on my ways, and turned my feet unto thy testimonies. 60. I made haste, and delayed not to keep thy commandments. 176. I have gone astray like a lost sheep.

Psa. 130.3. If thou, Lord, shouldest mark iniquities, O Lord, who shall stand?

Isa. 6.5. Woe *is* me! for I am undone: because I *am* a man of unclean lips, and I dwell in the midst of a people of unclean lips: for mine eyes have seen the King, the Lord of hosts.

Isa. 26.13. O Lord our God, *other* lords beside thee have had dominion over us: *but* by thee only will we make mention of thy name.

Isa. 38.15. What shall I say? he hath both spoken unto me, and himself hath done *it:* I shall go softly all my years in the bitterness of my soul.

Isa. 59.12. Our transgressions are multiplied before thee, and our sins testify against us: for our transgressions *are* with us; and *as for* our iniquities, we know them. *v.* 13-15.

Isa. 64.5. Behold, thou art wroth; for we have sinned: in those is continuance, and we shall be saved. 6. But we are all as an unclean *thing*, and all our righteousnesses *are* as filthy rags; and we all do fade as a leaf; and our iniquities, like the wind, have taken us away. 7. And *there is* none that calleth upon thy name, that stirreth up himself to take hold of thee: for thou hast hid thy face from us, and hast consumed us, because of our iniquities.

Jer. 3.21. A voice was heard upon the high places, weeping and supplications of the children of Israel: for they have perverted their way, *and* they have forgotten the Lord their God. 22. Return, ye backsliding children, *and* I will heal your backslidings. Behold, we come unto thee; for thou art the Lord our God. 25. We lie down in our shame, and our confusion covereth us: for we have sinned against the Lord our God, we and our fathers, from our youth even unto this day, and have not obeyed the voice of the Lord our God.

Jer. 8.14. The Lord our God hath put us to silence, and given us water of gall to drink, because we have sinned against the Lord. 15. We looked for peace, but no good *came*; *and* for a time of health, and behold trouble!

Jer. 14.7. O Lord, though our iniquities testify against us, do thou *it* for thy name's sake: for our backslidings are many; we have sinned against thee. 20. We acknowledge, O

Lord, our wickedness, *and* the iniquity of our fathers: for we have sinned against thee.

Jer. 31.18. I have surely heard Ephraim bemoaning himself *thus;* Thou hast chastised me, and I was chastised, as a bullock unaccustomed *to the yoke:* turn thou me, and I shall be turned; for thou *art* the Lord my God. 19. Surely after that I was turned, I repented; and after that I was instructed, I smote upon *my* thigh: I was ashamed, yea, even confounded, because I did bear the reproach of my youth.

Lam. 3.40. Let us search and try our ways, and turn again to the Lord. 41 Let us lift up our heart with *our* hands unto God in the heavens. 42. We have transgressed and have rebelled: thou hast not pardoned.

Dan. 9.5. We have sinned, and have committed iniquity, and have done wickedly, and have rebelled, even by departing from thy precepts and from thy judgments: 6. Neither have we hearkened unto thy servants the prophets, which spake in thy name to our kings, our princes, and our fathers, and to all the people of the land. 7. O Lord, righteousness *belongeth* unto thee, but unto us confusion of faces, as at this day. *v.* 5-19.

Dan. 10.12. From the first day that thou didst set thine heart to understand, and to chasten thyself before thy God, thy words were heard, and I am come for thy words.

Hos. 6.1. Come, and let us return unto the Lord: for he hath torn, and he will heal us; he hath smitten, and he will bind us up. *v.* 2.

Hos. 14.3. Asshur shall not save us; we will not ride upon horses: neither will we say any more to the work of our hands, Ye *are* our gods. 8. Ephraim *shall say,* What have I to do any more with idols? I have heard *him,* and observed him.

Jonah 3.10. God saw their works, that they turned from their evil way; and God repented of the evil, that he had said that he would do unto them; and he did *it* not.

Mic. 7.9. I will bear the indignation of the Lord, because I have sinned against him, until he plead my cause, and execute judgment for me: he will bring me forth to the light, *and* I shall behold his righteousness.

Luk. 15.17. And when he came to himself, he said, How many hired servants of my father's have bread enough, and to spare, and I perish with hunger! 18. I will arise, and go to my father, and will say unto him, Father, I have sinned against Heaven, and before thee, 19. And am no more worthy to be called thy son: make me as one of thy hired servants. 20. And he arose and came to his father.

1 Cor. 15.9. I am the least of the apostles, that am not meet to be called an apostle, because I persecuted the church of God.

2 Cor. 7.9. Ye sorrowed to repentance: for ye were made sorry after a godly manner, that ye might receive damage by us in nothing. 10. For godly sorrow worketh repentance to salvation not to be repented of: but the sorrow of the world worketh death. 11. For behold this selfsame thing, that ye sorrowed after a godly sort, what carefulness it wrought in you, yea, *what* clearing of yourselves, yea, *what* indignation, yea, *what* fear, yea, *what* vehement desire, yea, *what* zeal, yea, *what* revenge!

1 Pet. 2.25. Ye were as sheep going astray;

but are now returned unto the Shepherd and Bishop of your souls.

See CONVICTION OF SIN — AFFLICTION, BENEFITS EXEMPLIFIED—PARDON, PRAYER FOR.

REPHAIM (giants, see Deu. 2.11,20. Deu. 3.11,13. Jos. 12.4. Jos. 13.12. Jos. 17.15). Giants in Ashteroth, conquered by Chedorlaomer, Gen. 14.5. Land of, promised to Abraham, Gen. 15.20.

————, VALLEY OF, Isa. 17.5. Jos. 18.16.

REPHIDIM. See ISRAELITES, p. 254.

REPROOF. Lev. 19.17. Thou shalt in any wise rebuke thy neighbour, and not suffer sin upon him.

Psa. 141.5. Let the righteous smite me; *it shall be* a kindness: and let him reprove me; *it shall be* an excellent oil, *which* shall not break my head.

Pro. 9.8. Rebuke a wise man, and he will love thee.

Pro. 13.18. He that regardeth reproof shall be honoured.

Pro. 15.5. He that regardeth reproof is prudent. 31. The ear that heareth the reproof of life abideth among the wise. 32. He that heareth reproof getteth understanding.

Pro. 17.10. A reproof entereth more into a wise man than an hundred stripes into a fool.

Pro. 19.25. Smite a scorner, and the simple will beware: and reprove one that hath understanding, *and* he will understand knowledge.

Pro. 21.11. When the scorner is punished, the simple is made wise: and when the wise is instructed, he receiveth knowledge.

Pro. 25.12. *As* an earring of gold, and an ornament of fine gold, *so is* a wise reprover upon an obedient ear. *v.* 23.

Pro. 26.5. Answer a fool according to his folly, lest he be wise in his own conceit.

Pro. 27.5. Open rebuke *is* better than secret love. 6. Faithful *are* the wounds of a friend.

Pro. 28.23. He that rebuketh a man afterwards shall find more favour than he that flattereth with the tongue.

Ecc. 7.5. *It is* better to hear the rebuke of the wise, than for a man to hear the song of fools.

Eph. 4.15. Speaking the truth in love, may grow up into him in all things, which is the head, *even* Christ.

Eph. 5.11. Have no fellowship with the unfruitful works of darkness, but rather reprove *them.* 13. All things that are reproved are made manifest by the light.

Phil. 3.1. To write the same things to you, to me indeed *is* not grievous, but for you *it is* safe.

1 The. 5.14. Warn them that are unruly.

1 Tim. 5.1. Rebuke not an elder, but intreat *him* as a father; *and* the younger men as brethren; 2. The elder women as mothers; the younger as sisters, with all purity. 20. Them that sin rebuke before all, that others also may fear.

2 Tim. 4.2. Reprove, rebuke, exhort, with all long-suffering and doctrine.

Tit. 1.13. Rebuke them sharply, that they may be sound in the faith.

Heb. 3.13. Exhort one another daily, while it is called To day; lest any of you be hardened through the deceitfulness of sin.

REPROOF, FIDELITY IN GIVING, EXAMPLES

OF: Jacob, Gen. 30.2. Moses, Ex. 10.29. Ex. 11.8. Ex. 16.7. Ex. 32.19-30. Lev. 10. 16-18. Num. 14.41. Num. 16.9-11. Num. 20.10. Num. 32.14. Deu. 1.12,26-43. Deu. 9.16-24. Deu. 29.2-4. Deu. 31.27-29. Deu. 32.15-18.

Israelites, Jos. 22.15-20. Jud. 20.12,13. Samuel, 1 Sam. 15.14-35. Jonathan, 1 Sam. 19.4,5. Nathan, 2 Sam. 12.1-9. Joab, 2 Sam. 19.1-7. 2 Sam. 24.3. 1 Chr. 21.3,6. Gad, 2 Sam. 24.13. A prophet of Judah, 1 Kin. 13. 1-10. Elijah, 1 Kin. 18.18-21. 1 Kin. 21. 20-24. 2 Kin. 1. Micaiah, 1 Kin. 22.14-28.

Elisha, 2 Kin. 3.13,14. 2 Kin. 5.26. 2 Kin. 8.11-13. 2 Kin. 13.19. Isaiah, 2 Kin. 20.17. Joash, 2 Kin. 12.7. Shemaiah, 2 Chr. 12.5. Abijah, 2 Chr. 13.8-11. Azariah, 2 Chr. 15.2. Hanani, 2 Chr. 16.7-9. Jehu, 2 Chr. 19.2. Zechariah, 2 Chr. 24.20. Azariah, 2 Chr. 26. 17,18. Oded, 2 Chr. 28.9-11.

Ezra, Ezra 10.10. Nehemiah, Neh. 5.6-13. Neh. 13. Daniel, Dan. 4.27. Dan. 5.17-24. Amos, Amos 7.12-17. John, Mar. 6.18. Stephen, Act. 7.51-53. Paul, Act. 23.3.

See LOVE AND ZEAL OF PAUL—ZEAL FOR GOD'S GLORY—PRAYER, INTERCESSORY.

REPROOF HATED. Pro. 9.7. He that reproveth a scorner getteth to himself shame: and he that rebuketh a wicked *man getteth* himself a blot. 8. Reprove not a scorner, lest he hate thee.

Pro. 10.17. He that refuseth reproof erreth.

Pro. 12.1. He that hateth reproof *is* brutish.

Pro. 15.10. Correction *is* grievous unto him that forsaketh the way: *and* he that hateth reproof shall die. 12. A scorner loveth not one that reproveth him: neither will he go unto the wise.

Amos 5.10. They hate him that rebuketh in the gate, and they abhor him that speaketh uprightly.

Jno. 7.7. The world cannot hate you; but me it hateth, because I testify of it, that the works thereof are evil.

Gal. 4.16. Am I therefore become your enemy, because I tell you the truth?

Rev. 11.10. They that dwell upon the earth shall rejoice over them, and make merry, and shall send gifts one to another; because these two prophets tormented them that dwelt on the earth.

REPROOF HATED, EXAMPLES OF: Israelites, Num. 14.9,10. Ahab, 1 Kin. 18.17. 1 Kin. 21.20. 1 Kin. 22.8. Herodias, Mar. 6.18,19. Luk. 3.19,20. Men of Nazareth, Luk. 4.29. Jews, Act. 5.33. Act. 7.54. See SAINTS, ENMITY TO.

REPTILES. See ADDER, ASP, CAMELEON, COCKATRICE, DRAGON, FROG, HORSE-LEECH, LEVIATHAN, LIZARD, SCORPION, SERPENT, SNAIL, TORTOISE, VIPER, CREEPING THINGS.

RESIGNATION. Job 5.17. Happy *is* the man whom God correcteth: therefore despise not thou the chastening of the Almighty.

Job 34.31. Surely it is meet to be said unto God, I have borne *chastisement,* I will not offend *any more. v.* 34.

Psa. 46.10. Be still, and know that I *am* God. Psa. 4.4.

Pro. 3.11. My son, despise not the chastening of the Lord; neither be weary of his correction.

Pro. 18.14. The spirit of a man will sustain his infirmity.

Ecc. 7.14. In the day of prosperity be joyful, but in the day of adversity consider.

Isa. 24.15. Glorify ye the Lord in the fires.

Jer. 51.50. Ye that have escaped the sword, go away, stand not still: remember the Lord afar off, and let Jerusalem come into your mind.

Lam. 3.39. Wherefore doth a living man complain, a man for the punishment of his sins?

Mic. 6.9. The Lord's voice crieth unto the city, and *the man of* wisdom shall see thy name: hear ye the rod, and who hath appointed it.

Mat. 6.10. Thy will be done in earth, as *it is* in heaven.

Luk. 21.19. In your patience possess ye your souls.

Rom. 12.12. Rejoicing in hope; patient in tribulation; continuing instant in prayer.

Phil. 2.14. Do all things without murmurings.

Col. 1.11. Strengthened with all might, according to his glorious power, unto all patience and long-suffering with joyfulness.

1 The. 3.3. No man should be moved by these afflictions: for yourselves know that we are appointed thereunto.

2 Tim. 2.3. Endure hardness, as a good soldier of Jesus Christ.

2 Tim. 4.5. But watch thou in all things, endure afflictions.

Heb. 12.3. Consider him that endured such contradiction of sinners against himself, lest ye be wearied and faint in your minds. 4. Ye have not yet resisted unto blood, striving against sin. 5. And ye have forgotten the exhortation which speaketh unto you as unto children, My son, despise not thou the chastening of the Lord, nor faint when thou art rebuked of him. 9. We have had fathers of our flesh which corrected *us*, and we gave *them* reverence: shall we not much rather be in subjection unto the Father of spirits, and live? *v.* 6-12.

Jas. 1.10. Let the rich (*rejoice*) in that he is made low: because as the flower of the grass he shall pass away.

Jas. 4.7. Submit yourselves therefore to God.

1 Pet. 1.6. Wherein ye greatly rejoice, though now for a season, if need be, ye are in heaviness through manifold temptations.

1 Pet. 4.12. Beloved, think it not strange concerning the fiery trial which is to try you, as though some strange thing happened unto you: 13. But rejoice, inasmuch as ye are partakers of Christ's sufferings; that, when his glory shall be revealed, ye may be glad also with exceeding joy. 19. Let them that suffer according to the will of God commit the keeping of their souls to *him* in well doing, as unto a faithful Creator.

RESIGNATION EXEMPLIFIED. Lev. 10.3. And Aaron held his peace.

Jud. 10.15. We have sinned: do thou unto us whatsoever seemeth good unto thee.

1 Sam. 3.18. It *is* the Lord: let him do what seemeth him good.

2 Sam. 12.23. Now he is dead, wherefore should I fast? can I bring him back again? I shall go to him, but he shall not return to me.

2 Sam. 15.26. If he thus say, I have no delight in thee: behold, *here am* I, let him do to me as seemeth good unto him.

2 Sam. 16.10. So let him curse, because the Lord hath said unto him, Curse David. Who shall then say, Wherefore hast thou done so? 12. It may be that the Lord will look on mine affliction, and that the Lord will requite me good for his cursing this day.

2 Sam. 24.14. David said unto Gad, I am in a great strait: let us fall now into the hand of the Lord; for his mercies *are* great: and let me not fall into the hand of man.

2 Kin. 4.26. *Is it* well with the child? And she answered, It *is* well.

2 Kin. 20.19. Good *is* the word of the Lord which thou hast spoken. And he said, *Is it* not *good*, if peace and truth be in my days? Isa. 39.8.

Neh. 9.33. Howbeit thou *art* just in all that is brought upon us; for thou hast done right, but we have done wickedly.

Est. 4.16. If I perish, I perish.

Job 1.21. Naked came I out of my mother's womb, and naked shall I return thither: the Lord gave, and the Lord hath taken away; blessed be the name of the Lord. 22. In all this Job sinned not, nor charged God foolishly.

Job 2.10. What? shall we receive good at the hand of God, and shall we not receive evil? In all this did not Job sin with his lips.

Psa. 39.9. I was dumb, I opened not my mouth; because thou didst *it*.

Psa. 103.10. He hath not dealt with us after our sins, nor rewarded us according to our iniquities.

Psa. 119.75. I know, O Lord, that thy judgments *are* right, and *that* thou in faithfulness hast afflicted me.

Jer. 10.19. Woe is me for my hurt! my wound is grievous: but I said, Truly this *is* a grief, and I must bear it.

Lam. 1.18. The Lord is righteous; for I have rebelled against his commandment.

Dan. 9.14. Therefore hath the Lord watched upon the evil, and brought it upon us: for the Lord our God *is* righteous in all his works which he doeth: for we obeyed not his voice.

Mic. 7.9. I will bear the indignation of the Lord, because I have sinned against him, until he plead my cause, and execute judgment for me: he will bring me forth to the light, *and* I shall behold his righteousness.

Luk. 23.40. Dost not thou fear God, seeing thou art in the same condemnation? 41. And we indeed justly; for we receive the due reward of our deeds: but this man hath done nothing amiss.

Act. 21.14. When he would not be persuaded, we ceased, saying, The will of the Lord be done.

Rom. 5.3. We glory in tribulations also.

2 Cor. 6.9. As unknown, and *yet* well known; as dying, and, behold, we live; as chastened, and not killed. 10. As sorrowful, yet alway rejoicing; as poor, yet making many rich; as having nothing, and *yet* possessing all things. *v.* 3-10.

2 Cor. 7.4. I am filled with comfort, I am exceeding joyful in all our tribulation.

2 The. 1.4. We ourselves glory in you in the churches of God, for your patience and faith in all your persecutions and tribulations that ye endure.

Jas. 5.11. Behold, we count them happy which endure. Ye have heard of the patience of Job, and have seen the end of the Lord ; that the Lord is very pitiful, and of tender mercy.

See AFFLICTION, BENEFITS OF—MURMUR-ING—PERSECUTION.

RESPONSIBILITY. See JUDGMENT ACCORDING TO PRIVILEGE AND WORKS—SIN, PUNISHMENT OF.

RESURRECTION. Job 14.12. Man lieth down, and riseth not : till the heavens be no more, they shall not awake, nor be raised out of their sleep. 13. O that thou wouldest hide me in the grave, that thou wouldest keep me secret, until thy wrath be past, that thou wouldest appoint me a set time, and remember me ! 14. If a man die, shall he live again ? all the days of my appointed time will I wait, till my change come. 15. Thou shalt call, and I will answer thee : thou wilt have a desire to the work of thine hands.

Job 19.25. I know that my redeemer liveth, and that he shall stand at the latter day upon the earth : 26. And though after my skin worms destroy this body, yet in my flesh shall I see God : 27. Whom I shall see for myself, and mine eyes shall behold, and not another ; though my reins be consumed within me.

Psa. 16.9. My heart is glad, and my glory rejoiceth : my flesh also shall rest in hope. 10. For thou wilt not leave my soul in hell ; neither wilt thou suffer thine Holy One to see corruption.

Psa. 17.15. As for me, I will behold thy face in righteousness : I shall be satisfied, when I awake, with thy likeness.

Psa. 49.15. God will redeem my soul from the power of the grave : for he shall receive me.

Isa. 25.8. He will swallow up death in victory ; and the Lord God will wipe away tears from off all faces.

Isa. 26.19. Thy dead men shall live, together with my dead body shall they arise. Awake and sing, ye that dwell in dust : for thy dew is as the dew of herbs, and the earth shall cast out the dead.

Eze. 37.12. Behold, O my people, I will open your graves, and cause you to come up out of your graves, and bring you into the land of Israel. v. 1-14.

Dan. 12.2. Many of them that sleep in the dust of the earth shall awake, some to ever-lasting life, and some to shame and everlasting contempt. 13. Go thou thy way till the end be : for thou shalt rest, and stand in thy lot at the end of the days.

Hos. 13.14. I will ransom them from the power of the grave ; I will redeem them from death : O death, I will be thy plagues ; O grave, I will be thy destruction.

Mat. 27.52. The graves were opened ; and many bodies of the saints which slept arose, 53. And came out of the graves after his resurrection, and went into the holy city, and appeared unto many.

Luk. 14.14. Thou shalt be recompensed at the resurrection of the just.

Luk. 20.35. They which shall be accounted worthy to obtain that world, and the resurrection from the dead, neither marry, nor are given in marriage : 36. Neither can they die

any more : for they are equal unto the angels ; and are the children of God, being the children of the resurrection. 37. Now that the dead are raised, even Moses shewed at the bush, when he calleth the Lord the God of Abraham, and the God of Isaac, and the God of Jacob. 38. For he is not a God of the dead, but of the living : for all live unto him. Mat. 22.30-32. Mar. 12.25-27.

Jno. 11.23. Jesus saith unto her, Thy brother shall rise again. 24. Martha saith unto him, I know that he shall rise again in the resurrection at the last day.

Act. 17.32. When they heard of the resur-rection of the dead, some mocked : and others said, We will hear thee again of this matter.

Act. 23.6. I am a Pharisee, the son of a Pharisee : of the hope and resurrection of the dead I am called in question. 8. The Sadducees say that there is no resurrection, neither angel, nor spirit ; but the Pharisees confess both.

Act. 24.15. There shall be a resurrection of the dead, both of the just and unjust.

Act. 26.8. Why should it be thought a thing incredible with you, that God should raise the dead ?

Rom. 4.17. God, who quickeneth the dead.

Rom. 8.19. The earnest expectation of the creature waiteth for the manifestation of the sons of God. 21. The creature itself also shall be delivered from the bondage of corruption into the glorious liberty of the children of God. 23. Not only they, but ourselves also, which have the firstfruits of the Spirit, even we our-selves groan within ourselves, waiting for the adoption, to wit, the redemption of our body.

1 Cor. 6.14. God hath both raised up the Lord, and will also raise up us by his own power.

1 Cor. 15.32. What advantageth it me, if the dead rise not ? let us eat and drink ; for to morrow we die. 40. There are also celestial bodies, and bodies terrestrial : but the glory of the celestial is one, and the glory of the terrestrial is another. 42. So also is the resurrection of the dead. It is sown in corruption ; it is raised in incorruption : 43. It is sown in dishonour ; it is raised in glory : it is sown in weakness ; it is raised in power : 44. It is sown a natural body ; it is raised a spiritual body. There is a natural body, and there is a spiritual body.

1 Cor. 15.46. That was not first which is spiritual, but that which is natural ; and after-ward that which is spiritual. 48. As is the earthy, such are they also that are earthy : and as is the heavenly, such are they also that are heavenly. 49. And as we have borne the image of the earthy, we shall also bear the image of the heavenly. 50. Now this I say, brethren, that flesh and blood cannot inherit the kingdom of God ; neither doth corruption inherit incorruption.

1 Cor. 15.52. In a moment, in the twink-ling of an eye, at the last trump : for the trumpet shall sound, and the dead shall be raised incorruptible, and we shall be changed. 53. For this corruptible must put on incor-ruption, and this mortal must put on immor-tality. 54. So when this corruptible shall have put on incorruption, and this mortal

shall have put on immortality, then shall be brought to pass the saying that is written, Death is swallowed up in victory. *v.* 12-54.

2 Cor. 1.9. We had the sentence of death in ourselves, that we should not trust in ourselves, but in God which raiseth the dead.

2 Cor. 5.1. A building of God, an house not made with hands, eternal in the heavens. 2. Earnestly desiring to be clothed upon with our house which is from heaven: 3. If so be that being clothed, we shall not be found naked. 4. For we that are in *this* tabernacle do groan, being burdened: not for that we would be unclothed, but clothed upon, that mortality might be swallowed up of life.

2 Cor. 13.4. We shall live with him by the power of God.

Eph. 4.30. Grieve not the Holy Spirit of God, whereby ye are sealed unto the day of redemption.

Phil. 3.11. If by any means I might attain unto the resurrection of the dead.

Col. 3.4. When Christ, *who is* our life, shall appear, then shall ye also appear with him in glory.

1 The. 4.14. We believe that Jesus died and rose again, even so them also which sleep in Jesus will God bring with him. 15. We which are alive *and* remain unto the coming of the Lord shall not prevent them which are asleep. 16. For the Lord himself shall descend from heaven with a shout, with the voice of the archangel, and with the trump of God: and the dead in Christ shall rise first: 17. Then we which are alive *and* remain shall be caught up together with them in the clouds, to meet the Lord in the air: and so shall we ever be with the Lord.

2 Tim. 2.18. Who concerning the truth have erred, saying that the resurrection is past already; and overthrow the faith of some.

Heb. 6.2. The doctrine of, . . . : . resurrection of the dead.

Heb. 11.35. Women received their dead raised to life again: and others were tortured, not accepting deliverance; that they might obtain a better resurrection.

Rev. 20.6. Blessed and holy *is* he that hath part in the first resurrection: on such the second death hath no power; but they shall be priests of God and of Christ, and shall reign with him a thousand years. 13. The sea gave up the dead which were in it; and death and hell delivered up the dead which were in them: and they were judged every man according to their works.

RESURRECTION. By Christ and the Holy Spirit. Jno. 5.21. As the Father raiseth up the dead, and quickeneth *them;* even so the Son quickeneth whom he will. 25. The hour is coming, and now is, when the dead shall hear the voice of the Son of God: and they that hear shall live. 28. The hour is coming, in the which all that are in the graves shall hear his voice, 29. And shall come forth; they that have done good, unto the resurrection of life; and they that have done evil, unto the resurrection of damnation.

Jno. 6.39. This is the Father's will which hath sent me, that of all which he hath given me I should lose nothing, but should raise it up again at the last day. 44. No man can come to me, except the Father which hath sent

me draw him: and I will raise him up at the last day. 54. Whoso eateth my flesh, and drinketh my blood, hath eternal life; and I will raise him up at the last day.

Jno. 11.25. I am the resurrection, and the life: he that believeth in me, though he were dead, yet shall he live.

Jno. 14.19. Because I live, ye shall live also.

Act. 4.2. They preached through Jesus the resurrection from the dead.

Rom. 8.10. If Christ *be* in you, the body *is* dead because of sin; but the Spirit *is* life because of righteousness. 11. If the Spirit of him that raised up Jesus from the dead dwell in you, he that raised up Christ from the dead shall also quicken your mortal bodies by his Spirit that dwelleth in you.

1 Cor. 15.23. Every man in his own order: Christ the firstfruits; afterward they that are Christ's at his coming.

2 Cor. 4.14. He which raised up the Lord Jesus shall raise up us also by Jesus, and shall present *us* with you.

Phil. 3.21. Who shall change our vile body, that it may be fashioned like unto his glorious body, according to the working whereby he is able even to subdue all things unto himself.

2 Tim. 1.10. Our Saviour Jesus Christ, who hath abolished death, and hath brought life and immortality to light through the gospel.

Rev. 1.18. I am he that liveth, and was dead; and, behold, I am alive for evermore, Amen; and have the keys of hell and of death.

See CHRIST'S SECOND COMING—JUDGMENT-DAY—SOUL OF MAN IMMORTAL.

REUBEN, eldest son of Jacob and Leah, Gen. 29.32. 1 Chr. 2.1. Brings mandrakes to his mother, Gen. 30.14. His incest, Gen. 35.22. Gen. 49.4. Forfeits the birthright, 1 Chr. 5.1. Intercedes for Joseph; his grief on missing him, Gen. 37.21,22,29,30. Reproaches his brothers before Joseph, Gen. 42.22. Offers his sons as sureties for Benjamin, Gen. 42.37. Jacob's last words to him, Gen. 49.3,4. His children, Gen. 46.9. Ex. 6.14. 1 Chr. 5.3-6.

————, TRIBE OF. Numbered at Sinai, Num. 1.20,21; and in the plains of Moab, Num. 26.7. Led the 2d division of Israel, and encamped south of the tabernacle, Num. 2.10. Num. 10.18. Blessing of Moses on, Deu. 33.6. Possess many cattle; their inheritance east of Jordan, on the conquest of Og, king of Bashan, Num. 32. Deu. 3.1-20. Jos. 13.15-23. Jos. 18.7.

Aid in conquering Palestine, Jos. 1.12-18. Jos. 4.12. Jos. 22.1-6. Assist in building the altar of witness, Jos. 22.10-29. Reproved for not aiding against Sisera, Jud. 5.15,16. Conquer the Hagarites, 1 Chr. 5.10,18-22. Invaded by Hazael, 2 Kin. 10.33. Taken captive by Tiglath, 2 Kin. 15.29. 1 Chr. 5.6,26. For things common to the tribes, see ISRAEL, TRIBES OF.

REVENGE. See MALICE — MURDER — FORGIVENESS.

REWARDS. See HEAVEN—JUDGMENT ACCORDING TO WORKS—GOD'S FAVOUR.

REZEPH, a town west of the Euphrates, conquered by Sennacherib, 2 Kin. 19.12. Isa. 37.12.

REZIN, king of Syria, 2 Kin. 15.37. Besieges Jerusalem; captures Elath; slain by Tiglath, 2 Kin. 16.5-9. Isa. 7.1-8. Prophecy against, Isa. c. 7, 8, & 9.

REZON, an Edomite, becomes king of Damascus; an enemy of Solomon, 1 Kin. 11. 23-25.

RHEGIUM, a city on the south-west coast of Italy, visited by Paul, Act. 28.13.

RHODA, a Christian female in Jerusalem, Act. 12.13-15.

RHODES, an island in the Mediterranean, visited by Paul, Act. 21.1.

RIBBAND, Num. 15.38; elsewhere translated *lace*, Ex. 28.28; *bracelets*, Gen. 38.18.

RIBLAH, a town in north Palestine, Num. 34.11. Jehoahaz imprisoned in, by Pharaoh, 2 Kin. 23.33. Zedekiah brought to Nebuchadnezzar in, 2 Kin. 25.6,20,21. Jer. 39.5,6. Jer. 52.9,26.

RICHES, Danger of. See Covetousness.

RICHES, Value of. Deu. 12.7. Ye shall eat before the Lord your God, and ye shall rejoice in all that ye put your hand unto, ye and your households, wherein the Lord thy God hath blessed thee.

Pro. 13.8. The ransom of a man's life *are* his riches.

Pro. 14.24. The crown of the wise *is* their riches.

Ecc. 2.24. *There is* nothing better for a man, *than* that he should eat and drink, and *that* he should make his soul enjoy good in his labour. This also I saw, that it *was* from the hand of God.

Ecc. 3.12. *There is* no good in them, but for *a man* to rejoice, and to do good in his life. 13. And also that every man should eat and drink, and enjoy the good of all his labour, it *is* the gift of God. 22. *There is* nothing better, than that a man should rejoice in his own works; for that *is his* portion.

Ecc. 5.18. *It is* good and comely *for one* to eat and to drink, and to enjoy the good of all his labour that he taketh under the sun all the days of his life, which God giveth him: for it *is* his portion. 19. Every man also to whom God hath given riches and wealth, and hath given him power to eat thereof, and to take his portion, and to rejoice in his labour; this *is* the gift of God. 20. For he shall not much remember the days of his life; because God answereth *him* in the joy of his heart.

Ecc. 7.11. Wisdom *is* good with an inheritance: and *by it there is* profit to them that see the sun. 12. For wisdom *is* a defence, *and* money *is* a defence: but the excellency of knowledge *is, that* wisdom giveth life to them that have it.

Ecc. 10.19. Money answereth all things.

Isa. 23.18. Her merchandise and her hire shall be holiness to the Lord: it shall not be treasured nor laid up; for her merchandise shall be for them that dwell before the Lord, to eat sufficiently, and for durable clothing.

Isa. 45.3. I will give thee the treasures of darkness, and hidden riches of secret places, that thou mayest know that I, the Lord, which call *thee* by thy name, *am* the God of Israel.

Mic. 4.13. I will consecrate their gain unto the Lord, and their substance unto the Lord of the whole earth.

Luk. 16.9. Make to yourselves friends of the mammon of unrighteousness; that, when ye fail, they may receive you into everlasting habitations. *v.* 1-12.

1 Tim. 6.17. Charge them that are rich in this world, that they be not highminded, nor trust in uncertain riches, but in the living God, who giveth us richly all things to enjoy; 18. That they do good, that they be rich in good works, ready to distribute, willing to communicate; 19. Laying up in store for themselves a good foundation against the time to come, that they may lay hold on eternal life.

See Liberality—Thankfulness—Covetousness—God's goodness in providence.

RIDDLE. Of Samson, Jud. 14.12-18. Of Ezekiel, Eze. 17. Of the queen of Sheba (hard questions), 1 Kin. 10.1. 2 Chr. 9.1. Translated dark sayings or sentences, Psa. 49.4. Psa. 78.2. Pro. 1.6. Dan. 8.23; proverb, Hab. 2.6. See Pro. 30.15. Isa. 21.12. Rev. 13.18. See Parables—Proverbs.

RIGHTEOUSNESS. See Holiness—Integrity—Obedience—Sanctification—Justification—Self-righteousness.

RIMMON (pomegranate, see 1 Sam. 14.2), a town or rock near Gibeah, where the Benjamites took refuge, Jud. 20.45-47. Jud. 21.13.

———, a Syrian idol, 2 Kin. 5.18.

RING. Of gold, set with gems, Song 5.14. Worn on the hand by men and women, Ex. 35.22. Num. 31.50. Isa. 3.21. Given by Pharaoh to Joseph in making him governor, Gen. 41.42. By Ahasuerus, for sealing decrees, to Haman, Est. 3.10,12; to Mordecai, Est. 8.2-10. Worn in the nose, Isa. 3.21. Pro. 11.22. Offerings of, Ex. 35.22. Num. 31.50. Of gold, Ex. 28.23. Of silver, Est. 1.6. Of brass, Ex. 27.4.

RIVER, The. See Nile.

RIVERS. Overflow of, Jos. 3.15. 1 Chr. 12.15. Jer. 50.44. Amos 8.8. Vegetation on, Ex. 2.3,5. Num. 24.6. Job 40.22. Psa. 1.3. Isa. 19.7. Isa. 32.20. Jer. 17.8. Eze. 47.7,12. Resort of wild animals, Psa. 42.1. Jer. 49.19. Zec. 11.3. Illustrative, Psa. 36.8. Psa. 46.4. Jno. 7.38. Symbolical, Eze. 47.1-12. Rev. 8.10. Rev. 16.4. Rev. 22.1,2.

See Abana, Ahava, Arnon, Chebar, Euphrates, Gihon, Gozan, Hiddekel, Nile, Pharpar, Pison, Sihor, Ulai. See also Palestine, rivers of.

RIZPAH, Saul's concubine; her maternal affection, 2 Sam. 21.8-11.

ROAD (inroad), 1 Sam. 27.10.

ROADS, Jos. 10.10. 1 Sam. 4.13. 1 Kin. 20.38. 2 Kin. 11.19. 2 Kin. 25.4. Public highways or causeways, Lev. 26.22. Deu. 2. 27. Jud. 20.31. 1 Sam. 6.12. 1 Chr. 26. 16,18. King's highway, Num. 20.17. Num. 21.22. Byways, Jud. 5.6. Paths in vineyards, &c., Num. 22.24. Mar. 4.4. Marked by heaps of stones, 1 Sam. 20.19 (*marg.*), Jer. 31. 21. Prepared for kings, &c., Isa. 40.3,4. Isa. 62.10. Mal. 3.1. Made to the cities of refuge, Deu. 19.2,3.

ROBBERY. See Dishonesty.

ROBE. See Dress.

ROCK, water brought from, Deu. 8.15. Illustrative, Deu. 32.4. 2 Sam. 23.3. Psa. 31.2. Psa. 40.2. Isa. 17.10. Isa. 32.2. 1 Cor. 10.4. Mat. 16.18. See MOUNTAINS—STONE—MERIBAH.

ROD OR STAFF. Of Moses, Ex. 4.2-4,17,20. Ex. 7.20. Ex. 14.16. Ex. 17.9. Num. 20. 8-11. Of Aaron, Ex. 7.9-12. Num. 17.3-10. Of the princes of tribes, Num. 17.2-9. Passing under the rod, Lev. 27.32. Jer. 33.13. Eze. 20.37. Illustrative, 2 Sam. 7.14. Job 21.9. Mic. 6.9. Psa. 23.4. Mic. 7.14. Psa. 74.2. Psa. 110.2. Isa. 10.5,15,24,26. Isa. 11.1,4. Pro. 14.3. Symbolical, Jer. 1.11. Rev. 11.1. See SCEPTRE.

ROE, ROEBUCK. See DEER.

ROLLS. See BOOKS—GENEALOGIES.

ROME, strangers from, at Jerusalem in Pentecost, Act. 2.10. Jews banished from, by Claudius, Act. 18.2. Paul's purpose to visit, Act. 19.21. Rom. 1.15. Act. 23.11. Paul a prisoner in, 2 years, Act. 28.14-21. Onesiphorus aids Paul in, 2 Tim. 1.16,17. Prophecies of, Dan. 2.31-43. Dan. 7, see Mat. 24.15. Dan. 12.11. Dan. 9.27. Converts in, Rom. 16.5-17. Phil. 1.12-18. Phil. 4.22. 2 Tim. 4.21.

Emperors of, see CESAR. Roman governors and kings of Palestine, see HEROD I., ARCHELAUS, HEROD II., LYSANIAS, PHILIP, PILATE, HEROD III., FELIX, FESTUS, AGRIPPA.

Roman law of citizenship, see CITIZENS. Right of appeal to Cesar, Act. 25.10,21. Treatment of prisoners, Act 25.16. Act. 28. 16,30.

ROOFS OF HOUSES. Flat, Jos. 2.6. Jud. 16.27. 1 Sam. 9.25. 2 Sam. 11.2. 2 Sam. 16.22. Isa. 15.3. Mat. 24.17. Luk. 12.3. Battlements round, Deu. 22.8. Prayers offered on, Act. 10.9. Idolatrous altars on, 2 Kin. 23.12. Jer. 19.13. Jer. 32.29. Zeph. 1.5. Booths made on, Neh. 8.16.

ROOM. See HOUSE.

ROPES AND CORDS, Jos. 2.15,21. Jud. 16.11,12. 2 Sam. 17.13. Jer. 38.6-13. Eze. 27.24. Jno. 2.15. Threefold, Ecc. 4.12. Used for tents, Ex. 35.18. Isa. 33.20. Isa. 54.2. Jer. 10.20 ; carts, Isa. 5.18 ; boats, Act. 27. 32 ; binding sacrifices, Psa. 118.27. Gen. 22. 9 ; in casting lots, Mic. 2.5. Put on the head in token of submission, 1 Kin. 20.31,32. Illustrative, Job 36.8. Psa. 2 3. Psa. 140.5. Pro. 5.22. Isa. 5.18. Hos. 11.4.

ROSE, Isa. 35.1. Of Sharon, Song 2.1.

RUBY, Lam. 4.7. Job 28.18. Pro. 20.15.

RUE, a plant, Luk. 11.42.

RUFUS, son of Simon, Mar. 15.21. A disciple, Rom. 16.13.

RULERS. Patriarchal, Gen. 4.13-15,23,24. Nimrod, Gen. 10.8-10. Abraham, Gen. 14. 13-24. Gen. 21.10,14. Melchizedek, Gen. 14. 18. Isaac, Gen. 21.21-32. Gen. 26.26-31. Judah, Gen. 38.24. Officers of Israel, Ex. 5. 15. Heads of houses, Ex. 6.14. Ishmael and descendants, Gen. 17.20. Esau, and Edomite dukes, Gen. 36.

Moses, Ex. 18.13-26. Princes of Israel, Num. 16.2. Rulers of thousands, &c., Ex. 18. 25,26. Deu. 1.15. Officers and judges, Deu. 16.18. Deu. 19.17,18. 2 Chr. 19.5-7. Ezr. 7.25. See ELDERS — ISRAELITES, TRIBES OF —

CAPTAIN. During and after the captivity, see GEDALIAH, ZERUBBABEL, NEHEMIAH. Under the Romans, see HEROD, AGRIPPA, PILATE, FELIX, FESTUS, TETRARCH.

See KINGS—PRIESTS, THE HIGH-PRIEST'S JUDICIAL AUTHORITY—PRIESTS—LEVITES—SANHEDRIM—SYNAGOGUE—JUSTICE, ADMINISTRATION OF.

RULERS. DIVINELY APPOINTED AND DETHRONED. 1 Sam. 10.25. Job 12.18-21. Psa. 47.9. Psa. 76.12. Psa. 107.40. Pro. 8. 15,16. Isa. 40.23. Eze. 17.22-24. Eze. 21. 25-27. Dan. 2.21. Hos. 13.11. Hag. 2.21,22. Rom. 13.1,2,4,16.

EXAMPLES OF : Seventy elders, Num. 11. 16,17. Joshua, Num. 27.18-23. Judah, 1 Chr. 5.2. Psa. 60.7. Saul, 1 Sam 9.16,17. 1 Sam. 10.1,24. 1 Sam. 15.17,26. David, 1 Sam. 15.28. 1 Sam. 16.1,12. 1 Chr. 28.4. Psa. 78.70,71. Solomon, 1 Kin. 2.15. 1 Chr. 22.9,10. 1 Chr. 28.5-7. 1 Chr. 29.25. 2 Chr. 2.11. Jeroboam, 1 Kin. 11.11-13,29-38. 1 Kin. 14.7,8. Baasha, 1 Kin. 16.2. Jehu, 1 Kin. 19.16. 2 Kin. 9.2. Hazael, 1 Kin. 19. 15. Eliakim, Isa. 22.21-24. Cyrus, Isa. 41. 2,25. Isa. 45.1-4. Isa. 46.11, Nebuchadnezzar, Dan. 4.

See GOD A KING — GOD'S PROVIDENCE OVERRULING. See NEXT SUBJECT.

RULERS, DUTIES OF. Gen. 41.33. Let Pharaoh look out a man discreet and wise, and set him over the land of Egypt.

Ex. 18.16. When they have a matter, they come unto me ; and I judge between one and another, and I do make *them* know the statutes of God, and his laws. 20. And thou shalt teach them ordinances and laws, and shalt shew them the way wherein they must walk, and the work that they must do. 21. Provide out of all the people able men, such as fear God, men of truth, hating covetousness ; and place *such* over them. Ezr. 7.25.

Ex. 23.3. Neither shalt thou countenance a poor man in his cause. 6. Thou shalt not wrest the judgment of thy poor in his cause. 7. Keep thee far from a false matter ; and the innocent and righteous slay thou not : for I will not justify the wicked. *v.* 8,9.

Lev. 19.15. Ye shall do no unrighteousness in judgment : thou shalt not respect the person of the poor, nor honour the person of the mighty : *but* in righteousness shalt thou judge thy neighbour.

Lev. 24.22. Have one manner of law, as well for the stranger, as for one of your own country : for I *am* the Lord your God.

Num. 27.16. Let the Lord, the God of the spirits of all flesh, set a man over the congregation, 17. Which may go out before them, and which may go in before them, and which may lead them out, and which may bring them in ; that the congregation of the Lord be not as sheep which have no shepherd.

Deu. 1.16. Hear the *causes* between your brethren, and judge righteously between *every* man and his brother, and the stranger *that is* with him. 17. Ye shall not respect persons in judgment ; *but* ye shall hear the small as well as the great ; ye shall not be afraid of the face of man ; for the judgment *is* God's.

Deu. 16.18. Judges and officers shalt thou make thee in all thy gates, which the Lord thy God giveth thee, throughout thy tribes and

they shall judge the people with just judgment.
19. Thou shalt not wrest judgment; thou shalt
not respect persons, neither take a gift: for a
gift doth blind the eyes of the wise, and
pervert the words of the righteous. 20. That
which is altogether just shalt thou follow,
that thou mayest live, and inherit the land
which the Lord thy God giveth thee.

Deu. 17.18. When he sitteth upon the
throne of his kingdom, that he shall write him
a copy of this law in a book out of *that which
is* before the priests the Levites: 19. And it
shall be with him, and he shall read therein
all the days of his life. *v.* 20. Jos. 1.8.

Deu. 19.18. The judges shall make diligent
inquisition.

Deu. 24.16. The fathers shall not be put
to death for the children, neither shall the
children be put to death for the fathers: every
man shall be put to death for his own sin.

Deu. 25.1. If there be a controversy between men, and they come unto judgment,
that *the judges* may judge them; then they
shall justify the righteous, and condemn the
wicked.

2 Sam. 23.3. He that ruleth over men *must
be* just, ruling in the fear of God. 4. And *he
shall be* as the light of the morning, *when* the
sun riseth.

2 Chr. 2.11. Therefore made he thee king,
to do judgment and justice.

2 Chr. 19.6. Take heed what ye do: for ye
judge not for man, but for the Lord, who *is*
with you in the judgment. 7. Wherefore now
let the fear of the Lord be upon you; take
heed and do *it*: for *there is* no iniquity with
the Lord our God, nor respect of persons, nor
taking of gifts.

Psa. 2.10. Be wise now therefore, O ye
kings: be instructed, ye judges of the earth.
11. Serve the Lord with fear, and rejoice with
trembling. *v.* 12.

Psa. 72.10. The kings of Tarshish and of
the isles shall bring presents: the kings of
Sheba and Seba shall offer gifts. 11. Yea, all
kings shall fall down before him.

Psa. 82.3. Defend the poor and fatherless:
do justice to the afflicted and needy. 4. Deliver the poor and needy: rid *them* out of the
hand of the wicked.

Psa. 148.11. Kings of the earth, princes,
and all judges of the earth. 13. Let them
praise the name of the Lord.

Pro. 16.10. A divine sentence *is* in the lips
of the king: his mouth transgresseth not in
judgment. 12. *It is* an abomination to kings
to commit wickedness: for the throne is established by righteousness. 13. Righteous lips
are the delight of kings; and they love him
that speaketh right.

Pro. 17.7. Excellent speech becometh not a
fool: much less do lying lips a prince.

Pro. 20.8. A king that sitteth in the throne
of judgment scattereth away all evil with his
eyes. 26. A wise king scattereth the wicked,
and bringeth the wheel over them. 28. Mercy
and truth preserve the king: and his throne
is upholden by mercy.

Pro. 25.2. The honour of kings *is* to search
out a matter. 3. The heaven for height, and
the earth for depth, and the heart of kings *is*
unsearchable. 5. Take away the wicked *from*
before the king, and his throne shall be established in righteousness. Pro. 24.23-26.

Pro. 28.2. For the transgression of a land
many *are* the princes thereof: but by a man
of understanding *and* knowledge the state
thereof shall be prolonged. 16. He that hateth
covetousness shall prolong *his* days.

Pro. 29.2. When the righteous are in authority, the people rejoice: but when the wicked
beareth rule, the people mourn. 14. The king
that faithfully judgeth the poor, his throne
shall be established for ever.

Pro. 31.4. *It is* not for kings, O Lemuel, *it
is* not for kings to drink wine; nor for princes
strong drink: 5. Lest they drink, and forget
the law, and pervert the judgment of any of
the afflicted. 8. Open thy mouth for the dumb
in the cause of all such as are appointed to
destruction. 9. Open thy mouth, judge righteously, and plead the cause of the poor and
needy.

Ecc. 8.4. Where the word of a king *is,
there is* power: and who may say unto him,
What doest thou?

Ecc. 10.17. Blessed *art* thou, O land, when
thy king *is* the son of nobles, and thy princes
eat in due season, for strength, and not for
drunkenness!

Isa. 16.5. In mercy shall the throne be
established: and he shall sit upon it in truth
in the tabernacle of David, judging, and seeking judgment, and hasting righteousness.

Isa. 28.6. For a spirit of judgment to him
that sitteth in judgment, and for strength to
them that turn the battle to the gate.

Isa. 49.23. Kings shall be thy nursing
fathers, and their queens thy nursing mothers.

Isa. 58.6. To loose the bands of wickedness,
to undo the heavy burdens, and to let the oppressed go free, and that ye break every yoke.

Isa. 60.17. I will also make thy officers
peace, and thine exactors righteousness.

Jer. 13.18. Say unto the king and to the
queen, Humble yourselves, sit down: for your
principalities shall come down, *even* the crown
of your glory.

Jer. 22.3. Execute ye judgment and
righteousness, and deliver the spoiled out of
the hand of the oppressor: and do no wrong,
do no violence to the stranger, the fatherless,
nor the widow, neither shed innocent blood in
this place. Jer. 21.12.

Zec. 7.10. Oppress not the widow, nor the
fatherless, the stranger, nor the poor.

Zec. 8.16. Speak ye every man the truth to
his neighbour; execute the judgment of truth
and peace in your gates.

Rom. 13.3. Rulers are not a terror to good
works, but to the evil. *v.* 1-16.

1 Tim. 2.2. For kings, and *for* all that are
in authority; that we may lead a quiet and
peaceable life in all godliness and honesty.

1 Pet. 2.14. Governors, as unto them that
are sent by him for the punishment of evildoers, and for the praise of them that do
well.

RULERS, GOOD AND WISE, EXAMPLES OF:
Joseph, Gen. 47. Moses, Ex. 18.13-18. Psa.
78.72. Elders of Israel, Num. 7. Joshua,
Jos. 23. Jos. 24. Deborah, Jud. 4.4. Gideon,
Jud. 8.23. Jephthah, Jud. 11.11. Samson,
Jud. 13.5. Samuel, 1 Sam. 12.3-5. Saul,
1 Sam. 11.13. 1 Sam. 14.37-52. David,
2 Sam. 4.8-12. 2 Sam. 8.15. Psa. 101.5-8.
Solomon, 1 Kin. 1.52. 1 Kin. 3. 1 Kin. 10.
6-8. Hiram, 1 Kin. 5.1. Rehoboam, 2 Chr.

11.23.   Asa, 1 Kin. 15.11.   Obadiah, 1 Kin. 18.3.   Jehoshaphat, 1 Kin. 22.43.   Jehu, 2 Kin. 10.30.   Amaziah (Judah), 2 Kin. 14.3. Uzziah, 2 Chr. 26.4,5.   Jotham, 2 Kin. 15.34. Hezekiah, 2 Kin. 18.3.   2 Kin. 20.20.   Josiah, 2 Kin. 22.2.   2 Kin. 23.25.   Jer. 22.15,16. Jehoiada, 2 Chr. 24.2,16,22.   Cyrus, Ezr. 1. Nehemiah, Neh. c. 4 & 5.   Hanani, Neh. 7.2. Ahasuerus, Est. 6.3,10.   Esther, Est. 9.29. Mordecai, Est. 10.3.   Ezra, Ezr. 7.25.   Job, Job 29.12-17.   Daniel, Dan. 6.2.   Zerubbabel, Hag. 1.12,14.

RULERS, INJUSTICE AND WICKEDNESS OF. Gen. 15.13. They shall afflict them four hundred years: 14. And also that nation, whom they shall serve, will I judge.

Ex. 3.9. The cry of the children of Israel is come unto me: and I have also seen the oppression wherewith the Egyptians oppress them.

Deu. 27.19. Cursed be he that perverteth the judgment of the stranger, fatherless, and widow.

1 Sam. 8.11. This will be the manner of the king that shall reign over you: He will take your sons, and appoint them for himself, for his chariots, and to be his horsemen.   18. And ye shall cry out in that day because of your king which ye shall have chosen you; and the Lord will not hear you in that day. v. 12-17.

2 Kin. 9.19. What hast thou to do with peace.

2 Chr. 28.19. The Lord brought Judah low because of Ahaz king of Israel; for he made Judah naked, and transgressed sore against the Lord.

Neh. 5.9. It is not good that ye do: ought ye not to walk in the fear of our God, because of the reproach of the heathen our enemies?

Neh. 9.37. It yieldeth much increase unto the kings whom thou hast set over us because of our sins; also they have dominion over our bodies, and over our cattle, at their pleasure, and we are in great distress.

Job 9.24. The earth is given into the hand of the wicked: he covereth the faces of the judges thereof.

Job 13.10. He will surely reprove you, if ye do secretly accept persons.

Job 24.22. He riseth up, and no man is sure of life.   24. They are exalted for a little while, but are gone and brought low; they are taken out of the way as all other, and cut off as the tops of the ears of corn.

Job 35.9. By reason of the multitude of oppressions they make the oppressed to cry: they cry out by reason of the arm of the mighty.

Psa. 10.2. The wicked in his pride doth persecute the poor: let them be taken in the devices that they have imagined.   17. Thou wilt cause thine ear to hear: 18. To judge the fatherless and the oppressed, that the man of the earth may no more oppress. v. 2-10.

Psa. 12.5. For the oppression of the poor, for the sighing of the needy, now will I rise, saith the Lord; I will set him in safety from him that puffeth at him.   8. The wicked walk on every side, when the vilest men are exalted.

Psa. 49.20. Man that is in honour, and understandeth not, is like the beasts that perish.

Psa. 58.2. Yea, in heart ye work wickedness; ye weigh the violence of your hands in the earth.

Psa. 72.4. He shall save the children of the needy, and shall break in pieces the oppressor.

Psa. 82.1. God standeth in the congregation of the mighty; he judgeth among the gods.   2. How long will ye judge unjustly, and accept the persons of the wicked? v. 6,7.

Psa. 94.20. Shall the throne of iniquity have fellowship with thee, which frameth mischief by a law?   21. They gather themselves together against the soul of the righteous, and condemn the innocent blood.

Psa. 110.5. The Lord at thy right hand shall strike through kings in the day of his wrath.

Pro. 3.31. Envy thou not the oppressor, and choose none of his ways.   32. For the froward is abomination to the Lord.

Pro. 17.15. He that justifieth the wicked, and he that condemneth the just, even they both are abomination to the Lord.   26. To punish the just is not good, nor to strike princes for equity.

Pro. 18.5. It is not good to accept the person of the wicked, to overthrow the righteous in judgment.

Pro. 22.16. He that oppresseth the poor to increase his riches, shall surely come to want. 22. Rob not the poor, because he is poor: neither oppress the afflicted in the gate: 23. For the Lord will plead their cause, and spoil the soul of those that spoiled them.

Pro. 24.24. He that saith unto the wicked, Thou art righteous; him shall the people curse, nations shall abhor him. v. 23.

Pro. 28.3. A poor man that oppresseth the poor is like a sweeping rain which leaveth no food.   15. As a roaring lion, and a ranging bear; so is a wicked ruler over the poor people.   16. The prince that wanteth understanding is also a great oppressor.   21. To have respect of persons is not good: for for a piece of bread that man will transgress.   28. When the wicked rise, men hide themselves: but when they perish, the righteous increase. v. 12.

Pro. 29.12. If a ruler hearken to lies, all his servants are wicked.

Pro. 30.21. The earth is disquieted,   22. For a servant when he reigneth.

Ecc. 3.16. I saw under the sun the place of judgment, that wickedness was there; and the place of righteousness, that iniquity was there. 17. I said in mine heart, God shall judge the righteous and the wicked.

Ecc. 4.1. I returned, and considered all the oppressions that are done under the sun: and behold the tears of such as were oppressed, and they had no comforter; and on the side of their oppressors there was power; but they had no comforter.   13. Better is a poor and a wise child than an old and foolish king, who will no more be admonished.   14. For out of prison he cometh to reign; whereas also he that is born in his kingdom becometh poor.

Ecc. 5.8. If thou seest the oppression of the poor, and violent perverting of judgment and justice in a province, marvel not at the matter: for he that is higher than the highest regardeth; and there be higher than they.

Ecc. 7.7. Surely oppression maketh a wise man mad; and a gift destroyeth the heart.

Ecc. 8.9. *There is* a time wherein one man ruleth over another to his own hurt.

Ecc. 10.5. There is an evil *which* I have seen under the sun, as an error *which* proceedeth from the ruler : 6. Folly is set in great dignity, and the rich sit in low place. 7. I have seen servants upon horses, and princes walking as servants upon the earth. 16. Woe to thee, O land, when thy king *is* a child, and thy princes eat in the morning ! *v.* 17.

Isa. 1.23. Thy princes *are* rebellious, and companions of thieves : every one loveth gifts, and followeth after rewards : they judge not the fatherless, neither doth the cause of the widow come unto them.

Isa. 3.12. *As for* my people, children *are* their oppressors, and women rule over them. O my people, they which lead thee cause *thee* to err, and destroy the way of thy paths. 14. The Lord will enter into judgment with the ancients of his people, and the princes thereof : for ye have eaten up the vineyard ; the spoil of the poor *is* in your houses. 15. What mean ye *that* ye beat my people to pieces, and grind the faces of the poor? saith the Lord God of hosts.

Isa. 5.7. He looked for judgment, but behold oppression ; for righteousness, but behold a cry.

Isa. 10.1. Woe unto them that decree unrighteous decrees, and that write grievances *which* they have prescribed ; 2. To turn aside the needy from judgment. 3. And what will ye do in the day of visitation ?

Isa. 14.5. The Lord hath broken the staff of the wicked, *and* the sceptre of the rulers. 6. He who smote the people in wrath with a continual stroke, he that ruled the nations in anger, is persecuted, *and* none hindereth. *v.* 4-20.

Isa. 28.14. Hear the word of the Lord, ye scornful men, that rule this people which *is* in Jerusalem.

Isa. 29.20. The terrible one is brought to nought, and all that watch for iniquity are cut off : 21. That make a man an offender for a word, and lay a snare for him that reproveth in the gate, and turn aside the just for a thing of nought.

Isa. 30.33. Tophet *is* ordained of old ; yea, for the king it is prepared ; he hath made *it* deep *and* large : the pile thereof *is* fire and much wood ; the breath of the Lord, like a stream of brimstone, doth kindle it.

Isa. 33.1. Woe to thee that spoilest, and thou *wast* not spoiled ; and dealest treacherously, and they dealt not treacherously with thee ! when thou shalt cease to spoil, thou shalt be spoiled.

Isa. 40.23. That bringeth the princes to nothing ; he maketh the judges of the earth as vanity. 24. The whirlwind shall take them away as stubble.

Isa. 47.6. Thou didst shew them no mercy : upon the ancient hast thou very heavily laid thy yoke.

Isa. 52.5. What have I here, saith the Lord, that my people is taken away for nought? they that rule over them make them to howl, saith the Lord.

Isa. 59.14. Judgment is turned away backward, and justice standeth afar off : for truth is fallen in the street, and equity cannot enter. 15. The Lord saw *it*, and it displeased him that *there was* no judgment.

Jer. 5.28. They overpass the deeds of the wicked : they judge not the cause, the cause of the fatherless, yet they prosper ; and the right of the needy do they not judge. 29. Shall I not visit for these *things* ? saith the Lord : shall not my soul be avenged on such a nation as this?

Jer. 34.17. Ye have not hearkened unto me, in proclaiming liberty, every one to his brother, and every man to his neighbour : behold, I proclaim a liberty for you, saith the Lord, to the sword, to the pestilence, and to the famine ; and I will make you to be removed into all the kingdoms of the earth.

Lam. 3.34. To crush under his feet all the prisoners of the earth, 35. To turn aside the right of a man before the face of the most High, 36. To subvert a man in his cause, the Lord approveth not.

Eze. 21.25. And thou, profane wicked prince of Israel, whose day is come, when iniquity *shall have* an end, 26. Thus saith the Lord God ; Remove the diadem, and take off the crown.

Eze. 22.6. The princes of Israel, every one were in thee to their power to shed blood. 27. Her princes in the midst thereof *are* like wolves ravening the prey, to shed blood, *and* to destroy souls, to get dishonest gain. 29. The people of the land have used oppression, and exercised robbery, and have vexed the poor and needy : yea, they have oppressed the stranger wrongfully.

Eze. 28.2. Because thine heart *is* lifted up, and thou hast said, *I am* a god, I sit *in* the seat of God, in the midst of the seas ; yet thou *art* a man, and not God, though thou set thine heart as the heart of God. *v.* 1-19.

Eze. 34.4. The diseased have ye not strengthened, neither have ye healed that which was sick, neither have ye bound up *that which was* broken, neither have ye brought again that which was driven away, neither have ye sought that which was lost ; but with force and with cruelty have ye ruled them. *v.* 1-31.

Eze. 45.9. Thus saith the Lord God, Let it suffice you, O princes of Israel : remove violence and spoil, and execute judgment and justice, take away your exactions from my people, saith the Lord God.

Hos. 5.10. The princes of Judah were like them that remove the bound : *therefore* I will pour out my wrath upon them like water.

Hos. 7.3. They make the king glad with their wickedness, and the princes with their lies.

Hos. 10.7. Her king is cut off as the foam upon the water.

Amos 3.10. They know not to do right, saith the Lord, who store up violence and robbery in their palaces. 11. Therefore he shall bring down thy strength from thee, and thy palaces shall be spoiled.

Amos 4.1. Hear this word, ye which oppress the poor, which crush the needy, which say to their masters, Bring, and let us drink. 2. The Lord God hath sworn by his holiness, that, lo, the days shall come upon you, that he will take you away.

Amos 5.11. Your treading *is* upon the poor, and ye take from him burdens of wheat : ye have built houses of hewn stone, but ye shall not dwell in them ; ye have planted pleasant vineyards, but ye shall not drink wine of them. *v.* 12.

Amos 6.12. Ye have turned judgment into gall, and the fruit of righteousness into hemlock.

Mic. 3.1. Hear, I pray you, O heads of Jacob, and ye princes of the house of Israel ; *Is it* not for you to know judgment? 2. Who hate the good, and love the evil ; who pluck off their skin from off them, and their flesh from off their bones : 3. Who also eat the flesh of my people, and flay their skin from off them ; and they break their bones, and chop them in pieces, as for the pot, and as flesh within the caldron. 4. Then shall they cry unto the Lord, but he will not hear them : he will even hide his face from them at that time, as they have behaved themselves ill in their doings.

Mic. 3.9. Ye heads of the house of Jacob, and princes of the house of Israel, that abhor judgment, and pervert all equity. 10. They build up Zion with blood, and Jerusalem with iniquity. 11. The heads thereof judge for reward, and the priests thereof teach for hire, and the prophets thereof divine for money : yet will they lean upon the Lord, and say, *Is* not the Lord among us?

Mic. 7.3. That they may do evil with both hands earnestly, the prince asketh, and the judge *asketh* for a reward ; and the great *man*, he uttereth his mischievous desire : so they wrap it up. 4. The best of them *is* as a brier ; the most upright *is sharper* than a thornhedge : the day of thy watchmen *and* thy visitation cometh ; now shall be their perplexity.

Hab. 1.4. The law is slacked, and judgment doth never go forth : for the wicked doth compass about the righteous ; therefore wrong judgment proceedeth.

Hab. 2.8. Because thou hast spoiled many nations, all the remnant of the people shall spoil thee. 12. Woe to him that buildeth a town with blood, and stablisheth a city by iniquity ! *v.* 5-13.

Hab. 3.13. Thou woundedst the head out of the house of the wicked, by discovering the foundation unto the neck.

Zeph. 1.8. I will punish the princes, and the king's children, and all *such as are* clothed with strange apparel.

Zeph. 3.3. Her princes within her *are* roaring lions ; her judges *are* evening wolves ; they gnaw not the bones till the morrow.

Act. 23.3. God shall smite thee, *thou* whited wall : for sittest thou to judge me after the law, and commandest me to be smitten contrary to the law?

Jas. 2.6. Do not rich men oppress you, and draw you before the judgment-seats? 9. If ye have respect to persons, ye commit sin, and are convinced of the law as transgressors.

See BRIBERY—POOR, NEGLECT OF.

RULERS, INJUSTICE AND WICKEDNESS OF, EXAMPLES OF : Potiphar, Gen. 39.20. Gen. 40.15. Pharaoh, Ex. *c.* 1 to 11. Adoni-bezek, Jud. 1.7. Abimelech, Jud. 9.1-5. Eli's sons, 1 Sam. 2.12. Samuel's sons, 1 Sam. 8.1-5. Saul, 1 Sam. 15.8-35. 1 Sam. 19. Hanun, 2 Sam. 10.4. David, 2 Sam. 24.3,4. Solomon, 1 Kin. 11.6. 1 Kin. 12.4. Jeroboam, 1 Kin. 12.26-33. 1 Kin. 13.33. Abijam, 1 Kin. 15.3. Nadab, 1 Kin. 15.26. Baasha, 1 Kin. 15.33,34. Asa, 2 Chr. 16.10. Zimri, 1 Kin. 16.19. Omri, 1 Kin. 16.25-27. Ahab, 1 Kin. 16.30-33.

1 Kin. 21. Ahaziah (Israel), 1 Kin. 22.52,53. Jehoram (Israel), 2 Kir. 3.2,3. Hazael, 2 Kin. 8.12. Jehoram (Judah), 2 Kin. 8.18. 2 Chr. 21. Ahaziah (Judah), 2 Chr. 22. Joash, 2 Chr. 24.2,17-25. Jehoahaz (Israel), 2 Kin. 13.1,2. Jehoash, 2 Kin. 13.10,11.

Jeroboam II., 2 Kin. 14.23,24. Zachariah, Menahem, Pekahiah, & Pekah, 2 Kin. 15. 9,18,24,28. Ahaz, 2 Kin. 16.2-4. 2 Chr. 28. 1-4. Hoshea, 2 Kin. 17.1,2. Manasseh, 2 Kin. 21.1-17. Amon, 2 Kin. 21.19-22. 2 Chr. 33.22,23. Jehoahaz (Judah), 2 Kin. 23.32. Jehoiakim, 2 Kin. 23.37. Jer. 22. 18-23. Jehoiachin, 2 Kin. 24.9. Jer. 22.24-30. Zedekiah, 2 Kin. 24.19. 2 Chr. 36.12,13. Jer. 38.5. Ahasuerus & Haman, Est. 3. Nebuchadnezzar, Dan. 2.1-13. Dan. 3.19. Belshazzar, Dan. 5.22,23. Darius, Dan. 6. 7-9. Herod I., Mat. 2.16-18. Herod II., Mar. 6.16-28. Luk. 13.31,32. Luk. 23.6-15. Herod III., Act. 12. Pilate, Mat. 27. Gallio, Act. 18.17. Ananias, Act. 23.2. Jewish rulers, Ezr. 9.2. Mat. 26.59.

See SANHEDRIM.

RULERS, OBEDIENCE TO, AND REBELLION AGAINST. See SUBJECTS.

RUSH. See BULRUSH—FLAG.

RUTH, a Moabitess, marries a son of Naomi ; returns to Israel, after his death, Ruth 1. Gathers corn in Boaz' field, Ruth *c.* 2 & 3. Marries Boaz, Ruth 4. Ancestress of Christ, Ruth 4.17. Mat. 1.5,16.

RYE, Ex. 9.32. Translated fitches, Eze. 4.9 ; and spelt (a kind of corn with very smooth ears), Isa. 28.25 (*marg.*).

S

SABAOTH (hosts or armies), Jas. 5.4. Compare 2 Chr. 18.18. Psa. 103.21.

SABBATH, THE. Gen. 2.2. On the seventh day God ended his work which he had made ; and he rested on the seventh day from all his work which he had made. 3. And God blessed the seventh day, and sanctified it : because that in it he had rested from all his work which God created and made.

Ex. 16.5. On the sixth day they shall prepare *that* which they bring in ; and it shall be twice as much as they gather daily. 22. To morrow *is* the rest of the holy Sabbath unto the Lord : bake *that* which ye will bake *to day*, and seethe that ye will seethe ; and that which remaineth over lay up for you to be kept until the morning. 24. And they laid it up till the morning, as Moses bade : and it did not stink, neither was their any worm therein. 25. And Moses said, Eat that to day ; for to day *is* a Sabbath unto the Lord : to day ye shall not find it in the field. 26. Six days ye shall gather it ; but on the seventh day, *which* is the Sabbath, in it there shall be none. 27. There went out *some* of the people on the seventh day for to gather, and they found none. 28. And the Lord said, How long refuse ye to keep my commandments and my laws? 29. See, for that the Lord hath given you the Sabbath, therefore he giveth you on the sixth day the bread of two days ; abide ye every man in his place, let no man go out of his place on the seventh day. 30. So the people rested on the seventh day.

Ex. 20.8. Remember the Sabbath day, to keep it holy. 9. Six days shalt thou labour, and do all thy work: 10. But the seventh day is the Sabbath of the Lord thy God: in it thou shalt not do any work, thou, nor thy son, nor thy daughter, thy manservant, nor thy maidservant, nor thy cattle, nor thy stranger that is within thy gates: 11. For in six days the Lord made heaven and earth, the sea, and all that in them is, and rested the seventh day: wherefore the Lord blessed the Sabbath day, and hallowed it.

Ex. 23.12. Six days thou shalt do thy work, and on the seventh day thou shalt rest: that thine ox and thine ass may rest, and the son of thy handmaid, and the stranger, may be refreshed.

Ex. 31.13. Verily my Sabbaths ye shall keep: for it is a sign between me and you throughout your generations; that ye may know that I am the Lord that doth sanctify you. 15. Six days may work be done; but in the seventh is the Sabbath of rest, holy to the Lord: whosoever doeth any work in the Sabbath day, he shall surely be put to death. 16. Wherefore the children of Israel shall keep the Sabbath, to observe the Sabbath throughout their generations, for a perpetual covenant. 17. It is a sign between me and the children of Israel for ever: for in six days the Lord made heaven and earth, and on the seventh day he rested, and was refreshed. v. 14. Num. 15.32-36.

Ex. 34.21. Six days thou shalt work, but on the seventh day thou shalt rest: in earing time and in harvest thou shalt rest.

Ex. 35.3. Ye shall kindle no fire throughout your habitations upon the Sabbath day.

Lev. 19.30. Ye shall keep my Sabbaths, and reverence my sanctuary: I am the Lord. v. 3.

Lev. 23.3. Six days shall work be done: but the seventh day is the Sabbath of rest, an holy convocation; ye shall do no work therein: it is the Sabbath of the Lord in all your dwellings. v. 31,32. See Lev. 16.31. Neh. 8.9-12.

Lev. 24.8. Every Sabbath he shall set it in order before the Lord continually, being taken from the children of Israel by an everlasting covenant. 1 Chr. 9.32.

Lev. 26.34. Then shall the land enjoy her Sabbaths, as long as it lieth desolate, and ye be in your enemies' land ; even then shall the land rest, and enjoy her Sabbaths. 35. As long as it lieth desolate it shall rest; because it did not rest in your Sabbaths, when ye dwelt upon it. v. 2,43. 2 Chr. 36.21.

Num. 28.9. And on the Sabbath day two lambs, &c. 10. This is the burnt-offering of every Sabbath, beside the continual burnt-offering, and his drink-offering.

Deu. 5.12. Keep the Sabbath day to sanctify it, as the Lord thy God hath commanded thee. 15. Remember that thou wast a servant in the land of Egypt, and that the Lord thy God brought thee out thence: therefore the Lord thy God commanded thee to keep the Sabbath day. v. 13,14.

2 Kin. 4.23. Wherefore wilt thou go to him to day? it is neither new moon, nor Sabbath.

Neh. 9.14. And madest known unto them thy holy Sabbath.

Neh. 10.31. If the people of the land bring ware or any victuals on the Sabbath day to sell, that we would not buy it of them on the Sabbath, or on the holy day.

Neh. 13.17. Then I contended with the nobles of Judah, and said unto them, What evil thing is this that ye do, and profane the Sabbath day? 18. Did not your fathers thus, and did not our God bring all this evil upon us, and upon this city? yet ye bring more wrath upon Israel by profaning the Sabbath. v. 15-22.

Psa. 92 (title). A psalm or song for the Sabbath day.

Psa. 118.24. This is the day which the Lord hath made; we will rejoice and be glad in it.

Isa. 1.13. The new moons and Sabbaths, the calling of assemblies, I cannot away with; it is iniquity, even the solemn meeting.

Isa. 56.2. Blessed is the man that doeth this, and the son of man that layeth hold on it; that keepeth the Sabbath from polluting it. 6. Every one that keepeth the Sabbath from polluting it, and taketh hold of my covenant: 7. Even them will I bring to my holy mountain, and make them joyful in my house of prayer.

Isa. 58.13. If thou turn away thy foot from the Sabbath, from doing thy pleasure on my holy day ; and call the Sabbath a delight, the holy of the Lord, honourable ; and shalt honour him, not doing thine own ways, nor finding thine own pleasure, nor speaking thine own words: 14. Then shalt thou delight thyself in the Lord ; and I will cause thee to ride upon the high places of the earth.

Isa. 66.23. From one Sabbath to another, shall all flesh come to worship before me, saith the Lord.

Jer. 17.21. Take heed to yourselves, and bear no burden on the Sabbath day, nor bring it in by the gates of Jerusalem; 22. Neither carry forth a burden out of your houses on the Sabbath day, neither do ye any work, but hallow ye the Sabbath day, as I commanded your fathers. 24. If ye diligently hearken unto me, saith the Lord, to bring in no burden through the gates of this city on the Sabbath day, but hallow the Sabbath day to do no work therein; 25. Then shall there enter into the gates of this city kings and princes sitting upon the throne of David. 27. If ye will not hearken unto me to hallow the Sabbath day, and not to bear a burden, even entering in at the gates of Jerusalem on the Sabbath day ; then will I kindle a fire in the gates thereof, and it shall devour the palaces of Jerusalem, and it shall not be quenched.

Lam. 1.7. The adversaries saw her, and did mock at her Sabbaths.

Lam. 2.6. He hath destroyed his places of the assembly: the Lord hath caused the solemn feasts and Sabbaths to be forgotten in Zion.

Eze. 20.12. I gave them my Sabbaths, to be a sign between me and them, that they might know that I am the Lord that sanctify them. 13. And my Sabbaths they greatly polluted: then I said, I would pour out my fury upon them in the wilderness, to consume them. v. 20,21.

Eze. 22.8. Thou hast despised mine holy things, and hast profaned my Sabbaths.

Eze. 23.38. They have defiled my sanctuary in the same day, and have profaned my Sabbaths.

Eze. 44.24. They shall keep my laws and my statutes in all mine assemblies; and they shall hallow my Sabbaths.

Eze. 46.1. The gate of the inner court that looketh toward the east shall be shut the six working days; but on the Sabbath it shall be opened. 3. Likewise the people of the land shall worship at the door of this gate before the Lord in the Sabbaths.

Hos. 2.11. I will also cause all her mirth to cease, her feast days, her new moons, and her Sabbaths, and all her solemn feasts.

Amos 8.5. When will the new moon be gone, that we may sell corn? and the Sabbath, that we may set forth wheat?

Mat. 12.8. The Son of man is Lord even of the Sabbath day.

Mat. 24.20. Pray ye that your flight be not in the winter, neither on the Sabbath day.

Mar. 2.27. The Sabbath was made for man, and not man for the Sabbath.

Mar. 6.2. When the Sabbath day was come, he began to teach in the synagogue.

Luk. 4.16. As his custom was, he went into the synagogue on the Sabbath day, and stood up for to read. 31. Came down to Capernaum, a city of Galilee, and taught them on the Sabbath days.

Luk. 6.6. It came to pass also on another Sabbath, that he entered into the synagogue and taught.

Luk. 13.10. He was teaching in one of the synagogues on the Sabbath.

Luk. 23.54. That day was the preparation, and the Sabbath drew on. 56. Rested the Sabbath day according to the commandment.

Act. 13.27. Because they knew him not, nor yet the voices of the prophets which are read every Sabbath day. 42. When the Jews were gone out of the synagogue, the Gentiles besought that these words might be preached to them the next Sabbath. 44. The next Sabbath day came almost the whole city together to hear the word of God. v. 14. Act. 15.21.

Act. 16.13. On the Sabbath we went out of the city by a river side, where prayer was wont to be made; and we sat down, and spake unto the women which resorted *thither*.

Act. 18.4. He reasoned in the synagogue every Sabbath. Act. 17.2.

Heb. 4.4. He spake in a certain place of the seventh *day* on this wise, And God did rest the seventh day from all his works.

See SYNAGOGUE.

SABBATH, THE. JEWISH LAW. Working on Sabbath punished with death, Ex. 31. 14,15. Ex. 35.2. Num. 15.35.

————, JEWISH MISCONCEPTIONS OF. Rebuked by Christ, Mat. 12.1-13. Mar. 2. 23-28. Mar. 3.1-6. Luk. 6.1-11. Luk. 13. 14-16. Luk. 14.1-6. Jno. 5.9-18. Jno. 7. 22,23. Jno. 9.14,16. Jno. 19.31.

————, FIRST DAY OR LORD'S DAY. Mar. 16.9. When *Jesus* was risen early the first *day* of the week.

Jno. 20.19. The same day at evening, being the first *day* of the week, when the doors were shut where the disciples were assembled for fear of the Jews, came Jesus and stood in the midst. 26. After eight days again his disciples were within, and Thomas with them : *then*

came Jesus, the doors being shut, and stood in the midst, and said, Peace *be* unto you.

Act. 20.7. Upon the first *day* of the week, when the disciples came together to break bread, Paul preached unto them, ready to depart on the morrow; and continued his speech until midnight.

1 Cor. 16.2. Upon the first *day* of the week let every one of you lay by him in store, as *God* hath prospered him. *v.* 1.

Rev. 1.10. I was in the Spirit on the Lord's day.

SABBATH-DAYS' JOURNEY, Act. 1.12. Supposed to be about 2000 cubits; the following texts are usually referred to, Ex. 16.29. Num. 35.5. Jos. 3.4.

SABBATICAL YEAR or SEVENTH YEAR. Called Year of Release, Deu. 15.9. Den. 31.10. Every 7th year the land left uncultivated, Ex. 23.11. Lev. 25.2-7. Hebrew servants released, Ex. 21.2. Deu. 15.12. Jer. 34.14. Debts cancelled, Deu. 15.1-3. Neh. 10.31. Law publicly read at the feast of tabernacles, Deu. 31.10-13. Neh. 8.18. Promise of plenty the year before, Lev. 25.20-22. Neglect of, punished by the 70 years' captivity, Lev. 26. 34,35. 2 Chr. 36.21. Jer. 34.14-22.

SABEANS, a nation descended from Seba, Gen. 10.7. Africans, Isa. 43.3. Their wealth and stature, Isa. 45.14. Conversion of, predicted, Psa. 72.10. The Sabeans, Joel 3.8, and Job 1.15, are the descendants of two different Shebas. See SHEBA.

SACKBUT, a kind of harp, Dan. 3.5,7,10,15. See HARP—PSALTERY.

SACKCLOTH. Worn round the loins in mourning, Gen. 37.34. 1 Kin. 20.32. Worn next the skin, 2 Kin. 6.30. Job 16.15. By women, Joel 1.8. Put on animals, Jonah 3.8.

SACRAMENTS. See BAPTISM—LORD'S SUPPER.

SACRIFICES. See OFFERINGS. Illustrative, Isa. 34.6. Eze. 39.17. Zeph. 1.7,8. Rom. 12.1. Phil. 2.17. Phil. 4.18. Sacrifice of praise, Heb. 13.15. Hos. 14.2. See OFFERINGS, THANKSGIVING-OFFERING.

SACRILEGE. See WORSHIP, PRESUMPTION IN.

SADDUCEES. Denied the resurrection and a future state, Mat. 16.6,11,12. Mat. 22. 23-34. Mar. 12.18. Luk. 20.27. Act. 23.7,8. Reproved by John, on coming to be baptized, Mat. 3.7-12 Oppose Christ, who confutes them, Mat. 16.1. Mat. 22.23-34. Mar. 12. 18-27. Luk. 20.27-40. In the Sanhedrim, persecute the apostles for teaching the resurrection, Act. 4.1-3. Act. 5.17,18,33. Act. 23.6-10.

SAFFRON, a perfume made from the yellow crocus, Song 4.14.

SAINTS. BLESSINGS GRANTED FOR THEIR SAKES. Gen. 18.26. If I find in Sodom fifty righteous within the city, then I will spare all the place for their sakes.

Gen. 19.29. When God destroyed the cities of the plain, God remembered Abraham, and sent Lot out of the midst of the overthrow, when he overthrew the cities in the which Lot dwelt. *v.* 21.

Gen. 30.27. I have learned by experience that the Lord hath blessed me for thy sake.

Gen. 39.5. The Lord blessed the Egyptian's house for Joseph's sake.

Pro. 11.11. By the blessing of the upright the city is exalted.

Jer. 5.1. If ye can find a man, if there be any that executeth judgment, that seeketh the truth, and I will pardon it.

Eze. 22.30. I sought for a man among them that should make up the hedge, and stand in the gap before me for the land, that I should not destroy it : but I found none.

Mic. 5.7. The remnant of Jacob shall be in the midst of many people as a dew from the Lord, as the showers upon the grass, that tarrieth not for man, nor waiteth for the sons of men.

Mat. 5.13. Ye are the salt of the earth : but if the salt have lost his savour, wherewith shall it be salted? it is thenceforth good for nothing, but to be cast out, and to be trodden under foot of men. 14. Ye are the light of the world.

Mat. 24.22. Except those days should be shortened, there should no flesh be saved : but for the elect's sake those days shall be shortened.

Act. 27.24. Fear not, Paul; thou must be brought before Cesar : and, lo, God hath given thee all them that sail with thee.

See CHILDREN OF SAINTS—PRAYER, INTER-
CESSORY, ANSWERED.

SAINTS—CHRISTIANS, CHARACTER OF.

1 Sam. 13.14. The Lord hath sought him a man after his own heart.

Ezr. 10.3. Those that tremble at the commandment of our God.

Psa. 1.1. Blessed is the man that walketh not in the counsel of the ungodly, nor standeth in the way of sinners, nor sitteth in the seat of the scornful. 2. But his delight is in the law of the Lord; and in his law doth he meditate day and night.

Psa. 4.3. The Lord hath set apart him that is godly for himself.

Psa. 15.1. Lord, who shall abide in thy tabernacle? who shall dwell in thy holy hill? 2. He that walketh uprightly, and worketh righteousness, and speaketh the truth in his heart. v. 3-5.

Psa. 24.6. This is the generation of them that seek him, that seek thy face. v. 3-5.

Psa. 64.10. The righteous shall be glad in the Lord, and shall trust in him; and all the upright in heart shall glory.

Psa. 87.5. Of Zion it shall be said, This and that man was born in her : and the highest himself shall establish her. 6. The Lord shall count, when he writeth up the people, that this man was born there.

Psa. 119.1 Blessed are the undefiled in the way, who walk in the law of the Lord. 2. Blessed are they that keep his testimonies, and that seek him with the whole heart. 3. They also do no iniquity : they walk in his ways.

Isa. 33.15. He that speaketh uprightly : he that despiseth the gain of oppressions, that shaketh his hands from holding of bribes, that stoppeth his ears from hearing of blood, and shutteth his eyes from seeing evil.

Isa. 51.1. Ye that follow after righteousness, ye that seek the Lord.

Isa. 54.13. All thy children shall be taught of the Lord ; and great shall be the peace of thy children.

Isa. 60.21. Thy people also shall be all righteous.

Isa. 62.12. They shall call them, The holy people, The redeemed of the Lord.

Isa. 63.8. He said, Surely they are my people, children that will not lie : so he was their Saviour.

Eze. 18.8. He that hath not given forth upon usury, neither hath taken any increase, that hath withdrawn his hand from iniquity, hath executed true judgment between man and man, 9. Hath walked in my statutes, and hath kept my judgments, to deal truly ; he is just, he shall surely live, saith the Lord God. v. 7.

Eze. 44.9. No stranger, uncircumcised in heart, nor uncircumcised in flesh, shall enter into my sanctuary, of any stranger that is among the children of Israel.

Zeph. 2.3. All ye meek of the earth, which have wrought his judgment.

Zec. 3.2. A brand plucked out of the fire. 8. Men wondered at.

Mat. 3.6. Were baptized of him in Jordan, confessing their sins.

Mat. 5.3. Blessed are the poor in spirit : for their's is the kingdom of heaven. 4. They that mourn. 5. The meek. 6. They which do hunger and thirst after righteousness. 7. The merciful. 8. The pure in heart. 9. The peacemakers : for they shall be called the children of God. 10. Blessed are they which are persecuted for righteousness' sake : for their's is the kingdom of heaven. 13. Ye are the salt of the earth. 14. Ye are the light of the world.

Mat. 7.16. Ye shall know them by their fruits. 17. Every good tree bringeth forth good fruit. 18. A good tree cannot bring forth evil fruit.

Mat. 12.50. Whosoever shall do the will of my Father which is in heaven, the same is my brother, and sister, and mother. v. 48,49. Luk. 8.19-21.

Mat. 13.38. The good seed are the children of the kingdom.

Luk. 6.45. A good man out of the good treasure of his heart bringeth forth that which is good ; for of the abundance of the heart his mouth speaketh.

Luk. 18.16. Suffer little children to come unto me, and forbid them not : for of such is the kingdom of God. Mat. 19.14. Mar. 10.14.

Jno. 3.21. He that doeth truth cometh to the light, that his deeds may be made manifest, that they are wrought in God.

Jno. 8.31. If ye continue in my word, then are ye my disciples indeed. 39. If ye were Abraham's children, ye would do the works of Abraham. 42. If God were your Father, ye would love me : for I proceeded forth and came from God. 47. He that is of God heareth God's words.

Jno. 10.4. The sheep follow him : for they know his voice. 27. My sheep hear my voice, and I know them, and they follow me.

Jno. 13.35. By this shall all men know that ye are my disciples, if ye have love one to another.

Jno. 15.14. Ye are my friends, if ye do whatsoever I command you.

Act. 2.38. Repent, and be baptized every one of you in the name of Jesus Christ for the remission of sins, and ye shall receive the gift of the Holy Ghost. 47. The Lord added to the church such as should be saved.

Act. 8.2. Devout men. 12. When they believed Philip preaching the things concerning the kingdom of God, and the name of Jesus Christ, they were baptized, both men and women. 37. They were pricked in their heart, and said unto Peter and to the rest of the apostles, Men *and* brethren, what shall we do?

Act. 10.47. Can any man forbid water, that these should not be baptized, which have received the Holy Ghost as well as we?

Act. 11.24. He was a good man, and full of the Holy Ghost and of faith.

Act. 16.14. Lydia, which worshipped God, heard *us*: whose heart the Lord opened, that she attended unto the things which were spoken of Paul. 15. And when she was baptized, and her household, she besought *us*, saying, If ye have judged me to be faithful to the Lord, come into my house.

Act. 18.8. Believed on the Lord with all his house: and many of the Corinthians hearing believed, and were baptized.

Rom. 1.7. To all that be in Rome, beloved of God, called *to be* saints.

Rom. 8.9. Ye are not in the flesh, but in the Spirit, if so be that the Spirit of God dwell in you. Now if any man have not the Spirit of Christ, he is none of his. 14. As many as are led by the Spirit of God, they are the sons of God. 16. The Spirit itself beareth witness with our spirit, that we are the children of God. 23. Ourselves also, which have the first-fruits of the Spirit.

Rom. 15.14. I myself also am persuaded of you, my brethren, that ye also are full of goodness, filled with all knowledge, able also to admonish one another.

1 Cor. 1.2. Unto the church of God which is at Corinth, to them that are sanctified in Christ Jesus, called *to be* saints, with all that in every place call upon the name of Jesus Christ our Lord, both their's and our's.

2 Cor. 5.17. If any man be in Christ, *he is* a new creature: old things are passed away; behold, all things are become new.

2 Cor. 8.5. First gave their own selves to the Lord, and unto us by the will of God.

Gal. 5.22. The fruit of the Spirit is love, joy, peace, long-suffering, gentleness, goodness, faith, 23. Meekness, temperance: against such there is no law. 24. And they that are Christ's have crucified the flesh with the affections and lusts.

Eph. 1.1. To the saints which are at Ephesus, and to the faithful in Christ Jesus. Phil. 1.1. Col. 1.2.

Phil. 2.15. Blameless and harmless, the sons of God, without rebuke, in the midst of a crooked and perverse nation, among whom ye shine as lights in the world.

Phil. 4.8. Whatsoever things are true, whatsoever things *are* honest, whatsoever things *are* just, whatsoever things *are* pure, whatsoever things *are* lovely, whatsoever things *are* of good report; if *there be* any virtue, and if *there be* any praise, think on these things. 2 Cor. 1.12.

1 The. 1.3. Your work of faith, and labour of love, and patience of hope in our Lord Jesus Christ, in the sight of God and our Father.

1 The. 5.5. Ye are all the children of light, and the children of the day: we are not of the night, nor of darkness. 27. The holy brethren.

2 Tim. 2.22. Them that call on the Lord out of a pure heart.

Philm. 5. Thy love and faith, which thou hast toward the Lord Jesus, and toward all saints.

Heb. 3.1. Holy brethren, partakers of the heavenly calling. 6. Christ as a son over his own house; whose house are we, if we hold fast the confidence and the rejoicing of the hope firm unto the end.

1 Pet. 2.9. Ye *are* a chosen generation, a royal priesthood, an holy nation, a peculiar people; that ye should shew forth the praises of him who hath called you out of darkness into his marvellous light: 10. Which in time past *were* not a people, but *are* now the people of God: which had not obtained mercy, but now have obtained mercy. 11. Strangers and pilgrims.

2 Pet. 1.1. Them that have obtained like precious faith with us through the righteousness of God and our Saviour Jesus Christ.

1 Jno. 2.3. Hereby we do know at we know him, if we keep his commandments. 5. Whoso keepeth his word, in him verily is the love of God perfected: hereby know we that we are in him. 13. I write unto you, fathers, because ye have known him *that is* from the beginning. I write unto you, little children, because ye have known the Father. 14. I have written unto you, young men, because ye are strong, and the word of God abideth in you, and ye have overcome the wicked one.

1 Jno. 3.6. Whosoever abideth in him sinneth not; whosoever sinneth hath not seen him, neither known him. 7. Little children, let no man deceive you: he that doeth righteousness is righteous, even as he is righteous. 9. Whosoever is born of God doth not commit sin; for his seed remaineth in him: and he cannot sin, because he is born of God. 14. We know that we have passed from death unto life, because we love the brethren. He that loveth not *his* brother abideth in death. 18. My little children, let us not love in word, neither in tongue; but in deed and in truth. 19. And hereby we know that we are of the truth, and shall assure our hearts before him.

1 Jno. 4.7. Beloved, let us love one another: for love is of God; and every one that loveth is born of God, and knoweth God. 8. He that loveth not knoweth not God; for God is love.

1 Jno. 5.1. Whosoever believeth that Jesus is the Christ is born of God: and every one that loveth him that begat loveth him also that is begotten of him.

Rev. 17.14. They that are with him *are* called, and chosen, and faithful.

See HOLINESS—OBEDIENCE—REGENERATION—SPIRITUAL DILIGENCE—SIN HATEFUL TO SAINTS—CHURCH, NAMES OF.

SAINTS, COMMUNION AND FELLOWSHIP OF. 1 Sam. 23.16. Jonathan arose, and went to David into the wood, and strengthened his hand in God.

Psa. 55.14. We took sweet counsel together, and walked unto the house of God in company.

Psa. 119.63. I am a companion of all them that fear thee, and of them that keep thy precepts.

Mal. 3.16. They that feared the Lord spake often one to another: and the Lord hearkened, and heard it, and a book of remembrance was written before him for them that feared the Lord, and that thought upon his name.

Luk. 22.32. When thou art converted, strengthen thy brethren.

Luk. 24.32. They said one to another, Did not our heart burn within us, while he talked with us by the way, and while he opened to us the scriptures? v. 17.

Act. 2.42. They continued stedfastly in the apostles' doctrine and fellowship, and in breaking of bread, and in prayers.

Act. 20.35. So labouring ye ought to support the weak, and to remember the words of the Lord Jesus, how he said, It is more blessed to give than to receive.

Rom. 14.19. Let us therefore follow after the things which make for peace, and things wherewith one may edify another.

Rom. 15.2. Let every one of us please his neighbour for his good to edification.

Gal. 2.9. They gave to me and Barnabas the right hands of fellowship.

Gal. 6.2. Bear ye one another's burdens, and so fulfil the law of Christ.

Col. 3.16. Teaching and admonishing one another in psalms, and hymns, and spiritual songs.

1 The. 4.18. Comfort one another with these words.

1 The. 5.11. Comfort yourselves together, and edify one another, even as also ye do. 14. We exhort you, brethren, warn them that are unruly, comfort the feeble-minded, support the weak, be patient toward all men.

Heb. 3.13. Exhort one another daily, while it is called To day; lest any of you be hardened through the deceitfulness of sin.

Heb. 10.24. Let us consider one another to provoke unto love and to good works: 25. Not forsaking the assembling of ourselves together, as the manner of some is; but exhorting one another.

Jas. 5.16. Confess your faults one to another, and pray one for another, that ye may be healed.

1 Jno. 1.3. That which we have seen and heard declare we unto you, that ye also may have fellowship with us. 7. If we walk in the light, as he is in the light, we have fellowship one with another.

See LOVE — ZEAL — UNION — WISDOM IN SPEECH—CHURCH-DISCIPLINE.

SAINTS, DEATH OF. See DEATH OF SAINTS.

SAINTS, ENMITY TO. Job 1.9. Satan answered, Doth Job fear God for nought? 11. But put forth thine hand now, and touch all that he hath, and he will curse thee to thy face. Job 2.4,5.

Job 12.4. I am as one mocked of his neighbour: the just upright man is laughed to scorn. v. 5.

Psa. 38.20. They also that render evil for good are mine adversaries; because I follow the thing that good is.

Psa. 42.3. My tears have been my meat day and night, while they continually say unto me, Where is thy God? 10. As with a sword in my bones, mine enemies reproach me; while they say daily unto me, Where is thy God?

Psa. 56.5. Every day they wrest my words: all their thoughts are against me for evil.

Psa. 69.10. When I wept, and chastened my soul with fasting, that was to my reproach. 11. I made sackcloth also my garment; and I became a proverb to them. 12. They that sit in the gate speak against me; and I was the song of the drunkards.

Pro. 29.10. The bloodthirsty hate the upright. 27. He that is upright in the way is abomination to the wicked.

Amos 5.10. They hate him that rebuketh in the gate, and they abhor him that speaketh uprightly.

Mat. 10.22. Ye shall be hated of all men for my name's sake. 25. If they have called the Master of the house Beelzebub, how much more shall they call them of his household?

Jno. 15.18. If the world hate you, ye know that it hated me before it hated you. 19. If ye were of the world, the world would love his own: but because ye are not of the world, but I have chosen you out of the world, therefore the world hateth you.

Jno. 17.14. I have given them thy word; and the world hath hated them, because they are not of the world, even as I am not of the world.

Act. 26.24. Paul, thou art beside thyself; much learning doth make thee mad.

Act. 28.22. As concerning this sect, we know that every where it is spoken against.

2 Tim. 3.3. Despisers of those that are good. 12. All that will live godly in Christ Jesus shall suffer persecution.

1 Pet. 4.4. They think it strange that ye run not with them to the same excess of riot, speaking evil of you. 6. Judged according to men in the flesh.

1 Jno. 3.1. The world knoweth us not, because it knew him not. 13. Marvel not, my brethren, if the world hate you.

See MALICE — PERSECUTION — REPROOF HATED.

SAINTS, EXAMPLE OF. 1 Kin. 9.4. Walk before me, as David thy father walked, in integrity of heart. 2 Chr. 7.17.

1 Chr. 28.9. Thou, Solomon my son, know thou the God of thy father, and serve him with a perfect heart and with a willing mind.

Jer. 22.15. Did not thy father eat and drink, and do judgment and justice, and then it was well with him?

Mat. 5.16. Let your light so shine before men, that they may see your good works, and glorify your Father which is in heaven. 2 Cor. 3.2,3.

Jno. 8.39. If ye were Abraham's children, ye would do the works of Abraham.

1 Cor. 11.1. Be ye followers of me, even as I also am of Christ.

Phil. 3.17. Be followers together of me, and mark them which walk so as ye have us for an ensample.

Phil. 4.9. Those things, which ye have both learned, and received, and heard, and seen in me, do.

1 The. 1.5. Ye know what manner of men we were among you for your sake. 6. And ye became followers of us, and of the Lord.

2 The. 3.7. Yourselves know how ye ought to follow us: for we behaved not ourselves disorderly among you; 8. Neither did we eat any man's bread for nought. 9. But to make ourselves an ensample unto you to follow us.

Heb. 6.12. Be not slothful, but followers of them who through faith and patience inherit the promises.

Heb. 11.2. By it the elders obtained a good report. 4. By faith Abel offered unto God a more excellent sacrifice than Cain: and by it he being dead yet speaketh. *v.* 1-40.

Heb. 12.1. Wherefore, seeing we also are compassed about with so great a cloud of witnesses, let us lay aside every weight, and the sin which doth so easily beset *us*, and let us run with patience the race that is set before us.

Heb. 13.7. Remember them which have the rule over you, who have spoken unto you the word of God : whose faith follow, considering the end of *their* conversation.

Jas. 5.10. Take, my brethren, the prophets, who have spoken in the name of the Lord, for an example of suffering affliction, and of patience.

1 Pet. 2.12. Having your conversation honest among the Gentiles: that, whereas they speak against you as evildoers, they may by *your* good works, which they shall behold, glorify God in the day of visitation.

See SAINTS, COMMUNION OF.

SAINTS, PRIVILEGES OF. See such titles as ADOPTION — GOD'S FAVOUR — CHRIST'S LOVE—CHURCH—PROMISES, &c.

SALAMIS, a city on the south-east coast of Cyprus; the gospel preached in, by Paul and Barnabas, Act. 13.4,5.

SALEM. See JERUSALEM.

SALIM, John baptized at, Jno. 3.23. See SHALIM.

SALMON. See ZALMON.

SALMONE, a promontory on the east of Crete, Act. 27.7.

SALOME, wife of Zebedee, mother of James and John, Mat. 27.56 with Mar. 15.40 & Mar. 16.1. Requests honours for her sons in Christ's kingdom, Mat. 20.20. Beholds the crucifixion, Mar. 15.40. Visits the sepulchre, Mar. 16.1.

SALT, Job 6.6. Used with all offerings, Lev. 2.13. Ezr. 6.9. Eze. 43.24. Mar. 9.49. Called the salt of the covenant of thy God, Lev. 2.13. A covenant of salt; an unchangeable covenant, Num. 18.19. 2 Chr. 13.5. A salt land, a barren land, Eze. 47.11. Zeph. 2.9. Partaking of, a bond of friendship, Ezr. 4.14 (*marg.*). Shechem sown with, Jud. 9.45. Waters of Jericho healed with, 2 Kin. 2.20,21. Obtained from salt-pits, Jos. 11.8 (*marg.*). Zeph. 2.9. Illustrative, Mar. 9.49,50. Col. 4.6.

————, CITY OF, near the Dead Sea, belonging to Judah, Jos. 15.62.

————, PILLAR OF. Lot's wife became, Gen. 19.26. Luk. 17.32.

———— SEA. See DEAD SEA.

————, VALLEY OF. Syrians defeated in,

by David, 2 Sam. 8.13 ; and Edomites by Amaziah, 2 Kin. 14.7.

SALUTATIONS, COURTESY, Lev. 19.32. Rom. 13.7. 1 Pet. 2.17. 1 Pet. 3.8. By embracing, Gen. 33.4. Gen. 45.14. Act. 20.37, see KISS. Giving the hand, Gal. 2.9. Placing the hand on the head, Gen. 48.14. Taking hold of the beard, 2 Sam. 20.9. Bowing and prostrating, Gen. 18.2. Gen. 19.1,2. Gen. 23.7,12. Gen. 33.3. Gen. 43.26,28. 1 Sam. 25.23. 2 Sam. 18.28. Est. 8.3. Mat. 2.11. Mar. 5.22. Rising from the seat, 1 Kin. 2.19. Job 29.8. On a journey, 2 Kin. 4.29. Luk. 10.4.

SALUTATIONS, EXAMPLES OF: Gen. 19.2. My lord. Gen. 24.31. Come in, thou blessed of the Lord. Gen. 43.29. God be gracious unto thee. Ex. 4.18. Go in peace. Jud. 19.20. Peace be with thee. Ruth 2.4. The Lord be with you. The Lord bless thee. 1 Sam. 15.13. Blessed be thou of the Lord. 1 Sam. 25.6. Peace *be* both to thee, and peace *be* to thine house, and peace *be* unto all that thou hast. 2 Sam. 15.20. Mercy and truth be with thee. 2 Sam. 18.28. All is well. 2 Sam. 20.9. Art thou in health, my brother? 1 Kin. 2.13. Comest thou peaceably? 2 Kin. 9.11. *Is* all well? 17. *Is it* peace? Psa. 118.26. Blessed be he that cometh in the name of the Lord. Psa. 129.8. We bless you in the name of the Lord. Mat. 26.49. Hail, Master. Mat. 28.9. All hail. Luk. 10.5. Peace be to this house. Jno. 20.21. Peace be unto you. 2 Jno. 10. God speed.

BY SUBJECTS. 1 Sam. 25.41. *Let* thine handmaid be a servant to wash the feet of the servants of my lord. 2 Sam. 9.8. What is thy servant that thou shouldest look upon such a dead dog as I? 2 Sam. 14.17. As an angel of God, so is my lord. 1 Kin. 1.31. Let my lord king David live for ever. (Neh. 2.3. Dan. 3.11.) 1 Chr. 12.18. Peace be to thine helpers. 2 Kin. 11.12. God save the king. (1 Kin. 1.39.) Act. 24.3. Most noble Felix.

IN LETTERS. Ezr. 7.12. Unto Ezra, perfect peace. Dan. 6.25. Peace be multiplied unto you. 1 Cor. 1.3. Grace be to you, and peace. (2 Jno. 3.) 1 Cor. 16.20. All the brethren greet you. 23. The grace of our Lord Jesus Christ be with you. 24. My love be with you all in Christ Jesus. 2 Cor. 13.13. All the saints salute you. 14. The grace of the Lord Jesus Christ, and the love of God, and the communion of the Holy Ghost, *be* with you all. Amen. Gal. 6.16. Peace *be* on them, and mercy, and upon the Israel of God. Eph. 6.23. Peace *be* to the brethren, and love with faith. 24. Grace be with all them that love our Lord Jesus Christ in sincerity. Col. 4.18. Remember my bonds. Grace be with you. 2 The. 3.16. The Lord of peace himself give you peace. The Lord be with you all. 1 Tim. 1.2. Unto Timothy, my own son in the faith, grace, mercy, and peace, from God our Father, and Jesus Christ our Lord. 2 Tim. 4.22. The Lord Jesus Christ be with thy spirit. Tit. 3.15. Greet them that love us in the faith. Heb. 13.25. Grace be with you all. Jas. 1.1. To the twelve tribes, greeting. 1 Pet. 5.14. Peace be with you all that are in Christ Jesus. 2 Pet. 1.2. Grace and peace be multiplied unto you. 2 Jno. 1. The elder unto the elect lady. 3 Jno. 1. Unto the well-beloved Gaius. Jude 2. Mercy unto you, and peace, and love be multiplied. Rev. 1.4. Grace *be* unto you, and peace, from him which is, and which was, and which is to come.

SALVATION OFFERED TO ALL. CALL OF THE GENTILES. Gen. 12.3. In thee shall all families of the earth be blessed.

Deu. 30.19. Choose life, that both thou and thy seed may live.

1 Sam. 12.20. Fear not: ye have done all this wickedness: yet turn not aside from following the Lord, but serve the Lord with all your heart.

2 Sam. 14.14. Neither doth God respect *any* person; yet doth he devise means that his banished be not expelled from him.

1 Kin. 8.41. Concerning a stranger, that *is* not of thy people Israel, but cometh out of a far country for thy name's sake. 43. Hear thou in heaven thy dwelling-place, and do according to all that the stranger calleth to thee for: that all people of the earth may know thy name, to fear thee, as *do* thy people Israel.

Psa. 68.18. Thou hast received gifts for men; yea, *for* the rebellious also, that the Lord God might dwell *among* them.

Psa. 91.16. With long life will I satisfy him, and shew him my salvation.

Psa. 98.2. The Lord hath made known his salvation: his righteousness hath he openly shewed in the sight of the heathen. 3. He hath remembered his mercy and his truth toward the house of Israel: all the ends of the earth have seen the salvation of our God.

Psa. 132.15. I will abundantly bless her provision: I will satisfy her poor with bread. 16. I will also clothe her priests with salvation: and her saints shall shout aloud for joy.

Pro. 1.20. Wisdom crieth without; she uttereth her voice in the streets: 21. She crieth in the chief place of concourse, in the openings of the gates: in the city she uttereth her words.

Pro. 8.1. Doth not wisdom cry? and understanding put forth her voice? 4. Unto you, O men, I call; and my voice *is* to the sons of man. 5. O ye simple, understand wisdom: and, ye fools, be ye of an understanding heart. *v.* 2,3.

Pro. 9.1. Wisdom hath builded her house. 3. She crieth upon the highest places of the city.

Isa. 1.18. Come now, and let us reason together, saith the Lord: Though your sins be as scarlet, they shall be as white as snow; though they be red like crimson, they shall be as wool. *v.* 1-6.

Isa. 2.5. O house of Jacob, come ye, and let us walk in the light of the Lord.

Isa. 25.6. In this mountain shall the Lord of hosts make unto all people a feast of fat things, a feast of wines on the lees, of fat things full of marrow, of wines on the lees well refined. 7. And he will destroy in this mountain the face of the covering cast over all people, and the vail that is spread over all nations.

Isa. 29.18. In that day shall the deaf hear the words of the book, and the eyes of the blind shall see out of obscurity, and out of darkness. 19. The meek also shall increase *their* joy in the Lord, and the poor among men shall rejoice in the Holy One of Israel. 24. They also that erred in spirit shall come to

understanding, and they that murmured shall learn doctrine.

Isa. 32.2. A man shall be as an hiding-place from the wind, and a covert from the tempest; as rivers of water in a dry place; as the shadow of a great rock in a weary land. 3. And the eyes of them that see shall not be dim, and the ears of them that hear shall hearken. 4. The heart also of the rash shall understand knowledge, and the tongue of the stammerers shall be ready to speak plainly.

Isa. 35.8. An highway shall be there, and a way, and it shall be called The way of holiness; the unclean shall not pass over it; but it *shall be* for those: the wayfaring men, though fools, shall not err *therein*.

Isa. 44.3. I will pour water upon him that is thirsty, and floods upon the dry ground; I will pour my Spirit upon thy seed, and my blessing upon thine offspring.

Isa. 46.12. Hearken unto me, ye stout-hearted, that *are* far from righteousness: 13. I bring near my righteousness; it shall not be far off, and my salvation shall not tarry: and I will place salvation in Zion for Israel my glory.

Isa. 51.4. Hearken unto me, my people; and give ear unto me, O my nation: for a law shall proceed from me, and I will make my judgment to rest for a light of the people. 5. My righteousness *is* near; my salvation is gone forth, and mine arms shall judge the people; the isles shall wait upon me, and on mine arm shall they trust.

Isa. 52.15. So shall he sprinkle many nations; the kings shall shut their mouths at him: for *that* which had not been told them shall they see; and *that* which they had not heard shall they consider.

Isa. 55.1. Ho, every one that thirsteth, come ye to the waters, and he that hath no money; come ye, buy, and eat; yea, come, buy wine and milk without money and without price. 2. Wherefore do ye spend money for *that which is* not bread? and your labour for *that which* satisfieth not? hearken diligently unto me, and eat ye *that which is* good, and let your soul delight itself in fatness. 3. Incline your ear, and come unto me: hear, and your soul shall live; and I will make an everlasting covenant with you, *even* the sure mercies of David. 6. Seek ye the Lord while he may be found, call ye upon him while he is near: 7. Let the wicked forsake his way, and the unrighteous man his thoughts: and let him return unto the Lord, and he will have mercy upon him; and to our God, for he will abundantly pardon.

Isa. 56.1. My salvation *is* near to come, and my righteousness to be revealed. 6. The sons of the stranger, that join themselves to the Lord, to serve him, and to love the name of the Lord, to be his servants, every one that keepeth the sabbath from polluting it, and taketh hold of my covenant; 7. Even them will I bring to my holy mountain, and make them joyful in my house of prayer: for mine house shall be called an house of prayer for all people. 8. The Lord God, which gathereth the outcasts of Israel, saith, Yet will I gather *others* to him, besides those that are gathered unto him.

Isa. 57.17. He went on frowardly in the way of his heart. 18. I have seen his ways, and will heal him : I will lead him also, and restore comforts unto him and to his mourners.

19. I create the fruit of the lips ; Peace, peace to *him that is* far off, and to *him that is* near, saith the Lord ; and I will heal him.

Isa. 61.1. The Lord hath anointed me to preach good tidings unto the meek : he hath sent me to bind up the broken-hearted, to proclaim liberty to the captives, and the opening of the prison to *them that are* bound ; 2. To proclaim the acceptable year of the Lord, and the day of vengeance of our God ; to comfort all that mourn : 3. To appoint unto them that mourn in Zion, to give unto them beauty for ashes, the oil of joy for mourning, the garment of praise for the spirit of heaviness ; that they might be called Trees of righteousness, The planting of the Lord, that he might be glorified.

Jer. 21.8. Thus saith the Lord ; Behold, I set before you the way of life, and the way of death.

Eze. 18.32. I have no pleasure in the death of him that dieth, saith the Lord God : wherefore turn *yourselves*, and live ye.

Joel 2.32. Whosoever shall call on the name of the Lord shall be delivered : for in mount Zion and in Jerusalem shall be deliverance, as the Lord hath said, and in the remnant whom the Lord shall call.

Amos 5.4. Seek ye me, and ye shall live.

Zec. 14.8. Living waters shall go out from Jerusalem ; half of them toward the former sea, and half of them toward the hinder sea : in summer and in winter shall it be.

Mat. 11.28. Come unto me, all *ye* that labour and are heavy laden, and I will give you rest. 29. Take my yoke upon you, and learn of me ; for I am meek and lowly in heart : and ye shall find rest unto your souls. 30. For my yoke *is* easy, and my burden is light.

Mat. 18.14. It is not the will of your Father which is in heaven, that one of these little ones should perish.

Mat. 21.31. Jesus saith unto them, Verily I say unto you, That the publicans and the harlots go into the kingdom of God before you.

Mat. 22.9. Go ye therefore into the highways, and as many as ye shall find, bid to the marriage. 10. So those servants went out into the highways, and gathered together all as many as they found, both bad and good : and the wedding was furnished with guests. 14. Many are called.

Mat. 23.37. O Jerusalem, Jerusalem, *thou* that killest the prophets, and stonest them which are sent unto thee, how often would I have gathered thy children together, even as a hen gathereth her chickens under *her* wings, and ye would not !

Mat. 24.14. This gospel of the kingdom shall be preached in all the world for a witness unto all nations.

Mar. 2.17. They that are whole have no need of the physician, but they that are sick : I came not to call the righteous, but sinners to repentance. Mat. 9.12. Luk. 5.31,32.

Mar. 16.15. Go ye into all the world, and preach the gospel to every creature. Mat. 28.19.

Luk. 2.10. I bring you good tidings of great joy, which shall be to all people. 31. Thou

hast prepared before the face of all people ; 32. A light to lighten the Gentiles, and the glory of thy people Israel.

Luk. 3.6. All flesh shall see the salvation of God.

Luk. 7.47. Her sins, which are many, are forgiven ; for she loved much.

Luk. 10.11. Be ye sure of this, that the kingdom of God is come nigh unto you.

Luk. 13.29. They shall come from the east, and *from* the west, and from the north, and *from* the south, and shall sit down in the kingdom of God. 30. There are last which shall be first, and there are first which shall be last.

Luk. 15.2. This man receiveth sinners, and eateth with them. (Luk. 14.16-24. Parable of the Great Supper. Luk. 15.4-10. Of the Lost Sheep, and the Lost Piece of Silver. Luk. 15.11-32. Of the Prodigal Son. Luk. 16.19-31. Of the Rich Man and Lazarus.)

Luk. 19.10. The Son of man is come to seek and to save that which was lost.

Luk. 24.47. Repentance and remission of sins should be preached in his name among all nations, beginning at Jerusalem.

Jno. 1.7. The same came for a witness, to bear witness of the Light, that all *men* through him might believe.

Jno. 3.16. For God so loved the world, that he gave his only-begotten Son, that whosoever believeth in him should not perish, but have everlasting life. 17. For God sent not his Son into the world to condemn the world ; but that the world through him might be saved. *v.* 14,15.

Jno. 4.14. Whosoever drinketh of the water that I shall give him shall never thirst ; but the water that I shall give him shall be in him a well of water springing up into everlasting life.

Jno. 5.40. Ye will not come to me, that ye might have life.

Jno. 6.37. All that the Father giveth me shall come to me ; and him that cometh to me I will in no wise cast out.

Jno. 7.37. Jesus stood and cried, saying, If any man thirst, let him come unto me, and drink.

Jno. 11.51. Jesus should die for that nation ; 52. And not for that nation only, but that also he should gather together in one the children of God that were scattered abroad.

Act. 1.8. Ye shall be witnesses unto me both in Jerusalem, and in all Judea, and in Samaria, and unto the uttermost part of the earth.

Act. 2.39. The promise is unto you, and to your children, and to all that are afar off, *even* as many as the Lord our God shall call.

Act. 5.20. Go, stand and speak in the temple to the people all the words of this life.

Act. 10.34. God is no respecter of persons : 35. But in every nation he that feareth him, and worketh righteousness, is accepted with him. *v.* 9-48.

Act. 11.17. Forasmuch then as God gave them the like gift as *he did* unto us, who believed on the Lord Jesus Christ ; what was I, that I could withstand God ? 18. Then hath God also to the Gentiles granted repentance unto life.

Act. 13.26. Men *and* brethren, children of the stock of Abraham, and whosoever among you feareth God, to you is the word of this salvation sent. 47. I have set thee to be a light of the Gentiles, that thou shouldest be for salvation unto the ends of the earth.

Act. 15.7. God made choice among us, that the Gentiles by my mouth should hear the word of the gospel, and believe. 8. God, which knoweth the hearts, bare them witness, giving them the Holy Ghost, even as *he did* unto us ; 9. And put no difference between us and them, purifying their hearts by faith.

Act. 20.21. Testifying both to the Jews, and also to the Greeks, repentance toward God, and faith toward our Lord Jesus Christ.

Act. 28.28. Be it known therefore unto you, that the salvation of God is sent unto the Gentiles, and *that* they will hear it.

Rom. 1.5. We have received grace and apostleship, for obedience to the faith among all nations, for his name : 14. I am debtor both to the Greeks, and to the Barbarians ; both to the wise, and to the unwise. 16. It is the power of God unto salvation to every one that believeth ; to the Jew first, and also to the Greek.

Rom. 2.26. If the uncircumcision keep the righteousness of the law, shall not his uncircumcision be counted for circumcision ?

Rom. 3.22. The righteousness of God *which is* by faith of Jesus Christ unto all and upon all them that believe : for there is no difference : 29. *Is he* the God of the Jews only ? *is he* not also of the Gentiles ? Yes, of the Gentiles also : 30. Seeing *it is* one God, which shall justify the circumcision by faith, and uncircumcision through faith.

Rom. 4.16. *It is* of faith, that *it might be* by grace ; to the end the promise might be sure to all the seed ; not to that only which is of the law, but to that also which is of the faith of Abraham ; who is the father of us all.

Rom. 5.16. The free gift *is* of many offences unto justification.

Rom. 9.24. Even us, whom he hath called, not of the Jews only, but also of the Gentiles.

30. The Gentiles, which followed not after righteousness, have attained to righteousness, even the righteousness which is of faith.

Rom. 10.4. Christ *is* the end of the law for righteousness to every one that believeth. 8. The word is nigh thee, *even* in thy mouth, and in thy heart : that is, the word of faith, which we preach ; 11. The scripture saith, Whosoever believeth on him shall not be ashamed. 12. For there is no difference between the Jew and the Greek : for the same Lord over all is rich unto all that call upon him. 13. For whosoever shall call upon the name of the Lord shall be saved.

Rom. 11.11. Through their fall salvation *is come* unto the Gentiles, for to provoke them to jealousy. 12. Now if the fall of them *be* the riches of the world, and the diminishing of them the riches of the Gentiles ; how much more their fulness ? *v.* 1-36.

Rom. 15.9. That the Gentiles might glorify God for *his* mercy ; as it is written, For this cause I will confess to thee among the Gentiles, and sing unto thy name. 16. That the offering up of the Gentiles might be acceptable, being sanctified by the Holy Ghost. *v.* 8-12.

Rom. 16.26. Now is made manifest, and by the scriptures of the prophets, according to the commandment of the everlasting God, made known to all nations for the obedience of faith.

1 Cor. 6.11. Such were some of you : but ye are washed, but ye are sanctified, but ye are justified in the name of the Lord Jesus, and by the Spirit of our God.

2 Cor. 5.20. We are ambassadors for Christ, as though God did beseech *you* by us : we pray *you* in Christ's stead, be ye reconciled to God.

2 Cor. 6.1. We then, *as* workers together *with him*, beseech *you* also that ye receive not the grace of God in vain.

Gal. 3.8. The scripture, foreseeing that God would justify the heataen through faith, preached before the gospel unto Abraham, *saying*, In these shall all nations be blessed. 13. Christ hath redeemed us from the curse of the law, being made a curse for us : for it is written, Cursed *is* every one that hangeth on a tree : 14. That the blessing of Abraham might come on the Gentiles through Jesus Christ ; that we might receive the promise of the Spirit through faith. 26. Ye are all the children of God by faith in Christ Jesus. 27. As many of you as have been baptized into Christ have put on Christ. 28. There is neither Jew nor Greek, there is neither bond nor free, there is neither male nor female : for ye are all one in Christ Jesus.

Eph. 1.9. According to his good pleasure which he hath purposed in himself : 10. That in the dispensation of the fulness of times he might gather together in one all things in Christ, both which are in heaven, and which are on earth ; *even* in him.

Eph. 2.1. You *hath he quickened*, who were dead in trespasses and sins. 3. And were by nature the children of wrath, even as others. 4. But God, who is rich in mercy, for his great love wherewith he loved us, 5. Even when we were dead in sins, hath quickened us together with Christ ; (by grace ye are saved). 8. By grace are ye saved through faith ; and that not of yourselves ; *it is* the gift of God : 9. Not of works, lest any man should boast. 14. He is our peace, who hath made both one, and hath broken down the middle wall of partition *between us* ; 15. Having abolished in his flesh the enmity, *even* the law of commandments *contained* in ordinances ; for to make in himself of twain one new man, *so* making peace. 17. Came and preached peace to you which were afar off, and to them that were nigh.

Eph. 3.6. The Gentiles should be fellow-heirs, and of the same body, and partakers of his promise in Christ by the gospel. 9. To make all *men* see what *is* the fellowship of the mystery, which from the beginning of the world hath been hid in God, who created all things by Jesus Christ.

Eph. 5.14. Awake thou that sleepest, and arise from the dead, and Christ shall give thee light.

Col. 1.5. The word of the truth of the gospel ; 6. Which is come unto you, as *it is* in all the world. 20. Having made peace through the blood of his cross, by him to reconcile all things unto himself ; by him, *I say*, whether *they be* things in earth, or things in heaven. 21. You, that were sometime alienated and enemies in *your* mind by wicked works, yet now hath he reconciled 22. In the body of his flesh through death, to present you holy and unblameable and unreproveable in his sight: 23. The hope of the gospel, which ye have heard, *and* which was preached to every creature which is under heaven. 26. The mystery which hath been hid from ages and from generations, but now is made manifest to his saints: 27. To whom God would make known what *is* the riches of the glory of this mystery among the Gentiles; which is Christ in you, the hope of glory.

Col. 3.11. There is neither Greek nor Jew, circumcision nor uncircumcision, Barbarian, Scythian, bond *nor* free: but Christ *is* all, and in all.

1 Tim. 1.13. Who was before a blasphemer, and a persecutor, and injurious: but I obtained mercy, because I did *it* ignorantly in unbelief. 15. This *is* a faithful saying, and worthy of all acceptation, that Christ Jesus came into the world to save sinners; of whom I am chief. 16. Howbeit for this cause I obtained mercy, that in me first Jesus Christ might shew forth all longsuffering, for a pattern to them which should hereafter believe on him to life everlasting.

1 Tim. 2.3. God our Saviour; 4. Who will have all men to be saved, and to come unto the knowledge of the truth. 5. For *there is* one God, and one mediator between God and men, the man Christ Jesus; 6. Who gave himself a ransom for all, to be testified in due time. 7. I am ordained a preacher, and an apostle, a teacher of the Gentiles in faith and verity.

1 Tim. 4.10. We trust in the living God, who is the Saviour of all men, specially of those that believe.

Tit. 2.11. The grace of God that bringeth salvation hath appeared to all men.

Tit. 3.3. We ourselves also were sometimes foolish, disobedient, deceived, serving divers lusts and pleasures, living in malice and envy, hateful, *and* hating one another. 4. But after that the kindness and love of God our Saviour toward man appeared, 5. Not by works of righteousness which we have done, but according to his mercy he saved us.

Heb. 3.7. As the Holy Ghost saith, To day if ye will hear his voice, 8. Harden not your hearts. Psa. 95.7.

Heb. 4.1. A promise being left *us* of entering into his rest. *v.* 1-9.

2 Pet. 3.9. The Lord is not slack concerning his promise, as some men count slackness; but is longsuffering to us-ward, not willing that any should perish, but that all should come to repentance.

1 Jno. 2.25. This is the promise that he hath promised us, *even* eternal life.

1 Jno. 5.11. God hath given to us eternal life; and this life is in his Son.

Jude 3. I gave all diligence to write unto you of the common salvation.

Rev. 3.17. Thou art wretched, and miserable, and poor, and blind, and naked: 18. I counsel thee to buy of me gold tried in the fire, that thou mayest be rich; and white raiment, that thou mayest be clothed, and *that* the shame of thy nakedness do not appear; and anoint thine eyes with eye-salve, that thou mayest see. 20. Behold, I stand at the door, and knock: if any man hear my voice, and open the door, I will come in to him, and will sup with him, and he with me.

Rev. 5.9. Thou wast slain, and hast redeemed us to God by thy blood out of every kindred, and tongue, and people, and nation.

Rev. 7.9. I beheld, and, lo, a great multitude, which no man could number, of all nations, and kindreds, and people, and tongues, stood before the throne, and before the Lamb, clothed with white robes, and palms in their hands.

Rev. 14.6. I saw another angel fly in the midst of heaven, having the everlasting gospel to preach unto them that dwell on the earth, and to every nation, and kindred, and tongue, and people.

Rev. 21.6. I will give unto him that is athirst of the fountain of the water of life freely.

Rev. 22.17. And the Spirit and the bride say, Come. And let him that heareth say, Come. And let him that is athirst come. And whosoever will, let him take the water of life freely.

SALVATION BY CHRIST. See CHRIST SAVIOUR—CHRIST'S DEATH, DESIGN OF—PARDON—GOSPEL. By faith, See FAITH, SAVING—FAITH IN CHRIST, SAVING—JUSTIFICATION. From God, see GOD SAVIOUR—GOD'S MERCY—GOD GLORIFIED BY THE CHURCH.

————, PRAYER FOR, see PARDON. To be sought, see DECISION—REPENTANCE—SPIRITUAL DILIGENCE. Not of works, see PRIVILEGES—WORKS—SELF-RIGHTEOUSNESS—OFFERINGS, INSUFFICIENCY OF.

SAMARIA, capital of the 10 tribes (see ISRAELITES, p. 255), Isa. 7.9. 1 Kin. 16.29. 1 Kin. 22.51. 2 Kin. 13.1,10. 2 Kin. 15.8. Built by Omri on a hill bought from Shemer, 1 Kin. 16.24. Hadad's streets in, 1 Kin. 20.34.

Besieged by Benhadad I. in Ahab's reign; his defeat, 1 Kin. 20. Ahab's death at, 1 Kin. 22.10,37,38. Elisha brings the Syrians to, 2 Kin. 6.20. Besieged by Benhadad II.; famine, 2 Kin. 6.24-33; and plenty, 2 Kin. 7. Ahab's family slain at, 2 Kin. 10.1-28; and Ahaziah, 2 Chr. 22.9. Taken by Shalmanezer, 2 Kin. 17.5,6. 2 Kin. 18.9,10. Colonised from Assyria, 2 Kin. 17.24-41. Ezr. 4.9,10.

Altars to Baal in, 1 Kin. 16.32; and groves, 2 Kin. 13.6. Temple of, &c., destroyed by Jehu, 2 Kin. 10.17-28; and Josiah, 2 Kin. 23.19.

Simon the sorcerer's influence at; Philip, Peter, and John visit; many converted, Act. 8.5-25.

————, a district of Palestine. Jesus visits; a Samaritan woman, and others converted, Jno. 4.1-42. He heals 10 lepers in, Luk. 17.11-19. The twelve forbidden to preach in, Mat. 10.5. Gospel to be preached in, Act. 1.8. Disciples dispersed in, Act. 8.1. Visited by Paul and Barnabas, Act. 8.25. Churches in, Act. 9.31. Towers of, see TERZAH, SHECHEM, SAMARIA.

SAMARITANS, idolatry of, 2 Kin. 17. 25-41. Oppose the rebuilding of Jerusalem, Ezr. c. 4 & 5. Neh. c. 4 & 6. Hatred between them and the Jews, Jno. 4.9. Jno. 8.48.

SAMOS, an island in the Egean Sea, Act. 20.15.

SAMOTHRACIA, an island in the Egean Sea, Act. 16.11.

SAMSON, a Judge 20 years, Jud. 16.31. Son of Manoah; his birth is predicted by an angel; the Spirit of the Lord moves him, Jud. 13. He kills a lion; marries a Philistine; his riddle; slays 30 Philistines, Jud. 14. His wife given to another; he sets fire to the Philistines' corn; slays 1000 with a jawbone; his prayer, Jud. 15. Carries off the gates of Gaza; deceived by Delilah; bound by the Philistines; his eyes put out; his prayer; killed in pulling down the temple of Dagon, Jud. 16. Heb. 11.32.

SAMUEL, son of Elkanah and Hannah; his mother's prayer; she takes him to Shiloh, 1 Sam. 1. He ministers there; his mother's visits, 1 Sam. 2.18-21. His reputation; his visions, 1 Sam. 2.26. 1 Sam. 3. 1 Sam. 4.1. Act. 3.24.

Judges Israel at Mizpeh; his prayer and sacrifice; Philistines defeated; peace with Amorites, 1 Sam. 7. Judges at Bethel, Gilgal, Mizpeh, and Ramah; builds an altar at Ramah, 1 Sam. 7.15-17. Makes his sons Judges; their corrupt government, 1 Sam. 8. 1-3. 1 Chr. 6.28. Displeased with Israel for asking a king, 1 Sam. 8.4-22. Blesses the people's sacrifice, 1 Sam. 9.6-13.

Entertains Saul; anoints him king, 1 Sam. 9.15-27. 1 Sam. 10.1-8. Summons Israel to Mizpeh to choose a king, 1 Sam. 10.17-24. Describes his duties, 1 Sam. 10.25, see 1 Sam. 8.11-18. Saul recognised as king, 1 Sam. 11.14. Samuel's address to Israel; his integrity; calls for thunder, 1 Sam. 12. Reproves Saul, 1 Sam. 13.11-15. Predicts the loss of his kingdom; slays Agag; mourns for Saul, 1 Sam. 15. 1 Sam. 16.1.

Anoints David, 1 Sam. 16.1-13. 1 Chr. 11.3. Receives him at Naioth, 1 Sam. 19.18-24.

Appoints porters for the tabernacle, 1 Chr. 9.22. His offerings, 1 Chr. 26.28. Keeps the passover, 2 Chr. 35.18. His piety, Psa. 99.6. Jer. 15.1. Heb. 11.32. Writings, 1 Chr. 29.29. Death and burial, 1 Sam. 25.1. 1 Sam. 28.3. The witch of Endor, 1 Sam. 28.3-20.

SANBALLAT, opposes the rebuilding of Jerusalem, Neh. 2.10,19. Neh. 4. Neh. 6. Neh. 13.28.

SANCTIFICATION AND SPIRITUAL BLESSINGS BY CHRIST. Psa. 68.18. Thou hast received gifts for men; yea, *for* the rebellious also, that the Lord God might dwell *among* them.

Psa. 72.6. He shall come down like rain upon the mown grass: as showers *that* water the earth. 17. *Men* shall be blessed in him: all nations shall call him blessed.

Isa. 40.11. He shall feed his flock like a shepherd: he shall gather the lambs with his arm, and carry *them* in his bosom, *and* shall gently lead those that are with young.

Mal. 3.2. He *is* like a refiner's fire, and like fullers' sope: 3. He shall sit *as* a refiner and purifier of silver: and he shall purify the sons of Levi, and purge them as gold and silver, that they may offer unto the Lord an offering in righteousness.

Mal. 4.2. Unto you that fear my name shall the Sun of righteousness arise with healing in his wings.

Jno. 1.16. Of his fulness have all we received, and grace for grace.

Jno. 8.36. If the Son therefore shall make you free, ye shall be free indeed.

Jno. 15.4. As the branch cannot bear fruit of itself, except it abide in the vine; no more can ye, except ye abide in me. 5. I am the vine, ye *are* the branches: He that abideth in me, and I in him, the same bringeth forth much fruit: for without me ye can do nothing.

Act. 3.26. Unto you first God, having raised up his Son Jesus, sent him to bless you, in turning away every one of you from his iniquities.

Rom. 7.24. O wretched man that I am! who shall deliver me from the body of this death? 25. I thank God through Jesus Christ our Lord.

Rom. 8.3. What the law could not do, God sending his own Son in the likeness of sinful flesh, and for sin, condemned sin in the flesh: 4. That the righteousness of the law might be fulfilled in us, who walk not after the flesh, but after the Spirit.

1 Cor. 1.4. I thank my God always on your behalf, for the grace of God which is given you by Jesus Christ; 5. That in every thing ye are enriched by him, in all utterance, and *in* all knowledge. 30. Of him are ye in Christ Jesus, who of God is made unto us wisdom, and righteousness, and sanctification, and redemption.

2 Cor. 1.20. All the promises of God in him *are* yea, and in him Amen, unto the glory of God by us.

2 Cor. 5.15. He died for all, that they which live should not henceforth live unto themselves, but unto him which died for them, and rose again.

2 Cor. 12.9. My grace is sufficient for thee: for my strength is made perfect in weakness. Most gladly therefore will I rather glory in my infirmities, that the power of Christ may rest upon me.

Gal. 1.4. Who gave himself for our sins, that he might deliver us from this present evil world, according to the will of God and our Father.

Gal. 2.20. I am crucified with Christ: nevertheless I live; yet not I, but Christ liveth in me: and the life which I now live in·the flesh I live by the faith of the Son of God, who loved me, and gave himself for me.

Gal. 6.14. God forbid that I should glory, save in the cross of our Lord Jesus Christ, by whom the world is crucified unto me, and I unto the world.

Eph. 1.3. Who hath blessed us with all spiritual blessings in heavenly *places* in Christ. 4. According as he hath chosen us in him before the foundation of the world, that we should be holy and without blame before him in love.

Eph. 2.7. In the ages to come he might shew the exceeding riches of his grace in *his* kindness toward us through Christ Jesus. 10. We are his workmanship, created in Christ Jesus unto good works. 16. That he might reconcile both unto God in one body by the cross, having slain the enmity thereby. 21. In whom all the building fitly framed together groweth unto an holy temple in the Lord.

Eph. 4.7. Unto every one of us is given grace according to the measure of the gift of Christ. 12. For the perfecting of the saints, for the work of the ministry, for the edifying of the body of Christ: 13. Till we all come in the unity of the faith, and of the knowledge of the Son of God, unto a perfect man, unto the measure of the stature of the fulness of Christ. 15. Speaking the truth in love, may grow up into him in all things, which is the head, *even* Christ. 16. From whom the whole body fitly joined together and compacted by that which every joint supplieth, according to the effectual working in the measure of every part, maketh increase of the body unto the edifying of itself in love.

Eph. 5.25. Christ also loved the church, and gave himself for it; 26. That he might sanctify and cleanse it with the washing of water by the word, 27. That he might present it to himself a glorious church, not having spot, or wrinkle, or any such thing; but that it should be holy and without blemish.

Eph. 6.10. My brethren, be strong in the Lord, and in the power of his might.

Phil. 1.11. Filled with the fruits of righteousness, which are by Jesus Christ.

Phil. 4.13. I can do all things through Christ which strengtheneth me. 19. My God shall supply all your need according to his riches in glory by Christ Jesus.

Col. 2.11. In whom also ye are circumcised with the circumcision made without hands, in putting off the body of the sins of the flesh by the circumcision of Christ. 19. Not holding the head, from which all the body by joints and bands having nourishment ministered, and knit together, increaseth with the increase of God.

2 The. 2.16. Our Lord Jesus Christ himself, 17. Comfort your hearts, and stablish you in every good word and work.

2 The. 3.3. The Lord is faithful, who shall stablish you, and keep *you* from evil.

2 Tim. 4.17. The Lord stood with me, and strengthened me.

Tit. 2.14. Who gave himself for us, that he might redeem us from all iniquity, and purify unto himself a peculiar people, zealous of good works.

Heb. 2.11. Both he that sanctifieth and they who are sanctified *are* all of one: for which cause he is not ashamed to call them brethren.

Heb. 9.14. How much more shall the blood of Christ, who through the eternal Spirit offered himself without spot to God, purge your conscience from dead works to serve the living God? Heb. 8.6-13.

Heb. 10.10. We are sanctified through the offering of the body of Jesus Christ once *for all*. 14. By one offering he hath perfected for ever them that are sanctified.

Heb. 13.12. Jesus also, that he might sanctify the people with his own blood, suffered without the gate. 21. Make you perfect in every good work to do his will, working in you that which is wellpleasing in his sight, through Jesus Christ.

Rev. 3.8. I know thy works: behold, I have set before thee an open door, and no man can shut it. 18. I counsel thee to buy of me gold tried in the fire, that thou mayest be rich; and white raiment, that thou mayest be clothed, and *that* the shame of thy nakedness do not appear; and anoint thine eyes with eye-salve, that thou mayest see.

Rev. 7.14. These are they which have washed their robes, and made them white in the blood of the Lamb.

SANCTIFICATION AND SPIRITUAL BLESSINGS FROM GOD. Gen. 49.24. His bow abode in strength, and the arms of his hands were made strong by the hands of the mighty *God* of Jacob.

Ex. 15.2. The Lord *is* my strength and song, and he is become my salvation.

Ex. 33.16. Wherein shall it be known here that I and thy people have found grace in thy sight? *is it* not in that thou goest with us? so shall we be separated, I and thy people, from all the people that *are* upon the face of the earth.

Lev. 21.8. I the Lord which sanctify you *am* holy. Ex. 31.13.

Deu. 33.25. Thy shoes *shall be* iron and brass; and as thy days, *so shall* thy strength *be*.

1 Sam. 2.4. The bows of the mighty men *are* broken, and they that stumbled are girded with strength.

Neh. 8.10. The joy of the Lord is your strength.

Job 17.9. The righteous also shall hold on his way, and he that hath clean hands shall be stronger and stronger.

Job 23.6. Will he plead against me with *his* great power? No; but he would put *strength* in me.

Psa. 18.1. I will love thee, O Lord, my strength. 2. The Lord *is* my rock, and my fortress, and my deliverer; my God, my strength, in whom I will trust; my buckler, and the horn of my salvation, *and* my high tower. 28. Thou wilt light my candle: the Lord my God will enlighten my darkness. 32. *It is* God that girdeth me with strength, and maketh my way perfect. 35. Thou hast also given me the shield of thy salvation: and thy right hand hath holden me up, and thy gentleness hath made me great. 36. Thou hast enlarged my steps under me, that my feet did not slip. Psa. 144.1,2.

Psa. 23.2. He maketh me to lie down in green pastures: he leadeth me beside the still waters. 3. He restoreth my soul: he leadeth me in the paths of righteousness for his name's sake.

Psa. 27.14. Wait on the Lord: be of good courage, and he shall strengthen thine heart: wait, I say, on the Lord.

Psa. 28.8. The Lord *is* their strength, and he *is* the saving strength of his anointed.

Psa. 29.11. The Lord will give strength unto his people.

Psa. 30.7. Lord, by thy favour thou hast made my mountain to stand strong: thou didst hide thy face, *and* I was troubled.

Psa. 31.24. Be of good courage, and he shall strengthen your heart, all ye that hope in the Lord.

Psa. 37.6. He shall bring forth thy righteousness as the light. 17. The Lord upholdeth the righteous. 24. Though he fall, he shall not be utterly cast down: for the Lord upholdeth *him with* his hand. 39. The salvation of the righteous *is* of the Lord: *he is* their strength in the time of trouble.

Psa. 52.8. I *am* like a green olive tree in the house of God: I trust in the mercy of God for ever and ever.

Psa. 55.22. Cast thy burden upon the Lord

and he shall sustain thee : he shall never suffer the righteous to be moved.

Psa. 61.5. Thou, O God, hast heard my vows : thou hast given *me* the heritage of those that fear thy name.

Psa. 63.8. My soul followeth hard after thee : thy right hand upholdeth me.

Psa. 66.9. Which holdeth our soul in life, and suffereth not our feet to be moved.

Psa. 68.28. Thy God hath commanded thy strength : strengthen, O God, that which thou hast wrought for us. 35. The God of Israel *is* he that giveth strength and power unto *his* people.

Psa. 71.16. I will go in the strength of the Lord God ; I will make mention of thy righteousness, *even* of thine only.

Psa. 73.23. I *am* continually with thee : thou hast holden *me* by my right hand. 26. My flesh and my heart faileth : *but* God *is* the strength of my heart, and my portion for ever.

Psa. 81.10. Open thy mouth wide, and I will fill it.

Psa. 84.5. Blessed *is* the man whose strength *is* in thee ; in whose heart *are* the ways *of them*. 11. The Lord God *is* a sun and shield : the Lord will give grace and glory : no good *thing* will he withhold from them that walk uprightly.

Psa. 89.17. Thou *art* the glory of their strength : and in thy favour our horn shall be exalted.

Psa. 92.12. The righteous shall flourish like the palm tree : he shall grow like a cedar in Lebanon. 13. Those that be planted in the house of the Lord shall flourish in the courts of our God. 14. They shall still bring forth fruit in old age ; they shall be fat and flourishing. Psa. 1.3.

Psa. 94.17. Unless the Lord *had been* my help, my soul had almost dwelt in silence. 18. When I said, My foot slippeth ; thy mercy, O Lord, held me up.

Psa. 105.4. Seek the Lord, and his strength.

Psa. 119.32. I will run the way of thy commandments, when thou shalt enlarge my heart. 102. I have not departed from thy judgments : for thou hast taught me.

Psa. 132.15. I will abundantly bless her provision : I will satisfy her poor with bread. 16. I will also clothe her priests with salvation : and her saints shall shout aloud for joy.

Psa. 138.3. In the day when I cried thou answeredst me, *and* strengthenedst me *with* strength in my soul. 8. The Lord will perfect *that which* concerneth me : thy mercy, O Lord, *endureth* for ever : forsake not the works of thine own hands.

Psa. 146.5. Happy *is he* that *hath* the God of Jacob for his help, whose hope *is* in the Lord his God.

Pro. 4.18. The path of the just *is* as the shining light, that shineth more and more unto the perfect day.

Pro. 10.29. The way of the Lord *is* strength to the upright.

Pro. 16.6. By the fear of the Lord men depart from evil.

Isa. 1.25. I will turn my hand upon thee, and purely purge away thy dross, and take away all thy tin.

Isa. 4.3. *He that is* left in Zion, and *he that* remaineth in Jerusalem, shall be called holy,

even every one that is written among the living in Jerusalem : 4. When the Lord shall have washed away the filth of the daughters of Zion, and shall have purged the blood of Jerusalem from the midst thereof by the spirit of judgment, and by the spirit of burning.

Isa. 6.6. Then flew one of the seraphims unto me, having a live coal in his hand, *which* he had taken with the tongs from off the altar : 7. And he laid *it* upon my mouth, and said, Lo, this hath touched thy lips ; and thine iniquity is taken away, and thy sin purged.

Isa. 26.12. Lord, thou wilt ordain peace for us ; for thou also hast wrought all our works in us.

Isa. 28.6. For a spirit of judgment to him that sitteth in judgment, and for strength to them that turn the battle to the gate.

Isa. 33.5. The Lord is exalted ; for he dwelleth on high : he hath filled Zion with judgment and righteousness. 6. Wisdom and knowledge shall be the stability of thy times, *and* strength of salvation : the fear of the Lord *is* his treasure.

Isa. 40.2. She hath received of the Lord's hand double for all her sins. 29. He giveth power to the faint ; and to *them that have* no might he increaseth strength. 31. They that wait upon the Lord shall renew *their* strength ; they shall mount up with wings as eagles ; they shall run, and not be weary ; *and* they shall walk, and not faint.

Isa. 41.10. Fear thou not ; for I *am* with thee ; be not dismayed ; for I *am* thy God : I will strengthen thee ; yea, I will help thee ; yea, I will uphold thee with the right hand of my righteousness. 13. For I the Lord thy God will hold thy right hand, saying unto thee, Fear not ; I will help thee. 14. Fear not, thou worm Jacob, *and ye* men of Israel ; I will help thee, saith the Lord, and thy redeemer, the Holy One of Israel. 17. *When* the poor and needy seek water, and *there* is none, *and* their tongue faileth for thirst, I the Lord will hear them, *I* the God of Israel will not forsake them. 18. I will open rivers in high places, and fountains in the midst of the valleys : I will make the wilderness a pool of water, and the dry land springs of water.

Isa. 44.3. I will pour water upon him that is thirsty, and floods upon the dry ground : I will pour my spirit upon thy seed, and my blessing upon thine offspring.

Isa. 45.8. Drop down, ye heavens, from above, and let the skies pour down righteousness : let the earth open, and let them bring forth salvation, and let righteousness spring up together ; I the Lord have created it. 24. Surely, shall *one* say, in the Lord have I righteousness and strength : *even* to him shall *men* come.

Isa. 54.17. This *is* the heritage of the servants of the Lord, and their righteousness *is* of me, saith the Lord.

Isa. 58.8. Then shall thy light break forth as the morning, and thine health shall spring forth speedily : and thy righteousness shall go before thee ; the glory of the Lord shall be thy rereward. 10. Then shall thy light rise in obscurity, and thy darkness *be* as the noon day. 11. And the Lord shall guide thee continually, and satisfy thy soul in drought, and make fat thy bones : and thou shalt be like a watered garden, and like a spring of water, whose waters fail not.

Jer. 31.12. They shall come and sing in the height of Zion, and shall flow together to the goodness of the Lord: and their soul shall be as a watered garden;. and they shall not sorrow any more at all. 14. I will satiate the soul of the priests with fatness, and my people shall be satisfied with my goodness, saith the Lord. 33. I will put my law in their inward parts, and write it in their hearts; and will be their God, and they shall be my people.

Eze. 16.14. Thy renown went forth among the heathen for thy beauty: for it *was* perfect through my comeliness, which I had put upon thee, saith the Lord God.

Dan. 11.32. The people that do know their God shall be strong, and do *exploits*.

Hos. 6.3. Then shall we know, *if* we follow on to know the Lord: his going forth is prepared as the morning; and he shall come unto us as the rain, as the latter *and* former rain unto the earth.

Hos. 14.5. I will be as the dew unto Israel: he shall grow as the lily, and cast forth his roots as Lebanon. 8. What have I to do any more with idols? I have heard *him*, and observed him: From me is thy fruit found. *v.* 6,7.

Hab. 3.19. The Lord God *is* my strength, and he will make my feet like hinds' *feet*, and he will make me to walk upon mine high places.

Zec. 10.12. I will strengthen them in the Lord; and they shall walk up and down in his name, saith the Lord.

Zec. 12.8. In that day shall the Lord defend the inhabitants of Jerusalem: and he that is feeble among them at that day shall be as David; and the house of David *shall be* as God, as the angel of the Lord before them.

Mar. 4.26. So is the kingdom of God, as if a man should cast seed into the ground; 27. And should sleep, and rise night and day, and the seed should spring and grow up, he knoweth not how.

Jno. 17.11. Holy Father, keep through thine own name those whom thou hast given me, that they may be one, as we *are*.

Act. 20.32. I commend you to God, and to the word of his grace, which is able to build you up, and to give you an inheritance among all them which are sanctified.

Rom. 9.23. That he might make known the riches of his glory on the vessels of mercy, which he had afore prepared unto glory.

Rom. 14.4. Yea, he shall be holden up: for God is able to make him stand.

Rom. 16.25. To him that is of power to stablish you according to my gospel.

1 Cor. 12.6. There are diversities of operations, but it is the same God which worketh all in all.

1 Cor. 13.10. But when that which is perfect is come, then that which is in part shall be done away. 12. For now we see through a glass, darkly; but then face to face: now I know in part; but then shall I know even as also I am known.

1 Cor. 15.10. By the grace of God I am what I am: and his grace which *was bestowed* upon me was not in vain; but I laboured more abundantly than they all: yet not I, but the grace of God which was with me.

2 Cor. 3.5. Our sufficiency *is* of God.

2 Cor. 5.5. He that hath wrought us for the selfsame thing *is* God, who also hath given unto us the earnest of the Spirit.

2 Cor. 9.8. God *is* able to make all grace abound toward you; that ye, always having all sufficiency in all *things*, may abound to every good work.

2 Cor. 10.4. The weapons of our warfare *are* not carnal, but mighty through God to the pulling down of strong holds.

Eph. 3.20. Him that is able to do exceeding abundantly above all that we ask or think, according to the power that worketh in us.

Phil. 1.6. Being confident of this very thing, that he which hath begun a good work in you will perform *it* until the day of Jesus Christ.

Phil. 2.13. It is God which worketh in you both to will and to do of *his* good pleasure.

Phil. 4.7. The peace of God, which passeth all understanding, shall keep your hearts and minds through Christ Jesus. 19. My God shall supply all your need according to his riches in glory by Christ Jesus.

Col. 1.11. Strengthened with all might, according to his glorious power, unto all patience and longsuffering with joyfulness. 12. Giving thanks unto the Father, which hath made us meet to be partakers of the inheritance of the saints in light.

1 The. 5.24. Faithful *is* he that calleth you, who also will do *it*.

Heb. 12.10. He for *our* profit, that *we* might be partakers of his holiness. 11. Now no chastening for the present seemeth to be joyous, but grievous: nevertheless afterward it yieldeth the peaceable fruit of righteousness.

Jas. 1.17. Every good gift and every perfect gift is from above, and cometh down from the Father of lights, with whom is no variableness, neither shadow of turning. *v.* 18.

1 Pet. 1.5. Who are kept by the power of God, through faith unto salvation ready to be revealed in the last time.

2 Pet. 1.2. Grace and peace be multiplied unto you through the knowledge of God, and of Jesus our Lord. 3. His divine power hath given unto us all things that *pertain* unto life and godliness, through the knowledge of him that hath called us to glory and virtue: 4. Whereby are given unto us exceeding great and precious promises: that by these ye might be partakers of the divine nature, having escaped the corruption that is in the world through lust.

1 Jno. 1.9. If we confess our sins, he is faithful and just to forgive us *our* sins, and to cleanse us from all unrighteousness.

1 Jno. 4.4. Ye are of God, little children, and have overcome them: because greater is he that is in you, than he that is in the world.

Jude 1. Them that are sanctified by God the Father, and preserved in Jesus Christ, *and* called. 24. Him that is able to keep you from falling, and to present *you* faultless before the presence of his glory with exceeding joy.

See REGENERATION.

SANCTIFICATION BY THE HOLY SPIRIT. See REGENERATION AND SANCTIFICATION BY THE HOLY SPIRIT.

———— BY THE SCRIPTURES. See WORD OF GOD SANCTIFYING.

SANCTIFICATION, PRAYER FOR. See SPIRITUAL BLESSINGS.

SANCTUARY. See TABERNACLE — TEMPLE—WORSHIP.

SANDAL. See SHOE.

SANHEDRIM or COUNCIL (Gr. *sunedrion*), always translated council, Mat. 5.22, the supreme council of the Jewish nation, *comp*. Num. 11.16. Consisted of priests, elders, scribes, Mat. 16.21. Mat. 26.3,57. Called senate, Act. 5.21; and elders, Act. 22.5. Mat. 2.4. Presided over by the high-priest, Mat. 26.57,62-65. Jno. 11.49. Not allowed to inflict capital punishment, Jno. 18.31.

Persecuted Christ, Mat. 26.59. Mar. 14.55. Mar. 15.1. Luk. 22.66. Jno. 11.47; and the apostles, Act. 4.1-22. Act. 5.21-41. Act. 6, 12,15. Act. 7.54-60. Act. 22.30. Act. 23. Act. 24.20.

An inferior court called a council, Mat. 5.22. Mar. 13.9. See COUNSELLOR.

SAPPHIRA, wife of Ananias; her falsehood and death, Act. 5.1-11.

SAPPHIRE, a precious stone in the highpriest's breastplate, Ex. 28.18. Value of, Job 28.6,16. Isa. 54.11. Eze. 28.13. Symbolical, Rev. 21.19.

SARAH, originally Sarai, and supposed to be the same as Iscah, Lot's sister, Gen. 11. 29-31, but see Gen. 20.12. Her beauty; taken into Pharaoh's house, Gen. 12.5,10-20. Taken by Abimelech, Gen. 20. Gives Hagar to Abraham; ill-treats her, Gen. 16.1-6. Gen. 21.9-11. Name changed to Sarah (princess); a son promised, her incredulity, Gen. 17.15-21. Gen. 18.9-15. Rom. 9.9. Birth of Isaac, Gen. 21.1-8. Gen. 24.36. Isa. 51.2. Death of, at the age of 127; buried in the cave of Machpelah, Gen. 23.1,2,19. Gen. 25.10. Her excellences, Heb. 11.11. 1 Pet. 3.5,6.

SARDIS, the capital of Lydia; epistle to the church in, Rev. 3.1-6.

SARDIUS or SARDINE, a cornelian, Eze. 28.13. Rev. 4.3. Set in the high-priest's breastplate, Ex. 28.17. Ex. 39.10. Symbolical, Rev. 21.20.

SARDONYX, a precious stone, symbolical, Rev. 21.20.

SAREPTA or ZAREPHATH, a Phenician town between Tyre and Sidon, Obad. 20. Elijah multiplies a widow's oil in, and raises her son, 1 Kin. 17.9-24. Luk. 4.26.

SARGON, king of Assyria, the predecessor of Sennacherib; sends Tartan against Ashdod, Isa. 20.1.

SATAN. Gen. 3.1. The serpent was more subtile than any beast of the field which the Lord God had made. And he said unto the woman, Yea, hath God said, Ye shall not eat of every tree of the garden? 4. And the serpent said unto the woman, Ye shall not surely die: 5. For God doth know that in the day ye eat thereof, then your eyes shall be opened, and ye shall be as gods, knowing good and evil. 14. Because thou hast done this, thou *art* cursed above all cattle, and above every beast of the field; upon thy belly shalt thou go, and dust shalt thou eat all the days of thy life: 15. And I will put enmity between thee and the woman, and between thy seed and her

seed; it shall bruise thy head, and thou shalt bruise his heel. Isa. 65.25.

1 Chr. 21.1. Satan stood up against Israel, and provoked David to number Israel.

Job 1.6. There was a day when the sons of God came to present themselves before the Lord, and Satan came also among them. 7. The Lord said unto Satan, Whence comest thou? Then Satan answered the Lord, and said, From going to and fro in the earth, and from walking up and down in it. 9. Satan answered the Lord, and said, Doth Job fear God for nought? 10. Hast not thou made an hedge about him, &c. 12. The Lord said unto Satan, Behold, all that he hath *is* in thy power; only upon himself put not forth thine hand.

Job 2.3. The Lord said unto Satan, Hast thou considered my servant Job; and still he holdeth fast his integrity, although thou movedst me against him, to destroy him without cause. 4. And Satan answered the Lord, and said, Skin for skin, yea, all that a man hath will he give for his life. 5. But put forth thine hand now, and touch his bone and his flesh, and he will curse thee to thy face. 6. The Lord said unto Satan, Behold, he *is* in thine hand; but save his life. 7. So went Satan forth from the presence of the Lord, and smote Job with sore boils from the sole of his foot unto his crown.

Psa. 109.6. Let Satan stand at his right hand.

Zec. 3.1. He shewed me Joshua the highpriest standing before the angel of the Lord, and Satan standing at his right hand to resist him. 2. And the Lord said unto Satan, The Lord rebuke thee, O Satan. Dan. 10.13.

Mat. 13.19. When any one heareth the word of the kingdom, and understandeth *it* not, then cometh the wicked *one*, and catcheth away that which was sown in his heart. 38. The tares are the children of the wicked *one*; 39. The enemy that sowed them is the devil. Mar. 4.15. Luk. 8.12.

Mat. 25.41. Everlasting fire, prepared for the devil and his angels.

Luk. 4.6. The devil said unto him, All this power will I give thee, and the glory of them: for that is delivered unto me; and to whomsoever I will I give it. 7. If thou therefore wilt worship me, all shall be thine. *v*. 1-13. Mat. 4.1-11.

Luk. 10.18. I beheld Satan as lightning fall from heaven.

Luk. 11.15. Some of them said, He casteth out devils through Beelzebub the chief of the devils. Mat. 12.24. Mar. 3.22.

Luk. 13.16. This woman . . . . . . whom Satan hath bound, lo, these eighteen years.

Luk. 22.31. Simon, Simon, behold, Satan hath desired *to have* you, that he may sift *you* as wheat. 53. This is your hour, and the power of darkness.

Jno. 8.38. Ye do that which ye have seen with your father. 41. Ye do the deeds of your father. 44. Ye are of *your* father the devil, and the lusts of your father ye will do. He was a murderer from the beginning, and abode not in the truth, because there is no truth in him. When he speaketh a lie, he speaketh of his own: for he is a liar, and the father of it.

Jno. 12.31. Now is the judgment of this world: now shall the prince of this world be cast out.

Jno. 13.2. The devil having now put into the heart of Judas Iscariot, Simon's *son*, to betray him. 27. After the sop Satan entered into him.

Jno. 14.30. The prince of this world cometh, and hath nothing in me.

Jno. 16.11. The prince of this world is judged.

Act. 5.3. Ananias, why hath Satan filled thine heart to lie to the Holy Ghost?

Act. 13.10. *Thou* child of the devil, *thou* enemy of all righteousness.

Act. 26.18. To turn them from the power of Satan unto God.

Rom. 16.20. The God of peace shall bruise Satan under your feet shortly.

2 Cor. 2.11. Lest Satan should get an advantage of us: for we are not ignorant of his devices.

2 Cor. 4.4. The god of this world hath blinded the minds of them which believe not.

2 Cor. 11.3. I fear, lest by any means, as the serpent beguiled Eve through his subtilty, so your minds should be corrupted from the simplicity that is in Christ. 14. Satan himself is transformed into an angel of light. *v.* 15.

2 Cor. 12.7. There was given to me a thorn in the flesh, the messenger of Satan to buffet me.

Eph. 2.2. Ye walked according to the prince of the power of the air, the spirit that now worketh in the children of disobedience.

Eph. 4.27. Neither give place to the devil.

Eph. 6.11. Stand against the wiles of the devil. 12. For we wrestle not against flesh and blood, but against principalities, against powers, against the rulers of the darkness of this world, against spiritual wickedness in high *places*. 16. Taking the shield of faith, wherewith ye shall be able to quench all the fiery darts of the wicked.

Col. 1.13. Who hath delivered us from the power of darkness.

Col. 2.15. Having spoiled principalities and powers, he made a shew of them openly, triumphing over them in it.

1 The. 2.18. We would have come unto you, even I Paul, once and again; but Satan hindered us.

1 The. 3.5. Lest by some means the tempter have tempted you, and our labour be in vain.

2 The. 2.9. Whose coming is after the working of Satan with all power and signs and lying wonders.

1 Tim. 3.6. Not a novice, lest being lifted up with pride he fall into the condemnation of the devil. 7. He must have a good report of them which are without; lest he fall into reproach and the snare of the devil.

1 Tim. 5.15. Some are already turned aside after Satan.

2 Tim. 2.26. *That* they may recover themselves out of the snare of the devil, who are taken captive by him at his will.

Heb. 2.14. That through death he might destroy him that had the power of death, that is, the devil.

Jas. 4.7. Resist the devil, and he will flee from you.

1 Pet. 5.8. Your adversary the devil, as a roaring lion, walketh about, seeking whom he may devour: 9. Whom resist stedfast in the faith.

2 Pet. 2.4. God spared not the angels that sinned, but cast *them* down to hell, and delivered *them* into chains of darkness, to be reserved unto judgment.

1 Jno. 2.13. Ye have overcome the wicked one.

1 Jno. 3.8. He that committeth sin is of the devil; for the devil sinneth from the beginning. For this purpose the Son of God was manifested, that he might destroy the works of the devil. 10. In this the children of God are manifest, and the children of the devil. 12. Not as Cain, *who* was of that wicked one, and slew his brother.

1 Jno. 5.18. He that is begotten of God keepeth himself, and that wicked one toucheth him not.

Jude 6. The angels which kept not their first estate, but left their own habitation, he hath reserved in everlasting chains, under darkness, unto the judgment of the great day. 9. Michael the archangel, when contending with the devil he disputed about the body of Moses, durst not bring against him a railing accusation, but said, The Lord rebuke thee. Zec. 3.1,2.

Rev. 2.10. The devil shall cast *some* of you into prison, that ye may be tried. 13. I know thy works, and where thou dwellest, *even* where Satan's seat *is:* Antipas *was* my faithful martyr, who was slain among you, where Satan dwelleth. 24. As many as have not this doctrine, and which have not known the depths of Satan.

Rev. 3.9. The synagogue of Satan, which say they are Jews, and are not, but do lie.

Rev. 9.11. They had a king over them, *which is* the angel of the bottomless pit, whose name in the Hebrew tongue *is* Abaddon, but in the Greek tongue hath *his* name Apollyon.

Rev. 12.9. The great dragon was cast out, that old serpent, called the Devil, and Satan, which deceiveth the whole world: he was cast out into the earth, and his angels were cast out with him. 10. And I heard a loud voice saying in heaven, Now is come salvation, and strength, and the kingdom of our God, and the power of his Christ: for the accuser of our brethren is cast down, which accused them before our God day and night. 11. They overcame him by the blood of the Lamb, and by the word of their testimony. 12. Woe to the inhabiters of the earth and of the sea! for the devil is come down unto you, having great wrath, because he knoweth that he hath but a short time.

Rev. 13.2. The dragon gave him his power, and his seat, and great authority.

Rev. 20.1. I saw an angel come down from heaven, having the key of the bottomless pit and a great chain in his hand. 2. And he laid hold on the dragon, that old serpent, which is the Devil, and Satan, and bound him a thousand years, 3. And cast him into the bottomless pit, and shut him up, and set a seal upon him, that he should deceive the nations no more, till the thousand years should be fulfilled: and after that he must be loosed a little season.

Rev. 20.7. When the thousand years are expired, Satan shall be loosed out of his prison, 8. And shall go out to deceive the nations which are in the four quarters of the earth, Gog and Magog, to gather them together to battle. 10. And the devil that deceived them was cast into the lake of fire and brimstone, where the beast and the false prophet *are*, and shall be tormented day and night for ever and ever.

See DEMONS—ANGELS, FALLEN.

SATAN, NAMES OF. Devil, 1 Pet. 5.8, &c., see ABADDON, APOLLYON, BELIAL, DRAGON, SERPENT.

SATYR, Isa. 13.21. Isa. 34.14. Usually translated goat, as Lev. 4.24; also devils; that is, idols in the form of a goat, Lev. 17.7. 2 Chr. 11.15.

SAUL, 1st king of Israel (40 years' reign), Act. 13.21. Son of Kish, the Benjamite, his stature, 1 Sam. 9.1,2. 1 Sam. 10.23. 1 Chr. 8.33. Sent to seek his father's asses; visits Samuel; entertained by him; anointed king; he prophecies; proverb concerning him, 1 Sam. 9. 1 Sam. 10.1-16. Chosen king by lot, 1 Sam. 10.17-27. Hos. 13.11.

Resides at Gibeah, 1 Sam. 11.4. 1 Sam. 14.2. 1 Sam. 15.34. Isa. 10.29. Summons Israel to war; defeats Nahash; acknowledged king; his magnanimity, 1 Sam. 11. His guard; wars with the Philistines; offers a burnt-offering; rebuked by Samuel; threatened with loss of his kingdom, 1 Sam. 13.

Philistines defeated; his curse on any one eating; builds an altar; casts lots; defeats Moab, Ammon, Edom, Zobah, and Amalek, 1 Sam. 14. Enlists soldiers, 1 Sam. 14.52. 1 Chr. 12.29.

Sent to destroy Amalek; spares Agag, &c.; reproved by Samuel, and the loss of his kingdom predicted, 1 Sam. 15. 1 Sam. 28.17-19. Troubled by an evil spirit; sends for David, 1 Sam. 16.14-23. His war with the Philistines; interview with David; Goliath slain, 1 Sam. 17.

Makes David a general; envies him; casts a javelin at him; promises Merab to him as wife; gives him Michal, 1 Sam. 18. Attempts David's life, 1 Sam. 19; and Jonathan's, 1 Sam. 20.24-34. Slays the priests, 1 Sam. 22.11-19. Pursues David; invasion of the Philistines, 1 Sam. 23. His skirt cut off by David, 1 Sam. 24. 1 Sam. 26. Slays the Gibeonites, 2 Sam. 21.1,2.

War with the Philistines; slays the wizards, &c.; seeks the witch of Endor, 1 Sam. 28. Slain at Gilboa; his armour hung up in Ashtaroth; his body fastened to the wall of Bethshan; carried away, and burnt by the men of Jabesh, 1 Sam. 31. 1 Chr. 10. 2 Sam. 1. 2 Sam. 2.4. 2 Sam. 21.12-14. David's lament for him, 2 Sam. 1.17-27. His offerings, 1 Chr. 26.28.

His sons and chief officers, 1 Sam. 14.49-51. 2 Sam. 2.8-10. 1 Chr. 8.33. 1 Chr. 9.39. His concubine, 2 Sam. 3.7.

SAW, 2 Sam. 12.31. Isa. 10.15.

SCALES. See BALANCES.

SCAPE-GOAT (Heb. *Azazel*). The live goat over which, in the Day of Atonement, the sins of Israel were confessed; after which it was led into an uninhabited land and let go, Lev. 16.20-34.

SCARLET. Colour of robes of honour, Dan. 5.7,16,29. 2 Sam. 1.24. Mat. 27.28. Rev. 18.12,16. Symbolical, Rev. 17.3,4.

SCEPTRE or ROD. Of a ruler, Gen. 49.10. Num. 24.17. Isa. 9.4. Isa. 14.5. Jer. 48.17. Eze. 19.14. Amos 1.5,8. Zec. 10.11. Golden,

Est. 4.11. Held out as a mark of favour by the king, and touched, Est. 5.2. Est. 8.4. Of iron, illustrative, Psa. 2.9. Rev. 2.27. Rev. 12.5. See ROD.

SCEVA, the Jew, 7 sons of, attempt to cast out devils; their punishment, Act. 19. 13-17.

SCHISM (Gr. *schisma*), 1 Cor. 12.25. Translated rent, Mat. 9.16. Mar. 2.21; division (of opinion), Jno. 7.43. Jno. 9.16. Jno. 10.19. 1 Cor. 1.10. 1 Cor. 11.18.

SCIENCE (Gr. *gnōsis*), 1 Tim. 6.20. Usually translated knowledge, as Luk. 11.52. Rom. 2.20. See PHILOSOPHY.

SCOFFING, SCORNING. See BLASPHEMY —INFIDELITY.

SCORPION, a large insect of the spider species, shaped somewhat like a lobster, and furnished with a sting at the end of the tail, Deu. 8.15. Luk. 10.19. Luk. 11.12. Rev. 9.3,5,10. Illustrative, Eze. 2.6. A kind of scourge so called, 1 Kin. 12.11,14.

SCOURGING, Lev. 19.20. Deu. 22.18. Pro. 20.30. Stripe to be given for stripe, Ex. 21.25. Stripes not to exceed forty; inflicted while lying on the ground, in presence of the Judge, Deu. 25.2,3. 2 Cor. 11.24. By masters, Ex. 21.20; by kings, Pro. 17.26. Jer. 37.15; by parents, Pro. 13.24. Pro. 23. 13,14; by the synagogue, Mat. 10.17. Act. 26.11; by the Romans, Mat. 20.19. Jno. 19.1. Illustrative, 1 Kin. 12.11. Job. 5.21. Job 9.23. Isa. 10.26.

SCRIBE. A writer or Scripturist, Jud. 5.14. 1 Chr. 24.6. Psa. 45.1. Jer. 8.8. Jer. 36. 26,32. Eze. 9.2,3. King's secretary, 1 Chr. 27.32. 2 Sam. 8.17. 2 Sam. 20.25. 1 Kin. 4.3. 2 Kin. 18.18-37. 2 Kin. 19.2. Jer. 36.12. Est. 3.12. Est. 8.9.

Treasurer, Neh. 13.13. 2 Kin. 12.10-12. 2 Kin. 22.1-14. Military secretary, 2 Kin. 25.19. 2 Chr. 26.11. Teacher of the law, Ezr. 7.6,11,12,21. Neh. 8.1-8,13. Mat. 7.29. Mat. 13.52. Mat. 17.10. Mat. 23.2,3. Lawyer or jurist, Mar 12.28 with Mat. 22.35.

Families of (Judah), 1 Chr. 2.55; of Zebulon, Jud. 5.14; of Levites, 2 Chr. 34.13. Samaritan scribe, Ezr. 4.9. Translated town-clerk, Act. 19.35. Were members of the sanhedrim, Mat. 2.4. Mar. 14.1. Luk. 22.66. Act. 23.9.

Disciples of Christ, Mat. 8.19. Mar. 12. 32-34. Opposition to Christ; reproved by him, Mat. 5.20. Mat. 9.3. Mat. 12.38. Mat. 15.1. Mat. 16.21. Mat. 23. Mat. 27.41. Jno. 8.3. Opposition to the apostles, Act. 4.5. Act. 6.12.

SCRIP. See PURSE.

SCRIPTURES. See WORD OF GOD.

SCROLL. See BOOKS.

SCYTHIAN, Col. 3.11.

SEA. Symbolical, Dan. 7.2,3. Rev. 8.8,9. Rev. 10.2,5,6,8. Rev. 13.1. Rev. 15.2. Rev. 16.3. Rev. 21.1. Molten sea, see LAVER. Seas, see MEDITERRANEAN—RED SEA— CILICIA—PALESTINE, SEAS OF.

SEAL or SIGNET, Gen. 38.18. Job 41.15. Worn as a ring or bracelet, Song 8.6. Jer. 22. 24. See RING. Engraved, Ex. 28.11,21,36. Ex. 39.6,14,30. 2 Tim. 2.19. Impressions of, in clay, Job 38.14. Used for signing decrees, 1 Kin. 21.8. Est. 8.8; and covenants, Neh. 9. 38. Neh. 10.1. Isa. 8.16. Jer. 32.9-12,44. For securing doors, Deu. 32.34. Dan. 6.17. Mat. 27.66; and fountains, Song 4.12; and books or rolls, Isa. 29.11. Dan. 12.4. Rev. 5.1. For secrecy, Rev. 10.4. Rev. 22.10. Illustrative, Jno. 3.33. Jno. 6.27. Rom. 15. 28. 2 Cor. 1.22. Eph. 1.13. Eph. 4.30. Rev. 7.3-8. Rev. 20.3.

SEBA. See SABEANS.

SEBAT, the 11th month (February), Zec. 1.7.

SECRETARY. See SCRIBE.

SECTS. See HERESY.

SECUNDUS, a companion of Paul from Ephesus, Act. 20.4-6.

SEDITION. See SUBJECTS' REBELLION.

SEED. See SOWING.

SEEKING GOD. See SPIRITUAL DILIGENCE.

SEER. See PROPHET.

SEIR, MOUNT. Extends from the Dead Sea southward, Deu. 1.2. Deu. 2.1,8. Jos. 11.17. Jos. 12.7. Inhabited by the Horites, Gen. 14. 6. Gen. 36.20-30. Deu. 2.12,22. By Edomites, Gen. 32.3. Gen. 33.14,16. Gen. 36.8,9. Num. 24.18. Deu. 2.4,5. Israel defeated in, Deu. 1.44. Wanderings by, Deu. 1.2. Deu. 2.1. Deu. 33.2. See EDOMITES.

SELAH (pause), a musical term; it occurs above 70 times, Psa. 3.2. Psa. 143.6. Hab. 3.3.

——— or SELA (the rock), by the Greeks called Petra (the rock); the capital of the Edomites in Mount Seir, Isa. 16.1. Captured by Amaziah, and called Joktheel, 2 Kin. 14.7, see Jos. 15.38. See EDOMITES.

SELEUCIA, a city of Syria on the coast; Paul visits, Act. 13.4.

SELF-CONFIDENCE, SELF-DECEPTION. See FALSE CONFIDENCE.

SELF-DENIAL. Gen. 22.12. Now I know that thou fearest God, seeing thou hast not withheld thy son, thine only *son* from me.

2 Sam. 24.24. Neither will I offer burnt-offerings unto the Lord my God of that which doth cost me nothing.

Mat. 5.30. And if thy right hand offend thee, cut it off, and cast *it* from thee: for it is profitable for thee that one of thy members should perish, and not *that* thy whole body should be cast into hell. *v.* 29. Mat. 18.8,9. Mar. 9.43-48.

Mat. 13.44. The kingdom of heaven is like unto treasure hid in a field; the which when a man hath found, he hideth, and for joy thereof goeth and selleth all that he hath, and buyeth that field. 45. Like unto a merchant man, seeking goodly pearls: 46. Who, when he had found one pearl of great price, went and sold all that he had, and bought it.

Mat. 19.12. There be eunuchs, which have made themselves eunuchs for the kingdom of heaven's sake. 21. If thou wilt be perfect, go *and* sell that thou hast, and give to the poor, and thou shalt have treasure in heaven: and come *and* follow me. 27. Behold, we have forsaken all, and followed thee; what shall we have therefore? 28. And Jesus said unto

them, Verily I say unto you, That ye which have followed me, in the regeneration when the Son of man shall sit in the throne of his glory, ye also shall sit upon twelve thrones, judging the twelve tribes of Israel. *v.* 29. Mat. 4.22. Mar. 1.20.

Mat. 21.3. Say, The Lord hath need of them; and straightway he will send them.

Mar. 10.29. There is no man that hath left house, or brethren, or sisters, or father, or mother, or wife, or children, or lands, for my sake, and the gospel's, 30. But he shall receive an hundredfold now in this time, houses, and brethren, and sisters, and mothers, and children, and lands, with persecutions; and in the world to come eternal life. *v.* 39,40. Luk. 18.29,30.

Luk. 5.27. He said unto him, Follow me. 28. And he left all, rose up, and followed him. *v.* 11. Mat. 9.9. Mar. 2.14.

Luk. 9.23. If any *man* will come after me, let him deny himself, and take up his cross daily, and follow me. 24. For whosoever will save his life shall lose it: but whosoever will lose his life for my sake, the same shall save it. 57. A certain *man* said unto him, Lord, I will follow thee whithersoever thou goest. 58. And Jesus said unto him, Foxes have holes. and birds of the air *have* nests; but the Son of man hath not where to lay *his* head. Mat. 8. 19,20. Mat. 16.24,25. Jno. 12.25.

Luk. 14.26. If any *man* come to me, and hate not his father, and mother, and wife, and children, and brethren, and sisters, yea, and his own life also, he cannot be my disciple. 27. And whosoever doth not bear his cross, and come after me, cannot be my disciple. 33. So likewise, whosoever he be of you that forsaketh not all that he hath, he cannot be my disciple. *v.* 28-32. Mat. 10.37-39.

Luk. 21.4. For all these have of their abundance cast in unto the offerings of God: but she of her penury hath cast in all the living that she had. *v.* 2,3. Mar. 12.43.

Act. 20.24. But none of these things move me, neither count I my life dear unto myself, so that I might finish my course with joy, and the ministry, which I have received of the Lord Jesus, to testify the gospel of the grace of God.

Act. 21.13. I am ready not to be bound only, but also to die at Jerusalem for the name of the Lord Jesus. Rom. 8.35,36.

Rom. 6.6. Our old man is crucified with *him*, that the body of sin might be destroyed, that henceforth we should not serve sin.

Rom. 13.14. But put ye on the Lord Jesus Christ, and make not provision for the flesh, to *fulfil* the lusts *thereof.*

1 Cor. 6.12. All things are lawful unto me, but all things are not expedient: all things are lawful for me, but I will not be brought under the power of any.

1 Cor. 8.9. Take heed lest by any means this liberty of your's become a stumbling-block to them that are weak. 10. For if any man see thee which hast knowledge sit at meat in the idol's temple, shall not the conscience of him which is weak be emboldened to eat those things which are offered to idols? 13. If meat make my brother to offend, I will eat no flesh while the world standeth, lest I make my brother to offend.

1 Cor. 9.12. If others be partakers of *this*

power over you, *are* not we rather? Nevertheless we have not used this power; but suffer all things, lest we should hinder the gospel of Christ. 15. I have used none of these things; neither have I written these things, that it should be so done unto me: for *it were* better for me to die, than that any man should make my glorying void. 18. That, when I preach the gospel, I may make the gospel of Christ without charge, that I abuse not my power in the gospel. 19. For though I be free from all *men*, yet have I made myself servant unto all, that I might gain the more. 23. This I do for the gospel's sake, that I might be partaker thereof with *you*. 25. Every man that striveth for the mastery is temperate in all things. Now they *do it* to obtain a corruptible crown; but we an incorruptible. 26. I therefore so run, not as uncertainly; so fight I, not as one that beateth the air: 27. But I keep under my body, and bring *it* into subjection: lest that by any means, when I have preached to others, I myself should be a castaway.

Gal. 2.20. I am crucified with Christ.

Gal. 5.16. Walk in the Spirit, and ye shall not fulfil the lust of the flesh. 24. They that are Christ's have crucified the flesh with the affections and lusts.

Gal. 6.14. God forbid that I should glory, save in the cross of our Lord Jesus Christ, by whom the world is crucified unto me, and I unto the world.

Phil. 3.7. But what things were gain to me, those I counted loss for Christ. 8. Yea doubtless, and I count all things *but* loss for the excellency of the knowledge of Christ Jesus my Lord: for whom I have suffered the loss of all things, and do count them *but* dung, that I may win Christ.

1 Pet. 2.11. Dearly beloved, I beseech *you*, as strangers and pilgrims, abstain from fleshly lusts, which war against the soul.

3 Jno. 7. For his name's sake they went forth, taking nothing of the Gentiles.

Rev. 12.11. They loved not their lives unto the death.

See PERSECUTION—DECISION—LIBERALITY—UNSELFISHNESS.

SELF-EXAMINATION. Job 13.23. How many *are* mine iniquities and sins? make me to know my transgression and my sin.

Psa. 4.4. Stand in awe, and sin not: commune with your own heart upon your bed, and be still.

Psa. 19.12. Who can understand *his* errors? cleanse thou me from secret *faults*.

Psa. 26.2. Examine me, O Lord, and prove me; try my reins and my heart.

Psa. 77.6. I commune with mine own heart: and my spirit made diligent search.

Psa. 139.23. Search me, O God, and know my heart: try me, and know my thoughts: 24. And see if *there be any* wicked way in me, and lead me in the way everlasting.

Jer. 17.9. The heart *is* deceitful above all *things*, and desperately wicked: who can know it?

Lam. 3.40. Let us search and try our ways, and turn again to the Lord.

1 Cor. 11.28. Let a man examine himself, and so let him eat of *that* bread, and drink of *that* cup. 31. For if we would judge ourselves, we should not be judged.

2 Cor. 13.5. Examine yourselves, whether ye be in the faith; prove your own selves. Know ye not your own selves, how that Jesus Christ is in you, except ye be reprobates?

Gal. 6.4. Let every man prove his own work, and then shall he have rejoicing in himself alone, and not in another.

SELFISHNESS. Num. 32.6. Shall your brethren go to war, and shall ye sit here?

Psa. 38.11. My lovers and my friends stand aloof from my sore; and my kinsmen stand afar off.

Pro. 24.11. If thou forbear to deliver *them that are* drawn unto death, and *those that are* ready to be slain; 12. If thou sayest, Behold, we knew it not; doth not he that pondereth the heart consider *it?* and he that keepeth thy soul, doth *not* he know *it?* and shall *not* he render to *every* man according to his works?

Hos. 10.1. Israel *is* an empty vine, he bringeth forth fruit unto himself.

Amos 6.6. They are not grieved for the affliction of Joseph.

Hag. 1.4. *Is it* time for you, O ye, to dwell in your cieled houses, and this house *lie* waste? 9. Because of mine house that *is* waste, and ye run every man unto his own house. 10. Therefore the heaven over you is stayed from dew, and the earth is stayed *from* her fruit.

Zec. 7.6. When ye did eat, and when ye did drink, did not ye eat *for yourselves*, and drink *for yourselves?*

Luk. 6.32. If ye love them which love you, what thank have ye? for sinners also love those that love them. 33. And if ye do good to them which do good to you, what thank have ye? for sinners also do even the same. 34. And if ye lend *to them* of whom ye hope to receive, what thank have ye? for sinners also lend to sinners, to receive as much again. *v.* 31,35.

Rom. 14.15. If thy brother be grieved with *thy* meat, now walkest thou not charitably. Destroy not him with thy meat, for whom Christ died.

Rom. 15.1. We then that are strong ought to bear the infirmities of the weak, and not to please ourselves. 2. Let every one of us please *his* neighbour for *his* good to edification. 3. Even Christ pleased not himself.

1 Cor. 10.24. Let no man seek his own, but every man another's *wealth*.

Gal. 6.2. Bear ye one another's burdens, and so fulfil the law of Christ.

Phil. 2.4. Look not every man on his own things, but every man also on the things of others. 20. I have no man likeminded, who will naturally care for your state. 21. For all seek their own, not the things which are Jesus Christ's.

2 Tim. 3.2. For men shall be lovers of their own selves. 3. Without natural affection.

Jas. 2.15. If a brother or sister be naked, and destitute of daily food, 16. And one of you say unto them, Depart in peace, be *ye* warmed and filled; notwithstanding ye give them not those things which are needful to the body; what *doth it* profit?

SELFISHNESS, EXAMPLES OF: Cain, Gen. 4.9. Lot, Gen. 13.10,11. Meroz, &c., Jud. 5.16,17,23. Men of Succoth, &c., Jud. 8.6,8. David's soldiers, 1 Sam. 30.22. Jonah, Jonah 4.10,11.

Priest and Levite, Luk. 10.31,32. Rich man, Luk. 16.19-21.

See Poor, unkindness to—Love—Un-selfishness.

SELF-RIGHTEOUSNESS. Num. 16.3. Ye take too much upon you, seeing all the congregation are holy, every one of them, and the Lord is among them.

Deu. 9.4. Speak not thou in thine heart, For my righteousness the Lord hath brought me in to possess this land : but for the wickedness of these nations the Lord doth drive them out from before thee. 5. Not for thy righteousness, or for the uprightness of thine heart, dost thou go to possess their land.

1 Sam. 2.9. By strength shall no man prevail.

Job 13.13. Hold your peace, let me alone, that I may speak, and let come on me what will. 19. Who is he that will plead with me? for now, if I hold my tongue, I shall give up the ghost. v. 1-19.

Job 22.2. Can a man be profitable unto God, as he that is wise may be profitable unto himself? 3. Is it any pleasure to the Almighty, that thou art righteous? or is it gain to him, that thou makest thy ways perfect?

Job 33.9. I am clean without transgression, I am innocent ; neither is there iniquity in me.

Job 35.2. Thinkest thou this to be right, that thou saidst, My righteousness is more than God's? 7. If thou be righteous, what givest thou him? or what receiveth he of thine hand? 8. Thy wickedness may hurt a man as thou art; and thy righteousness may profit the son of man.

Pro. 14.12. There is a way which seemeth right unto a man, but the end thereof are the ways of death.

Pro. 16.2. All the ways of a man are clean in his own eyes ; but the Lord weigheth the spirits.

Pro. 20.6. Most men will proclaim every one his own goodness.

Pro. 21.2. Every way of a man is right in his own eyes : but the Lord pondereth the hearts.

Pro. 28.13. He that covereth his sins shall not prosper.

Pro. 30.12. There is a generation that are pure in their own eyes, and yet is not washed from their filthiness. 13. There is a generation, O how lofty are their eyes ! and their eyelids are lifted up.

Isa. 28.17. The hail shall sweep away the refuge of lies, and the waters shall overflow the hiding-place. 20. The bed is shorter than that a man can stretch himself on it : and the covering narrower than that he can wrap himself in it.

Isa. 50.11. Behold, all ye that kindle a fire, that compass yourselves about with sparks : walk in the light of your fire, and in the sparks that ye have kindled. This shall ye have of mine hand ; ye shall lie down in sorrow.

Isa. 65.5. Which say, Stand by thyself, come not near to me ; for I am holier than thou. These are a smoke in my nose, a fire that burneth all the day.

Jer. 2.23. How canst thou say, I am not polluted, I have not gone after Baalim? see thy way in the valley, know what thou hast done. 35. Thou sayest, Because I am innocent,

surely his anger shall turn from me. Behold, I will plead with thee, because thou sayest, I have not sinned.

Jer. 7.4. Trust ye not in lying words, saying, The temple of the Lord, The temple of the Lord, The temple of the Lord, are these.

Jer. 8.8. How do ye say, We are wise, and the law of the Lord is with us?

Jer. 17.5. Cursed be the man that trusteth in man, and maketh flesh his arm, and whose heart departeth from the Lord.

Eze. 33.24. They that inhabit those wastes of the land of Israel speak, saying, Abraham was one, and he inherited the land : but we are many ; the land is given us for inheritance.

Hos. 12.8. In all my labours they shall find none iniquity in me that were sin.

Amos 6.13. Ye which rejoice in a thing of nought, which say, Have we not taken to us horns by our own strength?

Hab. 2.4. His soul which is lifted up is not upright in him.

Zeph. 3.11. I will take away out of the midst of thee them that rejoice in thy pride, and thou shalt no more be haughty because of my holy mountain.

Mat. 7.22. Many will say to me in that day, Lord, Lord, have we not prophesied in thy name? and in thy name have cast out devils? and in thy name done many wonderful works? 23. And then will I profess unto them, I never knew you: depart from me, ye that work iniquity.

Mat. 9.11. When the Pharisees saw it, they said unto his disciples, Why eateth your Master with publicans and sinners? Mar. 2.16. Luk. 5.30.

Mat. 16.6. Take heed and beware of the leaven of the Pharisees and of the Sadducees. Mar. 8.15.

Mat. 19.16. Good Master, what good thing shall I do, that I may have eternal life? 20. The young man saith unto him, All these things have I kept from my youth up : what lack I yet? Mar. 10.20.

Mat. 21.31. The publicans and the harlots go into the kingdom of God before you. 32. For John came unto you in the way of righteousness, and ye believed him not : but the publicans and the harlots believed him : and ye, when ye had seen it, repented not afterward, that ye might believe him.

Mat. 22.12. Friend, how camest thou in hither not having a wedding garment? And he was speechless. 13. Then said the king to the servants, Bind him hand and foot, and take him away, and cast him into outer darkness ; there shall be weeping and gnashing of teeth.

Mat. 23.29. Ye build the tombs of the prophets, and garnish the sepulchres of the righteous. 30. And say, If we had been in the days of our fathers, we would not have been partakers with them in the blood of the prophets. 31. Wherefore ye be witnesses unto yourselves, that ye are the children of them which killed the prophets.

Luk. 7.39. This man, if he were a prophet, would have known who and what manner of woman this is that toucheth him : for she is a sinner. v. 40-47.

Luk. 10.29. He, willing to justify himself, said unto Jesus, And who is my neighbour?

Luk. 15.2. The Pharisees and scribes murmured, saying, This man receiveth sinners, and eateth with them. 29. Lo, these many years do I serve thee ; neither transgressed I at any time thy commandment ; and yet thou never gavest me a kid, that I might make merry with my friends.

Luk. 16.15. Ye are they which justify yourselves before men ; but God knoweth your hearts : for that which is highly esteemed among men is abomination in the sight of God.

Luk. 18.9. He spake this parable unto certain which trusted in themselves that they were righteous, and despised others. *v.* 9-14,21.

Jno. 7.47. Are ye also deceived ? 48. Have any of the rulers or of the Pharisees believed on him ? 49. But this people who knoweth not the law are cursed.

Jno. 8.33. We be Abraham's seed, and were never in bondage to any man : how sayest thou, Ye shall be made free ? 41. Then said they to him, We be not born of fornication ; we have one Father, *even* God.

Jno. 9.39. Jesus said, For judgment I am come into this world, that they which see not might see ; and that they which be might be made blind. 40. And *some* of the Pharisees which were with him heard these words, and said unto him, Are we blind also ? 41. Jesus said unto them, If ye were blind, ye should have no sin : but now ye say, We see ; therefore your sin remaineth.

Rom. 2.17. Thou art called a Jew, and restest in the law, and makest thy boast of God, 19. And art confident that thou thyself art a guide of the blind, a light of them which are in darkness, 20. An instructor of the foolish, a teacher of babes, which hast the form of knowledge and of the truth in the law.

Rom. 3.27. Where *is* boasting then ? It is excluded. By what law? of works? Nay : but by the law of faith.

Rom. 10.3. They being ignorant of God's righteousness, and going about to establish their own righteousness, have not submitted themselves unto the righteousness of God.

Rom. 11.19. Thou wilt say then, The branches were broken off, that I might be graffed in. 20. Well ; because of unbelief they were broken off, and thou standest by faith. Be not highminded, but fear : 21. For if God spared not the natural branches, *take heed* lest he also spare not thee.

2 Cor. 1.9. We had the sentence of death in ourselves, that we should not trust in ourselves, but in God.

Rev. 3.17. Thou sayest, I am rich, and increased with goods, and have need of nothing ; and knowest not that thou art wretched, and miserable, and poor, and blind, and naked.

See FALSE CONFIDENCE — HYPOCRISY — PRIDE—PRIVILEGES—WORKS.

SENATE, the sanhedrim, Act. 5.21. Senator, an elder, Psa. 105.22. See SANHEDRIM —ELDER.

SENEH, a rock guarding the passage of Michmash, 1 Sam. 14.4.

SENIR. See HERMON.

SENNACHERIB, king of Assyria, invades

Judah ; receives tribute from Hezekiah, 2 Kin. 18.13-16. 2 Kin. 19.8. Sends Rabshakeh, &c., to Jerusalem ; his blasphemy, 2 Kin. 18.17-37. 2 Kin. 19. 2 Chr. 32. Isa. *c.* 36 & 37. His army destroyed by an angel ; assassinated by his sons, 2 Kin. 19.35-37. Isa. 37.36-38.

SENSUALITY. See WORLDLINESS — DRUNKENNESS.

SEPHAR, MOUNT, the eastern limit of Joktan, Gen. 10.30.

SEPHARAD, a region to which the Jewish exiles were taken, Obad. 20.

SEPHARVAIM, a city in Mesopotamia, conquered by the Assyrians, from which colonists were brought to Samaria ; idolatry of the Sepharvites, 2 Kin. 17.24,31. 2 Kin. 18.34. 2 Kin. 19.13. Isa. 36.19. Isa. 37.13.

SEPULCHRE. See BURIAL-PLACES.

SERAIAH, the high-priest at the capture of Jerusalem ; slain by Nebuchadnezzar, at Riblah, 2 Kin. 25.18-21. Jer. 52.24-27. Ezra's father, Ezr. 7.1 with 1 Chr. 6.14, but see Neh. 11.11.

—— conspires against Gedaliah, 2 Kin. 25.23. Jer. 40.8,9.

——, chamberlain of Zedekiah, intrusted with a prophecy by Jeremiah, Jer. 51.59-64 (*v.* 59 *marg.*).

SERAPHIM (burning ones), Isa. 6.2,6. See 2 Kin. 2.11. 2 Kin. 6.17.

SERGEANT (rod-holder or lictor), one who carried the Roman *baton,* or bundle of rods, Act. 16.35,38.

SERGIUS PAULUS, proconsul of Cyprus, converted by Paul, on seeing Elymas struck blind, Act. 13.7-12.

SERPENT, Gen. 49.17. Deu. 32.24. Job 26.13. Psa. 140.3. Pro. 30.19. Ecc. 10.8. Amos 9.3. Mat. 7.10. Rev. 9.19. Moses' rod changed to, Ex. 4.3. Ex. 7.15. Sent against the Israelites, Num. 21.6,7. Deu. 8.15. 1 Cor. 10.9.

Poison of, Psa. 58.4. Biting of, Pro. 23.32. Licking the dust, Gen. 3.15. Isa. 65.25. Mic. 7.17. Cunning of, Mat. 10.16. Charming of, Psa. 58.4,5. Ecc. 10.11. Power given against, Mar. 16.18. Luk. 10.19. The devil called, Rev. 12.9,14,16. Rev. 20.2. See Gen. 3.1-14. 2 Cor. 11.3.

See ADDER, ASP, COCKATRICE, CREEPING THINGS, DRAGON, SCORPION, VIPER.

—— OF BRASS, set up by Moses, Num. 21.8,9. Worshipped by Israelites ; destroyed by Hezekiah, 2 Kin. 18.4. Christ compared to, Jno. 3.14,15.

SERVANTS. Psa. 123.2. As the eyes of servants *look* unto the hand of their masters, *and* as the eyes of a maiden unto the hand of her mistress.

Pro. 13.17. A wicked messenger falleth into mischief : but a faithful ambassador *is* health.

Pro. 17.2. A wise servant shall have rule over a son that causeth shame, and shall have part of the inheritance among the brethren.

Pro. 25.13. As the cold of snow in the time of harvest, *so is* a faithful messenger to them that send him : for he refresheth the soul of his masters.

Pro. 26.6. He that sendeth a message by

the hand of a fool cutteth off the feet, *and* drinketh damage.

Pro. 27.18. Whoso keepeth the fig tree shall eat the fruit thereof: so he that waiteth on his master shall be honoured.

Pro. 29.19. A servant will not be corrected by words; for though he understand he will not answer. Job 19.15,16.

Pro. 30.21. The earth is disquieted. 22. For a servant when he reigneth. 23. And an handmaid that is heir to her mistress.

Zeph. 1.9. I will punish all those that leap on the threshold, which fill their masters' houses with violence and deceit.

Mal. 1.6. A son honoureth *his* father, and a servant his master.

Mat. 8.9. I say to this *man*, Go, and he goeth; and to another, Come, and he cometh; and to my servant, Do this, and he doeth *it*.

Mat. 24.45. Who then is a faithful and wise servant, whom his Lord hath made ruler over his household, to give them meat in due season? 46. Blessed *is* that servant, whom his lord when he cometh shall find so doing. 47. Verily I say unto you, That he shall make him ruler over all his goods. 48. But and if that evil servant shall say in his heart, My lord delayeth his coming; 49. And shall begin to smite *his* fellow-servants, and to eat and drink with the drunken; 50. The Lord of that servant shall come in a day when he looketh not for *him*, and in an hour that he is not aware of, 51. And shall cut him asunder, and appoint *him* his portion with the hypocrites: there shall be weeping and gnashing of teeth.

Luk. 16.12. If ye have not been faithful in that which is another man's, who shall give you that which is your own? 13. No servant can serve two masters: for either he will hate the one, and love the other; or else he will hold to the one, and despise the other.

Luk. 17.7. Which of you, having a servant plowing or feeding cattle, will say unto him by and by, when he is come from the field, Go and sit down to meat? 8. And will not rather say unto him, Make ready wherewith I may sup, and gird thyself, and serve me, till I have eaten and drunken; and afterward thou shalt eat and drink. 9. Doth he thank that servant because he did the things that were commanded him? I trow not.

Jno. 13.16. The servant is not greater than his lord; neither he that is sent greater than he that sent him.

1 Cor. 4.2. It is required in stewards, that a man be found faithful.

1 Cor. 7.21. Art thou called *being* a servant? care not for it: but if thou mayest be made free, use *it* rather. 22. For he that is called in the Lord, *being* a servant, is the Lord's freeman: likewise also he that is called, *being* free, is Christ's servant. 23. Ye are bought with a price; be not ye the servants of men.

Eph. 6.5. Servants, be obedient to them that *are your* masters according to the flesh, with fear and trembling, in singleness of your heart, as unto Christ; 6. Not with eyeservice, as menpleasers; but as the servants of Christ, doing the will of God from the heart; 7. With good will doing service, as to the Lord, and not to men: 8. Knowing that whatsoever good thing any man doeth, the same shall he receive of the Lord, whether *he be* bond or free.

Col. 3.22. Servants, obey in all things *your* masters according to the flesh; not with eyeservice, as menpleasers; but in singleness of heart, fearing God: 23. And whatsoever ye do, do *it* heartily, as to the Lord, and not unto men; 24. Knowing that of the Lord ye shall receive the reward of the inheritance: for ye serve the Lord Christ. 25. But he that doeth wrong shall receive for the wrong which he hath done: and there is no respect of persons.

1 Tim. 6.1. Let as many servants as are under the yoke count their own masters worthy of all honour, that the name of God and *his* doctrine be not blasphemed. 2. And they that have believing masters, let them not despise *them*, because they are brethren; but rather do *them* service, because they are faithful and beloved, partakers of the benefit.

Tit. 2.9. *Exhort* servants to be obedient unto their own masters, *and* to please *them* well in all *things*; not answering again; 10. Not purloining; but shewing all good fidelity; that they may adorn the doctrine of God our Saviour in all things.

1 Pet. 2.18. Servants, *be* subject to *your* masters with all fear; not only to the good and gentle, but also to the froward. 19. For this *is* thankworthy, if a man for conscience toward God endure grief, suffering wrongfully. 20. For what glory *is it*, if, when ye be buffeted for your faults, ye shall take it patiently? but if, when ye do well, and suffer *for it*, ye take it patiently, this *is* acceptable with God.

SERVANTS, BAD, EXAMPLES OF: Abimelech's servants, Gen. 21.25. Ziba, 2 Sam. 16.1-4 with 2 Sam. 19.26,27. Jeroboam, 1 Kin. 11.26. Gehazi, 2 Kin. 5.20. Zimri, 2 Kin. 9.31. Servants of Joash, 2 Kin. 12.19-21; and of Amon, 2 Kin. 21.23. Onesimus, Philm. 11.

SERVANTS, GOOD, EXAMPLES OF: Jacob, Gen. 30.29,30. Gen. 31.6,36-42. Joseph, Gen. 39.6,23. David, 1 Sam. 18.14. 1 Sam. 19.4. Elisha, 2 Kin. 2.1-6. Onesimus, Philm. 11. Servants of Abraham, Gen. 24; of Boaz, Ruth 2.4; of Jonathan, 1 Sam. 14.7; of David, 2 Sam. 12.18. 2 Sam. 15.15,21; of Naaman, 2 Kin. 5.2,3,13; of Nehemiah, Neh. 4.16,23; of Cornelius, Act. 10.7. See SUBJECTS.

See MASTERS—KINGS, OFFICERS OF.

SERVANTS, BOND, LAWS REGARDING. Stealing and selling a man, punished with death, Ex. 21.16. Deu. 24.7. 1 Tim. 1.10. Rev. 18.13. Heathen only, to be bought as slaves for life, Lev. 25.44-46. 1 Kin. 9.22. Hebrews might be sold for 6 years; dismissed with abundance, Deu. 15.12,14,18; violation of this law, Jer. 34.10-22.

When selling themselves for life, had the ear bored with an awl, Deu. 15.16,17. Ex. 21.6, see Psa. 40.6. Not to be enslaved for life when poor, Lev. 25.39,40,42; this law violated, 2 Kin. 4.1. Neh. 5.5. Strangers allowed to buy Hebrews; redeemable at any time; to be treated as a yearly hired servant; free at the jubilee, Lev. 25.47-55. Neh. 5.8.

Born in the house, Ex. 21.4. Pro. 29.21. Jer. 2.14. Sold by parents, Ex. 21.7. Sold for theft, Ex. 22.3; and for debt, Mat. 18.25. Captives in war enslaved, Deu. 20.14. 2 Kin. 5.2. 2 Chr. 28.8,10. Voluntary bondage, Lev. 25.47. Deu. 15.16,17. Jos. 9.11-21.

A male servant freed on the 7th year; if married, his wife freed also, unless she was given to him by his master, Ex. 21.2-4. A female, if bought for a wife, or taken captive for a wife, could not be re-sold; if married, and a second wife taken, must have full maintenance; otherwise set free, Ex. 21.7-11. Deu. 21.10-14.

If unfaithful, scourged, Lev. 19.20. If smitten to death, the master punished, Ex. 21. 20,21. If the master put out an eye or tooth, the servant freed, Ex. 21.26,27. When gored, the master recompensed, Ex. 21.32. A runaway not to be restored, Deu. 23.15,16, see Gen. 16.6. 1 Kin. 2.39,40. Phil. 10.21.

Took part in all festivals, Deu. 12.12,18. Deu. 16.11,14. Deu. 29.10-13; on being circumcised, Ex. 12.44. Gen. 17.13,27. Ezr. 2. 65. Rested on Sabbath, Ex. 20.10. Ex. 23.12. Deu. 5.14. Freed at the end of the 6th year, Ex. 21.1-11. Deu. 15.12; at the jubilee, Lev. 25.41,54.

Enjoyed the fruits of the land at the jubilee, Lev. 25.6. To be instructed, Deu. 31.10-13.

Christian servants encouraged, 1 Cor 7. 21.22. 1 Cor. 12.13. Gal. 3.28. Eph. 6.8.

SERVANTS, BOND, EXAMPLES OF: Gen. 12.16. Gen. 30.43. Gen. 32.5. 1 Sam. 30.13. Born in the house, Gen. 14.14. Gen. 17.13,27. Ecc. 2.7. Bought, Gen. 17.13,27. Gen. 37. 28,36. Gen. 39.17. Deu. 28.68. Est. 7.4. Eze. 27.13. Rev. 18.13. Taken captive, Gen. 43.18. 2 Kin. 5.2. Given as a present, Gen. 20.14.

Intermarriage of, with master and family, 1 Chr. 2.34,35. Gen. 30.3,9. Gen. 16.1,2,6. In places of trust, Gen. 24.2-10. Gen. 39.4-6. Pro. 30.23. Dan. 1.19.

Israelites enslaved in Egypt, Ex. 1.14. Ex. 5.7-14. Deu. 6.12,21. In Babylon, 2 Chr. 36.20. Gibeonites enslaved, Jos. 9.23. Canaanites, 1 Kin. 9.21.

SERVANTS, HIRED. Hired by the day, Mat. 20.2. Job. 7.2; the year, Lev. 25.53; for longer periods, Gen. 29.15-18; in the market-place, Mat. 20.1-3. Wages paid in kind, Gen. 30.31,32. 2 Chr. 2.10; in money, Mat. 20.2. To be paid promptly, Lev. 19.13. Deu. 24.14,15. See MASTERS.

SETH, Adam's 3d son; his descendants, Gen. 4.25,26. Gen. 5.3-8. 1 Chr. 1.1. Luk. 3.38.

SEVEN. Peculiar occurrences of the number seven. 7 days, Gen. 2.3. Gen. 7.4,10. Gen. 8.10,12. Ex. 7.25. Jud. 14.12. 1 Sam 10.8. 1 Sam. 11.3. 1 Sam. 13.8. 1 Kin. 8.65. Eze. 3.15. Act. 20.6. Act. 21.4. Act. 28.14. Feasts lasted 7 days, Ex. 12.15. Lev. 23.34,42. Priests and altars consecrated 7 days, Ex. 29. 30,35,37. Defilement lasted 7 days, Lev. 12.2. Lev. 13.4; and fasting, 1 Sam. 31.13. Lamb to remain 7 days with dam, Ex. 22.30. Mourning 7 days, Gen. 50.10. Job 2.13; and feasting, Est. 1.5.

7 years' service, Gen. 29.18. Famine, 2 Sam. 24.13. 2 Kin. 8.1. Madness of Nebuchadnezzar, Dan. 4.23. 7 weeks, Dan. 9.25. 70 weeks, Dan. 9.24. 7 Sabbaths for Pentecost, Lev. 23.15. 7 Sabbaths of years for jubilee, Lev. 25.8.

7 animals given and offered, Gen. 7.2. Gen. 21.28. Lev. 23.18. Num. 29.32. 1 Chr.

15.26. 7 altars with 7 bulls and 7 rams offered, Num. 23.1.

Blood sprinkled 7 times, Lev. 4.6. Lev. 14.7; and oil, Lev. 14.16. Priests with 7 trumpets encompass Jericho 7 times on the 7th day, Jos. 6.4. Elijah's servant goes 7 times, 1 Kin. 18.43. Naaman dips 7 times, 2 Kin. 5.10.

Bowing 7 times, Gen. 33.3. Praising God 7 times, Psa. 119.164. Punishment 7 times, Lev. 26.18,21. 70 and 7 fold, Gen. 4.24. Restoration 7 fold, Pro. 6.31. Forgiveness 70 times 7, Mat. 18.22. Furnace heated 7 times, Dan. 3.19. Silver purified, Psa. 12.6. Saul's 7 sons put to death, 2 Sam. 21.6.

7 chamberlains, Est. 1.10,14. Ezr. 7.14. Maidens, Est. 2.9. Sons, Ruth 4.15. 1 Sam. 2.5. Jer. 15.9. Wise men, Pro. 26.16. Women, Isa. 4.1. Shepherds, Mic. 5.5. Poor men, Ecc. 11.2. 7 deacons, Act. 6.3. Churches, Rev. 1.4.

Fleeing 7 ways, Deu. 28.25. 7 troubles, Job 5.19. Sins, Pro. 6.16. Pro. 24.16 Pillars, Pro. 9.1. Streams, Isa. 11.15. Days' light, Isa. 30.26. Withes and locks, Jud. 16.7,13.

7 lamps, Ex. 25.37. Rev. 1.12. 7 evil spirits, Mat. 12.45. Devils, Mat. 16.9. 7 spirits, Rev. 1.4. Rev. 3.1. Rev. 4.5. Rev. 5.6. 7 angels with trumpets, Rev. 8.2; with 7 last plagues, Rev. 15.1.

7 kine and ears, Gen. 41.2-7. Eyes, Zec. 3.9. Zec. 4.10. Rev. 5.6. Stars, Amos, 5.8. Rev. 1.16. Seals, Rev. 5.1. Thunders, Rev. 10.3. 7000 slain, Rev. 11.13. 7 heads, crowns, mountains, and kings, Rev. 12.3. Rev. 17. 9,10.

SHAALBIM or SHAALABBIN, Jos. 19.42; an Amoritish town given to Dan, Jud. 1.35. 1 Kin. 4.9. 2 Sam. 23.32.

SHADRACH or HANANIAH, a pious friend of Daniel; delivered from the fiery furnace, and made governor by Nebuchadnezzar, Dan. 1.6-20. Dan. 2.17,49. Dan. 3.

SHALIM, a city of Shechem whose people were massacred by Jacob's sons, Gen. 33.18. Gen. 34. See SHAALBIM, SALIM. Land of Shalim, 1 Sam. 9.4.

SHALISHA, a district near Mount Ephraim, 1 Sam. 9.4. Baal-shalisha, 2 Kin. 4.42.

SHALLUM, 15th king of Israel; slays king Zachariah; reigns one month; slain by Menahem, 2 Kin. 15.10-13.

————, son of Josiah. See JEHOAHAZ.

SHALMANESER, king of Assyria, makes Hoshea king of Israel tributary; imprisons him; takes Samaria; deports the Israelites; colonises Samaria from Assyria, 2 Kin. 17. 3-6,24-27. 2 Kin. 18.9-12.

SHAMGAR, a Judge of Israel; defeats the Philistines, Jud. 3.31. Jud. 5.6.

SHAMIR, residence of Tola the Judge, in Mount Ephraim, Jud. 10.1,2. Jos. 15.48.

SHAMMAH, one of David's chiefs, defeats the Philistines, 2 Sam. 23.11,12.

SHAPHAN, a scribe appointed by Josiah to repair the temple; brings the book of the law to him, 2 Kin. 22. 2 Chr. 34.8-20.

SHAREZER. See ADRAMMELECH.

SHARON, a district between Carmel and Cesarea; its herds, 1 Chr. 27.29; roses, Song

2.1; fertility, Isa. 35.2. Isa. 65.10. Isa. 33.9. Christians in, Act. 9.35.

SHAVEH, the king's dale, north of Jerusalem; the king of Sodom and Melchizedek meet Abraham at, Gen. 14.17,18. Absalom's pillar in, 2 Sam. 18.18.

SHAVING. See BALDNESS—BEARD.

SHEBA, son of Raamah, Gen. 10.7. 1 Chr. 1.9; of Joktan, Gen. 10.28. 1 Chr. 1.22; of Jokshan, son of Abraham and Keturah, Gen. 25.3. 1 Chr. 1.32.

———, and the SABEANS, a country and people of Arabia-Felix. Queen of, visits Solomon, 1 Kin. 10.1-13. 2 Chr. 9.1-12. Gold, spices, and precious stones of, 2 Chr. 9.9. Psa. 72.15. Isa. 60.6. Jer. 6.20. Merchants of, Eze. 27.22,23. Eze. 38.13. Joel 3.8. People of, invade Uz, Job 1.15. Job 6.19. Prophecies of, Psa. 72.10,15. Isa. 60.6. Jer. 6. 20. See SABEANS.

———, his rebellion against David, and death, 2 Sam. 20.

SHEBNA, treasurer under Hezekiah; reproved, and his captivity predicted, Isa. 22. 15-19. Afterwards scribe, 2 Kin. 18.18-26,37. 2 Kin. 19.2. Isa. 36.3,11,22. Isa. 37.2.

SHECHEM or SYCHEM, a district in Samaria, 1 Chr. 7.28. Psa. 60.6. Psa. 108.7. Abraham visits, Gen. 12.6; and Jacob, Gen. 33.18,19. Jos. 24.32. Act. 7.16. Jacob hides idols in, Gen. 35.4. Joseph's brethren in, Gen. 37.12,14.

———, a Levitical city of refuge in Mount Ephraim, Jos. 20.7. Jos. 21.21. Jud. 21.19. Joshua makes a covenant with Israel in; and is buried in, Jos. 24.1-25,32. People of, make Abimelech king; and quarrel with him; he defeats them, Jud. 8.31. Jud. 9.1-49,57. Rehoboam crowned at, 1 Kin. 12.1. Jeroboam's residence, 1 Kin. 12.25. Ishmael slays men from, Jer. 41.5. Jesus visits (Sychar), Jno. 4.5,39-42. Idol of, see BAAL-BERITH.

———, son of Hamor, prince of Shechem; defiles Dinah; circumcision of; murdered and his city destroyed by Jacob's sons, Gen. 33. 18-20. Gen. 34. Gen. 49.6.

SHEEP, LAMB, Deu. 14.4. Great flocks of, Gen. 13.5. Gen. 24.35. Gen. 26.14. Gen. 29.2. Gen. 32.14. Job 1.3. Job 42.12. 2 Kin. 3.4. 1 Chr. 27.31. 2 Chr. 32.29. Bashan noted for, Deu. 32.14. Bozrah, Mic. 2.12. Kedar, Eze. 27.21. Nebaioth, Isa. 60.7. Sharon, Isa. 65.10. Jacob's experiment with, Gen. 30.32-40. Sheep-shearing, Gen. 31.19. Gen. 38.12-17. Song 4.2; feasting at, 1 Sam. 25.11,36. 2 Sam. 13.23. Given in tribute, 1 Chr. 5.21. 2 Chr. 17.11. Offered in sacrifice by Abel, Gen. 4.4. Noah, Gen. 8.20. Abraham, Gen. 22.13. See OFFERINGS. First fleece of, given to the priest, Deu. 18.4. Parable of the ewe-lamb, 2 Sam. 12.1-4; lost sheep, Luk. 15.4-7. Illustrative, 1 Chr. 21.17. Psa. 74.1. Isa. 53.7. Jer. 13.20. Jer. 50.6. See SHEPHERDS.

SHEKEL, value in silver, 2/4; in weight, 20 gerahs (10 dwt.), Ex. 30.13. Lev. 27.25, see Eze. 45.12. 3000 equal to 100 talents, Ex. 38.25-27. Shekel of the sanctuary, Ex. 30.13. Num. 7.85. After the king's weight, 2 Sam. 14.26. Of silver, Gen. 23.15,16. Of brass, 1 Sam.17.5. Iron, 1 Sam. 17.7. Gold, 1 Chr.

21.25. 2 measures of barley sold for, 2 Kin. 7. 1,16. Food of Ezekiel, 20 shekels (10 oz.) in weight a day, Eze. 4.10. A half shekel (bekah), Ex. 30.13,15. Quarter shekel, 1 Sam. 9.8.

SHEM, son of Noah, Gen. 5.32. Gen. 6.10. Gen. 9.18. 1 Chr. 1.4. Saved in the ark, Gen. 7.13. Blessed for his dutiful conduct, Gen. 9.23-27. His descendants, Gen. 10. 1,21-32. Gen. 11.10-26. 1 Chr. 1.17-54. Luk. 3.36.

SHEMAIAH, a prophet; forbids Rehoboam to invade Israel, 1 Kin. 12.22-24. 2 Chr. 12. 5-8. Writes Rehoboam's history, 2 Chr. 12.15.

———, a false prophet, and enemy of Jeremiah, Jer. 29.24-32.

SHEMEBER, king of Zeboiim; defeated by Chedorlaomer, Gen. 14.2-12.

SHEMER, owner of the hill on which Samaria was built, 1 Kin. 16.24.

SHEMINITH (octave or bass?), 1 Chr. 15.21. Titles of Psalms 6 & 12.

SHENIR. See HERMON.

SHEPHATIAH, an enemy of Jeremiah, Jer. 38.1-6.

SHEPHERDS and HERDMEN. Carried a scrip, 1 Sam. 17.40; a rod, Lev. 27.32. Psa. 23.4. Zec. 11.7-10. 1 Sam. 17.40; a sling, 1 Sam.17.49. Dwelt in tents, 2 Chr. 14.15. Song 1.8. Isa. 38.12. Had watch-towers, 2 Chr. 26.10. Mic. 4.8.

Dug wells and watered the flocks, Gen. 21. 25. Gen. 29.2-10. Ex. 2.16-19. Watched and defended the flocks, Gen. 31.40. Ex. 22. 12. 1 Sam. 17.34,35. Song 1.7. Luk. 2.8. Kept them in folds, Num. 32.16. 1 Sam. 24.3. 2 Sam. 7.8. Jno. 10.1.

Numbered them, Lev. 27.32. Jer. 33.13. Knew them by name, Jno. 10.3-5. Went before them, Psa. 78.52,53. Jno. 10.3,4. The sheep kept apart from the goats, Eze. 34.17. Mat. 25.32. Used dogs, Job 30.1.

Abel a shepherd, Gen. 4.2. Chiefs and their families were shepherds, Gen. 29.9. Ex. 2.16. Ex. 3.1. 1 Sam. 16.11. Shepherds of the kings, 1 Chr. 27.29-31. Were an abomination to the Egyptians, Gen. 46.34. The angels appeared to shepherds, Luk. 2.8-20.

Illustrative, Gen. 49.24. Psa. 23.1. Psa. 80.1. Isa. 44.28. Eze. 34.2. Mat. 26.31. Jno. 10.2. Heb. 13.20. 1 Pet. 2.25. Translated pastors, Jer. 2.8. Jer. 3.15. Jer. 12.10. Eph. 4.11. See SHEEP.

SHERIFF, a Chaldean lawyer or prefect, Dan. 3.2,3.

SHESHACH, a name of Babylon, Jer. 25. 26. Jer. 51.41.

SHESHAN, his daughter married to a freed Egyptian slave, 1 Chr. 2.31,34,35.

SHESHBAZZAR. See ZERUBBABEL.

SHETH (tumult); that is, enemies of Israel, Num. 24.17; compare Jer. 48.45.

SHETHAR-BOZNAI, an opponent of the Jews in building the temple, Ezr. 5.3-6. Ezr. 6.6.13.

SHEW-BREAD, called hallowed bread, 1 Sam. 21.6. Made of fine flour, in 12 cakes, 2-10ths to each cake, sprinkled with frankincense; renewed every Sabbath, and set on the table; eaten by the priests only, Lev. 24. 5-9. Ex. 25.30. 2 Chr. 2.4. 2 Chr. 13.11.

Neh. 10.33. Mat. 12.4. Heb. 9.2. Eaten by David, 1 Sam. 21.6. Mar. 2.26. Prepared by Levites, 1 Chr. 9.32. 1 Chr. 23.29.

SHEW-BREAD, TABLE OF. Of shittim-wood, 2 cubits long, 1 broad, 1½ high; covered with gold, with a border of crowns round about; a ring in each corner, for staves of shittim-wood overlaid with gold, Ex. 25.23-28. Ex. 37.10-15. Set in the holy place, on the north side, Ex. 26.35. Ex. 40.22. Heb. 9.2. Covered with a blue cloth, on which was set the shew-bread, with various golden vessels, Num. 4.7. Ex. 25.29,30. Ex. 37.16. Lev. 24.5-8. Anointed, Ex. 30.26,27. Directions for its removal, Num. 4.7. Tables made by Solomon, 1 Kin. 7.48,50. 2 Chr. 4.19.

SHIBBOLETH, pronounced SIBBOLETH by the Ephraimites, Jud. 12.6.

SHIELD, TARGET, BUCKLER, Jud. 5.8. 2 Sam. 1.21. 2 Chr. 14.8. 2 Chr. 17.17. 2 Chr. 26.14. Jer. 46.3. Eze. 38.4. Of brass, 1 Kin. 14.27. Of gold, 2 Sam. 8.7. 1 Kin. 10.16,17. Of wood, Eze. 39.9,10. With studs, Job 15.26. Armouries of, 1 Kin. 10.17. 2 Chr. 11.12. 2 Chr. 32.5,27. Illustrative, Gen. 15.1. Deu. 33.29. Psa. 18.2, &c.

SHIGGAION or SHIGIONOTH, a song or psalm (title), Psa. 7. Hab. 3.1.

SHILOH, prophetic name of Christ, Gen. 49.10.

———, a city of Ephraim, north of Bethel, Jud. 21.19. Tabernacle at, Jos. 18.1. Jud. 18.31. Jud. 20.18,26,27. 1 Sam. 1.3. 1 Sam. 2.14. Psa. 78.60. Jer. 7.12. Ark taken from, 1 Sam. 4.3,4. Casting of the lot at, Jos. 18. 8-10. Jos. 19.51.

Head-quarters of Joshua, Jos. 21.1,2. Jos. 22.9. Israelites assemble at, Jos. 22.12. Yearly feast at; stratagem to give the Benjamites wives, Jud. 21.12-23. Hannah prays at, and brings Samuel to, 1 Sam. 1.3,9,24. Revelations to Samuel in, 1 Sam. 3.21.

Eli's death at, 1 Sam. 4.12-22. Ahiah priest at, 1 Sam. 14.3. Ahijah the prophet's residence, 1 Kin. 14.2. Its destruction, Jer. 7.12,14. Jer. 26.6,9. Worshippers from, Jer. 41.5.

SHIMEI, a Benjamite who cursed David, 2 Sam. 16.5-13. Pardoned by David, 2 Sam. 19.16-23. Forbidden by Solomon to leave Jerusalem; and put to death for breaking his parole, 1 Kin. 2.36-46.

SHINAR. See BABYLONIA.

SHIPS, Job 9.26. Mar. 4.36-38. Act. 21.2. Sails, masts, tackling, and rudder of, Isa. 33.23. Eze 27.5-7. Act. 27.17,19,40. Oars used, Jonah 1.13. Mar. 6.48, see OARS. Hold of, Jonah 1.5. Helm of, Jas. 3.4. Figure-head of, Act. 28.11. Anchors used, Act. 27. 29,30,40. Heb. 6.19. Carried boats, Act. 28. 30,32. Ferry-boat, 2 Sam. 19.18.

Of Egypt, Deu. 28.68; Dan. Jud. 5.17; Tarshish, 1 Kin. 22.48; Chaldeans; Isa. 43.14; Chittim, Num. 24.24. Dan. 11.30; Tyre, 2 Chr. 8.18. 1 Kin. 10.11; Solomon, 1 Kin. 9.26,27; Jehoshaphat, 1 Kin. 22.48. Adramyttium, Act. 27.2; Alexandria, Act. 27.6. Built at Ezion-geber, 2 Chr. 20.36. Of fir, Eze. 27.5,9. Shipmaster, Jonah 1.6. Act. 27.11. Pilot, Eze. 27.8,27-29. Sailors, 1 Kin. 9.27. Act. 27.30.

SHISHAK, king of Egypt, protects Jeroboam, 1 Kin. 11.40. Sacks Jerusalem, 1 Kin. 14.25,26. 2 Chr. 12.2-9.

SHITTIM or SHITTAH (the acacia), Isa. 41.19. The ark, tabernacle, &c., made of, Ex. 25.5-28. Ex. 26.15-37. Ex. 37. Ex. 38.1-6.

———, in Moab; Israelites idolatry, &c. in, Num. 25. Num. 33.49. Mic. 6.5. Spies sent from, Jos. 2.1.

———, VALE OF, west of Jordan, Joel 3.18.

SHOCHOH or SOCHOH, a city of Judah, Jos. 15.35. David defeats Goliath near, 1 Sam. 17.1. Fortified by Rehoboam, 2 Chr. 11.7. Taken by Philistines, 2 Chr. 28.18.

SHOE or SANDAL, Mat. 3.11. Mar. 6.9. Act. 12.8. Women's, of badgers' skin, Eze. 16.10. Latchet of, Gen. 14.23. Isa. 5.27. Mar. 1.7. Putting off in worship, Ex. 3.5. Jos. 5.15. Loosing from the foot on refusing to marry a brother's widow, Deu. 25.9,10. Ruth 4.7,8. Casting, a mark of conquest, Psa. 60.8. Put off in mourning, Isa. 20.2. Eze. 24.17. A pair of, given for a slave, Amos 2.6. Amos 8.6.

SHOSHANNIM or SHUSHAN, a musical instrument resembling a lily; Shoshannim Eduth, lyric pipe, titles of Psalms 45, 60, 69, 80.

SHOVEL, Ex. 27.3. Jer. 52.18. Corn winnowed with, Isa. 30.24.

SHRINE (Gr. naos), a silver model of a temple, Act. 19.24.

SHULEMITE (Shunemite?), Song 6.13.

SHUNEM, a town of Issachar, Jos. 19.18. Philistines pitch near, 1 Sam. 28.4. Elisha restores a boy to life in, 2 Kin. 4. Abishag belonged to, 1 Kin. 1.3.

SHUR or ETHAM, desert of, Ex. 15.22 with Num. 33.8. Hagar wanders in, Gen. 16.7.

———, a city on the confines of Egypt and Palestine, Gen. 16.7. Gen. 20.1. Gen. 25.18. 1 Sam. 15.7. 1 Sam. 27.8.

SHUSHAN (Susa), capital of Persia, Neh. 1.1. Est. c. 1 to 9. Daniel's vision in, Dan. 8.2. Colonists from, in Samaria, Ezr. 4.9. See SHOSHANNIM.

SHUTTLE, Job 7.6.

SIBMAH, a town of Reuben, Num. 32.38. Jos. 13.19; also a vine district, Isa. 16.8,9. Jer. 48.32.

SICKLE, Deu. 16.9. Deu. 23.25. Jer. 50. 16 (marg. scythe), Mar. 4.29. Illustrative, Joel 3.13. Rev. 14.14-19.

SICKNESS. See AFFLICTION—DISEASES.

SIDDIM VALE OF (now covered by the Dead Sea), full of slime pits; the Sodomites, &c., defeated in, Gen. 14.3-10.

SIDON. See ZIDON.

SIEGE. By intrenchments, Deu. 20.20. Isa. 37.33. Battering-rams, 2 Sam. 20.15. Eze. 4.2. Eze. 26.8-12. Emptying moats, Isa. 19.6. Isa. 37.25. Raising forts, Isa. 29.3. Peace to be offered ; humanity enjoined, Deu. 20.10-12,19,20. Siege of Jericho, Jos. 6 ; Rabbah, 2 Sam. 11.1 ; Abel, 2 Sam. 20.15 Samaria, 1 Kin. 20.1. 2 Kin. 6.24. 2 Kin. 17.5 ; Tirzah, 1 Kin. 16.17 ; Gibbethon,

1 Kin. 15.27; Jerusalem, 2 Kin. 16.5. 2 Kin. 24.10,11. 2 Kin. 25.1-3. 2 Chr. 32.3-6.

SIEVE, Amos 9.9. Illustrative, Isa. 30.28. Luk. 22.31.

SIGN, a proof, Luk. 2.12. 2 Cor. 12.12. A portent or presage, Mat. 16.3,4. Mat. 24.3. A miracle, Jno. 4.48; and so translated, Jno. 2.11. Jno. 3.2, &c.

SIGNET. See SEAL.

SIHON, king of the Amorites, conquers the Moabites, Num. 21.26-30. Refuses Israel passage; slain, and his land occupied by them, Num. 21.21-25. Deu. 2.24-37. Deu. 3.2-9. See AMORITES.

SIHOR, (1) The Nile, Jer. 2.18. Isa. 23.3, see NILE. (2) The river of Egypt, Jos. 13.3. 1 Chr. 13.5, see RIVER OF EGYPT. (3) Sihor Libnath, a stream entering the sea near Carmel, Jos. 19.26.

SILAS or SILVANUS, sent by the apostles to Antioch with Paul and Barnabas, Act. 15. 22-34. Paul's fellow-labourer and companion in his 2d journey through Asia Minor, &c., Act. 15.40. Act. 17.4-10. 1 The. 1.1. 2 The. 1.1. Imprisoned at Philippi; released by an angel, Act. 16.19-40.

Remains at Berea with Timothy, Act. 17.14. Joins Paul at Corinth, Act. 17.15 with Act. 18.5. 2 Cor. 1.19. His character and prophetical gifts, Act. 15.22,32. 1 Pet. 5.12.

SILK, Pro. 31.22. Eze. 16.10,13. Rev. 18. 12. Often translated fine linen; see LINEN.

SILOAH, SHILOAH, or SILOAM (sent), a fountain or pool in Jerusalem, Neh. 3.15. Isa. 8.6. Jesus cures a blind man by washing in, Jno. 9.1-11.

————, TOWER OF, Luk. 13.4.

SILVANUS. See SILAS.

SILVER, the ordinary currency, Gen. 13.2. Gen. 20.16. Amos 8.6. Mat. 26.15. Mat. 10.9. Translated money, Gen. 17.12. Gen. 23.13 with v. 15,16. Mar. 14.11, &c. Provided by David for the temple, 1 Chr. 29.2-7. Abundance of, in Solomon's time, 1 Kin. 10. 27. Treasury of, 2 Chr. 32.27. From Tarshish, 2 Chr. 9.21. Eze. 27.12. Palace of, Song 8.9. Pictures of, Pro. 25.11. Studs, Song 1.11.

Articles made of, see BASON, CHAIN, CUP, IDOLS, JEWELS, LAMP, PIECE OF SILVER, RING, SHEKEL, TABLE, TRUMPET.

Workers in, 2 Chr. 2.14. Act. 19.24. Refining of, Pro. 17.3. Pro. 25.4. Eze. 22.18-22. Jer. 6.29,30. See REFINER—FURNACE.

SILVERLING, Isa. 7.23. See PIECE OF SILVER.

SIMEON, son of Jacob and Leah, Gen. 29. 33. Gen. 35.23. Ex. 1.2. 1 Chr. 2.1. His cruelty to the Shechemites, Gen. 34.25-30. Gen. 49.5-7. Imprisoned by Joseph till his brethren's return, Gen. 42.24,36. Gen. 43.23. Jacob's last words to, Gen. 49.5-7. His sons, Gen. 46.10. Ex. 6.15. 1 Chr. 4.24-27.

————, TRIBE OF, numbered at Sinai, Num. 1.22,23. Num. 2.13; and in the plains of Moab, Num. 26.14. Marched and encamped under the standard of Reuben, south of the tabernacle, Num. 2.12. Num. 10.18,19. Their inheritance, Jos. 19.1-9. Jud. 1.3-17. A portion of, emigrate to Gedor, 1 Chr. 4. 28-43. Portion of, keep the passover, 2 Chr.

15.9. Idols of, destroyed by Josiah, 2 Chr. 34.6. For things common to the tribes, see ISRAEL, TRIBES OF.

SIMEON, a pious, aged man who blessed Jesus in the temple, Luk. 2.25-35.

SIMEON, NIGER (black), a teacher at Antioch, Act. 13.1. (Supposed to be the same as Simon the Cyrenian.)

SIMON, an apostle called Zelotes, or the Canaanite (Cananite), both signifying the zealot, Mat. 10.4. Mar. 3.18. Luk. 6.15. Act. 1.13. Supposed to be the son of Cleophas and Mary, and the brother of James and Joses, Mat. 13.55. Mar. 6.3.

SIMON THE CYRENIAN, compelled to carry the cross, Mat. 27.32. Mar. 15.21. Luk. 23.26.

SIMON THE LEPER, made a feast for Jesus after the raising of Lazarus, Mat. 26.6. Mar. 14.3. Jno. 12.2.

SIMON MAGUS, a magician, baptised by Philip, Act. 8.9-13. Offers money for spiritual gifts, and is rebuked by Peter, Act. 8.18-24.

SIMON PETER. See PETER.

SIMON, a Pharisee, invites Jesus to his house, where a woman washes his feet with her tears, Luk. 7.36-44.

SIMON THE TANNER, Peter lodges with, at Joppa, Act. 9.43. Act. 10.6.

SIN, CONFESSION OF, see REPENTANCE. Conviction of, see CONVICTION. Sin to be forsaken, see HOLINESS, REPENTANCE, SELF-DENIAL.

SIN, FRUITS OF. ITS CONSEQUENCES. Num. 16.38. These sinners against their own souls.

Deu. 29.18. A root that beareth gall and wormwood.

Job 4.8. They that plow iniquity, and sow wickedness, reap the same.

Job 5.2. Wrath killeth the foolish man, and envy slayeth the silly one.

Job 13.26. Thou makest me to possess the iniquities of my youth.

Job 20.11. His bones are full *of the sin* of his youth, which shall lie down with him in the dust.

Psa. 5.10. Let them fall by their own counsels; cast them out in the multitude of their transgressions.

Psa. 9.15. The heathen are sunk down in the pit *that* they made: in the net which they hid is their own foot taken. 16. The wicked is snared in the work of his own hands.

Psa. 10.2. Let them be taken in the devices that they have imagined.

Psa. 94.23. He shall bring upon them their own iniquity, and shall cut them off in their own wickedness.

Psa. 141.10. Let the wicked fall into their own nets.

Pro. 1.31. Therefore shall they eat of the fruit of their own way, and be filled with their own devices.

Pro. 3.35. Shame shall be the promotion of fools.

Pro. 5.22. His own iniquities shall take the wicked himself, and he shall be holden with the cords of his sins. 23. He shall die without instruction; and in the greatness of his folly he shall go astray.

Pro. 8.36. He that sinneth against me wrongeth his own soul: all they that hate me love death.

Pro. 10.24. The fear of the wicked, it shall come upon him.

Pro. 11.5. The wicked shall fall by his own wickedness. 6. Transgressors shall be taken in *their own* naughtiness. 18. The wicked worketh a deceitful work. 19. He that pursueth evil *pursueth it* to his own death. 27. He that seeketh mischief, it shall come unto him.

Pro. 12.12. The wicked desireth the net of evil *men*. 13. The wicked is snared by the transgression of *his* lips. 14. The recompence of a man's hands shall be rendered unto him. 21. The wicked shall be filled with mischief. 26. The way of the wicked seduceth them.

Pro. 13.6. Wickedness overthroweth the sinner. 15. The way of transgressors *is* hard.

Pro. 22.8. He that soweth iniquity shall reap vanity.

Pro. 27.8. As a bird that wandereth from her nest, so *is* a man that wandereth from his place.

Pro. 29.6. In the transgression of an evil man *there is* a snare.

Isa. 3.9. Woe unto their soul! for they have rewarded evil unto themselves. 11. Woe unto the wicked! *it shall be* ill *with him:* for the reward of his hands shall be given him.

Isa. 57.20. The wicked *are* like the troubled sea, when it cannot rest, whose waters cast up mire and dirt. 21. *There is* no peace, saith my God, to the wicked.

Jer. 2.17. Hast thou not procured this unto thyself, in that thou hast forsaken the Lord thy God, when he led thee by the way? 19. Thine own wickedness shall correct thee, and thy backsliding shall reprove thee.

Jer. 4.18. Thy way and thy doings have procured these *things* unto thee; this *is* thy wickedness, because it is bitter, because it reacheth unto thine heart.

Jer. 7.19. *They provoke* themselves to the confusion of their own faces.

Jer. 14.16. I will pour their wickedness upon them.

Jer. 21.14. I will punish you according to the fruit of your doings.

Jer. 31.30. Every man that eateth the sour grape, his teeth shall be set on edge.

Eze. 11.21. *As for them* whose heart walketh after the heart of their detestable things and their abominations, I will recompense their way upon their own heads, saith the Lord God. Eze. 22.31.

Hos. 8.7. They have sown the wind, and they shall reap the whirlwind.

Hos. 10.13. Ye have plowed wickedness, ye have reaped iniquity; ye have eaten the fruit of lies.

Hos. 13.9. O Israel, thou hast destroyed thyself.

Mic. 7.13. The land shall be desolate because of them that dwell therein, for the fruit of their doings.

Act. 9.5. It is hard for thee to kick against the pricks.

Rom. 7.5. When we were in the flesh, the motions of sins, which were by the law, did work in our members to bring forth fruit unto death.

Gal. 6.8. He that soweth to his flesh, shall of the flesh reap corruption.

SIN, FRUITS OF. ITS HEREDITARY CONSEQUENCES. Ex. 20.5. Visiting the iniquity of the fathers upon the children unto the third and fourth *generation* of them that hate me. Ex. 34.7.

Lev. 26.39. Also in the iniquities of their fathers shall they pine away.

Num. 14.33. Your children shall wander in the wilderness forty years, and bear your whoredoms, until your carcases be wasted in the wilderness.

Job 5.4. His children are far from safety, and they are crushed in the gate, neither *is there* any to deliver *them.*

Job 18.19. He shall neither have son nor nephew among his people, nor any remaining in his dwellings. *v.* 17.

Job 21.19. God layeth up his iniquity for his children: he rewardeth him, and he shall know *it.*

Psa. 21.10. Their fruit shalt thou destroy from the earth, and their seed from among the children of men.

Psa. 37.28. The seed of the wicked shall be cut off.

Psa. 109.9. Let his children be fatherless, and his wife a widow. 10. Let his children be continually vagabonds, and beg; let them seek *their bread* also out of their desolate places.

Pro. 14.11. The house of the wicked shall be overthrown.

Isa. 14.20. The seed of evildoers shall never be renowned. 21. Prepare slaughter for his children for the iniquity of their fathers, that they do not rise, nor possess the land, nor fill the face of the world with cities. 22. For I will rise up against them, saith the Lord of hosts, and cut off from Babylon the name, and remnant, and son, and nephew, saith the Lord.

Jer. 32.18. Recompensest the iniquity of the fathers into the bosom of their children after them. Isa. 65.7.

Lam. 5.7. Our fathers have sinned, *and are* not; and we have borne their iniquities. Rom. 5.12-21.

SIN, HATEFUL TO GOD. Gen. 6.6. It repented the Lord that he had made man on the earth, and it grieved him at his heart. 7. And the Lord said, I will destroy man; for it repenteth me that I have made them.

Gen. 18.20. Because the cry of Sodom and Gomorrah is great, and because their sin is very grievous. Gen. 19.13.

Num. 22.32. I went out to withstand thee, because *thy* way is perverse before me.

Deu. 25.16. All that do such things, *and* all that do unrighteously, *are* an abomination unto the Lord thy God.

Deu. 32.19. When the Lord saw *it,* he abhorred *them,* because of the provoking of his sons, and of his daughters.

2 Sam. 11.27. The thing that David had done displeased the Lord.

1 Kin. 14.22. Judah did evil in the sight of the Lord, and they provoked him to jealousy with their sins which they had committed.

Psa. 5.4. Thou *art* not a God that hath pleasure in wickedness: neither shall evil dwell with thee. 5. The foolish shall not stand in thy sight: thou hatest all workers of iniquity. 6. Thou shalt destroy them that speak leasing: the Lord will abhor the bloody and deceitful man.

Psa. 10.3. The covetous, *whom* the Lord abhorreth.

Psa. 11.5. The wicked, and him that loveth violence, his soul hateth.

Psa. 78.59. When God heard *this*, he was wroth, and greatly abhorred Israel.

Psa. 95.10. Forty years long was I grieved with *this* generation.

Psa. 106.40. The wrath of the Lord kindled against his people, insomuch that he abhorred his own inheritance.

Pro. 3.32. The froward *is* abomination to the Lord. Pro. 11.20.

Pro. 6.16. These six *things* doth the Lord hate: yea, seven *are* an abomination unto him. *v.* 17-20.

Pro. 15.9. The way of the wicked *is* an abomination unto the Lord. 26. The thoughts of the wicked *are* an abomination to the Lord.

Pro. 21.27. The sacrifice of the wicked *is* abomination: how much more, *when* he bringeth it with a wicked mind?

Isa. 43.24. But thou hast made me to serve with thy sins, thou hast wearied me with thine iniquities.

Jer. 25.7. That ye might provoke me to anger with the works of your hands to your own hurt.

Jer. 44.4. Oh, do not this abominable thing that I hate. 21. Did not the Lord remember them, and came it *not* into his mind? 22. So that the Lord could no longer bear, because of the evil of your doings, *and* because of the abominations which ye have committed.

Hos. 4.1. The Lord hath a controversy with the inhabitants of the land, because *there* is no truth, nor mercy, nor knowledge of God in the land. Mic. 6.1,2.

Hab. 1.13. *Thou art* of purer eyes than to behold evil, and canst not look on iniquity.

Zec. 8.17. All these *are things* that I hate, saith the Lord.

Luk. 16.15. That which is highly esteemed among men is abomination in the sight of God.

Rev. 2.6. Thou hatest the deeds of the Nicolaitanes, which I also hate. *v.* 15.

See GOD HOLY — GOD JEALOUS — GOD'S JUSTICE — CHRIST'S HOLINESS — SIN SEPARATES FROM GOD.

SIN, HATEFUL TO SAINTS. Gen. 39.9. How then can I do this great wickedness, and sin against God?

Job 1.1. One that feared God, and eschewed evil.

Job 21.16. The counsel of the wicked is far from me. Job 22.18.

Psa. 26.9. Gather not my soul with sinners, nor my life with bloody men. *v.* 5.

Psa. 84.10. I had rather be a doorkeeper in the house of my God, than to dwell in the tents of wickedness.

Psa. 101.3. I will set no wicked thing before mine eyes: I hate the work of them that turn aside; *it* shall not cleave to me. 7. He that worketh deceit shall not dwell within my house: he that telleth lies shall not tarry in my sight. *v.* 4-8.

Psa. 119.104. I hate every false way. 113. I hate *vain* thoughts. 163. I hate and abhor lying. *v.* 128.

Psa. 120.5. Woe is me, that I sojourn in Mesech, *that* I dwell in the tents of Kedar!

Psa. 139.19. Depart from me therefore, ye bloody men. 21. Do not I hate them, O Lord, that hate thee? and am not I grieved with those that rise up against thee? 22. I hate them with perfect hatred: I count them mine enemies.

Pro. 8.13. The fear of the Lord *is* to hate evil: pride, and arrogancy, and the evil way, and the froward mouth, do I hate.

Pro. 29.27. An unjust man *is* an abomination to the just.

Jer. 9.2. Oh that I had in the wilderness a lodging-place of wayfaring men, that I might leave my people, and go from them! for they *be* all adulterers, an assembly of treacherous men.

Rom. 7.24. O wretched man that I am! who shall deliver me from the body of this death?

2 Pet. 2.7. Just Lot, vexed with the filthy conversation of the wicked: 8. For that righteous man dwelling among them, in seeing and hearing, vexed *his* righteous soul from day to day with *their* unlawful deeds.

Jude 23. Others save with fear, pulling *them* out of the fire; hating even the garment spotted by the flesh.

Rev. 2.2. Thou canst not bear them which are evil.

See HOLINESS — TEMPTATION — ZEAL FOR GOD'S GLORY — REPROOF.

SIN AGAINST THE HOLY GHOST. See HOLY SPIRIT, SINS AGAINST.

SIN, LOVE OF — SINNER'S CHARACTER. Gen. 13.13. The men of Sodom *were* wicked, and sinners before the Lord exceedingly. Gen. 18.20.

Lev. 18.25. The land is defiled: therefore I do visit the iniquity thereof upon it, and the land itself vomiteth out her inhabitants. Ezr. 9.11.

Deu. 9.13. Behold, it *is* a stiffnecked people. 24. Ye have been rebellious against the Lord from the day that I knew you.

Deu. 32.32. Their vine *is* of the vine of Sodom, and of the fields of Gomorrah: their grapes *are* grapes of gall, their clusters *are* bitter: 33. Their wine *is* the poison of dragons, and the cruel venom of asps.

1 Sam. 2.25. If one man sin against another, the judge shall judge him: but if a man sin against the Lord, who shall intreat for him?

1 Sam. 24.13. Wickedness proceedeth from the wicked.

1 Kin. 21.20. Thou hast sold thyself to work evil in the sight of the Lord.

2 Chr. 28.10. *Are there* not with you, even with you, sins against the Lord your God? 22. In the time of his distress did he trespass yet more against the Lord: this *is that* king Ahaz.

Job 14.4. Who can bring a clean *thing* out of an unclean? not one.

Job 15.16. How much more abominable and filthy *is* man, which drinketh iniquity like water?

Job 20.12. Though wickedness be sweet in his mouth, *though* he hide it under his tongue; 13. *Though* he spare it, and forsake it not; but keep it still within his mouth.

Job 22.5. *Is* not thy wickedness great? and thine iniquities infinite?

Psa. 5.9. *There is* no faithfulness in their mouth their inward part *is* very wickedness.

Psa. 36.1. *There is* no fear of God before his eyes. 2. For he flattereth himself in his own eyes, until his iniquity be found to be hateful. 3. He hath left off to be wise, *and* to do good. 4. He deviseth mischief upon his bed; he setteth himself in a way *that is* not good; he abhorreth not evil.

Psa. 49.20. Man *that is* in honour, and understandeth not, is like the beasts *that* perish.

Psa. 119.155. Salvation *is* far from the wicked; for they seek not thy statutes.

Pro. 1.29. They hated knowledge, and did not choose the fear of the Lord: 30. They would none of my counsel: they despised all my reproof.

Pro. 2.13. Who leave the paths of uprightness, to walk in the ways of darkness; 14. Who rejoice to do evil, *and* delight in the frowardness of the wicked; 15. Whose ways *are* crooked, and *they* froward in their paths.

Pro. 4.16. They sleep not, except they have done mischief; and their sleep is taken away, unless they cause *some* to fall.

Pro. 10.23. *It is* as sport to a fool to do mischief.

Pro. 13.19. *It is* abomination to fools to depart from evil.

Pro. 14.9. Fools make a mock at sin.

Pro. 27.22. Though thou shouldest bray a fool in a mortar among wheat with a pestle, *yet* will not his foolishness depart from him.

Pro. 28.4. They that forsake the law praise the wicked.

Ecc. 3.18. They themselves are beasts.

Ecc. 8.11. The heart of the sons of men is fully set in them to do evil.

Isa. 1.4. Ah sinful nation, a people laden with iniquity, a seed of evildoers, children that are corrupters: they have forsaken the Lord, they have provoked the Holy One of Israel unto anger, they are gone away backward. *v.* 5,6.

Isa. 3.9. The shew of their countenance doth witness against them; and they declare their sin as Sodom, they hide *it* not.

Isa. 5.18. Them that draw iniquity with cords of vanity, and sin as it were with a cart rope.

Isa. 24.5. The earth also is defiled under the inhabitants thereof.

Isa. 30.1. Woe to the rebellious children, saith the Lord, that take counsel, but not of me; and that cover with a covering, but not of my spirit, that they may add sin to sin.

Isa. 32.6. The vile person will speak villany, and his heart will work iniquity, to practise hypocrisy, and to utter error against the Lord.

Isa. 57.20. The wicked *are* like the troubled sea, when it cannot rest, whose waters cast up mire and dirt. 21. *There is* no peace, saith my God, to the wicked.

Isa. 59.3. Your hands are defiled with blood, and your fingers with iniquity; your lips have spoken lies, your tongue hath muttered perverseness. 4. None calleth for justice, nor *any* pleadeth for truth: they trust in vanity, and speak lies; they conceive mischief, and bring forth iniquity. 8. The way of peace they know not; and *there is* no judgment in their goings: they have made them crooked paths: whosoever goeth therein shall not know peace.

Isa. 63.19. Thou never bearest rule over them; they were not called by thy name.

Jer. 2.22. Though thou wash thee with nitre, and take thee much sope, *yet* thine iniquity is marked before me, saith the Lord God.

Jer. 3.5. Behold, thou hast spoken and done evil things as thou couldest.

Jer. 4.22. My people *is* foolish, they have not known me; they *are* sottish children, and they have none understanding: they *are* wise to do evil, but to do good they have no knowledge.

Jer. 5.4. I said, Surely these *are* poor; they are foolish: for they know not the way of the Lord, *nor* the judgment of their God. 5. I will get me unto the great men, and will speak unto them; for they have known the way of the Lord, *and* the judgment of their God: but these have altogether broken the yoke, *and* burst the bonds.

Jer. 6.7. As a fountain casteth out her waters, so she casteth out her wickedness. 15. Were they ashamed when they had committed abomination? nay, they were not at all ashamed, neither could they blush.

Jer. 8.6. I hearkened and heard, *but* they spake not aright: no man repented him of his wickedness, saying, What have I done? every one turned to his course, as the horse rusheth into the battle. *v.* 12.

Jer. 9.3. They bend their tongues *like* their bow *for* lies: but they are not valiant for the truth upon the earth; for they proceed from evil to evil, and they know not me, saith the Lord.

Jer. 11.8. They obeyed not, nor inclined their ear, but walked every one in the imagination of their evil heart. 15. When thou doest evil, then thou rejoicest. *Jer.* 13.10.

Jer. 14.10. Thus have they loved to wander, they have not refrained their feet.

Jer. 17.1. The sin of Judah *is* written with a pen of iron, *and* with the point of a diamond: *it is* graven upon the table of their heart.

Jer. 30.12. Thy bruise *is* incurable, *and* thy wound *is* grievous. 13. *There is* none to plead thy cause, that thou mayest be bound up: thou hast no healing medicines.

Eze. 16.47. Yet hast thou not walked after their ways, nor done after their abominations: but, as *if that were* a very little *thing,* thou wast corrupted more than they in all thy ways.

Eze. 20.16. They despise my judgments, and walked not in my statutes, but polluted my sabbaths: for their heart went after their idols.

Hos. 4.8. They eat up the sin of my people, and they set their heart on their iniquity.

Hos. 7.3. They make the king glad with their wickedness, and the princes with their lies. 9. Strangers have devoured his strength, and he knoweth *it* not: yea, gray hairs are here and there upon him, yet he knoweth not.

Hos. 9.10. *Their* abominations were according as they loved.

Hos. 13.12. The iniquity of Ephraim *is* bound up; his sin *is* hid.

Amos 5.10. They hate him that rebuketh in the gate, and they abhor him that speaketh uprightly.

Mic. 3.2. Who hate the good, and love the evil.

Mic. 7.3. That they may do evil with both hands earnestly.

Zeph. 3.5. The unjust knoweth no shame. 7. They rose early, *and* corrupted all their doings.

Hag. 2.14. Every work of their hands; and that which they offer there *is* unclean. *v.* 13.

Mat. 9.36. Sheep having no shepherd.

Mat. 13.38. The tares are the children of the wicked *one*.

Mar. 4.11. Them that are without.

Luk. 19.10. The Son of man is come to seek and to save that which was lost.

Jno. 8.34. Whosoever committeth sin is the servant of sin. 44. Ye are of *your* father the devil, and the lusts of your father ye will do.

Act. 8.21. Thou hast neither part nor lot in this matter: for thy heart is not right in the sight of God.

Act. 13.10. O full of all subtilty and all mischief, *thou* child of the devil, *thou* enemy of all righteousness, wilt thou not cease to pervert the right ways of the Lord?

Rom. 1.29. Being filled with all unrighteousness, fornication, wickedness, covetousness, maliciousness; full of envy, murder, debate, deceit, malignity; whisperers, 30. Backbiters, haters of God, despiteful, proud, boasters, inventors of evil things, disobedient to parents, 31. Without understanding, covenant-breakers, without natural affection, implacable, unmerciful: 32. Who, knowing the judgment of God, that they which commit such things are worthy of death, not only do the same, but have pleasure in them that do them.

Rom. 8.7. The carnal mind *is* enmity against God: for it is not subject to the law of God, neither indeed can be. 8. So then they that are in the flesh cannot please God.

Eph. 2.3. We all had our conversation in times past in the lusts of our flesh, fulfilling the desires of the flesh and of the mind; and were by nature the children of wrath, even as others. 12. At that time ye were without Christ, being aliens from the commonwealth of Israel, and strangers from the covenants of promise, having no hope, and without God in the world.

Eph. 4.19. Who being past feeling have given themselves over unto lasciviousness, to work all uncleanness with greediness.

Eph. 5.12. It is a shame even to speak of those things which are done of them in secret.

Phil. 2.15. A crooked and perverse nation.

1 The. 5.7. They that sleep in the night; and they that be drunken are drunken in the night.

2 Tim. 3.2. Lovers of their own selves, covetous, boasters, proud, blasphemers, disobedient to parents, unthankful, unholy, 3. Without natural affection, trucebreakers, false accusers, incontinent, fierce, despisers of those that are good, 4. Traitors, heady, highminded, lovers of pleasures more than lovers of God; 5. Having a form of godliness, but denying the power thereof. 6. Silly women laden with sins, led away with divers lusts, 7. Ever learning, and never able to come to the knowledge of the truth. 13. Evil men and seducers shall wax worse and worse, deceiving, and being deceived.

Tit. 1.15. Unto them that are defiled and unbelieving *is* nothing pure; but even their mind and conscience is defiled. 16. They profess that they know God; but in works they deny *him*, being abominable, and disobedient, and unto every good work reprobate.

Jas. 1.21. Filthiness and superfluity of naughtiness.

1 Pet. 3.19. Spirits in prison.

2 Pet. 2.13. They that count it pleasure to riot in the day time. 14. Having eyes full of adultery, and that cannot cease from sin; beguiling unstable souls: an heart they have exercised with covetous practices; cursed children. 19. While they promise them liberty, they themselves are the servants of corruption.

Jude 12. These are spots in your feasts of charity, when they feast with you, feeding themselves without fear: clouds *they are* without water, carried about of winds; trees whose fruit withereth, without fruit, twice dead, plucked up by the roots; 13. Raging waves of the sea, foaming out their own shame; wandering stars, to whom is reserved the blackness of darkness for ever.

See MAN'S NATURAL STATE — SIN, ITS NATURE AND ORIGIN.

SIN. NATIONAL SIN, PUNISHMENT OF. Pro. 14.34. Pro. 25.2. Isa. 19.4. Jer. 12.17. Jer. 25.31-33. Jer. 46.28. Jer. 50.14. Dan. 5.26-28. Jonah 1.2. Nah. 3.1.

EXAMPLES OF. The flood, Gen. 7.23. Sodom, &c., Gen. 18.20. Eze. 16.49,50. Egypt, Ex. *c.* 7 to 14. Canaanites, Deu. 9.5. Israelites, Lev. 26.14-39. Deu. 32.30. 2 Sam. 21.1. 2 Sam. 24.1. 2 Kin. 24.3,4,20. 2 Chr. 36.21. Neh. 9.36,37. Isa. 1.21-23. Isa. 3.4,8. Isa. 5. Isa. 59.1-15. Jer. 2. Jer. 5. Jer. 6. Jer. 9. Jer. 23. Jer. 30.11-15. Lam. 4.6. Eze. 2. Eze. 7. Eze. 22. Eze. 24.6-14. Eze. 33.25,26. Eze. 36.16-20. Eze. 39.23,24. Eze. 44.4-14. Hos. 4.1-11. Hos. 6.8-10. Hos. 7.1-7. Hos. 13. Amos *c.* 2 & 5. Mic. 6. Mic. 7.2-6.

See WAR—FAMINE—PESTILENCE—BACKSLIDING OF ISRAEL—IDOLATRY OF ISRAEL—GOD KING—GOD'S PROVIDENCE OVERRULING. See also BABYLON, ISRAELITES, &c., PROPHECIES AGAINST.

SIN. ITS NATURE AND ORIGIN. Deu. 29.18. A root that beareth gall and wormwood.

2 Chr. 12.14. He did evil, because he prepared not his heart to seek the Lord.

Psa. 95.10. It *is* a people that do err in their heart.

Pro. 4.23. Keep thy heart with all diligence; for out of it *are* the issues of life.

Pro. 24.9. The thought of foolishness *is* sin.

Isa. 44.20. A deceived heart hath turned him aside.

Jer. 7.24. Walked in the counsels *and* in the imagination of their evil heart.

Jer. 17.9. The heart *is* deceitful above all *things*, and desperately wicked: who can know it?

Eze. 20.16. They despised my judgments, for their heart went after their idols.

Mat. 5.28. Whosoever looketh on a woman to lust after her hath committed adultery with her already in his heart.

Mat. 12.33. Either make the tree good, and his fruit good; or else make the tree corrupt, and his fruit corrupt: for the tree is known by his fruit. 34. O generation of vipers, how can ye, being evil, speak good things? for out of the abundance of the heart the mouth speaketh. 35. A good man out of the good treasure of the heart bringeth forth good things: and an evil man out of the evil treasure bringeth forth evil things. Mat. 7.17,18. Luk. 6.45.

Mat. 15.19. Out of the heart proceed evil thoughts, murders, adulteries, fornications, thefts, false witness, blasphemies: 20. These are *the things* which defile a man.

Jno. 14.24. He that loveth me not keepeth not my sayings.

Rom. 14.23. Whatsoever is not of faith is sin.

1 Cor. 5.6. Know ye not that a little leaven leaveneth the whole lump?

Heb. 3.13. Lest any of you be hardened through the deceitfulness of sin.

Heb. 12.15. Lest any root of bitterness springing up trouble *you*, and thereby many be defiled.

Jas. 1.14. Every man is tempted, when he is drawn away of his own lust, and enticed. 15. Then, when lust hath conceived, it bringeth forth sin.

Jas. 4.1. From whence *come* wars and fightings among you? *come they* not hence *even* of your lusts that war in your members? 2. Ye lust, and have not: ye kill, and desire to have, and cannot obtain. 17. To him that knoweth to do good, and doeth *it* not, to him it is sin.

2 Pet. 1.4. The corruption that is in the world through lust.

1 Jno. 3.4. Sin is the transgression of the law. .6. Whosoever sinneth hath not seen him, neither known him. 8. He that committeth sin is of the devil; for the devil sinneth from the beginning. 10. In this the children of God are manifest, and the children of the devil.

1 Jno. 5.17. All unrighteousness is sin.

See SIN, LOVE OF.

SIN. ORIGINAL SIN. See FALL, THE—MAN'S NATURAL STATE.

———, PRAYER AGAINST. See TEMPTATION, PRAYER IN.

SIN, PUNISHMENT OF. Gen. 2.17. In the day that thou eatest thereof thou shalt surely die.

Gen. 3.17. Cursed *is* the ground for thy sake. 19. In the sweat of thy face shalt thou eat bread, till thou return unto the ground; for out of it wast thou taken: for dust thou *art*, and unto dust shalt thou return. *v.*16-18.

Gen. 4.7. If thou doest not well, sin lieth at the door.

Gen. 6.3. My spirit shall not always strive with man. *v.* 7.

Ex. 32.33. Whosoever hath sinned against me, him will I blot out of my book. 34. In the day when I visit I will visit their sin upon them.

Ex. 34.7. That will by no means clear *the guilty*. Ex. 20.5.

Lev. 26.21. I will bring seven times more plagues upon you according to your sins. *v.* 14-39.

Num. 15.31. That soul shall utterly be cut off; his iniquity *shall be* upon him.

Num. 32.23. Be sure your sin will find you out.

Deu. 7.10. Repayeth them that hate him to their face, to destroy them: he will not be slack to him that hateth him, he will repay him to his face.

Deu. 11.26. Behold, I set before you this day a blessing and a curse. 28. A curse, if ye will not obey the commandments of the Lord your God. Deu. 30.15,19.

Deu. 28.20. The Lord shall send upon thee cursing, vexation, and rebuke, in all that thou settest thine hand unto for to do, until thou be destroyed, and until thou perish quickly; because of the wickedness of thy doings, whereby thou hast forsaken me. *v.* 15-68.

Deu. 31.29. Evil will befall you in the latter days; because ye will do evil in the sight of the Lord, to provoke him to anger through the work of your hands.

Deu. 32.35. Their foot shall slide in *due* time: for the day of their calamity *is* at hand, and the things that shall come upon them make haste. 41. If I whet my glittering sword, and mine hand take hold on judgment; I will render vengeance to mine enemies, and will reward them that hate me. 42. I will make mine arrows drunk with blood, and my sword shall devour flesh. *v.* 30.

Jud. 5.31. So let all thine enemies perish, O Lord.

1 Sam. 2.9. The wicked shall be silent in darkness. 10. The adversaries of the Lord shall be broken to pieces; out of heaven shall he thunder upon them.

1 Sam. 3.11. I will do a thing in Israel, at which both the ears of every one that heareth it shall tingle. 12. When I begin, I will also make an end.

1 Sam. 12.25. If ye shall still do wickedly, ye shall be consumed, both ye and your king.

2 Sam. 3.39. The Lord shall reward the doer of evil according to his wickedness.

1 Kin. 21.20. Because thou hast sold thyself to work evil in the sight of the Lord. 21. Behold, I will bring evil upon thee, and will take away thy posterity.

2 Kin. 22.13. Great *is* the wrath of the Lord that is kindled against us, because our fathers have not hearkened unto the words of this book.

1 Chr. 10.13. Saul died for his transgression which he committed against the Lord.

1 Chr. 15.13. The Lord our God made a breach upon us.

Job 4.9. By the blast of God they perish, and by the breath of his nostrils are they consumed.

Job 5.3. I have seen the foolish taking root: but suddenly I cursed his habitation. *v.* 4,5.

Job 8.20. Neither will he help the evil doers. 22. They that hate thee shall be clothed with shame; and the dwelling-place of the wicked shall come to nought.

Job 10.14. If I sin, then thou markest me, and thou wilt not acquit me from mine iniquity. 15. If I be wicked, woe unto me.

Job 11.20. The eyes of the wicked shall fail, and they shall not escape, and their hope *shall be as* the giving up of the ghost.

Job 15.20. The wicked man travaileth with pain all *his* days, and the number of years is hidden to the oppressor. 21. A dreadful sound *is* in his ears: in prosperity the destroyer shall come upon him. 22. He believeth not that he shall return out of darkness, and he is waited for of the sword. 23. He wandereth abroad for bread, *saying*, Where *is it?* he knoweth that the day of darkness is ready at his hand. 24. Trouble and anguish shall make him afraid; they shall prevail against him, as a king ready to the battle. *v.* 28-30.

Job 18.17. His remembrance shall perish from the earth, and he shall have no name in the street. 18. He shall be driven from light into darkness, and chased out of the world. *v.* 5-21.

Job 19.29. Be ye afraid of the sword: for wrath *bringeth* the punishments of the sword.

Job 20.14. His meat in his bowels is turned, *it is* the gall of asps within him. 23. *God* shall cast the fury of his wrath upon him, and shall rain *it* upon him while he is eating. 26. All darkness *shall be* hid in his secret places: a fire not blown shall consume him; it shall go ill with him that is left in his tabernacle. *v.* 8-13.

Job 21.17. How oft is the candle of the wicked put out! and *how oft* cometh their destruction upon them! *God* distributeth sorrows in his anger! 18. They are as stubble before the wind, and as chaff that the storm carrieth away. 19. God layeth up his iniquity for his children: he rewardeth him, and he shall know *it*. 20. His eyes shall see his destruction, and he shall drink of the wrath of the Almighty. *v.* 30.

Job 31.3. *Is* not destruction to the wicked? and a strange *punishment* to the workers of iniquity? Job 27.13-23.

Job 36.17. Thou hast fulfilled the judgment of the wicked: judgment and justice take hold *on thee.* *v.* 6,12,18.

Psa. 1.4. The ungodly *are* not so: but *are* like the chaff which the wind driveth away. 5. Therefore the ungodly shall not stand in the judgment, nor sinners in the congregation of the righteous. *v.* 6.

Psa. 3.7. Thou hast smitten all mine enemies *upon* the cheek bone; thou hast broken the teeth of the ungodly.

Psa. 9.5. Thou hast rebuked the heathen, thou hast destroyed the wicked, thou hast put out their name for ever and ever. 6. Their memorial is perished with them.

Psa. 10.15. Break thou the arm of the wicked and the evil *man*: seek out his wickedness *till* thou find none.

Psa. 11.6. Upon the wicked he shall rain snares, fire and brimstone, and an horrible tempest: *this shall be* the portion of their cup.

Psa. 21.9. Thou shalt make them as a fiery oven in the time of thine anger: the Lord shall swallow them up in his wrath, and the fire shall devour them. 12. Thou shalt make ready *thine arrows* upon thy strings against the face of them.

Psa. 31.17. Let the wicked be ashamed, *and* let them be silent in the grave. Psa. 25.3.

Psa. 32.10. Many sorrows *shall be* to the wicked.

Psa. 34.16. The face of the Lord *is* against them that do evil, to cut off the remembrance of them from the earth. 21. Evil shall slay the wicked: and they that hate the righteous shall be desolate.

Psa. 36.12. There are the workers of iniquity fallen: they are cast down, and shall not be able to rise.

Psa. 37.17. The arms of the wicked shall be broken. 20. The wicked shall perish, and the enemies of the Lord *shall be* as the fat of lambs: they shall consume; into smoke shall they consume away. 22. *They that be* cursed of him shall be cut off. 38. The transgressors shall be destroyed together: the end of the wicked shall be cut off. *v.* 2,10,13-22,34-38.

Psa. 39.11. Thou with rebukes dost correct man for iniquity, thou makest his beauty to consume away like a moth.

Psa. 50.22. Consider this, ye that forget God, lest I tear *you* in pieces, and *there be* none to deliver. Psa. 52.1.

Psa. 55.19. God shall hear, and afflict them.

Psa. 56.7. Shall they escape by iniquity? in *thine* anger cast down the people, O God.

Psa. 58.6. Break their teeth, O God, in their mouth: break out the great teeth of the young lions, O Lord. 7. Let them melt away as waters *which* run continually: *when* he bendeth *his bow to shoot* his arrows, let them be as cut in pieces. *v.* 8,9.

Psa. 59.5. Awake to visit all the heathen: be not merciful to any wicked transgressors.

Psa. 68.1. Let God arise, let his enemies be scattered: let them also that hate him flee before him. 2. As smoke is driven away, *so* drive *them* away: as wax melteth before the fire, *so* let the wicked perish at the presence of God. 6. The rebellious dwell in a dry *land*. 21. God shall wound the head of his enemies, *and* the hairy scalp of such an one as goeth on still in his trespasses.

Psa. 73.18. Thou didst set them in slippery places: thou castedst them down into destruction. 19. How are they *brought* into desolation, as in a moment! they are utterly consumed with terrors. 20. As a dream when *one* awaketh; *so*, O Lord, when thou awakest, thou shalt despise their image. *v.* 27.

Psa. 75.8. In the hand of the Lord *there is* a cup, and the wine is red; it is full of mixture; and he poureth out of the same; but the dregs thereof, all the wicked of the earth shall wring *them* out, *and* drink *them*. 10. All the horns of the wicked also will I cut off.

Psa. 78.49. He cast upon them the fierceness of his anger, wrath, and indignation, and trouble, by sending evil angels *among them*. 50. He made a way to his anger. *v.* 65,66.

Psa. 89.10. Thou hast scattered thine enemies with thy strong arm. 32. I visit their transgression with the rod, and their iniquity with stripes.

Psa. 91.8. With thine eyes shalt thou behold and see the reward of the wicked.

Psa. 92.7. When the wicked spring as the grass, and when all the workers of iniquity do flourish; *it is* that they shall be destroyed for ever. 9. Lo, thine enemies, O Lord, for, lo, thine enemies shall perish; all the workers of iniquity shall be scattered.

Psa. 94.13. Until the pit be digged for the wicked. *v.* 1-4.

Psa. 97.3. A fire goeth before him, and burneth up his enemies round about.

Psa. 104.35. Let the sinners be consumed out of the earth, and let the wicked be no more.

Psa. 106.43. They were brought low for their iniquity.

Psa. 107.17. Fools because of their transgression, and because of their iniquities, are afflicted. 33. He turneth 34. A fruitful land into barrenness, for the wickedness of them that dwell therein.

Psa. 119.118. Thou hast trodden down all them that err from thy statutes: for their deceit is falsehood. 119. Thou puttest away all the wicked of the earth like dross. 155. Salvation is far from the wicked. v. 21.

Psa. 129.4. He hath cut asunder the cords of the wicked.

Psa. 132.18. His enemies will I clothe with shame.

Psa. 139.19. Surely thou wilt slay the wicked, O God.

Psa. 145.20. All the wicked will he destroy.

Psa. 146.9. The way of the wicked he turneth upside down.

Psa. 147.6. He casteth the wicked down to the ground.

Pro. 3.33. The curse of the Lord is in the house of the wicked.

Pro. 10.3. He casteth away the substance of the wicked. 7. The name of the wicked shall rot. 14. The mouth of the foolish is near destruction. 28. The expectation of the wicked shall perish. 29. Destruction shall be to the workers of iniquity. 30. The wicked shall not inhabit the earth. v. 25,27.

Pro. 11.8. The righteous is delivered out of trouble, and the wicked cometh in his stead. 21. Though hand join in hand, the wicked shall not be unpunished. 23. The expectation of the wicked is wrath. v. 31.

Pro. 12.2. A man of wicked devices will he condemn. 3. A man shall not be established by wickedness. 7. The wicked are overthrown, and are not.

Pro. 13.2. The soul of the transgressors shall eat violence. 5. A wicked man is loathsome, and cometh to shame. 21. Evil pursueth sinners. 23. There is that is destroyed for want of judgment. 25. The belly of the wicked shall want. v. 9.

Pro. 14.12. There is a way which seemeth right unto a man, but the end thereof are the ways of death. 19. 'he evil bow before the good; and the wicked at the gates of the righteous. v. 32.

Pro. 16.4. The Lord hath made all things for himself: yea, even the wicked for the day of evil. v. 5,25.

Pro. 18.3. When the wicked cometh, then cometh also contempt, and with ignominy reproach.

Pro. 21.12. God overthroweth the wicked for their wickedness. 15. Destruction shall be to the workers of iniquity. v. 16.

Pro. 22.12. He overthroweth the words of the transgressor.

Pro. 24.16. The wicked shall fall into mischief. 20. There shall be no reward to the evil man; the candle of the wicked shall be put out. 22. Their calamity shall rise suddenly; and who knoweth the ruin of them both?

Pro. 26.10. The great God that formed all things both rewardeth the fool, and rewardeth transgressors.

Pro. 28.18. He that is perverse in his ways shall fall at once.

Pro. 29.16. When the wicked are multiplied, transgression increaseth: but the righteous shall see their fall.

Ecc. 7.17. Be not over much wicked, neither be thou foolish: why shouldest thou die before thy time?

Ecc. 8.13. It shall not be well with the wicked, neither shall he prolong his days, which are as a shadow; because he feareth not before God. v. 10.

Ecc. 9.12. As the fishes that are taken in an evil net, and as the birds that are caught in the snare; so are the sons of men snared in an evil time, when it falleth suddenly upon them. v. 3.

Isa. 1.20. Ye shall be devoured with the sword. 24. I will ease me of mine adversaries, and avenge me of mine enemies. 28. The destruction of the transgressors and of the sinners shall be together, and they that forsake the Lord shall be consumed.

Isa. 5.24. As the fire devoureth the stubble, and the flame consumeth the chaff, so their root shall be as rottenness, and their blossom shall go up as dust.

Isa. 8.22. Behold trouble and darkness, dimness of anguish; and they shall be driven to darkness.

Isa. 10.3. What will ye do in the day of visitation, and in the desolation which shall come from far? to whom will ye flee for help? and where will ye leave your glory?

Isa. 11.4. He shall smite the earth with the rod of his mouth, and with the breath of his lips shall he slay the wicked.

Isa. 13.9. Behold, the day of the Lord cometh, cruel both with wrath and fierce anger, to lay the land desolate: and he shall destroy the sinners thereof out of it. 11. I will punish the world for their evil, and the wicked for their iniquity.

Isa. 24.6. The curse devoured the earth. 17. Fear, and the pit, and the snare, are upon thee, O inhabitant of the earth. 18. And it shall come to pass, that he who fleeth from the noise of the fear shall fall into the pit; and he that cometh up out of the midst of the pit shall be taken in the snare: for the windows from on high are open, and the foundations of the earth do shake. 20. The transgression thereof shall be heavy upon it; and it shall fall, and not rise again.

Isa. 26.21. The Lord cometh out of his place to punish the inhabitants of the earth for their iniquity.

Isa. 28.19. From the time that it goeth forth it shall take you: for morning by morning shall it pass over, by day and by night: and it shall be a vexation only to understand the report.

Isa. 29.5. The multitude of the terrible ones shall be as chaff that passeth away: yea, it shall be at an instant suddenly.

Isa. 30.14. He shall break it as the breaking of the potter's vessel that is broken in pieces; he shall not spare.

Isa. 33.11. Your breath, as fire, shall devour you. 12. And the people shall be as the burnings of lime: as thorns cut up shall they be burned in the fire. v. 14.

Isa. 47.14. Behold, they shall be as stubble; the fire shall burn them; they shall not deliver themselves from the power of the flame: there shall not be a coal to warm at, nor fire to sit before it. 15. They shall wander every one to his quarter; none shall save thee.

Isa. 50.11. This shall ye have of mine hand; ye shall lie down in sorrow.

Isa. 57.21. *There is* no peace, saith my God to the wicked. *v.* 20. Isa. 48.22.

Isa. 59.9. We wait for light, but behold obscurity; for brightness, *but* we walk in darkness. 10. We grope for the wall like the blind, and we grope as if *we had* no eyes: we stumble at noon day as in the night; *we are* in desolate places as dead *men.* 11. We roar all like bears, and mourn sore like doves: we look for judgment, but *there is* none; for salvation, *but* it is far off from us.

Isa. 63.10. He was turned to be their enemy, *and* he fought against them.

Isa. 64.5. Thou art wroth; for we have sinned. 6. We all do fade as a leaf; and our iniquities, like the wind, have taken us away. 7. Thou hast hid thy face from us, and hast consumed us, because of our iniquities.

Isa. 65.6. I will not keep silence, but will recompense, even recompense into their bosom. 7. Your iniquities, and the iniquities of your fathers together, saith the Lord.

Isa. 65.13. My servant shall eat, but ye shall be hungry: behold, my servant shall drink, but ye shall be thirsty: behold, my servant shall rejoice, but ye shall be ashamed · 14. Behold, my servant shall sing for joy of heart, but ye shall cry for sorrow of heart, and shall howl for vexation of spirit. 20. The sinner *being* an hundred years old shall be accursed.

Isa. 66.6. The Lord that rendereth recompence to his enemies. 15. The Lord will come with fire, and with his chariots like a whirlwind, to render his anger with fury, and his rebuke with flames of fire. 16. For by fire and by sword will the Lord plead with all flesh: and the slain of the Lord shall be many. 24. They shall go forth, and look upon the carcases of the men that have transgressed against me: for their worm shall not die, neither shall their fire be quenched; and they shall be an abhorring unto all flesh. *v.* 14.

Jer. 4.4. Lest my fury come forth like fire, and burn that none can quench *it.*

Jer. 5.9. Shall I not visit for these *things?* saith the Lord: and shall not my soul be avenged on such a nation as this?

Jer. 8.12. They were not at all ashamed, neither could they blush; therefore shall they fall among them that fall: in the time of their visitation they shall be cast down, saith the Lord. 14. The Lord our God hath put us to silence, and given us water of gall to drink. *v.* 13. Jer. 6.15.

Jer. 11.11. I will bring evil upon them, which they shall not be able to escape; and though they shall cry unto me, I will not hearken unto them.

Jer. 12.3. Pull them out like sheep for the slaughter, and prepare them for the day of slaughter. 13. They have sown wheat, but shall reap thorns. *v.* 4.

Jer. 13.16. Give glory to the Lord your God, before he cause darkness, and before your feet stumble upon the dark mountains, and, while ye look for light, he turn it into the shadow of death, *and* make *it* gross darkness. 22. For the greatness of thine iniquity are thy skirts discovered, *and* thy heels made bare.

Jer. 14.10. The Lord doth not accept them;

he will now remember their iniquity, and visit their sins.

Jer. 16.18. I will recompense their iniquity and their sin double.

Jer. 21.5. I myself will fight against you with an outstretched hand and with a strong arm, even in anger, and in fury, and in great wrath.

Jer. 30.14. I have wounded thee with the wound of an enemy, with the chastisement of a cruel one, for the multitude of thine iniquity *because* thy sins were increased. 15. Why criest thou for thine affliction? thy sorrow *is* incurable for the multitude of thine iniquity: *because* thy sins were increased, I have done these things unto thee. 23. The whirlwind of the Lord goeth forth with fury, a continuing whirlwind: it shall fall with pain upon the head of the wicked. 24. The fierce anger of the Lord shall not return, until he have done *it,* and until he have performed the intents of his heart: Jer. 23.19.

Jer. 48.44. He that fleeth from the fear shall fall into the pit; and he that getteth up out of the pit shall be taken in the snare.

Lam. 1.14. The yoke of my transgressions is bound by his hand: they are wreathed, *and* come up upon my neck: he hath made my strength to fall. *v.* 5-9.

Lam. 3.39. Wherefore doth a living man complain, a man for the punishment of his sins?

Lam. 4.22. The punishment of thine iniquity is accomplished.

Lam. 5.16. The crown is fallen *from* our head: woe unto us, that we have sinned! 17. For this our heart is faint; for these *things* our eyes are dim.

Eze. 3.19. He shall die in his iniquity.

Eze. 5.13. I will cause my fury to rest upon them.

Eze. 7.4. Mine eyes shall not spare thee, neither will I have pity: but I will recompense thy ways upon thee, and thine abominations shall be in the midst of thee. 5. Thus saith the Lord God; An evil, an only evil, behold, is come. 6. An end is come, the end is come: it watcheth for thee; behold, t is come. 7. The time is come, the day of trouble *is* near. 25. Destruction cometh; and they shall seek peace, and *there shall be* none. *v.* 8,9.

Eze. 18.4. The soul that sinneth, it shall die. 13. He shall not live: he shall surely die; his blood shall be upon him. 24. In his trespass that he hath trespassed, and in his sin that he hath sinned, in them shall he die. *v.* 18,26.

Eze. 21.24. Because ye have made your iniquity to be remembered, in that your transgressions are discovered, so that in all your doings your sins do appear; because, *I say,* that ye are come to remembrance, ye shall be taken with the hand. 32. Thou shalt be for fuel to the fire; thy blood shall be in the midst of the land; thou shalt be no *more* remembered: for I the Lord have spoken *it.* *v.* 23,31.

Eze. 22.14. Can thine heart endure, or can thine hands be strong, in the days that I shall deal with thee? 20. *As* they gather silver, and brass, and iron, and lead, and tin, into the midst of the furnace, to blow the fire upon it, to melt *it*; so will I gather *you* in mine anger and in my fury, and I will leave *you there,* and melt you.

Dan. 9.11. The curse is poured upon us. *v.* 12-14. Zec. 1.2.

Dan. 12.2. Some to shame *and* everlasting contempt.

Hos. 5.5. Israel and Ephraim fall in their iniquity ; Judah also shall fall with them. 9. Ephraim shall be desolate in the day of rebuke.

Hos. 7.13. Woe unto them ! for they have fled from me : destruction unto them ! because they have transgressed against me.

Hos. 8.1. *He shall come* as an eagle against the house of the Lord. 11. Because Ephraim hath made many altars to sin, altars shall be unto him to sin. 13. Now will he remember their iniquity, and visit their sins.

Hos. 9.7. The days of visitation are come, the days of recompence are come ; Israel shall know *it.* 15. For the wickedness of their doings I will drive them out of mine house, I will love them no more. *v.* 9.

Hos. 10.8. The thorn and the thistle shall come up on their altars ; and they shall say to the mountains, Cover us ; and to the hills, Fall on us. *v.* 10.

Hos. 12.14. Therefore shall he leave his blood upon him, and his reproach shall his Lord return unto him.

Hos. 13.1. When he offended in Baal, he died. 3. They shall be as the morning cloud, and as the early dew that passeth away, as the chaff *that* is driven with the whirlwind out of the floor, and as the smoke out of the chimney.

Hos. 14.1. Thou hast fallen by thine iniquity. 9. The ways of the Lord *are* right, and the just shall walk in them : but the transgressors shall fall therein.

Joel 2.2. A day of darkness and of gloominess, a day of clouds and of thick darkness, as the morning spread upon the mountains : a great people and a strong ; there hath not been ever the like, neither shall be any more after it, *even* to the years of many generations. *v.* 1.

Joel 3.13. Put ye in the sickle, for the harvest is ripe : come, get you down ; for the press is full, the fats overflow.

Amos 5.19. As if a man did flee from a lion, and a bear met him ; or went into the house, and leaned his hand on the wall, and a serpent bit him. 20. *Shall* not the day of the Lord *be* darkness, and not light? even very dark, and no brightness in it? Amos 9.1-4.

Mic. 6.13. Therefore also will I make *thee* sick in smiting thee, in making *thee* desolate because of thy sins. Mic. 1.5.

Nah. 1.2. He reserveth *wrath* for his enemies. 8. With an overrunning flood he will make an utter end of the place thereof, and darkness shall pursue his enemies. 9. He will make an utter end : affliction shall not rise up the second time. 10. They shall be devoured as stubble fully dry. Hab. 1.12.

Hab. 3.12. Thou didst march through the land in indignation, thou didst thresh the heathen in anger.

Zeph. 1.12. I will search Jerusalem with candles, and punish the men that are settled on their lees. 15. That day *is* a day of wrath, a day of trouble and distress, a day of wasteness and desolation, a day of darkness and gloominess, a day of clouds and thick darkness. 17. They shall walk like blind men,

because they have sinned against the Lord : and their blood shall be poured out as dust, and their flesh as the dung. *v.* 13-18.

Zeph. 3.8. The day that I rise up to the prey : all the earth shall be devoured with the fire of my jealousy.

Mal. 4.1. Behold, the day cometh, that shall burn as an oven ; and all the proud, yea, and all that do wickedly, shall be stubble : and the day that cometh shall burn them up, saith the Lord of hosts, that it shall leave them neither root nor branch. 3. Ye shall tread down the wicked ; for they shall be ashes under the soles of your feet.

Mat. 3.10. The ax is laid unto the root of the trees : therefore every tree which bringeth not forth good fruit is hewn down, and cast into the fire.

Mat. 5.19. Whosoever therefore shall break one of these least commandments, and shall teach men so, he shall be called the least in the kingdom of heaven. *v.* 26-30.

Mat. 7.23. Then will I profess unto them, I never knew you : depart from me, ye that work iniquity. *v.* 19,26,27.

Mat. 15.13. Every plant, which my heavenly Father hath not planted, shall be rooted up.

Mat. 18.7. Woe unto the world because of offences ! woe to that man by whom the offence cometh !

Mat. 21.41. He will miserably destroy those wicked men.

Mat. 23.33. *Ye* serpents, *ye* generation of vipers, how can ye escape the damnation of hell?

Mat. 24.51. Shall cut him asunder, and appoint *him* his portion with the hypocrites : there shall be weeping and gnashing of teeth.

Mat. 25.46. These shall go away into everlasting punishment. *v.* 41.

Mat. 26.24. Woe unto that man by whom the Son of man is betrayed ! it had been good for that man if he had not been born. Mar. 14.21. Luk. 22.22.

Luk. 6.49. The ruin of that house was great.

Luk. 12.5. Fear him, which after he hath killed hath power to cast into hell ; yea, I say unto you, Fear him.

Luk. 17.2. It were better for him that a millstone were hanged about his neck, and he cast into the sea, than that he should offend one of these little ones. *v.* 1.

Luk. 19.27. But those mine enemies, bring hither, and slay *them* before me.

Luk. 20.18. Whosoever shall fall upon that stone shall be broken ; but on whomsoever it shall fall, it will grind him to powder. Mat. 21.44.

Luk. 23.30. Then shall they begin to say to the mountains, Fall on us ; and to the hills, Cover us. 31. For if they do these things in a green tree, what shall be done in the dry ?

Jno. 5.14. Sin no more, lest a worse thing come unto thee. 29. They that have done evil, unto the resurrection of damnation.

Jno. 8.21. Ye shall seek me, and shall die in your sins. *v.* 11.

Jno. 17.12. None of them is lost, but the son of perdition.

Act. 1.25. Judas by transgression fell, that he might go to his own place. *v.* 18.

Rom. 1.18. The wrath of God is revealed

from heaven against all ungodliness and unrighteousness of men. *v.* 32.

Rom. 5.12. Death passed upon all men, for that all have sinned. 21. Sin hath reigned unto death.

Rom. 6.21. The end of those things *is* death. 23. The wages of sin *is* death. *v.* 16.

Rom. 8.2. The law of sin and death. 6. To be carnally minded *is* death. 13. For if ye live after the flesh, ye shall die. 20. The creature was made subject to vanity. 22. The whole creation groaneth and travaileth in pain together.

Rom. 9.22. Vessels of wrath fitted to destruction.

Rom. 11.22. The severity of God : on them which fell, severity.

Rom. 14.23. He that doubteth is damned if he eat.

1 Cor. 3.17. If any man defile the temple of God, him shall God destroy.

1 Cor. 5.13. Them that are without, God judgeth.

1 Cor. 6.9. The unrighteous shall not inherit the kingdom of God.

1 Cor. 10.5. They were overthrown in the wilderness.

Gal. 3.10. Cursed *is* every one that continueth not in all things which are written in the book of the law.

Eph. 5.6. Because of these things cometh the wrath of God upon the children of disobedience. Col. 3.6. Gal. 5.19-21.

1 The. 5.3. When they shall say, Peace and safety ; then sudden destruction cometh upon them, as travail upon a woman with child ; and they shall not escape.

1 Tim. 5.24. Some men's sins are open beforehand, going before to judgment ; and some *men* they follow after.

Heb. 2.2. Every transgression and disobedience received a just recompence of reward.

Heb. 10.31. *It is* a fearful thing to fall into the hands of the living God. *v.* 27,30.

Jas. 1.15. Sin, when it is finished, bringeth forth death.

1 Pet. 3.12. The face of the Lord *is* against them that do evil.

1 Pet. 4.17. What shall the end be of them that obey not the gospel of God? 18. And if the righteous scarcely be saved, where shall the ungodly and the sinner appear?

2 Pet. 2.5. Bringing in the flood upon the world of the ungodly. 6. Turning the cities of Sodom and Gomorrha into ashes condemned *them* with an overthrow, making *them* an ensample unto those that after should live ungodly. *v.* 9.

Jude 13. To whom is reserved the blackness of darkness for ever. *v.* 4,6,15.

Rev. 18.5. Her sins have reached unto heaven, and God hath remembered her iniquities.

Rev. 19.15. The winepress of the fierceness and wrath of Almighty God.

Rev. 21.27. There shall in no wise enter into it any thing that defileth, neither *whatsoever* worketh abomination, or *maketh* a lie.

See SIN, FRUITS OF—SINS, NATIONAL—DEATH OF SINNERS—HELL—JUDGMENT—GOD'S JUSTICE—CHRIST JUDGE. Also such titles as BACKSLIDING, FALSEHOOD, &c.

SIN, REPROOF OF. See REPROOF—ZEAL.

SIN SEEN AND MARKED BY GOD AND CHRIST. Gen. 3.11. Who told thee that thou *wast* naked? Hast thou eaten of the tree, whereof I commanded thee that thou shouldest not eat?

Gen. 4.10. The voice of thy brother's blood crieth unto me from the ground.

Gen. 18.13. The Lord said unto Abraham, Wherefore did Sarah laugh, saying, Shall I of a surety bear a child, which am old?

Ex. 16.8. The Lord heareth your murmurings which ye murmur against him. Num. 14.27. Deu. 1.34.

Num. 12.2. They said, Hath the Lord indeed spoken only by Moses? hath he not spoken also by us? And the Lord heard *it.*

Deu. 31.21. I know their imagination which they go about, even now, before I have brought them in.

Deu. 32.34. *Is* not this laid up in store with me, *and* sealed up among my treasures?

Job 10.14. If I sin, then thou markest me, and thou wilt not acquit me from mine iniquity. Jos. 7.16-20.

Job 11.11. He knoweth vain men : he seeth wickedness also ; will he not then consider *it?*

Job 13.27. Thou lookest narrowly unto all my paths ; thou settest a print upon the heels of my feet.

Job 14.16. Thou numberest my steps : dost thou not watch over my sin? 17. My transgression *is* sealed up in a bag, and thou sewest up mine iniquity.

Job 20.27. The heaven shall reveal his iniquity ; and the earth shall rise up against him.

Job 34.21. His eyes *are* upon the ways of man, and he seeth all his goings. 22. *There is* no darkness, nor shadow of death, where the workers of iniquity may hide themselves. Job. 24.23.

Psa. 69.5. O God, thou knowest my foolishness ; and my sins are not hid from thee. Psa. 44.21.

Psa. 90.8. Thou hast set our iniquities before thee, our secret *sins* in the light of thy countenance.

Psa. 94.11. The Lord knoweth the thoughts of man, that they *are* vanity.

Ecc. 5.8. If thou seest the oppression of the poor, and violent perverting of judgment and justice in a province, marvel not at the matter : for *he that is* higher than the highest regardeth ; and *there be* higher than they.

Isa. 29.15. Woe unto them that seek deep to hide their counsel from the Lord, and their works are in the dark, and they say, Who seeth us? and who knoweth us?

Jer. 2.22. Though thou wash thee with nitre, and take thee much sope, *yet* thine iniquity is marked before me, saith the Lord God.

Jer. 16.17. Mine eyes *are* upon all their ways : they are not hid from my face, neither is their iniquity hid from mine eyes. Eze. 21.24.

Hos. 5.3. I know Ephraim, and Israel is not hid from me : for now, O Ephraim, thou committest whoredom, *and* Israel is defiled.

Hos. 7.2. They consider not in their hearts *that* I remember all their wickedness : now their own doings have beset them about ; they are before my face.

Amos 5.12. I know your manifold transgressions and your mighty sins.

Amos 9.8. The eyes of the Lord God *are* upon the sinful kingdom, and I will destroy it from off the face of the earth. *v.* 2-4.

Hab. 2.11. The stone shall cry out of the wall, and the beam out of the timber shall answer it.

Mal. 2.14. The Lord hath been witness between thee and the wife of thy youth, against whom thou hast dealt treacherously.

Mat. 10.26. There is nothing covered, that shall not be revealed; and hid, that shall not be known.

Mat. 22.18. Jesus perceived their wickedness, and said, Why tempt ye me, *ye* hypocrites?

Mat. 26.46. Rise, let us be going: behold, he is at hand that doth betray me.

Luk. 6.8. He knew their thoughts, and said to the man which had the withered hand, Rise up.

Jno. 4.19. The woman saith unto him, Sir, I perceive that thou art a prophet. *v.* 17,18.

Jno. 5.42. I know you, that ye have not the love of God in you.

Jno. 6.64. There are some of you that believe not. For Jesus knew from the beginning who they were that believed not, and who should betray him.

Jno. 13.11. He knew who should betray him; therefore said he, Ye are not all clean.

See GOD OMNISCIENT—CHRIST OMNISCIENT —JUDGMENT ACCORDING TO WORKS.

SIN SEPARATES FROM GOD—ANSWERS TO PRAYERS OF SINNERS DENIED—SPIRITUAL DESERTION. Ex. 33.3. I will not go up in the midst of thee; for thou *art* a stiffnecked people: lest I consume thee in the way.

Deu. 1.45. Ye returned, and wept before the Lord; but the Lord would not hearken to your voice, nor give ear unto you.

Deu. 3.26. But the Lord was wroth with me for your sakes, and would not hear me: and the Lord said unto me, Let it suffice thee; speak no more unto me of this matter. *v.* 23-25.

Deu. 31.17. My anger shall be kindled against them in that day, and I will forsake them, and I will hide my face from them, and they shall be devoured, and many evils and troubles shall befall them; so that they will say in that day, Are not these evils come upon us, because our God *is* not among us?

Deu. 32.20. I will hide my face from them, I will see what their end *shall be:* for they *are* a very froward generation, children in whom *is* no faith.

Jos. 7.10. The Lord said unto Joshua, Get thee up; wherefore liest thou thus upon thy face? 11. Israel hath sinned. 12. Neither will I be with you any more, except ye destroy the accursed from among you.

1 Sam. 28.6. The Lord answered him not, neither by dreams, nor by Urim, nor by prophets. *v.* 15,16.

2 Chr. 24.20. Why transgress ye the commandments of the Lord, that ye cannot prosper? because ye have forsaken the Lord, he hath also forsaken you.

Job 11.13. If thou prepare thine heart, and stretch out thine hands toward him; 14. If iniquity *be* in thine hand, put it far away, and let not wickedness dwell in thy tabernacles.

Job 13.24. Wherefore hidest thou thy face, and holdest me for thine enemy? *v.* 16.

Job 23.3. Oh that I knew where I might find him! *that* I might come *even* to his seat! 8. Behold, I go forward, but he *is* not *there;* and backward, but I cannot perceive him: 9. On the left hand, where he doth work, but I cannot behold *him:* he hideth himself on the right hand, that I cannot see *him.*

Job 27.9. Will God hear his cry when trouble cometh upon him?

Job 29.2. Oh that I were as *in* months past, as *in* the days *when* God preserved me. *v.* 3-5.

Job 30.20. I cry unto thee, and thou dost not hear me: I stand up, and thou regardest me *not.*

Job 35.12. They cry, but none giveth answer, because of the pride of evil men. 13. Surely God will not hear vanity, neither will the Almighty regard it.

Psa. 66.18. If I regard iniquity in my heart, the Lord will not hear *me.*

Psa. 78.59. When God heard *this,* he was wroth, and greatly abhorred Israel: 60. So that he forsook the tabernacle of Shiloh, the tent *which* he placed among men.

Pro. 1.24. Because I have called, and ye refused; I have stretched out my hand, and no man regarded. 28. Then shall they call upon me, but I will not answer; they shall seek me early, but they shall not find me: 29. For that they hated knowledge, and did not choose the fear of the Lord. *v.* 24-30.

Pro. 15.8. The sacrifice of the wicked *is* an abomination to the Lord. 29. The Lord *is* far from the wicked. Pro. 21.27.

Pro. 28.9. He that turneth away his ear from hearing the law, even his prayers *shall be* abomination.

Isa. 1.15. And when ye spread forth your hands, I will hide mine eyes from you: yea, when ye make many prayers, I will not hear: your hands are full of blood.

Isa. 2.6. Thou hast forsaken thy people the house of Jacob, because they be replenished from the east, and they please themselves in the children of strangers.

Isa. 59.2. Your iniquities have separated between you and your God, and your sins have hid *his* face from you, that he will not hear. *v.* 1.

Isa. 64.7. Thou hast hid thy face from us, and hast consumed us, because of our iniquities.

Jer. 2.29. Wherefore will ye plead with me? ye all have transgressed against me, saith the Lord.

Jer. 5.25. Your iniquities have turned away these *things,* and your sins have withholden good *things* from you.

Jer. 11.14. Pray not thou for this people, neither lift up a cry or prayer for them: for I will not hear *them* in the time that they cry unto me for their trouble. *v.* 11. Jer. 7.16.

Jer. 14.8. O the hope of Israel, the saviour thereof in time of trouble, why shouldest thou be as a stranger in the land, and as a wayfaring man *that* turneth aside to tarry for a night? 10. Thus have they loved to wander, they have not refrained their feet, therefore the Lord doth not accept them; he will now remember their iniquity, and visit their sins. *v.* 11,12.

Jer. 15.1. Though Moses and Samuel stood before me, *yet* my mind *could* not *be* toward this people: cast *them* out of my sight, and let them go forth.

Jer. 16.5. Enter not into the house of mourning, neither go to lament nor bemoan them: for I have taken away my peace from this people, saith the Lord, *even* lovingkindness and mercies.

Lam. 3.44. Thou hast covered thyself with a cloud, that *our* prayer should not pass through.

Eze. 8.17. Is it a light thing to the house of Judah that they commit the abominations which they commit here? 18. Therefore will I also deal in fury: mine eyes shall not spare, neither will I have pity: and though they cry in mine ears with a loud voice, *yet* will I not hear them.

Eze. 14.3. These men have set up their idols in their heart, and put the stumblingblock of their iniquity before their face: should I be inquired of at all by them? 14. Though these three men, Noah, Daniel, and Job, were in it, they should deliver *but* their own souls by their righteousness, saith the Lord God. Eze. 20.3,4,31.

Hos. 5.6. They shall go with their flocks and with their herds to seek the Lord; but they shall not find *him;* he hath withdrawn himself from them. 15. I will go *and* return to my place, till they acknowledge their offence, and seek my face.

Hos. 7.1. When I would have healed Israel, then the iniquity of Ephraim was discovered, and the wickedness of Samaria.

Hos. 9.12. Yea, woe also to them when I depart from them!

Amos 3.3. Can two walk together, except they be agreed?

Amos 9.7. *Are ye* not as children of the Ethiopians unto me, O children of Israel? saith the Lord.

Mic. 3.4. Then shall they cry unto the Lord, but he will not hear them: he will even hide his face from them at that time, as they have behaved themselves ill in their doings.

Hab. 1.2. O Lord, how long shall I cry, and thou wilt not hear! *even* cry out unto thee *of* violence, and thou wilt not save!

Zec. 7.13. It is come to pass, *that* as he cried, and they would not hear; so they cried, and I would not hear, saith the Lord of hosts.

Mat. 6.5. Thou shalt not be as the hypocrites *are:* for they love to pray standing in the synagogues and in the corners of the streets, that they may be seen of men. Verily I say unto you, They have their reward.

Mar. 11.26. If ye do not forgive, neither will your Father which is in heaven forgive your trespasses.

Luk. 13.25. When once the master of the house is risen up, and hath shut to the door, and ye begin to stand without, and to knock at the door, saying, Lord, Lord, open unto us; and he shall answer and say unto you, I know you not whence ye are.

Luk. 18.14. I tell you, This man went down to his house justified *rather* than the other: for every one that exalteth himself shall be abased.

Jno. 9.31. God heareth not sinners: but if any man be a worshipper of God, and doeth his will, him he heareth.

Jas. 1.6. Let him ask in faith, nothing wavering. For he that wavereth is like a wave of the sea driven with the wind and tossed. 7. For let not that man think that he shall receive any thing of the Lord.

Jas. 4.3. Ye ask, and receive not, because ye ask amiss, that ye may consume *it* upon your lusts.

See HYPOCRISY—DOUBT—SIN HATEFUL TO GOD.

SIN, UNIVERSAL. See MAN'S NATURAL STATE—FALL, THE.

SIN, ZEAL AGAINST. See ZEAL FOR GOD'S GLORY.

SIN, DESERT OF; between Elim and Sinai; Israelites murmur in, for bread; manna given, Ex. 16. Ex. 17.1. Num. 33.11,12.

—— (Pelusium), a strong city of Egypt, Eze. 30.15.

SIN MONEY, 2 Kin. 12.16. Lev. 5.15,16,18. Num. 18.9.

SIN-OFFERING. See OFFERING, p. 329.

SINAI or HOREB, MOUNT. (*Sinai* is the name given to the *Mount*, with one exception. In Exodus, this name seems to have been nearly supplanted by *Horeb*, after the forty years' wandering; compare Ex. 20 with Deu. 5. Ex. 19.16-19 with Deu. 4.10-13.) Situation of, Ex. 16.1. Deu. 1.2.

Israelites encamp before, Ex. 19.2. Moses ascends, Ex. 19.3,20; with the seventy, Ex. 24.1,2,9-11; with Joshua, Ex. 24.12,13,15,18. Ex. 32.15,17; alone, Ex. 34.2. God reveals Himself to him, Ex. 34.5,6. Moses' face shines on descending, Ex. 34.29.

Approach to, forbidden, Ex. 19.12,13,21-24. Ex. 34.3. Heb. 12.20. Clouds, darkness, lightnings, and thunder on (Sinai), Ex. 19. 9,16-19. Ex. 20.18. Ex. 24.15-17. Deu. 33.2. Jud. 5.5. Psa. 68.8,17. Heb. 12.18-21. (Horeb), Deu. 4.10-13,33,36. Deu. 5.4.

Law given from (Sinai), Ex. 20. Lev. 7.38. Lev. 25.1. Lev. 26.46. Lev. 27.34. Num. 3.1. Num. 28.6. Neh. 9.13. Act. 7.30,38. (Horeb), Deu. 4.15. Deu. 5.2-6. Deu. 29.1. Mal. 4.4. Two tables given on (Sinai), Ex. 31.18. (Horeb), 1 Kin. 8.9. Moses intercedes for Israel on, Ex. 32.7-14.

Horeb called Mount of God; Moses sees the burning bush, Ex. 3.1-6. Rock in Horeb smitten, Ex. 17.6. Israelites worship golden calf at, Deu. 9.8. Ex. 33.6. Elijah flees to, 1 Kin. 19.8. Allegory of Sinai, Gal. 4.24,25.

SINAI, WILDERNESS OF. See ISRAELITES, HISTORY OF, p. 254.

SINCERITY. See SPIRITUAL DILIGENCE—PRAYERFULNESS—WORSHIP, REVERENCE IN, &c.—INTEGRITY—HYPOCRISY.

SINGING. See MUSIC.

SINIM (China), prophecy of, Isa. 49.12.

SINITES, descendants of Canaan, Gen. 10. 17. 1 Chr. 1.15.

SINNERS, CHARACTER OF. See SIN, LOVE OF.

——, DEATH OF. See DEATH OF SINNERS.

—— DREAD OF GOD. See CONVICTION.

SINNERS' Hatred of Reproof. See Reproof hated.

————, Joy of, short; their Misery. See Conviction — Worldliness — Sin, Fruits of — Sin, punishment of.

————, Prayers of, rejected. See Sin separates from God.

————, Punishment of. See Sin, punishment of.

————, Salvation offered to. See Salvation — God's mercy — Pardon — Repentance.

————, Temporal Prosperity of. See God's providence misunderstood.

SION, Mount, see Hermon. Sion, see Zion.

SIRION. See Hermon.

SISERA, general of king Jabin, of Canaan; defeated by Deborah, and slain by Jael, Jud. 4. Jud. 5.20,24-30. 1 Sam. 12.9. Psa. 83.9.

SITNAH (hatred), a well dug by Isaac, Gen. 26.21.

SIVAN (3d month (June), Est. 8.9.

SKIN. Coats of, Gen. 3.21. Of rams and badgers for the tabernacle, Ex. 25.5. Num. 4.8-14.

SLANDER. See Falsehood — Speaking evil.

SLAVE. See Servants, bond.

SLIME (Asphalt or bitumen), used at Babel, Gen. 11.3. Moses' ark daubed with, Ex. 2.3. Vale of Siddim full of, Gen. 14.10. See Pitch.

SLING, Pro. 26.8. 1 Sam. 17.40,50. 1 Sam. 25.29. 2 Chr. 26.14. Slingers, 2 Kin. 3.25.

SLOTH. See Idleness.

SMITH, 1 Sam. 13.19. 2 Kin. 24.14. Isa. 54.16. Jer. 24.1. See Goldsmith — Silver.

SMYRNA, a city of Ionia; epistle to the church in, Rev. 1.11. Rev. 2.8-11.

SNAIL, Lev. 11.30. Psa. 58.8.

SNARE or Gin, Amos 3.5. Illustrative, Job 18.8,10. Psa. 91.3. Jer. 5.26.

SNOW. In Palestine, 2 Sam. 23.20. In Uz, Job 6.16. Job 9.30. On Lebanon, Jer. 18.14.

SNUFFERS. Of the temple, 1 Kin. 7.50. 2 Kin. 12.13. 2 Kin. 25.14. Jer. 52.18.

SO, king of Egypt; Hoshea, king of Israel, seeks his aid against Assyria, 2 Kin. 17.4.

SOAP (potash or soda), Jer. 2.22. Mal. 3.2.

SOBRIETY. See Temperance.

SODOM, Gen. 10.19. Lot dwells in, Gen. 13.10-12. Gen. 19.1. King of, defeated and rescued by Abraham, Gen. 14. Abraham intercedes for, Gen. 18.16-33. Wickedness of; its destruction by fire; Lot saved, Gen. 13.13. Gen. 19. Deu. 23.22. Deu. 29.23. Isa. 1. 9,10. Isa. 3.9. Isa. 13.19. Jer. 23.14. Jer. 49.18. Jer. 50.40. Lam. 4.6. Eze. 16.46-56. Amos 4.11. Zeph. 2.9. Mat. 10.15. Luk. 17.28,29. Rom. 9.29. 2 Pet. 2.6. Jude 7. Symbolical, Rev. 11.8.

————, Vine of, illustrative, Deu. 32.32.

SODOMITES, those who imitated the licentiousness of Sodom, Deu. 23.17. 1 Kin.

14.24. Rom. 1.26,27. Destroyed, 1 Kin. 15. 12. 1 Kin. 22.46. 2 Kin. 23.7.

SOLDIERS. Levies of, Num. 31.4. Jud. 20.10. Mercenaries, Jud. 9.4. 2 Sam. 10.6. 1 Chr. 19.7,8. 2 Chr. 25.6. Men 20 years old liable to serve, Num. 1.3. Num. 26.2. Exemptions, Deu. 20.5-9. Deu. 24.5. Discipline of, Mat. 8.9. 2 Tim. 2.3,4.

A devout soldier, Act. 10.7. Soldiers at Christ's crucifixion, &c., Mat. 27.27,54,66. Mat. 28.4,11-15. Jno. 19.23-34. Preserve order, Act. 21.32-35. Guard prisoners, Act. 12.4-19. Act. 21.32-35. Act. 23.23,31. Act. 27.31,32,42. Act. 28.16. Illustrative, 2 Tim. 2.3.

See Armour-bearer — Captain — Centurion — Guards — Standard-bearer — Italian band — Legion — Quaternion — Armies — Arms.

SOLOMON (peace), 3d king of Israel (40 years' reign); son of David and Bathsheba, 2 Sam. 5.14. 2 Sam. 12.24. 1 Chr. 3.5. 1 Chr. 14.4. Mat. 1.6. Named Jedediah (beloved of the Lord) by Nathan, 2 Sam. 12. 24,25. Neh. 13.26. Prophecies of his birth and reign, 1 Chr. 22.9,10. 2 Sam. 7.12-16. 1 Chr. 17.11-14. 1 Chr. 28.6,7. Psa. 132.11.

David appoints him his successor; he is proclaimed and anointed king, 1 Kin. 1.13,17, 32-40. 1 Chr. 23.1. 1 Chr. 28.5; a second time, 1 Chr. 29.22-25. Sole king, 1 Kin. 2.12. David's charge to him, 1 Kin. 2.1-9. 1 Chr. 22.7-16. 1 Chr. 28.9-21.

Spares Adonijah, 1 Kin. 1.50-53. Puts him to death, 1 Kin. 2.12-25; also Joab, 1 Kin. 2. 28-34; and Shimei, 1 Kin. 2.36-46.

His prayer for wisdom answered; God appears in a dream, 1 Kin. 3.5-14. 2 Chr. 1.7-12. His second vision, 1 Kin. 9.1-9. 2 Chr. 7. 12-22.

His wisdom and fame, 1 Kin. 4.29-34. 1 Kin. 10.3,4,8,23,24. 1 Chr. 29.24,25. 2 Chr. 9.2-7,22,23. Ecc. 1.16. Mat. 12.42. Adjudges the case of the two harlots, 1 Kin. 3.16-28. Piety, 1 Kin. 5.3. Sacrifices in high places, 1 Kin. 3.3; at Gibeon, 1 Kin. 3.4. 2 Chr. 1.2-6; at Jerusalem, 1 Kin. 3.15. 1 Kin. 9.25. 2 Chr. 8.12,13.

Builds the temple, 1 Kin. 3.1. 1 Kin. c. 5 to 7. 1 Kin. 9.10. 1 Chr. 6.10. 2 Chr. c. 2 to 4. 2 Chr. 7.11. Act. 7.47. Brings up the ark, &c., 1 Kin. 8.1-11. 2 Chr. 5. Dedication of the temple; his prayer, 1 Kin. 8. 2 Chr. 6. Regulates the temple worship, 2 Chr. 8.14,15. 2 Chr. 35.4. Neh. 12.45, see Temple.

Marries Pharaoh's daughter, 1 Kin. 3.1. Receives Gezer as a dowry, 1 Kin. 9.16. Builds a house for her, 1 Kin. 7.8-12. 1 Kin. 9.24. 2 Chr. 8.11. Prosperity of Israel, 1 Kin. 4.20,25. 2 Chr. 1.1. Extent of his dominions, 1 Kin. 4.21,24. 1 Kin. 8.65. 2 Chr. 9.26. His tributaries, 1 Kin. 4.21. 1 Kin. 9.20,21. 2 Chr. 8.7,8. Officers, 1 Kin. 2.35. 1 Kin. 4.1-19. 2 Chr. 8.8-10. Provision of his house, 1 Kin. 4.22,23,27. 1 Kin. 10.5. His horses and chariots, 1 Kin. 4.26,28. 1 Kin. 10.26. 2 Chr. 1.14. 2 Chr. 9.25.

Cities, &c., built by him, 1 Kin. 9.15-19,24. 2 Chr. 8.1-6. Ecc. 2.4-7. Wall of Jerusalem, 1 Kin. 3.1. 1 Kin. 9.15. His house, 1 Kin. 3.1. 1 Kin. 7.1. 1 Kin. 9.10. 2 Chr. 7.11. 2 Chr. 8.1. House of the forest of Lebanon,

1 Kin. 7.2-8, see HIRAM. His pools, his gardens, &c., Ecc. 2.4-6. Song 8.11.

His throne, 1 Kin. 7.7; of ivory, 1 Kin. 10.18-20. 2 Chr. 9.17-19. Porch of judgment, 1 Kin. 7.7. Harps, &c., 1 Kin. 10.12. 2 Chr. 9.11. Ecc. 2.8. Shields, 1 Kin. 10.14,15. Drinking vessels, 1 Kin. 10.21. 2 Chr. 9.20. Splendour of his court, 1 Kin. 10.5. Mat. 6.29.

His wealth, 1 Kin. 10.14,15,23. Enriched by trade in gold, &c., with Ophir and Tarshish, 1 Kin. 9.26-28. 1 Kin. 10.11,12,22. 2 Chr. 8.17,18. 2 Chr. 9.10,21,22. With Egypt, &c., 1 Kin. 10.28,29. 2 Chr. 1.16,17. 2 Chr. 9.13,14,28.

Visited by the queen of Sheba, 1 Kin. 10.1-13. 2 Chr. 9.1-12. His proverbs, 1 Kin. 4.32. Pro. 1.1. Pro. 10.1. Pro. 25.1. Songs, 1 Kin. 4.32. Song of Solomon.

Silver abundant, 1 Kin. 10.27. 2 Chr. 1.15. 2 Chr. 9.27. Gold, &c., brought by the queen of Sheba, 1 Kin. 10.10. 2 Chr. 9.1,9; and in tribute, 1 Kin. 10.25. 2 Chr. 9.13,14,24. From Hiram, 1 Kin. 9.14. Oppressive taxes, 1 Kin. 12.4. 2 Chr. 10.4.

Marries numerous heathen wives; his idolatry, 1 Kin. 11.1-8. 2 Kin. 23.13. Neh. 13.26. Warned of the division of the kingdom, 1 Kin. 11.9-13. Rebellion of Hadad, 1 Kin. 11.14,21,22; and Rezon, 1 Kin. 11. 23-25. Promotes, but afterwards seeks to kill Jeroboam, 1 Kin. 11.26-28,40.

Psalms for Solomon, Psa. 72 & 127 (title). His son, Rehoboam, by Naamah, the Ammonitess, 1 Kin. 14.31. 1 Chr. 3.10. Reigns 40 years; death and burial, 1 Kin. 11.42,43. 2 Chr. 9.30,31. History of, written by prophets, 2 Chr. 9.29.

SON. Besides its ordinary meaning, it is used for grandson, 2 Sam. 19.24. Descendant, Mat. 1.1,20. As a name of affection, 1 Sam. 3.6. Ex. 4.22. 1 Tim. 1.2; and of humility, 2 Kin. 8.9. It occurs in such phrases as, Son of the morning, Isa. 14.12. Son of Belial, 1 Sam. 2.12. The Hebrew word for son, *ben* or *bar*, is incorporated with names, as Benoni, son of sorrow, Gen. 35.18. Barjona, son of Jonas, Mat. 16.17.

SONGS. Song of the well, Num. 21.17. War-song, Num. 21.27-30. Of the bow, 2 Sam. 1.19-27. Of Solomon, one thousand and five, 1 Kin. 4.32.

SOOTHSAYER. See SORCERY.

SOP, a bit, or morsel, Jno. 13.26,27.

SOPATER OF BEREA. Accompanies Paul to Asia, Act. 20.4-6. Perhaps the same as Paul's kinsman, Sosipater, Rom. 16.21.

SORCERY. Consulting cups, Gen. 44.5. Dreams, Deu. 13.1-5. Jer. 23.25-32. Jer. 27.9. Jer. 29.8. Zec. 10.2. Entrails of animals, Eze. 21.21. Arrows, Eze. 21.21,22. Familiar spirits, Lev. 20.6,27. 1 Chr. 10. 13. 2 Chr. 33.6. Isa. 8.19. Isa. 19.3. Isa. 29.4. Images or teraphim, 2 Kin. 23.24. Eze. 21.21. Rods, Hos. 4.12. The dead, see NECROMANCY. Consulting the stars, see ASTROLOGY.

Books of, Act. 19.19. Practice of muttering, Isa. 8.19. Isa. 29.4. Payment for, Num. 22.7. Mic. 3.11. Act. 16.16. Divination, enchantment, charms, soothsaying, witchcraft, observing of times forbidden, and punishment threatened, Lev. 19.26-28,31. Lev. 20.6. Deu. 18.9-14. 1 Sam. 15.23. Isa. 8.19. Isa. 19.3,11,12. Isa. 44.25. Isa. 47. 9-13. Jer. 10.2. Jer. 14.14. Jer. 27.9. Jer. 29.8,9. Eze. 12.23,24. Eze. 13.6-9,18-23. Eze. 21.29. Eze. 22.28. Mic. 3.6,7. Mic. 5.12. Zec. 10.2. Mal. 3.5. Mat. 24.24. Gal. 4.9-11. Gal. 5.19,20. 2 The. 2.9. Rev. 9.21. Rev. 13.13,14. Rev. 16.14. Rev. 18.23. Rev. 19.20. Rev. 21.8. Rev. 22. 15. Punished with death by the law, Ex. 22.18. Lev. 20.27. Deu. 13.5. See Jos. 13.22. 1 Sam. 28.3,9. 2 Kin. 23.24.

Practised by Joseph, Gen. 44.5,15. Pharaoh's magicians, Ex. 7.11,22. Ex. 8.7,18. Balaam, Num. 22.6. Num. 23. Num. 24.1. Jos. 13.22. Philistines, 1 Sam. 6.2-9. Isa. 2.6. Saul and the witch of Endor, 1 Sam. 28.7. Jezebel, 2 Kin. 9.22. Israel, 2 Kin. 17.17. Manasseh, 2 Kin. 21.6. Nebuchadnezzar, Eze. 21.21,22. Dan. 2.2,10,27. Dan. 4.7. Belshazzar, Dan. 5.7,15. Ninevites, Nah. 3.4,5. Simon Magus, Act. 8.9-11. Elymas, Act. 13.8. Damsel at Philippi, Act. 16.16. Sons of Sceva and Ephesians, Act. 19.13,14,18,19.

See MAGICIANS — PROGNOSTICATORS — MINISTERS, UNFAITHFUL.

SOREK, a vale; the residence of Delilah, Jud. 16.4.

SOSIPATER. See SOPATER.

SOSTHENES, chief ruler of the synagogue in Corinth, successor of Crispus, beaten by the Greeks, Act. 18.8,17; with Paul, 1 Cor. 1.1.

SOUL OF MAN, IMMORTAL. Gen. 5.24. Enoch walked with God: and he *was* not; for God took him.

2 Sam. 12.23. Now he is dead, wherefore should I fast? can I bring him back again? I shall go to him, but he shall not return to me.

2 Kin. 2.11. Elijah went up by a whirlwind into heaven.

Job 14.13. O that thou wouldest hide me in the grave, that thou wouldest keep me secret, until thy wrath be past, that thou wouldest appoint me a set time, and remember me!

Psa. 21.4. He asked life of thee, *and* thou gavest *it* him, *even* length of days for ever and ever.

Psa. 49.8. The redemption of their soul *is* precious, and it ceaseth for ever.

Psa. 121.8. The Lord shall preserve thy going out and thy coming in from this time forth, and even for evermore.

Ecc. 3.21. Who knoweth the spirit of man that goeth upward, and the spirit of the beast that goeth downward to the earth?

Ecc. 12.7. Then shall the dust return to the earth as it was: and the spirit shall return unto God who gave it.

Isa. 25.8. He will swallow up death in victory.

Mat. 10.28. Fear not them which kill the body, but are not able to kill the soul: but rather fear him which is able to destroy both soul and body in hell.

Mat. 16.26. What is a man profited, if he shall gain the whole world, and lose his own soul? or what shall a man give in exchange for his soul?

Luk. 9.25. What is a man advantaged, if

he gain the whole world, and lose himself, or be cast away?

Luk. 20.36. Neither can they die any more: for they are equal unto the angels; and are the children of God, being the children of the resurrection.

Rom. 6.23. The gift of God *is* eternal life through Jesus Christ our Lord.

1 Cor. 15.53. This corruptible must put on incorruption, and this mortal *must* put on immortality. 54. So when this corruptible shall have put on incorruption, and this mortal shall have put on immortality, then shall be brought to pass the saying that is written, Death is swallowed up in victory.

1 Tim. 4.8. Having promise of the life that now is, and of that which is to come.

2 Tim. 1.10. Our Saviour Jesus Christ, who hath abolished death, and hath brought life and immortality to light through the gospel.

Tit. 1.2. Eternal life, which God, that cannot lie, promised before the world began.

Heb. 11.5. Enoch was translated that he should not see death; and was not found, because God had translated him.

1 Jno. 2.25. This is the promise that he hath promised us, *even* eternal life.

See RESURRECTION — HEAVEN — HELL — JUDGMENT.

SOWING. Illustrative, Hos. 8.7. Psa. 126.5. Pro. 11.18. Isa. 32.20, &c. Parable of the sower, Mar. 4.3-9.

SPAIN, Rom. 16.24,28. See TARSHISH.

SPAN, from the end of the thumb to the end of the little finger expanded, 9 or 10 inches, Ex. 28.16. Ex. 39.9.

SPARROW, Psa. 102.7. Psa. 84.3. Generally translated bird; used in sacrifice, Lev. 14.4-53 (see *marg.*). Two sold for a farthing, Mat. 10.29. Luk. 12.6.

SPEAKING EVIL—FOOLISH SPEAKING.
Job 13.5. Oh that ye would altogether hold your peace! and it should be your wisdom.

Job 16.4. I also could speak as ye *do:* if your soul were in my soul's stead, I could heap up words against you. *v.* 3.

Job 19.18. Yea, young children despised me: I arose, and they spake against me.

Job 38.2. Who *is* this that darkeneth counsel by words without knowledge?

Psa. 35.21. They opened their mouth wide against me, *and* said, Aha, aha, our eye hath seen *it*.

Psa. 41.5. Mine enemies speak evil of me, When shall he die, and his name perish? 6. And if he come to see *me*, he speaketh vanity: his heart gathereth iniquity to itself; *when* he goeth abroad, he telleth *it*. 7. All that hate me whisper together against me: against me do they devise my hurt.

Psa. 64.3. Who whet their tongue like a sword, *and* bend *their bows to shoot* their arrows, *even* bitter words: 4. That they may shoot in secret at the perfect.

Psa. 69.12. They that sit in the gate speak against me; and I *was* the song of the drunkards. 26. They persecute *him* whom thou hast smitten; and they talk to the grief of those whom thou hast wounded.

Psa. 70.3. Let them be turned back for a reward of their shame that say, Aha, aha.

Psa. 102.8. Mine enemies reproach me all the day.

Psa. 106.33. They provoked his spirit, so that he spake unadvisedly with his lips.

Psa. 119.23. Princes also did sit *and* speak against me.

Psa. 140.3. They have sharpened their tongues like a serpent; adders' poison *is* under their lips. 11. Let not an evil speaker be established in the earth.

Pro. 4.24. Put away from thee a froward mouth, and perverse lips put far from thee.

Pro. 6.16. Doth the Lord hate. 19. He that soweth discord among brethren. *v.* 12-19.

Pro. 10.8. A prating fool shall fall. 11. Violence covereth the mouth of the wicked. 19. In the multitude of words there wanteth not sin. 32. The mouth of the wicked *speaketh* frowardness.

Pro. 12.6. The words of the wicked *are* to lie in wait for blood. 13. The wicked is snared by the transgression of *his* lips. 16. A fool's wrath is presently known. 18. There is that speaketh like the piercings of a sword. 23. The heart of fools proclaimeth foolishness.

Pro. 13.3. He that openeth wide his lips shall have destruction. *v.* 2.

Pro. 14.3. In the mouth of the foolish *is* a rod of pride.

Pro. 15.1. Grievous words stir up anger. 2. The mouth of fools poureth out foolishness. 4. A wholesome tongue *is* a tree of life: but perverseness therein *is* a breach in the spirit. 7. The lips of the wise disperse knowledge: but the heart of the foolish *doeth* not so. 14. The mouth of fools feedeth on foolishness. 28. The mouth of the wicked poureth out evil things.

Pro. 16.27. An ungodly man diggeth up evil: and in his lips *there is* as a burning fire. 28. A froward man soweth strife: and a whisperer separateth chief friends.

Pro. 17.9. He that repeateth a matter separateth *very* friends. 20. He that hath a perverse tongue falleth into mischief.

Pro. 18.2. A fool hath no delight in understanding, but that his heart may discover itself. 6. A fool's lips enter into contention, and his mouth calleth for strokes. 7. A fool's mouth *is* his destruction, and his lips *are* the snare of his soul. 13. He that answereth a matter before he heareth *it*, it *is* folly and shame unto him. 21. Death and life *are* in the power of the tongue: and they that love it shall eat the fruit thereof. 23. The poor useth intreaties; but the rich answereth roughly. *v.* 8.

Pro. 19.28. The mouth of the wicked devoureth iniquity.

Pro. 20.19. He that goeth about *as* a talebearer revealeth secrets. Pro. 11.13.

Pro. 22.12. He overthroweth the words of the transgressor.

Pro. 24.2. Their heart studieth destruction, and their lips talk of mischief. 7. Wisdom *is* too high for a fool: he openeth not his mouth in the gate.

Pro. 25.23. The north wind driveth away rain: so *doth* an angry countenance a backbiting tongue.

Pro. 26.4. Answer not a fool according to his folly, lest thou also be like unto him. 7. The legs of the lame are not equal: so *is* a parable in the mouth of fools. 9. *As* a thorn goeth up into the hand of a drunkard, so *is* a parable in the mouth of fools. 20. Where no wood is, *there* the fire goeth out: so where *there is* no talebearer, the strife ceaseth. 21. As coals *are* to burning coals, and wood to fire; so *is* a contentious man to kindle strife. 22. The words of a talebearer *are* as wounds, and they go down into the innermost parts of the belly. *v.* 23.

Pro. 29.11. A fool uttereth all his mind: but a wise *man* keepeth it in till afterwards. 20. Seest thou a man *that is* hasty in his words? *there is* more hope of a fool than of him.

Pro. 30.10. Accuse not a servant unto his master, lest he curse thee, and thou be found guilty.

Ecc. 5.3. A dream cometh through the multitude of business; and a fool's voice *is known* by multitude of words. 7. In the multitude of dreams and many words *there are* also *divers* vanities: but fear thou God.

Ecc. 10.3. When he that is a fool walketh by the way, his wisdom faileth *him*, and he saith to every one *that* he *is* a fool. 11. The serpent will bite without enchantment; and a babbler is no better. 13. The begin̅ning of the words of his mouth *is* foolishness: and the end of his talk *is* mischievous madness. 14. A fool also is full of words. *v.* 2,12,20.

Isa. 6.5. Woe *is* me! for I am undone; because I *am* a man of unclean lips, and I dwell in the midst of a people of unclean lips.

Isa. 32.6. The vile person will speak villany, and his heart will work iniquity, to practise hypocrisy, and to utter error against the Lord.

Jer. 8.6. I hearkened and heard, *but* they spake not aright.

Jer. 20.10. I heard the defaming of many, fear on every side. Report, *say they*, and we will report it.

Mat. 5.22. Whosoever shall say to his brother, Raca, shall be in danger of the council: but whosoever shall say, Thou fool, shall be in danger of hell fire. 37. Let your communication be, Yea, yea; Nay, nay: for whatsoever is more than these cometh of evil.

Mat. 12.34. O generation of vipers, how can ye, being evil, speak good things? for out of the abundance of the heart the mouth speaketh. 35. An evil man out of the evil treasure bringeth forth evil things.

Mat. 12.36. Every idle word that men shall speak, they shall give account thereof in the day of judgment. 37. For by thy words thou shalt be justified, and by thy words thou shalt be condemned.

Act. 23.5. Thou shalt not speak evil of the ruler of thy people. Ex. 22.28. Job 34.18.

1 Cor. 6.10. Nor revilers, nor extortioners, shall inherit the kingdom of God.

Eph. 4.29. Let no corrupt communication proceed out of your mouth. 31. Let all bitterness, and wrath, and anger, and clamour, and evil speaking, be put away from you, with all malice.

Eph. 5.4. Neither filthiness, nor foolish talking, nor jesting, which are not convenient: but rather giving of thanks.

Col. 3.8. Now ye also put off all these; blasphemy, filthy communication out of your mouth.

2 The. 3.11. We hear that there are some

which walk among you disorderly, working not at all, but are busybodies.

1 Tim. 5.13. They learn *to be* idle, wandering about from house to house; and not only idle, but tattlers also and busybodies, speaking things which they ought not.

Tit. 3.2. Speak evil of no man.

Jas. 1.26. If any man among you seem to be religious, and bridleth not his tongue, but deceiveth his own heart, this man's religion *is* vain. *v.* 19.

Jas. 3.5. Even so the tongue is a little member, and boasteth great things. Behold, how great a matter a little fire kindleth! 6. And the tongue *is* a fire, a world of iniquity: so is the tongue among our members, that it defileth the whole body, and setteth on fire the course of nature; and it is set on fire of hell. 8. But the tongue can no man tame; *it is* an unruly evil, full of deadly poison. 9. Therewith bless we God, even the Father; and therewith curse we men, which are made after the similitude of God. 10. Out of the same mouth proceedeth blessing and cursing. My brethren, these things ought not so to be. *v.* 2-12.

Jas. 4.11. Speak not evil one of another, brethren. He that speaketh evil of *his* brother, and judgeth his brother, speaketh evil of the law, and judgeth the law.

1 Pet. 2.1. Laying aside all malice, and all evil speakings.

1 Pet. 3.9. Not rendering evil for evil, or railing for railing: but contrariwise blessing. 10. He that will love life, and see good days, let him refrain his tongue from evil. Psa. 34.13.

1 Pet. 4.15. Let none of you suffer as a busybody in other men's matters.

2 Pet. 2.10. Presumptuous *are they*, selfwilled, they are not afraid to speak evil of dignities.

Jude 10. These speak evil of those things which they know not. *v.* 8.

SPEAKING EVIL, EXAMPLES OF: Laban's sons, Gen. 31.1. Joseph, Gen. 37.2. Miriam and Aaron, Num. 12.1. Israelites, Ex. 17.2,3. Num. 16.3,13,41. Michal, 2 Sam. 6.20. Saul, 1 Sam. 20.30,31. Princes of Ammon, 2 Sam. 10.3. Chaldeans, Dan. 3.8. Dan. 6.13. Jews, Mat. 11.18,19. Jno. 8.48.

See BLASPHEMY—FALSEHOOD—FLATTERY —UNCHARITABLENESS.

SPEAKING WITH WISDOM. See WISDOM —PRUDENCE.

SPEAR, JAVELIN, or LANCE, 1 Sam. 17.7. 1 Sam. 18.10. 2 Chr. 23.9. Jer. 50.42.

SPEECH. See WISDOM IN SPEECH— SPEAKING EVIL.

SPICES. From Gilead, Gen. 37.25. Palestine, Gen. 43.11. Sheba, 1 Kin. 10.2,10. Eze. 27.22. From gardens, Song 4.13-16. Mountains, Song 8.14. Given in presents, 1 Kin. 10.10. Mat. 2.11. Used in the sacred oil, Ex. 25.6. Ex. 35.8. 1 Chr. 9.29. 2 Kin. 20.13. In burial, 2 Chr. 16.14. Luk. 23.56. Luk. 24.1. Jno. 19.39,40.

See ANOINTING—INCENSE—OIL, SACRED— OINTMENT—PERFUMES—ALOES—BDELLIUM —CASSIA—CINNAMON—FRANKINCENSE— GALBANUM—MYRRH—ONYCHA—SPIKE-NARD.

SPIDER, Pro. 30.28.   Web of, Job 8.14. Isa. 59.5.

SPIES, Gen. 42.9. Num. 21.32. Num. 13. Jos. 2.1. 1 Sam. 8.57. 2 Sam. 15.10. Pharisees, Luk. 20.20. In the church, Gal. 2.4.

SPIKENARD, a valuable perfume, Song 1.12. Song 4.13,14. Mary anoints Christ's head with, Mar. 14.3. Jno. 12.3.

SPINDLE, Pro. 31.19.

SPINNING by women, Ex. 35.25,26. Pro. 31.19.

SPIRITUAL BLESSINGS. SANCTIFICATION, PRAYER FOR. 1 Kin. 8.57. The Lord our God be with us. 58. That he may incline our hearts unto him, to walk in all his ways, and to keep his commandments.

Neh. 1.11. Let now thine ear be attentive to the prayer of thy servants, who desire to fear thy name.

Psa. 17.5. Hold up my goings in thy paths, *that* my footsteps slip not.

Psa. 19.12. Who can understand *his* errors? cleanse thou me from secret *faults.*

Psa. 27.9. Hide not thy face *far* from me; put not thy servant away in anger: thou hast been my help; leave me not, neither forsake me, O God of my salvation.

Psa. 51.2. Wash me throughly from mine iniquity, and cleanse me from my sin. 7. Purge me with hyssop, and I shall be clean: wash me, and I shall be whiter than snow. 10. Create in me a clean heart, O God; and renew a right spirit within me. 12. Restore unto me the joy of thy salvation; and uphold me *with thy* free spirit.

Psa. 56.13. Thou hast delivered my soul from death: *wilt* not *thou deliver* my feet from falling, that I may walk before God in the light of the living?

Psa. 61.7. O prepare mercy and truth, *which* may preserve him.

Psa. 68.28. Strengthen, O God, that which thou hast wrought for us.

Psa. 71.18. Forsake me not; until I have shewed thy strength unto *this* generation, *and* thy power to every one *that* is to come.

Psa. 80.17. Let thy hand be upon the man of thy right hand, upon the son of man *whom* thou madest strong for thyself. 18. So will not we go back from thee: quicken us, and we will call upon thy name. 19. Turn us again, O Lord God of hosts, cause thy face to shine; and we shall be saved.

Psa. 85.6. Wilt thou not revive us again: that thy people may rejoice in thee?

Psa. 86.11. Teach me thy way, O Lord; I will walk in thy truth: unite my heart to fear thy name. 16. O turn unto me, and have mercy upon me; give thy strength unto thy servant, and save the son of thine hand-maid.

Psa. 90.12. So teach *us* to number our days, that we may apply our hearts unto wisdom. 16. Let thy work appear unto thy servants, and thy glory unto their children. 17. And let the beauty of the Lord our God be upon us: and establish thou the work of our hands upon us: yea, the work of our hands establish thou it.

Psa. 118.25. Save now, I beseech thee, O Lord: O Lord, I beseech thee, send now prosperity.

Psa. 119.5. O that my ways were directed to keep thy statutes! 10. With my whole heart have I sought thee: O let me not wander

from thy commandments. 17. Deal bountifully with thy servant, *that* I may live, and keep thy word. 25. My soul cleaveth unto the dust: quicken thou me according to thy word. 28. My soul melteth for heaviness: strengthen thou me according unto thy word. 32. I will run the way of thy commandments, when thou shalt enlarge my heart. 33. Teach me, O Lord, the way of thy statutes; and I shall keep it *unto* the end. 34. Give me understanding, and I shall keep thy law; yea, I shall observe it with *my* whole heart. 35. Make me to go in the path of thy commandments; for therein do I delight. 36. Incline my heart unto thy testimonies, and not to covetousness. 37. Turn away mine eyes from beholding vanity; *and* quicken thou me in thy way.

Psa. 119.40. Quicken me in thy righteousness. 77. Let thy tender mercies come unto me, that I may live: for thy law *is* my delight. 88. Quicken me after thy lovingkindness; so shall I keep the testimony of thy mouth. 116. Uphold me according unto thy word, that I may live: and let me not be ashamed of my hope. 117. Hold thou me up, and I shall be safe: and I will have respect unto thy statutes continually. 122. Be surety for thy servant for good. 133. Order my steps in thy word: and let not any iniquity have dominion over me. 149. Hear my voice according unto thy lovingkindness: O Lord, quicken me according to thy judgment. 156. Great *are* thy tender mercies, O Lord: quicken me according to thy judgments. *v.* 107,154,159.

Psa. 125.4. Do good, O Lord, unto *those that be* good, and to *them that are* upright in their hearts.

Psa. 139.23. Search me, O God, and know my heart: try me, and know my thoughts: 24. And see if *there be any* wicked way in me, and lead me in the way everlasting.

Psa. 143.10. Teach me to do thy will; for thou *art* my God: thy spirit *is* good; lead me into the land of uprightness. 11. Quicken me, O Lord, for thy name's sake.

Song 1.4. Draw me, we will run after thee.

Jer. 31.18. Turn thou me, and I shall be turned; for thou *art* the Lord my God.

Lam. 5.21. Turn thou us unto thee, O Lord, and we shall be turned; renew our days as of old.

Hab. 3.2. O Lord, revive thy work in the midst of the years, in the midst of the years make known; in wrath remember mercy.

Mar. 9.24. Lord, I believe; help thou mine unbelief.

Luk. 11.1. Lord, teach us to pray, as John also taught his disciples.

Luk. 17.5. The apostles said unto the Lord, Increase our faith.

Jno. 17.11. Holy Father, keep through thine own name those whom thou hast given me, that they may be one, as we *are.*

Eph. 3.16. That he would grant you, according to the riches of his glory, to be strengthened with might by his Spirit in the inner man; 17. That Christ may dwell in your hearts by faith; that ye, being rooted and grounded in love.

Phil. 1.9. I pray, that your love may abound yet more and more in knowledge and *in* all judgment. 10. That ye may approve things that are excellent; that ye may be sincere and without offence till the day of Christ; 11. Being filled with the fruits of righteousness, which are by Jesus Christ, unto the glory and praise of God.

Col. 2.2. That their hearts might be comforted, being knit together in love, and unto all riches of the full assurance of understanding, to the acknowledgment of the mystery of God, and of the Father, and of Christ.

Col. 4.12. That ye may stand perfect and complete in all the will of God.

1 The. 3.10. Night and day praying exceedingly that we might see your face, and might perfect that which is lacking in your faith. 12. And the Lord make you to increase and abound in love one toward another, and toward all men, even as we do toward you: 13. To the end he may stablish your hearts unblameable in holiness before God, even our Father, at the coming of our Lord Jesus Christ with all his saints.

1 The. 5.23. The very God of peace sanctify you wholly; and I pray God your whole spirit and soul and body be preserved blameless unto the coming of our Lord Jesus Christ.

2 The. 1.11. We pray always for you, that our God would count you worthy of this calling, and fulfil all the good pleasure of his goodness, and the work of faith with power.

2 The. 2.16. Now our Lord Jesus Christ himself, and God, even our Father, which hath loved us, and hath given us everlasting consolation, and good hope through grace, 17. Comfort your hearts, and stablish you in every good word and work.

2 The. 3.5. The Lord direct your hearts into the love of God, and into the patient waiting for Christ. 16. Now the Lord of peace himself give you peace always by all means. The Lord be with you all.

Heb. 13.20. Now the God of peace, that brought again from the dead our Lord Jesus, that great Shepherd of the sheep, through the blood of the everlasting covenant, 21. Make you perfect in every good work to do his will, working in you that which is well-pleasing in his sight, through Jesus Christ.

1 Pet. 5.10. The God of all grace, who hath called us unto his eternal glory by Christ Jesus, after that ye have suffered a while make you perfect, stablish, strengthen, settle you.

See TEMPTATION, PRAYER IN—PRAYER, INTERCESSORY—SANCTIFICATION.

SPIRITUAL BLINDNESS, IGNORANCE. Ex. 5.2. Pharaoh said, Who is the Lord, that I should obey his voice to let Israel go? I know not the Lord, neither will I let Israel go.

Deu. 29.2. Ye have seen all that the Lord did before your eyes in the land of Egypt. 4. Yet the Lord hath not given you an heart to perceive, and eyes to see, and ears to hear, unto this day.

Deu. 32.28. They are a nation void of counsel, neither is there any understanding in them. 29. O that they were wise, that they understood this, that they would consider their latter end!

Jud. 2.10. There arose another generation after them, which knew not the Lord, nor yet the works which he had done for Israel.

Jud. 16.20. He wist not that the Lord was departed from him.

Job 21.14. They say unto God, Depart from us; for we desire not the knowledge of thy ways.

Job 22.13. How doth God know? can he judge through the dark cloud? 14. Thick clouds are a covering to him, that he seeth not; and he walketh in the circuit of heaven.

Psa. 5.5. The foolish shall not stand in thy sight.

Psa. 10.5. Thy judgments are far above out of his sight.

Psa. 14.1. The fool hath said in his heart, There is no God. 4. Have all the workers of iniquity no knowledge?

Psa. 50.21. Thou thoughtest that I was altogether such an one as thyself.

Psa. 73.22. So foolish was I, and ignorant: I was as a beast before thee.

Psa. 79.6. Pour out thy wrath upon the heathen that have not known thee.

Psa. 82.5. They know not, neither will they understand; they walk on in darkness.

Psa. 92.5. O Lord, how great are thy works! and thy thoughts are very deep. 6. A brutish man knoweth not; neither doth a fool understand this.

Psa. 94.7. They say, The Lord shall not see, neither shall the God of Jacob regard it. 8. Understand, ye brutish among the people: and ye fools, when will ye be wise?

Psa. 95.10. It is a people that do err in their heart, and they have not known my ways.

Pro. 1.7. Fools despise wisdom and instruction. 22. How long, ye simple ones, will ye love simplicity? and the scorners delight in their scorning, and fools hate knowledge? 29. They hated knowledge, and did not choose the fear of the Lord: 30. They would none of my counsel: they despised all my reproof.

Pro. 4.19. The way of the wicked is as darkness: they know not at what they stumble.

Pro. 10.21. Fools die for want of wisdom.

Pro. 13.18. Poverty and shame shall be to him that refuseth instruction.

Pro. 17.16. Wherefore is there a price in the hand of a fool to get wisdom, seeing he hath no heart to it?

Pro. 19.2. That the soul be without knowledge, it is not good. 3. The foolishness of man perverteth his way: and his heart fretteth against the Lord.

Pro. 28.5. Evil men understand not judgment.

Ecc. 7.25. To know the wickedness of folly, even of foolishness and madness.

Ecc. 9.12. Man also knoweth not his time: as the fishes that are taken in an evil net, and as the birds that are caught in the snare; so are the sons of men snared in an evil time, when it falleth suddenly upon them.

Isa. 1.3. The ox knoweth his owner, and the ass his master's crib: but Israel doth not know, my people doth not consider.

Isa. 5.13. Therefore my people are gone into captivity, because they have no knowledge. 20. Woe unto them that call evil good and good evil; that put darkness for light, and light for darkness; that put bitter for sweet, and sweet for bitter!

Isa. 6.9. Hear ye indeed, but understand not; and see ye indeed, but perceive not. 10. Make the heart of this people fat, and make their ears heavy, and shut their eyes; lest they see with their eyes, and hear with their ears, and understand with their heart, and convert, and be healed.

Isa. 9.2. The people that walked in darkness have seen a great light: they that dwell in the land of the shadow of death, upon them hath the light shined.

Isa. 26.10. Let favour be shewed to the wicked, *yet* will he not learn righteousness: in the land of uprightness will he deal unjustly, and will not behold the majesty of the Lord. 11. Lord, *when* thy hand is lifted up, they will not see.

Isa. 27.11. It *is* a people of no understanding: therefore he that made them will not have mercy on them, and he that formed them will shew them no favour.

Isa. 29.10. The Lord hath poured out upon you the spirit of deep sleep, and hath closed your eyes: the prophets and your rulers, the seers hath he covered. 11. And the vision of all is become unto you as the words of a book that is sealed, which *men* deliver to one that is learned, saying, Read this, I pray thee: and he saith, I cannot; for it *is* sealed: 12. And the book is delivered to him that is not learned, saying, Read this, I pray thee: and he sayeth, I am not learned.

Isa. 40.21. Have ye not known? have ye not heard? hath it not been told you from the beginning? have ye not understood from the foundations of the earth?

Isa. 42.7. To open the blind eyes, to bring out the prisoners from the prison, *and* them that sit in darkness out of the prison-house. 18. Hear, ye deaf; and look, ye blind, that ye may see. 19. Who *is* blind, but my servant? or deaf, as my messenger *that* I sent? who *is* blind as *he that is* perfect, and blind as the Lord's servant? 20. Seeing many things, but thou observest not; opening the ears, but he heareth not.

Isa. 44.18. They have not known nor understood: for he hath shut their eyes, that they cannot see; *and* their hearts, that they cannot understand. 19. And none considereth in his heart, neither *is there* knowledge nor understanding. 20. He feedeth on ashes: a deceived heart hath turned him aside, that he cannot deliver his soul, nor say, *Is there* not a lie in my right hand?

Isa. 56.10. His watchmen *are* blind: they are all ignorant, they *are* all dumb dogs.

Isa. 60.2. Darkness shall cover the earth, and gross darkness the people.

Jer. 2.8. The priest said not, Where *is* the Lord? and they that handle the law knew me not.

Jer. 4.22. My people *is* foolish, they have not known me; they *are* sottish children, and they have none understanding: they *are* wise to do evil, but to do good they have no knowledge.

Jer. 5.4. I said, Surely these *are* poor; they are foolish: for they know not the way of the Lord, *nor* the judgment of their God. 5. I will get me unto the great men; and will speak unto them; for they have known the way of the Lord, *and* the judgment of their God: but these have altogether broken the yoke, *and* burst the bonds. 21. Hear now this, O foolish people, and without understanding; which have eyes, and see not; which have ears, and hear not.

Jer. 8.7. The stork in the heaven knoweth her appointed times; and the turtle and the crane and the swallow observe the time of their coming; but my people know not the judgment of the Lord. 9. The wise *men* are ashamed, they are dismayed and taken: lo, they have rejected the word of the Lord; and what wisdom *is* in them?

Jer. 9.3. They proceed from evil to evil, and they know not me, saith the Lord. 6. Through deceit they refuse to know me, saith the Lord.

Jer. 16.10. They shall say unto thee, Wherefore hath the Lord pronounced all this great evil against us? or what *is* our iniquity? or what *is* our sin that we have committed against the Lord our God?

Jer. 17.9. The heart *is* deceitful above all *things*, and desperately wicked: who can know it?

Dan. 12.10. None of the wicked shall understand.

Hos. 4.1. *There is* no truth, nor mercy, nor knowledge of God in the land. 6. My people are destroyed for lack of knowledge: because thou hast rejected knowledge, I will also reject thee, that thou shalt be no priest to me. 14. The people *that* doth not understand shall fall.

Hos. 5.4. They will not frame their doings to turn unto their God: and they have not known the Lord.

Hos. 7.11. Ephraim also is like a silly dove without heart.

Mic. 4.12. They know not the thoughts of the Lord, neither understand they his counsel.

Mat. 6.23. If thine eye be evil, thy whole body shall be full of darkness. If therefore the light that is in thee be darkness, how great *is* that darkness!

Mat. 13.19. When any one heareth the word of the kingdom, and understandeth *it* not, then cometh the wicked *one*, and catcheth away that which was sown in his heart.

Mar. 4.15. Luk. 8.12.

Mat. 15.14. They be blind leaders of the blind. And if the blind lead the blind, both shall fall into the ditch.

Mat. 16.3. Ye can discern the face of the sky; but can ye not *discern* the signs of the times?

Mat. 22.29. Ye do err, not knowing the scriptures, nor the power of God. Mar. 12.24.

Mat. 23.24. *Ye* blind guides, which strain at a gnat, and swallow a camel.

Mar. 6.52. They considered not *the miracle* of the loaves: for their heart was hardened.

Luk. 11.52. Woe unto you, lawyers! for ye have taken away the key of knowledge: ye enter not in yourselves, and them that were entering in ye hindered.

Luk. 12.48. He that knew not, and did commit things worthy of stripes, shall be beaten with few *stripes*. 57. Yea, and why even of yourselves judge ye not what is right?

Luk. 19.42. If thou hadst known, even thou, at least in this thy day, the things *which belong* unto thy peace! but now they are hid from thine eyes.

Luk. 23.34. Then said Jesus, Father, forgive them; for they know not what they do.

Jno. 1.5. The light shineth in darkness; and the darkness comprehended it not. 10.

He was in the world, and the world was made by him, and the world knew him not.

Jno. 3.4. How can a man be born when he is old? can he enter the second time into his mother's womb, and be born? 7. Marvel not that I said unto thee, Ye must be born again. 19. This is the condemnation, that light is come into the world, and men loved darkness rather than light, because their deeds were evil. 20. Every one that doeth evil hateth the light, neither cometh to the light, lest his deeds should be reproved. 31. He that is of the earth is earthly, and speaketh of the earth. *v.* 9-12.

Jno. 4.10. If thou knewest the gift of God, and who it is that saith to thee, Give me to drink; thou wouldest have asked of him, and he would have given thee living water. 22. Ye worship ye know not what. *v.* 11,15.

Jno. 6.52. How can this man give us *his* flesh to eat? 60. Many of his disciples, when they had heard *this*, said, This is an hard saying; who can hear it?

Jno. 7.28. He that sent me is true, whom ye know not.

Jno. 8.15. Ye judge after the flesh. 19. Ye neither know me, nor my Father: if ye had known me, ye should have known my Father also. 27. They understood not that he spake to them of the Father. 33. We be Abraham's seed, and were never in bondage to any man: how sayest thou, Ye shall be made free? 43. Why do ye not understand my speech: *even* because ye cannot hear my word. 52. Now we know that thou hast a devil. Abraham is dead, and the prophets; and thou sayest, If a man keep my saying, he shall never taste of death. 55. Yet ye have not known him; but I know him: and if I should say, I know him not, I shall be a liar like unto you. 57. Thou art not yet fifty years old, and hast thou seen Abraham?

Jno. 9.29. We know that God spake unto Moses; *as for* this *fellow*, we know not from whence he is. 30. Why, herein is a marvellous thing, that ye know not from whence he is, and *yet* he hath opened mine eyes. 39. Jesus said, For judgment I am come into this world, that they which see not might see, and that they which see might be made blind. *v.* 30-38.

Jno. 12.38. Lord, who hath believed our report? and to whom hath the arm of the Lord been revealed?

Jno. 14.17. The Spirit of truth; whom the world cannot receive, because it seeth him not, neither knoweth him.

Jno. 15.21. They know not him that sent me.

Jno. 16.3. These things will they do unto you, because they have not known the Father, nor me.

Jno. 17.25. O righteous Father, the world hath not known thee.

Act. 3.17. Now, brethren, I wot that through ignorance ye did *it*, as *did* also your rulers.

Act. 13.27. They that dwell at Jerusalem, and their rulers, because they knew him not, nor yet the voices of the prophets which are read every sabbath-day, they have fulfilled *them* in condemning *him*.

Act. 17.23. I found an altar with this inscription, TO THE UNKNOWN GOD. Whom therefore ye ignorantly worship, him declare I unto you.

Act. 19.2. We have not so much as heard whether there be any Holy Ghost.

Act. 26.18. To open their eyes, *and* to turn *them* from darkness to light, and *from* the power of Satan unto God.

Rom. 1.19. That which may be known of God is manifest in them; for God hath shewed *it* unto them. 20. For the invisible things of him from the creation of th world are clearly seen, being understood by the things that are made, *even* his eternal power and Godhead; so that they are without excuse: 21. When they knew God, they glorified *him* not as God, neither were thankful; but became vain in their imaginations, and their foolish heart was darkened. 22. Professing themselves to be wise, they became fools. 28. They did not like to retain God in *their* knowledge.

Rom. 2.4. Despisest thou the riches of his goodness and forbearance and longsuffering: not knowing that the goodness of God leadeth thee to repentance?

Rom. 8.26. We know not what we should pray for as we ought.

Rom. 11.25. Blindness in part is happened to Israel, until the fulness of the Gentiles be come in.

1 Cor. 1.18. The preaching of the cross is to them that perish foolishness. 20. Where *is* the wise? where *is* the scribe? where *is* the disputer of this world? hath not God made foolish the wisdom of this world? 21. The world by wisdom knew not God.

1 Cor. 2.8. Which none of the princes of this world knew: for had they known *it*, they would not have crucified the Lord of glory. 14. The natural man receiveth not the things of the Spirit of God: for they are foolishness unto him: neither can he know *them*, because they are spiritually discerned. 15. He that is spiritual judgeth all things, yet he himself is judged of no man.

1 Cor. 13.9. We know in part, and we prophesy in part.

1 Cor. 15.34. Some have not the knowledge of God: I speak *this* to your shame.

2 Cor. 3.14. Their minds were blinded: for until this day remaineth the same vail untaken away in the reading of the old testament. 15. Even unto this day, when Moses is read, the vail is upon their heart.

2 Cor. 4.3. If our gospel be hid, it is hid to them that are lost: 4. In whom the God of this world hath blinded the minds of them which believe not, lest the light of the glorious gospel of Christ, who is the image of God, should shine unto them.

Eph. 4.18. Having the understanding darkened, being alienated from the life of God through the ignorance that is in them, because of the blindness of their heart.

Eph. 5.8. Ye were sometimes darkness, but now *are ye* light in the Lord.

1 The. 4.5. The Gentiles which know not God.

2 The. 1.8. In flaming fire, taking vengeance on them that know not God, and that obey not the gospel of our Lord Jesus Christ.

2 Tim. 3.7. Ever learning, and never able to come to the knowledge of the truth.

2 Tim. 3.13. Evil men and seducers shall wax worse and worse, deceiving, and being deceived.

Tit. 1.16. They profess that they know God; but in works they deny *him*.

Heb. 5.11. Ye are dull of hearing. 12. For

when for the time ye ought to be teachers, ye have need that one teach you again which be the first principles of the oracles of God; and are become such as have need of milk, and not of strong meat.

1 Pet. 1.14. Not fashioning yourselves according to the former lusts in your ignorance.

2 Pet. 1.9. He that lacketh these things is blind, and cannot see afar off, and hath forgotten that he was purged from his old sins.

2 Pet. 3.16. In which are some things hard to be understood, which they that are unlearned and unstable wrest, as *they do* also the other scriptures, unto their own destruction.

1 Jno. 2.4. He that saith, I know him, and keepeth not his commandments, is a liar, and the truth is not in him. 9. He that saith he is in the light, and hateth his brother, is in darkness even until now. 11. But he that hateth his brother is in darkness, and walketh in darkness, and knoweth not whither he goeth, because that darkness hath blinded his eyes. 1 Jno. 1.6.

1 Jno. 3.1. The world knoweth us not, because it knew him not. 6. Whosoever sinneth hath not seen him, neither known him.

1 Jno. 4.8. He that loveth not, knoweth not God; for God is love.

3 Jno. 11. He that doeth evil hath not seen God.

Jude 10. These speak evil of those things which they know not.

Rev. 3.17. Thou sayest, I am rich, and increased with goods, and have need of nothing; and knowest not that thou art wretched, and miserable, and poor, and blind, and naked.

See MAN'S IGNORANCE — GOD'S PROVIDENCE MISUNDERSTOOD—APOSTLES' IMPERFECT KNOWLEDGE — IMPENITENCE — MAN'S NATURAL STATE.

SPIRITUAL DESERTION. See SIN SEPARATES FROM GOD—DOUBT.

SPIRITUAL DESTITUTION. RELIGIOUS PRIVILEGES WITHDRAWN. 2 Chr. 15.3. For a long season Israel *hath been* without the true God, and without a teaching priest, and without law.

Psa. 74.8. They have burned up all the synagogues of God in the land. 9. We see not our signs: *there is* no more any prophet: neither *is there* among us any that knoweth how long.

Pro. 29.18. Where *there is* no vision, the people perish.

Lam. 2.6. He hath violently taken away his tabernacle, as *if it were of* a garden: he hath destroyed his places of the assembly: the Lord hath caused the solemn feasts and sabbaths to be forgotten in Zion, and hath despised in the indignation of his anger the king and the priest. 7. The Lord hath cast off his altar, he hath abhorred his sanctuary, they have made a noise in the house of the Lord, as in the day of a solemn feast. 9. The law *is* no *more;* her prophets also find no vision from the Lord. Jer. 7.12.

Eze. 3.26. I will make thy tongue cleave to the roof of thy mouth, that thou shalt be dumb, and shalt not be to them a reprover: for they *are* a rebellious house.

Eze. 7.26. Then shall they seek a vision of the prophet; but the law shall perish from the priest, and counsel from the ancients.

Hos. 2.11. I will also cause all her mirth to cease, her feast-days, her new moons, and her sabbaths, and all her solemn feasts.

Joel 1.9. The meat-offering and the drink-offering is cut off from the house of the Lord; the priests, the Lord's ministers, mourn. *v.* 13.

Amos 8.11. I will send a famine in the land, not a famine of bread, nor a thirst for water, but of hearing the words of the Lord. 12. And they shall wander from sea to sea, and from the north even to the east, they shall run to and fro to seek the word of the Lord, and shall not find *it.*

Mic. 2.5. Thou shalt have none that shall cast a cord by lot in the congregation of the Lord. 6. Prophesy ye not, *say they to them that* prophesy: they shall not prophesy to them, *that* they shall not take shame.

Mat. 9.36. When he saw the multitudes, he was moved with compassion on them, because they fainted, and were scattered abroad, as sheep having no shepherd. 37. Then saith he unto his disciples, The harvest truly *is* plenteous, but the labourers *are* few: 38. Pray ye therefore the Lord of the harvest, that he will send forth labourers into his harvest.

SPIRITUAL DILIGENCE, SEEKING GOD, SPIRITUALITY, HEAVENLY - MINDEDNESS, SINCERITY. Deu. 6.5. Love the Lord thy God with all thine heart, and with all thy soul, and with all thy might.

Deu. 18.13. Thou shalt be perfect with the Lord thy God.

Jos. 22.5. Take diligent heed to do the commandment and the law, which Moses the servant of the Lord charged you, to love the Lord your God, and to walk in all his ways, and to keep his commandments, and to cleave unto him, and to serve him with all your heart and with all your soul. Deu. 10.12.

Jos. 24.14. Serve him in sincerity and in truth: and put away the gods which your fathers served on the other side of the flood, and in Egypt; and serve ye the Lord. 22. Ye *are* witnesses against yourselves that ye have chosen you the Lord, to serve him. And they said, *We are* witnesses. *v.* 23. 1 Sam. 7.3.

1 Sam. 12.24. Only fear the Lord, and serve him in truth with all your heart. *v.* 20.

1 Kin. 8.23. Who keepest covenant and mercy with thy servants that walk before thee with all their heart. 61. Let your heart therefore be perfect with the Lord our God, to walk in his statutes, and to keep his commandments.

1 Chr. 22.19. Now set your heart and your soul to seek the Lord your God.

1 Chr. 28.9. Know thou the God of thy father, and serve him with a perfect heart and with a willing mind: for the Lord searcheth all hearts, and understandeth all the imaginations of the thoughts: if thou seek him, he will be found of thee.

2 Chr. 15.2. The Lord *is* with you, while ye be with him; and if ye seek him, he will be found of you.

Ezr. 8.22. The hand of our God *is* upon all them for good that seek him; but his power and his wrath *is* against all them that forsake him.

Psa. 1.2. His delight *is* in the law of the Lord; and in his law doth he meditate day and night. 3. And he shall be like a tree planted by the rivers of water.

Psa. 22.26. They shall praise the Lord that seek him: your heart shall live for ever.

Psa. 24.6. This *is* the generation of them that seek him, that seek thy face.

Psa. 27.14. Wait on the Lord: be of good courage, and he shall strengthen thine heart: wait, I say, on the Lord.

Psa. 34.10. They that seek the Lord shall not want any good *thing*.

Psa. 37.4. Delight thyself also in the Lord; and he shall give thee the desires of thine heart. 7. Rest in the Lord, and wait patiently for him. 9. Those that wait upon the Lord, they shall inherit the earth. 34. Wait on the Lord, and keep his way, and he shall exalt thee to inherit the land.

Psa. 51.6. Behold, thou desirest truth in the inward parts: and in the hidden *part* thou shalt make me to know wisdom.

Psa. 69.32. Your heart shall live that seek God.

Psa. 70.4. Let all those that see . thee rejoice and be glad in thee: and let such as love thy salvation say continually, Let God be magnified.

Psa. 81.10. Open thy mouth wide, and I will fill it.

Psa. 105.4. Seek the Lord, and his strength: seek his face evermore.

Psa. 119.2. Blessed *are* they that keep his testimonies, *and that* seek him with the whole heart.

Pro. 2.3. If thou criest after knowledge, *and* liftest up thy voice for understanding; 4. If thou seekest her as silver, and searchest for her as *for* hid treasures; 5. Then shalt thou understand the fear of the Lord, and find the knowledge of God.

Pro. 8.17. I love them that love me; and those that seek me early shall find me. 34. Blessed *is* the man that heareth me, watching daily at my gates, waiting at the posts of my doors.

Pro. 11.28. The righteous shall flourish as a branch.

Pro. 12.12. But the root of the righteous yieldeth *fruit*.

Pro. 15.24. The way of life *is* above to the wise, that he may depart from hell beneath.

Ecc. 9.10. Whatsoever thy hand findeth to do, do *it* with thy might; for *there is* no work, nor device, nor knowledge, nor wisdom, in the grave, whither thou goest.

Ecc. 12.1. Remember now thy Creator in the days of thy youth, while the evil days come not, nor the years draw nigh, when thou shalt say, I have no pleasure in them.

Isa. 8.19. Should not a people seek unto their God?

Isa. 30.18. Therefore will the Lord wait, that he may be gracious unto you, and therefore will he be exalted, that he may have mercy upon you: for the Lord *is* a God of judgment: blessed *are* all they that wait for him.

Isa. 40.31. They that wait upon the Lord shall renew *their* strength; they shall mount up with wings as eagles.

Isa. 49.23. Thou shalt know that I *am* the

Lord: for they shall not be ashamed that wait for me.

Isa. 55.6. Seek ye the Lord while he may be found, call ye upon him while he is near.

Jer. 29.13. Ye shall seek me, and find *me*, when ye shall search for me with all your heart. Deu. 4.29.

Jer. 50.4. The children of Israel shall come, they and the children of Judah together, going and weeping: they shall go, and seek the Lord their God.

Lam. 3.25. The Lord *is* good unto them that wait for him, to the soul *that* seeketh him. 26. *It is* good that *a man* should both hope and quietly wait for the salvation of the Lord. 41. Let us lift up our heart with *our* hands unto God in the heavens.

Hos. 10.12. Sow to yourselves in righteousness, reap in mercy; break up *your* fallow ground: for *it is* time to seek the Lord, till he come and rain righteousness upon you.

Hos. 12.6. Turn thou to thy God: keep mercy and judgment, and wait on thy God continually.

Joel 2.12. Turn ye *even* to me with all your heart, and with fasting, and with weeping, and with mourning: 13. And rend your heart, and not your garments, and turn unto the Lord your God: for he *is* gracious and merciful, slow to anger, and of great kindness, and repenteth him of the evil.

Amos 4.12. Because I will do this unto thee, prepare to meet thy God, O Israel.

Mat. 5.6. Blessed *are* they which do hunger and thirst after righteousness: for they shall be filled. Luk. 6.21.

Mat. 6.20. Lay up for yourselves treasures in heaven, where neither moth nor rust doth corrupt, and where thieves do not break through nor steal: 21. For where your treasure is, there will your heart be also. 22. The light of the body is the eye: if therefore thine eye be single, thy whole body shall be full of light. 33. Seek ye first the kingdom of God, and his righteousness.

Mat. 7.13. Enter ye in at the strait gate: 14. Because strait is the gate, and narrow *is* the way, which leadeth unto life, and few there be that find it.

Mat. 13.11. It is given unto you to know the mysteries of the kingdom of heaven, but to them it is not given. 12. For whosoever hath, to him shall be given, and he shall have more abundance. Mat. 25.28,29. Mar. 4.10,11. Luk. 8.10

Luk. 10.42. One thing is needful: and Mary hath chosen that good part, which shall not be taken away from her.

Luk. 12.33. Sell that ye have, and give alms; provide yourselves bags which wax not old, a treasure in the heavens that faileth not, where no thief approacheth, neither moth corrupteth. *v.* 31-35.

Luk. 13.24. Strive to enter in at the strait gate: for many, I say unto you, will seek to enter in, and shall not be able.

Luk. 16.16. Since that time the kingdom of God is preached, and every man presseth into it.

Luk. 17.21. The kingdom of God is within you.

Luk. 20.38. He is not a God of the dead, but of the living: for all live unto him.

Jno. 4.23. The hour cometh, and now is,

when the true worshippers shall worship the Father in spirit and in truth: for the Father seeketh such to worship him. 24. God is a Spirit: and they that worship him must worship him in spirit and in truth.

Jno. 6.27. Labour not for the meat which perisheth, but for that meat which endureth unto everlasting life, which the Son of man shall give unto you.

Jno. 11.9. If any man walk in the day, he stumbleth not, because he seeth the light of this world. 10. But if a man walk in the night, he stumbleth, because there is no light in him.

Jno. 12.35. Walk while ye have the light, lest darkness come upon you: for he that walketh in darkness knoweth not whither he goeth. 36. While ye have light, believe in the light, that ye may be the children of light.

Act. 17.27. That they should seek the Lord, if haply they might feel after him, and find him.

Rom. 8.6. To be spiritually minded is life and peace.

Rom. 13.11. Knowing the time, that now it is high time to awake out of sleep: for now is our salvation nearer than when we believed. v. 12.

1 Cor. 5.8. Let us keep the feast, not with old leaven, neither with the leaven of malice and wickedness; but with the unleavened bread of sincerity and truth.

1 Cor. 7.29. Brethren, the time is short: it remaineth, that both they that have wives be as though they had none; 30. And they that weep, as though they wept not; and they that rejoice, as though they rejoiced not; and they that buy, as though they possessed not; 31. And they hat use his world, as not abusing it: for the fashion of this world passeth away.

1 Cor. 9.24. Know ye not that they which run in a race run all, but one receiveth the prize? So run, that ye may obtain. v. 27.

Gal. 5.16. Walk in the Spirit, and ye shall not fulfil the lusts of the flesh. 25. If we live in the Spirit, let us also walk in the Spirit.

Eph. 5.16. Redeeming the time, because the days are evil. 19. Singing and making melody in your heart to the Lord.

Eph. 6.14. Stand therefore, having your loins girt about with truth.

Phil. 1.10. Be sincere and without offence till the day of Christ.

Phil. 2.12. Work out your own salvation with fear and trembling. 13. For it is God which worketh in you both to will and to do of his good pleasure.

Phil. 3.3. We are the circumcision, which worship God in the spirit. 14. I press toward the mark for the prize of the high calling of God in Christ Jesus. 15. Let us therefore, as many as be perfect, be thus minded.

Phil. 4.5. Let your moderation be known unto all men. The Lord is at hand.

Col. 3.1. If ye then be risen with Christ, seek those things which are above, where Christ sitteth on the right hand of God. 2. Set your affection on things above, not on things on the earth. 3. For ye are dead, and your life is hid with Christ in God.

Col. 4.5. Walk in wisdom toward them that are without, redeeming the time.

1 Tim. 6.19. Laying up in store for themselves a good foundation against the time to come, that they may lay hold on eternal life. v. 12.

2 Tim. 1.6. I put thee in remembrance that thou stir up the gift of God which is in thee.

2 Tim. 2.4. No man that warreth entangleth himself with the affairs of this life; that he may please him who hath chosen him to be a soldier.

Heb. 3.7. Wherefore (as the Holy Ghost saith), To-day if ye will hear his voice, 8. Harden not your hearts. Psa. 95.7.

Heb. 4.11. Let us labour therefore to enter into that rest, lest any man fall after the same example of unbelief.

Heb. 6.11. We desire that every one of you do shew the same diligence to the full assurance of hope unto the end: 12. That ye be not slothful, but followers of them who through faith and patience inherit the promises.

Heb. 11.6. He is a rewarder of them that diligently seek him.

Heb. 12.12. Lift up the hands which hang down, and the feeble knees; 13. And make straight paths for your feet.

1 Pet. 2.2. As new-born babes, desire the sincere milk of the word, that ye may grow thereby.

1 Pet. 3.21. Not the putting away of the filth of the flesh, but the answer of a good conscience toward God.

2 Pet. 3.14. Seeing that ye look for such things, be diligent that ye may be found of him in peace, without spot, and blameless. 2 Pet. 1.10,11.

1 Jno. 3.21. If our heart condemn us not, then have we confidence toward God.

See DECISION—HOLINESS.

SPIRITUAL DILIGENCE, SEEKING GOD, SPIRITUALITY, HEAVENLY - MINDEDNESS, SINCERITY, EXEMPLIFIED.

Gen. 49.18. I have waited for thy salvation, O Lord.

2 Sam. 24.24. Neither will I offer burnt-offerings unto the Lord my God of that which doth cost me nothing.

1 Kin. 3.6. He walked before thee in truth, and in righteousness, and in uprightness of heart with thee. 1 Kin. 9.4.

1 Kin. 15.14. Asa's heart was perfect with the Lord all his days.

1 Chr. 29.17. As for me, in the uprightness of mine heart I have willingly offered all these things.

2 Chr. 15.15. All Judah rejoiced at the oath: for they had sworn with all their heart, and sought him with their whole desire.

2 Chr. 19.3. There are good things found in thee, in that thou hast taken away the groves out of the land, and hast prepared thine heart to seek God.

2 Chr. 26.5. As long as he sought the Lord, God made him to prosper.

2 Chr. 30.18. The good Lord pardon every one 19. That prepareth his heart to seek God, the Lord God of his fathers.

2 Chr. 31.21. In every work that he began in the service of the house of God, and in the law, and in the commandments, to seek his God, he did it with all his heart, and prospered.

Job 16.19. My witness is in heaven, and my record is on high.

Psa. 7.10. My defence *is* of God, which saveth the upright in heart.

Psa. 17.1. Give ear unto my prayer, *that goeth* not out of feigned lips. *v. 3.*

Psa. 25.5. Thou *art* the God of my salvation; on thee do I wait all the day. 15. Mine eyes *are* ever toward the Lord; for he shall pluck my feet out of the net.

Psa. 27.8. *When thou saidst,* Seek ye my face; my heart said unto thee, Thy face, Lord, will I seek.

Psa. 33.20. Our soul waiteth for the Lord : he *is* our help and our shield.

Psa. 39.12. I *am* a stranger with thee, *and* a sojourner, as all my fathers *were.* Ex. 2.22.

Psa. 40.1. I waited patiently for the Lord. 8. I delight to do thy will, O my God : yea, thy law *is* within my heart.

Psa. 42.1. As the hart panteth after the water-brooks, so panteth my soul after thee, O God. 2. My soul thirsteth for God, for the living God : when shall I come and appear before God?

Psa. 44.20. If we nave forgotten the name of our God. 21. Shall not God search this out? Jos. 22.22.

Psa. 52.9. I will wait on thy name; for *it is* good before thy saints.

Psa. 57.7. My heart is fixed, O God, my heart is fixed ; I will sing and give praise.

Psa. 62.1. Truly my soul waiteth upon God : from him *cometh* my salvation.

Psa. 63.1. O God, thou *art* my God ; early will I seek thee : my soul thirsteth for thee, my flesh longeth for thee in a dry and thirsty land, where no water is. 8. My soul followeth hard after thee : thy right hand upholdeth me.

Psa. 69.3. Mine eyes fail while I wait for my God.

Psa. 84.2. My soul longeth, yea, even fainteth for the courts of the Lord : my heart and my flesh crieth out for the living God.

Psa. 86.11. Teach me thy way, O Lord ; I will walk in thy truth : unite my heart to fear thy name. 12. I will praise thee, O Lord my God, with all my heart : and I will glorify thy name for evermore. Psa. 9.1.

Psa. 94.19. In the multitude of my thoughts within me thy comforts delight my soul.

Psa. 118.17. I shall not die, but live, and declare the works of the Lord.

Psa. 119.10. With my whole heart have I sought thee : O let me not wander from thy commandments. 20. My soul breaketh for the longing *that it hath* unto thy judgments at all times. *v. 19.*

Psa. 123.1. Unto thee lift I up mine eyes, O thou that dwellest in the heavens. 2. Behold, as the eyes of servants *look* unto the hand of their masters, *and* as the eyes of a maiden unto the hand of her mistress ; so our eyes *wait* upon the Lord our God, until that he have mercy upon us.

Psa. 130.5. I wait for the Lord, my soul doth wait, and in his word do I hope. 6. My soul *waiteth* for the Lord more than they that watch for the morning : *I say, more than* they that watch for the morning.

Psa. 143.5. I meditate on all thy works ; I muse on the work of thy hands. 6. I stretch forth my hands unto thee : my soul *thirsteth* after thee, as a thirsty land.

Isa. 26.8. In the way of thy judgments, O Lord, have we waited for thee ; the desire of *our* soul *is* to thy name, and to the remembrance of thee. 9. With my soul have I desired thee in the night ; yea, with my spirit within me will I seek thee early.

Jer. 12.3. Thou, O Lord, knowest me : thou hast seen me, and tried mine heart toward thee.

Hab. 2.1. I will stand upon my watch, and set me upon the tower, and will watch to see what he will say unto me.

Jno. 9.4. I must work the works of him that sent me, while it is day : the night cometh.

Jno. 12.21. Sir, we would see Jesus.

Jno. 17.14. They are not of the world, even as I am not of the world.

Rom. 1.9. God is my witness, whom I serve with my spirit in the gospel of his Son.

Rom. 7.22. I delight in the law of God after the inward man.

2 Cor. 4.18. We look not at the things which are seen, but at the things which are not seen.

Phil. 1.21. To me to live is Christ.

Phil. 3.12. Not as though I had already attained, either were already perfect ; but I follow after, if that I may apprehend that for which also I am apprehended of Christ Jesus. 13. Brethren, I count not myself to have apprehended : but *this* one thing *I do,* forgetting those things which are behind, and reaching forth unto those things which are before, 14. I press toward the mark for the prize of the high calling of God in Christ Jesus. 20. Our conversation is in heaven ; from whence also we look for the Saviour, the Lord Jesus Christ.

Heb. 10.34. Took joyfully the spoiling of your goods, knowing in yourselves that ye have in heaven a better and an enduring substance.

Heb. 11.10. He looked for a city which hath foundations, whose builder and maker *is* God. 13. These all died in faith, not having received the promises, but having seen them afar off, and were persuaded of *them,* and embraced *them,* and confessed that they were strangers and pilgrims on the earth. 14. For they that say such things declare plainly that they seek a country. 16. They desire a better *country,* an heavenly. 25. Choosing rather to suffer affliction with the people of God, than to enjoy the pleasures of sin for a season ; 26. Esteeming the reproach of Christ greater riches than the treasures in Egypt : for he had respect unto the recompence of reward. 27. He endured, as seeing him who is invisible.

Heb. 13.14. Here have we no continuing city, but we seek one to come.

1 Jno. 1.3. Truly our fellowship *is* with the Father, and with his Son Jesus Christ.

3 Jno. 2. Beloved, I wish above all things that thou mayest prosper and be in health, even as thy soul prospereth.

See DECISION—LOVE TO GOD—PRAYERFULNESS—WORD OF GOD LOVED.

SPIRITUAL PEACE AND JOY. Ex. 33.14. My presence shall go *with thee,* and I will give thee rest.

Deu. 33.29. Happy *art* thou, O Israel : who *is* like unto thee, O people saved by the Lord.

1 Sam. 2.1. My heart rejoiceth in the Lord, mine horn is exalted in the Lord : my mouth is enlarged over mine enemies ; because I rejoice in thy salvation.

1 Chr. 16.27. Glory and honour *are* in his presence ; strength and gladness *are* in his place.

Neh. 8.10. The joy of the Lord is your strength.

Neh. 12.43. God had made them rejoice with great joy.

Job 8.21. Till he fill thy mouth with laughing, and thy lips with rejoicing.

Job 22.21. Acquaint now thyself with him, and be at peace : thereby good shall come unto thee. 26. Then shalt thou have thy delight in the Almighty, and shalt lift up thy face unto God.

Job 33.26. He will be favourable unto him : and he shall see his face with joy.

Job 34.29. When he giveth quietness, who then can make trouble ?

Psa. 1.1. Blessed *is* the man that walketh not in the counsel of the ungodly.

Psa. 4.7. Thou hast put gladness in my heart, more than in the time *that* their corn and their wine increased.

Psa. 5.11. Let all those that put their trust in thee rejoice : let them ever shout for joy, because thou defendest them : let them also that love thy name be joyful in thee.

Psa. 9.2. I will be glad and rejoice in thee : I will sing praise to thy name, O thou most High.

Psa. 13.5. My heart shall rejoice in thy salvation.

Psa. 16.5. The Lord *is* the portion of mine inheritance and of my cup : thou maintainest my lot. 6. The lines are fallen unto me in pleasant *places* ; yea, I have a goodly heritage. 8. I have set the Lord always before me : because *he is* at my right hand, I shall not be moved. 9. Therefore my heart is glad, and my glory rejoiceth : my flesh also shall rest in hope. 11. Thou wilt shew me the path of life : in thy presence *is* fulness of joy ; at thy right hand *there are* pleasures for evermore.

Psa. 17.15. As for me, I will behold thy face in righteousness : I shall be satisfied, when I awake, with thy likeness.

Psa. 19.8. The statutes of the Lord *are* right, rejoicing the heart.

Psa. 20.5. We will rejoice in thy salvation, and in the name of our God we will set up *our* banners.

Psa. 21.1. The king shall joy in thy strength, O Lord ; and in thy salvation how greatly shall he rejoice ! 6. Thou hast made him most blessed for ever : thou hast made him exceeding glad with thy countenance.

Psa. 23.2. He maketh me to lie down in green pastures : he leadeth me beside the still waters.

Psa. 25.13. His soul shall dwell at ease.

Psa. 27.6. Now shall mine head be lifted up above mine enemies round about me : therefore will I offer in his tabernacle sacrifices of joy ; I will sing, yea, I will sing praises unto the Lord.

Psa. 28.7. The Lord *is* my strength and my shield ; my heart trusted in him, and I am helped : therefore my heart greatly rejoiceth ; and with my song will I praise him.

Psa. 29.11. The Lord will bless his people with peace.

Psa. 30.5. His anger *endureth but* a moment ; in his favour *is* life : weeping may endure for a night, but joy *cometh* in the morning. 11. Thou hast turned for me my mourning into dancing : thou hast put off my sackcloth, and girded me with gladness. *v.* 12.

Psa. 32.11. Be glad in the Lord, and rejoice, ye righteous : and shout for joy, all *ye that are* upright in heart. *v.* 1,2.

Psa. 33.21. Our heart shall rejoice in him, because we have trusted in his holy name.

Psa. 34.8. O taste and see that the Lord *is* good : blessed *is* the man *that* trusteth in him.

Psa. 35.9. My soul shall be joyful in the Lord : it shall rejoice in his salvation.

Psa. 36.8. They shall be abundantly satisfied with the fatness of thy house ; and thou shalt make them drink of the river of thy pleasures.

Psa. 37.4. Delight thyself also in the Lord ; and he shall give thee the desires of thine heart. 11. The meek shall inherit the earth ; and shall delight themselves in the abundance of peace. 37. Mark the perfect *man*, and behold the upright : for the end of *that* man *is* peace.

Psa. 40.16. Let all those that seek thee rejoice and be glad in thee : let such as love thy salvation say continually, The Lord be magnified. Psa. 70.4.

Psa. 42.4. I had gone with the multitude, I went with them to the house of God, with the voice of joy and praise.

Psa. 43.4. Then will I go unto the altar of God, unto God my exceeding joy : upon the harp will I praise thee, O God my God.

Psa. 45.15. With gladness and rejoicing shall they be brought : they shall enter into the king's palace.

Psa. 46.4. *There is* a river, the streams whereof shall make glad the city of God.

Psa. 53.6. When God bringeth back the captivity of his people, Jacob shall rejoice, *and* Israel shall be glad. Psa. 14.7.

Psa. 63.5. My soul shall be satisfied as *with* marrow and fatness ; and my mouth shall praise *thee* with joyful lips : 6. When I remember thee upon my bed, *and* meditate on thee in the *night* watches. 7. Because thou hast been my help, therefore in the shadow of thy wings will I rejoice. 11. The king shall rejoice in God ; every one that sweareth by him shall glory.

Psa. 64.10. The righteous shall be glad in the Lord, and shall trust in him ; and all the upright in heart shall glory.

Psa. 65.4. Blessed *is the man whom* thou choosest, and causest to approach *unto thee, that* he may dwell in thy courts : we shall be satisfied with the goodness of thy house, *even* of thy holy temple.

Psa. 68.3. Let the righteous be glad ; let them rejoice before God : yea, let them exceedingly rejoice.

Psa. 69.32. The humble shall see this, and be glad.

Psa. 71.23. My lips shall greatly rejoice when I sing unto thee ; and my soul, which thou hast redeemed.

Psa. 73.25. Whom have I in heaven *but thee?* and *there is* none upon earth *that* I desire beside thee. 26. My flesh and my heart faileth: *but* God *is* the strength of my heart, and my portion for ever.

Psa. 84.4. Blessed *are* they that dwell in thy house: they will be still praising thee. 5. Blessed *is* the man whose strength *is* in thee; in whose heart *are* the ways *of them.* 7. They go from strength to strength, *every one of them* in Zion appeareth before God.

Psa. 85.8. I will hear what God the Lord will speak: for he will speak peace unto his people, and to his saints.

Psa. 89.15. Blessed *is* the people that know the joyful sound: they shall walk, O Lord, in the light of thy countenance. 16. In thy name shall they rejoice all the day: and in thy righteousness shall they be exalted.

Psa. 92.4. Thou, Lord, hast made me glad through thy work: I will triumph in the works of thy hands.

Psa. 94.12. Blessed *is* the man whom thou chastenest, O Lord, and teachest him out of thy law.

Psa. 97.11. Light is sown for the righteous, and gladness for the upright in heart. 12. Rejoice in the Lord, ye righteous.

Psa. 100.1. Make a joyful noise unto the Lord, all ye lands. 2. Serve the Lord with gladness: come before his presence with singing.

Psa. 104.34. My meditation of him shall be sweet: I will be glad in the Lord.

Psa. 105.3. Glory ye in his holy name: let the heart of them rejoice that seek the Lord. 43. He brought forth his people with joy, *and* his chosen with gladness.

Psa. 106.3. Blessed *are* they that keep judgment, *and* he that doeth righteousness at all times.

Psa. 112.1. Blessed *is* the man *that* feareth the Lord, *that* delighteth greatly in his commandments. 7. He shall not be afraid of evil tidings: his heart is fixed, trusting in the Lord. 8. His heart *is* established, he shall not be afraid.

Psa. 118.15. The voice of rejoicing and salvation *is* in the tabernacles of the righteous.

Psa. 119.1. Blessed *are* the undefiled in the way, who walk in the law of the Lord. 2. Blessed *are* they that keep his testimonies, *and that* seek him with the whole heart. 14. I have rejoiced in the way of thy testimonies, as *much as* in all riches. 16. I will delight myself in thy statutes: I will not forget thy word. 55. I have remembered thy name, O Lord, in the night. 111. Thy testimonies have I taken as an heritage for ever: for they *are* the rejoicing of my heart. 162. I rejoice at thy word, as one that findeth great spoil. 165. Great peace have they which love thy law: and nothing shall offend them.

Psa. 125.5. Peace *shall be* upon Israel.

Psa. 126.5. They that sow in tears shall reap in joy. 6. He that goeth forth and weepeth, bearing precious seed, shall doubtless come again with rejoicing, bringing his sheaves *with him.*

Psa. 132.16. I will also clothe her priests with salvation: and her saints shall shout aloud for joy.

Psa. 138.5. They shall sing in the ways of the Lord.

Psa. 149.2. Let Israel rejoice in him that made him: let the children of Zion be joyful in their king. 5. Let the saints be joyful in glory: let them sing aloud upon their beds.

Pro. 3.17. Her ways *are* ways of pleasantness, and all her paths *are* peace. 24. When thou liest down, thou shalt not be afraid: yea, thou shalt lie down, and thy sleep shall be sweet. *v.* 13-18.

Pro. 8.32. Hearken unto me, O ye children: for blessed *are they that* keep my ways. 34. Blessed *is* the man that heareth me, watching daily at my gates, waiting at the posts of my doors.

Pro. 10.28. The hope of the righteous *shall be* gladness.

Pro. 13.9. The light of the righteous rejoiceth. 19. The desire accomplished is sweet to the soul.

Pro. 14.14. A good man shall be satisfied from himself.

Pro. 19.23. He that hath it shall abide satisfied.

Pro. 29.6. The righteous doth sing and rejoice.

Isa. 9.3. They joy before thee according to the joy in harvest, *and* as *men* rejoice when they divide the spoil.

Isa. 12.2. Behold, God *is* my salvation; I will trust, and not be afraid: for the Lord JEHOVAH *is* my strength and *my* song; he also is become my salvation. 3. With joy shall ye draw water out of the wells of salvation.

Isa. 25.9. Lo, this *is* our God; we have waited for him, and he will save us: this *is* the Lord; we have waited for him, we will be glad, and rejoice in his salvation.

Isa. 26.3. Thou wilt keep *him* in perfect peace, *whose* mind is stayed *on thee:* because he trusteth in thee. 12. Lord, thou wilt ordain peace for us; for thou also hast wrought all our works in us.

Isa. 27.5. Let him take hold of my strength, *that* he may make peace with me; *and* he shall make peace with me.

Isa. 28.12. This *is* the rest *wherewith* ye may cause the weary to rest; and this *is* the refreshing.

Isa. 29.19. The meek also shall increase *their* joy in the Lord, and the poor among men shall rejoice in the Holy One of Israel.

Isa. 30.29. Ye shall have a song, as in the night *when* a holy solemnity is kept; and gladness of heart, as when one goeth with a pipe to come into the mountain of the Lord, to the mighty One of Israel.

Isa. 32.2. A man shall be as an hiding-place from the wind, and a covert from the tempest; as rivers of water in a dry place, as the shadow of a great rock in a weary land. 17. The work of righteousness shall be peace; and the effect of righteousness quietness and assurance for ever.

Isa. 35.1. The wilderness and the solitary place shall be glad for them; and the desert shall rejoice, and blossom as the rose. 2. It shall blossom abundantly, and rejoice even with joy and singing. *v.* 8-10.

Isa. 41.16. Thou shalt rejoice in the Lord, *and* shalt glory in the Holy One of Israel.

Isa. 44.23. Sing, O ye heavens; for the Lord hath done *it:* shout, ye lower parts of the earth: break forth into singing, ye mountains, O forest, and every tree therein : for the Lord hath redeemed Jacob, and glorified himself in Israel. Isa. 49.13. Isa. 52.9.

Isa. 45.25. In the Lord shall all the seed of Israel be justified, and shall glory.

Isa. 48.18. O that thou hadst hearkened to my commandments ! then had thy peace been as a river, and thy righteousness as the waves of the sea.

Isa. 51.11. The redeemed of the Lord shall return, and come with singing unto Zion ; and everlasting joy *shall be* upon their head : they shall obtain gladness and joy ; *and* sorrow and mourning shall flee away.

Isa. 54.10. My kindness shall not depart from thee, neither shall the covenant of my peace be removed, saith the Lord, that hath mercy on thee. 13. All thy children *shall be* taught of the Lord ; and great *shall be* the peace of thy children.

Isa. 55.2. Hearken diligently unto me, and eat ye *that which is* good, and let your soul delight itself in fatness. 12. Ye shall go out with joy, and be led forth with peace : the mountains and the hills shall break forth before you into singing, and all the trees of the field shall clap *their* hands.

Isa. 56.7. Them will I bring to my holy mountain, and make them joyful in my house of prayer.

Isa. 57.19. I create the fruit of the lips ; Peace, peace to *him that is* far off, and to *him that is* near, saith the Lord ; and I will heal him.

Isa. 60.20. Thy sun shall no more go down ; neither shall thy moon withdraw itself : for the Lord shall be thine everlasting light, and the days of thy mourning shall be ended.

Isa. 61.3. To appoint unto them that mourn in Zion, to give unto them beauty for ashes, the oil of joy for mourning, the garment of praise for the spirit of heaviness. 7. *For* confusion they shall rejoice in their portion : therefore in their land they shall possess the double : everlasting joy shall be unto them. 10. I will greatly rejoice in the Lord, my soul shall be joyful in my God ; for he hath clothed me with the garments of salvation, he hath covered me with the robe of righteousness, as a bridegroom decketh *himself* with ornaments, and as a bride adorneth *herself* with her jewels.

Isa. 64.5. Thou meetest him that rejoiceth and worketh righteousness ; *those that* remember thee in thy ways.

Isa. 65.14. My servants shall sing for joy of heart. 18. Be ye glad and rejoice for ever *in that* which I create : for, behold, I create Jerusalem a rejoicing, and her people a joy. 25. They shall not hurt nor destroy in all my holy mountain, saith the Lord.

Isa. 66.10. Rejoice ye with Jerusalem, and be glad with her, all ye that love her : rejoice for joy with her, all ye that mourn for her : 11. That ye may suck, and be satisfied with the breasts of her consolations ; that ye may milk out, and be delighted with the abundance of her glory. 12. Behold, I will extend peace to her like a river, and the glory of the Gentiles like a flowing stream. 14. Your heart shall rejoice, and your bones shall flourish like an herb : and the hand of the Lord shall be known toward his servants.

Jer. 15.16. Thy words were found, and I did eat them ; and thy word was unto me the joy and rejoicing of mine heart : for I am called by thy name, O Lord God of hosts.

Jer. 31.12. They shall come and sing in the height of Zion, and shall flow together to the goodness of the Lord, for wheat, and for wine, and for oil, and for the young of the flock and of the herd : and their soul shall be as a watered garden ; and they shall not sorrow any more at all. 13. Then shall the virgin rejoice in the dance, both young men and old together : for I will turn their mourning into joy, and will comfort them, and make them rejoice from their sorrow. 14. And I will satiate the soul of the priests with fatness, and my people shall be satisfied with my goodness, saith the Lord. 25. I have satiated the weary soul, and I have replenished every sorrowful soul. 26. Upon this I awaked, and beheld ; and my sleep was sweet unto me.

Jer. 33.6. I will bring it health and cure, and I will cure them, and will reveal unto them the abundance of peace and truth. 11. The voice of joy, and the voice of gladness, the voice of the bridegroom, and the voice of the bride, the voice of them that shall say, Praise the Lord of hosts : for the Lord *is* good ; for his mercy *endureth* for ever : *and* of them that shall bring the sacrifice of praise into the house of the Lord.

Hos. 2.15. I will give her her vineyards from thence, and the valley of Achor for a door of hope : and she shall sing there, as in the days of her youth.

Joel 2.23. Be glad then, ye children of Zion, and rejoice in the Lord your God.

Nah. 1.15. Behold upon the mountains the feet of him that bringeth good tidings, that publisheth peace !

Hab. 3.18. I will rejoice in the Lord, I will joy in the God of my salvation.

Zeph. 3.14. Sing, O daughter of Zion ; shout, O Israel ; be glad and rejoice with all the heart, O daughter of Jerusalem.

Hag. 2.9. In this place will I give peace, saith the Lord of hosts.

Zec. 2.10. Sing and rejoice, O daughter of Zion : for, lo, I come, and I will dwell in the midst of thee, saith the Lord.

Zec. 9.9. Rejoice greatly, O daughter of Zion ; shout, O daughter of Jerusalem : behold, thy King cometh unto thee.

Zec. 10.7. Their children shall see *it*, and be glad ; their heart shall rejoice in the Lord.

Mat. 5.3. Blessed *are* the poor in spirit. 4. Blessed *are* they that mourn : for they shall be comforted. 5. Blessed *are* the meek. 6. Blessed *are* they which do hunger and thirst after righteousness : for they shall be filled. 7. Blessed *are* the merciful. 8. Blessed *are* the pure in heart : for they shall see God. 9. Blessed *are* the peace-makers. 10. Blessed *are* they which are persecuted for righteousness' sake. 12. Rejoice, and be exceeding glad ; for great *is* your reward in heaven. Luk. 6.23.

Mat. 13.44. The kingdom of heaven is like unto treasure hid in a field ; the which when a man hath found, he hideth, and for joy thereof goeth and selleth all that he hath, and buyeth that field.

Luk. 1.47. My spirit hath rejoiced in God my Saviour. 79. The way of peace.

Luk. 2.10. Behold, I bring you good tidings of great joy, which shall be to all people.

Luk. 10.20. But rather rejoice, because your names are written in heaven.

Luk. 11.28. Yea, rather, blessed *are* they that hear the word of God, and keep it.

Luk. 14.15. Blessed *is* he that shall eat bread in the kingdom of God.

Luk. 24.32. Did not our heart burn within us, while he talked with us by the way, and while he opened to us the scriptures? 52. They worshipped him, and returned to Jerusalem, with great joy: 53. And were continually in the temple, praising and blessing God.

Jno. 14.27. Peace I leave with you, my peace I give unto you: not as the world giveth, give I unto you. Let not your heart be troubled, neither let it be afraid.

Jno. 15.11. These things have I spoken unto you, that my joy might remain in you, and *that* your joy might be full.

Jno. 16.22. I will see you again, and your heart shall rejoice, and your joy no man taketh from you. 24. Ask, and ye shall receive, that your joy may be full. 33. These things I have spoken unto you, that in me ye might have peace. In the world ye shall have tribulation: but be of good cheer; I have overcome the world.

Jno. 17.13. These things I speak in the world, that they might have my joy fulfilled in themselves.

Jno. 20.19. Came Jesus, and stood in the midst, and saith unto them, Peace *be* unto you. 20. Then were the disciples glad, when they saw the Lord. 29. Blessed *are* they that have not seen, and *yet* have believed.

Act. 2.46. Did eat their meat with gladness and singleness of heart.

Act. 5.41. They departed from the presence of the council, rejoicing that they were counted worthy to suffer shame for his name.

Act. 8.8. There was great joy in that city. 39. He went on his way rejoicing.

Act. 10.36. Preaching peace by Jesus Christ.

Act. 13.52. The disciples were filled with joy, and with the Holy Ghost.

Act. 16.25. At midnight Paul and Silas prayed, and sang praises unto God. 34. And rejoiced, believing in God with all his house.

Act. 20.24. Neither count I my life dear unto myself, so that I might finish my course with joy.

Rom. 2.10. Glory, honour, and peace, to every man that worketh good; to the Jew first, and also to the Gentile.

Rom. 4.7. Blessed *are* they whose iniquities are forgiven, and whose sins are covered. 8. Blessed *is* the man to whom the Lord will not impute sin.

Rom. 5.1. Being justified by faith, we have peace with God through our Lord Jesus Christ. 2. By whom also we have access by faith into this grace wherein we stand, and rejoice in hope of the glory of God. 11. We also joy in God through our Lord Jesus Christ, by whom we have now received the atonement.

Rom. 8.6. To be spiritually minded *is* life and peace.

Rom. 12.12. Rejoicing in hope.

Rom. 14.17. The kingdom of God is not meat and drink; but righteousness, and peace, and joy in the Holy Ghost.

2 Cor. 1.24. Are helpers of your joy: for by faith ye stand.

2 Cor. 6.10. As sorrowful, yet alway rejoicing; as poor, yet making many rich; as having nothing, and *yet* possessing all things.

2 Cor. 7.4. I am filled with comfort, I am exceeding joyful in all our tribulation.

2 Cor. 8.2. In a great trial of affliction the abundance of their joy and their deep poverty abounded unto the riches of their liberality.

Gal. 5.22. The fruit of the Spirit is love, joy, peace.

Gal. 6.14. God forbid that I should glory, save in the cross of our Lord Jesus Christ, by whom the world is crucified unto me, and I unto the world.

Eph. 2.14. He is our peace.

Eph. 5.18. Be filled with the Spirit; 19. Speaking to yourselves in psalms and hymns and spiritual songs, singing and making melody in your heart to the Lord.

Phil. 1.25. I know that I shall abide and continue with you all for your furtherance and joy of faith.

Phil. 3.1. Finally, my brethren, rejoice in the Lord. 3. We are the circumcision, which worship God in the spirit, and rejoice in Christ Jesus, and have no confidence in the flesh.

Phil. 4.4. Rejoice in the Lord alway: *and* again I say, Rejoice. 6. Be careful for nothing: but in every thing by prayer and supplication, with thanksgiving, let your requests be made known unto God. 7. And the peace of God, which passeth all understanding, shall keep your hearts and minds through Christ Jesus. 9. The God of peace shall be with you.

Col. 1.11. Strengthened with all might, according to his glorious power, unto all patience and longsuffering with joyfulness.

Col. 3.15. Let the peace of God rule in your hearts, to the which also ye are called in one body; and be ye thankful.

1 The. 1.6. Having received the word in much affliction, with joy of the Holy Ghost.

1 The. 5.16. Rejoice evermore.

Heb. 3.6. Whose house are we, if we hold fast the confidence and the rejoicing of the hope firm unto the end.

Heb. 4.3. We which have believed do enter into rest.

1 Pet. 1.6. Ye greatly rejoice, though now for a season (if need be) ye are in heaviness through manifold temptations. 8. In whom though now ye see *him* not, yet believing, ye rejoice with joy unspeakable and full of glory: 9. Receiving the end of your faith, *even* the salvation of *your* souls.

1 Pet. 4.13. Rejoice, inasmuch as ye are partakers of Christ's sufferings; that, when his glory shall be revealed, ye may be glad also with exceeding joy.

1 Jno. 1.4. These things write we unto you, that your joy may be full.

Rev. 19.9. Blessed *are* they which are called unto the marriage supper of the Lamb.

Rev. 22.14. Blessed *are* they that do his commandments.

See God's favour—Hope—Love to God —Resignation—Thankfulness—Praise —Contentment.

SPIRITUAL Strength. See Sanctification.

—— Understanding. See Wisdom.

SPIRITUALITY. See Spiritual Diligence—Spiritual blessings, prayer for.

SPOONS. Of the tabernacle, Ex. 25.29.
Num. 4.7.

SPRING. Promise of, Gen. 8.22. Described, Psa. 65.10. Pro. 27.25. Song 2.11-13.
See Sowing.

SPRINGS. See Wells.

STACTE (Heb. *Nataf*), an unknown spice,
Ex. 30.34.

STANDARD, Banner, Ensign, Num. 1.
52. Num. 2.2. Psa. 20.5. Song 6.4,10.
Jer. 4.21.

STANDARD-BEARER, Song 5.10 (marg.).
Isa. 10.18. Illustrative, Song 2.4. Isa. 5.26.
Isa. 11.10.

STARS. Jud. 5.20. Job 25.5. Act. 27.
20. 1 Cor. 15.41. The eleven stars, Gen. 37.9.
Seven stars, Amos 5.8. Planets, 2 Kin. 23.5.
Constellations, Isa. 13.10. Morning-star, Job
38.7. Rev. 2.28. Rev. 22.16. Wandering stars,
Jude 13. See Arcturus, Chiun, Day-star,
Mazzaroth, Orion, Pleiades.

Star in the east at Christ's birth, Mat. 2.
2-10. Stars worshipped, Deu. 4.19. 2 Kin.
17.16. 2 Kin. 21.3. Jer. 19.13. Amos 5.
26. Zeph. 1.5. Act. 7.43. Illustrative and
symbolical, Num. 24.17. Rev. 1.16,20. Rev.
12.1. Darkening, &c., of, Job 9.7. Ecc. 12.2.
Isa. 13.10. Isa. 34.4. Eze. 32.7. Dan. 8.10.
Joel 2.10. Joel 3.15. Mat. 24.29. Mar. 13.
25. Luk. 21.25. Rev. 6.13. Rev. 8.10-12.
Rev. 9.1. Rev. 12.4.

STAR-GAZERS. See Astrologers.

STEDFASTNESS. See Decision—Persecution.

STEEL, bows of, 2 Sam. 22.35. Generally
translated brass, as Isa. 45.2.

STEPHANAS, a minister at Corinth; one
of the first converts; baptized by Paul, 1 Cor.
1.16. 1 Cor. 16.15,17.

STEPHEN, one of the seven; his character,
preaching, miracles; confutes the Jews;
accused of blasphemy, Act. 6. His defence,
prayer, martyrdom, and burial, Act. 7. Act.
8.1,2. Act. 22.20.

STEWARD, Gen. 15.2. Gen. 43.19.
1 Chr. 28.1. Luk. 8.3. Illustrative, Luk. 12.
42. Luk. 16.1-8. 1 Cor. 4.1,2. Tit. 1.7.
1 Pet. 4.10.

STOCKS, putting the feet in, as a punishment, Job 13.27. Job 33.11. In prisons, Jer.
20.2. Act. 16.24.

STOICS, a school of philosophers at Athens,
Act. 17.18.

STOMACHER, a wide mantle, Isa. 3.24.

STONE. For weights, Lev. 19.36 (marg.).
Deu. 25.13 (marg.). Knife of, Jos. 5.2
(marg.). See Altars, Burial-places,
Corner-stone, Foundations, Idols, Sling,
Tables, House, Cities, Mason.

Illustrative, Gen. 49.24. Eze. 36.26. Zec.
12.3. Mat. 21.44. 1 Pet. 2.4. Rev. 2.17.
Symbolical, Dan. 2.34. Zec. 3.9.
Memorial stones. See Pillars—Abel—

Bohan—Ezel. Precious stones, see Jewels
—Precious stones.

STONING, Jewish capital punishment, Ex.
19.13. Deu. 13.10. Deu. 17.5. Deu. 22.21.
Examples, Num. 15.36. Jos. 7.25. 1 Kin.
21.13. Act. 7.59. See Witness.

STOOL, 2 Kin. 4.10. Seat, 1 Sam. 1.9.

STOREHOUSE. See Treasury—Barn.

STORK, Lev. 11.19. Psa. 104.17. Zec. 5.
9. Migration of, Jer. 8.7.

STRANGERS, to be treated with justice,
Deu. 1.16. Deu. 24.14,17. Deu. 27.19. Jer.
7.6. Jer. 22.3. Eze. 22.29. Mal. 3.5.
Kindness to Edomites, &c., enjoined, Deu.
23.7. Jews allowed to purchase, as slaves,
Lev. 25.44,45; and to take usury from, Deu.
23.20; but not allowed to make kings of, Deu.
17.15. Partially exempt from Jewish law,
Deu. 14.21. See Feasts, Gleanings, Hospitality, Inhospitality, Proselyte,
Travelling.

STREET of Damascus, called straight,
Act. 9.11. Streets of Jerusalem. See Jerusalem.

STRENGTH, Spiritual. See Sanctification.

STRIFE, Schism. Gen. 13.8. Let there
be no strife, I pray thee, between me and thee,
and between my herdmen and thy herdmen;
for we *be* brethren.

Gen. 45.24. See that ye fall not out by the
way.

Psa. 55.9. Destroy, O Lord, *and* divide
their tongues: for I have seen violence and
strife in the city.

Pro. 3.30. Strive not with a man without
cause, if he hath done thee no harm.

Pro. 10.12. Hatred stirreth up strifes: but
love covereth all sins.

Pro. 13.10. Only by pride cometh contention: but with the well advised *is* wisdom.

Pro. 15.18. A wrathful man stirreth up
strife: but *he that is* slow to anger appeaseth
strife.

Pro. 16.28. A froward man soweth strife:
and a whisperer separateth chief friends.

Pro. 17.1. Better *is* a dry morsel, and quietness therewith, than an house full of sacrifices
with strife. 14. The beginning of strife *is as*
when one letteth out water: therefore leave
off contention, before it be meddled with.
19. He loveth transgression that loveth strife.

Pro. 18.6. A fool's lips enter into contention, and his mouth calleth for strokes. 19.
A brother offended *is harder to be won* than a
strong city: and *their* contentions *are* like the
bars of a castle.

Pro. 20.3. *It is* an honour for a man
to cease from strife: but every fool will be
meddling.

Pro. 21.19. *It is* better to dwell in the
wilderness, than with a contentious and an
angry woman.

Pro. 22.10. Cast out the scorner, and contention shall go out; yea, strife and reproach
shall cease.

Pro. 23.29. Who hath contentions? who
hath babbling? who hath wounds without
cause? who hath redness of eyes? 30. They
that tarry long at the wine; they that go to
seek mixed wine.

Pro. 25.8. Go not forth hastily to strive,

est *thou know not* what to do in the end thereof, when thy neighbour hath put thee to shame. 24. *It is* better to dwell in the corner of the housetop, than with a brawling woman and in a wide house.

Pro. 26.17. He that passeth by *and* meddleth with strife *belonging* not to him, *is like* one that taketh a dog by the ears. 21. *As* coals *are* to burning coals, and wood to fire; so *is* a contentious man to kindle strife.

Pro. 28.25. He that is of a proud heart stirreth up strife.

Pro. 30.33. Surely the churning of milk bringeth forth butter, and the wringing of the nose bringeth forth blood: so the forcing of wrath bringeth forth strife.

Isa. 58.4. Ye fast for strife and debate, and to smite with the fist of wickedness: ye shall not fast as *ye do this* day, to make your voice to be heard on high.

Hab. 1.3. Spoiling and violence *are* before me: and there are *that* raise up strife and contention.

Mat. 5.39. Resist not evil: but whosoever shall smite thee on thy right cheek, turn to him the other also. 40. And if any man will sue thee at the law, and take away thy coat, let him have *thy* cloke also. *v.* 25.

Mat. 12.25. Every kingdom divided against itself is brought to desolation; and every city or house divided against itself shall not stand.

Mat 18.15. If thy brother shall trespass against thee, go and tell him his fault between thee and him alone: if he shall hear thee, thou hast gained thy brother. 16. But if he will not hear thee, *then* take with thee one or two more, that in the mouth of two or three witnesses every word may be established. 17. And if he shall neglect to hear them, tell *it* unto the church: but if he neglect to hear the church, let him be unto thee as an heathen man and a publican.

Luk. 12.58. When thou goest with thine adversary to the magistrate, *as thou art* in the way, give diligence that thou mayest be delivered from him; lest he hale thee to the judge, and the judge deliver thee to the officer, and the officer cast thee into prison. 59. I tell thee, thou shalt not depart thence, till thou hast paid the very last mite.

Rom. 13.13. Let us walk honestly, as in the day; not in strife and envying.

Rom. 14.1. Him that is weak in the faith receive ye, *but* not to doubtful disputations. 19. Let us therefore follow after the things which make for peace, and things wherewith one may edify another. 21. *It is* good neither to eat flesh, nor to drink wine, nor *any thing* whereby thy brother stumbleth, or is offended, or is made weak.

Rom. 16.17. Mark them which cause divisions and offences contrary to the doctrine which ye have learned; and avoid them. 18. For they that are such serve not our Lord Jesus Christ, but their own belly; and by good words and fair speeches deceive the hearts of the simple.

1 Cor. 1.10. I beseech you, brethren, by the name of our Lord Jesus Christ, that ye all speak the same thing, and *that* there be no divisions among you; but *that* ye be perfectly joined together in the same mind and in the same judgment. 11. For it hath been declared unto me of you, my brethren, by them

which are of the house of Chloe, that there are contentions among you. 12. Every one of you saith, I am of Paul; and I of Apollos; and I of Cephas; and I of Christ. 13. Is Christ divided? was Paul crucified for you? or were ye baptised in the name of Paul?

1 Cor. 3.1. I, brethren, could not speak unto you as unto spiritual, but as unto carnal, *even* as unto babes in Christ. 3. For ye are yet carnal: for whereas *there is* among you envying, and strife, and divisions, are ye not carnal, and walk as men? 4. For while one saith, I am of Paul; and another, I *am* of Apollos; are ye not carnal? 21. Let no man glory in men. For all things are your's.

1 Cor. 4.6. Learn in us not to think *of men* above that which is written, that no one of you be puffed up for one against another. *v.* 7.

1 Cor. 6.7. There is utterly a fault among you, because ye go to law one with another. Why do ye not rather take wrong? why do ye not rather *suffer yourselves to* be defrauded? *v.* 1-6.

1 Cor. 11.16. But if any man seem to be contentious, we have no such custom, neither the churches of God. 17. Ye come together not for the better, but for the worse. 18. For first of all, when ye come together in the church, I hear that there be divisions among you. 19. For there must be also heresies among you, that they which are approved may be made manifest among you.

2 Cor. 12.20. I fear, lest, when I come, I shall not find you such as I would, and *that* I shall be found unto you such as ye would not: lest *there be* debates, envyings, wraths, strifes, backbitings, whisperings, swellings, tumults.

Gal. 5.10. He that troubleth you shall bear his judgment, whosoever he be. 15. If ye bite and devour one another, take heed that ye be not consumed one of another. 19. The works of the flesh are manifest, which are 20. Hatred, variance, emulations, wrath, strife, seditions, heresies.

Phil. 1.15. Some indeed preach Christ even of envy and strife; and some also of good will: 16. The one preach Christ of contention, not sincerely, supposing to add affliction to my bonds.

Phil. 2.3. *Let* nothing *be done* through strife or vainglory; but in lowliness of mind let each esteem other better than themselves. 14. Do all things without murmurings and disputings.

1 Tim. 1.6. Some having swerved have turned aside unto vain jangling; 7. Desiring to be teachers of the law; understanding neither what they say, nor whereof they affirm.

1 Tim. 2.8. I will therefore that men pray every where, lifting up holy hands, without wrath and doubting.

1 Tim. 3.3. No striker, not greedy of filthy lucre; but patient, not a brawler.

1 Tim. 6.3. If any man teach otherwise, and consent not to wholesome words, *even* the words of our Lord Jesus Christ, and to the doctrine which is according to godliness; 4. He is proud, knowing nothing, but doting about questions and strifes of words, whereof cometh envy, strife, railings, evil surmisings, 5. Perverse disputings of men of corrupt minds, and destitute of the truth, supposing that gain

is godliness : from such withdraw thyself. 20. Avoiding profane *and* vain babblings, and oppositions of science falsely so called : 21. Which some professing have erred concerning the faith.

2 Tim. 2.14. Charging *them* before the Lord that they strive not about words to no profit, *but* to the subverting of the hearers. 23. Foolish and unlearned questions avoid, knowing that they do gender strifes. 24. The servant of the Lord must not strive ; but be gentle unto all *men*, apt to teach, patient. 25. In meekness instructing those that oppose themselves.

Tit. 3.2. Put them in mind . . . . to be no brawlers. 9. Avoid foolish questions, and genealogies, and contentions, and strivings about the law ; for they are unprofitable and vain.

Jas. 3.14. If ye have bitter envying and strife in your hearts, glory not, and lie not against the truth. 15. This wisdom descendeth not from above, but *is* earthly, sensual, devilish. 16. For where envying and strife *is*, there *is* confusion and every evil work.

Jas. 4.1. From whence *come* wars and fightings among you ? *come* they not hence, *even* of your lusts that war in your members ? 2. Ye lust, and have not : ye kill, and desire to have, and cannot obtain : ye fight and war.

Strife—Schism—Examples of : Herdmen, Gen. 13.6,7. Gen. 26.20-22. Laban and Jacob, Gen. 31.36. Israelites, Ex. 2.13. Lev. 24.10. Deu. 1.12. Jephthah and his brethren, Jud. 11.2 ; and Ephraimites, Jud. 12.1-6. Israel and Judah, 2 Sam. 19.41-43. Disciples, Mar. 9.34. Luk. 22.24. Jews, Jno. 10.19. Christians at Antioch, Act. 15.2. Paul and Barnabas, Act. 15.38,39. Pharisees and Sadducees, Act. 23.7-10. Corinthians, 1 Cor. 1.11,12. 1 Cor. 6.6.

See Schism — Anger — Malice —Envy— Ministers unfaithful.

STRIFE, Jewish Law regarding, Ex. 21.18-27.

SUBJECTS, Duties and Rights of. Ex. 22.28. Thou shalt not revile the gods, nor curse the ruler of thy people. Act. 23.5.

Num. 27.20. Thou shalt put *some* of thine honour upon him, that all the congregation of the children of Israel may be obedient.

Ezr. 6.10. That they may pray for the life of the king, and of his sons.

Ezr. 7.26. Whosoever will not do the law of thy God, and the law of the king, let judgment be executed speedily upon him, whether *it be* unto death, or to banishment, or to confiscation of goods, or to imprisonment.

Ezr. 10.8. Whosoever would not come within three days, according to the counsel of the princes and the elders, all his substance should be forfeited, and himself separated from the congregation of those that had been carried away.

Job 34.18. *Is it fit* to say to a king, Thou *art* wicked? *and* to princes, Ye *are* ungodly ?

Pro. 14.28. In the multitude of people *is* the king's honour : but in the want of people *is* the destruction of the prince. 35. The king's favour *is* toward a wise servant : but his wrath is *against* him that causeth shame.

Pro. 16.14. The wrath of a king *is as* mes-

sengers of death : but a wise man will pacify it. 15. In the light of the king's countenance *is* life ; and his favour *is* as a cloud of the latter rain.

Pro. 17.11. An evil *man* seeketh only rebellion : therefore a cruel messenger shall be sent against him.

Pro. 19.10. Delight is not seemly for a fool : much less for a servant to have rule over princes. 12. The king's wrath *is* as the roaring of a lion ; but his favour *is* as dew upon the grass. Pro. 20.2.

Pro. 22.11. He that loveth pureness of heart, *for* the grace of his lips the king *shall be* his friend.

Pro. 23.1. When thou sittest to eat with a ruler, consider diligently what *is* before thee : 2. And put a knife to thy throat, if thou *be* a man given to appetite. 3. Be not desirous of his dainties : for they *are* deceitful meat.

Pro. 24.21. My son, fear thou the Lord and the king : *and* meddle not with them that are given to change.

Pro. 25.6. Put not forth thyself in the presence of the king, and stand not in the place of great *men* : 7. For better *it is* that it be said unto thee, Come up hither ; than that thou shouldest be put lower in the presence of the prince whom thine eyes have seen.

Pro. 25.15. By long forbearing is a prince persuaded, and a soft tongue breaketh the bone.

Ecc. 8.2. I *counsel thee* to keep the king's commandment, and *that* in regard of the oath of God. 3. Be not hasty to go out of his sight : stand not in an evil thing ; for he doeth whatsoever pleaseth him. 4. Where the word of a king *is, there is* power : and who may say unto him, What doest thou ?

Ecc. 10.4. If the spirit of the ruler rise up against thee, leave not thy place ; for yielding pacifieth great offences. 20. Curse not the king, no, not in thy thought ; and curse not the rich in thy bedchamber : for a bird of the air shall carry the voice, and that which hath wings shall tell the matter.

Jer. 29.7. Seek the peace of the city whither I have caused you to be carried away captives, and pray unto the Lord for it : for in the peace thereof shall ye have peace.

Mat. 17.24. They that received tribute *money* came to Peter, and said, Doth not your master pay tribute ? 25. He saith, Yes. *v.* 26,27.

Mat. 22.21. Render therefore unto Cesar the things which are Cesar's ; and unto God the things that are God's. Mar. 12.17. Luk. 20.25.

Act. 16.37. They have beaten us openly uncondemned, being Romans, and have cast *us* into prison ; and now do they thrust us out privily ? nay verily ; but let them come themselves and fetch us out.

Act. 19.36. Ye ought to be quiet, and to do nothing rashly. *v.* 35-41.

Act. 25.16. It is not the manner of the Romans to deliver any man to die, before that he which is accused have the accusers face to face, and have licence to answer for himself concerning the crime laid against him. *v.* 5,10. Act. 24.18,19.

Rom. 13.1. Let every soul be subject unto the higher powers. For there is no power but of God : the powers that be are ordained of God. 2. Whosoever therefore resisteth the power, resisteth the ordinance of God: and they that resist shall receive to themselves damnation. 3. For rulers are not a terror to good works, but to the evil. Wilt thou then not be afraid of the power? do that which is good, and thou shalt have praise of the same. 5. Ye must needs be subject, not only for wrath, but also for conscience' sake. 6. For this cause pay ye tribute also: for they are God's ministers, attending continually upon this very thing. 7. Render therefore to all their dues: tribute to whom tribute *is due*; custom to whom custom; fear to whom fear; honour to whom honour.

1 Tim. 2.1. I exhort therefore, that, first of all, supplications, prayers, intercessions, *and* giving of thanks, be made for all men; 2. For kings, and *for* all that are in authority; that we may lead a quiet and peaceable life in all godliness and honesty.

Tit. 3.1. Put them in mind to be subject to principalities and powers, to obey magistrates.

1 Pet. 2.13. Submit yourselves to every ordinance of man for the Lord's sake : whether it be to the king, as supreme; 14. Or unto governors, as unto them that are sent by him for the punishment of evildoers, and for the praise of them that do well. 15. For so is the will of God. 17. Fear God. Honour the king.

2 Pet. 2.10. Them that walk after the flesh in the lust of uncleanness, and despise government. Presumptuous *are they*, self-willed, they are not afraid to speak evil of dignities. 2 Tim. 3.1-4.

Jude 8. These *filthy* dreamers despise dominion, and speak evil of dignities.

See CITIZENS—CHURCH AND COUNTRY, LOVE OF.

SUBJECTS, LOYAL, EXAMPLES OF : Israelites, Jos. 1.16-18. 2 Sam. 3.36,37. 2 Sam. 15. 23,30. 2 Sam. 18.3. 2 Sam. 21.17. 1 Chr. 12.38. David, 1 Sam. 24.6-10. 1 Sam. 26. 6-16. 2 Sam. 1.14. Hushai, 2 Sam. 17.15,16. David's soldiers, 2 Sam. 18.12,13. 2 Sam. 23. 15,16. Joab, 2 Sam. 19.5,6. Barzillai, 2 Sam. 19.32. Jehoiada, 2 Kin. 11.4-12. Mordecai, Est. 2.21-23.

SUBJECTS, TREASON AND REBELLION OF, EXAMPLES OF : Miriam and Aaron, Num. 12. 1-11. Korah, &c., Num. 16. Num. 26.9. Shechemites, Jud. 9.22. Ephraimites, Jud. 12.1-4. Israelites, 1 Sam. 10.27. 1 Kin. 12. 16-19. Absalom, 2 Sam. 15.10-13. Ahithophel, 2 Sam. 17.1-4. Sheba, 2 Sam. 20.1,2. Adonijah, 1 Kin. 1.5-7. Hadad and Jeroboam, 1 Kin. 11.14-26. Baasha, 1 Kin. 15.27. Zimri, 1 Kin. 16.9. Servants of Joash, 2 Kin. 12. 19-21. 2 Kin. 14.5 ; of Amaziah, 2 Kin. 14. 19 ; of Amon, 2 Kin. 21.23. Shallum, 2 Kin. 15.10. Menahem, 2 Kin. 15.14. Pekah, 2 Kin. 15.25. Hoshea, 2 Kin. 15.30. Sennacherib's sons, 2 Kin. 19.37. Ishmael, Jer. 40.14-16. Jer. 41. Bigthan, &c., Est. 2.21. Jews, Eze. 17.12-20. Barabbas, Mar. 15.7. Theudas, &c., Act. 5.36,37. An Egyptian, Act. 21.38.

SUCCOTH (booths). Jacob builds a house at, Gen. 33.17. In Gad, Jos. 13.27. Princes of, refuse to aid Gideon ; slain by him, Jud. 8. 4-8,13-17. Temple vessels cast near, 1 Kin. 7.46.

————, VALLEY OF, Psa. 60,6.

SUCCOTH, the first encampment of the Israelites on leaving Egypt, Ex. 12.37. Ex. 13.20. Num. 33.5.

———— BENOTH, a Babylonian idol worshipped by the colonists in Samaria, 2 Kin. 17.30.

SUICIDE. See MURDER, SELF.

SUKKIIMS, a tribe of Ethiopians, allied with Shishak against Judah, 2 Chr. 12.3.

SUMMER. Promise of, Gen. 8.22. Drought of, Psa. 32.4. Signs of, Mat. 24.32. Summer-fruits, 2 Sam. 16.1. Mic. 7.1, &c. Summer-house, Amos 3.15.

SUN. Created on the 4th day, Gen. 1. 14-18. Worshipped, Deu. 4.19. Deu. 17.3. Job 31.26-28. Jer. 8.2. Eze. 8.16. Horses and chariots dedicated to, 2 Kin. 23.11. Miracles connected with, Ex. 10.21-23. Jos. 10.12,13. 2 Kin. 20.11. Luk. 23.44,45. Illustrative and symbolical, Psa. 84.11. Mal. 4.2. Jud. 5.31. Isa. 30.26. Isa. 60.19,20. Jer. 15.9. Rev. 1.16. Rev. 12.1. Rev. 19.17. Darkening, &c., of, Ecc. 12.2. Isa. 5.30. Isa. 24.23. Eze. 32.7. Joel 2.10,31. Joel 3.15. Amos 8.9. Mic. 3.6. Mat. 24.29. Mar. 13. 24. Luk. 21.25. Luk. 23.45. Act. 2.20. Rev. 6.12. Rev. 8.12. Rev. 9.2. Rev. 16.8.

SUPERSTITION FORBIDDEN, Lev. 19. 26-28. Lev. 21.5. Deu. 14.1. Jer. 10.2. See SORCERY—IDOLATRY.

SUPERSTITION, EXAMPLES OF : Micah, Jud. 17.13. Israelites, 1 Sam. 4.3. Philistines, 1 Sam. 5.5. Syrians, 1 Kin. 20.23. Jews, Jer. 44.18. Sailors, Jonah 1.7. The disciples, Mat. 14.26. Luk. 24.39. Jno. 9.2. Jews, Mat. 15.2. Mar. 7. 2-5,8,9. Luk. 11.38. Act. 5.15. Rhoda, Act. 12. 14,15. Melitians, Act. 28.3. Ephesians, Act. 19. 18,19. See SABBATH, JEWISH MISCONCEPTIONS OF.

SUPPER. See FEASTS—LORD'S SUPPER.

SURETY, Gen. 44.32. Pro. 6.1. Pro. 11. 15. Pro. 22.6.

SUSANNA, a woman who ministered to Christ, Luk. 8.3.

SWALLOW, Pro. 26.2. Psa. 84.3. Isa. 38.14. Migration of, Jer. 8.7.

SWAN, Lev. 11.18. Deu. 14.16.

SWEARING. See OATHS—BLASPHEMY.

SWINE, Lev. 11.7. Deu. 14.8. Isa. 65.4. Isa. 66.3,17. Wild, Psa. 80.13. Ferocity of, Mat. 7.6. Feeding of, Luk. 15.15,16. Herd of, drowned, Luk. 8.32,33.

SWORD, Gen. 27.40. 1 Chr. 21.5. Luk. 22.36,38,52. Pro. 18.10,11, &c. Dagger, Jud. 3.16. Goliath's, 1 Sam. 21.9. Gideon's watchword, 'The sword of the Lord,' Jud. 7.20. Illustrative, Deu. 32.41. Psa. 17.13. Psa. 57.4. Zec. 13.7. Luk. 2.35. Symbolical, Gen. 3.24. Jos. 5.13.

SYCAMINE TREE (the mulberry), Luk.17.6.

SYCOMORE, a kind of fig (Amos 7.14, *marg*). 1 Kin. 10.27. 1 Chr. 27.28. Psa. 78. 47. Luk. 19.4.

SYCHAR (drunkards, see Isa. 28.1,7). A name of Shechem, Jno. 4.5.

SYCHEM. See SHECHEM.

SYENE, a city on the south of Egypt, Eze. 29.10. Eze. 30.6.

SYMBOLS, TYPES. Tree of life, Gen. 2.9. Gen. 3.24. Rev. 22.2. Rainbow, Gen. 9. 12,13. Circumcision, Gen. 17.11. Rom. 4.11. Passover, Ex. 12.3-28. Pillar of cloud, Ex. 13.21,22. Thunder, &c., on giving of the law, Ex. 19.9-20. Heb. 12.18,19. Gal. 4.24-26. Sprinkling of blood, Ex. 24.8. Cherubim over the mercy-seat, Ex. 37.7-9. Psa 80.1. Heb. 4.16. Brazen serpent, Num. 21.8,9. Jno. 3.14.

Praying toward the temple, 1 Kin. 8.29. Dan. 6.10. Smiting commanded by a prophet, 1 Kin. 20.35,37. Joash shooting with a bow, 2 Kin. 13.15-19. Abundant harvest, 2 Kin. 19.29. Isaiah's children, Isa. 8.18. Isaiah walking naked and barefoot, Isa. 20.2-4. Shadow on the dial, Isa. 38.8.

Almond rod, Jer. 1.11. Seething pot, Jer. 1.13. Breaking of potter's vessel, Jer. 19. Good and bad figs, Jer. 24. Yokes sent to the king of Edom, Jer. 27.1-11. Hananiah breaks Jeremiah's yoke, Jer. 28.10. Jeremiah's title-deeds, Jer. 32.1-16. Book cast into Euphrates, Jer. 51.63.

Siege portrayed on a tile, Eze. 4.1-3. Ezekiel lying on his side, Eze. 4.4-8. Unclean food, Eze. 4.9-17. Ezekiel's beard, Eze. 5.1-4. Digging through a wall, Eze. 12.1-16. Eating bread with carefulness, Eze. 12.17-20. Boiling pot, Eze. 24.1-5. Mourning forbidden, Eze. 24.15-18. Two sticks, Eze. 37.15-28.

Handwriting on the wall, Dan. 5.5,24-28. Hosea's wife and children, Hos. c. 1 to 3. Star in the east, Mat. 2.2. Smitten rock, 1 Cor. 10.4. Ex. 17.6. Salt, Col. 4.6. Mosaic law, Heb. c. 7 to 10. Compare the sacrifices, p. 324-329. See VISIONS, SUN, MOON, STARS.

SYMBOLICAL NAMES. See AHOLAH and AHOLIBAMAH, JEZREEL, JESHURUN, LO-AMMI, LO-RUHAMMI, BEULAH, HEPHZIBAH, MAHER-SHALAL-HASHBAZ. See NAMES.

SYMBOLICAL PERIODS AND NUMBERS. See PROPHETIC PERIODS.

SYMPATHY. See LOVE—POOR, KINDNESS TO.

SYNAGOGUE signifies an assembly; so translated, Jas. 2.2; a congregation, Act. 13.43.

Services of, on Sabbath; Reading the Scriptures, Act. 13.27. Act. 15.21. Exposition, addresses, and preaching, by Christ, Luk. 4.15-33. Mat. 4.23. Mat. 9.35. Mat. 13.54. Mar. 1.39. Luk. 13.10. Jno. 18.20; by the apostles, Act. 9.20. Act. 13.5,15-44. Act. 14.1. Act. 17.2,10. Act. 18.4,19,26. Prayer in, Mat. 6.5. See Neh. 8.1-8. Neh. 9.3,5. See WORSHIP.

Several in Jerusalem, Act. 6.9; and Damascus, Act. 9.2,20. In foreign cities, Act. 14.1. Act. 17.1,10. Act. 18.4. One built by Jairus, Luk. 7.5. Christ healed in, Mat. 12.9-13. Luk. 13.11-14. Alms given in, Mat. 6.2.

Chief ruler of, Act. 18.8,17. Ruler, Mar. 5.22. Luk. 8.41. Luk. 13.14. Act. 13.15; or elder, Luk. 7.3. Minister, Luk. 4.20. Chief seats in, Mat. 23.6. Seats, Act. 13.14. Jas. 2.3.

Courts of justice, Luk. 12.11. Act. 9.2. Had power to scourge and imprison, Mat. 10.17. Mat. 23.34. Act. 26.11. Act. 22.19; to excommunicate, Jno. 9.22,34. Jno. 12.42. Jno. 16.2. See SANHEDRIM.

SYNAGOGUE OF SATAN. Rev. 2.9. Rev. 3.9.

SYNTYCHE, a Philippian Christian female, Phil. 4.2.

SYRACUSE, a city on the south-east coast of Sicily; Paul 3 days at, Act. 28.12.

SYRIA, Heb. *Aram*—as in Gen. 10.22. Gen. 22.21. Num. 23.7. 1 Chr. 2.23; translated Mesopotamia, see MESOPOTAMIA. Chushan-rishathaim, king of, invades Canaan, Jud. 3.10. Different cotemporary kings of, 2 Sam. 8.3,5. 2 Sam. 10.6. See ZOBAH, HAMATH, GESHUR, MAACAH.

Tributary to Saul, David, Solomon, see ZOBAH, HADADEZER, TOI, TALMAI, REZON.

Independent, and wars of, with Israel and Judah, see ZOBAH, BENHADAD I., II., III., HAZAEL, REZIN. Conquered by Jeroboam, 2 Kin. 14.25-28. Conquered and incorporated with Assyria, 2 Kin. 16.5-9. Isa. 7.1. 2 Kin. 17.24. 2 Kin. 18.34; with Chaldea, 2 Kin. 24.2. Jer. 39.5.

A Roman province, including Palestine, Mat. 4.24. Luk. 2.2,3; and Phenicia, Mar. 7.26. Act. 21.3. Governed by Romans, see CYRENIUS, ARETAS. Paul's visits to the churches in, Act. 15.41. Act. 18.18. Act. 21.3. Gal. 1.21.

Language of, 2 Kin. 18.26. Ezr. 4.7. Dan. 2.4. Idols of, see ASHIMA, RIMMON, TAMMUZ. Merchandise of, Eze. 27.16.

Towns of, see ANTIOCH, APHEK, ARPHAD, BETH-EDEN, DAMASCUS, HAMATH, HADRACH, HELBON, HOBAH, REHOB, REZEPH, SELEUCIA.

Rivers, see ABANA, PHARPAR. Plain of Aven, Amos 1.5.

Prophecies of, Isa. 7.8-16. Isa. 8.4-7. Isa. 17.1-3. Jer. 49.23-27. Amos 1.3-5. Zec. 9.1.

SYRO-PHENICIAN WOMAN, called a Greek, or Gentile, or woman of Canaan; her daughter cured by Jesus, Mar. 7.24-30. Mat. 15.21-28.

T

TAANACH, a royal Canaanitish city; conquered by Joshua, Jos. 12.21. Given to Manasseh out of Issachar, Jos. 17.11. 1 Kin. 4.12. 1 Chr. 7.29. Imperfectly subdued, Jud. 1.27. A Levitical city, Jos. 21.25. Barak's victory near, Jud. 5.19.

TABERAH (burning), a station where the Israelites were punished by fire for murmuring, Num. 11.1-3. Deu. 9.22.

TABERNACLE [signifies a tent, 1 Chr. 17.5. Figurative use of the word, 2 Cor. 5.1. 2 Pet. 1.13. Heb. 8.2. Heb. 9.11].

Called the sanctuary, Ex. 25.8. Tabernacle of the congregation, Ex. 27.21. 2 Chr. 5.5; of testimony or witness, Ex. 38.21. Num. 1. 50. Num. 17.7,8. 2 Chr. 24.6. Act. 7.44. Temple of the Lord, 1 Sam. 1.9. 1 Sam. 3.3. House of the Lord, Jos. 6.24. 1 Sam. 1. 7,24.

Made by Moses after a divine pattern, Ex. 25.9,40. Ex. 26.30. Ex. 39.32,42,43. Heb. 8.5; by men divinely gifted, Ex. 31.1-11. Ex. 35.30-35. From freewill-offerings, Ex. 25.1-8. Ex. 35.4-29. Ex. 36.3-7. Cost of, 29 talents, 730 shekels of gold; 100 talents,

1775 shekels of silver; 70 talents, 2400 shekels of brass, Ex. 38.24-31.

FRAME-WORK, 10 cubits high, 30 cubits long, 9 broad, Ex. 26.16-22. Pillars and boards of shittim-wood, boards double at the corners, overlaid with gold, sockets of silver, joined by gold rings and transverse bars, Ex. 26.15-37. Ex. 36.20-34.

CURTAINS. The frame covered with curtains of fine twined linen, with blue, purple, and scarlet, with embroidered cherubim, in 10 pieces looped together with gold hooks, each piece 28 cubits long by 4 broad; in all (10 by 4), 40 cubits; 10 cubits covering the west end, and 30 reaching to the front; the pieces (28 cubits long), lying across, and hanging within half a cubit of the ground, on each side, Ex. 26.1-6. Ex. 36.8-13.

Over the 1st curtain was a curtain of goat's hair, in 11 pieces looped together with brass hooks, each piece 30 cubits long by 4 broad, Ex. 26.7-11; in all (11 by 4), 44 cubits; 10 cubits covering the west end, the side folds lapped over protecting the west end; 30 cubits reaching to 'he front; the pieces lying across and touching the ground on each side; and 4 cubits hanging over the front, Ex. 26.7-13. Ex. 36.14-18.

Over the 2d curtain was a covering of rams' skins dyed red, and over this a covering of badgers' skin, Ex. 25.5. Ex. 26.14. Ex. 35.7,23. Ex. 36.19. Ex. 39.34. Num. 4.25.

THE DOOR, facing the east (Ex. 26.22); a frame of 5 pillars of shittim-wood overlaid with gold, sockets of brass, hooks of gold, and a curtain of blue purple and scarlet, and fine twined linen with needle-work (the full breadth of the tabernacle being 9 cubits), Ex. 26.36,37. Ex. 36.37,38.

The tabernacle divided into the holy place and the most holy; separated by a vail (see VAIL).

THE MOST HOLY PLACE (dimensions not given), the inner apartment, containing the ark and mercy-seat, Ex. 26.33,34. Ex. 40.20,21. Heb. 9.3-5. See ARK, MERCY-SEAT.

THE HOLY PLACE (dimensions not given), contained the table of shew-bread, candle-stick, and altar of incense, Ex. 26.33,35. Ex. 40.22-26. Heb. 9.2,6. See ALTAR OF INCENSE, CANDLESTICK, SHEW-BREAD.

COURT OF THE TABERNACLE, an enclosure of curtains of fine twined linen on pillars, of which the sockets were brass, the hooks and fillets silver, the pins brass; length 100 cubits, breadth 50, height 5 cubits, Ex. 27.9-15,17. Ex. 38.9-16. Ex. 40.8.

The entrance on the east, a gateway of 4 pillars with curtains of blue purple and scarlet, and fine twined linen wrought with needle-work, 20 cubits wide, Ex. 27.16. Ex. 38.18. Ex. 40.33. This court contained the altar of burnt-offering, and the laver of brass before the door of the tabernacle, Ex. 40.29,30. See ALTAR OF BURNT-OFFERING—LAVER.

Tabernacle vessels, anointed and held sacred, Ex. 40.9,10. Lev. 8.11. Num. 18.3. Lev. 21.5. Directions for removing, Num. 4.7-15. Brought to the temple, 1 Kin. 8.4. 2 Chr. 5. 5. Of gold for the altar of incense, shew-bread table, and candlestick, Ex. 25.29,38. Ex. 37. 16,23. Of brass for the altar of burnt-offering, Ex. 27.3-7. Ex. 38.3-7. Lev. 6.28. 1 Sam. 2.13,14.

Levites took down and set up, Num. 1.51. Num. 4. Levites only entered, Num. 1.51. Num. 18.3-5,22. Punishment for defiling, Lev. 15.31. Num. 19.13,20. Eze. 5.11. Eze. 23.38. All offerings brought to, Lev. 17.4. Deu. 12.5,6,11-14. Offerings of gold laid up in, Num. 31.54. Jos. 6.19,24. No man to be in when the high-priest entered the holy place, Lev. 16.17. Worship at, Num. 20.6. Num. 25.6. 1 Sam. 1.10,26. 1 Sam. 2.22. Psa. 27. 4. See ENQUIRING OF GOD. The place of judgment, Num. 27.2. The congregation of Israel assembled at, Num. 10.3. Num. 16. 19,42,43. The tribes encamped round the court, 3 on each side, Num. 2.

TABERNACLE, HISTORICAL NOTICES OF. Set up by Moses at Sinai 1st day of 1st month, 2d year, Ex. 40.17-33. Anointed with oil, Ex. 30.26. Ex. 40.9. Lev. 8.10. Num. 7.1. Sprinkled with blood, Lev. 16.15-20. Heb. 9. 21. Filled with the cloud, Ex. 40.34-38. See CLOUD OF GLORY. Offerings of the princes at its dedication, Num. 7.

Went before Israel to search out a resting-place, Num. 2.17. Num. 9.15-17. Num. 10. 33-36. Jos. 3.3-6. See CLOUD OF GLORY.

70 elders receive the Spirit in, Num. 11. 16,24,25. 12 rods of the tribes laid up in, Num. 17. The Lord speaks to Moses in, Lev. 1.1. Num. 1.1. Num. 7.89; to Moses and Joshua, Deu. 31.14,15; reproves Aaron, &c., Num. 12.4-10.

Set up at Gilgal, Jos. 4.18,19; at Shiloh, Jos. 18.1. Jos. 19.51. Jud. 20.18,26,27. 1 Sam. 2.14; at Nob in Saul's reign, 1 Sam. 21.1-6; at Gibeon in David and Solomon's reigns, 1 Chr. 16.39. 1 Chr. 21.29. Solomon's offering at, 2 Chr. 1.3-6. Brought to the temple by Solomon, 2 Chr. 5.5 with 2 Chr. 1. 3,5,6. 1 Kin. 8.4.

TABERNACLE OF THE CONGREGATION, previous to the erection of *the* tabernacle, Ex. 33.7.

———, a new tent for the ark alone (see 2 Sam. 7.6. 1 Chr. 17.5), erected by David in Mount Zion, 2 Chr. 1.4. 1 Chr. 15.1. 1 Chr. 16.1. 2 Sam. 6.17. 1 Kin. 1.39. 1 Kin. 2.28.

TABERNACLES, FEAST OF. See FEASTS.

TABLE, Jud. 1.7. 1 Sam. 20.29,34. 2 Kin. 4.10. Jno. 2.15. Of silver in the temple, 1 Chr. 28.16. Of shew-bread, see SHEW-BREAD. Table of the Lord, signifying altar, Mal. 1.7,12; Lord's supper, 1 Cor. 10.21.

TABLES OF STONE; two containing the law, given by God to Moses; broken, Ex. 24.12. Ex. 31.18. Ex. 32.15-19. Deu. 4.13. Deu. 9.9-11; two given a second time, Ex. 34.1. Deu. 10.1-4. Placed in the ark, Deu. 10.5. 1 Kin. 8.9. Heb. 9.4.

TABLE or TABLET, used for writing on, Isa. 30.8. Hab. 2.2. Luk. 1.63. Illustrative, Pro. 3.3. Jer. 17.1. 2 Cor. 3.3.

TABLET (signifying necklace of gold beads), Ex. 35.22. Num. 31.50. (Signifying smelling bottles), Isa. 3.20.

TABOR, MOUNT, on the confines of Zebulun and Naphtali, Jos. 19.22. Psa. 89.12. Jer. 46.18. Barak's army assemble at, Jud. 4. 6.12,14. Battle between Gideon and Zebah at, Jud. 8.18.

TABOR, a Levitical city of Zebulun, 1 Chr. 6.77.

——, a plain in Benjamin, 1 Sam. 10.3.

TABRET. See TIMBREL.

TACHES, loops or hooks, Ex. 26.6.

TADMOR, a city built in the wilderness by Solomon, 1 Kin. 9.18. 2 Chr. 8.4.

TAHAPANES, a city in Egypt, Jer. 2.16. Pharaoh's palace in, Jer. 43.9. Johanan takes Jeremiah, &c., to, Jer. 43.7-9. Jer. 44.1. Prophecy of, Jer. 46.14. Eze. 30.18.

TAHPENES, wife of Pharaoh; her sister given by him in marriage to Hadad, 1 Kin. 11.19,20.

TALENT, a weight equal to 3000 shekels (125 lbs.), Ex. 38.25,26. Value of a talent of gold at £4 an oz., £5475; of silver at 5s., £342, 3s. 9d. Parables of, Mat. 18.24. Mat. 25.15.

TALMAI, king of Geshur, Absalom's maternal grandfather, 2 Sam. 3.3. 2 Sam. 13.37. 1 Chr. 3.2.

TAMAR, wife of Judah's sons, and mother of Pharez and Zarah, Gen. 38. Ruth 4.12. 1 Chr. 2.4.

——, daughter of David, sister of Absalom, 2 Sam. 13. 1 Chr. 3.9.

TAMMUZ, a Syrian idol, Jewish women weeping for, Eze. 8.3,14.

TAPESTRY, Pro. 7.16. Pro. 31.22.

TAPPUAH, a city in Judah, on the confines of Ephraim and Manasseh, Jos. 12.17. Jos. 16.8. Jos. 17.8.

TARES, a weed resembling wheat; parable of, Mat. 13.25-30.

TARGET. See SHIELD.

TARSHISH (probably Spain), peopled by descendants of Tarshish, son of Javan, Gen. 10.4,5. 1 Chr. 1.7. Merchants of, Eze. 38.13. Silver brought from, Jer. 10.9. Ships of, Psa. 48.7. Isa. 2.16. Solomon with Hiram brought gold, &c., from, 1 Kin. 10.22. 2 Chr. 9.21. Jehoshaphat's ships of Tarshish made at Ezion-geber, to go to Ophir, 1 Kin. 22.48 with 2 Chr. 20.36 (this probably an eastern Tarshish; India?).

Commerce of Tyre with, Isa. 23.1-14. Eze. 27.12. Jonah attempts to flee to, Jonah 1.3. Jonah 4.2. Prophecies of, Psa. 72.10. Isa. 60.9. Isa. 66.19.

TARSUS, a city of Cilicia, birthplace of Paul, Act. 9.11. Act. 21.39. Act. 22.3. Paul escapes to, from Jerusalem. Act. 9.30. Barnabas fetches Paul from, Act. 11.25,26.

TARTAK, an idol worshipped by the Avites in Samaria, 2 Kin. 17.31.

TARTAN, a general of Sargon, king of Assyria; takes Ashdod, Isa. 20.1; of Sennacherib, sent against Hezekiah, 2 Kin. 18.17.

TATNAI, Persian governor of Samaria; reports the building of the temple, Ezr. 5. Is commanded by Darius to assist the Jews, and obeys, Ezr. 6.1-13.

TAXES. See TRIBUTE—PUBLICANS.

TEACHER, 1 Cor. 12.28,29. Eph. 4.11. See MINISTERS.

TEBETH, the 10th month (January), Est. 2.16. Eze. 29.1.

TEIL-TREE, Isa. 6.13. Elsewhere translated oak. See OAK.

TEKEL, signifies weighed, Dan. 5.25,27.

TEKOAH, a city of Benjamin, Jer. 6.1. Neh. 3.5,27. A woman of, intercedes for Absalom, 2 Sam. 14.2-9. Fortified by Rehoboam, 2 Chr. 11.6. Amos dwelt in, Amos 1.1.

——, WILDERNESS OF; Jehoshaphat's victory in, 2 Chr. 20.20-24.

TEL-ABIB, in Mesopotamia; the Israelites dwell in, during the captivity, Eze. 3.15.

TELEM, or TELAIM, a city in Judah, Jos. 15.24. Saul's army gathered at, 1 Sam. 15.4.

TEMA, a son of Ishmael, Gen. 25.15. 1 Chr. 1.30. His descendants, an Arabian tribe, Job 6.19. Isa. 21.14. Prophecy of, Jer. 25.23. See Gen. 36.34. 1 Chr. 1.45.

TEMAN, a district of Idumea, peopled by descendants of Teman, son of Eliphaz, the son of Esau, and one of the dukes of Edom, Gen. 36.11,15,42. 1 Chr. 1.36,53. Jos. 12.3 (marg.). Job 2.11. Hab. 3.3. Prophecies of, in connection with Idumea, Jer. 49.7,20. Eze. 25.13. Amos 1.12. Obad. 9.

TEMPERANCE, SOBRIETY. Rom. 13.14. Make not provision for the flesh, to *fulfil* the lusts *thereof*.

1 Cor. 9.25. Every man that striveth for the mastery is temperate in all things. Now they *do it* to obtain a corruptible crown, but we an incorruptible. 27. But I keep under my body, and bring *it* into subjection; lest that by any means, when I have preached to others, I myself should be a castaway. Dan. 1.3-21.

Phil. 4.5. Let your moderation be known unto all men. The Lord *is* at hand.

1 The. 5.6. Let us watch and be sober. 8. Let us, who are of the day, be sober.

1 Tim. 2.9. That women adorn themselves in modest apparel, with shamefacedness and sobriety.

1 Tim. 3.2. A bishop then must be blameless, sober, of good behaviour; 3. Not given to wine. 8. Likewise *must* the deacons *be* grave, not given to much wine. 11. So *must their* wives *be* grave, sober. Tit. 1.7,8.

Tit. 2.2. That the aged men be sober, grave, temperate. 3. The aged women likewise, that *they be* in behaviour as becometh holiness, not given to much wine. 4. That they may teach the young women to be sober. 6. Young men likewise exhort to be sober minded. 12. Teaching us that, denying ungodliness and worldly lusts, we should live soberly, righteously, and godly, in this present world. *v.* 7.

1 Pet. 1.13. Gird up the loins of your mind, be sober.

1 Pet. 4.7. The end of all things is at hand: be ye therefore sober.

1 Pet. 5.8. Be sober, be vigilant; because your adversary the devil, as a roaring lion, walketh about, seeking whom he may devour.

2 Pet. 1.6. Add to knowledge temperance.

See DRUNKENNESS—WORLDLINESS—SELF-DENIAL—HOLINESS.

TEMPLE, THE. 1 Kin. 6.17. Called temple of the Lord, 2 Kin. 11.10. Thy holy temple, Psa. 79.1. The house of the Lord, 2 Chr. 23.5,12; of the God of Jacob, Isa. 2.3; of my glory, Isa. 60.7; of prayer, Isa. 56.7. Mat. 21.13; of sacrifice, 2 Chr. 7.12; of their sanctuary,

2 Chr. 36.17. Mountain of the Lord's house, Isa. 2.2. Holy and beautiful house, Isa. 64.11. Holy house, 1 Chr. 29.3. Holy mount, Isa. 27.13. Palace for the Lord, 1 Chr. 29.1,19. Sanctuary, 2 Chr. 20.8. Tabernacle of witness, 2 Chr. 24.6. Zion, and Mount Zion, Psa. 74.2. Psa. 84.7. By Christ, my Father's house, Jno. 2.16.

Projected by David, who was not permitted to build it, 2 Sam. 7.2-12. 1 Kin. 5.3. 1 Chr. 22.7,8. 1 Chr. 28.2,3. Psa. 132.2-5.

Preparations for building by David, 1 Chr. 22. 1 Chr. 28.14-18. 1 Chr. 29.1-5. 2 Chr. 3.1. 2 Chr. 5.1. 2 Sam. 8.7,11. Freewill-offerings of the people, 1 Chr. 29.6-9. Workmen and Tyrian builders employed by David, 1 Chr. 22.2-16. 1 Chr. 29.2-5; by Solomon, 1 Kin. 5.8-18. Brazen vessels cast in the plain of Jordan, 1 Kin. 7.46.

Made after a divine pattern given by David to Solomon, 1 Chr. 28.11-19. Its beauty, Isa. 64.11.

Built on Mount Moriah, in the threshing-floor of Ornan, 2 Chr. 3.1. 1 Chr. 21.28-30. 1 Chr. 22.1. See Gen. 22.2,4.

Begun by Solomon 480 years after the Exodus (B.C. 1012), in the 2d month of the 4th year of his reign, 1 Kin. 6.1,37. 2 Chr. 3.2; by God's appointment, 1 Chr. 17.12. 1 Chr. 28. 6,10. Finished in 7 years and 6 months, 1 Kin. 6.38. No hammer or tool heard in building it, 1 Kin. 6.7. 1 Kin. 5.17,18. (Destroyed by Nebuchadnezzar (B.C. 588), 2 Kin. 25.9.)

Designed for the worship of God, and sacrifices, 1 Kin. 8.13,21. 1 Chr. 29.1,2. 2 Chr. 2.4-6. Isa. 56.7. Mar. 11.17. Prophecies read in, Jer. 36.5-10. Sacredness of, Jno. 2. 14-16. God's presence in, 1 Kin. 8.10,11. 1 Kin. 9.3. 2 Kin. 21.7. 2 Chr. 5.13,14. 2 Chr. 7.1-3,16. Eze. 10.4. Prayer made towards, 1 Kin. 8.38. Jonah 2.4. Dan. 6.10. Prayer in, 1 Kin. 8. 2 Kin. 19.14,15. 2 Chr. 30.27. Isa. 56.7. Jer. 7.2. Jer. 26.2. Eze. 46.2,3,9. Zec. 7.2,3. Isa. 27.13. Zec. 8. 21,22, see WORSHIP. Weapons stored in, 2 Kin. 11.10. Was a place of refuge, 2 Kin. 11.15. Neh. 6.10,11.

The Temple was 60 cubits long, 20 broad, 30 high, 1 Kin. 6.2. 2 Chr. 3.3. Great hewn costly stones for the foundation, 1 Kin. 5. 17,18. Walls of stone, hewn in the quarry, 1 Kin. 6.7. Covered with beams and boards of cedar, 1 Kin. 6.9. Garnished with precious stones and gold, 2 Chr. 3.6-7. 1 Kin. 7.50.

Was divided into (1) the Oracle, (2) the Holy Place, (3) the Porch, (4) the Chambers.

THE ORACLE, or Most Holy Place, 1 Kin. 6.19. 1 Kin. 8.6. Called most holy house, 2 Chr. 3.8. Inner house, 1 Kin. 6.27. Holiest of all, Heb. 9.3. 20 cubits in length, breadth, and height, 1 Kin. 6.16,20. 2 Chr. 3.8. Floored and wainscoted with cedar, 1 Kin. 6.16. With figures of cherubims, palm-trees, and open flowers, v. 29. Walls overlaid with gold, v. 20,21; and floor, v. 30. A door, between the oracle and the holy place, of olive-tree, in 2 leaves, with carvings of cherubims, palm-trees, and open flowers; the lintels and posts 5 sided (v. 31, marg.); all overlaid with gold, v. 31,32. 2 Chr. 4.22. Also a partition of gold chains, 1 Kin. 6.21; and a vail of blue, purple, and crimson and fine linen, with wrought cherubims, 2 Chr. 3.14. Had no windows, see 1 Kin. 8.12.

The gold in the oracle was 600 talents; the nails, 50 shekels, 2 Chr. 3.8,9.

The oracle contained the ark, 1 Kin. 6.19. 1 Kin. 8.6. 2 Chr. 5.2-10; with the cherubim, 1 Kin. 6.23-28. 2 Chr. 3.10-13. 2 Chr. 5.7,8. See ARK, CHERUBIM, VAIL, MERCY-SEAT.

THE HOLY PLACE, 1 Kin. 8.8,10. Called the greater house, 2 Chr. 3.5. Temple, 1 Kin. 6.17. 20 cubits broad, 40 long, 1 Kin. 6.17. Floor of fir; walls and ceiling lathed with fir, and wainscoted with cedar, v. 15. (2 Chr. 3.5.) Carved with knops and open flowers, v. 18; overlaid with gold, v. 21,22. (2 Chr. 3. 5,7.) Floor covered with gold (?) v. 30. Door of fir, in 2 leaves, carved with cherubims, palm-trees, and open flowers, and covered with gold fitted upon the carved work, v. 34,35. Door-posts four-sided, v. 33. (marg.). Windows of, narrow, v. 4.

The Holy Place contained the table of shew-bread, 1 Kin. 7.48. 2 Chr. 29.18. Several tables of gold and silver, 1 Chr. 28.16. 2 Chr. 4.18,19. 10 candlesticks of gold, with snuffers, &c., 1 Kin. 7.49,50. 1 Chr. 28.15. 2 Chr. 4. 7,20-22. Silver lamps, 1 Chr. 28.15. Altar of incense, its censers, spoons, &c., 1 Kin. 6.20. 1 Kin. 7.48,50. 1 Chr. 28.17,18. 2 Chr. 4. 19,22. Vessels of the tabernacle (?) 2 Chr. 5.5. 1 Kin. 8.4. See CANDLESTICK, SHEW-BREAD, ALTAR OF INCENSE, CENSER.

THE PORCH, or Entrance Tower, before the temple, on the east (Eze. 8.16); same breadth as the temple, 20 cubits; 10 cubits deep, 1 Kin. 6.3; height, 120 cubits, 2 Chr. 3.4. Overlaid, within, with gold, 2 Chr. 3.4. Doors of, 2 Chr. 29.7. Ezekiel's vision in, Eze. 8.16. Priests called to weep by, Joel 2.17.

In the porch, the pillars, Jachin and Boaz, 1 Kin. 7.21. 2 Kin. 11.14. 2 Kin. 23.3; 12 cubits in circumference, 18 high, with a capital of 5 cubits, with various mouldings and cornices, all of brass, 1 Kin. 7.15-22. 2 Chr.3.15-17. Jer. 52.20-23. 2 Kin. 25.17. 2 Chr. 4.12,13.

CHAMBERS, as wings, built round the temple, on the south, west, and north, and forming a part of the building, 1 Kin. 6.5-10. 2 Kin. 11.2,3. See TREASURIES.

Round the whole building was a court, called the court of the priests, and outside this a court called the great court.

THE COURT OF THE PRIESTS, 2 Chr. 4.9. called inner court, 1 Kin. 6.36. Surrounded the whole temple; having a wall of 3 rows of hewn stone and a row of cedar beams, 1 Kin. 6.36. 2 Chr. 4.9. 1 Kin. 7.12. Door of, overlaid with brass, 2 Chr. 4.9.

The Court of the priests contained, altar of burnt-offering, 2 Chr. 15.8. Brazen sea, 2 Chr 4.2-5,10. 1 Kin. 7.39. 10 lavers, 1 Kin. 7.38,39. 2 Chr. 4.6. See ALTAR OF BURNT-OFFERING, SEA, LAVER.

THE GREAT COURT, 2 Chr. 4.9; surrounding the whole temple; called the court of the Lord's house; people assembled in, for worship, Jer. 19.14. Jer. 26.2. Wall of 3 rows of hewn stones, with 1 row of cedar beams, 1 Kin. 7.12. Door of, overlaid with brass, 2 Chr. 4.9.

The king's ascent, 1 Kin. 10.5. 2 Chr. 9.4. King's entry, 2 Kin. 16.18. Third entry, Jer. 38.14. Covert for the Sabbath, 2 Kin. 16.18 with 2 Kin. 11.5-7. The causeway, 1 Chr. 26.

16,18. Terrace, 2 Chr. 9.11. Higher gate, 2 Kin. 15.35. New gate, Jer. 26.10. Jer. 36.10.

HISTORICAL NOTICES OF. Dedication of, by Solomon; his prayer, sacrifices, and a feast 14 days, 1 Kin. 8. 2 Chr. c. 5 to 7. The glory of the Lord fills the house, 1 Kin. 8. 10,11. 2 Chr. 5.13,14. 2 Chr. 7.1-3.

Pillaged by Shishak, 1 Kin. 14.25,26. Treasure from, given by Asa to Benhadad, 1 Kin. 15.18. Repaired by Joash, 2 Chr. 24.7-14. 2 Kin. 12.4-14. Treasures from, given to Hazael, 2 Kin. 12.18. Pillaged by Jehoash, 2 Kin. 14.14. Ahaz removes the brazen altar; makes a new one after a Syrian pattern, 2 Kin. 16.10-17. Treasures given by Ahaz to Assyrians, 2 Kin. 16.8,17,18. Purified, and worship restored by Hezekiah, 2 Chr. 29. Treasures given by him to Assyria, 2 Kin. 18.15,16. Idolatrous altars built in, and a grove set up by Manasseh, 2 Kin. 21.4-7. 2 Chr. 33.4-7. Repaired and purified by Josiah, 2 Kin. 22. 3-7. 2 Chr. 34.8-13.

Pillaged, and Solomon's golden vessels cut in pieces by Nebuchadnezzar, 2 Kin. 24.13. 2 Chr. 36.7. The temple burnt; the pillars of brass, and brazen sea, after being broken; the pots, shovels, snuffers, spoons, and all vessels of brass; the fire-pans, bowls, gold and silver vessels; and the candlesticks carried to Babylon [B.C.588], 2 Kin. 25.9-17. 2 Chr. 36.19. Psa. 79.1. Isa. 64.11. Jer. 52.13,17-23. Lam. 2.7. Lam. 4.1. Ezr. 1.7. Drunk out of, by Belshazzar, Dan. 5.2,3. 5400 vessels of gold and silver, restored by Cyrus to the second temple, Ezr. 1.7-11.

TEMPLE. THE SECOND TEMPLE. Cyrus [B.C. 536], by divine command appoints the building of it, and provides gold and silver, &c.; 5400 vessels of the former temple returned, Ezr. 1. Ezr. 5.6-17. Ezr. 6.3-5. Isa. 44.28. Contributions by the people, Ezr. 1. 5,6. Ezr. 2.68,69. Neh. 7.70-72.

Altar of burnt-offering set up, and sacrifices offered, before the foundation of the temple was laid, Ezr. 3.2-6.

Built on the former site, Ezr. 5.11,15. 60 cubits high, 60 broad, of stones and timber, Ezr. 6.3-5. Cedar-trees brought from Lebanon by Tyrians, Ezr. 3.7.

Foundation laid [B.C. 536] by Zerubbabel, Joshua, &c., with praise, Ezr. 3.8-11. Lamentations of the old men who had seen the first house, Ezr. 3.12,13. Hag. 2.3. Samaritans request to aid in building refused, Ezr. 4.1-3. They attempt to stop it, Ezr. 4.4,5. Obtain a decree for this purpose, from Ahasuerus, Ezr. 4.6-24.

Building resumed [B.C. 520] in the reign of Darius; encouraged by Haggai and Zechariah; Tatnai's letter to Darius; his decree in its favour, Ezr. 4.24. Ezr. 5. Ezr. 6. Lukewarmness of the Jews in building reproved, Hag. 1.2-9. Blessed for their zeal, Hag. 2. 15,19. Zec. 8.9. Finished [B.C. 515, 70 years after the destruction of the first temple], Ezr. 6.14,15. Dedication of, Ezr. 6.15-18.

Decree in favour of, and gifts by Artaxerxes, Ezr. 7.11-28. Ezr. 8.25-34.

Prophecies of its restoration, Isa. 44.28. Dan. 8.13,14. Hag. 1. Hag. 2. Zec. 1.16. Zec. 4.8-10. Zec. 6.12-15. Zec. 8.9-15. Of Christ's coming to it, Hag. 2.7. Mal. 3.1.

Herod repairs the temple; 46 years spent in rebuilding, Jno. 2.20. Mar. 13.1. Luk. 21.5. Beauty of, Mar. 24.1. The gate beautiful, Act. 3.10. Solomon's porch, Jno. 10.23. Act. 3. 11. Act. 5.12. The treasury, Mar. 12.41.

Desecration of, by the Jews, Jno. 2.15-17. Mat. 21.12,13. No Gentile allowed to enter, Act. 21.27-30. Act. 24.6. Partition-wall between Jew and Gentile, Eph. 2.13,14.

Jews sworn by, Mat. 23.16-22. Prayers offered in, Luk. 1.10. Luk. 2.37. Luk. 18.10. Act. 3.1. Act. 22.17. Beggars at gate of, Act. 3.10. Captains of, Luk. 22.52. Act. 4.1. Act. 5.24,26. Anna dwelt in, Luk. 2.37.

Christ presented in, Luk. 2.1-39; at 12 years of age, Luk. 2.46. Taken to the pinnacle of, Mat. 4.5. Teaches in, Mar. 11.27-33. Mar. 12. 35. Mar. 14.49. Jno. 5.14-47. Jno. 7.14,28. Jno. 8.2. Jno. 10.23. Jno. 18.20. Miracles in, Mat. 21.14,15. Purifies, Jno. 2.15-17. Mat. 21.12,13. Vail of, rent at his death, Mat. 27.51.

Zacharias' vision of Gabriel in, Luk. 1.8-22. Judas throws down the silver in, Mat. 27.5. Disciples assemble in, Luk. 24.53. Act. 2.46. Preach in, Act. 3. Act. 5.20,21,42. Miracle of Peter, Act. 3.1-10. Paul's trance in, Act. 22.17. Paul seized in, Act. 21.26-31.

Prophecies of its destruction, Dan. 8.11,12. Dan. 11.30,31. Mat. 24. Mar. 13.2. Luk. 21.6.

TEMPLE, described by Ezekiel, Eze. c. 40 to 48.

————, illustrative, Psa. 11.4. Psa. 18.6. Jer. 7.4. Mat. 26.61. 1 Cor. 3.16,17. 2 Cor. 6.16. Eph. 2.21. 2 The. 2.4. Rev. 3.12. Symbolical, Rev. 11. Rev. 14.15,17. Rev. 15. 5-8. Rev. 16.1-17.

TEMPLES, IDOLATROUS. Of Dagon at Ashdod, 1 Sam. 5.2; of the calves at Bethel, 1 Kin. 12.31-33; of Rimmon at Damascus, 2 Kin. 5.18; of Baal at Samaria, 2 Kin. 10. 21,27; at Babylon, 2 Chr. 36.7. Dan. 1.2; of Diana at Ephesus, Act. 19.27.

TEMPORAL BLESSINGS FROM GOD. See GOD'S GOODNESS IN PROVIDENCE—RICHES—THANKFULNESS.

TEMPORAL BLESSINGS, PRAYER FOR. Gen. 27.28. God give thee of the dew of heaven, and the fatness of the earth, and plenty of corn and wine: 29. Let people serve thee, and nations bow down to thee.

Gen. 28.20. If God will be with me, and will keep me in this way that I go, and will give me bread to eat, and raiment to put on, 21. So that I come again to my father's house in peace, then shall the Lord be my God. v. 3,4.

Gen. 48.16. The Angel which redeemed me from all evil, bless the lads; and let my name be named on them, and the name of my fathers Abraham and Isaac; and let them grow into a multitude in the midst of the earth.

Deu. 1.11. The Lord God of your fathers make you a thousand times so many more as ye are, and bless you, as he hath promised you.

Deu. 26.15. Look down from thy holy habitation, from heaven, and bless thy people Israel, and the land which thou hast given us.

Deu. 33.11. Bless, Lord, his substance, and accept the work of his hands: smite through the loins of them that rise against him, and of them that hate him, that they rise not again. 13. Blessed of the Lord be his land, for the precious things of heaven, for the dew, and for the deep that coucheth beneath. 16. And for the precious things of the earth, and fulness thereof; and for the good will of him that dwelt in the bush : let the blessing come upon the head of Joseph. 24. Let Asher be blessed with children; let him be acceptable to his brethren, and let him dip his foot in oil. v. 14,15.

1 Kin. 8.36. Give rain upon thy land, which thou hast given to thy people for an inheritance. v. 33-50.

1 Chr. 4.10. Oh that thou wouldest bless me indeed, and enlarge my coast, and that thine hand might be with me, and that thou wouldest keep me from evil, that it may not grieve me !

1 Chr. 17.27. Let it please thee to bless the house of thy servant, that it may be before thee for ever : for thou blessest, O Lord, and it shall be blessed for ever.

Psa. 28.9. Save thy people, and bless thine inheritance : feed them also, and lift them up for ever.

Psa. 36.11. Let not the foot of pride come against me, and let not the hand of the wicked remove me.

Pro. 30.8. Give me neither poverty nor riches; feed me with food convenient for me.

Mat. 6.11. Give us this day our daily bread.

Rom. 1.10. Making request (if by any means now at length I might have a prosperous journey by the will of God) to come unto you.

1 The. 3.11. Now God himself and our Father, and our Lord Jesus Christ, direct our way unto you.

3 Jno. 2. Beloved, I wish above all things that thou mayest prosper and be in health, even as thy soul prospereth.

Temporal Blessings, Prayer for, Examples of : Abraham, Gen. 15.2-4. Abraham's servant, Gen. 24.12. Laban, Gen. 24.60. Isaac, Gen. 25.21. Hannah, 1 Sam. 1. 11. Elijah, 1 Kin. 17.20,21. 1 Kin. 18.42,44. Jas. 5.17,18. Ezra, Ezr. 8.21-23. Nehemiah, Neh. 1.11. Neh. 2.4. Neh. 6.9.

See Affliction, Prayer in—Prayer.

TEMPTATION. Deu. 7.25. The graven images of their gods shall ye burn with fire : thou shalt not desire the silver or gold that is on them, nor take it unto thee, lest thou be snared therein : for it is an abomination to the Lord thy God. v. 26.

Deu. 13.3. Thou shalt not hearken unto the words of that prophet, or that dreamer of dreams : for the Lord your God proveth you.

2 Chr. 32.31. God left him, to try him, that he might know all that was in his heart.

Psa. 119.165. Great peace have they which love thy law : and nothing shall offend them.

Pro. 1.10. My son, if sinners entice thee, consent thou not. 15. My son, walk not thou in the way with them ; refrain thy foot from their path. 17. In vain the net is spread in the sight of any bird. v. 10-17.

Pro. 2.11. Discretion shall preserve thee, understanding shall keep thee : 12. To deliver

thee from the way of the evil man, from the man that speaketh froward things.

Pro. 3.21. Keep sound wisdom and discretion. 23. Then shalt thou walk in thy way safely, and thy foot shall not stumble.

Pro. 4.5. Get wisdom, get understanding : forget it not ; neither decline from the words of my mouth. 6. Forsake her not, and she shall preserve thee : love her, and she shall keep thee. 14. Enter not into the path of the wicked, and go not in the way of evil men. 15. Avoid it, pass not by it, turn from it, and pass away.

Pro. 6.27. Can a man take fire in his bosom, and his clothes not be burned? 28. Can one go upon hot coals, and his feet not be burned?

Pro. 14.27. The fear of the Lord is a fountain of life, to depart from the snares of death. Pro. 13.14.

Ecc. 7.26. I find more bitter than death the woman, whose heart is snares and nets, and her hands as bands : whoso pleaseth God shall escape from her ; but the sinner shall be taken by her.

Mat. 26.41. Watch and pray, that ye enter not into temptation : the spirit indeed is willing, but the flesh is weak. Luk. 22.40.

1 Cor. 10.13. There hath no temptation taken you but such as is common to man : but God is faithful, who will not suffer you to be tempted above that ye are able ; but will with the temptation also make a way to escape, that ye may be able to bear it.

2 Cor. 6.7. By the armour of righteousness on the right hand and on the left.

Gal. 5.16. Walk in the Spirit, and ye shall not fulfil the lust of the flesh. 17. For the flesh lusteth against the Spirit, and the Spirit against the flesh : and these are contrary the one to the other : so that ye cannot do the things that ye would.

Eph. 4.27. Neither give place to the devil.

Eph. 6.10. Be strong in the Lord, and in the power of his might. 11. Put on the whole armour of God, that ye may be able to stand against the wiles of the devil. 13. Wherefore take unto you the whole armour of God, that ye may be able to withstand in the evil day, and having done all, to stand. 14. Stand therefore, having your loins girt about with truth, and having on the breastplate of righteousness ; 15. And your feet shod with the preparation of the gospel of peace ; 16. Above all, taking the shield of faith, wherewith ye shall be able to quench all the fiery darts of the wicked. 17. And take the helmet of salvation, and the sword of the Spirit, which is the word of God.

2 The. 3.3. The Lord is faithful, who shall stablish you, and keep you from evil.

Heb. 2.18. In that he himself hath suffered, being tempted, he is able to succour them that are tempted.

Heb. 3.13. Exhort one another daily, while it is called To-day ; lest any of you be hardened through the deceitfulness of sin.

Heb. 4.15. We have not an high-priest which cannot be touched with the feeling of our infirmities ; but was in all points tempted like as we are, yet without sin.

Heb. 12.3. Consider him that endured such contradiction of sinners against himself, lest ye be wearied and faint in your minds.

4. Ye have not yet resisted unto blood, striving against sin.

Jas. 1. 2. My brethren, count it all joy when ye fall into divers temptations; 3. Knowing *this*, that the trying of your faith worketh patience. 4. But let patience have *her* perfect work, that ye may be perfect and entire, wanting nothing. 12. Blessed *is* the man that endureth temptation: for when he is tried, he shall receive the crown of life, which the Lord hath promised to them that love him. 14. Every man is tempted, when he is drawn away of his own lust, and enticed. 15. Then when lust hath conceived, it bringeth forth sin: and sin, when it is finished, bringeth forth death. 16. Do not err, my beloved brethren.

Jas. 4. 7. Resist the devil, and he will flee from you.

1 Pet. 5. 8. Be sober, be vigilant; because your adversary the devil, as a roaring lion, walketh about, seeking whom he may devour: 9. Whom resist stedfast in the faith, knowing that the same afflictions are accomplished in your brethren that are in the world.

2 Pet. 2. 9. The Lord knoweth how to deliver the godly out of temptations.

2 Pet. 3. 17. Seeing ye know *these things* before, beware lest ye also, being led away with the error of the wicked, fall from your own stedfastness.

1 Jno. 4. 4. Ye are of God, little children, and have overcome them: because greater is he that is in you, than he that is in the world.

Rev. 3. 10. Because thou hast kept the word of my patience, I also will keep thee from the hour of temptation, which shall come upon all the world, to try them that dwell upon the earth.

Rev. 12. 11. They overcame him by the blood of the Lamb, and by the word of their testimony; and they loved not their lives unto the death.

See WATCHFULNESS—SATAN—EVIL COMPANY.

TEMPTATION, EXAMPLES OF: Eve, Gen. 3. 6. Balaam, Num. 22. 17-19. Achan, Jos. 7. 21. Solomon, 1 Kin. 11. 4. David, 1 Chr. 21. 1.

TEMPTATION, PRAYER AGAINST. 1 Chr. 4. 10. Oh that thou wouldest bless me indeed, and enlarge my coast, and that thine hand might be with me, and that thou wouldest keep *me* from evil, that it may not grieve me!

Psa. 17. 5. Hold up my goings in thy paths, *that* my footsteps slip not.

Psa. 19. 13. Keep back thy servant also from presumptuous *sins;* let them not have dominion over me: then shall I be upright, and I shall be innocent from the great transgression.

Psa. 25. 21. Let integrity and uprightness preserve me; for I wait on thee.

Psa. 56. 13. Thou hast delivered my soul from death: *wilt not thou deliver* my feet from falling, that I may walk before God in the light of the living?

Psa. 119. 29. Remove from me the way of lying: and grant me thy law graciously. 37. Turn away mine eyes from beholding vanity; *and* quicken thou me in thy way. 117. Hold thou me up, and I shall be safe: and I will have respect unto thy statutes continually.

Psa. 139. 23. Search me, O God, and know my heart; try me, and know my thoughts; 24. And see if *there be any* wicked way in me, and lead me in the way everlasting.

Psa. 141. 3. Set a watch, O Lord, before my mouth; keep the door of my lips. 4. Incline not my heart to *any* evil thing, to practise wicked works with men that work iniquity: and let me not eat of their dainties.

Pro. 30. 7. Two *things* have I required of thee; deny me *them* not before I die: 8. Remove far from me vanity and lies: give me neither poverty nor riches; feed me with food convenient for me: 9. Lest I be full, and deny *thee*, and say, Who *is* the Lord? or lest I be poor, and steal, and take the name of my God *in vain*.

Mat. 6. 13. And lead us not into temptation; but deliver us from evil.

Luk. 22. 31. And the Lord said, Simon, Simon, behold, Satan hath desired *to have* you, that he may sift *you* as wheat: 32. But I have prayed for thee, that thy faith fail not: and when thou art converted, strengthen thy brethren.

Jno. 17. 15. I pray not that thou shouldest take them out of the world, but that thou shouldest keep them from the evil.

2 Cor. 13. 7. I pray to God that ye do no evil.

See SPIRITUAL BLESSINGS, PRAYER FOR.

TEMPTATION RESISTED. Gen. 39. 9. How then can I do this great wickedness, and sin against God?

Job. 31. 1. I made a covenant with mine eyes; why then should I think upon a maid?

Psa. 17. 4. By the word of thy lips I have kept *me from* the paths of the destroyer.

Psa. 73. 2. As for me, my feet were almost gone; my steps had well nigh slipped. *v.* 15-23.

Psa. 94. 18. When I said, My foot slippeth; thy mercy, O Lord, held me up.

Psa. 119. 101. I have refrained my feet from every evil way, that I might keep thy word. 110. The wicked have laid a snare for me: yet I erred not from thy precepts.

Luk. 4. 8. And Jesus answered and said unto him, Get thee behind me, Satan: for it is written, Thou shalt worship the Lord thy God, and him only shalt thou serve. *v.* 1-13. Mat. 4. 1-11. Mar. 1. 13.

See SIN HATEFUL TO SAINTS—HOLINESS.

——, WARNING AGAINST GIVING. Mat. 18. 6. But whoso shall offend one of these little ones which believe in me, it were better for him that a millstone were hanged about his neck, and *that* he were drowned in the depth of the sea. 7. Woe unto the world because of offences! for it must needs be that offences come; but woe to that man by whom the offence cometh! Deu. 13. 1-17.

Rom. 14. 13. Judge this rather, that no man put a stumblingblock or an occasion to fall in *his* brother's way. 2 Sam. 11. 13. 1 Kin. 13. 15-19. Hab. 2. 15.

Rom. 14. 15. If thy brother be grieved with *thy* meat, now walkest thou not charitably. Destroy not him with thy meat, for whom Christ died. *v.* 21.

1 Cor. 8. 11. Through thy knowledge shall the weak brother perish, for whom Christ died? *v.* 12, 13.

See EVIL COMPANY—MINISTERS, UNFAITHFUL.

TEN STRINGED INSTRUMENT, Psa. 92.3. Psa. 144.9. See HARP.

TENTS, Gen. 35.21. Jud. 4.21. ·Isa. 40. 22. Isa. 54.2. Jer. 10.20. Door of, Gen. 18.1. Invented by Jabal, Gen. 4.20. Dwelt in; by the patriarchs, Gen. 9.21. Gen. 12.8. Gen. 13.5. Gen. 25.27. Gen. 26.25. Heb. 11.9; by Israelites in the wilderness, Ex. 18.7. Num. 2. Num. 24.5; people in Palestine, Jud. 4.11,17. Jud. 8.11; Midianites, Jud. 6.5. Hab. 3.7. Arabians, Isa. 13.20; Kedarites, Psa. 120.5. Song 1.5. Jer. 49.29; Rechabites, Jer. 35.7,10. Separate, for women, Gen. 24.67. Gen. 31. 33,34. Israel worshipped at the doors of, Ex. 33.8,10. Wept at, Num. 11.10. Used in war, 1 Sam. 4.10. 1 Sam. 17.54. 2 Kin. 7. 7,10; by shepherds, Isa. 38.12. Jer. 6.3. For cattle, 2 Chr. 14.15. 'To your tents, O Israel,' a cry of disaffection, 2 Sam. 20.1. 1 Kin. 12.16. Paul, &c., tentmakers, Act. 18.3. See TABERNACLE, BOOTH, CORD, CURTAIN, NAIL.

TERAH, father of Abraham, leaves Ur for Haran, Gen. 11.24-32. Act. 7.2-4. Worshipped idols, Jos. 24.2,14.

TERAPHIM, household gods, Gen. 31.19 (marg.) with v. 30; resembling a man (marg. image or teraphim), 1 Sam. 19.13-16. Stolen from Laban by Rachel, Gen. 31.19,30-35. Of Micah, Jud. 17.5; stolen by Danites, Jud. 18.14,17-20. Consulted by diviners, Eze. 21. 21 (marg.). Zec. 10.2 (marg.). Hos. 3.4. Destroyed by Josiah, 2 Kin. 23.24.

TERESH, Ahasuerus's chamberlain; seeks to kill him; is slain, Est. 6.2.

TERTIUS, Paul's secretary, Rom. 16.22.

TERTULLUS, a Roman advocate, pleads against Paul, Act. 24.1-8.

TESTAMENT (Gr. diatheke), Heb. 9. 16,17. A covenant, often thus translated, Gal. 3.17. The Abrahamic covenant, Luk. 1. 72,73 with Gen. 15.1-18. Gen. 17.1-19. Act. 7.8. The Mosaic covenant, Heb. 8.9. Heb. 9.4,20 with Ex. 24.3-12. Mosaic writings, 2 Cor. 3.14. The gospel dispensation, 2 Cor. 3.6. Gal. 4.24. Heb. 7.22. Heb. 8.6,8,10. Heb. 9.15. Heb. 10.16,29. Heb. 12.24. Heb. 13.20. The Lord's supper, Mat. 26.28. Mar. 14.24. Luk. 22.20. 1 Cor. 11.25. See COVENANTS—WILLS.

TETRARCH (ruler of the fourth part of a province), in N. T., a title of any governor, Mat. 14.1 with v. 9. See LYSANIAS, HEROD, PHILIP.

THADDEUS. See JUDE.

THANKFULNESS ENJOINED. Gen. 35.1. Make there an altar unto God, that appeared unto thee when thou fleddest from the face of Esau.

Ex. 13.3. Remember this day, in which ye came out from Egypt. v. 3-16. Ex. 12. 14,17,42.

Ex. 16.32. Fill an omer of it to be kept for your generations; that they may see the bread wherewith I have fed you in the wilderness. v. 32-34.

Deu. 5.15. Remember that thou wast a servant in the land of Egypt, and that the Lord thy God brought thee out thence through a mighty hand and by a stretched out arm:

therefore the Lord thy God commanded thee to keep the sabbath day.

Deu. 8.2. Thou shalt remember all the way which the Lord thy God led thee these forty years in the wilderness. 10. When thou hast eaten and art full, then thou shalt bless the Lord thy God for the good land which he hath given thee. 18. Thou shalt remember the Lord thy God: for it is he that giveth thee power to get wealth.

Deu. 12.18. Thou must eat them before the Lord thy God, and thou shalt rejoice before the Lord thy God in all that thou puttest thine hands unto.

Deu. 16.10. Keep the feast of weeks unto the Lord thy God with a tribute of a freewill-offering of thine hand, which thou shalt give unto the LORD thy God, according as the Lord thy God hath blessed thee: 11. And thou shalt rejoice before the Lord thy God. v. 12-15.

Deu. 26.5. Thou shalt speak and say before the Lord thy God, A Syrian ready to perish was my father, and he went down into Egypt. 10. And now, behold, I have brought the first-fruits of the land, which thou, O Lord, hast given me. And thou shalt set it before the Lord thy God, and worship before the Lord thy God. v. 5-11. Lev. 23.14,42. Ex. 34. 26. Lev. 19.24. Num. 15.19-21. Num. 31.28-30.

Jud. 5.11. They that are delivered from the noise of archers in the places of drawing water, there shall they rehearse the righteous acts of the Lord, even the righteous acts toward the inhabitants of his villages in Israel.

Psa. 48.11. Let mount Zion rejoice, let the daughters of Judah be glad, because of thy judgments.

Psa. 50.14. Offer unto God thanksgiving; and pay thy vows unto the most High: 15. I will deliver thee, and thou shalt glorify me.

Psa. 98.1. O sing unto the Lord a new song; for he hath done marvellous things: his right hand, and his holy arm, hath gotten him the victory.

Psa. 100.4. Enter into his gates with thanksgiving, and into his courts with praise: be thankful unto him, and bless his name.

Psa. 105.5. Remember his marvellous works that he hath done; his wonders, and the judgments of his mouth. 44. They inherited the labour of the people; 45. That they might observe his statutes, and keep his laws. Praise ye the Lord.

Psa. 107.1. O give thanks unto the Lord; for he is good: for his mercy endureth for ever. 2. Let the redeemed of the Lord say so, whom he hath redeemed from the hand of the enemy. 21. Oh that men would praise the Lord for his goodness, and for his wonderful works to the children of men ! 22. And let them sacrifice the sacrifices of thanksgiving, and declare his works with rejoicing. 32. Let them exalt him also in the congregation of the people, and praise him in the assembly of the elders. 42. The righteous shall see it, and rejoice: and all iniquity shall stop her mouth. 43. Whoso is wise, and will observe these things, even they shall understand the loving-kindness of the Lord. Psa. 106.1.

Psa. 118.4. Let them now that fear the Lord say, that his mercy endureth for ever. v. 1-3.

Psa. 135.3. Praise the Lord; for the Lord *is* good.

Psa. 145.7. They shall abundantly utter the memory of thy great goodness, and shall sing of thy righteousness.

Psa. 147.12. Praise the Lord, O Jerusalem; praise thy God, O Zion. 13. For he hath strengthened the bars of thy gates; he hath blessed thy children within thee. *v.* 14-18.

Pro. 3.9. Honour the Lord with thy substance, and with the firstfruits of all thine increase.

Ecc. 5.18. *It is* good and comely *for one* to eat and to drink, and to enjoy the good of all his labour that he taketh under the sun all the days of his life, which God giveth him: for it *is* his portion. 20. Because God answereth *him* in the joy of his heart. *v.* 19.

Ecc. 7.14. In the day of prosperity be joyful.

Isa. 48.20. With a voice of singing declare ye, tell this, utter it *even* to the end of the earth; say ye, The Lord hath redeemed his servant Jacob.

Joel 2.26. Ye shall eat in plenty, and be satisfied, and praise the name of the Lord your God, that hath dealt wondrously with you.

Mic. 6.5. O my people, remember now what Balak king of Moab consulted, and what Balaam answered him; that ye may know the righteousness of the Lord. Isa. 51.1,2.

Mal. 1.5. Your eyes shall see, and ye shall say, The Lord will be magnified from the border of Israel.

Mar. 5.19. Go home to thy friends, and tell them how great things the Lord hath done for thee, and hath had compassion on thee. Luk. 8.38.

Rom. 14.6. He that eateth, eateth to the Lord, for he giveth God thanks; and he that eateth not, to the Lord he eateth not, and giveth God thanks.

Eph. 5.4. Nor foolish talking, nor jesting, which are not convenient: but rather giving of thanks. 20. Giving thanks always for all things unto God and the Father in the name of our Lord Jesus Christ.

Phil. 4.6. In every thing by prayer and supplication with thanksgiving let your requests be made known unto God.

Col. 1.12. Giving thanks unto the Father, which hath made us meet to be partakers of the inheritance of the saints in light.

Col. 2.7. Stablished in the faith, as ye have been taught, abounding therein with thanksgiving.

Col. 3.15. Be ye thankful. 17. Whatsoever ye do in word or deed, *do* all in the name of the Lord Jesus, giving thanks to God and the Father by him.

Col. 4.2. Continue in prayer, and watch in the same with thanksgiving.

1 The. 5.18. In every thing give thanks: for this is the will of God in Christ Jesus concerning you.

1 Tim. 2.1. I exhort therefore, that giving of thanks, be made for all men.

1 Tim. 4.3. Meats, which God hath created to be received with thanksgiving of them which believe and know the truth. 4. For every creature of God *is* good, and nothing to be refused, if it be received with thanksgiving:

5. For it is sanctified by the word of God and prayer.

Heb. 13.15. By him therefore let us offer the sacrifice of praise to God continually, that is, the fruit of *our* lips giving thanks to his name.

Jas. 1.9. Let the brother of low degree rejoice in that he is exalted.

THANKFULNESS, EXAMPLES OF : Eve, Gen. 4.1,25. Noah, Gen. 8.20. Melchizedek, Gen. 14.20. Lot, Gen. 19.19. Sarah, Gen. 21.6,7. Abraham's servant, Gen. 24.27,35. Laban, &c., Gen. 24.50. Isaac, Gen. 26.22. Leah, Gen. 29.32-35. Rachel, Gen. 30.6. Jacob, Gen. 31. 42. Gen. 33.5. Gen. 35.3,7. Joseph, Gen. 41.51,52. Gen. 45.5-8. Gen. 48.9. Gen. 50. 19-21. Moses, Ex. 18.3,4,8. Num. 20.14-16. Jethro, Ex. 18.10. Israel, Ex. 4.31. Num. 21.17. Num. 31.49-54. Jos. 4. 1 Kin. 8.6. 1 Chr. 29.22. Joshua, Jos. 4.9,20-24. Jos. 14. 10,11. Jos. 24.16-18. Deborah, &c., Jud. 5. Samson, Jud. 15.18. Hannah, 1 Sam. 1.27,28. Samuel, 1 Sam. 7.12. 1 Sam. 12.6-12. David, 2 Sam. 5.12-20. 2 Sam. 6.21. 1 Chr. 22.18. 1 Chr. 28.4. Solomon, 1 Kin. 3.6. 1 Kin. 5. 4,5. Queen of Sheba, 1 Kin. 10.9. Hiram, 2 Chr. 2.12. Asa, 2 Chr. 14.7. Jehoshaphat's army, 2 Chr. 20.27,28. Cyrus, Ezr. 1.2. Ezr. 7.6,9,28. Ezr. 8.31. Levites, Neh. 9.4-38. Nehemiah, Neh. 2.8,18. Neh. 7.5. Neh. 9. 7,35. Jews, Neh. 12.43. Mordecai, Est. 4.14. Shepherds, &c., Luk. 2.20,38. Blind men, lepers, &c., Mat. 9.31. Luk. 5.25. Luk. 8.39. Luk. 13.13. Luk. 17.15,16. Luk. 18.43. Act. 3.8. Peter, Act. 12.11.

THANKFULNESS EXEMPLIFIED. Gen. 32.10. I am not worthy of the least of all the mercies, and of all the truth, which thou hast shewed unto thy servant ; for with my staff I have passed over this Jordan; and now I am become two bands.

Gen. 48.15. The God which fed me all my life long unto this day, 16. The Angel which redeemed me from all evil, bless the lads. *v.* 11.

Ex. 15.1. I will sing unto the Lord, for he hath triumphed gloriously : the horse and his rider hath he thrown into the sea. 13. Thou in thy mercy hast led forth the people *which* thou hast redeemed : thou hast guided *them* in thy strength unto thy holy habitation. *v.* 1-21. Deu. 3.24.

Deu. 32.10. He found him in a desert land, and in the waste howling wilderness ; he led him about, he instructed him, he kept him as the apple of his eye. *v.* 7-14. Deu. 4.32-40. Deu. 8.15,16. Deu. 9.26. Deu. 10.22. Deu. 33.3. Jos. 2.24.

2 Sam. 4.9. The Lord liveth, who hath redeemed my soul out of all adversity.

2 Sam. 7.18. Who *am* I, O Lord God ? and what *is* my house, that thou hast brought me hitherto ? 19. And this was yet a small thing in thy sight, O Lord God ; but thou hast spoken also of thy servant's house for a great while to come. And *is* this the manner of man, O Lord God ?

1 Kin. 8.56. Blessed *be* the Lord, that hath given rest unto his people Israel, according to all that he promised : there hath not failed one word of all his good promise.

1 Chr. 17.19. O Lord, for thy servant's sake, and according to thine own heart, hast thou done all this greatness.

1 Chr. 29.14. For all things *come* of thee, and of thine own have we given thee.

Ezr. 7.27. Blessed be the Lord God of our fathers, which hath put such a thing as this in the king's heart, to beautify the house of the Lord.

Ezr. 9.8. Now for a little space grace hath been shewed from the Lord our God, to leave us a remnant to escape, and to give us a nail in his holy place, that our God may lighten our eyes, and give us a little reviving in our bondage. v. 9.

Neh. 1.10. These are thy servants and thy people, whom thou hast redeemed by thy great power, and by thy strong hand.

Job 23.14. He performeth the thing that is appointed for me: and many such things are with him.

Psa. 4.1. Thou hast enlarged me when I was in distress.

Psa. 9.1. I will praise thee, O Lord, with my whole heart; I will shew forth all thy marvellous works. 4. For thou hast maintained my right and my cause.

Psa. 13.6. I will sing unto the Lord, because he hath dealt bountifully with me.

Psa. 18.6. In my distress I called upon the Lord, and cried unto my God: he heard my voice out of his temple, and my cry came before him, even into his ears. 16. He sent from above, he took me, he drew me out of many waters. 19. He brought me forth also into a large place; he delivered me, because he delighted in me. 35. Thou hast also given me the shield of thy salvation: and thy right hand hath holden me up, and thy gentleness hath made me great. 36. Thou hast enlarged my steps under me, that my feet did not slip. 43. Thou hast delivered me from the strivings of the people; and thou hast made me the head of the heathen. 2 Sam. 22.

Psa. 22.4. Our fathers trusted in thee: they trusted, and thou didst deliver them. 5. They cried unto thee, and were delivered: they trusted in thee, and were not confounded. 9. Thou art he that took me out of the womb: thou didst make me hope when I was upon my mother's breasts. 10. I was cast upon thee from the womb: thou art my God from my mother's belly. 23. Ye that fear the Lord, praise him. 24. For he hath not despised nor abhorred the affliction of the afflicted; neither hath he hid his face from him; but when he cried unto him, he heard. 25. My praise shall be of thee in the great congregation.

Psa. 23.5. Thou preparest a table before me in the presence of mine enemies: thou anointest my head with oil; my cup runneth over.

Psa. 26.6. So will I compass thine altar, O Lord: 7. That I may publish with the voice of thanksgiving, and tell of all thy wondrous works.

Psa. 27.6. Now shall mine head be lifted up above mine enemies round about me: therefore will I offer in his tabernacle sacrifices of joy.

Psa. 28.7. The Lord is my strength and my shield; my heart trusted in him, and I am helped: therefore my heart greatly rejoiceth; and with my song will I praise him.

Psa. 30.1. I will extol thee, O Lord; for thou hast lifted me up, and hast not made my foes to rejoice over me. 2. O Lord my God, I cried unto thee, and thou hast healed me. 3.

O Lord, thou hast brought up my soul from the grave: thou hast kept me alive, that I should not go down to the pit. 11. Thou hast turned for me my mourning into dancing: thou hast put off my sackcloth, and girded me with gladness; 12. To the end that my glory may sing praise to thee, and not be silent. O Lord my God, I will give thanks unto thee for ever.

Psa. 31.7. I will be glad and rejoice in thy mercy: for thou hast considered my trouble; thou hast known my soul in adversities; 8. And hast not shut me up into the hand of the enemy: thou hast set my feet in a large room. 21. Blessed be the Lord: for he hath shewed me his marvellous kindness in a strong city. v. 22.

Psa. 34.4. I sought the Lord, and he heard me, and delivered me from all my fears. v. 5, 6.

Psa. 35.9. My soul shall be joyful in the Lord: it shall rejoice in his salvation. 10. All my bones shall say, Lord, who is like unto thee, which deliverest the poor from him that is too strong for him, yea, the poor and the needy from him that spoileth him? v. 18.

Psa. 40.2. He brought me up also out of an horrible pit, out of the miry clay, and set my feet upon a rock, and established my goings. 3. And he hath put a new song in my mouth, even praise unto our God. 5. Many, O Lord my God, are thy wonderful works which thou hast done, and thy thoughts which are to usward: they cannot be reckoned up in order unto thee: if I would declare and speak of them, they are more than can be numbered.

Psa. 41.11. By this I know that thou favourest me, because mine enemy doth not triumph over me. 12. And as for me, thou upholdest me in mine integrity, and settest me before thy face for ever.

Psa. 44.1. We have heard with our ears, O God, our fathers have told us, what work thou didst in their days, in the times of old. 2. How thou didst drive out the heathen with thy hand, and plantedst them. 7. Thou hast saved us from our enemies, and hast put them to shame that hated us. 8. In God we boast all the day long, and praise thy name for ever. v. 3.

Psa. 48.3. God is known in her palaces for a refuge. 8. As we have heard, so have we seen in the city of the Lord of hosts, in the city of our God.

Psa. 54.6. I will freely sacrifice unto thee: I will praise thy name, O Lord; for it is good. 7. For he hath delivered me out of all trouble.

Psa. 55.18. He hath delivered my soul in peace from the battle that was against me.

Psa. 56.12. I will render praises unto thee. 13. For thou hast delivered my soul from death.

Psa. 59.16. I will sing of thy power; yea, I will sing aloud of thy mercy in the morning; for thou hast been my defence and refuge in the day of my trouble. 17. Unto thee, O my strength, will I sing: for God is my defence, and the God of my mercy.

Psa. 61.3. Thou hast been a shelter for me, and a strong tower from the enemy.

Psa. 66.5. Come and see the works of God. 6. He turned the sea into dry land: they went through the flood on foot: there did we rejoice in him. 8. O bless our God, ye people, and make the voice of his praise to be heard : 9. Which holdeth our soul in life, and suffereth not our feet to be moved. 12. We went through fire and through water: but thou broughtest us out into a wealthy place. 16. Come and hear, all ye that fear God, and I will declare what he hath done for my soul. v. 5-16.

Psa. 68.9. Thou, O God, didst send a plentiful rain, whereby thou didst confirm thine inheritance, when it was weary. 10. Thy congregation hath dwelt therein: thou, O God, hast prepared of thy goodness for the poor. 19. Blessed be the Lord, who daily loadeth us with benefits, even the God of our salvation. v. 11,12.

Psa. 71.7. I am as a wonder unto many; but thou art my strong refuge. 15. My mouth shall shew forth thy righteousness and thy salvation all the day; for I know not the numbers thereof. 16. I will go in the strength of the Lord God : I will make mention of thy righteousness, even of thine only. 17. O God, thou hast taught me from my youth: and hitherto have I declared thy wondrous works. 23. My lips shall greatly rejoice when I sing unto thee ; and my soul, which thou hast redeemed. 24. My tongue also shall talk of thy righteousness all the day long. v. 6.

Psa. 74.12. God is my King of old, working salvation in the midst of the earth. Psa. 76.3-6. Psa. 77.14-20.

Psa. 78.54. He brought them to the border of his sanctuary, even to this mountain, which his right hand had purchased. v. 12-66. Psa. 80.8-11. Psa. 105. Psa. 106. Psa. 114.

Psa. 79.13. We thy people and sheep of thy pasture will give thee thanks for ever: we will shew forth thy praise to all generations.

Psa. 85.1. Lord, thou hast been favourable unto thy land · thou hast brought back the captivity of Jacob.

Psa. 86.13. Great is thy mercy toward me, and thou hast delivered my soul from the lowest hell.

Psa. 89.1. I will sing of the mercies of the Lord for ever: with my mouth will I make known thy faithfulness to all generations.

Psa. 92.1. It is a good thing to give thanks unto the Lord, and to sing praises unto thy name, O most High : 2. To shew forth thy lovingkindness in the morning, and thy faithfulness every night. 4. For thou, Lord, hast made me glad through thy work : I will triumph in the works of thy hands.

Psa. 98.1. O sing unto the Lord a new song ; for he hath done marvellous things: his right hand, and his holy arm, hath gotten him the victory. 2. The Lord hath made known his salvation : his righteousness hath he openly shewed in the sight of the heathen. 3. He hath remembered his mercy and his truth toward the house of Israel : all the ends of the earth have seen the salvation of our God.

Psa. 102.18. This shall be written for the generation to come : and the people which shall be created shall praise the Lord. 19. For he hath looked down from the height of his sanctuary ; from heaven did the Lord behold the earth ; 20. To hear the groaning of the prisoner; to loose those that are appointed to death.

Psa. 103.1. Bless the Lord, O my soul: and all that is within me, bless his holy name. 2. Bless the Lord, O my soul, and forget not all his benefits : 3. Who forgiveth all thine iniquities ; who healeth all thy diseases ; 4. Who redeemeth thy life from destruction ; who crowneth thee with lovingkindness and tender mercies.

Psa. 107.6. They cried unto the Lord in their trouble, and he delivered them out of their distresses. 7. And he led them forth by the right way, that they might go to a city of habitation. v. 1-43.

Psa. 116.6. The Lord preserveth the simple : I was brought low, and he helped me. 7. Return unto thy rest, O my soul ; for the Lord hath dealt bountifully with thee. 8. For thou hast delivered my soul from death, mine eyes from tears, and my feet from falling. 12. What shall I render unto the Lord for all his benefits toward me? 13. I will take the cup of salvation, and call upon the name of the Lord. 14. I will pay my vows unto the Lord now in the presence of all his people. 17. I will offer to thee the sacrifice of thanksgiving, and will call upon the name of the Lord.

Psa.118.5. I calledᵁupon the Lord in distress: the Lord answered me, and set me in a large place. 13. Thou hast thrust sore at me that I might fall: but the Lord helped me. 14. The Lord is my strength and song, and is become my salvation. 18. The Lord hath chastened me sore : but he hath not given me over unto death. 19. Open to me the gates of righteousness : I will go in to them, and I will praise the Lord. 21. I will praise thee : for thou hast heard me, and art become my salvation.

Psa. 119.65. Thou hast dealt well with thy servant, O Lord, according unto thy word. 108. Accept, I beseech thee, the freewill offerings of my mouth, O Lord, and teach me thy judgments.

Psa. 124.6. Blessed be the Lord, who hath not given us as a prey to their teeth. 7. Our soul is escaped as a bird out of the snare of the fowlers: the snare is broken, and we are escaped. 8. Our help is in the name of the Lord, who made heaven and earth. v. 1-5.

Psa. 126.1. When the Lord turned again the captivity of Zion, we were like them that dream. 2. Then was our mouth filled with laughter, and our tongue with singing : then said they among the heathen, The Lord hath done great things for them. 3. The Lord hath done great things for us ; whereof we are glad. Psa. 129. 1-3.

Psa. 136.23. Who remembered us in our low estate: for his mercy endureth for ever : 24. And hath redeemed us from our enemies : for his mercy endureth for ever. v. 11-24. Hab. 3.3-15.

Psa. 138.2. I will worship toward thy holy temple, and praise thy name for thy lovingkindness and for thy truth : for thou hast magnified thy word above all thy name.

Psa. 139.14. I will praise thee ; for I am fearfully and wonderfully made : marvellous are thy works ; and that my soul knoweth right well. 17. How precious also are thy thoughts unto me, O God ! how great is the sum of them ! 18. If I should count them, they are more in number than the sand : when I awake, I am still with thee.

Psa. 140.7. O God the Lord, the strength

of my salvation, thou hast covered my head in the day of battle.

Psa. 143.5. I remember the days of old; I meditate on all thy works; I muse on the work of thy hands. 10. Thou *art* my God: thy spirit *is* good.

Psa. 144.1. Blessed *be* the Lord my strength, which teacheth my hands to war, *and* my fingers to fight: 2. My goodness, and my fortress; my high tower, and my deliverer; my shield, and *he* in whom I trust; who subdueth my people under me.

Psa. 148.14. He also exalteth the horn of his people, the praise of all his saints; *even* of the children of Israel, a people near unto him. Psa. 147.19,20.

Isa. 25.1. O Lord, thou *art* my God; I will exalt thee, I will praise thy name; for thou hast done wonderful *things*; *thy* counsels of old *are* faithfulness *and* truth. 9. Lo, this *is* our God; we have waited for him, and he will save us: this *is* the Lord; we have waited for him, we will be glad and rejoice in his salvation. *v.* 4. Isa. 26.15.

Isa. 38.20. The Lord *was ready* to save me: therefore we will sing my songs to the stringed instruments all the days of our life in the house of the Lord.

Isa. 52.9. Break forth into joy, sing together, ye waste places of Jerusalem: for the Lord hath comforted his people, he hath redeemed Jerusalem. Isa. 49.13.

Isa. 63.7. I will mention the lovingkindnesses of the Lord, *and* the praises of the Lord, according to all that the Lord hath bestowed on us, and the great goodness toward the house of Israel, which he hath bestowed on them according to his mercies, and according to the multitude of his lovingkindnesses. *v.* 12-14.

Jer. 20.13. Sing unto the Lord, praise ye the Lord: for he hath delivered the soul of the poor from the hand of evildoers.

Jer. 31.11. The Lord hath redeemed Jacob, and ransomed him from the hand of *him that was* stronger than he. 12. They shall come and sing in the height of Zion, and shall flow together to the goodness of the Lord, for wheat, and for wine, and for oil, and for the young of the flock and of the herd.

Dan. 2.23. I thank thee, and praise thee, O thou God of my fathers, who hast given me wisdom and might, and hast made known unto me now what we desired of thee.

Dan. 4.2. I thought it good to shew the signs and wonders that the high God hath wrought toward me. 34. I blessed the most High, and I praised and honoured him that liveth for ever, whose dominion *is* an everlasting dominion, and his kingdom *is* from generation to generation.

Dan. 6.22. My God hath sent his angel, and hath shut the lions' mouths, that they have not hurt me.

Luk. 1.46. My soul doth magnify the Lord, 47. And my spirit hath rejoiced in God my Saviour. 48. For he hath regarded the low estate of his handmaiden. 49. For he that is mighty hath done to me great things; and holy *is* his name. 68. Blessed *be* the Lord God of Israel; for he hath visited and redeemed his people, 69. And hath raised up an horn of salvation for us in the house of his servant David.

Luk. 2.29. Lord, now lettest thou thy servant depart in peace, according to thy word: 30. For mine eyes have seen thy salvation.

Act. 2.46. They, continuing daily with one accord in the temple, and breaking bread from house to house, did eat their meat with gladness and singleness of heart, 47. Praising God.

Act. 28.15. Whom when Paul saw, he thanked God, and took courage.

2 Cor. 1.10. Who delivered us from so great a death, and doth deliver: in whom we trust that he will yet deliver *us.*

Phil. 2.27. He was sick nigh unto death: but God had mercy on him.

1 Tim. 1.12. I thank Christ Jesus our Lord, who hath enabled me, for that he counted me faithful, putting me into the ministry.

2 Tim. 3.11. What persecutions I endured: but out of *them* all the Lord delivered me.

2 Tim. 4.17. Notwithstanding the Lord stood with me, and strengthened me.

Rev. 12.10. Now is come salvation, and strength, and the kingdom of our God, and the power of his Christ: for the accuser of our brethren is cast down, which accused them before our God day and night.

See PRAISE.

THANKFULNESS TO MAN. See GRATITUDE.

THANK-OFFERING. See OFFERINGS.

THANKSGIVING. See PRAISE—PRAYER AT MEALS.

THEATRE, Act. 19.29,31.

THEBEZ, a town near Shechem; Abimelech killed in besieging it, Jud. 9.50-56. 2 Sam. 11.21.

THEFT. See DISHONESTY.

THEOPHILUS. Luke dedicates his gospel and the Acts to him, Luk. 1.3. Act. 1.1.

THESSALONICA, a city of Macedonia; Paul preaches in; his success; riot raised by the Jews, Act. 17.1-10. Phil. 4.16. Jews from, persecute him in Berea, Act. 17.11-13. Converts from, with Paul, Act. 20.4. Act. 27. 2. Demas in, 2 Tim. 4.10. See EPISTLES TO THE THESSALONIANS.

THEUDAS, a Jewish insurgent, slain with his followers, Act. 5.36.

THIEF, PENITENT, on the cross, Luk. 24. 39-43. Mat. 27.44. Mar. 15.32.

THISTLE, Gen. 3.18. Job 31.40. Translated thorns, 2 Chr. 33.11. Brambles, Isa. 34. 13. Parable of, 2 Chr. 25.18.

THOMAS, an apostle, called Didymus (the twin), Mat. 10.3. Mar. 3.18. Luk. 6.15. Act. 1.13. Proposes to go with Jesus to Bethany, Jno. 11.16. Questions Jesus, Jno. 14.5. Doubts Christ's resurrection, Jno. 20. 24,25. His confession of belief, Jno. 20.27-29. Is present at the miraculous draught of fishes, Jno. 21.2.

THORN, Job. 41.2. Pro. 26.9. Hedge of, Mic. 7.4. Illustrative, Num. 33.55. 2 Cor. 12.7. See THISTLE.

THREE TAVERNS, a place between Puteoli and Rome, where Paul was met by Roman disciples, Act. 28.15.

THRESHING, Ruth 2.17; with instruments of wood, 2 Sam. 24.22; of iron, Amos 1 3; with sharp instruments with teeth, Isa. 41.15. By treading with cattle, Deu. 25.4. Hos. 10.11. Isa. 25.10; by bruising with a cart-wheel, Isa. 28.27,28. Illustrative, Jer. 51. 33. Amos 1.3. Mic. 4.12,13.

———— FLOOR. Of Atad, Gen. 50.10,11. Gideon, Jud. 6.37-40. Boaz, Ruth 3.2-14. Nachon, 2 Sam. 6.6. Araunah, 2 Sam. 24. 16-25. Granaries in, Deu. 15.14. 1 Sam. 23.1. 2 Kin. 6.27. Hos. 9.2. Joel 2.24. See BARN.

THRONE. Of kings, Gen. 41.40. Ex. 11.5. 1 Kin. 2.19. Jonah 3.6; near the gate, 1 Kin. 22.10. Est. 5.1. Solomon's ivory throne, &c., 1 Kin. 10.18-20. 2 Chr. 9.17-19. 1 Kin. 7.7. Sitting on, signifying ruling and honour, 1 Kin. 1.13. Zec. 6.13. Rev. 20.4. Illustrative, 2 Chr. 18.18. Psa. 9.4,7. Jer. 17.12. Mat. 25.31. Rev. 3.21. Symbolical, Eze. 1. 26. Eze. 10.1. Rev. 4.2-10. Rev. 20.11.

THUMMIM. See URIM.

THUNDER, Psa. 29. Psa. 46.6. Psa. 77. 17,18. Psa. 104.7. Job 40.9. Thunderbolts, Psa. 78.48. Miraculous, Ex. 9.23-34. Ex. 19. 16. 1 Sam. 7.10. Symbolical, Rev. 4.5. Rev. 10.3. Rev. 11.19.

THYATIRA, a city of Lydia in Asia Minor; Lydia from, converted at Philippi, Act. 16. 14,15. Epistle to the lukewarm church in, Rev. 1.11. Rev. 2.18-29.

THYINE, an aromatic wood, Rev. 18.12.

TIBERIAS, CITY OF, Jno. 6.23. Sea of, See GALILEE, SEA OF.

TIBERIUS CESAR, emperor of Rome at the time of Christ's crucifixion, Luk. 3.1. Mat. 22.17,21. Luk. 23.2. Jno. 19.12,15.

TIBNI, an unsuccessful aspirant to the throne of Israel after Zimri's death, 1 Kin. 16. 21,22.

TIDAL, king of nations; his invasion of Canaan in Abraham's time, Gen. 14.1-16.

TIGLATH or TILGATH-PILESER, king of Assyria, takes the Gileadites captive, 2 Kin. 15.29. 1 Chr. 5.6,26. Bribed by Ahaz to attack Damascus; captures it, slays Rezin, 2 Kin. 16.5-9, but see 2 Chr. 28.20,21. Interview with Ahaz, 2 Kin. 16.10.

TIMBREL, or TABRET (a tambourine), used by Miriam, with dancing, Ex. 15.20,21; by Jephthah's daughter, with dancing, Jud. 11.34; by prophets, 1 Sam. 10.5; by women, with dancing, to meet Saul, &c., 1 Sam. 18.6; by David, in bringing up the ark, 2 Sam. 6.5. 1 Chr. 13.8; women playing on, Psa. 68.25. Used in dances, feasts, &c., Gen. 31.27. Job 21.12. Isa. 5.12. Isa. 24.8. Isa. 30.32; by women, Jer. 31.4; in praise, Psa. 81.2; with dancing, Psa. 149.3. Psa. 150.4. Made by Tyrians, Eze. 28.13.

TIME, computed by the heavenly bodies, Gen. 1.14; by sun-dials, 2 Kin. 20.9-11. Eras of time. Nativity of the patriarchs, Gen. 7.11. Gen. 8.13. The Exodus, from Egypt, Ex. 19.1. Ex. 40.17. 1 Kin. 6.1. The jubilee, Lev. 25.15. Accession of kings, 1 Kin. 15.1. Isa. 36.1. Jer. 1.2,3. Dan. 8.1. Luk. 3.1. Building of the temple, 1 Kin. 9.10. The captivity, Eze. 1.1. Eze. 33.21. Eze. 40.1.

Divisions of, see HOUR, DAY, NIGHT, WEEK, MONTH, YEAR, COCK-CROWING, PROPHETIC PERIODS. Time, signifying a year; times, 2 years, Dan. 7.25. Dan. 12.7. Rev. 12.14. Value of, see DEATH, PREPARATION FOR—SPIRITUAL DILIGENCE.

TIMNATH, Gen. 38.12-14. A town of Judah, Jos. 15.10. Samson's wife in, Jud. 14. Captured by Philistines, 2 Chr. 28.18.

TIMNATH-HERES, or SERAH, a city in Mount Ephraim; given to Joshua, Jos. 19.50; Joshua buried in, Jos. 24.30. Jud. 2.9.

TIMOTHY, his parentage, education, and early piety, Act. 16.1. 2 Tim. 1.5. 2 Tim. 3.15. Circumcised by Paul at Lystra; becomes his fellow-labourer, Act. 16.2,3. 1 Tim. 1.18. 1 Tim. 6.12. 1 Tim. 4.14. 2 Tim. 1.6. Act. 17.15. Act. 18.5. Act. 19.22. Act. 20.4. Rom. 16.21. 2 Cor. 1.1,19. Remains with Silas at Berea, Act. 17.14. Sent by Paul to preach at Corinth, 1 Cor. 4.17. 1 Cor. 16. 10,11; at Philippi, Phil. 2.19; at Thessalonica, 1 The. 3.2,6; at Ephesus, 1 Tim. 1.3. Imprisoned with Paul at Rome, Phil. 2.19-23 with Heb. 13.23. Paul's affection for him, Phil. 2.22. 1 Tim. 1.2. 2 Tim. 1.2-4. See the epistles to Timothy.

TIMON, one of the seven chosen at Jerusalem, Act. 6.5.

TIN, Num. 31.22. Plummet of, Zec. 4.10 (marg.).

TIPHSAH (1) a city on west bank of the Euphrates, possessed by Solomon, 1 Kin. 4.24. (2) A city in Samaria, sacked by Menahem, 2 Kin. 15.16.

TIRES, crescent-shaped ornaments, Isa. 3.18.

TIRHAKAH, king of Ethiopia, wars with Sennacherib, 2 Kin. 19.9. Isa. 37.9.

TIRSHATHA (governor), a Persic title of Zerubbabel, Ezr. 2.63. Neh. 7.65,70; of Nehemiah, Neh. 8.9. Neh. 10.1.

TIRZAH, a Canaanitish town, Jos. 12.24. Its beauty, Song 6.4. Capital of the 10 tribes, 1 Kin. 14.17. 1 Kin. 15.21,33. 1 Kin. 16. 6,9,15. Besieged by Omri, 1 Kin. 16,17. Menahem in, 2 Kin. 15.14,16.

TITHES or TENTHS. Of spoil taken in war, paid by Abraham to Melchizedek, Gen. 14.20. Heb. 7.2-6. Jacob vows a tenth of all his property to God, Gen. 28.22.

Of seed, fruit, the herd and flock holy unto the Lord, whether good or bad, Lev. 27.30-33. Called heave-offerings, Num. 18.24. To be given to the Levites, Num. 18.21-23. Neh. 10.37. Heb. 7.5-9. If commuted (converted into money), a fifth to be added, Lev. 27.31.

One-tenth of the best of the above given by the Levites to the priests, called a heave-offering, Num. 18.26-32. Neh. 10.38.

A second tenth of seed and fruit (not cattle or sheep), to be eaten before the Lord at the temple by the family, servants, and the Levites, Deu. 12.6,7,17-19. Deu. 14.22,23. Might be turned into money; and oxen, sheep, wine, or strong drink bought with it, and eaten before the Lord, Deu. 14.24-27. Every third year eaten at home, with the Levite, the stranger, the fatherless, and widow, Deu. 14.28,29. Amos 4.4. Deu. 26.12-15.

Kept in chambers of the temple, Neh. 10. 38,39. Neh. 12.44. Neh. 13.5,12. Mal. 3.10. 2 Chr. 31.11.

Paid in Hezekiah's reign, 2 Chr. 31.5-10. Under Nehemiah, Neh. 13.12. By a Pharisee, Luk. 18.12. Of mint, &c., Mat. 23. 23. Luk. 11.42. Withheld, Neh. 13.10. Mal. 3.8.

Idolatrous tithes and gifts, 2 Kin. 23.11. Dan. 11.38. Amos 4.4,5.

TITUS, a Greek convert, Gal. 2.3. Sent by the church of Antioch to Jerusalem with Paul and Barnabas, Gal. 2.1-3 with Act. 15. 1,2. Companion and fellow-labourer of Paul; Paul's love for him, 2 Cor. 2.13. 2 Cor. 7. 6,7,13-15. 2 Cor. 8.23. Tit. 1.4. Sent by Paul to Corinth, 2 Cor. 8.6,16-23. 2 Cor. 12. 18. Left by Paul in Crete, Tit. 1.5. Directed to join him at Nicopolis, Tit. 3.12. Is with him at Rome, and departs to Dalmatia, 2 Tim. 4.10. His disinterestedness, 2 Cor. 12.18.

TOB, Jephthah's retreat east of Jordan, Jud. 11.3-5.

TOBIAH, an Ammonite and Samaritan; one of the Jews' enemies who opposed the building of Jerusalem, Neh. 2.10,19. Neh. 4. 7. Neh. 6. Marries the high-priest's daughter in the absence of Nehemiah, who afterwards expels him from the temple, Neh. 13.4-9.

TOBIJAH, comes with gifts to Jerusalem, Zec. 6.9-11.

TOGARMAH (Armenia), peopled by Gomer's son, Togarmah, Gen. 10.3. 1 Chr. 1.6. Trade with Tyre, Eze. 27.14. Eze. 38.6. See ARMENIA.

TOI, king of Hamath, in friendship with David, 2 Sam. 8.9,10. Called Tau, 1 Chr. 18.9.

TOLA, a Judge, Jud. 10.1,2.

TOLL. See TRIBUTE.

TOMBS. See BURIAL-PLACES.

TONGS. For the tabernacle, Ex. 25.38. Num. 4.9; for the temple. 1 Kin. 7.49.

TONGUE, Jud. 7.5. Illustrative, Isa. 45. 23. 1 Jno. 3.18. A particular language, Gen. 10.5,20,21. People speaking a particular language, Isa. 66.18. Rev. 7.9, see LANGUAGE. Confusion of tongues, Gen. 11.1-10.

Gift of tongues at Pentecost, Act. 2.1-18,33. Given to Cornelius, &c., Act. 10.46; disciples at Ephesus, Act. 19.6; Paul, 1 Cor. 14.18. Corinthians, 1 Cor. 12.10,28,30. 1 Cor. 14. Interpretation of tongues, 1 Cor. 14.

TOOLS. See IMPLEMENTS.

TOPAZ, a precious stone, Eze. 28.13. Rev. 21.20. In the high-priest's breastplate, Ex. 28.17. Ex. 39.10. Of Ethiopia, Job. 28.19.

TOPHET, HIGH-PLACES OF, in the valley of the son of Hinnom, or Jehoshaphat, where children were passed through the fire to Molech by the Jews, Jer. 7.31,32. Jer. 19.6,11-13. Jer. 32.35; by Ahaz, 2 Chr. 28.3; Manasseh, 2 Chr. 33.6. Defiled by Josiah, 2 Kin. 23.10. The place of punishment, Isa. 30.33.

TORCH. See LAMP.

TORTOISE, Lev. 11.29.

TOW, Jud. 16.9. Isa. 1.31. See FLAX.

TOWEL, Jno. 13.4,5.

TOWERS. See FORTRESS, BABEL, EDAR, SHECHEM, HANANEEL, MEAH, MILLO, OPHEL, SILOAM.

TOWNS. See CITIES—VILLAGES.

TOWN-CLERK. See SCRIBES.

TRACHONITIS, a province south of Anti-libanus, Philip tetrarch of, Luk. 3.1.

TRADE. See ARTS—COMMERCE.

TRADITIONS. Inspired teachings, 1 Cor. 11.2 (marg.), 2 The. 2.15. 2 The. 3.6. Human ordinances, Mat. 15.2-6. Mar. 7.3-9. Col. 2. 8. 1 Pet. 1.18. See WORD OF GOD, THE ONLY RULE.

TRANCE. Of Balaam, Num. 24.4,16 ; of Peter, Act. 10.10 ; of Paul, Act. 22.17.

TRANSFIGURATION. Of Christ, Mat. 17.2. Mar. 9.2. Luk. 9.29. Translated, transformed, Rom. 12.2. Changed, 2 Cor. 3.18.

TRAP, Jos. 23.13. Job 18.10. Jer. 5.26.

TRAVELLING, mode of, see CAMEL, ASS, MULE, HORSE, CART, CHARIOT, LITTER, SHIP. Travellers carried food and water, Gen. 21.14. Jud. 19.19. 1 Sam. 9.7. Lodged in private houses, Gen. 18.2-8. Gen. 24.32-34. Jud. 19.12-21. Job 31.32, see INN. Rested at noon, Gen. 18.1-5. Jno. 4.6. By wells, Gen. 24.11. Ex. 15.27. Jno. 4.6. See TENT. Of rank, had running footmen, 2 Sam. 15.1. 1 Kin. 18.46. See HOSPITALITY.

TREACHERY. See HYPOCRISY AND TREACHERY.

TREASON. See SUBJECTS, TREASON OF.

TREASURIES. Of the tabernacle and temple, 1 Chr. 28.11,12. For dedicated things and offerings, Num. 31.54. Jos. 6.19,24. 1 Kin. 7.51. 2 Kin. 12.18. For money, 2 Kin. 12.4-14. 2 Kin. 22.4,5. Mat. 27.6. Mar. 12. 41,43. Luk. 21.1. Jno. 8.20. Chambers for tithes, meat-offerings, and first-fruits, Neh. 10.38,39. Neh. 13.5,9,12. Mal. 3.10. Under the care of priests and Levites, 1 Chr. 9.26. 1 Chr. 26.20-28. Neh. 12.44. Neh. 13.13.

—— or STOREHOUSES. Of kings, 2 Kin. 20.13. 1 Chr. 27.25,27,28. 2 Chr. 32. 27,28. Est. 3.9. Records kept in, Ezr. 5. 17. Ezr. 6.1. Under the charge of treasurers, Ezr. 1.8. Ezr. 7.20,21. Of idol temples, Dan. 1.2.

TREASURE CITIES. Royal, Ex. 1.11. 1 Kin. 9.19. 2 Chr. 8.4,6. 2 Chr. 17.12.

TREES. See PLANTS.

TRESPASS-OFFERING. See OFFERINGS.

TRIALS. See AFFLICTION — TEMPTA-TION.

TRIBES. See ISRAEL, TRIBES OF.

TRIBUTE. From conquered nations, Jos. 16.10. Jud. 1.30-33. 2 Kin. 15.19. By sub-jects, 1 Sam. 8.10-17. 2 Kin. 23.35. Paid to the Romans, Mat 17.24-27. Mat. 22.15-22. Luk. 2.1-5.

Paid in money, Mat 22.19,20 ; gold and silver, 2 Chr. 36.3 ; horses, sheep, spices, &c., 2 Kin. 3.4. 2 Chr. 27.5 ; labour, 1 Kin. 5. 13,14. 1 Kin. 9.21.

Collected by officers, 2 Sam. 20.24. 1 Kin. 4.6,7; by publicans, under the Romans, Luk. 2.3. Luk. 3.12,13. Luk. 5.27.

Not to be oppressive, Deu. 17.17. Priests and Levites exempted from, Ezr. 7.24. Duty of paying, Rom. 13.6,7. See PUBLICAN.

TRINITY. See GOD THE FATHER, SON, AND HOLY SPIRIT.

TROAS, a city in Asia Minor, south from Troy; Paul's vision in, Act. 16.8-11. 2 Cor. 2.12. He restores Eutychus, Act. 20.5-12. 2 Tim. 4.13.

TROGYLLIUM, a town on the coast of Asia Minor, visited by Paul, Act. 20.15.

TROPHIMUS, an Ephesian Christian, and companion of Paul, Act. 20.4. Act. 21.29. 2 Tim. 4.13.

TRUMPET, CORNET, HORN. Used in war, Job 39.24,25. Jer. 4.19. Jer. 6.1,17. Jer. 42.14. Jer. 51.27. Eze. 7.14. Amos 2.2. Amos 3.6. Zeph. 1.16. 1 Cor. 14.8. To summon soldiers, by Ehud, Jud. 3.27; by Gideon, Jud. 6.34; Saul, 1 Sam. 13.3; Joab, 2 Sam. 2.28. 2 Sam. 18.16. 2 Sam. 20.22; Absalom, 2 Sam. 15.10; Sheba, 2 Sam. 20.1; Nehemiah, Neh. 4.18,20. By Gideon's soldiers, Jud. 7.8-22.

Sounded at the fall of the walls of Jericho, Jos. 6.4-20. Sounded at the proclamation of Solomon, 1 Kin. 1.34,39; of Jehu, 2 Kin. 9.13; Joash, 2 Kin. 11.14.

Used by David, &c., in bringing up the ark, 2 Sam. 6.5,15. 1 Chr. 13.8. 1 Chr. 15.28. At the covenant under Asa, 2 Chr. 15.14.

Levites appointed by David to use, at the tabernacle, 1 Chr. 16.42. 1 Chr. 25.5. Sounded at Jehoshaphat's triumph, 2 Chr. 20.28.

Employed by priests (silver trumpets?); seven priests appointed by David to blow before the ark, 1 Chr. 15.24; two others, 1 Chr. 16.6; 120 with singing at the dedication of the temple, 2 Chr. 5.12.13. 2 Chr. 7.6; in Abijah's war, 2 Chr. 13.12,14. On the Day of Atonement, 2 Chr. 29.26-28. At the foundation of the 2d temple, Ezr. 3.10,11. At the dedication of the wall, Neh. 12.35,41.

Blown at the Jubilee on the Day of Atonement, Lev. 25.9. Used in praise, Psa. 47.5. Psa. 98.6. Psa. 150.3; in idolatrous worship, Dan. 3.7,10,15; in rejoicings, Rev. 18.22. Sound of, at Sinai, Ex. 19.13-19. Ex. 20.18. Heb. 12.19.

Illustrative, Isa. 27.13. Eze. 33.3. Joel 2.1. Zec. 9.14. Mat. 6.2. Symbolical, Mat. 24.31. 1 Cor. 15.52. 1 The. 4.16. Rev. 1.10. Rev. 4.1. Rev. 8. Rev. 9.1-14. Rev. 10.7. Rev. 11.15.

TRUMPET, SILVER. Two used by priests for calling assemblies; in the march of the Israelites; in war; on feast-days, and over the sacrifices, Num. 10.1-10. Psa. 81.3,4. Phinehas used, in the war with Midian, Num. 31.6. See ABOVE.

TRUMPETS, FEAST OF. See FEASTS.

TRUST. See FAITH. Trust in man, see FALSE CONFIDENCE.

TRUTHFULNESS. See INTEGRITY.

TRYPHENA AND TRYPHOSA, female disciples in Rome, Rom. 16.12.

TUBAL, a people descended from Japheth's son, Gen. 10.2. 1 Chr. 1.5. Trade of, Eze. 27.13. Prophecies of, Isa. 66.19. Eze. 32.26. Eze. 38.2. Eze. 39.1.

TUBAL-CAIN, inventor of the art of forging metals, Gen. 4.22.

TURTLE-DOVE. See DOVE.

TUTOR, Gal. 4.2.

TYCHICUS, a native of Asia; an assistant and companion of Paul, Act. 20.4. Tit. 3.12. Sent by Paul to Colosse, Col. 4.7,8; and from Rome to Ephesus, Eph. 6.21,22. 2 Tim. 4.12.

TYPES. See SYMBOLS—VISIONS—OFFERINGS.

TYRANNUS, an Ephesian in whose school Paul preached, Act. 19.9.

TYRANNY. See RULERS' TYRANNY.

TYRE, a city of Phenicia, called the daughter of Zidon, Isa. 23.12. Its antiquity and splendour, Isa. 23.7,8. Zec. 9.3. Commerce, 1 Kin. 9.26-28. 1 Kin. 10.11. Isa. 23. Eze. 27. Eze. 28. Zec. 9.2. Pleasant site, Hos. 9.13. Strength, Jos. 19.29. 2 Sam. 24.7. North boundary of Asher, Jos. 19.29; in David's reign, 2 Sam. 24.7. King of, his friendship with Israel, see HIRAM. Enmity to Israel, Psa. 83.7. Joel 3.4-6. Nebuchadnezzar's siege of, Eze. 29.18. Eze. 26.7.

Jesus preaches near; miracle in, Mat. 15.21-28. Mar. 7.24-31. People from, come to hear him, Mar. 3.8. Luk. 6.17. Paul visits disciples in, Act. 21.3,4. Tyrians displease Herod; their flattery; his death, Act. 12.20-23.

Prophecies of, Psa. 45.12. Psa. 87.4. Isa. 23. Jer. 25.22. Jer. 27.1-11. Jer. 47.4. Eze. c. 26 to 28. Joel 3.4-8. Amos 1.9,10. Zec. 9.2-4.

U

ULAI (modern Kerah or Karasu), a river of Chaldea, flowing by Shushan (Susa), Daniel's vision by, Dan. 8.2.

UNBELIEF AND PRESUMPTION. Deu. 18.19. Whosoever will not hearken unto my words which he shall speak in my name, I will require it of him.

Deu. 32.20. I will hide my face from them, I will see what their end *shall be*: for they are a very froward generation, children in whom *is* no faith.

Job 7.20. I have sinned; what shall I do unto thee, O thou preserver of men? why hast thou set me as a mark against thee, so that I am a burden to myself? 21. And why dost thou not pardon my transgression, and take away mine iniquity?

Job 31.35. Oh that one would hear me! behold, my desire *is, that* the Almighty would answer me. Job 9.34,35.

Job 33.10. Behold, he findeth occasions against me, he counteth me for his enemy, 11. He putteth my feet in the stocks, he marketh all my paths. v. 12,13.

Job 38.2. Who *is* this that darkeneth counsel by words without knowledge? 3. Gird up now thy loins like a man; for I will demand of thee, and answer thou me. v. 1-41. Job 42.3.

Job 40.2. Shall he that contendeth with the Almighty instruct *him?* he that reproveth God, let him answer it. v. 1-24.

Psa. 78.32. For all this they sinned still,

and believed not for his wondrous works. 41. Yea, they turned back and tempted God, and limited the Holy One of Israel.

Psa. 95.9. Your fathers tempted me, proved me, and saw my work. 10. Forty years long was I grieved with *this* generation, and said, It *is* a people that do err in their heart, and they have not known my ways : 11. Unto whom I swear in my wrath that they should not enter into my rest. Psa. 106.7,24.

Isa. 7.9. If ye will not believe, surely ye shall not be established. 12. Ahaz said, I will not ask, neither will I tempt the Lord. 13. And he said, Hear ye now, O house of David ; *Is it* a small thing for you to weary men, but will ye weary my God also ?

Isa. 8.15. Many among them shall stumble, and fall, and be broken, and be snared, and be taken.

Isa. 28.12. He said, This *is* the rest *wherewith* ye may cause the weary to rest ; and this *is* the refreshing : yet they would not hear.

Isa. 53.1. Who hath believed our report ? and to whom is the arm of the Lord revealed ? 2. When we shall see him, *there is* no beauty that we should desire him. 3. He is despised and rejected of men ; a man of sorrows, and acquainted with grief : and we hid as it were *our* faces from him ; he was despised, and we esteemed him not.

Jer. 7.27. Thou shalt speak all these words unto them ; but they will not hearken to thee : thou shalt also call unto them ; but they will not answer thee.

Jer. 8.9. Lo, they have rejected the word of the Lord ; and what wisdom *is* in them ?

Hos. 8.12. I have written to him the great things of my law, *but* they were counted as a strange thing.

Zec. 8.6. If it be marvellous in the eyes of the remnant of this people in these days, should it also be marvellous in mine eyes ? saith the Lord of hosts.

Mal. 1.2. I have loved you, saith the Lord : Yet ye say, Wherein hast thou loved us ?

Mat. 7.26. Every one that heareth these sayings of mine, and doeth them not, shall be likened unto a foolish man, which built his house upon the sand : 27. And the rain descended, and the floods came, and the winds blew, and beat upon that house ; and it fell : and great was the fall of it. Luk. 6.46-49.

Mat. 8.12. The children of the kingdom shall be cast out into outer darkness : there shall be weeping and gnashing of teeth.

Mat. 10.14. Whosoever shall not receive you, nor hear your words, when ye depart out of that house or city, shake off the dust of your feet. 15. Verily I say unto you, It shall be more tolerable for the land of Sodom and Gomorrha in the day of judgment, than for that city.

Mat. 11.16. Whereunto shall I liken this generation ? It is like unto children sitting in the markets, and calling unto their fellows, 17. And saying, We have piped unto you, and ye have not danced ; we have mourned unto you, and ye have not lamented. 18. For John came neither eating nor drinking, and they say, He hath a devil. 19. The Son of man came eating and drinking, and they say, Behold a man gluttonous, and a winebibber, a friend of publicans and sinners. Luk. 7.31-35.

Mat. 13.13. Therefore speak I to them in parables : because they seeing, see not ; and hearing, they hear not ; neither do they understand. 58. He did not many mighty works there because of their unbelief. *v.* 3-14. Isa. 6.9,10.

Mat. 17.17. O faithless and perverse generation, how long shall I be with you ? how long shall I suffer you ?

Mat. 21.32. John came unto you in the way of righteousness, and ye believed him not ; but the publicans and the harlots believed him : and ye, when ye had seen *it*, repented not afterward, that ye might believe him. 44. Whosoever shall fall on this stone shall be broken : but on whomsoever it shall fall, it will grind him to powder.

Mat. 22.5. They made light of *it*, and went their ways, one to his farm, another to his merchandise. *v.* 1-14. Luk. 14.16-24.

Mar. 6.6. He marvelled because of their unbelief. *v.* 7.

Mar. 16.16. He that believeth not shall be damned.

Luk. 8.12. Those by the way-side are they that hear ; then cometh the devil, and taketh away the word out of their hearts, lest they should believe and be saved. 18. Take heed therefore how ye hear : for whosoever hath, to him shall be given, and whosoever hath not, from him shall be taken even that which he seemeth to have. Mar. 4.24,25.

Luk. 10.16. He that heareth you heareth me ; and he that despiseth you despiseth me ; and he that despiseth me despiseth him that sent me.

Luk. 12.46. The Lord of that servant will come in a day when he looketh not for *him*, and at an hour when he is not aware, and will cut him in sunder, and will appoint him his portion with the unbelievers.

Luk. 13.34. O Jerusalem, Jerusalem, which killest the prophets, and stonest them that are sent unto thee ; how often would I have gathered thy children together, as a hen *doth gather* her brood under *her* wings, and ye would not !

Luk. 16.31. If they hear not Moses and the prophets, neither will they be persuaded, though one rose from the dead.

Luk. 18.8. When the Son of man cometh, shall he find faith on the earth ?

Luk. 19.42. If thou hadst known, even thou, at least in this thy day, the things *which belong* unto thy peace ! but now they are hid from thine eyes.

Luk. 22.67. Art thou the Christ ? tell us. And he said unto them, If I tell you, ye will not believe.

Luk. 24.25. O fools, and slow of heart to believe all that the prophets have spoken. *v.* 11,15-25,37-39.

Jno. 1.11. He came unto his own, and his own received him not.

Jno. 3.11. We speak that we do know, and testify that we have seen ; and ye receive not our witness. 12. If I have told you earthly things, and ye believe not, how shall ye believe if I tell you *of* heavenly things ? 18. He that believeth not is condemned already, because he hath not believed in the name of the only-begotten Son of God. 19. And this is the condemnation, that light is come into the world, and men loved darkness rather than light, because their deeds were evil. 32. What he hath seen and heard, that he testifieth ; and no man receiveth his testimony. 36. He that believeth not the Son shall not see life ; but the wrath of God abideth on him.

Jno. 4.48. Except ye see signs and wonders, ye will not believe.

Jno. 5.38. Ye have not his word abiding in you : for whom he hath sent, him ye believe not. 40. Ye will not come to me, that ye might have life. 43. I am come in my Father's name, and ye receive me not : if another shall come in his own name, him ye will receive.

Jno. 5.44. How can ye believe, which receive honour one of another, and seek not the honour that *cometh* from God only ? 46. Had ye believed Moses, ye would have believed me : for he wrote of me. 47. If ye believe not his writings, how shall ye believe my words ?

Jno. 6.36. Ye also have seen me, and believe not. 64. There are some of you that believe not. For Jesus knew from the beginning who they were that believed not.

Jno. 8.24. If ye believe not that I am *he*, ye shall die in your sins. 45. Because I tell *you* the truth, ye believe me not. 46. If I say the truth, why do ye not believe me ? 47. He that is of God heareth God's words : ye therefore hear *them* not, because ye are not of God. *v.* 21.

Jno. 10.25. I told you, and ye believed not : the works that I do in my Father's name, they bear witness of me. 26. Ye believe not, because ye are not of my sheep.

Jno. 12.37. Though he had done so many miracles before them, yet they believed not on him. 47. If any man hear my words, and believe not, I judge him not : for I came not to judge the world, but to save the world. 48. He that rejecteth me, and receiveth not my words, hath one that judgeth him : the word that I have spoken, the same shall judge him in the last day.

Jno. 14.17. The Spirit of truth ; whom the world cannot receive, because it seeth him not, neither knoweth him.

Jno. 15.20. If they have kept my saying, they will keep yours also. 21. All these things will they do unto you for my name's sake, because they know not him that sent me. 23. He that hateth me hateth my Father also.

Jno. 16.3. And these things will they do unto you, because they have not known the Father, nor me. 8. He will reprove the world 9. Of sin, because they believe not on me. *v.* 2.

Jno. 20.27. Be not faithless, but believing.

Act. 13.40. Beware therefore, lest that come upon you, which is spoken of in the prophets ; 41. Behold, ye despisers, and wonder, and perish : for I work a work in your days, a work which ye shall in no wise believe, though a man declare it unto you. 46. Seeing ye put it from you, and judge yourselves unworthy of everlasting life, lo, we turn to the Gentiles. Hab. 1.5.

Act. 18.6. When they opposed themselves, and blasphemed, he shook *his* raiment, and said unto them, Your blood *be* upon your own heads ; I *am* clean : from henceforth I will go unto the Gentiles.

Act. 19.9. When divers were hardened,

and believed not, but spake evil of that way before the multitude, he departed from them, and separated the disciples.

Act. 22.18. They will not receive thy testimony concerning me.

Rom. 1.18. The wrath of God is revealed from heaven against all ungodliness and unrighteousness of men, who hold the truth in unrighteousness.

Rom. 9.31. Israel, which followed after the law of righteousness, hath not attained to the law of righteousness. 32. Wherefore ? Because *they* sought *it* not by faith, but as it were by the works of the law.

Rom. 10.14. How then shall they call on him in whom they have not believed ? and how shall they believe in him of whom they have not heard ? 16. They have not all obeyed the gospel. For Esaias saith, Lord, who hath believed our report ? 21. But to Israel he saith, All day long I have stretched forth my hands unto a disobedient and gainsaying people.

Rom. 11.7. What then ? Israel hath not obtained that which he seeketh for ; but the election hath obtained it, and the rest were blinded. 20. Because of unbelief they were broken off. 30. As ye in times past have not believed God, yet have now obtained mercy through their unbelief ; 31. Even so have these also now not believed, that through your mercy they also may obtain mercy. 32. For God hath concluded them all in unbelief, that he might have mercy upon all.

Rom. 14.23. He that doubteth is damned if he eat, because he *eateth* not of faith : for whatsoever *is* not of faith is sin.

1 Cor. 1.18. The preaching of the cross is to them that perish foolishness. 22. The Jews require a sign, and the Greeks seek after wisdom : 23. But we preach Christ crucified, unto the Jews a stumblingblock, and unto the Greeks foolishness.

1 Cor. 10.9. Neither let us tempt Christ, as some of them also tempted, and were destroyed of serpents.

2 Cor. 2.16. To the one *we are* the savour of death unto death.

2 Cor. 4.3. If our gospel be hid, it is hid to them that are lost : 4. In whom the god of this world hath blinded the minds of them which believe not, lest the light of the glorious gospel of Christ, who is the image of God, should shine unto them.

Phil. 3.18. Many walk, of whom I have told you often, and now tell you even weeping, *that they are* the enemies of the cross of Christ : 19. Whose end *is* destruction.

2 The. 1.8. Taking vengeance on them that know not God, and that obey not the gospel of our Lord Jesus Christ : 9. Who shall be punished with everlasting destruction from the presence of the Lord, and from the glory of his power.

2 The. 2.10. With all deceivableness of unrighteousness in them that perish ; because they received not the love of the truth, that they might be saved. 11. And for this cause God shall send them strong delusion, that they should believe a lie : 12. That they all might be damned who believe not the truth, but had pleasure in unrighteousness.

2 The. 3.2. All *men* have not faith.

1 Tim. 1.13. Who was before a blasphemer,

and a persecutor, and injurious : but I obtained mercy, because I did it ignorantly in unbelief.

2 Tim. 2.12. If we deny him, he also will deny us : 13. If we believe not, yet he abideth faithful : he cannot deny himself.

Tit. 1.15. Unto them that are defiled and unbelieving is nothing pure ; but even their mind and conscience is defiled.

Heb. 2.3. How shall we escape, if we neglect so great salvation.

Heb. 3.12. Take heed, brethren, lest there be in any of you an evil heart of unbelief, in departing from the living God. 16. Some, when they had heard, did provoke : howbeit not all that came out of Egypt by Moses. 17. But with whom was he grieved forty years? was it not with them that had sinned, whose carcases fell in the wilderness? 18. And to whom sware he that they should not enter into his rest, but to them that believed not? 19. So we see that they could not enter in because of unbelief.

Heb. 4.1. Let us therefore fear, lest, a promise being left us of entering into his rest, any of you should seem to come short of it. 2. For unto us was the gospel preached, as well as unto them : but the word preached did not profit them, not being mixed with faith in them that heard it. 6. They to whom it was first preached entered not in because of unbelief : 11. Let us labour therefore to enter into that rest, lest any man fall after the same example of unbelief.

Heb. 11.31. By faith the harlot Rahab perished not with them that believed not.

Heb. 12.25. See that ye refuse not him that speaketh. For if they escaped not who refused him that spake on earth, much more shall not we escape, if we turn away from him that speaketh from heaven.

Jas. 1.6. But let him ask in faith, nothing wavering : for he that wavereth is like a wave of the sea driven with the wind and tossed. 7. For let not that man think that he shall receive any thing of the Lord.

1 Pet. 2.4. A living stone, disallowed indeed of men. 7. Unto them which be disobedient, the stone which the builders disallowed, the same is made the head of the corner, 8. And a stone of stumbling, and a rock of offence, even to them which stumble at the word, being disobedient : whereunto also they were appointed.

1 Pet. 4.17. What shall the end be of them that obey not the gospel of God ?

1 Jno. 2.22. Who is a liar but he that denieth that Jesus is the Christ? He is antichrist, that denieth the Father and the Son. 23. Whosoever denieth the Son, the same hath not the Father.

1 Jno. 4.3. Every spirit that confesseth not that Jesus Christ is come in the flesh is not of God : and this is that spirit of antichrist, whereof ye have heard that it should come ; and even now already is it in the world.

1 Jno. 5.10. He that believeth not God hath made him a liar ; because he believeth not the record that God gave of his Son. 12. He that hath not the Son of God hath not life.

Jude 5. The Lord, having saved the people out of the land of Egypt, afterward destroyed them that believed not.

Rev. 21.8. But the fearful, and unbelieving, shall have their part in the lake which burneth with fire and brimstone : which is the second death.

See INFIDELITY—MIRACLES, UNBELIEF IN —WORD OF GOD, UNBELIEF IN—CHRIST, JEWS' RECEPTION OF—SPIRITUAL BLINDNESS —IMPENITENCE—DOUBT.

UNBELIEF AND PRESUMPTION, EXAMPLES OF : Lot's children, Gen. 19.14. Egyptians, Ex. 9.21,25. Moses. Ex. 5.22,23. Num. 20. 12. Israelites, Ex. 16.3,6. Num. 14.3,11,12. Deu. 6.16. Deu. 9.23. Spies, Num. 13.31. Num. 14.36,37. David, 2 Sam. 6.8. Sons of the prophets, 2 Kin. 2.16-18. Naaman, 2 Kin. 5.12. A lord, 2 Kin. 7.2,17. Job's friends, Job 42.7,8. Gadarenes, Mat. 8.34. Priests, Mat. 21.15. Disciples, Mat. 28.17. Mar. 6. 52. Mar. 16.11,13,14. Thomas, Jno. 20.25. Zacharias, Luk. 1.18-20. Pharisees, Luk. 7. 30. Christ's kinsmen, Mar. 3.21. Jno. 7.3-5. Jews, Luk. 11.29. Jno. 6.41,42,66. Jno. 9.29. Jno. 11.46. Act. 3.13,14. Act. 4.2. Act. 14. 2. Act. 28.24-28. Rom. 15.31.

UNCHARITABLENESS. Mat. 7.1. Judge not, that ye be not judged. 2. For with what judgment ye judge, ye shall be judged : and with what measure ye mete, it shall be measured to you again. 3. And why beholdest thou the mote that is in thy brother's eye, but considerest not the beam that is in thine own eye? 4. Or how wilt thou say to thy brother, Let me pull out the mote out of thine eye; and, behold, a beam is in thine own eye? 5. Thou hypocrite, first cast out the beam out of thine own eye ; and then shalt thou see clearly to cast out the mote out of thy brother's eye. Luk. 6.37-42.

Jno. 7.24. Judge not according to the appearance, but judge righteous judgment.

Rom. 2.1. Thou art inexcusable, O man, whosoever thou art that judgest : for wherein thou judgest another, thou condemnest thyself ; for thou that judgest doest the same things.

Rom. 14.2. One believeth that he may eat all things : another, who is weak, eateth herbs. 3. Let not him that eateth despise him that eateth not ; and let not him which eateth not judge him that eateth : for God hath received him. 4. Who art thou that judgest another man's servant? to his own master he standeth or falleth. Yea, he shall be holden up : for God is able to make him stand. 10. Why dost thou judge thy brother? or why dost thou set at nought thy brother? for we shall all stand before the judgment-seat of Christ. 13. Let us not therefore judge one another any more : but judge this rather, that no man put a stumblingblock or an occasion to fall in his brother's way.

1 Cor. 4.5. Judge nothing before the time, until the Lord come, who both will bring to light the hidden things of darkness, and will make manifest the counsels of the hearts ; and then shall every man have praise of God.

1 Cor. 13.5. Charity doth not behave itself unseemly, seeketh not her own, is not easily provoked, thinketh no evil ; 6. Rejoiceth not in iniquity, but rejoiceth in the truth.

Jas. 4.11. Speak not evil one of another, brethren. He that speaketh evil of his brother, and judgeth his brother, speaketh evil of the law, and judgeth the law : but if thou judge the law, thou art not a doer of the law, but a judge. 12. There is one lawgiver, who is able to save and to destroy: who art thou that judgest another?

UNCHARITABLENESS, EXAMPLES OF: Eliab, 1 Sam. 17.28. The princes of Ammon, 2 Sam. 10.3. Bildad, Job 8. Eliphaz, Job 15. Job 22. Job 42.7,8. Zophar, Job 11.1-4. Job 20. Nathanael, Jno. 1.46. The Jews, Act. 21.28.

See SPEAKING EVIL—LOVE.

UNCIRCUMCISION, a name for the Gentiles, Eph. 2.11.

UNCLEANNESS. See DEFILEMENT — PURIFICATION—UNCLEAN ANIMALS, Lev. 11. Deu. 14.

UNCTION (anointing), illustrative, 1 Jno. 2.20,27.

UNDERSTANDING, SPIRITUAL. See WISDOM.

UNFRUITFULNESS. Pro. 24.11. If thou forbear to deliver *them that are* drawn unto death, and *those that are* ready to be slain; 12. If thou sayest, Behold, we knew it not; doth not he that pondereth the heart consider *it?* and he that keepeth thy soul, doth *not* he know *it?* and shall *not* he render to *every* man according to his works?

Hos. 10.1. Israel is an empty vine, he bringeth forth fruit unto himself.

Mat. 3.10. Now also the axe is laid unto the root of the trees: therefore every tree which bringeth not forth good fruit is hewn down, and cast into the fire. Luk. 3.10.

Mat. 13.12. Whosoever hath, to him shall be given, and he shall have more abundance: but whosoever hath not, from him shall be taken away even that he hath. *v.* 13.

Mat. 21.43. The kingdom of God shall be taken from you, and given to a nation bringing forth the fruits thereof. *v.* 33-43. See parable of the vineyard, Isa. 5.5-7; of the talents, Mat. 25.14-30; the wicked husbandmen, Mar. 12.1-12; the barren fig-tree, Luk. 13.6-9; the pound, Luk. 19.20-27.

Mat. 25.30. Cast ye the unprofitable servant into outer darkness: there shall be weeping and gnashing of teeth. 42. I was an hungred, and ye gave me no meat: I was thirsty, and ye gave me no drink: 43. I was a stranger, and ye took me not in: naked, and ye clothed me not: sick, and in prison, and ye visited me not. 45. Inasmuch as ye did *it* not to one of the least of these, ye did *it* not to me.

Jno. 15.2. Every branch in me that beareth not fruit he taketh away.

2 Pet. 1.9. But he that lacketh these things is blind, and cannot see afar off, and hath forgotten that he was purged from his old sins.

See LUKEWARMNESS—JUDGMENT, ACCORDING TO PRIVILEGE—HYPOCRISY.

UNGODLINESS. See GODLESSNESS.

UNICORN, Job 39.9-12. Psa. 29.6. Psa. 92.10. Isa. 34.7. Illustrative, Num. 24.8. Deu. 33.17. Psa. 22.21.

UNION TO CHRIST. Mat. 25.40. Verily I say unto you, Inasmuch as ye have done *it* unto one of the least of these my brethren, ye have done *it* unto me.

Jno. 6.53. Except ye eat the flesh of the Son of man, and drink his blood, ye have no life in you. 56. He that eateth my flesh, and drinketh my blood, dwelleth in me, and I in him. *v.* 51-57.

Jno. 14.20. At that day ye shall know that I *am* in my Father, and ye in me, and I in you.

Jno. 15.4. Abide in me, and I in you. As the branch cannot bear fruit of itself, except it abide in the vine; no more can ye, except ye abide in me. 5. I am the vine, ye *are* the branches: He that abideth in me, and I in him, the same bringeth forth much fruit: for without me ye can do nothing. 7. If ye abide in me, and my words abide in you, ye shall ask what ye will, and it shall be done unto you. *v.* 1-8.

Jno. 17.21. That they all may be one; as thou, Father, *art* in me, and I in thee, that they also may be one in us: that the world may believe that thou hast sent me. 22. And the glory which thou gavest me I have given them; that they may be one, even as we are one: 23. I in them, and thou in me, that they may be made perfect in one. 26. I have declared unto them thy name, and will declare *it:* that the love wherewith thou hast loved me may be in them, and I in them.

Act. 9.4. Saul, Saul, why persecutest thou me?

Rom. 6.3. So many of us as were baptized into Jesus Christ were baptized into his death? 4. Therefore we are buried with him by baptism into death; that like as Christ was raised up from the dead by the glory of the Father, even so we also should walk in newness of life. 5. For if we have been planted together in the likeness of his death, we shall be also *in the likeness of his* resurrection: 6. Knowing this, that our old man is crucified with *him,* that the body of sin might be destroyed, that henceforth we should not serve sin. 8. Now, if we be dead with Christ, we believe that we shall also live with him. 11. Likewise reckon ye also yourselves to be dead indeed unto sin, but alive unto God through Jesus Christ our Lord.

Rom. 7.4. My brethren, ye also are become dead to the law by the body of Christ; that ye should be married to another, *even* to him who is raised from the dead, that we should bring forth fruit unto God. Psa. 45.9-16. Song *c.* 1 to 8.

Rom. 8.1. *There is* therefore now no condemnation to them which are in Christ Jesus. 10. If Christ *be* in you, the body *is* dead because of sin; but the Spirit *is* life because of righteousness. 17. If children, then heirs; heirs of God, and joint-heirs with Christ; if so be that we suffer with *him,* that we may be also glorified together.

Rom. 11.17. Thou, being a wild olive tree, wert graffed in among them, and with them partakest of the root and fatness of the olive tree.

Rom. 12.5. We, *being* many, are one body in Christ, and every one members one of another.

1 Cor. 1.30. Of him are ye in Christ Jesus, who of God is made unto us wisdom, and righteousness, and sanctification, and redemption.

1 Cor. 3.23. Ye are Christ's.

1 Cor. 6.13. Now the body *is* not for fornication, but for the Lord; and the Lord for

the body. 14. And God hath both raised up the Lord, and will also raise up us by his own power. 15. Know ye not that your bodies are the members of Christ? 17. He that is joined unto the Lord is one spirit.

1 Cor. 10.16. The cup of blessing which we bless, is it not the communion of the blood of Christ? The bread which we break, is it not the communion of the body of Christ?

1 Cor. 12.12. As the body is one, and hath many members, and all the members of that one body, being many, are one body: so also *is* Christ. 27. Now ye are the body of Christ, and members in particular.

1 Cor. 15.48. As *is* the heavenly, such *are* they also that are heavenly. 49. And as we have borne the image of the earthy, we shall also bear the image of the heavenly. *v.* 20-23.

2 Cor. 5.17. If any man *be* in Christ, *he is* a new creature: old things are passed away; behold, all things are become new. 21. He hath made him *to be* sin for us, who knew no sin; that we might be made the righteousness of God in him.

2 Cor. 11.2. I have espoused you to one husband, that I may present *you as* a chaste virgin to Christ.

2 Cor. 13.5. Know ye not your own selves, how that Jesus Christ is in you, except ye be reprobates?

Gal. 2.20. I am crucified with Christ: nevertheless I live; yet not I, but Christ liveth in me: and the life which I now live in the flesh I live by the faith of the Son of God, who loved me, and gave himself for me.

Eph. 1.4. He hath chosen us in him before the foundation of the world, that we should be holy and without blame before him in love: 5. Having predestinated us unto the adoption of children by Jesus Christ to himself, 6. He hath made us accepted in the Beloved: 7. In whom we have redemption through his blood. 22. The church, 23. Which is his body, the fulness of him that filleth all in all.

Eph. 2.5. When we were dead in sins, hath quickened us together with Christ, (by grace ye are saved;) 6. And hath raised *us* up together, and made *us* sit together in heavenly *places* in Christ Jesus. *v.* 20-22.

Eph. 3.17. That Christ may dwell in your hearts by faith; that ye, being rooted and grounded in love.

Eph. 4.16. From whom the whole body fitly joined together and compacted by that which every joint supplieth, according to the effectual working in the measure of every part, maketh increase of the body unto the edifying of itself in love.

Eph. 5.30. We are members of his body, of his flesh, and of his bones. 32. This is a great mystery: but I speak concerning Christ and the church.

Phil. 3.8. I have suffered the loss of all things, and do count them *but* dung, that I may win Christ, 9. And be found in him; 10. That I may know him, and the power of his resurrection, and the fellowship of his sufferings, being made conformable unto his death; 11. If by any means I might attain unto the resurrection of the dead. 12. I follow after, if that I may apprehend that for which also I am apprehended of Christ Jesus.

Col. 1.18. He is the head of the body, the church. 24. For his body's sake, which is

the church. 27. Christ in you, the hope of glory.

Col. 2.6. As ye have therefore received Christ Jesus the Lord, *so* walk ye in him; 7. Rooted and built up in him. 10. Ye are complete in him, which is the head of all principality and power: 11. In whom also ye are circumcised with the circumcision made without hands, in putting off the body of the sins of the flesh by the circumcision of Christ: 12. Buried with him in baptism, wherein also ye are risen with *him* through the faith of the operation of God, who hath raised him from the dead. 13. You, being dead in your sins and the uncircumcision of your flesh, hath he quickened together with him, having forgiven you all trespasses. 19. The Head, from which all the body by joints and bands having nourishment ministered, and knit together, increaseth with the increase of God. 20. Dead with Christ from the rudiments of the world.

Col. 3.1. If ye then be risen with Christ, seek those things which are above. 3. Ye are dead, and your life is hid with Christ in God. 4. When Christ, *who is* our life, shall appear, then shall ye also appear with him in glory. 11. Christ is all and in all.

1 The. 1.1. The Church of the Thessalonians *which is* in God the Father and *in* the Lord Jesus Christ.

1 The. 5.9. God hath not appointed us to wrath, but to obtain salvation by our Lord Jesus Christ, 10. Who died for us, that, whether we wake or sleep, we should live together with him.

2 Tim. 2.11. If we be dead with *him*, we shall also live with *him*: 12. If we suffer, we shall also reign with *him*.

Heb. 2.11. Both he that sanctifieth and they who are sanctified *are* all of one: for which cause he is not ashamed to call them brethren.

Heb. 3.6. Christ as a Son over his own house; whose house are we, if we hold fast the confidence and the rejoicing of the hope firm unto the end. 14. We are made partakers of Christ, if we hold the beginning of our confidence steadfast unto the end.

1 Pet. 2.4. To whom coming, *as unto* a living stone, disallowed indeed of men, but chosen of God, *and* precious, 5. Ye also, as lively stones, are built up a spiritual house.

1 Pet. 4.13. Rejoice, inasmuch as ye are partakers of Christ's sufferings; that, when his glory shall be revealed, ye may be glad also with exceeding joy.

1 Jno. 2.6. He that saith he abideth in him, ought himself also so to walk, even as he walked. 24. If that which ye have heard from the beginning shall remain in you, ye also shall continue in the Son, and in the Father. 28. Little children, abide in him; that, when he shall appear, we may have confidence, and not be ashamed before him at his coming.

1 Jno. 3.6. Whosoever abideth in him sinneth not. 24. He that keepeth his commandments dwelleth in him, and he in him. And hereby we know that he abideth in us, by the Spirit which he hath given us.

1 Jno. 4.13. Hereby know we that we dwell in him, and he in us, because he hath given us of his Spirit.

1 Jno. 5.12. He that hath the Son hath life; *and* he that hath not the Son of God

hath not life. 20. We are in him that is true, *even* in his Son Jesus Christ.

2 Jno. 9. He that abideth in the doctrine of Christ, he hath both the Father and the Son.

Rev. 19.7. The marriage of the Lamb is come, and his wife hath made herself ready. 8. And to her was granted that she should be arrayed in fine linen, clean and white : for the fine linen is the righteousness of saints. 9. And he saith unto me, Write, Blessed *are* they which are called unto the marriage supper of the Lamb.

Rev. 21.9. The bride, the Lamb's wife.

See FAITH—CHRIST, HEAD OF THE CHURCH —ADOPTION—LIKENESS TO CHRIST.

UNION OF SAINTS. Psa. 132.1. Behold, how good and how pleasant *it is* for brethren to dwell together in unity !

Isa. 52.8. Thy watchman shall lift up the voice ; with the voice together shall they sing: for they shall see eye to eye, when the Lord shall bring again Zion.

Mat. 23.8. One is your Master, *even* Christ ; and all ye are brethren.

Act. 4.32. The multitude of them that believed were of one heart and of one soul : neither said any *of them* that ought of the things which he possessed was his own ; but they had all things common.

Rom. 12.16. Be of the same mind one toward another.

Rom. 14.19. Let us therefore follow after the things which make for peace, and things wherewith one may edify another.

Rom. 15.5. The God of patience and consolation grant you to be like-minded one toward another, according to Christ Jesus ; 6. That ye may with one mind *and* one mouth glorify God, even the Father of our Lord Jesus Christ.

1 Cor. 1.10. I beseech you, brethren, by the name of our Lord Jesus Christ, that ye all speak the same thing, and *that* there be no divisions among you ; but *that* ye be perfectly joined together in the same mind and in the same judgment.

2 Cor. 13.11. Be perfect, be of good comfort, be of one mind, live in peace ; and the God of love and peace shall be with you.

Eph. 4.3. Endeavouring to keep the unity of the Spirit in the bond of peace.

Phil. 1.27. Stand fast in one spirit, with one mind striving together for the faith of the gospel.

Phil. 2.2. Fulfil ye my joy, that ye be like-minded, having the same love, *being* of one accord, of one mind. Phil. 4.2.

Phil. 3.15. If in anything ye be otherwise minded, God shall reveal even this unto you. 16. Whereto we have already attained, let us walk by the same rule, let us mind the same thing.

1 The. 5.13. Be at peace among yourselves.

1 Pet. 3.8. Finally, *be ye* all of one mind, having compassion one of another, love as brethren, *be* pitiful, *be* courteous.

See LOVE.

UNITY OF THE CHURCH. See CHURCH.

UNKINDNESS. See HYPOCRISY AND TREACHERY — INHOSPITALITY — POOR, NEGLECT OF.

UNSELFISHNESS, MAGNANIMITY, GENEROSITY, EXAMPLES OF : Abraham, Gen.

13.9. Gen. 14.23,24. King of Sodom, Gen. 14.21. Children of Heth, Gen. 23.6,11. Judah, Gen. 44.33,34. Moses, Num. 11.29. Num. 14.12-19. Gideon, Jud. 8.22,23. Saul, 1 Sam. 11.12,13. Jonathan, 1 Sam. 23.17,18. David, 1 Sam. 24.17. 2 Sam. 15.19,20. 2 Sam. 23.16,17. 1 Chr. 21.17. Psa. 69.6. Araunah, 2 Sam. 24.22-24. Nehemiah, Neh. 5.14-18. Jews, Esth. 9.15. Daniel, Dan. 5.17. Jonah, Jonah 1.12,13. Joseph, Mat. 1.19. Paul, 1 Cor. 10.33. Phil. 1.18. Phil. 4.17. 2 The. 3.8. Philm. 13,14. Priscilla & Aquila, Rom. 16.3,4.

See SELFISHNESS—LOVE.

UPHARSIN, part of the verb *peres,* signifying to divide, Dan. 5.25,28.

UPHAZ (Ophir?), a gold country, Jer. 10.9. Dan. 10.5.

UPPER CHAMBER. See HOUSE.

UPRIGHTNESS. See INTEGRITY.

UR OF THE CHALDEES, the native country of Abraham, whence he emigrated to Haran, Gen. 11.28,31. Gen. 15.7. Neh. 9.7. Act. 7.4.

URBANE, a Roman disciple and assistant of Paul, Rom. 16.9.

URIAH, the Hittite, one of David's captains, 2 Sam. 23.39. 1 Chr. 11.41. Slain while besieging Rabbah ; and Bathsheba, his wife, taken by David, 2 Sam. 11. 1 Kin. 15.5.

URIJAH, high-priest ; makes a new altar by Ahaz's orders, 2 Kin. 16.10-16. Attests one of Isaiah's prophecies, Isa. 8.2.

———, a prophet, slain by Jehoiakim for prophesying against Judea and Jerusalem, Jer. 26.20-23.

URIM AND THUMMIM (the words signify Light and Truth), their exact nature unknown ; put in the breastplate of judgment, and worn on the high-priest's heart, when he went in before the Lord, Ex. 28.30. Lev. 8.8. Eleazar to ask counsel for Joshua, after the judgment of Urim, before the Lord, Num. 27.21. See 1 Sam. 30.8. Confined to the high-priest, Deu. 33.8. Saul obtained no answer by, 1 Sam. 28.6. Wanting to the high-priests after the captivity, Ezr. 2.63. Neh. 7.65.

See ENQUIRING OF GOD.

USURY. The Jews forbidden to take, from their brethren, Ex. 22.25. Lev. 25.36. Deu. 23.19. Psa. 15.5. Pro. 28.8. Eze. 18.13. Rebuked for exacting, Neh. 5.1-13. Allowed to take from foreigners, Deu. 23.20.

UZ, a country connected with Edom, Jer. 25.20. Lam. 4.21. Job dwelt in, Job 1.1. See Gen. 10.23. Gen. 22.21. Gen. 36.28. 1 Chr. 1.17,42.

UZZAH, a Levite, struck dead for touching the Ark, when driving the cart which conveyed it, 2 Sam. 6.6-8. 1 Chr. 13.9-11.

UZZIAH or AZARIAH, 9th king of Judah (52 years' reign) ; son of Amaziah, 2 Kin. 14.21. 2 Kin. 15.1,2. 2 Chr. 26.1. Seeks God in the days of Zechariah ; consequent prosperity, 2 Chr. 26.4,5,15. 2 Kin. 15.3. His conquests, 2 Kin. 14.22. 2 Chr. 26.6-8. Fortifies Jerusalem, and has a large army, 2 Chr. 26.9,11-15. Promotes agriculture, 2 Chr. 26.10.

Attempts to offer incense, and is struck with leprosy, 2 Chr. 26.16-21. 2 Kin. 15.5. His son Jotham made regent, 2 Kin. 15.5. 2 Chr. 26.21. His death, 2 Kin. 15.7. 2 Chr. 26.23. Chronicles of his reign written by Isaiah, 2 Chr. 26.22. Earthquake in his reign, Amos 1.1. Zec. 14.5.

V

VAIL (veil), different words are so translated (1.) Ruth 3.15 (*marg.*), apron. Translated wimples, Isa. 3.22. (2.) The vail put on the face of Moses, Ex. 34.33-35. 2 Cor. 3.13-16. (3.) Of Rebecca, Gen. 24.65; of Tamar, Gen. 38.14,19. (4.) Song 5.7. Isa. 3.23.

VAIL OF THE TABERNACLE, between the holy place and the most holy; of twined linen, blue, purple, and scarlet, with cherubim, hung by golden hooks with silver sockets from four pillars of shittim-wood, overlaid with gold, Ex. 26.31-33. Ex. 36.35,36. Heb. 9.3. Called the vail of the covering, and used to cover the ark, Num. 4.5. Ex. 35.12. Ex. 39.34. Ex. 40.21.

VAIL OF THE TEMPLE, 2 Chr. 3.14. Rent at Christ's death, Mat. 27.51. Mar. 15.38. Luk. 23.45. Illustrative, Heb. 10.20.

VALLEYS AND PLAINS. See DURA, SHINAR, PALESTINE, VALLEYS OF.

VANITY. See PRIDE.

VASHTI, wife of Ahasuerus; her feast; refuses to appear before the king; divorced, Esth. 1.

VAT. See WINE-PRESS.

VESSELS OF THE TEMPLE AND TABERNACLE. See TABERNACLE—TEMPLE.

VESTRY (wardrobe), 2 Kin. 10.22.

VIAL. Of oil, 1 Sam. 10.1. Translated, box, 2 Kin. 9.1,3. Symbolical, Rev. 5.8. Rev. 15.7. Rev. 16.1-17. Rev. 17.1. Rev. 21.9.

VILLAGES or UNWALLED TOWNS, Deu.3.5. 1 Sam. 6.18. Esth. 9.19. Belonging to cities, Jos. 15.44-47. Jos. 21.12. Neh. 11.25,30. Law respecting their redemption, Lev. 25.31.

VINE. Kinds of, Isa. 27.2. Eze. 17.6. Wild, Deu. 32.32. 2 Kin. 4.39. Jer. 2.21. Hos. 9.10.

Cultivated by Noah, Gen. 9.20. Cultivated in Canaan, Gen. 49.11. Deu. 8.8. 2 Kin. 18. 32. By the Canaanites, Num. 13.24. Deu. 6.11. Jos. 24.13. By Edomites, Num. 20.17. Amorites, Num. 21.22. Philistines, Jud. 15.5. Moabites at Sibmah, Isa. 16.8,9. Jer. 48.32.

By Israelites at Abel, Jud. 11.33 (*marg.*). Baal-hamon, Song 8.11. Carmel, 2 Chr. 26.10. Engedi, Song 1.14. Jezreel, 1 Kin. 21.1. Lebanon, Hos. 14.7. Samaria, Jer. 31.5. Shechem, Jud. 9.27. Shiloh, Jud. 21.20,21. Timnath, Jud. 14.5.

Planted on hills, 2 Chr. 26.10. Isa. 5.1. Jer. 31.5; in valleys, Song 6.11; by water, Eze. 17.5. Eze. 19.10; against houses, Psa. 128.3. Mic. 4.4.

Pruned and dressed, Lev. 25.3,11. Deu. 28. 39. 2 Kin. 25.12. 2 Chr. 26.10. Isa. 5.6. Blossoms of, fragrant, Song 2.13. Hos. 14.7 (*marg.*). Wood of, burned, Eze. 15.2-5.

Forbidden to be planted or fruit of eaten by Nazarites, Num. 6.3,4. See NAZARITES; or by RECHABITES, Jer. 35.7-9.

Illustrative, Deu. 32.32. Psa. 128.3. Jer. 2.21. Eze. 15. Hos. 10.1. Symbolical, Rev. 14.18-20.

Parables of, Jud. 9.12,13. Psa. 80.8-14. Eze. 17.6-10. Eze. 19.10-14. Jno. 15.1-5. See WINE—VINEYARDS.

VINEGAR (a sour wine), Num. 6.3. Ruth 2.14. Psa. 69.21. Pro. 10.26. Pro. 25.20. Offered to Christ on the cross, Mat. 27.34,48. Jno. 19.29 with Mar. 15.23.

VINEYARDS, OLIVE-YARDS, AND GARDENS. Cottages and towers built in, Isa. 1.8. Isa. 5.2. Mat. 21.33. Wine-press in, see WINE-PRESS. Pools in, Ecc. 2.4-6. Song 4. 15. Placed by rivers, Num. 24.6. Watered with the foot, Deu. 11.10. Boundaries of, see LANDMARKS, FENCE. Let out, and the rent paid in money, Song 8:11,12. Isa. 7.23; in produce, Mat. 21.34. Of kings under officers, 1 Chr. 27.26-31.

Parables of, Isa. 5.1-7. Isa. 27.2,3. Jer. 12. 10. Mat. 20.1-16. Mat. 21.28-31,33-41. Luk. 13.6-9.

VINTAGE, Jer. 6.9. A time of joy, Jud. 9.27. Isa. 16.10. Jer. 48.33. See FIRST-FRUITS—HARVEST.

VIOL, same as Psaltery. See PSALTERY.

VIPER, a kind of serpent, Job 20.16. Isa. 30.6. Isa. 59.5. Fastens on Paul's hand, Act. 28.3. Illustrative, Mat. 3.7. Mat. 23.33.

VIRTUE. (1.) Excellence, Phil. 4.8. 2 Pet. 1.5. (2.) Power, Luk. 6.19. Luk. 8.46.

VISIONS, SYMBOLS. Abraham's vision of the smoking furnace, Gen. 15.1-17. Jacob's ladder, Gen. 28.12. Jacob's dream of the cattle, Gen. 31.11-13. Dreams of Joseph, Gen. 37.5-10; of Pharaoh's baker and butler, Gen. 40; of Pharaoh, Gen. 41.

God appears to Jacob at Beersheba, Gen. 46. 2. The burning bush, Ex. 3.2. Appearance of God's glory on Sinai, Ex. 24.10,17. Ex. 19.18. Heb. 12.18-21. Ex. 32.18-23. See CLOUD OF GLORY.

Balaam's vision in a trance, Num. 24.4,16. The cake of barley-bread, Jud. 7.13. Solomon's vision at Gibeon, 1 Kin. 3.5-15. Elijah's vision at Horeb, 1 Kin. 19.11-13. Horses and chariots of fire, 2 Kin. 2.11. 2 Kin. 6.17. Vision of a spirit, Job 4.12-16.

The vision of Jehovah in the temple, Isa. 6. 1-7. Rod of an almond-tree, Jer. 1.11. A seething-pot set towards the north, Jer. 1.13. Roll of a book, Eze. 2.9. Eating a roll, Eze. 3.1-3. Vision of the temple, Eze. 8. A man with a writer's ink-horn, Eze. 9. Coals of fire scattered over Jerusalem, Eze. 10.2-7. The valley of dry bones, Eze. 37.1-14. Vision of a city, and temple with its ordinances, Eze. c. 40 to 48.

A man measures the city and temple, Eze. 40. Vision of the glory of God, 4 cherubims and 4 wheels, Eze. 43.2-7. Eze. 1. Eze. 3. 12-14,23. Eze. 8.2-4. Eze. 9.3. Eze. 10. Eze. 11.22,23.

Healing waters, Eze. 47.1-12. Nebuchadnezzar's dream of an image, Dan. 2; of a great tree, Dan. 4.10-18. Daniel's vision of the 4 beasts, Dan. 7. The Ancient of days sitting on a throne, Dan. 7.9,13.

The ram, he-goat, and little horn, Dan. 8. The angel by the banks of Hiddekel, Dan. 10. Dan. 12.5-7. Grasshoppers, Amos 7.1,2. Fire, Amos 7.4. Plumb-line, Amos 7.7,8. Basket of summer-fruit, Amos 8.1,2. The temple to be smitten, Amos 9.1.

Different coloured horses, Zec. 1.8-11. Four horns, and carpenters, Zec. 1.18-21. A man with a measuring-line, Zec. 2.1-3. Joshua, the high-priest, Zec. 3.1-5. The golden candlestick, Zec. 4. Zec. 5.1-4. The flying roll, Zec. 5.1-4.

The ephah, talent of lead, and women with wings, Zec. 5.5-11. The brass mountains and 4 chariots, Zec. 6.1-8. Descent of the Spirit like a dove on Christ, Mat. 3.16. Mar. 1.10. Luk. 3.22. Jno. 1.32-34. Transfiguration of Christ; appearance of Moses and Elijah, Mat. 17.1-9. Luk. 9.28-36.

Cloven tongues of fire at Pentecost, Act. 2.2,3. Stephen's vision of Christ, Act. 7. 55,56. Paul's visions of Christ, Act. 9.3-6. Act. 18.9. Act. 22.17,18. Act. 23.11. Vision of Christ to Ananias, Act. 9.10. Vision of Ananias to Paul, Act. 9.12.

Cornelius' vision of an angel, Act. 10.3. Peter's vision of unclean beasts, Act. 10.9-18. Vision of a man of Macedonia to Paul, Act. 16.9. Paul caught up into Paradise, 2 Cor. 12.1-4.

Christ walking among the seven golden candlesticks, and holding seven stars in his hand, Rev. 1.10-20. A door opened in heaven, Rev. 4.1. A rainbow round about the throne, Rev. 4.2,3. 24 elders, Rev. 4.4. 7 lamps of fire burning before the throne, Rev. 4.5. Sea of glass, Rev. 4.6.

Four living creatures, Rev. 4.6-8. Book with 7 seals, Rev. 5.1-5. Golden vials full of odours, Rev. 5.8. The opening of the 6 seals, Rev. 6. 4 horses with their riders, Rev. 6. 2-8. Earthquake, and convulsion of the heavenly bodies, Rev. 6.12-14.

Four angels holding the 4 winds, Rev. 7.1. The sealing of the 144,000, Rev. 7.2-8. Sounding of the 7 trumpets, Rev. c. 8 to 11. Silence in heaven for half an hour, Rev. 8.1. The opening of the 7th seal, Rev. 8.1. Incense offered on the golden altar, Rev. 8.3.

The censer filled with fire, Rev. 8.5. Hail and fire mingled with blood, Rev. 8.7. Mountain cast into the sea, Rev. 8.8,9. Star falling on the 3d part of waters, Rev. 8.10,11. The 3d part of sun and moon and stars darkened, Rev. 8.12.

A star falling from heaven, Rev. 9.1. Opening of the bottomless pit, Rev. 9.2. Locusts like unto horses, Rev. 9.3-11. Four angels loosed from the Euphrates, Rev. 9.14. An army of horsemen, Rev. 9.16-19. An angel having a little book open, Rev. 10.1-3,5,6,8. Seven thunders utter their voices, Rev. 10.3,4. The little book eaten, Rev. 10.9,10. Measurement of the temple, Rev. 11.1,2. The two witnesses, Rev. 11.1-12. The court given to the Gentiles, Rev. 11.2. Two olive-trees, and two candlesticks, Rev. 11.4.

The beast out of the bottomless pit, Rev. 11.7. Fall of the tenth part of the city, Rev. 11.13. The second and third woes, Rev. 11.14. The seventh angel sounds his trumpet, Rev. 11.15-19. The temple of God opened in heaven, Rev. 11.19.

A woman clothed with the sun; birth of the man-child, Rev. 12. A red dragon with 7 heads and 10 horns, Rev. 12.3-17. War in heaven, Rev. 12.7-9. The beast rising out of the sea, Rev. 13.1-10. The beast coming out of the earth having two horns, Rev. 13.11-18.

Image of the beast whose deadly wound was healed, Rev. 13.14,15. The Lamb on Mount Zion with the 144,000, and their new song, Rev. 14.1-5. The angel having the everlasting gospel, Rev. 14.6,7. The angel proclaiming the fall of Babylon, Rev. 14. 8-13.

The Son of man with sharp sickle, Rev. 14. 14-16. The angel reaping the harvest, Rev. 14.14-20. An angel coming out of the temple, Rev. 14.17-19. An angel having power over fire, Rev. 14.18. The vine of the earth cast into the wine-press, Rev. 14.18-20.

Angels with the seven last plagues, Rev. 15. A sea of glass mingled with fire, Rev. 15.2. Temple of the tabernacle of the testimony opened, Rev..15.5. The sore upon the men who had the mark of the beast, Rev. 16.2. Sea turned into blood, Rev. 16.3.

The seven angels pour out the seven vials, Rev. 16. The rivers and springs become blood, Rev. 16.4-6. Men scorched with great heat, Rev. 16.8,9. The seat of the beast filled with darkness, Rev. 16.10,11. Water of the Euphrates dried up, Rev. 16.12.

Three unclean spirits like frogs, Rev. 16. 13,14. The kings of the earth at Armageddon, Rev. 16.14-16. A great earthquake, and hail-storm, Rev. 16.17-21. An earthquake dividing the city into three parts, Rev. 16. 19,20.

The woman on the scarlet-coloured beast with 7 heads and 10 horns; judgment of the great whore, Rev. 17. Destruction of Babylon the great, Rev. 18. A stone cast into the sea by an angel, Rev. 18.21. The Word of God riding on a white horse, Rev. 19.11-16.

An angel standing in the sun, Rev. 19. 17-21. The fowls gathered to eat the flesh of the slain army; the beast and false prophet cast into the lake of fire, Rev. 19.20. Satan bound for 1000 years, Rev. 20.1-3. The souls of the martyrs reign with Christ 1000 years, Rev. 20.4.

The first resurrection, Rev. 20.4-6. Satan loosed, and deceiving the nations, Rev. 20. 7-10. Gog and Magog besieging the camp of the saints, Rev. 20.8,9. The devil cast into the lake of fire, Rev. 20.10. The lake of fire and brimstone, Rev. 20.10.

A great white throne, Rev. 20.11. The opening of the book of life, Rev. 20.12. Death and hell cast into the lake of fire, Rev. 20.14. New Jerusalem descending from God; its measurement, foundation, &c., Rev. 21.

A pure river of water of life from the throne, Rev. 22.1. The tree of life bearing 12 manner of fruits, Rev. 22.2.

See DREAMS—SYMBOLS—ANGELS, APPEARANCES OF—PROPHETS, INSPIRATION OF.

VOLCANO, Jer. 51.25. Neh. 1.5,6. Symbolical, Rev. 8.8.

VOLUNTARY OFFERINGS. See OFFERINGS, VOLUNTARY.

VOWS, Lev. 23.38. Psa. 22.25. Psa. 56.12. Psa. 61.5,8. Psa. 65.1. Psa. 66.13. Psa. 116.14,18. Psa. 132.2. Isa. 19.21. Persons vowed to God, redeemed, Lev. 27.1-8.

Clean beasts vowed must be perfect, Lev. 22. 18,21-23. Mal. 1.14; not redeemable, Lev. 27.9,10,26; sacrificed, Num. 15.3,8; at the tabernacle, Deu. 12.6,11,17,26; and eaten by the people, Lev. 7.16,17. Unclean beasts must be redeemed or sold, Lev. 27.11-13,27. Houses, &c., how redeemed, and when not redeemable, Lev. 27.14-25.

Things devoted not redeemable, Lev. 27. 28,29. Belonged to the priest, Lev. 27.21,28. Num. 18.14. Eze. 44.29 (marg.). Devoted cities, &c., destroyed, Num. 21.1-3. Jos. 6. 17-26. 1 Sam. 15.3.

Vows were voluntary, Deu. 23.22. Ecc. 5.5. Act. 5.4. Were binding, Num. 30. 2,4,7,11,12. Deu. 23.21-23. Jud. 11.35. Job 22.27. Psa. 50.14. Psa. 76.11. Pro. 20.25. Ecc. 5.4-7. Jonah 2.9. Nah. 1.15.

In certain cases not binding, Num. 30.3-13. Punishment for violating, Jos. 7.15. Things forbidden to be vowed, Deu. 23.18. Mar. 7.11-13.

Vows, EXAMPLES OF : Jacob, Gen. 28. 20-22. Jephthah, Jud. 11.30,31. Micah's mother, Jud. 17.2,3. Hannah, 1 Sam. 1.11. Elkanah, 1 Sam. 1.21. Mariners, Jonah 1.16. Jonah, Jonah 2.9.

See NAZARITE VOW—RECHABITES—DEDICATION—LIBERALITY—DECISION EXEMPLIFIED.

VULTURE. Three words are so translated: (1.) Job 28.7. Translated, kite, Lev. 11.14. Deu. 14.13. (2.) Lev. 11.14. (3.) Deu. 14.13. Isa. 34.15.

W

WAFER, a thin cake, Ex. 29.23. Num. 6.19.

WAGES. See SERVANTS, HIRED.

WAGGON. See CART.

WALKING WITH GOD. See SPIRITUAL DILIGENCE—GOD'S FAVOUR—PRAYERFULNESS.

WALLS OF CITIES, Amos 7.7. With gates and bars, Deu. 3.5. 2 Chr. 8.5 (see GATES). Battlements of, Jer. 5.10. Towers of, 2 Chr. 14.7. 2 Chr. 26.9. Isa. 25.12. Broad walls, Jer. 51.58. 2 Kin. 6.26,30. House built on, Jos. 2.15. Double walls, 2 Kin. 25.4. Isa. 22.11. 2 Sam. 20.15 (marg.). Dedicated, Neh. 12.27.

Soldiers on, Sam. 11.20,24. Eze. 27.11. Standards on, Jer. 51.12. Watchmen on, Song 5.7. Isa. 62.6. Bodies of enemies fastened to, 1 Sam. 31.11,12. Idolatrous rites on, 2 Kin.3.27. See JERUSALEM—FENCE—HOUSE. Illustrative, Psa. 62.3. Eze. 13.10-15. Zec. 2.5.

WAR, DESCRIPTION OF ; ITS EVILS. 2 Sam. 2.26. Job 5.20. Psa. 79.1-3. Isa. 3.5,25,26. Isa. 5.29,30. Isa. 6.11,12. Isa. 9.5,19-21. Isa. 16.9,10. Isa. 18.6. Isa. 19.2-16. Isa. 32.13,14. Isa. 33.8,9. Isa. 34.7-15. Jer. 4.19-31. Jer. 5.16,17. Jer. 6.24-26. Jer. 7.33,34. Jer. 8.16,17. Jer. 9.10-21. Jer. 10.20. Jer. 14.18. Jer. 15.8,9. Jer. 19.7-9. Jer. 46.3-12. Jer. 47.3. Jer. 48.28,33. Jer. 51.30-58. Lam. c. 1 to 5. Eze. 39.17-19. Hos. 10.14. Hos. 13.16. Joel 2.2-10. Amos 1.13. Amos 8.3. Nah. 2.10. Nah. 3.3,10.

Luk. 21.20-26. Rev. 19.17,18. See PEACE, NATIONAL—ARMIES—CHARIOTS.

WAR, A JUDGMENT FROM GOD, Lev. 26.17,31-39. Deu. 28.25-68. Deu. 32.30. Jud. 2.14. 2 Kin. 15.37. 1 Chr. 5.22,26. 1 Chr. 21.12. 2 Chr. 15.6. Psa. 44.9-16. Psa. 60. 1-3. Psa. 105.25. Isa. 5.1-8,26. Isa. 19.2. Isa. 34.4,5. Isa. 43.28. Isa. 45.7. Jer. 12. 7,12. Jer. 46.15-17,21. Jer. 47.6,7. Jer. 50. 25. Amos 3.6. Amos 4.11. Zec. 8.10.

WASHINGS. See ABLUTION—PURIFICATION.

WATCHES. See NIGHT.

WATCHFULNESS. Ex. 23.13. In all things that I have said unto you be circumspect.

Ex. 34.12. Take heed to thyself, lest thou make a covenant with the inhabitants of the land whither thou goest, lest it be for a snare in the midst of thee.

Deu. 4.9. Only take heed to thyself, and keep thy soul diligently, lest thou forget the things which thine eyes have seen, and lest they depart from thy heart all the days of thy life. 23. Take heed unto yourselves, lest ye forget the covenant of the Lord your God, which he made with you.

Deu. 11.16. Take heed to yourselves, that your heart be not deceived, and ye turn aside.

Jos. 22.5. Take diligent heed to do the commandment and the law.

Jos. 23.11. Take good heed therefore unto yourselves, that ye love the Lord your God.

1 Kin. 2.4. If thy children take heed to their way, to walk before me in truth with all their heart, and with all their soul, there shall not fail thee a man on the throne of Israel.

Job 36.21. Take heed, regard not iniquity.

Psa. 4.4. Stand in awe, and sin not : commune with your own heart upon your bed, and be still.

Psa. 119.9. Wherewithal shall a young man cleanse his way ? By taking heed thereto according to thy word.

Pro. 4.23. Keep thy heart with all diligence ; for out of it are the issues of life. 25. Let thine eyes look right on, and let thine eyelids look straight before thee. 26. Ponder the path of thy feet, and let all thy ways be established.

Pro. 16.17. The highway of the upright is to depart from evil : he that keepeth his way preserveth his soul.

Pro. 28.26. He that trusteth in his own heart is a fool : but whoso walketh wisely, he shall be delivered.

Mal. 2.15. Take heed to your spirit, and let none deal treacherously.

Mat. 25.13. Watch therefore, for ye know neither the day nor the hour wherein the Son of man cometh. v. 1-13.

Mat. 26.40. What, could ye not watch with me one hour ? 41. Watch and pray, that ye enter not into temptation : the spirit indeed is willing, but the flesh is weak. Mar. 14.38. Luk. 22.46.

Mar. 4.24. Take heed what ye hear : with what measure ye mete, it shall be measured to you ; and unto you that hear shall more be given. Luk. 8.18.

Luk. 11.35. Take heed therefore that the light which is in thee be not darkness.

Luk. 12.15. Take heed, and beware of covetousness. 35. Let your loins be girded about, and *your* lights burning; 36. And ye yourselves like unto men that wait for their lord, when he will return from the wedding; that when he cometh and knocketh, they may open unto him immediately. 37. Blessed *are* those servants, whom the lord when he cometh shall find watching: verily I say unto you, that he shall gird himself, and make them to sit down to meat, and will come forth and serve them. 38. And if he shall come in the second watch, or come in the third watch, and find *them* so, blessed are those servants. 39. And this know, that if the goodman of the house had known what hour the thief would come, he would have watched, and not have suffered his house to be broken through. 40. Be ye therefore ready also: for the Son of man cometh at an hour when ye think not. Mat. 24.42-47. Mar. 13.33-37.

Luk. 21.8. Take heed that ye be not deceived: for many shall come in my name. 36. Watch ye therefore, and pray always, that ye may be accounted worthy to escape all these things that shall come to pass, and to stand before the Son of man.

Rom. 13.11. Knowing the time, that now *it is* high time to awake out of sleep: for now *is* our salvation nearer than when we believed.

Rom. 14.16. Let not then your good be evil spoken of.

1 Cor. 3.10. I have laid the foundation, and another buildeth thereon. But let every man take heed how he buildeth thereupon.

1 Cor. 8.9. Take heed lest by any means this liberty of your's become a stumblingblock to them that are weak.

1 Cor. 10.12. Let him that thinketh he standeth take heed lest he fall. 1 Cor. 9.27.

1 Cor. 16.13. Watch ye, stand fast in the faith, quit you like men, be strong.

Eph. 5.15. See then that ye walk circumspectly, not as fools, but as wise.

Eph. 6.13. Take unto you the whole armour of God, that ye may be able to withstand in the evil day, and having done all, to stand. 18. Praying always with all prayer and supplication in the Spirit, and watching thereunto with all perseverance and supplication for all saints.

1 The. 5.4. Ye, brethren, are not in darkness, that that day should overtake you as a thief. 6. Let us not sleep, as *do* others; but let us watch and be sober.

2 Tim. 4.5. Watch thou in all things.

Heb. 2.1. We ought to give the more earnest heed to the things which we have heard, lest at any time we should let *them* slip.

Heb. 3.12. Take heed, brethren, lest there be in any of you an evil heart of unbelief, in departing from the living God.

Heb. 4.1. Let us therefore fear, lest, a promise being left *us* of entering into his rest, any of you should seem to come short of it.

Heb. 12.15. Looking diligently lest any man fail of the grace of God ; lest any root of bitterness springing up trouble *you*, and thereby many be defiled.

1 Pet. 1.13. Gird up the loins of your mind, be sober, and hope to the end for the grace that is to be brought unto you at the revelation of Jesus Christ. 17. Pass the time of your sojourning *here* in fear.

1 Pet. 4.7. The end of all things is at hand : be ye therefore sober, and watch unto prayer.

1 Pet. 5.8. Be sober, be vigilant ; because your adversary the devil, as a roaring lion, walketh about, seeking whom he may devour.

2 Pet. 3.17. Seeing ye know *these things* before, beware lest ye also, being led away with the error of the wicked, fall from your own stedfastness.

1 Jno. 5.18. He that is begotten of God keepeth himself, and that wicked one toucheth him not.

2 Jno. 8. Look to yourselves, that we lose not those things which we have wrought, but that we receive a full reward.

Rev. 3.2. Be watchful, and strengthen the things which remain, that are ready to die: for I have not found thy works perfect before God. 3. Remember therefore how thou hast received and heard, and hold fast, and repent. If therefore thou shalt not watch, I will come on thee as a thief, and thou shalt not know what hour I will come upon thee.

Rev. 16.15. Behold, I come as a thief. Blessed *is* he that watcheth, and keepeth his garments, lest he walk naked, and they see his shame.

See DECISION — PRUDENCE — SPIRITUAL DILIGENCE—TEMPTATION—SELF-DENIAL.

WATCHMEN, Neh. 4.9. Isa. 21.8. On city-walls, 2 Sam. 18.24,25. 2 Sam. 13.34. Isa. 62.6. Jer. 51.12. On watch-towers and hills, 1 Sam. 14.16. 2 Kin. 9.17. 2 Chr. 20. 24. Isa. 21.5-8. Jer. 31.6. See FORTRESS. In the streets of cities, Psa. 127.1. Song 3.3. Song 5.7. Around the temple, 2 Kin. 11.6,7. The watch changed, Neh. 7.3. Negligence punished with death, Eze. 33.6. Signal given by trumpet, Eze. 33.3-6. Illustrative, Isa. 52.8. Isa. 56.10. Eze. 3.17. Hos. 9.8.

WATER. Irrigation, Deu. 11.10. Pro. 21. 1. Isa. 58.11. Pouring out before the Lord, 1 Sam. 7.6. Water of separation, Num. 19. See ABLUTION — PURIFICATION. Miracles connected with water, Jud. 15.19. 2 Kin. 3. 17-22. Mat. 14.28. Jno. 2.1-11. See WELLS—JORDAN—NILE—RED SEA.

Illustrative, Psa. 69.1. Pro. 5.15. Isa. 43. 2. Isa. 55.1. Jer. 51.13. Eze. 36.25. Jno. 7.38. 1 Cor. 3.6. Symbolical, Isa. 8.7. Rev. 8.11. Rev. 12.15. Rev. 16.4. Rev. 17.1,15. Waterspout, illustrative, Psa. 42.7.

WAX, Psa. 22.14. Psa. 68.2. Psa. 97.5. Mic. 1.4.

WEAPONS. See ARMS.

WEASEL, Lev. 11.29.

WEAVER'S BEAM, Jud. 16.14. 2 Sam. 21.19. 1 Chr. 11.23. Translated shuttle, Job 7.6.

WEAVING, Ex. 28.32. Ex. 35.35. Ex. 39.22,27. 2 Kin. 23.7. Isa. 19.9. Isa. 38.12.

WEEK, the Hebrew word signifies seven (see seven) ; first mentioned, Gen. 29.27; but see Gen. 1.31. Gen. 2.2,3. Gen. 8.10,12. See DAY—FEAST OF WEEKS.

WEIGHTS, MEASURES, MONEY. See ACRE, ASS, BATH, BEKAH, BUSHEL, CAB,

COR, CUBIT, DAY'S JOURNEY, DRAM, EPHAH, FARTHING, FATHOM, FINGER-BREADTH, FIRKIN, FURLONG, GERAH, HAND-BREADTH, HIN, HOMER, LOG, MANEH, MEASURE, MILE, MITE, OMER, PALM, PENNY, PIECE OF SILVER, POUND, REED, SABBATH-DAY'S JOURNEY, SEAH, SHEKEL, SPAN, TALENT.

Required to be just, Lev. 19.35,36. Deu. 25.13-15. Pro. 11.1. Pro. 16.11. Pro. 20. 10,23. Mic. 6.10,11. See BALANCES—PURSE.

WELLS, POOLS, AND FOUNTAINS, made by Abraham, Gen. 21.25-30. Isaac, Gen. 26. 15-22,32,33. Jacob, Jno. 4.6. Solomon, Ecc. 2.6. Uzziah, 2 Chr. 26.10. Hezekiah, see GIHON.

For watering flocks, Gen. 24.10-20. Gen. 29.1-10. Ex. 2.16-19. For fish, Song 7.4. Isa. 19.10.

Public property, Gen. 24.13. 2 Kin. 20.20. Private property, Gen. 21.25,30. 2 Sam. 17. 18. Sealed, Song 4.12.

Miracles connected with, Ex. 7.19. Ex. 15. 23-25. Ex. 17.6,7. Num. 20.10,11. 2 Kin. 2.21. Jno. 5.2. Jno. 9.7. Christ at Jacob's well, Jno. 4.1-26.

Illustrative, Pro. 16.22. Isa. 12.3. Jer. 2. 13. Jno. 4.14. Rev. 7.17. Wells without water, Jer. 15.18. 2 Pet. 2.17. See BEER-ELIM, MARAH, MERIBAH, SHUR—PALESTINE, WELLS OF.

WHALE, Gen. 1.21. Job 7.12. Mat. 12. 40. The original signifies a monster; translated great fish, Jonah 1.17. A serpent, Ex. 7.9. Dragon, Jer. 51.34.

WHEAT, 1 Kin. 5.11. Psa. 81.16. Psa. 147.14. Rev. 6.6. In offerings, 1 Chr. 21.23. Num. 18.12. Of Minnith, Eze. 27.17. Illustrative, Jer. 12.13. Jer. 23.28. Mat. 3.12. Jno. 12.24. Parables, Mat. 13.25. Luk. 16.7.

WHEELS. Illustrative, Ecc. 12.6. Symbolical, Eze. 1.15-21. Eze. 3.13. Eze. 10. 9-19. Eze. 11.22. Potter's wheel, Jer. 18.3.

WHIP, 1 Kin. 12.11. Pro. 26.3. Nah. 3.2.

WHIRLWIND, Pro. 1.27. Pro. 10.25. From the south, Job 37.9. Isa. 21.1. Zec. 9. 14. Elijah taken up in, 2 Kin. 2.1,11. God answered Job in, Job 38.1. Illustrative, Hos. 8.7. Eze. 1.4. See WIND.

WHISPERER, a secret slanderer, Rom. 1. 29. 2 Cor. 12.20.

WICKED, THE. See SIN—SINNERS.

WIDOWS AND ORPHANS. Ex. 22.22. Ye shall not afflict any widow, or fatherless child. 23. If thou afflict them in any wise, and they cry at all unto me, I will surely hear their cry; 24. And my wrath shall wax hot, and I will kill you with the sword; and your wives shall be widows, and your children fatherless.

Deu. 10.18. He doth execute the judgment of the fatherless and widow.

Deu. 14.29. The stranger, and the fatherless, and the widow, which are within thy gates, shall come, and shall eat and be satisfied; that the Lord thy God may bless thee in all the work of thine hand which thou doest.

Deu. 24.17. Thou shalt not pervert the judgment of the stranger, nor of the fatherless; nor take a widow's raiment to pledge.

Deu. 27.19. Cursed be he that perverteth the judgment of the stranger, fatherless, and widow.

Job 22.9. Thou hast sent widows away empty, and the arms of the fatherless have been broken. Job 6.27. Eze. 22.7.

Job 24.3. They drive away the ass of the fatherless; they take the widow's ox for a pledge. 9. They pluck the fatherless from the breast, and take a pledge of the poor. 21. He evil-entreateth the barren that beareth not, and doeth not good to the widow.

Job 29.12. If I delivered the poor that cried, and the fatherless, and him that had none to help him. 13. The blessing of him that was ready to perish came upon me: and I caused the widow's heart to sing for joy.

Job 31.16. If I have withheld the poor from their desire, or have caused the eyes of the widow to fail; 17. Or have eaten my morsel myself alone, and the fatherless hath not eaten thereof; 18. For from my youth he was brought up with me, as with a father, and I have guided her from my mother's womb. v. 21.

Psa. 10.14. Thou art the helper of the fatherless. 17. Thou wilt cause thine ear to hear: 18. To judge the fatherless and the oppressed, that the man of the earth may no more oppress.

Psa. 27.10. When my father and my mother forsake me, then the Lord will take me up.

Psa. 68.5. A father of the fatherless, and a judge of the widows, is God in his holy habitation.

Psa. 82.3. Defend the poor and fatherless.

Psa. 94.6. They slay the widow and the stranger, and murder the fatherless.

Psa. 146.9. The Lord relieveth the fatherless and widow.

Pro. 15.25. He will establish the border of the widow.

Pro. 23.10. Remove not the old landmark; and enter not into the fields of the fatherless: 11. For their redeemer is mighty; he shall plead their cause with thee.

Isa. 1.17. Judge the fatherless, plead for the widow. 23. They judge not the fatherless, neither doth the cause of the widow come unto them. Jer. 5.28.

Isa. 10.2. That widows may be their prey, and that they may rob the fatherless!

Jer. 7.6. Oppress not the stranger, the fatherless, and the widow. Jer. 22.3. Zec. 7.10.

Jer. 49.11. Leave thy fatherless children, I will preserve them alive; and let thy widows trust in me.

Hos. 14.3. In thee the fatherless findeth mercy.

Mal. 3.5. I will be a swift witness against those that oppress the widow, and the fatherless.

Mat. 23.14. Ye devour widows' houses, and for a pretence make long prayer: therefore ye shall receive the greater damnation. Mar. 12.40.

Luk. 7.12. There was a dead man carried out, the only son of his mother, and she was a widow. v. 11-15.

Luk. 18.3. There was a widow in that city; and she came unto him, saying, Avenge me of mine adversary.

Act. 6.1. There arose a murmuring of the Grecians against the Hebrews, because their widows were neglected in the daily ministration.

Act. 9.39. All the widows stood by him weeping, and shewing the coats and garments which Dorcas made while she was with them.

1 Cor. 7.8. I say therefore to the unmarried and widows, It is good for them if they abide even as I.

1 Tim. 5.3. Honour widows that are widows indeed. 4. But if any widow have children or nephews, let them learn first to shew piety at home, and to requite their parents: for that is good and acceptable before God. 5. She that is a widow indeed, and desolate, trusteth in God, and continueth in supplications and prayers night and day. 16. If any man or woman that believeth have widows, let them relieve them, and let not the church be charged; that it may relieve them that are widows indeed. *v.* 11. Lam. 5.3.

Jas. 1.27. Pure religion and undefiled before God and the Father is this, To visit the fatherless and widows in their affliction, *and* to keep himself unspotted from the world.

WIDOWS. Vows of, binding, Num. 30.9. Gleanings to be left for them, Deu. 24.19-21. To share in the tithes and public rejoicings, Deu. 14.28,29. Deu. 16.11,14. Deu. 26.12,13. When priests' daughters, to be supported by their father, Lev. 22.13. Not to marry a priest, Lev. 21.14.

When childless, to be married by their husband's next of kin, Deu. 25.5,6. Ruth 4. 4,5. Mat. 22,24. Allowed to marry again, Rom. 7.3. 1 Cor. 7.39. See MARRIAGE. Wore mourning, Gen 38.14,19. 2 Sam. 14.2,5.

WILDERNESS. See DESERTS.

WILLS, Gen. 49.1. 1 Kin. 2.1. Gal. 3. 15 *(marg.).* Heb. 9.16,17. See INHERITANCE —TESTAMENT.

WILLOW, Lev. 23.40. Psa. 137.2. Eze. 17.5.

WIMPLE, a vail, Isa. 3.22.

WIND, 1 Kin. 19.11. North, Job. 37.9,22. Pro. 25.23. Song 4.16. South, Job 37.17. Luk. 12.55. East, Gen. 41.6. Job 27.21. Eze. 19.12. Jonah 4.8. West, Ex. 10.19. Luk. 12.54. Euroclydon, Act. 27.14. Pestilential, 2 Kin. 19.7,35. Jer. 4.11. See WHIRLWIND.

WINDOW, Gen. 6.16. Gen. 26.8. Jos. 2. 15,21. 1 Kin. 6.4. Act. 20.9.

WINE, made by Noah, Gen. 9.21. Of Palestine, Deu. 33.28. Jer. 31.12. Lebanon, Hos. 14.7. Helbon, Eze. 27.18. Moab, Isa. 16.8-10. Jer. 48.32,33.

Fermenting of, Job 32.19. Pro. 23.31,32. Mar. 2.22. Refining of, Isa. 25.6. Jer. 48.11. Squeezed from the grape, Gen. 40.11. See WINE-PRESS. Kept in jars, Jer. 48.12. Skins, Jos. 9.4,13. Job 32.19. Mat. 9.17. Cellars, 1 Chr. 27.27.

Intoxicating, Gen. 9.21. Gen. 19.32. 1 Sam. 25.37. 2 Sam. 13.28. Pro. 20.1. Pro.

21.17. Pro. 31.4. Isa. 5.11. Isa. 28.7. Jer. 23.9. Hos. 4.11. Hos. 7.5. Hab. 2.5. Act. 2.13. Eph. 5.18.

Red, Psa. 75.8. Pro. 23.31. Isa. 27.2. Mingled, Pro. 9.2. Mixed, Pro. 23.30. Spiced, Song 8.2. Scented, Hos. 14.7. Mixed with water, Isa. 1.22. Sour, Hos. 4.18. Juice or blood of the grape, Gen. 40.11. Gen. 49.11. New, Pro. 3.10. Sweet, Mic. 6.15. Strong wine or strong drink, Lev. 10.9. Num. 28.7. Pro. 20.1. Isa. 5.11. Wines on the lees, Isa. 25.6; or dregs, Psa. 75.8. Lees of wine, Jer. 48.11. Old wine, Luk. 5.39. Wine of pomegranates, Song 8.2. See VINEGAR.

Forbidden to priests, on entering the tabernacle, Lev. 10.9. Eze. 44.21; to Nazarites (see NAZARITES); to Samson's mother, Jud. 13.4,14. Israelites in the wilderness had none, Deu. 29.6. Daniel refused, Dan. 1.5,8,16. Dan. 10.3. Recommended to Timothy, 1 Tim. 5.23. Drink-offerings of, see OFFERING, DRINK-OFFERING. Banquet of, Est. 5.6. Est. 7.2. Christ changes water into wine, Jno. 2.9,10. Illustrative, Isa. 55.1. Jer. 51. 7. Rev 14.8. Rev. 16.19. See CUP-BEARER —TITHE—FIRST-FRUITS.

WINE-PRESS, VAT or FAT, Num. 18.27. Deu. 15.14. Jud. 6.11. Joel 2.24. Joel 3. 13. Hag. 2.16. In vineyards, Isa. 5.2. Mat. 21.33. Treading of, Neh. 13.15. Isa. 16.10. Illustrative, Isa. 63.23. Lam. 1.15. Rev. 19.15.

WINNOWING. See SHOVEL—SIEVE—THRESHING.

WINTER, Gen. 8.22. Pro. 20.4. Song 2. 11. Mat. 24.20. Act. 27.12. Act. 28.11. Tit. 3.12. See SNOW, ICE. Winter-house, Jer. 36.22. Amos 3.15.

WISDOM—KNOWLEDGE OF GOD—SPIRITUAL UNDERSTANDING. Ex. 8.10. That thou mayest know that *there is* none like unto the Lord our God.

Ex. 18.11. Now I know that the Lord *is* greater than all gods. Psa. 135.5.

Deu. 32.29. Oh that they were wise, *that* they understood this, *that* they would consider their latter end!

1 Chr. 28.9. Know thou the God of thy father, and serve him with a perfect heart and with a willing mind.

Job 4.3. Thou hast instructed many, and thou hast strengthened the weak hands. 4. Thy words have upholden him that was falling, and thou hast strengthened the feeble knees.

Job 5.27. Lo this, we have searched it, so it *is*; hear it, and know thou *it* for thy good.

Job 8.8. Enquire, I pray thee, of the former age, and prepare thyself to the search of their fathers. 10. Shall not they teach thee, *and* tell thee, and utter words out of their heart?

Job 12.7. Ask now the beasts, and they shall teach thee; and the fowls of the air, and they shall tell thee. 9. Who knoweth not in all these that the hand of the Lord hath wrought this? *v.* 8.

Job 22.21. Acquaint now thyself with him, and be at peace: thereby good shall come unto thee.

Job 42.5. I have heard of thee by the hearing of the ear: but now mine eye seeth thee.

Psa. 2.10. Be wise now therefore, O ye kings; be instructed, ye judges of the earth.

Psa. 9.10. They that know thy name will put their trust in thee. 16. The Lord is known by the judgment *which* he executeth.

Psa. 76.1. In Judah *is* God known: his name *is* great in Israel.

Psa. 107.43. Whoso *is* wise, and will observe these *things*, even they shall understand the loving-kindness of the Lord.

Psa. 111.10. The fear of the Lord *is* the beginning of wisdom: a good understanding have all they that do *his commandments*.

Pro. 1.5. A wise *man* will hear, and will increase learning; and a man of understanding shall attain unto wise counsels. 7. The fear of the Lord *is* the beginning of knowledge: *but* fools despise wisdom and instruction. *v.* 5-9.

Pro. 2.2. Incline thine ear unto wisdom, *and* apply thine heart to understanding; 3. Yea, if thou criest after knowledge, *and* liftest up thy voice for understanding; 4. If thou seekest her as silver, and searchest for her as *for* hid treasures; 5. Then shalt thou understand the fear of the Lord, and find the knowledge of God. 9. Then shalt thou understand righteousness, and judgment, and equity; *yea*, every good path. 10. When wisdom entereth into thine heart, and knowledge is pleasant unto thy soul; 11. Discretion shall preserve thee, understanding shall keep thee: 12. To deliver thee from the way of the evil *man*. 20. That thou mayest walk in the way of good *men*, and keep the paths of the righteous.

Pro. 3.13. Happy *is* the man *that* findeth wisdom, and the man *that* getteth understanding. 14. For the merchandise of it *is* better than the merchandise of silver, and the gain thereof than fine gold. 15. She *is* more precious than rubies: and all the things thou canst desire are not to be compared unto her. 16. Length of days *is* in her right hand; *and* in her left hand riches and honour. 17. Her ways *are* ways of pleasantness, and all her paths *are* peace. 18. She *is* a tree of life to them that lay hold upon her: and happy *is every one* that retaineth her. 21. My son, let not them depart from thine eyes: keep sound wisdom and discretion: 22. So shall they be life unto thy soul, and grace to thy neck. 23. Then shalt thou walk in thy ways safely, and thy foot shall not stumble. 24. When thou liest down, thou shalt not be afraid: yea, thou shalt lie down, and thy sleep shall be sweet. 35. The wise shall inherit glory; but shame shall be the promotion of fools.

Pro. 4.5. Get wisdom, get understanding: forget *it* not; neither decline from the words of my mouth. 6. Forsake her not, and she shall preserve thee: love her, and she shall keep thee. 7. Wisdom *is* the principal thing; *therefore* get wisdom: and with all thy getting get understanding. 8. Exalt her, and she shall promote thee: she shall bring thee to honour, when thou dost embrace her. 9. She shall give to thine head an ornament of grace: a crown of glory shall she deliver to thee. 13. Take fast hold of instruction; let *her* not go: keep her; for she *is* thy life. *v.* 20-22.

Pro. 6.22. When thou goest, it shall lead thee; when thou sleepest, it shall keep thee; and *when* thou awakest, it shall talk with thee.

23. For the commandment *is* a lamp; and the law *is* light; and reproofs of instruction *are* the way of life. *v.* 20,21.

Pro. 7.2. Keep my commandments, and live; and my law as the apple of thine eye. 3. Bind them upon thy fingers, write them upon the table of thine heart. 4. Say unto wisdom, Thou *art* my sister; and call understanding *thy* kinswoman.

Pro. 8.10. Receive my instruction, and not silver; and knowledge rather than choice gold. 11. For wisdom *is* better than rubies; and all the things that may be desired are not to be compared to it. 32. Now therefore hearken unto me, O ye children: for blessed *are they that* keep my ways. 33. Hear instruction, and be wise, and refuse it not. 34. Blessed *is* the man that heareth me, watching daily at my gates, waiting at the posts of my doors. 35. Whoso findeth me findeth life, and shall obtain favour of the Lord. *v.* 1-36.

Pro. 9.9. Give *instruction* to a wise *man*, and he will be yet wiser: teach a just *man*, and he will increase in learning. 10. The fear of the Lord *is* the beginning of wisdom: and the knowledge of the holy *is* understanding. 11. By me thy days shall be multiplied, and the years of thy life shall be increased. 12. If thou be wise, thou shalt be wise for thyself: but *if* thou scornest, thou alone shalt bear *it*.

Pro. 10.8. The wise in heart will receive commandments. 14. Wise *men* lay up knowledge. 23. A man of understanding hath wisdom.

Pro. 11.9. Through knowledge shall the just be delivered. 14. Where no counsel *is*, the people fall: but in the multitude of counsellers *there* is safety.

Pro. 12.1. Whoso loveth instruction loveth knowledge. 8. A man shall be commended according to his wisdom. 15. He that hearkeneth unto counsel *is* wise.

Pro. 13.14. The law of the wise *is* a fountain of life, to depart from the snares of death. 15. Good understanding giveth favour. 16. Every prudent *man* dealeth with knowledge.

Pro. 14.6. A scorner seeketh wisdom, and *findeth it* not: but knowledge *is* easy unto him that understandeth. 16. A wise *man* feareth, and departeth from evil. 18. The prudent are crowned with knowledge. 33. Wisdom resteth in the heart of him that hath understanding.

Pro. 15.14. The heart of him that hath understanding seeketh knowledge. 21. A man of understanding walketh uprightly. 33. The fear of the Lord *is* the instruction of wisdom. *v.* 22-24.

Pro. 16.16. How much better *is it* to get wisdom than gold! and to get understanding rather to be chosen than silver! 20. He that handleth a matter wisely shall find good. 22. Understanding is a wellspring of life unto him that hath it: but the instruction of fools *is* folly.

Pro. 17.10. A reproof entereth more into a wise man than an hundred stripes into a fool. 24. Wisdom *is* before him that hath understanding: but the eyes of a fool *are* in the ends of the earth.

Pro. 18.15. The heart of the prudent getteth knowledge; and the ear of the wise seeketh knowledge.

Pro. 19.8. He that getteth wisdom loveth

his own soul: he that keepeth understanding shall find good. 20. Hear counsel, and receive instruction, that thou mayest be wise in thy latter end.

Pro. 21.11. When the scorner is punished, the simple is made wise: and when the wise is instructed, he receiveth knowledge. 22. A wise *man* scaleth the city of the mighty, and casteth down the strength of the confidence thereof.

Pro. 22.17. Bow down thine ear, and hear the words of the wise, and apply thine heart unto my knowledge. 18. For *it is* a pleasant thing if thou keep them within thee; they shall withal be fitted in thy lips. 19. That thy trust may be in the Lord, I have made known to thee this day, even to thee. 20. Have not I written to thee excellent things in counsels and knowledge. 21. That I might make thee know the certainty of the words of truth; that thou mightest answer the words of truth to them that send unto thee?

Pro. 23.12. Apply thine heart unto instruction, and thine ears to the words of knowledge. 19. Hear thou, my son, and be wise, and guide thine heart in the way. 23. Buy the truth, and sell *it* not; *also* wisdom, and instruction, and understanding.

Pro. 24.3. Through wisdom is an house builded; and by understanding it is established: 4. And by knowledge shall the chambers be filled with all precious and pleasant riches. 5. A wise man is strong; yea, a man of knowledge increaseth strength. 13. The honeycomb, *which is* sweet to thy taste: 14. So *shall* the knowledge of wisdom *be* unto thy soul: when thou hast found *it*, then there shall be a reward, and thy expectation shall not be cut off.

Pro. 28.5. They that seek the Lord understand all *things*.

Ecc. 2.13. I saw that wisdom excelleth folly, as far as light excelleth darkness. 14. The wise man's eyes *are* in his head.

Ecc. 7.11. Wisdom *is* good with an inheritance: and *by it there is* profit to them that see the sun. 12. For wisdom *is* a defence, *and* money *is* a defence: but the excellency of knowledge *is, that* wisdom giveth life to them that have it. 19. Wisdom strengtheneth the wise more than ten mighty *men* which are in the city.

Ecc. 8.1. Who *is* as the wise *man?* and who knoweth the interpretation of a thing? a man's wisdom maketh his face to shine, and the boldness of his face shall be changed. 5. A wise man's heart discerneth both time and judgment.

Ecc. 9.15. There was found in it a poor wise man, and he by his wisdom delivered the city; yet no man remembered that same poor man. 16. Then said I, Wisdom *is* better than strength: nevertheless the poor man's wisdom is despised, and his words are not heard. 18. Wisdom *is* better than weapons of war: but one sinner destroyeth much good. *v.* 13,14.

Ecc. 10.2. A wise man's heart *is* at his right hand; but a fool's heart at his left. 10. If the iron be blunt, and he do not whet the edge, then must he put to more strength: but wisdom *is* profitable to direct. *v.* 3.

Isa. 11.9. The earth shall be full of the knowledge of the Lord, as the waters cover the sea

Isa. 29.24. They also that erred in spirit shall come to understanding, and they that murmured shall learn doctrine.

Isa. 33.6. Wisdom and knowledge shall be the stability of thy times, *and* strength of salvation: the fear of the Lord *is* his treasure.

Jer. 9.23. Let not the wise *man* glory in his wisdom, neither let the mighty *man* glory in his might, let not the rich *man* glory in his riches: 24. But let him that glorieth glory in this, that he understandeth and knoweth me.

Jer. 31.34. They shall all know me, from the least of them unto the greatest of them, saith the Lord.

Dan. 11.32. The people that do know their God shall be strong, and do *exploits*. 33. And they that understand among the people shall instruct many.

Dan. 12.3. They that be wise shall shine as the brightness of the firmament. 4. Many shall run to and fro, and knowledge shall be increased. 10. None of the wicked shall understand; but the wise shall understand.

Hos. 6.3. Then shall we know, *if* we follow on to know the Lord. 6. I desired the knowledge of God more than burnt-offerings.

Hos. 14.9. Who *is* wise, and he shall understand these *things?* prudent, and he shall know them?

Zec. 11.11. So the poor of the flock that waited upon me knew that it *was* the word of the Lord.

Mat. 7.24. Whosoever heareth these sayings of mine, and doeth them, I will liken him unto a wise man, which built his house upon a rock.

Mat. 25.4. The wise took oil in their vessels with their lamps.

Mar. 12.34. When Jesus saw that he answered discreetly, he said unto him, Thou art not far from the kingdom of God.

Luk. 7.35. Wisdom is justified of all her children. Mat. 11.19.

Luk. 11.34. The light of the body is the eye: therefore when thine eye is single, thy whole body also is full of light; but when *thine eye* is evil, thy body also *is* full of darkness. 35. Take heed therefore that the light which is in thee be not darkness. 36. If thy whole body therefore *be* full of light, having no part dark, the whole shall be full of light, as when the bright shining of a candle doth give thee light. Mat. 6.22.

Jno. 4.10. If thou knewest the gift of God, and who it is that saith to thee, Give me to drink; thou wouldest have asked of him, and he would have given thee living water. 22. Ye worship ye know not what: we know what we worship: for salvation is of the Jews.

Jno. 7.17. If any man will do his will, he shall know of the doctrine, whether it be of God, or *whether* I speak of myself.

Jno. 8.32. Ye shall know the truth, and the truth shall make you free.

Jno. 10.4. When he putteth forth his own sheep, he goeth before them, and the sheep follow him: for they know his voice. 14. I am the good shepherd, and know my *sheep*, and am known of mine.

Jno. 17.3. This is life eternal, that they might know thee the only true God, and Jesus Christ, whom thou hast sent. 7. They have known that all things whatsoever thou hast given me are of thee. 8. For I have given unto them the words which thou gavest me; and they have received *them*, and have known surely that I came out from thee, and they have believed that thou didst send me. 25. O righteous Father, the world hath not known thee: but I have known thee, and these have known that thou hast sent me.

Rom. 2.18. Knowest *his* will, and approvest the things that are more excellent, being instructed out of the law.

Rom. 15.14. I myself also am persuaded of you, my brethren, that ye also are full of goodness, filled with all knowledge, able also to admonish one another.

Rom. 16.19. I would have you wise unto that which is good, and simple concerning evil.

1 Cor. 2.6. We speak wisdom among them that are perfect: yet not the wisdom of this world, nor of the princes of this world, that come to nought: 7. But we speak the wisdom of God in a mystery, *even* the hidden *wisdom*, which God ordained before the world unto our glory. 15. He that is spiritual judgeth all things, yet he himself is judged of no man. 16. For who hath known the mind of the Lord, that he may instruct him? But we have the mind of Christ.

1 Cor. 3.18. Let no man deceive himself. If any man among you seemeth to be wise in this world, let him become a fool, that he may be wise.

1 Cor. 13.11. When I was a child, I spake as a child, I understood as a child, I thought as a child: but when I became a man, I put away childish things.

1 Cor. 14.20. Brethren, be not children in understanding: howbeit in malice be ye children, but in understanding be men.

2 Cor. 2.11. Lest Satan should get an advantage of us: for we are not ignorant of his devices.

2 Cor. 8.7. Ye abound in every *thing*, *in* faith, and utterance, and knowledge.

Gal. 4.9. After that ye have known God, or rather are known of God.

Eph. 4.13. Till we all come in the unity of the faith, and of the knowledge of the Son of God, unto a perfect man, unto the measure of the stature of the fulness of Christ.

Eph. 5.17. Be ye not unwise, but understanding what the will of the Lord *is*.

Phil. 3.1. To write the same things to you, to me indeed *is* not grievous, but for you *it is* safe. 8. I count all things *but* loss for the excellency of the knowledge of Christ Jesus my Lord: for whom I have suffered the loss of all things, and do count them *but* dung, that I may win Christ. 10. That I may know him, and the power of his resurrection, and the fellowship of his sufferings, being made conformable unto his death.

Col. 1.6. Since the day ye heard *of it*, and knew the grace of God in truth.

Col. 3.10. Have put on the new *man*, which is renewed in knowledge after the image of him that created him. 16. Let the word of Christ dwell in you richly in all wisdom.

1 The. 5.4. Ye, brethren, are not in darkness, that that day should overtake you as a thief. 5. Ye are all the children of light, and the children of the day: we are not of the

night, nor of darkness. 21. Prove all things; hold fast that which is good.

1 Tim. 2.4. Who will have all men to be saved, and to come unto the knowledge of the truth.

1 Pet. 3.15. *Be* ready always to *give* an answer to every man that asketh you a reason of the hope that is in you.

2 Pet. 1.2. Grace and peace be multiplied unto you through the knowledge of God, and of Jesus our Lord, 3. His divine power hath given unto us all things that *pertain* unto life and godliness, through the knowledge of him that hath called us to glory and virtue. 5. Add to virtue knowledge. 8. If these things be in you, and abound, they make *you that ye shall* neither *be* barren nor unfruitful in the knowledge of our Lord Jesus Christ. 12. I will not be negligent to put you always in remembrance of these things, though ye know *them*, and be established in the present truth.

2 Pet. 2.20. They have escaped the pollutions of the world through the knowledge of the Lord and Saviour Jesus Christ.

2 Pet. 3.18. Grow in grace, and *in* the knowledge of our Lord and Saviour Jesus Christ.

1 Jno. 2.3. Hereby we do know that we know him, if we keep his commandments. 13. I write unto you, fathers, because ye have known him *that is* from the beginning. I write unto you, little children, because ye have known the Father. 21. I have not written unto you because ye know not the truth, but because ye know it, and that no lie is of the truth.

1 Jno. 3.19. Hereby we know that we are of the truth, and shall assure our hearts before him.

1 Jno. 4.6. We are of God: he that knoweth God heareth us; he that is not of God heareth not us. Hereby know we the spirit of truth, and the spirit of error.

See GOD'S FAVOUR.

WISDOM, SPIRITUAL UNDERSTANDING, &c., FROM CHRIST. Isa. 42.6. I will give thee for a covenant of the people, for a light of the Gentiles; 7. To open the blind eyes, to bring out the prisoners from the prison, *and* them that sit in darkness out of the prison-house.

Isa. 53.11. By his knowledge shall my righteous servant justify many.

Mat. 11.27. Neither knoweth any man the Father, save the Son, and *he* to whomsoever the Son will reveal *him*.

Luk. 1.78. The dayspring from on high hath visited us, 79. To give light to them that sit in darkness and *in* the shadow of death, to guide our feet into the way of peace.

Luk. 21.15. I will give you a mouth and wisdom, which all your adversaries shall not be able to gainsay nor resist.

Luk. 24.32. Did not our heart burn within us, while he talked with us by the way, and while he opened to us the scriptures? 45. Then opened he their understanding, that they might understand the scriptures.

Jno. 1.4. In him was life; and the life was the light of men. 9. *That* was the true Light, which lighteth every man that cometh into the world. 17. The law was given by Moses, *but* grace and truth came by Jesus Christ. 18.

No man hath seen God at any time; the only-begotten Son, which is in the bosom of the Father, he hath declared *him*.

Jno. 8.12. I am the light of the world: he that followeth me shall not walk in darkness, but shall have the light of life. 19. If ye had known me, ye should have known my Father also. 31. If ye continue in my word, *then* are ye my disciples indeed; 32. And ye shall know the truth, and the truth shall make you free.

Jno. 9.5. As long as I am in the world, I am the light of the world. 39. For judgment I am come into this world, that they which see not might see.

Jno. 12.45. He that seeth me seeth him that sent me. 46. I am come a light into the world, that whosoever believeth on me should not abide in darkness.

Jno. 14.6. I am the way, and the truth, and the life: no man cometh unto the Father, but by me. 7. If ye had known me, ye should have known my Father also: and from henceforth ye know him, and have seen him.

Jno. 15.15. I have called you friends; for all things that I have heard of my Father I have made known unto you.

Jno. 17.6. I have manifested thy name unto the men which thou gavest me out of the world. 26. I have declared unto them thy name, and will declare *it*: that the love wherewith thou hast loved me may be in them, and I in them.

Jno. 18.37. For this cause came I into the world, that I should bear witness unto the truth. Every one that is of the truth heareth my voice.

1 Cor. 1.30. Of him are ye in Christ Jesus, who of God is made unto us wisdom.

Eph. 5.8. Ye were sometimes darkness, but now *are* ye light in the Lord.

2 Tim. 2.7. The Lord give thee understanding in all things.

1 Jno. 5.20. We know that the Son of God is come, and hath given us an understanding, that we may know him that is true, and we are in him that is true, *even* in his Son Jesus Christ.

See WORD OF GOD ENLIGHTENING.

WISDOM, SPIRITUAL UNDERSTANDING, &c., FROM GOD. Ex. 4.11. Who hath made man's mouth? or who maketh the dumb, or deaf, or the seeing, or the blind? have not I the Lord? 12. Now therefore go, and I will be with thy mouth, and teach thee what thou shalt say.

Deu. 4.35. Unto thee it was shewed, that thou mightest know that the Lord he is God; *there* is none else beside him. *v.* 36.

Deu. 8.18. Remember the Lord thy God: for *it* is he that giveth thee power to get wealth.

Deu. 29.4. The Lord hath not given you an heart to perceive, and eyes to see, and ears to hear, unto this day.

Deu. 32.10. He led him about, he instructed him.

1 Kin. 3.12. Lo, I have given thee a wise and an understanding heart; so that there was none like thee before thee, neither after thee shall any arise like unto thee. 1 Kin. 4. 29. 1 Kin. 5.12. 1 Kin. 10.24.

Job 11.5. Oh that God 6. Would shew thee the secrets of wisdom, that *they are* double to that which is!

Job 28.12. Where shall wisdom be found? and where *is* the place of understanding? 23. God knoweth the place thereof. 28. And unto man he said, Behold, the fear of the Lord, that *is* wisdom; and to depart from evil *is* understanding. *v.* 12-28.

Job 32.8. The inspiration of the Almighty giveth them understanding.

Job 33.16. He openeth the ears of men, and sealeth their instruction.

Job 35.11. Who teacheth us more than the beasts of the earth, and maketh us wiser than the fowls of heaven.

Job 36.22. Who teacheth like him?

Job 37.7. He sealeth up the hand of every man; that all men may know his work.

Job 38.36. Who hath put wisdom in the inward parts? or who hath given understanding to the heart?

Psa. 16.7. I will bless the Lord, who hath given me counsel: my reins also instruct me in the night seasons.

Psa. 19.1. The heavens declare the glory of God, and the firmament sheweth his handywork. 2. Day unto day uttereth speech, and night unto night sheweth knowledge.

Psa. 25.8. Good and upright *is* the Lord: therefore will he teach sinners in the way. 9. The meek will he guide in judgment: and the meek will he teach his way. 12. What man *is* he that feareth the Lord? him shall he teach in the way *that* he shall choose. 14. The secret of the Lord *is* with them that fear him; and he will shew them his covenant.

Psa. 32.8. I will instruct thee and teach thee in the way which thou shalt go: I will guide thee with mine eye.

Psa. 36.9. With thee *is* the fountain of life: in thy light shall we see light.

Psa. 51.6. In the hidden *part* thou shalt make me to know wisdom.

Psa. 71.17. O God, thou hast taught me from my youth: and hitherto have I declared thy wondrous works.

Psa. 94.10. He that teacheth man knowledge, *shall not he know?* 12. Blessed *is* the man whom thou chastenest, O Lord, and teachest him out of thy law.

Psa. 112.4. Unto the upright there ariseth light in the darkness.

Pro. 2.6. The Lord giveth wisdom: out of his mouth *cometh* knowledge and understanding. 7. He layeth up sound wisdom for the righteous.

Pro. 3.6. In all thy ways acknowledge him, and he shall direct thy paths. *v.* 5.

Ecc. 2.26. *God* giveth to a man that *is* good in his sight wisdom, and knowledge.

Isa. 28.26. His God doth instruct him to discretion, *and* doth teach him.

Isa. 30.21. Thine ears shall hear a word behind thee, saying, This *is* the way, walk ye in it, when ye turn to the right hand, and when ye turn to the left.

Isa. 42.16. I will bring the blind by a way *that* they knew not; I will lead them in paths *that* they have not known: I will make darkness light before them, and crooked things straight.

Isa. 48.17. I *am* the Lord thy God which teacheth thee to profit, which leadeth thee by the way *that* thou shouldest go.

Isa. 54.13. All thy children *shall be* taught of the Lord.

Isa. 58.11. The Lord shall guide thee continually.

Jer. 24.7. I will give them an heart to know me, that I *am* the Lord. 2 Chr. 33.13.

Dan. 1.17. God gave them knowledge and skill in all learning and wisdom.

Dan. 2.21. He giveth wisdom unto the wise, and knowledge to them that know understanding: 22. He revealeth the deep and secret things.

Mat. 11.25. Thou hast hid these things from the wise and prudent, and hast revealed them unto babes.

Mat. 13.11. It is given unto you to know the mysteries of the kingdom of heaven.

Mat. 16.17. Flesh and blood hath not revealed *it* unto thee, but my Father which is in heaven.

Jno. 6.45. They shall be all taught of God. Every man therefore that hath heard, and hath learned of the Father, cometh unto me. Isa. 54.13.

Act. 14.17. He left not himself without witness, in that he did good, and gave us rain from heaven, and fruitful seasons, filling our hearts with food and gladness.

Rom. 1.19. That which may be known of God is manifest in them; for God hath shewed *it* unto them. 20. For the invisible things of him from the creation of the world are clearly seen, being understood by the things that are made, *even* his eternal power and Godhead.

2 Cor. 4.6. God, who commanded the light to shine out of darkness, hath shined in our hearts, to *give* the light of the knowledge of the glory of God in the face of Jesus Christ.

Eph. 1.9. Having made known unto us the mystery of his will, according to his good pleasure, which he hath purposed in himself.

Phil. 3.15. If in any thing ye be otherwise minded, God shall reveal even this unto you.

Col. 1.26. The mystery which hath been hid from ages and from generations, but now is made manifest to his saints: 27. To whom God would make known what *is* the riches of the glory of this mystery among the Gentiles.

2 Tim. 1.7. God hath not given us the spirit of fear; but of power, and of love, and of a sound mind.

Jas. 1.5. If any of you lack wisdom, let him ask of God, that giveth to all *men* liberally, and upbraideth not; and it shall be given him.

Jas. 3.17. The wisdom that is from above is first pure, then peaceable, gentle, *and* easy to be entreated, full of mercy and good fruits, without partiality, and without hypocrisy.

See PROPHETS, INSPIRATION OF—GOD PROTECTOR AND GUIDE.

WISDOM, SPIRITUAL UNDERSTANDING, &c., FROM THE HOLY SPIRIT. Gen. 41.38. Can we find *such a one* as this *is*, a man in whom the Spirit of God *is? v.* 39.

Ex. 31.3. I have filled him with the Spirit of God, in wisdom, and in understanding, and in knowledge, and in all manner of workmanship. *v.* 6. Ex. 35.31-35. Ex. 36.1.

Neh. 9.20. Thou gavest also thy good Spirit to instruct them.

Pro. 1.23. I will pour out my Spirit unto you, I will make known my words unto you.

Isa. 11.2. The Spirit of the Lord shall rest upon him, the spirit of wisdom and understanding, the spirit of counsel and might, the spirit of knowledge and of the fear of the Lord: 3. And shall make him of quick understanding in the fear of the Lord.

Luk. 12.12. The Holy Ghost shall teach you in the same hour what ye ought to say.

Jno. 14.26. The Holy Ghost, whom the Father will send in my name, he shall teach you all things, and bring all things to your remembrance, whatsoever I have said unto you.

Jno. 16.13. When he, the Spirit of truth, is come, he will guide you into all truth: for he shall not speak of himself; but whatsoever he shall hear, *that* shall he speak: and he will shew you things to come. 14. He shall glorify me: for he shall receive of mine, and shall shew *it* unto you.

Act. 6.3. Look ye out among you seven men of honest report, full of the Holy Ghost and wisdom.

1 Cor. 2.9. Neither have entered into the heart of man, the things which God hath prepared for them that love him. 10. But God hath revealed *them* unto us by his Spirit: for the Spirit searcheth all things, yea, the deep things of God. 12. We have received, not the spirit of the world, but the Spirit which is of God; that we might know the things that are freely given to us of God. 13. Not in the words which man's wisdom teacheth, but which the Holy Ghost teacheth. 14. The natural man receiveth not the things of the Spirit of God: for they are foolishness unto him; neither can he know *them*, because they are spiritually discerned.

1 Cor. 12.8. To one is given by the Spirit the word of wisdom; to another the word of knowledge by the same Spirit. *v.* 10.

Eph. 1.17. That the God of our Lord Jesus Christ, the Father of glory, may give unto you the spirit of wisdom and revelation in the knowledge of him.

1 Jno. 2.20. Ye have an unction from the Holy One, and ye know all things. 27. The anointing which ye have received of him abideth in you, and ye need not that any man teach you; but as the same anointing teacheth you of all things, and is truth, and is no lie, and even as it hath taught you, ye shall abide in him.

See PROPHETS, INSPIRATION BY THE HOLY SPIRIT.

WISDOM FROM THE SCRIPTURES. See WORD OF GOD ENLIGHTENING.

WISDOM, SPIRITUAL UNDERSTANDING, &c., PRAYER FOR. Ex. 33.13. I pray thee, if I have found grace in thy sight, shew me now thy way, that I may know thee, that I may find grace in thy sight. 18. I beseech thee, shew me thy glory. Gen. 24.12-27.

1 Kin. 3.7. I *am but* a little child: I know not *how* to go out or come in. 9. Give therefore thy servant an understanding heart to judge thy people, that I may discern between good and bad: for who is able to judge this thy so great a people? 2 Chr. 1.10.

1 Kin. 8.36. Teach them the good way wherein they should walk. 2 Chr. 6.27.

Job. 34.32. *That which* I see not teach thou me.

Psa. 5.8. Lead me, O Lord, in thy rightcousness because of mine enemies; make thy way straight before my face.

Psa. 25.4. Shew me thy ways, O Lord; teach me thy paths. 5. Lead me in thy truth, and teach me: for thou *art* the God of my salvation; on thee do I wait all the day.

Psa. 27.11. Teach me thy way, O Lord, and lead me in a plain path, because of mine enemies.

Psa. 31.3. For thy name's sake lead me, and guide me.

Psa. 39.4. Lord, make me to know mine end, and the measure of my days, what it *is*; *that* I may know how frail I *am*.

Psa. 43.3. O send out thy light and thy truth: let them lead me; let them bring me unto thy holy hill.

Psa. 86.11. Teach me thy way, O Lord; I will walk in thy truth: unite my heart to fear thy name.

Psa. 90.12. So teach *us* to number our days, that we may apply *our* hearts unto wisdom.

Psa. 119.12. Blessed *art* thou, O Lord: teach me thy statutes. 18. Open thou mine eyes, that I may behold wondrous things out of thy law. 19. I *am* a stranger in the earth: hide not thy commandments from me. 27. Make me to understand the way of thy precepts: so shall I talk of thy wondrous works. 33. Teach me, O Lord, the way of thy statutes; and I shall keep it *unto* the end. 34. Give me understanding, and I shall keep thy law; yea, I shall observe it with *my* whole heart. 66. Teach me good judgment and knowledge: for I have believed thy commandments. 68. Thou *art* good, and doest good; teach me thy statutes.

Psa. 119.73. Thy hands have made me and fashioned me: give me understanding, that I may learn thy commandments. 80. Let my heart be sound in thy statutes; that I be not ashamed. 124. Deal with thy servant according unto thy mercy, and teach me thy statutes. 125. I *am* thy servant; give me understanding, that I may know thy testimonies. 135. Make thy face to shine upon thy servant; and teach me thy statutes. 144. Give me understanding, and I shall live. 169. Let my cry come near before thee, O Lord: give me understanding according to thy word. 171. My lips shall utter praise, when thou hast taught me thy statutes. *v.* 26.

Psa. 139.24. Lead me in the way everlasting.

Psa. 143.8. Cause me to hear thy lovingkindness in the morning; for in thee do I trust: cause me to know the way wherein I should walk; for I lift up my soul unto thee. 10. Teach me to do thy will; for thou *art* my God: thy Spirit *is* good; lead me into the land of uprightness.

Eph. 1.17. That the God of our Lord Jesus Christ, the Father of glory, may give unto you the spirit of wisdom and revelation in the knowledge of him: 18. The eyes of your understanding being enlightened; that ye may know what is the hope of his calling, and what the riches of the glory of his inheritance in the saints, 19. And what *is* the exceeding greatness of his power to us-ward who believe, according to the working of his mighty power.

Eph. 3.18. That ye may be able to compre-

hend with all saints what *is* the breadth, and length, and depth, and height; 19. And to know the love of Christ, which passeth knowledge, that ye might be filled with all the fulness of God.

Phil. 1.9. I pray, that your love may abound yet more and more in knowledge and *in* all judgment; 10. That ye may approve things that are excellent; that ye may be sincere and without offence till the day of Christ.

Col. 1.9. We also, do not cease to pray for you, and to desire that ye might be filled with the knowledge of his will in all wisdom and spiritual understanding; 10. Being fruitful in every good work, and increasing in the knowledge of God.

Col. 2.2. That their hearts might be comforted, being knit together in love, and unto all riches of the full assurance of understanding, to the acknowledgment of the mystery of God, and of the Father, and of Christ.

1 The. 3.11. Now God himself and our Father, and our Lord Jesus Christ, direct our way unto you.

2 Tim. 2.7. Consider what I say; and the Lord give thee understanding in all things.

WISDOM AND KINDNESS IN SPEECH, EXCELLENCE OF—EXEMPLIFIED. Job 16.5. I would strengthen you with my mouth, and the moving of my lips should asswage *your grief.*

Job 27.4. My lips shall not speak wickedness, nor my tongue utter deceit.

Psa. 15.1. Lord, who shall abide in thy tabernacle? 2. He that speaketh the truth in his heart. 3. *He that* backbiteth not with his tongue.

Psa. 17.3. I am purposed *that* my mouth shall not transgress.

Psa. 37.30. The mouth of the righteous speaketh wisdom, and his tongue talketh of judgment.

Psa. 39.1. I said, I will take heed to my ways, that I sin not with my tongue: I will keep my mouth with a bridle, while the wicked is before me.

Psa. 71.24. My tongue also shall talk of thy righteousness all the day long.

Psa. 77.12. I will meditate also of all thy work, and talk of thy doings.

Psa. 105.2. Talk ye of all his wondrous works.

Psa. 119.13. With my lips have I declared all the judgments of thy mouth. 27. Make me to understand the way of thy precepts: so shall I talk of thy wondrous works. 46. I will speak of thy testimonies also before kings, and will not be ashamed. 172. My tongue shall speak of thy word: for all thy commandments *are* righteousness.

Psa. 141.3. Set a watch, O Lord, before my mouth; keep the door of my lips.

Psa. 145.5. I will speak of the glorious honour of thy majesty, and of thy wondrous works. 6. And *men* shall speak of the might of thy terrible acts: and I will declare thy greatness. 7. They shall abundantly utter the memory of thy great goodness, and shall sing of thy righteousness. 11. They shall speak of the glory of thy kingdom, and talk of thy power; 12. To make known to the sons of men his mighty acts, and the glorious majesty of his kingdom.

Pro. 10.11. The mouth of a righteous *man*

is a well of life.   13. In the lips of him that hath understanding wisdom is found. 19. In the multitude of words there wanteth not sin : but he that refraineth his lips *is* wise.   20. The tongue of the just *is as* choice silver :   21. The lips of the righteous feed many. *3*1. The mouth of the just bringeth forth wisdom. 32. The lips of the righteous know what is acceptable.

Pro. 11.12. A man of understanding holdeth his peace.   13. A talebearer revealeth secrets : but he that is of a faithful spirit concealeth the matter.

Pro. 12.6.   The mouth of the upright shall deliver them.   14. A man shall be satisfied with good by the fruit of *his* mouth.   16. A prudent *man* coVereth shame.   17. *He that* speaketh truth sheweth forth righteousness. 18. The tongue of the wise *is* health.   19. The lip of truth shall be established for ever.   23. A prudent man concealeth knowledge.

Pro. 13.2. A man shall eat good by the fruit of *his* mouth.   3. He that keepeth his mouth keepeth his life.

Pro. 14.3. The lips of the wise shall preserve them.   5. A faithful witness will not lie.

Pro. 15.1. A soft answer turneth away wrath.   2. The tongue of the wise useth knowledge aright.   4. A wholesome tongue *is* a tree of life.   7. The lips of the wise disperse knowledge.   23. A man hath joy by the answer of his mouth : and a word *spoken* in due season, how good *is it !*   26. *The words* of the pure *are* pleasant words.   28. The heart of the righteous studieth to answer.

Pro. 16.21. The wise in heart shall be called prudent : and the sweetness of the lips increaseth learning.   23. The heart of the wise teacheth his mouth, and addeth learning to his lips.   24. Pleasant words *are as* an honeycomb, sweet to the soul, and health to the bones.

Pro. 17.27. He that hath knowledge spareth his words : *and* a man of understanding is of an excellent spirit.   28. Even a fool, when he holdeth his peace, is counted wise: *and* he that shutteth his lips *is esteemed* a man of understanding.

Pro. 18.4. The words of a man s mouth *are as* deep waters, *and* the wellspring of wisdom *as* a flowing brook.   20. A man's belly shall be satisfied with the fruit of his mouth ; *and* with the increase of his lips shall he be filled. 21. Death and life *are* in the power of the tongue : and they that love it shall eat the fruit thereof.

Pro. 19.1. Better *is* the poor that walketh in his integrity, than *he that is* perverse in his lips, and is a fool.   22. A poor man *is* better than a liar.

Pro. 20.15. There is gold, and a multitude of rubies : but the lips of knowledge *are* a precious jewel.

Pro. 21.23. Whoso keepeth his mouth and his tongue keepeth his soul from troubles.

Pro. 22.11. He that loveth pureness of 'heart, *for* the grace of his lips the king *shall* be his friend.

Pro. 25.11. A word fitly spoken *is like* apples of gold in pictures of silver.   *v.* 15.

Pro. 26.5. Answer a fool according to his folly, lest he be wise in his own conceit.

Pro. 29.11. A fool uttereth all his mind . but a wise *man* keepeth it in till afterwards.

Pro. 31.26. She openeth her mouth with wisdom ; and in her tongue *is* the law of kindness.

Ecc. 3.7. A time to keep silence, and a time to speak.

Ecc. 9.17. The words of wise *men are* heard in quiet more than the cry of him that ruleth among fools.

Ecc. 10.12. The words of a wise man's mouth *are* gracious.

Ecc. 12.11. The words of the wise *are* as goads, and as nails fastened *by* the masters of assemblies.

Amos 5.13. The prudent shall keep silence in that time ; for it *is* an evil time.

Zeph. 3.13. The remnant of Israel shall not do iniquity, nor speak lies.

Mat. 12.37. By thy words thou shalt be justified, and by thy words thou shalt be condemned.   *v.* 36.

Luk. 6.45. A good man out of the good treasure of his heart bringeth forth that which is good ; for of the abundance of the heart his mouth speaketh.

Eph. 4.25. Speak every man truth with his neighbour : for we are members one of another.   29. Let no corrupt communication proceed out of your mouth, but that which is good to the use of edifying, that it may minister grace unto the hearers.   Zec. 8.16.   Eph. 5.4.

Col. 4.6. Let your speech *be* alway with grace, seasoned with salt, that ye may know how ye ought to answer every man.

Jas. 1.19. Let every man be swift to hear, slow to speak, slow to wrath.   *v.* 26.

Jas. 3.2. If any man offend not in word, the same *is* a perfect man, *and* able also to bridle the whole body.   13. Who *is* a wise man and endued with knowledge among you? let him shew out of a good conversation his works with meekness of wisdom.

See INTEGRITY—SAINTS, COMMUNION OF.

WISDOM, NATURAL, KNOWLEDGE, LEARNING. Job 5.13. He taketh the wise in their own craftiness, and the counsel of the froward is carried headlong.

Job 11.12. Vain man would be wise, though man be born *like* a wild ass's colt.

Job 12.11. Doth not the ear try words? Job 34.13.

Pro. 18.1. Through desire a man, having separated himself, seeketh *and* intermeddleth with all wisdom.   Job 28.

Ecc. 1.18. In much wisdom *is* much grief : and he that increaseth knowledge increaseth sorrow.   *v.* 13-18.   Ecc. 2.15,16.

Ecc. 7.16. Be not righteous over much ; neither make thyself over wise : why shouldest thou destroy thyself?   17. Be not over much wicked, neither be thou foolish : why shouldest thou die before thy time?   23. All this have I proved by wisdom : I said, I will be wise ; but it *was* far from me.   24. That which is far off, and exceeding deep, who can find it out?   25. I applied mine heart to know, and to search, and to seek out wisdom, and the reason *of things,* and to know the wickedness of folly, even of foolishness *and* madness.

Ecc. 12.12. Of making many books *there is* no end ; and much study *is* a weariness of the flesh.

Isa. 29.14. The wisdom of their wise *men* shall perish, and the understanding of their prudent *men* shall be hid

Isa. 47.10. Thy wisdom and thy knowledge, it hath perverted thee; and thou hast said in thine heart, I *am*, and none else besides me.

Jer. 8.9. The wise *men* are ashamed, they are dismayed and taken: lo, they have rejected the word of the Lord; and what wisdom *is* in them?

Jer. 9.23. Thus saith the Lord, Let not the wise *man* glory in his wisdom.

Jer. 49.7. *Is* wisdom no more in Teman? is counsel perished from the prudent? is their wisdom vanished?

Luk. 16.8. The children of this world are in their generation wiser than the children of light.

Rom 1.22. Professing themselves to be wise, they became fools, 23. And changed the glory of the uncorruptible God into an image made like to corruptible man.

1 Cor. 1.17. not with wisdom of words, lest the cross of Christ should be made of none effect. 19. For it is written, I will destroy the wisdom of the wise, and will bring to nothing the understanding of the prudent. 20. Where *is* the wise? where *is* the scribe? where *is* the disputer of this world? hath not God made foolish the wisdom of this world? 21. For after that, in the wisdom of God, the world by wisdom knew not God, it pleased God by the foolishness of preaching to save them that believe. 22. For the Jews require a sign, and the Greeks seek after wisdom. 26. Not many wise men after the flesh, not many mighty, not many noble, *are called:* 27. But God hath chosen the foolish things of the world to confound the wise.

1 Cor. 2.1. I, brethren, when I came to you, came not with excellency of speech or of wisdom, declaring unto you the testimony of God. 4. My speech and my preaching *was* not with enticing words of man's wisdom, but in demonstration of the Spirit and of power: 5. That your faith should not stand in the wisdom of men, but in the power of God. 6. Howbeit we speak wisdom among them that are perfect: yet not the wisdom of this world, nor of the princes of this world, that come to nought. 13. Which things also we speak, not in the words which man's wisdom teacheth.

1 Cor. 3.18. If any man among you seemeth to be wise in this world, let him become a fool, that he may be wise. 19. The wisdom of this world is foolishness with God. For it is written, He taketh the wise in their own craftiness. 20. And again, the Lord knoweth the thoughts of the wise, that they are vain.

1 Cor. 8.1. Knowledge puffeth up, but charity edifieth.

2 Cor. 1.12. Not with fleshly wisdom, but by the grace of God, we have had our conversation in the world, and more abundantly to you-ward.

Col. 2.8. Beware lest any man spoil you through philosophy and vain deceit, after the tradition of men, after the rudiments of the world, and not after Christ.

1 Tim. 6.20. Keep that which is committed to thy trust, avoiding profane *and* vain babblings, and oppositions of science falsely so called.

Jas. 3.15. This wisdom descendeth not from above, but *is* earthly, sensual, devilish.

WISDOM, EXAMPLES OF: Jethro, Num. 10.31. Solomon, 1 Kin. 3.16-28. 1 Kin. 4.

30-34. Ethan, &c., 1 Kin. 4.31. Men of Issachar, 1 Chr. 12.32. A king, Dan. 8.25. Daniel, Dan. 6.3. Moses, Act. 7.22.

See PRUDENCE.

WISE MEN. See MAGI.

WITCHCRAFT. See SORCERY.

WITNESSES. Lev. 5.1. Two required, Num. 35.30. Deu. 17.6. Deu. 19.15. Mat. 18.16. 2 Cor. 13.1. 1 Tim. 5.19. Heb. 10.28. Witnesses of bargains, Ruth 4.1-9. Jer. 32.10-12; of marriage, Ruth 4.10. Isa. 8.2. Criminals stoned by, Deu. 17.7. Act. 7.58. Symbolical, Rev. 11.3. False witness, see FALSEHOOD.

WIVES. See WOMEN.

WIZARD. See SORCERY.

WOLF, Gen. 49.27. Jer. 5.6. Eze. 22.27. Mat. 10.16. Jno. 10.12. Illustrative, Isa. 11. 6. Zeph. 3.3. Mat. 7.15. Act. 20.29.

WOMEN, WIVES. Creation of woman, Gen. 1.27. Gen. 2.21,22. Relation to man, Gen. 2.18,20. 1 Cor. 11.3-12. Fall of, curse on, Gen. 3.1-16. 2 Cor. 11.3. 1 Tim. 2.14. Promise to, Gen. 3.15.

Had separate tents or apartments, Gen. 24.67. Gen. 31.33. Est. 2.9,11. Veiled the face, Gen. 24.65, see VAIL. Wore long hair, 1 Cor. 11.5-15. Worshipped in the tabernacle, Ex. 38.8. 1 Sam. 2.22. Joined in temple-music, 1 Chr. 25.5,6. Ezr. 2.65. Celebrated national victories, Ex. 15.20. 1 Sam. 18.6. Attended funerals as mourners, Jer. 9.17,20. Domestic duties of, Gen. 18.6. Pro. 31.15-18. Mat. 24.41. Spun, Ex. 35.25,26. 1 Sam. 2.19. Pro. 31.19-24. Gleaned, Ruth 2.8. Kept vineyards, Song 1.6. Tending sheep, Gen. 29.9. Ex. 2.16. Drew water, Gen. 24.11-16. 1 Sam. 9.11. Jno. 4.7.

Vows of, when binding, Num. 30.3-16. Inheritance of, Num. 27.8. Num. 36. Unfaithfulness of wives tested by the water of jealousy, Num. 5.14, see ADULTERY. Punishment for injuring a woman, Ex. 21.22-25.

Government by, Isa. 3.12. To be slain by a woman a disgrace, Jud. 9.54. See QUEEN —PROPHETESS— DEACONESS— MARRIAGE— DRESS.

Gen. 2.18. God said It *is* not good that the man should be alone; I will make him an help meet for him. 23. Adam said, This *is* now bone of my bones, and flesh of my flesh: she shall be called Woman, because she was taken out of Man.

Gen. 3.16. Thy desire *shall be* to thy husband, and he shall rule over thee.

Est. 1.20. All the wives shall give to their husbands honour, both to great and small. 22. Every man should bear rule in his own house.

Pro. 11.16. A gracious woman retaineth honour.

Pro. 12.4. A virtuous woman *is* a crown to her husband.

Pro. 14.1. Every wise woman buildeth her house.

Pro. 19.14. A prudent wife *is* from the Lord. Pro. 18.22.

Pro. 31.10. Who can find a virtuous woman? for her price *is* far above rubies. 11. The heart of her husband doth safely trust in her, so that he shall have no need of spoil. 28. Her children arise up, and called her blessed; her husband, *also*, and he praiseth her. 29. Many daughters have done virtuously, but thou excellest them all. 30. Favour *is* deceitful, and beauty *is* vain : *but* a woman *that* feareth the Lord, she shall be praised. 31. Give her of the fruit of her hands ; and let her own works praise her in the gates. *v.* 1-31.

1 Cor. 7.10. Let not the wife depart from *her* husband. 13. And the woman which hath an husband that believeth not, and if he be pleased to dwell with her, let her not leave him. 14. For the unbelieving husband is sanctified by the wife, and the unbelieving wife is sanctified by the husband : else were your children unclean ; but now are they holy. 16. For what knowest thou, O wife, whether thou shalt save *thy* husband ? Or how knowest thou, O man, whether thou shalt save *thy* wife ? *v.* 1-17,28-40.

1 Cor. 11.3. The head of the woman *is* the man. 5. Every woman that prayeth or prophesieth with *her* head uncovered dishonoureth her head : for that is even all one as if she were shaven. 7. The woman is the glory of the man. 8. For the man is not of the woman ; but the woman of the man. 9. Neither was the man created for the woman ; but the woman for the man. 11. Neither is the man without the woman, neither the woman without the man, in the Lord. 12. For as the woman *is* of the man, even so *is* the man also by the woman ; but all things of God. *v.* 3-15.

1 Cor. 14.34. Let your women keep silence in the churches : for it is not permitted unto them to speak ; but *they are commanded* to be under obedience, as also saith the law. 35. And if they will learn any thing, let them ask their husbands at home ; for it is a shame for women to speak in the church.

Eph. 5.22. Wives, submit yourselves unto your own husbands, as unto the Lord. 23. For the husband is the head of the wife, even as Christ is the head of the church : and he is the saviour of the body. 24. Therefore as the church is subject unto Christ, so *let* the wives *be* to their own husbands in every thing. 33. The wife *see* that she reverence *her* husband.

Col. 3.18. Wives, submit yourselves unto your own husbands, as it is fit in the Lord.

1 Tim. 2.9. That women adorn themselves in modest apparel, with shamefacedness and sobriety ; not with broided hair, or gold, or pearls, or costly array ; 10. But (which becometh women professing godliness) with good works. 11. Let the woman learn in silence with all subjection. 12. But I suffer not a woman to teach, nor to usurp authority over the man, but to be in silence. 13. For Adam was first formed, then Eve. 14. And Adam was not deceived, but the woman being deceived was in the transgression. 15. She shall be saved in childbearing, if they continue in faith and charity and holiness with sobriety.

1 Tim. 3.11. Even so *must their* wives *be* grave, not slanderers, sober, faithful in all things.

1 Tim. 5.9. Let not a widow be taken into the number under threescore years old, having been the wife of one man. 10. Well reported of for good works ; if she have brought up children, if she have lodged strangers, if she have washed the saints' feet, if she have relieved the afflicted, if she have diligently followed every good work. 14. I will therefore that the younger women marry, bear children, guide the house, give none occasion to the adversary to speak reproachfully.

Tit. 2.3. The aged women likewise, that *they be* in behaviour as becometh holiness, not false accusers, not given to much wine, teachers of good things ; 4. That they may teach the young women to be sober, to love their husbands, to love their children. 5. *To be* discreet, chaste, keepers at home, good, obedient to their own husbands, that the word of God be not blasphemed.

1 Pet. 3.1. Likewise, ye wives *be in* subjection to your own husbands ; that, if any obey not the word, they also may without the word be won by the conversation of the wives. 2. While they behold your chaste conversation *coupled* with fear. 3. Whose adorning let it not be that outward *adorning* of plaiting the hair, and of wearing of gold, or of putting on of apparel ; 4. But *let it be* the hidden man of the heart, in that which is not corruptible, *even the ornament* of a meek and quiet spirit, which is in the sight of God of great price. 5. For after this manner in the old time the holy women also, who trusted in God, adorned themselves, being in subjection unto their own husbands : 6. Even as Sara obeyed Abraham, calling him lord : whose daughters ye are, as long as ye do well, and are not afraid with any amazement.

WOMEN AND WIVES, GOOD, EXAMPLES OF : Deborah, Jud. 4.4. Manoah's wife, Jud. 13.23. Naomi and Ruth, Ruth 1.8,16,17. Ruth 3.11. Hannah, 1 Sam. 1.10-28. Abigail, 1 Sam. 25.3. Jehoshabeath, 2 Chr. 22.11. Esther, Est. 4.15-17. Mary, Luk. 1.26-38. Elizabeth, Luk. 1.6. Anna, Luk. 2.37. Syrophenician, Mat. 15.27,28. A widow, Mar. 12.42. Mary and Martha, Mar. 14.3-9. Luk. 10.42. Jno. 11.5. Mary Magdalene, &c., Mar. 16.1. Luk. 8.3. A woman who had been a sinner, Luk. 7.37-47. A Samaritan, Jno. 4.28,29. Dorcas, Act. 9.36. Lydia, Act. 16.14. Priscilla, Act. 18.26. Phebe, Rom. 16.1,2. Mary, Rom. 16.6. Lois and Eunice, 2 Tim. 1.5. Philippians, Phil. 4.3. See PROPHETESS.

WOMEN AND WIVES, SINS AND ERRORS. Pro. 11.22. *As* a jewel of gold in a swine's snout, *so is* a fair woman which is without discretion.

Pro. 12.4. A virtuous woman *is* a crown to her husband : but she that maketh ashamed *is* as rottenness in his bones.

Pro. 14.1. Every wise woman buildeth her house : but the foolish plucketh it down with her hands.

Pro. 21.19. *It is* better to dwell in the wilderness, than with a contentious and an angry woman.

Pro. 25.24. *It is* better to dwell in the corner of the housetop, than with a brawling woman and in a wide house.

Pro. 27.15. A continual dropping in a very rainy day and a contentious woman are alike. 16. Whosoever hideth her hideth the wind, and the ointment of his right hand, *which* bewrayeth *itself*. Pro. 19.13.

Pro. 30.23. An odious *woman* when she is married ; and an handmaid that is heir to her mistress.

Ecc. 7.28. One man among a thousand have

I found; but a woman among all those have I not found. *v.* 27.

Isa. 3.16. Because the daughters of Zion are haughty, and walk with stretched forth necks and wanton eyes, walking and mincing *as* they go, and making a tinkling with their feet. 18. In that day the Lord will take away the bravery of *their* tinkling ornaments. *v.* 16-24.

Isa. 32.9. Rise up, ye women that are at ease; hear my voice, ye careless daughters; give ear unto my speech. 10. Many days and years shall ye be troubled, ye careless women. *v.* 11.

Eze. 13.18. Woe to the *women* that sew pillows to all armholes, and make kerchiefs upon the head of every stature to hunt souls! Will ye hunt the souls of my people, and will ye save the souls alive *that come* unto you?

2 Tim. 3.6. Which creep into houses, and lead captive silly women laden with sins, led away with divers lusts.

WOMEN AND WIVES, SINS AND ERRORS, EXAMPLES OF: Eve, Gen. 3.6. 1 Tim. 2.14. Sarah, Gen. 18.12. Gen. 21.10. Lot's wife, Gen. 19.26. Luk. 17.32. Lot's daughters, Gen. 19.31-38. Rebekah, Gen. 27.13. Rachel, Gen. 30.1. Gen. 31.34. Dinah, Gen. 34,1,2. Tamar, Gen. 38.14-24. Potiphar's wife, Gen. 39.7. Zipporah, Ex. 4.25. Miriam, Num. 12. Samson's wife, Jud. 14.16,17. Delilah, Jud. 16.4-20. Michal, 2 Sam. 6.16. Bathsheba, 2 Sam. 12.10. Solomon's wives, 1 Kin. 11.4. Neh. 13.26. Jezebel, 1 Kin. 21. 2 Kin. 9. 30-37. Athaliah, 2 Kin. 8.18,26,27. 2 Kin. 11.1-3,13-16. 2 Chr. 24.7. Noadiah, Neh. 6. 14. Haman's wife, Est. 5.14. Est. 6.13. Job's wife, Job 2.9. Job 19.17. Herodias and her daughter, Mar. 6.18-28. Sapphira, Act. 5.2-10. Jezebel, Rev. 2.20.

WOOL. Spun for clothing, Lev. 13.47-52. Eze. 34.3. Hos. 2.5,9. Forbidden to be mixed with linen, Deu. 22.11. Exported from Damascus, Eze. 27.18. First fleece given to the priest, Deu. 18.4.

WORD OF GOD ENLIGHTENING—WISDOM FROM. Deu. 4.6. This *is* your wisdom and your understanding in the sight of the nations, which shall hear all these statutes, and say, Surely this great nation *is* a wise and understanding people.

Psa. 19.7. The testimony of the Lord *is* sure, making wise the simple. 8. The statutes of the Lord *are* right, rejoicing the heart : the commandment of the Lord *is* pure, enlightening the eyes. *v.* 1-14.

Psa. 94.12. Blessed *is* the man whom thou chastenest, O Lord, and teachest him out of thy law.

Psa. 119.18. Open thou mine eyes, that I may behold wondrous things out of thy law. 98. Thou through thy commandments hast made me wiser than mine enemies : for they *are* ever with me. 99. I have more understanding than all my teachers : for thy testimonies *are* my meditation. 100. I understand more than the ancients, because I keep thy precepts. 104. Through thy precepts I get understanding. 105. Thy word *is* a lamp unto my feet, and a light unto my path. 130. The entrance of thy words giveth light ; it giveth understanding unto the simple. Pro. 6.23.

Pro. 1.1. The proverbs of Solomon. 2. To know wisdom and instruction ; to perceive the words of understanding ; 3. To receive the instruction of wisdom, justice, and judgment, and equity ; 4. To give subtilty to the simple, to the young man knowledge and discretion.

Jer. 8.9. The wise *men* are ashamed, they are dismayed and taken : lo, they have rejected the word of the Lord ; and what wisdom *is* in them?

Mar. 12.24. Do ye not therefore err, because ye know not the scriptures, neither the power of God?

1 Cor. 10.11. They are written for our admonition, upon whom the ends of the world are come.

2 Tim. 3.15. From a child thou hast known the holy scriptures, which are able to make thee wise unto salvation through faith which is in Christ Jesus. 16. All scripture *is* given by inspiration of God, and *is* profitable for doctrine, for reproof, for correction, for instruction in righteousness.

WORD OF GOD. ITS EXCELLENCE. To BE READ AND RECEIVED. Deu. 4.8. What nation *is there so* great, that hath statutes and judgments *so* righteous as all this law, which I set before you this day? 10. I will make them hear my words, that they may learn to fear me all the days that they shall live upon the earth, and *that* they may teach their children. Deu. 5.1.

Deu. 6.6. These words, which I command thee this day, shall be in thine heart : 7. And thou shalt teach them diligently unto thy children, and shalt talk of them when thou sittest in thine house, and when thou walkest by the way, and when thou liest down, and when thou risest up. 8. And thou shalt bind them for a sign upon thine hand, and they shall be as frontlets between thine eyes. 9. And thou shalt write them upon the posts of thy house, and on thy gates. Ex. 13.9. Deu. 11. 18.

Deu. 17.18. When he sitteth upon the throne of his kingdom, he shall write him a copy of this law in a book. 19. And it shall be with him, and he shall read therein all the days of his life : that he may learn to fear the Lord his God, to keep all the words of this law and these statutes, to do them.

Deu. 30.11. This commandment which I command thee this day, it *is* not hidden from thee, neither *is* it far off. 14. But the word *is* very nigh unto thee, in thy mouth, and in thy heart, that thou mayest do it. *v.* 12,13.

Deu. 31.11. Thou shalt read this law before all Israel in their hearing. 12. Gather the people together, men, and women, and children, and thy stranger that *is* within thy gates, that they may hear, and that they may learn, and fear the Lord your God, and observe to do all the words of this law : 13. And *that* their children, which have not known *anything*, may hear, and learn to fear the Lord your God. 19. Write ye this song for you, and teach it the children of Israel : put it in their mouths, that this song may be a witness for me against the children of Israel. 21. For it shall not be forgotten out of the mouths of their seed : 26. Take this book of the law, and put it in the side of the ark of the covenant of the Lord your God, that it may be there for a witness against thee. *v.* 9.

Deu. 32.2. My doctrine shall drop as the rain, my speech shall distil as the dew, as the small rain upon the tender herb, and as the showers upon the grass : 46. Set your hearts unto all the words which I testify among you this day, which ye shall command your children to observe to do, all the words of this law.

Deu. 33.3. They sat down at thy feet ; every one shall receive of thy words.

Jos. 1.8. This book of the law shall not depart out of thy mouth ; but thou shalt meditate therein day and night, that thou mayest observe to do according to all that is written therein : for then thou shalt make thy way prosperous, and then thou shalt have good success.

Jos. 3.9. Come hither and hear the word of the Lord your God.

1 Chr. 16.15. Be ye mindful always of his covenant ; the word *which* he commanded to a thousand generations.

Neh. 9.29. And testifiedst against them, that thou mightest bring them again unto thy law : yet they dealt proudly, and hearkened not unto thy commandments, but sinned against thy judgments (which if a man do, he shall live in them).

Job 22.22. Receive, I pray thee, the law from his mouth, and lay up his words in thine heart.

Psa. 12.6. The words of the Lord *are* pure words : *as* silver tried in a furnace of earth, purified seven times.

Psa. 18.30. The word of the Lord is tried. 2 Sam. 22.31.

Psa. 19.11. By them is thy servant warned: *and* in keeping of them *there is* great reward. *v.* 7-9.

Psa. 78.1. Give ear, O my people, *to* my law : incline your ears to the words of my mouth. 7. That they might set their hope in God, and not forget the works of God, but keep his commandments : 8. And might not be as their fathers, a stubborn and rebellious generation.

Psa. 93.5. Thy testimonies are very sure.

Psa. 102.18. This shall be written for the generation to come : and the people which shall be created shall praise the Lord.

Psa. 119.86. All thy commandments *are* faithful. 96. Thy commandment *is* exceeding broad. 128. I esteem all *thy* precepts *concerning* all *things* to be right. 129. Thy testimonies *are* wonderful. 138. Thy testimonies *that* thou hast commanded *are* righteous and very faithful. 140. Thy word *is* very pure. 142. Thy righteousness *is* an everlasting righteousness, and thy law *is* the truth. 144. The righteousness of thy testimonies *is* everlasting. 151. All thy commandments *are* truth. 152. Concerning thy testimonies, I have known of old that thou hast founded them for ever. 160. Thy word *is* true *from* the beginning : and every one of thy righteous judgments *endureth* for ever. 172. All thy commandments *are* righteousness.

Psa. 147.15. He sendeth forth his commandment *upon* earth : his word runneth very swiftly. *v.* 19,20.

Pro. 6.21. Bind them continually upon thine heart, *and* tie them about thy neck. 22. When thou goest, it shall lead thee ; when thou sleepest, it shall keep thee ; and *when* thou awakest, it shall talk with thee. 23. For

the commandment *is* a lamp ; and the law *is* light ; and reproofs of instruction *are* the way of life.

Pro. 30.5. Every word of God *is* pure.

Ecc. 5.1. Keep thy foot when thou goest to the house of God, and be more ready to hear, than to give the sacrifice of fools.

Ecc. 12.10. Acceptable words: and *that which was* written *was* upright, *even* words of truth. 11. The words of the wise *are* as goads, and as nails fastened *by* the masters of assemblies, *which* are given from one shepherd.

Isa. 8.16. Bind up the testimony, seal the law among my disciples.

Isa. 40.8. The grass withereth, the flower fadeth : but the word of our God shall stand for ever.

Isa. 55.10. As the rain cometh down, and the snow from heaven, and returneth not thither, but watereth the earth, and maketh it bring forth and bud, that it may give seed to the sower, and bread to the eater : 11. So shall my word be that goeth forth out of my mouth : it shall not return unto me void, but it shall accomplish that which I please, and it shall prosper *in the thing* whereto I sent it.

Jer. 13.15. Hear ye, and give ear ; be not proud : for the Lord hath spoken.

Jer. 22.29. O earth, earth, earth, hear the word of the Lord.

Jer. 23.28. What *is* the chaff to the wheat saith the Lord. 29. *Is* not my word like as a fire ? saith the Lord ; and like a hammer *that* breaketh the rock in pieces ?

Jer. 36.6. Read in the roll, which thou hast written from my mouth, the words of the Lord in the ears of the people in the Lord's house upon the fasting day.

Eze. 3.10. All my words that I shall speak unto thee receive in thine heart, and hear with thine ears. *v.* 3.

Dan. 10.21. The scripture of truth.

Hos. 6.5. Therefore have I hewed *them* by the prophets ; I have slain them by the words of my mouth : and thy judgments *are as* the light *that* goeth forth.

Hab. 2.2. Write the vision, and make *it* plain upon tables, that he may run that readeth it.

Zec. 7.7. *Hear* the words which the Lord hath cried by the former prophets.

Mat. 7.24. Whosoever heareth these sayings of mine, and doeth them, I will liken him unto a wise man, which built his house upon a rock : 25. And the rain descended, and the floods came, and the winds blew, and beat upon that house ; and it fell not : for it was founded upon a rock. *v.* 26,27. Luk. 6.47.

Mat. 11.15. He that hath ears to hear, let him hear.

Mar. 1.15. Repent ye, and believe the gospel.

Luk. 11.28. Yea rather, blessed *are* they that hear the word of God, and keep it.

Luk. 16.29. They have Moses and the prophets ; let them hear them. 31. If they hear not Moses and the prophets, neither will they be persuaded, though one rose from the dead.

Jno. 5.39. Search the scriptures : for in them ye think ye have eternal life : and they are they which testify of me.

Jno. 17.20. Neither pray I for these alone, but for them also which shall believe on me through their word.

Jno. 20.31. These are written, that ye might believe that Jesus is the Christ, the Son of God ; and that believing ye might have life through his name.

Rom. 3.1. What advantage then hath the Jew ? 2. Chiefly, because that unto them were committed the oracles of God.

Rom. 4.23. It was not written for his sake alone, that it was imputed to him ; 24. But for us also.

Rom. 10.17. Faith *cometh* by hearing, and hearing by the word of God. *v.* 14-18.

Rom. 12.2. Prove what *is* that good, and acceptable, and perfect, will of God.

Rom. 15.4. Whatsoever things were written aforetime were written for our learning, that we through patience and comfort of the scriptures might have hope.

1 Cor. 2.13. Which things also we speak, not in the words which man's wisdom teacheth, but which the Holy Ghost teacheth ; comparing spiritual things with spiritual.

Eph. 6.17. Take the sword of the Spirit, which is the word of God.

Phil. 4.9. Those things, which ye have both learned, and received, and heard, and seen in me, do : and the God of peace shall be with you.

Col. 3.16. Let the word of Christ dwell in you richly in all wisdom ; teaching and admonishing one another in psalms and hymns and spiritual songs.

1 The. 4.1. As ye have received of us how ye ought to walk and to please God, *so* ye would abound more and more. 2. For ye know what commandments we gave you by the Lord Jesus.

1 The. 5.20. Despise not prophesyings. 27. I charge you by the Lord that this epistle be read unto all the holy brethren. Col. 4.16.

2 Tim. 2.15. A workman that needeth not to be ashamed, rightly dividing the word of truth.

Heb. 2.1. We ought to give the more earnest heed to the things which we have heard, lest at any time we should let *them* slip.

Heb. 4.2. Unto us was the gospel preached, as well as unto them : but the word preached did not profit them, not being mixed with faith in them that heard *it.* 12. The word of God *is* quick, and powerful, and sharper than any two-edged sword, piercing even to the dividing asunder of soul and spirit, and of the joints and marrow, and *is* a discerner of the thoughts and intents of the heart.

Jas. 1.19. Let every man be swift to hear. 21. Receive with meekness the ingrafted word, which is able to save your souls. 22. But be ye doers of the word, and not hearers only, deceiving your own selves. 25. But whoso looketh into the perfect law of liberty, and continueth *therein,* he being not a forgetful hearer, but a doer of the word, this man shall be blessed in his deed.

2 Pet. 1.19. We have also a more sure word of prophecy ; whereunto ye do well that ye take heed, as unto a light that shineth in a dark place. 20. No prophecy of the scripture is of any private interpretation.

2 Pet. 3.1. This second epistle, beloved, I now write unto you ; in *both* which I stir up your pure minds by way of remembrance ; 2. Be mindful of the words which were spoken

before by the holy prophets, and of the commandment of us the apostles of the Lord and Saviour. 15. As our beloved brother Paul also according to the wisdom given unto him hath written unto you. *v.* 16.

1 Jno. 1.4. These things write we unto you, that your joy may be full.

1 Jno. 5.13. These things have I written unto you that believe on the name of the Son of God ; that ye may know that ye have eternal life, and that ye may believe on the name of the Son of God.

Jude 3. Beloved, when I gave all diligence to write unto you of the common salvation, it was needful for me to write unto you, and exhort *you* that ye should earnestly contend for the faith which was once delivered unto the saints. *v.* 17.

Rev. 1.3. Blessed *is* he that readeth, and they that hear the words of this prophecy, and keep those things which are written therein.

Rev. 2.7. He that hath an ear, let him hear what the Spirit saith unto the churches.

Rev. 22.6. These sayings are faithful and true.

See GOSPEL—LAW.

WORD OF GOD AND GOSPEL, EXCELLENCE OF. LOVED AND RECEIVED. Job 23.12. Neither have I gone back from the commandment of his lips ; I have esteemed the words of his mouth more than my necessary *food.*

Psa. 1.2. His delight *is* in the law of the Lord ; and in his law doth he meditate day and night.

Psa. 19.10. More to be desired *are they* than gold, yea, than much fine gold : sweeter also than honey and the honeycomb. *v.* 8.

Psa. 37.31. The law of his God *is* in his heart ; none of his steps shall slide.

Psa. 40.8. I delight to do thy will, O my God : yea, thy law *is* within my heart.

Psa. 85.8. I will hear what God the Lord will speak : for he will speak peace unto his people, and to his saints.

Psa. 119.11. Thy word have I hid in mine heart, that I might not sin against thee. 14. I have rejoiced in the way of thy testimonies, *as much as* in all riches. 15. I will meditate in thy precepts, and have respect unto thy ways. 16. I will delight myself in thy statutes : I will not forget thy word. 19. I *am* a stranger in the earth : hide not thy commandments from me. 20. My soul breaketh for the longing *that it hath* unto thy judgments at all times. 23. Princes also did sit *and* speak against me : but thy servant did meditate in thy statutes. 24. Thy testimonies also *are* my delight *and* my counsellers.

Psa. 119.30. I have chosen the way of truth : thy judgments have I laid *before me.* 31. I have stuck unto thy testimonies : O Lord, put me not to shame. 35. Make me to go in the path of thy commandments ; for therein do I delight. 40. Behold, I have longed after thy precepts. 45. I will walk at liberty : for I seek thy precepts. 46. I will speak of thy testimonies also before kings, and will not be ashamed. 47. And I will delight myself in thy commandments, which I have loved. 48. My hands also will I lift up unto thy commandments, which I have loved ; and I will meditate in thy statutes.

Psa. 119.50. This *is* my comfort in my affliction : for thy word hath quickened me. 51. The proud have had me greatly in derision ; *yet* have I not declined from thy law. 52. I remembered thy judgments of old, O Lord ; and have comforted myself. 54. Thy statutes have been my songs in the house of my pilgrimage. 61. The bands of the wicked have robbed me : *but* I have not forgotten thy law. 66. I have believed thy commandments. 70. I delight in thy law. 72. The law of thy mouth *is* better unto me than thousands of gold and silver. 77. Let thy tender mercies come unto me, that I may live : for thy law *is* my delight.

Psa. 119.78. They dealt perversely with me without a cause : *but* I will meditate in thy precepts. 83. I am become like a bottle in the smoke ; *yet* do I not forget thy statutes. 92. Unless thy law *had been* my delights, I should then have perished in mine affliction. 93. I will never forget thy precepts : for with them thou hast quickened me. 97. O how love I thy law ! it *is* my meditation all the day. 98. Thou through thy commandments hast made me wiser than mine enemies : for they *are* ever with me. 99. For thy testimonies *are* my meditation. 103. How sweet are thy words unto my taste ! *yea, sweeter* than honey to my mouth !

Psa. 119.109. My soul *is* continually in my hand : yet do I not forget thy law. 111. Thy testimonies have I taken as an heritage for ever: for they *are* the rejoicing of my heart. 113. I hate *vain* thoughts: but thy law do I love. 115. Depart from me, ye evildoers : for I will keep the commandments of my God. 119. I love thy testimonies. 127. I love thy commandments above gold : yea, above fine gold. 129. Thy testimonies *are* wonderful : therefore doth my soul keep them. 131. I opened my mouth, and panted : for I longed for thy commandments. 140. Thy word *is* very pure: therefore thy servant loveth it. 141. I *am* small and despised : *yet* do not I forget thy precepts.

Psa. 119.143. Trouble and anguish have taken hold on me : *yet* thy commandments *are* my delights. 148. Mine eyes prevent the *night* watches, that I might meditate in thy word. 153. Consider mine affliction, and deliver me : for I do not forget thy law. 157. Many *are* my persecutors and mine enemies: *yet* do I not decline from thy testimonies. 159. Consider how I love thy precepts. 161. Princes have persecuted me without a cause : but my heart standeth in awe of thy word. 162. I rejoice at thy word, as one that findeth great spoil. 163. I hate and abhor lying : *but* thy law do I love. 165. Great peace have they which love thy law : and nothing shall offend them. 167. My soul hath kept thy testimonies ; and I love them exceedingly. 173. I have chosen thy precepts. 174. I have longed for thy salvation, O Lord ; and thy law *is* my delight.

Isa. 2.3. Many people shall go and say, Come ye, and let us go up to the mountain of the Lord, to the house of the God of Jacob ; and he will teach us of his ways, and we will walk in his paths.

Jer. 15.16. Thy words were found, and I did eat them ; and thy word was unto me the joy and rejoicing of mine heart.

Eze. 3.3. Then did I eat *it ;* and it was in my mouth as honey for sweetness.

Mat. 13.23. He that received seed into the good ground is he that heareth the word, and understandeth *it ;* which also beareth fruit, and bringeth forth, some an hundredfold, some sixty, some thirty. Mar. 4.8,20. Luk. 8.8,15.

Luk. 24.32. Did not our heart burn within us, while he talked with us by the way, and while he opened to us the scriptures ?

Rom. 6.17. Ye have obeyed from the heart that form of doctrine which was delivered to you.

2 Cor. 9.13. They glorify God for your professed subjection unto the gospel of Christ.

Eph. 1.13. In whom ye also *trusted,* after that ye heard the word of truth, the gospel of your salvation.

1 Thes. 1.5. Our gospel came not unto you in word only, but also in power, and in the Holy Ghost, and in much assurance. *v.* 9,10.

1 Thes. 2.13. When ye received the word of God which ye heard of us, ye received *it* not *as* the word of men, but as it is in truth, the word of God, which effectually worketh also in you that believe.

2 Tim. 2.9. The word of God is not bound.

WORD OF GOD LOVED, EXAMPLES : Ezra, Ezr. 7.10. Jews, Neh. 8.1-3. Elnathan, &c., Jer. 36.25. Jews, Mar. 12.37. Luk. 5.1. Luk. 6.17. Luk. 8.40. Luk. 12.1. Luk. 19. 48. Luk. 21.38. Jno. 4.29,39. Jno. 7.31. Jno. 8.2,30. Jno. 10.42. Act. 2.41,42. Act. 4.4. Act. 6.7. Act. 12.24. Eunuch, Act. 8. 28. Cornelius, Act. 10.33. People of Antioch, Lystra, &c., Act. 13.42,44,48,49. Act. 14.27. Act. 15.3. Bereans, &c., Act. 17.4,11,12. Apollos, Act. 18.24. Ephesians, Act. 19.20. 1 Cor. 16.9. Corinthians, Act. 19.20. 1 Cor. 11.2. Athenians, Act. 17.34. Philippians, Phil. 1.4,5.

See WORSHIP LOVED.

WORD OF GOD. INSPIRATION OF THE SCRIPTURES. Ex. 20.1. God spake all these words, saying.

Ex. 24.4. Moses wrote all the words of the Lord. 12. The Lord said unto Moses, Come up to me into the mount, and be there : and I will give thee tables of stone, and a law, and commandments which I have written ; that thou mayest teach them. Ex. 25.21. Ex. 31. 18. Ex. 32.16.

Ex. 34.27. The Lord said unto Moses, Write thou these words : for after the tenor of these words I have made a covenant with thee and with Israel. 32. Afterward all the children of Israel came nigh : and he gave them in commandment all that the Lord had spoken with him in mount Sinai. Lev. 26.46.

Lev. 24.12. They put him in ward, that the mind of the Lord might be shewed them.

Num. 33.2. Moses wrote their goings out according to their journeys by the commandment of the Lord.

Deu. 4.5. I have taught you statutes and judgments, even as the Lord my God commanded me. *v.* 14.

Deu. 11.18. Lay up these my words in your heart.

Deu. 31.19. Write ye this song for you, and teach it the children of Israel : put it in their mouths, that this song may be a witness for me against the children of Israel. *v.* 22.

2 Kin. 17.13. The Lord testified against Israel, and against Judah, by all the prophets, *and by* all the seers, saying, Turn ye from your evil ways, and keep my commandments *and* my statutes, according to all the law which I commanded your fathers, and which I sent to you by my servants the prophets.

2 Chr. 33.18. The words of the seers that spake to him in the name of the Lord God of Israel, behold, they are *written* in the book of the kings of Israel.

Job 23.12. The commandment of his lips; the words of his mouth.

Psa. 18.30. The word of the Lord is tried.

Psa. 78.5. He established a testimony in Jacob, and appointed a law in Israel, which he commanded our fathers, that they should make them known to their children.

Psa. 99.7. He spake unto them in the cloudy pillar; they kept his testimonies, and the ordinance *that* he gave them.

Psa. 147.19. He sheweth his word unto Jacob, his statutes and his judgments unto Israel.

Ecc. 12.11. Nails fastened *by* the masters of assemblies, *which* are given from one shepherd.

Isa. 34.16. Seek ye out of the book of the Lord, and read.

Jer. 30.2. Thus speaketh the Lord God of Israel, saying, Write thee all the words that I have spoken unto thee in a book.

Jer. 36.2. Take thee a roll of a book, and write therein all the words that I have spoken unto thee against Israel, and against Judah, and against all the nations, from the day I spake unto thee, from the days of Josiah, even unto this day. *v.* 27-32. Jer. 51.60-62.

Eze. 11.25. Then I spake unto them of the captivity all the things that the Lord had shewed me.

Dan. 10.21. I will shew thee that which is noted in the scripture of truth.

Hos. 8.12. I have written to him the great things of my law.

Mat. 22.31. Have ye not read that which was spoken unto you by God, saying, 32. I am the God of Abraham, &c.

Luk. 1.3. It seemed good to me also, having had perfect understanding of all things from the very first, to write unto thee in order, most excellent Theophilus, 4. That thou mightest know the certainty of those things, wherein thou hast been instructed. 70. He spake by the mouth of his holy prophets, which have been since the world began. *v.* 1,2.

Rom. 3.2. Unto them were committed the oracles of God. Heb. 5.12.

1 Cor. 14.37. Let him acknowledge that the things that I write unto you are the commandments of the Lord.

Col. 3.16. Let the word of Christ dwell in you.

1 The. 2.13. Not *as* the word of men, but as it is in truth, the word of God.

1 The. 4.1. As ye have received of us how ye ought to walk and to please God, *so* ye would abound more and more. 2. For ye know what commandments we gave you by the Lord Jesus.

1 Tim. 6.3. Wholesome words, *even* the words of our Lord Jesus Christ.

2 Tim. 3.16. All scripture *is* given by inspiration of God.

Heb. 1.1. God, who at sundry times and in divers manners spake in time past unto the fathers by the prophets.

Heb. 4.12. The word of God is quick, and powerful.

2 Pet. 3.2. The words which were spoken before by the holy prophets, and of the commandment of us the apostles of the Lord and Saviour. 15. Our beloved brother Paul also according to the wisdom given unto him hath written unto you.

1 Jno. 1.5. This then is the message which we have heard of him, and declare unto you, that God is light.

Rev. 1.1. The Revelation of Jesus Christ, which God gave unto him, to shew unto his servants things which must shortly come to pass; and he sent and signified *it* by his angel unto his servant John: 2. Who bare record of the word of God, and of the testimony of Jesus Christ, and of all things that he saw. 19. Write the things which thou hast seen, and the things which are, and the things which shall be hereafter. *v.* 11.

Rev. 19.10. The testimony of Jesus is the spirit of prophecy.

See GOSPEL FROM GOD—LAW FROM GOD.

WORD OF GOD. INSPIRATION OF THE SCRIPTURES BY THE HOLY SPIRIT. Isa. 59. 21. My Spirit that *is* upon thee, and my words which I have put in thy mouth, shall not depart out of thy mouth.

Zec. 7.12. The words which the Lord of hosts hath sent in his Spirit by the former prophets.

Act. 1.16. This scripture must needs have been fulfilled, which the Holy Ghost by the mouth of David spake before.

Act. 28.25. Well spake the Holy Ghost by Esaias the prophet unto our fathers.

1 Cor. 2.12. We have received, not the spirit of the world, but the Spirit which is of God; that we might know the things that are freely given to us of God. 13. Which things also we speak, not in the words which man's wisdom teacheth, but which the Holy Ghost teacheth.

Eph. 6.17. The sword of the Spirit, which is the word of God.

Heb. 3.7. Wherefore, as the Holy Ghost saith, To-day if ye will hear his voice.

Heb. 9.8. The Holy Ghost this signifying, that the way into the holiest of all was not yet made manifest.

1 Pet. 1.11. Searching what, or what manner of time the Spirit of Christ which was in them did signify, when it testified beforehand the sufferings of Christ, and the glory that should follow. 12. Things, which are now reported unto you by them that have preached the gospel unto you with the Holy Ghost sent down from heaven.

2 Pet. 1.21. The prophecy came not in old time by the will of man: but holy men of God spake *as they were* moved by the Holy Ghost.

See APOSTLES—PROPHETS' INSPIRATION—PROPHECY.

WORD OF GOD. THE ONLY RULE OF FAITH AND DUTY. Ex. 19.9. The Lord said unto Moses, Lo, I come unto thee in a thick cloud, that the people may hear when I speak with thee, and believe thee for ever.

Ex. 25.9. According to all that I shew thee, *after* the pattern of the tabernacle, and the pattern of all the instruments thereof, even so shall ye make *it. v.* 40. Ex. 27.8.

Deu. 12.32. What thing soever I command you, observe to do it: thou shalt not add thereto, nor diminish from it. Deu. 4.2.

Deu. 29.29. Those *things which are* revealed *belong* unto us and to our children for ever, that *we* may do all the words of this law.

1 Chr. 15.13. For because ye *did it* not at the first, the Lord our God made a breach upon us, for that we sought him not after the due order. *v.* 2.12. Lev. 10.1-3.

Pro. 30.6. Add thou not unto his words, lest he reprove thee, and thou be found a liar.

Isa. 8.20. To the law and to the testimony: if they speak not according to this word, *it is* because *there is* no light in them.

Jer. 23.36. The burden of the Lord shall ye mention no more; for every man's word shall be his burden: for ye have perverted the words of the living God, of the Lord of hosts our God.

Eze. 44.5. The Lord said unto me, Son of man, mark well, and behold with thine eyes, and hear with thine ears all that I say unto thee concerning all the ordinances of the house of the Lord, and all the laws thereof; and mark well the entering in of the house, with every going forth of the sanctuary.

Mat. 15.3. Why do ye also transgress the commandment of God by your tradition? 9. In vain they do worship me, teaching *for* doctrines the commandments of men. Mar. 7.7.

Act. 4.19. Whether it be right in the sight of God to hearken unto you more than unto God, judge ye.

Act. 10.15. The voice *spake* unto him again the second time, What God hath cleansed, *that* call not thou common.

Act. 11.17. Forasmuch then as God gave them the like gift as *he did* unto us, who believed on the Lord Jesus Christ, what was I, that I could withstand God?

Act. 17.11. They received the word with all readiness of mind, and searched the scriptures daily, whether those things were so.

Act. 26.22. I continue unto this day, witnessing both to small and great, saying none other things than those which the prophets and Moses did say should come.

1 Cor. 11.2. I praise you, brethren, that ye remember me in all things, and keep the ordinances, as I delivered *them* to you.

Gal. 1.8. Though we, or an angel from heaven, preach any other gospel unto you than that which we have preached unto you, let him be accursed.

Col. 2.18. Let no man beguile you of your reward in a voluntary humility and worshipping of angels, intruding into those things which he hath not seen, vainly puffed up by his fleshly mind.

1 The. 2.13. Ye received *it* not *as* the word of men, but as it is in truth, the word of God.

2 The. 2.15. Stand fast, and hold the traditions which ye have been taught, whether by word, or our epistle.

1 Tim. 6.3. If any man teach otherwise, and consent not to wholesome words, *even* the words of our Lord Jesus Christ, and to the doctrine which is according to godliness; 4. He is proud, knowing nothing.

2 Tim. 1.13. Hold fast the form of sound words, which thou hast heard of me, in faith and love which is in Christ Jesus.

Tit. 1.14. Not giving heed to Jewish fables, and commandments of men, that turn from the truth.

1 Pet. 4.11. If any man speak, *let him speak* as the oracles of God.

Rev. 22.18. I testify unto every man that heareth the words of the prophecy of this book, If any man shall add unto these things, God shall add unto him the plagues that are written in this book: 19. And if any man shall take away from the words of the book of this prophecy, God shall take away his part out of the book of life, and out of the holy city, and *from* the things which are written in this book.

See MINISTERS UNFAITHFUL.

WORD OF GOD SANCTIFYING. Psa. 1.2. But his delight *is* in the law of the Lord; and in his law doth he meditate day and night. 3. He shall be like a tree planted by the rivers of water, that bringeth forth his fruit in his season; his leaf also shall not wither; and whatsoever he doeth shall prosper.

Psa. 17.4. Concerning the works of men, by the word of thy lips I have kept *me from* the paths of the destroyer.

Psa. 19.7. The law of the Lord *is* perfect, converting the soul: 8. The statutes of the Lord *are* right, rejoicing the heart: the commandment of the Lord *is* pure, enlightening the eyes.

Psa. 37.31. The law of his God *is* in his heart; none of his steps shall slide.

Psa. 119.9. Wherewithal shall a young man cleanse his way? by taking heed *thereto* according to thy word. 11. Thy word have I hid in mine heart, that I might not sin against thee. 50. This *is* my comfort in my affliction: for thy word hath quickened me. 93. I will never forget thy precepts: for with them thou hast quickened me. 104. Through thy precepts I get understanding: therefore I hate every false way.

Mic. 2.7 Do not my words do good to him that walketh uprightly?

Mat. 13.33. The kingdom of heaven is like unto leaven, which a woman took, and hid in three measures of meal, till the whole was leavened.

Jno. 6.63. It is the Spirit that quickeneth; the flesh profiteth nothing: the words that I speak unto you, *they* are spirit, and *they* are life.

Jno. 8.31. If ye continue in my word, *then* are ye my disciples indeed; 32. And ye shall know the truth, and the truth shall make you free.

Jno. 15.3. Ye are clean through the word which I have spoken unto you.

Jno. 17.17. Sanctify them through thy truth: thy word is truth. 19. That they also might be sanctified through the truth.

Act. 15.9. Put no difference between us and them, purifying their hearts by faith.

Act. 20.32. I commend you to God, and to the word of his grace, which is able to build you up, and to give you an inheritance among all them which are sanctified.

Act. 26.18. Them which are sanctified by faith that is in me.

Eph. 5.26. That he might sanctify and cleanse it with the washing of water by the word.

1 The. 2.13. Ye received it not as the word of men, but (as it is in truth) the word of God, which effectually worketh also in you that believe.

1 Tim. 4.6. Nourished up in the words of faith and of good doctrine.

2 Tim. 3.16. All scripture is given by inspiration of God, and is profitable for doctrine, for reproof, for correction, for instruction in righteousness; 17. That the man of God may be perfect, throughly furnished unto all good works.

Tit. 1.1. The truth which is after godliness.

Jas. 1.18. Of his own will begat he us with the word of truth. 21. The ingrafted word, which is able to save your souls.

1 Pet. 1.22. Ye have purified your souls in obeying the truth through the Spirit. 23. Being born again, not of corruptible seed, but of incorruptible, by the word of God, which liveth and abideth for ever.

1 Pet. 2.2. As new-born babes, desire the sincere milk of the word, that ye may grow thereby.

2 Pet. 1.4. Exceeding great and precious promises: that by these ye might be partakers of the divine nature.

1 Jno. 2.14. Ye are strong, and the word of God abideth in you, and ye have overcome the wicked one.

See GOSPEL.

WORD OF GOD, UNBELIEF IN. Psa. 50.17. Thou hatest instruction, and castest my words behind thee.

Pro. 1.29. They hated knowledge, and did not choose the fear of the Lord: 30. They would none of my counsel: they despised all my reproof.

Pro. 13.13. Whoso despiseth the word shall be destroyed.

Isa. 5.24 Their root shall be as rottenness, and their blossoms shall go up as dust: because they have cast away the law of the Lord of hosts, and despised the word of the Holy One of Israel.

Isa. 30.9. This is a rebellious people, lying children, children that will not hear the law of the Lord: 10. Which say to the seers, See not; and to the prophets, Prophesy not unto us right things, speak unto us smooth things, prophesy deceits: 11. Get you out of the way, turn aside out of the path, cause the Holy One of Israel to cease from before us.

Isa. 53.1. Who hath believed our report? and to whom is the arm of the Lord revealed?

Jer. 6.10. To whom shall I speak, and give warning, that they may hear? behold, their ear is uncircumcised, and they cannot hearken: behold, the word of the Lord is unto them a reproach; they have no delight in it. Isa. 28.9-14.

Jer. 8.9. The wise men are ashamed, they are dismayed and taken: lo, they have rejected the word of the Lord; and what wisdom is in them?

Hos. 8.12. I have written to him the great things of my law, but they were counted as a strange thing.

Mic. 2.6. Prophesy ye not, say they to them that prophesy: they shall not prophesy to them, that they shall not take shame. Amo. 2.12.

Luk. 16.31. If they hear not Moses and the prophets, neither will they be persuaded though one rose from the dead. Luk. 24.25.

Jno. 3.20. Every one that doeth evil hateth the light, neither cometh to the light, lest his deeds should be reproved.

Jno. 5.46. Had ye believed Moses, ye would have believed me: for he wrote of me. 47. But if ye believe not his writings, how shall ye believe my words?

Jno. 8.37. Ye seek to kill me, because my word hath no place in you. 45. Because I tell you the truth, ye believe me not.

1 Cor. 1.18. The preaching of the cross is to them that perish foolishness. 22. For the Jews require a sign, and the Greeks seek after wisdom: 23. But we preach Christ crucified, unto the Jews a stumblingblock, and unto the Greeks foolishness.

2 Tim. 3.8. These also resist the truth: men of corrupt minds, reprobate concerning the faith.

2 Tim. 4.3. The time will come when they will not endure sound doctrine; but after their own lusts shall they heap to themselves teachers, having itching ears; 4. And they shall turn away their ears from the truth, and shall be turned unto fables.

1 Pet. 2.8. A stone of stumbling, and a rock of offence, even to them which stumble at the word, being disobedient.

2 Pet. 3.16. Some things hard to be understood, which they that are unlearned and unstable wrest, as they do also the other scriptures, unto their own destruction.

Rev. 22.19. If any man shall take away from the words of the book of this prophecy, God shall take away his part out of the book of life, and out of the holy city, and from the things which are written in this book.

WORD OF GOD, UNBELIEF IN, EXAMPLES OF: Jehoiakim, Jer. 36. Amaziah, Amo. 7. 10-17. Jews, Act. 13.45,46,50. Act.14.2-6,19. Act. 17.5-9,13. Act. 18.6,12. Act. 19.9. Act. 20.3. 1 Cor. 16.9. Alexander, 2 Tim. 4.14,15.

See INFIDELITY—UNBELIEF—MINISTERS UNFAITHFUL.

WORKS, INSUFFICIENCY OF, TO SALVATION. Job 9.2. How should man be just with God? 3. If he will contend with him, he cannot answer him one of a thousand. 20. If I justify myself, mine own mouth shall condemn me: if I say, I am perfect, it shall also prove me perverse.

Job 25.4. How then can man be justified with God? or how can he be clean that is born of a woman?

Job 40.14. Then will I also confess unto thee that thine own right hand can save thee. v. 12,13.

Psa. 49.7. None of them can by any means redeem his brother, nor give to God a ransom for him: 8. (For the redemption of their soul is precious, and it ceaseth for ever.)

Psa. 143.2. Enter not into judgment with thy servant: for in thy sight shall no man living be justified.

Isa. 43.26. Put me in remembrance: let us plead together: declare thou, that thou mayest be justified.

Isa. 57.12. I will declare thy righteousness, and thy works ; for they shall not profit thee.

Isa. 59.16. He saw that there was no man, and wondered that there was no intercessor.

Isa. 64.6. We are all as an unclean thing, and all our righteousnesses are as filthy rags ; and we all do fade as a leaf ; and our iniquities, like the wind, have taken us away.

Eze. 7.19. Their silver and their gold shall not be able to deliver them in the day of the wrath of the Lord : they shall not satisfy their souls, neither fill their bowels : because it is the stumblingblock of their iniquity.

Eze. 33.12. The righteousness of the righteous shall not deliver him in the day of his transgression. 13. When I shall say to the righteous, that he shall surely live; if he trust to his own righteousness, and commit iniquity, all his righteousnesses shall not be remembered ; but for his iniquity that he hath committed, he shall die for it.

Dan. 9.18. We do not present our supplications before thee for our righteousnesses, but for thy great mercies.

Mat. 5.20. Except your righteousness shall exceed the righteousness of the scribes and Pharisees, ye shall in no case enter into the kingdom of heaven. Luk. 18.9-14.

Luk. 17.10. When ye shall have done all those things which are commanded you, say, We are unprofitable servants: we have done that which was our duty to do.

Act. 13.39. By him all that believe are justified from all things, from which ye could not be justified by the law of Moses.

Rom. 3.20. By the deeds of the law there shall no flesh be justified in his sight : for by the law is the knowledge of sin. 21. But now the righteousness of God without the law is manifested, being witnessed by the law and the prophets. 28. A man is justified by faith without the deeds of the law.

Rom. 4.14. If they which are of the law be heirs, faith is made void, and the promise made of none effect : 15. Because the law worketh wrath : for where no law is, there is no transgression.

Rom. 8.3. For what the law could not do, in that it was weak through the flesh, God sending his own Son in the likeness of sinful flesh, and for sin condemned sin in the flesh.

Rom. 9.11. The children being not yet born, neither having done any good or evil, that the purpose of God according to election might stand, not of works, but of him that calleth. 16. It is not of him that willeth, nor of him that runneth, but of God that sheweth mercy. 31. Israel, which followed after the law of righteousness, hath not attained to the law of righteousness. 32. They sought it not by faith, but as it were by the v rks of the law. For they stumbled at that stumblingstone.

Rom. 11.6. If by grace, then is it no more of works: otherwise grace is no more grace. But if it be of works, then is it no more grace : otherwise work is no more work.

Gal. 2.16. Knowing that a man is not justified by the works of the law, but by the faith of Jesus Christ, even we have believed in Jesus Christ, that we might be justified by the faith of Christ, and not by the works of the law : for by the works of the law shall no flesh be justified. 19. I through the law am dead to the law, that I might live unto God.

21. I do not frustrate the grace of God : for if righteousness come by the law, then Christ is dead in vain.

Gal. 3.10. As many as are of the works of the law are under the curse : for it is written, Cursed is every one that continueth not in all things which are written in the book of the law to do them. 11. But that no man is justified by the law in the sight of God, it is evident : for, The just shall live by faith. 12. And the law is not of faith : but, The man that doeth them shall live in them. v. 1-29.

Gal. 4.9. After that ye have known God, or rather are known of God, how turn ye again to the weak and beggarly elements, whereunto ye desire again to be in bondage? v. 1-11.

Gal. 5.2. If ye be circumcised, Christ shall profit you nothing. 4. Christ is become of no effect unto you, whosoever of you are justified by the law ; ye are fallen from grace. 11. If I yet preach circumcision, why do I yet suffer persecution? then is the offence of the cross ceased. 18. If ye be led of the Spirit, ye are not under the law. v. 6.

Eph. 2.9. Not of works, lest any man should boast.

Phil. 3.4. Though I might also have confidence in the flesh. If any other man thinketh that he hath whereof he might trust in the flesh, I more : 5. Circumcised the eighth day, of the stock of Israel, of the tribe of Benjamin, an Hebrew of the Hebrews ; as touching the law, a Pharisee ; 6. Concerning zeal, persecuting the church ; touching the righteousness which is in the law, blameless. 9. Not having mine own righteousness, which is of the law, but that which is through the faith of Christ, the righteousness which is of God by faith. v. 3,7,8.

Col. 2.20. If ye be dead with Christ, from the rudiments of the world, why, as though living in the world, are ye subject to ordinances? 23. Which things have indeed a shew of wisdom in will worship, and humility, and neglecting of the body ; not in any honour to the satisfying of the flesh. v. 21,22.

2 Tim. 1.9. Who hath saved us, and called us with an holy calling, not according to our works, but according to his own purpose and grace.

Tit. 3.5. Not by works of righteousness which we have done, but according to his mercy he saved us. v. 4.

Jas. 2.10. Whosoever shall keep the whole law, and yet offend in one point, he is guilty of all. 11. For he that said, Do not commit adultery, said also, Do not kill. Now, if thou commit no adultery, yet if thou kill, thou art become a transgressor of the law.

See SELF-RIGHTEOUSNESS—PRIVILEGES—JUSTIFICATION—FALSE-CONFIDENCE—MAN'S NATURAL STATE.

WORKS, GOOD, ENJOINED. See OBEDIENCE.

WORLD. See EARTH.

WORLDLINESS, WORLDLY PLEASURES, SENSUALITY. 1 Sam. 8.19. They said, Nay ; but we will have a king over us ; 20. That we also may be like all the nations.

Job. 20.5. The triumphing of the wicked is short, and the joy of the hypocrite but for a moment.

Job 21.11. They send forth their little ones like a flock, and their children dance. 12. They take the timbrel and harp, and rejoice at the sound of the organ. 13. They spend their days in wealth, and in a moment go down to the grave.

Psa. 4.6. *There be* many that say, Who will shew us *any* good? Lord, lift thou up the light of thy countenance upon us. 7. Thou hast put gladness in my heart, more than in the time *that* their corn and their wine increased.

Psa. 49.18. While he lived he blessed his soul: and *men* will praise thee, when thou doest well to thyself.

Psa. 106.14. Lusted exceedingly in the wilderness, and tempted God in the desert. 15. And he gave them their request; but sent leanness into their soul.

Pro. 14.13. Even in laughter the heart is sorrowful; and the end of that mirth *is* heaviness.

Pro. 15.21. Folly *is* joy to *him that is* destitute of wisdom.

Pro. 21.17. He that loveth pleasure *shall be* a poor man: he that loveth wine and oil shall not be rich.

Pro. 23.20. Be not among winebibbers; among riotous eaters of flesh: 21. For the drunkard and the glutton shall come to poverty: and drowsiness shall clothe *a man* with rags.

Pro. 27.1. Boast not thyself of to morrow; for thou knowest not what a day may bring forth. 7. The full soul loatheth an honeycomb.

Ecc. 1.8. The eye *is* not satisfied with seeing, nor the ear filled with hearing. *v.* 11. Pro. 30.15.

Ecc. 2.1. I said in mine heart, Go to now, I will prove thee with mirth, therefore enjoy pleasure: and, behold, this also *is* vanity. 3. I sought in mine heart to give myself unto wine, yet acquainting mine heart with wisdom. 10. And whatsoever mine eyes desired I kept not from them, I withheld not my heart from any joy; for my heart rejoiced in all my labour: and this was my portion of all my labour. 11. Then I looked on all the works that my hands had wrought, and on the labour that I had laboured to do: and, behold, all *was* vanity and vexation of spirit, and *there was* no profit under the sun. *v.* 1-12,16. Ecc. 8.15.

Ecc. 6.11. Seeing there be many things that increase vanity, what *is* man the better? 12. For who knoweth what *is* good for man in *this* life, all the days of his vain life which he spendeth as a shadow? for who can tell a man what shall be after him under the sun?

Ecc. 7.2. *It is* better to go to the house of mourning than to go to the house of feasting: for that *is* the end of all men; and the living will lay *it* to his heart. 3. Sorrow *is* better than laughter: for by the sadness of the countenance the heart is made better. 4. The heart of the wise *is* in the house of mourning; but the heart of fools *is* in the house of mirth. 5. *It is* better to hear the rebuke of the wise, than for a man to hear the song of fools. 6. For as the crackling of thorns under a pot, so *is* the laughter of the fool: this also *is* vanity.

Ecc. 10.16. Woe to thee, O land, when thy king *is* a child, and thy princes eat in the morning! 17. Blessed *art* thou, O land, when thy king *is* the son of nobles, and thy princes eat in due season, for strength, and not for drunkenness! 19. A feast is made for laughter, and wine maketh merry: but money answereth all *things.*

Ecc. 11.9. Rejoice, O young man, in thy youth; and let thy heart cheer thee in the days of thy youth, and walk in the ways of thine heart, and in the sight of thine eyes: but know thou, that for all these *things* God will bring thee into judgment. 10. Therefore remove sorrow from thy heart, and put away evil from thy flesh: for childhood and youth *are* vanity.

Isa. 22.12. In that day did the Lord God of hosts call to weeping, and to mourning, and to baldness, and to girding with sackcloth: 13. And behold joy and gladness, slaying oxen, and killing sheep, eating flesh, and drinking wine: let us eat and drink; for to morrow we shall die. 1 Cor. 15.32.

Isa. 24.7. The new wine mourneth, the vine languisheth, all the merryhearted do sigh. 8. The mirth of tabrets ceaseth, the noise of them that rejoice endeth, the joy of the harp ceaseth. 11. *There is* a crying for wine in the streets; all joy is darkened, the mirth of the land is gone. *v.* 7-11.

Isa. 28.4. The glorious beauty, which *is* on the head of the fat valley, shall be a fading flower, *and* as the hasty fruit before the summer; which *when* he that looketh upon it seeth, while it is yet in his hand he eateth it up.

Isa. 32.10. Many days and years shall ye be troubled, ye careless women: for the vintage shall fail, the gathering shall not come. 11. Tremble, ye women that are at ease; be troubled, ye careless ones: strip you, and make you bare, and gird *sackcloth* upon *your* loins.

Isa. 47.7. Thou saidst, I shall be a lady for ever: *so* that thou didst not lay these *things* to thy heart, neither didst remember the latter end of it. 8. Therefore hear now this, *thou that art* given to pleasures, that dwellest carelessly, that sayest in thine heart, I *am,* and none else beside me; I shall not sit *as* a widow, neither shall I know the loss of children: 9. But these two *things* shall come to thee in a moment in one day, the loss of children, and widowhood.

Hos. 9.1. Rejoice not, O Israel, for joy, as *other* people: for thou hast gone a whoring from thy God. 11. *As for* Ephraim, their glory shall fly away like a bird, from the birth, *and* from the womb, and from the conception.

Amos 6.3. Ye that put far away the evil day, and cause the seat of violence to come near; 4. That lie upon beds of ivory, and stretch themselves upon their couches, and eat the lambs out of the flock, and the calves out of the midst of the stall; 5. That chant to the sound of the viol, *and* invent to themselves instruments of musick, like David; 6. That drink wine in bowls, and anoint themselves with the chief ointments; but they are not grieved for the affliction of Joseph. 7. Therefore now shall they go captive with the first that go captive, and the banquet of them that stretched themselves shall be removed.

Amos 8.10. I will turn your feasts into

mourning, and all your songs into lamentation.

Mic. 2.10. Arise ye, and depart; for this *is* not *your* rest: because it is polluted, it shall destroy *you*, even with a sore destruction.

Mic. 6.14. Thou shalt eat but not be satisfied.

Hag. 1.6. Ye have sown much, and bring in little; ye eat, but ye have not enough; ye drink, but ye are not filled with drink; ye clothe you, but there is none warm; and he that earneth wages earneth wages *to put it* into a bag with holes.

Mat. 6.25. Therefore I say unto you, Take no thought for your life, what ye shall eat, or what ye shall drink; nor yet for your body, what ye shall put on. Is not the life more than meat, and the body than raiment?

Mat. 10.39. He that findeth his life shall lose it.

Mat. 16.26. What is a man profited, if he shall gain the whole world, and lose his own soul? or what shall a man give in exchange for his soul? Mar. 8.35-38.

Mat. 24.38. As in the days that were before the flood they were eating and drinking, marrying, and giving in marriage, until the day that Noe entered into the ark, 39. And knew not until the flood came, and took them all away; so shall also the coming of the Son of man be. Luk. 17.26-33.

Luk. 8.14. That which fell among thorns are they, which, when they have heard, go forth, and are choked with cares and riches and pleasures of *this* life, and bring no fruit to perfection. Mat. 13.22. Mar. 4.19.

Luk. 12.19. I will say to my soul, Soul, thou hast much goods laid up for many years; take thine ease, eat, drink, *and* be merry. *v.* 15-30.

Luk. 16.25. Son, remember that thou in thy lifetime receivedst thy good things, and likewise Lazarus evil things: but now he is comforted, and thou art tormented. *v.* 19-24.

Luk. 21.34. Take heed to yourselves, lest at any time your hearts be overcharged with surfeiting, and drunkenness, and cares of this life, and *so* that day come upon you unawares.

Jno. 4.13. Whosoever drinketh of this water shall thirst again.

Jno. 5.44. How can ye believe, which receive honour one of another, and seek not the honour that *cometh* from God only?

Jno. 12.43. They loved the praise of men more than the praise of God.

1 Cor. 7.29. Brethren, the time *is* short: it remaineth, that both they that have wives be as though they had none. 31. Use this world, as not abusing *it*: for the fashion of this world passeth away.

1 Cor. 10.6. These things were our examples, to the intent we should not lust after evil things, as they also lusted.

Phil. 3.19. Whose end *is* destruction, whose god *is their* belly, and *whose* glory *is* in their shame, who mind earthly things.

Col. 3.2. Set your affection on things above, not on things on the earth. *v.* 5.

1 Tim. 5.6. She that liveth in pleasure is dead while she liveth.

2 Tim. 2.4. No man that warreth entangleth himself with the affairs of *this* life; that he may please him who hath chosen him to be a soldier.

2 Tim. 2.22. Flee also youthful lusts.

2 Tim. 3.4. Lovers of pleasures more than lovers of God. 6. And lead captive silly women, laden with sins, led away with divers lusts.

Tit. 2.12. Denying ungodliness and worldly lusts, we should live soberly, righteously, and godly, in this present world.

Tit. 3.3. We ourselves also were sometimes foolish, disobedient, deceived, serving divers lusts and pleasures.

Heb. 11.25. To enjoy the pleasures of sin for a season.

Jas. 4.4. Ye adulterers and adulteresses, know ye not that the friendship of the world is enmity with God? whosoever therefore will be a friend of the world is the enemy of God. 9. Be afflicted, and mourn, and weep: let your laughter be turned to mourning, and *your* joy to heaviness.

Jas. 5.5. Ye have lived in pleasure on the earth, and been wanton; ye have nourished your hearts, as in a day of slaughter.

1 Pet. 1.14. As obedient children, not fashioning yourselves according to the former lusts in your ignorance. 24. For all flesh *is* as grass, and all the glory of man as the flower of grass. The grass withereth, and the flower thereof falleth away.

1 Pet. 2.11. Dearly beloved, I beseech *you* as strangers and pilgrims, abstain from fleshly lusts, which war against the soul.

1 Pet. 4.3. The time past of *our* life may suffice us to have wrought the will of the Gentiles, when we walked in lasciviousness, lusts, excess of wine, revellings, banquetings, and abominable idolatries: 4. Wherein they think it strange that ye run not with *them* to the same excess of riot, speaking evil of *you*.

2 Pet. 2.13. Shall receive the reward of unrighteousness, *as* they that count it pleasure to riot in the day time. Spots *they are* and blemishes, sporting themselves with their own deceivings while they feast with you. 18. When they speak great swelling *words* of vanity, they allure through the lusts of the flesh, *through much* wantonness, those that were clean escaped from them who live in error.

1 Jno. 2.15. Love not the world, neither the things *that are* in the world. If any man love the world, the love of the Father is not in him. 16. For all that *is* in the world, the lust of the flesh, and the lust of the eyes, and the pride of life, is not of the Father, but is of the world. 17. The world passeth away, and the lust thereof: but he that doeth the will of God abideth for ever.

1 Jno. 4.5. They are of the world: therefore speak they of the world, and the world heareth them.

Jude 12. These are spots in your feasts of charity, when they feast with you, feeding themselves without fear. 19. These be they who separate themselves, sensual, having not the Spirit. *v.* 16.

WORLDLINESS AND SENSUALITY, EXAMPLES OF: Esau, Gen. 25.30-34. Heb. 12.16. Israelites, Num. 11.33,34. Psa. 78.18,29-31. Eli's sons, 1 Sam. 2.12-17. Herod, Mat. 14.6,7. Cretians, Tit. 1.12.

See ADULTERY—DRUNKENNESS—SLOTH—COVETOUSNESS—TEMPERANCE.

WORLDLY WISDOM. See WISDOM, NATURAL.

WORM. Ex. 42.7. Jno. 1.46. Illustrative, Job 25.6. Isa. 41.14. Isa. 66.24.

WORMWOOD. Illustrative, Deu. 29.18. Pro. 5.4. Lam. 3.19. Translated hemlock, Amos 6.12. Symbolical, Rev. 8.11.

WORSHIP. PUBLIC WORSHIP. Attitudes in praise and prayer, see PRAISE—PRAYER. Prayer at the ninth hour, Act. 3.1. Shoes put off, Ex. 3.5. Jos. 5.15. Covering the head, 1 Kin. 19.13. 1 Cor. 11.4-15.

The scriptures read publicly, Deu. 31.11-13. Jos. 8.33-35. 2 Kin. 23.2. 2 Chr. 17.9. Neh. 8.1-8,13,18. Jer. 36.6. The people stood and responded by saying Amen, and promising obedience, Neh. 8.5,6. Ex. 24.7. Deu. 27. 12-26.

Blessing pronounced on the people, Lev. 9. 22,23. Num. 6.23-27. Jos. 8.33. 1 Chr. 23. 13. 2 Sam. 6.18. 1 Kin. 8.14,55. 2 Chr. 30.27. The people responded Amen, or Hallelujah, in prayer and praise, 1 Chr. 16.36. Psa. 106.48. 1 Cor. 14.16. See AMEN.

Women worshipped separately in the temple (?), Ex. 38.8. 1 Sam. 2.22; with men in the Synagogue and in Christian assemblies, Luk. 11.27. Luk. 13.10,11. Act. 1.14,15. Not allowed to teach, 1 Cor. 14.34. Proselytes worshipped separately, Act. 21.28,29. Eph. 2.14. Rev. 11.2, see PROSELYTES. Children attended, see CHILDREN.

Reading the scriptures, preaching, and prayer—in the temple, Mat. 21.23, see TEMPLE, p. 462; in the Synagogue, see SYNAGOGUE; by the sea-side, Mar. 2.13; in the wilderness, Mar. 1.3,4; in a school, Act. 19.9; in an upper chamber, Act. 20. 7-9; in a house, Act. 28.30. Prayer in the tabernacle, 1 Sam. 1.9-18,26; in the temple, Luk. 2.37. Luk. 1.10. See TEMPLE.

Reading the scriptures and preaching standing, Act. 1.15. Act. 5.20,25. Act. 2.14; on a pulpit in the street, Neh. 8.3-8; in the temple, Jer. 7.2. Jer. 17.19. Jer. 19.14. Jno. 7.37; in the synagogue, Luk. 4.16-27. Act. 13.16; on Mars Hill, Act. 17.22. Preaching sitting in a boat, Luk. 5.3. Mat. 13.2; on a hillside, Mat. 5.1; in the temple, Jno. 7.37.

WORSHIP OF CHRIST, see CHRIST, WORSHIP OF. Of God, see GOD THE ONLY GOD. In heaven, see PRAISE IN HEAVEN.

WORSHIP ENJOINED. PROMISES OF GOD'S PRESENCE IN. Gen. 35.1. God said unto Jacob, Arise, go up to Beth-el, and dwell there: and make there an altar unto God. 2 Sam. 24.18.

Ex. 5.1. Thus saith the Lord God of Israel, Let my people go, that they may hold a feast unto me in the wilderness.

Ex. 12.47. All the congregation of Israel shall keep it.

Ex. 20.24. In all places where I record my name I will come unto thee, and I will bless thee.

Ex. 25.8. Let them make me a sanctuary; that I may dwell among them. v. 22. Num. 17.4.

Ex. 29.43. There I will meet with the children of Israel, and the tabernacle shall be sanctified by my glory. Ex. 40.34,35.

Lev. 19.30. Ye shall keep my sabbaths, and reverence my sanctuary: I am the Lord.

Deu. 6.13. Thou shalt fear the Lord thy God, and serve him, and shall swear by his name.

Deu. 12.5. Unto the place which the Lord your God shall choose out of all your tribes to put his name there, even unto his habitation shall ye seek, and thither thou shalt come. v. 11. Deu. 16.6. Deu. 26.2.

Deu. 31.11. When all Israel is come to appear before the Lord thy God, in the place which he shall choose, thou shalt read this law before all Israel in their hearing. 12. Gather the people together, men, and women, and children, and thy stranger that is within thy gates, that they may hear, and that they may learn, and fear the Lord your God, and observe to do all the words of this law; 13. And that their children, which have not known any thing, may hear, and learn to fear the Lord your God, as long as ye live in the land whither ye go over Jordan to possess it. Neh. 8. 14-18.

Deu. 33.19. They shall call the people unto the mountain; there they shall offer sacrifices of righteousness.

2 Kin. 17.36. Him shall ye fear, and him shall ye worship.

2 Chr. 5.13. It came even to pass, as the trumpeters and singers were as one, to make one sound to be heard in praising and thanking the Lord; and when they lifted up their voice with the trumpets and cymbals and instruments of musick, and praised the Lord, saying, For he is good; for his mercy endureth for ever: that then the house was filled with a cloud, even the house of the Lord; 14. So that the priests could not stand to minister by reason of the cloud: for the glory of the Lord had filled the house of God. 1 Kin. 8.10,11.

2 Chr. 7.1. When Solomon had made an end of praying, the fire came down from heaven, and consumed the burnt-offering and the sacrifices; and the glory of the Lord filled the house. 15. Mine eyes shall be open, and mine ears attent unto the prayer that is made in this place. 16. For now have I chosen and sanctified this house, that my name may be there for ever: and mine eyes and mine heart shall be there perpetually. 1 Kin. 9.3.

2 Chr. 30.27. The priests the Levites arose and blessed the people: and their voice was heard, and their prayer came up to his holy dwelling place, even unto heaven.

Psa. 36.8. They shall be abundantly satisfied with the fatness of thy house; and thou shalt make them drink of the river of thy pleasures.

Psa. 45.11. He is thy Lord; and worship thou him.

Psa. 65.4. Blessed is the man whom thou choosest, and causest to approach unto thee, that he may dwell in thy courts: we shall be satisfied with the goodness of thy house, even of thy holy temple.

Psa. 76.11. Vow, and pay unto the Lord your God: let all that be round about him bring presents unto him that ought to be feared.

Psa. 77.13. Thy way, O God, is in the sanctuary: who is so great a God as our God?

Psa. 84.4. Blessed are they that dwell in thy house: they will be still praising thee.

Psa. 92.13. Those that be planted in the house of the Lord shall flourish in the courts of our God. 14. They shall still bring forth fruit in old age ; they shall be fat and flourishing.

Psa. 96.8. Give unto the Lord the glory *due unto* his name : bring an offering, and come into his courts. 9. O worship the Lord in the beauty of holiness : fear before him, all the earth.

Psa. 97.7. Worship him, all *ye* gods.

Psa. 99.5. Exalt ye the Lord our God, and worship at his footstool ; *for* he *is* holy.

Psa. 132.13. The Lord hath chosen Zion ; he hath desired *it* for his habitation. 14. This *is* my rest for ever : here will I dwell ; for I have desired it.

Isa. 4.5. The Lord will create upon every dwelling-place of Mount Zion, and upon her assemblies, a cloud and smoke by day, and the shining of a flaming fire by night : for upon all the glory *shall be* a defence.

Isa. 12.6. Cry out and shout, thou inhabitant of Zion : for great *is* the Holy One of Israel in the midst of thee.

Isa. 17.7. At that day shall a man look to his Maker, and his eyes shall have respect to the Holy One of Israel.

Isa. 30.29. Ye shall have a song, as in the night *when* the holy solemnity is kept ; and gladness of heart, as when one goeth with a pipe to come into the mountain of the Lord, to the mighty One of Israel.

Isa. 56.7. Even them will I bring to my holy mountain, and make them joyful in my house of prayer : their burnt-offerings and their sacrifices *shall be* accepted upon mine altar ; for mine house shall be called an house of prayer for all people.

Joel 2.15. Blow the trumpet in Zion, sanctify a fast, call a solemn assembly : 16. Gather the people, sanctify the congregation, assemble the elders, gather the children, and those that suck the breasts : let the bridegroom go forth of his chamber, and the bride out of her closet. 17. Let the priests, the ministers of the Lord, weep between the porch and the altar, and let them say, Spare thy people, O Lord, and give not thine heritage to reproach.

Nah. 1.15. O Judah, keep thy solemn feasts, perform thy vows.

Zeph. 3.18. I will gather *them that are* sorrowful for the solemn assembly, *who* are of thee, *to whom* the reproach of it *was* a burden.

Hag. 1.8. Go up to the mountain, and bring wood, and build the house ; and I will take pleasure in it, and I will be glorified, saith the Lord.

Zec. 14.17. Whoso will not come up of *all* the families of the earth unto Jerusalem to worship the King, the Lord of hosts, even upon them shall be no rain. *v.* 18,19.

Mal. 3.3. That they may offer unto the Lord an offering in righteousness. 4. Then shall the offering of Judah and Jerusalem be pleasant unto the Lord, as in the days of old, and as in former years.

Mat. 8.4. Go thy way, shew thyself to the priest, and offer the gift that Moses commanded, for a testimony unto them. Mar. 1. 44. Luk. 5.14.

Mat. 18.19. If two of you shall agree on earth as touching anything that they shall ask,

it shall be done for them of my Father which is in heaven. 20. For where two or three are gathered together in my name, there am I in the midst of them.

Act. 2.1. When the day of Pentecost was fully come, they were all with one accord in one place. 2. And suddenly there came a sound from heaven as of a rushing mighty wind, and it filled all the house where they were sitting. 3. And there appeared unto them cloven tongues like as of fire, and it sat upon each of them. 4. And they were all filled with the Holy Ghost, and began to speak with other tongues, as the Spirit gave them utterance. See Act. 1.

1 The. 5.20. Despise not prophesyings.

Heb. 10.25. Not forsaking the assembling of ourselves together, as the manner of some *is*; but exhorting *one another* : and so much the more, as ye see the day approaching.

Rev. 11.1. The angel stood, saying, Rise, and measure the temple of God, and the altar, and them that worship therein.

Rev. 14.7. Fear God, and give glory to him ; for the hour of his judgment is come : and worship him that made heaven, and earth, and the sea, and the fountains of waters.

Rev. 15.4. Who shall not fear thee, O Lord, and glorify thy name? for *thou* only *art* holy : for all nations shall come and worship before thee ; for thy judgments are made manifest.

Worship, Examples of : Abraham, Gen. 21.33. Jacob, Gen. 32. Gen. 35.14,15. Israelites, Deu. 26.10. Jos. 18.1. Elkanah, 1 Sam. 1.3. Samuel and people, 1 Sam. 7. David, &c., 2 Sam. 6. 1 Chr. c. 13 & 16. 1 Chr. 29.10-20. Solomon, &c., 2 Chr. c. 1, 5 to 7. Jehoshaphat, &c., 2 Chr. 20.3-18. Hezekiah, &c., 2 Chr. 30.12,13,22,23. Ezra, Nehemiah, & Jews, Ezr. 3. Ezr. 6.22. Neh. c. 8 to 10 & 12. Sons of God, Job 1.6. Job 2.1. Jews, Luk. 1.10. Christ, Luk. 2.41,42. Luk. 4.16. Greeks, Jno. 12.20. Christians in Jerusalem, Act. 1.14. Act. 2.1,42,46. Act. 4.24. Act. 12.12. Ethiopian, Act. 8.27. Apostles, Act. 3.1. Act. 11.26. Act. 13. 3,14,15. Act. 16.13,16. Act. 18.21. Act. 19.9. Act. 20.7,16,36. Act. 24.11.

See Praise—Prayer—Sabbath—Synagogue — Feasts — Offerings — Altars — Tabernacle—Temple.

WORSHIP Loved. Ex. 15.2. He *is* my God, and I will prepare him an habitation ; my father's God, and I will exalt him.

1 Chr. 29.3. I have set my affection to the house of my God.

Neh. 10.39. We will not forsake the house of our God.

Psa.5.7. As for me, I will come *into* thy house in the multitude of thy mercy : *and* in thy fear will I worship toward thy holy temple.

Psa. 26.8. Lord, I have loved the habitation of thy house, and the place where thine honour dwelleth.

Psa. 27.4. One *thing* have I desired of the Lord, that will I seek after ; that I may dwell in the house of the Lord all the days of my life, to behold the beauty of the Lord, and to enquire in his temple.

Psa. 42.4. When I remember these *things*, I pour out my soul in me : for I had gone with the multitude ; I went with them to the house of God, with the voice of joy and praise, with a multitude kept holy-day.

Psa. 55.14. We took sweet counsel together, and walked unto the house of God in company.

Psa. 63.1. O God, thou art my God; early will I seek thee: my soul thirsteth for thee, my flesh longeth for thee in a dry and thirsty land, where no water is; 2. To see thy power and thy glory, so as I have seen thee in the sanctuary.

Psa. 66.13. I will go into thy house with burnt-offerings: I will pay thee my vows, 14. Which my lips have uttered, and my mouth hath spoken, when I was in trouble.

Psa. 84.1. How amiable are thy tabernacles, O Lord of hosts! 2. My soul longeth; yea, even fainteth for the courts of the Lord: my heart and my flesh crieth out for the living God. 10. A day in thy courts is better than a thousand: I had rather be a door-keeper in the house of my God, than to dwell in the tents of wickedness. v. 3.

Psa. 95.6. O come, let us worship and bow down: let us kneel before the Lord our Maker.

Psa. 122.1. I was glad when they said unto me, Let us go into the house of the Lord.

Psa. 132.7. We will go into his tabernacles: we will worship at his footstool.

Psa. 138.2. I will worship toward thy holy temple, and praise thy name for thy loving-kindness.

Isa. 2.3. Many nations shall come, and say, Come, and let us go up to the mountain of the Lord, and to the house of the God of Jacob; and he will teach us of his ways, and we will walk in his paths. Mic. 4.2.

Zec. 8.21. The inhabitants of one city shall go to another, saying, Let us go speedily to pray before the Lord, and to seek the Lord of hosts: I will go also. v. 22.

Act. 10.33. Now therefore are we all here present before God, to hear all things that are commanded thee of God.

See PRAISE—THANKFULNESS—PRAYER-FULNESS—LIBERALITY—ZEAL.

WORSHIP, PRESUMPTION AND SACRILEGE PUNISHED. Nadab and Abihu, Lev. 10. 1,2. Num. 3.4. Korah, &c., Num. 16.35. Eli's sons, 1 Sam. 2.13-36. Bethshemites, 1 Sam. 6.19. Saul, 1 Sam. 13.9-14. Uzzah, 2 Sam. 6.6,7. Manasseh, 2 Kin. 21.7. Uzziah, 2 Chr. 26.16-21. Ahaz, 2 Chr. 28.24. Jews, Eze. 8.10-16. Nebuchadnezzar, Dan. 1.2. Belshazzar, Dan. 5.1-6,22-31. The little horn, Dan. 8.11-13. Tyre, &c., Joel 3.5. Antichrist, 2 The. 2.4.

See BLASPHEMY—WORSHIP, REVERENCE IN.

WORSHIP, REVERENCE, SINCERITY, AND PURITY REQUIRED. Gen. 35.2. Put away the strange gods that are among you, and be clean, and change your garments: 3. And let us arise, and go up to Beth-el: and I will make there an altar unto God.

Ex. 3.5. Draw not nigh hither: put off thy shoes from off thy feet, for the place whereon thou standest is holy ground. v. 6. Jos. 5.15.

Ex. 19.10. Sanctify them to day and to morrow, and let them wash their clothes, 11. And be ready against the third day: for the third day the Lord will come down in the sight of all the people upon mount Sinai. 21.

Go down, charge the people, lest they break through unto the Lord to gaze, and many of them perish. v. 12,13,22-24.

Ex. 24.1. Come up unto the Lord, thou, and Aaron, Nadab and Abihu, and seventy of the elders of Israel; and worship ye afar off. 2. And Moses alone shall come near the Lord: but they shall not come nigh; neither shall the people go up with him.

Ex. 28.34. Bells of gold between them round about: 35. And it shall be upon Aaron to minister: and his sound shall be heard when he goeth in unto the holy place before the Lord, and when he cometh out, that he die not.

Ex. 30.19. Aaron and his sons shall wash their hands and their feet thereat: 20. When they go into the tabernacle of the congregation, they shall wash with water, that they die not; or when they come near to the altar to minister. 33. Whosoever compoundeth any like it, or whosoever putteth any of it upon a stranger, shall even be cut off from his people. v. 38.

Ex. 33.4. When the people heard these evil tidings, they mourned: and no man did put on him his ornaments.

Ex. 34.8. Moses made haste, and bowed his head toward the earth, and worshipped.

Lev. 10.3 I will be sanctified in them that come nigh me.

Lev. 16.2. Speak unto Aaron thy brother, that he come not at all times into the holy place within the vail before the mercy seat, which is upon the ark; that he die not.

Num. 1.51. The stranger that cometh nigh shall be put to death.

Num. 4.15. But they shall not touch any holy thing, lest they die. 20. They shall not go in to see when the holy things are covered, lest they die.

Num. 18.5. Keep the charge of the sanctuary, and the charge of the altar: that there be no wrath any more upon the children of Israel. v. 3,22.

Psa. 5.7. In thy fear will I worship toward thy holy temple.

Psa. 26.6. I will wash mine hands in innocency: so will I compass thine altar, O Lord: 7. That I may publish with the voice of thanksgiving, and tell of all thy wondrous works.

Psa. 29.2. Worship the Lord in the beauty of holiness.

Psa. 48.9. We have thought of thy loving-kindness, O God, in the midst of thy temple.

Psa. 89.7. God is greatly to be feared in the assembly of the saints, and to be had in reverence of all them that are about him.

Psa. 93.5. Holiness becometh thine house, O Lord, for ever.

Ecc. 5.1. Keep thy foot when thou goest to the house of God, and be more ready to hear, than to give the sacrifice of fools: for they consider not that they do evil. 2. Be not rash with thy mouth, and let not thine heart be hasty to utter any thing before God: for God is in heaven, and thou upon earth: therefore let thy words be few.

Isa. 56.6. The sons of the stranger, that join themselves to the Lord, to serve him, and to love the name of the Lord, to be his servants, every one that keepeth the sabbath from polluting it, and taketh hold of my covenant;

7. Even them will I bring to my holy mountain, and make them joyful in my house of prayer: their burnt-offerings and their sacrifices *shall be* accepted upon mine altar; for mine house shall be called an house of prayer for all people.

Isa. 66.1. Thus saith the Lord, The heaven *is* my throne, and the earth *is* my footstool: where *is* the house that ye build unto me? and where *is* the place of my rest? 2. For all those *things* hath mine hand made, and all those *things* have been, saith the Lord: but to this *man* will I look, *even to him that is* poor and of a contrite spirit, and trembleth at my word.

Jer. 7.11. Is this house, which is called by my name, become a den of robbers in your eyes? Behold, even I have seen *it*, saith the Lord.

Eze. 22.8. Thou hast despised mine holy things, and hast profaned my sabbaths.

Amos 5.23. Take thou away from me the noise of thy songs; for I will not hear the melody of thy viols. 24. But let judgment run down as waters, and righteousness as a mighty stream.

Hab. 2.20. But the Lord *is* in his holy temple: let all the earth keep silence before him,

Mar. 11.15. Jesus went into the temple, and began to cast out them that sold and bought in the temple, and overthrew the tables of the moneychangers, and the seats of them that sold doves; 16. And would not suffer that any man should carry *any* vessel through the temple. 17. And he taught, saying unto them, Is it not written, My house shall be called of all nations the house of prayer? but ye have made it a den of thieves. 25. When ye stand praying, forgive, if ye have aught against any. Mat 5.23. Mat. 21,13. Jno. 2.13-17.

Jno. 4.23. The hour cometh, and now is, when the true worshippers shall worship the Father in spirit and in truth: for the Father seeketh such to worship him. 24. God *is* a Spirit: and they that worship him must worship *him* in spirit and in truth.

Act. 17.24. God that made the world and all things therein, seeing that he is Lord of heaven and earth, dwelleth not in temples made with hands; 25. Neither is worshipped with men's hands, as though he needed any thing, seeing he giveth to all life, and breath, and all things.

1 Cor. 11.13. Judge in yourselves: is it comely that a woman pray unto God uncovered? 20. When ye come together therefore into one place, *this* is not to eat the Lord's supper. 21. For in eating every one taketh before *other* his own supper: and one is hungry, and another is drunken. 22. What? have ye not houses to eat and to drink in? or despise ye the church of God, and shame them that have not? What shall I say to you? shall I praise you in this? I praise *you* not.

1 Cor. 14.15. What is it then? I will pray with the spirit, and I will pray with the understanding also: I will sing with the spirit, and I will sing with the understanding also. 16. Else when thou shalt bless with the spirit, how shall he that occupieth the room of the unlearned say Amen at thy giving of thanks, seeing he understandeth not what thou say-

est? 17. For thou verily givest thanks well, but the other is not edified.

Phil. 3.3. We are the circumcision, which worship God in the spirit.

1 Tim. 2.8. I will therefore that men pray everywhere, lifting up holy hands, without wrath and doubting.

Heb. 12.28. Let us have grace, whereby we may serve God acceptably with reverence and godly fear. *v.* 29.

1 Pet. 2.5. Ye also, as lively stones, are built up a spiritual house, an holy priesthood, to offer up spiritual sacrifices, acceptable to God by Jesus Christ.

See SIN SEPARATES FROM GOD—PRAYER BY DIVINE AID.

WRITER. See SCRIBE.

WRITING, IMPLEMENTS OF, see INK, INK-HORN, PEN, TABLET. On paper, see PAPER, PARCHMENT. On stone or rock, Deu. 27.3. Jos. 8.32. Job 19.24, see TABLES OF STONE. In books or rolls, see BOOKS, LETTERS.

Y

YARN, 1 Kin. 10.28.

YEAR OF JUBILEE, see JUBILEE. Of release, see SABBATICAL YEAR.

YEARS. See MONTHS—DAY.

YOKE, Num. 19.2. 1 Sam. 11.7. Illustrative, Lev. 26.13. Lam. 3.27. Lam. 1.14. Mat. 11.29,30. Act. 15.10.

YOUTH. See CHILDREN.

Z

ZACCHEUS, chief of the publicans, at Jericho; seeks to see Jesus, who invites himself to his house; Christ's commendation of him, Luk. 19.1-10.

ZACHARIAH, 14th king of Israel, son and successor of Jeroboam II. (reigns 6 months); his wicked reign; murdered by Shallum; the last king of the dynasty of Jehu, 2 Kin. 14.29. 2 Kin. 15.8-12; fulfilling 2 Kin. 10.30.

ZACHARIAS, father of John the Baptist; a priest of the course of Abia; of the line of Eleazar, Luk. 1.5. 1 Chr. 24.4,10. His character, Luk. 1.6. Dwelt at Hebron, Luk. 1.23,39,40,65 with Jos. 21.10,11. His vision in the temple; Gabriel predicts the birth of John; he is struck dumb for incredulity; his dumbness removed when he named the child John; inspired by the Holy Ghost; his song, Luk. 1.7-23,62-79. See ELIZABETH—JOHN.

ZADOK, son of Ahitub; of the line of Phinehas, 1 Chr. 6.8,52,53. High-priest in David's reign, jointly with Abiathar, 2 Sam. 19.11. 2 Sam. 20.25. 1 Kin. 4.4. 1 Chr. 15.11. 1 Chr. 16.39; who is called Ahimelech, 2 Sam. 8.17. 1 Chr. 18.16. 1 Chr. 24.3-6,31. 1 Chr. 27.17. He and Abiathar carry the ark on David's flight from Absalom; return to the city; their sons, Ahimaaz and Jonathan, carry news of the rebellion, 2 Sam. 15.24-36. 2 Sam. 17.15,17-21, see AHIMAAZ. Anoints Solomon, 1 Kin. 1.8,26,32-45. Sole high-priest after the deposition of Abiathar, 1 Kin. 2.35. 1 Chr. 29.22.

ZALMON, or SALMON, a mountain near Shechem, Jud. 9.48. Psa. 68.14.

ZALMUNNA, king of Midian, conquered and slain by Gideon, Jud. 8.5-21. Psa. 83.11.

ZAMZUMMIMS, or ZUZIMS, a race of giants; dispossessed by the Ammonites, Deu. 2.20,21, see Gen. 14.5.

ZAREPHATH. See SAREPTA.

ZARETAN, ZARTANAH, ZARTHAN, or ZEREDA, a town west of the Jordan, opposite Adam, Jos. 3.16. 1 Kin. 4.12. 1 Kin. 7.46. 1 Kin. 11.26.

ZEAL. ZEAL FOR THE CONVERSION OF SINNERS. Psa. 60.4. Thou hast given a banner to them that fear thee, that it may be displayed because of the truth.

Psa. 90.3. Declare his glory among the heathen, his wonders among all people. 10. Say among the heathen *that* the Lord reigneth.

Prov. 11.30. The fruit of the righteous *is* a tree of life; and he that winneth souls *is* wise.

Isa. 43.12. *Ye are* my witnesses, saith the Lord, that I *am* God. *v.* 10. Isa. 44.8.

Isa. 58.12. *They that shall be* of thee shall build the old waste places: thou shalt raise up the foundations of many generations; and thou shalt be called, The repairer of the breach, The restorer of paths to dwell in.

Isa. 60.1. Arise, shine; for thy light is come, and the glory of the Lord is risen upon thee.

Isa. 62.6. I have set watchmen upon thy walls, O Jerusalem, *which* shall never hold their peace day nor night: ye that make mention of the Lord keep not silence. 7. And give him no rest, till he establish, and till he make Jerusalem a praise in the earth.

Dan. 12.3. They that be wise shall shine as the brightness of the firmament; and they that turn many to righteousness as the stars for ever and ever.

Mic. 5.7. The remnant of Jacob shall be in the midst of many people as a dew from the Lord, as the showers upon the grass, that tarrieth not for man, nor waiteth for the sons of men.

Hab. 2.2. Write the vision, and make *it* plain upon tables, that he may run that readeth it.

Hag. 2.4. Be strong, O Zerubbabel, saith the Lord; and be strong, O Joshua, son of Josedech, the high-priest; and be strong, all ye people of the land, saith the Lord, and work: for I *am* with you, saith the Lord of hosts: 5. *According* to the word that I covenanted with you when ye came out of Egypt, so my spirit remaineth among you: fear ye not.

Mat. 5.13. Ye are the salt of the earth: but if the salt have lost his savour, wherewith shall it be salted? it is thenceforth good for nothing, but to be cast out, and to be trodden under foot of men. 14. Ye are the light of the world. A city that is set on an hill cannot be hid. 15. Neither do men light a candle, and put it under a bushel, but on a candlestick; and it giveth light unto all that are in the house. 16. Let your light so shine before men, that they may see your good works, and glorify your Father which is in heaven. Mar. 4.21,22. Luk. 8. 16,17.

Luk. 22.32. When thou art converted strengthen thy brethren.

Act. 10.42. He commanded us to preach unto the people, and to testify that it is he which was ordained of God *to be* the Judge of quick and dead.

1 Cor. 14.12. Forasmuch as ye are zealous of spiritual *gifts*, seek that ye may excel to the edifying of the church.

1 Cor. 15.58. My beloved brethren, be ye stedfast, unmoveable, always abounding in the work of the Lord, forasmuch as ye know that your labour is not in vain in the Lord.

Gal. 4.18. *It is* good to be zealously affected always in a good *thing*, and not only when I am present with you.

Gal. 6.9. Let us not be weary in well doing: for in due season we shall reap, if we faint not. 2 The. 3.13.

Eph. 6.15. Your feet shod with the preparation of the gospel of peace.

Phil. 2.5. Let this mind be in you, which was also in Christ Jesus. 15. Shine as lights in the world; 16. Holding forth the word of life; that I may rejoice in the day of Christ, that I have not run in vain, neither laboured in vain. *v.* 6-9.

Col. 4.5. Walk in wisdom toward them that are without, redeeming the time.

Tit. 2.3. The aged women likewise, that *they be* teachers of good things.

Tit. 3.1. Be ready to every good work.

Jas. 5.19. Brethren, if any of you do err from the truth, and one convert him; 20. Let him know, that he which converteth the sinner from the error of his way shall save a soul from death, and shall hide a multitude of sins.

3 Jno. 8. We therefore ought to receive such, that we might be fellow-helpers to the truth.

Jude 3. Earnestly contend for the faith which was once delivered unto the saints. 22. Of some have compassion, making a difference: 23. And others save with fear, pulling *them* out of the fire; hating even the garment spotted by the flesh.

Rev. 3.19. As many as I love, I rebuke and chasten: be zealous therefore, and repent.

Rev. 22.17. The Spirit and the bride say, Come. And let him that heareth say, Come.

ZEAL, EXAMPLES OF: Asa, 2 Chr. 14.4. Jehoshaphat, 2 Chr. 17.7-9. 2 Chr. 19.4. Hezekiah, 2 Chr. *c.* 30 & 31. Josiah, 2 Kin. 23.2,3. 2 Chr. 34.29-33. Priests, 1 Chr. 9.13. Ezr. 8.17,18. Ezra and Nehemiah, Ezr. 7.10. Ezr. *c.* 9 & 10. Neh. 8. Shepherds, Luk. 2. 17,18. Anna, Luk. 2.38. Andrew and Philip, Jno. 1.41-46. Samaritan woman, Jno. 4. 28-30,39. Peter, Act. 2.14-40. Act. 3.12-26. John, see JOHN THE BAPTIST. Paul and Barnabas, Act. 11.22-26, see ZEAL OF PAUL. Phebe, &c., Rom. 16.1-12.

ZEAL. ZEAL FOR THE CONVERSION OF SINNERS, EXEMPLIFIED. Num. 10.29. We are journeying unto the place of which the Lord said, I will give it you: come thou with us, and we will do thee good: for the Lord hath spoken good concerning Israel.

Num. 11.29. Enviest thou for my sake? would God that all the Lord's people were prophets, *and* that the Lord would put his spirit upon them!

1 Kin. 8.43. Hear thou in heaven thy dwelling-place, and do according to all that the stranger calleth to thee for: that all people

of the earth may know thy name, to fear thee, as *do* thy people Israel. *v.* 42. 2 Chr. 6.33.

1 Kin. 22.14. *As* the Lord liveth, what the Lord saith unto me, that will I speak.

Job 6.10. I have not concealed the words of the Holy one.

Psa. 40.9. I have preached righteousness in the great congregation : lo, I have not refrained my lips, O Lord, thou knowest. 10. I have not hid thy righteousness within my heart ; I have declared thy faithfulness and thy salvation : I have not concealed thy lovingkindness and thy truth from the great congregation.

Psa. 51.13. *Then* will I teach transgressors thy ways ; and sinners shall be converted unto thee.

Psa. 67.1. God be merciful unto us, and bless us ; *and* cause his face to shine upon us; 2. That thy way may be known upon earth, thy saving health among all nations. *v.* 5. Psa. 105.1.

Psa. 71.17. O God, thou hast taught me from my youth : and hitherto have I declared thy wondrous works. 18. Now also, when I am old and grayheaded, O God, forsake me not, until I have shewed thy strength unto *this* generation, *and* thy power to every one *that is* to come.

Ecc. 12.9. Moreover, because the Preacher was wise, he still taught the people knowledge; yea, he gave good heed, and sought out, *and* set in order many proverbs.

Ecc. 12.10. The Preacher sought to find out acceptable words : and *that which was* written *was* upright, *even* words of truth.

Isa. 2.3. Many nations shall come, and say, Come, and let us go up to the mountain of the Lord, and to the house of the God of Jacob ; and he will teach us of his ways, and we will walk in his paths. 5. O house of Jacob, come ye, and let us walk in the light of the Lord.

Isa. 6.8. I heard the voice of the Lord, saying, Whom shall I send, and who will go for us? Then said I, Here *am* I ; send me.

Isa. 62.1. For Zion's sake will I not hold my peace, and for Jerusalem's sake I will not rest, until the righteousness thereof go forth as brightness, and the salvation thereof as a lamp *that* burneth.

Jer. 17.16. As for me, I have not hastened from *being* a pastor to follow thee : neither have I desired the woeful day ; thou knowest: that which came out of my lips was *right* before thee.

Jer. 18.20. Remember that I stood before thee to speak good for them, *and* to turn away thy wrath from them.

Jer. 20.9. Then ,I said, I will not make mention of him, nor speak any more in his name. But *his word* was in mine heart as a burning fire shut up in my bones, and I was weary with forbearing, and I could not *stay*. Jer. 26.12-15.

Eze. 44.15. The priests the Levites, the sons of Zadok, that kept the charge of my sanctuary when the children of Israel went astray from me, they shall come near to me to minister unto me.

Mic. 3.8. Truly I am full of power by the spirit of the Lord, and of judgment, and of might, to declare unto Jacob his transgression, and to Israel his sin.

Mar. 5.20. And he departed, and began to

publish in Decapolis how great things Jesus had done for him : and all *men* did marvel. *v.* 19.

Mar. 16.20. They went forth, and preached every where, the Lord working with *them*, and confirming the word with signs following.

Luk. 1.16. Many of the children of Israel shall he turn to the Lord their God. 17. And he shall go before him in the spirit and power of Elias, to turn the hearts of the fathers to the children, and the disobedient to the wisdom of the just ; to make ready a people prepared for the Lord. *v.* 15.

Act. 4.13. When they saw the boldness of Peter and John, and perceived that they were unlearned and ignorant men, they marvelled ; and they took knowledge of them, that they had been with Jesus. 18. And they called them, and commanded them not to speak at all nor teach in the name of Jesus. 19. But Peter and John answered and said unto them, Whether it be right in the sight of God to hearken unto you more than unto God, judge ye. 20. For we cannot but speak the things which we have seen and heard. 31. They were all filled with the Holy Ghost, and they spake the word of God with boldness. 33. With great power gave the apostles witness of the resurrection of the Lord Jesus : and great grace was upon them all. *v.* 2,8-12.

Act. 5.42. Daily in the temple, and in every house, they ceased not to teach and preach Jesus Christ. *v.* 21,25,29-32.

Act. 6.4. But we will give ourselves continually to prayer, and to the ministry of the word. 10. They were not able to resist the wisdom and the spirit by which he spake.

Act. 8.4. Therefore they that were scattered abroad went every where preaching the word. 35. Philip opened his mouth, and began at the same scripture, and preached unto him Jesus. *v.* 4,12,25,30,40. Act. 11. 19,20,24,26.

Act. 18.25. This man was instructed in the way of the Lord ; and being fervent in the spirit, he spake and taught diligently the things of the Lord, knowing only the baptism of John. 26. He began to speak boldly in the synagogue : whom when Aquila and Priscilla had heard, they took him unto *them*, and expounded unto him the way of God more perfectly. 27. And when he was disposed to pass into Achaia, the brethren wrote, exhorting the disciples to receive him : who, when he was come, helped them much which had believed through grace : 28. For he mightily convinced the Jews, *and that* publickly, shewing by the scriptures that Jesus was Christ. *v.* 24.

2 Cor. 8.5. · They first gave their own selves to the Lord, and unto us by the will of God. 18. We have sent with him the brother, whose praise *is* in the gospel throughout all the churches.

Phil. 1.14. Many of the brethren in the Lord, waxing confident by my bonds, are much more bold to speak the word without fear. *v.* 12-18.

Phil. 2.22. Ye know the proof of him, that, as a son with the father, he hath served with me in the gospel. 26. He longed after you all, and was full of heaviness, because that ye had heard that he had been sick. 30. For the work of Christ he was nigh unto death, not regarding his life, to supply your lack of service toward me. 1 Cor. 16.10.

Phil. 4.3. I intreat thee also, true yokefellow, help those women which laboured with me in the gospel, with Clement also, and *with* other my fellow-labourers, whose names *are* in the book of life.

Col. 4.7. A beloved brother, and a faithful minister and fellow-servant in the Lord. 11. *My* fellow-workers unto the kingdom of God. Eph. 6.21. Col. 1.7.

1 The. 1.3. Your work of faith, and labour of love, and patience of hope in our Lord Jesus Christ, in the sight of God and our Father. 7. Ye are ensamples to all that believe in Macedonia and Achaia. 8. For from you sounded out the word of the Lord not only in Macedonia and Achaia, but also in every place your faith to God-ward is spread abroad.

1 The. 3.2. Sent Timotheus, our brother, and minister of God, and our fellow-labourer in the gospel of Christ, to establish you, and to comfort you concerning your faith.

2 Pet. 1.12. I will not be negligent to put you always in remembrance of these things, though ye know *them*, and be established in the present truth. 13. Yea, I think it meet, as long as I am in this tabernacle, to stir you up by putting *you* in remembrance. 15. Moreover I will endeavour that ye may be able after my decease to have these things always in remembrance.

2 Pet. 2.5. Noah the eighth *person*, a preacher of righteousness.

3 Jno. 7. For his name's sake they went forth, taking nothing of the Gentiles.

See PRAYER, INTERCESSORY—CHURCH AND COUNTRY, LOVE OF—LIBERALITY AND ZEAL —ZEAL FOR GOD'S GLORY—REPROOF, FIDELITY IN—CHRIST'S ZEAL—SAINTS, COMMUNION OF—MINISTERS.

ZEAL OF PAUL; HIS PREACHING. Act. 9.20. Straightway he preached Christ in the synagogues, that he is the Son of God. *v.* 20-29.

Act. 14.22. Confirming the souls of the disciples, *and* exhorting them to continue in the faith, and that we must through much tribulation enter into the kingdom of God. *v.* 1-28.

Act. 15.26. Men that have hazarded their lives for the name of our Lord Jesus Christ. *v.* 30-36,41.

Act. 16.31. They said, Believe on the Lord Jesus Christ, and thou shalt be saved, and thy house. 32. And they spake unto him the word of the Lord, and to all that were in his house. *v.* 10,13,17.

Act. 17.2. Paul, as his manner was, went in unto them, and three sabbath days reasoned with them out of the scriptures. 3. Opening and alleging, that Christ must needs have suffered, and risen again from the dead ; and that this Jesus, whom I preach unto you, is Christ. 16. His spirit was stirred in him, when he saw the city wholly given to idolatry. 17. Therefore disputed he in the synagogue with the Jews, and with the devout persons, and in the market daily with them that met with him. *v.* 22-31.

Act. 18.5. Paul was pressed in the spirit, and testified to the Jews *that* Jesus *was* Christ. 6. And when they opposed themselves, and blasphemed, he shook *his* raiment, and said

unto them, Your blood *be* upon your own heads ; I *am* clean : from henceforth I will go unto the Gentiles. *v.* 4,19,23. Act. 13.16-52.

Act. 20.18. I have been with you at all seasons, 19. Serving the Lord with all humility of mind, and with many tears, and temptations, which befell me by the lying in wait of the Jews : 20. *And* how I kept back nothing that was profitable *unto you*, but have shewed you, and have taught you publickly, and from house to house, 21. Testifying both to the Jews, and also to the Greeks, repentance toward God, and faith toward our Lord Jesus Christ.

Act. 20.22. Now, behold, I go bound in the spirit unto Jerusalem, not knowing the things that shall befall me there : 23. Save that the Holy Ghost witnesseth in every city, saying that bonds and afflictions abide me. 24. But none of these things move me, neither count I my life dear unto myself, so that I might finish my course with joy, and the ministry, which I have received of the Lord Jesus, to testify the gospel of the grace of God.

Act. 20.26. Wherefore I take you to record this day, that I *am* pure from the blood of all men. 27. For I have not shunned to declare unto you all the counsel of God. 31. Therefore watch, and remember, that, by the space of three years, I ceased not to warn every one night and day with tears. 33. I have coveted no man's silver, or gold, or apparel. 34. Yea, ye yourselves know, that these hands have ministered unto my necessities, and to them that were with me. *v.* 7,25. Act. 19.8-10,21. Act. 21.13.

Act. 24.25. He reasoned of righteousness, temperance, and judgment to come. *v.* 14-25.

Act. 26.19. I was not disobedient unto the heavenly vision : 20. But shewed first unto them of Damascus, and at Jerusalem, and throughout all the coasts of Judea, and *then* to the Gentiles, that they should repent and turn to God, and do works meet for repentance.

Act. 26.22. Having therefore obtained help of God, I continue unto this day, witnessing both to small and great, saying none other things than those which the prophets and Moses did say should come : 23. That Christ should suffer, *and* that he should be the first that should rise from the dead, and should shew light unto the people, and to the Gentiles. 29. Paul said, I would to God, that not only thou, but also all that hear me this day, were both almost, and altogether such as I am, except these bonds. *v.* 1-29.

Act. 28.23. When they had appointed him a day, there came many to him into *his* lodging ; to whom he expounded and testified the kingdom of God, persuading them concerning Jesus, both out of the law of Moses, and *out of* the prophets, from morning till evening. 30. Paul dwelt two whole years in his own hired house, and received all that came in unto him, 31. Preaching the kingdom of God, and teaching those things which concern the Lord Jesus Christ, with all confidence. *v.* 24-28.

Rom. 1.1. Paul, a servant of Jesus Christ, called *to be* an apostle, separated unto the gospel of God. 14. I am debtor both to the Greeks, and to the Barbarians ; both to the wise, and to the unwise. 15. So, as much as in me is, I am ready to preach the gospel to you that are at Rome also. *v.* 9-13.

Rom. 9.1. I say the truth in Christ, I lie not, my conscience also bearing me witness in the Holy Ghost. 2. That I have great heaviness and continual sorrow in my heart. 3. For I could wish that myself were accursed from Christ for my brethren, my kinsmen according to the flesh.

Rom. 10.1. Brethren, my heart's desire and prayer to God for Israel is, that they might be saved. Rom. 11.13,14.

Rom. 15.19. From Jerusalem, and round about unto Illyricum, I have fully preached the gospel of Christ. 20. Yea, so have I strived to preach the gospel, not where Christ was named, lest I should build upon another man's foundation. *v.* 15-32. 2 Cor. 10.14-16.

1 Cor. 1.17. Christ sent me not to baptize, but to preach the gospel: not with wisdom of words, lest the cross of Christ should be made of none effect. 23. We preach Christ crucified, unto the Jews a stumblingblock, and unto the Greeks foolishness.

1 Cor. 2.1. I, brethren, when I came to you, came not with excellency of speech, or of wisdom, declaring unto you the testimony of God: 2. For I determined not to know any thing among you, save Jesus Christ, and him crucified. 3. And I was with you in weakness, and in fear, and in much trembling. 4. And my speech and my preaching *was* not with enticing words of man's wisdom, but in demonstration of the Spirit and of power. 13. Which things also we speak, not in the words which man's wisdom teacheth, but which the Holy Ghost teacheth; comparing spiritual things with spiritual. *v.* 6,7.

1 Cor. 3.1. I, brethren, could not speak unto you as unto spiritual, but as unto carnal, *even* as unto babes in Christ. 2. I have fed you with milk, and not with meat: for hitherto ye were not able *to bear it,* neither yet now are ye able. *v.* 5-7.

1 Cor. 4.16. Labour, working with our own hands: being reviled, we bless; being persecuted, we suffer it: 13. Being defamed, we intreat: we are made as the filth of the world *and are* the offscouring of all things unto this day. *v.* 1-21.

1 Cor. 9.16. Though I preach the gospel, I have nothing to glory of: for necessity is laid upon me; yea, woe is unto me, if I preach not the gospel! 18. What is my reward then? *Verily* that, when I preach the gospel, I may make the gospel of Christ without charge, that I abuse not my power in the gospel. 19. Though I be free from all *men,* yet have I made myself servant unto all, that I might gain the more. 22. To the weak became I as weak, that I might gain the weak: I am made all things to all *men,* that I might by all means save some. 23. And this I do for the gospel's sake. 27. I keep under my body, and bring *it* into subjection: lest that by any means, when I have preached to others, I myself should be a castaway. *v.* 12,15,17,20,21.

1 Cor. 10.33. I please all *men* in all *things,* not seeking mine own profit, but the *profit* of many, that they may be saved.

1 Cor. 11.1. Be ye followers of me, even as I also *am* of Christ.

1 Cor. 13 1. Though I speak with the tongues of men and of angels, and have not charity, I am become *as* sounding brass, or a tinkling cymbal.

1 Cor. 15.3. I delivered unto you first of all that which I also received, how that Christ died for our sins according to the scriptures. 10. By the grace of God I am what I am: and his grace which *was bestowed* upon me was not in vain; but I laboured more abundantly than they all: yet not I, but the grace of God which was with me. 11. Whether *it were* I or they, so we preach, and so ye believed. 31. I protest by your rejoicing which I have in Christ Jesus our Lord, I die daily. *v.* 1-32.

2 Cor. 1.12. Our rejoicing is this, the testimony of our conscience, that in simplicity and godly sincerity, not with fleshly wisdom, but by the grace of God, we have had our conversation in the world, and more abundantly to you-ward. *v.* 17-19,24.

2 Cor 2.17. We are not as many, which corrupt the word of God: but as of sincerity, but as of God, in the sight of God speak we in Christ. *v.* 12-16.

2 Cor. 3.6. Who also hath made us able ministers of the new testament; not of the letter, but of the spirit: for the letter killeth, but the spirit giveth life. 12. Seeing then that we have such hope, we use great plainness of speech.

2 Cor. 4.1. Seeing we have this ministry, as we have received mercy, we faint not; 2. But have renounced the hidden things of dishonesty, not walking in craftiness, nor handling the word of God deceitfully; but by manifestation of the truth commending ourselves to every man's conscience in the sight of God. 5. We preach not ourselves, but Christ Jesus the Lord; and ourselves your servants for Jesus' sake. 13. We having the same spirit of faith, according as it is written, I believed, and therefore have I spoken; we also believe, and therefore speak. *v.* 8-15.

2 Cor. 5.11. Knowing therefore the terror of the Lord, we persuade men; but we are made manifest unto God; and I trust also are made manifest in your consciences. 13. Whether we be beside ourselves, *it is* to God: or whether we be sober, *it is* for your cause. 14. For the love of Christ constraineth us; because we thus judge, that if one died for all, then were all dead: 20. We are ambassadors for Christ, as though God did beseech *you* by us: we pray *you* in Christ's stead, be ye reconciled to God. *v.* 18.

2 Cor. 6.3. Giving no offence in any thing that the ministry be not blamed. 4. In all *things* approving ourselves as the ministers of God, in much patience, in afflictions, in necessities, in distresses, 5. In stripes, in imprisonments, in tumults, in labours, in watchings, in fastings: 6. By pureness, by knowledge, by long suffering, by kindness, by the Holy Ghost, by love unfeigned, 7. By the word of truth, by the power of God, by the armour of righteousness on the right hand and on the left. *v.* 8-10.

2 Cor. 7.2. Receive us; we have wronged no man, we have corrupted no man, we have defrauded no man.

2 Cor. 10.3. Though we walk in the flesh, we do not war after the flesh.

2 Cor. 11.9. And when I was present with you, and wanted, I was chargeable to no man: for that which was lacking to me the brethren

which came from Macedonia supplied; and in all *things* I have kept myself from being burdensome unto you, and *so* will I keep *myself. v.* 7,12,23-33.

2 Cor. 12.10. I take pleasure in infirmities, in reproaches, in necessities, in persecutions, in distresses for Christ's sake. 14. I will not be burdensome to you: for I seek not your's, but you: 15. I will very gladly spend and be spent for you; though the more abundantly I love you, the less I be loved. 21. Lest, when I come again, my God will humble me among you, and *that* I shall bewail many which have sinned already, and have not repented. *v.* 17-19.

2 Cor. 13.8. We can do nothing against the truth, but for the truth. *v.* 6-9.

Gal. 1.10. Do I now persuade men, or God? or do I seek to please men? for if I yet pleased men, I should not be the servant of Christ. 15. When it pleased God, who separated me from my mother's womb, and called *me* by his grace, 16. To reveal his Son in me, that I might preach him among the heathen; immediately I conferred not with flesh and blood.

Gal. 2.2. I went up by revelation, and communicated unto them that gospel which I preach among the Gentiles, but privately to them which were of reputation, lest by any means I should run, or had run, in vain. Gal. 3.1.

Gal. 4.19. My little children, of whom I travail in birth again until Christ be formed in you. *v.* 11.

Gal. 5.11. I, brethren, if I yet preach circumcision, why do I yet suffer persecution? then is the offence of the cross ceased.

Eph. 6.20. For which I am an ambassador in bonds; that therein I may speak boldly, as I ought to speak. *v.* 17. Phil. 1.17. Phil. 4.11,12,17.

Phil. 1.18. What then? notwithstanding, every way, whether in pretence, or in truth, Christ is preached; and I therein do rejoice, yea, and will rejoice. 20. According to my earnest expectation and *my* hope, that in nothing I shall be ashamed, but *that* with all boldness, as always, *so* now also Christ shall be magnified in my body, whether *it be* by life, or by death. 24. To abide in the flesh *is* more needful for you. 25. And having this confidence, I know that I shall abide and continue with you all for your furtherance and joy of faith. 27. That whether I come and see you, or else be absent, I may hear of your affairs, that ye stand fast in one spirit, with one mind striving together for the faith of the gospel. *v.* 22,23. Phil. 2.16,17.

Col. 1.28. Whom we preach, warning every man, and teaching every man in all wisdom; that we may present every man perfect in Christ Jesus. 29. I also labour, striving according to his working, which worketh in me mightily. *v.* 24.

Col. 2.1. I would that ye knew what great conflict I have for you, and *for* them at Laodicea, and *for* as many as have not seen my face in the flesh.

1 The. 1.5. Ye know what manner of men we were among you for your sake. 6. And ye became followers of us, and of the Lord.

1 The. 2.2. Even after that we had suffered before, and were shamefully entreated, as ye know, at Philippi, we were bold in our God to speak unto you the gospel of God with much contention. 3. Our exhortation *was* not of deceit, nor of uncleanness, nor in guile: 4. As we were allowed of God to be put in trust with the gospel, even so we speak; not as pleasing men, but God, which trieth our hearts. 5. For neither at any time used we flattering words, as ye know, nor a cloke of covetousness; God *is* witness.

1 The. 2.6. Nor of men sought we glory, neither of you nor *yet* of others, when we might have been burdensome, as the apostles of Christ. 8. Being affectionately desirous of you, we were willing to have imparted unto you, not the gospel of God only, but also our own souls, because ye were dear unto us. 9. For ye remember, brethren, our labour and travail: for labouring night and day, because we would not be chargeable unto any of you, we preached unto you the gospel of God. 10. Ye *are* witnesses, and God *also*, how holily and justly and unblameably we behaved ourselves among you that believe: 11. Ye know how we exhorted and comforted and charged every one of you, as a father *doth* his children. 2 Tim. 1.3,7,11-13.

2 The. 3.7. Yourselves know how ye ought to follow us: for we behaved not ourselves disorderly among you; 8. Neither did we eat any man's bread for nought; but wrought with labour and travail night and day, that we might not be chargeable to any of you: 9. Not because we have not power, but to make ourselves an ensample unto you to follow us. Phil. 3.17.

1 Tim. 4.10. We both labour and suffer reproach, because we trust in the living God. 2 Tim. 2.9,10.

2 Tim. 3.10. Thou hast fully known my doctrine, manner of life, purpose, faith, longsuffering, charity, patience.

Heb. 13.18. Pray for us: for we trust we have a good conscience, in all things willing to live honestly.

See LOVE AND ZEAL OF PAUL—PERSECUTION OF PAUL—PRAYER, INTERCESSORY, OF PAUL.

ZEAL FOR GOD'S GLORY, SINS OF OTHERS HATED AND LAMENTED. Ex. 32.31. Oh, this people have sinned a great sin, and have made them gods of gold. 32. Yet now, if thou wilt forgive their sin—; and if not, blot me, I pray thee, out of thy book which thou hast written.

Deu. 9.18. I fell down before the Lord, as at the first, forty days and forty nights: I did neither eat bread, nor drink water, because of all your sins which ye sinned, in doing wickedly in the sight of the Lord, to provoke him to anger. *v.* 19.

1 Sam. 17.26. Who *is* this uncircumcised Philistine, that he should defy the armies of the living God?

Psa. 69.9. The zeal of thine house hath eaten me up; and the reproaches of them that reproach thee are fallen upon me. 1 Chr. 16. 35.

Psa. 94.16. Who will rise up for me against the evildoers? *or* who will stand up for me against the workers of iniquity?

Psa. 101.8. I will early destroy all the wicked of the land; that I may cut off all wicked doers from the city of the Lord.

Psa. 119.53. Horror hath taken hold upon me because of the wicked that forsake thy law. 126. *It is* time for *thee*, Lord, to work : *for* they have made void thy law. 136. Rivers of waters run down mine eyes, because they keep not thy law. 139. My zeal hath consumed me, because mine enemies have forgotten thy words. 158. I beheld the transgressors, and was grieved : because they kept not thy word. Psa. 9.19,20. Psa. 74.10,18-23. Psa. 115.1,2.

Pro. 28.4. They that forsake the law praise the wicked : but such as keep the law contend with them.

Isa. 59.17. He put on righteousness as a breastplate, and an helmet of salvation upon his head ; and he put on the garments of vengeance *for* clothing, and was clad with zeal as a cloak.

Jer. 13.17. If ye will not hear it, my soul shall weep in secret places for *your* pride ; and mine eye shall weep sore, and run down with tears, because the Lord's flock is carried away captive.

Eze. 6.11. Smite with thine hand, and stamp with thy foot, and say, Alas for all the evil abominations of the house of Israel !

Eze. 9.4. Set a mark upon the foreheads of the men that sigh and that cry for all the abominations that be done in the midst thereof.

Mic. 7.1. Woe is me ! 2. The good man is perished out of the earth : and *there is* none upright among men.

Hab. 1.2. O Lord, how long shall I cry, and thou wilt not hear ! *even* cry out unto thee *of* violence, and thou wilt not save ! *v.* 3,4.

Mar. 3.5. When he had looked round about on them with anger, being grieved for the hardness of their hearts.

Mar. 6.6. He marvelled because of their unbelief.

Mar. 8.12. He sighed deeply in his spirit, and saith, Why doth this generation seek after a sign ?

Luk. 9.41. Jesus answering, said, O faithless and perverse generation, how long shall I be with you, and suffer you ? Bring thy son hither.

Luk. 19.41. When he was come near, he beheld the city, and wept over it. *v.* 42. Mat. 23.37.

2 Cor. 12.21. Lest, when I come again, my God will humble me among you, and *that* I shall bewail many which have sinned already.

Eph. 4.26. Be ye angry and sin not.

Phil. 3.18. For many walk, of whom I have told you often, and now tell you even weeping, *that they* are the enemies of the cross of Christ. Act. 20.31.

Jude 3. Earnestly contend for the faith which was once delivered unto the saints.

ZEAL FOR GOD'S GLORY, &c. EXAMPLES OF : Moses, Ex. 11.8. Ex. 32.19,20. Joshua, Jos. 7.6. Samuel, 1 Sam. 15.11,35. 1 Sam. 16.1. Elijah, 1 Kin. 19.10. Elisha, 2 Kin. 8.11. Ezra, Ezr. 9.3-15. Nehemiah, Neh. 4.5. Neh. 13.7-9,15-28. Hezekiah, Isa. 37.1. Paul and Barnabas, Act. 14.14,15. Act. 17.16. Ephesians, Rev. 2.2,3,6.

See SIN HATED—REPROOF, FIDELITY IN—LOVE AND ZEAL OF PAUL.

ZEAL FOR GOD'S GLORY—ZEAL IN PUNISHING SIN, EXAMPLES OF : Moses and Levites, Ex. 32.20,26-29. Deu. 33.9. Phinehas, Num.

25.11-13. Psa. 106.30,31. Israelites, Jos. 22. 11-20. Jud. 20. Samuel, 1 Sam. 15.33. David, 2 Sam. 1.14. 2 Sam. 4.9-12. Elijah, 1 Kin. 18.40. Jehu, 2 Kin. 10.15-28. Jehoiada, 2 Kin. 11.18. Josiah, 2 Kin. 23.20.

See IDOLATRY, p. 244. REPROOF, FIDELITY IN.

ZEBAH, a king of Midian, defeated and slain by Gideon, Jud. 8.5-21. Psa. 83.11.

ZEBEDEE, husband of Salome, and father of James and John, Mat. 4.21. Mat. 20.20. Mat. 27.56. Mar. 1.20 with Mar. 15.40 & Mar. 16.1.

ZEBOIM, one of the cities of the plain, Gen. 10.19. King of, defeated by Chedorlaomer, Gen. 14.2,8. Destroyed with Sodom, &c., Deu. 29.23. Hos. 11.8. Gen. 19.24-29. Jer. 20.16.

ZEBUL, an officer left by Abimelech in charge of Shechem ; his prudence and fidelity, Jud. 9.29-41.

ZEBULUN, son of Jacob and Leah, Gen. 30.19,20. Gen. 35.23. Ex. 1.3. 1 Chr. 2.1. Blessed by Jacob, Gen. 49.13. His sons, Gen. 46.14.

————, TRIBE OF, numbered at Sinai, Num. 1.30,31 ; and in the plains of Moab, Num. 26.26,27. Marched and encamped under the standard of Judah, east of the tabernacle, Num. 2.3,7. Num. 10.14,16. Inheritance of, Gen. 49.13. Jos. 19.10-16 ; imperfectly subdued, Jud. 1.30. Levitical cities in, Jos. 21. 34,35. 1 Chr. 6.77. Blessing of Moses on, Deu. 33.18,19.

Assisted Barak, Jud. 4.6,10. Jud. 5.14,18 ; Gideon, Jud. 6.35 ; David, 1 Chr. 12.33,40. Furnished scribes to Israel, Jud. 5.14. Kept Hezekiah's passover, 2 Chr. 30.11,18 Carried captive to Assyria, 2 Kin. 15.29 with Isa. 9.1. Christ preached in the land of, Mat. 4.13-16. For things common to the tribe, see ISRAEL, TRIBES OF.

ZECHARIAH, high-priest in the reign of Joash, king of Judah ; son or grandson of Jehoiada. Stoned by the king's order for prophesying against Jerusalem, 2 Chr. 24.20-22,25. Mat. 23.35. Luk. 11.51.

ZECHARIAH, KING. See ZACHARIAH.

ZECHARIAH, a prophet in Uzziah's reign, 2 Chr. 26.5.

ZECHARIAH the prophet, son of Berechiah, and grandson of Iddo ; prophesied when young, Zec. 2.4 ; in the reign of Darius, to encourage the Jews in rebuilding the Temple, Ezr. 4.24. Ezr. 5.1. Ezr. 6.14. Zec. 1.1,7. Zec. 7.1. Supposed to be the priest mentioned in Neh. 12.16.

ZEDEKIAH, or MATTANIAH, 19th king of Judah (reigns 11 years) ; third son of Josiah, and uncle of Jehoiachin ; made king by Nebuchadnezzar, and his name changed from Mattaniah, 2 Kin. 24.17,18 with 1 Chr. 3.15. 2 Chr. 36.10 (*marg.*). Jer. 37.1.

Rebels against Nebuchadnezzar, 2 Kin. 24. 20. 2 Chr. 36.13. Jer. 52.3. Eze. 17.12-21. Seeks aid from Egypt ; Jeremiah prophesies his captivity and death at Babylon, Jer. 21. Jer. 24.8-10. Jer. 27.12-22. Jer. 32.3-5. Jer. 34. Jer. 37.7-10,17. Jer. 38.14-28. Eze. 12. 10-16. Eze. 17.12-21. 2 Chr. 36.12.

Imprisons Jeremiah, Jer. 32.2,3. Jer. 37.

15-21. Jer. 38.5-28. Asks Jeremiah's counsel and prayers, Jer. 21.1-3. Jer. 37.3. Jer. 38. 14-27.

His impenitence and wicked reign, 2 Kin. 24.19,20. 2 Chr. 36.12,13. Jer. 37.2. Jer. 52.2. His weakness and cowardice, Jer. 38. 5,19,24-26.

Nebuchadnezzar besieges Jerusalem, takes Zedekiah captive to Babylon, slays his sons, puts out his eyes, and sends Nebuzar-adan to destroy the temple and city; takes many captives this the third and last captivity (B.C. 588), 2 Kin. 25. 2 Chr. 36.17-20. Jer. 1.3. Jer. 32.1,2. Jer. 39.1-10. Jer. 51.59. Jer. 52.4-30.

ZEDEKIAH, a false prophet, urges Ahab to go up against Ramoth-gilead; opposes the prophet Micaiah, 1 Kin. 22.11-25. 2 Chr. 18. 10-24.

————, a false prophet, predicts deliverance from Nebuchadnezzar's army; prophecy by Jeremiah of his death, Jer. 29.21-23.

ZEEB, a Midianitish prince, slain by Gideon, Jud. 7.25. Jud. 8.3. Psa. 83.11.

ZELOPHEHAD'S daughters claim his inheritance, and obtain it on condition of marrying within their own tribe, Num. 27.1-11. Num. 36. Jos. 17.3-6.

ZEMARIM, a hill in Mount Ephraim, whence Abijah addressed Jeroboam's army, 2 Chr. 13.4.

ZENAS the lawyer, Tit. 3.13.

ZEPHANIAH the prophet, in the reign of Josiah, king of Judah, Zeph. 1.1.

————, the Second Priest in Zedekiah's reign, sent by the king to ask Jeremiah's prayers, Jer. 21.1,2. Jer. 37.3. Shews Jeremiah the letter of Shemaiah the false prophet, Jer. 29.25-29. Taken to Babylon by Nebuzaradan, 2 Kin. 25.18. Jer. 52.24. His son or grandson a priest after the captivity, Zec. 6. 10,14.

ZEPHATHAH, a valley of Dan, 2 Chr. 14. 10 with Jos. 15.44. Asa's victory over Zerah in, 2 Chr. 14.9-15.

ZERAH, king of the Ethiopians, defeated by Asa, 2 Chr. 14.9-15.

ZEREDA. See ZARETAN.

ZERESH, wife of Haman, counsels Mordecai's death, Est. 5.10-14. Est. 6.13.

ZERUBBABEL, or SHESHBAZZAR, son or grandson of Salathiel, the son of Jehoiachin, Ezr. 3.2,8 with 1 Chr. 3.17-19. Mat. 1.12. Luk. 3.27. Leader of the first colony of Jews returning from captivity, Ezr. 1.8-11. Ezr. 2. Neh. 12. Builds the altar, temple, &c., Ezr. 3.2-8. Ezr. 4.2,3. Ezr. 5.2,14-16. Hag. 1. 12-14. Hag. 2. Prophecies concerning, Hag. 2. Zec. 4.6-10.

ZERUIAH, sister of David, and mother of Joab, Abishai, and Asahel, 2 Sam. 2.18. 2 Sam. 3.39. 2 Sam. 16.9,10. 2 Sam. 17.25. 1 Chr. 2.16.

ZIBA, Saul's servant; his conduct to Mephibosheth, 2 Sam. 9. 2 Sam. 16.1-4. 2 Sam. 19.26-29.

ZICHRI, a general of Pekah, who slew Ahaz's son and the princes of Judah, 2 Chr. 28.7.

ZIDON or SIDON, a city of Phenicia, north boundary of the Canaanites, Gen. 10.19, see v. 15, and 1 Chr. 1.13. North boundary of Asher, Jos. 19.28 (but see Gen. 49.13); in David's reign, 2 Sam. 24.6. Land of, promised to Israel, Jos. 13.6. People not dispossessed, Jud. 1.31. Jud. 3.3. Oppressed Israel, Jud. 10.12. Supply cedar-wood to David, 1 Chr. 22.4; to Solomon, 1 Kin. 5.6; for the second temple, Ezr. 3.7. Eth-baal, king of, his daughter Jezebel marries Ahab, see JEZEBEL.

Merchants of, Isa. 23.2,4,12. Zec. 9.2. Mariners of, Eze. 27.8. Peaceful character of Sidonians, Jud. 18.7.

Prophecies against, Jer. 25.22. Jer. 27.3-11. Jer. 47.4. Eze. 28.21-23. Eze. 32.30. Joel 3.4-8.

Jesus preaches near, and works a miracle, Mat. 15. 21-28. Mar. 7.24-31. People of, come to hear him, Mar. 3.8. Luk. 6.17. Paul visits disciples at, Act. 27.3. Sidonians displease Herod; they flatter him; his death, Act. 12. 20-23.

Idols of, see ASHTAROTH—BAAL.

ZIF, the second month (May); the foundation of the temple laid in, 1 Kin. 6.1,37.

ZIKLAG, a city of Judah, Jos. 19.5. Subject to the Philistines, whose king, Achish, gave it to David for a residence, 1 Sam. 27.5,6. 1 Chr. 12.1. Burnt by the Amalekites, 1 Sam. 30. David mourns for Saul at, 2 Sam. 1. Rebuilt after the captivity, Neh. 11.28.

ZILPAH, Leah's handmaid, Gen. 29.24. Given by her to Jacob; the mother of Gad and Asher, Gen. 30.9-13. Gen. 35.26. Gen. 37.2. Gen. 46.18.

ZIMRI a chief of Simeon, slain by Phinehas for taking a Midianitish woman; the plague stayed by his death. Num. 25.6-8,14.

————, 5th king of Israel, captain of king Elah's chariots, murders his master and succeeds to the throne; slays all of the house of Baasha, 1 Kin. 16.9-13. 2 Kin. 9.31. Tirzah, his capital, taken by Omri, who is chosen king by Israel; Zimri sets fire to his palace; his wickedness and death, 1 Kin. 16. 16-20.

ZIN, a desert south of Palestine, and west of Idumea. Num. 34.3,4. Jos. 15.1,3. Kadesh situated in, Num. 13.21. Num. 20.1. Num. 27.14. Num. 33.36. Deu. 32.51.

ZION, MOUNT, a stronghold taken by David from the Jebusites, and called the city of David, 2 Sam. 5.6-9. 2 Sam. 6.12-16. 1 Kin. 8.1. See JERUSALEM.

ZIPH, wilderness of, in the neighbourhood of a town of Judah, Jos. 15.55. 2 Chr. 11.8. David hides in, and meets Jonathan in, 1 Sam. 23.14-24; takes the spear from Saul's bolster in, 1 Sam. 26. The inhabitants inform Saul of David's hiding-place, 1 Sam. 23.19. 1 Sam. 26.1. Psa. 54 (title).

ZIPPORAH, daughter of Reuel or Jethro, married to Moses, Ex. 2.16-22. Reproaches Moses on account of circumcision, Ex. 4.25,26. Is sent back to her father, who afterwards brings her to Moses at Sinai, Ex. 18.2-6. Miriam and Aaron quarrel with Moses on her account, Num. 12.1.

ZIZ, a cliff ; Ammonites defeated at, 2 Chr. 20.16.

ZOAN, a city of Egypt, Psa. 78.12,43. Isa. 19.11,13. Isa. 30.4. Built 7 years after Hebron, Num. 13.22. Prophecy against, Eze. 30.14 (marg. Tanis).

ZOAR (little), a small city in the plain of Jordan, Gen. 13.10. Deu. 34.3. Anciently called Bela ; its king defeated by Chedorlaomer, Gen. 14.2,8. Spared at the prayer of Lot, who dwelt in it for some time, Gen. 19. 20-23,30. Belonged to the Moabites, Isa. 15.5. Jer. 48.34.

ZOBAH (Hobah, Gen. 14.15 (?)), a Syrian kingdom ; king of, defeated by Saul, 1 Sam. 14.47. Hadadezer king of, defeated by David; chariots and horses taken ; shields of gold and much brass afterwards used for temple vessels,

2 Sam. 8.3-8,12. 1 Kin. 11.23,24. People of, at war with Toi, king of Hamath, 1 Chr. 18. 9,10. Hired by Ammonites against-David, and defeated, 2 Sam. 10.6-19. 1 Chr. 19.6-19. Psa. 60 (title). Defeated by Solomon, 2 Chr. 8.3. See SYRIA.

ZOPHAR, the Naamathite, one of Job's three friends, Job 2.11. His speeches to Job, Job 11. Job 20. Is reproved by God, and commanded to offer a sacrifice, Job 42.7-9.

ZORAH, a town of Dan, Jos. 19.41. The birthplace and burial-place of Samson, Jud. 13.2,25. Jud. 16.31. The Danites send men from, to seek an inheritance, Jud. 18.

ZUPH, LAND OF, 1 Sam. 9.5. See 1 Chr. 6.35, and 1 Sam. 1.1.

ZUR, a Midianitish chief, slain by the Israelites, Num. 25.15,18. Jos. 13.21.

ZUZIMS or ZAMZUMMIMS, a race of giants ; dispossessed by the Ammonites, Deu. 2.20,21. See Gen. 14.5.

INDEX OF DOCTRINAL
AND PRACTICAL SUBJECTS

It is not thought necessary to give an Index of the other subjects,
as *The Compact Topical Bible* is arranged alphabetically.